Philo of Alexandria: *On the Change of Names*

Philo of Alexandria Commentary Series

General editor

Gregory E. Sterling

Associate editor

David T. Runia

Editorial Board

Ellen Birnbaum – René Bloch
Michael Cover – John Dillon – Albert Kees Geljon
Annewies van den Hoek – Maren Niehoff

VOLUME 8

The titles published in this series are listed at *brill.com/pacs*

Philo of Alexandria:
On the Change of Names

Introduction, Translation, and Commentary

By

Michael B. Cover

BRILL

LEIDEN | BOSTON

Library of Congress Cataloging-in-Publication Data

Names: Cover, Michael, 1982- author, editor, translator. | Philo, of Alexandria. De mutatione nominum. English. 2023.
Title: On the change of names / Philo of Alexandria ; introduction, translation, and commentary by Michael B. Cover.
Other titles: Philo of Alexandria: On the change of names | Philo of Alexandria commentary series ; 8.
Description: Boston : Brill, 2023. | Series: Philo of Alexandria commentary series, 1570-095X ; 8 | Includes bibliographical references and index.
Identifiers: LCCN 2023040245 (print) | LCCN 2023040246 (ebook) | ISBN 9789004687431 (hardback) | ISBN 9789004687424 (ebook)
Subjects: LCSH: Philo, of Alexandria. De mutatione nominum. | Abraham (Biblical patriarch)
Classification: LCC B689.D413 C68 2023 (print) | LCC B689.D413 (ebook) | DDC 222/.11–dc23/eng/20231108
LC record available at https://lccn.loc.gov/2023040245
LC ebook record available at https://lccn.loc.gov/2023040246

Typeface for the Latin, Greek, and Cyrillic scripts: "Brill". See and download: brill.com/brill-typeface.

ISSN 1570-095X
ISBN 978-90-04-68743-1 (hardback)
ISBN 978-90-04-68742-4 (e-book)
DOI 10.1163/9789004687424

Copyright 2024 by Michael B. Cover. Published by Koninklijke Brill NV, Leiden, The Netherlands.
Koninklijke Brill NV incorporates the imprints Brill, Brill Nijhoff, Brill Schöningh, Brill Fink, Brill mentis, Brill Wageningen Academic, Vandenhoeck & Ruprecht, Böhlau and V&R unipress.
Koninklijke Brill NV reserves the right to protect this publication against unauthorized use. Requests for re-use and/or translations must be addressed to Koninklijke Brill NV via brill.com or copyright.com.

This book is printed on acid-free paper and produced in a sustainable manner.

PRINTED BY DRUKKERIJ WILCO B.V. - AMERSFOORT, THE NETHERLANDS

for Susanna Quaile Cover

Χάρις λιπαροκρήδεμνος
καλή

(*Il.* 18.382–383)

∴

Contents

General Introduction to the Philo of Alexandria Commentary Series XI
Preface and Acknowledgements XVIII
Abbreviations XXIII
List of Figures and Tables XXXIII

Introduction 1
1 The Place of *De Mutatione Nominum* in the Allegorical Commentary 2
  1.1 (*A Short*) *History of Scholarship on the Division of the Allegorical Commentary* 3
  1.2 De Mutatione Nominum *within the Allegorical Commentary and the Abrahamic Cycle* 6
2 The Genre, *Sitz im Leben*, and Rhetorical Structure of the Treatise 13
  2.1 *Genre and* Sitz im Leben 13
  2.2 *Rhetorical Structure* 15
  2.3 *The Partitions of the Treatise* 17
  2.4 *Thematic and Figural Movements of the Treatise* 18
  2.5 *Aporiae et Quaestiones* 19
3 Chapters of the Treatise 20
4 Exegetical Structure of the Treatise 22
5 Use of Scripture 31
6 The Main Themes of the Treatise 36
  6.1 *Perfection* 36
  6.2 *Emotions, Bad and Good* 36
  6.3 *Theological Epistemology: The Nature and Names of God* 37
  6.4 *Grace and the Covenant* 38
  6.5 *Hebrew and Greek Etymologies; Philosophy of Language* 38
  6.6 *Doxography* 39
  6.7 *The Allegorical Purpose of Scriptural Names and Their Changes* 40
  6.8 *Arithmological Exegesis* 40
  6.9 *Virtue, Individual and Generic* 41
  6.10 *Abraham's Faith and Doubt* 41
  6.11 *The Problem of Rhetoric and Sophism in Jewish Wisdom Literature* 41
  6.12 *Isaac and Ishmael as an Allegorical Binary* 42
  6.13 *Time and Eschatology* 42
7 Title and Previous Scholarship on the Treatise 42

8   The Text   45
9   Parallel Exegesis and *Nachleben*   45
    Bibliography   47

Translation: Philo of Alexandria, *On the Change of Names*   71

Notes to the Text and Translation   118

Commentary   129

TRANSLATION
Philo of Alexandria,
On the Change of Names

Part One   73
1   Abraham as Seer and Hearer of God (§§ 1–38)   73
2   Philo's Theology of Covenant (§§ 39–53)   79
3   Abraham's Great Fall (§§ 54–56)   81
4   Different Forms of Covenant (§§ 57–59)   82

Part Two   83
5   On the Change of Names (§§ 60–129)   83

Part Three   94
6   The Birth of Isaac (§§ 130–153)   94
7   Abraham's Laughter (§§ 154–174)   98
8   The Faith and Doubt of Abraham (§§ 175–200)   101
9   The Life of Ishmael (§§ 201–251)   106
10   Sarah's Child (§§ 252–260)   114
11   You Will Call His Name Joy (§§ 261–263)   115
12   God Alone Is the Appropriate Time (§§ 264–269)   116
13   God's Departure (§ 270)   117
     Notes to the Text and Translation   118

CONTENTS IX

Commentary

Part One   131
1   Abraham as Seer and Hearer of God (§§ 1–38)   131
2   Philo's Theology of the Covenant (§§ 39–53)   190
3   Abraham's Great Fall (§§ 54–56)   221
4   Different Forms of Covenant (§§ 57–59)   231

Part Two   239
5   On the Change of Names (§§ 60–129)   239

Part Three   370
6   The Birth of Isaac (§§ 130–153)   370
7   Abraham's Laughter (§§ 154–174)   409
8   The Faith and Doubt of Abraham (§§ 175–200)   442
9   The Life of Ishmael (§§ 201–251)   496
10   Sarah's Child (§§ 252–260)   551
11   You Will Call His Name Joy (§§ 261–263)   565
12   God Is the Appropriate Time (§§ 264–269)   573
13   God's Departure (§ 270)   584

Index of References to Scripture   588
Index of References to Philo   597
Index of References to Other Ancient Sources   609
Index of Modern Authors   617
Index of Selected Greek Terms   620
Index of Subjects and Names   624

General Introduction to the Philo of Alexandria Commentary Series

Philo of Alexandria (c. 20 BCE–c. 50 CE) was a member of one of the most prominent families of the large and influential Jewish community in Alexandria. We know more about his brother and his family than we do about Philo. His brother, Gaius Julius Alexander, held a responsible governmental position (Josephus, *A.J.* 18.159, 259; 19.276–277, 20.100) and may have been a substantial property owner (*CPJ* 420a and 420b) as well as the manager of the Egyptian estates of Julia Augusta, the mother of the emperor Tiberius (*CPJ* 420b). He had probably become known to the emperor's family through Herodian intermediaries (Josephus, *A.J.* 19.276–277). His *praenomen* and *nomen* suggest that the family was associated in some way with Gaius Julius Caesar. It may be that Caesar granted Roman citizenship to Alexander's grandfather for assistance during the Alexandrian War (48–47 BCE). Alexander made the most of his position and contacts and became exceptionally wealthy (Josephus, *A.J.* 20.100). He once loaned 200,000 drachmas to Agrippa I (Josephus, *A.J.* 18.159–160). He covered nine of the temple doors in Jerusalem with gold and silver (*B.J.* 5.201–205), an act of patronage that attests his immense resources as well as his commitment to Judaism. The rabbis later report that he had a Torah scroll with the names of God in gold letters (Sop. 1.9 and Sep. Torah 1.9).

Alexander's social and economic standing is confirmed by the roles of his two sons. The archive of Nicanor suggests that Marcus Julius Alexander, Alexander's younger son, was active in the import-export business that moved goods from India and Arabia through Egypt to the West. He married Berenice, the daughter of Herod Agrippa I and later partner of the emperor Titus, but died prematurely c. 43 CE (Josephus, *A.J.* 19.276–277). His older brother Tiberius Julius Alexander had one of the most remarkable careers of any provincial in the first two centuries of the Roman Empire. Tiberius moved through a series of lower posts until he held governorships in Judea, Syria, and Egypt. When he backed Vespasian in the Flavian's bid for the throne, his career quickly rose to its apex: he served as Titus's chief of staff during the First Jewish revolt in 66–70 CE (Josephus, *B.J.* 5.45–46; 6.237) and as prefect of the praetorian guard in Rome after the war (*CPJ* 418b). While his career strained his relationship with his native Judaism to the breaking point (Josephus, *A.J.* 20.100; Philo, *Prov.* and *Anim.*), it attests the high standing of the family.

The most famous member of this remarkable family was paradoxically probably the least known in wider circles during his life. This is undoubtedly due to the contemplative nature of the life that he chose. His choice was not total. He may have had some civic function in the Jewish community. At least this would help to explain why the Alexandrian Jewish community selected him to serve on the first Jewish delegation to Rome after the pogrom in Alexandria in 38 CE, a delegation that probably included his brother and older nephew (*Legat.* 182, 370; *Anim.* 54). The political arena was not, however, where his heart lay; he gave his heart to the life of the intellect (*Spec.* 3.1–6). He undoubtedly received a full education that included training in the gymnasium, the ephebate, and advanced lectures in philosophy and rhetoric. His philosophical training was of enormous importance to his intellectual formation. While he knew and made use of different philosophical traditions such as Stoicism and Pythagoreanism, his basic orientation was Platonic. Middle Platonism (c. 80 BCE–c. 220 CE) had become a vibrant intellectual movement in Alexandria in the first century BCE, especially in the work of Eudorus (fl. 25 BCE). Philo became convinced that Plato and Moses understood reality in similar ways, although he was unequivocal about who saw it most clearly. His commitment to Judaism is evident in his training in the LXX: he knew it with the intimacy of one who lived with it from the cradle. He also knew the works of some of his Jewish literary predecessors such as Aristobulus, Pseudo-Aristeas, and Ezekiel the tragedian. He was aware of a significant number of other Jewish exegetes to whom he alluded in his commentaries, but always anonymously (*Opif.* 26, 77, and *Migr.* 89–93). The most probable social setting for his literary work is a private school in which he offered instruction in much the same way that philosophers and physicians did. This was likely in his own private residence, but a setting in a house of prayer (synagogue) cannot be ruled out.

One of the ways that he taught was through writing. His treatises constitute one of the largest Greek corpora that has come down to us from antiquity. We know that he wrote more than seventy treatises: thirty-seven of these survive in Greek manuscripts and nine (as counted in the tradition) in a rather literal sixth-century Armenian translation. We also have excerpts of another work in Greek and fragments of two more in Armenian. The lost treatises are known from references to them in the extant treatises, gaps in his analyses of the biblical texts in the commentary series, and *testimonia*.

The treatises fall into five major groups: three separate commentary series, the philosophical writings, and the apologetic writings. The three commentary series are Philo's own literary creations; the philosophical and apologetic series are modern constructs that group conceptually similar but literarily independent treatises.

The heart of the Philonic enterprise lay in the three commentary series. Each of these was an independent work with a distinct rationale and form.

Philo set each series apart through explicit statements about the design of the series (for the Exposition of the Law), the use of secondary prefaces to link treatises together (for the Allegorical Commentary and Exposition of the Law), distinct approaches to the biblical text (for all three series), the literary forms of the treatises in the series (for all three series), and the different implied audiences (for all three series). The most elementary of the three is the twelve (six in the manuscript tradition) book *Questions and Answers on Genesis and Exodus* that cover Gen 2:4–28:9 and Exod 6:2–30:10. As the title suggests, Philo used a question and answer format to write a running commentary on the biblical text. The questions are often formulaic, but demonstrate a close reading of the biblical text which is cited in the question. The answers typically introduce both literal and allegorical interpretations. Philo rarely used secondary or tertiary texts in these answers. While earlier Jewish authors such as Demetrius (FF 2 and 5) and Aristobulus (F 2) used the question and answer device within larger works, they did not write zetematic works. The closest literary parallel to Philo's commentary series is the series of zetematic works which Plutarch composed. The pedagogical character of the format and the listing of multiple interpretations suggest that Philo's *Questions and Answers* were written for beginning students in his school who needed to learn how to read the text closely as well as become familiar with the range of possible interpretations.

The Allegorical Commentary shares some features in common with the *Questions and Answers*, but is profoundly different. Like the *Questions and Answers* these treatises use the question and answer technique in a running commentary. Unlike the *Questions and Answers*, the format is no longer explicit but is incorporated in a more complex form of exegesis. Literal readings are generally downplayed, although Philo sometimes includes them when he thinks they can contribute to the understanding of the text. The main focus, however, is on allegorical interpretations which are expanded through the introduction of secondary, or even tertiary, biblical texts (lemmata). While these expansions may give the treatises a meandering feel, in fact there is almost always a thematic unity that makes the treatise coherent. The scope is also different than in the QG and QE; the Allegorical Commentary provides a running commentary on Genesis 2:1–18:4 with some treatments of later texts in Genesis in the final treatises. Philo was by no means the first Jewish author to use allegory: earlier Jewish writers such as Aristobulus and Pseudo-Aristeas had used allegorical interpretation; however, they did not write allegorical commentaries. Philo's allegorical commentaries are closer in form to commentaries in the philosophical tradition, e.g., the Platonic *Anonymous Theaetetus Commentary*, Plutarch's *On the Generation of the Soul in the Timaeus*, and Porphyry's *On the Cave of Nymphs*. Yet even here there are considerable differences; for example, Philo's treatises have more thematic unity than his pagan counterparts. Philo also offered some hints that he saw a larger unity to his allegorical treatment of Genesis. He linked six of the treatises together with secondary prefaces. In particular, he linked four of the five treatises that dealt with the story of Noah together (*Agr., Plant., Ebr., Sobr.*). This suggests that Philo may have thought of the larger structure of the Allegorical Commentary in biographical terms: he devoted three treatises to Cain (*Sacr., Det., Post.*), five to Noah (*Gig./Deus, Agr., Plant., Ebr.* 1–2, *Sobr.*), and five to Abraham (*Migr., Her., Congr., Fug., Mut.*). Cain represented the embodiment of self-love; Noah, who represented justice or perfection, was part of Philo's first triad of virtuous ancestors; and Abraham, who represented virtue through learning, was part of Philo's second triad of ancestors. Philo prefaced these biographically oriented works with treatments on creation and the primeval history (*Leg.* 1–3 [originally 4 or 5 books], *Cher.*) and concluded it with a work on dreams that addresses multiple texts throughout Genesis (*Somn.* 1–2 [originally 5 books]). His work on *Conf.* is a transitional text moving from Noah to Abraham. The goal of this allegorical interpretation was the ascent of the soul or the experience of God achieved through virtue and contemplation. If the *Questions and Answers* were for beginning students, the Allegorical Commentary was most likely composed for advanced students or other exegetes in the Jewish community. It certainly places much greater demands on the reader, as any modern reader who has worked through these treatises can attest.

The third series, the Exposition of the Law, is different yet. It is not a running commentary, but a systematic exposition of the entire Pentateuch. Unlike the *Questions and Answers* and Allegorical Commentary, the Exposition of the Law rarely cites the biblical text—except for an occasional word or phrase—but paraphrases or summarizes it and provides a commentary on the summary. The treatment may include both literal and allegorical readings and in some cases regularly alternates between them, especially in the biographies. The scope of the Exposition of the Law is also quite different: it extends beyond Genesis and Exodus to include the entire Torah. Philo wrote an introduction to the Exposition in the form of a biography in the two volume *Life of Moses*. The work is similar in function to Porphyry's *Life of Plotinus* which introduces readers to the *Enneads*. Philo organized his understanding of the law in three parts (*Praem.* 1–3; cf. also *Abr.* 2–5; *Mos.* 2.45–47). The first part dealt with creation, demonstrating the harmony between the cosmos and the law (*Opif.*). The second part is the historical or biographical section that consists of biographies that show how the ancestors embodied the law before it was given to Moses (*Abr., Ios.* [the works on Isaac and Jacob are lost]). The third and most complex part is the legislative. Just like some later rabbis, Philo worked through the decalogue

(*Decal.*) and then used each of the ten commandments as a heading to subsume the remaining legislation in the Torah (*Spec.* 1–4). Unlike the later rabbis, he added a series of appendices under the headings of virtues (*Virt.*). He brought the series to a conclusion in a treatise *On Rewards and Punishments* in direct imitation of the end of Deuteronomy. The series was probably intended for a broader audience—both Jews and interested pagan readers—that included but was not limited to the school. It may be that Philo offered public lectures at his school or in a house of prayer.

If the three commentary series accentuate Philo's role within the Jewish community, the last two groups of his treatises reflect his efforts to relate to the larger world. The philosophical works use Greek sources and philosophical genres to address some of the major philosophical issues Philo and his students confronted. So, he wrote two dialogues (*Prov.* 1–2, *Anim.*) that featured his nephew, Tiberius Julius Alexander; two discourses that examined a famous Stoic proposition (*Prob.* and the lost *Improb.*), a thesis that set out arguments pro and contra (*Aet.* 1 and 2 [lost]), and an arithmology (*Num.* [only extant as an Armenian fragment]). The biblical text recedes and is replaced by citations from non-Jewish authors. These were probably for advanced students in his school.

The apologetic works were probably written—for the most part—in connection with the events of 38–41 CE. They were designed to assist Philo in his efforts to represent the Jewish community to the authorities. He wrote a work that was probably intended to help him with the embassy (*Hypoth.* [only extant in two Greek fragments]), a treatise holding out exemplars of Judaism (*Contempl.* and a parallel treatment on the Essenes now lost), and a five-volume treatment of the mistreatment of the Jews by Roman authorities who were punished by God (*Flacc., Legat.* [the five volumes were probably 1. Introduction and Pilate; 2. Sejanus, 3. Flaccus, 4. Embassy, 5. Palinode]). These works were likely intended for non-Jews or Jews dealing with non-Jews who probably comprised the largest audience.

This expansive corpus is the single most important source for our understanding of Second Temple Judaism in the diaspora. While some of the esoteric and philosophical aspects of his writings reflect a highly refined circle in Alexandria, the corpus as a whole preserves a wide range of exegetical and social traditions which enable us to reconstruct a number of beliefs and practices of Jews in the Roman empire. The difficulty that we face is the limited evidence from other Jewish communities.

This can be partially solved by expanding the comparisons to early Christian writings which were heavily indebted to Jewish traditions. As is the case with virtually all Second Temple Jewish texts composed in Greek, Philo's corpus was not preserved by Jews but by Christians who found his writings so irresistibly attractive that they gave him a *post mortem* conversion. In some *Catenae* he is actually called "Philo the bishop." A number of important early Christian authors are deeply indebted to him: Clement of Alexandria, Origen, Didymus, Gregory of Nyssa, and Ambrose in particular. While there is no solid evidence to show that New Testament authors knew his writings, they certainly knew some of the same exegetical traditions that he attests. His writings therefore serve both as a witness to exegetical traditions known and used by first-century Christians and as a source for some second-century and later Christians.

One of the factors that made Philo so attractive to Christians was the way that he combined Greek philosophy, especially Middle Platonism, with exegesis. The eclectic nature of his thought and the size of his corpus make his writings a particularly important source for our understanding of several Hellenistic philosophical traditions. The combination of Middle Platonism and Jewish exegesis also makes Philo important for the study of Gnosticism, especially for those scholars who argue that the second-century Christian Gnostic systems had significant antecedents in Jewish circles.

It is remarkable that in spite of the obvious importance of these writings and their complexity, no series of commentaries has been devoted to them. The present series is designed to fill that void. Each commentary will offer an introduction, a fresh English translation, and a commentary proper. The commentary proper is organized into units/chapters on the basis of an analysis of the structure of each treatise. Each unit/chapter of the commentary will address the following concerns: the context and basic argument of the relevant section, detailed comments on the most important and difficult phrases, passages where Philo treats the same biblical text, the *Nachleben* of Philo's treatment, and suggestions for further reading when appropriate. There will be some variation within the series to account for the differences in the genres of Philo's works; however, readers should be able to move from one part of the corpus to another with ease. We hope that in this way these commentaries will serve the needs of both Philonists who lack sustained analyses of individual treatises and those scholars and students who work in other areas but consult Philo's works.

Most of the volumes in this series will concentrate on Philo's biblical commentaries. It may seem strange to write and read a commentary on a commentary; however, it is possible to understand the second commentary to be an extended form of commentary on the biblical text as well. While Philo's understanding of the biblical text is quite different from our own, it was based on a careful reading of the text and a solid grasp of Greek philosophy. His commentaries permit us to understand how one of the most influential interpreters of the biblical text in antiquity read the text. The fact that his reading is so different from ours is in part the fascination of reading him. He challenges us to enter into a different world and to see the text from another perspective.

Gregory E. Sterling
Yale Divinity School

Preface and Acknowledgements

The twenty-first century reader, opening a Greek treatise by the first-century Jewish statesman, philosopher, and exegete, Philo of Alexandria, bearing the title *De mutatione nominum* (*On the Change of Names*), might naturally have questions about the scope of the work. From the shorter Latin title, one might rightly infer that the treatise has something to do with scriptural etymologies and the symbolic significance of Hebrew names being changed. Several examples spring to mind—for example, Abram's change of name to Abraham, and Sarai's change of name to Sarah in the Priestly covenantal narrative of Genesis 17. Ancient Jewish and pagan readers in Alexandria's museum, library, private schools, or prayer houses—many of them untutored in Hebrew—would have been fascinated and perplexed by the transliterated names, which leave so prominent a mark upon the narrative surface of the Jewish Scriptures in Greek.[1] *De mutatione nominum*, on this reading of its title, might include an alphabetical list of etymologies of Hebrew names paired with Greek interpretations, with special attention to doublets. Indeed, the sands of Egypt have given us such lists, called onomastica.[2] Jerome, in the preface to his *De nominibus hebraicis*, even attributes such a list to Philo on the authority of Origen.[3]

This first impression would not be entirely off the mark. Hebrew etymologies do appear throughout Philo's *œuvre* and play an especially important role in *De mutatione nominum*. So prominent is etymology in certain sections of the present treatise, that it might fairly be called the work's dominant "technique."[4] But etymology is never an end for Philo; it is always an instrument in service of allegorical exegesis.[5] And etymology is not primarily what the present treatise is about.

The treatise's lengthier and more cumbersome Greek title, *On Those Whose Names Are Being Changed, and For What Purposes They Are Being Changed* (περὶ τῶν μετονομαζομένων καὶ ὧν ἕνεκα μετονομάζονται), might give a more

---

1 A similar interest in foreign names in Greek philosophical literature is evinced by Plutarch's Platonizing etymologies in *De Iside et Osiride*. For a recent study of this text, in comparison with *De mutatione nominum*, see Brenk 2023.
2 For the onomastica, see Shaw 2015; Rokeah 1968.
3 Jerome, *Heb. nom.*, Pref. 1 (PCW 1:103).
4 I borrow the notion of "technique," the rhetorical device which gives a composition its tone and rhythm, from Stuart Gilbert's (1952) study of James Joyce's *Ulysses*, in which each of the novel's eighteen chapters is analyzed in terms of a dominant rhetorical "technic."
5 Runia 2004; Long 1997.

accurate impression: that the work is comprised of a catena of disconnected allegories, drawn from Jewish and perhaps also pagan narratives about patriarchs and matriarchs, heroes, and gods, whose names have changed or whose polyonymous characters warrant further explanation. Ancient works of philosophical criticism, including Plato's *Cratylus* and the Roman Stoic Cornutus's *Epidrome*, attend to such concerns, with both authors offering various catalogues of names and their symbolic etymologies. *De mutatione nominum* might include an allegorical interpretation of the names changed in the Septuagint—particularly the Pentateuch. This is in fact what Philo does in the fifth and longest chapter of this treatise. But this does not explain the work as a whole nor illuminate its purpose.

I begin my preface to this commentary on Philo's *De mutatione nominum* with two possible misperceptions about its scope, with the hope that I may entice potential readers to take a deeper look at it. It is true, as Samuel Taylor Coleridge famously opined, that "Philo has not been used half enough;"[6] and his works have been appreciated as the literary critical and theological masterpieces that they are even less. This is especially the case for Philo's Allegorical Commentary, the series of exegetical treatises on the Pentateuch, to which *De mutatione nominum* belongs. This commentary series is Philo's densest, richest, and most complicated, both philosophically and literarily. Before the Allegorical Commentary can be used in studies of ancient philosophy, rabbinic Judaism, and early Christianity, it must first be read and understood in its own right as an integral part of the history of Western philosophy, exegesis, and religions.

Although *De mutatione nominum* has had previous annotators, no one has offered a complete modern commentary on the treatise in any language. The editor of its 1587 *editio princeps*, the Augsburg humanist David Hoeschel, published a lengthy series of annotations in Latin as an appendix to the text, which are still useful to the reader and merit special consideration for the philosophical and Christian parallels that Hoeschel included.[7] They also warrant attention for the light they shed on the theological use of Philo in the context of sixteenth century interconfessional humanism.[8] In the twentieth century, Jacques Cazeaux, (*La trame et la chaîne* [1983]) mapped out the allegorical deep structure of the first chapter of the treatise (§§ 1–38), but did not assess the entire

---

6 Sterling 2004.
7 *De mutatione nominum* is missing from Adrien Turnèbe's 1552 *editio princeps* of Philo's works, as it did not appear in the manuscripts available to him in Paris. For additional annotators of the treatise, see 7. The Title, Text, and Previous Scholarship on the Treatise below.
8 See Cover 2024a.

work. A few years later, David Runia (1988), following in the path of Valentin Nikiprowetzsky (1977), contributed to the analysis of the treatise's structure in an essay on Philo's use of aporetic questions. Finally, at the 2016 SBL Annual Meeting in San Antonio, TX, the Philo of Alexandria Seminar devoted a panel to this treatise, including papers by Greg Sterling, Jim Royse, Fred Brenk, and Michel Barnes. I draw gratefully on these and the other works mentioned in the introduction.

My interest in writing a study of a treatise from the Allegorical Commentary dates back to my earliest encounters with Philo's writings as a student at Yale Divinity School in a graduate seminar with John J. Collins and Steven Fraade. Having just made the leap from Classics to the study of early Judaism, I became intrigued by the fusion of Septuagintal and Platonizing thought in Philo. What began as suspicion at Philo's allegorizing program became, over time, admiration for the complexity of his architectonic project—in equal parts philosophy, exegesis, and literary criticism. It was especially helpful for me, under the guidance of Greg Sterling at Notre Dame, to encounter the work of the Philo Institute and *The Studia Philonica Annual*. In contradistinction to Harry Wolfson (1947), whose work remains invaluable, scholars in this line have viewed Philo primarily as a tradent of Jewish tradition and as a philosophical exegete, rather than as a systematic philosopher; as a thinker at default conservative and anthological, rather than innovative and *sui generis*. Such a view enabled me to see in starker relief the true originality of the Allegorical Commentary. I was also interested, when this project was first being proposed, in writing a commentary on an Abrahamic treatise. This was an instinctual decision, for which I became increasingly grateful the more I wrote and learned about the Platonist allegorical readers of Homer and their interest in the psychological allegoresis of Odysseus's marriage, wandering, and *nostos*. There is an argument to be made that, to Philo's mind, Odysseus's heroic itinerary maps more closely onto Abraham's than onto that of any other Jewish patriarch. Hence, in electing to work on Abraham, I found myself at the center of Philo's allegorical multiverse.

As a New Testament scholar, my interests in this particular treatise were simultaneously piqued by certain exegetical and theological points of overlap—not least Philo's discussion of the faith (and doubt) of Abraham in chapter eight. This sub-treatise on faith and divine grace can fruitfully be read alongside key chapters (3–4) in Paul's Epistle to the Romans, just as Philo's little "bread from heaven" homily on Exod 16:4 in chapter ten illuminates Jesus's "bread of life" discourse in John 6. Despite the clear "usefulness" of *De mutatione nominum* for New Testament and early Christian studies, however, my fascination with Philo's writings remains non-instrumental; this treatise and my commentary on it are ends unto themselves.

Preface and Acknowledgements

This project could not have been begun or completed without the help and support of many people, institutions, and foundations. My thanks go first to Greg Sterling, editor of the Brill PACS series, who suggested *De mutatione nominum* as a possibility, accepted my proposal, and then read this commentary cover to cover at least three times. Greg saved me from numerous errors, improved the structure, content, and readability of the work, and has encouraged me on all fronts. David Runia has also been an unofficial mentor, first suggesting to me the theme of "perfection" in the treatise and discussing various Philonic topics over the years. A huge debt of gratitude is owed to the Alexander von Humboldt Foundation for a post-doctoral research fellowship to work on this commentary, and to my academic host during that first year as a *Humboldtianer*, Lutz Doering of the Institutum Judaicum Delitzschianum (IJD) at the University of Münster. Professor Doering not only provided me with a spacious second-floor office and access to Münster's numerous libraries, in which to research and write, but twice invited me to present my research at the joint IJD-New Testament research seminar; hosted an interdisciplinary workshop on the aims of commentary writing; and co-hosted with me, in May of 2019, an international conference on the theme of "Philo and Philosophical Discourse," again with academic support from the Humboldt Foundation. Heartfelt thanks are also due to Professor Emeritus Folker Siegert, who came out of *Ruhestand* to read Philo's Armenian corpus with me weekly during the year in Münster. Some of the fruits of our labors are present in the Parallel Exegesis sections of this commentary. Thanks are also due to colleagues at my home institution, Marquette University: Heidi Bostic and Rick Holz, deans of the Helen Way Klingler College of Arts and Sciences; Bob Masson, Susan Wood, Danielle Nussberger, and Conor Kelly, chairs of the Theology Department; and Jeanne Hossenlopp, vice president for research, have all given me time and financial support to work on this commentary. My colleagues at Marquette, including Michel Barnes, Josh Burns, Deirdre Dempsey, Julian Hills, Andrei Orlov, Sharon Pace, Marcus Plested, and Jeanne-Nicole Mellon Saint-Laurent have provided valuable feedback. Conversations with David Lincicum and especially Courtney Friesen have provided inspiration and encouragement. Thanks also to doctoral students Luke Beavers, Paul Cox, Vance Halfaker, and Tyler Stewart, who have helped with various aspects of this project. Marlou Meems and the staff at Brill have been a pleasure to work with.

The final and most consequential note of thanks goes to my wife, Susanna, and to our four daughters, Elizabeth, Lucia, Helen, and Phoebe. Each of them has patiently supported and encouraged this project in untold ways. This was especially true in 2018, when the Cover family journeyed from Wauwatosa,

Wisconsin, to Münster, Germany, for a Humboldt year, with Elizabeth attending the Wartburg Grundschüle, Lucia going to the Kita around the corner, and Helen keeping her mother company at our little house in Gievenbeck. If I may be afforded a bit of poetic license: "with these graceful companions over the past nine years, *we* have fashioned many cunning and delightful things" (cf. *Il.* 18.400: τῇσι παρ' εἰνάετες χάλκευον δαίδαλα πολλά).

This work is dedicated to Susanna Quaile Cover—whose change of name continues to increase my virtue and joy on a daily basis.

Michael B. Cover
Wauwatosa, WI

Abbreviations

Abbreviations of Philonic Treatises

Abr.	*De Abrahamo*
Aet.	*De aeternitate mundi*
Agr.	*De agricultura*
Cher.	*De Cherubim*
Conf.	*De confusione nominum*
Congr.	*De congressu eruditionis gratia*
Contempl.	*De vita contemplativa*
Decal.	*De Decalogo*
Deo	*De Deo*
Det.	*Quod deterius potiori insidiari soleat*
Deus	*Quod Deus sit immutabilis*
Ebr.	*De ebrietate*
Flacc.	*In Flaccum*
Fug.	*De fuga et inventione*
Gig.	*De gigantibus*
Her.	*Quis rerum divinarum heres sit*
Hypoth.	*Hypothetica*
Ios.	*De Iosepho*
Leg. 1–3	*Legum allegoriae* 1, 2, 3
Legat.	*Legatio ad Gaium*
Migr.	*De migratione Abrahami*
Mos. 1–2	*De vita Mosis* 1, 2
Mut.	*De mutatione nominum*
Num.	*De numeris*
Opif.	*De opificio mundi*
Plant.	*De plantatione*
Post.	*De posteritate Caini*
Praem.	*De praemiis et poenis*
Prob.	*Quod omnis probus liber sit*
Prov. 1–2	*De providentia* 1, 2
QE 1–2	*Quaestiones et solutiones in Exodum* 1, 2
QG 1–4	*Quaestiones et solutiones in Genesin* 1, 2, 3, 4
Sacr.	*De sacrificiis Abelis et Caini*
Sobr.	*De sobrietate*
Somn. 1–2	*De somniis* 1, 2

Spec. 1–4   De specialibus legibus 1, 2, 3, 4
Test. 1–2   De testamentis 1, 2
Virt.   De virtutibus

Abbreviations of Other Ancient Authors

Aeschylus
Prom.   Prometheus vinctus

Alexander Polyhistor
Frag.   Fragmenta (FHG 3)

Ambrose
Abr.   De Abraham
Isaac   De Isaac vel anima
Exp. Ps. 118 Expositio Psalmi CXVIII
Jac.   De Jacob et vita beata
Jos.   De Joseph patriarcha

Andreas of Caesarea
Comm. Apoc.   Commentarii in Apocalypsin

Andronicus of Rhodes
Pass.   De passionibus (περὶ παθῶν)

Anonymous
Frag. lex. Graec.   Fragmentum lexici Graeci (Cod. Paris. gr. 3027)
Tab. Ceb.   Tabula of Cebes

Apostolic Fathers
Herm.   Shepherd of Hermas

Aristophanes
Thesm.   Thesmophoriazusae

Aristotle
De an.   De anima
Cat.   Categoriae
Cael.   De caelo

Eth. eud.   *Ethica eudemia*
Eth. nic.   *Ethica nicomachea*
[*Mag. mor.*]   *Magna moralia*
Pol.   *Politica*
Top.   *Topica*

Astrampsychus
Sort. Astr.   *Sortes Astrampsychi*

Athanasius
C. Ar.   *Orationes contra Arianos*
Inc.   *De incarnatione*
[*Nav. praec.*]   *In navitatem praecursoris*

Augustine
Civ.   *De civitate Dei*

Bacchylides
Epigr.   *Epigrammata*

Basil of Caesarea
[*En. in proph. Isa.*]   *Enarratio in prophetam Isaiam*

Cocondrius
Trop.   *De tropis*

Cyril of Alexandria
Ador. cult.   *De adoratione et cultu in spiritu et veritate*
Comm. Jo.   *Commentarii in Ioannem*
Contr. Jul.   *Contra Julianum imperatorem*
Epist. pasch.   *Epistulae paschales*
Frag. Rom.   *Fragmenta in sancti Pauli epistulam ad Romanos*
Glaph. Pent.   *Glaphyra in Pentateuchum*

Cyril of Jerusalem
Catech. illum.   *Catacheses ad illuminandos* 1–18

Damascius
Princ.   *De principiis*

Didymus the Blind
Comm. Job	Commentarii in Job
Comm. Ps.	Commentarii in Psalmos
Comm. Zacch.	Commentarii in Zacchariam
In Gen.	In Genesim
Frag. Ps.	Fragmenta in Psalmos
[Trin.]	De Trinitate

Dio Chrysostom (Dio of Prusa)
Or.	Orationes

Dionysius of Halicarnassus
Ant. rom.	Antiquitates romanae
Is.	De Isaeo
[Rhet.]	Ars rhetorica

Epictetus
Diatr.	Diatribai

Epiphanius
Anchor.	Ancoratus
Pan.	Panarion

Euripides
Hel.	Helena

Eusebius of Caesarea
Comm. Is.	Commentarius in Isaiam
Comm. Ps.	Commentarius in Psalmos
Dem. ev.	Demonstratio evangelica
Ecl. proph.	Eclogae propheticae
Frag. Luc.	Fragmenta in Lucam
Hist. eccl.	Historia ecclesiastica
Praep. ev.	Praeparatio evangelica
Quaest. ev. Steph.	Quaestiones evangelicae ad Stephanum

Eusebius of Emesa
Comm. in Gen.	Commentarii in Genesim

Evagrius
Exp. Prov.   Expositio in Proverbia Salomonis

Galen
Comm. nat. hom.   In Hippocratis de natura hominis commentaria tria

George Kedrenos (Cedrenus)
Comp. hist.   Compendium historiarum

Gregory of Nyssa
Antirrhet. adv. Apoll.   Antirrheticus adversus Apollinarium
Eun. 1–3   Contra Eunomium 1, 2, 3
Hom. opif.   De hominis opificio
[*Lib. cogn. Dei*]   [Liber de cognitione Dei]
Vit. Moys. 1–2   De vita Moysis 1, 2

Hagiographiae et Martyria
Vit. Mar. Mag.   Vita sanctae Mariae Magdalenae (BHG 1161x)
Mart. Gur. Sam.   Martyrium sanctorum Guriae et Samonae (BHG 735)
Vit. Theod.   Vita Theodosii (BHG 1776)

Herodotus
Hist.   Historiae

Hesychius
Comm. brev.   Commentarius brevis (*in* Psalmos)

Hippodamus
[*Resp.*]   De respublica (περὶ πολιτείας)

Hippolytus
Ben. Is. Jac.   De benedictionibus Isaaci et Jacobi

Homer
[*Hymn.*]   Hymni
Il.   Iliad
Od.   Odyssey

Irenaeus
Frag. deperdit.   Fragmenta deperditorum operum
Haer.   Adversus haereses

Isocrates
Trapez.   Trapeziticus (Or. 17)

Jerome
Nom. hebr.   De nominibus hebraicis (Liber nominum)

John Chrysostom
Catech. illum.   Catacheses ad illuminandos
Hom. Gen.   In Genesim (hom. 1–67)
In 1 Cor.   In epistulam I ad Corinthos
Mut.   De mutatione nominum (hom. 1–4)
[Sim. reg.]   In illud: Simile est regnum caelorum grano sinapis

John of Damascus
[Anon. dial. Jud.]   Anonymus dialogus cum Judaeis

Josephus
A.J.   Antiquitates judaicae

Justin Martyr
Apol. 1–2   Apologia 1, 2
[Cohort. gent.]   Cohortatio ad gentiles
Dial.   Dialogus cum Tryphone

Libanius
Progymn.   Progymnasmata

Lucian
Hist. conscr.   Quomodo historia conscribenda sit

Ps.-Macarius
Serm.   Sermones 64 (collectio B)

Maximus the Confessor
[Capit. gnost.]   Capita gnostica
Exp. Ps. 59   Expositio in Psalmum LIX

Menander
Sent.   Sententiae/Monostichoi

New Testament Apocrypha
Acts John   Acts of John

Nilus of Ancyra
Ep.   Epistulae

Origen
Adnot. Deut.	Adnotationes in Deuteronomium
Cels.	Contra Celsum
Comm. Cant.	Commentarius in Canticum canticorum
Comm. Jo.	Commentarii in evangelium Joannis
Comm. Matt.	Commentarium in evangelium Matthaei
Comm. Rom.	Commentarii in Romanos
Engastr.	De engastrimytho
Frag. Jer.	Fragmenta in Jeremiam
Frag. Luc.	Fragmenta in Lucam
Hom. Gen.	Homiliae in Genesim
Hom. Jer.	Homiliae in Jeremiam
Hom. Jes. nav.	In Jesu Nave homiliae xxvi
Hom. Lev.	Homiliae in Leviticum
Hom. Luc.	Homiliae in Lucam
Hom. Ps.	Homiliae in Psalmos
Princ.	De principiis
Sel. Gen.	Selecta in Genesim
Sel. Num.	Selecta in Numeros

Philodemus
Ir.   De ira

Plato
Apol.	Apologia
Charm.	Charmides
Crat.	Cratylus
[Epin.]	[Epinomis]
Leg.	Leges/Laws
Phaedr.	Phaedrus
Phileb.	Philebus

Pol.	Politicus/Statesman
Prot.	Protagoras
Resp.	Respublica/Republic
Symp.	Symposium
Theaet.	Theaetetus
Tim.	Timaeus

Plotinus
Enn.	Enneades/Enneads

Plutarch
Adv. Col.	Adversus Colotem
Cim.	Cimon
Crass.	Crassus
Is. Os.	De Iside et Osiride
Quaest. conviv.	Quaestionum convivialum libri IX
Stoic. rep.	De Stoicorum repugnantiis

Posidippus
Epigr.	Epigrammata

Porphyry
Antr. nymph.	De antro nympharum

Proclus
In Plat. rem publ.	In Platonis rem publicam

Procopius
Comm. Gen.	Commentarii in Genesim

Quintilian
Inst.	Institutio oratoria

Rabbinic Literature
Gen. Rab.	Genesis Rabbah
Mek.	Mekilta d'Rabbi Ishmael

Seneca
Ep.	Epistulae

Sextus Empiricus
Math.   *Adversus mathematicos*

Sophocles
Ant.   *Antigone*
Oed. tyr.   *Oedipus tyrannus*

Stobaeus
Ecl.   *Eclogae*

Theodoret
Quaest. Oct.   *Quaestiones in Octateucum*

Theodotus
Exc.   *Excerpta ex Theodoto* (see Clement of Alexandria, *Strom.* 8)

Theophrastus
Caus. plant.   *De causis plantarum*

Tryphon (Grammaticus)
Trop.   *De tropis*

Vergil
Aen.   *Aeneid*

Other Abbreviations

ANF	Ante-Nicene Fathers
BHG	Bibliotheca Hagiographica Graeca
BiPa	*Biblia Patristica: Index des citations et allusions bibliques dans la littérature patristique*, ed. J. Allenbach et al.
BiPaSup	*Biblia Patristica: Supplément, Philon d'Alexandrie*
CCSG	Corpus Christianorum. Series graeca.
CSEL	Corpus Scriptorum Ecclesiasticorum Latinorum
Diels-Kranz	H. Diels and W. Kranz. *Die Fragmente der Vorsokratiker*. 11th ed. Berlin: Weidemann, 1964.
FGrH	*Die Fragmente der griechischen Historiker*, ed. F. Jacoby
FHG	Fragmenta historicorum Graecorum, ed. K. Müller
GCS	Die griechischen christlichen Schriftsteller

GCSNF	Die griechischen christlichen Schriftsteller, Neue Folge
GNO	Gregorii Nysseni opera
L&S	Long, A.A., and Sedley, D.N. *The Hellenistic Philosophers*. 2 vols. Cambridge: Cambridge University Press, 1987.
Lausberg	Lausberg, H. *Handbuch der literarischen Rhetorik*. 2 vols. München: Hueber, 1960.
NBHL	Awetikʻean, G., Siwrmēlean, S., and Awgerian, M. *Nor Baṙgirkʻ Haykazean Lezui*. 2 vols. Venice: San Lazzaro Press, 1836–1837.
OGIS	*Orientis Graeci Inscriptiones Selectae*, ed. W. Dittenberger
PAPM	Les œuvres de Philon d'Alexandrie
PCW	*Philonis Judaei opera quae supersunt*, ed. L. Cohn, P. Wendland, and S. Reiter
PG	Patrologia Graeca [*Patrologiae cursus completus*], ed. J.-P. Migne
PL	Patrologia Latina
PLCL	*Philo*, Loeb Classical Library, 10 vols, ed. F.H. Colson, G.H. Whitaker, and J.W. Earp
PLCLSup	*Philo*, Loeb Classical Library, 2 supplements, ed. R. Marcus
PO	Patrologia Orientalis
PTA	Papyrologische Texte und Abhandlungen
PTS	Patristische Texte und Studien
RR	Radice, R., and Runia, D.T. *Philo of Alexandria: An Annotated Bibliography*, 4 vols. Leiden: Brill, 1988–2022.
SC	Sources chrétiennes
SIG	*Sylloge inscriptionum graecarum*, ed. Dittenberger
Smyth	Smyth, Herbert Weir. *Greek Grammar*. Cambridge, MA: Harvard University Press, 1920.
SVF	*Stoicorum Veterum Fragmenta*, ed. H. von Arnim
TEG	Traditio Exegetica Graeca

Figures and Tables

Figures

8.1　Exodus Tabernacle Court, Sanctuary, and Holy of Holies　476

Tables

1　Narrative Cycles of the Allegorical Commentary　9
2　Chapters of the Treatise　21
3　Biblical / Classical Quotations and Major Scriptural Allusions in *De mutatione nominum*　31
2.1　References to the *Exhortations* (or **Encouragements*)　197
2.2　Philo's Divisions of *Deuteronomy*　197
3.1　Structure of Parts ONE and TWO of *De mutatione nominum*　221
5.1　Synopsis of *QG* 3.43 and *Mut.* 60–76　262
5.2　The Arithmological Significance of Abram and Abraham (mod. 9)　265
6.1　Pattern of Exegesis in *Mut.* 133　375
6.2　The Effects of Virtue and Vice　404
8.1　References to Gen 32 in *De mutatione nominum*　461
8.2　The Interpretation of Gen 32 in *De mutatione nominum*　462
8.3　Gen 17:17bβ in MT and LXX　470
8.4　Philo's Mock Wisdom Poem　486
9.1　Deut 33 in *De mutatione nominum*　513

Introduction

Around the year 8 CE, Publius Ovidius Naso published a poem that was destined to become his magnum opus. Its success was as universal as its scope and as unlikely as its topic, heralded in the poem's simple yet cryptic title: *Metamorphoses*. In his preface, Ovid announces his audacious bid to unite all of history, from the world's beginning to his own day ("ab origine mundi / ad mea ... tempora" [*Met.* 1.3–4]), in a single literary work. The thread, by which this disparate "torrent of stories" was to be unified,[1] was "the change of forms" ("mutatae ... formae" [*Met.* 1.1])—cosmic, mythological, and historical. If there was something of Heraclitean flux to the scope of this project, it was also one redolent of Genesis, Hesiod, and Lucretius in its bid for permanence (*Met.* 15.871–879). No doubt, a tale beginning with creation and flood would have interested many in the ancient world, in Rome and beyond.

Change was in the air at the turn of the era, and as Ovid's new poem was making its rounds, likely sometime in the years between 8 CE and 38 CE a Jewish exegete and philosopher named Philo of Alexandria would write and publish his own great multi-volume work, to begin "in principio" and likewise, at a critical moment, to take up the theme of change. This larger project, a running interpretation of the book of Genesis, has come to be called the Allegorical Commentary. Like many monotheistic Jews, Philo was chary of too much dabbling in literal stories about anthropomorphic divinities who changed their forms, though he creatively engages these from time to time.[2] And so, when he came to the theme of transformation, he opted for an angle arguably more at home in the Jewish Scriptures—not the change of forms, but the change of names (ἡ τῶν ὀνομάτων ἀλλαγή τε καὶ μετάθεσις [*Mut.* 130]).

This expressly more text-based, Jewish angle on the Ovidian theme of change, which comes down under the title *De mutatione nominum*, was as Philo himself tells us (*Mut.* 60–65) motivated in part by in-house, apologetic considerations. Apparently some of Philo's more cantankerous Alexandrian colleagues, in a spate of *odium philologicum*, had taken to criticizing Philo's school and allegorical project (if not the Pentateuch itself) on account of such underwhelming metamorphoses as Abram's change of name to Abraham in Genesis 17. Philo was certainly attentive to such criticisms; but *De mutatione nominum* is animated primarily by a constructive spirit, relatively free of ire

---

1 Feeney 2004, xiii.
2 Alesse and de Luca 2019.

and self-defense, and fired instead by a creative genius not unlike that of the author of the *Metamorphoses*. While there is no reason to ask about any genetic connections between Ovid's *Met.* and Philo's *Mut.*, both bear witness, in their own genre and idiom, to a common literary, political, philosophical, and theological interest in the possibilities, mechanics, and meaning of change in the early Roman principate.

1 The Place of *De mutatione nominum* in the Allegorical Commentary

De mutatione nominum is a treatise about perfection—its pursuit by human beings, its elusiveness, and ultimately its reception as a gift of divine grace. Through scriptural commentary on Gen 17, Philo paints a portrait of the ethical perfecting of the Abram soul as he approaches the symbolic age of one hundred, when his wife Sarai will give birth to Isaac, the symbol of spiritual joy. This dawning perfection is adumbrated in the scriptural narrative by the change of Abram's name to Abraham and Sarai's name to Sarah. From Philo's perspective, this soul's perfection is even at this stage in the narrative only partially realized through faith and hope and awaits the fullness of perfection in a noetic eternity.

From a formal point of view, the treatise is self-contained, but also serves as the culmination of an extended allegoresis of the migrations, covenants, and trials of Abraham and his family, which Philo has been elaborating through a sequential exegesis of Gen 12–17 in four preceding treatises: *De migratione Abrahami*, *Quis rerum divinarum heres sit*, *De congressu eruditionis gratia*, and *De fuga et inventione*. *De mutatione nominum* was likely followed by a sixth Abrahamic treatise, usually referred to as *De Deo*,[3] which survives only in an Armenian fragment and focuses on Abraham and Sarah's vision of the three men in Genesis 18.[4]

The question of the place of *De mutatione nominum* within the Philonic corpus involves understanding the structure of the Allegorical Commentary

---

3   Terian 2016 argues that this title is a misnomer, suggesting *De visione trium angelorum ad Abraham*.
4   So Terian 2016, 90, 91 n. 37. See also Royse 2009, 44; Geljon and Runia 2013, 2; Siegert 1988 and 1998. Eusebius, *Hist. eccl.* 2.18.1 lists the five extant Abrahamic allegorical treatises in the following order (cf. the accepted critical sequence): (4) *De fuga et inventione*, (3) *De congressu eruditionis gratia*, (2) *Quis rerum divinarum heres sit*; (5) *De mutatione nominum*, "in which he also says that he composed a first and second book *On the Covenants*"; (1) *De migratione Abrahami*. For the structure of the Allegorical Commentary as a whole, see Sterling 2018.

as well as the relationship between the various treatises in that series devoted to the Abrahamic cycle.[5] Philo himself never indicates explicitly the existence of sub-groups or cycles of treatises, but thinks of the Allegorical Commentary in the first place as a single work of sequential exegesis (at least until that project seemingly breaks down in *De somniis*),[6] a point demonstrated recently by Greg Sterling in two studies of Philo's secondary prefaces and the structure of the Allegorical Commentary (Sterling 2012, 2018). Despite this, scholars of the Allegorical Commentary have recognized the possibility of subdividing Philo's magnum opus according to a number of organizing principles. Here, after a (short) *Forschungsbericht* on the question, I offer a defense of my categorization of *De mutatione nominum* as part of an Abrahamic cycle within the Allegorical Commentary.

1.1 (A Short) History of Scholarship on the Division of the Allegorical Commentary

One of the earliest attempts to partition the Allegorical Commentary—that of Louis Massebieau and Émile Bréhier—periodized the series by way of its politics. Using the upheavals in Alexandria under the Roman governor Flaccus and their aftermath (as related by Philo himself in the *In Flaccum* and the *Legatio ad Gaium*) as chronological touchstones, Massebieau and Bréhier divide the Allegorical Commentary into four subgroupings, which do not depend on biblical characters or narrative cycle, but instead on Philo's political comments. According to this taxonomy (Massebieau and Bréhier 1906, 171), group one (*Legum allegoriae* to *Quod Deus sit immutabilis*) represents Philo's thought during the relative tranquility that Alexandrian Jews enjoyed under the first two Roman emperors, Augustus and Tiberius. Group two, *De agricultura* to *De confusione linguarum*, consists of those treatises written during the comparatively more turbulent and violent years in the run up to the Alexandrian riots of 38 CE under Flaccus, and their immediate aftermath. Group three, *De migratione Abrahami* to *De fuga et inventione* (Massebieau curiously fails to mention

---

5 In my presentation at the SBL Annual Meeting in 2016, I adopted the analogical term "cycle" from the study of epic poetry (Nagy 2005) to describe Philo's episodic focus. In studies of the archaic period, "cycle" (κύκλος) could refer to both Homeric and non-Homeric compositions (such as the "Cypria" and the "Little Iliad"), although Aristotle in the *Poetics* (1459a37–b16) restricts it to the latter. This epic metaphor was already being used by Cazeaux 1989.
6 In my view, the sequential principle was never enough to account for the thematic focus in many treatises of the Allegorical Commentary. The majority of Philonic scholars would agree that *De somniis* 1–2 still belongs to the Allegorical Commentary. For the alternative view, that in *De somniis* Philo begins a new series or adopts a radically different method, see the introductory "Presentación" in Martín 2016.

De mutatione nominum as part of the third or fourth series),[7] was prepared during "a time of profound peace" under Claudius. Group four, consisting solely of the two volumes of *De somniis*, reflects awareness of past Jewish persecutions. It is critical to note that these divisions are made without regard to narrative cycles, but depend instead on authorial tone as indicative of the broader political climate. The theory is intriguing, as it picks up on subtleties in tone and topic in Philo's treatises, but has proven methodologically difficult to sustain and few scholars have followed it uncritically.

The next major effort to partition the Allegorical Commentary was made by Maximilian Adler. Adler used exegetical rather than historical criteria to the subdivide the series. Recognizing that Philo's compositional method was not uniform, Adler (1929, 10–11) provided a five-fold typology of Philonic exegesis, ranging from concise, word for word exegesis of a single text (Type A) to more complex varieties of commentary (Types B–E). Using this fivefold typology, Adler makes the striking observation that whereas the exegesis in *Legum allegoriae* 1 belongs largely to type A, appearing somewhat "pedantic" (Adler 1929, 67), *Legum allegoriae* 2 through *Quod Deus sit immutabilis* are comprised primarily of the "mixed" types of exegesis, and contain considerably longer digressions on secondary texts. This suggested to Adler that *Legum allegoriae* 2 through *Quod Deus sit immutabilis* evince a methodological advance over *Legum allegoriae* 1. Adler nevertheless recognizes *Legum allegoriae* 1 through *Quod Deus sit immutabilis* as the first part of the Allegorical Commentary. The exegetical pace then slows dramatically with *De agricultura–De ebrietate*, with the first two books (*De agricultura* and *De plantatione*) focusing on just a single verse (Gen 9:20ab).[8] Using this exegetical distinction, Adler recognized here a "second group" of treatises,[9] and so forth. Adler thus made an advance on Massebieau and Bréhier, but he did not focus extensively on themes in the treatises (which determine extent of the scriptural lemmata) or the biblical cycles themselves.

A critical reorientation in the study of the Allegorical Commentary was made by Valentin Nikiprowetzky (1977). Nikiprowetzky argued that the unity of Philo's works was to be conceived primarily in terms of his method as an

---

[7] The failure of Massebieau and Bréhier to identify *Mut.* either with group three or group four is odd. Massebieau (1889, 28–29) clearly knows *De mutatione nominum* as the last treatise on Gen 17:1–22 prior to "une lacune très vaste," but it would seem that its shared characteristics with both groups precluded its being clearly assigned to either hypothetical period of composition.

[8] Royse 2009, 44, suggests that *Agr.* and *Plant.* focus on Gen 9:20ab; *Ebr.* on Gen 9:21; and *Sobr.* on Gen 9:24–27.

[9] Ibid.

exegete and that the basic sense units of the Allegorical Commentary could be understood in terms of rhetorical *quaestiones et solutiones*, using the example of Philo's QGE as an analogue.[10] On Nikiprowetzky's reading, the question of cycles or groupings of treatises becomes less central. Famously, Nikiprowetzky challenged the thematic unity of the individual Philonic treatise, suggesting that so central was Philo's exegetical principle of sequential exegesis, that each treatise possessed only a lose thematic coherence. True discursive unity resided only in the individual "chapter": the allegorical interpretation of a question or series of questions posed to a primary biblical lemma. While this analysis holds in some cases and helps significantly to illuminate the structure of various treatises, Philo does not consistently follow a *quaestio/solutio* model throughout the Allegorical Commentary as he does in the QGE.

An important counterpoint to Nikiprowetzky's analysis of the Allegorical Commentary was offered by Jacques Cazeaux. Turning away from the *quaestio et solutio* to narrative cycles, in his work *La trame et la chaîne* (1983) Cazeaux presented a literary, exegetical, and structuralist study of the five extant Abrahamic treatises from the Allegorical Commentary (*De migratione Abrahami–De mutatione nominum*). In diametrical opposition to Nikiprowetzky, Cazeaux argued for "the continuity of Philo's commentary," even across several treatises (1983, 3). As a test case, he studied "five treatises of Philo, which take for their explicit object the "movement" ("geste") of Abraham" (Ibid.). In focusing on Abraham's journey, Cazeaux chose the biblical character and the underlying allegorical narrative as his analytical criteria, rather than Philo's politics, his type of exegesis, or the *quaestio et solutio*. Six years later, Cazeaux published a second study of the Allegorical Commentary, extending his conclusions to the Noahic cycle (Cazeaux 1989). Here again, he aimed to demonstrate the continuity of *Gig.-Deus* through *De sobrietate*.

Cazeaux's monographs, however controversial,[11] took an important step toward refocusing attention on narrative cycles within the Allegorical Commentary. His attention to Abraham's movement, however, reveals that his interest is more on the underlying allegory than on the biblical text itself. One model of balancing these two positions—though with a decided preference for the method of Nikiprowetzky—is evinced in the 2013 and 2019 PACS commentaries by Geljon and Runia. In introducing *De agricultura*, Geljon and Runia

---

10 For the relationship between the QGE and the Allegorical Commentary, see Sterling 1991 and Terian 1991.
11 Cazeaux's work has been criticized on a number of fronts, not least for its ignoring of non-francophone scholarship. See Runia 1984, 1987; Dillon 1992.

suggest (along with Cazeaux 1989) that "*Agr.* belongs to the group of six treatises [*Gig.–Deus–Sobr.*] … that deal with the story of Noah as told in Gen 6:13 to 9:20." Against Massebieau and Adler, Geljon and Runia argue that *Gig.-Deus*—despite the absence of anti-Roman polemics and its "middle" exegetical pattern that mirrors *Legum allegoriae* 2 through *De posteritate Caini*—belongs with the *Agr.–Sobr.* pentad of treatises, in a seven-treatise Noahic "group." While thus attending to the Noahic cycle, their commentaries on *De agricultura* and *De plantatione* nevertheless take the *quaestio* and Philo's other explicit statements as the most important formal markers in each treatise. I have charted a slightly different middle-ground in assessing the structure of the Allegorical Commentary (2023d [2017]), placing greater emphasis on thematic development within cycles and positing the idea of "hinge-treatises." See also Sterling (2018b), who although maintaining that Philo conceived of the Allegorical Commentary as a single work, suggests that it is nonetheless arranged biographically, with an introduction and conclusion.

1.2 De mutatione nominum *within the Allegorical Commentary and the Abrahamic Cycle*

The foregoing review of scholarship, while only partial,[12] illustrates the central questions to be addressed when positioning *De mutatione nominum* within the Allegorical Commentary and the narrower "Abrahamic cycle." The following remarks represent my own approach to the issues.

First, following the insights of Sterling (2012 and 2018), it seems best not to posit any hard and fast breaks between the various groups or subsections of the series, but to think rather in terms of organic development within different clusters or cycles. As a rule, Philo begins each cycle using a relatively basic exegetical pattern, but then develops new techniques, scope, and density as the cycle ensues. For example: in the Adamic cycle, Philo begins by focusing on the primary biblical lemma in *Legum allegoriae* 1; in *Legum allegoriae* 2 and 3, he offers more amplifications by way of secondary and tertiary lemmata. *Legum allegoriae* 1–3 (+4), nonetheless, remain a single multi-volume treatise and the outset of the Adamic cycle. Similarly, *Gig.-Deus* looks exegetically more like the treatises which precede it than those which follow it; this need not signify that it does not belong to a Noahic cycle. Just as, in the Adamic cycle, Philo develops more complex exegetical patterns in the later treatises, so in the Noahic

---

12 Additional studies omitted in this survey include Morris 1973; Goulet 1987; Thorne 1989; Gershowitz and Kovelman 2002.

cycle, Philo begins with a more typical commentary format, but becomes more adventuresome and thematically focused in the second and third treatises.

This notion of organic or soft boundaries between sections of the Allegorical Commentary addresses one of the arguments against the analysis of this series into smaller narrative clusters: that Philo himself does not explicitly name such an organizational schema (as he will in the Exposition, which possesses clear subdivisions). Despite this formal silence, several additional kinds of indirect evidence suggest Philo is thinking in terms of patriarchal cycles in the Allegorical Commentary.

The first, and to my mind the strongest, argument for positing Philo's own division of his scriptural allegories into patriarchal cycles arises from analogy with contemporary Platonism. It has long been observed that Philo's charting the itinerary of the soul in the Allegorical Commentary mirrors similar Platonist allegories of Homeric heroes, particularly Odysseus (for Philo's knowledge of Homer and his exegetes, see Niehoff 2011, 2012; Roskam 2017). The most famous example of such an allegoresis occurs in the Neo-Platonist Porphyry's *De antro nympharum*—a treatise that has sometimes been heralded as the first work of literary criticism. Both Thomas Tobin, SJ, and Katell Berthelot point out that such an allegoresis of Odysseus as a symbol of the soul striving to depart the body and return to the ideal realm is present in Philo's later contemporary, Plutarch of Chaeronea.[13]

So similar are the Platonist and Philonic allegories of the soul that most presume that Philo has borrowed the Platonizing approach to Odysseus and applied it to the biblical patriarchs. The question follows: which of the patriarchs first prompted Philo to see an Odyssean analogy? In her study of Philo and Porphyry, Berthelot suggests that Moses serves as the primary analogy to Odysseus in Philo's thought.[14] In particular, Moses's exodus from Egypt mirrors Odysseus's exodus from the "wet" world of the sense-perceptible to the "dry" heart of Ithaca, or the ideal realm. While this makes good sense, there is another possibility. I would propose that Abraham provides just as good—if not a better—analogue to Odysseus as Moses. Not only does Abraham have an

---

13 Plutarch, *Quaest. conviv.* 9 (745d–f); Tobin 1983, 151; Berthelot 2012, 162–163. Berthelot traces this tradition further back to Plato in *Crat.* 403c–d.
14 Berthelot 2012, 169–171, esp. 171: "It is easier to read the story of the Exodus than the stories of the migrations of Abraham and Jacob, for instance, through the lens of the journey of the soul."

exodus in miniature[15]—the odyssey that leads him from Ur to Haran to Canaan, allegorically signifying the departure from the sense-perceptible realm. In addition, as Berthelot notes, the same allegoresis that the Platonists applied to Penelope and her maidservants—interpreted as symbols of wisdom and the preliminary fields of study—is applied by Philo to Abraham's wife and her maidservant, Sarah and Hagar.[16] This suggests that Abraham, rather than Moses, may first have struck an Odyssean chord in Philo's mind. The pattern might then be extended, *mutatis mutandis*, to Jacob, Moses, and others.[17] Of course, it may be overly exacting to look for a singular point of analogy. Odysseus's enigmatic epithet, "of many turnings" (πολύτροπος),[18] provides a warrant for the discovery of his likeness in the various characters, who populate the Pentateuch. Philo encourages his students to discover multiple psychic "manners" (τρόποι) in various scriptural actors, as well as multiple τρόποι represented beneath a single psychic symbol (like Moses).

A second argument supporting Philo's recognition of an Abrahamic cycle arises from his clusters of secondary lemmata. As scholars since Adler have recognized, Philo has a penchant for stringing together groups of secondary biblical texts and developing a composite allegoresis. Sometimes these groups are a miscellany, drawn from various books and authors; at other times, Philo concatenates texts related to a single figure or narrative. Looking to the beginning of the Allegorical Commentary, where one might expect to find some clues to its overall plan and scope, one finds constellations or catenae composed from sequentially selected Abrahamic texts.[19]

Third, it is not only the Abraham cycle which appears in these early clusters, but also the rhetorical technique and theological themes of *De muta-*

---

15 In addition to the migration out of Ur, contemporary biblical scholars have long recognized echoes of the Exodus in Abraham's sojourn in Egypt in Gen 12:10–20; see Levenson 1993, 85–86.
16 Berthelot 2012, 159–160. This allegory is attributed in Ps.-Plutarch (*Lib. ed.* 7d) to Bion of Borysthenes (3rd century BCE). Cf. Philo, *Cher.* 3; *Congr.* 71–88.
17 I omit here the thorny question of whether Philo inherited this analogy between Odysseus and Abraham from earlier Jewish allegorists, or whether this is his own original contribution. Whatever the origin of this tradition, it stands at the center of Philo's great allegorical project. The very fact that some Alexandrian Jew at some point had to make such an analogy between Abraham and Odysseus (in a kind of anticipation of Auerbach) suggests that at a deep-structural level—and more likely, at the level of Philo's own compositional intentionality—the allegories of the Pentateuch were divided in terms of patriarchal groups or cycles.
18 Homer, *Od.* 1.1.
19 See, e.g., Philo, *Leg.* 3.217–219; *Leg.* 3.39–43 (Gen 15:5; 24:7, 63); *Leg.* 3.83–87 (Gen 12:1; 17:17, 19); *Leg.* 3:244–245; *Cher.* 3–10.

tione nominum. This supports the hypothesis that Philo already had his Abrahamic end in sight when he began to explicate Genesis. In particular, if one traces Philo's use of the verb "to have one's name changed" (μετονομάζεσθαι) in the Allegorical Commentary,[20] one finds only six uses of it prior to the Abrahamic treatises. Five of these (*Leg.* 3.244; *Cher.* 4, 7) appear in clusters of Abrahamic secondary and tertiary lemmata mentioned above. In *Cher.* 4, the verb is applied to both Abram and Sarai simultaneously—a fact suggesting that Philo had already read Gen 17:5 and Gen 17:15 together as topically related (cf. *QG* 3.43 and *QG* 3.53, which interpret them separately). The verb "to change one's name" (μετονομάζεσθαι), moreover, occurs near the beginning of three "cycles" of the series: the cycle on Adam and Creation (*Leg.* 3), the cycle on Noah (*Gig.* 62–63); and the cycle on Abraham (*Migr.* 201). Philo thus signals the phenomenon of name change as a critical leitmotif throughout his the Allegorical Commentary, while planning to demonstrate its significance more fully when he reaches the exposition of Gen 17.

Charting earlier intimations of an Abrahamic cycle allows one to organize the extant (and probably missing)[21] treatises of the Allegorical Commentary into a series of four cycles, often with a hinge treatise spanning the gaps in the primary lemmata. This pattern breaks down partially in *De somniis*, which looks both to the theme of dreams as well as several patriarchal figures, but is still recognizable:

TABLE 1   Narrative cycles of the allegorical commentary

Nr	Title	Cycle	1° Lemma
1a	[*Legum allegoriae* 1a] (missing?)[22]	Adam	[Gen 1:1–31]
1b	*Legum allegoriae* 1b (extant *Leg.* 1)	Adam	Gen 2:1–17
2	*Legum allegoriae* 2	Adam	Gen 2:18–3:1a
3	*Legum allegoriae* 3	Adam	Gen 3:8b–19
4	[*Legum allegoriae* 4]	Adam	[Gen 3:20–23]

---

20   *Leg.* 3.15 (Jacob); *Leg.* 3.244 (Abram); *Cher.* 4 (Abram & Sarai), 7 (Abram); *Gig.* 62–63 (Abram); *Migr.* 201 (Jacob). The verb is used eight times in *Mut.* (65, 76, 77, 81, 83, 87, 88, 121), all within the central second part of the treatise, *Mut.* 60–129.

21   In the table, I give only the most commonly accepted missing treatises, and do not presume that every verse had a commentary attached to it. For a more fulsome series of speculations, see Royse 2009.

22   Tobin (2000, 40–41) suggests a *lacuna* here. Royse (2000, 2; 2009, 40) would combine *Leg.* 1–2 into a single first treatise, and place a missing treatise between the extant *Leg.* 2 and *Leg.* 3, while also positing a missing *Leg.* 4. Against Tobin, he thinks *Legum allegoriae* began

TABLE 1   Narrative cycles of the allegorical commentary (*cont.*)

Nr	Title	Cycle	1° Lemma
5	*De cherubim*	Hinge	Gen 3:24, 4:1
6	*De sacrificiis Abelis et Caini*	Cain	Gen 4:2–4
7	*Quod deterius potiori insidiari soleat*	Cain	Gen 4:8–15
8	*De posteritate Caini*	Cain	Gen 4:16–25
9	*De gigantibus*[23]	Hinge	Gen 6:1–4
10	*Quod Deus sit immutabilis*	Hinge	Gen 6:4–12
11	[*De testamentis* 1] (missing)	Noah	[Gen 6:13–22?][24]
12	[*De testamentis* 2] (missing)	Noah	[Gen 9:8–17?]
13	*De agricultura*	Noah	Gen 9:20a[25]
14	*De plantatione*	Noah	Gen 9:20b
15	*De ebrietate* 1	Noah	Gen 9:21

with the exposition of Gen 2:1. Sterling (2012) supports Royse's view of *Leg.* 4, which would have treated up to Gen 3:20–23. In the table, I have preferred to keep things simple, indicating that at least two treatises seem to be missing and that there are four books in the *Legum allegoriae*.

23   Since the commentary of Winston and Dillon (1983), most scholars hold that *Gig.* and *Deus* originally formed a single treatise.

24   Royse (2009, 41) gives Gen 6:13–9:19 as the hypothetical verse range for both treatises. I do not think that this entire range would have been covered. There are, within this range, two verses or pericopes in which the word διαθήκη is mentioned: Gen 6:18 and Gen 9:8–17. Given the length of the primary lemma in *Gig.*-*Deus* (12 verses), and the fact that Augustine (*Faust.* 12.39) seems to know an exegesis from Philo, in which he allegorically interprets the "door" of Gen 6:16 (see QG 2.6; Eusebius, *Hist. eccl.* 2.18.3, knows a two-volume work *De testamentis* [περὶ διαθηκῶν], but does not appear to possess a copy, or else why would he attribute the existence of the treatise to Philo's own testimony in *Mut.*?) as well as some of the ark's other measurements, I would propose *exempli gratia* a Hypothetical Arrangement 1: that *Test.* 1 covered God's instructions to Noah in Gen 6:13–22 (10 verses), while *Test.* 2 focused on God's covenant with Noah after the flood in Gen 9:8–17 (10 verses). Alternatively (Hypothetical Arrangement 2), Philo might have treated *both* discussions of the Noahide covenant (Gen 6:13–22; 9:8–17) in *Test.* 1, and then turned to the covenants with Abraham, Isaac, and Jacob in *Test.* 2. Based on the catalogue of name changes in *Mut.* 60–129, there is no reason to speculate that Philo looked to covenants beyond the Pentateuch.

25   The Noahic cycle probably consisted originally a quintet of scrolls comprising a single treatise; see Sterling 2012; 2018; Geljon and Runia 2013, 3. Cf. Massebieau and Bréhier (1906), esp. 171, 177), who partition *Agr.*–*Conf.* as a group. Adler (1929, 49) interprets *Agr.* and *Plant.* as a single book, and further conjectures (1929, 59) that *Plant.* 139–177 constitutes the lost first book of *De ebrietate*—which is doubtful. This would result in a division of the Noahic group into four sub-clusters: (1) *Gig.*-*Deus*; (2) [*Test.* 1–2]; (3) *Agr.*–*Plant.*; (4) *Ebr.*

TABLE 1   Narrative cycles of the allegorical commentary (cont.)

Nr	Title	Cycle	1º Lemma
16	[*De ebrietate* 2] (missing)	Noah	[Gen 9:22–23?][26]
17	*De sobrietate*	Noah	Gen 9:24–27[27]
18	*De confusione linguarum*	Hinge	Gen 11:1–9
19	*De migratione Abrahami*	Abraham	Gen 12:1–6
20	*Quis rerum divinarum heres sit*	Abraham	Gen 15:2–18
21	*De fuga et inventione*	Abraham	Gen 16:6–14
22	*De mutatione nominum*	Abraham	Gen 17:1–5+15; 16–22
23	*De Deo* (fragmentary)	Abraham	Gen 18:2 [18:1–8?][28]
24	[*De somniis* 1a] (missing)	Hinge—Abimelech?	[Gen 20:3–8?
		Isaac, dream 1?	Gen 26:1–5?
		Isaac, dream 2?	Gen 26:24–25?][29]
25	*De somniis* 1b (extant *Somn.* 1)	Jacob	Gen 28:12–15; Gen 31:11–13
26	*De somniis* 2	Joseph	Gen 37:7, 9; Gen 40:9–11, 16–17; Gen 41:11–17, 22–24

[1 and 2]   1 and 2–*Sobr*. Adler (1929, 67) ultimately divides Philo's early works into two groups on the basis of their broad exegetical patterns: (1) *Leg.–Gig.*; (2) *Agr.–Sobr*. This misses the "hinge" function of *Gig.-Deus.*

[26]   Royse 2009, 42.

[27]   Royse (Ibid.) notes that "*De sobrietate* is exceptionally short; it is likely that it and *De confusione linguarum* originally formed one book, and that Philo simply skipped treatment of Gen 10." This judgment overlooks the secondary preface in *Sobr.* 1, which considers it a continuation of a previous treatise on Noah's drunkenness and ensuing nakedness. While Royse's suggestion is not impossible, I prefer to treat *Sobr.* as more closely linked with *Ebr.* (Eusebius, *Hist. eccl.* 2.18.2, knows *Sobr.* as a separate treatise and lists it between *Ebr.* 1–2 and *Conf.*; he does not, however, treat it clearly as "of a piece" with either treatise.)

[28]   Some longer pericope was treated, but we have little clue how much. Given Philo's treatment of Sarah's laughter (Gen 18:12) in *Mut.* 166–167, it seems not unreasonable to hypothesize, *exempli gratia*, a lemmatic range from Gen 18:1–8 before Sarah is introduced.

[29]   Royse (2009, 45), following Massebieau, suggests that the first (Abimelech) and third (Isaac, dream two) of these pericopes was treated, as well as the dream of Laban in Gen 31:24. Torallas Tovar (2002 [1995], 353–355) rejects the dream of Abimelech, and suggests only the first dream of Isaac at Gen 26:2–5 fits the required dream-category delineated by Philo. In a later article (2003, 44), Torallas Tovar argues that the missing treatise dealt with dreams in "Genesis 26," beginning with part of Gen 26:1 and giving no *terminus*—thus potentially leaving room for the inclusion of Isaac's second dream as well.

While the connection between *De mutatione nominum* and the preceding Abrahamic treatises is transparent enough, a few final words need to be said about its relationship to the treatises in the Allegorical Commentary that follow, particularly *De Deo* and *De somniis*. Unfortunately, not much is known about *De Deo* (given its fragmentary nature) nor about the full extent of the Abrahamic Cycle. The remaining verses of Gen 17, as well as Gen 18:1 through Gen 28:9 were treated by Philo in the QGE. Did Philo's sequential allegory of Abraham extend to Gen 25:8 (cf. QG 4.153) and the death of the patriarch? While this seems possible, we do not have sufficient evidence to answer in the affirmative or the negative. It is worth recalling that the Noahic cycle has large gaps and may in fact have been left unfinished by Philo.

The relationship between *De mutatione nominum* and *De somniis* also remains unclear. On the one hand, the presence of *De Deo* indicates that whatever features it shares with the latter cycle on dreams, it does not function as a "hinge treatise" proper, in the manner of *De cherubim*, *Gig.-Deus*, and *De confusione linguarum*. It is tempting to wonder, in light of Royse's (2009, 45) suggestion that the lost *De somniis* 1a contained the dreams of Abimelech and Isaac (but not, I think, Laban),[30] whether in fact this treatise had a hinge function, transitioning from the Abraham cycle to the Dreams cycle.

Limiting ourselves to the evidence at hand, *De mutatione nominum* does have certain noteworthy affinities with *De somniis*. The first and most obvious similarity is that the central section of *De mutatione nominum* (as the whole of *De somniis*) does not follow a single primary lemma, but moves thematically between related pericopes. Philo also skips over a full nine verses of the primary lemma in *De mutatione nominum*. His stated rationale for his omission of Gen 17:6–17:14 indicates that he has already treated this material in the lost *De testamentis* (*On Covenants*); however, Philo also suggests in this same critical passage that returning to this content would distract from the thematic unity of the present treatise—a thing which Philo is at pains to avoid (ἅμα μὴ βουλόμενος ἀπαρτᾶν τὸ συμφυὲς τῆς πραγματείας, "neither do I wish to disturb the natural unity of the subject matter" [§ 53]). Is Philo's range of exegetical patterns evolving here in §§ 60–129 (as it also appears to do in *Legum allegoriae* 2 and in *De agricultura*) and paving the way for *De somniis*? Goulet thought so, noting that Philo had "abandoned his project of a running commentary on the Pentateuch" (1987, 330). While this might be the case, one should not forget that Philo also appears to follow a more thematic model earlier in the series in the missing two books *De testamentis*. We would need to

---

30 For an *exempli gratia* reconstruction of the lost *Somn.* 1a, see Torallas Tovar 2003; 2014.

know more about this double treatise from the Noahic cycle before drawing any conclusions about the character of *De mutatione nominum* and *De somniis*.

2 The Genre, *Sitz im Leben*, and Rhetorical Structure of the Treatise

> Philon pratique en fait l'art de composer et même, dans la perspective réelle de sa pensée qui est celle des *quaestiones et solutiones*, il le pratique d'une façon parfaitement cohérente et rigoureuse, avec une logique sans faille. C'est un auteur clair.
>
> VALENTIN NIKIPROWETZKY

> La continuité du discours philonien reste souvent inaperçue.
>
> JACQUES CAZEAUX

2.1 *Genre and* Sitz im Leben

The questions of the exegetical structure of *De mutatione nominum* and its literary unity are intertwined with the question of its genre. It is generally agreed, among Philonists, that the treatises in the Allegorical Commentary belong to the genus ὑπόμνημα—"memorandum" or "commentary"—a genre which offers sequential comments on a text on a separate medium from the text being commented upon (distinguishing a commentary from the *scholium*). Philo's treatises in this series proceed by the alternation of lemmatic citation and allegorical interpretation. This pattern is similar to that followed in the earlier QGE—albeit there, Philo begins with the literal interpretation, ignores the thematic principle that governs the treatises of the Allegorical Commentary, and does not adduce and interpret as many secondary (and tertiary) lemmata. The Exposition of the Law—though still a commentary in many portions, eschews for the most part the explicit citation of scriptural lemmata.

While the question of genre might thus seem to be an open and shut case, some further qualifications are in order. Several peculiarities in these treatises differentiate them from the genre of commentary, plain and simple, as it is witnessed in the nearly contemporaneous *Anonymous Theaetetus Commentary*, written perhaps by a member of the school or wider circle of Eudorus in Alexandria (Cover 2015, 134–135), as well as in the QGE. First, in the Allegorical Commentary, Philo is not content only to interpret one primary lemma after another in sequence, as though his sole intention is to explain the text at hand. In addition, he weaves in secondary lemmata drawn from the Pentateuch (or less frequently, from the prophets, the writings, and classical literature). These secondary texts often lead to independent exegeses of their own—and, not infrequently, to the adduction of *tertiary* lemmata, or texts which pertain to the exegetical, philosophical, and theological questions of the secondary discussion, and rather less directly relate to the primary text. Secondary discussions in Philo's allegorical treatises often become something like Russian Matryoshka dolls, with a representation of Jacob or the high priest nested inside a representation of Abraham.

To push this analogy a little further: what is curious about Philo's Alexandrian nested dolls is that in many cases, the inner ones, instead of getting smaller, seem to grow bigger—sometimes taking over the chapter or the treatise, so that the link to the primary biblical lemma from Genesis is all but lost. In Philo's "middle treatises" (Runia 1984, 239), among which *De mutatione nominum* can be numbered, one witnesses an interchange between focus on the primary allegoresis surrounding Abraham's perfection at the birth of Isaac and secondary and tertiary expansions.

There are several explanations for such "labyrinthine complexity in the Allegorical Commentary" (Geljon and Runia 2013, 7). In addition to Philo's "strongly associative mind" (Runia 1987, 130)—a characteristic which is often viewed more as a flaw than a strength by Philo's detractors—one can mention three additional factors that may have inspired Philo to build such an intricate and multi-tiered palace of side-chapels. The first is that despite writing "commentaries" (ὑπομνήματα) in a Platonizing tradition for a private school context, Philo was influenced by the rhetoric and forms of the Alexandrian Jewish "prayer houses" (προσευχαί), including both synagogue instruction and preaching. The great Göttingen *Alttestamentler*, Johann David Michaelis, is reported to have said that "the academic lecture and the homily ("der academische und der Canzelvortrag") are so different that, if done well, they will in time only corrupt one another" (Michaelis 1768–1776, 1.130; trans. Legaspi 2010, 27) and this seems to have been true for Philo's allegorical treatises as well.

In addition to being influenced by the forms and themes of the prayer houses in his own compositional habitus, Philo also took it upon himself to record and anthologize (often anonymously) the traditions of his Jewish peers and predecessors, on whose shoulders he stood when composing his allegories of the Pentateuch. The monograph of Richard Goulet (1987), the work of the Philo Institute, and Tobin's Harvard dissertation, *The Creation of Man* (1983), stand out as three signal contributions to the unfinished task of the source criticism of the Philonic corpus—a project which has fallen out of vogue less because of its unimportance than because of its methodological challenges.

A third factor, unrelated to Philo's Jewish matrix, that affected the shape of his literary output arose from the milieu of the Second Sophistic, the major currents of which were just beginning during the principates of Gaius and Claudius. This revival of Greek rhetoric—of which Philo's Atticism is a premonition, if not a result—led to an increasing fusion of genres (Adams 2020). One feels this especially in the slightly later treatises of the priest and Platonist, Plutarch, who like Philo used a variety of different genres (including his famous parallel biographies and ethical monographs) to explore pressing issues, infusing each with his own hallmark philosophical concerns, and developing many genres in new and creative ways (Brenk 2017). A similar spirit is also at play in Philo's transformation of the genre of philosophical commentary. These works present at once an extended running commentary on the Pentateuch, as well as distinct thematic treatises (cf. *Mut.* 53) on particular subjects. The writings are thus a fusion of the philosophical "commentary" (ὑπόμνημα) and the thematic "treatise" (σύγγραμμα). Geljon and Runia's (2013, 9) remarks in their introduction to the genre of *De agricultura* can again be applied, *mutatis mutandis*, to *De mutatione nominum*: "There are no good parallels in extant Greek literature for the kind of treatise (*Mut.*) represents." A later Platonist work like Porphyry's *De antro nympharum*, which also presents an eschatological vision of the soul, of John Chrysostom's *De mutatione nominum*, may approach it, even as these also both differ in numerous ways. "Philo may well represent a unique achievement in the long history of allegorical interpretation" (Ibid.).

2.2 Rhetorical Structure

Philo's pioneering development of a *sui speciei* type of commentary-monograph leaves the critic with more questions than answers. It opens afresh the perennial problem of the unity of Philo's treatises, as they oscillate between episodic exegesis and unified thematic exploration. Advocates of placing heavier weight on either end of this spectrum can be found in two French Philonists of the last generation: Nikiprowetzky and Cazeaux, who supply the twin epigraphs of the present section. This commentary has been influenced by both of their approaches. Their views, discussed in section one of the introduction and expressed pithily in the two citations, as thesis and antithesis, can be briefly recapitulated as follows: Nikiprowetzky championed the position that Philo's treatises are arranged fundamentally as a series of implicit or explicit questions and answers posed of particular biblical lemmata. The backbone of the Allegorical Commentary is thus something like (but not identical to) the series of *quaestiones et solutiones* found in Philo's first commentary series on the Pentateuch bearing that same title. Each *quaestio* and its *solutio*—a basic rhetorical unit which Nikiprowetzky calls "chapters"—possesses a thematic unity. Beyond that, Philo's allegorical treatises can make no further claim to topical coherence.

An alternative to Nikiprowetzky's way of reading Philo is articulated in several studies by Cazeaux.[31] Cazeaux (1983) reads Philo as a philosophically eclectic thinker, and takes as his critical starting point "the total coherence of the literary composition and structure of (Philo's) treatises" (Runia 1984, 211). Like Nikiprowetzky, Cazeaux agrees that the unity of Philo's thought lies in the chapter rather than the treatise (Runia 1984, 213)—although the two scholars disagree as to what exactly comprises a chapter. For Cazeaux, moreover, what appear like contradictions in Philo's writings are winks and nods—proddings toward a *lectio divina* (1989, 3–5), stumbling blocks to entice the reader to look beyond appearances to the architectonic deep structural unity that governs each of Philo's chapters and unites them at a conceptual and mythic level. Appealing to the metaphors of weaving and tapestry—"the weft and the warp"—Cazeaux offers a structuralist analysis of Philo's exegesis, which interprets the Alexandrian's writings more as myth than philosophy. Whereas Nikiprowetzky called attention to Philo's words, understanding him to speak the language of philosophy and answering the challenge of contradictions in Philo's thought by recontextualizing him as an exegete, Cazeaux put greater emphasis on the pregnant silences and unspoken allegorical connections that ripple just below the surface of Philo's writings, taking him to speak the idiolect of Scripture.

In analyzing the structure of this treatise, I begin with the surface-level agreement between Nikiprowetzky and Cazeaux that the fundamental unit of *De mutatione nominum* is the chapter. In section three below, I lay out this exegetical structure and provide a table illustrating how my analysis differs from or agrees with previous commentators on the treatise. I have used the parallel chapters in the *QGE*, which Philo probably composed first, as a heuristic guide.[32]

---

[31] The outline of Cazeaux's method, derived from his most important work, *La trame et la chaîne* (1983), is taken from Runia (1984, 211–226). Both Nikiprowetzky's and Cazeaux's works are treated in this essay.

[32] Cazeaux argued vigorously against the value of the *QGE* for illuminating the structure of the treatises of the Allegorical Commentary (1989, 3, 270–275). See esp. his note of caution at 3: "It would be improper ('abusif') to pass without method from one series to another, from *Quaestiones* to the treaties (of the Allegorical Commentary). The former can supply a 'grammar,' but the latter are matters of 'style' and creation." With this one can more or less agree. However, Cazeaux's conclusion at the end of his study—that "the treatises (of the Allegorical Commentary) and their corresponding *Quaestiones* evolved separately" (1989, 271)—is suspect. If the *QGE* can be seen as "*membra disjecta* of the later composition" (ibid.), they are still related in some organic way—illuminating Philo's divisions of pericopes and the traditional materials with which he worked.

While privileging Philo's exegetical structure and taking the chapter as an analytical starting point, the commentator must still try and understand the thematic flow of *De mutatione nominum* by addressing two additional questions: (1) does the treatise have any other major partitions, beyond the chapter structure? and (2) do chapters other than the fifth one (from which the treatise derives its name) bear any direct relationship to the commentary's thematic center? The first question is posed from the horizon of Nikiprowetzky's method; the second, from the angle of Cazeaux's. Below, I will take up these two questions sequentially, before turning to a third way of analyzing the treatise from a rhetorical angle.

2.3 The Partitions of the Treatise

Scholars have long been convinced of the thematic unity *De mutatione nominum*, despite certain appearances to the contrary. Roger Arnaldez, for example, opens his PAPM edition (1964) with the following description:

> Despite an apparent disorder—common, incidentally, to almost all of Philo's treatises—*De mutatione nominum* is in truth perfectly well-centered and all of its contents, including those which present as digressions, relate to a central idea …. The change of name is the symbol of a radical change of life for the soul, which passes from the world of becoming to the world of eternity, from physical nature to the Perfect Nature, from existence among the common herd to the state of election—in a word, from the simple, natural reality, which is the human condition to the spiritual reality, which is the human being after the Image, God's human being.

Of course, thematic focus is not literary unity; further questions abound. From the formal perspective, one might begin by asking whether the treatise divides into two or three basic units. Privileging either the exegetical structure (the position of Nikiprowetzky) or thematic coherence (that of Cazeaux), one might divide the treatise fundamentally into two parts: comments on Gen 17:1–5 + 15 (§§ 1–129) and Gen 17:16–22 (§§ 130–270). Arnaldez (1964, 27–30) does just this, calling part one (§§ 1–129) "On the Change of Names" and part two (§§ 130–270) "The Birth of Isaac." This division has the advantage of drawing on Philo's own titles for units of the text at § 130.

Attending to the title—which Arnaldez considers "the key to the work" (1964, 24)—it remains to be seen whether the phrase "the change of names" (ἡ τῶν ὀνομάτων ἀλλαγή) in § 130 refers to the entirety of chapters one through five, or simply to the fifth chapter. In my opinion, Philo's use of this title refers only to the work's fifth and longest chapter (§§ 60–129). Chapter five is set apart not only by its theme, but also by Philo's use of different principles of invention and exegesis (e.g., skipping from Gen 17:5 to Gen 17:15) than he uses in the more formulaic sections that frame it on both sides. These rhetorical cues suggest a division of the treatise into three parts: Part one (§§ 1–59); part two (§§ 60–129); and part three (§§ 130–270). Philo uses a clear transitional phrase at § 130. The transition at § 60 is more fluid and depends on the citation of a new primary lemma. (For more on the lemmatic divisions of the treatise, see section four of the introduction below.) The tripartition is supported by the independent judgment of Kraus Reggiani (1994).

2.4   Thematic and Figural Movements of the Treatise

Accepting this tripartite division of *De mutatione nominum*, the question arises whether the title of the treatise is fully explained by the fifth eponymous chapter, or whether it indicates a more pervasive theme throughout the work. Nikiprowetzky might wish the critic to maintain a prudential silence on this point. Cazeaux, to the contrary, given his structuralist inclinations and theory that cycles and itineraries of biblical characters formed symbolic deep structures, saw further unities at play in the unfolding of a psychic drama. Arnaldez (1964, 11, 19), similarly, understood the treatise as mystical work focused on "ontological Virtue" and her ability to "transfigure the being of the soul."

My own position inclines toward the middle of these two poles. Looking at the treatise as a whole, one sees a persistent focus (at least in the first two parts) on the problem of names and language, and their significance for the allegorical project. This linguistic focus provides the "technique" of the treatise and one of its unifying thematics. In part one, Philo meditates on the names of God and the ultimate ineffability of "The One Who Is" (τὸ ὄν). As Dillon points out (1996 [1977], 155), Philo is the first thinker in the history of Platonism to claim that God is "unnamable, unutterable, and incomprehensible under any form." Runia observes that "there is, strictly speaking, no exegetical constraint on Philo (in the primary lemma) to introduce the theme of the naming of God" (1988, 76). He goes on to suggest that Philo's development of a theory of divine/Mosaic *catachresis* or "misuse of language" in the giving of divine names is "the single most interesting part" of the section and, one could argue, of the entire treatise (Ibid.). It would thus seem that Philo's discussion of divine names in part one (§§ 1–59) of *De mutatione nominum* is meant as an intentional complement to the discussion of human name change in part two.

The question of the thematic coherence of the first two parts of the treatise with the third (§§ 130–270), while less easily resolved, can still be answered in the affirmative. Given that Philo leaps ahead in the primary lemma, one might wonder whether parts one and two form a thematic and exegetical unit, while the chapters in part three set out in a different direction. Philo's account of his omission of Gen 17:6–14, however, militates against this position. He tells the reader that he has forgone commenting on these, so as not to replicate what he had already said in *De testamentis*, and additionally, because he does not wish to harm the "natural unity of the subject matter of the treatise (τὸ συμφυὲς τῆς πραγματείας)" (§ 53). Philo thus reads the text of Moses as possessing a thematic unity, which he attempts to unfold across all three parts of the present treatise.

This unity resides in part in the continuation of allegorical narrative of the Abraham soul's perfection. Key figures from parts one and two, including Moses (§ 134), Sarah (§§ 137, 255), Isaac (§§ 137, 261), Abraham (§§ 166, 270), and Israel (§ 189), continue their symbolic development; and several new etymological figures, including Hannah (§ 143), Arphaxat (§ 189), Hamor and Shechem (§ 193), Dinah (§ 194), Simeon and Levi (§ 200), Ishmael (§ 202), Reuben (§ 210), Leah (§§ 132, 254), and Hagar (§ 255) are introduced.

In addition, although there are no name changes proper mentioned in part three, Philo nevertheless attends to the subject of name change in two indirect ways. First, he highlights the allegorical significance of a biblical figure whose name does not change: Isaac. (The stability of Isaac's name as "God-given" is already thematized in chapter five [§ 88].) Philo then turns to the multiple significances of the name Ishmael (§ 202), and hence to the mutability of the psychic types that Ishmael may represent. In terms of technique, Philo's treatment of the name "Ishmael" is similar to that of the name "Moses" in part two (§§ 125–129; see § 207). His focus on the names of Abraham's two sons in chapters nine through eleven gives the treatise structural balance: Philo's central chapter on Abraham's name change (part two) is flanked by a discussion of God, who in his transcendence has no name (part one); and by a discussion of Ishmael and Isaac, the two sons of Abraham, whose names signify stable and unstable gifts of God (part three).

2.5 *Aporiae et Quaestiones*

One further structural feature of *De mutatione nominum* merits comment: Philo's use of exegetical *aporiae* or questions. Runia (1988, 74) charts seven of these posed of the primary biblical lemma (Gen 17), which fall, interestingly, in parts one and three, but not in part two.

Part one
Aporia 1   §§ 1–2
Aporia 2   §§ 3–6

Aporia 3   §§ 7–17
Aporia 4   §§ 18–26
Aporia 5   §§ 27–33

Part three
Aporia 6   §§ 175–187
Aporia 7   §§ 218–232

"We have thus seven *aporiae*, a suitably Philonic number, but only a limited selection of all the questions and themes raised in this single treatise" (Ibid.). Runia is right to consider this a "limited selection"; it could be argued that every primary lemma in the treatise is approached with at least one implicit question in mind. The whole of part two, for example, which consists of chapter five, might be described as a discussion of one major *aporia* posed of Gen 17:5: "why is it that God changes Abram's name to Abraham, given that the gift of a letter seems below God's dignity or concern?" Further *aporiae* pertaining the primary lemmata of part three may be discovered by the discerning reader. Philo also raises a number of explicit exegetical *aporiae*, framed as direct or indirect questions, about his secondary texts (see, e.g., the series of three explicit *quaestiones* embedded in chapter five [§§ 81–82]; and those in chapter nine [§§ 236, 246, 250]). I have rendered these explicit in the detailed comments.

3   Chapters of the Treatise

Scholars have attempted to analyze *De mutatione nominum* into constituent subdivisions in various ways. The table below represents major divisions in German (Willy Theiler), French (Roger Arnaldez), Italian (Clara Kraus Reggiani), and Modern Hebrew (Ḥava Schur) versions. I have not included Karl Ernst Richter's divisions (included by Colson in PLCL), on the grounds that Richter's paragraphs are pre-critical (see Cover 2021). Cazeaux has been placed last, out of chronological sequence, because he only analyzed the first chapter of the treatise.

A brief note about my process for determining the limits of a chapter will help orient the reader. The standard method, pioneered by Nikiprowetzky (1977), is to recognize a chapter as the unit of exegesis dependent on the interpretation of a single pericope. Ambiguity enters in where there is doubt about how Philo divided a pericope. One simple way to resolve this ambiguity is to identify a chapter as beginning with the explicit citation of a new pericope. This works in most cases, and I follow this principle in all chapters other than

INTRODUCTION

chapter two, six, and twelve (each of which might be divided into two or three chapters) and chapters ten and eleven (which might be combined or differently bifurcated).

My divergence, in these instances, stems in part from the fact that Philo does not always cite every part of the primary lemma that he interprets; and in part, from an *a priori* decision to use Philo's pericope divisions in the *Quaestiones ad Genesin* as a heuristic guide to the structure of the *entire* treatise. His divisions of pericopes from Genesis and Exodus in the *QGE* form a part of his school tradition. If the Allegorical Commentary likewise stemmed from his private school, then it can be reasonably concluded that he did not come to the text of Genesis *tabula rasa*, but had such prior divisions of the text in mind. My reading of *De mutatione nominum* in light of such divisions has revealed key thematic connections between adjacent sections, which the more rigid division of chapters would have overlooked. Consequently, I have labeled such contiguous units "chapters." Readers of this commentary, who wish to follow a chapter structure emerging from the explicit pericope citations in *De mutatione nominum* alone, are advised to note that, on this principle, there could be as many as eighteen chapters (dividing chapters two, six, and twelve). The boundaries of such smaller chapter units can be easily ascertained from the table.

TABLE 2   Chapters of the treatise

Chapter	Cover	Schur (2012)	Kraus Reggiani (1994)	Arnaldez (1964)	Cohn/Theiler (1962)	Cazeaux (1983)
1	1–38 (1–2) 3–10 11–17 18–26 27–29 30–38	1–38	1–14 15–38	1–2 3–17 18–38	1–38	1–2 3–12 13–17 18–27 28–38
2	39–53	39–46 47–51 52–53	39–46 47–51 52–53	39–46 47–51 52–53	39–46 47–51a 51b–53	
3	54–56	54–56	54–56	54–57	54–56	
4	57–59	57–59	57–59	57–59	57–59	
5	60–129	60–129	60–129	60–129	60–129	

TABLE 2   Chapters of the treatise (cont.)

Chapter	Cover	Schur (2012)	Kraus Reggiani (1994)	Arnaldez (1964)	Cohn/Theiler (1962)	Cazeaux (1983)
6	130–153	130–147	130–140	130–147	130–147	
			141–147			
		148–153	148–150	148–150	148–150	
			151–153	151–153	151–153	
7	154–174	154–174	154–175	154–175	154–174	
8	175–200	175–200	176–200	176–200	175–200	
9	201–251	201–251	201–252	201–252	201–252	
10	252–260	252–263	253–262	252–260	253–260	
11	261–263			261–262 (sic?)	261–262	
			263		263	
12	264–269	264–269	264–266	264–269	264–266	
			267–269		267–269	
13	270	270	270	270	270	

4 Exegetical Structure of the Treatise (MBL = Gen 17:1–5 + 15, 16–22)[33]

The clearest way to observe Philo's train of thought in *De mutatione nominum*, which gives rise to the chapter structure in section three, is to attend to his shifting focus between various scriptural lemmata (Greek plural of "lemma"), or citations of short phrases intended for interpretation. The outline below sets out this schema in a highly compressed form, which will become most useful once the reader has mastered the key of abbreviations. This schema has been adapted from that of Runia 1984/1987, with several modifications. It is an attempt at precision, in a context where precision is not entirely possible. It is hoped, nevertheless, that the resulting analysis will be of assistance to the reader.

The main text interpreted by Philo in the treatise is called the "main" or "primary biblical lemma" (MBL).[34] Philo may either quote the lemma *verbatim*,

---

33   Geljon and Runia (2013, 2) suggest Gen 17:1–22 in its entirety. Cf. Colson (PLCL 5:128), who is slightly more circumspect in his "Analytical Introduction," limiting the lemma to Gen 17:1–5, 15–22.

34   Throughout the commentary, I speak of a "primary biblical lemma," but have adopted

paraphrase it, or allude to it. The reader should learn to detect the structuring presence of MBLs in the Allegorical Commentary, whether or not they are explicitly cited. Often, their full scope is only revealed in the exegesis.

While commenting on a primary lemma, Philo often adduces one or more secondary biblical lemmata (SBLs) from the same or another scriptural book to amplify his discussion. SBLs are deployed for at least four different purposes in the Allegorical Commentary: (1) rhetorical proof; (2) amplification of a foregoing allegorical theme; (3) anticipation of a forthcoming lemma or theme; or (4) to contextualize the literal or allegorical sense of the MBL. Lemmata in the third and especially the fourth category are somewhat distinct from the other SBLs and can often function structurally as a MBL. For clarity, they warrant the separate abbreviations of "anticipatory biblical lemmata" (SBL^A) and "contextualizing (secondary) biblical lemmata" (SBL^C; see Cover 2023d/2017 and 2015, 55; Runia 1991, 51), respectively.

In addition to Philo's SBLs, in this commentary I use the abbreviation SCL for a "secondary classical lemma," including those from Homer or Plato. While scholars disagree as to whether Homer and Plato occupy a similar place of authority or inspiration in Philo's mind as some other scriptural texts (the prophets, for example), formally speaking, these lemmata play an important role in Philo's commentaries and deserve to be noted.

Not infrequently, Philo's discussions of SBLs become very complex. In these contexts, additional lemmata are adduced, which pertain to the secondary-level discussion. Per the conventions of the PACS series, these are labeled TBLs ("tertiary biblical lemmata"). Greek words in the outline are those which serve as catchwords between scriptural passages.

Key of Abbreviations

MBL	Main or Primary Biblical Lemma
SBL	Secondary Biblical Lemma
SBL^C	Contextualizing Secondary Biblical Lemma
SBL^A	Anticipatory Secondary Biblical Lemma
SCL	Secondary Classical Lemma
TBL	Tertiary Biblical Lemma
TCL	Tertiary Classical Lemma

"main biblical lemma" (MBL) for consistency with other PACS volumes on the Allegorical Commentary.

Part One

Chapter One: Abraham as Seer and Hearer of God (cf. QG 3.39)

§§ 1–38	MBL Gen 17:1
§§ 1–2a	MBL Gen 17:1a ("Abraham came to be ninety-nine")
§ 2a	SBL Num 18:26–32
§§ 2b–10	MBL Gen 17:1bα ("Was seen")
§ 7	SBL Exod 20:21
§ 8–9	SBL Exod 33:13–23
§§ 11–17	MBL Gen 17:1bβ ("The Lord")
§§ 11–12	SBL Exod 3:14–15
§ 13b	SBL Exod 6:3
§ 14	SBL Gen 32:29
§ 15	MBL Gen 17:1bαβ
§ 17	MBL Gen 17:1bαβ
§§ 18–38	MBL Gen 17:1cα ("I am your God")
§ 18–26	MBL Gen 17:1cα[35] ("I am *your* God")
§ 19	SBL Exod 7:1
§ 20	SBL Exod 7:17
§ 20	SBL Exod 6:29
§ 21	SBL Exod 9:29–30
§ 23	MBL Gen 17:1cα
§ 23	SBL Gen 35:11
§ 23	SBL Exod 20:2
§ 23	SBL Deut 4:1
§ 25	SBL Deut 33:1
§§ 27–38	MBL Gen 17:1cα ("I am your *God*")
§ 27	MBL Gen 17:1cα
§ 29	MBL Gen 17:1cα
§ 30	SBL Gen 2:7
§ 30	TBL Gen 2:17/3:22
§ 31	SBL Gen 1:26
§ 31	MBL Gen 17:1cα

---

35 Cazeaux (1983, 477) recognizes a similar division, but begins the new section at § 28; this, however, overlooks Philo's return to the MBL in § 27. Philo focuses on "your" before "God," commenting on Abraham as the subject of the vision before turning to the divine object.

INTRODUCTION

§ 34	SBL Gen 5:24
	SBL^A Gen 5:24a (see § 39, Gen 17:1c)
§ 38	SBL Gen 5:24b

Chapter Two: Philo's Theology of Covenant (cf. *QG* 3.40)

§§ 39–53	MBL Gen 17:1cβ
§§ 39–46	MBL Gen 17:1cβ ("Be well-pleasing before me")
§ 39	MBL Gen 17:1cβ
§ 40	MBL Gen 17:1cβ
§ 40	SBL Exod 20:12; Deut 5:16
§ 41	SBL Gen 48:15
§ 42	SBL Deut 12:28
§ 43	TBL Exod 26:33
§ 43	TBL Exod 25:10
§ 43	TBL Exod 28:4; Lev 6:10; 16:4
§ 44	SBL Gen 32:28
§§ 47–51a	MBL Gen 17:1cγ ("Be blameless")
§ 47	MBL Gen 17:1cβ
§ 47	MBL Gen 17:1cγ
§ 48	SBL Job 14:14
§ 51	MBL Gen 17:1cγ
§§ 51b–53	MBL Gen 17:2 ("I will set my covenant …")
§ 52	MBL Gen 17:2

Chapter Three: Abraham's Great Fall (cf. *QG* 3.41)

§§ 54–56	MBL Gen 17:3 ("Abraham fell upon his face")
§ 54	MBL Gen 17:3
§ 54	SCL The Delphic Maxim (e.g., Xenophon, *Mem.* 4.2.24)
§ 56	MBL Gen 17:3b
§ 56	SBL Gen 2:7

Chapter Four: Different Forms of Covenant (cf. *QG* 3.42)

§§ 57–59	MBL Gen 17:4 ("And I, behold my covenant is with you")
§ 57	MBL Gen 17:4
§ 58	MBL Gen 17:4b

Part Two

Chapter Five: On the Change of Names (cf. *QG* 3.43 [Gen 17:5]; *QG* 3.53 [Gen 17:15])

§§ 60–129	MBL Gen 17:5, 15	
§§ 60–76	MBL Gen 17:5 ("Your name ... Abraham")	(a) Abram/Abraham
§ 60	MBL Gen 17:5	
§ 60	SCL Heraclitus, D-K fr. 123	
§ 61	MBL/SBL^c Gen 17:15	
§ 63	SBL Gen 2:19	
§§ 77–80	MBL/SBL^c Gen 17:15	(b) Sarai/Sarah
§§ 81–82	SBL Gen 32:28(29)	(c) Jacob/Israel
§ 87	SBL Gen 32:24(25)	
§§ 89–91	SBL Gen 41:41–49	(d) Joseph's Names
§ 89	SBL Gen 30:24	
§§ 92–96	SBL Gen 35:18bc	(e) Benjamin's Names
§ 94	SBL Gen 35:18b	
§ 96	SBL Gen 35:16, 19	
§§ 97–102	SBL Gen 48:5	(f) Ephraim/Manasseh Reuben/Simeon
§§ 103–120	SBL Exod 2:16–22	(g) Jethro/Raguel
§ 104	SBL Exod 18:17–26	
§ 106	SBL Exod 2:16aα	
§ 107	TBL Num 25:3	
§ 108	TBL Num 25:7–8, 12–13	
§ 109	TBL Num 31:49	
§ 110	SBL Exod 2:16aβ	
§ 111	SBL Exod 2:16b	
§ 112	SBL Exod 2:17a	
§ 113	SBL Exod 2:17b	
§ 114	SBL Exod 2:18a	
§ 115	TBL Ps 22:1 LXX	
§ 116	SBL Exod 2:18b	
§ 117	SBL Exod 2:19a	
§ 118	SBL Exod 2:19a	
§ 119	SBL Exod 2:20	
§ 120	SBL Exod 2:21	
§§ 121–122	SBL Num 13:16b	(h) Hoshea/Joshua
§§ 123–124	SBL Num 14:24 (cf. Num 13:6)	(i) Caleb

INTRODUCTION   27

§§ 125–129	SBL Catena	(j) Moses
§ 125	SBL Deut 33:1	
§ 125	SBL Exod 7:1	
§ 126	SBL Exod 24:1	
§ 128	SBL Deut 33:1	
§ 128	SBL Exod 7:1	

MBLs omitted: Gen 17:6–14. Cf. *QG* 3.44 (Gen 17:6); *QG* 3.45 (Gen 17:8); *QG* 3.46 (Gen 17:10–11); *QG* 3.47 (Gen 17:10); *QG* 3.48 (Gen 17:12); *QG* 3.49 (Gen 17:12); *QG* 3.50 (Gen 17:12); *QG* 3.52 (Gen 17:14)

Part Three

Chapter Six: The Birth of Isaac (cf. *QG* 3.54)

§§ 130–140	MBL Gen 17:16aα
§ 130	MBL Gen 17:15
§ 130	MBL Gen 17:16a ("I will give to you from her a child")
§ 132	SBL Gen 29:31
§§ 134–136	SBL Gen 38:15–26
§ 134	SBL Gen 38:15
§ 134	TBL Exod 3:6
§ 134	TBL Exod 34:33–35
§ 134	SBL Gen 38:18, 25a
§ 135	SBL Gen 38:25b
§ 136	SBL Gen 38:26
§§ 137–138	SBL^c Gen 21:6 (Sarah)
§ 137	SBL^c Gen 21:6a (Sarah)
§ 138	SBL^c Gen 21:6b
§ 139	TBL Hos 14:9–10
§§ 141–144	MBL Gen 17:16aβ ("From her")
§ 141	MBL Gen 17:16aαβ
§ 143	SBL^c Gen 11:30
§ 143	TBL 1 Kgdms 2:5
§§ 145–147	MBL Gen 17:16aγ ("A child")
§ 145	MBL Gen 17:16aβγ
§§ 148–150	MBL Gen 17:16b ("I will bless her, and she will be for nations")
§ 148	MBL Gen 17:16b
§§ 151–153	MBL Gen 17:16c ("Also kings of nations will be from her")

§ 151   MBL Gen 17:16c
§ 152   SBL[c] Gen 23:6

Chapter Seven: Abraham's Laughter (cf. *QG* 3.55)

§§ 154–174   MBL Gen 17:17a
   § 154   MBL Gen 17:17a ("And Abraham fell ... and laughed")
   § 166   SBL[c] Gen 18:12 ("[Sarah] laughed in herself")
   § 168   TBL Exod 4:14
   § 169   TBL Isa 57:21; cf. Isa 48:22
   [§§ 170–174]   TBL Gen 45:16–18
   § 171   TBL Gen 45:16
   § 173   TBL Gen 45:18a
   § 173   TBL[c] Gen 37:36; 39:1, 20–23
   § 174   TBL Gen 45:18b

Chapter Eight: The Faith and Doubt of Abraham (cf. *QG* 3.56)

§§ 175–200   MBL Gen 17:17b
   § 175   MBL Gen 17:17a
   § 176   MBL Gen 17:17b
   §§ 177–187   MBL Gen 17:17bα
   § 177   MBL Gen 17:17bα ("[Abraham] said in thought")
   § 177   SBL[c] Gen 15:4, 6
   § 178   MBL Gen 17:17bα
   § 179   SCL Homer, *Od.* 7.36
   § 183   SBL Deut 32:4
   § 186   SBL[c] Gen 15:6a
   § 187   SBL Gen 32:25(26), 31(32)
   §§ 188–200   MBL Gen 17:17bβα
   § 188   MBL Gen 17:17bβ ("If a child will be born to this hundred-year-old man")
   § 189   SBL Gen 11:10 (num. 100)
   § 190   SBL Gen 21:33 (num. 100)
   § 190   SBL Gen 26:12 (num. 100)
   § 190   SBL Exod 27:9 (num. 100)
   § 191   SBL Num 18:28 (num. 100)
   § 192   SBL Exod 26:33 (num. 90)
   § 193   MBL Gen 17:17bα ("Said in thought")
   [§§ 193–200]   SBL Gen 34:2–25

INTRODUCTION

§ 194	SBL Gen 34:2, 3 (Shechem)
§ 195	TCL *unde*? ("Silence is half of evil")
§ 195	TBL Gen 4:7 ("Be silent")
§ 200	SBL Gen 34:25 (Simeon and Levi)
§ 200	TBL Gen 49:5
§ 200	TBL Deut 33:8

Chapter Nine: The Life of Ishmael (cf. *QG* 3.57)

§§ 201–251	MBL Gen 17:18
§§ 201–209a	MBL 17:18a ("This Ishmael")
§ 201	MBL Gen 17:18a
§ 202	SBL Num 24:16
§ 203	SBL Num 31:8
§ 204	MBL Gen 17:18a
§ 204	TBL Deut 23:1–2
§ 206	SBL Deut 21:20
[§§ 207–209a]	SBL Exod 6:26–27
§ 207	SBL Exod 6:26–27
§ 208	TBL Exod 4:10–16; 7:11,22; 8:3
§ 209a	SBL Exod 6:26
§§ 209b–215	MBL 17:18b
§ 209b	MBL Gen 17:18b ("Let him live")
§ 210	SBL Deut 33:6
§ 211	SCL Homer, *Od.* 19.163
§§ 211–212	SCL Plato, *Theaet.* 191c–194d
§ 215	SBL Gen 46:30
§§ 216–251	MBL 17:18c
[§§ 216–217]	
§ 216	MBL Gen 17:18[ab]c ("Before you")
[§§ 218–232]	
§ 218	SBL Gen 15:6
§ 220	SBL Num 6:21
§ 223	TBL Gen 1:27; see Wis 7:26
§ 224	SBL Num 13:24(17–33)
§ 228	SBL Gen 18:24, 32
§ 228	TBL Lev 25:10
§ 230	SBL Gen 27:38
§ 232	SBL Num 11:33
[§§ 233–251]	SBL Lev 5:6–12

§ 233	SBL Lev 5:6, 7
§ 234	SBL Lev 5:11–12a
§ 237	TBL Deut 30:11–14
§ 243	TCL Democritus fr. 105
§ 245	SBL Lev 5:6–12
§ 249	SBL Lev 5:12
§ 250	SBL Lev 5:7, 11

Chapter Ten: Sarah's Child (cf. QG 3.58)

§§ 252–260	MBL Gen 17:19a
§ 252	MBL Gen 17:18
§§ 253–254	MBL Gen 17:19aα
§ 253	MBL Gen 17:19a ("Yes")
§§ 254–255	SBL Gen 29:31
§§ 255–260	MBL Gen 17:19aβ
§ 255	MBL Gen 17:19aβ ("Behold Sarah ... will bear a son")
§ 259	SBL Exod 16:4
§ 260	SBL Exod 16:23

Chapter Eleven: You Will Call His Name Joy (cf. QG 3.59)

§§ 261–263	MBL Gen 17:19b, 20, 21a
§ 261	MBL Gen 17:19a
§ 261	MBL Gen 17:19b ("Will bear you a son")
§ 263	MBL Gen 17:20 ("I have blessed him ... twelve nations")
§ 263	MBL Gen 17:21a ("But my covenant I will establish with Isaac")

Chapter Twelve: God Alone is the Appropriate Time (cf. QG 3.60)

§§ 264–266	MBL Gen 17:21b
§ 264	MBL Gen 17:21b ("At this acceptable time")
§ 265	SBL Num 14:9
§ 266	TBL Lev 26:12
§§ 267–269	MBL Gen 17:21c
§ 267	MBL Gen 17:21c ("In the other year")
§ 268	SBL Gen 26:12

INTRODUCTION 31

Chapter Thirteen: God's Departure (No par. in *QGE*)

§ 270   MBL Gen 17:22 ("God finished speaking to him")

MBL Omitted: Gen 17:23–27. Cf. *QG* 3.61 (Gen 17:24–25); *QG* 3.62 (Gen 17:27)

5   Use of Scripture

The foregoing exegetical structure leaves a number of details about Philo's exegetical poetics unspoken. In addition to (1) the level of the lemma (primary, secondary, anticipatory, etc.), the reader may wish to pay attention to (2) the content of each lemma; (3) its type, either (C) citation or close verbal paraphrase or oblique (A) allusion; and (4) Philo's mode of transition (MOT) between various lemmatic levels. **Citation** or close verbal paraphrase refers to texts where Philo cites one or more distinct word from a particular pericope or clearly intends to reference a particular scriptural text through the use of an introductory formula. Citations are printed in bold in the translation. ***Allusions*** refer to biblical stories or events reference by Philo in a less direct way, usually without replicating a distinct word from the referenced pericope. Allusions are printed in bold and italics in the translation.

TABLE 3   Biblical / classical quotations and major scriptural allusions in *De mutatione nominum*

Nr	§	Level	Text	Content	Type	MOT
1	1	MBL	Gen 17:1a–cα	Abraham was 99 … your God	C	
2	2a	SBL	Num 18:26–32	The Levitical tithe	A	T
(= 1)	2b	MBL	Gen 17:1b	The Lord was seen	C	
3	7	SBL	Exod 20:21	Moses entered into darkness	C	T
4	8	SBL	Exod 33:13	Moses's request to see God	C	L
5	9	SBL	Exod 33:23	God's response	C	L
6	11	SBL	Exod 3:14a	I am The One Who Is	C	T
7	12	SBL	Exod 3:15 (4×)	The meaning of "Lord God"	C	L
8	13	SBL	Exod 6:3	"Lord" not told to patriarchs	C	L
9	14	SBL	Gen 32:29*bis*	Jacob and the Angel	C	T
(= 1)	15	MBL	Gen 17:1b	The Lord was seen	C	
(= 1)	17	MBL	Gen 17:1b	The Lord was seen	C	
(= 1)	18	MBL	Gen 17:1cα	I am your God	C	
10	19	SBL	Exod 7:1	A god to Pharaoh	C	L
11	20	SBL	Exod 7:17	The Lord says	C	T
12	20	SBL	Exod 6:29	The Lord spoke	C	T
13	21	SBL	Exod 9:29–30	Several "Lord" texts	C	T

TABLE 3   Biblical / classical quotations and major scriptural allusions in *De mutatione nominum* (*cont.*)

Nr	§	Level	Text	Content	Type	MOT
(= 1)	23	MBL	Gen 17:1cα	I am your God	C	
14	23	SBL	Gen 35:11	I am your God	C	L
15	23	SBL	Exod 20:2	I am the Lord your God	C	L
16	23	SBL	Deut 4:1	The Lord God	C	L
17	25	SBL	Deut 33:1	God's human being	C	L
(= 1)	27	MBL	Gen 17:1cα	I am your God	C	
(= 1)	29	MBL	Gen 17:1cα	I am your God	C	
18	30	SBL	Gen 2:7	God molded	C	T
19	30	TBL	Gen 2:17/3:22	Distinction of good and evil	A	T
20	31	SBL	Gen 1:26	According to our image	C	T
(= 1)	31	MBL	Gen 17:1cα	I am your God	C	
21	34	SBL[A]	Gen 5:24ab	Enoch pleasing, not found	C	TL
(= 21)	38	SBL	Gen 5:24bc	Enoch not found, translated	C	TL
22	39	MBL	Gen 17:1cβ	Be pleasing before me	C	
(= 22)	40	MBL	Gen 17:1cβ	Be pleasing before me	C	
23	40	SBL	Exod 20:12; Deut 5:16	Honor your parents	C	T
24	41	SBL	Gen 48:15	Israel's fathers pleasing	C	L
25	42	SBL	Deut 12:28	Please God (from Moses)	C	L
26	43	TBL	Exod 26:33	Division of the tabernacle	A	T
27	43	TBL	Exod 25:10	Double gilding of the ark	A	T
28	43	TBL	Exod 28:4; Lev 6:10; 16:4	Linen vestment within, mottled vestment without	A	T
29	44	SBL	Gen 32:28	Jacob strong with God/humans	A	T
(= 22)	47	MBL	Gen 17:1cβ	Be pleasing before me	C	
30	47	MBL	Gen 17:1cγ	Be blameless	C	
31	48	SBL	Job 14:14	Who is clean from filth?	C	T
(= 30)	51	MBL	Gen 17:1cγ	Be blameless	C	
32	52	MBL	Gen 17:2	Covenant between me …	C	
33	54	MBL	Gen 17:3	Abraham fell on his face	C	
34	54	SCL	Delphic max.	Know yourself	C	T
(= 33)	56	MBL	Gen 17:3b	Abraham fell on his face	C	
(= 18)	56	SBL	Gen 2:7	Adam formed as a living being	C	L
35	57	MBL	Gen 17:4	And I, behold my covenant …	C	
(= 35)	58	MBL	Gen 17:4b	My covenant is with you	C	
36	60	MBL	Gen 17:5	Abram to Abraham	C	
37	60	SCL	Heraclitus	Nature loves to hide herself	A	T
38	61	SBL[C]	Gen 17:15	Sarai to Sarah	A	T
39	63	SBL	Gen 2:19	Adam named animals	C	L
(= 38)	77	MBL/SBL[C]	Gen 17:15	Sarai to Sarah	A	T
40	81	SBL	Gen 32:28(29)	Jacob to Israel	A	T
41	87	SBL	Gen 32:24(25)	Jacob wrestles a "human being"	A	T
42	89	SBL	Gen 41:45	Joseph/Psonthomphanek	A	T
43	89	SBL	Gen 30:24	Joseph means "addition"	A	T

INTRODUCTION   33

TABLE 3   Biblical / classical quotations and major scriptural allusions in *De mutatione nominum* (*cont.*)

Nr	§	Level	Text	Content	Type	MOT
44	92	SBL	Gen 35:18bc	Benjamin/Son of Pain	C	T
(= 44)	94	SBL	Gen 35:18b	Son of Pain	C	T
45	96	SBL	Gen 35:16, 19	Rachel died in childbirth	C	T
46	97	SBL	Gen 48:5	Ephraim and Manasseh	C	T
47	104	SBL	Exod 18:17–26	Jethro counsels Moses	AC	T
48	106	SBL	Exod 2:16aα	From "Midian"	A	T
49	107	TBL	Num 25:3	Baal Peor	A	T
50	108	TBL	Num 25:7–8, 12–13	The zeal of Phinehas	CA	L
51	109	TBL	Num 31:49	No one was lost	C	T
(= 48)	110	SBL	Exod 2:16aα	From "Midian"	C	T
52	110	SBL	Exod 2:16aβ	Raguel had seven daughters	C	T
53	111	SBL	Exod 2:16b	They water his sheep	C	T
54	112	SBL	Exod 2:17a	Local shepherds disturb them	C	T
55	113	SBL	Exod 2:17b	Moses rescues them	C	T
56	114	SBL	Exod 2:18a	The daughters return to Raguel	C	T
57	115	TBL	Ps 22:1 LXX	The Lord shepherds me	C	L
58	116	SBL	Exod 2:18b	Raguel asks why they lingered	C	T
59	117	SBL	Exod 2:19a	Moses, human being / Egyptian	C	T
(= 59)	118	SBL	Exod 2:19a	Moses, human being / Egyptian	C	T
60	119	SBL	Exod 2:20	Raguel asks why they left Moses	C	T
61	120	SBL	Exod 2:21	Moses invited, marries Zipporah	CA	T
62	121	SBL	Num 13:16b	Hoshea to Joshua	A	T
63	123	SBL	Num 14:24	Another spirit in Caleb	C	T
(= 17)	125	SBL	Deut 33:1	Moses, God's human being	C	T
(= 10)	125	SBL	Exod 7:1	Moses, God to Pharaoh	C	T
64	126	SBL	Exod 24:1	Moses simply "Moses"	A	T
(= 17)	128	SBL	Deut 33:1	Moses, God's human being	C	T
(= 10)	128	SBL	Exod 7:1	Moses, God to Pharaoh	C	T
(= 38)	130	MBL	Gen 17:15	Sarai to Sarah	A	
65	130	MBL	Gen 17:16a	I will give to you … a child	C	
66	132	SBL	Gen 29:31	Leah's womb opened	C	T
67	134	SBL	Gen 38:15	Tamar's face veiled	C	T
68	134	TBL	Exod 3:6	Moses turns to bush	A	T
69	134	TBL	Exod 34:33–35	Moses veils his face	A	L
70	134	SBL	Gen 38:18	Judah gives tokens	C	T
71	134	SBL	Gen 38:25a	Tamar requests the tokens	C	T
72	135	SBL	Gen 38:25b	Necklace, staff, scepter	C	T
73	136	SBL	Gen 38:26	Tamar justified	C	T
74	137	SBL[C]	Gen 21:6a	Sarah receives laughter	C	T
75	138	SBL[C]	Gen 21:6b	And bids others to rejoice	C	T
76	139	TBL	Hos 14:9–10	Fruit from God for the wise	C	T
(= 65)	141	MBL	Gen 17:16aα	I will give to you	C	
(= 65)	141	MBL	Gen 17:16aβ	From her	C	

TABLE 3 Biblical / classical quotations and major scriptural allusions in *De mutatione nominum* (*cont.*)

Nr	§	Level	Text	Content	Type	MOT
77	143	SBL^C	Gen 11:30	Sarah was barren	C	T
78	143	TBL	1 Kgdms 2:5	A barren woman bore seven	C	T
(= 65)	145	MBL	Gen 17:16aβ	From her	C	
(= 65)	145	MBL	Gen 17:16aγ	A child	C	
79	148	MBL	Gen 17:16b	She will be for the nations	C	
80	151	MBL	Gen 17:16c	Kings … will be from her	C	
81	152	SBL^C	Gen 23:6	Abraham a king from God	C	L
82	154	MBL	Gen 17:17a	Abraham falls and laughs	C	
83	166	SBL^C	Gen 18:12	Sarah laughs in herself	C	L
84	168	SBL	Exod 4:14	Aaron will rejoice in himself	C	L
85	169	SBL	Isa 57:21	The impious do not rejoice	C	L
86	171	TBL	Gen 45:16	Pharaoh rejoices	C	L
87	173	SBL^C	Gen 45:18a	Bring your possessions	C	T
88	173	TBL	Gen 37:36; 39:1, 20–23	Potiphar, eunuch and butcher	C	T
89	174	TBL	Gen 45:18b	Pharaoh gives goods	C	T
(= 82)	175	MBL	Gen 17:17a	Abraham falls and laughs	C	
90	176	MBL	Gen 17:17b	Abraham said in thought	C	
(= 90)	177	MBL	Gen 17:17b	Abraham said in thought	C	
91	177	SBL^C	Gen 15:4, 6	Abraham's faith	C	T
(= 90)	178	MBL	Gen 17:17bα	Abraham said in thought	C	
92	179	SCL	*Od.* 7.36	A wing or a notion	C	T
93	183	SBL	Deut 32:4	God is faithful	C	L
(= 91)	186	SBL^C	Gen 15:6a	Abraham's belief	C	T
94	187	SBL	Gen 32:25(26), 31(32)	Jacob limped	C	T
(= 90)	188	MBL	Gen 17:17bβ	Abraham 100, Sarah 90	A	
95	189	SBL	Gen 11:10	Noah 100	C	L
96	190	SBL	Gen 21:33	Abraham's 100-fold field	C	L
97	190	SBL	Gen 26:12	Isaac finds 100 measures	C	L
98	190	SBL	Exod 27:9	100 cubits in tabernacle	C	L
(= 2)	191	SBL	Num 18:28	Levitical tithe	A	L
(= 26)	192	SBL	Exod 26:33	The tabernacle curtain	A	L
(= 90)	193	MBL	Gen 17:17bα	Abraham said in thought	C	
99	194	SBL	Gen 34:2–3	Shechem's rape of Dinah	C	T
100	195	TCL	*unde*?	Silence (destroys) half of evil	C	T
101	195	TBL	Gen 4:7	You sinned, keep silent	C	T
102	200	SBL	Gen 34:25	Simeon and Levi avenge	A	T
103	200	TBL	Gen 49:5	Simeon and Levi identified	A	T
104	200	TBL	Deut 33:8	Simeon enrolled in Levi	A	T
105	201	MBL	Gen 17:18	Let this Ishmael live	C	
106	202	SBL	Num 24:16	Balaam hears and knows God	C	T
107	203	SBL	Num 31:8	Perished among wounded	C	T
(= 105)	204	MBL	Gen 17:18a	This Ishmael	C	

INTRODUCTION 35

TABLE 3   Biblical / classical quotations and major scriptural allusions in *De mutatione nominum* (*cont.*)

Nr	§	Level	Text	Content	Type	MOT
108	204	TBL	Deut 23:1–2	Eunuchs not admitted	A	T
109	206	SBL	Deut 21:20	This son disobeys	C	L
110	207	SBL	Exod 6:26–27	This Aaron and Moses	C	L
111	208	TBL	Exod 4:10–16; 7:11; 8:3	Moses mind, Aaron speech		
(= 110)	209a	SBL	Exod 6:26	This Aaron and Moses	C	L
(= 105)	209b	MBL	Gen 17:18b	Let (this Ishmael) live	C	
112	210	SBL	Deut 33:6	Let Reuben live	C	L
113	211	SCL	*Od.* 19.163	From an oak or mute stone	C	T
114	211–212	SCL	*Theaet.* 191c–194d	The waxy tablet heart	A	T
115	215	SBL	Gen 46:30	You are still alive	C	L
(= 105)	216	MBL	Gen 17:18c	(Let Ishmael live) before God	C	
(= 105)	218	MBL	Gen 17:18ab	Let this Ishmael live	C	
(= 91)	218	SBL	Gen 15:6	Abraham's faith	C	T
116	220	SBL	Num 6:21	The power of hands	C	T
117	223	TBL	Gen 1:27; see Wis 7:26	Image and fragment of God	A	T
118	224	SBL	Num 13:24	Moses's spies	AC	T
119	228	SBL	Gen 18:24, 32	Abraham prays for Sodom	AC	T
120	228	TBL	Lev 25:10	Release into freedom	A	T
121	230	SBL	Gen 27:38	Esau requests second blessing	C	T
122	232	SBL	Num 11:23	Will the hand of the Lord fail?	C	L
123	233	SBL	Lev 5:6, 7	Sheep and turtle doves	C	T
124	234	SBL	Lev 5:11–12a	Flour	C	T
125	237	TBL	Deut 30:11–14	Works in mouth, heart, hands	C	L
126	243	TCL	Democr. 105	A word is shadow of an act	C	L
(= 123/124)	245	SBL	Lev 5:6–12	Sheep, doves, flour	C	T
(= 124)	249	SBL	Lev 5:12b	The memorial offering	C	T
(= 123)	250	SBL	Lev 5:7	Sheep and turtle doves	C	T
(= 124)	250	SBL	Lev 5:11	If he should not find	C	T
(= 105)	252	MBL	Gen 17:18	Let this Ishmael live	C	
127	253	MBL	Gen 17:19a	Yes, Sarah will bear	C	
(= 66)	254	SBL	Gen 29:31a	Leah hated by scoffers	C	T
(= 66)	255	SBL	Gen 29:31b	Her womb was opened	C	T
(= 127)	255	MBL	Gen 17:19aβ	Sarah will bear you a son	C	
128	259	SBL	Exod 16:4	Bread from heaven	C	T
129	260	SBL	Exod 16:23	Wilderness sabbaths	A	T
(= 127)	261	MBL	Gen 17:19a	Yes, Sarah will bear	C	
130	261	MBL	Gen 17:19b	You will call the name	C	
131	263	MBL	Gen 17:20	Ishmael's blessing	C	
132	263	MBL	Gen 17:21a	Isaac's covenant	C	
133	264	MBL	Gen 17:21b	At this appropriate time	C	

TABLE 3   Biblical / classical quotations and major scriptural allusions in *De mutatione nominum* (*cont.*)

Nr	§	Level	Text	Content	Type	MOT
134	265	SBL	Num 14:9	Appropriate time departed	C	L
135	266	TBL	Lev 26:12	I will walk among you	C	L
136	267	MBL	Gen 17:21c	In the other year	C	
137	268	SBL	Gen 26:12	In this year	C	L
138	270	MBL	Gen 17:22	God finished speaking	C	

6   The Main Themes of the Treatise

In *De mutatione nominum*, Philo ruminates exegetically on a number of themes. The following sections discuss his major interpretive priorities, as well as other topics that may be of help to the reader, roughly in the order of their appearance in the treatise.

6.1   *Perfection*

The central theme of *De mutatione nominum* is psychological and moral perfection. Abraham's change of name, his turning one-hundred years old, and the promised birth of Isaac constitute the three-fold symbol of this perfection. Philo's selection of Abraham to illustrate this final stage in the soul's journey is determined by the centrality of Abraham in the Jewish tradition, Abraham's narrative similarities to Odysseus (in Platonist readings of Homer), his role as the first elected patriarch of Israel, arithmological exegesis, and words of the Septuagintal text. As the anthropological culmination of the Abrahamic cycle, Philo's choice of this theme makes sense within the broader exegetical series in which it occurs. Abraham's first steps in this direction are charted in *De migratione Abrahami*. One suspects that *De Deo*, which follows *De mutatione nominum*, depicted a complementary picture of Abraham's contemplative perfection—the natural pairing with the ethical perfection depicted in this penultimate treatise of the cycle.

6.2   *Emotions, Bad and Good*

Part and parcel with the theme of noetic perfection is the right ordering of the emotions. From the first to the final chapters of this treatise, Philo attends to both good and bad emotions, including fear and grief on the negative side, and hope and joy on the positive side. That Isaac is interpreted as "joy" in the first section of chapter one highlights the centrality of this good emotion for the treatise—one which finds its birth in the perfected Abrahamic soul. For more on this important topic, see Weisser 2021, 265–368.

6.3 Theological Epistemology: The Nature and Names of God

Early in the first chapter of *De mutatione nominum*, Philo turns to one of the most fascinating topics of the treatise, which is of major importance for the history of philosophy and theology: the possibility of human knowledge of God. Epistemological questions are posed to the biblical text and its quasi-mythical depiction of God's appearance to Abraham and revelation of the divine name. Philo becomes the first witness in the history of Platonism to make the absolute claim that God in unknowable and ineffable (Dillon 1977, 155)—two positions which have a very long *Nachleben* in Jewish and Christian tradition. For Philo, God has no "proper" name—a clever and subversive reading of the apparent scriptural title, κύριος ("Lord"). Even more uniquely (Runia 1988b, 86), Philo argues that the divine names in the Septuagint are given as a form of rhetorical κατάχρησις ("misuse"). Such intentional misuse of language cannot indicate God's nature; rather, it exhibits God's graciousness in facilitating the creature's approach to him in prayer, while simultaneously pinpointing aspects of God's action in the world through the divine powers. Even these powers, Philo goes on to say, are not completely knowable.

A related categorical claim that Philo makes about God in the first chapter of this treatise is worth noting. Commensurate with God's unknowability is his total transcendence. While this *theologoumenon* is well-known from elsewhere in Philo's writings, here the Alexandrian makes a more specific claim: that this transcendent God cannot *properly* receive predicates of relation vis-à-vis the created order (§ 27). Because relation necessarily involves passibility, God can only receive predicates of relation in a spurious fashion (ὡσανεὶ πρός τι, "as if in relation (to something else)," [§ 28]); neither he nor his powers can be said to be πρός τι ("in relation") to anything in creation, properly speaking.

In later chapters of the treatise, Philo will continue to explore the limitations of human epistemology from a psychological angle. In particular, he will mesh Plato's tripartite soul with the Stoic eight-part soul and develop an intriguing ethical interpretation of Plato's "wax tablet" from the *Theaetetus*, as he charts the variety of human psychic types and their respective mechanics of change.

6.4 *Grace and the Covenant*

Philo's understanding of the catachrestic self-naming of God in Scripture is related in this treatise to his discussion of God's covenant with Abraham in Gen 17. Unfortunately, much of Philo's thought on this particular theme is omitted from the present treatise, as he tells us in § 53 that he has previously discussed it at length in the now lost two-volume *De testamentis*. Vestiges of his thought are recoverable in chapters two through four, and these repay careful study by those interested in this topic.

6.5 *Hebrew and Greek Etymologies; Philosophy of Language*

Etymology, while a salient feature of all of Philo's allegorical writings, serves as the primary "technique" of the current treatise; his use of it is on display throughout. (I follow the standard view that Philo knew little to no Hebrew, and hence had to rely on a bilingual onomasticon in deriving his etymologies of Hebrew names. The reader will be interested to find several new suggestions about the origins of such etymologies, particularly the possible Greek etymology of Levi given in the comments on § 200.) As Graabe (1987) has shown, Philo is predominantly interested in Hebrew etymologies, but attests a few Greek and Latin ones as well. A brief history of the discourse on language in Greek philosophy will help orient the reader to understanding Philo's unique use of etymology.

Although ancient Greek discourse on language is attested already in the Homeric poems, with their interest in the difference between divine and human names for the same objects (*Il.* 20.74), for practical purposes Greek philosophy of language begins in earnest with the *Cratylus* of Plato. In this dialogue, Socrates is invited to adjudicate a debate about the nature of language. Hermogenes, the first partner in the debate, argues that names and language are purely "conventional," bearing no relationship to the thing they represent; the eponymous Cratylus, by contrast, argues for the "natural" view: that names are inherently bound to the thing itself—and hence, that there are more and less accurate names. Socrates's own mediating position in this dialogue is notoriously unclear. He endorses some natural connection between names and things, as evidenced particularly by etymologies.

Among the Hellenistic schools of philosophy, it was the Stoics who followed Socrates's etymological enthusiasm most closely. Stoics traced the epistemic value of words—made plain through etymology—to their preservation of an "ancient wisdom." On the Stoic theory, the oldest and earliest human beings, being closer to the first principle, articulated through names and speech a system of wisdom which has never been surpassed. A part of the work of philosophy, according to the Stoics, is to recover this wisdom through the sifting of ancient sources. The earlier the sources, the better (Boys-Stones 2001). In several passages—including one in *De mutatione nominum*—Philo seems to rely on this Stoic theory of ancient wisdom, which might be called "primitivist."

Philo, however, was hardly a Stoic, and his theory of language and use of etymologies cannot be traced solely along these lines (Long 1997). In the imperial period, the Platonic Academy turned from scepticism toward dogmatism under the leadership of Antiochus of Ascalon and developed a new theory of language that was to affect Philo's approach to Jewish Scripture. (For the "mystical" Jewish elements in Philo's understanding of language, see Niehoff 1995.) According to the Middle Platonists, the Stoic understanding of language needed to be supplemented (or perhaps even "altered") by a new proposition: that Plato, despite being a relatively recent author, had understood, recorded, and systemized the "ancient wisdom" better than anyone (Boys-Stones 2001, 115). Scholarship is divided as to whether Middle Platonists understood Plato's supreme wisdom to derive from a supernatural font of revelation, from a more successful natural sifting of the ancient sources of wisdom, or from both. Different authors give differing accounts, and it is not impossible to suppose that Plato received the ancient wisdom through natural and supernatural pathways simultaneously.

Philo's conception of Mosaic language and wisdom takes the Middle Platonist's Plato as a model and paradigm. Mosaic wisdom, like Plato's, springs from twin sources, natural and supernatural. Moses, however, was not only older than Plato, and hence better acquainted with the ancient wisdom (as well as the source of Plato's knowledge); he also possessed a mind more brightly illuminated by the divine Logos and thus had learned even better than the Athenian the truths there were to be had by the human intellect, both moral and speculative. Under this double guarantee of wisdom, the words of Moses in the Pentateuch become for Philo the singularly most important channels for discerning wisdom and truth. Every word, including the Hebrew names, are shafts to be mined for moral and theological gold and related to the "things themselves."

6.6 *Doxography*

Although Philo read many of Plato's treatises in the original and had access to some of the best private and public libraries in antiquity, there is evidence that he also made use of summaries and collections of philosophical "opinions" (δόξαι) on various topics in the composition of his scriptural commentaries and other writings. These compendia are traditionally called "doxographies" (Mansfeld 2022). Many ancient authors composed such doxographies—Clement of Alexandria and Diogenes Laertius being two well-known representatives. In the nineteenth century, Hermann Diels postulated that many of the extant doxographies stemmed from a first- or second-century CE work, known as the *Placita* (or "doctrines") of Aëtius. Diels offered a reconstruction of the *Placita* in two columns in his *Doxographi Graeci* (1879). Jaap Mansfeld and David Runia have now published a new and completely revised edition of Aëtius with a reconstructed text in a single column (Mansfeld and Runia 2020); this has become the scholarly standard. Due to its early date, and probable independence, the *Placita* of Aëtius is crucial for students wishing to understand Philo's use of the doxographical tradition (Inwood 2021).

The density of references to doxographical writings is especially high in two later treatises in the Allegorical Commentary, *De mutatione nominum* (§§ 10, 67) and *De somniis*. As Runia writes: "The cluster of doxographical texts in these two treatises is certainly striking and suggests that Philo may have made a special study of doxographical texts at the time of writing these two works" (Runia 2008, 29). Runia's analysis echoes the earlier estimation of Willy Theiler that in six cases, *De mutatione nominum* owes its unique philosophical vocabulary to Eudorus of Alexandria, who in turn drew on Antiochus of Ascalon (Alesse 2008, 3; Theiler 1965). In addition to the growing importance of the thematic principle in composition of *De mutatione nominum* and *De somniis*, this doxographical density provides another indicator of the kinship between the two treatises. Reference to doxographical tradition in the present treatise will be highlighted in the detailed comments.

6.7 *The Allegorical Purpose of Scriptural Names and Their Changes*

While the Stoics often stopped in their quest for the "ancient wisdom" at the literal and cosmological level (see, e.g., Cornutus's *Epidrome*), Philo follows the Middle Platonists in moving beyond the etymologies of words, both Hebrew and Greek, to their allegorical "undersenses" pertaining to the soul (Tobin 2000). On the basis of etymological-symbolic identifications of their protagonists, Philo developed sustained allegorical interpretations of the Pentateuchal narrative cycles.

He undertook this project in part out of theological conviction, but also in a defensive maneuver against contemporary Jewish or pagan philosophers, who ridicule the narrative name changes in the Pentateuch on grounds derived from Plato's *Cratylus* itself. Philo's aim is to appeal to commonalities with such Platonists and argue for the symbolic relevance of name changes, understood as part of an extended allegory of the soul.

6.8 *Arithmological Exegesis*

Less central than etymological allegoresis, but nevertheless present in *De mutatione nominum*, are the vestiges of arithmological interpretations of various

Pentateuchal names. Of particular interest is an apparent Jewish tradition related to the change of names from Abram to Abraham, suppressed in the current treatise, but more prominent in the parallel exegesis of Gen 17:5 in QGE. The reader with interests in ancient Jewish and Neopythagorean arithmology will want to attend to the relevant sections in the commentary on chapter five.

6.9   Virtue, Individual and Generic
Many scholars agree that *De mutatione nominum* narrates a story of the soul's journey toward perfection in virtue. For some, however, including Roger Arnaldez, such a description of the theme of the treatise is too narrowly anthropological. In his introduction to the PAPM edition, which rewards revisiting, Arnaldez argues that in keeping with the treatise's focus on divine grace, *De mutatione nominum* is not only about the perfection of human virtue, but also and perhaps even primarily about Virtue as "a reality at the order of the Idea" with "an ontological value" (1964, 11; 19). In this, Arnaldez emphasizes the theology motifs of the treatise. Further aspects of his reading along these lines are presented in the detailed comments.

6.10   Abraham's Faith and Doubt
Alongside the philosophical and literary essays in chapters one and five, perhaps the most interesting section in the treatise from the point of view of the history of religions is Philo's essay on Abraham's faith and doubt in chapter eight. In the general introduction to that chapter, I suggest that this little theological subtreatise is a Philonic masterpiece, which deserves to be read alongside certain chapters of Paul's epistles as a signal discussion of human and divine "faithfulness" (πίστις) in antiquity. Of special interest is Philo entertainment of the thesis that faith and doubt—of a certain kind—may exist simultaneously in the Abraham soul. Such "wavering" (ἐνδοιασμός) on Abraham's part is not "lack of faith" (ἀπιστία) proper, but a natural hesitation, resulting from his created condition. To demand completely unwavering "faith" (πίστις), of the variety possessed by God, from any human being is in Philo's view misguided. God is "faithful" in an unwavering fashion—all creatures tremble and shudder, clothed in the rags of their own ontological nothingness, and are faithful only by imperfect analogy.

6.11   The Problem of Rhetoric and Sophism in Jewish Wisdom Literature
Another Platonizing characteristic of the present treatise is Philo's invective against "sophism." Particularly noteworthy in chapter eight is his targeting of the Jewish gnomic wisdom tradition itself (§ 197). Philo goes so far as to write

a seven-line mock wisdom poem—not quite metrical—in the style of Ps.-Phocylides to reveal its potential for rhetorical misuse. Even the form of poetry that would seem to be welcome in Plato's *Republic* admits the possibility of distortion. Far better, from Philo's point of view, is Platonizing allegoresis of Moses and Homer, which requires more extensive study and philosophical knowledge.

6.12   *Isaac and Ishmael as an Allegorical Binary*

Philo most commonly interprets Isaac as a symbol of the self-taught nature, placing him in a triad of psychological types along with Abraham and Jacob. Ishmael, by contrast, is usually treated negatively as a symbol of the sophist (the child of Hagar, or the preliminary studies). In chapters nine through eleven of the present treatise, however, Philo develops the allegorical significance of two brothers, Ishmael and Isaac, in relation to one another in a different, more positive direction. Ishmael becomes the soul that progresses by "hearing"—an interpretation derived from the Hebrew etymology of his name, "to hear" (שׁמע). This Ishmael soul that "hears" and learns anticipates the Isaac soul, which gives birth to Israel, the soul that "sees." The two half-brothers represent differing stages of the soul's perfection—the one who is in the middle and the one who has become perfect.

6.13   *Time and Eschatology*

It is neither unintentional nor unfitting that the final themes addressed by Philo in this treatise on psychological perfection relate to time and eternity. Philo's novel interpretation of *Tim*. 37d—inspired by Aristotle—is on display, casting the difference between his eschatology and that of Apocalyptic Judaism into clear relief. In particular, the Greek word "appropriate time" or "moment" (καιρός) is given a Platonist reading, which aligns it not with a temporal season but with the eternal Lord and Logos. Similarly, Isaac's birth is depicted as occurring not in the literally succeeding "other year," but in the noetic realm—that which is truly "other" from all materially bounded space-time. With these fascinating and pregnant meditations, Philo leaves the reader awaiting both the eschatological perfection of the soul, and his further theological meditations on God, which he offered in *De Deo*.

7   Title and Previous Scholarship on the Treatise

The longer title of the treatise, *On Those Whose Names Are Being Changed, and For What Purposes They Are Being Changed* (περὶ τῶν μετονομαζομένων καὶ ὧν

INTRODUCTION

ἕνεκα μετονομάζονται),[36] is contained in the Augustana manuscript of the treatise (*Codex Monacensis Gr.* 459), from which David Hoeschel made the *editio princeps*. It is also attested in Eusebius's catalogue of Philonic treatises (*Hist. eccl.* 2.18.3). The shorter Latin title, *De mutatione nominum*, might abbreviate the former part of this title (περὶ τῶν μετονομαζομένων; "On Those Whose Names Are Being Changed"), but more likely arises independently from Philo's own summary of chapter five in § 130, "On the Change of Names" (περὶ τῆς τῶν ὀνομάτων ἀλλαγῆς). Whether the double or single title circulated with the work originally is impossible to determine,[37] but the longer title looks to be an expansion or clarification of a shorter title that did not convey the full scope of the treatise's contents.

Among Philo's works listed by Eusebius, *De mutatione nominum* is one of the few treatises given a composite or double title.[38] Formally speaking, the closest analogue is the title given to *Spec.* 1.162–256: "On the Animals for Reli-

---

36 It is also possible to interpret the καί in the title of this treatise as epexegetical ("that is" rather than "and"). This would give the translation: "Concerning those whose names are being changed, i.e., *for what purposes* they are being changed." I interpret the καί as conjunctive. It suggests Philo's goal of discussing two related subjects: (1) the kinds of *souls* whose names change, particularly Abram and Sarai in the direction of perfection; and (2) the various allegorical significances of those name changes as signs of differing kinds of movements toward perfection or imperfection.

37 By "double title," I mean a title which includes more than one discrete question (see the foregoing note) conjoined by a καί or ἤ ("and" or "or"). Admittedly, not all composite titles gathered under this rubric will evince an identical relationship between the two parts of their title. A full consideration of such composite titles and their varieties would require an independent study.

38 The list of Philonic treatises by Eusebius is not complete. Treatises which could conceivably be understood as having composite titles, in addition to *De mutatione nominum*, include *De sobrietate* ("On Things for Which the Sober Mind Prays and Curses," περὶ ὧν νήψας ὁ νοῦς [*sive* Νῶε] εὔχεται καὶ καταρᾶται), *Quis rerum divinarum heres sit* ("On Who is the Heir of Divine Things or On the Division into Equals and Opposites," περὶ τοῦ τίς ὁ τῶν θείων ἐστὶ κληρονόμος ἢ περὶ τῆς εἰς τὰ ἴσα καὶ ἐναντία τομῆς), *De Abrahamo* ("On the Life of the Wise Man Who Has Been Perfected according to Righteousness or [On] the Unwritten Laws," περὶ βίου σοφοῦ τοῦ κατὰ δικαιοσύνην τελειωθέντος ἢ νόμων ἀγράφων), *Gig.-Deus* ("On Giants or On the Fact that the Divine Is Not Changed," περὶ γιγάντων ἢ περὶ τοῦ μὴ τρέπεσθαι τὸ θεῖον), *Spec.* 1.162–256 ("On the Animals for Religious Services and What the Species of Sacrifices Are," περὶ τῶν εἰς τὰς ἱερουργίας ζῴων καὶ τίνα τὰ τῶν θυσιῶν εἴδη), *De praemiis et poenis* ("On the Rewards Set Out in the Law for the Good, and the Punishments and Curses [Established] for the Wicked," περὶ τῶν προκειμένων ἐν τῷ νόμῳ τοῖς μὲν ἀγαθοῖς ἄθλων τοῖς δὲ πονηροῖς ἐπιτιμίων καὶ ἀρῶν), *De animalibus* ("Alexander, or On Whether Irrational Animals Have Reason," ὁ Ἀλέξανδρος ἢ περὶ τοῦ λόγον ἔχειν τὰ ἄλογα ζῷα), and *De vita contemplativa* ("On the Contemplative Life or [On] Suppliants," περὶ βίου θεωρητικοῦ ἢ ἱκετῶν).

gious Services and What the Species of Sacrifices Are" (περὶ τῶν εἰς τὰς ἱερουργίας ζῴων καὶ τίνα τὰ τῶν θυσιῶν εἴδη), which has a secondary question conjoined without an additional preposition "on" (περί). As with the title of the present treatise, this title suggests two closely related questions. Other Philonic treatises in the Allegorical Commentary transmitted with a composite Greek title in the MSS tradition include *De cherubim*, *De sacrificiis Abelis et Caini*, and *De posteritate Caini*, the last of which provides the nearest parallel, with a genitive plural object ("On Names" or "On Offspring") supplemented by a second indirect question ("Why" or "How").[39] It would seem that Philo (or a later student) was fond of such double titles, even if he used them relatively sparingly.

I have benefited from numerous previous studies of *De mutatione nominum*. In addition to Hoeschel's *Notatiunculae*, which make important steps toward a first modern commentary and deserve further study, despite their uneven value, I have aimed to incorporate regular references to the notes of Francis Colson (England) and Roger Arnaldez (France). The annotated translations of Clara Kraus Reggiani (Italy), José Pablo Martín (Argentina); and Ḥava Schur (Israel) also repay consultation. For structural analysis, I have drawn on the essays of Cazeaux (1983) and Runia (1988). Lester Grabbe's monograph on Philo's Hebrew etymologies has been indispensable (followed in part by the unpublished work of Frank Shaw [SBL 2015]). Those interested further in Philo's philosophy of language may be referred to the studies of Klaus Otte (1968), John Dillon (1978), Maren Niehoff (1995), Anthony Long (1997), David Runia (2004: see the special section on "Etymology and Allegory" in *SPhiloA* 16 [2004]: 96–187), David Robertson (2008), and Harold Attridge (2017). A special session on *De mutatione nominum* was held by the Philo of Alexandria Seminar at the SBL Annual Meeting on 21 Nov 2016, with papers by James Royse, Gregory E. Sterling, Frederick Brenk, SJ, and Michel Barnes: I have drawn deeply from these essays (Barnes 2016 [cf. Cover 2022], Royse 2016, Sterling 2018; Brenk 2023/2016).

---

39   *De cherubim* ("On the Cherubim and the Flaming Sword and the First Offspring from the Man Cain," περὶ τῶν χερουβεὶμ καὶ τῆς φλογίνης ῥομφαίας καὶ τοῦ κτισθέντος πρώτου ἐξ ἀνθρώπου Κάϊν); *De sacrificiis Abelis et Caini* ("On the Birth of Abel and the Sacrifices of Him and His Brother Cain," περὶ γενέσεως Ἄβελ καὶ ὧν αὐτός καὶ ὁ ἀδελφὸς αὐτοῦ Κάϊν ἱερουγοῦσιν); *De posteritate Caini* ("On the Offspring of the Pseudo-Wise Man Cain and How He Became a Wanderer," περὶ τῶν τοῦ δοκησισόφου Κάϊν ἐγγόνων καὶ ὡς μετανάστης γίγνεται).

INTRODUCTION 45

8 The Text

De mutatione nominum is among the most poorly attested treatises in the Allegorical Commentary.[40] It was not contained in the manuscripts used by Adrien Turnèbe for his 1552 *editio princeps* of Philo's works, but waited, along with *Leg.* 2 and *Somn.* 2, to see the modern light of day in David Hoeschel's 1587 *Opuscula tria*.[41] The principal witnesses to *De mutatione nominum* are families A and B. Cohn and Wendland (PCW 3:xvii–xix) also list a number of helpful parallels from John of Damascus. The additional manuscripts (Cantabrigiensis Collegii S. Trinitatis B.9.6, Oxoniensis Collegii Novi 143, and Coislinianus 43) collated at the request of Thomas Mangey seem to have helped little and are largely derivative (Sterling 2021; Cover 2022a). James Royse (2016) made an investigation of these three manuscripts recently and found nothing new of interest. There is no Armenian translation of the work. Hoeschel himself made a few emendations to the text of A (see Cover 2022a and 2023c). Mangey and Jeremiah Markland likewise have offered some brilliant emendations *ex ingenio*. The PCW text also includes a number of helpful emendations by both editors, and Colson adds some of his own in the Loeb. I have followed PCW, and noted any divergences in the Notes to the Text and Translation.

9 Parallel Exegesis and Nachleben

This commentary follows other volumes in the PACS series by including, after the detailed comments, sections charting Parallel Exegesis and *Nachleben* of each passage. Neither is meant to be exhaustive; both are meant to be illuminative. The first catalogues the most important parallels to a given chapter of *De mutatione nominum* within the Philonic corpus. As the reader will discover, the particularities and contingencies of any Philonic interpretation are greatly clarified by comparing it with texts, in which the same scriptural passage is interpreted in light of a different theme. Because, in the case of *De mutatione nominum*, we are fortunate enough to have parallels from *QG* 3.39–60, I have

---

40 Of the three major codex families / text types of Philo's works established by Cohn and Wendland (A, H, UF; see PCW, "Prolegomena," 1:xxxi) *De mutatione nominum* appears regularly only in the A family, but does not appear in the H or UF families. One codex, Vaticano-Palatinus graecus 311 (H), has the treatise appended to the corpus, but transcribed by another hand. PCW, "Prolegomena," 1:xiv.

41 Turnèbe 1552; Hoeschel 1587. On these early editions, see Sterling 2023; Cover 2021b and 2023c.

foregrounded these wherever possible. These parallels, which Philo likely composed before the present treatise, showcase the uniqueness and innovations of the Allegorical Commentary. Parallels from within the Allegorical Commentary, by contrast, will prove to the reader the open-endedness, or as Runia (1984, 1987) has put it, the "modesty" of Philo's allegorical interpretation of any given scriptural pericope. While these parallels share a family resemblance, they are seldom identical and depend upon context.

Even less exhaustive are the *Nachleben* sections. To chart the reception of Philo in a satisfactory manner would require a separate article, or indeed a separate book. Thankfully, a new edited volume is in preparation (Friesen, Lincicum, and Runia 2023), to complement the work that has already been done (Geljon 2002; Van den Hoek 2000, 1998; Rogers 2017; Runia 2012, 1995a, 1993). Traditionally in the PACS commentaries, *Nachleben* has only referred to instances where Philonic influence or reception is clear. I have found it necessary to broaden the parameters. In the *Nachleben* sections of this commentary, I have made a selection of major parallel themes and issues, as they are received especially in the Alexandrian tradition (Clement, Origen, Eusebius, and Cyril), as well as in John Chrysostom's four homilies, *De mutatione nominum*. I have occasionally included passages from the Cappadocian Fathers and later Greek authors as well. In the Latin west, I have focused almost exclusively on Ambrose, *vel Philo latinus*, with the occasional reference to Jerome. Elsewhere, I have explored Philo's reception in Origen, Gregory of Nyssa, and Augustine at greater length, as well as his relationship to the New Testament (Cover 2015, 296–303; 2018a; 2020b; 2022c; 2023a). The reader may consult these studies for more sustained treatments of Philo's influence and reception in early Christianity.

Consequently, in many of the passages adduced in the *Nachleben* sections, conclusive evidence of the reception of a particular Philonic passage is not demonstrable. More distant parallels of the same texts are sometimes given to demonstrate the uniqueness of a Philonic tradition that did not make it into the interpretive mainstream. To assist the reader, I have evaluated each parallel from [A–D] (adopting the model of Van den Hoek 1988, 2000), with [A] meaning "certainty" of Philonic reception, [B] meaning non-demonstrable probability, [C] meaning possibility, and [D] indicating a shared philosophical or exegetical commonplace, but no more. Combined judgments (e.g., [A/B], [B/C]) are sometimes given, including where I depart from Van den Hoek's estimation. NB: these rankings are meant only as general indicators of the likelihood of genetic dependence between two specific traditions, not as judgments of whether a certain author (or textual tradition) read or receives Philo. Thus, different parts of the same text may receive different rankings. Parallels to the

New Testament are also included in the *Nachleben*, though these never indicate genetic connection, as I agree with the critical consensus that no New Testament author was directly familiar with Philo's works.

Bibliography

Select Critical Editions of Philo
De mutatione nominum and QGE

Turnèbe [Turnebus], A. 1552. ΦΙΛΩΝΟΣ ΙΟΥΔΑΙΟΥ ΕΙΣ ΤΑ ΤΟΥ ΜΩΣΕΩΣ ΚΟΣΜΟΠΟΙ-ΗΤΙΚΑ, ΙΣΤΟΡΙΚΑ, ΝΟΜΟΘΕΤΙΚΑ; ΤΟΥ ΑΥΤΟΥ ΜΟΝΟΒΙΒΛΙΑ, *sive Philonis Iudaei in libros Mosis: de mundi opificio, historicos, de legibus; eiusdem libri singulares*. Paris: Regius. [The *editio princeps* of Philo's works, which lacked *Mut.*]

Hoeschel, D. 1587. *Philonis Iudaei opuscula tria: 1, Quare quorundam in sacris literis mutata sint nomina; 2, De formatione Euae ex Adami latere; & de utriusque lapsu; 3, Somniorum Iosephi, Pharonis, picernaeque ac pistoris, allegorica expositio: Graeca nunc primum edita, studio & opera Davidis Hoeschelii A.M. eiusdemque Notatiunculis alicubi illustrata*. Frankfurt: Joannes Wechelus. [Containing the *editio princeps* of *Mut.*]

Aucher, J.B. 1826. *Philonis Judaei paralipomena Armena: libri videlicet quatuor in Genesin, libri duo in Exodum, sermo unus de Sampsone, alter de Jona, tertius de tribus angelis Abraamo apparentibus*. Venice: Typis Coenobii PP. Armenonorum in Insula S. Lazari. [The Armenian text of the QG.]

Cohn, L., Wendland, P., and Reiter, S., eds. 1896–1930. *Philonis Alexandrini opera quae supersunt*. 7 vols. Berlin: George Reimer. [*Mut.* is printed in volume 3, edited by Wendland and appearing in 1898.]

Texts, Translations, and Notes
De mutatione nominum

Arnaldez, R. 1964. *De mutatione nominum*. PAPM 18. Paris: Cerf.

Colson, F.H., Whitaker, G.H., and Earp, J.W. 1929–1943. *Philo*. 10 vols. Loeb Classical Library. Cambridge, MA: Harvard University Press.

Kraus Reggiani, C. 1994. "Il Mutamento dei Nomi." Pages 997–1075, esp. 999–1003. *Filone di Alessandria: Tutti i Trattati del Commentario Allegorico alla Bibbia*. Edited by R. Radice. Milan: Rusconi.

Martín, J.P., ed. 2012. *Filón de Alejandría: Obras Completas*. Volume III. Madrid: Trotta.

Schur, H. 2012. "On the Change of Names" (על שנוי השמות). Pages 5:227–278 in *Philo of Alexandria: Writings* [Heb.]. 5 vols. Edited by Y. Amir and M. Niehoff. Jerusalem: Bialik Institute and Israel Academy of Sciences and Humanities.

Theiler, W. 1962. "Über die Namensänderung." Pages 6:104–162 in *Philo von Alexandria:*

die Werke in deutscher Übersetzung. Edited by L. Cohn and I. Heinemann. 2nd ed. 7 vols. Berlin: De Gruyter. [PCH.]

QGE
Marcus, R. 1953. *Philo.* Loeb Classical Library. 2 supplements. Cambridge, MA: Harvard University Press.
Petit, F. 1978. *Quaestiones: Fragmenta Graeca.* PAPM 33. Paris: Cerf.

Other Ancient Texts and Translations

NB: *Ancient authors not listed below are taken from the* Thesaurus Linguae Graecae *database.*

Ambrose
Petschenig, M. 1913. *Ambrosius: Expositio de psalmo CXVIII.* CSEL 62. Vienna: Tempsky. [*Exp. Ps. 118*]
Schenkl, C. 1896. *Ambrosius: Hexameron, De paradiso, De Cain, De Noe, De Abraham, De Isaac, De bono mortis.* CSEL 32.1. Vienna: Tempsky. [*Abr.*]
Schenkl, C. 1897. *Ambrosius: De Iacob, De Ioseph, De patriarchis, De fuga saeculi, De interpellatione Iob et David, De apologia prophetae David, De Helia, De Nabuthae, De Tobia.* CSEL 32.2. Vienna: Tempsky. [*Jac., Jos.*]

Andreas of Caesarea
Schmidt, J. 1955. *Studien zur Geschichte des griechischen Apokalypse-Textes. Text und Einleitung.* Münchener theologische studien 1. Munich: Zink. [*Comm. Apoc.*].

Anonymous
Hermann, H. 1801. *De emendanda ratione Graecae grammaticae,* Part 1. Leipzig: Fleischer. [*Frag. lex. Graec.*]
Prächter, K. 1893. *Cebetis tabula.* Leipzig: Teubner. [Tab. Ceb.]

Astrampsychus
Browne, G.M. 1983. *Sortes Astrampsychi, vol. 1.* Teubner. Leipzig: Teubner.
Stewart, R. 2001. *Sortes Astrampsychi, vol. 2.* Teubner. Munich-Leipzig: K.G. Saur.

Athanasius
Kannengiesser, C. 1973. *Sur l'incarnation du verbe.* SC 199. Paris: Cerf. [*Inc.*]

Ps.-Athanasius
Migne, J.-P. 1857–1866. PG 28. Paris: Migne. [*Nav. praec.*]

Clement of Alexandria
Harl, M., Marrou, H.-I., Matray, C., and Mondésert, C. 1960–1970. *Clément d'Alexandrie. Le pedagogue*. 3 vols. SC 70, 108, 158. Paris: Cerf. [*Paed.*]
Früchtel, L., Stählin, O., and Treu, U. 1960–1970. *Clemens Alexandrinus*. 2 vols. GCS 52 [15], 17. Berlin: Akademie-Verlag. [*Strom.*]

Cyril of Alexandria
Burns, W.H., and Évieux, P. 1991. *Cyrille d'Alexandrie. Lettres Festales (Lettres 1–6), Tome 1*. SC 372. Paris: Cerf. [*Epist. pasch.*]
Migne, J.-P. 1857–1866. PG 68, 69. Paris: Migne. [*Ador. cult., Glaph. Pent.*]
Pusey, P.E. 1872. *Sancti patris nostri Cyrilli archiepiscopi Alexandrini in D. Joannis evangelium*. 3 vols. Oxford: Clarendon Press. [*Comm. Jo., Frag. Rom.*]

Cyril of Jerusalem
Reischl, W.C., and Rupp, J. 1848–1860. *Cyrilli Hierosolymorum archiepiscopi opera quae supersunt omnia*. 2 vols. Munich: Lentner. [*Cat. ill.*]

Damascius
Ruelle, C.É. 1889–1899. *Damascii successoris dubitationes et solutiones*: Vol. 1–2. Paris: Klincksieck.

Didymus the Blind
Doutreleau, L., and Nautin, P. 1976–1978. *Didyme l'Aveugle. Sur la Genèse 1–2*. SC 233, 244. Paris: Cerf. [*In Gen.*]
Doutreleau, L., Gesche, A., and Gronewald, M. 1969. *Didymos der Blinde. Psalmenkommentar, part 1*. Papyrologische Texte und Abhandlungen 7. Bonn: Habelt. [*Comm. Ps. 20–21*]
Doutreleau, L. 1962. *Didyme l'Aveugle sur Zacharie*. 3 vols. SC 83, 84, 85. Paris: Cerf. [*Comm. Zacch.*]
Gronewald, M. 1969. *Didymos der Blinde: Psalmenkommentar, Part 3*. PTA 8. Bonn: Habelt. [*Comm. Ps. 29–34*]
Henrichs, A. 1968. *Didymos der Blinde. Kommentar zu Hiob, parts 1–2*. Papyrologische Texte und Abhandlungen 1, 2. Bonn: Habelt. [*Comm. Job*]
Mühlenberg, E. 1975–1977. *Psalmenkommentare aus der Katenenüberlieferung*. 2 vols. PTS 15, 16. Berlin: De Gruyter. [*Frag. Ps.*]

Ps.-Didymus the Blind
Migne, J.-P. 1857–1866. PG 39. Paris: Migne. [*Trin.*]

Dio Chrysostom
von Arnim, J. 1893–1896. *Dionis Prusaensis quem vocant Chrysostomum quae exstant omnia*. 2 vols. Berlin: Weidmann.

Epiphanius
Holl, K. 1915–1933. *Epiphanius, Bände 1–3: Ancoratus und Panarion*. GCS 25, 31, 37. Leipzig: Hinrichs. [*Pan.*]

Eusebius of Caesarea
Heikel, I.A. 1913. *Eusebius Werke, Band 6: Die Demonstratio evangelica*. GCS 23. Leipzig: Hinrichs. [*Dem. ev.*]
Bardy, G. 1952–1958. *Eusèbe de Césarée. Histoire ecclésiastique*. 3 vols. SC 31, 41, 55. Paris: Cerf. [*Hist. eccl.*]
Gaisford, T. 1842. *Eusebii Pamphili episcopi Caesariensis eclogae propheticae*. Oxford: Oxford University Press. [*Ecl. proph.*]
Migne, J.-P. 1857–1866. PG 22, 24. Paris: Migne. [*Comm. Ps., Frag. Luc., Quaest. ev. Steph.*]
Mras, K. *Eusebius Werke, Band 8: Die Praeparatio evangelica*. GCS 43.1 and 43.2. Berlin: Akademie-Verlag. [*Praep. ev.*]
Ziegler, J. 1975. *Eusebius Werke. Band 9: Der Jesajakommentar*. GCS. Berlin: Akademie-Verlag. [*Comm. Is.*]

Eusebius of Emesa
Petit, F., Van Rompay, L., and Weitenberg, J.J.S. 2011. *Eusèbe D'Émèse. Commentaire de la Genèse*. TEG 15. Louvain: Peeters. [*Comm. Gen.*]

Evagrius
Tischendorf, C. 1860. *Notitia editionis codicis bibliorum Sinaitici*. Leipzig: Brockhaus, 1860. [*Exp. Prov.*]

George Kedrenos (Cedrenus)
Bekker, I. 1838–1839. *Georgius Cedrenus Joannis Scylitzae ope*. 2 vols. Corpus scriptorum historiae Byzantinae. Bonn: Weber.

Gregory of Nyssa
Jaeger, W. 1960–1992. *Gregorii Nysseni opera*. Leiden: Brill. [*Eun., Hom. opif., Vit. Moys.*]
Mueller, G. 1958. *Gregorii Nysseni opera*. Vol. 3.1. Leiden: Brill. [*Antirrhet. adv. Apoll.*]

Ps.-Gregory of Nyssa
Migne, J.-P. 1857–1866. PG 130. Paris: Migne. [*Lib. cogn. Dei*]

Hagiographiae et Martyria
Halkin, F. 1987. "Une vie grecque de sainte Marie-Madeleine (BHG 1161x)." *Analecta Bollandiana* 105: 6–16. [*Vit. Mar. Mag.*]
Von Dobschütz, E., and von Gebhardt, O. 1911. *Die Akten der edessenischen bekenner Gurjas, Samonas und Abibos*. TUGAL 37.2. Leipzig: Hinrichs. [*Mart. Gur. Sam.* BHG 735]
Usener, H. 1890. *Der heilige Theodosios: Schriften des Theodoros und Kyrillos*. Leipzig: Teubner, 1890. [*Vit. Theod.* BHG 1776]

Hesychius
Jagic, V. 1917. *Supplementum Psalterii Bononiensis. Incerti auctoris explanatio Graeca*, Vienna: Holzhausen. [*Comm. brev.*]

Ps.-Hippodamus
Thesleff, H. 1965. *The Pythagorean Texts of the Hellenistic Period*. Åbo: Åbo Akademi. [*Resp.*]

Hippolytus
Brière, M., Mariès, L., and Mercier, B.C. 1954. *Hippolyte de Rome. Sur les bénédictions d'Isaac, de Jacob et de Moïse*. PO 27, fasc. 1–2. Paris: Firmin-Didot et Companie. [*Bened. Is. Jac.*]

Irenaeus
Harvey, W.W. 1857. *Sancti Irenaei episcopi Lugdunensis libri quinque adversus haereses*, vol. 1–2. Cambridge: Cambridge University Press. [*Frag. deperdit.; Haer.* 1]

Jerome
Migne, J.-P. 1845. PL 23. Paris: Migne. [*Nom. hebr.*]

John Chrysostom
Migne, J.-P. 1857–1866. PG 51, 53, 54, 61. Paris: Migne [*Hom. Gen, In 1 Cor., Mut.*]
Wenger, A. 1970. *Jean Chrysostome. Huit catéchèses baptismales*. 2nd ed. SC 50. Paris: Cerf. [*Cat. ill.*]

Ps.-John Chrysostom
Migne, J.-P. 1857–1866. PG 64. Paris: Migne [*Sim. regn.*]

Ps.-John of Damascus
Declerck, J.H. 1994. *Anonymus dialogus cum Iudaeis saeculi ut videtur sexti*. CCSG 30. Turnhout: Brepols. [*Anon. dial. Jud.*]

Josephus
Niese, B. 1887–1890. *Flavii Iosephi opera.* 4 vols. Berlin: Weidmann. [*A.J.*]

Justin Martyr
Goodspeed, E.J. 1915. *Die ältesten Apologeten.* Göttingen: Vandenhoeck & Ruprecht. [*Apol.* 1–2, *Dial.*]
Minns, D., and Parvis, P. 2009. *Justin, Philosopher and Martyr: Apologies.* OECT. Oxford: Oxford University Press. [*Apol.* 1–2]

Ps.-Justin Martyr
Otto, J.C.T. 1879. *Corpus apologetarum Christianorum saeculi secundi, vol. 3.* 3rd ed. Jena: Mauke. [*Cohort. gent.*]

Ps.-Macarius
Berthold, H. 1973. *Makarios/Symeon Reden und Briefe.* 2 vols. GCS. Berlin: Akademie, 1973. [*Serm.*]

Maximus the Confessor
van Deun, P. 1991. *Maximi confessoris opuscula exegetica duo.* CCSG 23. Turnhout: Brepols. [*Exp. Ps. 59*]

Ps.-Maximus the Confessor
Levrie, K. 2017. *Maximi Confessoris Capita de duabus Christi naturis, necnon Pseudo-Maximi Confessoris Capita gnostica.* CCSG 89. Turnhout: Brepols. [*Capit. gnost.*]

Nilus of Ancyra
Migne, J.-P. 1857–1866. PG 79. Paris: Migne. [*Ep.*]

Origen
Borret, M. 1967–1969. *Origène. Contre Celse.* 4 vols. SC 132, 136, 147, 150. Paris: Cerf. [*Cels.*]
Baehrens, W.A. 1899–1955. *Origenes Werke: Vol. 6–8.* GCS 29, 30, 33. Leipzig: Teubner. [*Comm. Cant., Hom. Gen., Hom. Ex., Hom. Lev., Hom. Num., Hom. Jes. nav. xxvi*]
Blanc, C. 1966–1992. *Origène. Commentaire sur saint Jean.* 5 vols. SC 120, 157, 222, 290, 385. Paris: Cerf. [*Comm. Jo.*]
Görgemanns, H., and Karpp, H. 1976. *Origenes vier Bücher von den Prinzipien.* Darmstadt: Wissenschaftliche. [*Princ.*]
Klostermann, E. 1901. *Origenes Werke: Vol. 3.* GCS 6. Leipzig: Hinrichs. [*Engastr., Frag. Jer.*]
Migne, J.-P. 1857–1866. PG 12, 14, 17. Paris: Migne. [*Adnot. Deut., Comm. Rom., Sel. Gen., Sel. Num.*]

Nautin, P. 1976–1977. *Origène. Homélies sur Jérémie*. 2 vols. SC 232, 238. Paris: Cerf. [*Hom. Jer.*]

Perrone L. 2015. *Origenes Werke: eine kritische Edition des Codex Monacensis Graecus 314, vol. 13, Die neuen Psalmenhomilien*. GCS, NF 19. Berlin: De Gruyter. [*Hom. Ps.* 314]

Rauer, M. 1959. *Origenes Werke: Vol. 9*. 2nd edition. GCS 49 [35]. Berlin: Akademie Verlag. [*Frag. Luc., Hom. Luc.*]

Plato

Burnet, I. 1976–1982. *Platonis opera*. 5 vols. OCT. Oxford: Oxford University Press.

Hamilton, E., and Cairns, H. 1961. *Plato: The Collected Dialogues, Including the Letters*. Bollingen Series 71. New York: Pantheon.

Plutarch

Hubert, C. 1938. *Plutarchi moralia, vol. 4*. Leipzig: Teubner. [*Quaest. conviv.*]

Sieveking, W. 1935. *Plutarchi moralia*. Vol. 2.3. Leipzig: Teubner. [*Is. Os.*]

Procopius

Metzler, K. 2015. *Prokop von Gaza: Eclogarum in libros historicos Veteris Testamenti epitome, Teil 1: Der Genesiskommentar*. GCSNF 22. Berlin: de Gruyter.

Theodoret

Fernández Marcos, N., and Sáenz-Badillos, A. 1979. *Theodoreti Cyrensis quaestiones in Octateuchum*. Textos y Estudios «Cardenal Cisneros» 17. Madrid: Poliglota Matritense. [*Quaest. Oct.*]

Theodotus

Sagnard, F. 1948. *Clément d'Alexandrie. Extraits de Théodote*. 2nd ed. SC 23. Paris: Cerf. [*Exc. Theod.*]

Studies and Instrumenta

Adams, S.A. 2020. *Greek Genres and Jewish Authors: Negotiating Culture in the Greco-Roman Era*. Waco, TX: Baylor University Press.

Adams, S.A. 2018. "Movement and Travel in Philo's *Migration of Abraham*: The Adaptation of Genesis and the Introduction of a Metaphor." *SPhiloA* 30: 47–70.

Adler, M. 1929. *Studien zu Philon von Alexandreia*. Breslau: M. and H. Marcus.

Alesse, F. and L. de Luca, eds. 2019. *Philo of Alexandria and Greek Myth: Narratives, Allegories, and Arguments*. SPhA 10. Leiden: Brill.

Alesse, F., ed. 2008. *Philo of Alexandria and Post-Aristotelian Philosophy*. SPhA 5. Leiden: Brill.

Alexandre, Jr., M. 1999. *Rhetorical Argumentation in Philo of Alexandria*. BJS 322; SPhilo-M 2. Atlanta: Scholars Press.

Alexandre, Jr., M. 1991. "The Art of Periodic Composition in Philo of Alexandria." *SPhiloA* 3: 135–150.

Allenbach, J. et al., eds. 1982. *Biblia Patristica. Supplément: Philon d'Alexandrie.* Paris: Éditions du Centre National de la Recherche Scientifique (CNRS).

Amir, Y. 1967. "Explanation of Hebrew Names in Philo." *Tarbiz* 18: 128–139. [Hebrew]

Anderson, G.A., and M. Bockmuehl, eds. 2018. *Creation ex nihilo: Origins, Development, Contemporary Challenges.* Notre Dame, IN: University of Notre Dame Press.

Anderson, G.A. 2013. *Charity: The Place of the Poor in Biblical Tradition.* New Haven: Yale University Press.

Anderson, G.A. 2009. *Sin: A History.* New Haven: Yale University Press.

Anderson, G.A. 2003. "Joseph and the Passion of Our Lord." Pages 198–215 in *The Art of Reading Scripture.* Edited by E.F. Davis and R.B. Hays. Grand Rapids: Eerdmans.

Appelbaum, A. 2018. "A Fresh Look at Philo's Family." *SPhiloA* 30: 93–113.

Arnaldez, R. 1963. "Les images du sceau et de la lumière dans la pensée de Philon." *L'Information littéraire* 15: 62–72.

Attridge, H. 2017. "Stoic and Platonic Reflections on Naming in Early Christian Circles: Or, What's in a Name?" Pages 277–295 in *From Stoicism to Platonism: The Development of Philosophy, 100 BCE to 100 CE.* Edited by T. Engberg-Pedersen. Cambridge: Cambridge University Press.

Attridge, H. 1989. *The Epistle to the Hebrews.* Hermeneia. Minneapolis: Fortress.

Auvinen, R. 2024. *Philo and the Valentinians.* SPhiloM 10. Atlanta: SBL Press.

Barclay, J.M.G. 2015. *Paul and the Gift.* Grand Rapids, MI: Eerdmans.

Barnes, M.R. 2016. "Divine Powers in *De mutatione nominum* and Patristic Reception." Paper presented in the Philo of Alexandria Seminar at the Society of Biblical Literature Annual Meeting, "Special Session: *De mutatione nominum*," 21 Nov 2016, San Antonio, TX.

Barnes, M.R. 2001. *The Power of God: Dunamis in Gregory Of Nyssa's Trinitarian Theology.* Washington, DC: The Catholic University of America Press.

Barthélemy, D. 1967. "Est-ce Hoshaya Rabba qui censura le 'Commentaire Allégorique?' A partir des retouches faites aux citations bibliques, étude sur la tradition textuelle du commentaire allégorique de Philon." Pages 45–78 in *Philon d'Alexandre: Lyon 11–15 septembre 1966.* Edited by R. Arnaldez, C. Mondésert, and J. Pouilloux. Paris: Editions du Centre National de la Recherche Scientifique.

Bedrossian, M. 1879. *New Dictionary Armenian—English.* Venice: S. Lazarus Armenian Academy.

Bekken, P.J. 2007. *The Word is Near You: A Study of Deuteronomy 30:12–14 in Paul's Letter to the Romans in a Jewish Context.* BZNW 144. Berlin: De Gruyter.

Bernstein, M.J. 1983. "כי קללת אלהים תלוי" (Deut 21:23): A Study in Early Jewish Exegesis." *JQR* 74: 21–45.

Berthelot, K. 2012. "Philo and the Allegorical Interpretation of Homer (with an emphasis on Porphryry's *De Antro Nympharum*)." Pages 155–174 in *Homer and the Bible in the Eyes of Ancient Interpreters*. Edited by M. Niehoff. Leiden: Brill.

Birnbaum, E. and J. Dillon. 2021. *Philo of Alexandria, On the Life of Abraham: Introduction, Translation, and Commentary*. PACS 6. Leiden: Brill.

Birnbaum, E. 2016. "What in the Name of God Led Philo to Interpret Abraham, Isaac, and Jacob as Learning, Nature, and Practice?" *SPhiloA* 28: 273–296.

Birnbaum, E. 1996. *The Place of Judaism in Philo's Thought: Israel, Jews, and Proselytes*. SPhiloM 2. Atlanta: Scholars Press.

Boccaccini, G. 1998. *Beyond the Essene Hypothesis: the Parting of the Ways between Qumran and Enochic Judaism*. Grand Rapids, MI: Eerdmans.

Böhm, C. 2017. *Die Rezeption der Psalmen in den Qumranschriften, bei Philo von Alexandrien und im Corpus Paulinum*. WUNT 2.437. Tübingen: Mohr Siebeck.

Böhm, M. 2017. "Zum Glaubensverständnis des Philo von Alexandrien: Weisheitliche Theologie in der 1. Hälfte des 1. Jh. n. Chr." Pages 159–182 in *Glaube: Das Verständnis des Glaubens im frühen Christentum und in seiner jüdischen und hellenistisch-römischen Umwelt*. Edited by J. Frey, B. Schliesser, and N. Ueberschaer. WUNT 1.373. Tübingen: Mohr Siebeck.

Borgen, P. 2014. *The Gospel of John: More Light from Philo, Paul and Archaeology: The Scriptures, Tradition, Exposition, Settings, Meaning*. NovTSup 154. Leiden: Brill.

Borgen, P. 1965. *Bread from Heaven: An Exegetical Study of the Concept of Manna in the Gospel of John and the Writings of Philo*. NovTSup 10. Leiden: Brill.

Borgen, P. 1963. "Observations on the Midrashic Character of John 6." *ZNW* 54: 232–240.

Bosman, P.R. 2006. "Conscience and Free Speech in Philo." *SPhiloA* 18: 33–47.

Bowersock, G. 1969. *Greek Sophists in the Roman Empire*. Oxford: Clarendon.

Boys-Stones, G.R. 2001. *Post-Hellenistic Philosophy: A Study of Its Development from the Stoics to Origen*. Oxford: Oxford University Press.

Brenk, F., SJ. 2017. "Plutarch: Philosophy, Religion, and Ethics." Pages 291–310 in *The Oxford Handbook of the Second Sophistic*. Edited by D.S. Richter and W.A. Johnson. Oxford: Oxford University Press.

Brenk, F., SJ. 2023. "A Name by Any Name? The Allegorizing Etymologies of Philo and Plutarch." Pages 217–243 in *Plutarch on Literature, Graeco-Roman Religion, Jews and Christians*. Brill Plutarch Series 11. Leiden: Brill. Originally presented in the Philo of Alexandria Seminar at the Society of Biblical Literature Annual Meeting, "Special Session: *De mutatione nominum*," 21 Nov 2016, San Antonio, TX.

Brisson, L. 1998 [1994]. *Plato the Myth Maker*. Translated by G. Naddaf. Chicago: University of Chicago Press.

Brooke, G.J. 1985. *Exegesis at Qumran: 4QFlorilegium in Its Jewish Context*. JSOTSup 29. Sheffield: JSOT Press.

Bultmann, R. 1951–1955 [1948–1952]. *Theology of the New Testament*. 2 vols. Translated by K. Grobel. New York: Scribners.

Burkhardt, H. 1988. *Die Inspiration heiliger Schriften bei Philo von Alexandrien.* Giessen: Brunner.

Cazeaux, J. 1989. *La trame et la chaîne, II: Le Cycle de Noé dans Philon d'Alexandrie.* ALGHJ 20. Leiden: Brill.

Cazeaux, J. 1983. *La trame et la chaîne: ou les structures littéraires et l'exégèse dans cinq des traités de Philon d'Alexandrie.* ALGHJ 15. Leiden: Brill.

Cohen, N.G. 2007. *Philo's Scriptures: Citations from the Prophets and Writings: Evidence for a Haftarah Cycle in Second Temple Judaism.* JSJSup 123. Leiden: Brill, 2007.

Cohen, N.G. 1997. "The Names of the Separate Books of the Pentateuch in Philo's Writings." *SPhiloA* 9: 54–78.

Collins, J.J. 2020. "Love of Neighbor in Hellenistic-Era Judaism." *SPhiloA* 32: 97–111.

Collins, J.J. 1980. "The Epic of Theodotus and the Hellenism of the Hasmoneans." *HTR* 73: 91–104.

Conroy, J.T. 2008. "'The Wages of Sin Is Death:' The Death of the Soul in Greek, Second Temple Jewish, and Early Christian Authors." PhD diss., The University of Notre Dame, 2008.

Córdova, N.N. 2018. *Philo of Alexandria's Ethical Discourse: Living in the Power of Piety.* Lanham: Lexington/Fortress.

Cover, M.B. 2024a. "Paris and Augsburg Revisited: David Hoeschel, *Bürgerhumanismus*, and the Interconfessional Completion of Turnèbe's Philo." *Philon d'Alexandrie dans l'Europe moderne: réceptions d'un corpus judéo-hellénistique (XVIe–XVIIIe s.).* Edited by F. Gabriel, S. Marculescu, and J. Weinberg. Études augustiniennes. Turnhout: Brepols, Forthcoming.

Cover, M.B. 2024b. "Symbolic Purity and Microcosmic Anthropology in Philo's Allegorical Commentary." In *Purity in Ancient Judaism and Early Christianity.* Edited by L. Doering, J. Frey, and L. von Bartenwerffer. WUNT. Tübingen: Mohr Siebeck, Forthcoming.

Cover, M.B. 2024c. "What's in a Name Change? Neopythagorean Arithmology and Middle Platonic Namewrights in Philo's Orchard of Philosophy." In *Philo of Alexandria and Philosophical Discourse.* Edited by M.B. Cover and L. Doering. Göttingen: Vandenhoeck & Ruprecht, Forthcoming.

Cover, M.B. 2023a. "Israel's Scriptures in Philo." Pages 162–187 in *Israel's Scriptures in Early Christian Writings: The Use of the Old Testament in the New.* Edited by M. Henze and D. Lincicum. Grand Rapids: Eerdmans.

Cover, M.B. 2023b. "Origen of Alexandria." *The Reception of Philo of Alexandria.* Edited by C.J.P. Friesen, D. Lincicum, and D.T. Runia. Oxford: Oxford University Press, Forthcoming.

Cover, M.B. 2023c. "Philo of Alexandria." In *T & T Clark Handbook to Hellenistic Jewish Literature in Greek.* London: Bloomsbury, Forthcoming.

Cover, M.B. 2023d. "The Poetics of Association: Secondary and Tertiary Texts in the Thematic Development of Philo's *De Cherubim*." *SPhiloA* 25: Forthcoming. Originally presented in the Philo of Alexandria Seminar at the Society of Biblical Literature Annual Meeting, "Special Session: *De mutatione nominum*," 21 Nov 2016, San Antonio, TX.

Cover, M.B. 2022a. "Of Dreams and Editions: Emendations, Conjectures, and Marginal Summaries in David Hoeschel's Copy of *De somniis* 2." Pages 243–268 in *Ancient Texts, Papyri, and Manuscripts: Studies in Honor of James R. Royse*. NTTSD 64. Edited by A.T. Farnes, S. Mackie, and D.T. Runia. Leiden: Brill.

Cover, M.B. 2022b. "Philo of Alexandria, Eunomius, and Gregory of Nyssa on Divine Names and Power(s)." Pages 103–122 in *New Narratives for Old: Reading Early Christian Theology Using the Historical Method*. Edited by A. Briggman and E. Scully. Washington, DC: Catholic University of America Press.

Cover, M.B. 2021a. "The Conversion and Return of Simon Peter." Pages 131–149 in *Celebrating the Work of Arthur Darby Nock: Choice, Change, and Conversion*. Edited by R.M. Calhoun, J. Kelhoffer, and C. Rothschild. WUNT 472. Tübingen: Mohr Siebeck.

Cover, M.B. 2021b. "Karl Ernst Richter's Schwickert Edition: The Art (and Science) of Introducing Philo." *SPhiloA* 33: 175–196.

Cover, M.B. 2020a. "Jewish Wisdom in the Contest of Hellenistic Philosophy and Culture: Pseudo-Phocylides and Philo of Alexandria." Pages 229–247 in *The Wiley-Blackwell Companion to Wisdom Literature*. Edited by M. Goff and S. Adams. Hoboken, NJ: Wiley-Blackwell.

Cover, M.B. 2020b. "Philo's 'Confessions': An Alexandrian Jew between Nothing and Something." *SPhiloA* 32: 113–135.

Cover, M.B. 2018a. "A New Fragment of Philo's *Quaestiones in Exodum* in Origen's Newly Discovered Homilies on the Psalms? A Preliminary Note." *SPhiloA* 30 (2018a): 15–29. Spanish Translation: "¿Un nuevo fragmento de *Quaestiones in Exodum* de Filón en *Homiliae in Psalmos* recientemente descubierto de Orígenes? Una nota preliminar." Translated by P. Druille. *Circe de clásicos y modernos* 24/2 (2020c): 129–143.

Cover, M.B. 2018b. Review of John M.G. Barclay. *Paul and the Gift* (Grand Rapids, MI: Eerdmans, 2015). In *SPhiloA* 30: 204–207. For an expanded version of this review, in dialogue with the author, see: https://syndicate.network/symposia/theology/paul-and-the-gift/

Cover, M.B. 2016a. "*Paulus als Yischmaelit?* The Personification of Scripture as Interpretive Authority in Paul and the School of Rabbi Ishmael." *JBL* 135: 611–631.

Cover, M.B. 2016b. "Sample Commentary on Philo's *De mutatione nominum*: Introduction and Chapter Five." Paper presented to the Philo of Alexandria Seminar at the SBL Annual Meeting, 19–22 Nov 2016, San Antonio, Texas.

Cover, M.B. 2015. *Lifting the Veil: 2 Corinthians 3:7–18 in Light of Jewish Homiletic and Commentary Traditions*, BZNW 210. Berlin: de Gruyter, 2015.

Cover, M.B. 2014. "The Sun and the Chariot: The *Republic* and the *Phaedrus* as Sources for Rival Platonic Paradigms of Psychic Vision in Philo's Biblical Commentaries." *SPhiloA* 26: 151–167.

Cover, M.B. 2010. "Reconceptualizing Conquest: Colonial Narratives and Philo's Roman Accuser in the *Hypothetica*." *SPhiloA* 22: 183–207

Cuomo, S. 2001. *Ancient Mathematics*. Sciences of Antiquity. London: Routledge.

Cuomo, S. 2000. *Pappus of Alexandria and the Mathematics of Late Antiquity*. Cambridge Classical Studies. Cambridge: Cambridge University Press.

Dawson, D. 1992. *Allegorical Readers and Cultural Revision in Ancient Alexandria*. Berkley, CA: University of California Press.

DelCogliano, M. 2010. *Basil of Caesarea's Anti-Eunomian Theory of Names: Christian Theology and Late-Antique Philosophy in the Fourth Century Trinitarian Controversy*. VCSup 103. Leiden: Brill.

Despotis, A. 2021. "Aspects of Cultural Hybridity in Philo's Apophatic Anthropology." *SPhiloA* 33: 91–108.

Diels, H. 1970 [1917]. *Philodemos über die Götter: Erstes und drittes Buch*. Abhandlungen der königlich preussischen Akademie der Wissenschaften, Philosophisch-Historische Klasse 7. Leipzig: Zentralantiquariat der Deutschen Demokratischen Republik.

Diels, H. 1879. *Doxographi Graeci*. Berlin: Weidmann.

Dillon, J.M. 1997. "The Pleasures and Perils of Soul-Gardening." *SPhiloA* 9: 190–197.

Dillon, J.M. 1996 [1977]. *The Middle Platonists, 80 B.C. to A.D. 220*. Rev. ed. Ithaca, NY: Cornell University Press.

Dillon, J.M. 1992. Review of Jacques Cazeaux, *La Trame et la Chaîne, II: le Cycle de Noë dans Philon d'Alexandrie* (Leiden: Brill, 1989) in *VC* 46: 83–87.

Dillon, J.M. 1978. "Philo of Alexandria and the *Cratylus*." *Liverpool Classical Monthly* 3: 37–42.

Doering, L. 2018. "'And Who is My Neighbour?' Revisiting the Love Commandment and the Golden Rule in Ancient Judaism." Paper delivered in the Early Jewish Theologies and the New Testament Seminar at the 73rd General Meeting of the SNTS, 8–10 Aug 2018, Athens, Greece.

Edwards, M. 2014. *Image, Word and God in the Early Christian Centuries*. Ashgate Studies in Philosophy and Theology in Late Antiquity. Farnham: Ashgate.

Elder, N. 2018. "'Wretch I Am!' Eve's Tragic Speech-in-Character in Romans 7:7–25." *JBL* 137: 143–163.

Engberg-Pedersen, T., ed. 2017. *From Stoicism to Platonism: The Development of Philosophy, 100 BCE to 100 CE*. Cambridge: Cambridge University Press.

Erbse, H., ed. 1969. *Scholia Graeca in Homeri Iliadem*. 7 vols. Berlin: De Gruyter.

Erginel, M.M. 2011. "Plato on the Psychology of Pleasure and Pain." *Phoenix* 65: 288–314.

Feeney, D. 2004. "Introduction" to David Raeburn, trans., *Ovid: Metamorphoses. A New Verse Translation*. London: Penguin.

Feldmeier, R. 2017. "Gotteserkenntnis durch Selbsterkenntnis: Philons *Migratio* in ihrem religionsgeschichtlichen Kontext." Pages 203–218 in H. Detering et al., *Abraham's Aufbruch: Philon von Alexandria, De migratione Abrahami.* SAPERE 30. Tübingen: Mohr Siebeck.

Fitzgerald, J.T., ed. 1996. *Friendship, Flattery, and Frankness of Speech: Studies on Friendship in the New Testament World.* NovTSup 82. Leiden: Brill.

Förster, N. 2000. "The Exegesis of Homer and Numerology as a Method for Interpreting the Bible in the Writings of Philo of Alexandria." Pages 91–98 in *Jewish Ways of Reading the Bible.* Edited by G.J. Brooke. Journal of Semitic Studies Supplement 11. Oxford: Oxford University Press.

Fraade, S.D. 1991. *From Tradition to Commentary: Torah and Its Interpretation in the Midrash Sifre to Deuteronomy.* Albany, NY: SUNY Press.

Francis, M. 2015. "Borderline Bad: Philo of Alexandria on the Distinction between Voluntary and Involuntary Sin." PhD diss., University of Notre Dame.

Friesen, C.J.P. 2019. "Heracles and Philo of Alexandria: The Son of Zeus between Torah and Philosophy, Empire and Stage." Pages 176–199 in *Philo of Alexandria and Greek Myth.* Edited by F. Alesse and L. de Luca. SPhA 10. Leiden: Brill.

Friesen, C.J.P. 2015. *Reading Dionysus: Euripides' Bacchae and the Cultural Contestations of Greeks, Jews, Romans, and Christians.* STAC 95. Tübingen: Mohr Siebeck.

Friesen, C.J.P., D. Lincicum, and D.T. Runia, eds. 2023. *The Reception of Philo of Alexandria.* Oxford: Oxford University Press, Forthcoming.

Gardiner, Q. and D. Baltzly. 2020. "Hermias on the Unity of the *Phaedrus*." Pages 68–83 in *Studies in Hermias' Commentary on Plato's Phaedrus.* Edited by J.F. Finamore, C.-P. Manolea, and S. Klitenic Wear. Studies in Platonism, Neoplatonism, and the Platonic Tradition 24. Leiden: Brill.

Geljon, A.C. and D.T. Runia. 2019. *Philo of Alexandria, On Planting: Introduction, Translation, and Commentary.* PACS 5. Leiden: Brill.

Geljon, A.C. and D.T. Runia. 2013. *Philo of Alexandria, On Cultivation: Introduction, Translation, and Commentary.* PACS 4. Leiden: Brill.

Geljon, A.C. and D.T. Runia. 2002. *Philonic Exegesis in Gregory of Nyssa's* De vita Moysis. BJS 333; SPhiloM 5. Providence, RI: Brown Judaic Studies.

Gershowitz, U. and A. Kovelman. 2002. "A Symmetrical Teleological Construction in the Treatises of Philo and in the Talmud." *Review of Rabbinic Judaism* 5: 228–246.

Gilbert, S. 1952. *James Joyces's Ulysses: A Study.* 2nd edition. New York: Alfred Knopf.

Goodenough, E.R. 1935. *By Light, Light: The Mystic Gospel of Hellenistic Judaism.* New Haven: Yale University Press.

Goodenough, E.R. 1938. *The Politics of Philo Judaeus: Practice and Theory; with a General Bibliography of Philo by Howard L. Goodhart and Erwin R. Goodenough.* New Haven: Yale University Press.

Goulet, R. 1987. *La philosophie de Moïse: Essai de reconstitution d'un commentaire philosophique préphilonien du Pentateuque.* Paris: J. Vrin.

Grabbe, L.L. 1988. *Etymology in Early Jewish Interpretation: The Hebrew Names in Philo.* BJS 115. Atlanta: Scholars Press.

Graver, M. 2008. "Philo of Alexandria and the Origins of the Stoic ΠΡΟΠΑΘΕΙΑΙ." Pages 197–221 in *Philo of Alexandria and Post-Aristotelian Philosophy.* SPhA 5. Leiden: Brill.

Graver, M. 2007. *Stoicism and Emotion.* Chicago: University of Chicago Press.

Hamerton-Kelly, R.G. 1972. "Sources and Traditions in Philo Judaeus: Prolegomena to an Analysis of His Writings." *SPhilo* 1: 3–26.

Harl, M. 1961. *Les œuvres de Philon d'Alexandrie: Quis Rerum Divinarum Heres Sit.* PAPM 15. Paris: Cerf.

Harris, J.R. 1887. "Hermas in Arcadia." *JBL* 7: 69–83.

Harris, J.R. 1886. *Fragments of Philo Judaeus.* Cambridge: Cambridge University Press.

Hay, D. 1991. "Philo's View of Himself as Exegete: Inspired But Not Authoritative." *SPhiloA* 3: 40–52.

Hay, D. 1991. "References to Other Exegetes." Pages 81–89 in *Both Literal and Allegorical: Studies in Philo of Alexandria's Questions and Answers on Genesis and Exodus.* Edited by idem. BJS 232. Atlanta: Scholars Press.

Hay, D. 1989. "*Pistis* as 'Ground for Faith' in Hellenized Judaism and Paul." *JBL* 108: 461–476.

Hay, D. 1979–1980. "Philo's References to Other Allegorists." *SPhilo* 6: 41–61

Hays, R. 1983. *The Faith of Jesus Christ: An Investigation of the Narrative Substructure of Galatians 3:1–4:11.* Chico, CA: Scholars Press.

Heath, M. 1989. "The Unity of Plato's *Phaedrus*." OSAP 7: 151–173.

Heath, T. 1921. *A History of Greek Mathematics.* Oxford: Clarendon.

Hilgert, E. 1985. "The Dual Image of Joseph in Hebrew and Early Jewish Literature." *BR* 30: 5–21.

Hirsch-Luipold, R. 2017. "Religiöse Tradition und individueller Glaube: Πίστις und πιστεύειν bei Plutarch als Hintergrund zum neutestamentlichen Glaubensverständnis." Pages 251–273 in *Glaube: Das Verständnis des Glaubens im frühen Christentum und in seiner jüdischen und hellenistisch-römischen Umwelt.* Edited by J. Frey, B. Schliesser, and N. Ueberschaer. WUNT 1.373. Tübingen: Mohr Siebeck.

Holladay, C. 1989. *Fragments from Hellenistic Jewish Authors: Volume II: Poets.* Texts and Translations: Pseudepigrapha Series 30. Chico, CA: Scholars Press.

Hornblower, S. 2014. "Lykophron and Epigraphy: The Value and Function of Cult Epithets in the *Alexandra*." *CQ* 64: 91–120.

Hrobon, B. 2013. "Shaping Up the Form of the Tabernacle." *VT* 63: 555–565.

Ierodiakonou, K. 1993. "The Stoic Division of Philosophy." *Phronesis* 38: 57–74.

Inwood, B. 2021. Review of *Aëtiana V*, by Jaap Mansfeld and David T. Runia, eds., *SPhiloA* 33: 31–35

Inwood, B. 1985. *Ethics and Human Action in Early Stoicism.* Oxford: Oxford University Press.

Jacobson, H. 1983. *The Exagogue of Ezekiel*. Cambridge: Cambridge University Press.
Jastram, D.N. 1991. "Philo's Concept of Generic Virtue." SBLSP 30: 323–347.
Jastram, D.N. 1989. *Philo's Concept of Generic Virtue*. PhD Diss., University of Wisconsin, Madison.
Kamesar, A., ed. 2009. *The Cambridge Companion to Philo*. Cambridge: Cambridge University Press.
Kamesar, A. 2004. "The *Logos Endiathetos* and the *Logos Prophorikos* in Allegorical Interpretation: Philo and the D-Scholia to the *Iliad*." GRBS 44: 163–181.
Kattan Gribetz, S. 2018. "*Zekhut Imahot*: Mothers, Fathers, and Ancestral Merit in Rabbinic Sources." JSJ 49: 263–296.
Katz, P. 1950. *Philo's Bible: The Aberrant Text of Bible Quotations in Some Philonic Writings and Its Place in the Textual History of the Greek Bible*. Cambridge: Cambridge University Press.
Keizer, H.M. 2000. "'Eternity Revisited': A Study of the Greek Word Αἰών." *Philosophia Reformata* 65 (2000): 53–71.
Konstan, D. 2006. *The Emotions of the Ancient Greeks: Studies in Aristotle and Classical Literature*. Toronto: University of Toronto Press.
Korsgaard, C.M. 2008. *The Constitution of Agency: Essays on Practical Reason and Moral Psychology*. Oxford: Oxford University Press.
Koskenniemi, E. 2019. *Greek Writers and Philosophers in Philo and Josephus: a Study of Their Secular Education and Educational Ideals*. SPhA 9. Leiden: Brill.
LaPorte, J. 1983. *Eucharistia in Philo*. Studies in the Bible and Early Christianity 3. New York: Edwin Mellon.
Lateiner, D. and D. Spatharas. 2016. *The Ancient Emotion of Disgust*. Oxford: Oxford University Press.
Lausberg, H. 1960. *Handbuch der literarischen Rhetorik: eine Grundlegung der Literaturwissenschaft*. 2 vols. München: M. Hueber.
Leonhardt-Balzer, J. 2001. *Jewish Worship in Philo of Alexandria*. TSAJ 84. Tübingen: Mohr Siebeck.
Levenson, J.D. 1993. *The Death and Resurrection of the Beloved Son: the Transformation of Child Sacrifice in Judaism and Christianity*. New Haven: Yale University Press.
Levison, J.R. 2009. *Filled with the Spirit*. Grand Rapids: Eerdmans.
Lévy, C. 2024. "Was Philo's Moses a Pyrrhonian Hero?" In *Philo and Philosophical Discourse*. Edited by M.B. Cover and L. Doering. Göttingen: Vandenhoeck & Ruprecht, Forthcoming.
Lévy, C. 2019. "Philo of Alexandria vs. Descartes: An Ignored Jewish Premonitory Critic of the *Cogito*." Pages 5–22 in *Sceptical Paths: Enquiry and Doubt from Antiquity to the Present*. Edited by G. Veltri et al. Berlin: de Gruyter.
Lévy, C. 2018. Review of *Philo of Alexandria: An Intellectual Biography*, by Maren Niehoff, *SPhiloA* 30: 183–190.

Lincicum, D. 2014. "Philo's Library." *SPhiloA* 26: 99–114.
Lincicum, D. 2013. "A Preliminary Index to Philo's Non-Biblical Citations and Allusions." *SPhiloA* 25: 139–167.
Lincicum, D. 2010. *Paul and the Early Jewish Encounter with Deuteronomy*. WUNT 2.284. Tübingen: Mohr Siebeck.
Litwa, M.D. 2014. "The Deification of Moses in Philo of Alexandria." *SPhiloA* 26: 1–27.
Long, A.A. 1997. "Allegory in Philo and Etymology in Stoicism: A Plea for Drawing Distinctions." *SPhiloA* 9: 198–210.
Long, A.A. and D.N. Sedley. 1987. *The Hellenistic Philosophers*. 2 vols. Cambridge: Cambridge University Press.
Lourié, B. 2016. "Temporality and a Metric for Created Natures in Gregory of Nyssa." *Scrinium* 12: 340–351.
Luck, G. 1953. *Der Akademiker Antiochos*. Bern: P. Haupt.
Mack, B. and E. Hilgert. 1972. "Introducing *Studia Philonica*." *SPhilo* 1: 1.
Malherbe, A.J. 2014. *Light from the Gentiles: Hellenistic Philosophy and Early Christianity. Collected Essays, 1959–2012*. Edited by C.R. Holladay, J.T. Fitzgerald, G.E. Sterling, and J. Thompson. NovTSup 150. Leiden: Brill.
Mansfeld, J. 2022. "Doxography of Ancient Philosophy," *The Stanford Encyclopedia of Philosophy* (Fall 2022 Edition). Edited by E.N. Zalta and U. Nodelman. https://plato.stanford.edu/archives/fall2022/entries/doxography-ancient/.
Mansfeld, J. 1988. "Philosophy in the Service of Scripture: Philo's Exegetical Strategies." Pages 70–102 in *The Question of Eclecticism*. Edited by J.M. Dillon and A.A. Long. Berkeley: University of California Press.
Mansfeld, J. and D.T. Ruina. 2020. *Aëtiana: Volume v.1–4. An Edition of the Text of the Placita with a Commentary and a Collection of Related Texts*. PhA 153.1–4. Leiden: Brill.
Martín, J.P. 2016. "Presentación." Pages 9–13 in *Filón de Alejandría: Obras Completas, Volume IV*. Edited by idem et al. Madrid: Trotta.
Massebieau, L. and É. Bréhier. 1906. "Essai sur la chronologie de la vie et des oeuvres de Philon." RHR 53: 25–64; 164–185; 267–289.
Massebieau, L. 1889. *Classement des Oeuvres de Philon*. Paris: Leroux.
McFarland, O. 2016. *God and Grace in Philo and Paul*. NovTSup 164. Leiden: Brill.
Méasson, A. 1986. *Du char ailé de Zeus à l'Arche d'Alliance: Images et mythes platoniciens chez Philon d'Alexandrie*. Paris: Études Augustiniennes.
Meier, J.P. 2009. *A Marginal Jew. Volume Four, Law and Love*. AYBRL. New Haven: Yale University Press.
Mendelson, A. 1982. *Secular Education in Philo of Alexandria*. HUCM 7. Cincinnati: Hebrew Union College Press.
Michaelis, J.D. 1768–1776. *Raisonnement über die protestantischen Universitäten in Deutschland*. 4 vols. Frankfurt and Leipzig.

Moehring, H. 1995. "Arithmology as an Exegetical Tool in the Writings of Philo of Alexandria." Pages 141–176 in *The School of Moses: Studies in Philo and Hellenistic Religion. In memory of Horst R. Moehring*. Edited by J.P. Kenney. BJS 304. SPhiloM 1. Atlanta: Scholars Press.

Montes-Peral, L.A. 1987. *Akataleptos Theos: der unfassbare Gott*. ALGHJ 16. Leiden: Brill.

Morgan, T. 2015. *Roman Faith and Christian Faith: Pistis and in the Early Roman Empire and Early Churches*. Oxford: Oxford University Press.

Morgan, T. 2007. *Popular Morality in the Hellenistic and Roman Worlds*. Cambridge: Cambridge University Press.

Morris, J. 1987 [1973]. "The Jewish Philosopher Philo." Pages 813–870 in *The History of the Jewish People in the Age of Jesus Christ (175 B.C.–A.D. 135)*. Edited by E. Schürer. Translated by T.A. Burkill et al. Revized by G. Vermes and F. Millar. Edinburgh: Clark.

Nagy, G. 2005. "The Epic Hero." Pages 71–89 in *A Companion to Ancient Epic*. Edited by J.M. Foley. Malden, MA: Wiley Blackwell.

Nagy, G. 1999. "Homer and Plato at the Panathenaia: Synchronic and Diachronic Perspectives." Pages 123–150 in *Contextualizing Classics: Ideology, Performance, Dialogue: Essays in Honor of John J. Peradotto*. Edited by T.M. Falkner, N. Felson, and D. Konstan. Lanham, MD: Rowman and Littlefield.

Najman, H. 2003. "Cain and Abel as Character Traits: A Study in the Allegorical Typology of Philo of Alexandria." Pages 107–119 in *Eve's Children: the Biblical Stories Retold and Interpreted in Jewish and Christian Traditions*. Edited by G. Luttikhuizen. Themes in Biblical Narrative 5. Leiden: Brill.

Niehoff, M.R. 2021. "Roger Arnaldez' Vision of Philo." Pages 82–88 in *Les études philoniennes: Regards sur cinquante ans de recherche (1967–2017)*. SPhA 13. Leiden: Brill.

Niehoff, M.R. 2020. "Paul and Philo on the Psalms: Towards a Spiritual Notion of Scripture." *NovT* 62: 392–415.

Niehoff, M.R. 2018. *Philo of Alexandria: An Intellectual Biography*. New Haven: Yale University Press.

Niehoff, M.R., ed. 2012. *Homer and the Bible in the Eyes of Ancient Interpreters*. Leiden: Brill.

Niehoff, M.R. 2011. *Jewish Exegesis and Homeric Scholarship in Alexandria*. Cambridge: Cambridge University Press.

Niehoff, M.R. 1995. "What is in a Name? Philo's Mystical Philosophy of Language." *JSQ* 2.3: 220–252.

Niehoff, M.R. 1992. *The Figure of Joseph in Post-Biblical Jewish Literature*. AGJU 16. Leiden: Brill.

Hernández, P.N. 2014. "Philo and Greek Poetry." *SPhiloA* 26: 135–149.

Nikiprowetzky, V. 1977. *Le commentaire de l'Écriture chez Philon d'Alexandrie: son caractère et sa portée: Observations philologiques*. ALGHJ 11. Leiden: Brill.

Nikiprowetzky, V. 1967. "La spiritualisation des sacrifices et le culte sacrificiel au temple de Jérusalem chez Philon d'Alexandrie." *Sem* 17: 97–116.

Nissen, A. 1974. *Gott und der Nächste im Antiken Judentum: Untersuchungen zum Doppelgebot der Liebe*. Tübingen: Mohr Siebeck.

Orlov, A.A. 2017. *Yahoel and Metatron: Aural Apocalypticism and the Origins of Early Jewish Mysticism*. TSAJ 169. Tübingen: Mohr Siebeck.

Orlov, A.A. 2013. *Heavenly Priesthood in the Apocalypse of Abraham*. Cambridge: Cambridge University Press.

Otte, K. 1968. *Das Sprachverständnis bei Philo von Alexandrien*. Tübingen: Mohr Siebeck.

Pearce, S. 2007. *The Land of the Body: Studies in Philo's Representation of Egypt*. WUNT 208. Tübingen: Mohr Siebeck.

Reydams-Schils, G. 2008. "Philo of Alexandria on Stoic and Platonist Psycho-Physiology: The Socratic Higher Ground." Pages 169–195 in *Philo of Alexandria and Post-Aristotelian Philosophy*. Edited by F. Alesse. SPhA 5. Leiden: Brill.

Reydams-Schils, G. 1995. "Stoicized Readings of Plato's Timaeus in Philo of Alexandria." *SPhiloA* 7: 85–102.

Robbins, F.E.. 1931. "Arithmetic in Philo Judaeus." *CP* 26: 345–361.

Rokeah, D. 1968. "A New Onomasticon Fragment from Oxyrhynchus and Philo's Etymologies." *JTS* 19: 70–82.

Roskam, G. 2017. "Nutritious Milk from Hagar's School: Philo's Reception of Homer." *SPhiloA* 29: 1–32.

Royse, J.R. 2021. "The Cohn-Wendland Critical Edition of Philo of Alexandria." *SPhiloA* 33: 197–207.

Royse, J.R. 2016. "The Text of *De mutatione nominum*." Paper delivered at the Philo of Alexandria Seminar at the SBL Annual Meeting, 21 Nov 2016, San Antonio, TX.

Royse, J.R. 2009. "The Works of Philo." Pages 32–64 in *The Cambridge Companion to Philo*. Edited by A. Kamesar. Cambridge: Cambridge University Press.

Runia, D.T. 2020. "The Virtue of Hope in the Writings and Thought of Philo." *SPhiloA* 32: 257–274.

Runia, D.T. 2019. "Is Philo Committed to the Doctrine of Reincarnation?" *SPhiloA* 31: 107–125.

Runia, D.T. 2012. "Philo in Byzantium: An Exploration." *VC* 70: 259–281.

Runia, D.T. 2008. "Philo and Hellenistic Doxography." Pages 13–54 in *Philo of Alexandria and Post-Aristotelian Philosophy*. Edited by F. Alesse. SPhA 5. Leiden: Brill.

Runia, D.T. 2004. "Etymology as an Allegorical Technique in Philo of Alexandria." *SPhiloA*: 101–121.

Runia, D.T. 2002. "The Beginning of the End: Philo of Alexandria and Hellenistic Theology." Pages 281–316 in *Traditions of Theology: Studies in Hellenistic Theology, Its Background and Aftermath*. Edited by D. Frede and A. Las. PhilAnt 89. Leiden: Brill.

Runia, D.T. 2001a. *On the Creation of the Cosmos according to Moses.* PACS 1. Leiden: Brill.

Runia, D.T. 2001b. "Philo's Reading of the Psalms." *SPhiloA* 13: 102–121.

Runia, D.T. 1995a. *Philo and the Church Fathers: A Collection of Papers.* VCSup 32. Leiden: Brill.

Runia, D.T. 1995b. "Why Does Clement of Alexandria Call Philo 'The Pythagorean'?" *VC* 49: 1–22.

Runia, D.T. 1993. *Philo in Early Christian Literature: A Survey.* CRINT 3. Assen: Van Gorcum.

Runia, D.T. 1991. "Secondary Texts in Philo's *Quaestiones*." Pages 47–79 in *Both Literal and Allegorical: Studies in Philo of Alexandria's Questions and Answers on Genesis and Exodus.* Edited by idem. BJS 232. Atlanta: Scholars Press.

Runia, D.T. 1988. "Naming and Knowing: Themes in Philonic Theology with Special Reference to the *De mutatione nominum*." Pages 69–91 in *Knowledge of God in the Graeco-Roman World.* Edited by R. Van den Broek, T. Baarda, and J. Mansfeld. Leiden: Brill.

Runia, D.T. 1987. "Further Observations on the Structure of Philo's Allegorical Treatises." *VC* 41: 105–138.

Runia, D.T. 1984. "The Structure of Philo's Allegorical Treatises: A Review of Two Recent Studies and Some Additional Comments." *VC* 38: 209–256.

Salvesen, A., S. Pearce, M. Frenkel, and D.J. Crowther, eds. 2020. *Israel in Egypt: The Land of Egypt as Concept and Reality for Jews in Antiquity and the Early Medieval Period.* AJEC 110. Leiden: Brill.

Schäfer, P. 2020. *Two Gods in Heaven: Jewish Concepts of God in Antiquity.* Princeton: Princeton University Press.

Schironi, F. 2012. "Greek Commentaries." *DSD* 19: 399–441.

Schliesser, B. 2011. *Was ist Glaube? Paulinische Perspektiven.* Zürich: Theologischer Verlag.

Schwartz, D.R. 2009. "Philo, His Family, His Times." Pages 9–31 in *The Cambridge Companion to Philo.* Edited by A. Kamesar. Cambridge: Cambridge University Press.

Scott, J. 2015. *Bacchius Iudaeus: A Denarius Commemorating Pompey's Victory over Judea.* NTOA 104. Göttingen: Vandenhoeck & Ruprecht.

Segal, A. 1977. *Two Powers in Heaven: Early Rabbinic Reports About Christianity And Gnosticism.* Leiden: Brill.

Shaw, F. 2015. "An Onomastic History: What Can Philo Provide?" Paper Delivered at the Philo of Alexandria Seminar at the Society of Biblical Literature Annual Meeting, Nov 2015 in Atlanta, Georgia.

Shroyer, M.J. 1936. "Alexandrian Jewish Literalists." *JBL* 55: 261–284.

Siegert, F. 1996–2015. "Early Jewish Interpretation in a Hellenistic Style." Pages I.1:130–198 in *Hebrew Bible / Old Testament: the History of Its Interpretation.* 3 vols. Edited by Magne Sæbø. Göttingen: Vandenhoeck & Ruprecht.

Siegert, F. 1998. "The Philonian Fragment *De Deo*: First English Translation." *SPhiloA* 10: 1–33.

Siegert, F. 1992. *Drei hellenistische Predigten II. Ps.-Philon, "Über Jona," "Über Jona" (Fragment) und "Über Simson."* WUNT 1.61. Tübingen: Mohr Siebeck.

Siegert, F. 1988. *Philon von Alexandrien: über die Gottesbezeichnung 'wohltätig verzehrendes Feuer' (De Deo): Rückübersetzung des Fragments aus dem Armenischen, deutsche Übersetzung und Kommentar.* WUNT 1.46. Tübingen: Mohr Siebeck.

Siegert, F. 1980. *Drei hellenistische Predigten I. Ps.-Philon, "Über Jona," "Über Simson," und "Über die Gottesbezeichnung 'wohltätig verzehrendes Feuer.'"* WUNT 1.20. Tübingen: Mohr Siebeck.

Siegfried, C.G.A. 1863. *Die hebräischen Worterklärungen des Philo und die Spuren ihrer Einwirkung auf die Kirchenväter.* Magdeburg: E. Baensch.

Sly, D. 1990. *Philo's Perception of Women.* BJS 209. Atlanta: Scholars Press.

Speiser, E.A. 1964. *Genesis.* AB 1. Garden City, NY: Doubleday.

Staehle, K. 1931. *Zahlenmystik bei Philon von Alexandreia.* Leipzig-Berlin: Teubner.

Sterling, G.E. 2024a. "Adrianus Turnebus and the *Editio Princeps* of Philo (1552)." *Philon d'Alexandrie dans l'Europe moderne: réceptions d'un corpus judéo-hellénistique (XVIe–XVIIIe s.).* Edited by F. Gabriel, S. Marculescu, and J. Weinberg. Études augustiniennes. Turnhout: Brepols, Forthcoming.

Sterling, G.E. 2024b. "Apophaticism and Skepticism in Philo of Alexandria." In *Scepticism in Philo.* Edited by C. Lévy and Z. Strauss. In Preparation.

Sterling, G.E. 2024c. "Philo's Library and the Libraries of Philosophical Schools." In *Philo and Philosophical Discourse.* Edited by M.B. Cover and L. Doering. Göttingen: Vandenhoeck & Ruprecht, Forthcoming.

Sterling, G.E. 2022a. "A Human *sui generis*: Philo of Alexandria's *De vita Moysis*." *JSJ* 73: 225–250.

Sterling, G.E. 2022b. "Did Ancient Philosophers Read Philo? Philo of Alexandria and Plotinus." Pages 37–63 in *At the Borders of the New Testament: Studies in Honor of Johan C. Thom.* Edited by G. Kotze and P. Bosman. NovTSup. Leiden: Brill.

Sterling, G.E. 2021. "The First Critical Edition of Philo: Thomas Mangey and the 1742 Edition." *SPhiloA* 33: 133–159.

Sterling, G.E. 2018a. "Dancing with the Stars: The Ascent of the Mind in Philo of Alexandria." Pages 155–166 in *Apocalypticism and Mysticism in Ancient Judaism and Early Christianity.* Edited by P.G.R. de Villiers, A. Yarbro Collins, and J.J. Collins. Ekstasis 7. Berlin: de Gruyter.

Sterling, G.E. 2018b. "The Structure of Philo's Allegorical Commentary." *TLZ* 143: 1225–1238.

Sterling, G.E. 2017. "'The Most Perfect Work': The Role of Matter in Philo of Alexandria." Pages 243–257 in *Light on Creation: Ancient Commentators in Dialogue and Debate on the Origin of the World.* Edited by G. Roskam and J. Verheyden. STAC 104. Tübingen: Mohr Siebeck.

Sterling, G.E. 2014. "From the Thick Marshes of the Nile to the Throne of God: Moses in Ezekiel the Tragedian and Philo of Alexandria." *SPhiloA* 26: 115–133.

Sterling, G.E. 2013a. "'A Man of the Highest Repute': Did Josephus Know the Writings of Philo?" *SPhiloA* 25: 101–113.

Sterling, G.E. 2013b. "Different Traditions or Emphases? The Image of God in Philo's *De Opificio Mundi*." Pages 41–56 in *New Approaches to the Study of Biblical Interpretation in Judaism of the Second Temple Period and in Early Christianity: Proceedings of the Eleventh International Symposium of the Orion Center for the Study of the Dead Sea Scrolls and Associated Literature, Jointly Sponsored by the Hebrew University Center for the Study of Christianity, 9–11 January, 2007*. Edited by G.A. Anderson, R. Clements, and D. Satran. STDJ 106. Leiden: Brill.

Sterling, G.E. 2012a. "Prolific in Expression and Broad in Thought: Internal References to Philo's Allegorical Commentary and Exposition of the Law." *Euphrosyne* 40: 55–76.

Sterling, G.E. 2012b. "The Interpreter of Moses: Philo of Alexandria and the Biblical Text." Pages 413–435 in *The Companion on Biblical Interpretation in Early Judaism*. Edited by M. Henze. Grand Rapids: Eerdmans.

Sterling, G.E. 2012c. "When the Beginning is the End: The Place of Genesis in the Commentaries of Philo of Alexandria." Pages 427–446 in *The Book of Genesis: Composition, Reception, and Interpretation*. Edited by C.A. Evans, J.N. Lohr, and D.L. Petersen. VTSup 152; FIOTL 6. Leiden: Brill.

Sterling, G.E. 2012d. "Which Version of the Greek Bible Did Philo Read?" Pages 89–127 in *Pentateuchal Traditions in the Late Second Temple Period: Proceedings of the International Workshop in Tokyo, August 28–31, 2007*. Edited by A. Moriya and G. Hatta. JSJSup 158. Leiden: Brill.

Sterling, G.E. 2006. "'The Queen of the Virtues': Piety in Philo of Alexandria." *SPhiloA* 18: 103–123.

Sterling, G.E. 2004. "The Place of Philo of Alexandria in the Study of Christian Origins." Pages 21–52 in *Philo und das Neue Testament: Wechselseitige Wahrnehmungen. I. Internationales Symposium zum Corpus Judaeo-Hellenisticum 1.–4. Mai 2003, Eisenach/Jena*. Edited by K.-W. Niebuhr and R. Deines. WUNT 172. Tübingen: Mohr Siebeck.

Sterling, G.E. 2001. "Mors philosophi: The Death of Jesus in Luke." *HTR* 94: 383–402.

Sterling, G.E. 1999. "'The School of Sacred Laws': The Social Setting of Philo's Treatises." *VC* 53 (1999): 148–164.

Sterling, G.E. 1997. "Prepositional Metaphysics in Jewish Wisdom Speculation and Early Christological Hymns." *SPhiloA* 9: 219–238.

Sterling, G.E. 1992. "*Creatio Temporalis, Aeterna, vel Continua*? An Analysis of the Thought of Philo of Alexandria." *SPhiloA* 4: 15–41.

Sterling, G.E. 1991. "Philo's *Quaestiones*: Prolegomena or Afterthought?" Pages 99–123 in *Both Literal and Allegorical: Studies in Philo of Alexandria's Questions and Answers on Genesis and Exodus*. Edited by D. Hay. BJS 232. Atlanta: Scholars Press.

Sterling, G.E. 1990. "Philo and the Logic of Apologetics. An Analysis of the *Hypothetica*." Pages 412–430 in *Society of Biblical Literature 1990 Seminar Papers*. SBLSP 29. Edited by D.J. Lull. Atlanta: Scholars Press.

Struck, P.T. 2004. *Birth of the Symbol: Ancient Readers at the Limits of Their Texts*. Princeton: Princeton University Press.

Taylor, C.C.W. 2016. "Aristotle on Practical Reason." *Oxford Handbooks Online*. Oxford: Oxford University Press. DOI: 10.1093/oxfordhb/9780199935314.013.52

Taylor, C.C.W. 2008. "Aristotle on the Practical Intellect." Pages 204–222 in *Pleasure, Mind, and Soul*. Oxford: Oxford University Press.

Taylor, J.E. and D.M. Hay. 2020. *Philo: On the Contemplative Life*. PACS 7. Leiden: Brill.

Terian, A. 2021. "Aucher's 1822 and 1826 Editions of *Philonis Judaei opera in Armenia conservata*: A History." *SPhiloA* 33: 161–173.

Terian, A. 2016. "*Philonis De visione trium angelorum ad Abraham*: A New Translation of the Mistitled *De Deo*." *SPhiloA* 28: 77–93 (esp. 94–107).

Terian, A. 1995. "Inspiration and Originality: Philo's Distinctive Exclamations." *SPhiloA* 7: 56–84.

Terian, A. 1991. "The Priority of the *Quaestiones* in Philo's Biblical Commentaries." Pages 29–46 in *Both Literal and Allegorical: Studies in Philo of Alexandria's Questions and Answers on Genesis and Exodus*. Edited by D. Hay. BJS 232. Atlanta: Scholars Press.

Terian, A. 1984. "A Philonic Fragment on the Decad." Pages 173–182 in *Nourished with Peace: Studies in Hellenistic Judaism in Memory of Samuel Sandmel*. Edited by F.E. Greenspahn et al. Chico, CA: Scholars Press.

Theiler, W. 1965. "Philon von Alexandria und der Beginn des kaiserzeitlichen Platonismus." Pages 199–218 in *Parusia: Studien zur Philosophie Platons und zur Problemgeschichte des Platonismus. Festgabe für J. Hirschberger*. Edited by K. Flasch. Frankfurt: Minerva.

Thorne, G. 1989. "The Structure of Philo's Commentary on the Pentateuch." *Dionysius* 13: 17–50.

Tigchelaar, E. 2008. "The Evil Inclination in the Dead Sea Scrolls, with a Re-edition of 4Q468i (4QSectarian Text?)." Pages 347–358 in *Empsychoi Logoi—Religious Innovations in Antiquity: Studies in Honour of Pieter Willem van der Horst*. Edited by P.W. van der Horst, A. Houtman, A. de Jong, and M.W.M. van de Weg. AJEC 73. Leiden: Brill.

Tsouona, V. 2007. *The Ethics of Philodemus*. Oxford: Oxford University Press.

Tobin, T.H., SJ. 2004. *Paul's Rhetoric in Its Contexts: The Argument of Romans*. Peabody, MA: Hendrickson.

Tobin, T.H., SJ. 2000. "The Beginning of Philo's *Legum allegoriae* I." *SPhiloA* 12: 29–43.

Tobin, T.H., SJ. 1985. *Timaios of Locri: On the Nature of the World and the Soul*. Texts and Translations 26. Graeco-Roman Religion Series 8. Chico, CA: Scholars Press.

Tobin, T.H., SJ. 1983. *The Creation of Man: Philo and the History of Interpretation.* CBQMS 14. Washington, DC: The Catholic Biblical Association of America.

Topchyan, A. and G. Muradyan. 2013. "Pseudo-Philo: *On Samson* and *On Jonah.*" In *Outside the Bible: Ancient Jewish Writings Related to Scripture.* Edited by L.H. Feldman, J.L. Kugel, and L.H. Schiffman. Philadelphia: Jewish Publication Society.

Torallas-Tovar, S. 2014. "Philo of Alexandria's Dream Classification." *Archiv für Religionsgeschichte* 15: 67–82.

Torallas-Tovar, S. 2003. "Philo of Alexandria on Sleep." Pages 41–52 in *Sleep.* Edited by T. Wiedemann and K. Dowden. Nottingham Classical Studies 8. Bari: Levante.

Torallas-Tovar, S. 2002. *El De somniis de Filón de Alejandria.* PhD diss., Complutense University of Madrid.

Van den Hoek, A. 2000. "Philo and Origen: A Descriptive Catalogue of their Relationship." *SPhiloA* 12: 44–121.

Van den Hoek, A. 1988. *Clement of Alexandria and His Use of Philo in the Stromateis: An Early Christian Reshaping of a Jewish Model.* VCSup 3. Leiden: Brill.

Van Inwagen, P. 2015. "What Difference Would (or Does) God's Existence Make?" Opening statement from debate at University of Toronto, Toronto, ON, 5 March 2015. https://andrewmbailey.com/pvi/Debate_Opening.pdf.

Vela, H. 2010. "Philo and the Logic of History." *SPhiloA* 22: 165–182.

Wasserman, E. 2008. *The Death of the Soul in Romans 7: Sin, Death, and the Law in Light of Hellenistic Moral Psychology.* WUNT 2.256. Tübingen: Mohr Siebeck.

Wasserman, E. 2007. "The Death of the Soul in Romans 7: Revisiting Paul's Anthropology in Light of Hellenistic Moral Psychology." *JBL* 126: 793–816.

Weisser, S. 2021. *Eradication ou moderation des passions: Histoire de la controverse chez Cicéron, Sénèque et Philon d'Alexandrie.* Philosophie hellénistique et romaine. Turnhout: Brepols.

Whitmarsh, T. 2005. *The Second Sophistic.* GR 35. Oxford: Oxford University Press.

Wilson, W.T. 2011. *Philo of Alexandria: On Virtues.* PACS 3. Leiden: Brill.

Winston, D. 1985. *Logos and Mystical Theology in Philo of Alexandria.* Cincinnati: Hebrew Union College Press.

Winston, D. and J.M. Dillon. 1983. *Two Treatises of Philo of Alexandria: A Commentary on De Gigantibus and Quod Deus Sit Immutabilis.* BJS 25. Chico, CA: Scholars Press.

Winter, B.W. 1997. *Paul and Philo among the Sophists.* SNTSMS 97. Cambridge: Cambridge University Press.

Wolfson, H.A. 1947. *Philo: Foundations of Religious Philosophy in Judaism, Christianity, and Islam.* Cambridge, MA: Harvard University Press.

Wyss, B., R. Hirsch-Luipold, and S. Hirschi, eds. 2017. *Sophisten in Hellenismus und Kaiserzeit: Orte, Methoden und Personen der Bildungsvermittlung.* STAC 101. Tübingen: Mohr Siebeck.

Yadin, Y. 1977. *The Temple Scroll.* 3 vols. Jerusalem: Israel Exploration Society.

Yadin-Israel, A. 2004. *Scripture as Logos: Rabbi Ishmael and the Origins of Midrash*. Divinations. Philadelphia: University of Pennsylvania Press.

Yli-Karjanmaa, S. 2016. "'Call Him Earth': On Philo's Allegorization of Adam in the *Legum allegoriae*." Pages 253–293 in *The Adam and Eve Story in the Hebrew Bible and in Ancient Jewish Writings, Including the New Testament*. Edited by A. Laato and L. Valve. Studies in the Reception History of the Bible 7. Winona Lake, IN: Eisenbrauns.

Yli-Karjanmaa, S. 2015. *Reincarnation in Philo of Alexandria*. SPhiloM 7. Atlanta: SBL Press.

Zaleski, R.A. 2020. "Between the Literal and the Allegorical: Biblical Paraphrase and the Mediation of Scripture in Philo of Alexandria's and Gregory of Nyssa's Lives of Moses." PhD diss., The University of Chicago.

Zeller, D. 1995. "The Life and Death of the Soul in Philo of Alexandria: The Use and Origin of a Metaphor." *SPhiloA* 7: 19–55.

Zeller, D. 1990. *Charis bei Philon und Paulus*. SBS 142. Stuttgart: Katholisches Bibelwerk.

TRANSLATION

Philo of Alexandria
On the Change of Names

∴

Part One

[Chapter 1]
Abraham as Seer and Hearer of God (§§ 1–38)

a   *The Meaning of Abraham's Age at the Time of the Annunciation and Birth of Isaac (§§ 1–2)*

(§ 1) **Abraham came to be ninety-nine years old, and the Lord was seen by Abraham and said to him, "I am your God."**[a] The number ninety-nine is a neighbor of one hundred, in which the self-taught class shone forth—Isaac, best of the good emotions, joy! For he is born in the hundredth year. (§ 2) And this is also signified by the first-fruit offering given to the priests of the Levitical tribe. For when they have received the tithes, they set aside from these, as if from their own fruits, *additional tithes*,[b] which when multiplied together with the first tithes produce the number one hundred. The number ten is a symbol of progress, while the number one hundred is a symbol of perfection. But he who is at the mean always hastens toward the summit, if he has a good nature to assist him. It is by this person (i.e., Abraham) that Moses says **the Lord** of the universe **was seen**.[c]

b   *Abraham as a Seer and Hearer of God (§§ 3–17)*

(b1)   Abraham as Seer: Vision of God

(§ 3) But do not think that such a visitation comes to Abraham through the eyes of the body. For these see only perceptible things and perceptible things admit of comparison and are filled up with ruin. The Divine, to the contrary, is peerless and incorruptible. Therefore, the faculty that receives the divine impression is the eye of the soul. (§ 4) Furthermore, whatever the eyes of the body see, they comprehend using light as a co-laborer, which differs both from the object seen and the seeing subject. But whatever the soul sees, it sees through itself without any other assistance. For knowable things are a light unto themselves. (§ 5) In the same way, we also learn the sciences. The mind, having applied its unbolted and unsleeping eye to decrees and theorems, sees them not by a counterfeit light, but by a legitimate illumination that shines forth from itself. (§ 6) Therefore, whenever you hear that *God* **was seen** *by a human being*,[d] know that this happens apart from perceptible light. For only by thought can the

---

[a] Gen 17:1.   [b] Num 18:26–30 (32).   [c] Gen 17:1bα.   [d] Gen 17:1bα.

knowable be comprehended. And God is the wellspring of the clearest light, such that whenever it dawns upon the soul, it projects shadowless and most resplendent rays.

(§ 7) Do not think, however, that The One Who Is—who is truly Being—can be comprehended by any human. For we have no organ in ourselves, by which we will be able to form an impression of This One, neither perception—for he is not perceptible—nor mind. Therefore Moses, the seer of the invisible nature, [that is, the seer-of-God]—for the divine oracles say that **he entered into the darkness**,[a] speaking in riddles about the invisible and bodiless Being—examining all things thoroughly, was seeking to see clearly the thrice-desired and only Good. (§ 8) But when he could find nothing, no form answering to that which was hoped for, he gives up on the teaching of others, flees to the One who was sought, and prays, saying **"Show yourself to me, let me see you with knowledge."**[b] Nevertheless, Moses does not attain the object of his petition, since the gift reckoned most fitting to the best class of mortals is knowledge of material and immaterial things that rank after The One Who Is. (§ 9) For it is said: **"You will see the things behind me, but my face will not be seen by you."**[c] This is because the things ranking after The One Who Is, both material and immaterial, may come to be comprehended, even if they are not already comprehended. Only the Former, on account of his nature, cannot be seen. (§ 10) Moreover, why is it amazing if The One Who Is should be incomprehensible to human beings, when in fact the mind in each of us is unknown to us? For who has seen the essence of the soul? Lack of clarity on this point has spawned myriad disputes among the sophists, who introduce opposing opinions or even opinions entirely contradictory from the start.

(b2)   Abraham as Hearer: The Title "Kyrios"
(§ 11) It follows, therefore, that the name "Lord" cannot truly be applied to The One Who Is. Do you not see that when the inquiry-loving prophet (i.e., Moses) is asking what he is to reply to those seeking his name, God says: **"I am The One Who Is,"**[d] which is the equivalent of saying that "my nature is to be, not to be spoken." (§ 12) But so that the human race should not be left entirely bereft of a means of addressing the highest Good, he allows them to use inexactly (as if The One Who Is could be addressed by this sort of name) the title **"Lord, the God"**[e] of the three natures—teaching, perfection, and practice—of which Abraham, Isaac, and Jacob are inscribed as symbols. For **"This,"** he says, **"is my name in this age,"**[f] as if it were appointed for our age but not for the eternity

---

[a] Exod 20:21.   [b] Exod 33:13.   [c] Exod 33:23.   [d] Exod 3:14a.   [e] Exod 3:15a.   [f] Exod 3:15b.

before "age." **"And a memorial,"**[a] he adds, not as a name that is established outside the bounds of memory and knowledge. Then again, it is a name **"for generated,"**[b] but not for ungenerated natures. (§ 13) Those who come to mortal birth have need of some loose approximation of the divine name, so that they might be equipped to approach God, even if not in reality, then at least by the best name. So also, a saying proclaimed by the mouth of the Ruler of the universe explains that he has not disclosed a proper name of his to anyone. **"I was seen,"** he says, **"by Abraham, Isaac, and Jacob, being their God. But my name, 'Lord' (*kurion*), I did not clearly disclose to them."**[c] After the transposition in the syntax has been reversed, the meaning would be something like: "I did not clearly disclose my proper (*kurion*) name to them, but my loosely approximate name," for the reasons stated above. (§ 14) Indeed, so ineffable is The One Who Is that not even his ministering powers speak a proper name to us. Thus, after the bout that the man of practice (i.e., Jacob) wrestled in order to acquire virtue, he says to the unseen Governor: **"Proclaim your name to me."**[d] But he (i.e., the ministering power) said in reply: **"Why do you ask this, my name?"**[e] And he does not disclose his personal and proper name. "For your need," he says, "is to be assisted by my honorable titles. But those symbols of the things that have come into being—the names—do not seek them in the case of incorruptible natures." (§ 15) Therefore, do not be perplexed if the most ancient of Essences is ineffable, when we are not able to address even his Word with a proper name. And indeed, if he is ineffable, he is also incomprehensible and imperceptible; so that the phrase **the Lord was seen by Abraham**[f] should be understood as spoken not to indicate that the Cause of all shone forth and manifested itself—for what human mind is sufficient to make room for the greatness of this impression?—but as an indication that one of the powers around it, the kingly, was seen. For this is the proper manner of address for a ruling principle and kingly office. (§ 16) Now our mind, when it used to Chaldeanize and go on about heavenly bodies, would speak reverently of the active powers of the world as if they were its causes. But when it departed from the Chaldean doctrine, it recognized that the world was under the reins and governance of a leader, of whose rule it had received an impression. (§ 17) Therefore it is said, not that The One Who Is **was seen**, but that the **Lord** (i.e., the kingly power) **was seen**.[g] This is like saying that the king was revealed, who although he was king from the beginning, was not yet recognized by the soul. Despite being slow in learning, this soul did not end up entirely ignorant, but received an impression of his rule and governance among the things that are.

---

[a] Exod 3:15c. [b] Exod 3:15d. [c] Exod 6:3. [d] Gen 32:29. [e] Ibid. [f] Gen 17:1b. [g] Gen 17:1b.

c   *Abraham, God's Human Being (§§ 18–38)*

(c1)   "I Am *Your* God"

(§ 18) After he had appeared to Abraham, the Ruler does yet more good for the hearer and seer, saying, "**I am *your* God.**"ᵃ "But," I might say, "out of all those that have come into existence, of whom are you not God?" In response, his Word-interpreter will teach me that he speaks here not about the cosmos, of which he is entirely both Craftsman and God, but about human souls, which he does not think all worthy of the same treatment. (§ 19) For it seems right that he be called "Lord" and "Master" of the wicked, "God" of those making moral advancements and improvements, and both "Lord" and "God" together, in the case of the very best and most perfect. For example, when he establishes Pharaoh as the furthest limit of impiety, he never calls himself Pharaoh's ["Lord" and] "God." Rather, he gives this name to the wise man Moses. Thus, he says: "**Behold, I give you as a god to Pharaoh.**"ᵇ On the other hand, he often uses the name "Lord" in the oracles spoken by him, (§ 20) uttering sayings like, **The Lord says these things**ᶜ and, in the beginning ⟨of the narrative⟩, **The Lord spoke to Moses saying, "I am the Lord. Tell Pharaoh the king of Egypt what I will say to you.**"ᵈ (§ 21) Later Moses says to Pharaoh, "**When I depart from the city, I will stretch out my hands to the Lord and the sounds of thunder will cease and the hail and rain will be no more, so that you may know that the earth**"—that is, every bodily and earthly substance—"**belongs to the Lord,**ᵉ **even you**"—that is, the portrait-bearing mind—"**and your servants**"—that is, the particular thoughts that attend you. "**For I know that in no way have you feared the Lord**"ᶠ—which is equal to saying, "you failed to fear not the one who is wrongly called a master, but he who is really Master." (§ 22) For no one who comes into being is truly a lord, even if he should acquire a territory that extends from one end of the earth to the other. Only the Ungenerated is truly a ruler, and the one who fears his rule and is awe-struck by it receives for himself the very useful prize of divine correction. An entirely lamentable destruction, on the other hand, awaits the one who is contemptuous of his rule and chastisement. (§ 23) In this way it has been demonstrated that he is "Lord" of the foolish, as he extends the proper fear of a ruler over them. But it is written that he is "God" of those who are becoming better, as is the case now in the verse under consideration, "**I am your God,**"ᵍ and again when he says, "**I am your God, increase and multiply.**"ʰ But he is called by both names with respect to the perfect—that is, "Lord and God" together. Thus, in the Ten Words, he says, "**I am the Lord your God,**"ⁱ and in a different place it says, "**the Lord God of your**

ᵃ Gen 17:1cα.   ᵇ Exod 7:1.   ᶜ Exod 7:17 (*et passim*).   ᵈ Exod 6:29.   ᵉ Exod 9:29.   ᶠ Exod 9:30.
ᵍ Gen 17:1b.   ʰ Gen 35:11.   ⁱ Exod 20:2.

fathers."ᵃ (§ 24) Indeed, it is just for the wicked person to be ruled by a despot, as by a lord, so that with reverence and groaning he may have the master's fear hanging over his head. The one who is making progress, by contrast, ought to be given benefits, as by a god, so that he may reach the good works of perfection. And the perfect person, for his part, ought both to be governed as by a lord and to be given benefits as by a god. For under the Lord's governance, he remains entirely unturned; and thanks to the beneficence of the latter, he is entirely God's human being. (§ 25) This is most clear in the case of Moses; for it says, **This is the blessing, which Moses, God's human being, gave.**ᵇ O man, thought worthy of such an entirely good and God-befitting gift-exchange: to give oneself in return for God's providential care! (§ 26) But do not think that one becomes a human being and becomes God's human being in the same manner. To be human is to be as God's possession. To be God's human being, by contrast, is to be as both his boast and benefit. So, if you wish to have God as the allotment of your mind, become first yourself a portion worthy of serving him. You will become so, if you flee all hand-made and self-willed laws.

(c2)   "I Am Your *God*"
(§ 27) Additionally, one should not be ignorant of the fact that the phrase, "**I am your God,**"ᶜ is spoken inexactly, not properly. For The One Who Is, insofar as he is Being, does not have predicates of relation. He possesses his own fullness and is sufficient for himself, and both before and after the generation of the cosmos he was in a like state. (§ 28) He is unturned and unchanged, needing no other at all, with the result that all things belong to him, while he belongs properly to nothing. Some of his powers, on the other hand, which he extended in creation for the good fashioning of the composite, do happen to be spoken of *as if* with respect to relation. These are the kingly and the beneficent powers. For a king rules someone and a benefactor assists someone, who is entirely other in being ruled and receiving a benefit. (§ 29) Kindred to these two is also the creative power, who is called "God." It was through this power that the begetting and fashioning Father set the universe in place, such that the phrase, "**I am your God,**"ᵈ is identical to the phrase, "I am Creator and Craftsman."

(§ 30) It is a very great gift to have as one's own architect the one who is also the Architect of the entire world. For he did not **mold** a soul for the wicked person, as vice is hateful to God.ᵉ Neither was the middle kind of soul molded through his instrumentality alone, according to the most holy Moses, since this kind of soul was about to receive, in the manner of wax, *the distinction of good*

ᵃDeut 4:1.   ᵇDeut 33:1.   ᶜGen 17:1cα.   ᵈGen 17:1cα.   ᵉGen 2:7.

and evil.[a] (§ 31) This is why it is said, "**Let us make a human being according to our image**,"[b] so that if it should receive the mold badly, it is clear that it was the craftsmanship of others. But if it receives the image well, this stems from the Fashioner of only beautiful and good things. Therefore, that human being is entirely good, to whom he says, "**I am your God**,[c] you have me alone as Maker, without the collaboration of others." (§ 32) At the same time, Moses also introduces the dogma often set out by him, teaching that God is the Craftsman of the good and the wise alone. Not only has this whole company willingly deprived itself of the plentiful possession of external things, but it has also disregarded things dear to the flesh. (§ 33) Well-conditioned and energetic are athletes who have built up their servant-body as a fortification against the soul, whereas those of *paideia's* party become pale, wasted away, and in a certain manner skeletonized, having allotted their body's exertions to the powers of their soul, and—to speak the truth—having resolved themselves into one, the form of the soul, becoming bodiless thoughts.

(§ 34) Actually, it stands to reason that the earth-like part of a person perishes and is dissolved when the mind chooses to become wholly and entirely **well-pleasing to God**. This class of person is rare and found with difficulty, but it is not impossible for him to exist. The following oracle, spoken about Enoch, makes this clear: **Now Enoch was well-pleasing to God, and he was not found**.[d] (§ 35) Where could someone who looked find such goodness? Over what sorts of seas must they sail? To what islands, what uncharted lands must they travel? (§ 36) Among barbarians or Greeks? Or is it not the case that even now, there are some of those fully initiated in philosophy who say that wisdom is non-existent, since the true sage is also non-existent? They say that no one from the beginning, from the creation of human beings until the present life, has been reckoned entirely blameless. For, they claim, it is also impossible for someone bound in a mortal body to be entirely happy. (§ 37) Whether these things are said rightly, we will see in time. At present, however, we will follow reason and say that wisdom is a thing that exists, as also is her lover, the sage. Nevertheless, his existence has escaped the notice of us ordinary people. For good did not wish to have congress with evil. (§ 38) Therefore it is said that the manner of life well-pleasing to God **was not found**,[e] since doubtless this manner of life does exist, although it is hidden and flees from sharing our common road toward the same goal. For this reason, it is also said that **Enoch has been translated**,[f] that is, that he was removed from his home country and set out on a migration from the mortal life for the immortal one.

---

[a] Cf. Gen 2:17.   [b] Gen 1:26.   [c] Gen 17:1bβ.   [d] Gen 5:24ab.   [e] Gen 5:24b.   [f] Gen 5:24c.

[Chapter 2]
Philo's Theology of Covenant (§§ 39–53)

a *Abraham, Follower of the Gentle Wisdom (§§ 39–46)*

(§ 39) Those people just described are sages who have gone wild, crazed by the divine madness. But there are others who are companions of the tame and gentle wisdom. Piety for them is practiced differently and does not overlook human affairs. The oracles bear witness to such a group, in which it is said to Abraham in the presence of God, "**Be well-pleasing before me**,"[a] that is, not only to me, but also to my works, while I judge as Overseer and Guardian. (§ 40) If you honor your parents or have mercy on the poor or are a benefactor to friends or guard your homeland or care for the common justice of all human beings, then you will **be** entirely **well-pleasing** to those in need and you will **be well-pleasing before God** as well. For with an unsleeping eye, he sees all deeds and he summons to himself those which are good with a choice grace and receives them as his own.

(§ 41) For this very reason, ⟨Israel⟩ the practicer will also clarify the same thing in prayer. Saying, "**God, to whom my fathers were well-pleasing**," he then adds, "**before him**."[b] He does this in order to make known the practical difference between being well-pleasing **to God** and being well-pleasing **before him**. The latter phrase (i.e., "before God") embraces both kinds of well-pleasing, the former (i.e., "to God") only being well-pleasing to God. (§ 42) So also Moses in his *Exhortations* advises the Israelites, saying, "**You shall do what is well-pleasing before the Lord your God**."[c] This is the equivalent of saying, "Do the sorts of things that will be worthy to be revealed to God and which, having seen, he will receive." For such deeds customarily extend a benefit to one's peers as well.

(§ 43) Prompted by this thought, *Moses was weaving the tabernacle with two curtained spaces*, setting a veil between both of them, so that the outer things might be distinguished from the inner things.[d] Likewise, *he gilded the holy law-guarding ark both within and without*,[e] and presented the high priest with two vestments, *the linen one for within the adytum*,[f] and *the many-colored one, with the long robe, for the outer sanctuary*.[g] (§ 44) These and things like them are symbols of a soul that is both being purified toward God in its inner thoughts and being cleansed in its outer words and deeds with respect to the perceptible cosmos and its manner of life.

---

[a] Gen 17:1cα. [b] Gen 48:15. [c] Deut 12:28. [d] See Exod 26:33. [e] See Exod 25:11. [f] See Lev 6:10, esp. Lev 16:4–5, 12. [g] See Exod 28:4–6.

Well-aimed, then, was the word spoken to Jacob, the triumphant wrestler about to be crowned with the victor's wreath. For the proclamation to him is similar in kind: "**You were strong with God and capable with human beings.**"[a] (§ 45) To be in good repute with each order of being, that of the ungenerated and that of the generated, does not belong to a small intellect, but, if one must speak truthfully, is the possession of the mind at the borderland between God and the world. It is entirely fitting that the excellent human being should be an attendant of God, for the Ruler of all and Father of what is generated is concerned for him. (§ 46) Who does not know that even before the generation of the world, God was sufficient for himself, and after the generation of the world, he remained the same, not changing? For what reason, then, was he making the things that are not? Is there any reason other than because he is good and loves to give gifts? Shall not we, who are slaves, follow the Master, marveling exceedingly at the Cause, while also not overlooking the nature that is common to us?

b   On Blamelessness (§§ 47–51a)
(§ 47) After he says, "**Be well-pleasing before me,**"[b] he adds: "**and be blameless,**"[c] employing a logical sequence. He would rather that you undertake good pursuits, so that you may be well-pleasing; but if you cannot achieve them, at least refrain from sins, so that you may not receive blame. For the one who is upright is worthy of praise, but the one who is not unjust cannot be blamed. (§ 48) Therefore, the most important prize, to be well-pleasing, belongs to the upright, while the second, to be blameless, belongs to those who do not sin. But perhaps for mortal creation, "not to sin" means one and the same thing as "being upright." "**For who,**" as Job says, "**is clean from filth, even if his life is but one day?**"[d] (§ 49) Indeed, boundless are the things which soil the soul, which cannot entirely be purged and washed clean. Inborn defects of necessity remain in every mortal thing. These are possible to lessen, but cannot be removed completely. (§ 50) Does someone seek a just, prudent, temperate, or entirely good and perfect person in this mixed life? Be content if you should find someone who is not unjust or not imprudent or not undisciplined or not entirely wicked. For the ways of the vices are attractive, while the complete possession of the virtues is impossible for a human being in our condition. (§ 51) Well-said, then, is God's command, "**Be blameless,**" since he considers being without sin and fault a great advantage toward happiness.

---

[a] Gen 32:28.   [b] Gen 17:1cβ.   [c] Gen 17:1cγ.   [d] Job 14:4.

PART ONE 81

c   *Philo on the Covenants and Grace (§§ 51B–53)*
To the one who has chosen to live in this manner, he also agrees to leave an inheritance in accordance with the covenants—one that is appropriate for God to give and for the wise person to receive. (§ 52) For he says, "**I will set my covenant between me and between you.**"[a] Covenants are written for the benefit of those worthy of a gift, with the result that a covenant is a symbol of grace, which God sets **between** himself, as the extender, and a human being, as the recipient. (§ 53) And the superabundance of God's beneficence is this: that there is nothing **in between** God and the soul, save this virgin grace. (I have written the entire treatise *On the Covenants* in two volumes and I now willingly skip over this, so that I do not repeat myself and also because I do not wish to disturb the natural unity of the subject matter of the treatise.)

[Chapter 3]
Abraham's Great Fall (§§ 54–56)

(§ 54) Next it is said, "**Abraham fell upon his face.**"[b] Was it not likely, in light of the divine promises, that he would both come to **know himself**[c] and the nothingness of the mortal race and also fall before the One who stands, as proof of the estimate that he had regarding himself and God? For Abraham saw that the One who stands ever the same moves all that is at rest, not through the movement of legs—for he does not have human form—but demonstrating that his being is unturned and unchanged. (§ 55) The human being, on the other hand, who is never firmly fixed in the same place, receives at different times various kinds of changes and tripping over his own heels, the unfortunate one—for his entire life is a slipping—falls a great fall.

(§ 56) Now, one person falls because he is involuntarily ignorant, but another because he is docile. It is on this latter account that it is also said that Abraham **fell upon his face**; that is, upon his senses, upon his speech, and upon his mind. He all but shouts and cries out, "Fallen is perception, since it is unable to perceive on its own, unless it should be raised up by the forethought of the Savior to apprehend bodily substances. Fallen also is speech, since it is unable to explain any of the intellectual substances, unless the One who fashioned and fine-tuned the vocal instrument, having opened the mouth and fixed the tongue, should strike the chords in a musical fashion. Fallen finally is king mind, since it is deprived of its impressions, unless the One who **formed him as a living**

---

[a] Gen 17:2. [b] Gen 17:3. [c] The Delphic maxim. See Xenophon, *Mem.* 4.2.24; Plato, *Phaedr.* 229e, inter alia.

being,[a] having raised him, should establish him in place and, having endowed him with swift-seeing pupils, should lead him to the vision of the bodiless realities."

[Chapter 4]
Different Forms of Covenant (§§ 57–59)

(§ 57) God, then, delights in the manner of life that flees itself and willingly falls a fall on account of the confession it makes concerning The One Who Is—that there is One, in truth, who stands, while those who follow after him are susceptible to all kinds of turnings and changes. And he audibly instructs it and gives it a share in his Reason, saying "**And I, behold my covenant is with you.**"[b] (§ 58) The saying suggests the following sort of thought: "There are many species of covenant, which apportion graces and gifts to those who are worthy; but I myself am the highest genus of covenants." For having shown himself (insofar as it is possible for the Non-Demonstrable One to be shown) with the words "**And I**," he then adds, "**behold my covenant**"; that is, "I am myself the source and wellspring of all graces." (§ 59) To some, God is accustomed to extend benefits through other agents: earth, water, air, sun, moon, sky, and other bodiless powers. But to others, he gives benefits through himself alone, setting himself aside as an inheritance for those who receive him. These, he also immediately deems worthy of another name.

---

[a] Gen 2:7.   [b] Gen 17:4a.

Part Two

[Chapter 5]
On the Change of Names (§§ 60–129)

a   *Abram–Abraham (§§ 60–76)*
(§ 60) For it is said that "**Your name will not be called Abram, but your name will be Abraham (Abraam).**"[a] Now, some quarrelsome people always wish to attach blame to the blameless, not so much to the material signs, as to the realities they represent. They wage a truceless war against the saints and present for slander all things that seem unfit to be preserved in Scripture—although these are symbols of nature, who always loves to hide herself—[b] disparaging them with "scrupulous" investigation. They do this with special vigor in the case of changes of names. (§ 61) Just recently, I heard a godless and impious man, who scoffed and railed thus: "Great indeed and superabundant are the gifts that Moses says the Leader of the Universe extends. For in Abram's case, by the addition of a letter, of the one alpha, [He causes him to abound by a letter]; and again, with another appendage of a rho, he thought that a marvelously great benefaction had been furnished … *insofar as he changed the name of Abram's wife Sarai (Sara) to Sarah (Sarra)*,[c] doubling the rho." And thus he went through many similar examples, stringing them together breathlessly and sneering. (§ 62) It was not long before he paid the price befitting his stupidity. By some small chance circumstance, he came to hanging ⟨himself⟩, so that this foul and ill-cleaned fellow did not end with a clean death. Worthily, then, lest another be snatched by the same errors, would we excise these suspicions, using natural reason to demonstrate that these things which have been said by Moses are deserving of all studious zeal.

(§ 63) God, after all, does not bestow letters, whether consonants or vowels or even names and appellations in their entirety. Thus, after he had created the plants and animals, he called to the human being as to a leader, whom he had distinguished from all the other creatures by his knowledge, so that he might place the appropriate names upon each. For Moses says, **And whatever Adam called it, this was the name of the creature thus called.**[d] (§ 64) If God did not think it fitting for him to undertake the placement of names in their entirety, but turned this work over to a wise man, the founder of the human race, should we suppose that later he himself was appending or retrofitting

---

[a] Gen 17:5.   [b] Heraclitus, D-K fr. 123.   [c] Gen 17:15.   [d] Gen 2:19.

portions of names, whether syllables or letters—and not vowels alone, but also consonants!—and that he did these things with the pretense of giving a gift or superabundant benefaction? (§ 65) It is not right to say this. Rather, these sorts of changes are markers of capacities, small indicators of great gifts, perceptible figures of noetic realities, clear tokens of hidden truths. These powers are discovered in the best doctrines, in guileless and pure conceptions, in improvements of the soul. Proof of this is easy to obtain, for those who begin with the person, whose name is now being changed in the text at hand.

(§ 66) For "Abram" is interpreted as "elevated father," but "Abraham" as "elect father of sound." We will know more clearly how these names differ from one another once we have first recalled what is signified by each of them. (§ 67) By "elevated" we mean allegorically the one who is lifting himself from the earth to the heights and gazing upon the things high in the air. He busies himself with reasoning about these lofty things, inquiring what the size of the sun is, what its courses are, how it divides the hours of the year as it comes and goes again with equally measured rotations. He also enquires about the light of the moon, about its phases, its waning, its waxing, and about the movement of the other stars—both those that are set and the wanderers (i.e., the planets). (§ 68) The examination of these things does not belong to the soul that is ill-natured and cannot beget, but is characteristic of those whose souls have a supremely good natural disposition and are able to produce complete and perfect offspring. For this reason, Moses also called the elevated reasoner "father," since this type of soul is not unable to beget wisdom.

(§ 69) The symbolic elements in the name "Abram" can be clarified in this manner; but those in the name "Abraham" are the following, as we will demonstrate. There are three parts: "father" and "elect" and "sound." We interpret "sound" to be externalized speech. For the voice box is an animal's sound organ, and the mind is its father. It is from reasoning, as from a spring, that the stream of speech flows forth. "Elect," for its part, specifies the mind of a sage. For whatever is best is in him. (§ 70) Thus, while according to the former characters (i.e., "Abram") the figure of the lover of learning and stargazer was sketched, according to the characters outlined just now (i.e., "Abraham") it is the philosopher who is specified—or better, the sage. May you no longer suppose, then, that the Divine bestows a change of names, but that through symbols, he gives a correction of character.

(§ 71) This man, who was formerly busying himself with the nature of heaven—whom some people call a mathematician—God called to a change of virtue, and both proved and named him a sage. And he named the remodeled manner of living "Abraham," as Hebrew speakers would say; or "elect father of sound," as would the Greeks. (§ 72) "For what reason," he asks, "do you seek the pathways and revolutions of stars? Why have you leapt up so high, from earth to aether? Is it only for this purpose, that you may busy yourself with the things there? But what would be the benefit of so lofty a business? What diminution of pleasure does it provide? What upsetting of desire? What dissolution of grief or fear? What kind of excision of the passions, which agitate and confuse the soul?" (§ 73) Just as there is no profit in trees, unless they bear fruit, in the same manner there is no benefit in natural science, unless it will lead to the acquisition of virtue; for this is its fruit.

(§ 74) Therefore, some of the ancients have even likened philosophical discourse to a field. They compare the division of physics to trees; logic, to walls and fences; and ethics, to fruit. They presume, thereby, that the circular walls have been constructed by the owners for the sake of guarding the fruit, and that the trees were fashioned for the sake of producing fruit. (§ 75) They also say that in philosophy, the study of physics and logic leads up to ethics, by which the character is improved through its desire to possess and make use of virtue. (§ 76) These are the sort of things we have been taught concerning him whose name was changed in word, but transformed in action from the investigation of nature to ethical philosophy, who has arisen from speculation about the cosmos to knowledge of its Maker, from which piety, the best of possessions, is acquired.

b   *Sarai (Sara)–Sarah (Sarra)* (*§ 77–80*)

(§ 77) We will speak now of matters concerning Abraham's wife, Sarai (*Sara*). **She too has her name changed to Sarah (*Sarra*)**[a] through the addition of a single letter, rho.[b] These are the names, but we must disclose the events signified. Sarai is interpreted to mean "my ruling principle," but Sarah means "ruling woman." (§ 78) The former is a symbol of specific virtue, whereas the latter is a symbol of generic virtue. To the extent that a genus differs from a species on account of the attenuation of the latter, so does the second name differ from the former. For the species is small and perishable, whereas the genus is manifold and imperishable. (§ 79) God wishes to give great and imperishable gifts instead of small and perishable ones, and this work befits him. For practical wisdom in the good human being is the ruling principle of that person only. The one who has this would not err, if he should claim, "The practical wisdom in me is my ruling principle." But that which impresses this particular virtue—generic practical wisdom—is no longer ruling principle of that specific person, but is the ruling principle itself. (§ 80) Therefore, the former specific ruling principle will perish with its possessor, while the latter generic ruling principle, which

---

[a] Gen 17:15.   [b] Gen 17:15.

imprints the specific virtue in the manner of a seal, once it has been freed of all that is mortal will continue on imperishable forever. Likewise, specific skills are destroyed with their possessors, whether they are geometricians, grammarians, or musicians. Generic skills, on the other hand, remain indestructible. Moses also teaches figuratively in this same passage that every virtue is a queen, both ruling and governing the affairs of life.

c Jacob–Israel (§§ 81–88)

(§ 81) It also happens that *Jacob's name is changed to Israel*[a] in a way that is not unrelated to the subject at hand. Why is this? Because Jacob is called "the one who trips at the heels,"[b] whereas Israel is called "the one who sees God." Now, it is the role of "the one who trips at the heels," who is practicing virtue, to move, shake, and remove the foundations of emotion, upon which he is situated, especially if there are any recalcitrant or fixed habits among them. These tasks are not easily accomplished without struggle or the dust of the arena, but only when one competes in the contests of practical wisdom, doing exercises of the soul and wrestling against the arguments that attempt to throw and throttle it. The work of "the one who sees God" is not to depart from the holy arena uncrowned, but to carry off the prizes awarded for victory. (§ 82) And what more blossom-bedecked and fitting crown could be woven for the victorious soul, than the one through which The One Who Is will be able to be seen with sharp clarity? Good indeed is the prize that is set before the practicing soul—to be given eyes to comprehend clearly the only object worthy of sight.

(§ 83) But it is worth puzzling over why Abraham, once his name has been changed, is thought worthy of the same appellation throughout subsequent narratives and is no longer called by his former name, whereas Jacob, although he has received the title Israel, is nonetheless again and again frequently named Jacob. It may be answered that these too represent characteristics, in which taught virtue differs from practicing virtue. (§ 84) For the one who has been improved by teaching—possessing, as he does, a well-apportioned nature that guards his retentiveness with the assistance of memory—makes use of this cognitive persistence, having fixedly laid hold of and firmly grasped the things that he has learned. The practicer, by contrast, whenever he has exercised intensely, catches his breath again and relaxes, gathering and recovering the power that had been enfeebled by toil, just as those who anoint their bodies for the games. For these, likewise weary from practice, lest their powers entirely leave them on account of the difficulty and intensity of their training, pour oil on themselves. (§ 85) Accordingly, the taught human being, through the assistance of an

---

[a] Gen 32:29.   [b] Cf. Gen 25:26.

immortal Prompter, holds this benefit "in his own halls," immortally, not being turned aside from them. The practicing human being, by contrast, has only his own willing capacity—and this he trains and disciplines, so that he may throw down the emotion belonging to generated being. But even if he reaches perfection, when he grows weary, he will return to his earlier class. (§ 86) This latter kind of person must bear more hardships, whereas the former is more fortunate. For the former has recourse to another as his teacher, while the latter seeks and inquires and keeps busy on his own initiative, investigating with zeal the things of nature and engaging in continuous and uninterrupted toil.

(§ 87) For this reason, Abraham, because he was going to remain in the same ethical state, had his name changed by the unturned God, so that he who was about to be stationed firmly might be fixed in place by the One who stands firm and carries himself in the same fashion. Jacob, on the other hand, had his name changed by an angel,[a] a minister of God, the Word, so that nothing that ranks after The One Who Is might be said to be a cause of unbending and unwavering stability, but of the harmony which in a musical instrument contains constrictions and relaxations of sounds for skillful mixture with the melody.

(§ 88) Of the three founders of an ethical class, the two extremes—Abraham and Jacob—have their names changed, but the middle, Isaac, always has the same appellation. Why is this? Because taught virtue and practiced virtue, on the one hand, receive external incentives for improvement. The one who is taught, for instance, desires the knowledge of which he is ignorant, while the one who uses training longs for the garlands and prizes that are set out for the soul that loves toil and contemplation. The self-taught and self-learning class, on the other hand, since it is established by nature rather than by the cultivation of character, carries itself from the beginning in a balanced, perfect, and even manner, with no number lacking from its fullness.

d   The Names of Joseph (§§ 89–91)

(§ 89) Not so for the administrator of bodily provisions, Joseph. He exchanges his name, *being called Zaphenath-paneah (Psonthomphanech) by the king of the land.*[b] What meaning these names have must be disclosed. Joseph is interpreted to mean "addition,"[c] and conventional goods are an appendage to natural ones: gold, silver, possessions, incomes, the ministries of servants, bountiful materials like heirlooms, furniture, and other surplus items—an inconceivable number of provisions made for pleasure. (§ 90) Joseph, the supplier and caregiver of these things, happens to be called by the fitting name, "addition," since

---

[a] See Gen 32:25.   [b] Gen 41:41–49, esp. 45.   [c] Gen 30:24.

he has attained presidency over the goods that are externally introduced and accrued to our natural endowments. The oracles testify to this, demonstrating that from his storehouse he supplies provisions for the entire land of the body, Egypt.

(§ 91) Joseph is known to be someone of this sort from the marks just mentioned. But what kind of person this Zaphenath-paneah (*Psonthomphanech*) is, let us now see. His name means: "mouth judging in answer." Indeed, every fool thinks that the person who has many possessions and is overflowing with external belongings is immediately also good at reasoning and speaking; that he is sufficient to reply to whatever someone asks; and that he is likewise sufficient at introducing fitting opinions through his own internal resources. This person puts practical wisdom entirely in the sphere of fortune, when he ought instead to have put fortune in the sphere of practical wisdom. For what is unstable ought to be guided by the reins of that which is firmly established.

e   *The Names of Benjamin (§§ 92–96)*

(§ 92) Again, in a most allegorical manner, Joseph's father names his co-maternal brother "**Benjamin**," but his mother names him "**son of pain**."[a] Benjamin means, etymologically, "son of days," and a day is illuminated by the perceptible light of the sun, to which we liken vain opinion. (§ 93) For vain opinion often possesses a certain observable brilliance in the panegyrics of vulgar multitudes, in written decrees, in the displays of busts and images, in crowns of purple and gold, in chariots, four-horse entourages, and processions before the crowds. He who is zealous for these things is aptly named "son of days," that is, "son of perceptible light and the brilliance surrounding vain opinion."

(§ 94) This truly accurate and proper name (i.e., Benjamin) is set upon the son by the elder reason—that is, his father. The suffering soul (i.e., his mother), for her part, gives him a name that corresponds to what she herself has experienced. For she calls him "**son of pain**."[b] Why? Because those carried along by vain opinions suppose they are happy, but in truth they are wretched. (§ 95) Many are the adverse winds that blow them: slander, envies, irresolvable discords, contentions that are not cured until death, ill-wills passed on through succession to children's children—a inheritance not to be coveted. (§ 96) Necessarily, then, the interpreter of God depicts Rachel, who gives birth to vain opinion, dying in her own throes of labor. For he says, **Rachel died giving birth to an unfortunate offspring**.[c] And this is really the death of the soul: the sowing and bearing of vain opinion, grounded in the senses.

---

[a] Gen 35:18c.   [b] Gen 35:18b.   [c] Gen 35:16, 19.

f Ephraim and Manasseh, Reuben and Simeon (§§ 97–102)

(§ 97) What comes next? Are not the children of Joseph, Ephraim and Manasseh, very much like the two older sons of Jacob, Reuben and Simeon, according to natural allegory? For Jacob says, "**Your two sons, who were born in Egypt before I came to Egypt, will be mine. Ephraim and Manasseh will be like Reuben and Simeon to me.**"[a] Let us see, therefore, in what manner the latter two are counterparts of the former. (§ 98) Reuben is a symbol of a good nature—for his name means "seeing son," since every mind that is possessed of cleverness and a good nature is visionary. Ephraim, on the other hand, as we have often said in other places, is a symbol of memory—for his name is understood to mean "the bearing of fruit," and the best fruit of the soul is memory. No two things are more kindred to one another than an active memory is to a good-natured mind. (§ 99) Now take the second pairing. Simeon is the name for learning and instruction—its interpretation is "obedience"—and it belongs to the one who has learned both to hear and to hold fast to the lessons that have been spoken. Manasseh, on the other hand, is a symbol of recollection. His name means "away from forgetting." (§ 100) It happens of necessity that the one who departs "from forgetting" proceeds first to recollection, since recollection belongs to learning. Often, objects of contemplation slip away from the learner, when he is not able to hold onto them on account of his weakness, but then rise again to the surface from their source. This experience of slipping away is called forgetting, while the latter experience of resurgence is called recollection. (§ 101) Is not memory, then, akin to a good nature? And is not recollection fittingly paired with learning? Moreover, the same relationship that Simeon has to Reuben (i.e., which learning has to nature), Manasseh has to Ephraim (i.e., recollection has to memory). (§ 102) Just as being good-natured is better than learning virtue—for the first is like seeing, whereas the second is like hearing; and hearing takes second place to vision—so also the faculty of memory is in every way superior to the faculty of recollection. For recollection is mingled with forgetting, whereas memory remains unmixed and unmingled from beginning to end.

g Jethro–Raguel (§§ 103–120)

(§ 103) Again, the father-in-law of the archprophet, Moses, is sometimes called Jethro by the oracles, while at other times he is called Raguel. He is called Jethro whenever pomposity thrives. For Jethro means "excessive" and pomposity is a thing excessive to a guileless life. It makes risible what is well-balanced and necessary for good living, while it reveres the inequalities of covetous

---

[a] Gen 48:5.

gain. (§ 104) This Jethro also honors human things before divine ones, customs before laws, the profane before the holy, mortal goods before immortal ones, seeming before being. He even *dares to offer himself unbidden to Moses in the office of counselor*, suggesting that the sage ought not teach that which alone is worth learning, **the commands of God and his law**,[a] but rather the contracts that men make with one another, which are usually causes of fictitious fellowship. And the great man obeys all his advice, thinking that it is fitting to give a little justice to the little, but great rewards to the great. (§ 105) Often, however, this seeming-sage changes and, abandoning the animals that he took to leading blindly, seeks again the divine flock and becomes a blameless member of it. He marvels at its Herdsman for his nature and admires him for the presidential power that he employs to provide for his own animals. For Raguel means "shepherded by God."

(§ 106) This much has been said by way of summary; the proofs now follow. Moses first introduces Raguel as an attendant of judgment and justice. For the appellation *Midian*,[b] interpreted etymologically, means "from judgment." The symbolic significance of this epithet is twofold. First, the name Midian signifies selection and separation, such as customarily happens with contenders in the so-called holy games. For many who appeared unfit for the competition were immediately eliminated by the judges. (§ 107) These people, who have been initiated into *the unholy rites of Baal Peor*[c] and opened wide all their bodily orifices to receive sensuous waves flowing in from the outside—for Baal Peor means "upper mouth of skin"—flood their governing mind and cast it out into the deepest abyss, so that it cannot swim back up nor even ascend even a little. (§ 108) This was what the mind suffered, until the peaceful and clear-piercing priest of God, **Phinehas**,[d] arrived as a champion, unbidden—for he is by nature a hater of wickedness and possessed by zeal for the good. **Taking a lance**, i.e., swift and sharpened reason, sufficient to search and investigate each matter, he was granted not to be deceived, but, making use of this stronger force, **impaled** emotion **through the womb**,[e] so that it might no longer give birth to any *God-sent evil (i.e., the plague)*.[f] (§ 109) It is also against these (i.e., the Midianites) that the greatest war is stirred up by the seeing race (i.e., Israel), in which **no one** of those who were contending **was lost**.[g] Rather, each returned unwounded and safe, bedecked with victors' crowns.

(§ 110) This was one of the things shown allegorically by the words **priest from Midian**.[h] The other is the discerning and judicial capacity, which through intermarriage between Moses and Zipporah is also appropriated to the pro-

---

[a] Exod 18:20. [b] Exod 2:16. [c] Num 25:3. [d] Num 25:12–13. [e] Num 25:7, 8. [f] Num 25:8.
[g] Num 31:49. [h] Exod 2:16.

PART TWO									91

phetic class. Therefore, he says, **the priest** of judgment and justice **had seven daughters**[a]—symbolically, the ⟨seven⟩ powers of the irrational part of the soul: the organs of procreation, the voice, and the five senses—who are shepherding the sheep of their father. (§ 111) Through these seven powers, the advancements and progress of their father mind are established by proximate impressions. These faculties, **coming** to what is their own—vision to colors and forms; hearing to sounds; smell to scents; taste to juices; and the rest, to what befits them—**draw up**, after a fashion, the external sense-perceptible objects, **until they fill the receptacles** of the soul, **from which they water the sheep of their father.**[b] The sheep I am interpreting as the most clean flock of reasoning, which embraces security and order together in the same fold. (§ 112) Beside these powers, however, the companions of envy and malice—rulers of the wicked herd—also **come**[c] and drive them away from their natural use. The seven shepherding powers lead external impressions within to the mind as to a judge and king, so that by making use of the best ruler they might be kept on the most excellent path. (§ 113) The other shepherds stand opposed to them, pursuing them and proclaiming the opposite, in order to draw out the mind and hand it over easily to the appearances. This continues until the virtue-loving manner, whose name is Moses, which had formerly seemed disengaged, **having arisen** and been inspired, will shield and **rescue them** from their captors, nourishing the father's flock with **thirst-slaking** words.[d] (§ 114) Having fled the onset of those who are wicked in thought and zealous for tangible goods alone, as in a tragedy, the seven powers come back no longer to Jethro, but to **Raguel.**[e] They have left behind their kinship with pomposity and associated themselves with lawful leadership, having thought it worthwhile to become a part of the holy flock, which is led by divine Reason, as the name makes clear. For Raguel means "shepherded by God." (§ 115) Since it is God's private flock that is being cared for, plenteous goods are readily available to those of his sheep, who are obedient and do not resist his governance. A song of this sort is also sung among the *Hymns*: **"The Lord shepherds me, and nothing will I lack."**[f]

(§ 116) Fittingly, therefore, the mind that has the divine Word as its shepherd and king will ask his seven daughters, "Why have you returned **today** hastening with such **swiftness**?[g] Formerly, when you were encountering perceptible things, you tarried outside and were scarcely returning, if you were caught by them. But now, having suffered I know not what, you have returned hastily, contrary to custom." (§ 117) They will reply that they themselves have not been the cause of their breathless, strenuous, recurrent racing to and from the percep-

---

[a] Exod 2:16a.   [b] Exod 2:16b.   [c] Exod 2:17a.   [d] Exod 2:17b.   [e] Exod 2:18a.   [f] LXX Ps 22:1.   [g] Exod 2:18b.

tible objects, but that this was the work of the **human being**[a] who had rescued them from the shepherds of the wild flock. They call Moses an **Egyptian**,[b] although he is not only a Hebrew, but a member of the purest tribe of Hebrews, which alone exercises priesthood. Raguel's daughters are not able to transcend their own nature. (§ 118) It would be desirable if the senses, situated as they are at the borderland of knowable and sense-perceptible objects, might strive after both of these, and not be led by the sense-perceptible objects alone. To suppose that they will ever be guided solely by the noetic realities, however, is a great naïveté. For this reason, they make reference to both kinds of objects, signifying that which can be contemplated by reason alone with the word **human being** and pointing to the sense-perceptible objects with the word **Egyptian**.[c] (§ 119) Having heard these things, again their father will inquire, "**Where is** the human being?[d] In what part of your members does the rational capacity dwell? **Why have you left him behind** so easily,[e] and not, upon encountering him, held fast to this possession, which is most beautiful and profitable for you? (§ 120) But if you failed to do this formerly, now **call him, so that he may eat** and be nourished by your improvements and affinities with him. And perhaps he will even **dwell** with us, and take in marriage the winged, god-borne, and prophetic class, whose name is **Zipporah** (*Sepphora*)."[f]

h   Hoshea–Joshua (§§ 121–123a)

(§ 121) These words will suffice regarding the story of Raguel and his daughters. But Moses also *changes the name of Hoshea (Ōsēa) to Joshua (Iēsous)*,[g] symbolically transforming, through this exchange of letters, the person predicated by a certain quality into a stable disposition. For Hoshea is interpreted as "this person is of a certain sort," whereas Joshua means "salvation of the Lord"—the name of the best stable disposition. (§ 122) For the stable dispositions are better than persons predicated by their correlative qualities. Thus, music exceeds the musician and medicine exceeds the doctor and every skill exceeds every practitioner, with regard to its eternality and power and unfailing excellence in handling the objects of its investigation. A stable disposition is infinite, actively self-fulfilling, and complete, whereas a person predicated by such-and-such a quality is perishable, passive, and incomplete. What is imperishable is better than what is perishable, the active cause is better than its passive object, and the complete is better than the incomplete. (§ 123a) Thus, the coinage of the one spoken of has been reminted into a better form.

---

[a] Exod 2:19aα.   [b] Exod 2:19aβ.   [c] Exod 2:19a.   [d] Exod 2:20a.   [e] Exod 2:20b.   [f] Exod 2:21.
[g] Num 13:16b.

i   Caleb (§§ 123B–124)

(§ 123b) Caleb, for his part, is entirely changed. For Moses says, **there came to be another spirit in him**,[a] as when the governing part of the soul changes into the pinnacle of perfection. (§ 124) Caleb, etymologically, means "all heart." This is a symbol that the soul is not half-way between two poles and vacillating back and forth, but that it has entirely and completely gone over to that which is trustworthy; and that if there were anything at all unpraiseworthy in the soul, that it has evicted this through words of repentance. Having thus been purged of all that stained it and made use of the lustrations and purifications of practical wisdom, it was standing on the verge of shining brightly.

j   The Many Names of Moses (§§ 125–129)

(§ 125) Now, it follows that the archprophet is a man of many names. For whenever he is depicted interpreting the revealed oracles, he is called *Moses*; and whenever in prayer he blesses the people, he is called **God's human being**;[b] and when Egypt is paying the just penalties for their impieties, he is called **god of Pharaoh**, the king of the land.[c] (§ 126) Why is this? With regard to the first name, because to transcribe laws for the benefit of those who will receive them is the work of one who can touch and always have at hand the divine things, and of one who has been called up by *the oracle-speaking Lawgiver*[d] and has received from him a great gift: the interpretation and exposition of the holy laws. For Moses interpreted means "receiving," but it is possible also that it means "touching," for the reasons which have been stated. (§ 127) With regard to the second name: to pray and to bless do not belong to any person who chances to be present, but to the human being who has not looked steadily on his kinship with becoming, but has attached himself to the Ruler and Father of all. (§ 128) It is desirable, if someone happens to make use of a blessing. But to do good for others—this was the promised reward of a greater and more perfect soul, the one that is, so to speak, truly God-seeing. He who possesses this kind of soul is fittingly called **God⟨'s human being⟩**.[e] Third, this same man is even called **god**, because he is wise and therefore ruler **of every fool**,[f] even if that fool should be well-established, boasting in his kingly scepter—not least of all in this case. (§ 129) For the Ruler of the universe wishes the guilty, even if some intolerably unjust people are going to be chastised, to have advocates who will plead for them—who, imitating the merciful power of the Father, will apply punishments in a way that expresses moderation and love for human beings. For to show kindness is characteristic of a **god**.

---

[a] Num 14:24; cf. Num 13:6.   [b] Deut 33:1.   [c] Exod 7:1.   [d] Exod 24:1.   [e] Deut 33:1.   [f] Exod 7:1.

Part Three

[Chapter 6]
The Birth of Isaac (§§ 130–153)

a   *"I Will Give to You" (§§ 130–140)*

(§ 130) Having said what was necessary regarding the change and transposition of names, we will turn now to the chapters which come next in course. The birth of Isaac follows most proximately. For once ***God has named Isaac's mother Sarah (Sarra) in place of Sarai (Sara)***,[a] he then says to Abraham, "**I will give to you ⟨from her⟩ a child.**"[b] (§ 131) Each part of this sentence warrants detailed investigation. The one who just now **gives**, properly speaking, gives something that is entirely his own. And if this statement is not false, Isaac would not be the human being, but a synonym for the best of the good emotions, joy, laughter within the mind, a son of God, who gives him as an appeasement of desire for the most peaceful souls.

(§ 132) Now, it is strange that one man should be a woman's husband, but that from another she should produce children, illegitimate and born in adultery. So then, at a later point, Moses writes that God is the husband of the virtue-loving thought, through the words which he says: **The Lord, seeing that Leah was hated, opened her womb.**[c] (§ 133) Having mercy and pity on virtue, which is hated by the mortal race, and on the soul that loves virtue, he renders barren … the nature that does ⟨not⟩ love the good, whereas he **opens** the spring of good childbearing, giving Leah the gift of healthy delivery.

(§ 134) Tamar too became pregnant from divine seeds. And although she did not see the One who sowed them—for at that time, it is said that **her face was veiled**,[d] just as ***Moses was, when he turned aside, intent on seeing God***[e]—she nevertheless inspected the symbols and tokens left behind. And judging within herself that a mortal does not **give** these,[f] she cried out, "**To whomsoever these things belong, from him I have conceived.**[g] (§ 135) Whose is the **ring**, the proof, the seal of the universe, the archetypal form, by which all things, being without form and symbolized without quality, were impressed into matter? Whose also is the **necklace**, fate, the necessary sequence and analogy, which possesses the uninterrupted chain of all things? And whose is the **staff**,[h] the mainstay, the unshaken, the unturned, establishment of mind, temperance, and instruction?

---

[a] Gen 17:15.   [b] Gen 17:16a.   [c] Gen 29:31.   [d] Gen 38:15.   [e] Exod 3:6; Cf. Exod 34:33–35.   [f] Gen 38:18.   [g] Gen 38:25a.   [h] Gen 38:25b.

© MICHAEL B. COVER, 2024 | DOI:10.1163/9789004687424_005

The scepter, the kingdom, whose are these? Do they not belong to God alone?" (§ 136) Therefore Judah, the thankful manner, delighted by her steadfast and godly reasoning, speaks frankly saying, "**She is justified, for I gave her to no mortal,**"[a] thinking that it would be impious to pollute divine things with profane ones.

(§ 137) So also Sarah, practical wisdom, after she brought forth the self-taught class in the manner of a mother, recalls that God sowed it within her. For after the child was born, she adds this interpretation, saying, "**The Lord made laughter for me.**"[b] This is the equivalent of saying, "He molded Isaac, he fashioned him, he begot him," since Isaac is the same as laughter. (§ 138) Not everyone is able to hear and understand this, on account of the great evil of superstition, which surges among us and floods cowardly and ignoble souls. Therefore, she adds, "**Whoever should hear this will rejoice with me.**"[c] There are few whose ears have been opened and attuned to the reception of these holy words, which teach that it is the proper work of God alone to sow and beget good things. All others have become deaf to these sayings. (§ 139) Indeed, I know an oracle to this effect, proclaimed once by a prophetic mouth as if through flame: "**From me, may your fruit be found. Who is wise, and will comprehend these things? Who is comprehending and will know them?**"[d] In these words, I intuited the unseen ⟨Word⟩, the One who invisibly echoes and strikes the instrument of the human voice, and I marveled at this, being also thoroughly overwhelmed by the content of the proclamation. (§ 140) For if there is any good among the things that are—or rather, the entire heaven and the cosmos, if it is necessary to speak the truth—it is the fruit of God, which is maintained in the manner of a tree by eternal and ever-blooming nature. It belongs to comprehending and wise men to know and confess these sorts of things, not to the insignificant.

b *"From Her" (§§ 141–144)*

(§ 141) What the phrase "**I will give to you**"[e] means has been stated above. The meaning of the next part of the verse, "**from her,**" must now be indicated.[f] Some take this to signify what comes into existence "outside of her," thinking it best to judge by right reason that the soul manifests nothing good, which properly belongs to her, but that everything is appended to her from the outside, according to the magnanimity of God, who showers down gifts. (§ 142) Others suggest that "**from her**" refers to immediate speed. They say that the phrase "**from her**" is the equivalent of "straightaway, immediately, unencum-

---

[a] Gen 38:26. [b] Gen 21:6a. [c] Gen 21:6b. [d] Hos 14:9–10. [e] Gen 17:16aα. [f] Gen 17:16aβ.

bered, without delay." Divine gifts typically arrive in this manner, outstripping even intervals of time. Third are those who say that "**from her**" signifies that virtue is the mother of the created good, who gets her offspring from no mortal father.

(§143) Now, to those who inquire about whether a barren woman gives birth—for the oracles, although they were relating at an earlier stage that Sarah is barren,[a] now agree that she will become a mother—the following must be said: A barren woman cannot naturally give birth, just as a blind person cannot see nor a deaf person hear. The soul, on the other hand, which has become barren of wicked deeds and has not given birth to excessive passions and evils, almost exclusively bears children well. She produces offspring most worthy of love, seven in number according to the song which is sung by grace—Hannah—who says, "**A barren woman gave birth to seven, but she who was many with children became weak.**"[b] (§144) She calls "many" the intellect that is borne along by mixed and confused arguments, which on account of the greatness of the tumultuous crowds around her gives birth to incurable evils. To the contrary, grace calls barren the intellect that has not admitted anything mortal as a productive seed, but snatching up and destroying conversations and liaisons with wicked things, embraces the seven and its most peaceful character. For she wishes to be pregnant with this good quality and to be called its mother.

c   "A Child" (§§145–147)

(§145) This was the meaning of the second part of the phrase, "**from her.**"[c] Let us now investigate the third part, "**a child.**"[d] First, it is worthy of amazement that God does not say that he will give many children, but that only one will be granted graciously. Why is this? Because the good is not naturally proved by its abundance, but by its power. (§146) Many things, as it happens, are musical and grammatical and geometrical and prudent and brave and temperate. But music itself, grammar itself, geometry itself, and still more, justice itself, temperance itself, practical wisdom itself, and courage itself—there is only one of each of these, which is the highest, differing in no way from the archetypal form, from which pattern those unspeakably many particular examples were molded. (§147) These comments will suffice on the topic of God's saying that he will give "*one*" offspring. Now, it should be added that he has not said "**child**" carelessly or without circumspection, but in order to establish that it is neither foreign, nor switched at birth, nor again adopted or illegitimate, but the legiti-

---

[a] Gen 11:30.   [b] 1 Sam (1 Reg) 2:5.11.   [c] Gen 17:16aβ.   [d] Gen 17:16aγ.

mate and noble offspring of the truly citizen soul. Thus, rather than "progeny" (*tokos*), "**child**" (*teknon*) is said, with an emphasis on affinity, by which children are naturally fitted to their parents.

d   *"I Will Bless Her, and She Will Be for Nations" (§§ 148–150)*
(§ 148) Then God says, "**I will bless her, and she will be for nations.**"[a] Not only does he clarify that generic virtue is divisible into suitable species and subspecies, as if into nations. He also suggests that just as there are "**nations**" of animals, so also there are in a certain respect "**nations**" of actions, to which it is a great benefit for excellence to be present. (§ 149) All things that are destitute and bereft of practical wisdom are liable to penalties, just as in those places where the sun does not shine, it is of necessity dark and gloomy. By excellence, to the contrary, the agrarian cares better for his plants. By excellence also does the charioteer drive his chariot in the hippodrome without crashing. Again, by excellence, the ship's captain pilots the vessel on her voyage. Excellence also prepares households, city, and country to be better governed, making men managers, statesmen, and keepers of the common weal. (§ 150) Excellence furthermore introduces the best laws and sows everywhere the seeds of peace. And by the opposite disposition to excellence, the opposite results naturally come to pass: war, lawlessness, corrupt political machinations, confusions, bad sailing, upheavals, and that most grievous sickness among the sciences, deceitful cunning, from which the title "perverse skills" in place of "skills" has been coined. Of necessity, then, will virtue spread abroad to "**nations**"—these great and numerous networks of animals and actions—to the benefit of those who receive them.

e   *"Kings of Nations Will Be from Her" (§§ 151–153)*
(§ 151) It is said next that "**also kings of nations will be from her.**"[b] Those whom ⟨virtue⟩ carries in her womb and issues forth are all rulers. They are not chosen for a short period of time by lot, by unstable action, and by the vote of human beings, who are in most cases paid-off. Rather, they are established as rulers forever by nature herself. (§ 152) This is not a myth of my fabrication, but derives from the most holy oracles, in which some people are introduced as saying to Abraham: "**You are a king from God among us.**"[c] They say this not after examining his material possessions—for what belongs to a man on the move and without a city in which to dwell, wandering through a vast, deserted, and intractable land?—but rather, because they recognize the kingly disposition of Abraham's thought, and thus confess in accordance with Moses that only

---

[a] Gen 17:16b.   [b] Gen 17:16c.   [c] Gen 23:6.

the sage is a king. (§153) For really, the prudent person is ruler of the imprudent, knowing what it is necessary to do and not to do; the temperate person is ruler of those with unchecked appetites, capable of distinguishing carefully between what one ought to choose and to abstain from; the courageous person is ruler of cowards, having learned when it is necessary to stand one's ground, and when this cannot be done safely; the just person is ruler of unjust people, aiming at impartial fairness when there are portions to be assigned; and the holy person is ruler of unholy people, being grasped by the best conceptions about God.

[Chapter 7]
Abraham's Laughter (§§154–174)

(§154) It was reasonable that the mind, swollen by these promises, would become uplifted. Therefore, in order to convict us, who are wont to put on airs even after the smallest accomplishments, he **falls and** immediately **laughs** the laughter of the soul.[a] He is sullen in face, but smiling in thought, since a great and unmixed joy has come to dwell within him. (§155) Both of these movements happen at the same time within the sage who is inheriting goods greater than his hope: to fall and to laugh. He falls on account of his belief that he should not boast through scorning his mortal nothingness; he laughs, to the contrary, on account of the firmness of his piety, reckoning that God alone is the cause of graces and goods. (§156) Therefore, let creation fall and be sullen with regard to its natural capacity—for on its own, it is unstable and destined for grief. But let creation be raised by God and laugh; for he alone is its stay and its joy.

(§157) Fittingly might someone be confused at this point as to how a person should be able to laugh, when in fact, according to our account, laughter has not yet come into existence. For Isaac is "laughter," and he has not yet come into being according to the present study. Moreover, just as one cannot see without eyes, nor hear without ears, nor smell without nostrils, nor make use of any of the senses apart from their respective sense organs, nor, for that matter, form mental conceptions apart from the reasoning faculty, so also it makes no sense that someone should laugh, without laughter having first been fashioned. (§158) What should be said to this objection? Just this: that nature foreshadows many things, which are about to happen, through certain symbols. Do you not see the chick, which, before it can ply the air, delights in fluttering its wings and

---

[a] Gen 17:17a.

stretching its digits, proclaiming beforehand its hope that it will be able to fly? (§159) Have you not seen a ram or a billy goat or a newly born ox? Although horns have not grown forth upon his head, whenever something provokes him, he will oppose it and charge to guard himself with those parts, from which nature produces his defensive weapons. (§160) Even in the bullfights, mature bulls do not immediately make a serious pass at their opponents, but first they circle about in a stately fashion and shake their necks occasionally and turn around quickly and look really bull-like; only then do they make a pass, taking up their work. Those people, whose custom it is to coin words, call this "getting charged up"—being a kind of charge before the charge.

(§161) The soul also experiences many things in a similar way. When good is hoped for, it becomes cheerful ahead of time, with the result that in a certain manner it rejoices before joy or makes merry before mirth. Perhaps someone would liken it also to what happens in plants. For these, too, when they are about to bear fruit, put forth buds and flowers and green shoots ahead of time. (§162) Consider the cultivated vine, how it has been wondrously adorned by nature with vines, tendrils, suckers, petals, and leaves, which ⟨all⟩ but hurling forth their voice betoken the joy of the tree on account of the fruit that it is about to bear. So also, the day at deep morning laughs ahead of time, when the sun is about to rise. Ray is herald of ray, and light comes forth before light, the dimmer before the more piercing. (§163) Likewise, joy attends the good which has already come, but hope attends the good that is expected in the future. We rejoice in what is arriving, but we hope for what is coming. This also happens in the opposite cases. The presence of evil begets sorrow, while the expectation of evil begets fear. And fear is nothing other than sorrow before sorrow, just as hope is joy before joy. For I think what fear is to sorrow, hope is to joy.

(§164) The senses also entail clear signs of the phenomenon under discussion. Smell, for instance, which takes place before tasting, tries ahead of time nearly everything pertaining to food and drink. For this reason, some people in the interest of clarity have accurately called smell a "foretaster." Hope likewise naturally tastes beforehand, as it were, the future good and recommends it to the soul, so that she might make it her firm possession. (§165) Again, when someone on a journey has grown hungry and thirsty and then suddenly espies water springs or trees of various kinds bowed down by cultivated fruits, although he has not yet eaten or drunk, nor drawn the water or plucked the fruit, nonetheless, in hope of their enjoyment he takes his fill of these beforehand. Accordingly, do we think that it is possible to feast on food that supplies bodily nourishment even before its actual consumption, but that the aliments of thought are not sufficient for us to delight in beforehand, even when feasting upon them is imminent?

(§ 166) Fittingly, therefore, did Abraham **laugh**, although laughter does not seem to have been sown in the mortal race—and not he alone, but his wife also laughs. As it is said a little later, **And Sarah laughed within herself, saying, "It has not yet happened to me up until now,**[a] that a good should come about automatically without assistance. But the One who promises this, **my Lord, is indeed older**[b] than all creation; it is necessary to believe him." (§ 167) At the same time, these verses reiterate that virtue is a delightful thing by nature, and the one who possesses it always rejoices, whereas vice is a sorrowful thing, and whoever possesses it becomes seriously distressed. And now, do we still wonder at those among the philosophers who say that virtue is a good emotion?

(§ 168) For behold, Moses may be discovered as the patron of this wise doctrine, introducing in the foregoing verse[c] the good mind as rejoicing and laughing. Likewise in another passage, it is not the good mind only, but also those who are approaching this same goal with him, who rejoice. There, God says to Moses, **"When Aaron sees you, he will rejoice in himself."**[d] For the advance vision of the good person by itself is enough to fill the intellect with gladness, having jettisoned that most hateful of psychic evils, sorrow. (§ 169) But no one wicked has been permitted to rejoice, as it is also sung in the prophetic verses: **"It does not belong to the impious to rejoice," says God.**[e] This saying is also truly a divine oracle: that the life of every bad person is sullen and sorrowful and full of heavy spirits, even if he should play at smiling with his face. (§ 170) For I would not say that the Egyptians truly rejoiced, when they heard that Joseph's brothers had come, but that play-acting they changed their appearance, in order to seem to rejoice. Never is a rebuke brought against fools to their delight, just as a doctor is not ineffectual when practicing upon a sick person. For hard work attends those things which are beneficial, but ease attends those which are harmful. And putting ease before toil, they are likely also repulsed by those who might procure them benefits. (§ 171) So when you hear that **Pharaoh rejoiced and all his retinue**[f] on account of the arrival of the brothers of Joseph, do not suppose that they truly had any delight, unless perhaps in this regard: that they expect to shift him (i.e., Joseph) from the goods of the soul, on which he was reared, to the insatiable desires of the body, once he had debased the ancient and ancestral coinage of kindred virtue. (§ 172) Having such hopes, the mind that loves pleasure does not think it enough to snare with lures of delights those who have only recently—in fact, just now—enrolled in the gymnasia of temperance. It thinks it a shame if it does not also lead astray the older reason, whose raving passions have passed their prime. (§ 173) For he says again,

---

[a] Gen 18:12a. [b] Gen 18:12b. [c] Gen 18:12; see § 166. [d] Exod 4:14. [e] Isa 48:22. [f] Gen 45:16.

extending detriments as if they were benefits, "**Bring your father and your possessions and come to me,**"ª that is, to Egypt and into the court of this fearful king. He it is who, when our paternal and truly good faculties have moved out in advance of the body (for they are by nature free), draws them back again by force to hand them over to a very bitter prison, appointing as guard, as the verse says, **Potiphar, the eunuch and chief butcher.**ᵇ He is called **eunuch** on account of his dearth of good members and the excision from himself of the procreative organs of the soul. Moreover, being no longer able to sow or plant anything that has value for *paideia*, he is called **chief butcher** because, in the manner of a butcher, he slaughters living creatures, cuts them up and divides them into portions and limbs, and then stalks among the lifeless corpses—not the bodies so much as the immaterial realities—rousing and titillating with superfluous seasonings the impulses to numberless passions, which he should instead have tamed and domesticated. (§ 174) Pharaoh also says, "**I will give to you from all the goods of Egypt, and you shall eat the marrow of the earth.**"ᶜ But we will respond to him, "We who look to the goods of the soul do not aim at acquiring some good for the body. For the three-fold desire of those goods, when it has been absorbed by the soul, is sufficient to render forgettable all those things which are dear to the flesh."

[Chapter 8]
The Faith and Doubt of Abraham (§§ 175–200)

(§ 175) The falsely named "joy" of fools is something of this sort; but the true joy has been spoken of earlier as befitting the good alone. Therefore, **falling, he laughed**ᵈ—falling not from God's want of strength, but from his own. For he stood with the support of the Unturned, but he fell away from his personal self-conceit. (§ 176) This is why, after his seemingly wise pretension had been brought low and his god-loving thought, which is fixed about the Unbending alone, had been raised up, **having laughed**, he immediately **said in thought, "Will a child be born to this hundred-year-old man? And will Sarah, being ninety years old, give birth?"**ᵉ (§ 177) Now do not think, noble reader, that his **speaking** this not with his mouth, but **in thought**ᶠ is set down superfluously—Moses has done this with studied intention. Why is this? Because it seems that, by asking "**Will a child be born to this hundred-year-old man,**"ᵍ Abraham has begun to waver concerning the birth of Isaac. Beforehand, however, it was said

---

ª Gen 45:18a. ᵇ Gen 39:1. ᶜ Gen 45:18b. ᵈ Gen 17:17a. ᵉ Gen 17:17b. ᶠ Gen 17:17bα. ᵍ Gen 17:17bβ.

that he believed, as this oracle spoken a little earlier clarified: "**This man (i.e., Eliezer of Damascus) will not inherit from you, but a child who will come forth from you.**"[a] Then immediately Moses adds: **And Abraham believed God, and it was reckoned to him as righteousness.**[b] (§178) Since, then, it did not follow for the one who had come to believe to waver in earnest, Moses does not make Abraham's wavering long-lasting, of the variety that reaches tongue and mouth. Instead, it remains fixed in his swift-moving thought. For he says, **he said in thought**,[c] and no other faculty praised for its swiftness of foot would have been able to outrun this, since thought has even outstripped all the winged natures. (§179) This is the reason, it seems to me, that the most revered of Greek poets (i.e., Homer) uses the phrase, **as if a wing or a notion.**[d] He clarifies the speed of thought's sharpness by setting "notion" after "wing" on account of its surpassing intensity. For thought advances by some ineffable motion over many terrains, both immaterial and material alike, and arrives in an instant at the bounds of earth and sea, compressing and traversing distances of unbelievable magnitude. In this same quantity of time, it also lifts off the earth, ascends from air to aether, and with great toil comes to stand at the furthest circuit of the fixed stars. (§180) Its hot and fiery aspect does not allow it to rest even here. Therefore, transcending many material bodies, it is borne beyond the boundary of this perceptible universe to the fixed region of the forms by kindred attraction. Thus, the change which happens in the good man (i.e., Abraham) is immediate, immeasurable, not perceptible but only noetic—in a certain manner, outside of time.

(§181) But perhaps someone would say, "Why is it, then, that he who has come to believe admits a trace or shade or whiff of doubt at all?" This person, it seems to me, would profess nothing other than that the generated is ungenerated; that the mortal is immortal; that the perishable is imperishable; and that a human being—if it is lawful to say it—is a god. (§182) For he claims that the faith, which a human being obtains, is necessarily so firm that it does not differ from the faithfulness pertaining to The One Who Is—a faithfulness which befits the divine essence and is complete in all respects. As Moses says in the *Greater Song*: "**God is faithful, and there is no injustice in him.**"[e] (§183) It is a great ignorance to think that a human soul is capable of making space for the unwavering and most securely fixed virtues of God. Indeed, it is lovely that images of these were able to be created, even as they are lesser than their archetypes by myriad and great degrees. And is this not suitable? (§184) For it is necessary that God's virtues be unmixed, since God himself is not compos-

---

[a] Gen 15:4. [b] Gen 15:6. [c] Gen 17:17bβ. [d] Homer, *Od.* 7.36. [e] Deut 32:4.

ite, being a simple nature. Human virtues, by contrast, had to be mixed, since we come into being as mixtures, with a divine and a mortal element blended together and harmonized with one another according to the logic of the perfect music. And that which is compounded out of multiple components has natural proclivities toward each of its constituent parts. (§185) Happy is the one who can devote, the greater part of his life toward the better and more divine portion. Of course, it would be impossible for him to spend his entire life in this way, because there inevitably comes a point when the rival counterweight of his mortal part confronts him like a wrestler and, lying in ambush, bides its time for those inopportune moments when reason should falter, so that it may overpower him by force. (§186) Therefore **Abraham did come fully to believe in God**,[a] but as a human being comes to believe, so that you might become acquainted with what is characteristic of a mortal nature and learn that its changeability was no different than that which stems from nature. And if his wavering is short and momentary, he ought to give thanks. For many others, flooded by the strength of the current of doubt, have been carried away entirely by its force. (§187) For, noble reader, according to the most holy Moses, there is no virtue in a mortal body that is nimble-footed, but whenever it meets something of about equal strength in conflict, it grows stiff and becomes a little lame. For he says, **The flat part of Jacob's thigh became stiff**, on account of which **he limped**.[b]

(§188) But perhaps someone of better courage might come forward and say that the utterance made by Abraham is not that of a doubter, but rather of one who prays that, "If the best of the good emotions, joy, should soon be begotten, may it be born *in conjunction with no other numbers than ninety and one hundred*."[c] In this way, the perfect good would be born to perfect numbers. (§189) Indeed, the numbers spoken of in this verse are perfect, especially according to the most holy Scriptures. Let us look at each of these numbers in turn. Shem, first of all, the son of the righteous **Noah** and ancestor of the visionary race (i.e., Israel) is said to have been **one hundred years old when he gave birth to Arphaxat**,[d] whose name means, "he confounded misery." It is a good offspring of the soul to disturb and confuse and destroy injustice, which is miserable and replete with evils. (§190) **Abraham** also **plants a field**,[e] making use of a one-hundred-fold rule to measure the land; Isaac **finds a hundred measures of barley**;[f] and **Moses** prepares the courtyard of the holy tabernacle at **one hundred cubits**,[g] as he measures the distance from east to west. (§191) There is finally the one-hundred-fold reckoning of the first fruit of the first fruit, which *the*

---

[a] Gen 15:6. [b] Gen 32:25(26), 31(32). [c] Gen 17:17bβ. [d] Gen 11:10. [e] Gen 21:33. [f] Gen 26:12.
[g] Exod 27:9.

*Levites offer to the consecrated high priests.*ᵃ For when they receive the tenths from the nation of Israel, it is said that they give the first fruits of it to the priests as from their own possessions, reckoned as a holy tenth of ⟨tenfold⟩ reckonings.

(§ 192) One could look and find many other places in the laws pertaining to this praise of the aforementioned number. At present, what we have said will more than suffice. If, however, you subtract a holy tenth from the one-hundred—a first offering to God, who is bearing, growing, and bringing to maturation fruits within the soul—you will leave another perfect number: ninety. How could it not be perfect, being a borderland between the first and the ⟨second⟩ tenth, according to which **the holy ⟨of holies⟩** is divided from **the sanctuary**, in the manner of **a middle curtain**,ᵇ by which things of the same genus are sorted according to their divisions into species?

(§ 193) The good man thus was speaking **in thought**ᶜ things that are truly good. The bad man, however, though from time to time he gives utterance to entirely good things, shamelessly does the most shameful things. This indeed is the case with Shechem (*Sychem*), the spawn of ignorance. He has Hamor (*Emōr*) for his father,ᵈ whose name, interpreted, means "ass" (*onos*). His own name, Shechem, means "shoulder" (*ōmos*), the symbol of toil. The toil, to which ignorance gives birth, is wretched and full of hardship, whereas the toil, to which the attentive and nimble mind is kin, is beneficial. (§ 194) Therefore the oracles say that Shechem **spoke according to the thought of the virgin**, after he had formerly **humbled her**.ᵉ Was not this phrase, **spoke according to the thought of the virgin**, pronounced deliberately and for no other purpose than to clarify that what had been done was the opposite of the words Shechem had spoken? For Dinah (*Deina*) is judgment, which cannot be bribed. She is justice, coregent with God. She is the ever-virgin. Indeed, Dinah can be interpreted both ways: as "judgment" or "justice." (§ 195) Those fools who attempt to corrupt her through their daily plots and pursuits avoid condemnation by using speech that seems to be good. They ought, however, to either do what follows from what they say, or if they act unjustly, keep silent. For it is said, **Silence ⟨destroys⟩ half of evil**. For this very reason, Moses, rebuking the one who thinks creation worthy of the foremost honors and the imperishable God worthy of second honors, says, **You sinned, keep silent.**ᶠ (§ 196) To boast and speak excessively about one's evils, like a tragic actor, doubles one's sin. And nearly all have experienced this. These people always say things dear and just to virgin virtue, yet they do not miss an opportunity to affront and harm her, if they are

---

ᵃ Num 18:28.   ᵇ Exod 26:33.   ᶜ Gen 17:17bβ.   ᵈ Gen 34:2.   ᵉ Gen 34:3, 2.   ᶠ Gen 4:7.

able. What city is there, which is not full of people who sing a hymn to virtue, ever-virgin? (§197) ⟨None!⟩ They rub the ears of their hearers raw, spewing out truisms, like:

> Practical wisdom is necessary, the lack of wisdom it is harmful.
> Temperance is a choice virtue, incontinence is hateful.
> Courage is worthy of endurance, cowardice is worthy of flight.
> Justice is beneficial, injustice holds no reward.
> Holiness is good, profanity is shameful.
> Piety is praiseworthy, impiety should be cursed.
> It is most appropriate for human nature to think and act and speak well, but to do each of these badly is most alien to us.

(§198) Forever stringing together these and similar maxims, they deceive the courts and council chambers and theatres and every human society and religious sodality. They are like those who put beautiful masks on the most shameful of faces, with the thought of not being discovered by those who see them. (§199) These theatrics are of no use. For some men will come, very vigorous and possessed by zeal for virtue. Stripping off these veils and curtains, which Shechem and Hamor have woven poorly with their speech, and gazing upon her, they will know the soul in its own nakedness as well as the ineffable secrets that are hidden in inner chambers of her nature. Then, dragging out all that is shameful and disgraceful within her into the clear light of day, they will show everyone what sort she really is, how shameful and laughable she is without her wrappings, and how she donned a false but lovely superficial form.

(§200) Those who are ready to ward off such base and unclean characters are two in number—**Simeon and Levi**[a]—but in judgment they are one. Therefore, also in the *Blessings*, their father Jacob was **numbering them in a single order**[b] on account of the harmony and singularity of their minds and their proclivity toward one and the same part. Moses no longer even mentions that they were two, but **enrolls the entirety of Simeon in Levi**[c] and mixing their two substances fashions, as it were, one entity stamped by a single form, unifying hearing (i.e., Simeon) with acting (i.e., Levi).

---

[a] Gen 34:14, esp. 25–26. [b] Gen 49:5. [c] Deut 33:8.

[Chapter 9]
The Life of Ishmael (§§ 201–251)

a   *"This Ishmael" (§§ 201–209a))*

(§ 201) When the excellent man (i.e., Abraham), through his own thought, now came to understand that the promise was articulating things full of reverence and piety, he experienced both movements simultaneously as well: faith toward God, and lack of faith toward what is generated. Fittingly, then, he says in prayer, **"Let this Ishmael live before you,"**[a] choosing each of these words—"**this** ⟨Ishmael⟩," "**let him live**," and "**before you**"—with an eye to the allegorical meanings, which they entailed. For more than a few people have been deceived by like-sounding terms used to signify different realities. (§ 202) What I mean by this must be examined. **Ishmael** is interpreted "hearing of God." Now, with regard to the divine teachings, there are some who hear to their own benefit, and others who hear to their own harm and that of others. Or do you not see the bird-augur Balaam? He is introduced as **hearing the words of God and gaining knowledge from the Most High.**[b] (§ 203) But what benefit did he accrue from this sort of hearing, from this sort of knowledge? For although he tried willfully to maim the best eye of the soul, which alone has been taught to see God, he was not able, due to the indomitable might of the Savior. Goaded on, nonetheless, by his own damaged mind and receiving many injuries, he perished in the midst of **wounded men**,[c] because by mantic sophistry he had debased the God-inspired prophecy. (§ 204) Therefore, the good man necessarily prays that **"this Ishmael"**[d] alone might be healthy, owing to the fact that there are also those who do not rightly hear the sacred instructions. Moses openly forbade these people from frequenting the assembly of the Ruler of all.[e] (§ 205) Those who are permanent eunuchs with regard to their generative thought-organs, or those who, being completely castrated, extol their own mind and sense-perception as the sole causes of human affairs, or those who are lovers of polytheism and honor with complete conviction the polytheistic band—these offspring of fornication, who do not know that the one husband and father of the virtue-loving soul is God—are these not fittingly driven away and banished?

(§ 206) The parents who accuse their son of drunkenness in the Scriptures seem to me to do something similar. For they say, **"This son of ours disobeys,"**[f] declaring by the addition of **"this"** that their other children are patient and temperate, governed by the demands of right reason and *paideia*. These are the

---

[a] Gen 17:18.   [b] Num 24:16.   [c] Num 31:8.   [d] Gen 17:18a.   [e] Deut 23:1–2.   [f] Deut 21:20.

most truthful parents of a soul, by whom it is most shameful to be accused and most glorious to be praised. (§ 207) And as regards the phrases, **It is this Aaron and Moses, whom God commanded to lead the sons of Israel out of Egypt**,[a] and **It is these who are disputing with king Pharoah**,[b] let us not think that **these** are spoken superfluously, or that the demonstratives do not reveal anything more than the proper names. (§ 208) For Moses is the purest sort of mind, and Aaron is its speech.[c] This mind is instructed to attend to holy things in a God-befitting way, and its speech interprets them with holiness. The sophists, on the other hand, aping their behavior and counterfeiting their esteemed currency, claim both to be able to think rightly about that which is best and to speak about it in a praiseworthy fashion.[d] Therefore, so that we may not deceived by exchanging the false coinage for the true on account of their similarity of character, God gave a touchstone, by which the two may be distinguished. (§ 209a) What is the touchstone? The leading out from the land of the body the visionary, contemplative, and philosophical mind. The one who is able to do this is **this Moses**.[e] The one who is not able to do this, who only says that he can, although he be clad in myriad reverent titles and names, is the object of laughter.

b "Let Him Live" (§§ 209b–215)

(§ 209b) Abraham, therefore, prays for Ishmael **to live** not because he himself is being converted toward the life with the body, but so that the divine hearing, sounding eternally in the soul, might raise Ishmael and rekindle the life within him. (§ 210) And whereas Abraham prays that the hearing of words and the learning of sacred doctrines (i.e., Ishmael) might **live**, as it has been said, the practicer Jacob prays the same for the good nature. For he says, "**Let Reuben live and not die**."[f] Does he pray for immortality and imperishability, a thing impossible for a human being? Surely not. What it is that he wishes to establish with these words must now be said. (§ 211) All things that can be heard and learned are built upon a nature receptive to *paideia*, as upon a pre-constructed foundation. If this kind of nature does not exist beforehand, however, all these things lose their benefit. Persons without such a nature would seem to differ nowise **from an oak or a mute stone**.[g] Nothing could be rightly adjoined with them, but everything rebounds and glances off, as from some solid surface. (§ 212) On the other hand, one can see that the souls of good natures have been mixed moderately, in the manner of smoothed wax, neither too hard nor too soft. These natures readily receive all audible and visual stimuli, perfectly impressing their

---

[a] Exod 6:26. [b] Exod 6:27. [c] See Exod 4:10–16. [d] Exod 7:11, 22; 8:3. [e] Exod 6:26. [f] Deut 33:6.
[g] Homer, *Od.* 19.163. Cf. Homer, *Il.* 22.126; Hesiod, *Theog.* 35.

forms on themselves as accurate images for memory. (§ 213) It was necessary, then, for the rational class to pray that the good-natured offspring might persist without sickness and imperishable. For few people have a share in the life that accords with virtue, which is the least false life. I do not mean few from the crowds, for none of these has fellowship with the true life; but few even if there are those for whom it is possible to flee human pursuits and live for God alone. (§ 214) For this reason also is the ascetic and courageous man greatly amazed, if some person being carried along in the midst of the river of life is not totally submerged by its current, but should be able to fight against so strongly flowing a current of wealth and repel the torrent of unbounded pleasure and not be snatched up in the storm of vain opinion. (§ 215) Therefore, it is not Jacob who addresses Joseph, so much as the holy Word who addresses every person in good bodily condition, who, although plying his trade among bounteous and abundant material goods, is carried away by none of them, when he says, "**You are still alive!**"[a] He speaks a wondrous phrase, which transcends the usual pattern of our life. For typically, once we have felt the slightest breeze of good fortune, we shake off our reefing ropes and become keenly puffed up. Putting on great and taut airs, we are borne toward the pleasures of the passions. Neither do we check these desires, once they have been released and let loose without limit, until we run ashore the whole vessel of our soul and end in shipwreck.

c *"Before You" (§§ 216–251)*

(§ 216) Therefore, it is entirely right that we pray for "**this Ishmael to live.**" He then adds, "**before God let him live,**"[b] indicating that the goal of happiness is for human thought to be worthy of the truly best Overseer and Guardian. (§ 217) For if the ward does not wander off when his school-slave is present; if an adviser being near benefits the learner; if, when an elder approaches, a youth dons reverence and temperance; and if a father and mother hinder a son, about to commit an injustice, although they are only seen by him in silence; how great indeed a superabundance of goods ought we reckon that person has at his disposal, who supposes that he is always being seen by God? Surely, ⟨if⟩ he looks out for the approval of the One who is present, with fear and trembling he will flee from acting unjustly with all his might.

(§ 218) When he prays that "**Ishmael might live,**"[c] however, he does not despair of the birth of Isaac, as I also said before, but **he has come to believe in God**[d] ⟨....⟩ For what God is able to give, human beings are not capable of receiv-

---

[a] Gen 46:30.   [b] Gen 17:18.   [c] Gen 17:18.   [d] Gen 15:6.

ing, since it takes little for him to give the most numerous and greatest things, whereas it is not easy for us to receive even the gifts that are extended. (§ 219) It is cause for gladness, then, if we should hold onto some of the goods that customarily and ordinarily result from work and cultivation, whereas there is no hope for us to approach those which are born automatically, entirely apart from human skill or ingenuity, and come into being readily on their own. For since these things are divine, it is necessary for more divine and unmixed natures, which have taken leave of what is mortal, to find them.

(§ 220) Nevertheless, Moses taught that thankful confessions ought to be made according to the **power of hands**,[a] with the rationally acute person presenting comprehension and practical wisdom as an offering, while the eloquent person consecrates all the excellences in speech, through song and prose *encomia* to The One Who Is. Next, according to his type, the naturalist will offer discoveries of the world; the ethicist, all moral philosophy; the craftsman and the scientist the theoretical findings of the arts and sciences. (§ 221) So also, a sailor and helmsman will dedicate a successful voyage; a farmer, a good production of crops; a herdsman, the healthy birth of livestock; a doctor, the health of those who were ailing. Likewise, the leader of an army will dedicate his might in battle and the statesman or the king will dedicate lawful presidency and governance. To put it concisely, he who is not a lover of himself will declare that the cause of all things, whatever is good for soul or body or external affairs, is God, the only true Cause.

(§ 222) Therefore, let no one who seems to be possessed of less resplendent and more modest gifts despair of hope and shrink from becoming a thankful suppliant of God. Even if he expects nothing more of the greater goods, let him nonetheless give thanks according to his own power for the gifts that he has already received. (§ 223) For he has received myriad: birth, life, nourishment, soul, sense perception, impressions, impulse, and reason. Reason especially, although it is a small word, signifies the most perfect and divine operation. It is a fragment of the soul of the universe, or to put it in more holy terms befitting those practice philosophy according to Moses, an impress corresponding to the divine image.[b]

(§ 224) Worthy also of praise are those *spies* sent by Moses, who undertook to pull up the whole tree of virtue, root and branch, and carry it back by its stump. But since they could not do this, they took instead a small vine and one **grape cluster**,[c] a proof and portion of the whole virtue of the land, which was all they had the strength to carry. (§ 225) Let us pray, then, to enjoy the full number of

---

[a] Num 6:21.   [b] Gen 1:27. See Wis 7:26.   [c] Num 13:24(17–33).

the virtues. But if this proves greater than our human nature can bear, let us be happy to obtain any one of the particular virtues: practical wisdom or courage or justice or love of human beings. Let the soul bear and give birth to one good, rather than becoming bereft and sterile with respect to them all. (§ 226) Will you yourself set these sorts commands on your own son: "If you do not treat your servants gently, neither should you share things with your peers. If you do not act respectfully toward your wife, neither should you honor your parents. If you disregard your mother and father, also act impiously toward God. If you delight in pleasure, do not refrain from hoarding silver. Do you want to acquire much wealth? Also court vain opinion." (§ 227) What then? Do you not think it worthwhile to walk a middle way in some respects, even if you are not able to do so in all? And, were you to deny this, would not your son say, "What are you saying, father? Do you wish your son to be either perfectly good or perfectly bad? Are you not glad if he should reach the middle regions before he reaches the heights?"

(§ 228) Was it not also for this reason that Abraham, in the time of the destruction of the people of Sodom, *beginning his prayer with a group of fifty ends with a group of* **ten**?[a] He implores and pleads that if, in some created being, there should not be found the all-perfect *release into freedom*[b]—of which the holy number fifty is a symbol—then at least the middle *paideia*, being reckoned as ten, might suffice for deliverance of the soul on the verge of condemnation. (§ 229) Those who have been educated have an advantage over those who are uneducated, and those who have been tutored in the general arts and letters have more opportunities for growth than those without schooling in instrument or muse, given that the former have been nourished nearly from their childhood by teachings about fortitude, self-control, and every virtue. Therefore, even if they have not been entirely scrubbed and cleansed from acting unjustly, as those bright from a fresh bath, nevertheless they have gradually and in a measured way begun to be washed.

(§ 230) Esau seems to say something similar to this to his father when he asks, **"Surely, you have not but one blessing, Father? Bless me too, Father."**[c] Different blessings have been distinguished for different types of people: perfect blessings for the perfect, intermediate blessings for the imperfect, as is also the case with bodies. Different exercises are used for healthy and sick bodies, and likewise different nourishments. And so it is with everything else pertaining to one's manner of living: not all treatments are the same, but some are fitting to one group, so that they do not become wholly sick, while other treatments are proper to another group, so that they might make the transition back to bet-

---

[a] Gen 18:24, 32.   [b] Lev 25:10.   [c] Gen 27:38.

ter health. (§ 231) Therefore, since there are many goods in nature, grant me, ⟨Lord⟩, that which most seems to befit me, even if it should be rather small, considering this alone: whether I will be able to bear readily what has been given. But grant also that it not be such a gift that I, unfortunate man that I am, will faint and collapse under its weight.

(§ 232) And what else do we suppose is displayed in the phrase, ⟨**Are you afraid**⟩ **that the hand of the Lord will not suffice?**[a] Is it not that the powers of The One Who Is extend everywhere for the sake of providing benefits not only to those of good reputation but also to those who seem to be more unimportant? To these he gives what is fitting, calculating and apportioning with his own standard of equality, in accordance with the proportions and measurements of each soul, the gift that is analogous to each.

(§ 233) I am also amazed not least of all by the law pertaining to those who put off their sins and resolve to repent. For it orders them to *bring*, as the first sacrificial animal, a blameless **female sheep.**[b] **But if**, it says, **his hand cannot acquire sufficient money for the sheep, he will bring for the sin that he has committed two turtledoves or two young doves, one as a sin offering and one as a whole burnt offering.**[c] (§ 234) **But if his hand should not find a yoke of turtledoves or two young doves, he will bring as the gift a tenth of an ephah of flour. He will not pour oil on it, nor will he set incense on it, because it is for sin. And he will bring it to the priest, and when he has received it from him, the priest will set the full handful as the memorial upon the altar.**[d] (§ 235) Therefore, one makes atonement by means of the three named manners of repentance: beasts or birds or fine wheat, in accordance with, I presume, the power of the one who is being cleansed and repenting. For small sins do not require great purifications, nor are great sins cleansed by small ones, but the purifications must be alike and equal to their corresponding sin.

(§ 236) Why precisely cleansing should be divided into three kinds is a matter worthy of investigation. It is roughly the case that both sins and their corrections turn out to be classifiable under three headings: thought, words, and deeds. For this reason, Moses also teaches in the *Exhortations* that the attainment of good is neither impossible nor overly difficult,[e] saying, (§ 237) **It is not necessary to fly up to heaven, nor to go to the ends of earth and sea to acquire it. Rather, the acquisition of the good is near; in fact, it is very near.**[f] Then he shows this, although not in a way that is clear to the eyes, saying that every work is **in your mouth and heart and hands**,[g] indicating symbolically "in words, in plans, in actions." For he insinuates that human happiness is established by

---

[a] Num 11:23.　[b] Lev 5:6.　[c] Lev 5:7.　[d] Lev 5:11–12a.　[e] Deut 30:11.　[f] Deut 30:12–14a.　[g] Deut 30:14b.

good counsel and good speech and good work, just as human misery is established by their opposites. (§ 238) In these same three places, both correction and sin take place: in heart, mouth, and hand. For some take the most informed counsel and say what is best and do what ought to be done. Now, among these three kinds of offense, the lightest is to plan what one ought not to, the heaviest is to do what is unjust with one's own hand, and the middle kind of offense is to speak what is unfitting. (§ 239) As it happens, moreover, the lightest kind of sin is also the most difficult to uproot. It is difficult to guide the turning of the soul toward rest, and one would more quickly stem the current of a swollen river than check the movement of a soul rushing about erratically. For an untold number of cares crash upon it, one upon another, in the manner of a deluge, carrying the soul along and agitating it and turning it every which way by force.

(§ 240) Now, the best and most perfect form of purification is this: not to entertain in one's heart anything out of place, but to be governed by peace and lawfulness, whose leader is justice. The second form of purification is not to sin with words, whether by lying or swearing false oaths or deceiving or playing the sophist or flattering or by opening one's mouth and wielding the tongue for libel of anyone. It is better for those given to such speech to set a bridle and an unbreakable chain about their mouths. (§ 241) Moreover, it is easy to see why speaking unfitting things is a heavier sin than thinking them. There are times when one entertains thoughts in one's heart, not by one's own agency but unwillingly. One is compelled to receive thoughts of things that one does not wish, and for such unwilling thoughts, there is no culpability. (§ 242) But a person speaks willingly, with the result that if he utters a word that ought not be spoken, he does injustice and is unhappy as well, since he did not by chance will to speak some gentler words. It is advantageous for him to prefer a very secure solitude. Then, when he is not able to be alone, he is presumably capable of maintaining a voluntary silence. (§ 243) In the same way, an unjust deed is a weightier sin than speaking unjustly. For they say, **A word is a shadow of an act.**[a] And if a shadow can harm, how is the act not more harmful?

Therefore, Moses exonerates the mind's judgment from complaints and charges, since judgment entertains many unwilled changes and turnings and is acted upon by numerous external thoughts that bombard it, more than it acts by its own volition. But whatever words proceed from the mouth, these Moses calls to defend themselves and receive chastisements, since he supposes that our speech is under our control. (§ 244) Now whereas the chastisements for words are more moderate, the chastisements for culpable actions are more severe. For Moses appoints great penalties for those who do great injustices

---

[a] Democritus frag. 105.

and execute in deed what they premeditate in senseless judgment and speak out loud with the advance declaration of the tongue.

(§ 245) Moses has called the purifications of these three—thought, word, and deed—a **sheep and *a pair* of turtledoves or young doves and a tenth of a holy measure of flour**,[a] considering it worthy that thought be purified by a **sheep**, speech by **birds**, and action by **flour**. (§ 246) Why is this? Because just as the mind is the best faculty in us, so also is the **sheep** best among the kinds of irrational animals, since a sheep is the tamest, giving forth yearly produce from itself for the assistance and adornment of human beings. For clothing wards off the harmful effects of icy cold and summer heat and shades our natural "unmentionables," while fostering the comely appearance of those who wear it.

(§ 247) Therefore, let the best of living animals, the **sheep**, be the symbol of the purification of our best part, thought. And let the **birds** stand for the purification of speech. For speech is light and winged by nature, borne along swifter than an arrow and darting every which way. A word, once it has been spoken, cannot be drawn back, but being carried outside and running with great swiftness, strikes the ears and coming through the whole faculty of hearing, immediately resounds. (§ 248) Now, speech is twofold—the true and the false. For this reason, it seems to me, it was likened it to ***a pair* of turtledoves or young doves**. The first of the birds, Moses says, ought to be for a sin offering, while the second must be sacrificed as a whole-burnt offering. This is because true speech is completely holy and perfect, whereas false speech has sinned and is in need of correction.

(§ 249) **Flour**, as I was saying, is a symbol of the purification of action. For this also comes to be purified not without skill and active thought, but by the hands of wheat-workers, who have made this work a regular practice. Therefore Moses also says, **The priest, having grasped the full handful, will also elevate its memorial**,[b] showing symbolically, through the word **handful**, "handwork" and "action." (§ 250) And very deliberately does Moses say concerning the hoofed-animal: **If the hand cannot acquire sufficient money for the sheep**,[c] but concerning the birds he says, **If he should not find**.[d] Why is this? Because great strength and overwhelming power are necessary to undo the ill turnings of thought, whereas lesser force is required to check the sins of words. (§ 251) A safeguard against all the sins which happen through speech, as I said earlier, is silence, which can easily be used by anyone at all. Many, however, through their talking and immoderate use of words do not find a limit to set upon their speech.

---

[a] Lev 5:6–12.   [b] Lev 5:12.   [c] Lev 5:7.   [d] Lev 5:11.

[Chapter 10]
Sarah's Child (§§ 252–260)

(§ 252) Since he has been reared and trained on these and similar divisions and specifications of realities, would it not see reasonable for the good man to pray that **"Ishmael might live,"**[a] in case somehow he is not able to beget Isaac? (§ 253) And what does the propitious God reply? To the one who asks for one thing, he gives two; and to the one who asks for the lesser thing, he gives the greater. For, Moses says, **He said to Abraham: "Yes, behold Sarah your wife will bear you a son."**[b] God's symbolic answer, **"Yes,"**[c] responds directly to Abraham's request. For what is more fitting than for God to assent to good things and agree to them quickly? (§ 254) But those things to which God assents, every fool rejects. The oracles introduce **Leah as hated.**[d] Therefore, she also has the sort of name that signifies this. For the interpretation of Leah is "rejected" and "hard-laboring," because we all defect from virtue and think that she is too often enjoining laborious rather than sweet commandments. (§ 255) But she was thought worthy of so great a favor by the Ruler of all, such that once **her womb had been opened** by him,[e] she received the seed of divine progeny, for the purpose of giving birth to lovely practices and actions. Learn then, O soul, that also **Sarah**—virtue—**will bear you a son,**[f] not only Hagar—the middle education. And while Hagar's offspring must be taught, Sarah's offspring is entirely self-taught.

(§ 256) Do not be amazed, then, if God, who brings forth all good things, also produces this latter kind ⟨of Isaac-soul⟩, rare on earth but abundant in heaven. You could learn why this is fitting from the other bodily members, of which the human being is composed. Do the eyes see because they have been taught? If not, then why? Do the nostrils smell through learning? Do hands touch or feet walk because of the commands or exhortations of headmasters? (§ 257) What about impulses and impressions—for these are the first movements and dispositions of the soul? Are these established by teaching? And does our mind learn to think and comprehend by frequenting the lectures of a sage? All these faculties eschew teaching and make use of self-propelling nature for their own proper activities. (§ 258) Why then do you still wonder, if God will also shower down virtue to be acquired without toil or difficulty, with no need for oversight, but complete and perfect from the beginning? But if you also wish to have a witness of this, will you find any more trustworthy than that of Moses? He says

---

[a] Gen 17:18; § 218, etc. *supra*.   [b] Gen 17:19a.   [c] Gen 17:19aα.   [d] Gen 29:31a.   [e] Gen 29:31b.
[f] Gen 17:19aβ.

that for other human beings, nourishments come from the earth, but that for one alone—the visionary class (i.e., Israel)—they come from heaven. (§ 259) On behalf of the nourishments of earth, human farmers work together; but God, who alone works through his own power without the collaboration of others, sends down like snow the nourishments from heaven. So indeed it is said, "**Behold, I rain down on you bread from heaven.**"[a] And what nourishment is rightly said to be rained down from heaven, except the heavenly wisdom? (§ 260) It is this nourishment that he, who has a plenteous abundance of practical wisdom and waters all things, sends down from above upon the souls which have a desire for virtue. This he does especially on the holy seventh day, *which Moses calls the Sabbath*.[b] For then, he says, the production of goods will take place automatically, rising up from the earth not by any skill, but blooming and bearing their respective fruits by means of self-begetting and self-perfecting nature.

[Chapter 11]
You Will Call His Name Joy (§§ 261–263)

(§ 261) "Virtue, therefore, **will bear you a son**,[c] noble, male, removed from all female emotion. And **you will call the name**[d] of your son the emotion that you feel for him (and you will feel it entirely): joy. As a result, you will also make his name a symbol of this emotion: laughter." (§ 262) Just as sorrow and fear have their own appropriate shouts, which the corresponding emotion coins by violence and force, so also good counsels and merriments compel the use of natural expressions. One could not find more proper and accurate phrases than these, even if one happens to be wise concerning appellations. (§ 263) Therefore, God says: "**I have blessed him, I will increase him, I will bring him to fullness, and he will beget twelve nations**,"[e] that is, the whole cyclical chorus of sophistic preliminary topics. "**But my covenant I will establish with Isaac.**"[f] Thus, he re-fashions the class of humans belonging to each virtue—taught virtue and self-taught virtue—with the weaker class partaking of learned virtue and the stronger class availing itself of the virtue that is ready to hand.

---

[a] Exod 16:14. [b] Exod 16:23. [c] Gen 17:19a. [d] Gen 17:19b. [e] Gen 17:20. [f] Gen 17:21a.

[Chapter 12]
God Alone Is the Appropriate Time (§§ 264–269)

a *"At This Appropriate Time"* (§§ 264–266)
(§ 264) **"And at this appropriate time, she will bear ⟨a son⟩ for you,"**[a] that is, wisdom will give birth to joy. What sort of **appropriate time** do you signify, O most-wonderful speaker? Do you mean the **appropriate time** that alone cannot be referenced from the horizon of creation? For he himself would be the true **Appropriate Time**, the dayspring of the universe, the good and timely fashioning of earth, heaven, and the natures which are between them, of all the animals and plants together. (§ 265) For this reason, Moses also dared to say about those who fled and did not wish to levy war in defense of virtue against her antagonists: **"The appropriate time has departed from them, but the Lord is among us."**[b] Here he confesses, although not in a straightforward manner, that God alone is the Appropriate Time, who stands far off from all impiety, but walks among souls that conquer in virtue. (§ 266) For he says, **"I will walk among you, and I will be your God."**[c] But those who say that the seasons of the year are "appropriate times" use the words inexactly and in an improper fashion, since they in no way clarify the natures of realities, but speak in the main at random.

b *"In the Other Year"* (§§ 267–269)
(§ 267) Augmenting the goodness of the one being born, God says that Isaac will be born **"in the other year,"**[d] indicating not the distance of time that is measured by lunar and solar circuits, but the distance that is placeless and foreign and really new, "other" than what is seen and perceived, numbered among the bodiless and noetic spaces, although it comprises the paradigm and archetype of time—namely, eternity. For eternity is described as the life of the noetic world, just as time is the life of the perceptible world. (§ 268) **In this year**, moreover, he who has sown the graces of God for the creation of more abundant goods **finds the grain increased one-hundred-fold**,[e] so that as many as possible of those who are worthy to partake may have a share in them. (§ 269) Now, it is the custom for the one who sows also to reap. Here, however, he was sowing to demonstrate that virtue is the enemy of jealousy and vice; and he is said "to find," but not "to reap." For he who made the ear of grain riper and full of good works was Another, who having prepared and made ready greater hopes and more abundant gifts, has set them out for those who seek to find.

---

[a] Gen 17:21bα.   [b] Num 14:9.   [c] Lev 26:12.   [d] Gen 17:21bβ.   [e] Gen 26:12.

[Chapter 13]
God's Departure (§ 270)

(§ 270) But the phrase, **God finished speaking to Abraham**,[a] is equal to saying: "He perfected the hearer himself, who had been formerly empty of wisdom, and filled him with immortal words." And when the student had become perfect, **the Lord departed from Abraham**.[b] This indicates not that they had been disjoined from one another; for the sage is by nature an attendant of God. Rather, it expresses God's wish to establish the volition of his student—that by demonstrating what he had learned apart from compulsion (now that the teacher was no longer present) and putting to use an intentional and self-controlled forethought, he might act through his own agency. For the teacher gives the student space for voluntary practice without external prompting, engraving within the soul a most secure form of unforgetting memory.

---

[a] Gen 17:22a. [b] Gen 17:22b.

Notes to the Text and Translation

§ 1 In Philo's citations of the Septuagint and his ensuing commentary, the textual witnesses use the spelling Ἀβραάμ ("Abraham") rather than Ἀβράμ ("Abram") for the name of the treatise's protagonist, regardless of whether the citation occurs before or after Gen 17:5. This may have been Philo's own convention—seeing as Abraham is a timeless psychic type—but as the question of name change is at issue in the present treatise, it is also possible that a later scribe has altered the spelling (at least in the citations) to reflect convention. In the translation, I follow PCW and always print the longer version of the name. For Philo's scriptural text, see Katz 1950; Sterling 2012d.

§§ 7–22 *The Greek text of §§ 7–22* has been eclectically reconstructed by Cohn and Wendland by using a number of significant variants to the A and B versions of the text, preserved in the *Sacred Parallels* of John of Damascus and lauded by Wendland as "utilissima" (PCW 1:lxiii). The relatively poor state of the codices can be ascertained from the number of occasions on which the testimony of John of Damascus is preferable to the later manuscript evidence. This is unfortunate, as it makes it difficult to understand with certainty the precise contours of Philo's thought on knowledge of God.

§ 12 *as if … by this sort of name*. The text is confused. The codices read ὡς ἐν ὀνόματι τῷ κυρίῳ, which might be translated "as by a name, 'the Lord'" or "as by the proper name." D reads: "as if The One Who Is by this sort of name" (ὡς ἂν ὁ ὢν ὀνόματι τοιούτῳ). Wendland follows the Damascene reading, but adds his own conjectures: "The One Who Is Ineffable by this sort of name" (ὁ ἀκατονόμαστος ὢν ὀνόματι τοιούτῳ). Objecting to the speculative nature Wendland's emendation *ex ingenio*, Colson follows the MSS, but corrects in light of the Damascene text to "as if by a proper name, 'The Lord God'" (ὡς ἂν ὀνόματι κυρίῳ τῷ «κύριος ὁ θεός»). Arnaldez calls the locus a "passage discuté" and adopts the D text (1964, 36). In the translation, I have tried to render the Damascene variant. The student will do well to consult the textual apparatus at this point.

§ 13 *a proper name of his*. The translation follows the conjecture of Hoeschel, "some name" (ὄνομά τι), which was accepted by Colson and Arnaldez (1964, 38). This simply splits up the MSS "by a name" (ὀνόματι) into two words. Wendland instead writes "the name" (τὸ ὄνομα), inspired by the Damascene text, but this reading might imply that God has a proper name "Lord"/the Tetragrammaton, only he did not disclose it. Philo's own view is that he has no proper name that a human could use. To this, Colson (PLCL 5:586) adds: "In the next sentence Philo seems to lay down that τὸ ὄνομά μου κύριον is not a natural way of expressing 'my proper name,' and it is unlikely that he would himself adopt this order of the words." More important is the argument from textual criticism. Splitting up the *lectio difficilior*, "by a name" (ὀνόματι), into two parts elegantly accounts for how the aberrant dative form arose. The result is in better keeping with Philo's thought.

§16 *would speak reverently*. The translation follows Mangey's emendation, ἣν περιέπων. The MSS read ἣν περιίππευων ("was riding around, was 'horsing' around"). The periphrastic form is unusual and points to the corruption of the text, which may have arisen from the Phaedran imagery in this passage. Wendland's conjecture, "spoke about" (περιεῖπεν), attempts to solve the problem, but does not fully satisfy Colson (PLCL, 5:150, n. 2): "περιέπειν is … 'to honor,' and if it is read we should expect τοῦ κόσμου ('of the world'), or as Mangey τὰ κόσμου ('elements of the world') governed by μετεωρολεσχῶν ('talking of lofty things')."

§23 *I am your God, increase and multiply*. Wendland's proposed restoration of the definite article here ("ὁ addidi") misses the point: it is not ⟨ὁ⟩ θεός ("The God," i.e., The One Who Is) but θεός ("God," i.e., God's beneficent power) who assists the progressing soul.

§24 *under the Lord's governance … the beneficence of the latter*. The referents of the Greek demonstratives, "this … and that" (οὗτος … ἐκεῖνος δέ), are obscure and can be interpreted in at least two different ways as the text stands.
(1)   This = God ("the unturned"), that = the perfect type
(2)   This = the progressing type, that = the perfect type
The reader has been led to expect some comment on the perfect type of soul, insofar as he is governed by the kingly and creative powers. The translation presented here thus follows Colson's (PLCL 5:154, n. 3) emendations, "in this way" (οὕτως) and "in that way" (ἐκείνως), in sense:
(3)   In this way = governed by the "Lord"; In that way = governed by "God"
This *locus* is a crux and the text is likely corrupt. While option three gives a good sense, stylistically the piling on of two adverbs "and in that way entirely" (ἐκείνως δὲ πάντως) resulting from Colson's emendation seems uncharacteristically cumbersome for Philo. Arnaldez, who accepts Colson's emendation, translates with greater specificity "ainsi gouverné … ainsi comblé ⟨de bienveillance⟩" (1964, 42–43, and n. 1). Philo uses "in that way" (ἐκείνως) very sparingly, and on

the two occasions in which he does employ the adverbial pair "In this way ... in that way" (οὕτως ... ἐκείνως, *Post.* 39 and 48), it highlights a negative and positive allegorical binary (as the MSS reading) rather than two complementary perfections. Even adopting Colson's emendation, many questions about the relationship of "Lord" and "God" to the perfect soul remain unanswered. Thus, Arnaldez, despite accepting Colson's reading (see above), notes in his introduction (1964, 14) that Philo "does not explicate this subject ⟨i.e., the meaning of the titles 'Lord and God' for the perfected soul⟩."

§ 48 *the most important prize*. Rendering the adjective πρεσβύτατον, after Wendland's conjecture. MSS and PCW have πρεσβυτικόν ("like an old man"). Colson (PLCL 5:166, n. a) observes that "the adjective seems to be only known in the sense of 'senile' or 'antiquated.' Probably, as Wendland suggests, read πρεσβύτατον." So also Arnaldez (1964, 55, n. 3).

§ 54 *moves ... unchanged*. The text between "moves ... demonstrating" (κινεῖ ... ἐμφαίνουσαν) is corrupt, and Mangey, Cohn, Wendland, and Colson each offer possible improvements. My translation follows largely the suggestions of English Classicist, Jeremiah Markland.

A first problem relates to the phrase "all that is at rest" (τὴν σύμπασιν στάσιν). This description of creation as "at rest" (στάσις) seems to be at odds with Philo's overall distinction in this pericope between creation as movement and God, "The One Who Stands" (ὁ ἑστώς), as unmoved. Mangey emends the MSS reading τὴν σύμπασιν στάσιν ("all that is at rest") to τὴν πᾶσαν σύστασιν ("all that is composite"). Wendland suggests "τὴν σύμπασαν φύσιν (vel γένεσιν)" ("All ⟨created⟩ nature or becoming"). Colson (PLCL 5:168, n. 1), in turn, suggests τὴν σύμπασιν τάσιν ("all extension" ⟨of divine being⟩, i.e., creation), drawing on *Post.* 30 as a precedent. Arnaldez (1964, 56, n. 2) prefers the "composite" (σύστασιν) of Mangey, combined with Colson's "according to extension" (κατὰ τάσιν). Of these four, Colson's conjecture would seem least intrusive (granted, the text has other problems), and a sigma could easily be added because of the surrounding context.

A second textual problem relates to the description of the metaphysics of God's motion. Markland supplies οὐ ⟨τὴν⟩ διὰ τῶν σκελῶν ⟨κίνησιν⟩ ("not through the movement of his legs"). Wendland, adapting Markland, suggests ⟨κινούμενος αὐτὸς κίνησιν⟩ οὐ ⟨τὴν⟩ διὰ τῶν σκελῶν ("God himself being moved not through the motion of legs ..."). Wendland's conjecture offers more of a paraphrase of Philo's meaning than an attempt to reconstruct the original text, and problematically inverts Aristotle, *Met.* 1072a, making God subject to "being moved."

A third textual problem, related to the second, concerns the feminine attributive participial chain τὴν ... ἐμφαίνουσαν ("that which is demonstrating ..."). Markland, rather ingeniously, suggests splitting the feminine accusative participle into two words, ἐμφαίνων οὐσίαν ("God, demonstrating his unmoving and unchanging being"), and adding an iota. These two words could have been combined into the feminine accusative participle through scribal assimilation in light of the foregoing feminine nouns and articles. On the emendation of Wendland, by contrast, the feminine participle remains, modifying κίνησιν ("movement"). The movement itself demonstrates the immovability of the Mover. Wendland complements the emendation of Cohn, who inserted the neuter definite article, after τήν, yielding τὴν ⟨τὸ⟩ ἄτρεπτον καὶ ἀμετάβλητον ἐμφαίνουσαν ("the nature which is demonstrating its unturned and unchanged ⟨character⟩"). Colson (PLCL 5:169, n. 1) tries to synthesize the best of the suggestions here as follows: κινεῖ τὴν σύμπασαν ⟨φύσιν or γένεσιν or σύστασιν κατὰ⟩ τάσιν ... ἀλλὰ ⟨τὸ⟩ ἄτρεπτον καὶ ἀμετάβλητον ἐμφαίνουσαν ("which moves the entire nature or creation or composition according to extension ... but which is demonstrating the unturned and unchanged character"). As mentioned above, the translation most nearly follows Markland.

§ 55 *falls a great fall.* PCW erroneously gives the infinitive "to fall" (πίπτειν) without marking it a conjecture. Colson (PLCL), and before him, Hoeschel (1587), read "falls" (πίπτει), which appears also in the Augustana manuscript (*Cod. Mon. Gr.* 459, 32R, line 6 from bottom).

§ 60 *"scrupulous."* Because of its lack of fit with what follows, Wendland suggests reading "without scrupulous investigation" (⟨δίχα⟩ ἀκριβοῦς ἐρευνῆς), following Cohn's similar emendation to "not with scrupulous investigation" (⟨οὐ⟩ μετὰ ἀκριβοῦς ἐρευνῆς) or "with non-scrupulous investigation" (μετ' ⟨οὐκ⟩ ἀκριβοῦς ἐρευνῆς). Colson (PLCL 5:172, n. 1) thinks one of these emendations necessary. My translation opts more simply to take the adjective ἀκριβής ("scrupulous," "sharp," "keen") as ironic.

§ 61 *great indeed ... insofar as he changed the name of Abram's wife Sarai.* PCW suggests that the MSS are defective here, lacking some crucial bit of the sentence—perhaps, as Wendland conjectures, a statement that God changed the name Abram to Abra(h)am. I have preserved the lacuna. For the textual difficulties with this second part of the sentence, see Colson (PLCL 5:174, n. 1; and 5:588–589).

[*he causes him to abound by a letter*]. Wendland bracketed the words στοιχείῳ περιττεύει, perhaps on stylistic grounds. Markland emended the text to "extraordinary letter" (στοιχείου περιττοῦ) so that it can modify the foregoing genitive ("the one extraordinary letter, alpha"). Colson (PLCL 5:588) rightly opines that Wendland's seclusion is "rather arbitrary" and adds two further possibilities, both with the infinitive: "with the result that it has an extra letter" (⟨ὡς⟩ στοιχείῳ περιττεύει⟨ν⟩) and "having an extra letter" (⟨τὸ⟩ στοιχείῳ περιττεύει⟨ν⟩), either one of which would work. I have translated the text as it stands, rendering "abound, have extra" (περιττεύει) in its causal sense (LSJ IV) and reading it as syntactically parallel to "it seemed he had furnished" (ἔδοξεν παρεσχῆσθαι), with "God" as the subject of both. If the difference in tenses between the two verbs is a problem, Markland's or Colson's emendations might be adopted. Arnaldez (1964, 61, n. 3) finds Colson's conjectures too speculative and prefers the emendation of Markland.

§ 62 *the same errors.* Colson (PLCL 5:175, n. a) observes: "This use of ὑπονοίας ["notions" = "errors"] is strange, though Wendland's suggestion of τὰς ⟨τοιαύτας⟩ ὑπ. ['these sorts of notions'] or Mangey's τὰς ⟨κακὰς⟩ ὑπ. ['the evil notions'] would make it more natural." See further Colson (PLCL 5:589). The translation "the same errors" draws on these insights.

§ 104 *ought not teach.* Philo appears to contradict the scriptural account. In contrast to the Septuagint, where Jethro bids Moses "bear witness to the commands of God and his law," Philo's Jethro bids just the opposite: Moses ought *not* (μή) teach divine commands, but "human contract law." In light of this apparent difficulty, Mangey (followed tentatively by Wendland) transposes the negative from § 104, 29 to § 104, 30, such that the text now reads "that he *ought* to teach the commands of God ... but *not* human contracts." While this emendation brings Philo's text into harmony with the LXX, it directly subverts his allegory of Jethro as one who honors "human things before divine, customs over laws" (§ 104). Colson (PLCL 5:194, n. a), followed by Arnaldez (1964, 78, n. 2) agrees. I have followed the reading of the MSS.

§ 113 *hand it over easily to the appearances.* "The text is obscure" (Colson, PLCL 5:200, n. a), and potentially corrupt; no emendation is entirely satisfactory. Colson's noble attempt to render the PCW text as it stands (PLCL 5:200, n. a) could work, but seems forced. The translation here, "to hand ⟨it⟩ [i.e., the mind] over easily to the appearances" (ἀγώγιμον παραδιδόναι τοῖς φαινομένοις [Cohn: πρὸς τὰ φαινόμενα, "to the appearances"]) follows the conjecture of Wendland in the apparatus (see also Cohn) and requires only minor alterations. Wendland takes ἀγώγιμον ("easily lead, pliable") to refer to the Jethro/Raguel mind, rather than to the plural sense perceptible objects. If one leaves the adjective in the plural "easily led things" (ἀγώγιμα), Mangey's intriguing suggestion that "appearances" (φαινόμενα) is a scribal mishearing of "shepherded things" (ποιμαινόμενα) becomes attractive. The homeoteleuton of both words (-αινόμενα) and the similarity of the initial sounds (ποιμ- / φ-, both bilabial consonants) make it plausible that a scribe misheard the rarer participle "shepherded animals" for the more common classical philosophical term, "appearances." This emendation is also defended by Colson (PLCL 5:589–590), although not included in his translation. On this reading, the shepherds "hand over the 'shepherded' sense material objects" to the mind more easily. Arnaldez (1964, 82, n. 2) retains "appearances" (φαινόμενα) and cites Colson's (PLCL 5:200, n. a) explanation of the unamended substantive participle, while also giving some consideration to Mangey's suggestion.

§ 121 *is interpreted*. Reading ἑρμηνεύεται with Colson and Grabbe (1988, 222), and taking CW ἐμηνεύεται as a printing error.

§ 122 *every skill*. The translation adopts the conjecture of Mangey, "every skill" (τέχνη πᾶσα), followed by Colson (PLCL 5:204, n. 2) and Arnaldez (1964, 87, n. 5), as opposed to "a sort of skill" (τέχνη ποιά) found in PCW and the MSS, on the grounds that it balances better with "every practitioner" (παντὸς τεχνίτου). It may be that the indefinite "of a sort" (ποιά) arose in the text because of the focus on "such-and-such a person" (ὁ ποιός) in § 121.

§ 128 *God⟨'s human being⟩*. All the MSS read "God" (θεός). PCW prints this, but indicates in the apparatus that "God's human being" (ἄνθρωπος θεοῦ) ought to be read. Colson (PLCL 5:208, n. 1) prefers to emend "God" (θεός) to "of God" (θεοῦ). Arnaldez (1964, 90, n. 2) adopts Colson's "of God" (θεοῦ), in which case the text would read similarly, "is fittingly called 'God's.'"

§ 131 *laughter within the mind, a son of God*. This translation follows Colson's repunctuation of the PCW text. Cohn and Wendland print "laughter, the immanent son of God" (γέλως, ὁ ἐνδιάθετος υἱὸς θεοῦ) or (after Drummond) "laughter, the ideal son of God." Colson (PLCL 5:208, n. 3) opines: "But can ἐνδιάθετος ('placed within') mean this? I understand it in its usual sense of opposition to προφορικός ('borne forth, externalized')." Critical to resolving this issue are the parallel phrases at *Migr.* 157 and *Mut.* 154, especially the former, in which Philo speaks of "the laughter which is immanent and good" (ὁ ἐνδιάθετος καὶ σπουδαῖος γέλως). On this basis, Colson repunctuates the phrase as "laughter within the mind, a son of God" (γέλως ὁ ἐνδιάθετος, υἱὸς θεοῦ) or "laughter of the heart, a son of God" (Colson PLCL). Arnaldez, responding in a learned note (1964, 92–93, n. 1), prefers the punctuation of PCW. As he summarizes: "In our translation, the joyous laughter is the Logos, in which a human being participates, by which he is saved. In that of Colson, ⟨joyous laughter⟩ is *a* son of God in the broad sense, where God is said to engender it in the soul of the sage." As is characteristic, Arnaldez prefers the ontologically more robust reading, while Colson keeps ethics and psychic progress in the fore.

§ 133 *he renders barren ... the nature that does ⟨not⟩ love the good*. Something may have fallen out of the text here. Cohn posits a lacuna and Wendland punctuates Philo's text to read, "he renders barren ... the nature which loves the good" (στεροῖ μέν ... τὴν φιλόκαλον φύσιν). Colson fills the lacuna: "he sends barrenness ⟨on the favorite and gives honour⟩ to the nature which loves excellence." Mangey suggests "world-loving" (φιλόκοσμον). The translation follows Colson's (PLCL 5:210, n. 1) alternative emendation of "loving the good" (φιλόκαλον) to "not loving the good" (ἀφιλόκαλον)—an adjective attested in Plutarch. Arnaldez (1964, 93, n. 3) relates the brilliant conjecture of his colleague, J. Taillardat, to restore an original "not" (οὐ) before "renders barren" (στεροῖ μέν), giving "he does not render barren the lover of virtue" (φιλαρέτου ⟨οὐ⟩ στεροῖ μέν). The "not" (οὐ) would have fallen out due to haplography. Arnaldez (Ibid.) justifies this complementary use of μέν ... δέ citing the precedent of Plato, *Tim*. 21a. I have left PCW's lacuna to signal the textual problem to the reader.

§ 135 *fate, the necessary sequence ... the uninterrupted chain of all things*. The translation and interpretation follow Wendland's emendation of the MSS, which reads "or [the world] fate" (ἢ [ὁ κόσμος] εἱμαρμένη) to "fate" (ἡ εἱμαρμένη). Colson (PLCL 5:210, n. 2) opines: "I see no reason to exclude ὁ κόσμος ['the world'], which naturally suggests 'order' as well as 'world'." He prints "the world, fate" (ὁ κόσμος, ἡ εἱμαρμένη) by metathesizing "or" (ἢ) and "the world" (ὁ κόσμος). If both terms are to be kept, another possibility would be to restore another disjunction (ἢ), giving "either the world or fate" (ἢ ὁ κόσμος ἢ εἱμαρμένη), as a string of two allegorical equivalences. Colson also suggests "natural consequence" (⟨ἡ⟩ ἀκολουθία).

§ 140 *if there is any good among the things that are*. Wendland conjectures a lacuna here as "heaven" (οὐρανός) and "world" (κόσμος), after the δέ particle, appear not to agree with the preceding dative, "among the things that are" (ἐν τοῖς οὖσι). I follow Colson (PLCL 2:212, n. 1) and Arnaldez (1964, 96, n. 2) in finding this suggestion over-exacting and unnecessary. Philo begins to speak of invisible realities in the dative, and then changes his syntax to speak of all goods, immaterial or immaterial. There is thus an anacoluthon, but not a lacuna.

§ 155 *to fall and to laugh*. Following the suggestion of Wendland, adopted by Colson. PCW and the MSS give "to laugh and to fall" (γελᾶν τε καὶ πίπτειν). Wendland's emendation brings the verbs into scriptural sequence, in which order they are subsequently interpreted in the exegesis.

§ 162 *which ⟨all⟩ but hurling forth their voice*. The translation follows the emendation of Wendland at § 166, 6, changing φωνὴν οὐκ ἀφιέντα ("not hurling forth their voice") to φωνὴν ⟨μονον⟩οὐκ ἀφιέντα ("⟨all⟩ but hurling forth their voice"). Some such emendation is necessary for sense.

§ 168 *he will rejoice in himself*. Philo's text of Exod 4:14 ("seeing you he will rejoice in him" [ἐν αὐτῷ]) agrees nearly with the Septuagint ("seeing you, he will rejoice in himself" [ἐν ἑαυτῷ]), with the exception that the final reflexive pronoun has been replaced by Philo with the third person pronoun. The reading "in him" (ἐν αὐτῷ), found in *Mut*. 168 and *Migr*. 79, might equally be punctuated "in himself" (ἐν αὑτῷ, so Colson, PLCL 4:176, n. c). This would be in keeping with Philo's citations of this verse in *Det*. 126 and 135, where the reflexive is attested. Colson himself (PLCL 4:563) hesitated to print "in him" (ἐν αὐτῷ) in *Mut*. 168 and *Migr*. 79, saying, "I feel very doubtful as to its correctness here and in *De Mut*." Further support of Colson's instinct to read "in himself" (ἐν αὑτῷ) in *Mut*. 168 comes from the exegetical structure of §§ 166–168. Looking at the two scriptural verses linked here, the SBLᶜ (Gen 18:12) and the SBL (Exod 4:14), it is striking that both include not merely a word for joy or laughter, but also a description of *internal* joy:

SBLᶜ: Gen 18:12	SBL: Exod 4:14
Sarah laughed in herself (ἐν ἑαυτῇ)	Aaron will rejoice in himself (ἐν ἑαυτῷ)

Thus, I have found it better to read "himself."

§ 191 *reckoned as a holy tenth of ⟨tenfold⟩ reckonings*. Although the sense seems clear enough, establishing the text of this passage has proved difficult for interpreters. The reading of the MSS, given in PCW, is likely corrupt: "as a holy tenth of words" or "a rational holy tenth" (ὡς δεκάτην λόγων ἱεράν). Mangey, sensing something amiss, conjectures "a holy tenth by a hundredfold reckoning" (δεκάτην ἑκατοστῷ λόγῳ ἱεράν)—an elegant solution as far as meaning goes, as it draws on the phrase "hundred-fold reckoning" (ἑκατοστὸς λόγος) used earlier in the treatise (§ 190). In text-critical terms, however, Mangey's solution does not explain why the final nu was dropped on "words/reckonings" (λόγων), nor why the word hundred-fold was omitted. Wendland, clearly unhappy with Mangey's placeholder, supplies either (1) "containing other tenths ⟨by a⟩ hundred⟨fold⟩ reckoning" (ἑτέρας δεκάτας ⟨ἑκατοστὸν⟩ λόγον περιεχούσας)—which is an ungrounded importation of § 2 into the present text; or (2) the more ingenious, but overly conjectural "a tenth as a holy first fruit" (δεκάτην ὡς ἀπαρχὴν ἱεράν—why metathesize the ὡς?). I have translated Colson's conjecture (PLCL 5:240, n. 1), "a holy tenth of tenfold reckonings" (δεκάτην ⟨δεκάτων⟩ λόγων ἱεράν), which is minimally intrusive and nicely mirrors Philo's "first fruit of first fruit" (ἀπαρχῆς ἀπαρχή) in the present section. Colson's emendation is accepted by Arnaldez (1964, 120, n. 3), who further comments: "The first tithe is offered on behalf of created goods in the realm of becoming; the second ⟨tithe⟩, for the created goods in the soul. In the same way, the veil of the tabernacle separates two regions: that which is reserved for God and the high priest, and that to which consecrated people have access, but which is veiled with regard to the profane (*Her.* 75; *Mos.* 2.87)." I am less convinced by Colson's judgment that the "the periphrasis with λόγος ('reckoning') for the ordinal is quite common," although the phrase is certainly grammatical enough given the parallel in "hundredfold reckoning."

§ 192 *between the first and the* ⟨*second*⟩ *tenth*. Philo's description of ninety as "being a borderland of the first and tenth" (μεθόριος ὢν πρώτης καὶ δεκάτης) requires clarification. The text is likely corrupt. I have translated Wendland's "first and ⟨second⟩ tenth" (πρώτης καὶ ⟨δευτέρας⟩ δεκάτης) from PCW, but it is far from clear what the best reading and correlated sense is. Colson (PLCL 5:240, n. 2) posits instead "being a borderland of the first and tenth decade" (πρώτης καὶ δεκάτης ⟨δεκάδος⟩), saying that he can "see no meaning" in Wendland's reading and agues instead that "ninety is certainly the borderland between ten and one hundred." This interpretation, however, would signify the interstice between the first decade (1–10) and the tenth (91–100), which ought to be a borderland of 80. Colson's translation also overlooks that Philo has used "tenth" (δεκάτη) as a substantive throughout this passage. Arnaldez (1964, 120–122, n. 4) considers this passage "very obscure" and cannot follow the reasoning of either Wendland or Colson ("Est-ce si certain?"). He attempts to read the text of the

MSS almost as it stands by importing the noun "first fruit" (ἀπαρχή) from § 191. According to this logic, the two tithes and the two classes of priest are in view. It is the first tithe (10/100) of the inferior class of Levitical priests and the second tithe (1/100) of the "consecrated priests" that Philo has in mind. Thus, Arnaldez argues, "it is not the number 90 which makes this separation, as Colson translates it; it is at the interior of the boundary defined by 90 (90/100), that the remaining 10/100 resolve into 1/100 and 9/100." This reading is ingenious, but ignores the basic point that Philo means to defend the number 90 (Sarah's age) and is no longer thinking of the tithes (as in § 191), but of sacred spaces (as in § 190). Better, then, is Wendland's suggestion that 90 leads up to the juncture between the "first tenth" (100–91), construed as the "holy of holies" (itself, 100 square cubits in area—10 × 10 [see Hrobon 2013, 556]) and the "second tenth" (90–81), which begins the remaining 90 units (9 tens).

the Holy ⟨of Holies⟩ is divided from the sanctuary. The MSS read "the sanctuary is divided from the sanctuary" (διακρίνεται τὰ ἅγια τῶν ἁγίων). Something like Colson's emendation (PLCL 5:240, n. 3), "The Holy ⟨of Holies⟩ is divided from the sanctuary" (τὰ ἅγια ⟨τῶν ἁγίων⟩ τῶν ἁγίων) is required, and Arnaldez (1964, 122, n. 4) accepts it as "useful."

§ 215 *"You are still alive!"* The Göttingen text of Gen 46:30, "for do you still live?" (ἔτι γὰρ σὺ ζῇς;), punctuates these words as a question. PCW follows suit, taking an additional cue from the sense of "wonder" (τεθαύμακεν, θαυμαστόν) that Philo attributes to Jacob/Israel. PLCL and NETS print a period instead. I have punctuated Jacob's statement with an exclamation point, as a middle ground, which keeps the sentence as declaratory but gives a heightened sense of wonder.

§ 216 *we pray for this Ishmael.* Wendland, not thinking that "we pray" (εὐχόμεθα) in the manuscripts at § 216 makes sense, emends to "he prays" (εὔχεται) in the main text of PCW. Cohn had previously suggested the hortatory subjunctive, "let us pray" (εὐχώμεθα). A parallel use of the first person plural indicative appears in QG 3.57a, "we do not despair" (ní hausuwutup), *pace* Aucher, who translates freely, "I do not despair" ("non despero"). I follow the MSS and the judgment of Colson (PLCL 5:255, n. a) as well as Marcus (see Parallel Exegesis from QG 3.57 on *Mut.* 216). Writes Colson: "The objection ... of Wendland to the first person ignores the fact that Philo constantly regards the stories and sayings of the Pentateuch as representing the spiritual experiences of every generation." Colson gives other examples at *Somn.* 1.143, 226 and *Somn.* 2.170. Colson further notes that "Cohn's εὐχώμεθα ('let us pray') does not fit in well with Philo's use of παγκάλως ('entirely right/good')."

§ 217 ⟨*if*⟩ *he looks out for the approval of the One who is present.* The text of the MSS, while not impossible to read as it stands, has seemed corrupt to most editors. The two finite verbs, "looks out" and "flees" (περιβλέπεται, ἀποδράσεται) lack a regular conjunction, if the participles "fearing and trembling" are read together; and the first καί is postponed. Mangey suggests, *ex ingenio*, turning the first verb into a participle (καὶ προσβλέποντος), to give "when ⟨God⟩ is watching." The conjecture is clever, but too free. Cohn suggests emending "both looks out" (καὶ περιβλέπεται) to "always looking out" (αἰεὶ περιβλεπόμενος), which elegantly solves both textual problems. Colson (PLCL 5:254, n. 3) develops Cohn's suggestion to read "if he always looks out" (ἀεὶ εἰ περιβλέπεται), which has much the same force but is harder to explain scribally. The most economic suggestion is thus to read "if he looks out" (εἰ περιβλέπεται), substituting only "if" (εἰ) for "and" (καί), as I have done in the translation. Arnaldez (1964, 134, n. 2) demurs, suggesting that Philo is using a "both ... and" (καί ... καί) construction.

§ 218 ⟨....⟩ Wendland proposes a lacuna here, on the grounds that the adapted citation of Gen 15:6 has a μέν *pendens* and seems to lack the second part of the expected explanation. Considering the generally poor status the manuscripts for this treatise, this editorial decision is warranted. Wendland points the reader to §178 as proof. Colson accepts the lacuna, noting (PLCL 5:254, n. 4) that it might be filled with "but he disbelieves in what is generated" (ἀπιστεῖ δὲ τῷ γενητῷ). Arnaldez (1964, 134, n. 2) supplies to the contrary: "but he does not believe that he is able to have a son" (this is followed, in nn. 2 and 3, by several fascinating comparisons between Abraham's situation and Teresa of Avila's "fourth residence" in the interior castle). Arnaldez's reading, while intriguing, is ill at ease with the Philo's understanding of Abraham's faith in chapter eight. Colson is nearer to the mark.

§ 229 *those bright from a fresh bath.* Colson (PLCL 5:260, n. 4) finds the conjunction δέ in "bright fresh from a bath" (φαιδρυνόμενοι δέ) "clearly corrupt," presumably on the grounds of its final position, and proposes "these" (οἵδε) as an alternative. He notes that "Mangey proposed δή ('now, just'), Wendland τελείως ('perfectly')."

§ 231 *grant me,* ⟨*Lord*⟩. Colson (PLCL) is probably right to supply the vocative "lord" ⟨sc. κύριε⟩, which might mean "sir/father" or "Lord" (indicating the divine power). He does not, however, emend the Greek text, which lacks the addressee.

Commentary

∴

Part One

[Chapter 1]
Abraham as Seer and Hearer of God (§§ 1–38)

Philo opens *De mutatione nominum* with a citation of the biblical lemma (Gen 17:1ab) that will serve as the text for the first chapter of the commentary (§§ 1–38). He will interpret the remainder of this verse (Gen 17:1c) in chapter two (§§ 39–53). The Septuagint text reads as follows:

> Abram came to be ninety-nine years old, and the Lord was seen by Abram and said to him, "I am your God." (NETS, adapted)

The immediately preceding treatise in the Allegorical Commentary, *De fuga et inventione*, ended with Gen 16:14 (Royse 2009, 43; Geljon and Runia 2013, 2). By foregoing any comment on Gen 16:15–16 and continuing the series at the beginning of a distinct narrative unit (corresponding, coincidentally, to the modern source-critical division between Gen 16 [J] and Gen 17 [P]), Philo makes a small break with the previous two treatises in the "Abraham cycle" (*De congressu eruditionis gratia* and *De fuga et inventione*), signaling that this last fully extant treatise on Abraham will take up a new subject and stand thematically on its own.

Philo comments on the primary biblical lemma in this first chapter sequentially, dividing it into three units: (a) Gen 17:1a: "Abram came to be ninety-nine years old" (§§ 1–2); (b) Gen 17:1bα: "and the Lord was seen by Abram" (§§ 3–17); (c) Gen 17:1bβ: "and said to him, 'I am your God.'" (§§ 18–38).

a *Abraham's Age at the Time of Isaac's Birth (§§ 1–2)*
    Analysis/General Comments

Philo begins by citing the primary biblical lemma (Gen 17:1ab)—the standard opening feature for treatise in this series. *Leg.* 1.1; 2.1; 3.1; *Cher.* 1; *Sacr.* 1; *Det.* 1; *Post.* 1; *Gig.* 1; *Deus* 1 (= *Gig.-Deus* 2.1); *Agr.* 1; *Migr.* 1; *Congr.* 1; *Fug.* 1; and §1 of the present treatise all follow this basic form and begin with a biblical citation. *Plant.* 1; *Ebr.* 1; *Sobr.* 1; *Her.* 1; *Fug.* 2; and *Somn.* 1.1 begin with secondary prefaces. *Conf.* 1 contains a brief transitional preface, but then commences a new thematic discussion. For more on Philo's secondary prefaces, and their importance for reconstructing the sequence of the Allegorical Commentary, see Sterling 2019; 2012a; and 2012b, esp. 433, nn. 44–45.

After the citation, Philo comments on the first part of the verse. His allegoresis of the number ninety-nine, which in its arithmological details may strike the reader as recondite and obscure, is meant like the overture in an opera to sound a festive introduction to the treatise's main theme: the perfection of the soul. Already at the beginning of the Abrahamic cycle (*Migr.* 198–207), Philo offered an arithmological allegory of Abram's age at the time of his departure from Haran: seventy-five (Gen 12:4). While the number seventy represents the noetic capacity of reason (*Migr.* 199) and is associated with the wisdom of Moses (*Migr.* 201), the number five represents the senses and the soul's immature affection for material and bodily things. The Abram soul thus begins its journey in a mixed psychological and ethical state, "at the borderland (μεθόριος) of the perceptible and intelligible, of the older and the newer, of the nature that is still perishable and the nature that is imperishable" (*Migr.* 198). Philo's opening of the present treatise with an arithmological discourse on the significance of the number ninety-nine (Gen 17:1) offers a backward glance at the Abram soul's point of departure (Gen 12:4), while looking forward to the coming perfection of the same at one hundred.

This section can be divided into four parts.

(1) A slightly modified text of Gen 17:1ab is cited, providing the primary lemma for Philo's first chapter, §§ 1–38 (§ 1a).

(2) Taking the first subsection of this lemma, Gen 17:1a, Philo explains that the significance of Abram's age of ninety-nine depends on its proximity to one hundred, a perfect number. It is in Abraham's hundredth year that Isaac—who symbolizes self-taught virtue and joy—will be born (§ 1b).

(3) Philo amplifies his interpretation of the perfection of the number one hundred by alluding to a secondary biblical lemma, Num 18:26–32, and the law of the "first fruit" (ἀπαρχή). The Levitical priest, who offers a "tithe of the tithe" as a second "first fruit," mathematically presents God with the product of the two tithes (10 × 10 = 100), one hundred, the perfect offering of the soul (§ 2a).

(4) The section closes by clarifying the analogy between the Abraham soul and the Levitical priest. In making a perfect tithe, the priest becomes a complementary image (alongside the centenarian Abraham) of the soul ascending to the height of virtue from some previous middle-ground. A paraphrase of Gen 17:1bα serves as the primary lemma for the subsequent section §§ 3–17 (§ 2b).

Although not a formal introduction, this first subsection offers an implicit proem to the treatise by establishing Abraham's fittingness to receive a vision of the Lord and the birth of Isaac. Philo introduces the reader not only to the first person whose name will be changed in the ensuing sections, but also begins to explain *why* Abra(ha)m was selected, touching implicitly upon the double subject of his treatise indicated in the long Greek title (see the Introduction 7. Title and Previous Scholarship).

This section also illustrates the theological artistry characteristic of Philo's exegesis. Employing one of the hallmarks of the Allegorical Commentary, Philo uses a secondary lemma to "flesh out" the psychological allegoresis of the primary biblical text. By subordinating Num 18:26–32, the legislation about priestly tithes, to the primary lemma of Gen 17:1a, Philo expands Abraham's portrait as a psychic paradigm, adorning the Genesis narrative with an allegory of the priestly cult. (Cf. *Leg.* 2.53–58, where Exod 33:7 is expanded by Lev 16:2–14 and Lev 10:1–5.)

Philo's priestly characterization of Abraham contributes to the catalogue of sacerdotal portraits of the patriarch in the Second Temple period, which developed from natural biblical pressures. In Gen 15 and 22, Abraham is depicted as offering sacrifices. His implicit priestly actions in these narratives are rendered explicit in another masterwork of Second Temple biblical interpretation, Jubilees. Here, Abraham offers sacrifices for all three major pilgrimage festivals (Jub. 13.8–9, 16; 14.8–11; 15.1–2; 22.1–6 [Weeks/First fruits]; 16.20–31 [Tabernacles]; 18.17–19 [Passover]) and gives cultic laws (Jub. 21.7–20). An early Christian work, the Epistle to the Hebrews (9:7), establishes a similar connection between Abraham and Levi at a more genetic level. Philo himself presents Abraham in the guise of cult hero and priest ("as a priest himself, he initiated the sacrificial ritual," ὥσπερ ἱερεὺς αὐτὸς κατήρχετο τῆς ἱερουγίας) at the Akedah in the Exposition of the Law (*Abr.* 198). In the Amoraic period, Rabbi Ishmael (among others) identifies Abraham as a high priest (Gen. Rab. 46:5; see also Gen. Rab. 43:6; 55:6–7); and there exists a rich tradition of Abraham's heavenly priesthood in the Jewish-Christian apocalyptic literature of the Common Era (Orlov 2013). For a "Levitical spirituality" running throughout Philo's Allegorical Commentary, see Harl 1967, 87 and 111.

Detailed Comments

(1) § 1a. ***Abraham came to be ninety-nine years old ... "I am your God."*** Philo's citation of Gen 17:1ab agrees with the LXX, with two small exceptions: the omission of the conjunctive particle δέ and the citation of the longer spelling of Abraham's name (Ἀβραάμ). This latter point is interesting, given that the central conceit of the treatise depends on Abraham initially having a shorter name at this point. Philo similarly speaks in an anticipatory fashion of "Abraham's" previous tarrying in Chaldea in *Gig.* 62 prior to discussing his change of name (*Gig.* 64). See the Notes to the Text and Translation.

(2) ***the number ninety-nine is a neighbor of one hundred.*** Arithmology is one of the best-known features of Philonic exegesis. His use has Neopythagorean roots (Royse 2009, 58; Moehring 1995; Runia 1995, 10). For early attestation of Philo's "affinity" with Pythagorean arithmology, see Clement of

Alexandria (*Strom.* 1.72.4; 2.100.3) and Eusebius (*Hist. eccl.* 1.12.9; 2.4.3). See also the Parallel Exegesis on §60. Philo composed an entire treatise, *De numeris*, which has been lost with the exception of one Armenian fragment on the number ten (Terian 1984). His interest in numbers was not only philosophical in origin, but arose out of exegetical necessity: the numbers in the Pentateuch, written by Moses, could not be superfluous. In §1, the number ninety-nine is honored because of its proximity to one hundred—the year in Abraham's life in which Isaac was born. It provides the thematic link between Abraham's age in Gen 17:1a and the priestly "tithe of a tithe" in Num 18:26–32. Philo will return to the number one hundred in §§176–177, 188–192, where he interprets the "one-hundred-year-old" (ἑκατονταέτης) of Gen 17:17.

the self-taught class. Isaac will be distinguished in perfection from the other two principal patriarchs of Genesis (Abraham and Jacob) because of his natural, self-taught adherence to virtue. By underscoring the uniqueness of Isaac in the overture to his treatise, Philo prepares the reader for a leitmotif that will return later: only Isaac will not have a change of name, because he signifies "the self-taught and self-learning race" (τό ... αὐτοδίδακτον καὶ αὐτομαθὲς γένος [§88]). For Philo's development of the three patriarchal types of soul in light of the three Platonist forms of education, see the note on §12.

shone forth. Isaac and self-taught wisdom are often depicted through the image of light, a Platonizing metaphor.

best of the good emotions. Philo's term "good emotions" (εὐπάθειαι, Lat. *constantiae*) is found in Stoic and Platonist ethics. Colson (PLCL 5:142) suggests that the phrase "good emotions" is "used in the strict Stoic sense of reasonable forms of πάθος." They are the opposites of the bad emotions or "passions" (πάθη, Lat. *perturbationes*). For classic statements on the passions and "good emotions," see Diogenes Laertius (7.116; SVF 3.431) and Cicero (*Tusc.* 4.10–14). The concept has its origins in Plato (*Phaedr.* 247d4; *Resp.* 347c7, 404d9, and 615a3). For a new treatment of the good emotions, see Weisser 2021.

The four chief passions for Cicero (*Tusc.* 4.11) are "pleasure, fear, desire, and grief" (laetitia, metus, libido, aegritudo), though he will often vary his terms. For Philo, "joy" (χαρά), "caution" (εὐλάβεια), and "will" (βούλησις), as good emotions, stand as the virtuous versions of vicious "pleasure" (ἡδονή), "fear" (φόβος), and "desire" (ἐπιθυμία), respectively. Philo pairs the fourth passion, "sorrow" (λύπη), with "remorse," "constraint," or "incitement" in QG 2.47 (see Parallel Exegesis). What differentiates a passion from a good emotion is, in the Greek tradition, the relative *rationality* of the soul's movement. Latin authors sometimes highlight the relative *stability* of the movement as a distinguishing factor as well. Thus, whereas Diogenes Laertius describes joy as a "well-reasoned elevation" (εὔλογος ἔπαρσις: Diogenes Laertius 7.115; *SVF* 3.431) and Andronicus defines pleasure as an "irrational elevation" (ἄλογος ἔπαρσις: Andronicus, *Pass.* 1; *SVF* 3.391), Cicero will speak of "joy" (gaudium) as the more stable (and rational) counterpart to "happiness *qua* pleasure" (laetitia): "for when the mind is moved by reason peacefully and constantly, then it is called joy" ("nam cum ratione animus movetur placide atque constanter, tum illud gaudium dicitur" [Cicero, *Tusc.* 4.13]). For further discussion, see Inwood 1985, 173–175; Graver 2007, 35–60; and Weisser 2021. Philo does not adopt the Stoic pattern with the exactitude of a disciple of Zeno or Chrysippus, but adapts the model freely. At times, he uses joy as the opposite of both pleasure and sorrow (Cf. *Leg.* 3.86, 107; *Cher.* 12; and *Det.* 119–120; Colson, PLCL 2:495). In another passage in the present treatise (§§ 163–164), hope rather that caution is considered the good emotion corresponding to fear.

joy. Philo adds the word "joy" at the end of this impressive sentence without a conjunction. Rhetorically, the asyndetic style highlights a key theme, which Philo will unpack later in the third part of the treatise (§§ 131, 154–165, 175, 188, 261–264). Why joy should be considered by Philo the "best" of the good emotions is not immediately clear from the philosophical fragments and handbooks, though the eudaimonistic telos is clearly in view. Diogenes Laertius (7.115; *SVF* 3.431) places it first in his list, but without an explicit rationale. For joy's superlative place among human goods, see also Philo, *Det.* 120; *Migr.* 157; *Congr.* 36; *Mut.* 131, 188. Philo's evaluation may be related to joy's identity as a good emotion in the present, as opposed to "caution" (εὐλάβεια) and "hope" (ἐλπίς), which look to the future (*Somn.* 1.71; 2.279), and to the "expansive" effect that joy has on the soul (*Migr.* 157; Wilson 2011, 178–179.)

Philo's interpretation of Isaac's name stems from Hellenistic Jewish exegetical tradition. It is undoubtedly a symbolic interpretation of the character, drawn from the verb "rejoice with" (συγχαρεῖται) in Gen 21:6 (*Det.* 123–124), and may represent a secondary etymology of the name as well (see *Leg.* 3.218). Philo's most common etymology of the Hebrew name "Isaac" (יצחק), drawn from a Greek-Hebrew onomasticon, is "laughter" (γέλως). The same Hebrew root, "to laugh" (צחק), underlies both Greek words in LXX Gen 21:6 (Gen 17:17; 18:12–15; Grabbe 1988, 171–172). Philo will interpret this etymology as symbolizing "joy of the mind" later in the present treatise (§ 131), describing laughter and joy as "synonyms."

(3) § 2a. *this is also signified by the first-fruit offering given to the priests.* Philo alludes to the law of priestly tithes, offering a loose paraphrase of LXX Num 18:26 (cf. *Spec.* 1.157). His implicit scriptural lemma extends at least from the mention of the Levite's "tenth from the tenth" (ἐπιδέκατον ἀπὸ τοῦ ἐπιδεκά-

του) in Num 18:26 to the reference to the "first fruit" (ἀπαρχή) in Num 18:30(32). By overlaying Abraham's siring of Isaac / joy at the age of one hundred with the law of the Levitical tithe of the first fruit, Philo gilds the spiritual progress of the Abraham soul with a priestly finish. Isaac / joy is a fruit of the sage's perfect sacrifice. For more on virtue as fruit, see §§ 74–75; Dillon 1997, 191 n. 3; Geljon and Runia 2013, 107.

The number ten is a symbol of progress ... one hundred is a symbol of perfection. In Neopythagorean arithmology, the number ten is called "the all-perfect" (ἡ παντέλεια). Philo modifies this tradition with the scriptural text in view. Ten becomes the symbol of moral "progress" (προκοπή), while one hundred supplants it as the symbol of "perfection" (τελειότης), just as the Levitical tithe transcends the tithe of first fruits. In this way, the teaching of Moses transcends the teaching of Pythagoras. For further analysis of the decade and "middle education" in Philo's œuvre, see Arnaldez 1964, 32–33, n. 1.

The mean always hastens toward the summit. The language of progress and completion is combined with the Aristotelian metaphor of middle and summit. For Aristotle, virtue could be described as both (1) the "mean" (μεσότης) between "surfeit" (ὑπερβολή) and "scarcity" (ἔλλειψις) as well as (2) a "height" or "summit" (ἀκρότης), with regard to its superlative goodness (Aristotle, *Eth. nic.* 6.17, 1107a2–8). Philo may have absorbed this Aristotelian concept of the "mean" through the writings of the Middle Platonist, Antiochus of Ascalon (Alesse 2008, 3; Theiler 1965; and Luck 1953, 26–29, 64–65). For evidence that the "summit" (ἀκρότης) had become part of several streams of Hellenistic philosophy in the first century BCE, see also the fragment of the Epicurean philosopher Philodemus, *De deis* (3.5; Diels 1970, 22):

> It is not that some are lacking, while others have excess, but all, both men and women, achieve the unsurpassable summit (τὴν ἀνυπέρε[κ]τον ἀκρότητ').

Here, Philodemus argues that the community of Epicureans all equally possess the "unsurpassable summit" of the good.

The Lord of the universe was seen. Philo's paraphrase of Gen 17:1aβ serves as the lemma for the subsequent section (§§ 3–17). The syntax of the paraphrase, "**The Lord** of the universe **was seen**" (ὀφθῆναι τὸν τῶν ὅλων κύριον), mirrors and expands the syntax of the biblical text, "The Lord was seen" (ὤφθη κύριος). The title "Lord of the universe" does not reflect the Semitizing Greek of the LXX (the title occurs only in 2 Macc 14:35), but stands in the stream of Platonizing Judaism, which linked the biblical Creator with the cosmic Demiurge of Plato's *Timaeus*.

Parallel Exegesis

The number ninety-nine. Philo treats the number one hundred only here in the Allegorical Commentary. He also discusses the significance of one hundred in his other two commentary series (*QG* 3.39, 56; *Decal.* 27). In all three series, the significance of one hundred is based on its being the square of "ten, the entirely perfect" (δεκὰς ἡ παντέλεια) in Pythagorean thought (*Decal.* 20). See Stobaeus (*Ecl.* 1.1.10) for the claim that the Pythagoreans used the phrase "the entirely perfect" (ἡ παντέλεια) as a kind of "divine name" for ten (Colson, PLCL 6:598). Philo supplements this Pythagorean interest in ten by adducing the ten words or headings (Exod 34:28) of the specific Mosaic laws in his extensive exegesis of the number in *De Decalogo*. In Philo's view, Pythagoras and Moses agree on its importance.

QG 3.39b begins by defining the symbolic significance of the number 99 with respect to its "neighbor" (հրահկից) 100. This is precisely the metaphor used in *Mut.* 1. Philo notes that Moses, "the theologian" (աստուածաբանն), calls this number "the holy of holies," on the analogy of the Levitical "tithe of the tithe." Lev 18:26 is alluded to as a secondary lemma, though with a less-detailed exegesis than in *Mut.* 2. (For the number 100 in connection with the Holy of Holies in the present treatise, see § 192.)

Philo's arithmological discussions are typically longer in the *QGE* than they are in the other two commentary series (Terian 1984, 181). Thus, in contrast to *Mut.* 1, which focuses solely on ninety-nine's proximity to one hundred, in *QG* 3.39b Philo adds a second interpretation: that ninety-nine "is not adorned" (ոչ ... զարդարեալ է) solely by virtue of the number that follows it. Rather, ninety-nine has a spiritual significance of its own, as it is the sum of fifty—the number of years in a Jubilee—and forty-nine—the seven weeks of sabbatical years that precede a Jubilee year (see Lev 25:1–17). The pentecostal year (50) is understood symbolically as the "release" for inanimate and animate beings. The "sabbatical years" (49) are understood as periods of psychological rest and memorials of natural or self-producing goods.

Philo's omission of this second arithmological argument in *Mut.* 1 reflects (1) the general redactional trend that arithmological exegeses are curtailed in the Allegorical Commentary; (2) the fact that this interpretation occurs at the beginning of a treatise and hence has an introductory character; and (3) most importantly, the focus on Abraham and the eschatological trajectory of the treatise, which moves toward the number 100. Given that the treatise is heading toward the birth of Isaac, it would have been self-defeating and distracting for Philo to include this second tradition on ninety-nine. His use of exegetical arithmology in *Mut.* 1–2 is an exercise in focus and economy.

shone forth. The verb "shine forth" (ἐπιλάμπω) is also used of Isaac's birth in *Cher.* 8; of self-taught wisdom in *Sacr.* 78; of "practical wisdom" (φρόνησις) in *Somn.* 1.82; and once more in *Mut.* 15 to refer to the epiphany of a divine power.

best of the good emotions. In QG 2.57, Philo gives a more complete catalogue of the bad and good emotions than he does in the Allegorical Commentary. He interprets Gen 9:3 (animals given as food) to imply pairs of poisonous and non-poisonous reptiles; these allegorically symbolize the various pairs of harmful and salutary passions (the bad and the good emotions):

> For alongside sensual pleasures there is the passion of joy. And alongside the desire for sensual pleasures, there is reflection. And alongside grief there is remorse and constraint. And alongside desire there is caution. (trans. Marcus, PLCLSup)

Notably, Philo here calls the good emotions "joys" (բերկրութիւն) rather than "good emotions," though this may be a translational equivalent. The Armenian *solutio* can be outlined as follows:

Passion (bad emotion)			Joy (good emotion)		
pleasure	հեշտ ցանկութեան	ἡδονή	joy	բերկրութիւն խնդութիւն	χαρά χαρμονή χαρμοσύνη
desire	ցանկութիւն	ἐπιθυμία	reflection willing	կամք խորհուրդ	ἐνθύμημα, βούλησις
grief	տրտմութիւն	λύπη	remorse constraint irritation	խայթումն զղծումն	πληγή, πλῆγμα παροξυσμός, παρόργισμα, παροργισμός
yearning (fear?)	փափաքումն	πόθος, ἔφεσις (φόβος?)	caution	երկեղա- ծութիւն	εὐλάβεια

The Armenian translator's use of pleonasm is striking, as he consistently gives two words for each good emotion, excepting the last. Of desire, Marcus (PLCLSup) wonders whether it is "possible Philo here contrasts ἐνθύμημα and ἐπιθυμία." "Willing" (βούλησις) as a rational form of intention is given in the Allegorical Commentary as the corresponding good emotion and might equally stand behind the Armenian. Especially interesting is the presence of several good emotions corresponding to "grief" (λύπη): "remorse," "constraint," or "irritating incitement" (παροξυσμός). (NHBL gives "incite" [παροξύνω] and "anger" [παροργίζω] as definitions of "irritate" [գձօտգնուցանեմ], whence I have derived these *Vorlagen*.) For "incitement," used in a positive, virtuous sense, see Heb 10:24 ("incitement to love and good deeds"). Note that the good emotion "caution" is usually opposed to "fear"; here, Philo gives instead "foolhardy appetition" or "yearning" (πόθος). Marcus (PLCLSup) renders this noun "desire" again, which is confusing since the underlying word is different from that found in the second pair of emotions.

Isaac ... joy. Philo's reference to Isaac as joy finds no parallel in QG 3.39. Cf. the immediately preceding QG 3.38, where the etymology and its interpretation (laughter and joy) appear; as well as QG 3.53 (happiness and joy); 4.17 (laughter); and 4.147 (laughter; joyful). This etymology of Isaac and its psychic interpretation (joy, happiness) surface throughout Philo's exegetical writings, especially the Allegorical Commentary (QG 3.53; *Leg.* 3.43, 86, 87, 218, 219; *Cher.* 8; *Det.* 123–124; *Plant.* 167–169; *Congr.* 36; *Mut.* 131, 188, 261; *Abr.* 201). In *Cher.* 8, Isaac stands for the people who "put to death" the passions—and thereby embrace the "good emotions" (εὐπάθειαι). Given the prominence of joy and "thanksgiving" (εὐχαριστία) in Philo's thought (LaPorte 1983), one might postulate that the association of Isaac and "joy" (χαρά) was a commonplace in his exegetical school. The only other scriptural figure frequently identified with joy in the Allegorical Commentary is Eden (*Leg.* 1.45; *Cher.* 12–13; *Plant.* 38).

Num 18:26–32. Philo's treatment of the Levitical tithe in QG 3.39b is shorter and less detailed than it is in *Mut.* 1–2. He alludes to Num 18:26–30 in QG 3.56 (par. *Mut.* 191), noting that "in the law, I see two tithes of first fruits distinguished" (յայրէևս տեսանեմ երկուս տասանորդս նախնեալս երախայրեաց որոշեցեալս). Philo thus carries traditions forward from QG 3.53, 56 and combines them with selective material from QG 3.39 in order to compose his opening sequence. The lemma is not cited elsewhere in the Allegorical Commentary, and is used by Philo in these first two series exclusively in connection with Abraham's age and the number one hundred. Parallel treatments of Num 18:26–32 include QG 3.56; PAPM 33, frag. B 17 (228.4); *Mut.* 191; *Spec.* 1.157; 4.98. At *Spec.* 1.157, the law is explicated literally, but with no recourse to the allegorical significance given in *Mut.* 2.

the number ten. See also *Decal.* 27 and the Armenian fragment from *De numeris* for Philo's interpretation of the decade.

Nachleben

There are numerous Christian expositions of Gen 17. It is interpreted selectively and allegorically by Origen in his *Hom. Gen.* 3, "On the Circumcision of Abraham" (*De circumcisione Abrahae*). The entire sermon, preserved in Latin, may fruitfully be read in parallel with the present treatise, even though Philo omits the critical verses on circumcision that concern his Alexandrian successor. Origen, for his part, omits the second half of Gen 17, with which Philo's treatise is largely occupied, and moves on to Gen 18 in *Hom. Gen.* 4. Also noteworthy, in the Greek tradition, is John Chrysostom's *De mutatione nominum*. These four homilies focus primarily on Saul's change of name to Paul in the Acts of the Apostles, but the Golden Mouth approaches this question by way of name changes in the Old Testament, including Abraham, Isaac, and Jacob. As a result of John's Antiochene provenance, his philosophy of language is only partially reflective of Philo's view. In the Latin West, the most immediate analogue to the present treatise is Ambrose's *De Abraham*, which like Gregory of Nyssa's *De vita Moysis*, is comprised of a literal paraphrase and an allegorical contemplation of the patriarch's life in two volumes.

All three of these works are more wide-ranging than Philo's *De mutatione nominum* and cover more of the scriptural text. Nevertheless, Philonic themes resound in each, in ways peculiar to their respective authors, which suggests a high probability of familiarity with Philo's treatise [A] or [B]. Origen, for instance, begins his third homily with the theological issues arising from the fact that (as Scripture indicates) "God speaks to human beings" ("Deum ... ad homines loqui"), and proposes "to begin with a little homily on this theme" ("his primo paucis sermocinandum"), before passing on to his main scriptural topic of circumcision. The reader of this prologue will immediately think of Philo's remarks on divine speech in *Mut.* 11–14, as well as his discourses on the incomprehensibility of God throughout chapter one (*Mut.* 7, 12). John Chrysostom, for his part, takes up a critical Philonic exegetical question: why some patriarchs' names change (like Abram and Jacob), while others' (like Isaac) do not. Similarly, book two of Ambrose's *De Abraham* is infused with Philonic traditions, transformed in light of the Milanese bishop's ecclesiological focus. For Ambrose, knowledge of *De mutatione nominum* is generally certain [A], though not in every detail.

What follows in these *Nachleben* sections is not an attempt at the complete reading of any early Christian text, but a more focused and atomistic catalogue of similar traditions, exegetical and philosophical, ranked in terms of probable knowledge of *De mutatione nominum* (see Introduction 9. Parallel Exegesis and *Nachleben*), which will both illustrate the importance of Philo's contribution and show which of his innovative interpretations proved too speculative or controversial to be taken up by later exegetes. NB: All translations in the *Nachleben*, unless otherwise noted, are mine.

§ 1. *one-hundred*. Didymus the Blind (*In Gen.* 250.12 [B]) offers an arithmological exegesis of Abraham's age in Gen 17:1 as resulting from the multiplication of two tens. Although the commentary is fragmentary, the passage includes references to "stability" (βέβαιον) and "perfection" (τελιότης), which reflect influence by Philo's commentary in *De mutatione nominum*.

Isaac ... joy. Origen knows the Septuagintal etymology of Isaac as "laughter" (*Cels.* 5.45 [C]); Jerome (*Nom. hebr.* 7.15 [C]) gives the etymology "laughter, or joy" ("risus, vel gaudium"), which likewise reflects the Philonic interpretation. More clearly dependent on Philo is Ambrose's interpretation of Isaac as "public happiness" and "perfect joy" ("publica laetitia," "perfecta iucunditas"); see *Abr.* 1.43 [A/B]: "that in Isaac she [Sarah] would give birth to universal joy" ("quod publicam esset in Isaac paritura laetitiam"); *Abr.* 2.85 [A]: "that birth of perfect enjoyment, whose name is Isaac" ("ille perfectae partus iucunditatis, cuius nomen est Isaac"); and *Isaac* 1.1 [A]: "for Isaac signifies 'laughter' in Latin, but 'laughter' is a symbol of joy" ("Isaac etenim risus Latine significatur, risus autem insigne laetitiae est"). These impressive examples show Ambrose's direct dependence on the Allegorical Commentary, including *De mutatione nominum*, in composing his patriarchal treatises.

Num 18:26–32. Philo's allegorical interpretation of the priestly tithe is received and redeployed with particular brilliance by Origen in the magisterial prologue to his John commentary. In a series of passages (*Comm. Jo.* 1.9, 12 [A/B]), Origen develops an allegoresis of this pericope, in which the tithe represents the spiritual offering of the ordinary Christian, whereas the Levitical tithe symbolizes the spiritual labors of the perfect, "those who are being consecrated to the divine Word and becoming devoted to the service of God alone" (οἱ δὲ ἀνακείμενοι τῷ θείῳ λόγῳ καὶ πρὸς μόνῃ τῇ θεραπείᾳ τοῦ θεοῦ γινόμενοι γνησίως, *Comm. Jo.* 1.9). This offering is made particularly in the interpretation of Scripture. The Gospels themselves also become "the first fruits of many first fruits" (*Comm. Jo.* 1.12–13 [A/B]), and their interpretation—Origen's principal occupation in Alexandria—is likened to the interpretation of Moses's writings (*Comm. Jo.* 1.14; see further 1.20, 23 [A/B]).

b   *The Lord's Appearance to Abraham* (§§ *3–17*)
     Analysis/General Comments

Philo's paraphrase of Gen 17:1bα ("It is by this person that Moses says the Lord of the universe was seen") in § 2 draws the reader's attention back to the primary biblical lemma. He will not quote the lemma in full again until § 15.

The relative pronoun, rendered as "by this person" in the paraphrase, allows Philo to postpone the discussion of Abraham's name until chapter five. In this second section of the first chapter (§§ 3–17), Philo sequentially interprets the first two words of the verse "The Lord was seen" (ὤφθη κύριος). It divides, accordingly, into two parts.

(1) Philo first interprets the verb "was seen," ὤφθη. Echoes of this verb, its cognates, and synonyms ("eye," "eyes," "seeing," "seen") sound throughout the section in §§ 3–4 (ὀφθαλμοί, ὁρῶσι, ὄμμα, ὁρωμένου, ὁρῶντος), § 5 (ὄμμα, εἶδεν), § 6 (ὀφθέντα), § 7 ("God-seer," θεόπτης), § 9 (ὄψει, ὀφθήσεται, ὁρᾶσθαι), and § 10 (εἶδεν), marking it as a distinct interpretive unit (§§ 3–10).

§§ 3–10 is divisible into two further subsections: (1A) §§ 3–6 highlights the unique capabilities of human noetic vision. (1B) §§ 7–10 focuses on its limitations. Philo first establishes that Abraham's seeing is not a physical but psychic/noetic in nature (1A §§ 3–6). To support this theory, he alludes to Plato, *Resp.* 508b–509e, and the notion of the "eye of the soul" (see *Resp.* 508b1, d4; 518c; 533d). Philo then clarifies (1B §§ 7–10) that God in his essence cannot been seen. Instead, Abram sees one of God's powers. Through this allegoresis, Philo illustrates two important conversions within the soul: (1) the turn from the visible to the invisible; and (2) from epistemological optimism to epistemological realism or scepticism.

To support this allegorical interpretation, Philo adduces Exod 20:21 (§ 7) and Exod 33:13–23 (§§ 8–9) as secondary lemmata. God's appearance to Abraham is likened to the theophany to Moses in the darkness of Sinai (Exod 20) and to God's showing his "back" when passing by Moses on the mountain (Exod 33). Moses's limited vision of God on Mount Sinai provides a correlative to Abraham's limited vision in Gen 17:1aβ.

(2) Having interpreted "was seen" (ὤφθη) in §§ 3–10, Philo proceeds to the next word, "Lord" (κύριος). "Lord" occurs in §§ 11, 12, 13 (3×), 14 (2×), 15 (3×), and 17. By detecting a literary transposition (*hyperbaton*) in Moses's syntax, Philo creatively misinterprets the divine title "Lord" (κύριος) as an adjective, insisting that it betokens the opposite of its plain sense: God has no "proper" (κύριον) name. Exod 3:14–15 (§§ 11–13), Exod 6:3 (§ 13), and Gen 32:29 (§ 14) are all adduced as secondary lemmata, linked to each other lexically through the word "name" (ὄνομα). Moses's restricted vision in Midian (E) and Egypt (P), as well as Jacob's frustrated theophany at the Jabbok, express the same doctrine of limited human vision found in Gen 17:1aβ (§§ 11–17).

Philo's exegetical poetics in this subsection of the treatise are more complex than the first (§§ 1–2). Fleshing out each word of the primary biblical lemma,

"The Lord was seen" (ὤφθη κύριος) with secondary texts, Philo coordinates visionary ("was seen," ὤφθη) and auditory (the name "Lord," κύριος) modes of revelation. He thus introduces a second key theme of his treatise: the revelatory significance of God-given names (§ 11). Exegetically speaking, the clusters of secondary lemmata in parts one (§§ 7–10) and two (§§ 11–17) are asymmetrically balanced with one another. Cluster one (§§ 7–10) has a relatively simple concatenation of two texts, which is outweighed by the three supplemental texts in cluster two (§§ 11–17). This gives the reader a sense of progressing deeper into the mysteries of divine Scripture. The two clusters also rhetorically and theologically complement each other. Rhetorically, Moses's second person singular aorist imperative, "reveal yourself to me" (ἐμφάνισόν μοι σεαυτόν [§ 8]), in cluster one is balanced by Jacob's second person singular aorist imperative "announce your name to me" (ἀνάγγειλόν μοι τὸ ὄνομά σου [§ 14]) in cluster two. Philo thus forges an exegetical link between Moses and Jacob. Juxtaposing the two theophanies, which focus on two different senses—vision and sound—Philo establishes the epistemic limitations of both. With sublime irony, Philo's opening chapter is devoted to the One who has no proper name in human language, and hence, cannot be properly addressed. The name that God gives humans for the purpose of prayer paradoxically establishes the opposite dogma: that his nature is ineffable (Exod 3:15; § 13).

Detailed Comments

(1a) § 3. *perceptible things*. The differentiation between "the perceptibles" (τὰ αἰσθητά) and "the intelligibles" (τὰ νοούμενα) comes from Platonic tradition (see *Tim.* 51.d5; *Resp.* 508c1).

impression. As was typical for Middle Platonists, Philo's account of vision includes technical terms from Epicurean and Stoic theories of sensation and epistemology, including "impression" (φαντασία). For the Epicurean account of sensation, see Epicurus's *Ep. Hdt.* 46–56 (L&S 15A6–9). For the Stoic account, see Diogenes Laertius 7.49–51 (SVF 2.52, 55, 61; L&S 39A). Impressions for the Stoics might be sensory or non-sensory (Diogenes Laertius 7.49–51; L&S 39A4); in this case, Philo speaks of the latter. For philosophical eclecticism in Philo arising from the exegetical nature of his writings, see Mansfeld 1988.

the eye of the soul. This Platonic phrase, drawn from *Resp.* 533d (τὸ τῆς ψυχῆς ὄμμα), is frequent in Philo. Arnaldez (1964, 33, n. 2) adds that the "eye of the soul" is also found in Aristotle, e.g., at *Eth. nic.* 12 1143b. Plato first uses the phrase in *Resp.* 518c6. The analogy of the sun and the Good in *Resp.* 508b–509e underlies *Mut.* 3–10. In fact, Philo's exposition draws words sequentially from this Platonic passage, suggesting that the text of the *Republic* functions analogously to a secondary biblical lemma (albeit with less prescriptive force).

§ 4. *light as a co-laborer*. Philo uses the metaphor of visible light, drawn from ancient physics. So Aëtius 4.12.3 (*SVF* 2.54): "The light shows itself and other things embraced by it" (τὸ φῶς αὐτὸ δείκνυσι καὶ τὰ ἄλλα τὰ ἐν αὐτῷ περιεχόμενα). For the Stoics, the term "impression" or "appearance" (φαντασία [§ 3]) is etymologically connected to "light" (φῶς: Aëtius 4.12.3; L&S 39B3). The description of light as a tool or "co-laborer" (συνεργός) is a favorite epithet of Philo's: see also *Cher.* 96; *Sacr.* 36; and *Spec.* 4.60. Alesse (2008, 3), following Willy Theiler, includes "co-laborer" (συνεργός) as a term that Philo may have taken from Antiochus of Ascalon by way of the school of Eudorus.

whatever the soul sees, it sees through itself. In this passage, Philo appears to alter Plato's description of cognitive vision in the *Republic* (esp. 508c1, e1–3), in which both minds and intelligible objects require the Good as a *tertium quid* to mediate apprehension. For Plato, the eye (of the soul) may be the "most like the sun" (ἡλιοειδέστατον) of human organs (*Resp.* 508b3), but it is not the sun itself. For Philo, in this passage, the external light required for bodily perception has no counterpart in the visionary process of the eye of the soul. In order to transform Plato's portrait of intellection and make the mind semi-autonomous, Philo introduces a direct analogy between the sun and the human mind (*Her.* 263; cf. *Somn.* 1.73–74). By identifying the soul as itself a little sun, Philo adapts the Platonic analogy to highlight the superiority of the soul's vision over bodily vision. Nevertheless, created intellect for Philo is not truly autonomous. Elsewhere, Philo argues that the eye of the soul still needs to be illumined by knowledge or wisdom in order to see clearly (e.g., *Congr.* 47). On this model, it is the all-illuminating Logos rather than the individual mind, which most resembles the sun.

knowable things are a light unto themselves. Philo's terms "the knowable things" (τὰ νοούμενα) and "light" (φέγγος) are drawn from *Resp.* 508c. The phrase "the knowable things" (τὰ νοούμενα), with a definite article, occurs in Plato's corpus only here and at *Tim.* 30d2. That intelligible objects could be seen without the illumination of the Good is a development not entirely consonant with Plato's epistemology in the *Republic* (see above), nor one which Philo will hold fast to elsewhere in the Allegorical Commentary.

§ 5. *sciences*. The "sciences" (ἐπιστῆμαι) in Platonic thought signify branches of knowledge whose certainty transcends the "arts" (τέχναι). In keeping with the primacy of "science/knowledge" (ἐπιστήμη) in Plato's line (*Resp.* 509d6–511e5), Philo often uses the term to indicate the soul's mastery of certain fields of knowledge with the greatest degree "fixity" (τὸ βέβαιον). See, e.g., *Congr.* 140: "Science (ἐπιστήμη) is greater than skill (τέχνη), as it has in addition a stability (τὸ βέβαιον) that cannot be shaken by argument." For stability or fixity as the key distinguisher of "science" (ἐπιστήμη) in Middle Platonic epistemology, and particularly for the incorporation of the Stoic notion that this kind of knowledge is "unable to be altered by logical argumentation" (ἀμετάπτωτος ὑπὸ λόγου), compare *Anon. Theat. Comm.* 15.19–23 (which ascribes the view to Zeno).

For these reasons, Philo sometimes distinguishes the noetic sciences from preliminary studies, including grammar, music, geometry, rhetoric, and dialectic (*Congr.* 15–18), which are not sciences in the proper sense (*Congr.* 140, 143, 145), but "middle skills" (αἱ μέσαι τέχναι) or "middle education" (ἡ μέση παιδεία). But cf. *Congr.* 14, where Philo can refer to the "preliminary studies" (προπαιδεύματα) as "the middle education in the median and universal sciences" (ἡ τῶν μέσων καὶ ἐγκυκλίων ἐπιστημῶν μέση παιδεία, *Congr.* 14).

its unbolted and unsleeping eye. Plato (*Resp.* 508d4–9) suggests that the eye of the soul needs to exert effort to "stay fixed" (ἀπερείσηται) on the forms; otherwise, it may become mixed with darkness. Philo presupposes the best-case scenario.

sees ... shines forth. Philo's aorist verbs "sees" (εἶδεν) and "shines forth" (ἐξέλαμψεν; cf. §1, ἐπέλαμψε) pick up on the aorist verbs of *Resp.* 508d6, "understands and recognizes" (ἐνόησέν τε καὶ ἔγνω). They are gnomic aorists, expressing a general truth (Smyth §§ 1931–1932). Philo uses this kind of aorist often in *De mutatione nominum* on account of its ability to blend past scriptural narration with timeless psychological allegory.

counterfeit light ... legitimate illumination. The distinction between illegitimate and legitimate light is used to differentiate the light of the moon and the sun, respectively, in *Somn.* 1.23, 53. It also echoes Philo's allegorical reading of the sons of Hagar and Sarah in *Congr.* 14. While "Ishmael" knowledge, which comes from hearing (*Mut.* 201–209) and is born of Hagar, is not legitimate, "Isaac" knowledge, which comes from seeing and is born of virtue (Sarah), is self-illuminating as the sun.

that shines forth from itself. Philo further transforms the Platonic account of noetic vision in the *Republic*. Whereas in the *Resp.* 508d, the soul looks up to the region "where truth and the existent 'shine down' (καταλάμπει)," here the soul "shines forth" (ἐξέλαμψεν) with its own sun-like brilliance. Both joy (*Mut.* 1) and knowledge (*Mut.* 5) "shine" for Philo from an internal principle, as well as from a source extrinsic to the soul of the wise person. Such semi-autonomous power in the soul results from God's gracious gift, as Philo will reiterate throughout the Allegorical Commentary (Lévy 2018; 2021; Cover 2020).

§ 6. *whenever you hear that God was seen.* A general Philonic hermeneutical guideline for all scriptural theophanies. Philo's paraphrase, "God, having been seen by a human being" (ὀφθεὶς θεὸς ἀνθρώπῳ; cf. Gen 17:1 above), rearticulates the primary biblical lemma in more universal theological and philosophical terms, allowing Philo to postpone the examination of the two names which follow: "Lord" (κύριος), which he will treat in §§ 11–17; and "Abraham" (Ἀβραάμ), which he will treat in §§ 60–129.

God is the wellspring of the clearest light. Philo's images of the "most pure light" (καθαρωτάτη αὐγή) and its "spring" (πηγή) echo Plato's optical metaphors for contemplation in the *Phaedrus*. See esp. *Phaedr.* 250c4 for the "pure light" and *Phaedr.* 245c9 for the God as "spring" of all movement.

shadowless and most resplendent rays. In Plato's famous allegory of the cave in *Resp.* 7, shadows represent the unrealities of the perceptible cosmos. Philo's "shadowless" rays, by contrast, proceed from the sun itself, not the deceptive shadow-casting fire. Philo allusively synthesizes images from the *Phaedrus* and the *Republic* (Méasson 1986; Cover 2014).

(1b) § 7. ***The One Who Is.*** Philo often uses the neuter substantive construction "That Which Is" (τὸ ὄν) rather than the masculine "The One Who Is" (ὁ ὤν) revealed in the Septuagint (Exod 3:14, cited below in § 11), to refer to the transcendent God. The former is standard in Platonism, the latter in Jewish texts. Owing to their classical education, Philo and Josephus routinely use both and, as a rule, I have not differentiated between these Philonic titles in the translation, nor do I usually in the commentary. In § 7, Philo may still be thinking of "That Which Is" (τὸ ὄν) in *Resp.* 508d5. See Cover 2014 for the suggestion that Philo reads "that which really is" (τὸ ὂν ὄντως) in *Phaedr.* 249c as a reference to God.

no organ. Not even the eye of the soul (see *Resp.* 508b2). Philo signals one of his most characteristic and novel doctrines within the history of philosophy and theology (Dillon 1996, 155): the complete transcendence of God, "The One Who Is" (τὸ ὄν) and the corresponding human epistemological limitation. For the metaphor of "seeing God" in Philo, see Cover 2014; Sterling 2018.

to form an impression. Philo redeploys the Stoic notion of the divine "impression" (φαντασία) from § 3, offsetting his positive statement there with a negative corollary. The eye of the soul cannot receive an impression of The One Who Is. Philo's use of this verb in close proximity to the verb "receive," "grasp," or "comprehend" (καταλαμβάνεσθαι) in § 7 brings to mind the Stoic notion of a "cognitive impression" (καταληπτικὴ φαντασία), the only infallible kind of impression in Stoic epistemology (Diogenes Laertius 7.54; *SVF* 2.105; L&S 40). By insisting that a cognitive impression of The One Who Is is impossible, Philo leaves open the possibility of some less certain knowledge of the Divine.

nor mind. Philo's epistemology here is very pessimistic, in some contrast with the immediately preceding sections (§§ 3–6).

the seer of the invisible nature. The Greek word "seer" (θεατής) recalls a spectator at the theater or at a one of the Panhellenic games (see Philo, *Contempl.*

42; *Legat.* 46), as well as the philosophical visionary. The word does not appear in the Septuagint. In *Mut.* 18, Abraham is designated as both "the hearer and seer" (ὁ ἀκροατὴς καὶ θεατής)—the phrase from which I have derived the title of this chapter. That the object of his vision is "invisible" (ἀειδής / ἀΐδής) highlights the paradox.

[*that is, the seer-of-God*]. Philo specifies Moses's role title "seer (θεατής) of the invisible nature" with the alliterative phrase "that is, seer-of-God" (καὶ θεόπτης). The alliteration of the phrase, θεατὴς καὶ θεόπτης, has a poetic, rhetorical quality not infrequent in Philo's florid prose. PCW questions its authenticity (see Notes to the Text and Translation).

divine oracles. One of Philo's favorite ways of referring to the writings of Moses. The term "oracle" (χρησμός) never occurs in the Septuagint, and the related verb "to speak an oracle" (χρησμολογεῖν) is found only once in Jer 45(38):4. Philo has borrowed the word from the world of Greco-Roman religion, where it is used by literary authors, including lyric (Pindar) and tragic (Aeschylus, Euripides) poets, historians (Herodotus), and philosophers (Plato, Plutarch), as well as in inscriptions (e.g., SIG 1044.49). The term might imply a variety of inspirational mechanics. Plutarch's treatise on the oracle at Delphi indicates that interest in ecstatic, mantic experience was flourishing in the first century, even if the gods themselves had become (relatively) taciturn. While some Jews (like Ben Sira) resisted the Hellenizing impulse to mix pagan accounts of mantic inspiration with traditional Jewish prophecy, Philo saw in such descriptions of oracular speech a ready-made lexicon ripe for theological reapplication, which he could fruitfully adopt to explain the anthropology and pneumatology of Mosaic inspiration (Levison 2009, 155–170). Presumably, they convey the intention of Moses the "lawgiver" (νομοθέτης), who knows how to set names (cf. Plato, *Crat.* 388e–389a).

he entered into the darkness. A paraphrase of LXX Exod 20:21, "And Moses entered into the darkness" (Μωϋσῆς δὲ εἰσῆλθεν εἰς τὸν γνόφον). In Philo's rewriting, the prepositional phrase is transposed to the beginning of the sentence (in indirect discourse), in order to highlight the negative aspect of Moses's vision. The darkness of Sinai stands as a parallel to the "invisible nature" imperfectly seen by Abraham. A more expansive version of this paraphrase is found in *Mos.* 1.158: "It is said that he entered into the darkness, where God was, that is into the invisible and unseeable and bodiless paradigmatic being of the things that are, wherein he perceived that which is unseen by mortal nature" (εἴς τε τὸν γνόφον, ἔνθα ἦν ὁ θεός, εἰσελθεῖν λέγεται, τουτέστιν εἰς τὴν ἀειδῆ καὶ ἀόρατον καὶ ἀσώματον τῶν ὄντων παραδειγματικὴν οὐσίαν, τὰ ἀθέατα φύσει θνητῇ κατανοῶν).

speaking in riddles. The divine oracles themselves are said to be "riddling" (αἰνιττόμενοι)—a good example of Atticism in Philo's prose. Moses's agency is implied by the passive: see similarly Porphyry, *Antr. nymph.* 1: "At some time the cave that is in Ithaca is riddled about by Homer" (ὅτι ποτὲ Ὁμήρῳ αἰνίττεται τὸ ἐν Ἰθάκῃ ἄντρον), cited by Struck (2004, 23). The cognate noun "riddle" (αἴνιγμα) and its coordinate term "symbol" (σύμβολον, see *Mut.* 12) are the two most common designations for an allegorical figure in ancient literary criticism. The terms are used as early as the pre-Socratic philosophers and are a special favorite of Platonic and Stoic commentators (Struck 2004, 3, n. 1; 23), including Heraclitus the Allegorist's *Quaestiones Homericae* and the Stoic Cornutus's *Compendium de graecae theologiae traditionibus*.

thrice-desired. Philo uses this unique adjective "thrice-desired" (τριπόθητος) eight times in his corpus, twice in this treatise (cf. *Mut.* 174), once in *Her.* 43 and once in *Post.* 12 (totaling 4 times in the Allegorical Commentary). It occurs in the fragments of the Hellenistic poets Moschus and Bion of Smyrna, as well as in the prose of the Second Sophistic (e.g., Lucian, *Hist. conscr.* 31). The prefix "thrice" is a superlative intensifier (synonym: "worthy to be loved", ἀξιέραστος, *Post.* 12), which has mostly lost its arithmological significance. Both in *Mut.* 7 and in *Post.* 12, Philo uses the adjective in descriptions of Moses's vision of God (in Exod 33 and Exod 20), which suggests a traditional relationship with the Sinai vision. Philo may also have gravitated toward the epithet "thrice-desired" in light of its correspondence with the three-fold nature of God's revelation to the Abrahamic soul (i.e., God and his two powers), noted at *Abr.* 123 and QG 4.8 (see Parallel Exegesis below). There may also be some connection with the roots of Hermetic thought, as witnessed in the adjective "thrice-greatest" (τρισμέγιστος).

only Good. Philo here identifies the God of the Pentateuch with Plato's Good. See *Resp.* 508e.

§ 8. *no form.* Philo enters into a centuries-long philosophical debate about the form of the Good. He means either that the Good has no "form" (ἰδέα), or more likely, that the form of the Good (= God) is unknowable by humans, including Moses. This would appear to contradict the plain sense of *Resp.* 508e2–3, which speaks of "the form of the Good" (ἡ τοῦ ἀγαθοῦ ἰδέα); earlier in the dialogue, however, Plato has Socrates admit some doubt as to whether the form of the Good "may be known sufficiently" (οὐχ ἱκανῶς ἴσμεν; *Resp.* 505a). In a later dialogue, the *Parmenides*, Plato problematizes Socrates's theory of forms in general, including the form of the Good (*Parm.* 130b). The form of the Good was vigorously attacked by Aristotle (*Eth. nic.* 1.6, 1096a23). Drawing on Plato's later dialogues and the critique of Aristotle, Plotinus suggests that the One or the Good transcends the Intellect (wherein reside the intelligible forms); hence, for Plotinus, if the Good is a form, it is a singular one standing apart from the multiplicity of the forms by virtue of its unity and simplicity (see *Enn.* 6.7)—a position anticipated not only by Philo but also by his near contemporary, the pagan Middle Platonist, Eudorus of Alexandria (Dillon 1996, 126–129).

giving up on the teaching of others. Philo suggests that the doctrine of the inaccessibility of the Good stems from earlier Platonist discourse. "The teaching of others" may reflect intellectual currents in Philo's time—such as Eudorus of Alexandria's "postulation of a supreme, utterly transcendent First Principle, which is also termed God" (Dillon 1996, 127–128). In Philo's account, Moses ignores such teaching (even if true) out of love and longing to see and know The One Who Is.

"show yourself to me, let me see you with knowledge." Philo quotes Exod 33:13 as a secondary lemma. His citation, "let me see you with knowledge" (γνωστῶς ἴδω σε), differs from the Göttingen LXX, "let me know you recognizably" (γνωστῶς εἴδω [= εἰδῶ?] σε), which would more accurately reflect the Hebrew "and I will know you" (ואדעך). Philo's reading could be the result of a scribal error in the Caesarean transmission (Katz 1950; Barthélemy 1967; Cover 2023b). It may also reflect an interpretive rewriting of the text, enabling Philo to link Exod 33:13 lexically not only with verbs of "vision" (ὄψει and ὀφθήσεται) in Exod 33:23 (§ 9), but also with the statement that God "was seen" (ὤφθη) in Gen 17:1, the primary lemma of this chapter (§1). Philo has taken advantage of the historical connection between the Greek verbs for "knowing" (οἶδα) and "seeing" (εἶδον) and transformed the Septuagintal text. For alternative interpretations of this lemma, see the Parallel Exegesis.

Material and immaterial things. Literally, "bodies together with things" (σωμάτων τε ὁμοῦ καὶ πραγμάτων) or "bodies and realities." The phrase, repeated in § 9, is a merism—a pair of nouns denoting the totality of a class (e.g., "goods and chattels" means the sum total of one's moveable and immoveable property). It usually signifies "all things in the created order" (*Det.* 68), though Philo can also speak of "divine immaterialities" (*Her.* 64). In *Mut.* 8, it might include the Logos or divine powers, which are properly speaking "after The One Who Is." The meaning of the two constituent units of the merism adopted here ("material and immaterial things") is proposed by Harl (1961, 330) and followed by Runia (2001, 352). Winston and Dillon (1983, 298) suggest a wider variety of potential meanings embraced by Philo's formula, and Goulet (1987, 297–299) draws on the phrase "bodiless realities" (ἀσωμάτων ... πραγμάτων) in *Mut.* 56 to suggest that the "realities" are not simply the "forms" (though this evidence might be read in support of Harl as well).

The use of the adverb "together" (ὁμοῦ) to bind the two parts of this merism is rare, occurring only in *De mutatione nominum* (§§ 8, 9, 179) and in *Fug.* 153. Conception of the "immaterial realities" has positive consequences. In *Agr.* 1–2,

Philo says that only those who are familiar with "the natures of the immaterial realities" (αἱ φύσεις τῶν πραγμάτων) use "proper appellations" (κύριαι προσρήσεις). Moses is one such person, and hence his lawgiving is replete with careful attention to names (cf. *Crat.* 389a), which are "penetratingly accurate" (εὐθυβολώτατοι) as to the nature of the thing, and "supremely revelatory" (ἐμφαντικώτατοι) of the same. Despite this perspicuity, Moses remains "in the dark" with regard to the name of God. He cannot know the "reality" (πρᾶγμα) of God's Being, and hence cannot know the proper name of God (see the note on §11 below).

that rank after The One Who Is. Both immaterial forms and their material imprints are metaphysically derivative, and thus ranked "after" (μετά) the transcendent Good or God. This need not mean a literal, temporal procession of the immaterial "realities" (πράγματα), since the forms—as thoughts of God—are eternally present to him.

§9. *for it is said.* Philo often uses an impersonal citation formula to introduce scriptural speech, whether God's, Moses's, or the verse itself.

"you will see things behind me, but my face will not appear to you." This citation from Exod 33:23 continues the story begun with the secondary lemma in §8 (Exod 33:13). Philo cites the LXX text of Exod 33:23b with only minor changes. The first two words of Exod 33:23b, "and then" (καὶ τότε), are omitted in order to turn God's response to Moses into of timeless statement about humanity's limited epistemological horizon.

§10. *if The One Who Is should be incomprehensible.* Philo is the first extant author in this history of philosophy to apply the adjective "incomprehensible" (ἀκατάληπτος) to God (Dillon 1996, 155; Montes-Peral 1987). It is one among several alpha-privative adjectives that Philo uses to cloak the transcendent One with grammatical darkness, expressive of human limitation. Philo's doctrine may derive in equal parts from God's transcendence in common Jewish tradition, as well as from his readings in Pyrrhonian scepticism (Lévy 2024). Philo is not anti-dogmatic by any stretch, but here gives to dogmatism its proper limits (see further, Despotis 2021).

the mind in each of us is unknown to us. Philo applies a sceptical stance to the Delphic-Socratic imperative, "know thyself" (e.g., Plato, *Prot.* 343b). See Despotis 2021.

myriad disputes among the sophists. Philo most likely refers to the arguments among Hellenistic Philosophical schools, not *rhetors* of the Second Sophistic. The presence of the latter kind of oratorical "sophists" in Philo's Alexandria has been suggested by Winter 1997, but remains contested (Wyss, Hirsch-Luipold, and Hirschi 2017). Runia (2008, 28) suggests that the current passage "presupposes the kind of doxography set out more fully in *Somn.* 1.30–32."

PART ONE

(2) § 11. *the name "Lord" (Kyrios) cannot truly be applied to The One Who Is.* Whereas §§ 3–10 discuss divine transcendence through the metaphor of limited vision, using an ocular paradigm of revelation, §§ 11–17 focus on divine ineffability, using the aural paradigm of revelation (on these two paradigms, see Orlov 2017). Philo achieves this by shifting his attention from "was seen" (ὤφθη) to the name "Lord" (κύριος) in his primary biblical lemma (Gen 17:1aβ). Importantly, his interpretation in § 11 includes the first occurrence of the word "name" in the treatise. The comment thus marks not only a shift in topic (to the relationship between names and ontology), but also offers an initial sounding of the central leitmotif of *De mutatione nominum*. The adverbial phrase "truly" or "in truth" (πρὸς ἀλήθειαν) potentially modifies either the main verb (because of its predicative position) or "The One Who Is" (cf. § 7). As mentioned in the detailed comment on § 8, Philo says that only those who are familiar with "the natures of realities" (αἱ φύσεις τῶν πραγμάτων) use "proper appellations" (κύριαι προσρήσεις) for them. Conversely, knowledge of a proper name reveals nature. Because of God's essence or "reality" (πρᾶγμα) is ineffable, he has no "proper name" in human language.

inquiry-loving prophet. The English translation misses an alliteration present in the Greek: a chiastic arrangement of aspirated and unaspirated bilabial plosives (φιλοπευστοῦντι τῷ προφήτῃ). This offers a good example of the poetic quality of Philo's prose.

I am The One Who Is. Philo adduces Exod 3:14–15 as a secondary lemma and sequentially interprets it in §§ 11–13. The transition between primary and secondary lemma is lexical, depending on the presence of the name κύριος in both texts. Before turning to a discussion of κύριος in Exod 3:15c, Philo looks at the first title of God in this pericope: "The One Who Is" (ὁ ὤν) in Exod 3:14. This is the biblical equivalent of Plato's "The One Who Is" (τὸ ὄν). Philo cites only the first unit of his pericope, Exod 3:14a. Below, the entire Göttingen LXX pericope is translated and compared with the shorter lemma that Philo cites (including some alternative Philonic meanings):

LXX Exod 3:14–15	§§ 11–13
¹⁴And God said to Moses, "I am The One Who Is." And he said, "Thus you will say to the sons of Israel, 'The One Who Is has sent me to you.'" ¹⁵ᵃAnd God said again to Moses,	"I am The One Who Is."

LXX Exod 3:14–15	§§ 11–13
b"Thus you will say to the sons of Israel,	
c 'The Lord God of your fathers,	The Lord God …
d The God of Abraham and the God of Isaac and the God of Jacob	… of Abraham … Isaac … Jacob
ehas sent me to you.'	
fThis is my name forever (αἰώνιον)	This is my name for this age (αἰώνιον)
gand a memorial for generations of generations."	and a memorial … for generated beings (γενεαί).

As is clear from his selective citation, Philo is primarily interested in the divine titles and their significance.

which is the equivalent of saying. A technical interpretive formula. "Equivalent" (ἴσον) is either predicated directly of the preceding "that" (ὅτι) clause or is an accusative absolute (Smyth § 2059). Other occurrences of this exegetical formula appear in the present treatise at §§ 21, 29, 48, 137, 142, 270.

my nature is to be, not to be spoken. The pithy, chiastic syntax of Philo's interpretation (Gk. εἶναι πέφυκα, οὐ λέγεσθαι) gives it a gnomic, proverbial tone. By suggesting that God's Being cannot be "spoken" (οὐ λέγεσθαι), Philo gives new expression to the transcendence of God's Being, this time in terms of human language. A few sections later, and in a subsequent treatise, Philo will express this using the terms "unspeakable" (ἄρρητος [§§ 14–15]) and "unnamable" (ἀκατονόμαστος [*Somn.* 1.67]), applying the former to the natures of both God and the Logos.

§ 12. **a means of addressing.** The Greek term "appellation" / "means of addressing" (πρόσρησις) is used in a number of contexts, including a sacral address to a deceased ancestor (see, e.g., Euripides, *Hel.* 1165–1166). For Plato in the *Politicus* (258a), the term is a synonym for "title" (κλῆσις); it is said that those who share an "appellation" have a kind of kinship (i.e., Socrates and "the young Socrates"), even if a non-ontological one: "The title or appellation which is homonymous with another name entails some form of kinship between the two named things" (ἡ κλῆσις ὁμώνυμος οὖσα καὶ ἡ πρόσρησις παρέχεταί τινα οἰκειότητα). "Name" (ὄνομα) is thus the more identity-binding term.

For Philo, "appellation" is sometimes a synonym for "name." In *Agr.* 1, for instance, he suggests a direct connection between knowledge of the nature of a thing and its "proper appellation" (κυρία πρόσρησις). In *Mut.* 12, however, Philo denies that "anything proper" (τις οἰκειότης, *Pol.* 258a) about God's nature is revealed by this "appellation," thereby distinguishing it from the "name," properly speaking. God reveals his "appellation" to facilitate dialogue with humans in prayer, not to reveal his essence.

he allows them to use inexactly. Philo introduces a very interesting verb, "to misuse or use inexactly" (καταχρῆσθαι). It implies an imprecise, analogous, or erroneous usage of language for the sake of utility. Philo uses the cognate noun, "misuse" or "accommodating use" (κατάχρησις), in § 13 to describe the character of God's speech to Moses in the burning bush. According to Runia 1988, Philo's theological use of this term—which is not often adopted by later theological authors—is "the single most interesting feature of ⟨this⟩ passage" and perhaps of the treatise as a whole. It deserves further study. (For Runia's own excellent treatment of the subject, see 1988, 76–81, 83–89.)

Lausberg notes that there are two forms of *catachrēsis* recognized by the grammarians: the metaphoric and the metonymic-synecdochic (Lausberg §§ 562, 577). The former is more relevant to Philo's usage in *Mut.* 12–13. Tryphon, the Alexandrian grammarian (first century BCE), defines metaphoric *catachrēsis* as "a word which is transferred from the object, which it first named properly and etymologically, to another object, which has no proper name of its own" (λέξις μετενηνεγμένη ἀπὸ τοῦ πρώτου κατονομασθέντος κυρίως τε καὶ ἐτύμως ἐφ' ἕτερον ἀκατονόμαστον κατὰ τὸ οἰκεῖον: *Trop.* P.192, 21). The use of "properly" (κυρίως) in Tryphon's definition is relevant, given Philo's playful use of the adjective "Lord/proper" (κύριος) in *De mutatione nominum*. Similarly Tryphon's "according to what is proper" (κατὰ τὸ οἰκεῖον) illuminates the way God's name in Philo differs in kind from the names of created objects (cf., however, Plato, *Crat.* 436a–d, in which Socrates suggests the possibility of fallible names). In Philo's context, Quintilian's (*Inst.* 8.6) metaphoric definition is also interesting: "*catachresis*, as we say rightly, is an abuse of language .... It applies what is linguistically near at hand to objects that have no name of their own" ("catachresis, quam recte dicimus, abusionem .... non habentibus nomen suum accommodat quod in proximo est"). See *Mut.* 11 and 14 for The One Who Is as the one "not having its own name" ("non habens nomen suum"). For the Logos's lack of a proper name, see *Mut.* 15.

as if ... by this sort of name. Commenting on Exod 3:15c, "The Lord God" (κύριος ὁ θεός)—the explicit lexical link between Exod 3:14–15 and Gen 17:1aβ—Philo asserts that while God does not reveal a "proper" (κύριον) name that might render intelligible his nature, he does give an ersatz name: "Lord (κύριος), the God of the three natures."

Lord, the God ... Abraham, Isaac and Jacob. Having commented on the first two divine names revealed in the secondary lemma, "The One Who Is" (ὁ ὤν,

Exod 3:14a) and "The Lord God" (κύριος ὁ θεός, Exod 3:15c), and noting that neither constitutes God's "proper," nature-revealing name, Philo turns to a third. Eliding Exod 3:15c with Exod 3:15d, he derives "the God ... of Abraham, Isaac, and Jacob." This name, which Philo will continue to explore through the adduction of Exod 6:3 (§ 13), is the divinely sanctioned "appellation" for human prayer.

of the three natures. Within the biblical title "the God of Abraham, Isaac, and Jacob," Philo sandwiches an allegorically charged paraphrase—"of the three natures." For Philo, the patriarchs are not primarily historical persons, but rather in the context of the Allegorical Commentary, symbols of natures or souls. For a similar technique of paraphrase, keyed into an allegorical expansion, see the detailed comments on § 2, "The Lord of the universe."

teaching, perfection, and practice. Philo's pedagogical triad, "teaching, perfection, and practice," is derived and adapted from educational patterns found in Plato and Aristotle. Philo famously notes in the Exposition of the Law that Abraham, Isaac, and Jacob are ethical paradigms and living laws, which Philo calls the second ethical triad or "the second triad of those who yearn for virtue" (ἡ ἑτέρα [τριὰς τῶν ἀρετὴν ἐπιποθησάντων])—the first triad being comprised of Enosh, Enoch, and Noah (*Abr.* 48). Abraham, Isaac, and Jacob represent the sages who obtain virtue "by learning, by nature, and by practice" (ὁ ... ἐκ διδασκαλίας καὶ ὁ αὐτομαθὴς καὶ ὁ ἀσκητικός), respectively (*Ios.* 1). Compare the opening question of Plato's *Meno* (70a): "Tell me, Socrates, is virtue taught? Or is it not taught, but practiced? Or is it neither practiced nor learned, but comes about in human beings by nature, or in some other fashion?" (Ἔχεις μοι εἰπεῖν, ὦ Σώκρατες, ἆρα διδακτὸν ἡ ἀρετή; ἢ οὐ διδακτὸν ἀλλ' ἀσκητόν; ἢ οὔτε ἀσκητὸν οὔτε μαθητόν, ἀλλὰ φύσει παραγίγνεται τοῖς ἀνθρώποις ἢ ἄλλῳ τινὶ τρόπῳ;). Colson (PLCL 5:586) also points to Aristotle's "educational triad" in passages like *Eth. nic.* 2 (1103a); *Eth. eud.* 1.1.4–5 (1214a); and *Pol.* 7 (1332a); cf. Diogenes Laertius 5.18; Birnbaum 2020.

symbols. Another of Philo's favorite words for the meaning of a text in his allegory of the soul. See the note above on § 7, "speaking in riddles."

this ... is my name in this age. Philo cites and interprets Exod 3:15 f. The NETS translation renders the text according to its Hebrew sense, "this is my everlasting name." Philo opts for an alternative meaning. Just as he transposes the name "Lord" (κύριος), rendering it as the adjective "proper," so here the adjective "eternal" (αἰώνιον) is given an alternative meaning. It should not be interpreted as "eternal"—which would suggest that the name reveals nature. Rather, through a philosophical *relecture* (which is completely possible in Greek), it comes to mean the opposite: "time-bound" or "dispensational"—i.e., "belonging to this 'age' alone." Similarly, Arnaldez notes that the word does not denote eternity:

"Αἰών has its first sense of 'for the duration of life'. Cf. Aristotle, Cael. 279a" (1964, 37, n. 3). Cf. *Mut.* 267, in which "age" (αἰών) is given its "second" Platonizing meaning of "eternity." Meditations on time and eternity—both contained in the word "age" (αἰών)—thus bookend *De mutatione nominum.*

and a memorial. Philo interprets to the penultimate excerpt of his secondary lemma, Exod 3:15gα. "Memorial" signifies the limited, functional scope of the name: to remind but not to reveal.

for generated ... natures. Philo cites the last excerpt of his secondary lemma, Exod 3:15gβ. He omits the cognate genitive, "unto generations of generations" (γενεῶν γενεαῖς) in the Septuagint, construing "generations" (γενεαῖς) alone as a dative of possession (or ethic dative) modifying an implicit noun, "natures." Rather than referring to the eternal establishment of the name of God for all eternity, Philo reads "generations" to signify its limited applicability to created, non-divine beings.

§ 13. *loose approximation.* For this concept, see the more detailed comments on § 12 above. The underlying term, *catachrēsis* (καταχρήσις), may signify one of several related literary devices, all of which involve a misappropriation or abuse of language.

if not in reality, then at least by the best name. Inability to comprehend the divine essence does not mean the loss of a relationship with God. The God-given appellations facilitate communication, however darkly. Philo distinguishes between "reality" (πρᾶγμα) and "name" (ὄνομα) rather than between reality and "body" (σῶμα), as in § 8. For this distinction, see Plato, *Crat.* 391b, 436a. In both polarities, ideal "reality" (πρᾶγμα) is contrasted with nominal or material "seeming."

the Ruler of the universe. Cf. "Lord of the universe" in § 2. Philo draws on the mythic vocabulary of the *Phaedrus* as well as the *Timaeus*, particularly the cosmic "ruler" (ἡγεμών).

not ... to anyone. Not even to Moses—a claim that is especially counterintuitive, given the secondary lemma that Philo is about to adduce (LXX Exod 6:3). According to Exod 6, God discloses to Moses the name which had been hidden from Abraham, Isaac, and Jacob. The passage, which is literally a revelation, is construed by Philo as an obfuscation.

I was seen ... but my name, 'Lord,' I did not clearly disclose to them. Philo adduces LXX Exod 6:3 as a secondary lemma modifying Gen 17:1aβ. The primary and secondary lemmata are linked through the shared aorist verb, "was seen" (ὤφθη[ν]). Exod 6:3 also shares thematic and lexical connections with the proceeding secondary lemma, Exod 3:14–15. Both passages speaking of (1) God's revelation of his name to Moses; particularly, (2) the name "Lord" (κύριος); (3) the reference to Abraham, Isaac, and Jacob; and (4) the catchword, "name" (ὄνομα). Philo's text of Exod 6:3 agrees with the Septuagint, except for the replacement of the masculine nominative singular κύριος (LXX) with the accusative masculine/neuter singular, κύριον. While this might be understood simply as a grammatical change due to indirect discourse (κύριον = accusative masculine singular, standing in a predicative relationship with τὸ ὄνομα), κύριος as a proper title could have been left in the nominative. Philo's change to indirect discourse allows him to make κύριον's grammatical gender ambiguous, in anticipation of his forthcoming *relecture* of the word as a neuter adjective meaning "proper," rather than as a masculine divine title.

after the transposition in the syntax has been reversed. To discover the desired sense, Philo suggests that Moses has used the rhetorical device of *hyperbaton* ("transposition"). According to the manuals, *hyperbaton* involves "the separation of two words which belong syntactically together by interposing a (one-or-more word) phrase that does not properly belong," often an article (Lausberg, 357; see §§ 716–718; § 462.3b; cf. Cocondrius, *Trop.* 3, p. 238, 11: "Hyperbaton is a transposition of the first and customary order of speech" [ὑπερβατόν ἐστι πρώτης καὶ συνήθους τάξεως λόγου μετακίνησις]). Philo "reverses" Moses's hyperbaton to reveal the "proper" meaning of the sentence. He first changes κύριος (LXX) to κύριον, and then repositions the article τό before κύριον to change the sentence "my name, 'Lord,' I did not clarify" (τὸ ὄνομα μου κύριον οὐκ ἐδήλωσα) into "I did not clarify my proper name" (ὄνομα μου τὸ κύριον οὐκ ἐδήλωσα). By re-placing the definite article, Philo moves κύριον from predicative to attributive position and renders it an adjective rather than a title. See Colson's notes (PLCL 5:149, n. c; 5:586) for more on this rhetorical device. For a parallel commentary text involving *hyperbaton*, see Cocondrius, *Trop.* 3, p. 238 11 (= Lausberg § 716), where the rhetor inserts the article τό (semantically) in *Il.* 12.177–178 to clarify that the adjective "stony" (λάϊνον) belongs with the more remote noun "wall" (τεῖχος), rather than with the immediately preceding noun, "fire" (πῦρ).

An important Philonic irony may be highlighted here. The translation "reversed" renders the participle μετατεθέντος. Its cognate noun, "transposition" (μετάθεσις), is used by Philo in *Mut.* 130 as a synonym for a "change" (ἀλλαγή) of name. Thus, while God does not have a proper name to change *per se*, reading divine ineffability into of the Pentateuch involves a nominal "transposition" (μετάθεσις) of another sort. There is a lightness, even a humor to Philo's rewriting of God's revealing of his name in this chapter, *pace* critics like Edwards (2013), who find the Alexandrian always humorless and severe.

§ 14. *so ineffable is The One Who Is*. Philo states positively what he has heretofore argued negatively: in having no "proper name" (κύριον ὄνομα), "The

One Who Is is ineffable" (τὸ ὄν ἄρρητόν ἐστιν). While a split-Demiurge tradition that separates "The One Who Is" (τὸ ὄν/ὁ ὤν) from a "second creator god" is common to both Philo and Numenius, the latter never explicitly applies the epithet "ineffable" (ἄρρητον) to his first God. The later sixth-century Platonist, Damascius, who retrieved certain aspects of Numenius's system, would use this title copiously for his highest God who was above the upper and lower One. (For the first and second "One," see Damascius, *Princ.* 3; for the "ineffable," see *Princ.* 6.25; and Dillon 1996, 123–124).

ministering powers. One of the hallmarks of Philo's theology is his doctrine of divine powers, which facilitate the worldly action of an otherwise transcendent God. Scholars from Hoeschel (1587) to Goodenough (1935) and beyond (Segal 1977; Radice 2009; Schäfer 2020) have offered various taxonomies of the interrelation of these powers, which generally divide under two primary headings (e.g., the creative and the kingly, correlated with the beneficent and the punitive, etc.; see *QE* 2.68). Some scholars speak of the Logos (Philo's "second god") as the first divine power "after" The One Who Is, into which all the other powers resolve. From a tradition-critical perspective, however, it is better to say that Logos language and power language have been redacted together (perhaps from Stoic and Platonizing/Aristotelian fonts, respectively) in Philo's thought. Thus Lebreton (1927, 198) speaks "of the powers and of the Logos" and treats both as species of "intermediaries"; Goodenough (1935, 123–125) and similarly Radice (2009, 136–142) give a philosophical origin for the powers and a partially scriptural one for the Logos. The use of the middle form "ministering" (ὑπηρετούμεναι) is odd; Colson (PLCL 5:148, n. 3) notes that "any use of the middle seems to be later than Philo," a point confirmed by LSJ.

With regard to the argument of *Mut.* 14: Following the proofs that God did not disclose his proper name to Moses or Abraham, Philo now argues *a minore ad maius* (cf. the Tannaitic middah, "light and heavy" [קל וחומר]) that if God's Word or ministering power did not disclose a proper name—neither God's nor his own—all the more should God himself remain nameless. God's ineffability extends, at least to a certain degree, to the Logos and his powers, even as the latter remain his intermediaries (see further Despotis 2021).

the man of practice wrestled. To illustrate the Logos's refusal to reveal a proper name, Philo adduces Gen 32:29–31 as a secondary biblical lemma. His text is identical with the Septuagint. Philo associates the "human being" of LXX Gen 32:25, with whom Jacob wrestles, with the Logos on account of the Logos's identity as the "image of God" used to create human nature. An appearance of the Logos to Israel in this passage is further suggested by the patriarch's name for the place, Peniel (Gen 32:30), which the Septuagint renders as "Form of God" (Εἶδος θεοῦ).

In Philo's recounting of patriarchal theophanies in this chapter, one can see a psychological hierarchy emerging (1. Isaac, 2. Abraham, 3. Jacob). Jacob's ascetical type ranks beneath Abraham's pedagogical type because Jacob's theophany (Gen 32) is associated only with the name of the Logos, whereas Abraham (Gen 17) is given an approximate name for "God" (ὁ θεός) himself. Isaac's type comes first, as it needs no training.

the unseen Governor. Philo refers to the Logos or ministering power as a "Governor" or "Overseer" (ἐπιστάτης). The term can have military overtones, but may also refer to a civic governor or the attendant at a cult temple (Goodenough 1935, "bodyguards" or "attendants").

his personal and proper name. The phrase "personal and proper name" (ὄνομα ἴδιον καὶ κύριον) occurs only in *Mut.* 14 and in *Deo* 4 (ականն անդա խվկ ևւ ուժր; see Terian 2016, 79, n. 5), the immediately following treatise in the Allegorical Commentary. This suggests some thematic connection between *De mutatione nominum* and *De Deo*. In *Deo* 4, it signifies that The One Who Is does not have a proper name; in *Mut.* 14, it suggests that the Logos and the powers, if they have proper names that can be known, do not share them.

honorable titles. Colson renders this "fair names." Perhaps a merism like "euphemisms and benedictions" would do better justice to the *double entendre* of εὐφημίαι, signifying both the catachrestic nature and religious purpose of the divine names in Philo's thought. The term may also refer to the silence before prayer (see *Migr.* 87–88, 115; as well as Aristophanes, *Thesm.* 295–310, where silence precedes the invocation of many names). In *Mut.* 14 Philo emphasizes the cataphatic aspect of such honorable titles.

symbols of the things that have come into being, the names. In contrast to "appellations" and "honorable titles," symbols and proper names provide a direct epistemic conduit to a thing's essence.

§15. *even his Word*. While §14 implies the reluctance of God's ministering power to speak the proper name of The One Who Is, in this section Philo adds the Logos's reluctance to speak even his own proper name.

one of the powers around it, the kingly. Philo returns to the word "Lord" (κύριος) of Gen 17:1aβ and gives it a positive explanation: whereas "the transcendent God" (ὁ θεός) has no "proper" name, the biblical text nonetheless indicates by "Lord" that the kingly power appeared to Abraham (this is clarified further in §17). For more on God's two principal powers, the creative ("God," θεός) and the kingly/legislative ("Lord," κύριος) see *QE* 2.68; and *Abr.* 119–122 (referenced by Arnaldez [1964, 38, n. 2]).

§16. *when it used to Chaldeanize and go on about heavenly bodies*. Philo alludes to Gen 11:28–32. Abram's threefold movement from Chaldea to Haran to the Land of Israel signifies the movement of the soul from a fixation on astrology, to knowledge of God through creation, to knowledge of God more directly (*Abr.* 68–80). A parallel tradition in Jub. 11–12 sees a movement from cultic idolatry (Ur) to astrology (Haran) to monotheism (the Land). Philo presents a Platonizing version of this common Jewish tradition. The verbs "Chaldeanize" (χαλδαΐζειν) and "go about the heavenly bodies" (μετεωρολεσχεῖν) warrant comment. The latter (μετεωρολεσχεῖν) is a satirical form of "practice astronomy" (μετεωρολογεῖν). For the nominal form, "stargazer" (μετεωρολέσχης), see *Mut.* 70; *Somn.* 1.161; *Prob.* 80. "To Chaldeanize" (χαλδαΐζειν) is as synonym for practicing astrology or the worship of cosmic powers (*Abr.* 77); it occurs only twelve times in a TLG search and appears to be a *verbum Philonicum*.

the reins and governance of a leader. Philo alludes to the divine charioteer of Plato's *Phaedrus*, often understood in Middle and Neoplatonic thought as the Logos, who leads the souls best able to rein in their "white and black horses" and to keep their eyes steadily fixed on the realm of the forms. See Plato, *Phaedr.* 246b2, 253e1 (the verb only occurs in these two Platonic *loci*); Méasson 1986; Cover 2014.

of whose rule it had received an impression. Arnaldez (1964, 40, n. 1) observes that Abraham's impression of the singular ἡ ἀρχή ("son pouvoir": "rule," "causal principle," "kingly power") demonstrates a critical step in his progress toward perfection. "The multiplicity of powers, when one considers them as primary causes, leads to polytheism. Monotheism corresponds to the unification of these multiple causes in a single God, of whom they are powers."

§ 17. *although he was king from the beginning.* The Greek lacks the predicate "king." This ellipsis has the effect of creating an even bolder ontological statement, that the kingly power "was (ὤν) from the beginning." Philo elsewhere describes the Logos and his powers in terms that suggest their creation (see Cover 2014).

Although king ... not yet recognized ... slow in learning ... not entirely ignorant. This phrase is elegantly crafted with two μέν ... δέ constructions, indicating the correlation between the kingly power's revelation and the soul's gradual education. Arnaldez (1964, 40, n. 2) explains: "God can only make himself known to a soul prepared to recognize him. The human being can intuit the existence of a unique first principle, but in order for him to surpass the image in which he himself is formed, he needs God to make himself visible."

but received an impression. The verb is passive (lit. "was impressed") and complemented with two accusatives of respect. This lends a kind of indirection to the apprehension of the divine impression (per § 7). Philo does not claim that the Logos himself (in his kingly aspect) was grasped by Abraham, but that his actions in the world led to an impression of him becoming discernable.

rule and governance among the things that are. The merism "rule and governance" (ἀρχὴ καὶ ἡγεμονία) represents both the totality of the kingly power's dominion as well as his temporal preeminence. Philo plays on both senses of the word "rule/beginning" (ἀρχή), using the noun in its both its regal (§ 16) and in its temporal (ἐξ ἀρχῆς [§ 17]) senses. It is possible that Philo also means to apply the title ἀρχή in its cosmogonic, sapiential sense to the kingly power as well. Cf. Prov 8:22.

Parallel Exegesis

§ 3. *the eye of the soul.* Philo uses the "eye of the soul" metaphor most frequently in the Allegorical Commentary: see *Sacr.* 36, 69 ("eyes," ὄμματα), 78; *Det.* 22; *Post.* 9, 118 (pl.), 167 ("eyes of thought," τοῖς διανοίας ὄμμασιν); *Deus* 181; *Plant.* 22 (pl.); *Ebr.* 44; *Sobr.* 3; *Migr.* 49, 165 (pl.), 191; *Her.* 89; *Congr.* 135; *Mut.* 3, 203; *Somn.* 1.117 (pl.), 1.164, *Somn.* 2.160 (pl.), but it also occurs in the Exposition of the Law and the philosophical works. In *Mut.* 3, Philo juxtaposes the singular vision of the soul's one eye—a symbol of the unity of the noetic realm—with the plural somatic eyes of the body, which correspond with the multiplicity of the material world. On at least six occasions, however, Philo can also speak of the "eyes" of the soul (see Plato, *Soph.* 254a10).

§ 4. *light as a co-laborer.* The description of light as a tool or "co-laborer" (συνεργός) is a favorite epithet of Philo's: see also *Cher.* 96; *Sacr.* 36; and *Spec.* 4.60.

it sees through itself. For the idea that intelligible objects are a light unto themselves, see *QE* 2.106.

§ 7. *Exod 20:21.* For Philo's interpretation of Exod 20:21 and the darkness of Sinai, *Post.* 13–16 is the most important parallel. There, Exod 20:21 is cited (with the verb in the future) and sandwiched between two references to Exod 33:13—the same lemma quoted below in *Mut.* 8. In contrast to *Mos.* 1.158, which remains optimistic about Moses's ability to "understand the things that are unseen by mortal nature" (τὰ ἀθέατα φύσει θνητῇ κατανοῶν), *Post.* 14 and *Mut.* 7 assert that Moses's request to see and understand God cannot be satisfied fully. In Philo's parallel explication of Gen 17:1b in *QG* 3.39, Exod 20:21 is not used as a secondary lemma. In *QE* 2.28, Moses's entry into the darkness in Exod 20:21 (as a secondary lemma) is likened to dwelling "in the forecourt" (i.e., of the tabernacle) (ի սրահն = αὐλῇ [Marcus, PLCLSup]; cf. LXX Exod 27:9; Ps 64:5; 83:3).

thrice-desired. In the detailed comments on *Mut.* 7, it was suggested that Philo's use of the adjective "thrice-desired" (τριπόθητος) may reflect God's three-fold revelation as The One Who Is, flanked (and mediated) by his two powers. Philo does *not* call God "thrice-desired" in *QG* 3.39a. He does, however, offer a parallel exegesis of Exod 33:13 (as a secondary lemma) in *QG* 4.8, much to the same effect. There, commenting on Gen 18:6–7, Philo interprets Sarah's "three measures of flour" as corresponding to Abraham's three-fold vision of God and his powers. "For indeed," writes Philo, "all things are measured by three" (բանզի արդարև էին երիւք չափին բոլորք)—an assertion which he defends with reference to Homer and Pythagoras (see Homer, *Il.* 15.189: "All things have been measured in threes" [τριχθὰ δὲ πάντα δέδασται]). Philo then clarifies that, on the one hand, "God alone is the measure of all things, both immaterial and sensible" (չափ ամենեցուն, եւ իմանալեացն եւ զգալեացն աստուած մի). The Armenian merism, "both immaterial and sensible" (եւ իմանալեացն եւ զգալեացն), may represent the Greek genitive, "both realities and bodies" (καὶ πραγμάτων καὶ σωμάτων). It also echoes the longer form of Protagoras's famous *homomensura*, cited by Plato (*Theaet.* 152a) and rebutted by Philo: "For he says somewhere that 'the human being is the measure of all things, of the being of those that are, and of the non-being of those that are not'" (φησὶ γάρ που «πάντων χρημάτων μέτρον ἄνθρωπον» εἶναι, «τῶν μὲν ὄντων ὡς ἔστι, τῶν δὲ μὴ ὄντων ὡς οὐκ ἔστιν»: trans. Cornford, in Hamilton and Cairns 1961, adapted; see Diels-Kranz 80b1). Nevertheless, Philo continues, "in his oneness, he is likened to a triad because of the weakness of the beholders" (որպէս ըստ միատրութեանն նմանեալ երրորդութեան յաղագս տեսողացն տկարութեան).

Having asserted this near-universal human experience of perceiving God as three, Philo adduces Exod 33:13 as a secondary lemma, noting Moses's request for vision of The One Who Is. Whether or not Moses receives such a vision, Philo does not say—but returning to the clearly achievable three-fold vision he then exclaims: "O thrice-happy and thrice-fortunate soul (Ով երիցս երանելոյ եւ երիցս բարեբաստիկ ոգւոյ), in which God has not disdained to dwell and move and to make his palace." As *Vorlage* to the Armenian here, one can suggest "thrice-blessed" (τρισμακάριος) and "thrice-fortunate" (τρισευδαίμων)—adjectives strikingly reminiscent of "thrice-desired" (τριπόθητος) in *Mut.* 7. Aucher renders the phrase "thrice-blessed and thrice-happy soul" (*ter beatam terque felicem animam*). All three adjectives occur in relatively close proximity in *Spec.* 1.31, 40. It thus seems reasonable to detect, in Philo's use of the adjective "thrice-desired," an intimation of his broader theory of Abram's three-fold vision of God, which is also given to the Moses-soul in *Mut.* 8.

§§ 8–9. *Exod 33:13–23*. Exod 33:13–23 appears frequently in Philo's other commentary series. Moses's request for a direct revelation of God in Exod 33:13 is interpreted in *Leg.* 3.101; *Post.* 13, 18; and *Fug.* 165. *Leg.* 3.101 simply relates

Moses's request—to which God seems to give an affirmative answer. In this passage, Philo holds open the possibility of some unmediated apprehension of The One Who Is, although not knowledge of his essence (see Cover 2014). *Post*. 13–18 offers a more pessimistic take, including God's negative response in Exod 33:23, even if Colson's textual conjecture rendering Moses's request as "useless" (ἄχρηστον) in *Post*. 16 doesn't convince (cf. *Praem*. 44, ἀμήχανον). *Fug*. 165 follows suit with *Post*. 13–18. In *Mut*. 8, we find Philo's most detailed negative assessment of human epistemic capacity, such that between *Leg*. 3.101 to *Mut*. 8 one finds an ever-growing pessimism on Philo's part that the Moses-soul is capable of seeing God directly. Such a negative view is confirmed by Philo's pessimistic stance in the Exposition of the Law, *Spec*. 1.41–50.

§ 10. *the mind in each of us is unknown to us*. Runia (2008, 28) hypothesizes that Philo alludes to a doxographical tradition "set out more fully in *Somn*. 1.30–32. There, Philo enumerates a series of questions about the soul—what it is made of, what its name means, where it resides in the body—which are meant to leave the reader with a sense of *aporia*."

§§ 11–12. *Exod 3:14–15*. Exod 3:14–15 is treated in an extended fashion only in §§ 11–12 in the Allegorical Commentary and in *Mos*. 1.75–76 in the Exposition of the Law. Philo will return to Exod 3:14 twice more in the present treatise (*Mut*. 57, 82). For Exod 3:14 as a secondary lemma more generally, see *QG* 4.2, 4, 8 (2×), 22; *QE* 1.20; 2.3 (2×), 11, 14, 16, 47, 51, 61, 62, 63 (2×), 66 (2×), 68 (2×), 122; *Cher*. 27; *Det*. 92, 139, 159, 160 (2×), 161; *Fug*. 110, 112; *Her*. 70; *Plant*. 26; *Sacr*. 9; *Deo* 5; *Somn*. 1.231, 234; 2.227, 237, 292. For the use of this lemma in the Exposition of the Law, see *Abr*. 51–52, 121; *Spec*. 1.81.

§ 12. *to use inexactly*. For Philo's other uses of the term *catachrēsis* and its verbal cognates, see Runia 1988, 85. Runia highlights seven passages in which Philo references linguistic "misuse" when speaking about God: *Sacr*. 101; *Post*. 168; *Mut*. 11–14, 27–28; *Deo* 4; *Somn*. 1.229; *Abr*. 120. In all these cases, Philo adopts a "hard line" (Runia 1988, 85) differentiation of name from essence. Runia suggests that Philo has not hit on this idea on his own, but adopted it from contemporary Platonism, although Scripture suggests an analogous idea.

§ 13. *Exod 6:3*. Philo paraphrases this lemma again in *Somn*. 1.230, and recapitulates the interpretation given in *Mut*. 13, that God grants catachrestic names: "When [Moses] had enquired whether The One Who Is has any name, he came to know full well that he has no proper name (κύριον μὲν οὐδέν), and that whatever name anyone may use of him he will use by license of language (καταχρώμενος)."

§ 14. *Gen 32:29(30)*. Philo interprets Jacob's request to see God in Gen 32:29(30) only here in his corpus. Jacob's change of name and the proclamation that Jacob will be "strong with God and powerful with human beings" in Gen 32:28(29) is a favorite of Philo's (see Parallel Exegesis on *Mut.* 44). For the use of the broader pericope, Gen 32:26–32, in *De mutatione nominum*, see the detailed comment on *Mut.* 187.

§ 15. *one of the powers around it, the kingly.* QG 3.39a catalogues the two powers of God (creative, kingly) in their economic/theological order. In *Mut.* 15 and 28, by contrast, Philo unfolds the two titles in their scriptural sequence in Gen 17. Gen 17:1 has only "Lord" as the subject of the theophany. Philo's discussion of the second power—and of both powers together—will not occur until *Mut.* 27–29 when the title "God" is more formally given (see the Parallel Exegesis for the following subsection).

Nachleben

§§ 6–7. *Exod 20:21.* Clement of Alexandria (*Strom.* 2.6.1 [A]; cf. *Strom.* 5.78.3 [B]) interprets Moses's entrance into the "darkness" (γνόφος) of Sinai in Exod 20:21 in ways that show dependence on Philo (Van den Hoek 1988, 181, 194). In the wider pericope, *Strom.* 2.5.3–2.6.4, Clement argues that God is "remote in his essence (κατ' οὐσίαν) ... but very near in his power (δυνάμει)" (*Strom.* 2.5.4; Van den Hoek 1988, 149). For *Strom.* 5.78.3 [B], which also interprets Exod 20:21, see the *Nachleben* on § 14 below.

comprehended. Cf. John 1:5: "The darkness did not comprehend it" (ἡ σκοτία αὐτὸ οὐ κατέλαβεν). The thought is similar, though with critical differences. Whereas Philo speaks of the first transcendent God, John speaks of the Logos. The inability to see, which in Philo's thought results from natural creaturely limitation, is simultaneously a result of sin and cosmic "darkness" for the author of the Fourth Gospel.

§ 8. *material and immaterial things.* The Philonic merism, "bodies and things" (σώματά τε ὁμοῦ καὶ πράγματα; or more simply καὶ σώματα καὶ πράγματα), is Middle Platonizing jargon, which has an important reverberation (if not a genetic influence) in Heb 10:1–5. There, the Law is said explicitly *not* to entail the form of immaterial "realities" (πράγματα, Heb 10:1), but rather the "body" (σῶμα) prepared for Jesus in the incarnation (Heb 10:5). See Attridge 1989 for this homiletic twist on the Platonic trope.

§ 10. *incomprehensible.* Dillon (1977, 155) notes that Philo is the first in the history of philosophy to apply the description "incomprehensible according to all forms/ideas" (κατὰ πάσας ἰδέας ἀκατάληπτος, *Somn.* 1.67) to God. (See the related term, also "incomprehensible" [ἀπερινόητος] in English at *Mut.* 15.) The Acts of John [D] (second century CE) follows suit in applying the descriptions "unutterable" (ἄφραστος; see Parallel Exegesis on *Mut.* 14) and "incomprehensible" (ἀκατάληπτος) to "the only God" (Acts John 79). Irenaeus (*Haer.* 1.2.1 [B/C]) relates a Valentinian tradition, in which the "first Father" is "incomprehensible" (ἀκατάληπτος) to all save his emanation, the primordial Mind. Runia (1988, 77) notes important developments of the philosophical details relative to divine incomprehensibility in Clement of Alexandria and Plotinus. See also Origen, *Hom. Exod.* 12.3 [C] (Van den Hoek 2000, 59). Later Christian authors of the Nicene and post-Nicene era, like Gregory of Nyssa, unfold the meaning of the description, speaking of "the incomprehensibility of the ⟨Divine⟩ essence" (τὸ ἀκατάληπτον τῆς οὐσίας [*Hom. opif.* 11] [B]). See especially Eusebius (*Praep. ev.* 3.6.6 [B])—the possessor of Philo's library and works—who speaks of God's "nature" (φύσις) as "unutterable and incomprehensible" (ἄρρητος ... καὶ ἀκατάληπτος) in completely Philonic terms.

§ 11. *The name "Lord" (Kyrios) cannot truly be applied.* One of Philo's more influential theological notions is the idea that God has no proper name, by which human beings might grasp his essence. This idea calls to mind the later Trinitarian debate between Gregory of Nyssa (and the Cappadocians) and Eunomius of Cyzicus, as to whether God the Father has an essence that can be known. Eunomius, using a "name reveals essence" paradigm, argues that the Father's essence is the Unbegotten (DelCogliano 2010). Gregory of Nyssa, by contrast, in passages such as *Hom. opif.* 11 [A/B], argues to the contrary that God has no name by which his essence can be known. For the question of Philonic influence on either Eunomius or Nyssen, see Cover 2022b.

my nature is to be, not to be spoken. In identifying God's "nature" (φύσις) and his Being, Philo stands as an indirect predecessor to Thomas Aquinas's more famous *respondeo* in ST 1a.3.3 [D]: "God is the same as his own essence or nature" ("Deus est idem quod sua essentia vel natura"). In his more inexact expression, Philo moves in the direction of a radical divine simplicity, in which God does not "have" being but "is" Being.

§ 12. *the God of the three natures.* In a very important passage in the *Contra Celsum*, Origen reveals his knowledge of Platonizing rewritings of the threefold divine name of Exod 3:14 and 6:3: "The God of the elect father of sound and the God of laughter and the God of him, who trips at the heels" (ὁ θεὸς πατρὸς ἐκλεκτοῦ τῆς ἠχοῦς καὶ ὁ θεὸς τοῦ γέλωτος καὶ ὁ θεὸς τοῦ πτερνιστοῦ, *Cels.* 5.45 [B]; Van den Hoek 2000, 51, ranks this passage [C]). This interpretation of the tri-fold name of God echoes Philo's etymologies of the name (*Mut.* 12) and the patriarchs (*Mut.* 66, 131, and 81, respectively). Origen agrees with Philo in rejecting the conventionalist view of names, which he attributes to Celsus; however, he also holds that calling God "the God of Abraham, Isaac, and Jacob" is more effective than calling him by an interpreted title, such as "the God of the three natures." In terms of his theory of names, Philo occupies a median position between Origen and Celsus, showing affinities with both.

§ 13. *loose approximation*. Runia (1988) notes that few later Christian commentators followed Philo in applying the term *catachrēsis* to the giving of divine names. He identifies two possible texts in which Philonic influence may be discerned: in Clement of Alexandria (*Strom.* 5.82.1 [B]; Van den Hoek 1988, 196, ranks this text a [C] with respect to *Legat.* 6) and in the anonymous (Ps.-Justin Martyr) *Cohortatio ad gentiles* 20–21 [B] by a contemporary of Origen. To these, we might add the more indirect statement by Origen (*Cels.* 5.4 [B]; unranked by Van den Hoek 2000) regarding the "discernment of proper naming and misuse [of language] with regard to prayer" (κατακούειν τῆς περὶ προσευχῆς κυριολεξίας καὶ καταχρήσεως), in a context that speaks of addressing God and the Word. Attridge (2017) suggests that this may have to do with the early Christian conviction that the Logos, at least, did have a proper name—Jesus (see Phil 2:10). For proper and catachrestic names with regard to human scriptural figures (such as Jethro/Raguel), see Didymus the Blind, *Comm. Ps.* 29–34, 184.15–23 [B].

§ 14. *ineffable*. Dillon (1996, 155) notes that Philo is the first in the history of philosophy to apply the description "unutterable" (ἄρρητος) to God. See also "unable to be named" (ἀκατονόμαστος) in *Somn.* 1.67. The adjective "unspeakable" (ἄφραστος) is given as a descriptor of "the only God" in the Acts John 79 [D]. Justin Martyr (*Dial.* 126.2 [C]), speaks of the "Son of the only and unbegotten and ineffable God" (τοῦ μόνου καὶ ἀγεννήτου καὶ ἀρρήτου θεοῦ υἱόν). Van den Hoek (1988, 194) notes the presence of "general Platonizing concepts" reminiscent of *Mut.* 14 (though their "dependence [is] not demonstrable") in Clement of Alexandria, *Strom.* 5.65.2 (Van den Hoek ranks [D]); as well as (more importantly) Clement's use of the adjective "ineffable" (ἄρρητος) to describe God in *Strom.* 5.78.3 [B]:

> And whenever Scripture says, "Moses entered into the darkness where God was" (Exod 20:21), this shows, to those who are able to understand, that God is invisible (ἀόρατος) and ineffable (ἄρρητος), while the doubt and ignorance of the majority is brought forth as real darkness (γνόφος δὲ ὡς ἀληθῶς) by the ray of truth.

Eusebius (*Praep. ev.* 3.6.6 [B]) speaks of the "unutterable and incomprehensible" nature of God in thoroughly Philonic terms. God's ineffability becomes especially important in the debate between the Cappadocians and Eunomius during the Trinitarian crisis of the fourth century CE (DelCogliano 2010; Cover 2022b), as to whether the essence of God can be known.

his ministering powers. Philo's theology of divine powers, while scriptural and partially adumbrating a multi-personal God (Hoeschel 1587), would cause problems for later rabbinic (Segal 1977) and Christian readers (Cover 2022b; 2024a). Barnes (2001) has traced how pro-Nicene theology identified the common essence of the three Trinitarian persons with their singular power.

§15. *even his Word.* That the Logos cannot be addressed by his proper name—that he is not "sayable" (ῥητός)—distinguishes Philo's Logos theology from the early Christian adaptation of a similar figure (cf. Phil 2:6–11).

§17. *although he was king from the beginning.* Philo's statement that the kingly power "was (ὤν) ⟨sc. king⟩ from the beginning" may be compared with Jesus's lacunose statement in John 18:5–6.

rule and governance over all that exists. Compare Philo's application of the title "beginning" (ἀρχή) in its Wisdom/cosmogonic sense to Col 1:18.

c   *Abram, God's Human Being (§§18–38)*
     Analysis/General Comments

After commenting on Gen 17:1a in §§1–2 and Gen 17:1b in §§3–17, Philo continues sequentially through the primary biblical lemma to interpret Gen 17:1cα, "I am your God," in §§18–38. By focusing on "Lord" (κύριος, God's kingly power) in §§3–17 and "God" (θεός, God's creative power) in §§18–38, Philo comments on both units of the divine title "the Lord God," before turning to the subject of human names in §§60–129. Having identified God's kingly power as the person revealed as "Lord" in Gen 17:1b (§17), Philo explains that the same transcendent One reveals himself as creative power, under the title, "God" (Gen 17:1c). This slippage of identities and speakers leads to a productive theological tension. At times, Philo identifies the divine speaker of Gen 17:1c as The One Who Is (§§22, 27), at other times, as the Logos speaking as creative power (§§18, 23). This tension is mirrored in the different ways Philo cites Gen 17:1. In §1, Philo uses the formula "the God of yours" (ὁ θεός σου), which usually indicates The One Who Is, due to the presence of the definite article. In §18, by contrast, Philo cites the verse as reading "your God" (θεὸς σός), which usually indicates the Logos or creative power. Philo understands both to be the speakers signified by the language of Scripture, even as they are differentiated at the philosophical level.

In his exegesis, Philo divides Gen 17:1cα into two major units, focusing first on the adjective "your" (§§18–26) and the second on the noun "God" (§§27–38).

(1) "I am *your* God" (ἐγώ εἰμι ὁ θεός σου / θεὸς σός). Philo first highlights the Logos's claim to be *Abraham's* God, as opposed to the God of all people. In doing so, he differentiates between two meanings of the title "God." In a first sense, "God" is the world Creator, the equivalent of the Platonic "Demiurge." The Logos is thus God of every human being and the entire

cosmos. But the phrase "your God" also signifies in a moral or tropological register. This is "God" as leader of the soul. In this sense, the title "God" is invoked with differing degrees of propriety by the wicked, by those making progress, and by perfect. God is "Lord" or "Despot" to the bad, like Pharaoh (§§ 19–22); he is "God" to the progressing, like Abraham and Jacob (§§ 23–24); and he is both "Lord and God" to the perfect—those like Moses (§ 24). To be "God's human being" as Abraham means to be advancing toward perfection, even if one has not attained it yet (§§ 18–26).

(2) "I am you *God*" (ἐγώ εἰμι ὁ θεός σου / θεὸς σός). Philo next attends to several problems related to the name "God." He begins by explaining that the title "God" (like the title "Lord" in the previous unit) does not properly refer to The One Who Is. This is because saying that "the transcendent God creates and blesses" applies to him predicates of "relation" (πρός τι [§ 27]). This could hypothetically jeopardize his unknowability and ineffability, and would open the door for divine passibility, as subjects in relation can be acted upon. Like contemporary and later Platonists, Philo is cautious not to apply predicates of relation to the supreme God. These belong, in his thought, only to God's powers. Even God's powers can be spoken of only "as if with respect to relation" (ὡσανεὶ πρός τι [§ 28]). This is perhaps Philo's most important philosophical phrase in the entire treatise. It captures his recognition that Moses in the Scriptures depicts God speaking and acting "as if" The One Who Is immediately engages with creation, even if properly and philosophically speaking such interactions are always carried out by intermediaries, who themselves retain some shadow of God's immutability ([2a] §§ 27–29).

Having established this cosmological point—that The One Who Is is Demiurge only in an improper sense—Philo next speaks of God's work in creation with an emphasis on moral education and progress. To have God as one's fashioner is not to be literally created, soul and body, by him; but to be morally perfected by his powers. So much are God's humans "created" by him that, through their moral efforts, they may be said to shed their bodies and become (insofar as this is possible) disembodied reasoners. It is as though they had been created without a body by the Demiurge alone, and not with the help of angelic assistants ([2b] §§ 30–38).

Philo's use of Scripture in (1) §§ 18–26 and (2) §§ 27–38 is far less elaborate than in the preceding part of the chapter. (1) §§ 18–26 are ornamented with three distinct *catenae* of secondary lemmata illustrating that God is "not God" to the bad, like Pharaoh (Exod 7:1, 17; 6:29; 9:29–30); that he is "God" to those making progress, like Abraham and Jacob (Gen 17:1; 35:11); and that he is "Lord and

God" to the perfect, like Moses (Exod 20:2; Deut 4:1; 33:1). These texts serve as scriptural proofs for Philo's argument, but they are not developed into longer discourses. (2) §§ 27–38 contain an even sparser set of secondary lemmata (Gen 2:7; 1:26; and 5:24), which amplify Philo's moral allegory of human creation and establish Enoch as a type of those who have been perfected as souls apart from their bodies.

Detailed Comments

(1) § 18. *the hearer and seer.* With this phrase, Philo supplies a pithy summation of God's twin modes of revelation to Abraham: speech and vision. The patriarch is both "hearer" (ἀκροατής) of the divine name (§§ 11–17) and "seer" (θεατής) of the Lord (§§ 18–38)—though not of the divine nature (§§ 3–10).

"I am your God." Philo's paraphrase of Gen 17:1cα in § 18, "I am your God" (ἐγώ εἰμι θεὸς σός) differs from the LXX and his initial citation of the verse in § 1, "I am the God of yours" (ἐγώ εἰμι ὁ θεός σου). The force of the definite article on the noun "God" is to specify The One Who Is. Philo's omission of the article in §§ 18, 23, and 27 suggests that the Logos or God's creative power is the more proper speaker of the revelatory statements to Abraham. The subject of the speech in Gen 17:1a in its entirety can only be unified in the person of the Logos, speaking first as kingly power, and second as creative power. Philo's Logos theology thus entails a kind of power-modalism.

I might say. Philo uses the first-person interjection, "I might say" (εἴποιμ' ἄν), twenty times in his extant Greek writings, being evenly distributed across the Allegorical Commentary and the Exposition of the Law. He employs the formula to introduce questions, to raise logical problems, or to otherwise respond to a biblical, real, or hypothetical speaker. Many of his questions in the Allegorical Commentary are posed to the words of Scripture themselves—as though to Moses, God, or some other character speaking in the Scriptures (*Opif.* 72; *Cher.* 75; *Det.* 4, 62; *Post.* 181; *Agr.* 149; *Ebr.* 84; *Conf.* 119; *Somn.* 1.183). Elsewhere, Philo makes a response to a real or imagined interlocutor (*Plant.* 71, 108; *Decal.* 88; *Spec.* 1.271, 278; 2.75, 96; 3.202; *Legat.* 195). The formula may reflect Philo's rhetoric in his private school. Justin Martyr uses the same formula to dispel Trypho's potentially problematic reading of Gen 18 (*Dial.* 57.2). Only in *Mut.* 18 does Philo allow himself to be explicitly corrected by another teacher or exegete—in this case, the Logos.

his Word-interpreter will teach me. Having posed a question to the scriptural words of Gen 17:1aγ ("I am your God") in the fashion of a diatribe, Philo introduces a respondent: the Logos, who comes as an "interpreter" (ὑποφήτης) and "will teach" (διδάξει) Philo how to understand the words of the Pentateuch. This personification of the Logos as teacher finds an echo in a later exegesis of the school of Rabbi Ishmael, in which the personified "Scripture" (הכתוב) "comes to teach" (בא ללמד) the rabbinic sage its own meaning (see Yadin 2004, 26; Mek. Pisḥa 11). This trope of self-interpreting Scripture may date back to Pharisaic exegesis, as witnessed in the letters of Paul (Cover 2016a). "Interpreter" (ὑποφήτης) is a rare word in Philo. In Homer, "interpreter" (ὑποφήτης) can designate the mundane-textual or oracular interpreter (*Il.* 16.235). The noun occurs three times in the *corpus Philonicum*. Only here and in *Somn.* 1.190 is it a descriptor of the Logos. In all three instances, the word refers to a class of mediators lower than The One Who Is (*Somn.* 1.190 sets the title "interpreter" in apposition to "attending angel" [ὀπαδὸς ἄγγελος]).

Craftsman. The divine Demiurge of Plato's *Timaeus* (29a3). Members of the Old Academy argued about the identity of the Demiurge. Speusippus identified him with a lower deity, ontologically inferior to the two first principles (the Monad and the Dyad). Xenocrates, conversely, associated the Demiurge with the Monad (Runia 1986, 42). Middle Platonists settled upon a schema in which, "The highest god is a transcendent νοῦς, reminiscent of Aristotle's Unmoved Mover. He creates only indirectly, by inciting a second god (i.e., the rational part of the cosmic soul) to action. Plato's Demiurge is thus split in two" (Runia 1986, 53). Philo adopts some version of this split-Demiurge theory throughout his writings. He sometimes identifies the Demiurge with the transcendent God: so *Leg.* 3.96, wherein God "fashioned the universe" (ἐκοσμοποίει) using the Logos as his "instrument" (ὄργανον). However, as Runia writes, "the description of God as Demiurge or maker is also implicitly qualified ... by the affirmation that God himself does not touch chaotic matter, but leaves that to his instrumental Logos" (Runia 1986, 423). In § 18, the case for identifying the "Demiurge" (δημιουργός) with The One Who Is would be stronger if Philo had cited the primary lemma in the same form that he does in § 1, "I am the God of you" (ἐγώ εἰμι ὁ θεός σου). His paraphrase, "your God" (θεὸς σός), in § 18, which removes the definite article, suggests instead that the Logos speaks here of his own role in creation as Demiurge. Similarly, in §§ 27–30, "The One Who Is" extends his powers in creation, but the title "Demiurge" is reserved "properly" for God's creative power.

§ 19. *The wicked.* Philo speaks of "the wicked" (φαῦλοι) as a group. Long and Sedley note that "this was the favored term ⟨of the Stoics⟩ for the for the immoral majority ... which means inferior or ordinary rather than vicious or wicked" (L&S 1:427). Given Philo's scriptural example of this class (Pharaoh), he seems to mean the term in a more negative sense here.

"Master." The double title "Master Lord" (δέσποτα κύριε) is a common Septuagintal rendering of the Hebrew "Lord God" (אדוני אלוהים). It occurs only twice in the Pentateuch (Gen 15:2, 8), but more frequently in prophetic and wisdom

literature. In the Platonic tradition, "master" (δεσπότης) has positive, negative, and neutral connotations. In the *Leges*, it can be paired with tyrannical rule rather than the rule of an affectionate parent (*Leg.* 589a). In the *Phaedrus*, by contrast, it is metaphorically applied in a positive way to a god (265c2). Philo has drawn on both traditions, and the title points in the first place to God's kingly (political) power. Philo also draws on the punitive connotations of the appellation, characterizing "Lord" (κύριος) as one with a capacity for divine coercion required to govern the "wicked."

both "Lord" and "God" together. Arnaldez (1964, 40, n. 3) sees a mystical progression in this threefold arrangement of types and titles. He argues that only the Lord (i.e., the legislative power) is visible to Abraham soul in perfection; the Logos (or creative power), is a step further removed. It is "heard" rather than "seen" and must be invoked through the name "God" (the creative power). Arnaldez continues: "In his ruling power, the Being One is most visible, and in it access to the beneficence of the Creator is revealed." This interpretation works best in the current context, but is perhaps overly schematized for the entire *corpus Philonicum*. While the powers are in some passages closer to humanity than the Logos, as Philo says in §§ 14–15, *both* divine powers, as well as the Logos, are in a certain sense ineffable. Moreover, there is no reason why God should not be equally visible in his creative power and his kingly power, for those with eyes to attend to creation (i.e., astronomy). Philo's point is more pedagogical than theological: the bad ignore God's "visibility" in his creative power, and *to them* the "Lord" is more apparent in his chastisements.

"behold, I give you as a god to Pharaoh." Philo's first secondary lemma in this *catena* is Exod 7:1. Whereas the Septuagint reads, "Behold, I *have* given you as a God to Pharaoh" (ἰδοὺ δέδωκά σε θεὸν Φαραώ), Philo's citation in § 19 (also *Sacr.* 9; *Det.* 161) renders the verb in the present tense: "Behold, I *give* you as a God to Pharaoh" (ἰδοὺ δίδωμί σε θεὸν Φαραώ). This change brings the allegorical significance of the statement into the present and renders its aspect ongoing rather than completed. In § 19, Philo's point centers on divine rhetoric: God chooses not to be named "god" to the wicked—that is, as Creator and Benefactor—but to emphasize instead his title "Lord." Recognizing God's regal and judicial power is the first stage in the divine pedagogy.

§ 20. *the Lord says these things*. Philo adduces the second (Exod 7:17 *et passim*) in a string of secondary lemmata, demonstrating how God exclusively uses the title "Lord" (κύριος) when speaking to Pharaoh. The formulaic phrase, "the Lord says these things" (τάδε λέγει κύριος), is found throughout Moses's confrontation with the Egyptian king (Exod 7:16, 17, 26; 8:16, 20; 9:1, 13; 10:3; 11:4). Philo's claim that God never refers to himself by the title "God" in these *formulae* is not quite accurate; in half of the foregoing cases (those with an asterisk), the introductory formula is actually, "The Lord God of the Hebrews says these things" (τάδε λέγει κύριος ὁ θεὸς τῶν Ἑβραίων). Upon closer inspection, this modified formula bears out Philo's point: God is "God" of the Hebrews—not of the Egyptians—just as he is the "God" of Abraham in an exclusive way.

in the beginning. Colson (PLCL) rightly translates "in the beginning" (ἐν ἀρχῇ) as signifying "at the beginning of his speech," presumably taking a cue from Wendland's note in the PCW apparatus, "ἐν ἀρχῇ, sc. orationis dei]," rather than "in the beginning" in a more absolute sense (*pace* Mangey, who conjectured that a citation of Prov 8:22 had been lost from the text).

"I am the Lord." Philo adduces Exod 6:29 as a third secondary lemma, to demonstrate that God consistently speaks only in the name of the "Lord" to Pharaoh from the beginning of his instructions to Moses.

§ 21. *"the earth ... belongs to the Lord ... in no way have you feared."* Philo ends the catena of secondary lemmata with an extended exegesis of Exod 9:29–30. Unlike his treatment of other texts in this subgroup, here he offers an allegorical interpretation of four discrete, sequential phrases from the lemma in a way that resembles the continuous pesharim found at Qumran. He inserts interpretive glosses inside the lemma itself, developing four different phrases.

The first phrase that Philo glosses is (1) "the earth" (Exod 9:29). He interprets this as bodily and earthly substances (heaven is not included), because Pharaoh is symbolically concerned primarily with the body and its goods. Philo turns next to two related phrases: (2) "as well as you;" (3) "and your servants" (Exod 9:30a). Unlike the Septuagintal text (which, like the NETS, is ambiguous), Philo interprets these nouns as appositives glossing the word "earth" (γῆ) in Exod 9:29, rather than as subjects of the verb "you have feared" (πεφόβησθε) of Exod 9:30c. This allows him to fill out the anthropological allegory. It is not just the earth (i.e., the body) which is the Lord's, but also "you" (i.e., the "mind") and "your servants" (i.e., the mind's "thoughts" [λογισμοί]). The whole of the human person, body and soul, is thus claimed by the Lord as his possession. Last, Philo interprets the phrase (4) "you failed to fear the Lord" as indicating that the Pharaoh soul rebels against God's kingly power, to whom all human beings owe allegiance.

the portrait-bearing mind. The verb "to bear a portrait" (ἀγαλματοφορέω) is a Philonic neologism, which Runia (2001, 141) calls "perhaps the most remarkable of all the so-called the *verba Philonica*." The ninth century CE lexicographer Photius defines the participle with reference to the Alexandrian: "Portrait-bearing: bearing portraits or imprints of things that have been thought within oneself; so Philo used ⟨the word⟩" (ἀγαλματοφορούμενος: ἀγάλματα ἤ⟨τοι⟩ τύπους τῶν νοηθέντων φέρων ἐν ἑαυτῷ. οὕτω Φίλων ἐχρήσατο). This definition and attribution date back to the second century CE figure, Eudemus Rhetoricus (περὶ λέξεων ῥητορικῶν, fol. 2b, line 1). The metaphor of moving statues, animated by causal forms, occurs in Plato, *Tim.* 37c7. There, the Craftsman views the composite cosmos as bearing an "image/portrait/type" (ἄγαλμα) of the invisible gods. Cf. *Symp.* 215b, in which Socrates is said to carry "divine statues/images" (ἀγάλματα ... θεῶν; Runia [2001, 141]) inside himself. Philo develops this Platonic metaphor on both the cosmic and microcosmic scales. As regards the human microcosm, Philo suggests that *the human mind* is the "image of the image" (*Opif.* 25) and carries a "portrait" (ἄγαλμα) of the Logos in its double aspect, both as rational subject and as passive ideas (*Opif.* 69, 82; *Somn.* 1.208). In *Mut.* 21, Philo further clarifies that *the human body* is sculpted by God with an awareness that it will enshrine this image of the image (*Opif.* 137; *Somn.* 1.32; *Mos.* 1.27). The ideas in the divine Mind, the Logos within the human mind, and the human mind within the human body are all described by Philo as "being born about as statues/images in a shrine" (ἀγαλματοφορούμενος/-α).

In the Allegorical Commentary, Philo places primary emphasis on the microcosmic dimensions of the divine statue imagery. In *Mut.* 21, Pharaoh, symbolizing the mind obsessed with bodily things, is reminded that the body is in fact the house of the soul. The body ("the earth") exists to assist the mind in its pursuit of virtue, rather than the mind existing to animate the body for pleasure.

the particular thoughts that attend you. Philo uses the compound "attending" or "spear-bearing" (δορυφοροῦντες) and its cognate "attendant" (δορυφόρος) ca. 47 times throughout his writings. The metaphor of armed guardians is a hallmark of Philo's anthropology and theology. He uses the word to describe, *inter alia*, the female entourage of personified Virtue (*Opif.* 139; *Sacr.* 28; *Migr.* 37) or Vice (*Deus* 113); the guiding role of sense perception vis-à-vis the mind (*Leg.* 1.59; *Conf.* 19); and the protective and mediatorial functions of God's two primary powers vis-à-vis The One Who Is (*Sacr.* 59; *Deus* 109). In *Mut.* 21, "particular thoughts" (κατὰ μέρος ... λογισμοί) are described as "attendants" of the Pharaoh mind (cf. *Migr.* 37 for "attendants" as particulars). These bodyguards defend Pharaoh in his recalcitrance and hardening against the Logos.

he who is really Master. "The one who is really Master" (ὁ ὄντως ὢν δεσπότης) refers in context to the kingly power rather than to "The One Who Truly Is" (ὁ ὄντως ὤν). The wording, nevertheless, suggests a very close ontological connection between The One Who Is and his powers.

§ 22. **only the Ungenerated is truly a ruler.** Philo apparently speaks of God's kingly power as "ungenerated" (ἀγένητος). The epithet is more commonly a title for The One Who Is, as Philo elsewhere in the Allegorical Commentary speaks of the Logos as "generated" (γενητός) or at the borderland of generation (*Leg.* 3.175; Cover 2014). Philo's primary point in *Mut.* 22 is to emphasize that God alone, rather than human beings, can rule and thereby bear the title "ruler" (ἡγεμών) "truly" or "without falsehood" (ἀψευδῶς).

§ 23. *"I am your God."* Philo now adduces two biblical lemmata as proofs that the soul making progress (or per § 23, "becoming better") is governed not by the "Lord" in the Pharaonic sense, but by "God." Just as the Divine speaks to Pharaoh almost exclusively as "Lord," so he speaks to Israel and the other patriarchs distinctively as "your God." Philo first reintroduces Gen 17:1cα, the primary biblical lemma for this section, using the form without a definite article, "your God" (θεὸς σός), to indicate that just as the "Lord" (the kingly power) rules the Pharaoh soul, so "God" (the beneficent power) oversees the spiritual progress undertaken by the Abraham soul.

"I am your God, increase and multiply." Philo next adduces Gen 35:11 as a secondary lemma. The text of Philo's quotation, "I am your God, increase and multiply" (ἐγὼ θεός σου, αὐξάνου καὶ πληθύνου), is identical to the Septuagint, with the exception that Philo again omits the definite article (cf. LXX: ἐγὼ ὁ θεός σου, αὐξάνου καὶ πληθύνου). Philo brings his citation of Gen 35:11 into conformity with his paraphrase of Gen 17:1cα and the allegorical significance he attributes to these titles.

By supplementing the Abrahamic story (Gen 17:1) with a parallel from the Jacob cycle (Gen 35:11), Philo discovers a link between the first and third members of this pedagogical triad. Abraham, the soul that progresses through teaching, and Jacob, the soul that progresses through practice, are similar in both having God as "your God." The passages, from which the two shorter lemmata are taken, show a series of narrative, thematic, and formulaic connections, which may partially account for Philo's foregrounding of Gen 35:11 at this early point of the commentary. In both (P) texts, God "was seen" (ὤφθη: Gen 17:1aβ; 35:9) by the patriarch; in both texts, God declares that he is "your God" (ὁ θεός σου: Gen 17:1cα; 35:11); and critically, in both texts, God draws the patriarch toward perfection by changing his name, using nearly identical formulae (Gen 17:5 ["And your name will not still be called Abram, but your name will be Abraham"]; Gen 35:10 ["⟨your name⟩ will not still be called Jacob, but your name will be Israel"]). This is the only time in *De mutatione nominum* that Philo interprets Gen 35:9–11. For Jacob's change of name to Israel, Philo will favor the JE parallel in Gen 32—a secondary lemma that is adduced in four different chapters and plays an architectonic role in the treatise (see the detailed comments on § 187).

the Ten Words. A biblical phrase (Exod 34:28) referring to the Decalogue. Turning from those who are making improvements to "the perfect" (§ 23), Philo shifts his scriptural focus from Abraham and Jacob to Moses and God's giving and reciting of the Law.

"I am the Lord your God." Philo adduces two secondary lemmata to prove that perfect souls know the Divine under the double title, "Lord and God." Both of these texts are drawn from the Moses cycle. Philo first adduces Exod 20:2—God's word to Moses (and all Israel) at the head of the Decalogue. In addition to revealing his twin appellation, in this and the subsequent citation God names himself with the definite article "the God of yours" (ὁ θεός σου; cf. "your God" [θεὸς σός] to those making progress). This indicates the even closer proximity to God experienced by the perfect.

"The Lord God of your fathers." Philo next adduces Deut 4:1, "the Lord God of your fathers." Although it occurs in a Mosaic text, the title "Lord God" is applied to a larger group than just the Moses soul. "Your fathers" include souls represented by Noah, Abraham, Jacob/Israel, and potentially even Adam. Philo views his patriarchal soul-types as dynamic symbols. Abraham and Jacob can be included among those making progress as well as the perfect, depending on the life-stage from which they are viewed. For Philo, Abraham's perfection arrives in his one-hundredth year with the birth of Isaac (§§1–2). It is noteworthy that the title "Lord God" is missing from the Abraham cycle until Gen 24:3, after Isaac is born, bound, and released.

§ 24. **wicked ... making progress ... perfect**. Philo reiterates his threefold typology of psychic progress (see § 19).

given benefits. The progressing and the perfected souls are both said to be "given benefits" (εὐεργετεῖσθαι) by God. This verb anticipates the discussion of God's "beneficent power" (ἡ εὐεργετικὴ δύναμις) in § 28. For Philo, the two principal powers are the creative and the kingly. Closely related to them are the beneficent and the merciful powers (extending from the creative power) and the punitive and legislative (extending from the kingly). For this sixfold schema, see the Greek fragment of *QE* 2.68 (Goodenough 1935, 24–25). While "bad" human souls in *Mut.* 24 are chastised by the "Lord," vis-à-vis the punitive aspect of his kingly power, the "progressing" are given benefits by "God," i.e., the creative power in his role as benefactor.

the perfect person ... ought ... to be governed. Arnaldez (1964, 42, n. 1) observes: "The perfect human being does not exhaust the Law; however, it less inspires fear in him than it witnesses to the love of God. ⟨This is⟩ an important mystical notion."

entirely unturned. God's kingly power establishes the perfect man as morally "unturned" (ἄτρεπτος), i.e., entirely unable to be changed for the worse. Readers familiar with Platonist allegories of the Homeric poems will hear an echo and improvement of the Odysseus soul, which begins its journey with the epithet "turned in many directions" (πολύτροπος [*Od.* 1.1]). In *De mutatione nominum*, the adjective "unturned" only refers to a human being in § 24. It is used to describe God at §§ 28, 54, 175, and esp. 87, in which God, the unchangeable and unmoved, gives an image of this quality to Abraham. In being made "entirely unturned," the perfect soul comes to resemble (with all creaturely qualifications) the kingly power, and even The One Who Is, who is likewise described as "unturned" (ἄτρεπτος [§ 28]).

God's human being. Whereas the kingly power gives the perfect person unshakeable virtue, the creative power makes him or her a new kind of human being. For Arnaldez, becoming "l'homme de Dieu," complemented by a theology of grace and adoption, is one of the principal themes of the work, a scarlet thread that runs throughout the treatise (1964, 12–14, 23–25). "The opposition 'human being—God's human being' has an unusually large significance: Philo's thought hangs upon it" (1964, 44, n. 2).

§ 25. *most clear in the case of Moses.* Although other figures are referred to as "God's human being" in the Septuagint, Moses is the only figure in the Pentateuch so named (Deut 33:1). Elsewhere, it may refer to a prophet or angel (e.g., Judg 13:8; 3 Kgdms 13:1). The Abraham soul is in the process of becoming such a human being, but has not attained this status.

this is the blessing, which Moses, God's human being, gave. Philo adduces Deut 33:1 as a secondary lemma to demonstrate that only the perfect soul may be called "God's human being." The text is nearly identical to the LXX, with the curious omission of the definite pronoun "the" (τοῦ) in the key phrase "God's human being" (ἄνθρωπος τοῦ θεοῦ). This change links the title more closely with the creative power, whom Philo understands Moses to refer to when "God" is anarthrous. Philo's secondary lemma comes from the introduction to Mosaic *Benedictions* (Deut 33; cf. *Det.* 67), one of the named subunits of Deuteronomy. On these divisions, see the detailed comment on § 42.

O man. The first of five Philonic ὤ-asides in the present treatise—a special subclass of sayings within the *corpus Philonicum*, which Terian (1995) argues stem from the Alexandrian himself. Some are autoreferential. In others, Philo speaks to an ideal reader or hearer. Other ὤ-asides in the present treatise appear in §§ 177, 187, 255, 264. In § 25, Philo addresses the Moses soul, God's human being.

entirely good and God-befitting gift-exchange. Philo uses the word "gift-exchange" (ἀντίδοσις) to describe Moses's interchange with God. In return for God's providential care, Moses gives his very self. This noun and the cognate verb, used only here in this treatise, provide a convenient place to introduce Philo's theology of grace. At first glance, the word "gift-exchange" (ἀντίδοσις), with its implication of reciprocal gift-giving, appears to entail a theology self-sufficiency and self-improvement. Moses's self-sacrifice wins him God's providential care. Philo's note of Moses's "worth" (ἀξιωθείς) might seem to corroborate this reading. Nothing, however, could be further from Philo's mind. Philo's theology is pervaded by the doctrine of grace (McFarland 2016; Barclay 2015). Consider, for example, *Cher.* 123, in which Philo describes the social ramifications of a gift in antiquity and suggests that all human givers are really "sellers":

> But God is no salesman (πωλητήρ), hawking his goods in the market, but a free giver (δωρητικός) of all things, pouring forth eternal fountains of graces (ἀενάους χαρίτων πηγὰς ἀναχέων), and seeking nothing in return. For he has no needs himself and no created being is sufficient to repay his gift (οὔτε τις τῶν γεγονότων ἱκανὸς ἀντιδοῦναι δωρεάν). (*Cher.* 123, trans. PLCL, adapted)

Philo can adopt the language of human gift-exchange with God without relinquishing his commitment to the priority of divine grace and the total disproportionality between the gift of the Giver and the "counter-gift" of the beneficiary. Divine providence, syntactically and theologically, proceeds and grounds the human gift of self: "in return for God's providential care, he gives himself" (θείας προνοίας ἀντιδοῦναι ἑαυτόν [§ 25]). For more on Philo's theology of grace and human worth and nothingness, set within the diverse landscape of Jewish theologies of grace in the Second Temple period and the New Testament, especially Paul, see Arnaldez 1964, 44, n. 1; Barclay 2015, 4, 212–238; Lévy 2018; and Cover 2018b, 2020b.

§ 26. *but do not think that one becomes a human being.* Philo contrasts the ordinary human being with "God's human being," responding to the *quaestio* in § 18 and continuing the conversation about the highest type of soul represented by Moses in § 25.

boast and benefit. The Greek merism, "boast and benefit" (αὔχημα καὶ ὠφέλημα), expresses the human soul's perfection in virtue and ontology. The first and last letters of the Greek alphabet, alpha and omega, appearing at the beginning of the two words, symbolize comprehensiveness. Philo appears to suggest that God might boast and receive some kind of benefit from the perfect. So foreign is such an idea to the Alexandrian's thought, however, that Colson (PLCL 5:156–157) has emended the structure of the sentence to say that "a human being belongs to God as his possession, ⟨whereas⟩ God belongs to a human being to be his glory and assistance." While this is possible, Colson's emendation misses the exegetical developments that Philo has been making in § 25. Moreover, in § 27, Philo will go on to address the very problem that Colson's emendation erases: how one might accidentally suspect that "God's human being" contributes something to the divine essence. The One Who Is "is full in-and-of himself and is sufficient for himself ... needing nothing else whatsoever, with the result that all things belong to and stem from him." Understanding "benefit" (ὠφέλημα) as a purely honorific title, Arnaldez (1964, 45, n. 2) suggests comparing SVF 3.23, 136.

handmade ... laws. "Handmade" (χειροποίητος) is a curious adjective with which to describe laws; it more often applied to physical structures (see *Opif.* 142). *Somn.* 2.125 supplies an antonym: θεήλατος ("God-caused" or "God-driven"). Philo uses "handmade" in *Mut.* 26 to distinguish the laws of Sinai, written with the finger of God (see Exod 31:18), from the laws carved by the human hand and devised by the human will, such as are followed by Pharaoh. The inferiority of the "hand-made" as opposed to the God-made is a standard trope in Second Temple Jewish rhetoric. See, e.g., *Opif.* 142, which compares the cosmic house/city (positively) to human hand-made copies.

(2) § 27. *inexactly, not properly.* Just as "Lord" is not a "proper name" (κύριον ὄνομα) of The One Who Is (§§ 11, 15), neither for Philo is "God." It, too, is a catachrestic appellation. For the term "by misuse of language" (καταχρηστικῶς), see the detailed comments on §§ 12–13.

The One Who Is ... does not have predicates of relation. "Relation" or πρός τι is one of the ten kinds of predication in Aristotle's *Categoriae*. It is the fourth category of the series after (1) "substance" (οὐσία); (2) "quantity" (ποσός); and (3) "quality" (ποιός); it is followed by (5) "place" (ποῦ); (6) "time" (ποτέ); (7) "position" (κεῖσθαι); (8) "state" (ἔχειν); (9) "activity" (ποιεῖν); and (10) "passivity" (πάσχειν). See Aristotle, *Cat.* 4. While "The One Who Is" (τὸ ὄν) may be "Being" (οὐσία) for Philo, this is only predicated inexactly. Philo further denies that any of the other nine categories can properly be used of him. To have relation requires that a substance be open to activity and passivity vis-à-vis other substances. This would compromise divine transcendence. Thus, while Philo might identify The One Who Is with the One (i.e., "quantity" [ποσός]) and "the Good" (i.e., "quality" [ποιός]) of Plato's *Republic*, he will also, on several occasions in the Exposition of the Law and in his apologetic works, prefer more apophatic statements that describe The One Who Is as "better than the Good and older than the Monad and more simple than the One" (ὃ καὶ ἀγαθοῦ κρεῖττον καὶ μονάδος πρεσβύτερον καὶ ἑνὸς εἰλικρινέστερον). See *Praem.* 40; *Contempl.* 2. For God as "without quality" (ἄποιος) in Philo, see Wolfson 1948, 2:101–110. As quantity and quality are not properly predicated of The One Who Is, all the more improper are predicates of relation.

§ 28. *unturned and unchanged.* Philo's description of divine immovability, particularly the adjective "unchanged" (ἀμετάβλητον), echoes Aristotle (see *Cael.* 279a: "the foremost and highest divinity must be entirely immutable" [τὸ θεῖον ἀμετάβλητον ἀναγκαῖον εἶναι πᾶν τὸ πρῶτον καὶ ἀκρότατον])—another example of the way Alexandrian Middle Platonism drew upon Peripatetic tradition.

as if with respect to relation. Wolfson's comments on the quasi-transcendence of divine powers, indicated in the remarkable phrase "as if with respect to relation" (ὡσανεὶ πρός τι), are worth quoting at length:

> Philo maintains that all those properties which indicate action, while they establish a relation, the relation [*sic*] is not to be understood to be a reciprocal relation: the suffering action by the patient indeed depends upon the agent, but the activity of the agent does not depend upon the patient. In the strictly logical sense, therefore, such a non-reciprocal relation is not a true relation; Philo consequently describes it as a *quasi*-relation (ὡσανεὶ πρός τι). It is called a relation only because in ordinary speech the activity of an agent upon a patient, analogous to that of God, who is the "Father" (πατήρ), "Maker" (ποιητής), and "Artificer" (δημιουγός) … upon the world, is called a relation and such a relation is reciprocal in the same was as "a king is king of someone and a benefactor is the benefactor of someone." In reality, however, the activity of God is not dependent upon anything outside of God. Like the essence of God, it is self-sufficient; it is an activity which is absolute and in the real sense not relative. (Wolfson 1948, 2:138)

In light of such concerns, it would have been easy enough to simply divert all locutions about God and creation to the Logos and his powers, but this would sever all link between The One Who Is and his powers/creation—a move later made by Numenius (see Dillon 1996, 369) and various Gnostic authors. Philo instead accepts more inexact expressions, defending the language of Scripture and the real, causal link between the ineffable God and the actions of his Word and powers in creating the universe. See the further notes on this topic by Colson (PLCL 5:587) and Arnaldez (1964, 46, n. 1).

kingly and beneficent powers. The two powers corresponding to the work of the "Lord" and "God" (see the comments on § 24). Both powers imply some kind of relation with the created order (as also, e.g., the "merciful" power in QE 2.68, which cannot exist without someone to pardon).

§ 29. ***creative power.*** The creative power can be said to be in "relation," insofar as God is Creator in relation to creation. It is described as "kindred" (συγγενής) to the kingly and merciful. Philo uses a schema similar to that found in QE 2.68, where the creative and merciful powers form one pair and the kingly and lawgiving-punitive form a second pair, identified with the twin titles "God" and "Lord," respectively. Arnaldez (1964, 46, n. 2) interprets Philo's comments on the creative power (*Mut.* 29) only after his discussion of the kingly and beneficent powers (*Mut.* 28), as supporting his own view that the creative power is higher up the ontological/mystical chain than the kingly power. See the detailed comments on § 19.

begetting and fashioning Father. I.e., The One Who Is, who creates "through" (διά) the instrumentality of the creative power. See Sterling 1997.

set the universe in place. Although anarthrous, "God" (θεός) most likely refers to the foregoing "Father" and transcendent One. The creative power cannot be the subject of the verb. As Colson notes (PLCL 5:158, n. a), Philo quietly etymologizes *theos* (θεός, God) here as stemming from the Greek verb *tithēmi* (τίθημι, to set)—a tradition found in Herodotus (*Hist.* 2.52) but not the *Crat.* 397d, where Plato gives the "running" (θεῖν) of the celestial bodies as his primary etymology. See Yli-Karjanmaa (2015, 110, n. 334). For Philo's Greek etymologies, see Runia 2004, 116–118; and Grabbe 1988, 237–238.

Creator and Craftsman. These two titles are construed as equivalents of "God" (θεός), the one who "sets" things in order. Given as a gloss of "I am your God," the titles are applied to the Logos/creative power in its demiurgic rather than its instrumental capacity. Cf. Philo's usage elsewhere (*Leg.* 1.77; 2.3), where "Father" and "Craftsman" are used of the transcendent "God" (ὁ θεός), not of his Logos "instrument" (ὄργανον). The instrumentality ("*through* this power" [διὰ ταύτης τῆς δυνάμεως]) and agency ("Creator and Craftsman" [ποιητὴς καὶ δημιουργός]) of God's creative power are both foregrounded in this passage. For the "split-Demiurge" in Philo, see the comment on "Craftsman" above in § 18.

§ 30. ***a very great gift.*** To become "God's human being" is a work of grace, not human self-sufficiency. See the detailed comment on "gift-exchange" in § 25.

one's own architect. Whereas §§ 27–29 offered a cosmological interpretation of the word "God" in LXX Gen 17:1cα, in §§ 30–38 Philo returns to the adjective "your" and further develops the moral aspect of his allegory. Key themes of §§ 18–26 (particularly §§ 24–26 on Moses as "God's human being") are resumed in § 30, now with a special focus on God as "Creator." The noun "architect" (ἀρχιτέκτων) refers to a master builder, bearing an antithetical relationship to the uncompounded "sculptor" (τέκτων). See the comment on "he did not mold" below. The highest God is *not* the molder of the lower-souled human being, but the architect of the spiritual human being. Philo alludes to traditional Jewish "physical" interpretations of Gen 1:26 and 2:7, which interpret the double creation as offering a Platonic anthropology (see *Opif.* 75, 134–135). To this natural allegory, he adds his own distinctive "moral" twist, distinguishing between merely molded and the inbreathed psychic types. As in *Leg.* 1.31–42, so in *Mut.* 30–38, Philo narrates his anthropology "both naturally and ethically" (καὶ φυσικῶς καὶ ἠθικῶς [*Leg.* 1.39]), with an emphasis on the ethical meaning of God's role as Creator. For more on the complexity of such protological allegorical traditions, see Tobin 1983.

he did not mold. Philo's use of the word "he molded" (διέπλασεν) echoes Gen 2:7 (ἔπλασεν), suggesting that the subsequent anthropology has the differentiation between the "molded" mind (Gen 2:7a) and the "inbreathed-spiritual" mind (Gen 2:7bc) in view (cf. Sterling 1995, 362–365). By negating the verb for molding, Philo argues that the defects of human minds are not attributable to God, but derive from his assistants in creation. In developing this anthropological model, Philo draws on the cosmogonic myth of Plato's *Timaeus* (41b–42d), in which a chief God and Demiurge creates human beings with the assistance of "lower gods"—in Philo's case, lower powers or angels (cf. the plural "us" of Gen 1:26–27). This solves, for both Plato and Philo, the so-called "ontological problem of evil." Nowhere in the *Timaeus*, however, is it ever implied that there is an entire race of human beings, in whose creation the Demiurge had no part. Philo is speaking primarily at the level of moral allegory rather than physical anthropology (although the latter is not excluded). God had no part in the process by which a soul becomes wicked. He is in no way their "Creator" in a moral sense, even if he does remain, in the literal sense, the Creator of the "immortal part" of all souls (cf. Plato, *Tim.* 41cd).

vice is hateful to God. The moral register of Philo's allegory is strengthened by his use of "vice" (κακία) rather than "evil" (κακόν) here. Cf. *Opif.* 75 where the cosmological is the primary concern and the moral problems play a subsidiary role: "It was necessary for the Father to be blameless for the evil in his offspring; now, vice and its activities are what is meant by evil" (ἔδει γὰρ ἀναίτιον εἶναι κακοῦ τὸν πατέρα τοῖς ἐκγόνοις· κακὸν δ' ἡ κακία καὶ αἱ κατὰ κακίαν ἐνέργειαι).

middle kind of soul. I.e., "the advancing kind." See the detailed comments on §§ 2 and 24 ("the advancing mind"). Arnaldez (1964, 43, n. 3) points to the "middle practical wisdom" (*Opif.* 154), "the middle education" and "middle moral life" in *Mut.* 227–228, 255, as related concepts.

nor ... molded through his instrumentality alone. I.e., through his own creative power. He had the help of "fellow workers" (συνεργοί, *Opif.* 75) and "subordinates" (ὑπηκοοί, Ibid.).

wax. The likening of the soul to a tablet made of "wax" (κηρός) is a famous Platonic image (see *Theaet.* 194c5, 8). Plato's Socrates traces the idea back to Homer, who imperfectly understood that "heart" (κέαρ / κῆρ) etymologically entailed a description of the soul as receiving wax-like impressions. See §§ 211–212 (and the related detailed comments) for Philo's further development of this psychological image.

the distinction of good and evil. The phrase "distinction of beautiful and shameful" (καλοῦ τε καὶ αἰσχροῦ διαφορά) alludes to Adam and Eve's acquisition of elicit knowledge of "good and evil" (καλὸν καὶ πονηρόν) in Gen 2:17, 3:22. The noun "distinction" (διαφορά) in context means something like "a portion," but also implies the capacity to distinguish between good and evil in one's discursive reasoning. Cf. the good and bad inclinations in rabbinic literature, which have precursors in the anthropology of several Qumran documents, including the "bad inclination" (יצר רע) in 1 QS 3.13–14 and beyond (see Tigchelaar 2008 for more examples), with a focus on the Hebrew verb for divine "molding."

§ 31. **"*let us make a human being according to our own image.*"** To further explicate his moral allegory of Gen 2:7, Philo adduces Gen 1:26 as a secondary lemma. His text is identical to the LXX, but as often omits the second prepositional phrase "and according to the likeness" (καὶ καθ' ὁμοίωσιν [cf. *Conf.* 169]). He does this, in part, because the Logos is metaphysically associated with the divine "image," and in part, because "likeness to god" (cf. *Theaet.* 176b1: ὁμοίωσις θεῷ) is reserved by Philo for the perfect (see *QG* 2.62). Here, by contrast, the progressing soul is in view. Those created according to the image alone (Gen 1:26aα), but not the likeness, are identified with those created with soul (Gen 2:7b) but not yet perfected in the spirit.

the craftsmanship of others. A remarkable Platonizing phrase, which would strike Philo's later Christian recipients as heretical, "silly," or "rash" (see *Nachleben*). The first person plural, "let us make," in Gen 1:26 suggests to Philo that God collaborates with lower helpers to "make," i.e., to assist a soul. Human moral successes are attributable to God, moral failures to "the craftsmanship of others." Philo's God adopts a strategy similar to Plato's Demiurge in *Tim.* 42d: he employs coworkers "so that he may be without blame for the vice of each of his creatures" (ἵνα τῆς ἔπειτα εἴη κακίας ἑκάστων ἀναίτιος). Philo's use of the verb "seem" (φαίνηται) rather than Plato's "be" (εἴη) suggests that he realizes the insufficiency of Plato's solution. Unlike the Athenian, who may draw upon a polytheistic mythology to totally exonerate the creative powers of the Demiurge, Philo's monotheism puts him in a stricter bind. (For Philo's debt to *Tim.* 41b–42d, see the detailed comments on § 30.)

Israelite tradition identifies these "others" with the divine council of Gen 1:26 and Gen 3:22. As monotheism rather than henotheism became the norm in Israel, Second Temple Jewish authors reinterpreted these figures as angels. Elsewhere in Philo's allegory, members of this "we" include God's own powers (see *Cher.* 27). Can The One Who Is be thus exonerated because of the insufficient work of his own creative Logos or powers? Or does Philo advert, instead, to God's partnership with created beings of some kind? It is worth stressing that Philo's emphasis here is on the moral rather than the cosmological allegory. For

Philo's relative lack of concern about the ontology of angels, see Dillon, "Philo's Doctrine of Angels," in Dillon and Winston 1983, 197–205.

that human being is entirely good, to whom he says, "I am your God." Philo reintroduces the primary lemma, Gen 17:1cα, as an example of the third type of soul that is entirely good. This stands in tension with his use of this citation in § 23, where the Abrahamic soul was an image of progress. The inconsistency may result from Philo's use of exegetical sources or from his desire to depict the Abrahamic soul both in its progressive and perfective dimensions.

§ 32. **at the same time.** The precise referent implied by the adverb "at the same time" (ἅμα) is unclear. It might mean "in addition to the immediately preceding lesson" about other craftsmen just mentioned. Alternatively, Colson (PLCL 5:158, n. c) finds a reference to other "lessons" in §§ 18 and 28.

God is the Craftsman of the good and the wise alone. Contrast the statement about "the craftsmanship of others" in § 31 (see the detailed comments).

this whole company. Philo refers to groups of Jewish sages with the term "thiasus" or "company" (θίασος). The term is derived from Greek religion, most famously from the cult of Dionysus, and reflects an earlier *interpretatio Graeca atque Romana* of Judaism. The analogy between Jewish religion and Dionysiac cult probably originated as a pagan characterization of Judaism (Scott 2015). Earlier scholars debated whether or not Philo transformed Judaism into a mystery religion (Goodenough 1935) or simply represented it in terms accessible to his Roman colleagues (Wolfson 1948). The latter, metaphorical position has prevailed. Philo—like other educated Jews—adopted the analogy as a positive identity marker. He often describes those advanced "initiates" in Jewish piety with the language of the Greek mysteries. Behind the ascetical description of this Jewish "company" (θίασος), Colson (PLCL 5:587) simultaneously hears the influence of Stoic "bands" of philosophers.

§ 33. **well-conditioned and energetic ... athletes.** Arnaldez (1964, 48, n. 1) observes that although Philo usually employs the image of the athlete metaphorically in a positive manner, here he uses it in a more literal and negative fashion to describe the psychological/ethical costs of pursuing bodily excellence and, inversely, the corporeal atrophying that accompanies serious study of philosophy and theology. Nevertheless, Arnaldez argues, such asceticism for Philo is not an end in itself. Bodies are not inherently negative, even as their limitations demonstrate the need of a higher wisdom. Arnaldez is rightly keen to absolve Philo of the charge of body-denying Gnosticism, arguing that the "but" (ἀλλὰ δέ) of § 32, which introduces an extensive devaluation of "all that is dear to the flesh," must be something of an exaggeration.

one, the form of the soul. The perfect human being, in imitation of The One Who Is, ultimately resolves his duality and becomes entirely "one" (ἕν) in the "form of soul" (εἶδος τῆς ψυχῆς). Philo means this both ontologically and morally—with an emphasis here on the latter. Ontologically, he suggests that the perfect human exists as mind or soul detached from the body, having reverted to the state of the "heavenly human", described in *Opif.* 134 as "an idea (ἰδέα) or genus (γένος) or seal (σφραγίς), noetic, bodiless, neither male nor female, naturally imperishable." Literally, this is possible for human beings only in death—as Philo famously describes God "transforming" Moses "who was a dual being, body and soul, entirely into a sun-like mind according to the nature of the unpartitioned Monad" (ὃς αὐτὸν δυάδα ὄντα, σῶμα καὶ ψυχὴν εἰς μονάδος ἀνεστοιχειου φύσιν ὅλον δι' ὅλων μεθαρμοζόμενος εἰς νοῦν ἡλιοειδέστατον, *Mos.* 2.288). For Philo, as for many later Greek Christian thinkers, eschatology reflects protology: a return to God-likeness in created singularity. Philo's concern in *Mut.* 33, however, is not eschatology, but moral allegory—the process by which the human being becomes entirely soulful and mind-like in his dispositions, such that the body is so devoted to the mind that it becomes "pale and wasted-away."

§ 34. *the earthlike part of a person.* For the "earthlike substance" and the "earthlike mind," see *Leg.* 1.31–32.

when the mind chooses. Philo's soteriology, which includes a notion human "predetermination" (προαιρεῖσθαι), is synergist: human freedom and divine providence are integrated. This statement should not be read apart from Philo's doctrine of grace (see the detailed comment on "gift-exchange" on § 25). Philo is not encouraging suicide, but living as though one had already left the body.

well-pleasing to God. The verb "to be well-pleasing" (εὐαρεστεῖν) anticipates the culminating secondary lemma of the chapter (§ 34), Gen 5:25: "Now Enoch was well-pleasing to God." This verse itself anticipates Gen 17:1cβ ("be well-pleasing before me"), the primary lemma of chapter 2 (§ 39), and is labeled an "anticipatory secondary lemma" (SBL^A).

now Enoch was well-pleasing ... he was not found. The text of the last secondary lemma in the section, Gen 5:24, agrees with the Septuagint, except on several inconsequential points. More importantly, Philo has omitted the final phrase of the verse, "because God translated him" (ὅτι μετέθηκεν αὐτὸν ὁ θεός), although he will interpret these words in § 38. This lemma serves as a hinge between the first and second chapters of *De mutatione nominum*. It is thematically related to Gen 17:1cα, but lexically linked to the primary lemma of the subsequent chapter (§ 39, Gen 17:1cβ): God's command that Abraham "be well-pleasing." Gen 5:24 is thus a rare example of an anticipatory biblical lemma (SBL^A). (For anticipatory lemmata earlier in the Abraham cycle, see *Migr.* 36 [Exod 15:25], which anticipates the formal citation of the lemma in *Migr.* 43 [Gen 12:1c].)

Philo divides the biblical lemma into three units: §34 ("Enoch was well-pleasing"); §§35–37 ("he was not found"); and §38 ("God translated him"). The contrast of Enoch and Abraham, as well as of Enoch and Moses, as different kind of sages was of great interest in wider Jewish tradition. All three figures are visionaries who journey to heaven (Orlov 2013). For Philo's potential knowledge of such Enochic traditions (despite his evident suppression of their more apocalyptic currents), see Stuckenbruck 2007. Colson (PLCL 5:587) notes that the phrase "he was not found" connects Enoch to the Stoic tradition as well: "This wording of the LXX suits Philo's argument admirably, since one phrase of theirs was that the wise man 'is until the present undiscovered' (μεχρὶ τοῦ νῦν ἀνεύρετός ἐστι, SVF 3.32, p. 216)." Enoch is the symbol of a "hidden sage" of a strongly ascetical variety. Philo will contrast him with the "gentler" wisdom of the more visible sage, Abraham, in §39.

Despite their descriptive similarities, Enoch is "well-pleasing" in a very different sense than Abraham and Jacob. Whereas Enoch's well-pleasing status makes him basically invisible to all save God, Jacob and Abraham are exemplars of a "well-pleasing" character that entails earthly responsibilities and makes their wisdom manifest to other human beings. The two psychic types, Enoch and Abraham, thus belong in separate chapters, despite their lexical connection.

§35. *over what sort of seas?* Philo's description of the quest for "the good person," in its maritime and ethnographic details, recalls the elusiveness of Odysseus. Philo's imagination has drifted to a Homeric register to amplify this picture of the hidden Enoch. Notably, at the outset of the poem (*Od.* 1.235–236), Odysseus is said to have been made "unseen" (ἄϊστον) by the gods, who have, as Telemachus laments, "caused him to pass from sight more than all human beings" (οἳ κεῖνον μὲν ἄϊστον ἐποίησαν περὶ πάντων / ἀνθρώπων). Such invisibility matches the invisibility of the sage in Stoic tradition.

§36. *the true sage is also non-existent.* Philo contests the strong Stoic view, paraphrased here, that no wise person has ever existed. He adopts a Platonist response to defend the Pentateuch's portraits of the patriarchal sages. For the Stoic position, see Plutarch, *Stoic. rep.* 1040f. (SVF 3.545; L&S 1:423, §66A), who cites Chrysippus; and cf. Epictetus, *Diatr.* 4.12.19 (SVF 3.763; L&S 1:425, §66F). For more moderate examples of the Stoic position, including that "a wise man like Phoenix appears once in 500 years" (Seneca, *Ep.* 42.1), see Colson (PLCL 5:587–588); and Arnaldez (1964, 50, n. 1), who points to parallels at Wis 9:5–6, 13–14. Philo's position aligns with this more moderate strain.

it is ... impossible for someone bound in a mortal body to be entirely happy. If there is no wisdom, Philo reasons, there can be no happiness. He then articulates an alternative position, in which wisdom (§37) and happiness (§185) do exist, but can only be experienced in proportion to the perfection of each given soul. Arnaldez (1964, 50, n. 1) suggests that Philo does not wish to preclude the possibility of perfection, but emphasizes that such a true sage "is the work of God alone."

§ 37. *his existence has escaped the notice of us ordinary people.* Countering the position that no truly wise person exists, Philo argues that sages do exist but are missed by ordinary human "bad/common" (φαῦλοι) folk—among whom Philo here rhetorically includes himself. While earlier he uses φαῦλοι to refer to the "wicked" like Pharoah (§ 19), here he adopts the more neutral Stoic technical connotation of "ordinary" or "inferior"—i.e., not yet perfect (L&S 1:427; see the detailed note on § 19).

§ 38. *Enoch has been translated.* Philo now explicitly adds Gen 5:24c to his secondary biblical lemma (cf. § 34) and comments upon it. He paraphrases LXX Gen 5:24c "for God translated him / put him elsewhere" (ὅτι μετέθηκεν αὐτὸν ὁ θεός), rendering it into the divine perfect passive "has been translated / moved" (μετατεθῆναι). The three μετα- compounds in this final period betoken "change of place, station, and home" (μετατεθῆναι, μεταναστῆναι, μετοικία) and recall the theme of ethical transformation, implicit in the title of the work, "Concerning Those Whose Names Are Being Changed" (καὶ ὧν ἕνεκα μετονομάζεται).

was removed from his home country. Philo supplements the theme of the vertical, heavenly ascent of Enoch with the horizontal Abrahamic theme of migration. Etymologically, the verb "was moved" (μεταναστῆναι) echoes and combines the Jewish notion of "resurrection" (ἀνίστημι) with the prepositional marker of the Greek concept of "transformation" (μεταμορφόω [cf. 2 Cor 3:18]) and Platonic "psychic transmigration" (μετεμψυχόομαι).

set out on a migration. I render μετοικία as "journey" (LSJ I) rather than "settlement" (LSJ II; Arnaldez 1964, "to found a colony").

Parallel Exegesis

§ 18. *Gen 17:1ca ("I am your God").* In addition to the parallels in QG 3.39–40, Philo also interprets Gen 17:1c earlier in the Allegorical Commentary at *Gig.* 63–64. Abraham's status is represented as already "improved" (βελτιωθείς), when God says, "I am your God." He stands on the cusp of having his name changed. See also *Decal.* 38 in the Exposition of the Law, where Philo explains God's desire to be "God" both to the just man, and to the world as well.

§ 19. *"Lord" and "Master" of the wicked; "God" of those making moral advancements.* Philo's interpretation of the title "Lord God" in QG 3.39a focuses on God's unique governing of the wise human being alone; he omits discussion of the wicked and the progressing. Neither the problem raised by Philo in

Mut. 18 (is not God the Creator and Governor of *all* generated things?), nor the three-fold differentiation of psychic types in *Mut.* 19, has a parallel here.

Exod 7:1 ("God to Pharaoh"). God's promise to make Moses "a god to Pharaoh" is an important verse for Philo. He interprets it variously to signify (1) that the wise man is governor of the foolish man, and in fact, divine (so *Det.* 161–162; *Mut.* 125, 128; *Prob.* 43); (2) that the mind is superior to the body (*Leg.* 1.40; *Migr.* 84); or (3) that the Logos is "god" in the world of becoming (*Sacr.* 9; *Somn.* 2.189). Only in *Mut.* 19 does Philo focus negatively on God's refusal to call himself "God" to Pharaoh, the wicked soul.

§ 25. *Deut 33:1 ("Moses, God's human being")*. Philo does not cite this verse as evidence of Moses's exemplary status outside of the present treatise (see the parallel interpretation in § 125).

§ 28. *the kingly and the beneficent powers*. Whereas in § 28, Philo treats the two principal powers in their scriptural order, "Lord" and "God," in QG 3.39a he follows instead the logical/economic ordering of "God" (Creator) and "Lord" (lawgiver). The theme of epistemic limitation vis-à-vis these powers, prominent in *De mutatione nominum*, is missing in QGE.

§ 30. *Gen 2:7 ("God molded the human being")*. Arguably one of the two most important anthropological passages in Scripture for Philo, which grounds a double theory of creation, the "heavenly" and "earthly" human being. *BiPaSup* list some 80 uses of the verse in the *corpus Philonicum*. See (as a representative sample from each series) QG 1.4; *Leg.* 1:31–42; *Plant.* 18–44; *Opif.* 134–144. *De opificio mundi*, with its theory of God's helpers in creation (*Opif.* 75), gives the cosmological basis, from which the present treatise derives its psychological allegory.

§ 31. *Gen 1:26aα ("let us make a human being according to our image")*. Along with Gen 1:27 and Gen 2:7 (see the preceding note), one of the most important scriptural passages for Philonic anthropology and Logos theology. Gen 1:26 (by itself) is adduced or paraphrased also at QG 2.62; *Conf.* 169, 179; *Fug.* 68, 71; *Mos.* 2.65; and frequently in *Opif.* (esp. 69, 71, and 75). From the theological perspective, Philo finds in the verse a theology of "the God before the Logos" (ὁ πρὸ τοῦ λόγου θεός [QG 2.62]). Anthropologically, Philo uses it to explore the divine element in the human being and the difficulty of becoming like God. In an early passage in the Allegorical Commentary, Philo cites the verse with reference to both "image and likeness" (*Conf.* 169). Later in the Abrahamic cycle (*Fug.* 68; *Mut.* 31), he omits the clause about the likeness, focusing on the image alone.

the craftsmanship of others. For parallels to this concept, see Arnaldez (1964, 14 and 46, n. 4), who adduces *Opif.* 72, *Conf.* 169, and *Fug.* 60. A similar list is given by Colson (PLCL 5:158, nn. b and d).

§ 34. *Gen 5:24 ("Enoch was well-pleasing to God ...")*. Arnaldez (1964, 49, n. 2) calls attention to the parallel treatment of Enoch in *Abr.* 17–18, in which the patriarch figures in Philo's first ethical triad as a symbol of "the one who finds grace/favor" (*Abr.* 17) and who is "translated" to a better kind of life (*Abr.* 18). The same lemma, Gen 5:24, is cited in both texts. Philo omits the etymology of Enoch's name, which is given in *Abr.* 17 as "graced" (κεχαρισμένος)—or better, as in *Post.* 35, as "your grace" (χάρις σου), since the name "Enoch" (חנוך) might be resolved into the Hebrew word for "grace," *ḥēn* (חן) and the second person singular suffix "your," *-kā* (ך־). See Grabbe 1988, 156–157; *Post.* 35, 41; *Conf.* 123.

Arnaldez points out a tension in Enoch's symbolic significance in the Allegorical Commentary in *De posteritate Caini*, arising from the two persons named Enoch in Gen 4:17 (the son of Cain) and Gen 5:18 (the son of Seth). Etymologically, the name is the same, but Philo will derive opposing allegorical significances from the same title in different contexts. In *Post.* 36, Enoch is the sophist, who sees everything as the gift of one's own mind ("your ⟨own⟩ gift" as symbol of self-sufficiency); in *Post.* 41–42, by contrast, Philo argues that the second Enoch (Gen 5:18) is the mind that recognizes that "your ⟨divine⟩ gift" means "God's gift" (i.e., "grace"). Despite their homonymy, Philo finds two different "Enochs" (compare *Mut.* 201–208, where he discerns two Ishmaels). The former, however, might be converted or re-enrolled from the family of Cain to the family of Seth (*Post.* 42). It is this latter kind of Enoch mind that Philo discusses in *Mut.* 34.

§ 38. *flees from sharing our common road.* The idea that the sage "flees" (ἀποδιδράσκων) common "synodality" (σύνοδος) with the masses is a theme Philo has already treated in the Abrahamic cycle. See *Fug.* 1–3, and esp. 20, where Jacob's flight from Laban is presented as the flight of the progressing soul from the wicked.

Nachleben

§ 18. *Gen 17:1cα ("I am your God")*. Origen (*Hom. Jer.* 9.3 [B/C]) adduces Gen 17:1cα as the first in a catena of secondary texts, to reinforce his interpretation of LXX Jer 11:4 ("you will be my people and I will be your God"). He comments: "He is not God of all, so much as he is God of those to whom he has given himself, just as he gave himself to that patriarch to whom he said, 'I am your God' (Gen 17:1)" (Οὐκ ἔστιν πάντων θεὸς ἀλλ' ἢ ἐκείνων οἷς χαρίζεται ἑαυτόν, ὥσπερ ἐχαρίσατο ἑαυτὸν τῷ πατριάρχῃ ἐκείνῳ ᾧ εἶπεν· «Ἐγὼ θεὸς σός»). See also Didymus the Blind (*In Gen.* 250.24–29 [B/C]), who in his comment on Gen 17:1, notes that although God is, properly speaking, God and Craftsman of the cosmos, he becomes "specially 'their God' [i.e., 'God of the saints'] according to their worship of him" (ἐξαιρέτως κατὰ λατρείαν αὐτῶν Θεὸς γινόμενος). Both interpretations show Philonic influence.

§ 19. *Exod 7:1 ("a god to Pharaoh")*. Ambrose also uses Exod 7:1 as a secondary lemma in the *Expositio Psalmi 118* and, like Philo, emends its tense, but for a slightly different purpose. Presenting Moses as an image of the soul approaching its spiritual completion, Ambrose notes that God says, "I will make you into god to king Pharao" ("Faciam te in deum regi Pharao"; *Exp. Ps. 118* 8.21 [C]). Cf. OL Exod 7:1, which reads "Behold, I have given you [have turned you] into a god for Pharaoh" ("Ecce dedi te in deum Pharaoni" [*alt*. posui, constitui]). For the broader context of this passage, see the following note.

§ 23. *Deut 4:1 ("the Lord God of your Fathers")*. For a similar use of Moses as a dynamic allegorical type, admitting various shades of virtue, rather than as a fixed symbol of ethical perfection, see Ambrose, *Exp. Ps. 118*, 8.21 [D]. The Milanese bishop calls the reader's attention to the point in Moses's life when God says, "take off your sandals" (Exod 3:5): "But consider when this was said to him ⟨by God⟩. It had not yet been said 'I will make you a god to Pharaoh the king' (Exod 7:1); at this point (Exod 3:5) he was a ⟨mere⟩ human being" ("Quando autem id dictum sit, considera. Nondum ei dictum erat: 'Faciam te in deum regi Pharao' [Exod 7:1]. Adhuc homo erat ....").

§ 25. *Deut 33:1 ("God's human being")*. Of *De mutatione nominum* as a whole, Arnaldez (1964, 12) notes: "It seems that rarely has Philo been so near to Christian ideas as in this treatise." Chief among his arguments for this claim is Philo's conception of "God's human being." With this schema, one approaches a Philonic analogue to Johannine "rebirth" (John 3:3–8) and Paul's "new Adam" (1 Cor 15:44–49). The parallel remains imperfect, however, for Philo lacks the apocalyptic and messianic dimensions of his Pauline and Johannine counterparts. As with other New Testament parallels, it is not a question of genetic dependence, but of shared Jewish tradition branching out in various directions. A case for genetic reception of Philo can be made in the case of Origen, who in his newly discovered homily on Ps 73(74):16 [B/C], notes that "Even Moses is with difficulty called 'God's human being' (Deut 33:1) at the end ⟨of his life⟩" (καὶ μόλις ἐχρημάτισε Μωϋσῆς ἐπὶ τέλει «ἄνθρωπος τοῦ θεοῦ» [*Hom. Ps.* 11.2.18]). This bears some resemblance to the Philonic reading of this verse offered in *Mut.* 25 and 125. Skipping forward several centuries to Amphilochius's *Iambi ad Seleucum*, we find the description "faithful Moses, God's human being, image of the virtuous life" (ὁ πιστὸς Μωϋσῆς, ὁ τοῦ θεοῦ ἄνθρωπος, εἰκὼν τοῦ κατ' ἀρετὴν βίου, *Iamb. Sel.* 219–220[B/C]). While the evidence does not admit a firm conclusion of dependence on Philo, the interpretation of this verse along Philonic lines had become mainstream in Greek Christian literature.

§ 26. *Handmade laws.* For parallel conceptualities in early Christian literature, see Mark 14:58; Acts 7:48; 17:24; 2 Cor 5:1; and Heb 9:11. Most germane to Philo's usage is the Deutero-Pauline concept of "a circumcision not made with human hands" (περιτομῇ ἀχειροποιήτῳ), which approximates Philo's partial allegorizing of circumcision in *Migr.* 92–93. Cf. Gal 3:19, "at the hand of a mediator" (ἐν χειρὶ μεσίτου) for Paul's earlier problematizing of the literal, hand-given sense of Sinai's Law.

§ 29. *set the universe in place.* Clement of Alexandria (*Strom.* 1.182.3 [B]) knows the same Herodotean etymology of "God" (θεός) from the verb "to place/set" (τίθημι) present in *Mut.* 29. Van den Hoek (1988, 180–181) concludes that "a reminiscence of Philo is likely," though she traces it to *Abr.* 121 or *Mos.* 2.99.

§ 31. *the craftsmanship of others.* Philo's Platonist solution to the "ontological problem of evil" presented an issue for his later Christian interpreters. *Inter alia*, it recalled to their minds the Valentinian position of a second Demiurge, ancillary to the fallen Sophia, who creates the material cosmos in error—an imperfect imitation of the heavenly archetype. Authors from Irenaeus onwards would refute this solution, on the grounds that it distances the Father of Jesus from the Creator of the Pentateuch, and renders matter the domain of an evil, secondary divinity. The anxieties about *Philo gnosticus vel Platonicus* are present already in the textual transmission of *De mutatione nominum.* One anonymous Byzantine scholiast, writing in the margins of the Augustana manuscript (*Codex Monacensis Graecus* 459), penned a poem playfully censuring Philo: "But, Friend, you are too silly here / in this place, as also elsewhere" (ἀλλ' ὦ φίλος λίαν ληρεῖς / ἐνθάδε ὡς καὶ ἐν ἀλλοῖς). While treating Philo as a "friend" (an evident pun on his name), the scholiast nevertheless suggests the insufficiency of Philo's scriptural interpretation. Hoeschel (1587, 218), the first modern editor of *Codex Monacensis Graecus* 459, was less light-hearted when he wrote of this same locus (§ 31): "Truly Philo wrote these words, as many others, while he was still uninitiated in the teaching of the Gospel. Nor is there any doubt, that having spoken with the divine Peter in Rome, and having conversed with the students of Mark the Evangelist in his own country, being led by God he learned to drink the mysteries of the sacred Scriptures from the Font itself and put away errors of this sort." See Cover 2024a for further analysis of both the Byzantine scholiast and Hoeschel.

§ 38. *flees from sharing our common road.* Philo's position on the relative difficulty (but not impossibility) of finding a sage to share the "common road" (σύνοδος) of humanity has an interesting parallel in the famous Road to Emmaus scene of Luke 24:13–27. In Luke's Gospel, Jesus shares many of the marks of a Stoic sage (Sterling 2001). In agreement with Philo, the presence of

Luke's sage (Jesus) is missed by those around him; in contrast to Philo, Luke's sage *does* condescend to share a common "road" with souls, like that of Cleopas, making progress in perfection.

Enoch has been translated. See similarly Heb 11:5–6, which paraphrases Enoch's "translation" in the aorist passive ("he was set elsewhere" [μετέτεθη]).

[Chapter 2]
Philo's Theology of Covenant (§§ 39–53)

The designation of §§ 39–53 as a single chapter follows from the treatment of this verse and a half as a single pericope in QG 3.40, as well as from the thematic coherence of the section. The *quaestio* is extant fully in Armenian and partially in a Greek paraphrase from Procopius. (For text and analysis of the Procopius fragment, see Marcus, PLCLSup 2:211; Petit 1978, 141.) In QG 3.40, Philo cites LXX Gen 17:1c–2 as a unit. In §§ 39–53, by contrast, he will introduce the chapter pericope piecewise in §§ 39, 47, and 52. Philo first interprets (a) Gen 17:1cβ, "be well-pleasing before me" (§§ 39–46); then (b) Gen 17:1cγ, "be blameless" (§§ 47–51a); and finally (c) Gen 17:2, "I will set my covenant in the midst of you and me" (§§ 51b–53). The piecewise nature of Philo's introduction of his lemma(ta) has led most modern commentators on this treatise, including Cohn, Arnaldez, Kraus Reggiani, and Schur, to postulate the existence of three chapters rather than one. Philo, however, clearly conceives of all three parts of the pericope—the human obligation (a) to be well-pleasing and (b) to be blameless; and (c) God's reciprocal gift of the covenant—as interlocking theological movements, which one might call Philo's theology of covenant.

In speaking of Philo's theology of covenant, I do not imply that Philo spells out the cultic and legal requirements for "getting in" and "staying in" a special relationship with Israel's God. We know that Philo held the literal observance of Sabbath, festivals, and circumcision to be important religious obligations for Jews (*Migr.* 92–93), but he passes over those subjects in silence here. (Would that his two volume *De testamentis*, which included his comments on Gen 17:10, had come down to us!) In chapter two, Philo takes up the more modest task of explicating the parameters of God's covenant from a philosophical and ethical perspective. While not abrogating the letter of the law, he nevertheless ignores its body to penetrate to its soul and the underlying theological anthropology that animates it. The very fact that Philo can do this—discuss the Abrahamic covenant of Genesis 17 from the level of psychic allegory—suggests that there was a universal edge to his covenantal thinking. Precisely how this

PART ONE 191

universal dimension relates to Philo's commitment to the particular laws prescribed to the Jewish people cannot be clearly ascertained from the surviving evidence.

a   *"Be Well-Pleasing before Me" (§§ 39–46)*
    Analysis/General Comments

At the opening of the second chapter, Philo shifts his focus away from the company of sages wildly possessed by God—entirely pleasing to him, but rare upon the earth, such as Enoch (§§ 32–34)—toward a more cultivated and common kind of sage, possessed of reason and typified by Abraham (§ 39). Both groups may say that God is "their God," but each is pleasing to him in a different way—the Enochic type, by way of its single-mindedness, the Abrahamic type, by way of its worship and philanthropy. Just as later in the Exposition of the Law, Enoch and Abraham will exemplify different triads of virtue (*Abr.* 17, 48), so here in the Allegorical Commentary they represent different kinds of inspiration, initiation, and ethics (see comment on § 39 below, pertaining to "Enochic Judaism."). Gen 5:24 ("Enoch was well-pleasing [εὐηρέστησεν] to God"), adduced in § 34 as a secondary anticipatory lemma to Gen 17:1bβ ("I am *your* God"), is now lexically linked to the primary lemma in the first subsection of chapter two, Gen 17:1cα ("be well-pleasing [εὐαρέστει] before me").

This first subsection on "being well-pleasing" (Gen 17:1cα) can be divided into three units:

(1) Using the rhetorical technique of *diairesis*, Philo divides his primary biblical lemma into two parts: "be well-pleasing" and "before me." To each of these, he ascribes an allegorical significance. "To be well-pleasing" signifies moral perfection toward God the Creator; this is the human covenantal obligation from an eschatological perspective. To be well-pleasing "before God" means that one's moral uprightness also extends to God's creatures and is seen and recognized by them as well. Philo offers a metaphysical reading of the preposition "in the face of" (ἐνώπιον), seeing it as a signifier of all that is "before God," to wit, all God's works in creation (§ 41). The first element of Philo's covenant theology is thus something like adherence to the "double love command" elsewhere in Jewish and Christian tradition (§§ 39–40).

(2) To supplement this portrait of the sage who is well pleasing to God and creation, Philo adduces two secondary lemmata, linked lexically through the phrase "before me" (ἐνώπιόν μου/αὐτοῦ): Gen 48:15 ("O God, to whom my fathers were pleasing before him") and Deut 12:28 ("you shall do what is well pleasing before the Lord your God"). Abraham's double approval before God and created beings is amplified by the example of "the

fathers" (mentioned by Jacob in a prayer) and the command given to the Israelites by Moses (§§ 41–42).

(3) In a third cluster of supplementary lemmata, Philo turns from law and exhortation to cultic allegory, offering symbolic interpretations of a variety of tabernacle implements and vestments. Moses designed these with inner and outer beauty to symbolize the sage's need to be well-pleasing in a double fashion, "within" toward God and "without" toward humanity. The allusions to Exod 26:33; 25:10; Lev 6:10; and Exod 28:4–6, are thematically connected to the discourse. Because they amplify Deut 12:28, they are classified as tertiary biblical lemmata (§§ 43–44a). In § 44b, Philo adduces one final secondary lemma, which is neither paraenesis nor mystagogy, but "proclamation" (κήρυγμα) in connection to the covenant. This lemma stems from the Jacob tradition (Gen 32:28), in which the patriarch is proclaimed to have "been strong with God, capable with human beings." This section concludes with a meditation on the gratuitous nature of God's gift in creation (§§ 43–46).

Detailed Comments

(1) § 39. *those people just described ... gone wild*. Arnaldez (1964, 51, n. 3) argues that this first group of "hermits are not perfect sages, nor Stoic sages: 'The sage will not live in the desert, for he is by nature sociable' (Diogenes Laertius 7.123)." Philo does not indicate whether, from his Jewish perspective, sociability is equally important, or whether his Abrahamic sages surpass the Enochic ones. One might infer this from the sequence of their presentation, as well as from Philo's description of the second ethical triad in the Exposition of the Law as "greater" than the first (*Abr.* 48).

the divine madness. Philo alludes to Plato's account of "love" (ἔρως) as a kind of divine madness in *Phaedr.* 244a. He attributes this ecstatic form of divine possession especially to followers of Enoch. Both Platonic and Enochic ascents are attributed to the love of God alone, which (to invoke a Platonic image) raptures them like Ganymede from the normal duties of life and elevates them to the exclusive service of God. Philo thus recognizes an implicit differentiation between Enochic and Abrahamic patterns of religion. (For the theory of an apocalyptic species of "Enochic Judaism" in the Second Temple period, as witnessed by 1 Enoch, see Boccaccini 1998.)

companions. Philo takes the word "companion" or "devotee" (ἑταῖρος) from Greek religion. Unlike the Enochic "company" (see § 32), which Philo presents in an ecstatic, Dionysiac guise, Abraham and his band—though equally inspired—exemplify a rational, moderate (Aristotelian) character, which results in their ready acceptance by the outside world.

the tame and gentle wisdom. Enoch and Abraham are said to be "devotees" (ἑταῖροι) of two kinds of wisdom, the wilder and the gentler. While it is possible that Philo refers to the heavenly and the earthly wisdoms (*Leg.* 1.43), respectively, the distinction is better understood in terms of the different human responses to the one Logos, which prompts them to differing patterns of practice and piety. In the description of Abraham's type, Arnaldez (1964, 51, n. 4) suggests that "here we find an echo of Philo's personal experience."

"be well-pleasing before me." Philo's citation of Gen 17:1cβ conforms with the Septuagint in most respects, although he apparently paraphrases or follows a text tradition that has "facing" (ἐνώπιον) instead of "opposite" (ἐναντίον, Göttingen LXX) as the preposition in the phrase "before me." Either Philo's text had "facing" (ἐνώπιον) in these verses, or Philo paraphrased "opposite" (ἐναντίον) as "facing" (ἐνώπιον) by accident of memory or because it fits his allegory better. For Philo's text, see Katz 1950; Sterling 2012d.

Philo illustrates the exhortation of the primary lemma (Gen 17:1cβ), to "be well-pleasing," with five specific commandments. Although they do not correspond exactly to Moses's second table in the Decalogue, the number five recalls them. The stipulations are roughly comparable as well, though given in a more philosophical Roman idiom, and represent obligations in Philo's ethical covenant. Unlike the commands of the second table of the Decalogue, Philo's five commands are joined by *disjunctions* ("or"), indicating that the list offers examples, each of which is a species of the behavior that satisfies the covenantal requirement. Formally speaking, they are written as descriptions rather than imperatives, though they are treated as commands below.

not only to me, but also to my works. This expression of humanity's double responsibility approximates the "double love command" found elsewhere in Jewish and Christian tradition. Cf. Ps.-Phocylides, *Sent.* 8; Mark 12:28–34; Rom 13:8–10; 14:18. For more on the (double) love command in early Judaism and in Philo, see Collins 2020; Doering 2018; Meier 2009. *Pace* Nissen (1974, 478), for whom the love commandments are "fremd und fern" from Philo's thinking. Collins (2020, 104) is right to suggest that this gives a "misleading" picture of Philo's thought.

§ 40. ***honor your parents.*** Philo begins his five covenantal stipulations by paraphrasing the commandment that serves as the hinge or "borderland" between the two tables of the Decalogue (*Her.* 171–172; *Decal.* 106). Philo's paraphrase follows that of other Hellenistic Jewish authors, including Ps.-Phocylides (*Sent.* 8), whose hexameter formulation, "honor God first, next your parents" (πρῶτα θεὸν τιμᾶν, μετέπειτα δὲ σεῖο γονῆας) closely mirrors Philo's "honoring … parents" (τιμῶν … γονεῖς). For Philo, the honoring of parents is simultaneously respecting God, because parents are *as* God to children

(*Decal.* 111). In Philo's halakhic discourse, the fifth commandment combines Moses's concern for piety (first table) and justice (second table)—the latter of which is the organizing factor of the four injunctions which follow. See the Parallel Exegesis.

have mercy on the poor. Philo's second commandment does not echo the Decalogue, but draws on the Jewish commitment to works of mercy. Philo's terse "being merciful to the poor" (πένητας ἐλεῶν) echoes the more expansive formulations in Ps.-Phocylides (*Sent.* 22–23), "Give to the poor person immediately; do not say, 'come back tomorrow.' Fill your hand. Give alms to the one in need" (πτωχῷ δ' εὐθὺ δίδου μὴ δ' αὔριον ἐλθέμεν εἴπῃς· πληρώσει σέο χεῖρ'. ἔλεον χρῄζοντι παράσχου); see also Prov 19:17 "the one who has mercy to the poor, lends to God" (δανίζει θεῷ ὁ ἐλεῶν πτωχόν) and m.'Abot 1.2. On this theme in Judaism and Christianity, see Anderson 2009 and 2013.

⟨**be**⟩ **a benefactor to friends ... guard your homeland.** Philo's third and fourth commandments in this philosophical "second table" do not stem exclusively from Jewish tradition, but reinforce traditional Roman imperial *mores*. "⟨Be⟩ a benefactor to friends" translates the sense of (e.g.) Lev 19:18 (a verse which Philo never cites!) into more philosophical terms (see Collins 2020, *pace* Nissen 1974, 478), but also reflects the customs of Roman imperial patronage. "Guard your homeland" exhorts citizens to natural civic duty, even as one may detect some distant echo of the Maccabean histories, about which Philo is generally silent.

care for the common justice of all human beings. Philo's fifth commandment, "care for the common justice of all human beings" (τῶν κοινῶν πρὸς ἅπαντας ἀνθρώπους δικαίων ἐπιμελούμενος) finds several close echoes in Ps.-Phocylides (*Sent.* 9–14, esp. 12), where the anonymous hexameter poet connects this obligation with the ninth commandment, Exod 20:16: "Flee false witness; arbitrate things with justice" (μαρτυρίην ψευδῆ φεύγειν· τὰ δίκαια βραβεύειν). The concern for "justice" in this injunction dovetails with Philo's understanding of the fifth commandment (see "honor your parents" above).

with an unsleeping eye. Philo uses the phrase "unsleeping eye" (ἀκοίμητος ὀφθαλμός) only here in his extant Greek corpus to refer to God's continual overseeing of the world. Cf. LXX Ps 120:4; see also Epictetus, *Diatr.* 14.12, who cites Posidonius's adverbial use of the adjective "unsleeping" (ἀκοίμητον) to describe the supervision of one's personal δαίμων (frag. 388.4; Epictetus, *Diatr.* 1.14); and Wis 7:10, which speaks of the "unsleeping light" of wisdom—a phrase resembling the later "unsleeping fire" in the *corpus Hermeticum*. Philo uses the related phrase "unsleeping eye" (ἀκοίμητον ὄμμα) in *Mut.* 5 to refer to the eye(s) of the human soul. Comparing these two *loci*, Arnaldez (1964, 52, n. 1) observes: "Here ⟨i.e., § 40⟩, it is God who knows no sleep; in § 5 it is mind. This alignment compels one to comprehend the importance that the relationship of the intellect to God has for the human being."

with a choice grace ... receives them as his own. Philo's theology of covenant is synergist: human actions are simultaneously the responsibility of their human agents and acknowledged by God as fruits of divine grace. The adjective "choice" (ἐξαιρετός) carries with it the connotation of "election," which is less particularistic in Philo's thought than in other Jewish discourses.

(2) § 41. ⟨*Israel*⟩ *the practicer.* Philo's most common epithet for the Jacob soul, which makes progress by training rather than purely cognitive teaching and learning. Here, however, it is applied to "Israel", the perfected "practicer" (ἀσκητής), as he blesses the sons of Joseph at the end of his life. See the notes on § 1 "the self-taught race" and § 12 "God of the three natures."

God, to whom my fathers were well-pleasing ... before him. Philo adduces Gen 48:15 as a secondary lemma, lexically linked to Gen 17:1cβ through the preposition "before" (ἐνώπιον). Philo (or his textual tradition) has replaced the scriptural preposition "opposite" (ἐναντίον) with "in the face of" (ἐνώπιον) in both of these texts. Philo understands the phrase "before me" (ἐνώπιον ἐμοῦ) as a "clarification" (ἀποδήλωσις) of the way in which Abraham and Isaac were well-pleasing. It is likely that Philo's allegory of this phrase derives from Greek rather than Hebrew exegetical tradition. In the Hebrew *Vorlage* of Gen 48:15, the phrase "before him" (לפניו) is required to limit the indeclinable relative pronoun "whom" (אשר). In Greek, where the relative pronoun can be declined in the dative case (ᾧ), the prepositional phrase becomes redundant ("*to whom* my fathers were well-pleasing *before him*") and triggers the allegorical interpretation.

the latter phrase ... both kinds of well-pleasing. I follow Cohn, Colson, and Kraus Reggiani in translating τὸ μέν as specifying "the last" or "the latter" prepositional phrase ("before him"). Philo offers a deep reading of this prepositional phrase, in which "before" (ἐνώπιον) signifies God's "works" (ἔργα) in creation, while "him" (αὐτοῦ) points to God himself. The two words of the lemma indicate the double object ("both" [ἀμφότερα]) of the soul's responsibility to be well-pleasing.

§ 42. ***so also Moses.*** Moses joins Abraham and Jacob among the "devotees" of the tame and gentle wisdom, who keep an eye on both the contemplation of the heavenly realm and moral perfection in the terrestrial-civic sphere. Philo thus constructs an Abrahamic-Israelite-Mosaic covenantal type which stands as a counterpoint to the Enochic model.

in his Exhortations. Philo speaks of Moses's *Exhortations* (Προτρεπτικοί) at several places in the Allegorical Commentary (Colson, PLCL 8:90, n. a). The phrase cannot fail to recall Aristotle's nearly homonymous work, as well as the "Exhortations" (προτρεπτικοὶ [λόγοι]) attributed to the Academic Antisthenes and the Stoics Posidonius and Perseus (Diogenes Laertius 6.1; 7.35, 91, 129; see further Wilson 2011, 149). Other philosophers reported by Diogenes Laertius to have authored works called "Exhortations" include the Socratic-Cyrenaic Aristippus (2.85), Aristotle (5.22), Theophrastus (5.49), and the Stoic Monimus (6.83). It is intriguing to speculate on the basis of this title whether Philo and his school considered some portion of the Pentateuch—perhaps Deuteronomy, in whole or in part—as the Mosaic equivalent of this kind of philosophical work, aimed at initiating neophytes in the particular ethical stipulations of a tradition and encouraging them to follow the school's way of life. Colson, thinking in this vein, translates the phrase "Moses in his Exhortations" (PLCL 5:163), indicating by the capitalization that Philo thinks here of an ancient work. In a related note on *Fug.* 170, Colson adds that Philo uses the phrase seven times in the Allegorical Commentary, and in six of the seven cases, refers to Deuteronomy. Thus, Colson suggests that "the Exhortations" was one of Philo's names for Deuteronomy (Colson, PLCL 5:102, n. a. See also Siegert 1996–2015, I.1.173; Geljon and Runia 2013, 171–172, 256).

While this is possible, several considerations point in a different direction. First, as noted by several scholars (Cohen 2007, 25–53; Burkhardt 1988, 73), Philo knows and uses more traditional names for at least four of the five books of Moses: "Genesis" (Γένεσις: *Aet.* 19; *Post.* 127; *Abr.* 1); "Exagogē" (Ἐξαγωγή: *Migr.* 15; *Her.* 14, 251; *Somn.* 1.117); "Leviticus" / "Levitical Book" (Λευιτικόν / *Λευιτικὴ βίβλος: *Leg.* 2.105; *Her.* 152; *Plant.* 26); and "Deuteronomy" (Δευτερονόμιον: *Leg.* 3.174 [Deut 8:3]; *Deus* 50 [Deut 30:15, 19]). Siegert (1996–2015, 173) suggests that Philo may also have known the title "Numbers" in *Mos.* 2.117, but this is a reference to Philo's fragmentary treatise, *De numeris*. Philo also occasionally calls Deuteronomy the "Appendix" (Ἐπινομίς). It is thus unlikely that Philo understood Moses's *Exhortations* to be simply identical with the book of Deuteronomy (So Cohen 1997, esp. 66–70; Wilson 2011, 149)

Naomi Cohen, pointing to *Fug.* 170 where Philo cites a passage from Leviticus as stemming from the "Exhortations," develops a counter-thesis: that this title refers not to Deuteronomy, but represents "a taxonomical category, and very likely also the name of an anthology containing passages of exhortation" (Cohen 1997, 70). She thus renders the phrase "hortatory discourse" (Cohen 1997, 67). Cohen is right that, as Philo conceived it, this hortatory discourse came to include more the Deuteronomy and functions as something of a "taxonomical category" in Philo's understanding of the scriptural anatomy. But this does not necessitate Philo's knowledge and use of multiple anthologies or compendia ("the *Exhortations*" and "the *Epinomis*"), as Cohen suggests.

TABLE 2.1   References to the *Exhortations*
(or *Encouragements)

Philonic text	Biblical text
Agr. 78	Deut 20:1
**Agr.* 84	Deut 17:15–16
Agr. 172	Deut 8:18
Fug. 142	Deut 4:29–30
Fug. 170	Lev 25:11
Mut. 42	Deut 12:28
Mut. 263	Deut 30:12–14
**Spec.* 4.131	Deut 12:8
Virt. 47	Deut 28:1, 2, 7; Lev 26:5

TABLE 2.2   Philo's Divisions of *Deuteronomy*

Philonic division	Biblical pericope	Philonic reference
The Exhortations	Deut 1–30	See Table 2.1
The Great(er) Song	Deut 32	*Leg.* 3.105; *Det.* 114; *Mut.* 182
The Benedictions	Deut 33	*QG* 4.123; *Det.* 67; *Mut.* 200 (cf. Gen 49)
The Head of the Law Giving	Deut 34	*Mos.* 2.290

To get a better sense of the contents Philo did include in this "work" called the *Exhortations*, it is helpful to recall the nine pericopes, in which Philo cites a biblical text as standing "in the *Exhortations*" (ἐν τοῖς προτρεπτικοῖς), or alternatively, *"In the *Encouragements*" (ἐν ταῖς παραινέσεσι).

Table 2.1 (above) shows that the title *Exhortations* most often references Deut 1–30. Philo has names for other parts of Deuteronomy as well, including "the Curses," which are a part of the *Exhortations* (see Philo, *Her.* 250; Siegert 1996–2015, 173), "the Great Song," "the Benedictions," and "the Head of the Law Giving." This suggests that Deuteronomy was divided by Philo and his school into four basic "orders" or divisions (see table 2.2 above).

That the *Exhortations* came to include several passages from Leviticus may represent an expansion of this "taxonomical category" to accommodate the needs of Philo's broader allegorical and halakhic projects, which reckoned with all five Mosaic books as a single, composite organism.

"You shall do what is well-pleasing before the Lord your God." Philo cites Deut 12:28—his next secondary lemma in the chain—in a loose fashion:

LXX Deut 12:28	§ 42
If you do what is good and pleasing before (ἐναντίον) the Lord your God.	You shall do what is well-pleasing before (ἐνώπιον) the Lord your God.

The three changes of Philo's paraphrase are (1) to turn the condition "if you make" (ἐὰν ποιήσῃς) into "you shall make" (ποιήσεις); (2) to combine "what is good and pleasing" (τὸ καλὸν καὶ τὸ ἀρεστόν) into "that which is well-pleasing" (τὸ εὐάρεστον) so that it more closely echoes the verb of his primary ("be well-pleasing," εὐαρέστει [§ 39]) and anticipatory ("was well-pleasing," εὐηρέστησε [§ 34]) biblical lemmata; and (3) to replace "opposite" (ἐναντίον) with "facing" (ἐνώπιον—see the General Comments on § 41). Philo does not shy from paraphrasing biblical citations for the sake of creating a more cohesive scriptural "multi-verse." For paraphrase as an allegorical tool in Philo, see Zaleski 2020.

he will receive. Philo reiterates the verb from § 40, which states that he "receives" as the gift of his own grace those human works which appear good in his sight and the sight of others.

(3) § 43. ***prompted by this thought.*** Philo adduces three tertiary lemmata in support of his interpretation of Deut 12:28. The Greek participle "prompted" (ὁρμηθείς) denotes poetic, mantic, and rhetorical inspiration in Homer and Plato, as much as it does cognitive impulse (see Nagy 1999, 140; Homer, *Od.* 8.499; Plato, *Ion* 434c3). Philo endorses the Middle Platonic idea that Moses was intentionally "weaving" moral allegories in relaying the cultic prescriptions at Sinai and (then again) at the Jordan. This contrasts with the Stoic view that earlier mythological poets accidentally related philosophical truths inherent in divine names, while confusing these with ornate fictions. For the Stoic view (and its Platonist reception), see Boys-Stones 2001, esp. 28–43.

Moses was weaving the tabernacle. Although it was Bezalel who served as foreman in the construction of the tabernacle (Exod 31:2), Philo presents Moses as its active artificer, insofar as Moses alone sees its eternal form. Philo's use of the verb "weave together" (συνυφαίνειν) merits special comment. The compound verb applies to the making of fabrics of all sorts and occurs only three times in the Pentateuch (Exod 28:28[32]; 36:10, 17 [39:3, 10]). All three pertain to the making of the high priestly vestments (on which, see below), not the embroidering of the tabernacle curtains. Related to these is 2 Chron 2:12–13, in which Huram (Gk. Chiram), the King of Tyre, sends Solomon an artificer named Huramabi (Gk. "Chiram ⟨is⟩ my father") to help him with the construction of the temple. Huramabi is described as:

> A wise man and possessing knowledge (ἀνὴρ σοφὸς καὶ εἰδὼς σύνεσιν) … knowing how to make things with gold and silver and bronze and iron, with stones and wood; and how to weave (ὑφαίνειν) in purple and hyacinth and flax-linen and scarlet; how to make engraved objects and think every thought (⟨εἰδὼς⟩ διανοεῖσθαι πᾶσαν διανόησιν).

This description of Huramabi, the wise temple-builder and weaver, is only one step removed from Philo's allegorizing of Moses's weaving wisdom in the soul and was likely an inspiration for Philo's paraphrase.

Philo's use of the verb "weave together" (συνυφαίνειν) may also echo classical tradition. Perhaps most important is the verb's singular occurrence in Plato (*Pol.* 305e), where the Eleatic Stranger offers his climactic definition of the political "science" as that which subsumes the sciences of the general, the judge, and the rhetor, "weaving them all together most rightly" (⟨ἐπιστήμη⟩ πάντα συνυφαίνουσα ὀρθότατα). Plato uses the weaving metaphor earlier in the same dialogue to derive his definition of statecraft (see *Pol.* 279b–287c). If Philo alludes to the *Statesman* here, he paints the Jewish lawgiver as a symbol of the ideal psychic disposition within the Abrahamic cohort, capable of seamlessly weaving together the works which please both God and humanity. At a further remove still, the verb "weave together" depicts Philo's own scriptural artistry, as the Alexandrian himself, in this catena of secondary and tertiary lemmata, weaves together two kinds of tradition, the halakhic and the cultic. Cf. Philo's antithetical use of "weave-together" (συνυφαίνειν) at *Mut.* 199 to denote the beguilements of the sophists; and Moses's weaving together four psychic powers in *Mos.* 2.7.

with two curtained spaces … distinguished from the inner things. Philo paraphrases Exod 26:33 (TBL) to illustrate how Moses inculcates wisdom, not only by deontological mandate but also by cultic symbolism. Allegoresis of religious cult is attested by other Middle Platonists like Plutarch, *De Iside et Osiride* (Brenk 2023). The synopsis on the next page illustrates echoes of the Septuagint in Philo's paraphrase.

In Philo's allegory, doing the work pleasing to God is symbolized by the holy of holies ("the inner things"), while doing works pleasing to other human beings is symbolized by "the holy place" ("the outer things"). Interiority and exteriority are depicted in all four tertiary lemmata surrounding the tabernacle, illustrating the symbolic coordination of works done externally with the body and works done interiorly in the mind.

LXX Exod 26:33	§ 43
33 And you will set the curtain (θήσεις τὸ καταπέτασμα) upon the posts and you will bring in there, within (ἐσώτερον) the curtain, the ark of the testimony; and the curtain will divide (διοριεῖ) for you between (ἀνὰ μέσον) the sanctuary and the holy of holies.	He wove the tabernacle together with two curtained spaces (δυσὶ ... ὁρίοις), setting a veil (κάλυμμα θείς) between (μέσον ἀμφοῖν) both of them, so that the outer things might be distinguished from the inner things (τῶν εἴσω).

he gilded the holy law-guarding ark both within and without. Philo next paraphrases Exod 25:11 (TBL), the double-gilding of the ark of the covenant. It shares with the preceding lemma the theme of inner and outer craftsmanship, which symbolizes the doubly pleasing aspect of the sage in Abraham's company. Moses, rather than Bezalel, is understood as the artificer, to maintain the consistency of the allegoresis. Philo's paraphrase, "he gilded it within and without" (ἔνδοθεν καὶ ἔξωθεν ἐχρύσωσε) shifts the scriptural future tense verb, "you shall gild" (χρυσώσεις), into the past tense, and cleverly reverses the sequence "outside and inside" (ἔξωθεν καὶ ἔσωθεν) in Exodus to reflect the priority of interiority (and service to God) in Philonic thought. Philo also follows the Deuteronomic tradition in placing the tablets within the ark—another sign of the covenantal character of this passage. Exod 25–30 knows nothing of this tradition; it first appears in Deut 10:1–2 and is echoed in Heb 9:4. The application of the feminine adjective "law-guarding" (νομοφυλακίς) to the ark is a Philonic *hapax* and is not recapitulated by Josephus. The adjective only occurs once prior to Philo in a first-century BCE inscription, as an epithet of Aphrodite at Cyrene (*Rendic. Linc.* 1925.420, per LSJ). It appears to be a variant of the more common epithet, "law guarding" (νομοφύλαξ), which is among other things an office in Plato's *Laws*.

presented the high priest with two vestments. Philo adduces a third example of cultic interiority and exteriority by weaving together accounts of the high priest's garments from Exod 28:4 and Lev 6:10. These represent a third, composite tertiary lemma in the sequence. The language of "two stoles" (διτταὶ ... στολαί) is taken from Exod 28:4, but this chapter does not distinguish which vestments are to be worn in which precinct, nor does it list only two garments, but rather six. The exchange of priestly vestments when entering the holy of holies is described in Lev 6:10: "then he will put off his stole and put on another stole" (καὶ ἐκδύσεται τὴν στολὴν αὐτοῦ καὶ ἐνδύσεται στολὴν ἄλλην). Colson (PLCL 5:166, n. a) observes: "for the general thought of this passage with the same illustration from the two robes and the words of Gen 32:28 [see § 44], cf. the fuller exposition in *Ebr.* 80–87."

the linen one for within the adytum. The editors of PCW point to Lev 6:10 as the source of this tradition, but Lev 16:4 and 12 are likely not far from Philo's mind as well. Earlier in the Allegorical Commentary, Philo makes much of the high priest's ritual of entrance (see *Leg.* 2.54–55). There, after donning the "linen tunic" (χιτών), the high priest is commanded to lead the goat for the Lord "within the curtain" (ἐσώτερον τοῦ καταπετάσματος [Lev 16:12]), a phrase which stitches together Philo's first (the tabernacle) and third (the vestments) cultic images in this sequence.

the many-colored one, with the long robe, for the outer sanctuary. Philo's description of the priest's more common vestment used for the "daily offering" (תמיד) is derived from Exod 28. The adjective "mottled, bunt" (ποικίλη) is used of the multicolored fabrics of Exod 28:5, 8, etc. The "foot-length undergarment" (ὁ ποδήρης) mentioned by Philo, with the pomegranates and golden bells, is found in this chapter as well (Exod 28:4, 27[31]). While Philo often uses the adjective "many-colored" in the Allegorical Commentary as a negative descriptor of the variegated pleasures of creation, which draw the mind away from the singular good of noetic contemplation (e.g., *Leg.* 2.75), in *Mut.* 43 he uses it positively. The multi-colored everyday garment allegorically represents the naturally differentiated pattern of ethical living amid quotidian contingencies required of the Abrahamic-Mosaic sage.

§ 44. *symbols of a soul.* For "symbol" (σύμβολον), see detailed comment on § 2. Abraham, Jacob, and Moses are here synthesized as a single type.

purified ... cleansed. Philo imbues the language of cultic holiness with moral significance frequently in the Allegorical Commentary (see *Leg.* 2.53; 3.100; Cover 2024b). Some have suggested that Philo's high valuation of the priesthood in his allegoresis suggests his priestly descent (Schwartz 2009), but this remains speculative.

the perceptible cosmos and its manner of life. "The perceptible cosmos" (ὁ αἰσθητὸς κόσμος) or "the visible cosmos" (ὁ ὁρατὸς κόσμος [cf. *Opif.* 16]), meaning material universe, as opposed to the "intelligible cosmos" (ὁ νοητὸς κόσμος) or the summation of the world of forms, contained in the Logos. For the latter concept in the Allegorical Commentary, see *Gig.* 61 and *Sobr.* 55.

Jacob, the triumphant wrestler. Philo leaves off the Mosaic exempla and returns to the secondary level of exposition with a paraphrase of Gen 32 and Jacob's symbolism of the ethical wrestler/athlete (see the detailed comment on § 41). The broader pericope alluded to, in which Jacob is said to have wrestled with a mysterious man at the Jabbok river all night and then have his name changed (Gen 32:25–26), is of central importance to the treatise. It is adduced by Philo four times, in chapters one (§ 14), two (§ 44), five (§ 81), and eight (§ 187). (For an analysis of these four texts together, see the detailed comment on § 187.) In the present section, Jacob symbolizes the sage eschatologically perfected after his struggle with God. This is in keeping with Philo's interpretation of Gen 48:15 earlier in this section (§ 41), where the patriarch Israel—Jacob in perfection—is referenced. Philo's three exempla of double blessing in this section—Abraham, Moses, and Jacob—represent the covenantal type of the devotees of "the gentler wisdom," with Moses standing in for Isaac in the ethical triad.

the victor's wreath. Philo decks the biblical allegory with a metaphor drawn from pagan athletics: the wreath at the Panhellenic Games. The transformation of this wreath into a symbol of wisdom was a favorite of other Hellenistic Jewish authors (e.g., 1 Cor 9:25) as well as philosophers and sophists (cf. Dio Chrysostom, *Or.* 8.15). Dio can also speak of the philosopher as competing in a tougher contest than that of wrestlers (*Or.* 8.12).

the proclamation. In Gen 32:29, the "man" at the Jabbok offers Jacob a description of the patriarch's past actions, which Philo calls a "proclamation" (κήρυγμα). The language is neither legal nor cultic, but offers an eschatological judgment on the Jacob soul that has become Israel, indicating that all who follow him will ultimately also receive the same proclamation.

"you were strong with God, and capable with human beings." Philo has only lightly modified the form of his secondary lemma, Gen 32:29b, simplifying the first verb from "prevail" (ἐνίσχυσας) to "be strong" (ἴσχυσας). Reading the latter verb as an aorist indicative (with the scribe of A, PCW, and Colson) rather than a participle (ἰσχύσας) with imperatival force, the verse pronounces the perfection of the Jacob soul. More importantly for the covenantal pattern, Jacob's "past perfection" grounds God's future promise to those who follow in his footsteps. While not quite adducing the "merits of the fathers," Philo does build into his covenantal theology a witness of God's past faithfulness in perfecting Jacob and a pledge of similar faithfulness to those whose souls follow Jacob's pattern of virtuous practice. For more on grace in Philo's covenant theology, see the detailed comments on § 25 ("gift-exchange"), § 40 ("choice grace"), and §§ 52–53.

§ 45. *each order of being.* Philo construes the goal of becoming doubly well-pleasing in ontological terms, invoking two "orders" (τάξεις) of being, the ungenerated and the generated. Given Philo's usage elsewhere (*Her.* 205), it may be more accurate to speak of three kinds of being in Philo's thought: the ungenerated (The One Who Is), those at the borderland (occupied or approached in different ways by the Logos and perfected souls), and the generated.

the mind at the borderland. Philo's middle kind of being at the borderland is here populated by the "mind" or "intellect" (διάνοια), situated between the generated and ungenerated. Elsewhere in the Allegorical Commentary, this space is said to be inhabited (more properly) by the Logos, who is situated "at the borderland" (μεθόριος) between "that which is becoming" (τὸ γενόμενον) and "the Maker" (ὁ πεποιηκώς), "neither uncreated as God nor created as you ⟨human beings⟩" (οὔτε ἀγένητος ὡς ὁ θεός, οὔτε γενητὸς ὡς ὑμεῖς) (*Her.* 205; cf. *Leg.* 3.175, where the Logos is probably construed as a distinctive member of the third order, that of "becoming" [τὸ γενόμενον]). It is only by assimilation to the Logos that created minds attain this ontological "order" (τάξις), as a form of Jewish-Platonic *theōsis*. (For deification in Philo, see Litwa 2014.)

attendant. Commenting on the word "attendant" (ὀπαδός), Arnaldez (1964, 53, n. 2) observes: "When the virtuous human being has seen in God the Father and Creator, he is covered with a virtue which participates in the attributes of God and which is beneficent as they are."

the Ruler of all and Father of what is generated. Although "ruler" (ἡγεμών) can sometimes refer to the Logos, Philo usually reserves the title Father exclusively for "The One Who Is" (τὸ ὄν), as here.

is concerned. God's care for the person is a central part of Philo's covenant theology and prompts him in § 46 to give a philosophical grounding for the theology of grace that he will develop later in this chapter.

§ 46. *before the generation of the world ... after the generation of the world.* While a simple reading of these phrases would suggest that Philo thinks of creation as a temporal event, the case is far from clear. The language is scriptural and traditional (LXX Prov 8:22–30), but leaves the philosophical details underdetermined. For the debate on whether Philo endorses a doctrine of *creatio temporalis*, *creatio perpetua*, or *creatio continua*, see Sterling 1992.

God was sufficient for himself. The sufficiency of God in Philo's thought stands in stark juxtaposition to human lack of self-sufficiency or nothingness. See Cover 2020b; Lévy 2018.

not changing. Philo here endorses one of the key tenets of classical theism: the immutability of God, on which he wrote an entire treatise (*Quod Deus sit immutabilis*). His expression of this concept with the words "not changing" (οὐ μεταβαλών) contrasts with the dynamic, changing quality of human souls, which undergo a "metabolic" process of transformation toward perfection (or the opposite; see, e.g., §§ 76, 105), which is symbolized in this treatise especially by their "change of names."

the things that are not. The phrase "the things that are not" (τὰ μὴ ὄντα) is a Jewish expression for creation, but does not necessarily entail a belief in *creatio ex nihilo*. See Sterling 2017; Anderson and Bockmuehl 2018.

is there any reason. Philo answers his own rhetorical question with an interrogative rather than a declarative sentence. He thus falls short of saying that God creates "because he is good" or "because he loves to give gifts." In this instance, the sceptical influence on his thought leads him to be cautious in answering a tricky philosophical problem (Lévy 2018).

because he is good. Colson (PLCL 5:588) suggests that the first part of Philo's answer to the question of the "why" of creation—that God created on account of his goodness—stems from a clever misreading or extension of *Tim.* 29de. Plato's point is that God's goodness entails the absence of envy; in *Mut.* 46, Philo is searching for a deeper answer to the question of why create anything at all if the transcendent God was entirely sufficient. Philosophically speaking, it is not clear that goodness in itself is a reason *for* creating something, if nothing was truly needed and God was entirely sufficient (Van Inwagen 2015).

he loves to give gifts. Philo's second answer to the question of why God creates carries more force. The negative form of the argument might be reframed as follows: (1) if the giving of gifts is good; and (2) God in his transcendence cannot give gifts; then (3) there must be some lack (insufficiency) in God. Philo, however, has also been careful to assert the total sufficiency of God before creation—a point which stems from the transcendence of "The One Who Is" (τὸ ὄν) and the impossibility of describing him with predicates of relation (§ 28). Rather than wade further into this problem here, Philo wisely leaves his entire answer in the form of a question.

Master ... Cause. Philo closes with two more names for God, "master" and "cause," which have equal resonance in Jewish Scripture and Roman households, on the one hand, and Greek philosophy, on the other. For "master" (δεσπότης), see the detailed comments on §§ 19, 22; for "cause" (αἴτιον), see those on § 15.

the nature that is common to us. Arnaldez (1964, 54, n. 1) takes this text as an occasion to recall the optimistic (and non-dualist) character of Philo's anthropology: "An important idea: creation is attributable to the goodness of God, therefore the creature is fundamentally good. The pessimistic critiques of sensible and corporeal nature elsewhere in Philo do not apply to the ontological reality of the human. Evil does not penetrate to the root (cf. Wis 11:24)."

Parallel Exegesis

§ 39. *Gen 17:1cβ ("be well pleasing")*. In §§ 39 and 47, Philo gives the commands to "be well-pleasing" and to "be blameless" distinct interpretations. To be "well-pleasing" is the higher goal, indicating the active practice of virtue and works of mercy. It remains realizable in the embodied state. This view of God's first command does not find a parallel in *QG* 3.40. Instead, Philo argues that to be "perfectly good" belongs only to incorporeal natures—a thought that Marcus (PLCLSup 1:229, n. d) suggests is most closely paralleled at *Mut.* 50. As a result, the command to be "well-pleasing" receives no independent exegesis in *QG* 3.40. It is considered a rough equivalent of the second command to "be blameless," which in *De mutatione nominum* is differentiated as a lesser "negative" kind of virtue, namely, the avoidance of vice. An undifferentiated interpretation of the two commands of Gen 17:1c is also found in *Gig.* 63–64, where they are jointly understood to represent the soul that "becomes God's companion and makes straight the path of its whole life, treading the true 'King's way' (Num 20:17), the way of the one sole almighty king, swerving and turning aside neither to the right nor to the left" (trans. Colson, PLCL).

the divine madness. "The divine madness" (ἡ ἔνθεος μανία) is a Philonic phrase, more often given in the combination, "the divine possession and madness" (ἡ ἔνθεος κατοκωχή τε καὶ μανία), as in *Migr.* 84; *Her.* 250, 264. The uncompounded form is also found at *Fug.* 168.

the tame and gentle wisdom. Colson (PLCL 5:162, n. b) adduces *Her.* 127 as a parallel to the description of divine Wisdom in *Mut.* 39 as "tame and gentle" (ἥμερος καὶ τιθασός). In that text, however, the description belongs properly to the turtledove, mentioned in Gen 15:9.

§ 40. *honor your parents … common justice.* Philo begins his five-fold list of covenantal stipulations with a paraphrase of Exod 20:12 and Deut 5:16, treating the command at the literal level. Within the Allegorical Commentary, Philo's nearest parallel to *Mut.* 40 is *Ebr.* 17, where he paraphrases the fifth commandment similarly as (1) "honor your parents" (τοὺς γονεῖς τιμᾶν) and sets it at the head of a chain of example-laws, which one can transgress passively and actively. This list also includes (2) to "save one's country" (τὴν πατρίδα σῴζειν); (3) to "do kindness to a neighbor" (ὁ … χαριζόμενός τισι); and (4) to "make use of the holy rites (ἱερουργίαι) and all else that pertains to piety." The list of five covenantal stipulations in *Mut.* 40 follows and expands a similar pattern, with non-scriptural laws pertaining to justice anthologized under the heading of the fifth commandment (*Her.* 171–172). Philo also offers an allegorical interpretation of the command at *Det.* 52–53, with the "father" symbolizing "mind" and "mother" symbolizing "sense-perception." Philo's primary treatment of this command is found in the Exposition of the Law at *Decal.* 106–120.

with an unsleeping eye. In *Ios.* 147, Philo speaks of the heavenly realm as cared for by "sleepless oversight." Philo uses the related phrase, "unsleeping eye" (ἀκοίμητον ὄμμα), in *Mos.* 1.185 and *Spec.* 1.49, 330 (*inter alia*), as well as "unsleeping eyes" (ἀκοίμητοι ὀφθαλμοί) at *Spec.* 4.139, to refer to the eye(s) of the human soul (see the comment on *Mut.* 5).

choice grace. The election of Abraham is described similarly in *Gig.* 64 as something "allotted beforehand" (προσκεκλήρωται) by God, which nevertheless requires the soul's active participation.

§ 41. *Gen 48:15 ("God, to whom my fathers were well-pleasing")*. Gen 48:15a, with its lexical link to the primary verb, "be well-pleasing" (εὐηρέστησαν), is specially quarried from the Scriptures for this context. The same is true of Deut 12:28 in § 42, which occurs nowhere else in the *corpus Philonicum*.

§ 43. *Exod 26:33*. The concatenation of these three Mosaic "doubles"—the tabernacle, the ark, and the priestly vestments—is given in a slightly different order at *Ebr*. 85. For the division of the tabernacle on its own in Exod 26:33, see *Mut*. 192; *QG* 4.80; and *QE* 2.91, 94, 104, and 106. In *QG* 4.80, Exod 26:33 is adduced as a secondary lemma following Abraham's request for a "double cave" in which to bury Sarah in Gen 23:9. Just as the "double-cave" symbolizes the interiority and exteriority of body and soul, so Moses makes the tabernacle a symbol of the duality of the noetic and sense-perceptible (see also *QE* 2.106). *QE* 2.91, by contrast, offers a cosmological (rather than anthropological) interpretation of the bifurcation, relating to sublunary and heavenly bodies and geographies (so also *QE* 2.94 and 104).

weaving together. See the similar use of the metaphor in *Somn*. 1.203–205.

Exod 25:11. For the double-gilding of the ark, along with both tabernacle and priestly vestments, see *Ebr*. 85. For the ark on its own, see *QE* 2.54. There, the double gilding is given literal, natural, and ethical interpretations. Most germane to the present text is Philo's statement that the double gilding of the ark points to a pure mind (on the inside) and virtuous actions (on the outside).

Exod 28:4; Lev 6:10, 16:4. For the priest's two vestments, along with tabernacle and ark, see *Ebr*. 85. For the two vestments, see *Somn*. 1.213–218 and *Spec*. 1.84–85, 94. In *Somn*. 1.213–218, the priest's change of vestment to enter the Holy of Holies becomes a sign of ethical purity. Lev 16:4 is a secondary lemma, amplifying Jacob's vision of three kinds of sheep in Laban's pasture (Gen 31:10), particularly the "thorough-white" (διάλευκοι) kind. These demonstrate the Jacob-soul's potential to reach ethical purity of the highest order. In *Spec*. 1.84, Philo suggests that the linen tunic worn by the high priest when entering the Holy of Holies is made of plant rather than animal fabric, as wool symbolizes animals subject to demise. Otherwise, the vestments' cosmological (rather than anthropological-ethical) significance is more to the fore in these passages from the Exposition of the Law.

§ 44. *Gen 32:28(29)*. This lemma—especially Jacob's change of name and the proclamation that Jacob will be "strong with God and powerful with human beings" is a favorite of Philo's as a secondary lemma. He uses it twice, at §§ 44 and 81–83. For the use of the broader pericope, Gen 32:26(27)–32(33), in *De mutatione nominum*, see the detailed comment on §187. In *QE* 2.108, Philo adduces Gen 32:28(29) and Jacob's two-fold strength in support of his interpretation of the two priestly shoulder-pieces of Exod 28:7 (cf. *Mut.* 44). Similarly, *Ebr.* 82–83 offers a sequential interpretation of Gen 32:28(29)–29(30), including a citation of Jacob's change of name and a paraphrase (*Ebr.* 83) of the Israel soul's dual strength with God and human beings. *Somn.* 1.131, with its reference to Jacob's acquiring "indomitable power" (δύναμις ἀκαθαίρετος), may allude to this verse.

§ 46. *because he is good*. See *Opif.* 21 for a similar explanation for the goodness of God as the cause of creation.

Nachleben
§ 39. *Gen 17:1cβ ("be well-pleasing before me")*. A favorite passage in the Alexandrian Christian tradition, even where a direct connection to *De mutatione nominum* is not ascertainable. Clement (*Paed.* 1.56.3 [C]) interprets Gen 17:1 to depict God as one who "prepares ⟨Abraham as⟩ a faithful child in a most teacherly fashion" (τοῦτον δὲ παιδαγωγικώτατα ὑποκατασκευάζει παῖδα πιστόν). Didymus, in his comments on this lemma (*In Gen.* 250.28–29 [C]), notes that the speaker of this command is "anointing ⟨the saint⟩ for the contest and preparation of courage" (ἀλείφων δὲ αὐτὸν εἰς ἀγῶνα καὶ παρασκευὴν ἀνδρείας). In *Comm. Zacch.* 2.23 [C], Didymus adduces Gen 17:1c as typical of the one who "delights in the Lord" (LXX Ps 36:4). He adds: "The one who accepts this good provision innocently and in a well-pleasing fashion (εὐαρέστως), trusting in the Judge who says, 'Be well-pleasing before me and become blameless' (Gen 17:1c), receives a crown of delight." Similarly, in *Comm. Ps.* 20–21, 41.21 [B], Didymus opines that "just as each of the saints is no longer said simply to be a human being, but God's human being, so also the soul that is exhibited as being well-pleasing to God (ἡ εὐαρεστεῖν προθεμένη θεῷ ψυχὴ) is not simply called a soul, but a soul of God," with evident connection to this Philonic theme and chapter.

the divine madness. Although clearly a reference to the *Phaedrus*, the precise phrase "the divine madness" (ἡ ἔνθεος μανία) appears to be a Philonic coinage. Libanius (*Progymn.* 6.1 [D]), Cyril of Alexandria (*Contr. Jul.* 2.4 [D]), and Proclus (*In Plat. rem publ.* 1.157 [D]) especially connect it with the inspiration of the Homeric singers. In the *Theologia Platonica*, Proclus invokes a similar phrase, "the divine mouth" (ἔνθεον στόμα), to discuss Plato's alternation between "enthusiastic" (ὁτὲ μὲν ἐνθεαστικῶς) and "dialectical/rational" (ὁτὲ δὲ διαλεκτικῶς) speech, giving the *Phaedrus* as a prime example of the former (*Theol. Plat.* 1.3.17–18 [D]).

§ 41. ⟨*Israel*⟩ *the practicer*. Later Alexandrian Christian authors adopt from Philo the identification of Jacob (rather than Israel) as the typical "practicer" (ἀσκητής). See esp. Didymus the Blind, *Frag. Ps.* 948 (Ps 97:3) [B/C].

§ 42. *in his Exhortations*. Later Christian authors do not usually use the title "Exhortations" (Προτρεπτικοί) with special reference to Moses's writings or Deuteronomy (see, e.g., Eusebius, *Praep. ev.* 11.4.6 [D], who speaks of the prophets after Moses). The title came to designate the rhetorical mode of various speakers, including Solomon, Jeremiah, and the Psalmist.

§ 43. *Exod 26:33* (*inner and outer curtain*). Christian tradition largely followed the path charted in Matt 27:51 and Heb 10:20 in interpreting the space within the temple veil as symbolic of the new Christian order. As such, a purely ethical allegory was foreclosed. Hebrews (like Philo), nevertheless, gives to entrance *within* the veil ethical importance, while the space outside the curtain is less important. Oblique echoes of Philo are detectable in later Alexandrian authors. Cyril, for example, invokes an interpretation of the inner and outer spaces delineated by the temple curtain, which although materially different from Philo's allegoresis, betrays a similar symbolic logic. In *Comm. Jo.* 1.522–523 [D], Cyril likens John the Baptist, nicknamed the "burning lamp" (ὁ λύχνος ὁ καιόμενος [cf. John 5:35]), to the "lamp" (λύχνος) of the tabernacle, which God commands the Levites to burn "outside the curtain" (ἔξωθεν τοῦ καταπετάσματος [Lev 24:3]). Cyril continues:

> In the foregoing discussion, we have interpreted the lantern in the holy tabernacle, which is giving light outside the curtain (ἔξωθεν τοῦ καταπετάσματος ὁ καταφωτίζων [Lev 24:2–3]), to be the blessed John; for he is nourished by purist oil, that is, the light of the Spirit. ⟨And he is⟩ indeed "outside the curtain" (ἔξω γεμὴν τοῦ καταπετάσματος), since his word is catechetical: "prepare the way of the Lord," he says, "make straight the paths of our God" (Matt 3:3). But the things within the curtain (τὰ δὲ ἔσω τοῦ καταπετάσματος), that is, the hidden mystery concerning Christ, ⟨John⟩ does not shine much light upon.

Like Philo, Cyril interprets the outer and inner spaces created by the tabernacle curtain as symbolizing ascending realms of importance. Whereas for Philo, both relate to human ethical obligations, to neighbor and to God, Cyril connects the space outside with works of repentance and moral catechesis preached by John, and the inner space with mystery of Christ's redemptive work toward God. The resemblance is general, but not genetic.

Exod 25:11 (*gilding the ark*). An unassigned fragment of Irenaeus of Lyons (*Frag. deperdit.* 8 [B/C]) attests something like the Philonic allegoresis of the ark's double gilding, albeit with a Christological twist:

For just as the ark was gilded within and without with pure gold (ὥσπερ γὰρ ἡ κιβωτὸς κεχρυσωμένη ἔσωθεν καὶ ἔξωθε χρυσίῳ καθαρῷ ἦν), so also the body of Christ was clean and shining. Within, it was adorned by the Logos (ἔσωθεν μὲν τῷ Λόγῳ κοσμούμενον); without, it was guarded by the Spirit (ἔξωθεν δὲ τῷ Πνεύματι φρουρούμενον). Therefore, from both of the natures (φύσεις) was his resplendency demonstrated (τὸ περιφανὲς ... παραδειχθῇ).

Exod 28:4; Lev 6:10; 16:4 (two sets of vestments). Cf. Origen, *Hom. Lev.* 4.6 [B/C]. There, Paul is presented as a high priest, capable of exchanging his linen stole, in which he teaches wisdom to the perfect, for the mottled garment, in which he addresses the common Christian (see 1 Cor 2:4–8). As with the previous two examples, this is not exactly the allegorical meaning that Philo derives from the verse, though the scriptural trigger is the same. Van den Hoek (2000, 90), who does not mention *Hom. Lev.* 4.6, ranks a similar passage in *Hom. Lev.* 6.3, which speaks of the priestly garments, at a [C], where the similarities with *Mut.* 43 are weaker.

§ 44. *proclamation*. It is illustrative to contrast Philo's covenantal "proclamation" (κήρυγμα), summarized by Gen 32:29, with Paul's use of the same root in 1 Corinthians, wherein it also plays a role in a Hellenistic Jewish covenantal framework (1 Cor 1:21; 2:4; 15:14; cf. 9:27; 11:4.). In both contexts, the faithfulness and perfection of a previous figure grounds the promise of future grace for a contemporary Jewish(-Christian) community. Whereas Philo's fellow Alexandrian Jews might take inspiration from the fact that the Jacob soul was eschatologically declared "strong with God and capable with human beings," Paul's ironic proclamation of "Jesus Christ and him crucified" intentionally subverts the conventional covenantal rhetoric of strength for a rhetoric of weakness (cf. 1 Cor 2:3).

§ 46. *things that are not*. Compare Rom 4:17, which describes God as "the One who makes life for the dead and calls the things that are not as though they are" (ὁ ζωοποιῶν τοὺς νεκροὺς καὶ καλῶν τὰ μὴ ὄντα ὡς ὄντα). Neither text, strictly speaking, requires a doctrine of *creatio ex nihilo*. See Sterling 2017.

b   *"Be Blameless" (§§ 47–51a)*
     Analysis/General Comments

In § 47, Philo treats the next part of the verse in sequence, Gen 17:1cγ, "be blameless." Moses "adds" (προσεπιλέγει) these words, he suggests, as a qualifying stipulation or codicil to what has come before in (a) §§ 39–46. The positive command, to "be well-pleasing" (Gen 17:1cβ), now receives a covenantal *caveat* in Gen 17:1cγ, in the form of a negative addendum not to merit blame. This softening of the first command takes into account the created limitations of human agents. To support this anthropological accommodation, Philo adduces, via a thematic connection, Job 14:4 as a secondary lemma. Job's question, "Who is clean from pollution, even if his life is but one day?" indicates that the goal of being "well-pleasing" is not attainable by the majority of people. Most do well, then, to avoid sin—and this is sufficient as a response to the grace of God, even if it does not lead to the "first prize."

Detailed Comments

§ 47. *"and be blameless."* Philo cites Gen 17:1cγ, the primary biblical lemma, in exact accordance with the Septuagint. See § 39.

employing a logical sequence. Philo implies that the two commands of the scriptural verse belong together in a single chapter, as also in QG 3.40. "employing a logical sequence" (lit. "in following and sequence," ἀκολουθίᾳ καὶ εἱρμῷ) is a hendiadys, which suggests that God's addition of "and be blameless" follows a soteriological logic.

the one who is upright. Colson (PLCL 5:588) observes: "Philo here uses κατορθόῦ [sic; read κατορθόω, 'be upright'] in a sense slightly different from the regular Stoic use. With them the κατορθώματα ('upright deeds') are actions done from a good motive and part of a generally virtuous course of conduct, and are opposed to καθήκοντα ('fitting deeds') of common duties; here it is opposed to simple abstention from evil doing."

the one who is not unjust cannot be blamed. Arnaldez (1964, 54, n. 2) observes: "A divergence with the doctrine of the sage in ancient Stoicism, in the distinction between positive and negative moral values: to do the good and to abstain from evil. There is a medial zone between perfect virtue and pure evil. Here lies ascetical morality and the religion of the Law."

§ 48. *mortal creation.* Philo distinguishes between "becoming" or "creation" (γένεσις) in general, which has no real being, and "mortal" human "becoming" (γένεσις ἡ θνητή), which is subject to ethical life and death. In Platonic anthropology, the soul is generally spoken of as immortal (*Mut.* 49; Plato, *Phaedr.* 245c5). In Middle Platonism, however, the mortality of the body gives rise to the analogous concept of soul death, on account of its enmeshment in vice. See Zeller 1995; Conroy 2008; Wasserman 2008.

perhaps ... "not to sin" means ... "being upright." Although Philo has distinguished between "being blameless" and "not sinning" as first- and second-prize behaviors, he now anthologizes an alternative theory that "not sinning" may in fact be tantamount to "being upright" for most (see QG 3.40 in the Parallel Exegesis). Philo ventures this thought with caution ("perhaps" [τάχα]), in order not to muddy his earlier position.

as Job says. This secondary lemma is one of Philo's seven or eight references to Job listed in the *BiPaSup* index (see the Parallel Exegesis), the only one in which Job is mentioned by name, and the only citation. References to named authors from the prophets and the writings are relatively infrequent, given Philo's sparse use of these texts. See further Sterling 2012b; Cohen 2007, 171–173.

"for who is clean ... his life is but one day." Philo adduces LXX Job 14:4 as a secondary lemma. The following synopsis shows Philo's differences from the Old Greek:

Job 14:4–5	§ 48
⁴ For who will be (ἔσται) clean from stain? No one. ⁵ And even if his life (ὁ βίος αὐτοῦ) should be one day upon the earth, even so his months are numbered by you, you have set it for a time, and surely he will not go beyond it.	For who ⟨is⟩ clean from stain even if life (ἡ ζωή) is one day?

Philo has edited the citation, so that the answer to Job's rhetorical question is suppressed. This leaves room for the possibility, but rarity, of human perfection. The removal of the phrase "upon the earth" prepares the way for Philo's psychological allegory.

§ 49. *soil.* Philo applies the language of cultic purity and impurity to the soul. Although the language is common in Philo, he uses this cluster of verbs, "to soil," "to purge," "to wash clean" (καταρρυπαίνειν, ἐκνίψασθαι, ἀπολούσασθαι) only in the Allegorical Commentary (*Cher.* 95; *Deus* 7; *Her.* 113; *Fug.* 41; *Mut.* 49, 124). See the comment on § 44.

which cannot entirely be purged and washed clean. Arnaldez (1964, 55, n. 4) suggests that Philo answers here the question "left in suspense in § 37": whether anyone can be purified in this life. Arnaldez does not take into account, however, Philo's earlier answer in § 38, where he holds open the possibility of perfection.

inborn defects. Philo speaks of "congenital corruptions" (συγγενεῖς κῆρες) in human nature that diminish its moral capacities. The word κῆρες in poetry means "fates" or "dooms" external to human beings (e.g., Homer, *Il.* 2.302). In prose, however, it indicates an interior anthropological fault, akin to "sins" (ἁμαρτίαι: see Plutarch, *Cim.* 2). Thus, Dionysus of Halicarnassus (*Ant. rom.*

2.3.7) can speak of "innate defects" (σύμφυτοι κῆρες), and Plutarch (*Crass.* 6.6) uses the identical phrase, "inborn defects" (συγγενεῖς κῆρες), to Philo. The most important predecessor to Philo's (and Plutarch's) usage in *Mut.* 49 is Plato, *Leg.* 937d: "Of the many fair things in human life, something like defects adhere in the natures (οἷον κῆρες ἐπιπεφύκασιν) of most of them, which pollute (καταμιαίνουσιν) and soil (καταρρυπαίνουσιν) them." For more on the theme of the "fall" of the Philonic soul, see the notes on chapter three (§§ 54–56) of the present treatise.

§ 50. *does someone seek ... in this mixed life.* Philo alludes (again) to the Stoic notion of the non-existence of the sage; see the detailed comment on § 36 above. This non-existence is limited to the "mixed life" (βίος πεφύρμενος) of the composite, imperfect human being, which is involved in daily affairs.

just, prudent, temperate, or entirely good. Philo lists three of the four cardinal virtues (courage is lacking). For the full set of four in the present treatise, see §§ 146 and 153; and, with holiness added as a fifth, § 197.

impossible for a human being in our condition. I.e., the embodied condition, with minds formed as "the molded man" in *Leg.* 1.31 (on the problem of double creation in Philo, see Tobin 1983; Winston 1985). Literally speaking, the "heavenly human being" of *Leg.* 1.31 points to a protological and eschatological (or ideal-formal) being. At the allegorical level, the heavenly human may symbolize the soul perfectly detached from the body (see *Leg.* 2.3); but Philo seems in *Mut.* 50 and elsewhere to suggest that embodied souls rarely if ever attain this psychic character.

§ 51a. *happiness.* Philo suggests here, as often throughout his corpus, that "happiness" (εὐδαιμονία) or the "happy life" (εὐδαίμων βίος) is the end toward which the virtuous soul is striving (see *Plant.* 49). This may be contrasted, on the one hand, with the "unfortunate life" (κακοδαίμων βίος, *Det.* 119). The designation of happiness as the supreme end (eudaimonism) of human existence was championed by most Hellenistic philosophical schools, including Neopythagoreans, Platonists, Peripatetics, and Stoics—although each school defines happiness differently. In § 50, Philo notes that "happiness" is the quality of a "second place" life—of the person who follows the mean and is "blameless." The highest good, belonging to the perfect soul that reaches the "pinnacle" (πρὸς ἀκρότητα; § 2) of virtue, is "joy (χαρά), the best of the good emotions" (§ 1). Philo thus forges a hierarchical distinction between joy and happiness, as first and second prizes. "Joy" represents the Abrahamic transcendence of mere Aristotelian "contentment."

Parallel Exegesis

§ 47. *be blameless*. In *De mutatione nominum*, God's injunction to "be blameless" (Gen 17:1cγ) expresses a second, lesser good than the first, to "be well-pleasing." QG 3.40a, by contrast, treats the two phrases as equivalents: "these statements relate and correspond (to each other) (եւ հակառակականգործութիւն ունի ասածեալն), for a character which pleases God does not incur blame, while one who is blameless and faultless in all things is altogether pleasing (to God)" (trans. Marcus, PLCLSup). The parallel citation of this text at *Gig.* 63—its only other citation in the Philonic corpus—does not treat the second command explicitly.

§ 48. *Job 14:4–5* ("*who is clean … his life is but one day*"). This is the only time in the *corpus Philonicum* that Philo adduces Job 14 or directly cites from the book. For possible additional references to Job, see the list from *BiPaSup* 90: QG 1.69 (Job 28:24); *Det.* 61 (Job 28:24); *Migr.* 136 (Job 38:4); *Spec.* 1.295 (Job 1:21); *Spec.* 2.192 (Job 25:2); and *Prob.* 65 (Job 28). Some of these, especially the references to God's inescapable eye (Job 28:24), are very loose and uncertain. The influence of Job 38:4 on *Migr.* 136, if not in letter then at least in spirit, seems more plausible. Cohen (2007, 171–173) does not treat any of these allusions, only the unique citation in *Mut.* 48.

§ 49. *inborn defects*. Only here in the Allegorical Commentary does Philo use the word κῆρες in the sense of natural "moral defects." In *Ebr.* 79 and *Somn.* 1.105, he applies it metaphorically to mean "plagues" or "pests." In the Exposition of the Law (*Spec.* 2.52; *Virt.* 193), he will align "the diseases of the body" (αἱ σώματος κῆρες) with "the greed of the soul" (αἱ ψυχῆς πλεονεξίαι).

§ 50. *this mixed life*. See *Her.* 45–46 for the three kinds of life, including the life focused on God, the life focused on the world of becoming, and the so-called "mixed life" (βίος μικτός), which is "a mixture of both preceding kinds" (μικτὸν ἀμφοῖν).

§ 51a. *a great advantage toward happiness*. In *De mutatione nominum*, Philo considers blamelessness "a great advantage *toward* a happy life (πρὸς εὐδαίμονα βίον)." In QG 3.40, by contrast, blamelessness "suffices for the happiness of the mortal nature" (շատ է մահկանացու բնութեան առ բարեխատութիւն). Marcus retroverts the Armenian word for "happiness" as "good fortune" (εὐτυχία) in Greek. The NBHL gives "success" (εὐπραγία), but *not* "happiness" (εὐδαιμονία). Cf. Bedrossian 1879, who gives a longer catalogue of definitions: "fortune, happiness, prosperity, chance, destiny." Philo may distinguish between blamelessness as a state that secures good fortune, and happiness, which only results from perfection. This would be in keeping with his differentiation of joy and happiness in *Mut.* 51 (see the detailed comment). Elsewhere in the Allegorical Commentary, both of these "good emotions" (εὐπάθειαι) are associated with Isaac and can be used as synonyms (*Cher.* 8; *Det.* 140).

Nachleben

§ 47. *Gen 17:1cγ ("be blameless")*. In a reversal of Philo's commentary arrangement, Didymus the Blind adduces Gen 17:1 as a secondary lemma in his *Commentarium in Job*, to explicate the meaning of Job 9:20. There, Job opines, "even if I should be blameless, I will turn out crooked" (ἐάν τε ὦ ἄμεμπτος, σκολιὸς ἀποβήσομαι). Didymus adduces Gen 17:1cγ (*Comm. Job* 251 [B]) to distinguish two kinds of blamelessness:

> "Blameless" (τὸ ἄμεμπτον [cf. Job 9:20]) signifies in two ways, the first of which results from doing nothing ⟨evil⟩ (τὸ μὲν τῷ μηδὲν ἐνεργεῖν), and the second from doing rightly (τὸ δὲ τῷ δικαιοπραγεῖ[ν]), which is praiseworthy, as also was said to Abraham: "be well-pleasing before me and be blameless" (Gen 17:1).

Intriguingly, Didymus recapitulates the two kinds of obedience discussed by Philo in chapter two of *De mutatione nominum*, the active "well-pleasing" and the passive "blamelessness," but understands these as two species of "blamelessness." The influence of Philo on this passage may be indirect, but shows at minimum that Didymus and the Alexandrian school were thinking very much along Philonic lines. Ambrose (*Abr.* 2.75–76 [B/C]) offers an ethical allegory of this command "be blameless" (for his literal interpretation, which is distant from Philo's mind, see *Abr.* 1.27 [D]), suggesting that God means the Abraham soul has not yet attained perfection, and must thereby attend to the teaching of wisdom. This is reminiscent of Philonic, but not so close as the parallel in Didymus.

refrain from sins. This section, as a whole, bears some similarity to Paul's covenantal discourse in Rom 3:9–20. In Rom 3, Paul adduces LXX Ps 14:1–3 in a way that mirrors Philo's use of Job 14:4. The critical difference is that while Philo suggests that to "refrain from sins" (τῶν γε ἁμαρτημάτων ἀπέχου [§ 47]) is possible, Paul finds, in a similar scriptural text, proof that all humanity, both Jews and Greeks, are "under sin" (Rom 3:9: ὑφ' ἁμαρτίαν). Philo and Paul thus each espouse a realist position on the capacity of human beings for perfection in virtue, but Paul's blend of apocalypticism and popular philosophy causes him to suggest that human beings are in an even more dire position than Philo suggests. See the following comment.

§ 48. *Job 14:4–5 ("who is clean ... his life is but one day")*. The verse is a favorite of Origen's, who uses it several times, inter alia, in his *Commentary on*

Romans. In *Comm. Rom*. 5.1 (1012C) [C], he adduces the lemma in support of his interpretation of Rom 3:23 and 5:12, which insist that "all have sinned," including the otherwise righteous Noah. This is in general keeping with Philo's use of the text to demonstrate the near impossibility of human perfection. His paraphrase, "no one is clear from stain, even if his life should be one day" ("nemo mundus a sorde, etiamsi unius diei fuerit vita eius") is similar to Philo's, but renders explicit the "no one," which Philo suppresses.

§ 49. ***inborn defects***. Philo's depiction of sin as an innate illness bears some resemblance to early Christian understandings of the "fall" (especially Origen's); however, there are still important differences. For Philo, there is no "hard" notion of a fall, mythologically speaking; the mind's proclivity toward the body is a natural and logical consequence of composite creation (*Leg*. 2.4–5; *Gig*. 28–29), which would have happened sooner or later. So Runia (2001, 356), commenting on *Opif*. 151 and *Gig*. 28–29: "Philo does not give the impression of regarding the descent into wickedness as a 'fall from grace,' i.e., a single event which might not have happened, but rather as a structural feature of the world of becoming." For the possibility of a "soft" fall in Philo, see Yli-Karjanmaa 2016.

c *"I Will Set My Covenant between Me and between You"* (§§ 51b–53)
    Analysis/General Comments

Turning from his evaluation of human moral potential and covenantal obligation (§§ 47–51a), Philo briefly lays out his understanding of the divine side of the covenant (§§ 51b–53). His elaboration of divine obligations is presented as an exegesis of the final part of the primary lemma, Gen 17:2: "I will set my covenant between me and between you." His interpretation exemplifies what for Barclay (2015, 238) is the defining aspect of Philo's theology of grace: the language of worth. "Covenants are written for the benefit of those worthy of a gift" (§ 52), says Philo. It is indeed tempting to see, in the flow of this chapter, a pattern of salvation that might be called "worth-righteousness," according to which those who strive to be "well-pleasing" and "blameless" and who have a natural capacity for the same are considered worthy of a divine gift as recompense. Several features, however, tell against a strong version of this construal of Philo's theology of covenant. Not least is the Philonic doctrine of human "nothingness," attested throughout the Allegorical Commentary. Additionally, the structure of the biblical lemma accounts for the sequence in which Philo has proceeded. Philo begins with human obligations (§§ 39–51a) because the text does, but this does not mean that he thinks of the covenant as a reward for services rendered. A more careful look at the chapter will reveal that Philo envisions grace as present from the very beginning and considers human avoidance of sin and obedience of the commandments as primarily a divine, and only secondarily as a human work—even if a subject's "worth" is indeed invoked.

Detailed Comments

§ 51b. *to the one who has chosen.* The human being has a role in accepting the stipulations of the covenant. Philo will clarify, however, in subsequent lines, the priority of divine grace in the covenantal structure.

to live in this manner. I.e., in a manner that is "well-pleasing" to God and to humanity ([a] §§ 39–46) or at least in the manner that is "blameless" ([b] §§ 47–51a).

in accordance with the covenants. Colson renders this phrase "a covenanted portion," but this loses the plural sense of "covenants" (διαθῆκαι). Like God's grace, the covenants precede human volition. In the cosmological perspective of QG 3.40, these covenants are none other than the "incorporeal words, ideas, and paradigms with which this entire universe has been made" (see the Parallel Exegesis). From anthropological horizon of the Allegorical Commentary, by contrast, Philo envisions each of the covenants as being a particular kind of grace, given in proportion to the needs and capacities of the human recipient. Abraham receives not the entirety of the covenants, but a singular covenant (or portion of grace) "appropriate" or "attuned" (ἁρμόζοντα) to his disposition. In the Exposition of the Law, Philo will say that each of the patriarchs allegorically symbolizes a mythologized "Grace" (*Abr.* 54). See Dillon and Birnbaum 2021, 195, who draw out the pedagogical connotations of the "Graces" in a Platonizing school context.

appropriate for God to give and the wise person to receive. This is the first of two expressions meant to construe God as the giver (or "extender") of the covenant and the wise human as the recipient. Philo speaks of a harmony between divine activity and human passivity.

§ 52. *I will set my covenant between me and between you.* Philo cites Gen 17:2a, the third part of the chapter's primary lemma, as the basis for his explication of God's covenantal grace. He omits the second part of this verse (Gen 17:2b, "and I will increase you greatly"), which he does interpret in QG 3.40. Philo's text of Gen 17:2a is identical to that of the Septuagint, with the exception that his text apparently reads "I will set" (θήσω) rather than "I will set for myself" (θήσομαι) as the verb of God's giving. Philo's text here is of the type represented in Göttingen LXX groups 15′ and 17′. The active rather than the middle form of the verb reinforces the completely active (and non-reciprocal: see § 27) work of God in establishing the covenant.

for the benefit of those worthy of the gift. The language of "human worth" is part of Philo's understanding of the covenant. This links him with other patterns of covenantal nomism in Second Temple Judaism, resembling in part the "merit of the fathers" theme associated especially with Abraham in rabbinic Judaism (cf. Rom 11:28; for the term and its development in the Tannaitic and Amoraic periods, see Kattan Gribetz 2018). Philo's explication of the nature of this "worth," however, remains underdetermined. He will not, for example, go as far as Jub. 12 and fill in the silences regarding Abraham's departure from Ur, which might merit his election. In *Abr.* 66–67, we are given a literal retelling of Abraham's departure, but this focuses on Abraham's psychic worth, rather than on actions (such as the burning of the idols) prior to his calling. Further complicating Philo's language of worth is the fact that in *Leg.* 1.34, *inter alia*, he suggests that God considered all human beings "worthy" of gifts of grace—even those who would not know how to use it. See further Cover 2018b; McFarland 2016; Barclay 2015; Zeller 1990.

a covenant is a symbol of grace. Philo interprets the covenant in § 51 in anthropocentric terms, as befits his focus on the allegory of the soul in the Allegorical Commentary. For a cosmological interpretation of the symbolism of the covenants, see QG 3.40 in the Parallel Exegesis. Philo will return to the theme of covenant in *Mut.* 57–59 (par. QG 3.41–42), giving an even fuller explication of the interrelation of various kinds of covenants.

himself, as the extender ... recipient. The second extender-recipient formulation of the Abrahamic covenant (cf. § 51). Philo sequentially interprets the biblical words "me ... and you" as indicating the active and passive parties, respectively, of the economy of salvation. Philo varies his vocabulary here, describing "God" (ὁ θεός) now as the "extender" (ὀρέγων) rather than simply as the one able "to give" (δοῦναι [§ 51]) the covenant. Arnaldez (1964, 56, n. 1) observes: "Note the conception of the covenant [l'alliance] (διαθήκη: testament) as intermediary and grace. Here, grace is a gift calibrated to the one who receives it. The veil that remains between the human being and God is nothing other than human finitude. But it is entirely fulfilled. Later on, God will give himself through participation in his intimate joy."

§ 53. *superabundance.* Literally, "superabundance of good work" (ὑπερβολή ... εὐεργεσίας). For "superabundance" as a "perfection" in Jewish theologies of grace, see the detailed treatment of Barclay 2015, 70–75. Whereas the transcendent "God" (ὁ θεός) remains the active extender of the covenant, Philo suggests that the covenant is also mediated by a passive overflowing of divine beneficence. This emanationist schema foreshadows the more developed Gnosticizing and Neo-Platonist systems developed by, e.g., Valentinus, Numenius, and Plotinus.

nothing between. Having interpreted "me and you" as God and the soul, Philo now turns his exegetical attention to the phrase "between" (ἀνὰ μέσον).

The middle term of the divine-human relationship is the covenant. While not explicitly the Logos, at an ontological level, the Logos is agent of the covenantal grace. For the ontological identity of the covenant, see the Parallel Exegesis.

virgin grace. A mythologizing personification. Although the phrase has classical echoes and antecedents, Philo is the first author in Greek literature to apply "virgin" as a particular epithet for "grace" (χάρις) or the "graces" (χάριτες). He more often speaks of God's "virgin graces" in the plural (see *Post*. 32; *Migr*. 31; *Fug*. 141; *Mos*. 2.7), implicitly likening the God of Israel to the Greek father-God, Zeus, or perhaps to Dionysus (see *Migr*. 31–35). Only in *Mut*. 53 does Philo speak of an individual grace and a singular (Abrahamic) human soul. This unique pairing may be modelled loosely on an allegorical reading Charis (Χάρις) as the consort of Hephaestus in Homer, *Il*. 18.382–383. Even more importantly for Philo's allegory of the soul, in *Od*. 8.18–19, Athena is said to "pour out wondrous grace upon Odysseus" (τῷ ... θεσπεσίην κατέχευε χάριν), the heroic analogue of Philo's Abraham. Philo has such Homeric parallels in mind and has transferred them to the Abraham cycle.

the entire treatise **On the Covenants** ***in two volumes***. Philo refers to a lost double-work in the Allegorical Commentary, *De testamentis*, which would have appeared between *Quod Deus sit immutabilis* and *De agricultura* in the Noahic cycle. It took some portion of Gen 6:13–9:19 as its primary lemma. As Royse (2009, 41) speculates, "presumably, Philo would have taken the occasion of the first covenant with Noah to discuss the various covenants that God makes with Abraham, Isaac, and Jacob." Geljon and Runia (2013, 3) wonder whether this double treatise included an analysis of the flood narrative. Given the allegoresis of this material in QG 2, this seems plausible. See further Massebieau 1889, 23; Cohn 1899, 397–398; PCW 2:xii; Morris 1987, 835. For "treatise" (πραγματεία) as a technical term in Aristotelian criticism, see Engberg-Pedersen 1999, 41: "Aristotle ... was the inventor of a distinct literary genre, the *pragmateia* or 'systematic or scientific treatise'." See, e.g., Aristotle, *Eth. nic.* 2.2: "since the present discussion/treatise is not about contemplation ..." (ἐπεὶ οὖν ἡ παροῦσα πραγματεία οὐ θεωρίας ἕνεκά ἐστι ...).

repeat myself. Philo gives two rationales for skipping Gen 17:6–14 as a primary lemma. First, he does not wish to "repeat" (παλινῳδεῖν) material that he has formerly treated, presumably in the lost treatise *De testamentis* (Royse 2009, 43). While this is likely Philo's meaning, the odd verb that Philo uses to speak of self-repetition in § 53 requires further comment. παλινῳδεῖν is a *hapax* in Philo's corpus. The root may mean either (1) "recant" or (2) "sing again" or "repeat." Its nominal cognate "palinode" (παλινῳδία) is most often used by Philo in the Allegorical Commentary its classical sense of "recantation" (*Post*. 179

(2×); *Somn.* 2.292; cf. *Legat.* 373, where "palinode" bespeaks Gaius's inversion of fortune). This is precisely how Plato uses the noun in the *Phaedrus*—a dialogue which exerted a strong influence on Philo's thought (Méasson 1986; Cover 2014)—when he famously "recants" his former speech on Love in exchange for a more accurate account (*Phaedr.* 243b; 257a; in the [ps.]-Platonic corpus, the verb appears only in the spurious [*Alc. maj.*] 148b, with the sense of "repent, unpray" [ἀνεύχομαι]). As evidence of the second meaning, "repeat," the LSJ lists the present Philonic passage (*Mut.* 53) as its principal proof, pointing also to the second century CE treatise of Sextus Empiricus, *Contra mathematicos* (7.202). It is tautological, however, to use Philo to prove Philo in arguing for the existence of this secondary meaning in the first century CE. Philo's sense remains ambiguous.

Is it possible that Philo's sole use of the verb "sing again" (παλινῳδεῖν) signals not merely his desire to avoid redundancy, but likewise his fear of contradicting himself—e.g., recanting a more universalistic interpretation of the covenants occasioned by Genesis 6:18 for a more particularist perspective derived from the current pericope (Gen 17:6–14; see *Migr.* 92–93, where he takes a particularist line)? Or, if Philo's position on the covenants doesn't change, is he perhaps exempting himself from having to litigate the tension between these two kinds of covenant, the universal and the particular? This especially might detract from the topical coherence of the present treatise—on which, see the following comment.

the natural unity of the subject matter. Philo's second rationale for refraining to comment on Gen 17:6–14 is that this would interrupt the discourse. The Greek phrase "natural unity" (lit. "the connaturality," τὸ συμφυές) expresses Philo's adherence to the Platonic idea that a speech or piece of writing ought to have an organic unity on the analogy of a living animal. It further indicates that Philo plans to limit the primary biblical lemma from Gen 17 to those verses pertaining to a particular πραγματεία—a word that simultaneously refers to the genre of the "scientific treatise" (Engberg-Pedersen 1999, 41) as well as to the "subject matter" of such a treatise. Philo fears that returning to topic of the covenant would derail the focus of the present treatise.

Parallel Exegesis
§ 51b. *Gen 17:2a ("I will set my covenant between me and between you").* As in *De mutatione nominum*, so in QG 3.40b, Philo connects human blamelessness and being well-pleasing with the establishment of the covenant (Gen 17:2a). In both texts, Abraham in some sense is "worthy" of the covenant through his moral conduct, even if divine grace establishes such worth at a more fundamental level.

Despite these basic similarities, the two passages also evince a number of striking differences. First, at the exegetical level, whereas in § 51b the "covenant" (Gen 17:2a) is the sole focus of God's recompense to the Abraham soul, in *QG* 3.40b, Philo interprets a second verse (Gen 17:2a: "and I will multiply you greatly"). This causes him to speak of God's promising a "double grace" (կրկնակ ... շնորհել; Aucher: *duplicem gratiam*; better, διπλᾶ ... χαρίζεσθαι) corresponding with the double merit of being both "well-pleasing" and "blameless," which are synonyms in *QG* 3.40a.

Second, from a metaphysical perspective, Philo is largely silent in §§ 51b–53 about the precise nature of the covenantal grace. Noting that he has more fully stated his position elsewhere, he contents himself with saying, "there is nothing between God and the soul, save this virgin grace." Much is left to be filled in, and we may get a glimpse at Philo's ontology of grace if we consider what he says about the covenant in *QG* 3.40b (Marcus, PLCLSup, adapted):

> The words "I will place my covenant between me and you" (Gen 17:2a) show that custody and guardianship belong to a truly noble and virtuous man. Now, the divine covenant consists of all incorporeal principles, forms, and measures for the whole of all the things of which this world was made.

In this earlier interpretation, Philo explains that the covenant promised to Abraham is not an agreement centered on the human person, but the noetic blueprints of the entire cosmos—its "incorporeal principles/words" (անմարմին բանք—οἱ ἀσώματοι λόγοι), its "forms" (տեսակք—τὰ εἴδη or αἱ ἰδέαι), and its measures (չափք—παραδείγματα), i.e., the Logos in his passive dimension as "Form of forms" (ἰδέα ἰδεῶν, *Migr.* 103).

Several features of Philo's missing covenantal theology in the Allegorical Commentary may be filled in by this passage. First, when Philo speaks of the soul being led to God by virgin Grace, we should not envision an unmediated access to The One Who Is. Rather, it is the eternal forms—themselves the paradigms from which all law comes—by which the human soul is guided. In Philo's Middle Platonic tradition, they are contained in the Logos. Second, in *QG* 3.40b, the covenanting soul is entrusted not merely with particular laws for the sake of its own perfection, but also becomes the guardian of the cosmic order. For Philo, as for later rabbis like Simeon the Just, the keeping of the covenant is not merely something of importance for Israel; it is that "upon which the entire world depends" ([עליו] אשר העולם עומד [עליו], m.'Abot 1.2). Despite clear differences, a shared emphasis on the law, the tabernacle/temple, and works of mercy links

Philo's allegorical interpretation of the covenants with the wisdom of the rabbinic sages.

Nachleben

§ 51b. *covenants*. For the use of the plural "covenants" in first century Judaism, see also Rom 9:4.

§ 52. *Gen 17:2a ("I will set my covenant ...")*. In commenting on this verse, Clement of Alexandria (*Paed.* 1.7.56 [D]) opines on the nature of the covenantal relationship established between God and Abraham: "Here is a communion of ⟨mutually⟩ attentive friendship" (φιλίας ἐνταῦθα ἐπιστατικῆς ἐστι κοινωνία). This reflects Philo's position on God's personal oversight of the sage's progress toward joy ("I am *your* God"), and human oversight of the covenantal "forms" or "ideas" (*QG* 3.40). The comments of Didymus the Blind on this lemma are too fragmentary to make out and are preserved primarily for Gen 17:2b.

[Chapter 3]
Abraham's Great Fall (§§ 54–56)

Previous commentators (See Introduction 3. Chapters of the Treatise) agree that §§ 54–56 comprise an independent third chapter. This decision rests in part upon a comparison with *QG* 3.41, which treats the same primary biblical lemma in a single *quaestio*. Given that chapter four will return to the theme of the covenant, there is some reason to consider chapters two, three, and four as a covenantal cluster, which focus on the grace given to the Abrahamic soul and its response. This cluster follows upon the magisterial first chapter, with its more theocentric focus on the divine name, and prepares the way for the central fifth, eponymous chapter of the treatise, "On the Change of Names."

TABLE 3.1   Structure of Parts I & II of *De mutatione nominum*

	Part I		Part II
Chapter 1 (§§ 1–38)	Chapter 2 (§§ 39–53)		Chapter 5 (§§ 60–129)
	Chapter 3 (§§ 54–56)		
	Chapter 4 (§§ 57–59)		

TABLE 3.1 Structure of Parts I & II of *De mutatione nominum* (cont.)

Part I		Part II
The initial theme of perfection announced; God the ineffable, invisible, imperceptible one	God's covenant with the Abraham soul	On those whose names are being changed

Chapter three may be divided into two further units, §§ 54–55 and § 56, as outlined in the general comments.

a   *"Abraham Fell"* (§§ 54–55)
     Analysis / General Comments

In this first section of chapter three, Philo cites the primary lemma, Gen 17:3a, "Abraham fell upon ⟨his⟩ face" (ἔπεσεν Ἀβραὰμ ἐπὶ πρόσωπον) and proceeds to interpret it sequentially.

(1) Philo begins with the first words of the lemma, "Abraham fell" (ἔπεσεν Ἀβραάμ). In § 54, he offers a philosophically rich explication of Abraham's falling, adducing Socrates's appropriation of the Delphic maxim, "know thyself" (γνῶθι σεαυτόν), as a secondary lemma. He also alludes to Aristotle's concept of the unmoved mover. Knowing himself as moveable rather than unmoved, Abraham falls (§§ 54–55a).

(2) Philo clarifies this interpretation. Using the rhetorical technique of *diairesis*, he distinguishes between two kinds of falling—one which happens accidentally through ignorance, the other which happens voluntarily through docility. Abraham falls in the second sense. He is image of the soul that makes progress through learning (§ 55b).

     Detailed Comments

(1) § 54. **Abraham fell upon his face.** Philo cites the primary lemma, Gen 17:3a. The text of his citation varies only slightly from the Septuagint, primarily by omission of the possessive pronoun, "his," restored in the translation.

that he would … come to know himself. Philo adduces the Greek maxim, "know thyself" (γνῶθι σεαυτόν), famous from its inscription on the shrine at Delphi. It serves as a secondary classical lemma. A version of the maxim is attested in Aeschylus (*Prom.* 309), but Philo's reference is inspired by Socratic tradition, as Plato refers to it in a number of his dialogues (e.g., *Charm.* 164d;

Phaedr. 229e; *Prot.* 343b; cf. *Leg.* 923a). Philo elides Jewish and philosophical tradition, presenting Abraham as the disciple of both scriptural and Socratic wisdom.

nothingness. A special emphasis of Philo's anthropology, especially in the Allegorical Commentary. Philo gives metaphysical content (or lack thereof) to the elusive "self-knowledge" recommended by Socrates. Self-knowledge is not only knowing that one is not wise, but also knowing one's created nothingness. Lévy (2018; 2024) argues that this emphasis on created nothingness stems from the Pyrrhonic sceptical tradition and differentiates the Socratic Philo from his Stoic peers, who focused more intently on the cultivation of the self. For Philo and the Sceptical tradition, see also Sterling 2024.

fall before the One who stands. It is atypical in Jewish literature to imagine God as standing; this is more commonly the posture of those who pray. God, by contrast, in the Septuagint and early Jewish literature, is more often depicted as sitting or enthroned (e.g., Isa 6). Philo's philosophical description is a backformation from the scriptural image of Abraham's falling. Human posture becomes a symbol of ontological hierarchy, with only the Creator capable of "standing," while all created beings "fall." For the philosophical significance of God's "stability" and "standing," see Sterling 2022b, esp. 49–52.

unturned and unchanged. Philo alludes to Aristotle's unmoved mover. A synthesis of Plato and Aristotle was undertaken by the Middle Platonists, though it was not as complete as later efforts. For parallels to Philo's terms, "unturned and unchanged" (ἄτρεπτον καὶ ἀμετάβλητον), see Aristotle, *Cael.* 288b: "It is necessary that the divine be entirely unchanged, entirely the first and the highest" (τὸ θεῖον ἀμετάβλητον ἀναγκαῖον εἶναι πᾶν τὸ πρῶτον καὶ ἀκρότατον); and Ps.-Aristotle (*Mund.* 392a), who speaks of "the ethereal and divine nature" (ἡ αἰθέριος καὶ θεία φύσις) as "unturned and unaltered and unsuffering" (ἄτρεπτος καὶ ἀνετεροίωτος καὶ ἀπαθής). Further passages on the "unmoved mover" include Aristotle, *Met.* 1012b: "The first mover is itself unmoved" (τὸ πρῶτον κινοῦν ἀκίνητον αὐτό); and idem, *Met.* 1072a: "there is something which, while unmoved, moves, being invisible and essence and activity" (ἔστι τι ὃ οὐ κινούμενον κινεῖ, ἀΐδιον καὶ οὐσία καὶ ἐνέργεια οὖσα). See the comments on §§ 24, 28, and 87. As Arnaldez (1964, 57 n. 3) observes, Philo has adapted Aristotle's concept to give "an original idea on the unmoved mover, which allows ⟨Philo⟩ to evade the consequences of Aristotelianism: the movement of the created world is a symbol of divine immutability, just as time is a symbol of eternity. God is not the generative cause of movement; he is its Creator. Unchanging insofar as he is Creator, he can do naught but create moveable beings which bear witness to his immutability."

he does not have human form. Philo stands in a long line of Jewish apologists and theologians, who argue against overly literal readings of the corporeal metaphors for God in Scripture. This tradition, known perhaps best from Philo's Jewish predecessor, Aristobulus (frag. 1), has its crystallization in the Hellenistic period. The earliest evidence for Jews adopting this strategy is the fourth century BCE anti-Jewish historian and sceptical (Pyrrhonist) philosopher, Hecataeus of Abdera, who writes mockingly of Moses, "he did not fashion any cult statue of gods at all, since he did not think that God was in human form" (ἄγαλμα δὲ θεῶν τὸ σύνολον οὐ κατεσκεύασε διὰ τὸ μὴ νομίζειν ἀνθρωπόμορφον εἶναι τὸν θεόν, *FrGH* 264 frag. 6).

(2) §55. *the unfortunate one ... falls a great fall.* Philo earlier describes all humanity categorically as "unfortunate"—fallen on account of its created nature (cf. *Leg.* 2). The fall described in *Mut.* 55, by contrast, is not related to this primal unhappiness, but rather its soteriological reverse. Abraham's recognition of created nothingness fosters humility and paves the way for psychic progress. In this sense, his fall can be called "great" in both quantitative and, paradoxically, qualitative senses (cf. the "felix culpa" motif in Christianity, which draws out the counterintuitive gains of unfortunate events under God's providence in a different way). From a rhetorical perspective, Philo's construction of this event as a "great fall" (μέγα πτῶμα) is typical of his theological language. He also develops elaborate allegory of the "great vow" (μεγάλη εὐχή: *Leg.* 1.17; *Deus* 87; *Agr.* 175; *Ebr.* 2; *Fug.* 115; *Spec.* 1.247) of the Nazirites and makes several references to the "great song" (μεγάλη ᾠδή: *Leg.* 3.105; *Det.* 114) of Moses. See also Philo's exegesis of Moses's "great vision" (μέγα ὅραμα) in Exod 3:3, according to a new fragment discovered in Origen's *Homiliae in Psalmos* (Cover 2018a).

Parallel Exegesis

The theory of a thematic link between chapters two and three of *De mutatione nominum* is strengthened by the evidence of *QG* 3.41, the parallel passage in the *Quaestiones*. Although treating Gen 17:3a as a separate lemma, Philo begins by announcing that "this present saying (Gen 17:3) is a development of the foregoing (Gen 17:1c–2)" (կազմած աղաշնոյն այժմու ասացեալդ է). Marcus retroverts the Armenian word կազմած as "preparation" (κατασκευή) in Greek, but then translates it as "development" in English, following Aucher's rendering, "constructio" ("construction"). However one interprets this noun, it points to a connection between the two chapters, insofar as Abraham's "fall" in chapter three is a direct response to the covenantal grace offered in chapter two.

§54. *Gen 17:3a ("Abraham fell upon his face").* Philo interprets the same primary lemma (Gen 17:3) in *QG* 3.41 as he does in chapter three, but with a different sequence and emphasis. In *Mut.* 54–56, Philo addresses the lemma sequentially. He focuses first on Abraham's "falling" (*Mut.* 54–55), and only then turns to the meaning of Abraham's "face" (*Mut.* 56). In *QG* 3.41, by contrast, Philo starts by identifying the meaning of the "face" (*QG* 3.41aα), and then offers a three-fold interpretation of Abraham's "fall" (*QG* 3.41aβ, b, c). First, "face" means the "sense(s)" (զգայութիւն / զգայութիւնք), which are the "beginning and font of passions." Mind does a good work in falling upon these (*QG* 3.41a), presumably to suppress them. Second, Abraham is said to fall in reverence, struck by the vision of The One Who Is and unable to keep looking at him (*QG* 3.41b). Third, this manifestation of The One Who Is reveals an ontological hierarchy: God has the ability to "stand" (կայ) firmly, whereas all created nature "vacillates and falls" (դեդեւի եւ անկանի; *QG* 3.41c). One sees here various bits or raw material that would be reworked in *Mut.* 54–56.

know himself. Philo adduces and interprets the Delphic maxim on numerous occasions in his writings. In six cases, he quotes the phrase directly as a second person singular reflexive imperative, "know thyself." Four of these direct citations (*Migr.* 8; *Fug.* 46; *Somn.* 1.57, 58) occur in the Allegorical Commentary, one in the Exposition of the Law (*Spec.* 1.44), and one in the apologetic treatises (*Legat.* 69). *Migr.* 8 is unique in citing the maxim with a present rather than aorist imperative, "continue knowing yourself for all time" (πάντα τὸν αἰῶνα γίνωσκε σεαυτόν). Self-knowledge, according to this paraphrase, is a life-long pursuit. The wisdom of Socrates can be likened and harmonized with the command of Moses in Exod 24:12 to "attend to thyself" (πρόσεχε σεαυτῷ). In other passages, however, Philo suggests that the Socratic quest for a more intimate understanding of one's identity is not enough and must be transcended for the contemplation of higher goods, chiefly God. In *Somn.* 1.57–58, for example, Philo says that the manner of soul "which the Hebrews call Terah, the Greeks call Socrates." The Abraham soul must take leave Terah (and his Socratic quest) to pursue the heavenly journey toward God. Philo can thus cite the Delphic maxim verbatim to varying effect, depending on the allegorical point that he is trying to make.

On eight other occasions, including *Mut.* 54, Philo cites the Delphic maxim in a third person form, often in the indicative or indirect discourse ("he knew himself"). These include *Deus* 162; *Migr.* 138; *Her.* 31; *Somn.* 1.58, 60, 212, and 220. The concentration of these references in the Abrahamic treatises in discussions of psychic nothingness (see *Her.* 31; *Somn.* 1.60, 212; and the following comment) is noteworthy. For Philo's Socratic self-(un)fashioning, see Cover 2020b, 123–124.

nothingness. The word "nothingness" (οὐδένεια/οὐδενία) occurs eleven times in the Philonic corpus, primarily in the Allegorical Commentary, but once in the Exposition as well (*Sacr.* 56; *Her.* 29, 31; *Congr.* 107; *Fug.* 82; *Mut.* 54, 155; *Somn.* 1.60, 212; 2.293; *Mos.* 1.273). See Cover 2020b; Lévy 2018.

the One who stands. Philo's third interpretation of Abraham's "fall" in *QG* 3.41c echoes *both* arguments of *Mut.* 54–55. Note particularly the reference to God's standing (կալ)—a theme which in *Mut.* 54 has been translated into a title, "the One who stands" (ὁ ἑστώς [2×]). This lexical connection is obscured by Marcus's translation, which renders the verb "remain" rather than "stand." In this instance, an exegetical observation in *QG* 3.41c—the contrasting Abraham's falling with God's "standing"—has in *De mutatione nominum* been developed into an ontology of God's solitary "standing" while all creation falls.

Nachleben

§ 54. *Gen 17:3a ("Abraham fell upon his face").* The closest parallel to Philo's interpretation of Abraham's fall may be that of Ambrose, who in *Abr.* 2.86 [A] (on Gen 17:17; cf. Philo, *Mut.* 175) lists as a possible interpretation of Abraham's fall "the fact that while all ⟨created⟩ things fall before God and are changed and pass away, Substance alone (i.e., God) stands always immutable" ("Simul quia cadunt ante Deum omnia, et mutantur et transeunt, sola illa immutabilis stat semper substantia"). Both human "fall" / "change" and divine "standing" are thematized by the Milanese bishop, suggesting dependence on Philonic tradition. John Chrysostom (*Hom. Gen.* 53.363 [B/C]) suggests that Abraham's fall stems from his awareness of God's "love of human beings, for him in particular" (ἡ περὶ αὐτὸν φιλανθρωπία), which excludes any explicit reference to Philo's interpretation of Gen 17:3, but certainly reflects the Philonic idea of God's love for and friendship with Abraham (*Her.* 21).

nothingness. The notion of human "nothingness" (οὐδένεια, οὐδενία), both ontologically and morally, in its Platonist, Pyrrhonist, and Philonic forms, will have a lasting influence in early Christian literature. Athanasius will make the idea of created nothingness the metaphysical foundational for his discussion of the incarnation in *Inc.* 4.4–5 [D]. Athanasius furthermore uses the phrase "according to my nothingness" (κατά γε τὴν ἐμὴν οὐθένειαν) to qualify his interpretation of the Acts of the Apostles in *C. Ar.* 2.15 [B/C]. In neither case is there direct reference to Genesis or the patriarchal tradition, but the autoreferential style of the latter is Philonic. Gregory of Nyssa also speaks of "human nothingness" (ἡ ἀνθρωπίνη οὐδένεια, ἡ τῶν ἀνθρώπων οὐθένεια, *Eun.* 2.1.100 [B]) several times, including in a description of the Son's state prior to his incarnation, during which he was "unapproachable by the scantiness of human nothingness" (τῇ βραχύτητι τῆς ἀνθρωπίνης οὐδενείας ἀχώρητος, *Antirrhet. adv. Apoll.* 3.1, p. 159[B]). Nyssen also speaks collectively of "our nothingness" in several places, bypassing the more self-indicting first person singular of Philo and

Athanasius. At *Eun.* 2.1.124 [B/C], Gregory states that "the great David ⟨was⟩ well apprised of our nothingness" (ὁ μέγας Δαβὶδ καλῶς ἐπεσκεμμένος ἡμῶν τὴν οὐθένειαν) when he penned LXX Ps 38:6 ("my substance is as nothing before you" [ἡ ὑπόστασίς μου ὡσεὶ οὐθὲν ἐνώπιόν σου]). Gregory's connection between the theme of human nothingness and the subjectivity of a scriptural sage is reminiscent of Philo's, but the direct connection with Socrates or Abraham is absent. We have evidence, then, that the Philonic trope worked its way into Alexandrian theological culture and thence to early Christian exegesis more broadly.

b *"Upon His Face"* (§ 56)
Analysis / General Comments
In the second section of chapter three, Philo turns to Gen 17:3b and in the prepositional phrase, "upon ⟨his⟩ face" (ἐπὶ πρόσωπον), discovers a threefold allegorical significance. Abraham recognizes the fallen character of his senses, his speech, and his mind. Philo adduces Gen 2:7 as a secondary lemma, arguing that the salvation of the fallen human mind is only achieved through gracious elevation by its first "molder."

Detailed Comments
§ 56. *involuntarily ignorant ... docile.* Using the rhetorical device of *diairesis*, Philo divides "falling" into two kinds of psychic action: those that fall out of ignorance (i.e., fall to their disadvantage), and those that fall as a necessary part of the pedagogical process. Abraham's fall belongs to the second category. On involuntary sin in Philo, see Francis 2015.

Abraham fell upon his face. Philo cites the second part of the primary biblical lemma, "upon ⟨his⟩ face" (ἐπὶ πρόσωπον), introduced in § 54. As was the case with the adjective "before" (ἐνώπιον) in chapter two, so here another "face" (ὤψ) compound functions as an exegetical trigger in Philo's allegoresis.

upon his senses, upon his speech, and upon his mind. Philo presents his allegorical interpretation of "upon ⟨his⟩ face" (ἐπὶ πρόσωπον, Gen 17:3) using a rhetorical tricolon, which is further vivified by the use of asyndeton. (On Philo's rhetorical style, see Manuel Alexandre, Jr. 1991.) Philo's interpretation of the phrase "upon ⟨his⟩ face" (ἐπὶ πρόσωπον) develops an allegoresis of the phrase "into the face" (εἰς τὸ πρόσωπον) in Gen 2:7 given earlier in the Allegorical Commentary. To his interpretation of "face" as symbolizing "senses" and "mind" (*Leg.* 1.39), Philo adds "speech" (ὁ λόγος) as a third intermediary power of the soul (*Mut.* 56). Human "speech" (ὁ λόγος) itself will be divided into two categories later in the treatise: the spoken word discussed in Philo's Stoicizing allegoresis of Raguel and his seven daughters (*Mut.* 110–120), and Abraham's "speaking in his mind" (εἶπε τῇ διανοίᾳ) as he considers the birth of Isaac (*Mut.* 176).

"fallen ... fallen ... fallen." Philo's asyndetic tricolon accentuates his threefold interpretation of "upon ⟨his⟩ face." This is explicated by the threefold cry of the Abraham soul, which returns to the verb of primary lemma "he fell" (ἔπεσεν) and renders it three times as a perfect "has/is fallen" (πέπτωκε). Each proclamation is complemented by the addition of a circumstantial participle, describing a psychic faculty, and an exceptive protasis beginning with "unless" (εἰ μή).

unable to perceive on its own. Although Philo will draw language from Stoic psychology and epistemology elsewhere in this treatise (e.g., §§ 110–111), his claim in § 56 that perception cannot function on its own represents an important break with that school's teaching. It was a central tenet of Stoic materialism that the senses could be counted on as "normally reliable" in conveying external data to the soul as "impressions" (L&S 1:240). Philo's assertion that the perceptive faculties are impotent without external divine mediation introduces a Platonizing-Jewish idea into his anthropology, which transcends the materialist immediacy of the Stoic system.

unless it should be raised up by ... the Savior. The title "savior" (σωτήρ) is derived from Jewish Scripture and tradition. It would have been politically resonant in Philo's context, in light of its adoption as an epithet by several Ptolemies in Alexandria (I and IX) as well as Augustus Caesar (Octavian) in the Priene Calendar Inscription (*OGIS* 458).

forethought. While Philo's reference to God's "forethought" in § 56 suggests that salvation is something given by God in the beginning (i.e., the inbreathing of human reason in creation), Philo elsewhere in the Abraham cycle (*Migr.* 124) suggests that the human mind requires continued support by God, lest the soul regress to unreason.

unable to explain ... the intellectual substances. Unlike the irrational "voice" (φωνή) mentioned by Philo in § 110, the anthropological "word" (λόγος) here referenced is speech as rational mediator of thought. Philo employs this concept again in § 208. The notion of speech as interpreter of thought recalls the Stoic distinction between an "immanent word" (λόγος ἐνδιάθετος) and an "externalized word" (λόγος προφορικός), with reason being "inner" contemplation and speech being "uttered" expression. Philo is the first ancient philosopher to give an extensive account of this notion (Kamesar 2004), even though it is not original to him.

fashioned and fine-tuned ... opened ... fixed ... strike. Philo uses a string of musical verbs to depict the human process of speech as dependent on God. Not only does God fashion the vocal "instrument" (φωνητήριον), but he also plays it as an unseen musician. The sentiment—particularly the need for the "mouth to be opened" (διανοίξας τὸ στόμα [§ 56])—is reminiscent of LXX Ps 50:17, "Lord, you will open my lips / and my mouth will proclaim your praise" (κύριε, τὰ χείλη μου ἀνοίξεις / καὶ τὸ στόμα μου ἀναγγελεῖ τὴν αἴνεσίν σου).

king mind. Philo uses this metaphor throughout the present treatise to signify a mind "rightly ruling" the senses and other irrational parts of the soul (§§ 56, 113, 116). This language has an antecedent in Plato (*Phileb.* 28c).

the One who formed him as a living being. With the single word "living-animal-former" (ζῳοπλάστης), Philo alludes to a longer sentence in Gen 2:7: "God formed the human being ⟨as⟩ clay from the earth and breathed into his face a breath of life, and the human being became a living soul" (ἔπλασεν ὁ θεὸς τὸν ἄνθρωπον χοῦν ἀπὸ τῆς γῆς καὶ ἐνεφύσησεν εἰς τὸ πρόσωπον αὐτοῦ πνοὴν ζωῆς, καὶ ἐγένετο ὁ ἄνθρωπος εἰς ψυχὴν ζῶσαν). The compound noun was coined sometime in the Hellenistic era. It appears in Posidippus (*Epigr.* 62, third century BCE), a comic poet in the court of the first two Ptolemies. Philo is the first recorded author to apply the noun to God on the basis of the Septuagintal text.

Parallel Exegesis

§ 56. *involuntarily ignorant ... docile.* Philo's division of "falling" into two categories may fruitfully be compared with his *diairesis* of "fleeing" into three categories (*Fug.* 3) and of "finding" into four (*Fug.* 120).

it is also said that Abraham fell upon his face. In QG 3.41a, the only exegetical parallel to this section, Philo underscores anthropological weakness by highlighting not created nature *per se* (he will mention this in his third proof in QG 3.41c), but human nature's dependence upon the senses, which are the gateway to the bad emotions. The face is a symbol of these senses and their transgressions. Falling upon the face represents Abraham's recognition that the senses need to be kept in check and cannot be given free rein over the soul's movements. Such falling is thus construed as "a good work" (բարեգործութիւն, which Marcus [PLCLSup] retroverts as εὐεργασία) of the Abraham soul. NB: Marcus (PLCLSup 1:230) suggests that God is the pronominal agent ("of him", ինզու) of this good work. This is unlikely, as Abraham is the subject of QG 3.41a. Aucher's translation ("⟨Abraham⟩ showing by good works" ["operibus bonis ... ostendens"]), while more paraphrastic than Marcus's, gives the better sense.

Philo's interpretation in *Mut.* 56 makes two improvements on QG 3.41a. First, while retaining the "natural" association of the face and the senses, he extends this allegorically to include speech and the mind as well (Cf. *Leg.* 1.39–41 for a psychological interpretation of God's breathing "into ⟨Adam's⟩ face" [εἰς τὸ πρόσωπον] in Gen 2:7.). Including the entirety of the human soul in Abraham's fall lays the foundation for further psychological allegory. Since it is not only the senses that have fallen, the act of falling can no longer be construed as a "good work" (εὐεργασία) of the mind. Rather, all the faculties of the soul, even the highest, stand in need of divine grace to operate in their most basic functions. Marcus's comment (PLCLSup 1:230, n. i) that in *Mut.* 56 "Philo more clearly says that God keeps the senses from erring" is thus a little off the mark. The point is rather that the human soul cannot fall upon its senses and transcend them through its own power, but requires divine grace to elevate each of its faculties, including the mind.

Savior. Philo refers to God as a "Savior" (σωτήρ) roughly 40 times in his corpus, in all three exegetical series and his apologetic works. In the Allegorical Commentary, God's soteriological power is sometimes linked to his beneficent power (*Leg.* 2.57; *Sobr.* 55) or his gracious power (*Migr.* 124)—both of which have ties with God's "creative power" (as opposed to his "legislative power").

speech ... unable to explain. While Philo's clearest explications of the Stoic distinction between the "immanent word" (λόγος ἐνδιάθετος) and the "externalized word" (λόγος προφορικός) are found in the Exposition of the Law (*Mos.* 2.127; *Spec.* 4.69), the idea is present in passages in the Allegorical Commentary as well (esp. *Migr.* 76–81; *Det.* 38–40). Its most typical allegorical use is as an exegesis of the internal word represented by Moses and the external speech represented by Aaron in their joint mission to Pharaoh.

king mind. Philo uses this image of mind as king on at least eleven occasions. Elsewhere in the Allegorical Commentary (the Noahic cycle) and the patriarchal treatises of the Exposition, "king mind" refers specifically to Pharaoh, or the mind that loves the body and keeps it as its special realm (*Agr.* 57; *Ebr.* 111, 220; *Abr.* 103; *Ios.* 151). In the present treatise, to the contrary, as well as in *De specialibus legibus*, Philo uses the same metaphor to signify a mind "rightly ruling" the senses and other irrational parts of the soul (*Spec.* 3.111; 4.92, 123).

the One who formed him as a living being. See also *Det.* 80, where Philo links the adjective "animal-former" (ζωοπλάστης) to a direct quotation of Gen 2:7. Philo uses this unique compound with some frequency (e.g., *Leg.* 2.73; 3.88; *Det.* 80).

Nachleben

"fallen." Philo's rendering of the verb of Gen 17:3 "he fell" (ἔπεσεν) as a perfect "has/is fallen" (πέπτωκε) has a formal, if not a material, parallel in Jewish and Christian exegetical tradition. It is common for both Semitic and Hellenophone authors to "re-point" (alter the tense of) a scriptural verb in an explication of its meaning. Thus, in John 6:31–35, the aorist verb "he gave" (ἔδωκεν, LXX Ps 78:24; John 6:31) is interpreted by the Fourth Evangelist by transforming it into the perfect ("he has given" [δέδωκεν], John 6:32a), the present ("he gives" [δίδωσιν], John 6:32b), the aorist active participle ("be giving" [δούς], John 6:33) and the aorist imperative ("give" [δός], John 6:34). See Cover 2015, 189–190; Borgen 1963.

[Chapter 4]
Different Forms of Covenant (§§ 57–59)

Chapter four (§§ 57–59) continues the covenantal themes of chapters two (§§ 39–53) and three (§§ 54–56). It simultaneously introduces the eponymous fifth chapter of *De mutatione nominum*, on the change of names of those who receive God as their particular form of covenant. The connection between this and the previous two chapters is understated in the present treatise, but its logic is explicit in the parallel passage QG 3.42, which begins "since he earlier (Վասն զի յառաջագոյն) spoke of the covenant, he ⟨now⟩ says ...." The primary scriptural lemma (Gen 17:4a), as well as content and theme, mirror §§ 52–53. The chapter divides into two exegetical subunits. In (a) §§ 57–58a, Philo cites Gen 17:4a and interprets the first words of the lemma (Gen 17:4aα: "and I" [κἀγώ]); in (b) §§ 58b–59, he cites and interprets Gen 17:4aβ ("behold my covenant" [ἰδοὺ ἡ διαθήκη μου]).

a   *"And I"* (§§ 57–58a)
      Analysis and General Comments

At the outset of chapter four, Philo summarizes his allegoresis of the Abrahamic soul up to this stage: the soul that flees, finds (cf. *De migratione Abrahami, Quis heres rerum divinarum heres sit, De fuga et inventione*), and falls (§§ 54–56), delights God and is worthy of receiving him as his personal covenant (§ 57). Although there are many kinds of covenant and many species of grace, both visible and invisible, it is only the Abrahamic soul and those who follow in his company, to whom God gives himself as covenant. This is remarkable, for unlike the other "species" (εἴδη) of covenant, God is the archetypal "genus" (γένος) of covenant (§ 58α). Philo derives this meaning from the first part of the primary biblical lemma, "and I" (κἀγώ, Gen 17:4aα). Section (a) divides into two smaller units:

(1) Philo first summarizes the manner of life symbolized by the Abrahamic soul; he concludes by citing the entire primary biblical lemma, Gen 17:4a (§ 57).
(2) Philo then offers an allegorical explication of the first part of Gen 17:4aα, "and I" (κἀγώ [§ 58a]).

Detailed Comments

(1) § 57. *delights*. Although he speaks of God "delighting" in the manner of life signified by Abraham, in Philo's technical view, God has no emotions. Like other philosophical interpreters of Moses, Philo must accommodate scriptural language suggesting that God has feelings with a theology of divine impassibility.

the confession ... concerning The One Who Is. Philo adds a new element to his covenantal structure, not present in chapter two (§§ 39–53): a "confession" (ὁμολογία). The noun "confession" is invoked twice in the Pentateuch (Lev 22:18; Deut 12:17), with only Leviticus speaking of a singular confession. Philo will adduce a verse similar to Lev 22:18/Num 6:21 later on in the treatise to expound this idea of "confession" (§ 220). Abraham's confession is not explicitly stated in Scripture, but may be inferred from the allegoresis of his actions (fleeing the self, falling before The One Who Is).

that there is One, in truth, who stands. The confession that it is God alone who stands (ontologically) recapitulates Philo's comment in § 54, with a significant addition: the notion of God's numerical singularity. Philo's description of God as "One" (ἕν) recalls both scriptural and Platonizing tradition. On the scriptural side, it recalls Deut 6:4: "Hear, O Israel: the Lord Our God is One" (Ἄκουε, Ἰσραήλ· κύριος ὁ θεὸς ἡμῶν κύριος εἷς ἐστιν). The Greek of Abraham's confession, "that there is One, in truth, who stands" (ὅτι πρὸς ἀλήθειαν ἑστὼς ἕν ἦν ἄρα) offers a textbook example of the "imperfect of truth just recognized." As Smyth (§ 1902) elaborates: "The imperfect, usually some form of εἶναι, with ἄρα, is often used to denote that a present fact or truth has just been recognized, although true before." The construction is common in Plato. In this case, Abraham has just recognized, through his vision of God, a theological doctrine and fallen down before it.

As to the neuter number "one" (ἕν, rather than Deuteronomy's masculine εἷς), there are several possibilities. Colson renders the word adverbially ("that it is he *alone* who stands"), presumably on the grounds that ἕν is neuter, while ἑστώς is masculine. Given, however, (1) the Neopythagorean influence on Philo's thought, with its interest in arithmology; (2) that Philo could have written "only" (μόνον) to achieve Colson's sense; (3) the presence of the emphatic particle ἄρα; and (4) the echo of Deut 6:4, it seems more likely that "One" (ἕν) is meant to carry some "confessional" weight (even if it is formally adverbial). In support of the stronger readings presented here, one might compare Philo's language in § 57 with a particularly important passage at the beginning of the Allegorical Commentary (*Leg.* 2.3):

> The "one" (τὸ ἕν) and the "monad" (ἡ μονάς) are, therefore, the standard for determining the category (τέτακται) to which God belongs. Rather, we should say, the One God (ὁ εἷς θεός) is the standard for the "monad." (PLCL, adapted)

In this passage, Philo expresses divine singularity with nouns in all three grammatical genders. His identification of God as ἕν in § 57 is in keeping with the theology of the Allegorical Commentary.

turnings and changes. Unlike God, who is One, all created things—particularly human souls, which are defined in Platonic thought by motion (cf. Plato, *Phaedr.* 245c5)—undergo change. Such turnings or conversions, sometimes for the worse, sometimes (as Philo is at pains to demonstrate in the present treatise) for the better, distinguish vacillating creation from divine stability. Philo's statement that all created beings "receive all kinds of turnings and changes" (τροπὰς καὶ μεταβολὰς παντοίας ἐνδεχομένων) echoes the language of Timaeus Locrus (94c), who describes the work of the Demiurge as ordering matter "from unbounded changes (ἐξ ἀορίστων μεταβολᾶν) ... so that it might not receive spontaneous alternations (ἱνά ... μὴ κατ' αὐτόματον τροπὰς δέχοιτο)." For the close affinity of this pseudonymous work with the cosmology of Philo's *œuvre*, see Tobin 1985.

A share in his Reason. Colson, in a footnote, translates this phrase, "gives him a share of the speech" (PLCL 5:170, n. a), but then renders it "a call to partnership" in the main translation. That λόγος here may refer more specifically to God's "word" or "reason" (rather than the audible speech) seems better, given Philo's identification of the covenant with the immaterial forms in QG 3.40.

"and I, behold my covenant is with you." Philo cites Gen 17:4a, the primary lemma, as it appears in the Septuagint, with two exceptions: (1) the first two words, "and I" (καὶ ἐγώ) are blended via *crasis* in Philo's citation (κἀγώ); and (2) Philo omits the verb in the phrase "⟨is⟩ with you" (μετὰ σοῦ ⟨ἐστιν⟩).

(2) § 58a. ***many species ... the highest genus of covenants.*** Philo interprets "and I" (κἀγώ) as God's identification of himself with the highest class of "covenant." Colson renders this phrase "many kinds ... the highest form," but this does not exactly capture Philo's distinction between of "species" (εἴδη) and

"genus" (γένος). There are many species of covenant and many kinds of grace, which result in differing covenantal patterns. Two have been discussed in the treatise: the one given to Enoch (§§ 34–39) and the one given to Abraham. Of these "covenantal species," Philo asserts, God (i.e., the Logos) is the "uppermost genus of covenants" (τὸ ἀνώτατον γένος διαθηκῶν).

having shown ... the Non-Demonstrable One. With pithy paradoxical precision, Philo summarizes his theological argument in the treatise thus far: "⟨God⟩ has shown ... that the Non-Demonstrable has been demonstrated as far as possible" (δείξας ... ὡς ἐνῆν δειχθῆναι τὸν ἄδεικτον). This recapitulation recalls the earlier negative dogma of chapter one (e.g., § 10), that God is "incomprehensible" (ἀκατάληπτον). In § 264, the same adjective, "undemonstrated" (ἄδεικτον), will be used to describe the God who "cannot be demonstrated" within time.

Parallel Exegesis

Chapter four (§§ 57–59) does not treat as long a primary biblical lemma as its parallel at *QG* 3.42. Only *QG* 3.42a ("And I, behold my covenant is with you"), which comments on Gen 17:4a, finds an analogue in the present section. In both treatises, Philo subdivides the lemma along similar lines, interpreting "and I" (κἀγώ, *QG* 3.42aα) first and then turning to "behold my covenant is with you" (*QG* 3.42aβ). The argument in the first part of both interpretations is similar: "and I" means that God himself is the archetypal form of the covenant, or the most effective kind of grace. Philo's interpretation of "behold my covenant" differs in the two series, although both play on connotations of seeing (i.e., "behold" [ἰδού]). In *QG* 3.42aβ, "behold" signifies Abraham's psychic ascent through both earth and heaven into the cosmic realm, seeing (insofar as this is possible) the "power" of God. In *Mut.* 58b–59, by contrast, "behold" signifies Abraham's discernment of the gracious efficaciousness of God as covenant among the other kinds of covenant, while remaining in the world.

§ 57. *the manner of life that flees itself.* The theme of "self-flight" has not yet been mentioned in *De mutatione nominum*. Philo looks back to the earlier treatises in the Abrahamic cycle, including *De fuga et inventione*, in which the verb "flee" (ἀποδιδράσκειν [cf. Gen 16:6, 8]) is given a three-fold *diairesis* (*Fug.* 3) and extended discussion. The closest antecedent to the phrase in *Mut.* 57, "the one who flees himself" (ὁ αὑτὸν ἀποδιδράσκων), is *Her.* 69, where in an interpretation of Gen 12:1 as a secondary lemma, the Abraham soul is exhorted to flee not only body (Ur) and senses (Haran), but also to "flee yourself and stand apart from yourself" (σαυτὴν ἀπόδραθι καὶ ἔκστηθι σεαυτῆς).

the confession ... concerning The One Who Is. Whereas Philo speaks of a "confession" (ὁμολογία) in *De mutatione nominum*, in the parallel place in *QG*

3.41b he will instead call this a "revelation" (յայտնութիւն)—a word that can render various Greek *Vorlagen*, including φανέρωσις, δήλωσις, ἐπιφάνεια, θεοφάνεια, and ἀποκάλυψις. The difference arises from the fact that in QG 3.41b, Philo is not yet focused on Abraham's acceptance of the covenant, as he is in *Mut.* 57, but in God's revelation to the sage.

that there is One, in truth, who stands. Philo offers a similar description of God as One in QG 3.41 (see Parallel Exegesis in chapter three). It is interesting to compare the phrasing of God as "one" (ἕν) in *Mut.* 57 with that of QG 3.41, which contains similar content: "the one (մին) stands firmly and intact, while the other one (հակ մին) vacillates and falls upon its place, the earth." While the Armenian repetition of the numeral "one" (մին) may represent an original Greek ὁ μέν ... ὁ δέ construction, it is possible that God's singularity was also thematized in the Greek *Vorlage*. Elsewhere, in his other commentary series, Philo will speak of God as "simpler than ⟨the⟩ one" (ἑνὸς εἰλικρινέστερον [*Praem.* 40]) and "older than the one" (ἑνὸς πρεσβύτερος [*QE* 2.68]). Moses (God is "one") and Platonic tradition (God is simpler than "one") sit partially at odds here.

turnings and changes. Philo's description of souls as receiving every sort of turning and change recalls the description of "created nature" in QG 3.41, which "vacillates" or "is shaken" (դեդեւի—σείεται, σαλεύεται).

§ 58. **many species of covenant.** In QG 3.42, Philo interprets the verse "and I, behold my covenant," as a warning to Abraham not to think of the covenant as something "in writing" (գրով). In QG 3.40, Philo had identified the "covenant" (ուխտ) as the plurality of incorporeal "words, ideas, and paradigms" of creation—a point that he here reiterates. In QG 3.42, Philo identifies the covenant with something higher as well—the "I" of God himself. He thereby implies that the ideas of creation are at home in the mind and Logos of God. Philo also emphasizes the "economic" side of such covenants, pointing out the myriad goods which come to human beings through material and immaterial objects created from the heavenly models.

the highest genus of covenants. For this phrase in *Mut.* 58, compare QG 3.42: "archetypal form of the covenant" (նախրանատիպ ուխտին կերպարան—τὸ ἀρχέτυπον διαθήκης εἶδος), after Marcus's retroversion (PLCLSup 1:231, n. g). The Armenian word "form" (կերպարան) may be better retroverted as "idea" (ἰδέα). While Philo thus postulates a categorical break between God as "covenant" and the "ideas" as covenants, he also construes them as a continuity. Just as the Logos is the "idea of ideas" (ἰδέα ἰδεῶν) in *Migr.* 103, so in *Mut.* 58, Philo comes close to saying what he spells out more clearly in QG 3.42: that the Logos is "the covenant of covenants" (ուխտ կտակարանացն—διαθήκη τῶν διαθηκῶν, per Marcus, PLCLSup 1:231, n. f).

having shown ... what cannot be shown. Philo explains the paradox of the demonstrated Non-Demonstrable One at greater length in QG 3.42. He notes that God had "shown (gnigtuy—δείξας [retroversion is mine, after *Mut.* 58]) himself clearly, not as he is, for this is impossible, but (insofar) as the eyes of the beholder are able to comprehend his genuine intellectual power (ɾnɪů ... qɯɪpnɪphɪůů hůɯůɯɪh—ἡ γνησία καὶ νοερὰ δύναμις, after Marcus, PLCLSup 1:232, n. e)." Philo's terser formulation of this idea in *Mut.* 58 underscores the paradox of divine revelation, which always has an apophatic (and "adeictic") character.

Nachleben
§ 57. *confession.* The "confession" (ὁμολογία) will come to play a central role in contemporaneous and later Christian covenantal texts, including 2 Cor 9:13 and especially Heb 3:1; 4:14; and 10:23.

§ 58a. *that there is One, in truth, who stands.* On God's "standing" in Christian tradition, see Ambrose (*Abr.* 2.86 [A]) in the *Nachleben* for § 54 ("Abraham fell").

Gen 17:4aα ("and I"). Philo's identification of the divine "I" of Gen 17:4 with the Abrahamic covenant is echoed in an intriguing passage by Clement of Alexandria (*Strom.* 1.182.2 [A/B]). Clement writes: "Moses seems to call the Lord a covenant, saying 'behold I, my covenant is with you' (Gen 17:4)" (Μωυσῆς δὲ φαίνεται τὸν κύριον διαθήκην καλῶν, «ἰδοὺ ἐγώ,» λέγων, «ἡ διαθήκη μου μετὰ σοῦ»). Although Clement and Philo divide Gen 17:4a along slightly different seams, Clement clearly knows the exegetical tradition first related here by Philo. According to Van den Hoek (1988, 180–181), who ranks this passage at [B], "a reminiscence of Philo is likely."

b   "Behold, My Covenant" (§§ 58b–59)
Analysis and General Comments
In § 58b, Philo adds a brief but important comment on Gen 17:4aβ, "behold my covenant." In § 59, he gives some examples of the varieties of divine covenants *qua* grace, both the lesser kind from the natural world, and the highest kind, in which God gives himself and changes the name of the covenantal partner.

Detailed Comments
§ 58b. *he then adds, "behold my covenant."* Following the pattern of QG 3.42, Philo divides Gen 17:4a into two parts. Having interpreted "and I" (κἀγώ [Gen 17:4aα]), he now turns to the second part of the primary biblical lemma: "behold my covenant" (ἰδοὺ ἡ διαθηκή μου [Gen 17:4aβ]). Saliently absent are the final words, "is with you" (μετὰ σοῦ ⟨ἐστιν⟩), which were cited in § 57. Philo thus lays

the primary emphasis on the genitive pronoun "my" (μου), indicating God's personal investment in and identity with the covenant given to the Abraham soul.

"I am myself the source and wellspring of all graces." Philo distinguishes God's covenant from the other covenants which flow from him as "source and wellspring" (ἀρχή τε καὶ πηγή). These natural images reinforce the genus-species distinction between God, as wellspring, and the various other covenants, which flow forth as rivers.

§ 59. *other agents: earth, water ... bodiless powers*. This passage demonstrates how wide a semantic range the word "gift/grace" (χάρις) has in Philo's thought. It encompasses natural created gifts from the material cosmos, as well as God's bodiless "powers" (δυνάμεις), i.e., his Logos and its various beneficent and punitive modalities. The cosmological sequence "earth, water, air, sun" is in ascending order and follows the standard Middle Platonic cosmology (see, e.g., Timaeus Locrus [95a]), which positions earth as the lowest, fire as the highest, and water and air in the middle. The change from "fire" to "sun" allows Philo to blend a Platonic cosmology with the Jewish tradition found in Gen 1, in which "sun, moon, and heaven" are the primary divisions. The bodiless powers may be Philo's representation of angels (but see Dillon and Winston 1983, 197–205).

to others ... through himself alone. God's gift of "his covenant"—that is, his genus and particular form of grace—is distinct from the other covenantal types, even those extended by various powers of the Logos. The idea that the Abraham soul should possess a unique "covenant of covenants," while other souls outside his company possess covenantal graces less directly identified with the God of the Pentateuch, reminds one of Deut 32:8–12, which says that, while other nations are allotted a governing angel, God himself cares directly for Israel.

these, he also immediately deems worthy of another name. Philo turns "with logical immediacy" (εὐθέως) from Gen 17:4a to Abraham's change of name in Gen 17:5, neglecting to comment on Gen 17:4b ("you will be the father of many nations"; cf. *QG* 3.42). This omission demonstrates (1) the thematic character of the treatises in the Allegorical Commentary, despite their being generically textual "commentaries" (ὑπομνήματα); and (2) the independence of the Allegorical Commentary from the *QGE*. Arnaldez (1964, 60, n. 1) observes that the phrase "another name" amounts to "a resumption of the distinction between the human being and God's human being, ⟨the latter of⟩ which receives divine graces immediately from God *alone*. One recalls the κλῆρος ("inheritance"). This distinction demands a ⟨differentiation⟩ of two names: the name of birth, and the name given to that one which goes through, so to speak, a new birth."

Parallel Exegesis

§ 58b. *Gen 17:4aβ ("behold").* There is a difference of emphasis between Philo's interpretation of the first word of Gen 17:4aβ, "behold" (ἰδού), in *De mutatione nominum* and QG 3.42. Whereas in *Mut.* 58b–59, the word suggests that the Abraham soul should consider how surpassing God's immediate grace is in comparison to the various other divine gifts of creation, in QG 3.42a "behold" points to Abraham's Phaedran ascent to the noetic realm, where he beholds (insofar as it is possible) the covenantal power of God in ideal form. In QG 3.42, Philo simultaneously reports ontological and ethical traditions, with a special emphasis on cosmology and theology; in the present treatise, his focus is on the ethical and anthropological ramifications of such interpretations.

source and wellspring. Philo's merism, "source and wellspring (ἀρχή τε καὶ πηγή) of all graces" in *Mut.* 58 finds an antithetical parallel in QG 3.41, where Philo speaks of "perception" (զգայութիւն—αἴσθησις) as "the source and spring (սկիզբն եւ աղբիւր) of evils."

Nachleben

§ 58b. *"behold my covenant."* For Clement of Alexandria's adoption of Philo's notion that God himself is identified with a covenant, see *Strom.* 1.182.2 [B], cited and discussed in the previous *Nachleben* section.

Part Two

[Chapter 5]
On the Change of Names (§§ 60–129)

Οὐκ ἄρα παντὸς ἀνδρός, ὦ Ἑρμόγενες, ὄνομα θέσθαι, ἀλλά τινος ὀνοματουργοῦ· οὗτος δ' ἐστιν, ὡς ἔοικεν, ὁ νομοθέτης, ὃς δὴ τῶν δημιουργῶν σπανιώτατος ἐν ἀνθρώποις γίγνεται.

It does not belong to every man, Hermogenes, to give a name, but to a certain kind: a namewright. And he, as it seems, is the lawgiver, who is indeed the rarest of craftsmen among humans.

PLATO, *Cratylus* 389a

The second and central part of *De mutatione nominum* is comprised of a single, topically organized chapter, which provides the basis for the work's Greek title, "On Those Whose Names Are Being Changed and for What Reason They Are Being Changed" (Eusebius, *Hist. eccl.* 2.18.3: περὶ τῶν μετονομαζομένων καὶ ὧν ἕνεκα μετονομάζονται). For the title(s) of the treatise, see Introduction 7. Title and Previous Scholarship on the Treatise.

In this chapter, Philo interprets two major biblical lemmata: Gen 17:5 and 17:15, skipping over the large intervening section of text. He thus makes a break with the form of a running commentary. Combining his allegories of Gen 17:5 and 17:15 (treated previously in QG 3.43 and 3.53), Abram's and Sarai's changes of name, Philo refrains from treating Gen 17:6–14—one of the longest gaps in a primary lemma in a treatise within the Allegorical Commentary. This gap is all the more salient because Philo treats the bypassed verses in QG 3.44–52. For these reasons, chapter five more nearly resembles an "exegetical monograph" (σύγγραμμα) or philosophical "treatise" (πραγματεία [see the detailed comment on *Mut.* 53]) than a "running commentary" (ὑπόμνημα) proper. (For the distinction between "commentary" [ὑπόμνημα] and "treatise" [σύγγραμμα], see Schironi [2012, esp. 407, 428–429], who discusses the dispute surrounding the genre of Didymus's *On Demosthenes* preserved in *P. Berol. inv.* 9780—a text discovered in the same house of Hermoupolis as the *Anonymous Theaetetus Commentary* [*P. Berol. Inv.* 9782].) The pacing of the chapter is reminiscent of the topical intensity of the *Agr.–Sobr.* sub-grouping and foreshadows the selective treatment of Scripture in *De somniis*, the final extant treatise in the Allegorical Commentary. Having interpreted these two primary lemmata, Philo then adduces a long series of secondary biblical texts to further explore the phenomenon of scriptural name change.

Several reasons are often given for Philo's break with his usual sequential treatment of primary biblical texts. Royse (2009, 43) suggests that "much of the material in (Gen) 17:1–22 is not discussed, because presumably it was covered in the lost *De testamentis* (*On the Covenants*)." This is surely a part of the answer, as Philo indicates in § 53 (on Gen 17:4; see the detailed comment). Philo's entire explanation in this section, however, warrants revisiting:

> I have written the entire treatise (λόγον) *On the Covenants* in two volumes and I now willingly pass over (ἑκὼν ὑπερβαίνω) ⟨that subject⟩ so that I do not repeat myself (ὑπὲρ τοῦ μὴ παλινῳδεῖν) and, also (ἅμα) because I do not wish to disturb the natural unity of the subject matter of the present treatise (μὴ βουλόμενος ἀπαρτᾶν τὸ συμφυὲς τῆς πραγματείας).

A careful reading of Philo's apology in § 53 shows that he gives not one but two reasons for passing over a further discussion of the covenants. Both reasons are linked "together" (ἅμα) to Philo's compositional "will" (ἑκών, βουλόμενος). Philo notes first that he has treated the subject of covenants earlier, and then states additionally that to return to this subject would "disturb" or "dismember" (ἀπαρτᾶν) the thematic unity of the current "topic/treatise" (πραγματεία). These two rationales require further comment.

Philo's first rationale—that he does not wish to return to the theme of covenants—has often been taken as sufficient for explaining the lacuna of Gen 17:6–14 in the present treatise: he has already interpreted these verses in *De testamentis*. If this is what Philo means, it is an odd rationale, since Philo's use of other texts from Genesis as secondary lemmata earlier in the Allegorical Commentary does not disqualify them from treatment as primary lemmata when they arise in sequence. In addition, elsewhere in the Allegorical Commentary, Philo has no trouble repeating his favorite allegorical ideas, sometimes in expanded, sometimes in contracted form. (For further issues raised by the odd verb "repeat myself" [παλινῳδεῖν], see the detailed comment on § 53.)

Philo's second rationale in § 53—that he does not wish to violate the thematic coherence of the treatise—has not received sufficient attention. His language is reminiscent of Plato's *Phaedrus*—specifically the discussion in that dialogue about the unity of a speech as the unity of a living animal (Plato, *Phaedr.* 264c). A properly ordered "speech" (λόγος) according to Socrates (265e2) is one that has a natural somatic order and that can be again divided "according to the natural joints and limbs" (κατ' ἄρθρα ᾗ πέφυκεν), rather than inelegantly as by an amateur butcher. For the adjective "connatural" (συμφυές [§ 53]) used in connection with bodily unity and disunity in Plato's corpus, see e.g., *Soph.* 247d3; *Tim.* 45d5; 64d7.

Philo's reason for skipping from Gen 17:5 to 17:15 is thus motivated as much by the thematic connections between those two verses as it is by the fact that he has apparently treated Gen 17:5 (and perhaps Gen 17:6–14) earlier. It is important to note, in this regard, that Philo's makes his apology for the leap in a comment on Gen 17:4, rather than after Gen 17:5 where the real *lacuna* in the primary biblical lemma occurs. Philo carefully prepares the way for this omission because his treatment of Gen 17:5 and 17:15 together as a unit in §§ 60–129 represents the thematic center of his speech and he does not want to interrupt it when he comes to Gen 17:5 (see § 77—the discourse is seamless). On the importance of the thematic principle in Philo's allegorical treatises, see further Sterling 2018b.

A third, unstated rationale motivating Philo's thematic leap from Gen 17:5 to Gen 17:15 is that these two texts traveled together as a pair of secondary lemmata earlier in the Allegorical Commentary (see, e.g., *Cher.* 4–8 and the other parallels below). Having treated Gen 17:5, Philo naturally introduces Gen 17:15 as a contextualizing secondary lemma (SBL^c). His "strongly associative mind" then embarks on a lengthy dissertation on this subject, and when he returns to the primary text, it not to Gen 17:6 but Gen 17:16: the contextualizing secondary lemma has become the primary biblical lemma.

In addition to these three compositional rationales for the special structure of chapter five, Philo provides a fourth clue, which may supply an external context for the selection of this particular theme. In the opening of this chapter (§ 60), Philo suggests that his topic (i.e., names) responds to a criticism leveled by a particular group of Alexandrian contemporaries, who apparently mock scriptural name changes from a philosophical perspective. Further discussion of the identity of these "quarrelsome" contemporaries is offered in an excursus in the detailed comments. Here, it will suffice to say that Philo has shaped this chapter partially in response to an ongoing struggle with a group of exegetical opponents in Alexandria—most likely scholars on the margins or outside of his Jewish community.

The structure of the chapter is as follows: Philo begins by interpreting two major biblical lemmata: Gen 17:5 (MBL) and Gen 17:15 (SBL^c/MBL). He then introduces a further series of secondary biblical lemmata to complement this initial pair. The chapter may be divided into ten subunits, based on the figures they interpret:

(a) Abram/Abraham (§§ 60–76)
(b) Sarai/Sarah (§§ 77–80)
(c) Jacob/Israel (§§ 81–88)
(d) Joseph/Psonthonphonek (§§ 89–91)
(e) Benjamin: Son of Days/Son of Grief (§§ 92–96)

(f) Ephraim/Manasseh :: Reuben/Simeon (§§ 97–102)
(g) Jethro/Raguel (§§ 103–120)
(h) Hoshea/Joshua (§§ 121–122)
(i) Caleb (§§ 123–124)
(j) Moses (§§ 125–129)

The order of this cast of characters follows roughly the Pentateuchal sequence (with the important exception of Moses) and can be subdivided into three main clusters. Sections (a)–(c) represent the core discussion rooted in the primary and contextualizing secondary lemmata (Gen 17:5, 15). Philo treats the three name changes in the Abraham-Jacob cycles. Isaac is mentioned in § 88 in answer to the question of why his name does *not* change. These psychic types are generally positive.

Sections (d)–(f) treat Rachel's two sons and the family of Joseph. Joseph and Benjamin are negative figures, whereas Ephraim and Manasseh are positive. This nominal quartet presents a kind of fall narrative: Israel's embroilment with Egypt.

A third group may be found in sections (h)–(j): Joshua, Caleb, Moses, the three leaders of Israel in the wilderness and saviors from Egypt. These are presented not in strict chronological order, but in order of their increasing perfection: Hoshea changes his name for the better; Caleb's name does not change, but he has an exchange of spirit (§ 123); and Moses anchors the list as the man of many names (actually three), which vary according to his different offices: prophet of oracles, human devoted to God, and surrogate god and sage to the foolish.

The foregoing analysis leaves only (g) Jethro/Raguel unaccounted for. This fascinating and lengthy section looks in part to continue the discussion begun in the discussion of (c) Jacob/Israel on why names sometimes change and then revert as the scriptural narrative continues. Given its lack of fit with the overall structure of the chapter and its high degree of exegetical development, it seems probable that section (g) stems from an independent interpretive tradition, which Philo has included here for its sheer exegetical merit, its philosophical sophistication, and in keeping with his anthological habit. This unit, which is of extreme interest for reconstructing the exegetical traditions of the Alexandrian Jewish schools and prayer houses, will be introduced more systematically below.

a   *Abram's Name Becomes Abra(h)am (§§ 60–76)*
       Analysis and General Comments

The first section of chapter five, (a) §§ 60–76, explains the symbolic meaning of Abram's (Ἀβράμ) change of name to Abraham (Ἀβραάμ). While not the

PART TWO   243

longest section in the chapter (cf. [f] Jethro/Raguel), it is arguably the most programmatic. Philo presents his lengthiest interpretation of the significance of Abraham's change of name in the Allegorical Commentary, expanding earlier presentations of this interpretive tradition, wherein Gen 17 serves as a secondary lemma (see *Cher.* 4; *Gig.* 62–64). He gives not only etymologies of Abram and Abraham, along with their allegoresis, but also comments on the social context of the debate in and around his private school (Sterling 1999), as well as offering further notes toward a philosophy of language in dialogue with Plato's *Cratylus*. Although the interpretation given in §§ 60–76 is shorter in length and scope than *QG* 3.43, the two sections can fruitfully be read synoptically (see Parallel Exegesis). The Abraham section divides into five units:

(1) Philo cites the first of two primary biblical lemmata in this chapter, Gen 17:5 (§ 60a).

(2) Before proceeding to an exegesis of this verse, Philo offers the autobiographical context catalyzing his notes on the phenomenon of name changes in the Scriptures. He references a group of "quarrelsome" contemporaries, who defame the Mosaic tradition and its Scriptures on account of such passages as Abraham's change of name. Apparently, such lampoons of scriptural tradition carried weight in the broader Alexandrian intellectual milieu, and Philo felt it his duty to match wits with these scornful exegetes and unveil the deep, "non-literal" meaning of these stories of name change in the Pentateuch (§§ 60b–62).

(3) Having cleared the stables, but still in advance of his exegesis of Gen 17:5, Philo offers one of his clearest statements of the philosophy of language (see Introduction 6d. Philosophy of Language). His theory can be located against the background of Plato's *Cratylus*. Philo suggests that language is neither purely revelatory of essences (*contra* Cratylus) nor completely conventional (*contra* Hermogenes), but a mixture of these extremes (cf. Plato, *Crat.* 383a–384d). Adducing Gen 2:19 as a secondary lemma, Philo notes that the first names in the Scriptures were not given by God, but by a rational animal (Adam) acting as his agent. The wise human being serves from the beginning as a kind of "logos" in miniature, assisting the divine Word by giving fitting names to things. Arguing from the greater to the lesser, Philo concludes that God would not forego giving "entire names" in creation, and then give single letters later on, as though these were a great boon. Rather, the divine name changes reported in Scripture signify improvements in human souls by infusion with divine powers or graces, which help them on the road to perfection (§§ 63–65).

(4) Philo turns at last to the primary lemma, Gen 17:5. He gives etymologies of "Abram" and "Abra(h)am" as "exalted father" and "elect father of sound,"

respectively. Philo then offers his standard allegoresis of the first of these etymologies: Abram, the "exalted father," symbolizes the soul enraptured with astronomy, searching the heavens for its Creator, but not yet turning inward to the ethical life and pursuit of self-knowledge (§§ 66–68).

(5) Philo offers the second etymology and its symbolic significance. Abram becoming Abraham, the "elect father of sound," represents the soul's empowerment by divine grace to turn from cosmic speculation and ascend along the pathways of ethical perfection and contemplation. In a fascinating rewriting and expansion of God's words in Gen 17:5, Philo has God enter into a protreptic dialogue with the Abraham soul, inviting him to the "orchard of philosophy," which has logic as its walls, physics as its trees, and ethics as its fruit. The empowerment to follow this kind of life is not presented solely as the work of the human will, but as an aspect of "election"—i.e., covenantal grace (§§ 69–76).

Detailed Comments

(1) § 60a. *"your name will not be called Abram, but ... Abraham."* Philo cites the primary biblical lemma, Gen 17:5a, as it appears in the Septuagint, omitting only the adverb "still/longer" (ἔτι) in the phrase "your name will no *longer* be called ...." As will be explained below, it is of critical importance to Philo's interpretation that the difference between these names is not the addition of a Hebrew "h" (Abram → Abraham) but the addition of a Greek "a" (Ἀβράμ → Ἀβραάμ).

(2) § 60b. *quarrelsome*. Philo names the group of antagonists who have occasioned his allegoresis of biblical name change in this chapter. This is the clearest autobiographical note in the treatise, and the one which best helps contextualize it against the backdrop of Philo's school and Alexandrian scholasticism. Unlike *De confusione linguarum*, in which Philo names his opponents at the very beginning of the treatise (*Conf.* 2–13), here, Philo has not foregrounded his polemical context but buried it at the center. For further study of the identity of these quarrelsome contemporaries, see Excursus A below.

the material signs ... the realities they represent. Philo suggests that his quarrelsome contemporaries are engaged in a polemic against the deeper realities intended by the Scriptures. Their exegesis sounds like a crude form of scriptural "literalism." For the contrast between "bodies" (σώματα) and "realities" (πράγματα), see the detailed comment on § 8 ("material and immaterial things"). Colson (PLCL 4:573) gives a series of texts, in which Philo juxtaposes these two terms.

a truceless war against the saints. The Greek adjective translated "truceless" (ἀκήρυκτος), when describing a war, can mean (1) "sudden" and "unheralded"; (2) "unacknowledged," as in the Cold War; or (3) "indefinite"—i.e., in which no heralds carrying terms of peace are admitted into the enemy camp. Colson (PLCL) takes Philo to use the word in the third sense here, rendering it "a war without end."

unfit to be preserved. Philo describes his scholarly rivals in terms that place them on the margins or outside of mainstream Alexandrian Judaism. One possible key to their critical activities is Philo's use of the verb "preserve" (διασῴ-ζειν). The verb might allude to the practices of Alexandrian literary critics, who athetized problematic lines of texts—famously, identifying interpolations in the Homeric poems. Are Philo's "quarrelsome" exegetes similarly suggesting that certain parts of Scripture be athetized as unworthy of Moses? If so, Philo seems to have rejected their practices as essentially heterodox and apostate—outside the bounds of acceptable critical scholarship on the Pentateuch. (See Niehoff 2011, 122–129.)

symbols of nature, who always loves to hide herself. Philo cites the saying of the Presocratic philosopher, Heraclitus—"Nature ... loves to hide herself" (φύσις ... κρύπτεσθαι φιλεῖ, Heraclitus, Marcovich fr. 8; DK fr. 123)—as a rationale for the existence of "undersenses" in both human language and revealed Scripture. In § 60, Philo has modified the original saying by adding the adverb, "always" (ἀεί), to emphasize that no part of Mosaic Scripture fails to entail a deeper meaning.

with "scrupulous" investigation. Philo presents his opponents as scholars who engage in the meticulous study of Scripture. This depiction seems at odds with the shallow and superficial nature of their exegesis reported in § 61. Barring a text critical solution (see the "Notes to the Text"), I have printed "scrupulous" in scare quotes to indicate an ironic tone. Arnaldez (1964, 60 n. 2), in a slightly different vein, argues that Philo suggests in all sincerity that his quarrelsome contemporaries do exacting scholarly labors, "to collect with care all the passages of the sacred text, at which they can scoff."

§ 61. ***just recently I heard.*** Philo reports that he has heard a criticism of this sort recently from an individual in Alexandria. In QG 3.43 and 3.53, by contrast, Philo simply notes this kind of attitude as stereotypical. This suggests that at the time of writing *De mutatione nominum*, there had been some recent agitation.

Sarai (Σάρα) to Sarah (Σάρρα), doubling the rho. Unlike the Hebrew text, where God changes Abram's and Sarai's names by giving them each the same letter, *he* (ה; see Niehoff 2011, 122)—a letter which is twice present in the Tetragrammaton—in the Septuagint, God's anomalous gift of the letters alpha (α) and rho (ρ) to Abram and Sarai lacks a similar revelatory rationale. Philo's quarrelsome contemporaries thus suggest athetizing the line (or, if they are pagans, ridicule the Pentateuch in its entirety). Philo, without recourse to Hebrew letters, must save these verses on their own merits, and does so primarily by appealing to the trustworthiness of the lawgiver, his etymologies, and their symbolic allegoresis.

stringing together. Philo's verb, "stringing together" (συνείρων), recalls Aristotle's "running style" (λέξις εἰρομένη), remarkable for its paratactic simplicity. Philo, who certainly prefers a more hypotactic, subordinated prose style, takes a rhetorical (as well as a theological) jab at his opponents here, insinuating that they are "prosaic" in both spheres.

breathlessly and sneering. The appearance of Greek roots related to "spirit" and "flesh" together in the description of Philo's antagonist here—"stringing together, breathlessly and sneering" (συνείρων ἀπνευστὶ καὶ ἐπισαρκάζων), or literally "in a spiritless manner and with attention to the flesh"—is rare in the *corpus Philonicum* and warrants further comment. "Breathless" (ἀπνευστί), a favorite adverb of Philo's, occurs some 18 times and almost always refers to the "winded" haste of a runner. The Logos himself may hasten "breathlessly" (ἀπνευστί) to separate holy and unholy thoughts in the mind of Moses (*Her.* 201). "Sneering" (ἐπισαρκάζων), by contrast, is a Philonic hapax, and occurs elsewhere in contemporaneous Greek literature only in the scholia to Homer and to Sophocles. On balance, given Philo's similar description of philosophers who "run breathlessly through their lectures, stringing together words" (διεξέρχονται δὲ ἀπνευστὶ συνείροντες ... λόγους) in *Congr.* 64, Colson's rendering of the pair as meaning stringing together words "without a moment's pause" and "sneering" is the most obvious translation. Nevertheless, given that the "flesh and spirit" polarity is etymologically present in this phrase, it is worth at least asking whether an anthropological significance is also intended. On this reading, Philo takes subtle aim at his exegetical opponent's literal reading of the Pentateuch, which ridicules God for the gift of single letters, while missing the "spirit" of the text. See further the Parallel Exegesis and *Nachleben*.

§ 62. *some small, chance circumstance*. Philo makes the point that the cause leading to one quarrelsome exegete's demise was minor and accidental—a little death, which according to divine justice, is attuned to his "belittling" of the Mosaic letter.

he came to hanging ⟨himself⟩. The Greek could be read "he came to the gallows" or "he came to hanging himself." In the first instance, he would have suffered the death penalty; in the second, he commits suicide. Colson (PLCL) renders the phrase "he hastened to hang himself," and this is perhaps the better rendering, although both kinds of death could lead to the "unclean" status that Philo attributes to him.

this foul and ill-cleaned fellow. Philo is speaking primarily of inner or noetic impurity and the impure mind that scoffs at the revelation of Moses. The adjective "foul" (μιαρός) may echo Deut 21:23, "do not pollute" (οὐ μιανεῖτε). Philo's second adjective, "ill-cleaned" (δυσκάθαρτος)—which he uses fourteen times in his extant Greek works—echoes Sophocles (*Ant.* 1284) and lends the whole scenario a tragic overtone.

did not end with a clean death. Philo's attribution of impurity to a hung corpse reflects a broader early Jewish halakhic discussion. The tradition that a hung corpse, if left hanging overnight, defiles, has its origin in the legislation in Deut 21:22–23:

> When someone is convicted of a crime punishable by death and is executed, and you hang him on a tree, his corpse must not remain as carrion ⟨i.e., overnight⟩ upon the tree. You shall bury him that same day. For anyone hung on a tree is under God's curse (כי קללת אלהים תלוי / κεκατηραμένος ὑπὸ θεοῦ πᾶς κρεμάμενος ἐπὶ ξύλου). You must not defile your/the land (לא תטמא את־אדמתך / οὐ μιανεῖτε τὴν γῆν) that the LORD your God is giving you for possession.

In Philo's case, the impurity of the scoffer's death is almost guaranteed if he is a suicide: having hung himself, there would be no one to take his body down. On the various interpretations of Deut 21:22–23 in Second Temple and Rabbinic Judaism, see Yadin 1977 (1:290; 2:204a–b) and Bernstein 1983 (esp. 30–32). For a more detailed study of the present Philonic pericope, see Cover 2024c.

using natural reason. Philo uses the verb "to reason naturally" (φυσιολογεῖν) only four times in his corpus, twice in the Allegorical Commentary (*Leg.* 3.61; *Mut.* 62) and twice in his philosophical treatise, *De aeternitate mundi* (75, 94). It may indicate philosophical speculation about the nature of the cosmos, as the theories of Chrysippus (*Aet.* 94). Here, however, it points more etymologically to the discussion of natural language which follows in *Mut.* 63.

§ 63. *God, after all, does not bestow letters.* Philo begins by accepting the quarrelsome exegete's key claim: that it is ludicrous for God to bestow letters according to the Pentateuch itself. Philo addresses this charge by setting it within the Pentateuch's own (J) narrative of creation in Gen 2. There, in contradistinction to Gen 1, God does not call or name anything, but leaves this task to the first human being (Gen 2:19).

whether consonants or vowels. Philo refers to the addition of a rho (consonant) to the name Sarai (Σάρα → Σάρρα) and an alpha (vowel) to the name Abram (Ἀβράμ → Ἀβραάμ). The problem is posed with reference to Greek-speaking Judaism. In Hebrew, God's change of both Sarai's and Abram's names involves the giving of the same consonant, *he* (ה), the most frequent letter in the Tetragrammaton. In the Hebrew text, their respective name changes clearly impart to Abram and Sarai a share in the divine name. Philo and other Alexandrian Jews seem to know this theological idea, but not its linguistic basis, and thus search for a way to preserve it as an interpretation of the Greek text.

plants and animals. This sequence of creatures recalls both J (Gen 2:8, 19) and P (Gen 1:11, 25) creation accounts. Philo's use of the word "plants" (φυτά) pinpoints Gen 2:8 (καὶ ἐφύτευσεν κύριος ὁ θεός) as the secondary lemma standing at the front of his mind.

the human being as to a leader. Philo routinely speaks of the Logos as a "leader" within the cosmos. Here, the human mind plays an analogous role as the first among creatures.

distinguished ... by his knowledge. Gen 2 does not speak of human possession of "knowledge" (ἐπιστήμη), but rather, the "the tree of knowing an acquaintance with good and evil" (τὸ ξύλον τοῦ εἰδέναι γνωστὸν καλοῦ καὶ πονηροῦ [Gen 2:9]).

so that he might place the appropriate names. Philo's turn of phrase, "so that he might place the appropriate names" (ἵνα ... τὰ οἰκεῖα ὀνόματα θῆται) echoes both Gen 2:20 and Plato's discourse on name-giving in the *Cratylus*. See especially Plato, *Crat.* 388e–389a, cited as the epigraph to this commentary chapter:

> It does not belong to every man, Hermogenes, to give a name (ὄνομα θέσθαι), but to a namewright (ὀνοματουργοῦ); and this, it would seem, is the lawgiver (ὁ νομοθέτης), who is the rarest of craftsmen (τῶν δημιουργῶν) among humans.

Philo construes both Adam and Moses as such Platonic "namewrights"—the rarest of human demiurges and lawgivers (i.e., "custom makers"), who are able to appropriately assign words to things. In the case of Moses, Philo recognizes a special connection between name-setting and lawgiving.

and whatever Adam ... the creature thus called. Philo adduces Gen 2:19c as a secondary lemma, to explicate the difference between divine name change in Gen 17:5, 15, and human name-giving. Philo's paraphrase differs slightly from the biblical lemma, to support his interpretation:

LXX Gen 2:19c	§ 63
And everything, which Adam called a living soul (ψυχὴν ζῶσαν), this ⟨was⟩ its name.	Whatever Adam called ⟨it⟩, this was the name of creature thus called (τοῦ κληθέντος ἦν).

Philo has cleaned up the Semitizing syntax of the Septuagint, omitting the direct object "living soul" (ψυχὴ ζῶσα), adding the verb "was" (ἦν), and inserting the objective genitive "of the one thus called" (τοῦ κληθέντος) to foreground the naming aspect of Adam's work.

§ 64. *a wise man.* In calling Adam a "wise man" or a "sage," Philo adverts to the Stoic idea that the earliest humans had a special proximity to truth, reflected in their name-giving (Boys-Stones 2001). Unlike some Stoics, Philo holds that there actually have been sages—at a minimum, in the Jewish Scriptures. The view that the earliest human beings played a special role in name-giving is also shared by Plato (*Crat.* 401b) and Pythagoras (Cicero, *Tusc.* 1.62). See Colson (PLCL 1:479 at *Mut.* 15). For other passages relevant to Philo's implicit philosophy of language, see *Leg.* 2.15; *Opif.* 148; and Introduction 6d. Philosophy of Language.

the founder of the human race. The Greek term, "founder" (ἀρχηγέτης), refers literally to the leader of a colony (as used, e.g., by Polybius and Dionysius of Halicarnassus). The metaphorical use found here was common in early Judaism. Philo uses it of Adam in *Opif.* 136. In *Mut.* 64, it refers more specifically to Adam's pioneering role in the giving of human language. In *Mut.* 88, he will use it even more freely to speak of "the three founders of our race," Abraham, Isaac, and Jacob.

retrofitting portions of names. The Greek verb rendered "retrofit" (μεθαρμό-ζειν, lit. "change to harmonize with") is chosen with Gen 17:5 and Gen 17:15 in mind, where letters are infixed in names rather than appended to the end of them. The verb is similar to "change a name" (μετονομάζειν) and complements the chapter's central theme.

not vowels alone, but also consonants. I.e., the alpha and the rho (see the comment above on § 63).

§ 65. *it is not right to say this.* Philo grants the quarrelsome exegete's argument in part: were the claim to be that there is some intrinsic value in the giving of individual "letters" (γράμματα), this would be beneath the dignity of the Mosaic God. In the parallel interpretation of Gen 17:5 in *QG* 3.43, Philo is less concerned about God giving literal letters (see the Parallel Exegesis).

markers of capacities ... tokens of hidden truths. In replying to the literalist interpretation of the quarrelsome exegete—that God has given Abram and Sara mere letters—Philo argues that the scriptural changes of name are in fact symbols or "signs" (Colson, PLCL) of deeper transformations in these souls' "powers" (δυνάμεις). On the noun translated as "marker" (χαρακτήρ), Colson (PLCL 5:589) notes: "The use of χαρακτήρ here, as compared to § 70 and § 83, all of which must stand together, is difficult. Ordinarily, χαρακτήρ, if it does not mean literally a stamp, is not a type or symbol, but a trait or characteristic, and this suits § 83, for the two kinds of virtue. It may with some forcing fit § 70, for though the names are the χαρακτῆρες they represent characteristics. But here this is not so, for the χαρακτῆρες which are small, sensible, and obscure must be the names and *not* what they represent." Colson's difficulty can be partially answered by recognizing that Philo playfully uses the term "characters" in a multivalent fashion. They are both "characters" in the ethical sense, but also letters. *Pace* Edwards (2013, 74), even when in earnest, Philo was not "a dogmatist without humour or rhetorical vivacity."

in the best doctrines ... in improvements of the soul. There are three spheres, Philo argues, in which the truth of his interpretation of the change of names can be found: (1) in "doctrine" (δόγμα); (2) in pure conceptions; and (3) in the improvements of the soul, rendered visible through ethical behavior. This threefold list mirrors the steps toward psychic perfection: (1) reading the doctrine of Moses leads, via allegory, to (2) clearer conceptions of reality, and ultimately to (3) the improvement in the soul.

whose name is now being changed. Philo uses the verb "to change one's name" (μετονομάζειν) for the first time in the treatise. Usually, a biblical person rather than their name is the subject of the verb "to be name changed" (μετονομάζεσθαι)—as the people themselves are the proper focus of Philo's psychic allegories. See, e.g., Philo, *Ios.* 121: "⟨God⟩ renamed him ..." (μετονομάζει δ' αὐτόν), where the masculine singular "him" (αὐτόν) can only refer to Joseph, not his name. Similarly, in *Mut.* 121, "But Moses also renamed Hosea into Joshua" (ἀλλὰ καὶ τὸν Ὡσηὲ μετονομάζει Μωυσῆς εἰς τὸν Ἰησοῦν), the presence of the masculine definite article (rather than neuter) before Hoshea and Joshua suggests that the people are undergoing fundamental changes (see Smyth § 1136). Philo's unique phraseology in *Mut.* 65, "whose name is now being changed in the text at hand" (τοῦ νυνὶ μετονομασθέντος) is noteworthy, as is the emphatic "just now" (νυνί), which underscores the presentism of Philo's psychic allegory and its role as a paradigm for the reader.

§ 66. ***"elevated father."*** Philo's first etymology in the treatise. The process of etymologization was used in Stoic and Platonist exegesis and has precedent in the Hebrew Bible and Septuagint. Philo's general practice in the Allegorical Commentary is to interpret a name by first providing an etymology, and then offering an interpretation of this etymology befitting his allegory of the soul (Long 1997). Philo's etymology of the name Abram, "elevated father" (PLCL; Grabbe 1988; Birnbaum and Dillon 2021)—or here, perhaps "elevating father" (μετέωρος πατήρ)—takes the name "Abram" (אברם) to be composed of two parts: *ab* (אב), meaning father, and *rām* (רָם), being the present active Qal participle of the root "rwm" (רום), "arise." The epithet "uplifted" has an active quality, reflected in Philo's Greek interpretation ("lifting," αἴροντα [§ 67]), but any connection to the active Hebrew participle is traditional. It is also curious that Philo's received etymology of Abram renders its lexical components in the reverse order of the Hebrew (unlike his etymology of Abraham). The allegorical explication of both parts of the name in §§ 67–68 follows this inverted syntax. The title "elevated father" has a curious antecedent in Herodotus (*Hist.* 3.124), in the dream of the daughter of Polycrates of Samos, wherein she sees her "father elevated in the air" (ὁ πατὴρ ἐν τῷ ἠέρι μετέωρος), washed by Zeus and anointed by the Sun. It is a bad omen, and appears unrelated to this tradition about Abram.

"elect father of sound." Philo's etymology of Abraham differs from the implicit biblical etymology given in Gen 17:5, "father of many nations" (אב המון גוים / πατὴρ πολλῶν ἐθνῶν). Philo may not have recognized that the biblical text offers an etymology (see Excursus B: Philo's Knowledge of Hebrew) and therefore does not see the linguistic affinity between *ab-hāmôn* (אב המון) and *Abrāhām* (אברהם). Philo's Greek etymology also improves on its Hebrew precursor, as it makes up for the seeming failure of the biblical etymology to account for the *resh* at the center of the name (might this have stood for *rabbim* [רבים, πολλῶν] in some etymological traditions?). According to George Brooke (1985, 20) and Lester Grabbe (1988, 127), Philo's Greek etymology is produced by a process called "notarikon," an analysis that isolates and etymologizes several Hebrew letters at a time, in this case two: *ab bārûr hāmôn* (אב ברור המון). This can be translated "elected father of sound" (πατὴρ ἐκλεκτὸς ἠχοῦς). Birnbaum and Dillon (2021, 223) give the related etymology *ab bārûr hemyâ* (אב ברור המיה). This suggests that Hebrew-speaking exegetes were working with the first part of the biblical etymology, "father of a crowd" (*ab-hāmôn*, אב המון), perhaps replacing *hāmôn* ("sound, crowd") with *hemyâ* ("sound"), and also dealing with the problem of the missing *resh* by finding the word "elect" (*bārûr*, ברור) hidden in the center of Abraham's name. Philo will offer an allegorical explication of all three verbal elements of this etymology in § 69.

§ 67. *lifting himself ... and gazing*. Philo's two active participles, "lifting" (αἴρων) and "gazing" (ἐπισκοπῶν) render the active voice and progressive aspect of the Hebrew active participle, "rām" (רָם). Philo could not have gleaned this from the adjective "in the air" (μετέωρος), which suggests, if anything, a passive and completed state. On the understanding that Philo knew little Hebrew, his grasp of the active element in the etymology suggests either (1) that he knows an oral tradition surrounding this name from Jewish astronomical circles; or, more simply, that (2) he has accidentally hit upon an agreement between Hebrew morphology and his own "realized" allegorical tense, which depicts the lives of the patriarchs as symbols of souls in action in the typological present.

he busies himself with reasoning about these lofty things. Philo, in poetic fashion, adds two compound synonyms to explicate "uplifting" (μετέωρος): "going about in the air" (μετεωροπόλος) and "reasoning in the air" (μετεωρολογικός). These signify the one who (astronomically speaking) "busies himself" and "reasons" with the heavenly bodies. Although Philo can speak positively about astronomy when viewed as a preliminary study (see *Congr.* 11, 51), there is always the danger of taking this "second best" (*Congr.* 51) for the perfect. Both varieties of astronomer can be seen in the Abram type, hence, the need for his name to be changed.

the size of the sun ... equally measured rotations. Philo offers a summary of the astronomical science, beginning with the observation of the sun. His reverence for the sun as the principal light and symbol of truth stems from Platonic tradition (*Resp.* 516b), as well as the sun's description as "the great light" in Gen 1:16a. Runia (2008, 28) considers this one of two clearly doxographical texts in *De mutatione nominum* (the other is § 10), noting that "Philo briefly indicates the scope of astronomy, alluding to various chapter titles from the *Placita* [of Aëtius], but without sceptical intent."

he also enquires about the light of the moon ... its waning, its waxing. Philo turns from the sun to the moon—a pattern that reflects Gen 1:16b.

and about the movement of the other stars. Following his secondary lemma, Philo moves from sun and moon to the stars in Gen 1:16c. These are comprised of "those with a set course" or the "fixed stars" (see *Opif.* 113; *Leg.* 1.8)—and the "wanderers" (i.e., Mercury, Venus, Mars, Jupiter, Saturn), which, in addition to the sun and moon, make up the seven planets in Philo's geocentric universe. See Runia 2001, 284.

§ 68. *the soul that ... cannot beget.* Both Abram and Abraham, in the Allegorical Commentary, are types of soul. Philo uses a hendiadys "ill-natured and cannot beget" (ἀφυὴς καὶ ἄγονος) to describe the soul with a natural deficit in acquiring scientific, philosophical, and ultimately, theological knowledge. The possibility of such natural deficiencies is explained in § 31.

to produce complete and perfect offspring. This perfect offspring is not the knowledge gained by astronomy, but the wisdom garnered from philosophical contemplation of unseen realities. Philo gives a nod to the "cosmic religion" of certain Platonists, who prized astronomy as the pursuit of "the fairest things that sight can see" (Ps.-Plato, *Epin.* 986c5–d4), without endorsing it unqualifiedly. See Runia 2001, 207–209. Arnaldez (1964, 64, n. 1) observes that Philo is elsewhere (*Migr.* 138) "more severe" in his critique of the astronomers, whereas in *Mut.* 68, he sees astronomy as a kind of steppingstone toward contemplation of God. Arnaldez traces both views of this science, the negative and the more positive, to Plato, *Resp.* 529b and 530a, respectively.

Moses also called the elevated reasoner "father." Having interpreted the first part of the etymology of Abram ("uplifted" [μετέωρος]) as "reasoning astronomically" (μετεωρολογικός) in § 67, in § 68 Philo offers an interpretation of the second element in string, "father" (πατήρ). This signifies that a soul with a natural proclivity for astronomy is not "non-generative" (ἄγονος) but "capable of begetting" (δυναμένη ... γεννᾶν).

§ 69. *those in the name "Abraham."* Philo continues, according to the plan set out in § 66, to interpret the etymology of Abram's new name, Abraham (Gk. *Abraam*), according to its Hebrew etymology.

there are three parts. Whereas the astronomer soul is signified by a name with only two verbal components, the soul of the philosopher-sage is signified by a name with three. The latter kind of soul maintains continuity with the former (through the shared element "father" [πατήρ]), but undergoes a transformative supplementation in character and power.

"father" and "elect" and "sound." Philo's etymology of Abraham hews more closely to the sequence of Hebrew words than his etymology of Abram. These elements, however, are not interpreted sequentially in the allegoresis. Philo begins with elements (3) "sound" and (1) "father", as these relate most directly to his Middle Platonic psychic allegory. (2) "Elect" is then dealt with in a more perfunctory manner.

we interpret "sound" to be externalized speech. Beginning with the third element in his etymology, Philo interprets "sound" (ἦχος) as "logos" (λόγος)—in particular, as "externalized speech" (λόγος προφορικός). This concept, derived from Stoicism but now integrated into Philo's Middle Platonic psychology, signifies the "word" (λόγος) in its audible "expression" (λέγειν). Its antipode, which Philo does not mention here, is the immanent reason or the "word which resides internally" (λόγος ἐνδιάθετος). For the pairing of both terms, see *Mos.* 2.127–129 in the explication of the Urim and Thummim on the breastplate of the high priest; also *Spec.* 4.69.

for the voice box is an animal's sound organ. Philo reports a tradition known as early as Aristotle about the physical production of sound in an ensouled body (Aristotle, *De an.* 420b: "The voice is a certain noise of the ensouled ⟨being⟩" [ἡ δὲ φωνὴ ψόφος τίς ἐστιν ἐμψύχου]). Philo is one of the first to use the phrase "sound organ" (φωνητήριον ⟨sc. ὄργανον⟩), though it appears also in Strabo, *Geogr.* 14.2.28.

the mind is its father. Rather than coordinating "externalized speech" (λόγος προφορικός) with "internal speech" (λόγος ἐνδιάθετος), Philo speaks in more Platonizing terms of the "mind" (νοῦς) as the immanent rational principle. Whereas in the etymological allegory of Abram, "father" (πατήρ) signifies the soul's capacity to beget sense-perceptive conclusions, in the allegory of Abraham's name, "father" signifies instead the rational "spring" and begetter of all speech.

the stream of speech. Plato in *Tim.* 75e speaks of "the stream of words" (τὸ δὲ λόγων νᾶμα). Philo adapts this metaphor as "the stream of *the* word" (τὸ τοῦ λόγου νᾶμα)—adding the title "mind" (νοῦς) to help articulate his analogy between the human mind and speech, on the one hand, and the two-fold Logos of God, on the other.

"elect" ... specifies the mind of a sage. The "elect" father is the soul that begets philosophical knowledge and thus properly warrants the title "philosopher"— or better, "sage" (cf. §70). The mere word "father," by contrast, references the soul capable of producing a derivative kind of wisdom, but not the best.

§70. *the lover of learning and stargazer.* Philo expands his allegorical description of the astronomer, symbolized by the name "Abram," with the terms "lover of learning" (φιλομαθής) and "stargazer" (μετεωρολέσχης). These names highlight the "natural-scientific" character of the astronomer, as well as his aloofness from earthly ethical concerns.

sketched. Philo's verb, "to sketch" or "figure" (σκιαγραφεῖν), is of Platonic provenance, and literally means "to write in shadows." It suggests the relative unreality of the name, in contrast to the reality of the allegorical referent.

the philosopher ... or better, the sage. Just as Abram is given two additional titles in this section (see above), so Abraham is given two new titles as well: "philosopher" (φιλόσοφος) and "sage" (σοφός). "Philosopher" is meant as a verbal contrast to Abram's "lover of learning" (φιλομαθής): instead of heavenly knowledge, Abraham loves heavenly wisdom. Philo then peels off the first part of the compound, "lover of *x*" (φίλο-), to arrive at an even more accurate signification of "Abraham": the soul that is religiously "wise" (σοφός).

no longer suppose ... that the Divine bestows a change of names. Philo reiterates his point from §§64–65: that God does not mean to take credit for changing Abraham's name, but rather for the ethical transformation of the astronomical soul into the soul of a philosopher-sage. This is in direct contrast to Philo's position in QG 3.43 (see the Parallel Exegesis), where Philo ascribes the giving of the letter alpha to divine providence and then catalogues its many "literal" benefits.

a correction of character. Philo's phrase, "correction of character," entails a *double entendre.* "Correction" (ἐπανόρθωσις) might describe both the process of scribal revision, including the changing of letters (γράμματα), as well as, in a pedagogical sense, the straightening out of "characters" or "moral dispositions" (ἤθη). God, according to §70, writes in the soul, but not with human letters. For a similarly playful turn, involving Abraham's "rewritten manner of life" (ὁ μεταχαραχθεὶς τρόπος), see §71.

§ 71. *mathematician*. This alternative name for an astronomer refers back to the scientific quality of Abram as "knowledge-loving" (φιλομαθής) in § 70. Astronomy was generally considered a sub-branch of mathematics or geometry.

manner of living. Abram and Abraham are types of souls and the "manners of living" (τρόποι) that flow forth from such souls.

§ 72. *"for what reason."* Philo constructs a "speech in character" (προσωποποιΐα) or *suasoria*, giving God a more expansive speaking part than is present in the Pentateuch. God addresses the Abram soul—but also to the reader of the commentary, who might be inclined to the sciences and only beginning the journey into philosophy. Philo often composes such speeches at the end of chapters or chapter subunits, giving an indirect window into the rhetorical and homiletical practices of the Hellenistic synagogue (see esp. Ps.-Philo, *De Jona*; Cover 2015; Siegert 1992; 1980). For the importance of Philo's works in uncovering such synagogue traditions embedded in Philo's commentaries, see Mack and Hilgert 1972.

"pleasure ... desire ... grief or fear." God, in Philo's speech-in-character, enumerates the four generic Stoic "passions" (πάθη): "pleasure" (ἡδονή), "desire" (ἐπιθυμία), "grief" (λύπη), and "fear" (φόβος); (Stobaeus 2.88,8–90,6; L&S § 65a). By the first century CE, these passions had passed into wider philosophical usage. Ps.-Andronicus of Rhodes, *De passionibus* (περὶ παθῶν, SVF 3.391), groups them into dissociative and appetitive pairs: the dissociative, "grief" (λύπη) and "fear" (φόβος); and the appetitive, "desire" (ἐπιθυμία) and "pleasure" (ἡδονή). Philo's arrangement follows a different logic, placing the emotions pertaining to the present (pleasure and grief) as the first element in each pair, and the emotions pertaining to the future (desire and fear) as the second. According to Ps.-Andronicus (SVF 3.391), a passion is defined as an "irrational movement of the soul" (ἄλογος ψυχῆς κίνησις). (1) "pleasure" (ἡδονή) is an "irrational swelling or elation" (ἄλογος ἔπαρσις); (2) "desire" (ἐπιθυμία) is an "irrational longing" (ἄλογος ὄρεξις); (3) "grief" (λύπη) is an "irrational contraction" (ἄλογος συστολή); and (4) "fear" (φόβος) is an "irrational avoidance" (ἄλογος ἔκκλισις). The sage, in Stoic and Philonic thought, is the one who ultimately cultivates both "lack of passion" (ἀπάθεια) and the "good emotions" (εὐπάθειαι). For the latter, see the detailed comments on "joy" in § 1. For a more detailed study of the passions in Roman Stoicism and Philo, see Weisser 2021.

"demolition ... upsetting ... dissolution ... excision." God, in Philo's speech-in-character, employs a variety of metaphors for the soul's process of ridding itself of the passions: "demolition" (καθαίρεσις), "upsetting or capsizing" (ἀνατροπή), "organic dissolution" (κατάλυσις), and "surgical excision" (ἐκτομή). Rhetorically, the alternation between "down" (κατά), "up" (ἀνά), and "out" (ἐξ)

prefixes on these nouns conveys both the confusion generated by the emotions and the psychic upheaval required to remove them. This is Philonic wordsmithing at its finest.

§ 73. *just as there is no profit in trees, unless they bear fruit.* God, in Philo's speech-in-character, offers an analogy for human virtues in the fruitfulness of a tree. This comparison stems from Jewish and philosophical commonplace. See the following comment.

the acquisition of virtue; for this is its fruit. According to Arnaldez (1964, 66, n. 1), "a comparison of Stoic origin (cf. Sextus Empiricus, *Math.* 7.12; SVF 2:15, n. 38)." The connection between fruit and virtue is common to broader Greek (Menander, *Sent.* 1.298: "The fruit of virtue is a well-ordered life" [καρπὸς γὰρ ἀρετῆς ἐστιν εὔτακτος βίος]) and Jewish thought.

§ 74. *some of the ancients ... a field.* Philo repeats a tradition that he has already related in *Leg.* 1.57 and *Agr.* 14 (Arnaldez 1964, 67, n. 2): that the "threefold" division of "discourse about philosophy" has been allegorized by "some of the ancients" according to the parts of a field or orchard. The "ancients" referred to are probably the Stoics. A similar division of philosophical "propositions and problems" into "three parts" (μέρη τρία)—"ethical propositions, physical propositions, and logical propositions" (αἱ μὲν γὰρ ἠθικαὶ προτάσεις εἰσίν, αἱ δὲ φυσικαί, αἱ δὲ λογικαί)—is recorded in Aristotle, *Top.* 105b (Colson, PLCL 1:477), but only the Stoic variant of this schema appearing in Diogenes Laertius (7.39–40; so Geljon and Runia 2012, 107; Colson, PLCL 1:477; 3:490) uses the illustration of the "all-productive field" (ἀγρὸς πάμφορος).

According to most philosophical textbooks, the typical Stoic ordering of this threefold division is logic (stage one, the wall), physics (stage two, the tree), ethics (stage three, the fruit) (Geljon and Runia 2012, 107). Aristotle presents these divisions in the reverse order. In fact, the situation is more complicated still. Critical analysis of the Stoic sources reveals that there were at least two Stoic sequences in circulation: (1) logic, physics, ethics; and (2) logic, ethics, physics (see Ierodiakonou 1993, 68–70). In the first Stoic sequence, the initiate is led ever closer to the true food of the soul. Pace Geljon and Runia (2012, 107), Philo does not explicitly present this first Stoic sequence in any of his works (*Leg.* 1.57; *Agr.* 14; *Ebr.* 202; *Mut.* 74; *Spec.* 1.336; *Virt.* 8), although it may be implied by the field analogy. In the second sequence, by contrast—Logic-Ethics-Physics (see *Leg.* 1.57, where virtue is at the zenith *despite* the sequence)—the student moves from basic propositions, to a study of the human microcosm, to a study of the cosmic macrocosm, ascending through the realities according to increasing orders of magnitude, and ending with the contemplation not of human life, but of the world. Stoic monism, it seems, does not *necessarily* have an ethical telos. Plutarch, moreover, criticized

Chrysippus for inconsistently adopting both of these sequences (Plutarch, *Stoic. rep.* 1035a–f; Ierodiakonou 1993, 68).

In § 74, Philo reorders the Stoic divisions of philosophy according to the exigencies of his allegory of the soul. Unlike either of the known Stoic sequences, physics (the trees) comes first. This is followed by logic (the walls) and ethics (the fruit and the true purpose of the field—i.e., moral philosophy). A possible rationale for this inversion is that Philo wishes to depict the transformation of the Abram soul (focused on physics) into the Abraham soul (focused on ethics) with the study of the words of Scripture (a focus on logic) forming the middle stage in the progression. This order better befits Philo's Platonist view of the inspired text as mediator of transformation, as opposed to the Stoic view of language, which grants it only a limited, primitivist authority.

Both here and in *Agr.* 14, Philo eschews taking full ownership of this division, preferring to attribute it to the "ancients." This may be because the category of physics does not adequately account for Philo's Platonic ontology, which includes metaphysical realities as well. Its usefulness in the present argument stems from the Stoic suggestion that everything is ordered toward ethics: particularly the natural sciences (physics), among which astronomy was numbered. This is the precisely the kind of conversion that Philo suggests God is producing in Abram: a turn away from astrophysics (the middle point of the journey) toward ethics and virtue (the end of philosophy).

philosophical discourse. Critically, as in Diogenes Laertius 7.39, it is "philosophical discourse" (ὁ κατὰ φιλοσοφίαν λόγος), not "philosophy" *per se*, which is divided into three. For the importance of the former phrase and its potential role in ancient pedagogy, see Ierodiakonou 1993, 58–61.

physics to trees. Although physics is second in many divisions of philosophical discourse, Philo mentions it first here because it represents the location of the Abram soul, which is occupied by astronomy and the natural sciences. A brief comparison with an alternative sequence in Diogenes Laertius will prove instructive. Diogenes (7.40) like Philo compares "the physical" division (τὸ φυσικόν) to "the earth or the trees" (ἡ δὲ γῆ ἢ τὰ δένδρα). Diogenes presents the trees third, after the wall and the fruit, which suggests that he is following the Logic-Ethics-Physics order (see detailed comment above on "some of the ancients"). In Diogenes's presentation, the fruit is the tree in microcosm or the necessary ethical preparation for true natural contemplation. For Philo in the Allegorical Commentary, by contrast, the telos is not the full tree or the cosmos, but the human "eating" of the fruit, i.e., ethics and virtue.

logic, to walls and fences. Logic, though always the first division in Stoic sequences, is placed curiously by Philo here between physics and ethics. Diogenes Laertius (7.40) likewise identifies "the logical" division (τὸ λογικόν) as "the wall surrounding" the orchard (ὁ μὲν περιβεβλημένος φραγμός). The rationale for Philo's transposition may be that the allegorical reading of the scriptural text (i.e., logic) is viewed by Philo as a kind of transformative stage, leading the Abram soul towards the fullness of philosophy and changing him into a sage.

ethics, to fruit. Philo places ethics last in his sequence, according to the most common Stoic model. Diogenes Laertius (7.40) likewise likens "the ethical" division (τὸ ἠθικόν) to "the fruit" (ὁ ... καρπός).

§ 75. *the study of physics and logic leads up to ethics.* Philo gives an ethically centered reading of the Stoic field of philosophy. As we have seen in the detailed comments above, however, there were other ways to order this symbolic sequence. In Peripatetic tradition, contemplation and ethics stand as mutual final ends, famously in tension with one another in Aristotle's *Ethica nicomachea*. Stoicism also knew this tension, and Diogenes Laertius (7.40), immediately prior to his metaphor of the fruitful field (outlined in the comments above), describes the division of philosophy according to the analogy of the egg: it consists in the shell (logic), the white (ethics), and the yolk (physics). In this alternative metaphor, the "innermost" part of the egg is not ethics but physics—the cosmic speculation in which the Abram soul is engaged in. In the Allegorical Commentary, Philo more often would transpose these, so that ethics is the yolk.

§ 76. *the investigation of nature to ethical philosophy.* This statement of Abram's change of occupation recapitulates the first and most common Stoic sequence, from physics to ethics.

from speculation about the cosmos to knowledge of its Maker. This second conversion in the Abraham soul, from physical cosmology to contemplation of God, comes as a surprise. It was not signaled by Philo's metaphor of the fruitful field. Here, the soul moves not only from physics to ethics, but also from physics to metaphysics—or better, from physics to theology and from attending to the world of becoming to contemplating The One Who Is. This shift of Abraham's attention from nature to supernature challenges the anthropocentric and ethics-final position that Philo seemed to be advocating as the end of philosophical discourse up to this point. Here, Stoic ethics and Middle Platonic contemplation stand in some degree of tension with one another.

piety, the best of possessions. Partially to resolve the apparent tension between ethics and contemplation, Philo introduces the key to his virtue theory: "piety" (εὐσέβεια). Piety, or reverence of God and divine law, is here called the greatest of possessions. Elsewhere, Philo understands it to be the queen of the virtues (*Spec.* 4.135; Sterling 2006; Córdova 2018). It is not one of the four cardinal virtues according to Platonic and Aristotelian tradition—which look more toward the human sphere—but stands above them as a kind of crown. It is the Greek equivalent of the Latin *pietas*—the traditional Roman virtue *par excellence* (Vergil, *Aen.* 1.10, 378). It is often paired with "holiness" (ὁσιότης) and was adopted by Philo to express religious virtue in Jewish terms that would simultaneously resonate with a Roman readership. No other cardinal virtue deals so clearly with human transcendent obligations. On the basis of the testimonia, some scholars, including Mangey, Cohn and Wendland, Colson, Royse, and Sterling (2006, 111–112) posit that Philo wrote an entire treatise *De pietate* ("On Piety")—now lost—which would have been part of *De virtutibus* and placed before the treatise on "love of human beings" (φιλανθρωπία [Wilson 2011, 13–15; Royse 2009, esp. 81–94]) between *Virt.* 50 and 51. For the potential fragments of this treatise, see Harris 1886, 10–11; Royse 1980. In §76, piety includes the virtue of attending to God and the metaphysical realm—shifting one's reverential vision from the created world to "knowledge of the Maker," as a virtue complementary to those more focused on the emotions and right action in the human sphere, "justice" or "love of humanity" (δικαιοσύνη or φιλανθρωπία; Sterling 2006, 119). See *Spec.* 2.63; cf. *Mut.* 39, where "piety" refers to attention to human beings as well.

Excursus A: The Identity of the Quarrelsome Exegetes
Who might Philo's "quarrelsome" exegetes (§60b) have been? There are at least five possibilities: (1) non-Jewish scholars; (2) Jewish literalists; (3) Jewish allegorizers; (4) Jewish "athetizers" of biblical texts; and (5) fictive opponents.

Hay (1979–1980, esp. 42–43), in his comprehensive list of Philo's references to (3) "other allegorists" (i.e., "non-literal" interpreters) throughout his corpus, tentatively considers §§62–76 evidence of such a group (though why he has not included §§60–61 in his range is not clear to me). He marks this, however, with a question mark—his critical *siglum* indicating that these may not refer to real exegetes, but (5) "to imaginary conversation partners Philo introduces to enliven his commentary."

Niehoff (2011, 77) is more optimistic than Hay about the possibility of recovering details of the various colleagues with whom Philo interacted in this passage, and in my judgment charts the better path. The fifth option, that of (5) fictive opponents, is ruled out by the anecdotal elements in §61, where Philo reports a recent criticism against his school's high valuation of scriptural name changes. Of the other four groups, it seems more likely that Jewish scholars would be making a "'scrupulous' investigation" (ἀκριβὴς ἔρευνα) of the Scriptures, whether for constructive or polemical purposes. If "scrupulous" (ἀκριβής) is to be taken in earnest (see the detailed comment on §61), can a particular

Jewish group be pinpointed? They do not seem to be (2) defenders of the literal sense of Scripture—at least, not the same pious "simpletons" (εὐήθεις, *Leg.* 1.91) of whom Philo often speaks—"uninitiated in allegory" (ἀλληγορίας ... ἀμύητοι, *Fug.* 179) and spiritual "microcitizens" (μικροπολῖται, *Somn.* 1.39), who remain fixated on Scripture's earthly referents. Their mocking of God's gift of single letters to Abram and Sarai and Philo's description of their exegesis as "spiritless" (ἀπνευστί) and "fleshy" (ἐπισαρκάζων) in § 61 might suggest a certain kind of literalism, and thus Shroyer argues that in addition to the more pious literalists, Philo also refers to "literalists of an extremely aggressive type" (1936, 277). So also Goulet (1987, 319), who presumes that Philo speaks to "an impious literalist," arguing that neither a Jewish allegorist nor a pagan seems likely in his mind.

Philo's complaint in § 60 that they attack not so much the material "bodies" (σώματα) of the text as their underlying "realities" (πράγματα), alternatively, suggests that the quarrelsome are (3) radical allegorizers. As stated above, this was the tentative position of Hay (Hay 1979–1980, 52; see further Hay 1991). Niehoff adds to Hay's position, accepting the critics described in §§ 60–61 as some kind of Jewish allegorizers (2011: 153–155), but also suggesting, on the basis of the verb "to preserve" (διασῴζειν [§ 60]), that they were also (4) proponents of the praxis of textual athetizing—the elimination of spurious interpolations. She traces this practice to Alexandrian Homeric scholarship (Niehoff 2011, 122–129).

Despite the strong likelihood that the quarrelsome exegetes represent a Jewish contingent of some kind, it is worth considering several cues that suggest some involvement with (1) non-Jewish scholars. In favor of this identification are the following points: (a) The criticisms are not against Philo's interpretation of the change of names, but against the literal sense of the biblical text itself. Jewish literalists and allegorists generally take the text seriously, whereas Philo's "quarrelsome" do not. (b) Philo describes their hostility against Scripture as an assault on "holy things," which might be read as an attack on Jewish cult and "holy people." (c) Most decisive are Philo's other uses of the adjective "quarrelsome" (φιλαπεχθήμων). The term is used only once elsewhere in the Allegorical Commentary (*Fug.* 5), but the context is different. The best parallels to Philo's usage in *Mut.* 60 occur in *De Abrahamo* and the *De vita Mosis*. Both treatises presume an external audience, lacking in *De mutatione nominum*. In *Mos.* 1.248, the adjective "quarrelsome" (φιλαπεχθήμων) is used to describe the Egyptians' attitude toward the "Hebrews"—a not-so-veiled reminder on Philo's part that contemporary Egyptian attitudes toward Jews since Flaccus have become all too reminiscent of their scriptural counterparts. In *Abr.* 178–183, the "quarrelsome people" (φιλαπεχθήμονες) are instead literary critics who find no reason to praise Abraham's near sacrifice of Isaac in Genesis 22. Comparing Abraham to figures like Agamemnon and those held "in highest reputation by the Greeks" (Ἑλλήνων ... οἱ δοκιμώτατοι: *Abr.* 180), who sacrifice their children when duty calls, these quarrelsome exegetes also invoke the practices of child-sacrifice by the Canaanites—which Moses outlaws—and the self-immolation of the Indian gymnosophists to render Abraham's faithfulness in Gen 22 a relatively lukewarm demonstration of piety. It is hard to imagine a pious Jew espousing such a critique of Abraham—and the invocation of Greek models as the highest exemplars suggests that some of Philo's borderline Jewish, apostate Jewish, or gentile Alexandrians may comprise part of the faction that he addresses here. This last was the position that I advanced in my presentation of chapter five to the SBL Philo of Alexandria Seminar (Cover 2016b), and it remains, to my mind, the most probable. The "esoteric" audience of the Allegorical Commentary, however, renders the parallels from the Exposition of the Law less probative. Birnbaum and Dillon (2021, 315–316) consider non-Jews, assimilationist Jews, and apostate Jews all as possibilities in *De Abrahamo*, but determine that the evidence is inconclusive. It may have been a mixed group.

Excursus B: Philo's Knowledge of Hebrew and Use of Onomastica

The view taken in this commentary is that Philo's Hebrew etymologies are derived from an onomasticon, several of which are extant in the papyri (see Rokeah 1968; Shaw 2015). The scholarly consensus that Philo did not know much Hebrew himself has recently been challenged, or at least problematized, by Bloch (2021), but there remains much evidence arguing against Philo's fluency in the language, even if he had some cursory familiarity. In addition to the multiple etymologies that appear in his commentaries (suggesting his use of traditional sources made by bilingual Jews), many of Philo's etymologies do not exactly fit his allegorical system and have to be adapted in ways that stretch their literal meaning or applicability. Even more tellingly, Philo's failure to refer to features of the Hebrew text—in cases other than names, where he had an onomasticon—to help explain numerous difficult passages (e.g., the letter *he* added to both Abram's and Sarai's names!) is further evidence that, while Philo used Hebrew resources when he had them, he was neither creatively generating them nor actively reading the Hebrew text itself. His argument that the Greek and Hebrew translations were "sisters, or rather one and the same, with regard both to realities and words" (*Mos.* 2.40) offers a rationale for ignoring the Hebrew. Thus, we may thus lightly modify Joseph Scaliger's judgment regarding the Alexandrian: *ille non Hebraismi imperitissimus fuit, sed tamen imperitus* ("He was not 'very unacquainted' with Hebrew, but he was unacquainted nonetheless." For Scaliger's original sentence, see Bloch 2021, 261). Scaliger's superlative "very unacquainted" ("imperitissimus") is hyperbolic, but points out the real difference between a Jew like Philo, on the one hand, and a Jew like Paul, on the other, who was educated in Palestine and likely did have some fluency in Hebrew or Aramaic (though these points are also debated).

Parallel Exegesis

Philo's interpretation of God's changing the name Abram to Abraham in §§ 60–76 runs parallel to the exegesis of Gen 17:5 in *QG* 3.43. His coordinated interpretation of Sarah's change of name in §§ 77–80 follows the model of the interpretation of Gen 17:15 in *QG* 3.53. While he introduces these exegeses independently in the *QG*—in both cases, mentioning a group of contemporaneous scholars who mock name changes as unbefitting of God—in *Mut.* 61, Philo combines the attacks on both Abram's and Sarai's name changes into a single charge and attributes it to the same group. For a more extensive treatment of these passages, see Cover 2024c.

The comparative exegetical structure of Mut. 60–76 and QG 3.43. A synoptic outline of the topics in each passage will facilitate comparative analysis:

TABLE 5.1 Synopsis of *QG* 3.43 and *Mut.* 60–76

	Topic	*QG* 3.43	*Mut.* 60–76
A	Citation of primary lemma	*QG* 3.43a	§ 60a
B	Description and rebuttal of some quarrelsome exegetes	*QG* 3.43b	§§ 60b–62
C1	Praise of the power of the letter alpha (ayb)	*QG* 3.43c	Missing
C2	Secondary lemma (Gen 2:19) and explication: That Adam, rather than God, bestows names	Missing	§§ 63–65a
D	Symbolic allegoresis of name change: transformation of the soul	*QG* 3.43d	§ 65b
E	Allegoresis of the etymologies of Abram and Abraham	*QG* 3.43e	§§ 66–71
F	Paraphrase of God's appeal to the Abram soul	Missing	§§ 72–73
G1	*Peroratio* A: Second rebuttal of the quarrelsome, including a praise of the letter alpha (ayb)	*QG* 3.43f.	Missing
G2	*Peroratio* B: The orchard of philosophy	Missing	§§ 74–76

As the table shows, Philo twice in his *solutio* in QG 3.43 (sections C1 and G1) offers a defense of God's gift of the letter and its literal "power" (զաւրութիւն). These proofs are missing, and in fact rejected, in *De mutatione nominum* and replaced with the adduction and interpretation of a secondary biblical lemma (Gen 2:19). This does not preclude Philo's use of an allegorical component in his *solutio* in QG 3.43e (E). His contextualization of both passages within the same debate with the "quarrelsome" makes his difference in apologetic approach noteworthy.

§ 60. *quarrelsome*. In QG 3.43, the group is addressed analogously as "uncultivated" and "uninitiated ... who do not belong to the divine chorus" (Philo QG 3.43 [Marcus, PLCLSup]). In QG 3.53 (Marcus, PLCLSup), members of the same group are referred to as "stupid people." Unlike in *Mut*. 62, where Philo's opponent comes to an abrupt and unclean death as a result of his disdain for divine law, in QG 3.43 and 53, it would appear that the debate is ongoing and that the "unclean" death has not yet occurred. This fact supplies evidence for the priority of the QGE, at least in this section. See Excursus A above for the possible identity of this group.

nature, who always loves to hide herself. Philo quotes the same proverb of Heraclitus in *Fug*. 179 to defend the presence of "allegory" (ἀλληγορία). Intriguingly, in the only other place in which he alludes to this aphorism (*Spec*. 4.51), Philo affirms the opposite interpretation: that nature does *not* always love to hide herself. In that context, however, Philo is not describing licit allegorical practices, but false prophets, who ascribe their own personal predictions to divine oracles.

§ 61. ***A godless and impious man***. Philo uses a string of less hostile terms in QG 3.43, speaking of these exegetes collectively as "uncultivated" (անէրախշուն ել անպար, ἄμουσος [Marcus, PLCLSup 1:234, n. a]), "inconsiderate" or "uninitiated," (անխորհուրդ, ἀμυήτος [Marcus, PLCLSup 1:234, n. b]) and "who do not belong to the divine chorus" (անաստուածպար). These epithets sound more like those used of naïve literalists in the Allegorical Commentary, which suggests that the crisis has not yet reached its fever point in the QGE.

great indeed and superabundant are the gifts. Philo sets a similar phrase on the lips of the quarrelsome exegetes in QG 3.43. However, whereas in QG 3.43 (see QG 3.53 as well) Philo defends "the gift of the letter," in *Mut*. 63–65 he defends instead the gift of powers in the soul.

the Leader of the Universe. In QG 3.43, the quarrelsome exegete uses a similar phrase in his mock-description of Jewish interpreter, who speaks of the "Leader and Lord of the Universe" (ὁ ἡγεμὼν καὶ κύριος τῶν ὅλων [so Marcus, PLCLSup 1:234, n. d]); cf. *Mut*. 61, "the leader of the universe" (ὁ ἡγεμὼν τῶν ὅλων). The two passages show literary or oral dependence and describe the same group.

by the addition of a letter, of the one alpha. The numerical specificity of the phrase "the one alpha" (τὸ ἓν ἄλφα; cf. *QG* 3.43: "one letter" [մի գիր]), lampoons Jewish arithmological speculation about the values of Greek scriptural names ("by the addition of the 1, alpha"). Three pieces of evidence support this conclusion. First, Sara's rho is not given an arithmological marker (τὸ ῥῶ [§ 61]), as though its value were also "one" (as alpha). Second, later in *QG* 3.43, Philo will claim that "⟨alpha⟩ is the brother of the number one" (⟨Այբն⟩ եղբայր է միականն)—a phrase which leads Marcus (PLCLSup 1:235, n. b) to comment: "Alpha as a numeral letter = 1." Third, from an Armenian fragment of *De numeris* (Terian 1984), we see that Philo did occasionally attribute arithmetic values to Greek words (there, he computes the numerical value of the word ἕν to be 55), using the standard Greek numerals (Smyth § 347).

This raises a question for the present passage: Is it possible that Philo (or his quarrelsome opponent) knows a tradition associated with the arithmological values of the names Abram / Abra(h)am? The possibility is intriguing, given the statement at *Post.* 173 that "the faithful Abraham is eponymous of the decad" (ἧς ⟨δεκάδος⟩ Ἀβραὰμ ὁ πίστος ἐπώνυμος) and that fact that *De mutatione nominum* begins with the addition of a single year to Abraham's life (from 99 to 100), which signifies his moral perfection (*Mut.* 1–2). At first blush, however, the answer appears to be negative. If one adds up the standard numerical significances of the Greek names Ἀβράμ and Ἀβραάμ (which Philo uses in *De numeris*), one arrives at the numbers 144 and 145, respectively. It is hard to see, initially, how moving from a square (12×12) to a less easily divisible number might function as a symbol of patriarchal perfection. On the other hand, adding the individual digits in each of these numbers leads to a quite fascinating result: 1+4+4 = 9; 1+4+5 = 10. A movement from 9 to 10 is significant and clearly a symbol of perfection in both Pythagorean and Jewish arithmology. The difference, moreover, is "one" or alpha.

The reduction of 144 and 145 to 9 and 10, respectively, invites the scholar to search the history of exegesis for alternative modes of reckoning the values of letters in antiquity. An important Neopythagorean and Jewish tradition involves calculating the numerical value of letters not according to their absolute value, but according to what is called, in contemporary mathematics, their *modulo* 9 values (hereafter, mod 9). According to Thomas Heath's *History of Greek Mathematics* (1921, 115), the use of mod 9 calculations in ancient arithmology dates at least as early as Hippolytus and Ps.-Iamblichus's commentary on Nicomachus of Gerasa. It would potentially be of Pythagorean or Neopythagorean origin. Something like a mod 9 schema is used in later Hebrew gematria under the heading *mispar qatan* ("small enumeration").

Put simply, the mod 9 value of any number is its remainder after being divided by nine. This modulus was specially designed for the decimal sys-

TABLE 5.2 The Arithmological Significance of Abram and Abraham, mod. 9

Greek Letter	Value (mod. 9)	Greek Letter	Value (mod. 9)
A	1	A	1
B	2	B	2
P	1(00)	P	1(00)
A	1	A	1
M	4(0)	A	1
		M	4(0)
Total Value	9	Total Value	10

tem admired by Pythagoras, Plato, and Philo. As table 5.2 shows, the mod 9 values for the names Ἀβράμ and Ἀβραάμ are 9 and 10, respectively.

Using mod 9 to derive the arithmetic equivalent of each letter, the addition of one alpha mathematically brings the calculated value of the patriarch's name from 9 to 10—a number of perfection, which has been thematized in the tithe discussed earlier in the treatise (§§ 1–2). Philo's Neopythagorean affinities and arithmological interest make this possibility worthy of consideration. It is critical to note, however, that whether or not such an arithmological tradition existed in the first century CE and whether or not Philo knew about it, he does not offer it in § 61—perhaps because it was already the subject of mockery. It is only residually visible in QG 3.43 and actively suppressed in *De mutatione nominum*, where Philo's strategy will be to point to the allegorical significances of Hebrew etymologies. See further (on ancient mathematics) Cuomo 2000; 2001; and Heath 1921. On Philo's arithmology, see Robbins 1931; Staele 1931; Terian 1984; Moehring 1995; and Förster 2000.

letter. Literally, "one element" (στοιχεῖον). Cf. QG 3.43: "one letter" (ܚܕ ܐܬܘܬܐ), which Marcus (PLCLSup 1:234, n. e) retroverts identically as ἓν γράμμα. Philo shifts away from the letter to the "element" and its signification in the Allegorical Commentary.

breathlessly and sneering. The pairing "breathless and sneering" (ἀπνευστὶ καὶ ἐπισαρκάζων) has an anthropological overtone to it, suggesting that Philo's opponents are fleshy and unspiritual in their exegesis. Although Philo more often speaks of the Platonic dichotomy of body and soul, at several moments—often on account of biblical pressure (see *Post.* 67; *Gig.* 19, 29; *Agr.* 44; *Her.* 55; *Virt.* 58)—he can also distinguish between flesh and spirit, construing them in either harmonious or adversarial relationship. The flesh-spirit antagonism is most strongly developed in *Gig.-Deus* (*Gig.* 19; *Deus* 2), where it appears to have an eschatological (though not an apocalyptic) connotation.

§ 63. ***Gen 2:19*** (*"whatever Adam called it"*). As noted above, Philo's adduction and interpretation of Gen 2:19 as a secondary lemma finds no parallel in QG 3.43 or elsewhere in his corpus. Philo interprets Gen 2:19 as a primary lemma, however, in QG 1.20–21; *Leg.* 2.14–15; and *Opif.* 148–150. In QG 1.20, Philo gives a Stoic account of names, whereby Adam the sage gives names accurately on account of his being the first to see them. The beginning of the Armenian *solutio*, lacking from the Greek fragment, says that names are given "by setting … but not by nature" (ηὐειγμ … այլ ոչ բունրեամբ). The Armenian instrumental cases might be retroverted either as τῷ θεῖναι … ἀλλ' οὐ φύσει or as θέσει … ἀλλ' οὐ φύσει, creating an oppositional account, which supports the conventionalist view. At the end of the same *solutio*, however, also preserved only in Armenian, Philo argues that the animals were struck by some "familiar and related" (յիրմէ բնաւանի և յազգակցէ) element in the names Adam gave. The Armenian adjectives may be retroverted as "proper" (οἰκεῖος) and "kindred" (συγγενής), the latter of which denotes natural affinity. Both convention and nature play a role in Adam's naming. In *Leg.* 2.14–15, Philo returns to the question of names and their origin, establishing the same priority of human "setting" (θέσις), but arguing that such human-given names ought to harmonize with the "reality" (πρᾶγμα) that they represent. In the Exposition of the Law, Philo articulates the relationship between nature in convention in name giving in an even more compatibilist way, arguing that God was "testing" (ἀπεπειρᾶτο [*Opif.* 149]) Adam, to see whether the names he would give would adequately reveal the "particular properties" (αἱ … ἰδιότητες [*Opif.* 149]) and "natures" of each animal (αἱ φύσεις [*Opif.* 150]).

§ 65. ***whose name is being changed.*** The verb "to change one's name" (μετονομάζειν) is used previously of Abram/Abraham in *Leg.* 3.244 and *Gig.* 62, in the expression "before his name was changed" (πρὶν μετονομασθῆναι). In *Cher.* 4, Philo mentions that Abram and Sara "had not yet received their change of name" (οὔπω μετωνομάσθησαν). These references show that Philo considered scriptural name changes to be significant events in his allegory of the soul prior to his conflict with the quarrelsome exegetes, and that he had been preparing for the present treatise from the inception of the Allegorical Commentary. For a similar "exemplary" passage, see *Cher.* 56, where Philo lays out a theory of language and then gives a scriptural example (names of Adam and Eve as allegories of mind and sense, via the etymologies "human" and "life").

§ 66. *"elevated father."* In addition to QG 3.43, this etymology also appears in *Leg.* 3.83; *Cher.* 4; *Gig.* 62; and *Abr.* 82. On the last, see Birnbaum and Dillon 2021, 223.

"*elect father of sound.*" The same etymology is used in *QG* 3.43, as well as the allegorical interpretation of "sound" (ἦχος) as the "externalized word" (ὁ προφορικὸς λόγος). In *QG* 3.43, this means that the "elect father of sound" is the true, philosophical orator and wise man, whose words effectively communicate the truths that are intended, as opposed to the sophistic "verbosity" of the quarrelsome, who mock the text of Scripture. This etymology of Abraham's name and its allegorical interpretation also appear in *Cher.* 7; *Gig.* 64; and *Abr.* 82. On the last, see Birnbaum and Dillon 2021, 223.

§ 67. *the size of the sun*. Compare *Somn.* 1.73, where Philo will elaborate the symbolic and allegorical multivalence of the sun (as opposed to the astronomical interests of the Abram soul mentioned here).

§ 73. *this is its fruit*. Philo may think back to his extended allegory of the trees of the Garden of Eden as virtues in *Leg.* 1.56. There, however, it is the trees, rather than the fruit, which metonymically stand for virtues. The use of the word ξύλον (*Leg.* 1.56, 59 [Gen 2:9]) rather than δένδρον (*Mut.* 73) for "tree" also diminishes the strength of the parallel. More influential for the present passage is the development of this arboreal allegory by Philo in the Noahic cycle of the Allegorical Commentary, esp. *Agr.* 8–16, which provides the background of the present metaphors.

Nachleben

§ 60a. *Gen 17:5 ("your name will be Abraham")*. God's change of Abraham's name, and the connection of this event with Abraham's departure from the flesh and readiness for the covenant, is treated by Origen (*Hom. Gen.* 3.3 [B/C]). Worthy of special note are Eusebius's comments in *Dem. ev.* 4.17.2 [A]:

> See in what manner the prophet did not think lightly about the nature of names (περὶ φύσεως ὀνομάτων), but in fact derives as many philosophical doctrines (πλεῖστα ... φιλοσοφήσας) as there are stories *about divine men whose names have been changed by him, and for what reason they are changed* (περὶ τῶν παρ' αὐτῷ μετονομαζομένων θείων ἀνδρῶν καὶ ὧν ἕνεκα μετονομάζονται). He introduces Abram receiving, as a prize from God for his virtue, the perfect title, "father Abraham" (ἡ πατρὸς Ἀβραὰμ ἐντελὴς προσηγορία)—the significance of which, it is not now the time to clarify.

Although Eusebius prescinds from offering an allegoresis of Abraham's name in this context, he lays out the Philonic principle at work in *De mutatione nominum*. The astute reader will not miss that Eusebius has in fact quoted the title of Philo's work, adding only the words "divine men" (which would not hold in Philo's context) and suggesting that Moses himself paid attention to these questions, valuing highly the revelatory "nature of names." See also John Chrysostom, *Mut.* 1.6 (123.19–22); 2.2 [126.28–34] [B/C], who in a series of homilies primarily about Saul/Paul, lists Abraham, Sarah, and Israel as Old Testament figures who have their names changed.

quarrelsome. Philo's description of those who disparage the words or Scripture, or read them too simply, is echoed obliquely by John Chrysostom in his second homily *De mutatione nominum* (*Mut.* 2.2 [126.5–11] [B/C]):

> In the case of the Holy Scriptures, some people, who read the letters simply (οἱ μὲν ἁπλῶς ἀναγινώσκοντες τὰ γράμματα), think that the letters are simple and that they have need of nothing else; but others, inspecting these things with the eyes of faith (οἱ δὲ τοῖς τῆς πίστεως ὀφθαλμοῖς αὐτὰ καταμανθάνοντες), as other ⟨craftsmen⟩ use the instruments of their skill, and entrusting their investigation to the fire of the Spirit, will easily see that all is gold.

As Philo, Chrysostom lays out two methods or approaches to the letters of Scripture. In both cases, it is literalism that is the problem, even though John and Philo would hardly agree what the right method of spiritual/symbolic reading entailed.

§ 60b. ***in Scripture.*** The phrase "in Scripture" (ἐν λόγῳ) should not be taken to suggest the New Testament Greek word for "Scripture" (γραφή), which Philo seldom uses in the singular to refer to inspired writings. He more often speaks of "oracles," "scriptures," or "word"—this last reflecting his Logos-centered hermeneutics. The New Testament "Scripture" (Γραφή), by contrast, stems from the Hellenistic Jewish milieu of Pharisaism and Palestinian Judaism (Cover 2016a). Philo's way of referring to the Scripture as *logos* was to impact the conception of Scripture in the Alexandrian catechetical school, including Clement and Origen. See Yadin-Israel 2004.

§ 61. ***breathlessly and sneering.*** Philo's use of the word "breathlessly" (ἀπνευστί), with its connotation of "spiritless" exegesis on behalf of his opponents, recalls several passages in the Pauline corpus. These include 2 Cor 3:12–18, in which Paul claims that the Spirit enables "unveiled" exegesis of the text of Moses. Extending this reading further, the Philonic *hapax* "sneering" (ἐπισαρκάζων) might connote "attending to the flesh, i.e., the letter" of Genesis, and not to the "undersense" intended by Moses to be signified by these changes of name. For the anthropological polarity of flesh and spirit in New Testament authors, see, e.g., Gal 4:29; 5:17; 1 Cor 3:1; Rom 7:14; 8:4–9; Mark 14:38. If Paul is confronting a group of Jewish-Christian allegorists in 2 Corinthians 3 (see Cover 2015, 254–257), his use of a similar invective—that their allegorical hermeneutic is insufficiently spiritual (see 2 Cor 3:17)—might confirm that Philo, too, is calling other Jewish allegorists "spiritless" (ἀπνευστί) in *Mut.* 61.

by the addition of a letter, of the one alpha. Justin Martyr highlights the "one alpha" added to Abram's name, and the "one rho" to Sarai's (*Dial.* 113.2 [B/C]). This verbal similarity, while by no means conclusive, counts in the ledger of cases where some direct contact between Justin and Philo is possible. For the "considerable" debate on the possibility of Justin's knowledge of Philo, see the even-handed treatment of Runia 1993, 97–105. For further analysis of this passage in Justin, see the *Nachleben* on *Mut.* 121.

§ 63. *Gen 2:19.* Origen never comments on this verse in his extant Greek writings (*BiPa* 3). The Philonic tradition resurfaces, however, in Gregory of Nyssa (*Eun.* 2.1.402 [B]), where the Cappadocian father adduces Gen 2:19 as evidence that God's gift of natural reason sufficed for Adam to generate names that had some natural affinity with the things they symbolize. He argues this against Eunomius's position that, without direct teaching of language, human beings would have existed in a confused and languageless state, without a way of referencing external (and abstract) objects (*Eun.* 2.1.398 [B]). For more on the connections between Philo's and Nyssen's theory of language, see Cover 2022b.

§ 64. *if God did not think it worthy.* Compare John Chrysostom's position, that when God gives names, it is important to ask why. "We are inquiring about the giving of names, which God sets upon the saints" (*Mut.* 2.2 (125.58–60) [B]: περὶ τῆς τῶν ὀνομάτων θέσεως ἐζητοῦμεν, ἅπερ ἐπέθηκε τοῖς ἁγίοις ὁ Θεός), he writes; and again: "whenever God gives a name, it is necessary to show all haste, that the cause may be found" (*Mut.* 2.2 [126.45–47] [B]: ὅταν δὲ ὁ Θεὸς ὀνομάζῃ, πᾶσαν ἐπιδείκνυσθαι σπουδὴν χρὴ ὡς εὑρεῖν τὴν αἰτίαν).

the founder of the human race. Philo's Greek term, "founder" (ἀρχηγέτης)— applied here to Adam—echoes the New Testament Epistle to the Hebrews (12:2), which uses a similar term, "pioneer" (ἀρχηγός), to describe the foundational role of Jesus for Christian faith.

§ 65. *these sorts of changes are markers of capacities.* Compare the defense of scriptural name changes made by Origen in *Sel. Gen.* 12.115 [B/C] and *Hom. Num.* 25.3 [B/C]. Van den Hoek (2000, 105) argues that while "Origen may have had Philo in mind, the parallel is not precise enough to prove it." She therefore ranks the passages at [C]. On account of the strong general similarities, I label these texts [B/C].

§ 66. *Gen 17:5a ("elevated father").* Clement of Alexandria knows the etymology of Abram as "elevated father," which he gives at *Strom.* 5.8.5 [A], interpreting it as a sign of Abram's erstwhile interest in astronomy (Van den Hoek 1988, 192). In Clement's own words:

This man, following the upper ⟨science⟩ (ἡ μετάρσιος ⟨ἐπιστήμη⟩) of things that happen in the air and the elevated philosophy (ἡ μετέωρος ... φιλοσοφία) of the movements of the heavenly bodies, was called Abram, which is interpreted "elevated father" (ὃ μεθερμηνεύεται «πατὴρ μετέωρος»).

See also Origen, *Sel. Gen.* 12.116; *Hom. Num.* 25.3 [B/C]; Eusebius, *Praep. ev.* 11.6.25–27 [A/B]; and especially *Dem. ev.* 4.17.2 [A], cited in full in the *Nachleben* for § 60a. For Ambrose's interpretation of Abram's name and change to Abraham, see the following note. The etymology also appears in Augustine, *Civ.* 16.28 [C/D].

Gen 17:5b (*"elect father of sound"*). Clement of Alexandria also knows the etymology of Abraham as "elect father of sound," which he gives at *Strom.* 5.8.5–6 [A] (Van den Hoek 1988, 192–193). His account of Abram's conversion to Abraham is worth recounting, as it includes Philo's pedagogical rationale, while subjecting it to other Christian traditions, and finally opting for Philo's anthropological allegory of the etymology.

> Later, looking up (ἀναβλέψας [cf. Gen 22:13]) to heaven—whether seeing the Son in the Spirit, as some say, or a glorious angel—or also in another place recognizing (εἴτε καὶ ἄλλως ἐπιγνούς, cf. Gen 17:1) God as better than creation and its every order, ⟨Abram⟩ receives the *alpha*—the knowledge of the one and only God—and is called "Abraham," becoming a sage and a lover of God in place of a natural philosopher (προσλαμβάνει τὸ ἄλφα, τὴν γνῶσιν τοῦ ἑνὸς καὶ μόνου θεοῦ, καὶ λέγεται Ἀβραάμ, ἀντὶ φυσιολόγου σοφὸς καὶ φιλόθεος γενόμενος). Now, ⟨Abraham⟩ is interpreted "elect father of sound"; for the sonorous word "resounds," and the mind is its "father," and the mind of the good human being has been "elected" (ἑρμηνεύεται μὲν γὰρ «πατὴρ ἐκλεκτὸς ἠχοῦς»· ἠχεῖ μὲν γὰρ ὁ γεγωνὸς λόγος, πατὴρ δὲ τούτου ὁ νοῦς, ἐξειλεγμένος δὲ ὁ τοῦ σπουδαίου νοῦς).

Siegfried (1863, 9) notes that Clement's "resounding word" may paraphrase Philo's "externalized word." Most ingenious in Clement's reception is the way he allows Abraham's transformative "vision" of the ram in Gen 22:13 to displace the more noetic "appearance" of Gen 17:1 as the catalyst for his change of name (Gen 17:5). This clearly results from a Christological pressure to focus on the Akedah as the transformative moment in Abraham's life. Nevertheless, Abraham could be said to "see" his son prefigured both in Gen 17:1 and 22:13, and it is the genius of Clement to elide these two visions. For the etymology, see also Origen, *Cels.* 5.45 [C] (Van den Hoek 2000, 51).

The interpretation of Abram's change of name to Abraham in Ambrose's *De Abraham* is likewise worth quoting:

> With the added syllable, his name changes ("mutat enim nomen, littera addita"), so that instead of "Abram," he is called "Abraham" [Genesis 17:5]; that is, instead of "false father" ("pater vanus"), as signified by the Latin interpretation ("sicut habet Latina interpretatio"), he is called "sublime father" ("pater sublimis"), "chosen father" ("pater electus"); or, instead of "father," he is called "father of a son" ("pater filii"). (*Abr.* 1.27 [A/B])

As Clement, Ambrose anthologizes an etymology like Philo's ("pater electus"; note, however, that "of sound" ["soni"] is missing) alongside another etymology of Abraham ("pater sublimis"). This latter looks quite a bit like the Latin equivalent of "elevated father," Philo's etymology of Abram. Ambrose's Latin interpretation of Abram, "false father" ("pater vanus"), if taken from the Hebrew, is perplexing, or at minimum, as Siegfried (1863, 9) calls it, "strange" ("seltsam"). "Ramus" in Latin means a twig or branch. In Pythagorean thought, it could point to the "branches" of a road leading to virtue and vice (Lewis and Short). But how this would lead to the interpretation "false" or "empty" is unclear.

§ 68. *not unable to beget wisdom.* Van den Hoek (1988, 188) cites Philo's claim that Abraham "was not unable to beget wisdom" (οὐκ ἄγονος σοφίας) as a potential antecedent to Clement of Alexandria, *Strom.* 3.99.1 [B]. There, the Christian Alexandrian catechist claims that the scriptural eunuch allegorically stands for "the one who is unable to beget truth" (ὁ ἄγονος ἀληθείας), the inverse of Abraham's condition in Philo. Both phrases may be traced back to the words "unable to beget wisdom" (ἄγονος σοφίας), which Socrates uses to describe himself in *Theaet.* 150C. Origen, *Comm. Matt.* 15.5 [B], echoes this allegorical interpretation (Van den Hoek 2000, 94), which is of interest in part due to its illustration of the continuity of Alexandrian exegetical tradition (with Clement serving as a mediator of Philo) and in part due to its potential relevance to Origen's own biography.

§ 73. *this is its fruit.* Cf. Gal 5:17–23, where there is a similar fusion of Jewish and philosophical fruit metaphors in the context of a discussion of theological virtues. See also Matt 7:16–20; Luke 6:43–45

§ 76. *ethical philosophy ... piety.* Just as Abraham is the pioneer of a new school of philosophy for Philo, so John Chrysostom in his *De mutatione nominum* conceives of Isaac—the typological forebear of the baptized Christian—as the symbol of a kind of philosophical excellence. At the end of his second homily (*Mut.*2.4.132 [D]), he exhorts his hearers, you who have been born according to Isaac, to imitate the meekness and gentleness and all the other philosophy of Isaac (μιμεῖσθαι τοῦ Ἰσαὰκ τὴν πραότητα καὶ τὴν ἐπιείκειαν καὶ τὴν ἄλλην ἅπασαν φιλοσοφίαν).

b   *Sarai's Name Becomes Sarah (§§ 77–80)*
          Analysis and General Comments
The second etymological allegory in chapter five concerns Abraham's wife, whose name is changed from Sarai (Σάρα) to Sarah (Σάρρα) in Gen 17:15. This pericope is treated as a separate chapter in QG 3.53, but included as part of the same Philonic chapter in *De mutatione nominum*. On Philo's omission of Gen 17:6–14, see the detailed comment on *Mut.* 53.

The etymological allegory of Sarah's name change in (b) §§ 77–80 is much shorter than Abraham's, and serves to develop the theme of the God's gift of power in the soul. The tandem references of Abraham's and Sarah's name changes together earlier in the Allegorical Commentary (*Cher.* 4) suggest that these two stories travelled as a scriptural pair. Gen 17:15 is most properly understood as a primary lemma, even though it simultaneously functions as a contextualizing secondary lemma (see Introduction 4. Exegetical Structure of the Treatise).

Philo argues that the change of name from Sarai (*Sara*) to Sarah (*Sarra*) symbolizes a transformation in virtue, from the specific to the generic. Sarah's name change further clarifies the nature of Abraham's transformation. God has given him (in Sarah) a stable and imperishable "prudence" (φρόνησις)—the governing power of all specific forms of practical wisdom. This short section can be subdivided into three subunits:

(1)   A Greek etymology of the two Hebrew names, Sarai and Sarah, drawn from an onomasticon (§ 77).
(2)   The primary allegoresis of these etymologies. Sarai's change to Sarah signifies a change from specific to generic virtue—with major benefit for the Abraham soul (§§ 78–80a).
(3)   A second allegory of Sarah's name: that all virtue has a regal character, ruling as a queen over the affairs of life (§ 80b).

          Detailed Comments
(1) § 77. ***Abraham's wife***. Philo highlights Sarah's relationship to Abraham as he weaves her into the developing allegory. As wisdom, she is not a psychic figure in her own right (as she is elsewhere), but a divine power or an excellence in the Abraham soul. For Sarah more generally, see Sly 1990.

she too has her name changed. Philo alludes to, but does not cite, Gen 17:15, which along with Gen 17:5 (§ 60) serves as one of the two primary biblical lemmata of the present chapter.

the addition of a single letter, rho. In Hebrew, Sarai's change of name to Sarah involves the replacement of a final *yod* (י) with a final *he* (ה), so that Sarah (like Abraham) receives a letter from God's own name (the Tetragrammaton) into her own. In the Greek of the Septuagint, however, Sarai's change of name involves God's seemingly incomprehensible addition of the letter rho (*Sara → Sarra*). In light of the arithmological significance of the number 100 in this treatise (see §§ 1–2, 188–192), it is worth noting that the Greek letter rho has 100 as its standard arithmological equivalent. Some connection between Abraham's becoming 100 and God's gift of a rho (100) to Sara may be present in the traditions binding these two passages, but it is not made explicit. See the Parallel Exegesis sections in this chapter for further traces of arithmological traditions in the *Quaestiones in Genesin*.

The phrase "of a single letter" mirrors the quarrelsome exegete's description of the addition of "the single letter alpha" to Abram's name in § 61. Philo intends to continue his apology for name changes in Mosaic Scripture. The specification in § 64, "not only vowels, but also consonants" (οὐ φωνήεντα μόνον, ἀλλὰ καὶ ἄφωνα), further proves the origin of this Philonic tradition in Greek-speaking Judaism. The addition of an alpha (Gen 17:5), a vowel, and a rho (Gen 17:15), a consonant, are taken as an alphabetical merism, indicating the totality of linguistic sounds.

the events signified. Or, as Colson renders it, "the facts" (τά ... τυγχάνοντα). He argues (PLCL 5:589) that Philo derives the substantive "happening" (τυγχάνον) from the threefold Stoic distinction between (1) the externalized "sound" (φωνή); (2) the "sayable" (λεκτόν) or "signified" (σημαινόμενον) in human thought; and (3) the "happening" or "event" (τυγχάνον), to which the signifier points (SVF 2.166). According to Sextus Empiricus (SVF 2.166), in Stoic logic, (1) the sound and the (3) happening belong to the category of "material things" (σώματα), whereas (2) the "sayable" is a logical-noetic "reality" (πρᾶγμα). In § 77, Philo adapts these Stoic distinctions in a Platonizing way: there are, on the one hand, (1) words or signifiers; and on the other hand, (3) psychic realities, which are (2) cognitively signified. Colson (PLCL 5:589) thus suggests that Philo collapses (2) the "signified" (σημαινόμενον) and (3) the "event" (τύγχανον) under the heading of "realities" (πράγματα), whereas (1) the name remains a "body" (σῶμα). (For the elimination of [2] the "signified" [σημαινόμενον] among Epicureans and the Stoics, see Plutarch, *Adv. Col.* 1119e; SVF 2.236.)

Sarai is interpreted to mean "my ruling principle." The Hebrew name Sarai (שׂרי) is interpreted as "my ruling principle" (ἀρχή μου), following a morphological analysis of the name into two parts: (1) the noun *śar* (שׂר > שׂרר), "prince[ss]"; and (2) *-y* (י-), being the first person singular pronominal suffix, "my."

Sarah means "ruling woman." The Hebrew name Sarah (שרה) is read as a feminine singular active Qal participle (שָׂרָה) of the geminate root *śrr* (but as though it were formed from the hollow root *śwr* [11-Weak]—perhaps on analogy with *rwm*, in the minds of the Hebrew etymologists of Genesis 17 on account of Abram's name). While Philo's interpretation of the string *rām* (רָם) in the name Abram (אברם) with the present active participle "lifting" (αἴρων) in §67 is accidental to his allegoresis, the present active interpretation of Sarah (שָׂרָה) in §78 as "ruling" (ἄρχουσα) is an explicit part of the Greek etymology.

(2) §78. ***specific virtue ... generic virtue.*** Philo allegorically interprets the etymologies "my ruling principle" (ἀρχή μου) and "ruling" (ἄρχουσα) as the difference between "particular virtue" (εἰδικὴ ἀρετή [cf. §79, ἡ ἐν εἴδει ⟨ἀρετή⟩]) and "generic virtue" (γενικὴ ἀρετή). Although the division of genus and species is Aristotelian, Philo deploys it (as he does of the "generic," asexual "first man" in *Opif.* 134) in a Platonizing fashion, speaking of the genus as having a kind of ideal, asomatic existence.

a genus differs from a species on account of the attenuation. Philo compares a genus with a species—which is, technically speaking, a category mistake—creating an analogy between scientific taxonomy and psychological metaphysics. The phrase "on accounts of the attenuation" (κατὰ τὸ ἔλαττον), which characterizes the derivative "species," suggests that a specific virtue is relatively small in breadth and "feeble" in its power when compared to the genus, insofar as it is bound to a particular person and not to a universal, immaterial form.

does the second name differ from the former. By "name," Philo includes not only (1) the "audible word," but also (2) its noumenal "signified" and (3) its "factual happening." See the detailed comment on §77 above.

small and perishable ... manifold and imperishable. By "species," Philo is not speaking of a taxonomic abstraction, but of an individuated subsistence. The genus is not merely "great" (μέγα)—the exact antonym of "small" (βραχύ)—in comparison, but "again, manifold" (πόλυ τε αὖ), extended over a variety of specific cases and dependent on none of them. The genus is "imperishable" (ἄφθαρτον), whereas a specific human person is not.

§79. ***God wishes to give great and imperishable gifts.*** In employing the verb for "gracious giving" (χαρίζεσθαι), Philo cross-references the covenantal language that he uses earlier in §40 and especially in his comments on Gen 17:2 (§§52–53, 57–59).

this work befits him. Philo uses the adjective "befitting" (ἐμπρέπες) to index a major question in his dispute with the quarrelsome exegete: what is an appropriate gift for God to give? He continues his argument from this §65 that the gift befitting God is not the change of a literal name or addition of a letter *per se*, but the correction of character and a new power in the soul.

practical wisdom. Philo names the "generic" and "specific" virtue of which he is thinking, "practical reason" (φρόνησις). Practical reason is one of the four cardinal virtues (e.g., Plato, *Phaed.* 69b). Although it is often associated with the thought of Aristotle, where it refers both to the exercise of practical reason *and* a knowledge of what the good entails (Taylor 2016; 2008), the noun occurs over 100 times in Plato's corpus in many dialogues, including the *Cratylus* and the *Statesman*. Philo deploys it in its broader sense, as a chief moral virtue encompassing an array of lower virtues.

ruling principle of that person only. I.e., "practical reason" (φρόνησις) as the ethical disposition of the individuated subsistence.

the practical wisdom in me is my ruling principle. Claiming one's own prudence as a personal ruling principle does not mean possession of the form. As Philo will go on to say, every person's particular virtue is impressed by its generic cause and type, and each genus of virtue flows from Goodness itself, which is the fountainhead of all the virtues (*Leg.* 1.63–65).

that which impresses this particular virtue. Generic virtues, including generic "practical wisdom" (φρόνησις), function as stamps or seals to shape the individual soul. For the mechanics of this impression of virtue on the human soul, see *Leg.* 1.61.

generic practical wisdom ... ruling principle itself. Philo speaks not of one generic virtue (i.e., "goodness"; cf. *Leg.* 1.59), but of multiple generic cardinal virtues, each of which has a specific stamped counterpart in the waxy souls of human beings. While this might read like a baroque Platonism, some such explanation is required by the scriptural text on which Philo's allegory is based.

§ 80a. *generic ruling principle ... imperishable forever*. Arnaldez (1964, 68–69, n. 1) opines: "Generic excellence is not the generic concept of virtue, but a truly existing idea ⟨of virtue⟩, capable of engendering the various virtues in the soul." For Arnaldez, this ideal virtue—another name for a power of God—is the central philosophical and theological actor of the treatise. The work treats not merely self-wrought human moral perfection, but God's real action which enables this. Cf. Arnaldez 1963. Some will find Arnaldez to over-emphasize the theological dimension of Philo's ethical allegory, but his view is worth considering. For a recent assessment of Arnaldez as a Philonist, see Niehoff 2021.

specific skills. Philo links his discussion of the difference between generic and specific "virtues" with the contrast of generic and specific "skills" (τεχναί). The discussion of the nature of such technical skills and who possesses them is a staple of Platonic thought, occurring in numerous dialogues, including the *Gorgias*, the *Cratylus*, and the *Statesman*. In this Platonic register, an "excellence" (ἀρετή in a general sense) and a "skill" (τεχνή) can be used as near synonyms (e.g., Plato, *Soph.* 224c).

geometricians, grammarians, or musicians. Plato often uses a similar tricolon in discussions of the "skills" (τεχναί). See, for example, the very similar list in the *Euthydemus* (290b–c), "The geometricians and the astronomers and the grammarians" (οἱ δ' αὖ γεωμέτραι καὶ οἱ ἀστρονόμοι καὶ οἱ λογιστικοί).

(3) § 80b. *every virtue is a queen.* A fitting allegorical conclusion to draw from either the name Sarai or Sarah, perhaps reflecting a second, related etymology ("queen" or "princess").

Parallel Exegesis

Unlike Philo's complex treatment of Abram's change of name in QG 3.43, his parallel treatment of Sarai's name change in QG 3.53—like its analogue in *Mut.* 77–80—is shorter and focused on the "inward facts" (Marcus, PLCLSup) of the change in the soul. After a brief mention of the "stupid people" who laugh at such name changes (QG 3.53a), Philo offers a symbolic interpretation: that God gives the Abraham soul the generic good in exchange for the particular (QG 3.53b). To illustrate this, he adduces the etymologies of Sarai and Sarah (Σάρα and Σάρρα in Greek), interpreting "my rule" (Sarai) as the particular, contingent virtue in a soul and "ruler" (Sarah) as generic virtue, surviving after individual subjects perish (QG 3.53c). He closes with the observation that such a change is "for the sake of the future birth" of Isaac, symbol of joy (QG 3.53d).

§ 77. *through the addition of a single letter rho.* Marcus (PLCLSup 1:254, n. d) observes that the translator has rendered the Armenian "numerical equivalent, 'hundred'" instead of the Greek word "rho." Aucher also notes the oddity, that the Armenian reads "century (for in Greek, R. ρ'. Signifies 100)." As Aucher's more accurate Latin translation makes clear, the Armenian word substituted for the "rho" is not the simple cardinal number "one hundred" (հարիւր), but the substantival adjective "of a century" (հարիւրեկին > հարիւրեակ, *centenarius*), which can denote, *inter alia*, one hundred years. The Armenian translator of the Hellenizing school thus records a possible Greek arithmological tradition linking God's gift of the number 100 (ρ') to Sarah with Abraham's perfection at the age 100.

events signified. Despite Philo's apparent conflation of the categories "signified" (σημαινόμενον) and "event" (τυγχάνον) in § 77, Colson (PLCL 5:589) points out that Philo does know the distinction between the two former categories, which he uses when describing the thought of the Stoics and Moses's advances on them (see *Leg.* 2.15).

my ruling principle ... ruling woman. The identical etymologies for Sarai and Sarah are given in QG 3.53; *Cher.* 5; and *Congr.* 2. In *Cher.* 5, the text is adduced as a supplemental lemma, and Sarah plays a more central role in the allegorical narrative. She represents specific, but not yet generic virtue, with whom

Hagar (the lower, preliminary studies) may still find a place, returning from her first flight (Gen 16), only to be expelled again once Sarah's virtue is perfected (Gen 21). In *Congr.* 2, Philo likewise offers a pedagogical allegoresis of the relationship between Sarai and Hagar, with regard to Sarai's encouraging congress between Abram and Hagar (Gen 16:1–2). For Sarah as "ruling woman," see also *Leg.* 3.244–245; *Her.* 258; and *Abr.* 99.

§ 78. *specific virtue ... generic virtue.* Philo's discussion of specific and generic virtue recalls his earlier allegoresis of the tree of life (Gen 2:9) in *Leg.* 1.59, where goodness is described as "the most generic virtue" (ἡ γενικωτάτη ἀρετή), from which the other particular virtues "derive their existence" (συνίστανται). See also his allegoresis of the four rivers of Eden in *Leg.* 1.63–67, where he defines "practical wisdom" (φρόνησις) in the particular as the virtue "concerned with what ought to be done, setting limits around these things" (περὶ τὰ ποιητέα ὅρους αὐτοῖς τιθεῖσα).

small and perishable ... manifold and imperishable. The same descriptors of the symbolic difference between specific and generic virtue are given by Philo in QG 3.53.

§ 80. *that every virtue is a queen, both ruling and governing.* Philo uses the word "queen" or "princess" (βασιλίς). Cf. QG 3.53, in which generic virtue is called "ruler and queen" (Marcus, PLCLSup; Arm. հշխան ... եւ դշխուհի). In *Spec.* 4.135, Philo speaks of piety as "queen of the virtues" (ἡγεμονίς)—presumably a princess among princesses. See Sterling 2006.

Nachleben

§ 77. *Gen 17:15a ("my ruling principle").* Clement of Alexandria (*Strom.* 1.31.1 [A/B]) repeats Philo's etymology of Sarai with a rare, explicit reference to the Alexandrian:

> Philo interprets Hagar as "sojourning" (παροίκησις); for here it is said, "Be not much with a foreign woman" (Prov 5:20). But Sarai he interprets as "my ruling principle" (ἀρχή μου). It is therefore possible for the one who has received the preliminary instruction to come to the most regal wisdom (ἔνεστιν οὖν προπαιδευθέντα ἐπὶ τὴν ἀρχικωτάτην σοφίαν ἐλθεῖν), from which the Israelite race (τὸ Ἰσραηλιτικὸν γένος) will grow.

Van den Hoek (1988, 36) finds it "noteworthy" that Philo is mentioned by name, but concludes that it is difficult to show that Clement has a particular passage in mind. In light of the connection between Hagar and the preliminary studies, however, some reference to *Leg.* 3.245 (which has Hagar as "sojourning" [παροίκησις]) and *Cher.* 5 or *Congr.* 2 seems more likely than *Mut.* 77. The reference to

Prov 5:20—"an essential text for Clement" (Van den Hoek 1988, 36) and one which Philo never cites—represents Clement's own recalibration of Hagar's role in the pedagogical allegory. In the Alexandrian tradition, see also Origen, *Hom. Gen.* 6.1 [C] (Van den Hoek 2000, 69).

Also worthy of note is Eusebius, who in the context of demonstrating Moses's concern with the nature of names and their changes, mentions Sarai's change of name to Sarah (*Dem. ev.* 4.17.3 [B/C]) after Abram's change to Abraham (*Dem. ev.* 4.17.2) in the catalogue "divine men" (θεῖοι ἄνδρες), whose titular alternations symbolize philosophical doctrines. See also John Chrysostom, *Mut.* 1.6 (123.19–22); 2.2 (126.28–34) [B/C].

Gen 17:5b (*"ruling woman"*). The etymological allegoresis of Sarah as "ruling woman" would have a more far-reaching *Nachleben* than that of Sarai. We find an early record of the etymology in a magical text dating from the second or third century CE, the *Sortes Astrampsychi* (4.86 [C/D]), where the title "Sarah, ruling woman" (Σάρρα ἄρχουσα) stands cryptically at the head of one of the fortunes. Nothing betrays Philonic influence. Ps.-Basil (*En. in proph. Isa.* 3.99.16 [C]) records a closer tradition, that "Sarah ⟨is⟩ strong and ruling (ἰσχύουσα καὶ ἄρχουσα) over the likes of Abraham, according to the command of the Lord, who says, 'everything that Sarah will say to you, listen to her'" (Gen 21:12; cf. Philo, *Leg.* 3.245 [B]). Even more strongly redolent of Philo is the comment of Didymus the Blind (*In Gen.* 114.5):

> Sarai (*Sara*), with only one rho appended (ἑνὸς προσγραφομένου ῥῶ), is interpreted "smallness" (μικρότης); this clarifies her introductory manner (ὁ εἰσαγωγικὸς τρόπος). But Sarah (*Sarra*) is "ruling woman" (ἄρχουσα), through which title is signified the perfection of virtue (ἡ τελειότης τῆς ἀρετῆς); for she is governing and most powerful (ἀρχικόν ... δυνατώτατον).

Here, the roles of Sarai and Hagar have been elided. "Smallness" (μικρότης) as an etymology of Sarai (*Sara*) is either gleaned inductively, by comparison with Sarah (*Sarra*, in which there are two rhos); or perhaps by way of the Hebrew adjective *ṣar* (צר), meaning "narrow." "Ruling woman" as the perfection of virtue is very Philonic. Ps.-John Chrysostom similarly knows the etymology of Sarah as "ruling and queen" (ἄρχουσα καὶ ἡγεμονίς, *Sim. regn.* 64.24.7 [C]) and "governing or ruling" (ἡγεμόνισσα ἢ ἄρχουσα, *Sim. regn.* 64.24.18 [C]). And Cyril of Alexandria (*Glaph. in Pent.* 69.125.48 [C]) knows the Philonic etymology.

In Philo's Latin reception, two passages from Ambrose's *De Abraham* merit mention. Less direct is Ambrose's reception of Sarah's etymology in the first book of *De Abraham* (1.31 [A/B]), which recounts the matriarch's life according to the letter:

Sarah, before the circumcision of her husband, is blessed with no mean requital by the addition of one letter ("in unius litterae adjectione") [cf. Genesis 17:15], so that she would possess the first principle of virtue and of grace ("principatum virtutis et gratiae"). (Trans. adapted from Tomkinson 2000)

Tomkinson's translation, which renders "first principle" ("principatum") as "makings," misses the connection between this word and the Greek "principle" (ἀρχή) or "ruling" (ἄρχουσα). Unmistakably Philonic, and in direct conversation with the Greek of *Mut.* 77–80, is Ambrose's account of Sarah's change of name in the second allegorical part of the book (2.85 [A]):

> Moreover, one letter is added ("una additur littera") to Sarai ("Sara"), i.e., "r," so that she is called "Sarah" ("Sarra") [Genesis 17:15]. It is fitting, as above, that she not be recompensed by the addition of a single letter ("non unius adjectione pensari litterae"). For the one letter is not the gift of God ("non enim munus Deo est una littera"), but the virtue of the letter ("sed virtus litterae"), which expresses the grace of the divine gift ("muneris divini gratiam"). For Sarai ("Sara") signifies "ἀρχὴ ἐμή," i.e., "my power" ("potestas mea") or "my sovereignty" ("principatus mei"); i.e., "beginning" or "the authority of a king." But Sarah ("Sarra") is, in Greek, ἄρχουσα; in Latin, "she who will rule" ("quae regat"). The one is mortal, the other immortal; the one is specific ("specialis"), the other generic ("generalis"). For, indeed, there is in me prudence, chastity, virtue, righteousness: these govern ("regunt") and rule ("dominantur") me alone and are mortal; for when I die, they are loosed and they, too, die. But what is generally called prudence, chastity, courage, and the other sovereign virtues ("virtutes principales"), but generally royal and certain immortal queens ("reginae quaedam immortales")—in these lie power ("potestas"), the immortal sovereignty ("principale"), just as the Church is Queen, who rules, not me alone, but all. Therefore, we see the specific changed into the general, the part into the whole, corruptibility into incorruptibility, all attributes which assuredly befit the Church: for reason is not specific but general, and salvation is not of the part but of the whole. (Trans. adapted from Tomkinson 2000)

A perusal of this interpretation will reveal numerous points of connection with the themes and argumentation of *Mut.* 77–80. It is on account of such passages that the Milanese bishop justly earns his epithet, *Philo latinus*. Ambrose's own ingenious addition is to elide Sarah as generic, ruling virtue with the universal role of the Church catholic, which governs not just the individual soul but the whole *corpus fidelium*. To Philo's ethical allegory, Ambrose adds an anagogical one. The passage is a masterpiece of reception.

c   *Jacob's Name Becomes Israel* (§§ 81–88)
    Analysis and General Comments

After his allegoresis of the name changes of (a) Abraham and (b) Sarah, Philo turns to a long series of secondary biblical lemmata that touch on other name changes in the Pentateuch. His goal is further to explore and defend Moses's literary and theological system by compounding examples of this narrative phenomenon. Philo starts with a second patriarch whose name is changed: (c) Jacob-Israel. While Abram-Abraham symbolizes the soul that acquires virtue through learning, Jacob-Israel symbolizes the soul that wins the prize of virtue through practice or ascesis. Moses signals this by relating God's renaming of Jacob, "the one who trips at the heels" (πτερνιστής)—that is, the one who enters the wrestling arena and attacks the foundational passions confusing the soul— as Israel, "the one who sees God," and wins the crown of virtue and contemplation (§§ 81–82).

Once Philo has two points of reference (Abraham and Israel) for the scriptural phenomenon that he is investigating, he raises several further questions that unpack the symbolic transformations of these two soul-types. First, Philo asks why Abraham's name, once changed, stays fixed, while Israel's does not (§§ 83–87). Second, Philo asks why the two extremes of the patriarchal triad, Abram and Jacob, have their names changed, but the middle member, Isaac, does not (§ 88).

Section (c) can be subdivided in to three units, each of which is occasioned by the same question, "why/for what reason?" (διὰ τί; [§§ 81, 83, 88]):

(1) Philo begins by asking "why" (διὰ τί; [§ 81]) Jacob's name is also changed to Israel, as Abram's and Sarai's names were changed. Drawing the etymologies of these names (Jacob, Israel) from his onomasticon (§ 81a), Philo offers an allegorical interpretation of their meanings, which symbolize the opening bouts (Jacob) and ultimate victory (Israel) of the soul-wrestler in the arena of virtue (§§ 81b–82).

(2) Philo then asks a second "why" question (διὰ τί; [§ 83]): Why does Abraham's name remain changed in Genesis, while Jacob-Israel's name vacillates in the subsequent narratives? This is not, according to Philo, an inconsistency (to say nothing of source critical hypotheses), but Moses's way of conveying the relative stability of the rational virtue acquired by learning, in comparison to the instability of the habitual virtues inculcated through practice (§§ 83–87).

(3) Philo asks a third "why" question: Why (διὰ τί; [§ 88]) do Abram's and Jacob's names change, but Isaac's does not? Philo answers that whereas the Abram and Jacob souls begin in a state of imperfection, the soul which is good by nature (Isaac) is begotten without need for improvement or increment; his virtue, like his number, is complete from the beginning (§ 88).

Detailed Comments

(1) § 81. *not unrelated to the subject at hand.* The noun "subject" (σκοπός) is a technical term in ancient literary criticism for the "point" or main theme of an ancient work (Heath 1989). Neoplatonists tried to discern the subject of given Platonic dialogues (Gardiner and Baltzly 2020), and Philo demonstrates a Middle Platonic concern for the same in his own treatises.

why is this? The first of three iterations of the scholastic question "on account of what?" (διὰ τί;) in this subunit, which provide its structural backbone (§§ 81, 83, 88). While it may be inaccurate to assert that the *quaestio* is the sole building block of the Allegorical Commentary (Nikiprowetzky 1977), these questions supply some of the clearest formal markers within the series.

is called. Philo alters his vocabulary for describing scriptural name change. Whereas the verb "is interpreted" (ἑρμενεύεται) is used in recounting the changes of (a) Abram and (b) Sarai (§§ 66, 78), in § 81, Philo introduces the etymologies from his onomasticon with the verb "is called" (καλεῖται). This change echoes the secondary biblical lemma that Philo has in mind, Gen 32:28(29), which states that the Jacob soul will "no longer be called" (οὐ κληθήσεται ἔτι) by this name.

"the one who trips at the heels." Philo's onomasticon glosses the name "Jacob" as "supplanter" (πτερνιστής) or "the one who trips up." This etymology stems from the Pentateuchal one, in which Jacob's name points to "his hand grabbing" his twin brother "Esau's heel" (καὶ ἡ χεὶρ αὐτοῦ ἐπειλημμένη τῆς πτέρνης Ἠσαῦ [Gen 25:26]) as he is born. The etymological link between the "heel" (עקב) and "Jacob" (יעקב) in Hebrew is lost in the Greek translation, even as the sense remains. The same etymology is echoed later in Gen 27:36, where Esau laments, "Justly has his name been called Jacob; for he has supplanted me again this second time" (δικαίως ἐκλήθη τὸ ὄνομα αὐτοῦ Ἰακώβ· ἐπτέρνικεν γάρ με ἤδη δεύτερον τοῦτο).

"the one who sees God." The interpretation of the name Israel as "the one who sees God" (ὁρῶν τὸν θεόν / ὁ τὸν θεὸν ὁρῶν) is one of Philo's favorite and best-known etymologies. It highlights the central role of sight in Platonic epistemology and appears most frequently in the Allegorical Commentary. There are a variety of hypotheses as to which Hebrew roots are involved. All agree

that "God" is taken from the last two letters of the name, *ʾēl* (אל). Two verbs for "seeing" are commonly hypothesized. (1) A first interpretation suggests that the seeing root is *rʾh* (ראה). On this analysis, *yiśrāʾēl* (ישראל) may be further analysed into the constituent morphemes (1a) *ʾîš rōʾeh ʾēl* (איש ראה אל), "a man seeing God"; or (1b) *yeṣer rōʾeh ʾēl* (יצר ראה אל), "form or *nous* seeing God." A third syntactic possibility along these lines would be to analyze the first component of the name Israel as the existential particle (יש): thus (1c): *yēš lirʾōt ʾēl* (יש לראות אל, "it is [possible] to see God"). Alternatively, the verb is sometimes understood to be from the root (2) *šwr* (שור), to be supplied with one of the subjects above in (1a) or (1b). See further Birnbaum and Dillon 2021, 197–198; Birnbaum 1996, 67–77; Grabbe 1988, 172–173.

who is practicing virtue. Philo allegorizes the etymology of Jacob as "supplanter" (πτερνιστής) to mean "practicing virtue" (ἀσκῶν ἀρετήν). This interpretation distances "supplanter" from any connotation of trickery. Deception could hardly be an image of the virtuous soul for Philo. Rather, he rereads the title as an athletic allusion, signifying "the one who trips at the heels" in wrestling (see his use of "wrestling" [παλαίειν] a little further on in this section).

the foundations of emotion. Just as the wrestler trips the heels of his opponent, so the Jacob soul practices virtue by supplanting "the foundations" (αἱ βάσεις) of his emotions.

not easily accomplished without struggle. Philo construes the Jacob soul as involved in a strenuous "contest" (ἀγωνία) for virtue. Cf. Dio Chrysostom (*Or.* 8.11, 26), who suggests that Diogenes the Cynic was also "contesting" (ἀγωνιούμενος) for the prizes of virtue at the time of the Isthmian games.

competes in the contests of practical wisdom. Just as the Abraham soul gains "practical wisdom" (φρόνησις) through learning and the conversion of his scientific energies toward the scriptural study of ethics, so the Jacob soul competes for the prizes of practical wisdom by training against the vices. Cf. Dio Chrysostom *Or.* 8.11–12.

doing exercises of the soul. I.e., to struggle against the emotions and the false understanding of sense-perception, and to train the eyes of the mind to see God, insofar as it is possible. Dio Chrysostom similarly describes the athletics of the sage as an active battle against the hardships of the body (*Or.* 8.13) and a passive flight from the delights of pleasure (*Or.* 8.20).

wrestling against the arguments … to throw and throttle. Philo personifies irrational "arguments" (λογισμοί) as enemies "to wrestle" (παλαίειν) against. Cf. Dio Chrysostom, *Or.* 8.12, where literal "wrestlers" (παλαίοντες) are mentioned as less difficult opponents than "hardships" which beset the body and soul. Philo's phrase "attempt to throw" renders the Greek "opposing wrestlers" (ἀντίπαλοι). Cf. Dio Chrysostom, who likens hardships and pleasure to athletic "antagonists" (ἀνταγωνισταί, *Or.* 8.11).

it. Although "soul" (ψυχή) or "practical wisdom" (φρόνησις) are both possible antecedents of "it" (αὐτή), "soul" is more proximate and most likely. Philo points to the kinds of arguments that threaten the praxis of practical wisdom, disturbing the soul through pleasure and other emotions.

the work of "the one who sees God" ... the prizes of victory. Philo extends his allegory to include the Israel soul as well as the Jacob soul. Whereas it is enough for the latter practicing soul to enter the ethical contest, improve himself, and trip up the "feet" of the passions, the Israel soul is the victor in the holy contest of virtue and must not leave uncrowned. This is in keeping with the Abram-Abraham pattern: the change of name signifies the perfection of the psychic type. For the metaphor of the "crown" of virtue, used by Philo in § 81, compare Dio Chrysostom's similar remarks (*Or.* 8.15) that he is competing not for ⟨crowns⟩ of celery, olive, or pine (common laurels at the Panhellenic games), but for "happiness" (εὐδαιμονία) and "virtue" (ἀρετή).

§ 82. *than one through which*. Whereas Dio Chrysostom (*Or.* 8.15) allegorizes the athletic crown as "virtue" and "happiness," Philo infuses his allegoresis with a speculative, instrumental aspect as well. The crown is a lens, mirror, or window "through which" (δι' οὗ) the victor is able "to contemplate" (θεωρεῖν) God.

The One Who Is will be able to be seen with sharp clarity. Philo suggests that the object of the Israel soul's vision is The One Who Is. While this cannot mean knowing God in his essence, in passages like this one Philo holds open the possibility of some other kind of vision or knowledge of the transcendent. The epistemic optimism of § 82 stands in some tension with passages like § 7, in which Philo states that The One Who Is cannot be seen or comprehended. For the complexity of this subject, see Cover 2014; Sterling 2018a.

the practicing soul. Although Philo more properly applies the title "practicing soul" (ἀσκητικὴ ψυχή) to Jacob (§ 81), here he extends it to the Israel soul as the perfected practicer—one who attains to the both practical and theoretical virtues.

(2) § 83. *it is worth puzzling over*. Philo introduces his question in this subunit with the Platonic trope of the *aporia* or "puzzlement." The term "aporetic" is used to describe the early dialogues of Plato, in which firm answers are not reached. These were foundational for the Sceptical Academy. In later dogmatic Platonism, the listener's or viewer's *aporiae* serve as opportunities for clarification by an authoritative figure. For a late Hellenistic example of this phrase, see the Tab. Ceb. 2.14.

why. The second of three identical "why" questions (διὰ τί; [§§ 81, 83, 88]) that Philo uses to frame this section of the treatise.

Abraham, once his name has been changed ... frequently named Jacob. Philo asks why, if the change of names is so important, Moses would change Abraham's name permanently, but allow Jacob's name, once converted to Israel in Gen 32:29, to revert back to Jacob on many occasions? This is a serious question, to which later source and literary criticisms would offer various answers. The name Jacob occurs roughly two hundred times in the Septuagint version of Genesis alone. Of these occurrences, 118 precede and include Jacob's change of name in Gen 32:29. This leaves approximately 82 instances of the name Jacob appearing after his name is changed to Israel. Comically—from the Philonic perspective (or that of his critics)—three of these recursions happen immediately after Jacob's name has been changed in Gen 32!

taught virtue differs from practicing virtue. Philo suggests that Moses has intentionally allowed the names of Jacob and Israel, but not of Abram and Abraham, to alternate for the sake of his allegory. The stable transmutation of the name Abraham and the capricious pendulum-swinging of the names Jacob and Israel signify the difference between the two types of soul, taught and practicing, and their relationship to the acquired virtues.

§ 84. ***possessing, as he does, a well-apportioned nature.*** The soul of the Abraham type, which is improved through learning and teaching, is naturally more suited to fixed and permanent improvement than the Jacob type of soul. As such, his soul is naturally more "fortunate" than the Jacob soul.

guards his retentiveness with the assistance of memory. The natural endowment, in which the Abraham soul exceeds the Jacob soul, is the pliability and retentiveness of his memory. Philo alludes to the image of the soul as a wax tablet in Plato, *Theaet.* 191c–d (a text and theme to which he will return later in *Mut.* 212). There, Socrates suggests that souls are like tablets possessing different amounts and qualities of wax. Some are composed of purer wax, others of less pure; some of harder wax, some of softer. The result is that the capacity for memory differs from nature to nature and from soul to soul.

makes use of this cognitive persistence. The taught soul relies on an accurate recollection of intellectual virtues, which enables him to retain his improvements. According to this description, there would be no possibility of akrasia or weakness of the will, only better or worse memories.

fixedly ... firmly. Philo sets the two adverbs, "fixedly ... firmly" (ἀπρίξ ... βεβαίως), in synthetic parallelism, to denote the finality of the transformation of the Abrahamic soul. The root "firm" (βέβαιος) refers properly to God in Philo's thought. Its catachrestic application to a human soul indicates an analogous firmness in a created subject, rooted in divine power and imperfectly imitating this divine characteristic.

the practicer, by contrast. I.e., the soul which vacillates between Jacob and Israel, between practice and winning the crown of virtue.

exercised intensely ... the power that had been enfeebled by toil. The Jacob soul's transformation through psychic exertion involves a correlated process of psychic relaxation, in which the soul must recover its weakened "power" (δύναμις). Due to this alternation of activity and rest, the perfection of the Jacob soul remains unstable and has a shelf-life. He may win the prize and be crowned with contemplative vision; but there is always another contest, and he will require a period of recovery before he is capable of exercising his faculties again.

those who anoint their bodies. Philo vivifies his image of the practicer soul and its alternations in virtue by adding the custom of anointing. Athletes used oil after exercising "lest ⟨their⟩ powers entirely leave them" on account of fatigue. See, e.g., the first-century CE bronze "Athlete from Ephesus" statue from the Roman gymnasium at the Ephesos Museum in Vienna (Inv. no. VI 3168) for an image. Philo's analogy depends on a medical model of bodily power, in which oil serves as a kind of retentive guard, trapping the heat and other energy that would otherwise have evaporated due to perspiration. The same fluctuation occurs in the soul that alternates between perfected exertion (Israel) and rest for reinvigoration (Jacob).

§ 85. ***an immortal Prompter.*** In contrast to the Jacob/Israel soul, the Abraham soul, which progresses by learning, has the help of a divine "reminder" or "prompter" (ὑποβολεύς). Plutarch (*Praec. ger. rei publ.* 813f.) uses this word in the latter sense, referring to a line "prompter" in the theater. The word first occurs in Greek literature in Philo. In *Mut.* 85, God is said to be the divine "Prompter" (ὑποβολεύς) of the Abrahamic mind, just as the human mind prompts speech. The Prompter's function is to help the Abrahamic soul maintain its perfection in virtue and contemplation, "so that it does not turn aside" (μὴ τρεπόμενος). In this regard, Philo's "Prompter" functions a little like the δαιμόνιον of Socrates (see Plato, *Apol.* 31d; *Phaedr.* 242b9), which steers him on the right course of life. Philo will return to the Abraham soul and his Prompter in the very last section of this treatise (*Mut.* 270), to offer a further expansion of the idea: that it is possible for the Prompter ultimately to depart the taught soul, without fear of ethical relapse, once a certain degree of stability has been reached.

only his own willing capacity. The Jacob soul has no divine Prompter, but must rely on its inner "willing capacity" (τὸ ἑκούσιον). Such a psychic capacity is referenced in Plato's dialogues (*Crat.* 420d4; *Pol.* 292c6) and receives its first systematic definition in Aristotle (see *Eth. nic.* 1111a–1113b). In this context, "the willing capacity" (τὸ ἑκούσιον) describes actions elected by "will" (βούλησις). See, e.g., Ps.-Aristotle, *Mag. mor.* 1.9.11 (1187a): "It seems it is the willing capacity ⟨that is operative⟩ in an issue concerning virtue or vice" (ἔοικεν οὖν ἐν τῷ κατ' ἀρετὴν καὶ κακίαν εἶναι τὸ ἑκούσιον). Another predecessor of Philo's use of "the willing capacity" (τὸ ἑκούσιον) as a faculty of the soul is the Epicurean philosopher, Philodemus. In his treatise *De ira*, in describing the coexistence of antithetical emotions in the same soul, Philodemus remarks that "the willing capacity (τὸ ἑκούσιον) moves us to anger just as it moves us to gratitude" (*Ir.* 46.30; trans. Tsouna 2007, 230 [adapted]).

if he reaches perfection ... returns to his earlier class. The practicing soul's dependence on the willing capacity leaves it subject to exhaustion and in a more unstable state of perfection than the taught soul. Philo describes Jacob and Israel here as distinct "classes" (γένη), even though they comprise a picture of a single type of soul. As Arnaldez (1964, 70, n. 1) summarizes:

> Philo does not therefore think that ascesis creates fixed habits which keep them safe from relapses. Jacob represents in the mystical life the phase of voluntary effort which can be rewarded with certain illuminations, but which ought to begin again; for the end of mysticism is a grace given and not the result of voluntary effort ....

This warning against positing a pure voluntarism in Philo's thought is well-articulated.

§ 86. ***must bear more hardships ... more fortunate.*** Philo spells out the difference between the Abraham and Jacob souls in a third way: the Abraham type is "more fortunate" (εὐτυχέστερος), whereas the Jacob soul is "more miserable" (τλητικώτερος) in enduring continuous cycles of training, composition, and exhaustion. The idea that certain souls might be more naturally fortunate and disposed to the life of virtue is a common conceit in Hellenistic and Roman philosophy (see, e.g., Tab. Ceb. 6.1–7.3). The adjective describing the Jacob soul, "more miserable" (τλητικώτερος), might likewise be translated "more patient in toil" (so Colson, PLCL), but the LSJ gives "distressed, miserable" (ταλαίπωρος) as synonyms, with reference to this instance in Philo. I have tried to find a middle ground between "patient" and "miserable," and settled on "bear⟨ing⟩ more hardships."

another as his teacher. Philo refers to the divine "Prompter" (ὑποβολεύς) as a "teacher" (διδάσκαλος). For the former title, see the detailed comment on § 85.

investigating with zeal the things of nature. Philo indicates that the Jacob soul's training is especially focused on the study of nature. This differentiation between the taught Abraham soul and practicing Jacob soul pinpoints two distinct pathways to God: Scripture and natural revelation, respectively. Not only their methods of progress, but also their respective objects of contemplation, contribute to their different pathways.

uninterrupted toil. Philo likens the training of the Jacob soul to "toil" or "labor" (πόνος). Dio Chrysostom (*Or.* 8.13) speaks of "hardships" (πόνοι) against which his soul struggles in the contest of virtue. The motif is probably Heraclean in origin (see *Or.* 8.28–29, in which Dio reports that "hardships" are especially associated with Heracles, both in myth and as a model for philosophical virtue). Philo elides the labors of Heracles with the labors of Jacob.

§ 87. ***had his name changed by the unturned God.*** Philo introduces another difference between the Abraham soul and the Jacob soul, which directly relates to the theme of the treatise: whereas the change of Abraham's name is scripturally attributed to God himself, Jacob's name was changed, according to Gen 32:24(25), by a "human being" (ἄνθρωπος)—a figure whom Philo identifies with the divine Logos or one of God's powers. Philo's formulation "the unmoved God" (ὁ ἄτρεπτος θεός)—the agent of Abraham's change of character—is a reference to Aristotle's unmoved mover (see the detailed comment on § 54). This attribution of direct action to "the unturned God" is at odds with the statement in chapter one of *De mutatione nominum*, that God has no relational predicates on account of his complete transcendence (see the note on § 28: ὡσανεὶ πρός τι). Philo is driven by exegetical rather than philosophical necessity to explain the difference between the two soul classes in this way.

he who was about to be stationed firmly. The ethical firmness of the Abraham soul (but not the Jacob soul) comes to mirror, at the created level, the unmoved Being of the Creator. See the detailed comments on § 24 ("entirely unturned") and § 84 ("fixedly ... firmly").

had his name changed by an angel. Unlike Abraham, whose name was permanently changed by the unmoved God, the Jacob soul undergoes ethical transformation through the agency of an angel. Philo derives this interpretation from Gen 32:24(25), in which Jacob is said to wrestle not with God but with a "human being" (ἄνθρωπος), and perhaps also from Jacob's imperative, "announce your name to me" (ἀνάγγειλόν μοι τὸ ὄνομά σου) in Gen 32:29(30). "Human being" (ἄνθρωπος) is a polyvalent trigger in Philonic allegory, often symbolizing the human mind or soul. In § 87, the key text underlying Philo's interpretation is Gen 32:30(31): "Jacob called the name of that place Vision/Form of God (Heb. "Peniel"), 'for I saw God face to face, and my soul was saved'" (ἐκάλεσεν Ιακὼβ τὸ ὄνομα τοῦ τόπου ἐκείνου Εἶδος θεοῦ· εἶδον γὰρ θεὸν πρόσωπον πρὸς πρόσωπον, καὶ ἐσώθη μου ἡ ψυχή). The title "Form of God" (Εἶδος θεοῦ) suggests to Philo an identity between the "human being" of Gen 32:34(35) and the "image of God," i.e., the Logos.

nothing that ranks after The One Who Is. Philo repeats the phrase "those after The One Who Is" (οἱ μετὰ τὸ ὄν), used earlier in the treatise at §§ 8–9. These are the only three occurrences of this phrase used to designate extra-divine noetic realities in the Philonic corpus. It is crucial that here, the Logos is taxonomically distinguished from the transcendent God, standing somewhere at the borderland of the created and uncreated. The precise metaphysical significance of the word "after," whether of time or of ontological taxis (Smyth § 1691), is left underdetermined by Philo.

the harmony ... constrictions and relaxations of sounds. Arnaldez (1964, 72, n. 1) observes: "Philo could be thinking here either of the Pythagorean doctrine of soul harmony or the ὁμολογουμένως ζῆν [agreeable living] of the Stoics. Whichever it is, this is only a step in the development of the soul. Beyond this, ⟨the soul⟩ achieves a simplicity in which it is entirely turned towards God." The goods given by the Logos to the Jacob soul are not simple, but many things in harmony, reflecting the order of the cosmos. This doctrine is in keeping with Philo's double theory of the Logos, who is both the singular storehouse of the forms as well as the author of their variegated extension into the ordered cosmos. Philo likens these second-tier goods to the harmony of notes in music. Just as the Jacob soul alternates between exertion and relaxation in the contest of virtue (§ 84), so his patron, the Logos, gives the best that can be given in this context: the harmonious interrelation of elements amid a world of multiplicity and a soul in flux.

§ 88. ***founders of an ethical class.*** Abraham, Isaac, and Jacob are understood by Philo in the Allegorical Commentary as three types of soul. The threefold categorization of virtue as acquired by teaching, practice, or nature is drawn from Plato, *Meno* 70a. For this schema, and Isaac as a symbol of the "self-taught class," see the detailed comments on § 1 and especially § 12.

Extremes ... middle. Philo construes the three patriarchal soul-types along a spatial spectrum, with Abraham and Jacob on either end and Isaac in the middle. Philo's language is reminiscent of that in § 2, where the mean and extremes were also invoked. The introduction of Isaac in § 88 has made his mind turn back to that initial discussion. Unlike § 2, however, where the language of the "mean" and the "extreme" (ἀκρότης) were used in an ascending sense, such that the middle was an intermediate stage and the extreme was the zenith of the ethical journey, in § 88 Philo uses the "mean" positively, in a Platonic adaptation of Aristotle, to specify perfection. Isaac's "middle" position is the ideal, situated between the "extremes" of the Abraham and Jacob classes, which are imperfect and improve by learning or training.

why is this? The third of three identical rhetorical "why" (διὰ τί;) questions, which frame this subunit on Jacob (§§ 81, 83, 88).

improvement. The Abraham and the Jacob souls, though different types or classes, are joined by their common need for ethical "improvement" (βελτίωσις). The Isaac soul does not share this need. Alongside Philo's explicit rationale for the stability of Isaac's name, there is also an implicit one related to the central theme of the treatise: that God himself tells Abraham what to name Isaac. Isaac, therefore, has already received his name from God (unlike Abram and Jacob). The Book of Jubilees knows a similar tradition, having the angel of the presence note that Isaac's name was "ordained and written on the heavenly tablets" (Jub. 16:3).

desires the knowledge of which he is ignorant. Improvement is garnered by the Abraham soul through its natural desire for knowledge. Philo's verb "desires" (ἐφίεται) is not that typically used for vicious "desiring" (ἐπιθυμεῖν), of the variety forbidden by the tenth commandment (Svebakken 2012), but a more general verb denoting purpose or intent. A verb of the same root is used in the opening lines of the *Odyssey* in describing Odysseus's "desiring" (*Od.* 1.6: ἱέμενός περ) to bring his companions home safely. In the Introduction, I argued that Philo considered Odysseus a special analogue to Abraham. Here, both figures of the soul evince a virtuous intentionality or will, a good emotion.

toil and contemplation. Just as the Abraham soul "desires" (ἐφίεται) knowledge, the Jacob soul "loves" (φιλεῖν) toil and contemplation, which serve as vehicles of his improvement. See §§ 81–87.

established by nature rather than by the cultivation of character. Both the learning of the Abraham soul and the practice of the Jacob soul are described by Philo as "cultivation" (ἐπιτήδευσις) of mind and character. The self-taught soul, by contrast, possesses virtue "by nature."

balanced, perfect, and even. Colson (PLCL 5:187, n. b) observes that "ἄρτιον here combines its ordinary sense of 'perfect' or 'complete' with its technical use for an 'even' number." Philo compares the Isaac soul to an even number, specifying that it is already "perfect" (τέλειος)—the end toward which the other two souls are striving. Contrast this with § 1, in which Isaac does not represent a soul-type, but rather the good emotion ("joy") of the Abrahamic soul upon *its* perfection. Like Moses, Isaac as a psychic type can be identified with few embodied souls, but stands as a perennial goal or ideal. While no clear arithmological significance can be discerned in the Greek name "Isaac" (Ἰσαάκ), it is worth mentioning that unlike "Abram" (Ἀβράμ)—who needs an alpha to become the perfect "Abraam" (Ἀβραάμ)—Isaac's name already has two alphas and stands in no need of an addition. Furthermore, the first two letters of Isaac's name, "Is-" (Ἰσ-), recall the Greek word "balanced" (ἴσος), which Philo uses in § 88 along with "even" (ἄρτιος) to describe the Isaac soul. These qualities are symbolized by the first even number, two. For the allegorical significance of Abraham's second alpha, and a possible arithmological symbolism in his Greek names, see the detailed comment and Parallel Exegesis on § 61.

Parallel Exegesis

§ 81. *Gen 32:28(29)* (*"your name shall no longer be called Jacob ...."*). Jacob's change of name to Israel, interpreted as an etymological allegory, is also discussed in *Ebr.* 82; *Migr.* 39, 200–201; and *Somn.* 1.129, 171.

"the one who trips at the heels." In *Leg.* 3.15, Jacob the "supplanter" (πτερνιστής) or "the one who trips at the heels" appears as the soul that has not yet become Israel. The title "supplanter" is also applied to Jacob, apart from explicit reference to Israel, at *QG* 4, frag. 163; *Leg.* 1.61; 2.89; 3.15, 93, and 180. In *Leg.* 2.99, the description is also applied to Dan, one of Jacob's sons, as one who is "biting at the horse heels" (Gen 49:17). See Grabbe 1988, 166.

"the one who sees God." Philo gives the etymological interpretation of Israel as "the one who sees God," apart from an explicit allegoresis of Jacob's name change, in *Conf.* 146; *Congr.* 51; *Her.* 78; *Fug.* 208; *Praem.* 44. The etymology is implicit in other passages as well: *QG* 3.49; 6.233; *Leg.* 2.34; *Conf.* 92; *Somn.* 2.44, 173; *Abr.* 57; *Legat.* 4. While thus most frequent in the Allegorical Commentary, the etymology also appears in the Exposition of the Law, the *QGE*, and the apologetic works, and has a wide distribution. See further Birnbaum 1996.

§ 85. *an immortal Prompter.* In *Migr.* 80–81, while interpreting the relationship of Moses and Aaron in their mission to Pharaoh, Philo speaks of the human mind as the "prompter" (ὑποβολεύς) of speech, and of God as the Prompter of the mind. In *Mos.* 2.37, an invisible "prompter" is said to have inspired and guided the translators of Septuagint independently to arrive at the same renderings of the Hebrew scriptures. And in *Praem.* 50, Philo speaks of the role of some inner "prompter" in every mental act of discovery.

willing capacity. Philo explains the origin of "the willing capacity" (τὸ ἑκούσιον) as a psychic faculty in *Conf.* 179, claiming that God delegated the creation of this "part" (μέρος) of the soul to his lesser colleagues, presumably on account of its capacity for both good and evil. "For the work of forming the voluntary element (τὸ ἑκούσιον) to balance (ἀντίπαλον) the involuntary had to be accomplished to render the whole complete" (*Conf.* 179, PLCL).

§ 87. *Gen 32:24(25), 29(30)* (*"had his name changed by an angel"*). Apart from the present passage, only *Sobr.* 65–66 relates Jacob's wrestling with "angels." But there, Colson (PLCL 3:478, n. a) rightly notes that the plural "angels" refers to Gen 32:1(2), rather than to an allegoresis of the singular "human being" of Gen 32:24(25), 29(30). Outside of these two passages, a specific connection between an angel and Jacob's change of name is not specified.

the unturned God. See similarly *Post.* 28, where Philo speaks of "The One Who Is, who is moving and turning other things, while he remains unmoved and unturned" (τὸ ὂν τὸ τὰ ἄλλα κινοῦν καὶ τρέπον ἀκίνητόν τε καὶ ἄτρεπτον).

§ 88. *why is this?* Cf. *Congr.* 34, in which Philo asks an analogous "why" (διὰ τί;) question about the uniqueness of Isaac: Why do Abraham and Jacob have multiple wives and concubines, but Isaac has only one wife and no concubines?

Nachleben
§ 81. *Jacob's name is changed to Israel.* The etymological allegoresis of Israel as the one who "sees God" was widely received in later Greek tradition. It appears in Clement of Alexandria's excerpts from the writings of the Valentinian Theodotus (*Exc. Theod.* 56.5 [C/D]; see Auvinen 2024) and was also adopted by Clement himself (*Paed.* 1.57.2; *Strom.* 1.31.4 [A/B]; Van den Hoek 1999, 36–38) and Origen, *Hom. Gen.* 15.3–4 [C] (Van den Hoek 2000, 72). For an allegorical interpretation of Jacob's change of name to Israel reminiscent of Philo, see Didymus the Blind, *In Gen.* 114.6–11 [A/B]:

> Jacob, interpreted "tripping at the heels" (πτερνιστὴς ἑρμηνευόμενος), represents the ⟨race⟩ that is practicing (τὸ ἀσκητικόν ⟨sc. γένος⟩) and opposed to the passions (πρὸς τὰ πάθη ἀντιστατικόν), whereas Israel, having his name changed by God (πρὸς τοῦ Θεοῦ μετονομαζόμενος)—which was done in no wise without purpose (μηδὲν εἰκαίως)—represents the contemplative ⟨class⟩ (τὸ θεωρητικόν) and the correction of the mind, according to which he sees God (Θεὸν ὁρᾷ); this happens after his ethical correction (μετὰ τὴν ἠθικὴν κατόρθωσιν). For Israel is interpreted "mind seeing God" (νοῦς γὰρ [ὁρῶ]ν Θεόν)

Aside from the more obvious correspondences, Didymus's claim that Israel's renaming involves an "ethical correction" (ἠθικὴ κατόρθωσις) of the Jacob character echoes Philo similar statement in *Mut.* 70 that Abraham's "correction" (ἐπανόρθωσις) of spelling betokens a transformation of his psychic type. See further Didymus's comments in *Frag. Ps.* 948 (Ps 97:3).

Likewise worthy of mention is Eusebius's description of this name change in his tacit précis of *De mutationum nominum* in *Dem. ev.* 4.17.3 [B/C]: "Jacob he endowed with the wrestler's prize (τῆς πάλης τὸ βραβεῖον), in virtue of his new name, Israel (διὰ τῆς τοῦ Ἰσραὴλ ἐπωνυμίας)." See also John Chrysostom, *Mut.* 1.6 (123.19–22); 2.2 (126.28–34).

In the Latin tradition, Ambrose gives the etymology of Israel's name (*Iac.* 2.1.3 [C]) as the people which "sees God through the inner eyes of the mind" ("Deum mentis internae oculis intueretur"), though his point here is to prove the "happiness" of Jacob even before his name was changed.

"the one who trips at the heels." Van den Hoek (1988, 198) notes that Philo's etymology of Jacob as "the one who trips at the heels" and the correlated allegorical interpretation of this name to signify the athlete of virtue is found also in Clement of Alexandria (*Strom.* 6.60.3 [B]). There, Clement speaks of "the sons of Jacob" as "those who trip up the activity of vice" (οἱ τῆς κακίας πτερνίσαντες τὴν ἐνέργειαν). Van den Hoek lists *Mut.* 81 as one of several Philonic texts that might have influenced Clement. She concludes: "The tradition passes on by way of Origen to later times" (cf. *Comm. Jo.* 1.35.260). See also Origen, *Cels.* 5.45 [C] (Van den Hoek 2000, 51) and the texts by Didymus the Blind in the previous note.

struggle. Just as Philo depicts Jacob as an athlete in a "struggle" or "contest" (ἀγωνία) of virtue, so Paul, in 1 Cor 10:25, likens the struggle of an apostle with that of one "who competes in an athletic contest" (ὁ ἀγωνιζόμενος).

prizes. For parallels to Philo's allegorical language of "prizes" (βραβεῖα) in the New Testament, see 1 Cor 9:24. For the "crown" image, see 1 Cor 9:25.

§ 83. ***Abraham, once his name has been changed ... frequently named Jacob.*** Origen (*Hom. Gen.* 15.4 [A]) takes note of the vacillation between the names Jacob and Israel in Scripture, and attempts to follow out the rationale for the alternations. This offers an intriguing example of Origen following one of Philo's literary-critical and allegorical principles further down the scriptural path with greater systematic rigor than his predecessor. Van den Hoek (2000, 72) ranks this passage a [C], but only considers the etymology of Israel, not the question of vacillation. See also *Hom. Gen.* 3.3 [B/C], where Origen differentiates God's speech to Abram from God's speech to Abraham. Van den Hoek (2000, 67) ranks this text a [B] in its reception of *Sobr.* 16–17.

§ 88. ***Isaac always has the same appellation.*** John Chrysostom (*Mut.* 2.3 [128.23–28] [B]) raises the same question as Philo. In trying to piece together why Saul's name does not immediately change to Paul in Acts, he looks to the Old Testament for clues and discovers an irregularity:

> In the Old Testament, God changed the name (ὁ Θεὸς μετωνόμασε) of Abraham and Jacob, but not of Joseph, nor Samuel, nor David, nor Elijah, nor Elisha, nor the rest of the prophets, but he left them stay with the appellation they had in the beginning (ἀφῆκεν αὐτοὺς ἐπὶ τῆς προσηγορίας μένειν τῆς ἐν ἀρχῇ). This is our first point of enquiry: why some ⟨of the saints⟩ have their names changed, while others do not.

Chrysostom is looking far beyond the Pentateuch, so his question is more complicated than Philo's, since the Alexandrian is enquiring only about the allegories of Moses. Several lines later (*Mut.* 2.3 [128.44–54] [A/B]), Chrysostom hits on the very problem that Philo wrestles with:

PART TWO   293

> Abram and Jacob had their names changed in the middle of their life (ἐν μέσῃ τῇ ἡλικίᾳ μετωνομάζοντο). For he used to be called (ἐκαλεῖτο) Abram, but came to be called (ἐκλήθη) Abraham; and Jacob used to be called Jacob, but came to be called Israel. With Isaac, however, it was not so, but he receives his name (τὸ ὄνομα δέχεται) before his struggles .... Thus God said to Abraham: "Your wife Sarah will bear a son, and you will call his name Isaac" (Gen 17:19).

After offering an etymological interpretation of Adam's name, Chrysostom returns to Isaac in *Mut.* 2.4 [130.51–57] [A/B]:

> Who then after Adam received his appellation by God before he was born (ὑπὸ τοῦ Θεοῦ προσηγορίαν ἔλαβε πρὶν ἢ γενέσθαι)? Isaac .... Why is this? (Διὰ τί;)

John's answer to this question is different than Philo's: he argues that Isaac's name was announced before his birth, on account of its meaning "laughter"—the laughter of faith at the power of God over nature and procreation. Philo's explanation, that it has to do with the stability of the self-taught class of soul, is nowhere to be seen.

d   *The Names of Joseph (§§ 89–91)*
Analysis and General Comments

Philo continues in scriptural sequence to the next patriarchal figure in Genesis, Joseph. Joseph will become the primary focus of Philo's allegorical attention in *De somniis* 2. In *De mutatione nominum*, he gives the name Joseph a negative interpretation as the soul that transgresses the limits of nature in its love of the body. A different and more positive assessment of Joseph appears in Philo's later treatise, *De Iosepho*, in the Exposition of the Law. For Joseph's various interpretations in Philo, see Hilgert 1985; Niehoff 1992.

Philo treats Joseph's "change of name"—which he finds in Gen 41:45, when the Egyptian king calls Joseph "Psonthomphanek"—using a similar exegetical pattern to the one he used when interpreting the stories of Abraham and Jacob. Instead of first offering an etymology of both names and then allegorizing their alternation as indicative of psychic progress, Philo gives each name its etymology and interpretation independently. In Joseph's case, the allegorical significance of the change of name itself remains implicit, but can be inferred from context. Whereas Abraham and Jacob change for the better, in Joseph's renaming by the Egyptian king, his soul-type moves from bad to worse—from excess to insolence. In the present treatise, Joseph serves as the lead figure of a second cluster of soul-types, which also includes Benjamin, Ephraim, and Manasseh. The first pair (Joseph and Benjamin) charts a more negative trajectory of psychic change than the first cluster, Abraham, Isaac, and Israel. At the same time, Joseph, Benjamin, Ephraim, and Manasseh simultaneously symbolize vectors of change *within* the Jacob/Rachel soul (much as Cain and Abel often represent types of "opinion" within the Adam/Eve soul).

Section (d) may be divided into three units:

(1) Philo begins by allusively adducing Gen 41:45(–49) as a secondary lemma, to contrast with the perfection embodied by the Abraham, Isaac, and Jacob souls. He then offers an etymology of Joseph, drawn from the onomasticon. The name means "addition," as one adds wealth to natural property (§ 89).

(2) Philo next offers a cursory allegoresis of "addition." Joseph represents the soul that acquires what is extraneous to its own needs. In particular, it has oversight of Egypt, which Philo understands allegorically as the "the land of the body" (§ 90).

(3) Philo turns to Joseph's second name: Psonthomphanek. Drawing again from the onomasticon, he offers the etymology, "mouth judging in answer." This represents the soul that conceives of itself as superior to others on account of its ability to provide for the body. The soul's regress from excess to insolence is not explicitly charted by Philo, but can be inferred from its juxtaposition with the foregoing changes (§ 91).

Detailed Comments

§ 89. *administrator of bodily provisions.* Philo identifies Joseph as the soul overly concerned with the body. His portrait of Rachel's oldest son is colored not only by scriptural imagery, but also by the *realia* of Hellenistic and Roman Alexandria and represents his complicated attitude toward Jewish life in the diaspora. The naming of Joseph as an "administrator (προστάτης) of bodily provisions" echoes Pharaoh's "establishment" of Joseph over all the land of Egypt in Gen 41:41 ("Behold, I am establishing you today over all the land of Egypt" [ἰδοὺ καθίστημί σε σήμερον ἐπὶ πάσης γῆς Αἰγύπτου]), but also reflects the local Egyptian political term "administrator" (προστάτης). See *P. Teb.* 81.19, which mentions an "administrator of the allotted income" (προστάτης τῆς κεχωρισμένης προςόδου)—the title of a type of revenue official in Hellenistic Egypt (2nd century BCE).

Joseph ... exchanges his name. Joseph's name is not "changed" (μετονομάζεσθαι: § 65 [Abram]; § 77 [Sara]; § 81 [Jacob]), but "exchanged" (ἀλλάττει). Although Philo can use the latter verb to indicate positive psychic transformation (see §123 and the "transformation" of Caleb), here it probably carries negative commercial overtones. Joseph's alternation between his Hebrew and Egyptian names represents a kind of bartering, both literally and allegorically, with Egyptian culture—and results in the opposite of an "improvement." The fact that he begins life with a Hebrew name and has an Egyptian one added cannot be a positive sign. As Arnaldez (1964, 17) notes: "The change of name does not take place uniquely in the case of progress, but equally on the road to perversion. Thus, Joseph is the name of attachment to the goods of this world; yet, the rich person believes, in the name of his riches, that he is capable of judging and adjudicating all things, as if wisdom is revealed from fortune, whereas it is the contrary that is true. This inversion of values is marked by the second name of Joseph, Psonthomphanech."

being called Zaphenath-paneah (Psonthomphanech). Philo alludes to Gen 41:45, but the secondary lemma he has in mind covers a wider range of verses (Gen 41:41–49). This is shown by the lexical connections between "establish" (καθίστημι [Gen 41:41]) and "administrator" (προστάτης [§89]), and "grain" (σῖτον [Gen 41:49]) and "supplies" (ἐσιτάρχει [§90]), both of which appear in Philo's paraphrase.

by the king of the land. While Abraham and Israel are renamed by God and his Logos, respectively, Joseph is renamed by Pharaoh, the king of Egypt. This has a negative significance in the allegory of his soul. The title "the king of the land" is not Pentateuchal, but may reflect an etymology of the name Pharaoh, derived from Demotic and reflected in the later Coptic noun, ⲡⲣⲣⲟ, which analyzes the old Egyptian title into two morphemes: (1) the definite article (ⲡ) followed by (2) the word "king" (ⲣⲣⲟ). For an alternative etymology of Pharaoh as "scattering," see *Somn.* 2.211 (Grabbe 1988, 212–213). The detail "land" stems from the scriptural record in Gen 41:41, where Pharaoh places Joseph "over all the land of Egypt" (ἐπὶ πάσης γῆς Αἰγύπτου). Philo does not use the Pentateuchal word for land, however, but its Hellenistic synonym, "land, space" (χώρα), reflecting the idiom of Hellenistic Judaism (cf. 1Macc 7:7), as well as the designation of rural Egypt outside of the cities as the chora.

Joseph is interpreted to mean "addition." Philo gives the etymology of the onomasticon, deriving "addition" from the Hebrew triliteral root *ysp* (יסף). The Greek word "addition" (πρόσθεμα) reflects the biblical etymology of Joseph given in the narrative of his naming by Rachel in Gen 30:24: "And she called his name Joseph, saying, 'Let God add another son for me'" (καὶ ἐκάλεσεν τὸ ὄνομα αὐτοῦ Ἰωσὴφ λέγουσα· «προσθέτω ὁ θεός μοι υἱὸν ἕτερον.»). The allegorical significance of Joseph's "addition" varies according to Philo's exegetical series, and even between treatises (see Parallel Exegesis). In §89, "addition" indicates the accumulation of superfluous wealth—exactly the opposite of the grain Joseph stores up in the biblical account, which is needed to prevent starvation. Allegorically, Philo correlates this kind of "addition" with the soul that cares inordinately for the comfort of the body and is consumed with the passion of pleasure. Rather than destroying pleasure, as Abraham and Jacob, or fleeing it as Diogenes the Cynic (cf. Dio Chrysostom, *Or.* 8), the Joseph soul embraces it. On the etymology, see Grabbe 1988, 174–175.

conventional goods are an appendage to natural ones. Following Colson's translation, to distinguish between "things ⟨given⟩ by nature" (τὰ φύσει) and "things given by human placement" (τὰ θέσει) or "convention." (For these two positions, see Plato's *Cratylus*.) Joseph is associated, etymologically *via* the "set" (θε-) root, especially with the accumulation of "conventional" rather than "natural" goods.

(2) § 90. *the fitting name, "addition."* In this next subsection, Philo offers a second allegoresis of the etymology "addition" (πρόσθεμα / προσθήκη). Rather than literal wealth, the acquisition of goods symbolizes the Joseph soul's undue attention to sense-perceptible stimuli, beyond what is required by nature to live and reason.

the oracles. Philo indicates that he is thinking of a secondary biblical lemma, Gen 41:41–49, which is interpreted sequentially (Gen 41:41 [§ 89]; Gen 41:45 [§ 89b]; Gen 41:49 [§ 90]). For the clues determining the range of this lemma, see the detailed comments on § 89.

from his storehouse he supplies. Philo paraphrases the biblical narrative, adding both the verb for "storing up" (θησαυρισάμενος) and the compound verb "to dole out grain" (σιταρχεῖν [cf. σῖτον in Gen 41:49])—i.e., "to pay the army." Philo construes Joseph allegorically as the soul that outfits the body and the passions for their assault upon the mind.

the entire land of the body, Egypt. Egypt, per the allegory developed by Philo earlier in the Abraham cycle, represents the land of the body, from which the virtuous soul ought to make an Exodus (e.g., *Migr.* 14–20). Contrariwise, the Joseph soul travels to this land and flourishes there. On the Egypt motif in Philo, see Salvesen et al. 2020; Adams 2018; Feldmeier 2017; Pearce 2007. Philo's allegorizing of the "land" (cf. Gen 45:45) as the human body trades on the Platonic understanding of "space" (χώρα) in *Tim.* 52b, where the noun appears as a synonym for the receptacle—a concept that adumbrates Aristotle's "matter" (ὕλη).

(3) § 91. *"mouth judging in answer."* Philo offers an etymology of the patriarch's Egyptian title, "Zaphenath-paneah" (*Psonthomphanech*). According to Speiser (1964, 311), the name derives from Egyptian, meaning "God speaks: he lives." Philo's etymologist apparently analyzes the name *ṣopnat paʻnēaḥ* (צפנת

פענח) into three parts, using near phonological equivalents: (1) ṣopnat (צפנת) = šāpaṭ (שפט), "to judge"; (2) *peh* (פה), "mouth"; (3) *bə* + *'ānâ* (ענה + ב) "in answering." Together, this yields in reverse order (3) "in answer" (ἐν ἀποκρίσει); (2) "mouth" (στόμα); (1) "judging" (κρῖνον). In fact, the sequence of the Greek etymology looks to be the work of someone reading the Hebrew morphemes from left to right instead of right to left:

ἐν ἀποκρίσει   στόμα   κρῖνον

For a slightly different account of this etymology, see Grabbe 1988, 220–221.

every fool. As the eye is the symbol of mind and virtuous soul in Philonic allegory, so the mouth—via its connection with deceptive rhetoric—is the symbol of the sophist and foolish soul.

overflowing with external belongings. Philo interprets Joseph's material surplus allegorically as "external stuffs" (αἱ ἐκτὸς οὐσίαι). The distinction of the "inner" and the "outer" is typical of popular Platonism in the first century Jewish authors (cf. 2 Cor 4:16).

good at reasoning and speaking. A clumsy but exact rendering of the Greek "well-reasoned" (εὐλόγιστος), which denotes excellence first in thought, then in speech, as two edges of the same ability. Philo clarifies the double aspect of the adjective in the following sentence. The soul signified by "mouth speaking in judgment" is assumed to be "sufficient" at answering public questions as well as presenting sound judgments "through his own internal reasoning" (δι' ἑαυτοῦ).

he puts practical wisdom entirely in the sphere of fortune. Philo lampoons the faulty reasoning of the fool, according to which the accumulation of possessions arises not from "practical wisdom" (φρόνησις), but from the blind gifts of "fortune" (τύχη), or in Philo vocabulary, "that which results from luck" (τὸ τυχηρόν). Cf. the Jacob soul (Joseph's father), who exemplifies practical reason (§ 81).

what is unstable. Philo's claim that "fortune" (τύχη) and "that which results from luck" (τὸ τυχηρόν) are "unstable" (ἄστατον) recalls the famous image of the Tabula of Cebes, in which "a certain blind Lady ⟨Fortune⟩ … is standing upon a kind of stone ball" (τυφλή τις … ἑστηκυῖα ἐπὶ λίθου τινὸς στρογγύλου), handing out benefits and then capriciously taking them back again (Tab. Ceb. 7.1). The old man interpreting the ekphrasis of the tablet understands the ball to symbolize the instability of Fortune's benefits: "what she gives is neither unshakeable nor certain" (οὐκ ἀσφαλὴς καὶ βεβαία ἐστὶν ἡ παρ' αὐτῆς δόσις, Tab. Ceb. 7.3).

guided by the reins of that which is firmly established. Or literally, "by the reins of what can stand." Philo mixes his metaphor, contrasting the instability of fortune with the fixity of the charioteer—a favorite image drawn from Plato's *Phaedrus*. His point is clear: mind and practical reason ought to govern one's process of coping with the caprices of fortune. Furthermore, only the one skilled at dealing with bad fortune privately should be esteemed worthy of making public judgments. To set up someone in the seat of judgment solely on account of external good fortune is to elevate a "mouth" rather than a "mind"—the Joseph rather than the Jacob type of soul.

Parallel Exegesis
§ 90. *Gen 30:24 ("Joseph ... 'addition'").* While Joseph is treated as a positive figure in the Exposition of the Law, throughout the Allegorical Commentary, Joseph's "addition" (πρόσθεμα / προσθήκη) is interpreted negatively. In *Somn.* 1.78, Joseph's name is associated with "the citizenship of the body." In *Somn.* 2.47, Joseph is said to symbolize "vainglory" (κενὴ δόξα), while later in the same treatise (*Somn.* 2.63–66), Philo gives a related etymology of Joseph's name, "addition" (προσθήκη), an extended pejorative explication: "addition" means "the enemy of simplicity and the friend of vanity." Such additions are then likened to parasitic tumors on trees, which hamper their growth and must be excised by the arborist. Thus, in Philo's allegory, Joseph's brothers rightly lamented to Joseph's father, "an evil beast has seized and eaten ⟨him⟩" (Gen 37:33 [*Somn.* 2.65]), i.e., "vice has consumed him." In the Exposition of the Law, a different etymology of Joseph's name is given: "addition of the Lord" (κυρίου πρόσθεσις). This paraphrases the whole of Rachel's statement in Gen 30:24 ("let God add to me ...."). Here, the name is understood positively (as are Rachel's utterance of these words in *Post.* 179), indicating that the constitutions and governments of human states are salutary "additions" and extensions of nature's "lordship all things" (τὸ κῦρος ἁπάντων [*Ios.* 28]). Philo will go on to say that "the political man is an addition to the one who is living in conformity with nature" (*Ios.* 31, PLCL). Colson (PLCL 6:155, n. b) adds that "the appendage 'of a lord' helps Philo in the political interpretation which he gives ⟨in *De Iosepho*⟩." In the Exposition, politics complements, but does not compete with, the life of the sage. It worth noting that in the course of three treatises, Philo uses three nouns for the etymology of Joseph's name, each derived from the command of Gen 41:45, "let God add" (προσθέτω ὁ θεός). While it is possible that the onomasticon had several entries, this variance of etymologies and symbolic equivalents also attests to a rich Jew-

ish interpretive tradition related to Joseph, of which Philo is both heir and anthologizer.

§ 91. *Gen 41:45 ("mouth judging in answer")*. Philo only interprets the name Zaphenath-paneah (*Psonthomphanech*) here in the Allegorical Commentary. In keeping with the positive representation of Joseph in the Exposition of the Law, in *Ios.* 121 Philo mentions that Pharaoh gave the patriarch another Egyptian name, without mentioning the title or offering an etymology. He merely notes that the name was "based on ⟨Joseph's⟩ art of dream interpretation" (ἀπὸ τῆς ὀνειροκριτικῆς), for which he was rightly famous and merited his marriage to Aseneth. "Mouth judging in answer" does in fact represent Joseph's ability to answer Pharaoh's question about his dreams of cows and wheat. Thus, the etymology of Zaphenath-paneah, given in § 91, probably underlies the tradition referenced in *Ios.* 121 as well. For other possible etymologies, see the *Nachleben*.

Nachleben

Philo's negative allegorical interpretation of Joseph was largely eclipsed in early Christianity by the positive typological value attached to Joseph, both as father of Jesus (the "just man" of Matt 1–2) and as a figure of Jesus himself (see Anderson 2003).

§ 90. *Gen 30:24 ("Joseph ... 'addition'")*. Philo's etymology of Joseph, "addition," is known by Christian authors, but not dwelt on in nearly the same length. Origen (*Hom. Jes. nav.* 436 [C]) gives the Philonic etymology, "addition of the Lord" (προσθήκη Κυρίου), echoing Philo, *Ios.* 121. See also Origen's *Hom. Jos.* 22.4 [C] (Van den Hoek 2000, 82). The same etymology also appears in Nilus of Ancyra's *Ep.* 90 [C]. Cyril of Alexandria gives a similar etymology of Joseph, "addition of God" (προσθήκη Θεοῦ), which hews even more closely to the text of Gen 30:24, at several points in the *Glaphyra in Pentateuchum* (213, 224, 232 [C]). In *Glaph. in Pent.* 224 [D], Cyril interprets the etymology along ecclesiological lines, similar to Ambrose's interpretation of Joseph's marriage to Aseneth (*Jos.* 7.40), saying that "the Church from the gentiles has been added to the flocks from Israel" (προστέθειται δὲ ταῖς ἐξ Ἰσραὴλ ἀγέλαις ἡ ἐξ ἐθνῶν Ἐκκλησία; see also *Glaph. in Pent.* 232 [D]). In *Glaph. in Pent.* 296 [D], Cyril gives an expanded etymology, "'addition *and augmentation* of God' (προσθήκη καὶ αὔξησις Θεοῦ); for always the holy throng is supplemented for the augmentation of the children of the Church" (ἀεὶ γὰρ εἰς αὔξησιν τῶν τῆς Ἐκκλησίας τέκνων ἡ ἁγία πληθὺς ἐπιδίδοται). Finally, in that same section (*Glaph. in Pent.* 296 [D]), commenting on the report in Acts 2:47 that "the Lord's was adding those being saved daily" (προσετίθει τοὺς σωζομένους καθ' ἡμέραν), Cyril comments: "here, as I was already saying before, the noetic Joseph could presumably be called to mind—that is, those who are in Christ, the 'addition of God'" (ταύτητοι, καθάπερ ἤδη προεῖπον, νοοῖτ' ἂν εἰκότως ὁ νοητὸς Ἰωσὴφ, τουτέστιν, οἱ ἐν Χριστῷ, προσθήκη Θεοῦ). In such texts, the Philonic interpretation of Joseph's material "addition" has been eclipsed by the ecclesial reading.

§ 91. *Gen 41:41–49 ("mouth judging in answer")*. Philo's interpretation of Zaphenath-paneah (*Psonthomphanech*) in *Ios.* 121 has been more widely received in the tradition than the etymology found in § 91. Josephus (*A.J.* 2.91 [D]) says that "the name signifies a finder of hidden things" (σημαίνει γὰρ τὸ ὄνομα κρυπτῶν εὑρετήν). Similarly, Origen (*Sel. Gen.* 12.136 [D]) notes "Psonthomphanech ... is interpreted, 'to whom the future was revealed'" (Ψομθομφανήχ ... ἑρμηνεύεται, ᾧ ἀπεκαλύφθη τὸ μέλλον). Eusebius of Emesa (*Comm. in Gen.* frag. 74 [D]) writes of the name: "the Syrian has 'the one who knows hidden things'" (ὁ Σύρος ἔχει «ὁ εἰδὼς τὰ κρυπτά»). Ambrose (*Jos.* 7.40 [D]) gives an allegorical and ecclesial interpretation of Pharaoh's gifts to Joseph and his marriage to Aseneth (the Church) in Gen 41:42–43, 45, but skips over Egyptian name.

e   *The Names of Benjamin (§§ 92–96)*
     Analysis and General Comments

After interpreting the two names of Joseph (Gen 41:41–49), Philo turns to Joseph's co-maternal brother, Benjamin—the second figure in this cluster. He discovers a similar allegorical significance in etymologies of Benjamin's two names in Gen 35:16–19, "son of days" and "son of pain," given by his father and mother, respectively. The titles represent the effects of vainglory, as recognized publicly by the masses and experienced privately by the soul. Joseph's symbolic identity as "vainglory" elsewhere in the Allegorical Commentary (*Migr.* 21; *Somn.* 2.47) is here transferred to his younger brother. Inversely from the allegoresis of the Joseph soul, which began with an internal defect (A: "addition") and then turned to public appearance (B: "mouth speaking in judgment"), Philo's allegoresis of Benjamin begins with public persona (B': "son of days" = popular appeal) and then turns to psychic effects (A': "son of pain" = soul-death). As was the case in §§ 89–91, so in §§ 92–96 Philo has a mid-length pericope in view, which he interprets in a sequential fashion.

While Joseph and Benjamin each represent psychic types on their own in this sub-chapter, Philo also treats the brothers as vices of the Jacob mind and the Rachel soul. More specifically: whereas in (1) and (2) §§ 92–93, Benjamin is a type of soul (i.e., "he who is zealous for these things"), in (3) and (4) §§ 94–96, Jacob becomes the rational capacity, Rachel becomes the ill-bearing soul, and Benjamin a synonym for vain opinion. As elsewhere in this treatise and the Allegorical Commentary, such minor slippages stem in part from Philo's anthologizing of various exegetical traditions and in part from atomistic attention to new scriptural details. In this case, the residual question "on account of what" (διὰ τί;) in § 94 reveals the tradition-historical seam between two psychic exegeses, one that focuses on the Benjamin soul and a second that focuses on the Rachel soul. In a certain sense, all of §§ 81–102 can be seen as a developed discussion of the Jacob soul (i.e., its subtypes, perfections, vices, and devolutions).

The unit divides into four sections:

(1) Philo introduces the two names of Joseph's younger brother in inverted scriptural sequence: "Benjamin" and "son of pain." He gives an etymology of "Benjamin" as "son of days" (Gen 35:18c), derived from the onomasticon, as a syntactic parallel to Rachel's "son of pain" (Gen 35:18b) (§ 92a).

(2) Philo allegorizes the name given by Jacob (the mind), "son of days." It signifies the soul that, though vainglorious, enjoys popular appeal. The sequence of thought is complex. First, the sun ("daylight") is interpreted as a symbol of sense perception, which leads to the notion of "empty opinion." Philo then notes that the mind so disposed to empty opinion often achieves a kind of ephemeral ("lasting for a day") glory in the approval of public opinion (§§ 92b–93).

(3) Philo offers an allegorical interpretation of Benjamin's second name, "son of pain," derived from the biblical text. Rachel, Benjamin's mother—a symbol of the entire soul, including the irrational part—speaks from her comprehensive experience of being guided by vain opinion. To be driven by opinion, rather than knowledge and prudence, causes the soul great pain, including envy without and ignorance within. Philo presents this attention to vain opinion as a congenital condition, which may be bequeathed to other souls (§§ 94–95).

(4) Philo extends the second etymological allegoresis ("son of pain") by giving an explanation of Rachel's death. The event is identified as "soul death"—the status of becoming entirely dependent upon the senses in decision-making, such that the "inner person" dies (§ 96).

Detailed Comments

(1) § 92a. *a most allegorical manner*. Rendering "most naturally" (φυσικώτατα), a common Philonic way of noting an allegorical composition. Here, the allegory is in part natural (in addition to ethical), as Benjamin's etymology, "son of days," will be developed according to several astronomical markers.

his co-maternal brother. Benjamin, like Joseph, is a symbol of vanity and the soul that follows it. While each brother may be a psychic type in his own right, Rachel's two sons also represent a certain pattern of breakdown within the Jacob soul. Leah's children, by contrast, who represent a more positive trajectory for the Jacob soul, will be taken up in §§ 97–102 in the discussions of Reuben, Simeon, Ephraim, and Manasseh.

"Benjamin" ... "son of pain." Philo alludes to a part of his secondary biblical lemma, Gen 35:18. Three observations are warranted: First, Philo has inverted the biblical sequence of the names, beginning with Gen 35:18c ("Benjamin") and then turning to Gen 25:18b ("son of pain"). He starts with the Hebrew name, whose meaning is less clear to the reader, and then moves to the etymologies. Second, as his comments about the death of Rachel in § 96 make plain, Philo has in mind not just Gen 35:18, but a longer implicit secondary lemma: Gen 35:16–19. Third, in beginning with Joseph's name exchange (Gen 45) and then turning to Benjamin's twin names (Gen 35), Philo follows birth order rather scriptural sequence. This demonstrates that he is thinking his way through the Jacob Cycle chronologically—a process which continues at least until § 102, when thematic considerations take the chapter in the direction of a third allegorical triad in §§ 103–129: Moses, Joshua, and Caleb.

Benjamin means, etymologically, "son of days." Ignorant of or eschewing the more accurate meaning of Benjamin, "son of the right hand," Philo analyzes the Hebrew into two components: (1) *ben* (בן), "son"; and (2) *yomim* (ימים), "days." Syntactically, this matches Rachel's name for Benjamin, "son of pain." The shift from "son of days" to "son of pain," in Philo's allegory, does not represent a positive reconfiguration of the Benjamin soul; rather, like the change from Joseph to Zaphenath-paneah, the two names present a narrative of decline from one state of vanity to another.

(2) § 92b. *a day is illuminated by the perceptible light of the sun.* Philo links the epithet "days" with solar light, drawing implicitly on Gen 1:16–18. This opens a wide range of semiotic possibilities, several of which he will exploit in the subsequent allegoresis. See the Parallel Exegesis for Philo's interpretation of the "sun" in *De somniis* 1.

to which we liken vain opinion. Philo first links the sun to the vain opinion of others. Just as the sun shines in the heavens, where all can see it, so those who acquire popular approval have a certain luminous quality and sense-perceptible appeal. Although this is not one of the four meanings given to the sun in *Somn.* 1.72–119 (see Parallel Exegesis), it resembles several of those interpretations.

§ 93. *written decrees ... busts and images ... crowns ... chariots ... four-horse entourages ... processions before the crowds.* In this litany of styles of pompous showmanship, Philo echoes the media of Roman imperial propaganda and triumph.

(3) § 94. *this truly accurate and proper name.* "Son of days"—the vain opinion of the crowd—is said properly to reflect the symbolic meaning of the name

"Benjamin" as a type or characteristic of the soul. On proper vs. improper naming, see the detailed comment on §14.

the elder reason—that is, his father. Philo's precise meaning is ambiguous. Colson takes "elder" (πρεσβύτερος) predicatively ("his father and head of the house"), but the adjective is in attributive position, modifying reason. I have therefore taken καὶ πατήρ epexegetically ("that is, his father") rather than conjunctively. Literally, the "father" referred to is Jacob. Allegorically, the identity of this "elder" logos admits of several interpretations. It might refer to (1) the divine Logos (see *Leg.* 3.218), in which case Philo means to say that the Logos has rightly inspired Moses to call this son of Jacob, "Benjamin." Alternatively, (2) it might suggest that the Jacob mind is "older" than the Benjamin mind in the scriptural record (both being kinds of "reason"). Third, (3) Philo may think of the mind/reason/word (Jacob) as the "rational faculty" (λογικόν) of the soul, prior to the addition of the irrational part (τὸ ἄλογον). Given Philo's interpretation of Rachel as the soul in its entirety, option three seems attractive.

the suffering soul (i.e., his mother). Having interpreted Gen 35:18c, Philo now turns to the second name of Benjamin, "son of pain," given to him by his mother Rachel in Gen 35:18b. Philo omits the first-person singular pronoun, "my" (μου), from the scriptural etymology "son of my pain/labor." Supporting figures in Philonic allegories, such as matriarchs and sons, are understood according to two principal patterns: (1) as virtues or characteristics in the soul; (2) as souls in their own right. Here, Rachel is allegorized according to Philo's second pattern, as a soul, in contrast to the naked paternal "mind" (νοῦς, i.e., Jacob). This identity derives in part from Gen 35:18a, "when she was sending forth her soul" (ἐν τῷ ἀφιέναι αὐτὴν τὴν ψυχήν). As the composite soul, Rachel is compounded of the sense-perceptible capacities, as well as speech and reproduction (see §110 below). She speaks of the detrimental effects that vain-opinion has in introducing emotions to the soul

"son of pain." In the narrative, the "pain" (ὀδύνη) in Benjamin's name refers to Rachel's hard labor in child-birth (Gen 35:16). In Philo's allegory, this pain becomes a symbol for the emotions in the soul.

why? Philo uses the question, "On account of what?" (διὰ τί;), as he did earlier in the Jacob section, to explore the significance of Benjamin's second name. The fact that Benjamin's symbolic significance shifts from being an independent soul-type ("the one who is zealous for vain opinion") to a vain opinion in the Rachel soul suggests that there is a source-critical or anthological seam here in Philo's commentary (see further the detailed comments on §96).

carried along by vain opinions. The metaphor "carried along" (φερόμενοι) is a nautical one, to be resumed in the next chapter ("the contrary winds" [§95]).

The allegory of the Odysseus soul may stand in the background, as well as Alexandria's maritime environs.

suppose they are happy, but in truth they are wretched. In addition to vainglory, the Benjamin soul also suffers from self-deceit. With its external and internal duplicitousness, it is worse-off than the Joseph soul, whose sophistry is primarily external, and denotes a truly tragic type.

§ 95. ***that are not cured until death.*** A rare window into Philo's psychic eschatology. Although there may be embodied sages, those who have suffered the wounds of vain opinion seldom recover before their souls are separated from their bodies.

(4) § 96. ***the interpreter of God.*** Philo's noun, "interpreter of God" (θεοφράδμων), is rare in his corpus and used to describe Moses in his role as author. It occurs only twice, here and at *Her.* 301, where it is used in parallel with the title "philosopher," suggesting a rational (rather than ecstatic) grasp of divine revelatory intention.

depicts Rachel. According to Philo, allegorical meaning is not derived from the genius of the interpreter; Moses himself is writing Scripture as an allegory of the soul.

Rachel died giving birth to an unfortunate offspring. Philo cites Gen 35:19, adding a verbal allusion to Gen 35:16 ("Rachel was giving birth and she suffered in labor" [ἔτεκεν Ῥαχὴλ καὶ ἐδυστόκησεν ἐν τῷ τοκετῷ]). As often, the full scope of Philo's implicit scriptural lemma extends beyond the cited verse. Benjamin's second name is tied to the experience of the mother, interpreting him to be a misfortunate kind of offspring of the soul.

the death of the soul. Philo alludes to the Platonic concept of soul death, which unlike bodily death negatively impacts the moral life in the present as well as during the soul's judgment and reincarnate body (according to the myth of Er; see Plato, *Resp.* 10). Whether Philo takes up the concept at a purely "moral-psychological" level, or whether he entertains with seriousness the doctrine's eschatological dimensions as well, is underdetermined. In the Allegorical Commentary, Philo is focused primarily on the present moral life. For soul-death in Philo, see Zeller 1995; Conroy 2008; Wasserman 2007, 2006. For the debate over Philo's commitment (or not) to the Platonic doctrine of reincarnation, see Runia 2019; Yli-Karjanmaa 2015.

Parallel Exegesis

§ 92. ***Gen 35:18c ("son of days").*** Outside *De mutatione nominum*, the names of Benjamin are only interpreted by Philo in *Somn.* 2.36, 41. In the first of these parallels, Philo gives a wholly different allegorical interpretation of this etymology:

Benjamin ⟨is a symbol of time⟩, both that of youth and of old age. For his name is interpreted to mean "son of days," and youth and old age are alike measured by days and nights (*Somn.* 2.36, PLCL [adapted]).

This allegory is given in Philo's interpretation of the names of Joseph's ten brothers, as the eleven "sheaves" he sees in his dream in Gen 37:7. In *Somn.* 2.41, Philo goes on to distinguish the symbolism of Benjamin from that of Joseph's other ten brothers. While the latter symbolize virtuous dispositions in the soul, Benjamin, as "days and time," symbolizes "the causes of nothing and everything"—a thoroughly ambivalent designation. Philo's ability to adduce completely different allegorical meanings from identical etymologies in *Mut.* 92 and *Somn.* 2.36–41 demonstrates his freedom as an exegete, as well as his habit of anthologizing multiple interpretive traditions.

the perceptible light of the sun. An important parallel to Philo's interpretation of the sun as "vainglory" and the opinion of the crowds may be found in *Somn.* 1.72–119. In *Somn.* 1.77, Philo notes that, "'sun' is often spoken with ⟨various⟩ symbolic meanings according to the holy word" (λέγεται δὲ πολλαχῶς κατὰ τὸν ἱερὸν λόγον ἐν ὑπονοίαις ἥλιος). In the ensuing section, he gives no fewer than five allegorical equivalents for the sun: (1) the light of the invisible God (*Somn.* 1.72); (2) the process of reasoning (*Somn.* 1.75); (3) the human mind under the influence of sense-perception (*Somn.* 1.77); (4) sense-perception itself (*Somn.* 1.79); and (5) the divine Word (*Somn.* 1.85). Interpretations (3) and (4) are especially related to the allegoresis in *Mut.* 92.

§ 94. **the suffering soul (*i.e., his mother*).** Rachel, though a frequent figure in Philo's corpus, is only presented as the hard-laboring and dying soul in the present treatise. She is a particularly mercurial symbol in Philo's allegorical network and her significance vacillates between negative and positive poles. In *Post.* 135, Philo identifies her as "sense perception," the enemy of Leah, who is virtue "apart from the passions." On the other hand, Rachel can also be Leah's coworker, a legitimate wife of the mind, and a symbol of virtue *within* the irrational soul (so *Congr.* 25–27 and Colson, PLCL 4:470–471, n. a).

Gen 35:18b ("son of pain"). Philo gives this etymology nowhere else in his extant writings. This suggests that Benjamin was a relatively minor figure in Philo's allegorical system, and that he chose these verses on thematic grounds for inclusion in the present treatise, on account of the two names.

§ 96. **the death of the soul.** For further elaborations of the death of the soul in the Allegorical Commentary, see *Leg.* 1.105–107.

Nachleben

§ 92. **Gen 35:18c ("son of days").** Philo's etymology, "son of days," is also given in the Testament of Benjamin (T.Ben 12.1 [D]), with the following explanation:

> For Rachel, after she bore Joseph, was sterile for twelve years; and she prayed to the Lord after a fast of twelve days and she conceived and bore me. Our father loved Rachel fervently and prayed to see two sons from her. For this reason, I was called "son of days," which is Benjamin (διὰ τοῦτο ἐκλήθην υἱὸς ἡμερῶν, ὅ ἐστι Βενιαμίν).

There is no case for a genetic relationship between these passages. Unlike Philo, the author of the Testament of Benjamin makes the epithet "of days" a positive descriptor, derived from Rachel's fast. It is noteworthy, however, that Philo's question in *Mut.* 92, "for what reason" (διὰ τί;), introducing the explanation of the name "son of pain," is echoed by the author of the Testament in the phrase "for this reason" (διὰ τοῦτο) to explain the title "son of days." Taken together, these two features suggest that both texts bear witness to a common Jewish tradition, which puzzled over the word "days" in the etymology of Benjamin's name.

Among Christian authors, the interpretation of the etymology "son of days" follows the positive tradition in the Testament of Benjamin, though the hagiographic details are missing. It appears, for example, in Didymus the Blind (*Comm. Zacch.* 5.103–104 [D]), who in his interpretation of the title "the gate of Benjamin" (Zech 14:10) notes:

> The gate of "Benjamin," which is translated "son of the right hand" or "son of days" (μεταλαμβανομένου [εἰς] τὸ δεξιᾶς ἢ ἡμερῶν υἱός), is the entrance into the divine mysteries and right doctrines, through which he who has been perfectly illuminated and is acting and thinking rightly (i.e., "in a right-handed manner," δεξ[ιῶς π]ρά[τ]των καὶ διανοούμενος) enters, being called "son of a right hand and son of days" (υἱὸς δεξιᾶς καὶ ἡμερῶν προσ-αγο[ρευό]μενος).

As this pericope reveals, even in Origenist circles, Philo's negative or neutral interpretations of the title "son of days" in the Allegorical Commentary have given way to something more positive and constructive. Evagrius (*Exp. in Prov.* 95.15 [D]) likewise knows both of these etymologies and considers "these names ... as indicators of the distinguished and pure states" (ἅτινα ὀνόματα διαφόρων καὶ καθαρῶν καταστάσεων ... διαγνωρίσματα) of Judah and Benjamin, spiritually speaking, among the twelve tribes. This point is antithetical to Philo's assessment of the title in both *De mutatione nominum* and *De somniis*. See further Andreas of Caesarea (*Comm. in Apoc.* 7.19), who gives the curious variant, "son of a day" (υἱὸς ἡμέρας).

§ 94. ***Gen 35:18b* ("*son of pain*")**. I do not find Philo's interpretation of the name "son of pain" as a reference to "soul death" in any of the consistently cited Greek or Latin Christian authors referenced in Introduction 9. Parallel Exegesis and *Nachleben*. Hippolytus (*Ben. Is. Jac.* 114 [D]) connects the name "son of pain" with Paul the apostle, scion of Benjamin, who would cause pain to his mother, the Church, in persecuting her. (For Paul's own repeated spiritual "labor pains" [ὠδίνω], see Gal 3:19). More positively, Cyril of Alexandria (*Glaph. Pent.* 69.213, 224 [D]) gives "son of pain" (υἱὸς ὀδύνης) in connection to Benjamin, relating this to Rachel's birth of the Church of the gentiles, after Leah's birth of the Church from the synagogue. Ambrose (*Jac.* 2.7.34 [D]), in yet another ecclesial reading, identifies the burial of Rachel as a type of the burial of all Christians with Christ (Rom 6:4); and finds in the "column" ("columna" [Gen 35:20]) marking her tomb a symbol of the pillar Church ("ecclesia"). Much as was the case of Joseph, so also in the case of Rachel, the Christian anagogical reading eclipses any potential use of a negative Philonic tradition.

Gen 35:16–19. Philo's omission of Gen 35:20, Jacob's setting up a pillar over Rachel's tomb, from his lemma is intentional and consequential. Later Alexandrian tradition will develop a positive allegorical importance for Rachel from this verse (see Origen, *Hom. Ps.* 15.1.1 [D]). That Philo has refrained from commenting on Gen 35:20 in the entirety of his corpus is important for the history of exegesis.

f   *Ephraim and Manasseh, Reuben and Simeon (§§ 97–102)*
        Analysis and General Comments

Having treated (d) Joseph (+ Rachel) and (e) Benjamin, Philo now inserts what appears to be a digression from the topic of name change. He makes a synthetic comparison of the symbolic etymologies of Joseph's eldest sons, Ephraim and Manasseh (memory and recollection, respectively) with Jacob's eldest sons, Reuben and Simeon (vision and hearing). Of this section, Colson writes, "Here, the mention of Joseph and his mother seems to lead Philo into an irrelevant interpolation of the analogy between Reuben and Simeon on the one hand and Ephraim and Manasseh on the other" (PLCL 5:133). Colson will further comment (PLCL 5:190, n. a) that §§ 97–102 "are obviously irrelevant, as none of the four persons discussed have any change of name. The only link is that they show how different names symbolize contrasting qualities. Possibly the thought is partly induced by the proximity of the two sons of Rachel, cf. the digression in *Her.* 252–266." These latter comments are better, but still only partly fair to Philo, and lack any clarifying explanation of the section's importance in the chapter. Colson is right that name change, *per se*, is not involved in any one of these four figures. However, the section is not an "interpolation," as though misplaced and not integral to Philo's theme in the chapter. Arnaldez's assessment (1967, 18) of Philo's use of these four figures is more constructive:

The Bible can, moreover, mark a change of state either by a change of name, or by the alignment of two characters together with one another. The significance is reinforced when four characters are distributed into two pairs, which correspond with one another word for word. This is the case with the two sons of Joseph, Ephraim and Manasseh, set alongside the two eldest sons of Jacob, Reuben and Simeon. Reuben corresponds with Ephraim, as the well-endowed nature which sees the truth ⟨corresponds⟩ to the memory which guards it. Manasseh, by contrast, corresponds to Simeon, as recollection ⟨corresponds⟩ to study by hearing. This new example is also intended to illustrate progress: the Simeon-Reuben pair, of a more speculative order; the Manasseh-Ephraim pair, of a more moral and religious order, for in the mind of a Jewish thinker recollection and memory evoke, before all, the commemoration of God.

Pace Colson, §§ 97–102 are thus not "irrelevant" to Philo's central theme in the treatise; quite the contrary.

In addition, these sections also provide an important answer to a question implicit in sections (d) and (e): why is it that the Jacob mind seems to have produced only vicious, vain, and opinionated offspring, rather than contemplative athletes of virtue or the virtuous by nature (as Abraham begets Isaac in §§ 1–2)? Philo's answer to this conundrum is already hinted at in § 92. By likening Benjamin to Joseph as "co-maternal brother" (ὁ ἀδελφὸς ὁ ὁμογάστριος), Philo suggests that it is only Jacob's immediate offspring by Rachel that are so ill-born. Rachel, as the sense-dependent soul (§ 96), bears the primary responsibility for Jacob's two vainglorious sons. It is the children of Leah, by contrast, who in Philo's extended allegory of the Jacob soul will redeem the sons of Rachel, as will Joseph's two sons, Ephraim and Manasseh. Allegorical genealogies do not progress in hereditary lineages but in typological ones. These chapters affirm that Jacob's upright sons and grandsons stem from *both* of his wives, and that his good offspring are likewise twice as numerous and his bad ones.

Viewing the emerging allegorical picture from within an even widen frame, Philo illustrates the difference between the practicing (Jacob) and the taught (Abraham) soul by way of allegories of their children. The semiotic vacillation of Jacob's six offspring (between bad and good qualities, and between vices and virtues) represents the relative instability of the practicing type and contrasts with the singular, self-taught stability signified by Abraham soul and his only son Isaac, who represents the best of the good emotions, joy. (But cf. Philo's further musings on Ishmael in chapter nine of the present treatise [§§ 201–251].)

The section divides into four units:

(1) Philo interrupts the thread of his discourse on name change to address an implicit problem, which is never explicitly stated: how can it be, if Jacob's children (Joseph and Benjamin) represent reprehensible characteristics, that two of *Joseph's* sons can then be claimed by Jacob as his own, in the same manner as Jacob's firstborn by Leah, Reuben and Simeon? Philo quotes, as a tertiary biblical lemma, Gen 48:5, as proof of this "Mosaic problem" (§ 97).

(2) Philo answers this question by comparing one son in each pair with his analogue in the other. He begins with Reuben and Ephraim. Reuben etymologically means "seeing son" and symbolizes a soul which is good by nature; Ephraim etymologically means "memory" and symbolizes the soul that naturally possesses an attentive mind (§ 98).

(3) Philo next considers the second pair, Simeon and Manasseh. Simeon etymologically means "hearing" (i.e., "learning" and "teaching") and symbolizes the soul that is steadfast in these practices. Manasseh etymologically means "recollection," and signifies the power in the soul to recover what it has forgotten (§§ 99–101a).

(4) Having suggested the fittingness of each diachronic pair—of the good-natured soul and memory and of the learning soul and recollection— Philo then draws a correspondence between each pair considered synchronically or "horizontally" with his own brother. Just as natural goodness/vision (Reuben) in a soul is better than the soul that improves by learning/hearing (Simeon), so having a fixed memory (Ephraim) is better than needing a dialectical process of recollection to recover and retain knowledge (Manasseh) (§§ 101b–102).

Detailed Comments

(1) § 97. *what comes next?* Philo's minimalist introductory question, "what next" (τί δ';), signals that the thematic flow of his treatise might naturally turn in several directions. In this case, he develops the allegory by attending to a problematic verse, Gen 48:5, in which Jacob will claim two of Joseph's sons as his own. Given the ethical differences between the Jacob and Joseph types, how can Moses have written this? What can the hidden allegorical significance be?

very much like ... according to natural allegory. Philo raises the issue of natural continuities. If psychic nature flows from psychic nature, what sense can there be in two of Joseph's sons being "thoroughly like" (ἐξωμοιοῦντο) two of Jacob's (by Leah) in nature? Asking this first question entails a second one: how can Jacob produce sons as bad (allegorically speaking) as Joseph and Benjamin;

while Joseph produces sons as good as Ephraim and Manasseh? Nothing less than the coherence of Moses's allegory is at stake in these questions.

the two older sons of Jacob. Philo continues developing his answer to the implicit problems. Whereas in §§ 92 and 96, he suggested that Jacob's children by Rachel (Joseph and Benjamin) are negative figures, Jacob's firstborn by Leah, like Joseph's firstborn by Aseneth (who is not referenced by Philo), are virtuous and positive figures. According to the allegorical logic, the "older sons" of each father signify his positive psychic potential.

"Your two sons ... will be like Reuben and Simeon to me." Philo cites, as a contextualizing secondary lemma, Gen 48:5. This is the verse that provides the "problem" that the subsection attempts to answer. I give Philo's text in parallel with the LXX:

Gen 48:5c	§ 97
Your two sons, who have been born to you in Egypt, before I came to you in Egypt, are mine. Ephraim and Manasseh will be as Reuben and Simeon to me.	Your two sons, who have been born in Egypt, before I came in Egypt, are mine. Ephraim and Manasseh will be as Reuben and Simeon to me.

As the synopsis demonstrates, Philo follows the Septuagint, but critically omits both references "to you" (i.e., Joseph). This shorter text has the effect of diminishing the connection of the two brothers to their natural father Joseph and supplanting it with Jacob's spiritual claim on the boys.

let us see. Philo uses here at § 97 the same verb that he does in § 91 (on the name Zaphenath-paneah)—"let us see" (θεασώμεθα). These are the only two instances of this hortatory verb form in the treatise, a point which suggests that this (f) and the foregoing subsection (d) on Joseph are of a piece and that Philo may be reworking a traditional block of Joseph material.

(2) § 98. *Reuben is a symbol of a good nature.* Philo begins with a symbolic allegory of Jacob's eldest son, mentioned in Gen 48:5. Instead of starting with an etymology, he begins with Reuben's symbolic significance. Alesse (2008, 3) follows Theiler in identifying "good nature" (εὐφυΐα) as one of the (Stoic, in this case) words Philo borrows from Antiochus of Ascalon, via the school of Eudorus.

his name means "seeing son." The onomasticon analyzes the Hebrew name *Rəʾûbēn* (ראובן) into two parts, (1) *rʾh* (ראה), "seeing"; and (2) *bēn* (בן), "son."

The etymologist probably reads the verb for seeing as an active participle *rō'eh* (רֹאֶה), "seeing," corresponding with the Greek participle, "seeing" (ὁρῶν).

every mind. Some masculine noun must be supplied with the adjective "every"; whether this is "human being" (ἄνθρωπος) or "mind" (νοῦς) makes little difference, as the former often symbolizes the latter in Philo's allegoresis.

cleverness and a good nature ... visionary. Intriguingly, Reuben's symbolic identity, "good nature" (εὐφυΐα), finds its closest analogues in Abraham (good nature and memory [§ 84]) or Isaac (§ 88), not Jacob/Israel. In being characterized as "visionary" (ὁρατικός), however, he takes on elements of Israel's symbolic significance as well. Reuben thus combines a variety of family traits in a single psychic type.

Ephraim ... memory ... "the bearing of fruit." As in the case with his presentation of the name of Reuben, so in the case of the name of Ephraim, Philo rhetorically foregrounds the symbolic meaning and gives the etymology second. The author of the onomasticon connects the Hebrew name *'Ep⟨h⟩rayim* (אפרים) with the Hebrew root *prh* (פרה), "be fruitful"—a tradition stemming from MT Gen 41:52. Hence, Philo understands Ephraim to mean "the bearing of fruit" (καρποφορία). This etymological connection is obscured by the Septuagint, which renders the Hiph'il verb "he caused me to be fruitful" (הפרני) as "he increased" (ηὔξησεν). See Grabbe 1988, 160–161. Both the Samaritan Targum and Syriac (Peshitta), on the contrary, make the etymological connection clearer by rendering the Hebrew Hiph'il as an Aramaic 'Aphel (both binyanim are causative). Foregrounding an initial aleph in the explanation "Ephraim, because he caused me to be fruitful" (אפרים הלא אפרתי or ܐܦܪܝܡ ܕܐܦܪܢܝ) increases the homophony between name and verb. The etymologist of the onomasticon may have been working within this trilingual tradition. Targums Onkelos, Neofiti, and Ps.-Jonathan, by contrast, use different Aramaic roots to render the Hebrew etymology.

as we have often said in other places. Philo interprets Ephraim as "memory" no fewer than five times in the Allegorical Commentary. See the Parallel Exegesis for examples.

the best fruit of the soul is memory. This may strike one as a curious conclusion for Philo. It is occasioned by the exigencies of the present allegorical interpretation. In § 1, Philo claims that the perfect offspring of the soul and first fruit of first fruits is "joy" (χαρά)—a primary theme of the treatise. Then, in § 74, when speaking of the "orchard of philosophical discourse," Philo states that the fruit of natural reasoning is "virtue" (ἀρετή). Here, by contrast, he says that the best fruit of the soul is "memory" (μνήμη). Such symbolic supersaturation is typical of Philo's commentaries. He does not necessarily contradict his earlier positions about the superlative quality of joy or the finality of virtue for the good life, but extends the metaphor of the word "fruit" (καρπός) to embrace a further concept. Memory is the "best fruit of the soul" in the sense that it guides the mind toward joy and virtue and plants them there firmly.

no two things are more kindred ... memory is to a good-natured mind. Philo's association of a good nature and memory is reminiscent of his description of the Abraham soul in § 84. Reuben and Ephraim together form a second expression of this soul in perfection.

(3) § 99. *now take the second pairing.* Having interpreted the names of the first two brothers in each of the pairs of Gen 48:5 (Reuben and Ephraim) and given their symbolic relationship to one another, Philo turns to the second diachronic pairing, Simeon and Manasseh.

Simeon is the name for learning and instruction. Following the exegetical pattern used above in explicating Reuben and Ephraim, Philo offers the symbolic meaning of each figure first and the etymology of the name second. Simeon stands for "learning" (μάθησις) and "teaching" (διδασκαλία). In this, Simeon symbolically resembles Abraham more than his father, Jacob.

its interpretation is "obedience." The etymologist understands the name *Šimʿôn* (שמעון) as a noun derived from the verbal stem *šmʿ* (שמע), "to hear," "to obey." From this comes the Greek equivalent, "obedient hearing" (εἰσακοή).

the one who has learned both to hear and to hold fast. Hearing, Philo says, is not tantamount to virtue; the learner must also retain the precepts he has heard, by committing them to memory.

Manasseh ... is a symbol of recollection. As Ephraim symbolized "memory" (μνήμη), similarly his brother Manasseh symbolizes "recollection" (ἀνάμνησις). "Memory" is better, as it represents a stable capacity or possession, and may constitute a new cognitive discovery. "Recollection" is worse, because it indicates a non-retentive mind, which vacillates between remembrance and forgetfulness (see § 102). This mind characterized by "recollection" (ἀνάμνησις) is "reminiscent" of the Jacob soul, as presented in § 84, in contradistinction to the Abrahamic mind which uses "memory" (μνήμη) proper.

It is worth emphasizing that Philo does not speak of "recollection" here in its standard Platonic definition (i.e., remembering something that a soul has forgotten from a previous incarnation: see *Meno* 80–86), but according to a more ordinary usage. For a discussion of Platonic recollection (and the tensions between them) as a topic in Alexandrian Middle Platonism, see the *Anonymous Theaetetus Commentary* (56.11–31).

his name means "away from forgetting." The etymologist of the onomasticon analyzes the Hebrew name *Mənaššeh* (מנשה) into two parts: (1) *min* (מן), "from"; (2) *nšh* (נשה), "to forget." This yields the rather wooden Greek equivalent, "from forgetting" (ἐκ λήθης), the symbolic meaning of which ("apart from forgetting," "not forgetting") ironically contradicts the Hebrew etymology in Gen 41:51: "God has made me forget" (נַשַּׁנִי). As was the case with the name of Ephraim, where the onomasticon pays rigid attention to the seemingly superfluous initial aleph, so here, the etymologist wishes to explain every letter of Manasseh's name in a maximal sense, including the initial mem—which in the Hebrew of Gen 41:51 is more likely the mem-prefix of a Pi'el participle or a mem as a nominal marker.

§ 100. *the one who departs "from forgetting" proceeds first to recollection.* Drawing on the prepositional force of "from" in his etymology of Manasseh, Philo constructs an epistemological itinerary for the Simeon-Manasseh soul, "out of forgetfulness" toward virtue and truth by way of recollection. The notion that forgetfulness confronts the soul upon embodiment is a Platonic one (see, e.g., *Phaed.* 73c–75e; *Symp.* 208a). Here, Philo speaks of the more usual process of forgetting when one tries to acquire a new subject of knowledge.

recollection belongs to learning. Cf. Plato, *Phaed.* 72e5: "For our learning happens to be nothing other than recollection" (ὅτι ἡμῖν ἡ μάθησις οὐκ ἄλλο τι ἢ ἀνάμνησις τυγχάνει οὖσα).

objects of contemplation slip away from the learner. Philo's suggestion that knowledge acquired by souls through contemplation may "slip away" (ἀπορρεῖ [§ 99]) echoes Plato's myth of the chariot soul in the *Phaedrus*. There, Socrates speaks of the causes whereby the wings of the soul, which in good health enable it to pursue the lives of the gods, likewise "slip away" (ἀπορρεῖ, *Phaedr.* 246d) on account of vice.

not able to hold onto them on account of his weakness. This description of the "weakness" (ἀσθένεια) of the learning type of mind is similar to the Aristotelian concept of "want of power" (ἀκρασία), or weakness of the will (Aristotle, *Eth. nic.* 1136a–b). Famously, Plato's Socrates asserts that there is no such thing as true "want of power" (*Prot.* 358bc); we simply mistake what is evil for good. Philo's language may be a sign of the influence of Aristotle on Middle Platonizing thought.

rise again to the surface. Whereas Philo's definition of forgetting as the "slipping away" (ἀπορρεῖ) of knowledge echoes Platonic language, his notion of recollection as a "floating up" again (ὑπαναπλεῖ) is a Middle Platonic addition, perhaps of Philo's own coinage. This rare double compound occurs only four times in Greek literature—all four in Philo's Allegorical Commentary (*Sacr.* 61; *Agr.* 132; *Fug.* 129; *Mut.* 100).

experience of slipping away is called forgetting. Philo renders explicit a connection between "slipping or ebbing away" (ἀπορροή) and "forgetting" (λήθη), which one finds more diffusely expressed in the *Phaedrus*, in Socrates's description of the soul's loss of its wings (*Phaedr.* 246d [ἀπορρεῖ]; 248c: [λήθη]).

experience of resurgence is called recollection. "Resurgence" or "flowing back again" (παλίρροια) is not a Platonic word, but one which Philo draws from his classical education to complement the noun "slipping away" (ἀπορροή). Philo demonstrates his own poetic ability to forge a new philosophical vocabulary, recasting of old words in new molds.

(4) § 101b. *the same relationship.* Having linked Reuben with Ephraim and Simeon with Manasseh in diachronic pairs, Philo now establishes a similar semantic "relationship" (λόγος) between each member of the fraternal pair.

> Reuben : Simeon :: Ephraim : Manasseh
> nature (φύσις) : learning (μάθησις) :: memory (μνήμη) : recollection (ἀνάμνησις)

As Reuben is to Simeon—i.e., as natural knowledge is better (§ 102) and more stable than learning—so Ephraim is to Manasseh—i.e., so memory is better and more stable than recollection of what is learned imperfectly and forgotten. On the latter pair, Arnaldez (1964, 76, n. 1) observes: "The distinction between memory and recollection is fundamental to Philo's thought. The present passage concludes with the ontological and mystical value of memory."

§ 102. *like seeing ... like hearing.* Philo explains the superiority of natural knowledge over learning—a priority which he has already espoused in his description of the Isaac soul in § 88 as deriving from the superiority of "nature" (φύσις) over "habituation" (ἐπιτήδευσις)—by aligning the former with seeing and the latter with hearing. The argument trades on the common Platonic hierarchy of sight over hearing, as the first and second senses. Arnaldez (1964, 78, n. 1) observes: "Philo always places seeing above hearing. Regarding the order of the progress of the soul, hearing can lead to seeing."

mingled with forgetting ... unmixed and unmingled. Philo further explains the superiority of nature (memory) over learning (recollection) in terms of their participation or non-participation in the process of forgetting. See the note § 99 ("Manasseh") above.

Parallel Exegesis

Philonic parallels to the individual interpretations of the four figures of this section, Ephraim, Manasseh, Reuben, and Simeon, are found in the comments below. Analysis reveals that Ephraim and Manasseh are related to various scriptural dyads: Esau and Jacob (*Sobr.* 27–29), Sarah and Hagar (*Congr.* 39–41), those who keep the first and second Passovers during the Exodus (*Leg.* 3.94), and so forth. Philo was thus able to take an allegorical molecule, like Ephraim-

Manasseh (memory-recollection), and recombine it with various other figures in his symbolic table of elements, according to exegetical need.

§ 97. *Gen 48:5 ("like Reuben and Simeon to me")*. This verse is only interpreted here in the *corpus Philonicum*.

§ 98. *Reuben ... a good nature*. Philo repeats the allegoresis of Reuben as a "good nature" (εὐφυΐα) in *Mut.* 210, and then again in *Somn.* 2.33. In *Mut.* 210, Reuben (seeing) is paired with Ishmael (hearing—a cipher for Simeon, who also represents hearing), as examples of the good and moderately good natures for whom the mind ought to pray. In *Somn.* 2.33—the allegorical catalogue of the eleven "sheaves" of Joseph's dream—Reuben's interpretation as "good nature" is paired again with the etymology "seeing son," and his goodness qualified: "he is not a perfect son, but in so far as he is a man with power to see and keenness of vision, as son well-endowed by nature" (trans. PLCL [adapted]).

"seeing son." This etymology of Reuben is given only in *Mut.* 98 and *Somn.* 2.33. See the above detailed comments for interpretation, and Grabbe 1988, 197–198.

Ephraim ... memory ... as we have often said in other places. Philo interprets Ephraim as a symbol of memory no fewer than five times in the Allegorical Commentary. In addition to *Mut.* 98, see *Leg.* 3.93; *Sobr.* 27–29; *Migr.* 205–206; and *Congr.* 40–41 (so Colson, PLCL 5:191, n. b). In *Leg.* 3.90–93, Philo explicitly addresses the question of the crossing of Jacob's hands in Gen 48:14. He goes on to say that recollection is "older" than "memory," since during the preliminary studies one often forgets what one has learned; memory is the fruit of learning perfected. In Philo's pithy formulation, "memory is the younger ⟨sister⟩ of recollection" (*Leg.* 3.93, PLCL [adapted]), and therefore better than recollection, because more stable. In an appendix to this interpretation (*Leg.* 3.94), Philo adds that Ephraim and Manasseh represent those who keep Passover in the first and second months (Num 9:11), respectively. In *Sobr.* 27–29, Ephraim and Manasseh, with their traditional etymologies and symbolisms, are paired with Jacob and Esau. Philo again highlights the superiority of the younger over the older in each fraternal pair. This same tradition resurfaces in *Migr.* 205–206, where Philo, commenting on the death of father of the five daughters of Zelophehad (Num 27:1–3), interprets their father as "recollection" (in tandem with their stemming from Manasseh) and his death as "forgetfulness." Finally, in *Congr.* 39–43, Philo aligns Ephraim and Manasseh with matriarchal wives and concubines, respectively (i.e., Sarah and Hagar, though their names are not explicitly mentioned), noting that Ephraim marries a legitimate wife (memory), whereas Manasseh (recollection) bears children by a Syrian concubine (Gen 46:20).

"the bearing of fruit." The etymology of Ephraim as "the bearing of fruit" (καρποφορία) appears also in *Leg.* 3.93; *Sobr.* 27–29; *Migr.* 205–206; *Congr.* 39–43.

The best fruit of the soul is memory. For the motif of memory as fruit, in connection with Gen 48:14, see especially *Leg.* 3.93: "Therefore quite rightly does the heel-tripper of the passions and practicer of virtue, Jacob, place his right hand on the fruit-bearing memory, Ephraim" (ὀρθότατα οὖν ὁ πτερνιστὴς τῶν παθῶν καὶ ἀσκητὴς ἀρετῆς Ἰακὼβ δεξιοῦται τὴν καρποφόρον μνήμην Ἐφραῒμ). Here, the relationship between virtue and memory is explicitly stated.

§ 99. *Simeon ... "learning" and "instruction" ... "obedience."* For the etymology of Simeon as "hearing of obedience" (εἰσακοή) and his symbolism of learning (μάθησις), see *Somn.* 2.34. Cf. *Ebr.* 94, where the similar etymology "hearing" (ἀκοή) is given; and the notes in Grabbe 1988, 209–210.

Manasseh ... is a symbol of "recollection." Philo invokes the important distinction between "memory" (μνήμη) and "recollection" (ἀνάμνησις), which only partially recalls the Platonic definition, at numerous points in the Allegorical Commentary. See the full list of parallel passages in the detailed comment on "Ephraim" above. This contrast between memory and recollection shares similar features with Philo's distinction between "finding" (εὕρεσις) and "finding again" (ἀνεύρεσις) in *Deus* 86–93.

his name means "away from forgetting." The etymology of Manasseh as "from forgetting" (ἐκ λήθης) appears also in *Leg.* 3.93; *Sobr.* 27–29; *Migr.* 205–206; *Congr.* 39–43.

§ 101. *the same relationship.* Arnaldez (1964, 76, n. 1) points to *Leg.* 3.91 and *Congr.* 39 for parallel treatments of the relationship of recollection and memory.

§ 102. *seeing ... hearing.* Arnaldez (1964, 78, n. 1) points to *Congr.* 144 and *Migr.* 38 for parallel treatments of seeing and hearing in Philo's epistemology. *Migr.* 38 makes the Platonic hierarchy of sight over hearing plain. A similar distinction of sight over hearing, represented by Reuben and Ishmael, respectively, occurs in the present treatise in *Mut.* 210

Nachleben

§ 98. *Reuben ... a good nature ... "seeing son."* I do not find Philo's allegory of Reuben as "a good nature" extant in the consistently consulted sources referenced in the Introduction 9. Parallel Exegesis and *Nachleben*. The etymology "seeing son" (ὁρῶν υἱός) is recorded, in the Greek tradition, by Nilus of Ancyra and seems to have grown in popularity thereafter. Nilus mentions it as the first of a series of patriarchal etymologies in *Ep.* 90 [C], addressed to one Akakios Memopialios: "You desire to know the interpretations of the names of the patriarchs. I will explain their meanings. Reuben is interpreted, 'seeing son' ('Ρουβὴν ἑρμηνεύεται, ὁρῶν υἱός)." Two similar etymologies can be found later in the writings of Andreas of Caesarea (*Comm. in Apoc.* 7.19 [C]): "seeing son" (ὁρῶν υἱός) or "son of vision" (υἱὸς ὁράσεως). In the Latin tradition, Jerome similarly gives both "seeing son" ("videns filius") and "son of vision" ("visionis filius"; Grabbe 1988, 198 [C]) as etymologies for Reuben.

Ephraim ... memory ... "the bearing of fruit." The interpretation of Ephraim as "the bearing of fruit" (καρποφορία) is known and used by Origen (e.g., *Comm. Jo.* 28.213 [B], 222; *Frag. Jer.* 56 [B]; *Hom. Ios.* 21.2 [B]), who is followed by Eusebius (*Ecl. proph.* 125.18 [B/C]) and Didymus the Blind (*Comm. Zacch.* 3.276 [B/C]). In *Comm. Jo.* 28.24.213, Origen gives the interpretation of Ephraim in close proximity to the etymology of Manasseh as "from forgetting" (either ἐκ λήθης or ἀπὸ λήθης). This suggests that the Philonic pair of etymologies traveled together in later Alexandrian tradition.

§ 99. Simeon ... learning and instruction ... "obedience." Philo's etymology "obedience of hearing" (εἰσακοή) finds a parallel in Origen, *Hom. Ios.* 14.2 [C] (Van den Hoek 2000, 84). Nilus of Ancyra (*Ep.* 90 [C]) knows a similar etymology: "obedience of God" (ὑπακοὴ Θεοῦ). Andreas of Caesarea (*Comm. Apoc.* 7.19 [C]) gives "obedience" (εἰσακουσμόν).

the one who has learned both to hear and to hold fast. "To hold fast" (προσέχειν) expresses the need to "stay in" God's gracious covenant with the soul. For parallel uses of this verb in covenantal and pedagogical contexts, see 1 Tim 4:13; Jas 1:22–25; 2 Pet 1:19.

Manasseh ... recollection ... "from forgetting." Origen and Didymus the Blind know a similar etymology of Manasseh, "from forgetting" (ἀπὸ λήθης). This is repeated by Andreas of Caesarea (*Comm. Apoc.* 7.19 [C]). Intriguingly, in Hesychius (*Comm. brev.* 107.9[D]) and Maximus the Confessor (*Exp. Ps.* 59 204–205[D]), the etymology of Manasseh has been reduced to "forgetting" (λήθη), exactly the opposite of its meaning in Philo.

g   *Jethro–Raguel (§§ 103–120)*
    Analysis and General Comments

Philo's interpretation of Moses's father-in-law, whose name alternates between Jethro and Raguel, is the longest treatment afforded to a character in chapter five. It is comprised of eighteen sections, making it roughly commensurate with the seventeen sections devoted to Abraham. Other major figures in this chapter are covered in significantly shorter units: Jacob's change of names is treated in eight sections, Ephraim and Manasseh (together) in six, Moses and Benjamin in five each, Sarah in four, Joseph in three, and Caleb and Joshua (each) in two.

The unique length of the Jethro/Raguel section is mirrored by its exegetical complexity. Only in his discussion of Raguel does Philo employ tertiary biblical lemmata (see §§ 107–109, 115) in this central chapter. In addition, the allegorical equivalents for the various figures in the scriptural narrative prove slippery, shifting as the exegesis proceeds. A final oddity, noted in the introduction to the chapter, is that (g) Raguel stands outside the three primary subgroups, which make up the backbone of the chapter: (a-c) Abraham, Sarah, and Jacob; (d-f) Joseph, Benjamin, and Ephraim/Manasseh (Reuben/Simeon); and (h-j) Joshua, Caleb, and Moses—although he belongs most nearly with the third. Combined with the structural and exegetical irregularities already mentioned, the evidence suggests that Philo has incorporated traditional material about Raguel into his commentary—perhaps, stemming from a homily or an independent treatise.

The plausibility of this suggestion is heightened when one considers the place that Raguel held in the popular imagination of Alexandrian Jews. As is well-known, Raguel was brought into the spotlight sometime in the second century BCE by the Hellenistic Jewish playwright Ezekiel the Tragedian. In his only extant play, the *Exagoge*, Ezekiel expanded the role of Raguel (frag. 3) in the Moses narrative, making him not just a local shepherd, but the priest-judge-ruler of the entire multi-ethnic "city" (frag. 4). Similar traditions about Raguel as a political leader are recorded by Alexander Polyhistor (frag. 14)—himself, a tradent of Ezekiel and numerous other Jewish authors—in Rome during the first century BCE. Raguel's most exalted and super-biblical role in extant drama, however, is that of dream interpreter. In a much-celebrated rewriting of the scriptural narrative, Ezekiel elevates Raguel's office in Midian from father-in-law to chief confidant and mentor of Moses. When the latter, still sojourning in Midian, has a dream of a throne on Mount Sinai (frag. 6), it is Raguel who, like Joseph or Daniel, comes forward to interpret (frag. 7) its meaning. (For the text and fragments, see Holladay 1989.)

Raguel's portrayal as a political leader and visionary in the popular Jewish imagination gives plausible grounds for further homiletic meditations on his person in Alexandrian prayer and study houses. In the detailed comments, I will suggest that Philo's interpretation of Raguel's change of name is a response both to the biblical figure and his expanded role in Ezekiel's play—the latter of which could have been known widely among non-Jewish Alexandrians. (For Philo's knowledge of the *Exagoge*, see Sterling 2014.) Philo's commentary both echoes and criticizes Raguel's popular dramatic portrait, offering what he thinks is the real theological intention of this story.

Viewed from the level of the chapter, the Raguel section serves two functions. On the one hand, it continues the analysis of scriptural name change, adding a new type. Unlike Abram–Abraham and Jacob–Israel, whose changes of name signify processes of ethical improvement, and unlike Joseph and Benjamin, whose alternative names represent related negative characteristics, the alternation between Jethro and Raguel demonstrates a third pattern: a figure whose twin names symbolize antithetical characteristics—"excess" or "superfluity" (Jethro), on the one hand, and the mind "shepherded by God" (Raguel), on the other. The second function of this subunit is to transition from two patriarchal clusters in Genesis, centering around Abraham and Joseph respectively, to a patriarchal triad drawn from the Exodus-Conquest: Moses, Joshua, and Caleb.

Philo arranges his argument in this subsection through both rhetorical and exegetical markers. At the rhetorical level, Philo explicitly (§ 106) divides the section into two subunits: (1) a "summary" (κεφάλαιον) of the meaning of the alternation between Jethro and Raguel (§§ 103–105); and (2) detailed "proofs" (πίστεις) supporting this interpretation (§§ 106–120). Plutarch (*An. procr.* 5 [1014a]) similarly divides his commentary on the *Timaeus* into (1) "train of thought" (διάνοια) and (2) detailed "exegesis and demonstration" (ἐξήγησις καὶ ἀπόδειξις). In point of fact, Philo's comments in the "summary" on Exod 2:16 and Exod 18 (esp. Exod 18:20, 22, and 24) turn out to provide support for the meaning of the name "Jethro" as well. The "proofs," to the contrary, offer an extended sequential exegesis Exod 2:16–21 as a secondary biblical lemma, to establish the meaning of the name Raguel. This is amplified by several tertiary biblical lemmata: the stories of the zeal of Phinehas in Num 25; the wars with the Midianites in Num 31 (§§ 107–109); and the "shepherding of God" via a citation of LXX Ps 22 (23):1 (§ 115).

The unique rhetorical features of this section suggest its origin as an independent piece of exegesis. Philo's swift, allusive, sequential movement through a biblical lemma of six verses presupposes the listeners' familiarity with the narrative and suggests that Philo may have borrowed or composed this in a homiletic style. (On synagogue traditions in Philo more generally, see Borgen 1965 and 2014; Hamerton-Kelly 1972.) Similar sequential exegeses may be found in the Pauline letters (esp. 2 Cor 3:7–18) and Ps.-Philonic homilies. Especially relevant for the present section is the fragment of the Ps.-Philonic homily *De Jona* (to be distinguished from the entire extant homily), which interprets a scene from the Jonah narrative at a similar pace. (For the Armenian text of the *De Jona* fragment with a translation, see Cover 2015, 202; and esp. Siegert 1992; 1980. For English translations of both homilies, see Topchyan and Gohar 2013.) The *De Jona* fragment also interweaves direct quotations from the Scriptures with rewritten narrative, as Philo does with Jethro/Raguel, his daughters, the shepherds, and Moses.

Philo's explicit rhetorical division of the section runs as follows:

(1) "Summary" (κεφάλαιον): Moses's father-in-law is sometimes called Jethro and sometimes called Raguel by the "oracles." This owes to a kind of fickleness of character, as well as an alternation of what he symbolizes at the allegorical level. He is first (in the biblical account) called Jethro (*Iothor* [Exod 2:16]), which means, etymologically, "excess" or "superfluity" (Hebrew: *yitrô* [יִתְרוֹ] = *yeter* [יֶתֶר], "excess"). "Jethro" thus symbolizes a pompous, immoderate lifestyle, which tempts and disturbs the otherwise moderate sage. (NB: there is a connection here with the "addition" represented by Joseph in the preceding patriarchal cluster.) The illustrative example of attention to "excess" comes in Exodus 18, when Jethro dissuades Moses from using an equal standard of measure for all cases, but encourages him to employ assistants to dole out judgments differently, depending on the gravity of the case. Often, however, Scripture gives another picture of Moses's father-in-law, one in which he gives up offering immoderate counsel and blind guidance to his own wards and become a member of God's flock. In these contexts, the oracles call him Raguel, with good etymological reason, since he himself represents the soul "shepherded by God" (Hebrew: *rəʿûʾēl* [רְעוּאֵל] = *rāʿûy ʾēl* [רְעוּי אֵל]) (§§ 103–105).

(2) "Proofs" (πίστεις): Raguel's role in symbolizing the soul which is part of the divine flock—and his differentiation from Jethro—can be understood by attending to the two etymological significances of his title "from Midian" (Exod 2:16): (a) "separation and setting apart" (§§ 106–109) and (b) "judgment and justice" (§§ 110–120).

  (a) "Midian" etymologically figures two things. First, "Midian" (Hebrew: *midyān* [מִדְיָן] = *min dîn* [מִן דִּין], lit. "from judgment") signifies the "separation" (ἔκκρισις) and "elimination" (ἀπόκρισις) of those souls, which are not fit for the contest of virtue. Unfit minds are figured scripturally by the initiates of Baal Peor, who are slain by another priest of justice and judgment, Phinehas (Num 25:3–13). Wielding the lance of reason, Phinehas—like the priest of Midian in Exodus—destroys the deceptive passions that confuse and disturb athletes of the mind—Israel, the "seeing class" (§§ 106–109).

  (b1) A second interpretation of "Midian"—"judgment"—arises from focusing on the nominal morpheme in the etymology and leaving aside the initial preposition. On this rendering, the title "Midian" signifies "the critical and judicial capacity" (τὸ κριτικὸν καὶ δικαστικὸν εἶδος) of the wise mind, when dealing with the reception and emission of material phenomena. The priest "from Midian" appropriates this judicial capacity to himself through the marriage of his daughter Zipporah (the prophetic class) to Moses (the reasoning capacity). Collectively, the seven daughters of this discriminating mind represent the faculties of "the irrational" (τὸ ἄλογον) part of the soul, as enumerated by the Stoics: the reproductive organ(s), speech, and the five senses. Their drawing water from the well represents the collection of impressions, which the mind must test and sift. The shepherds who come to harass the seven faculties represent vicious modes of living, which attempt to draw the mind away from noetic realities into the world of appearances. Against this assault, the virtuous way of life, represented in this allegory by Moses, rescues the irrational faculties and sends them back to their father, mind, where he can exercise his critical and judicial function without being tempted by the vices. When the seven return, it is not to Jethro (Exod 2:16), "excessive" pomposity, but to Raguel (Exod 2:18), the mind that is "shepherded by God." Members of this herd have all they need. The same message is signified succinctly in LXX Psalm 22:1 "the Lord shepherds me, and nothing will I lack" (§§ 110–115).

(b2) Having completed his proofs regarding the change of name from Jethro to Raguel, which took Exod 2:16–18a as its focal (secondary) lemma, Philo now extends his allegory of the soul to include Raguel's dialogue with his daughters in Exod 2:18b–21. The mind wonders why the irrational faculties have hurried home so swiftly, when their wont is to delay for a long time among perceptible objects. The seven indicate that they have come home because they have somehow encountered a new pair of objects, signified by Moses's epithets, "the human being" and "the Egyptian." These titles represent intelligible (νοητά) and sense-perceptible (αἰσθητά) objects, respectively. The irrational capacities of the soul, stationed as they are at the borderland between these two epistemological divisions, ought to be governed by both. Mind asks the seven to invite this human being— now, symbolizing the rational capacity—home, so that it might be wed with winged prophecy (i.e., speech), Zipporah (§§ 116–120).

Detailed Comments

(1) § 103. *father-in-law*. Philo uses the Greek word "father-in-law" (πενθερός) in place of the Septuagintal word "kinsman" (γαμβρός). See Exod 3:1; Alexander Polyhistor, *frag.* 4.96. Philo's reticence to refer to Raguel as Moses's "kinsman" (*pace* the conjecture of Wendland and Mangey at *Her.* 44) is likely due to the fact that it is an ambiguous term—applying to anyone related by marriage (see *Spec.* 1.111, where γαμβροί and πενθεροί are used of "sons-in-law" and "fathers-in-

law," respectively). Symmachus uses "father-in-law" (πενθερός) in his recension of Exodus, as does Josephus in *A.J.* 3.63. If Eusebius is faithful to his source, this may also have been the way Ezekiel Tragicus referred to Raguel in the *Exagoge* (frag. 7)—a probability strengthened by the fact that "father-in-law" is stock vocabulary in Sophocles and Euripides. In choosing this word for his paraphrase, Philo follows classical and popular Alexandrian Jewish tradition.

the archprophet. Moses is depicted as the first in a fellowship of prophets. The designation "archprophet" (ἀρχιπροφήτης) is rare in the Philonic corpus and in Greek literature more broadly. It occurs only ten times in the TLG canon, being used by Philo at §§ 103 and 125 (the last section of chapter five, on the names of Moses), and in *Somn.* 2.189 in a discussion of Moses's role of "god to Pharaoh." That these three occurrences appear in the last two extant treatises of the Allegorical Commentary and in Mosaic contexts suggests that the coinage is relatively new, even for Philo.

Philo's uses this title in § 103 to clarify the relative prophetic powers of Moses and Raguel. In popular portraiture—particularly Ezekiel's *Exagoge* (frag. 7)— Raguel is made to interpret a dream to Moses, much as Joseph interprets the dream of Pharaoh. Moreover, in §§ 110 and 120, Philo himself (or a tradition that he has inherited) identifies Raguel's daughter Zipporah as "the prophetic class." Lest these portraitures be misunderstood, Philo insists that Moses is the archprophet and has no need for anyone to interpret his dreams for him.

sometimes ... other times. Shaw (2015, 36–39) suggests that Philo sometimes uses the phrase "sometimes ... other times" (τότε μέν ... τότε δέ) in a technical sense, to report differing etymologies for the same name in the onomastica. Here, however, as in the case of Jacob/Israel, Philo is interested in the fact that Moses's father-in-law is called by several names in Scripture, and that unlike Abram/Abraham, there is not a unidirectional change, but a seemingly intentional alternation on Moses's part, to signify distinct allegorical narratives. Philo's exegesis of Exod 2:16–21 (§§ 110–120) in the "proofs" will demonstrate this in detail.

pomposity. Following the exegetical pattern used in the Ephraim-Manasseh section, Philo offers the symbolic allegory of Jethro ahead of his etymology. Jethro symbolizes "pomposity" (τῦφος)—the state of the soul deluded by its own "excess." Similarities between the symbolic meanings of "Jethro" and "Joseph" may be detected here.

Jethro means "excessive." Philo's etymologist construes the Hebrew name *yitrô* (יִתְרוֹ) and its alternative spelling *yeter* (יֶתֶר, cf. Exod 4:18) as cognate with the noun *yeter* (יֶתֶר), "surplus", meaning "excessive" (περισσός). We find this etymology in several extant onomastica, including "Iether | excessive" (Ιεθερ | περισσός, *P.Oxy.* 2745, 15) and "Iōthor | excessiveness" (Ιωθωρ | περισσεία, Vat.

os 179, 17). The fact that Philo adopts the sigmatic spelling for "excessive" (περισ-σός), followed immediately by his own preferred Atticized spelling (περιττός) as if a gloss, provides strong evidence that he has relied upon an onomasticon and has not developed this and other etymologies from his own knowledge of Hebrew. For more details on Jethro in the onomastica, see Amir 1967; Rokeah 1968; Grabbe 1988, 168–169; and Shaw 2015, 38–39.

covetous gain. Philo's charge that Jethro reveres the "immoderate acquisition" (πλεονεξία) of goods is deduced from reading of Exod 18:1–12 with the foregoing etymological interpretation of Jethro as "excessive" in mind. Jethro thus emerges as the symbolic counterpart of Joseph. Although unstated, the logic of Philo's exegesis might be expressed as follows: Jethro did not wish to expose his family to the dangers of the Exodus; thus, he does not accompany Moses to Egypt. Only after God's deliverance—and Moses's significant increase of fame and wealth (see Exod 18:1: "Jethro *heard* all that Moses had done for his people"; Exod 18:9: "Jethro was amazed by all the *goods*"; cf. Exod 12:26)—does Jethro believe that the God of Israel is greater than the other gods (Exod 18:11: "now I have come to recognize" [νῦν ἔγνων ...]) and offer him sacrifices (Exod 18:12). His later allegiance to Moses is motivated not by faith but by "covetous gain."

§ 104. *This Jethro.* The allegorical subject is still the masculine nominative singular "pomposity" (τῦφος), as in the previous sentence; but the demonstrative "this one" (οὗτος) refers back to the scriptural figure, "Jethro." Cf. the discussion of demonstrative pronouns as markers of symbolic "pairs" in Philo's discussion of "this Ishmael" in § 201.

unbidden ... in the office of counselor. Philo adduces Exod 18:17–26 allusively as a secondary lemma. In interpreting it, he follows a similar exegetical pattern to the one he used in his exegesis of the names of Joseph (§§ 89–91 [Gen 41:41–49]) and Benjamin (§§ 92–96 [Gen 35:16–19]). Philo's description of Jethro as a self-appointed "counselor" (σύμβουλος) of Moses echoes Jethro's words in Exod 18:19: "now then, hear me and I will counsel you and God will be with you" (νῦν οὖν ἄκουσόν μου, καὶ συμβουλεύσω σοι, καὶ ἔσται ὁ θεὸς μετὰ σοῦ). This offer strikes Philo as the height of pomposity, since Jethro presumes a connection between Moses's heeding of his counsel and God's assistance. Indeed, God's earlier promise in Exod 3:12, "I will be with you" (ἔσομαι μετὰ σοῦ), makes it clear that his commitment to Moses is conditioned only on the latter's obedience to the deity and God's faithfulness to Abraham.

ought not teach ... the commands of God and the law. Philo's paraphrase of Jethro's advice paves the way for an extended allegory of the secondary biblical lemma, Exod 18:17–26. He draws on Exod 18:20: "and you shall attest to them the commands (τὰ προστάγματα) of God and his law (τὸν νόμον αὐτοῦ)."

Philo's paraphrase, in which Jethro counsels Moses just the opposite—*not* to teach these commands thoroughly—warrants some comment. Rejecting a severe text-critical solution as "untenable" (see the "Notes on the Text"), Colson (PLCL, 5:194, n. a), followed by Arnaldez (1964, 78, n. 2), argues instead that:

> Philo apparently gets his interpretation by stopping short at v. 17 of Ex. xviii, and ignoring the rest. Moses has said that he teaches the people "the ordinances of God and the law," and Jethro replies οὐκ ὀρθῶς ποιεῖς ["you do not do rightly'"].

While Colson's solution is on the right track, it still leaves some gaps. Colson wrongly supposes that Philo's quotation is from Exod 18:16 rather than Exod 18:20, ignoring the clear allusion to Exod 18:19 in § 104. Philo is treating the biblical lemma sequentially, and his focus here is on Exod 18:20. A closer look at Exod 18:16 and 18:20 together will help clarify Philo's exegetical rationale:

> Gen 18:16 [Moses]: I teach (συμβιβάζω) them the commands (τὰ προστάγματα) of God and his law.

> Gen 18:20 [Jethro]: You shall attest (διαμαρτυρῇ) to them the commands (τὰ προστάγματα) of God and his law, and you shall indicate (σημανεῖς) to them the ways (τὰς ὁδούς), in which they are to go, and the works (τὰ ἔργα), which they are to do.

Jethro's explicit criticism of Moses in Exod 18:17 (noted by Colson) is complemented by the subtle reconfiguration of Moses's words in Exod 18:20. Jethro suggests that Moses refocus his pedagogical attention on "ways and works"— a practical summary of legal customs—rather than on the commands and law of God *per se*. Moses might still "attest" or "bear witness" (διαμαρτυρεῖσθαι) to the former divine precepts and Torah, but he need not "teach" them (LXX: συμβιβάζει [§ 104: ἀναδιδάσκειν]) exclusively or as thoroughly as before.

the great man obeys all his advice. An allusion to Exod 18:24. Colson (PLCL 5:195, n. b) cannot imagine that Philo really means that Moses follows Jethro's advice; thus, he renders the subject in the plural as "the great one(s) of the earth." This circumvents the plain meaning of the text. It is worth noting that Philo never says Jethro is speaking to Moses in his allegory, but to "the sage" and "the great one." Moses here most likely symbolizes the generic sage-in-formation, who might be persuaded by a bad counsellor (cf. *Leg.* 1.45, in which Moses without Aaron is the symbol of a "bad person" [φαῦλος]!). Like

Odysseus, who is "much-turned" (πολύτροπος), Moses is a figure of many symbolic significances in the Allegorical Commentary. His depiction is more stable and uniformly perfected in the Exposition of the Law.

a little justice to the little, but great rewards to the great. Jethro encourages distinguishing cases and treating "lighter" ones with a lesser attention or seriousness. Compared with Exod 18:22 and 26, where Jethro distinguishes between "the weighty matter" (τὸ ῥῆμα τὸ ὑπέρογκον) and "the light matter" (τὸ ῥῆμα τὸ ἐλαφρόν) or "small matters of judgment" (τὰ βραχέα τῶν κριμάτων), Philo's paraphrases, "the small things" (τὰ μικρά) and "the great things" (τὰ μεγάλα), better align with the Hebrew, "the small matter" (הדבר הקטן) and "the great matter" (הדבר הגדל [MT Exod 18:22]). The LXX translation adds the nuance of "light and heavy," mirroring later rabbinic middah, qal va-ḥomer (קל וחמר). Colson (PLCL 5:195, n. c) suggests that Philo may be thinking also of Deut 1:17; 24:13–16.

§105. *changes.* Jethro's change of name to Raguel (between Exod 2:16 and 2:18) is understood by Philo as signifying a shift in the character of mind from the excessive, pompous soul to the soul that is pastured by God (see the comment on §114). The verb for "change" (μεταβάλλων) denotes a real alteration of character, rather than a mere change of name.

leading. Lit. "holding the reins" (ἡνιοχεῖν). The metaphor, more appropriate to the equestrian than the shepherd, anticipates the forthcoming Phaedran allegory of the soul in the "proofs" (§§106–120), in which Jethro/Raguel will symbolize "mind" (νοῦς). Philo has already used this verb twice in this treatise: in chapter one (§16), to describe the transformation of the Abraham soul from Chaldean astronomer to seer of the true Governor of the world; and earlier in chapter five (§92), to illustrate the correct disposition of the soul, which—unlike Joseph—subjects fortune to the reins of prudence. Given the similarities between the symbolic meanings of Joseph ("addition") and Jethro ("surplus"), one sees in Philo's development of the Jethro-Raguel allegory a thematic continuation of the Joseph study. The Raguel soul makes the transformation that the Joseph soul cannot. Accepting the teaching of Abraham, that the Logos is the leader of the cosmos (§16; cf. §115), he allows his life to be guided by the precepts of wisdom rather than the vicissitudes of fortune (§92).

seeks again. Philo's participle, "re-seeking" (ἀναζητήσας), uses the same prepositional prefix as the noun "recollection" (ἀνάμνησις), which he applies to the soul's recovery of virtue in the immediately preceding pericope on the names Ephraim and Manasseh (§§99–102). The Platonic compound has apparently inspired a number of Philonic spin-offs, both lexically and conceptually. For Philo as a creative wordsmith, see Nieto Hernández 2014.

a blameless member. The Greek word translated "member" (μέρος) is used as a technical term in Platonism for a soul's affiliation with a particular heavenly being or deity (see, e.g., the phrase "affiliated souls" [μερικαὶ ψυχαί] in the following note).

Herdsman. In Pythagorean and Platonist traditions, the term "herdsman" (ἀγελάρχης) comes to designate a being charged with psychic leadership. See, e.g., Ps.-Hippodamus (3rd BCE–2nd CE), *Resp.* 101.11, on the importance of psychic "lawgivers and ... herdsmen" (νομοθέται καί ... ἀγελάρχαι) of human ethical perfection. Proclus (*In Tim.* 3.265), commenting on *Tim.* 42d, will also speak of the younger deities as "herdsmen" (ἀγελάρχαι) of the "souls belonging to their portion" (μερικαὶ ψυχαί) of the cosmos. Philo uses the term in both its literal (*Mos.* 1.63) and metaphorical sense. Here, God (or more properly, the divine Logos [see §116]) is envisioned as a shepherd of souls.

"shepherded by God." The translator of the onomasticon understands the Hebrew name Raguel (רְעוּאֵל) to be derived from the Hebrew root *rʿh* (רעה), "to shepherd/pasture," rather than the identical root meaning "friend" (רֵעַ). The composer of the onomasticon resolves the name into two parts: (1) the Qal passive participle *rāʿûy* (רָעוּי), "shepherded," and (2) the subjective genitive *ʾēl* (אֵל), "God," giving the construct chain *rāʿûy-ʾēl* (רְעוּי אֵל), meaning "shepherded by God." If Philo knew the alternative etymology, "friend of God," he opted for "shepherding of/shepherded by (ποιμασία) God" because he wished to emphasize the corrected soul's dependence upon God, and because, in his allegorical system, it is Moses who primarily deserves the title "friend of God" (see *Her.* 21). On this passage, Arnaldez (1964, 79, n. 3) observes: "The Jethro-Raguel dichotomy is that between human authority, which is conventional and abusive, and the authority of the true shepherd of human beings, God. Goodenough has noted the political importance of this passage. Here, Jethro leaves his flocks—human society founded on error—to seek out the true flock, the people of God guided by the Law."

(2a) §106. ***summary ... proofs.*** Philo follows his "summary" (κεφάλαιον) of the allegory in §§103–105 with more detailed "proofs" (πίστεις) in §§106–120. These can be subdivided into three sections (see general comments above). Aristotle (*Rhet.* 1.2.2) first introduced "proofs" as a central part of rhetorical composition, and he is followed in the Latin tradition by Quintilian (*Inst.* 5.1.1), who makes "proofs" (*probatio*[*nes*]) the *sine qua non* of forensic speech. The coordination of "summary" and "proofs" as a technical pair occurs in Greek rhetorical theorists contemporaneous with Philo. Dionysus of Halicarnassus (*Is.* 14), for instance, speaks of multiple "summaries" (κεφάλαια), each of which is divisible into a number of "proofs" (πίστεις); and the spurious *Ars rhetorica* (10.6) attributed to him suggests that proofs be creatively reintroduced according to the exigencies of the rhetorical context, even if this diverges from the order in which they were presented in the summary. Quintilian (*Inst.* 5.7.35) has a special section on how to use *oracula*—a Latin equivalent for "oracles" (χρησμοί), which Philo applies to scriptural witnesses (see §103)—and other sacred texts as rhetorical proofs. Because Philo has already offered an etymological allegory of "Jethro" in the summary, his proofs are focused on the biblical text supporting his etymology for Raguel ("shepherding of God"), but also creatively address some additional content from the secondary biblical lemma.

an attendant. Philo's word "attendant" (θεραπευτής) is an interpretive paraphrase of the Septuagintal word "priest" (ἱερεύς). He also uses the Greek word "attendant/worshipper" (θεραπευτής) to describe the famous Jewish contemplatives who lived on the shores of Lake Mareotis (see Philo, *De vita contemplativa*; Taylor and Hay 2020). Here, the word means more generally the cult attendant of a shrine or holy place. It is striking that Philo describes Raguel in such humble terms, given that in popular portraiture, he was priest, king (tyrant), and dream interpreter (see Ezekiel, *Exagoge*, frag. 4.6–8 and frag. 7)—roles which Philo would attribute primarily to Moses.

appellation. In §§106–115, Philo interprets Exod 2:16–2:18a sequentially and selectively. He gives two etymological allegories for the geographic name, "Midian," which he takes as a title or epithet of the priest. Philo uses the noun "appellation" (προσηγορία) to describe such a title only here in the Allegorical Commentary, preferring the compound "designation" (πρόσρησις), which he uses five times (§§12, 15, 59, 83, 88) in the present treatise to designate proper names—both God's lack of a proper name, and those new names that God gives to those on the road of spiritual progress. It is noteworthy that although "Midian" receives an extended analysis in the proofs, this title is not listed as one of the priest's names in the summary. This may result simply from closer attention to the secondary lemma; or, Philo may have anthologized additional exegetical material.

Midian ... means "from judgment." Philo's onomasticon offers a Hebrew etymology of the Canaanite place name *Midyān* (מִדְיָן), derived from analyzing the word into two parts, *min dîn* (מִן דִּין), "from judgment." For this etymology, see Grabbe 1988, 180–181.

the symbolic significance of this epithet is twofold. This is the first time in chapter five—and in the treatise as a whole—that Philo offers *two* allegorical explanations of a single etymology. The offering of multiple opinions on a given scriptural question is a hallmark of Philo's exegesis, particularly in the QGE. The anthological character of his interpretation reinforces the judgment that Philo is drawing on a commentary tradition—possibly one previously developed in his own private school—and weaving it into the present discourse. See Colson (PLCL 5:196, n. a).

"selection" and "separation." Philo's first etymology understands "Midian" to symbolize acts of "separation" (ἔκκρισις) and "setting apart" (ἀπόκρισις). The overall connotation is negative, signifying souls which have been eliminated from the contest of holiness. Philo's second interpretation of Midian ("discerning" and "judging" [§ 110]; see comment below), by contrast, will be more positive. Philo could thus creatively use the data of his onomasticon to serve his own allegorical project and does not shy away from attributing multiple symbolic significances to the same signifier (cf. *Somn.* 1.77 and the detailed comment on *Mut.* 92b above for the allegorical polyvalence of the word "sun").

the so-called holy games. As an example of the kind of "separating out" he is talking about, Philo alludes to the practice of judges in athletic contests. The "holy games" refer to pagan athletic contests, which might have taken place on a variety of occasions, ranging from funerals to the four great Panhellenic festivals (Olympia, Isthmia, Delphi, and Nemea). Such games had sacral as well as civic significance. Philo often likens the life of virtue to the contest of an athlete, and this example from the games motivates the ethical allegory which follows in §§ 107–108.

§ 107. ***the unholy rites of Baal Peor.*** To further illustrate the meaning of the first interpretation of Midian as "selection and separation," Philo develops an extended allegory of a tertiary lemma: Num 25:3–13. Num 25:3 recounts Israel's conflict with the Midianites who worshipped the pagan god Baal Peor. The transition to this tertiary lemma is primarily thematic, but there are lexical tie-ins as well: Raguel and Phinehas are both priests (Exod 2:16; Num 25:7, 11) and the unholy initiates are, paradoxically, Midianites (Num 25:6, 14–15; cf. Num 31:1–3, 49). For the "Midianite" connection between secondary and tertiary lemma, see the note on § 109 below.

all their bodily orifices. The Greek word for "orifices" (στόμια) echoes the forthcoming etymology of Baal Peor as "upper mouth of skin" (ἀνωτέρω στόμα δέρματος). Openings for Philo typically symbolize the mechanics of the physical world and sense perception (see, e.g., *Migr.* 188).

sensuous waves. Plato, in the *Phaedr.* 255c, speaks of a "stream" or "wave" (ῥεῦμα) of ethereal "desire" (ἵμερος) that flows between the eyes of a lover and beloved (allegorizing the Zeus and Ganymede story), facilitating the ascent of the soul. While Philo can also speak of psychic "desire" (ἵμερος) positively, here the sensuous influxes disrupt the upward journey of the "mind" (νοῦς) and pull it down into the baser realm of sense-perceptible objects.

Baal Peor means "upper mouth of skin." The etymology from Philo's onomasticon, "upper mouth of skin" (ἀνωτέρω στόμα δέρματος), depends upon an analysis of the Canaanite name Baal Peor (Βεελφεγώρ, בעל פעור) into three components: (1) "upon" or "lord" (ba'al, בַּעַל), giving "upper"; (2) "mouth" (peh, פֶּה); and (3) "skin" ('ôr, עוֹר). Etymologizing "Baal" as "upper" according to the Hebrew preposition "upon" ('al, עַל), rather than (correctly) as "Lord," demonstrates the etymologist's preference for prepositional etymology (see similarly the prepositional etymology of "Manasseh" in the comment on § 99). See also Grabbe 1988, 141–142. On the interpretation of the etymology, Colson (PLCL 5:196, n. c) opines: "I take the application to be that δέρμα ("skin") indicates the body, and … that in this case the body has usurped the superiority which belongs to the mind." Arnaldez (1964, 80, n. 1) much to this same effect, adds: "⟨Philo⟩ could also think of the root פער (p'r), 'to open wide the mouth' and 'to defecate,' which would explicate τὰ τοῦ σώματος στόμια ('the orifices of the body')." This etymology and its allegoresis are strikingly similar to those given by Philo to Zaphenath-paneah—another non-Hebrew name given a Hebrew etymology—in the Joseph allegory in § 91.

governing mind. An allusion to the mind's role in governing and guiding the well-ordered tripartite soul—namely, its appetitive and spirited divisions. See Plato, *Phaedr.* 252e3; cf. Philo, *Leg.* 2.6, where mind is presented as "the governing faculty of the soul" (τὸ ἡγεμονικὸν τῆς ψυχῆς), as Philo blends Stoic terminology with this Platonic schema (Dillon 1996, 174).

§ 108. *peaceful and clear-piercing priest of God.* Philo continues the allegorical interpretation of the tertiary lemma with an allusion to Num 25:12–13. God grants Phinehas his "covenant of peace" in return for the priest's violent but holy zeal. The adjective "resplendent, clear" (τρανός, var. τρανής) is more difficult to derive from the scriptural account. Colson (PLCL 5:197, n. d) considers this "a strange use of τρανός." It indicates the brightness of the reason symbolized by Phinehas. One might have rendered τρανός as "glancing," to capture in one English word both Phinehas's "brightness" as well as his connection with the "sharpness" of metal weaponry (i.e., the "lance"), were it not for the fact that swords "glance" (as they reflect) obliquely. Phinehas's spear and the Logos, by contrast, pierce directly. I have thus settled for the compound adjective "clear-piercing."

Phinehas. Philo gives no explicit etymology of Phinehas's name, but the ensuing allegory depends upon its analysis into two parts, meaning "muzzle of the mouth" (στόματος φιμός [*Post.* 182]; Heb. *peh ḥāsam*, פֶּה חָסַם). See Grabbe 1988, 214. In contrast to Baal Peor, the unbridled "mouth" (§ 107)—that is, the sense perceptions given free rein over the mind—Phinehas represents the muzzling or bridling of that same "mouth" and its proper subjugation to the charioteer reason.

At the allegorical level, it can be no accident that Philo has woven together the narratives of Raguel, the discerning priest of Midian, and Phinehas, the priest who "separates" the female Midianite "passions" from the visionary mind, symbolized by the Israelites (see § 109). These secondary (Exod 2) and tertiary lemmata (Num 25, 31) are linked lexically through the words "priest" and "Midian," and symbolically through the similar roles played by Raguel and Phinehas. Phinehas's defense against the emotions is furthered replicated in Moses's allegorical role in the following well-scene (see §§ 110–120), where he defends the seven daughters of Raguel—symbols of the irrational faculties of the soul—against the assaults of the shepherd-vices (§§ 112–113).

unbidden. This same adjective, "unbidden" (αὐτοκέλευστος)—which might be more literally translated "self-ordered" or "self-appointed"—is used positively here of Phinehas's precipitous action. Earlier in the same section (§ 104), it is used of negatively of Jethro's self-appointment as the counsellor of Moses. At the end of this treatise (§ 270), as well as in several other treatises in the Allegorical Commentary (*Det.* 11; *Conf.* 59), its positive sense comes out through pairing with another compound adjective, "willing the work" (ἐθελουργός). This double use of "unbidden" (αὐτοκέλευστος), in both its negative (§ 104) and positive (§ 108) senses within the same allegoresis, highlights the contrast between the foolish intervention of Jethro ("excessive" pomposity) and the salvific intervention of the lance of reason, symbolized by Phinehas, for the sake of the Israel mind.

lance ... swift and sharpened reason. Continuing his allegory of Phinehas, Philo alludes to the priest's "lance" (σειρομάστης) and the narrative of the surrounding events in Num 25:7–8. Although his allusions to the lemma are not sequential (Num 25:3, 12–13, 7–8), Philo still follows the flow of the biblical narrative. For the image of human "reason" (λόγος) as a "sharpened and swift" (ἠκονημένος καὶ ὀξύς) weapon used to excise the passions, cf. *Cher.* 31, where human reason is similarly likened to a "knife" (μάχαιρα) and the role of the divine Logos as "cutter" (τομεύς [*Her.* 133]; Dillon 1996, 160).

§ 109. *it is also against these (i.e., the Midianites)*. To further illustrate the symbolic war between reason and the passions, Philo quotes Num 31:49. He thus extends his allegoresis of Num 25:3–13 to embrace the larger narrative cycle of Israel's ongoing warfare with the Midianites. His reluctance to name Phinehas's and Israel's enemies as "Midianites" (I have supplied the gloss) is an intentional allegorical "blanc" or silence (Cazeaux 1983, 1), required by the positive value of "Midian" in the interpretation of the secondary lemma. Were Philo to name the Midianites in his expositions of Numbers, it would cause complications for correlation of his (3°-level) allegoresis of the priest of Israel who fights Midianites, and his (2°-level) allegoresis of the priest of Midian as discriminating reason (§§ 111–120). In the secondary level narrative, Moses himself takes a Midianite wife! Philo thus speaks not of Midianites, but only of their allegorical referents.

the seeing race (i.e., Israel). Philo recapitulates his etymology of Israel as the class of people who are capable of "seeing God" (ὁρῶν τὸν θεόν), comprised of the components *ʾîš rōʾeh ʾēl* (איש ראה אל[א]) or *šûr ʾēl* (שור אל). For a fuller treatment of the etymology of this name, see the detailed comment on § 81.

no one of those who were contending was lost. Colson (PLCL 5:198, n. a) references his own notes on the word translated "lost" (διεφώνησεν, Num 31:49) at *Conf.* 56 and *Ebr.* 11. In those two texts, Philo plays on the "sound" morpheme in the Greek verb. "Here," he continues, "there is no allusion to the original meaning of the word, and the derived sense 'is lost' [or, *mutatis mutandis*, 'perished'] may be given in the translation."

bedecked with victors' crowns. The reference to laurels echoes the athletic imagery used to explain the Israel soul earlier in the treatise. See the detailed comments on §§ 81–82.

(2b1) § 110. *the other ⟨thing shown⟩.* Philo turns to his second symbolic interpretation of the etymology of "Midian." He illustrates this by offering an elaborate allegoresis of the remainder of the secondary lemma, Exod 2:16–21.

the discerning and judicial capacity. Whereas Philo's first interpretation of "Midian" focused on the disjunctive, discriminatory, and ultimately purgative aspect of the etymology *"from* judgment" (מן; ἔκ-κρισις, ἀπό-κρισις), the second etymological significance emphasizes the priest's role as symbol of and capacity for right "judgment" and "justice" (*dîn*, דין; κρίσις, δίκη). Whether this represents a secondary etymology in Philo's onomasticon (one which omitted an initial *mem* in its analysis) or simply a second allegorical interpretation of the same etymology remains unclear. Colson renders the Greek word εἶδος not as "capacity" or "form," but as "type." In context, the word signifies a role, faculty, or function of the soul. It is also possible that the word "form" (εἶδος) has taxonomical overtones, referring to the "discerning and judging species/aspect" belonging to a prophetic "class."

which through intermarriage … also is appropriated to the prophetic class. Philo says that the discerning and judicial capacity is appropriated to the prophetic class by way of intermarriage. There are two opposing ways to identify the figures in this statement. First, looking back on the previous exegesis, "the priest from Midian" might symbolize the "judicial capacity," while Moses, the "archprophet" (§ 103), might symbolize the "prophetic class." Philo, however, identifies Zipporah with "the prophetic class" in § 120. This leads to a second possible identification of the figures in § 110: Zipporah is the "prophetic class," and Moses is the "discerning and judicial capacity" (τὸ κριτικὸν καὶ δικαστικὸν εἶδος). On this reading, the priest "from Midian" lacks (i.e., stands "apart from") such a discerning capacity, until it is "appropriated" (οἰκειοῦται) to him via Zipporah in intermarriage.

This second interpretation is supported by two additional points: first, Philo's allegory of Raguel and his seven daughters is framed by a ring composition, with the themes of "the prophetic class" and Moses's marriage to Zipporah appearing in both §§ 110 and 120. It would make sense if Zipporah were the prophetic class in both statements. Second, Moses is identified in § 119 as "the rational capacity" (τὸ λογικὸν εἶδος), echoing the phrase "the judging capacity" (τὸ κριτικὸν καὶ δικαστικὸν εἶδος) in § 110. On this reading, Zipporah is consistently a "class" and Moses is consistently a "form" or "capacity." This second interpretation of Philo's statement does not remove all inconsistencies from the exegesis. In particular, it leaves a rift between Moses's identification as "archprophet" in § 103, and his apparent dissociation from at least one form of prophecy prior to his marriage to Zipporah in §§ 110, 120. Such a minor discrepancy might well result from Philo's use of a different Raguel source in (2b) §§ 110–120. It is far superior to the problems created by the first reading, and is thus the view adopted in this commentary.

the priest ... had seven daughters. In his allegoresis, Philo will quote and allude to an extended pericope from Exodus, sequentially and selectively. He only uses only one citation formula, "he says" (φησίν), in § 110. The following synopsis sets Philo's major references to the secondary lemma in parallel columns with the Göttingen Septuagint, omitting a fair amount of Philonic paraphrase and interpretation.

Exod 2:16–21	§§ 110–120
[16] The priest of Midian (Μαδιάν) had seven daughters, shepherding the sheep of their father [Jethro]; when they got there (παραγενόμεναι), they drew (ἤντλουν) water until they filled (ἕως ἔπλησαν) their receptacles, to water the sheep of their father.	§ 110 The priest of Midian (Μαδιάμ) had seven daughters, shepherding the sheep of the father [...]; when they get there (παραγενόμεναι), they draw (ἀντλοῦσι) water until they fill (ἕως ἂν πληρώσωσι) their receptacles, to water the sheep of the father.
[17] But the shepherds, who also came (παραγενόμενοι δέ), were driving them away (ἐξέβαλον). Then Moses, having arisen (ἀναστάς), rescued them (ἐρρύσατο) and drew water for them and watered (ἀπότισεν) their sheep.	§ 112 But the companions of envy also come (παραγενόμενοι δ') are driving them out (ἐλαύνουσιν). § 113 Then Moses arising (ἀναστάς) will rescue them (ῥύσεται) and nourish the flock with thirst-slaking (ποτίμοις) words.

Exod 2:16–21	§§ 110–120
¹⁸ They returned (παραγένοντο) to Raguel their father; he said to them, "What is the reason you hastened to return today" (τί ὅτι ἐταχύνατε τοῦ παραγενέσθαι)?	§ 114 They arrive home (ἀφικνοῦνται) to Raguel § 116 "For what reason have you arrived home with much haste?" (διὰ τί μετὰ πολλοῦ τάχους ἀφῖχθε)
¹⁹ And they said to him, "An Egyptian human being rescued us (ἐρρύσατο) from the shepherds, and drew water for us and watered the sheep."	§§ 117–118 "An Egyptian human being having rescued us (ῥυσάμενος)."
²⁰ But he said to his daughters, "And where is he? Why have you thus abandoned the human being (ἵνα τί οὕτως καταλελοίπατε)? Call him, then, so that he may eat bread (ὅπως φάγῃ ἄρτον)."	§ 119 "Where is ⟨the human being⟩"? "Why have you thus … abandoned (ἵνα τί … οὕτω καταλελοίπατε)? § 120 Call him, so that he may eat (ὅπως ἂν φάγῃ)."
²¹ So Moses dwelt with the person, and he gave his daughter Zipporah to Moses as a wife.	… Zipporah.

As the synopsis demonstrates, Philo follows the scriptural text closely. The key differences come in the change of several of the verbs from the aorist to the present tense, in order to convey realized allegorical action. As was the case with the Ephraim-Manasseh section (§§ 97–102), this passage also involves the coordination of four etymologies—albeit, this time drawn from the same biblical story. Philo interprets the names Jethro, Raguel, Moses, and Zipporah, as well as their actions in the narrative, making this one of Philo's most impressive and detailed allegorical exegeses in the treatise. The whole system illustrates a fifth etymology: how the priest "from Midian" (Exod 2:16a) came to appropriate the faculties of "discernment" (κρίσις) and the exercise of "justice" (δίκη), through the marriage of his daughter.

the priest of judgment and justice. Philo inserts his second etymological interpretation of "Midian" ("judgment and justice") within the quotation of Exod 2:16. According to § 120, however, Raguel only appropriates the judicial capacity for the irrational part of his soul through Moses's marriage to Zipporah.

powers of the irrational part of the soul. The priest's seven daughters symbolize seven powers of "the irrational" (τὸ ἄλογον) part of the soul: the five (passive) senses along with the active, productive capacities of speech and procreation. The inspiration for this allegoresis is Stoic psychology, which likened the soul to an octopus, with one rational and seven irrational "parts" (Aelius Aristides 4.21.1–4; SVF 2.836; L&S 53H). This Stoic language is elsewhere combined by Philo with a Neopythagorean valuation of the number seven, such as that found in *Opif.* 117. Earlier in the Allegorical Commentary, he also says that "the irrational part of the soul is sense perception and the passions that it begets" (τὸ δὲ ἄλογον αἴσθησίς ἐστιν καὶ τὰ ταύτης ἔκγονα πάθη [*Leg.* 2.6]), with no mention of specific faculties. Philo's psychology thus fluctuates, drawing on a blend of Platonic, Neopythagorean, Stoic, and scriptural vocabularies (Dillon 1996, 174).

§ 111. ***advances***. Translating προβάσεις—the "advances" of sense-perceptible phenomena—which interprets the daughters' sheep according to a Greek etymology. Thus Colson (PLCL 5:198, n. b) suggests that Philo "evidently alludes to the idea that πρόβατον ("sheep") is derived from προβαίνω ("advance"), cf. *Sacr.* 112."

their father mind. The father of the seven daughters is allegorically identified with "mind" (νοῦς)—the Platonic name for the rational governor of the "irrational" (ἄλογον) part of the soul. This Stoic bipartite terminology (Reydams-Schils 2008, 185) elides with Philo's anthropological allegory of the molded human (Gen 2:7) in *Leg.* 2.5–6, composed of clay and divine breath. It is important that Philo does not yet name this father-mind. (The name "Jethro" may or may not have appeared in his text of Exod 2:16.) He will reserve the etymology for his exegesis of Exod 2:17 (§ 114), in which the significance of both the names Jethro and Raguel, and the meaning of their scriptural alternation, can be revealed with fullest rhetorical force.

these faculties ... draw up. Philo portrays the sense perceptions as female capacities drawing up their appropriate objects. This lends an active dimension to "sense perception" (αἴσθησις), as a complement to its passive portrayal in a text like *Leg.* 2.38–39: "Sense-perception makes its investigations through passive experience in a female manner .... Vision ⟨for example⟩ is affected by visible objects, which move it" (ἐν δὲ τῷ πάσχειν γυναικὸς τρόπον ἡ αἴσθησις ἐξετάζεται .... ἡ ὄψις πάσχει ὑπὸ τῶν κινούντων αὐτὸν ὁρατῶν.). In the allegory of the seven daughters, by contrast, it is mind that is passive ("in a certain manner" [τρόπον τινά]), waiting for the senses to bring back impressions. Philo's attention to the biblical text motivates different expressions of soul mechanics.

the rest, to what befits them. Philo does not specify how speech or the reproductive organs "draw up" sense perceptions.

sense-perceptible objects. The term is drawn from Stoic epistemology. For "perceptions" (καταλήψεις), see further Dillon 1996, 145.

receptacles of the soul. English syntax cannot capture how Philo deftly inserts his allegorical gloss ("the soul") in attributive position between the biblical article "the" and its noun "receptacles": αἱ τῆς ψυχῆς δεξαμεναί.

flock of reasoning. Philo identifies the sheep—the "advances" of sense-perceptible objects—as belonging to "reasoning" (λογισμός). In Stoic psychology (see Aëtius, SVF 2.836; LS § 53H), "reasoning" (λογισμός) is a name for "the rational/governing" (τὸ ἡγεμονικόν) part of the soul and its activity, which Philo has assigned to Raguel. Colson (PLCL 5:199, n. c) cross-references Philo's parallel exposition of the connection between sheep and rational thoughts in § 246 (interpreting Lev 5:6–7). This suggests a "stock" symbolic equivalence for sheep in Philo's allegorical repertoire.

§ 112. *rulers of the wicked herd*. The pseudo-shepherds have their own flock, but attempt to meddle in Raguel's reasoning process by disturbing his seven daughters. Although both the daughters and these "rulers" are literally shepherds, they symbolize different kinds of things on the allegorical plane. The "rulers" true figurative counterpart is Moses. Just as Moses will symbolize the "virtue-loving manner" (τρόπος [§ 113]), so these shepherds represent a manner of life that is vicious and wills things irrationally by following the "appearances" (φαινόμενα).

also come. Philo echoes verbatim the participles from Exod 2:16 and 2:17, which might be translated in context "come" or "stand near" (παραγενόμεναι [f.] and παραγενόμενοι [m.]). The repetition of this verb in Exod 2:16, 17, and 18 (παρεγένοντο) with varying subjects suggested to Philo the significance of this threefold sequence of movements.

away from their natural use. For Philo, "sense perception" (αἴσθησις), when rightly governed by "mind" (νοῦς), is a useful and in fact necessary component in virtuous living. For the molded human being, sense-perception may truly be a "helper" (βοηθός [*Leg.* 2.8–9]). When it attempts to play a more dominant role in the willing process, however, it leads the molded human being toward vicious acts contrary to their "natural use" (ἡ κατὰ φύσιν χρῆσις). The description of specific actions "contrary to nature" (παρὰ φύσιν) in antiquity ranges from sexual deviance (Plutarch, *Amat.* 751d–e) to usury (Aristotle, *Eth. nic.* 5.5; *Pol.* 1.10) and seems to have been a philosophical commonplace originating with Plato. For further comment on "the double function of the sensations," see Arnaldez 1963, 67.

the mind, as to a judge and king. This phrase echoes the second etymology of Midian: the priest-father-reason, in his role of proffering right "judgment" (κρίσις) and administering "justice" (δίκη). In Exod 2:16, Jethro/Raguel is merely a "priest." Under the influence of Exodus 18 and other popular currents, his role was expanded in the Second Temple period. Alexandrian Jews would have known the characterization of Raguel by Ezekiel the Tragedian as the "king" (τύραννος) and "commander" (στρατηλάτης), who "rules" (ἄρχει) and "judges" (κρίνει) people from many nations in Midian (frag. 4). See also Alexander Polyhistor (frag. 14.92–93), which speaks of "Raguel as the ruler of the climes" ('Ραγουῆλος ὁ τῶν τόπων ἄρχων) of Arabia.

§ 113. *draw out the mind*. Philo's allegory follows the literal action of the shepherds in Exod 17:2: "they drove ⟨Raguel's daughters⟩ *out*" (ἐξέβαλον αὐτάς). His natural-unnatural binary (see § 112) is now given spatial expression. Reasoning ought to take place "within" the mind, where sense-perceptible impressions can be rightly adjudicated. Vice aims for the opposite: to draw the mind "out" of itself, in pursuit of its irrational powers, into the realm of appearances, where it is easily confused and alienated. The middle verb "to draw for one's own purposes" (ἐπισπᾶσθαι) represents the shepherds' vicious inversion of the proper task of the senses: "to draw" (ἀντλεῖν) impressions within the soul to be adjudicated by the mind.

the virtue-loving manner. Colson (PLCL 5:201) erroneously renders this phrase "the *mind* who loves virtue and is inspired by God." There is no reason to render "manner" (τρόπος) as "mind." Colson's translation, moreover, introduces confusion into the allegorical schema: "mind" is consistently identified with the father of the seven daughters (§§ 111, 112, 116). It is better then to consider Moses and the shepherds as opposing "manners" or ways of life (the virtuous and the vicious), which safeguard and threaten (respectively) the natural cooperation of mind and sense perception. The fact that Moses is a singular "manner," while the shepherds are multiple "manners," maps well onto Philo's ethics in the Allegorical Commentary, in which virtue is singular and vice is plural (see *Leg.* 1.101–104, esp. 103: "for the reception and application of virtue, one needs reasoning alone" [εἰς ἀρετῆς ἀνάληψιν τε καὶ χρῆσιν ἑνὸς μόνου δεῖ τοῦ λογισμοῦ]). It is also worth noting that Philo's description of the previously dormant Moses manner in § 113 ("until the heretofore quiet ⟨Moses⟩ manner, having arisen ..." [μέχρις «ἀναστὰς» ὁ τέως ἠρεμεῖν τρόπος ...]) syntactically mirrors the erstwhile dormancy of Phinehas in § 108 ("until the peaceful, clear-piercing priest of God ..." [ἕως ὁ εἰρηνικὸς καὶ ἱερεὺς τοῦ θεοῦ τρανός ...]). The descriptions cross-reference each other and demonstrate Philo's efforts to rhetorically unify previously independent traditions.

whose name is Moses. Philo uses the phrase "whose name is X" (ὄνομα X, without the copula, where X = proper name) only twice in *De mutatione nominum*, both times in this allegory of Raguel and his daughters. He distributes it evenly, applying it to Moses in part one (b1: §§ 110–115) and to Zipporah in part two (b2: §§ 116–120). Not only does this contribute to the balance of the two halves of the exegesis, but it highlights the importance of the symbolic marriage between Moses and Zipporah, as rational virtue and inspired prophecy, respectively.

In Zipporah's case, the use of the formula is followed by the explicit use of an etymology (§ 120). This raises the question of whether there is also an implicit etymological component in Philo's identification of Moses as the "inspired and virtue-loving manner." Two explicit Hebrew etymologies of Moses's name will be given in § 126: "receiving" and "groping." Philo also offers an Egyptian etymology of the name in *Mos.* 1.17 (from "water"). These are the only etymologies listed by Grabbe (1988, 188–189), who concludes: "Philo clearly differs from the LXX ⟨etymology⟩ [Exod 2:10] in both *Mut.* and *Vita Moses* and cannot have relied on it as his source." § 113 may provide contrary evidence, that Philo did in fact know the scriptural etymology ("to draw"). There are two ways Philo could have arrived at this: first, he could have known this from his onomasticon; alternatively, LXX Exod 2:10 might have provided him with a clue. There, it is reported that Pharaoh's daughter "called his name 'Moses,' saying, 'out of the water I drew him up'" (ἐπωνόμαζεν δὲ τὸ ὄνομα αὐτοῦ Μωυσῆν λέγουσα «Ἐκ τοῦ ὕδατος αὐτὸν ἀνειλόμην»). Looking at this text, Philo might have concluded (correctly) that Moses's name is etymologically connected to the Hebrew verb for "drawing" water (מָשָׁה). Once Philo understood Moses's name in connection with the concept of "drawing" (ἄντλησις) from the water, the link with Moses's role in the well scene of Exod 2 becomes transparent. The seven daughters of Raguel (non-Israelite women) were also "drawing water after a certain manner" (ἀντλοῦσι τρόπον τινά [§ 111; cf. Exod 2:16]), which left them susceptible to attack by the shepherds. Noting that Moses scattered those shepherds and their perverse "drawing" (ἐπισπᾶσθαι [§ 113]), and then took up the task of drawing water on the daughters' behalf (Exod 2:17), Philo seems to understand Moses symbolically as an alternative "manner ⟨of drawing⟩" (τρόπος ⟨ἀντλήσεως⟩ [§ 113]), which safeguards the senses from further assaults of vice.

thirst-slaking words. Or "the waters of reason." As opposed to the vicious modes of discernment promoted by the shepherds, Moses represents the "manner" (τρόπος) that waters the flock on the intelligible objects (cf. § 118), mirroring their father mind. Philo, the poetic wordsmith (see detailed comment on § 105), uses the adjective "thirst-slaking" (πότιμος) to echo the biblical verb "he watered" (ἐπότισεν).

§ 114. ***those who are ... zealous for tangible goods alone.*** Lit. "for things draped around" (περίαπτα). According to Colson (PLCL 5:201, n. b; cf. Arnaldez 1964, 82–83, n. 3), the noun may have both metaphorical-ethical (cf. Aristotle, *Eth. nic.* 10.8) and literal (as § 199: "garments" or "wraps," set in apposition to περικαλύμματα) connotations. Here, both significances are felt. Those concerned with externals (the sense-perceptible phenomena) are, as it were, living "outside" the mind, with a primary concern for the body and pleasure, which enclose the seat of reason.

as in a tragedy. Philo extends the literal significance of "externalities" (περίαπτα) to apply to theatrical masks and costumes (cf. §§ 198–199; Colson, PLCL 5:201, n. b). Those concerned with the externalities are "hypocrites," engaged only with surface appearances and the pleasure of sense perception. Philo does not always use "tragedy" in this negative sense. In *Leg.* 2.75, he can speak of a kind of neutral, necessary pleasure received by the mind's intercourse with the senses as they hear words and music on the tragic and comic stage—a possibility he seems also to defend in *Mut.* 220 as well. In *Mut.* 114 and 199 (as in *Post.* 165), to the contrary, Philo considers the pleasure engendered by actors and the stage as leading to vice. His criticism is reminiscent of Plato's banishment of poetry and actors from the *Republic*. (For Philo's "ambivalence" to Greek drama, see Friesen 2019 and 2015, esp. 86–94, 197–206.)

Philo's mind may turn to the theatrical analogy in this instance because, as noted earlier, the story of Raguel's daughters and Zipporah's marriage to Moses was staged in the Alexandrian theater by Ezekiel Tragicus in his *Exagoge* (frags. 3, 4, and 5). The play likely included a chorus of Raguel's seven daughters (Jacobson 1983, 24). Philo's critique of the theater betrays a pedagogical worry: those who simply attend to the life of Moses for entertainment and enjoyment pay attention only to the "trappings" (περίαπτα) of Scripture. This is insufficient for the life of virtue. To really understand the philosophy of Moses, one must attend instead to the "undersense" (ὑπόνοια), the allegorical significance of the story, which is lost on the theater-going crowd.

come back no longer to Jethro, but to Raguel. This interpretation suggests that Philo's scriptural text had the name of Jethro printed in Exod 2:16—following the version attested in Codex Alexandrinus and Cyril of Alexandria. The allegorical movement of the daughters from the "sheep of their father Jethro" in Exod 2:16 to "their father Raguel" in Exod 2:18 depends on the Alexandrian text type for the presence of a "change of name." The Göttingen edition omits the proper name from its eclectic edition. In this climactic phrase, Philo weaves together his allegories of the names Jethro (Exod 2:16) and Raguel (Exod 2:18). In the "summary" (κεφάλαιον), Philo had etymologized these names as "excessive" (περισσός [§ 103]) and "shepherded of God" (ποιμασία θεοῦ [§ 105]), respectively. These identities are now applied to two kinds of mind within the allegorical narrative.

they have left behind. Philo's verb echoes Raguel's question to the daughters in Exodus 2:20, inquiring about their abandonment of Moses ("why have you thus abandoned the human being?" [καὶ ἵνα τί οὕτως καταλελοίπατε τὸν ἄνθρωπον;]). Philo uses the verb to indicate the daughters' flight from the shepherds, who had distracted their reasoning process, and their swift return to Raguel-νοῦς. That Moses and the shepherds can both be objects of abandonment by the senses suggests that they are the same category of thing (namely "manners" [τρόποι]) in Philo's allegoresis.

lawful leadership. Colson (PLCL 5:590) argues that the Stoic connection between "right reason" (λόγος ὀρθός) and the rule of "law" (νόμος) stands behind this association of Raguel with the adjective "lawful" (νόμιμος; see SVF 3.613, 614). This is clearly a reversal of Jethro's subversion of the laws of Torah in § 104.

the holy flock. Whereas in the "summary" (κεφάλαιον), it is the father Jethro who abandons his role as "seeming sophist" (δοκησίσοφος) to rejoin "the divine flock" (ἡ θεία ἀγέλη [§ 105]), here in the proofs, the allegory is more complex and includes a reconfigured cast of characters. The sophists are played by the shepherds, sensuous hypocrites who disturb the reasoning process; the daughter-senses rejoin of the "holy flock" (ἡ ἱερὰ ἀγέλη [§ 114]); Raguel remains the soul "shepherded by God."

divine Reason. Philo identifies the "God" referred to in the etymology of Raguel, "shepherded by God" (ποιμασία θεοῦ), as the divine Logos. This aligns with Philo's typical allegoresis, where the arthrous title "the God" (ὁ θεός) points to the ineffable and transcendent One Who Is (see §§ 13–14), while the anarthrous title "God" (θεός) signifies the "second God," the Logos. His interpretation reveals a connection between the Raguel soul and the Jacob-Israel soul, both of which are said to be perfected through the guidance of the Logos (see the detailed comments above on § 87, "had his named changed by an angel"; and § 105, "guided").

Raguel means "shepherded by God." For the passive interpretation of the phrase "shepherded by God" (ποιμασία θεοῦ), see the detailed comment on § 105. Arnaldez (1964, 84, n. 1), who translates the phrase "pastoral action of God," notes: "if Philo has a political ulterior motive (Goodenough), his commentary leads definitively to a moral distinction: a flock of instincts, which has only the appearance of law; and a flock of senses at the service of thought, directed by the divine light (cf. *Fug.* 10)."

§ 115. *in the Hymns*. Although Philo can apply the plural term "*Hymns*" (ὕμνοι) to various collections of biblical poetry (see, e.g., *Leg.* 3.26 [Gen 49]; *Agr.* 79–83 [Exod 15]), the precise phrase that he uses here, "in the *Hymns*" (ἐν ὕμνοις), is a technical formula applied to quotations from the Psalms. It appears only in the Allegorical Commentary. Nine out of ten times, it introduce a Psalm pericope or catena: *Plant.* 29 (Ps 93:9); *Conf.* 39 (Ps 30:19); *Conf.* 52 (Ps 79:7); *Migr.* 157 (Ps 79:6; 41:4); *Fug.* 59 (Ps 113:25); *Mut.* 115 (Ps 22:1); *Somn.* 1.75 (Ps 26:1); *Somn.*

2.242 (Ps 36:4); *Somn.* 2.245 (Ps 64:10). The last, *Flacc.* 122, contains no particular scriptural reference, but describes the worship practices of the Alexandrian Jews. Philo intimates that the author(s) of the *Hymns* is not Moses, but that the collection is connected to his school. In § 115, Philo alludes to a song in this anthology "being sung." Elsewhere, he describes the psalmist actively and anonymously as "the inspired man" (ὁ θεσπέσιος ἀνήρ [*Plant.* 29, Ps 93:9]) or "one of those acquainted with Moses" (τῶν Μωυσέως γνωρίμων τις [*Conf.* 39, Ps 30:19]; cf. *Somn.* 2.245 [Ps 64:20]). For Philo's divisions of the Scriptures—particularly the Pentateuch—see the note on § 42 ("the *Exhortations*"). For the Psalms in Philo's exegesis, see Burkhardt 1988; Runia 2001; Cohen 2007; Böhm 2017; and Niehoff 2020.

"the Lord shepherds me." To amplify Raguel's identity as the mind shepherded by the divine Logos, Philo quotes Ps 22(23):1 as a tertiary lemma. Like the anarthrous "God" (θεός), which signifies the Logos, so the title "Lord" (κύριος) found in the Psalm points to the Logos, particularly in his exercise of God's "kingly power" (βασιλικὴ δύναμις [§ 15]). Raguel is construed as the speaker of the Psalm: the "me" refers to the individual mind within the "holy flock."

(2b2) § 116. *fittingly, therefore.* The etymology of Raguel, which ended the "summary" (κεφάλαιον [§ 105]), is reprised at § 115. Somewhat surprisingly, Philo now extends the allegoresis to the subsequent dialogue between Raguel and his daughters (Exod 2:18b–21). In doing so, he returns to the theme of "intermarriage" (ἐπιγαμία) introduced in part one of the Raguel "proof" ([2b1] § 110).

divine Word as its shepherd and king. Depicting the "Word" (λόγος) as shepherd and king demonstrates its paradigmatic similarity to the human "mind" (νοῦς), which is in a derivative way also "king and judge" (§ 112).

will ask. To "learn by inquiry" (πυνθάνομαι) in a Socratic sense, often used by Philo to describe the give-and-take between scriptural characters. Here, in the context of the allegory, Philo crafts a dialogue between "self and soul"—or better, between the rational and irrational parts of the soul. The noun "inquiry" (πεῦσις) is one of the terms Philo uses to denote the epistemological process of question and answer (e.g., *Mos.* 2.188). The future verb, "will ask" (πεύσεται), here and in § 119 is rare in Philo (3×), and denotes the mind's cross-examination of the senses in moral discernment.

why have you returned today … with such swiftness? Philo paraphrases Raguel's question to his daughters at Exod 2:18b, both to improve its style and to clarify its allegorical significance. He Atticizes, as is his wont, using "today" (τήμερον) in place of the Hellenistic koine form (σήμερον). In this case, it is Raguel himself who asks the scholastic question "on account of what" (διὰ τί; cf. §§ 81, 83, 88).

having suffered I know not what. Raguel rephrases his question in a way that highlights the passive nature of the senses "suffering" (παθοῦσαι) in their tasks of impression-gathering and processing. Cf. § 111, where they are depicted quasi-actively.

§ 117. *the human being ... an Egyptian.* According to Exod 2:19aα, Raguel's daughters do not learn the name of Moses, but describe him as "an Egyptian person" (ἄνθρωπος Αἰγύπτιος). Philo understands this description to include two discrete titles or epithets, "human being" and "Egyptian," and proceeds to explain them in sequence. This process of *diairesis* and symbolic analysis is similar to his earlier twofold allegoresis of the epithet "Midian," which is explicitly described as "twofold" (διττὸν δὲ τοῦτο [§ 106]). In both cases, distinguishing these epithets from the proper names of a scriptural character allows Philo to expand his allegoresis without complicating earlier interpretations. Despite his strategy, however, Philo cannot forgo the chance first to offer a literal correction of the second title given to Moses by the daughters. Moses was not, is not, and never will be an "Egyptian." Nor is he merely one of the Hebrews (generally), but from the "most pure tribe" (i.e., Levi), which alone serves as priests. One may hear some echoes of the struggles between Jews and the native Egyptian population in Alexandria—particularly those which played a role in the pogrom of 38 CE—surfacing in Philo's corrective remark.

which alone exercises priesthood. Philo's high regard for the Levitical priesthood in this passage may corroborate later theories (e.g., Jerome, *Vir. ill.* 11) that the Alexandrian was from a priestly family (see Schwartz 2009, 11; Appelbaum 2018). Philo's insistence on Levitical priestly exclusivity betrays a tension with Raguel's priesthood in popular portraiture (see the detailed comment on § 106) in the *Exagoge*. Drawing on the biblical account (Exod 2:16), Ezekiel Tragicus emphasizes the priestly and visionary capacities of Raguel (see frag. 4). Ezekiel's Zipporah boasts to Moses (whose identity is as yet unknown to her): "There is one ruler of the land, who is both lord and sole commander (στρατηλάτης μόνος). / A priest rules this city and judges men, / who is father of both me and these maidens." Against Ezekiel's rendition of Zipporah's boast, Philo's insistence that Moses is "not only a Hebrew" (οὐ μόνον Ἑβραῖον), but a scion of that "purest tribe, which alone exercises priesthood (ὃ ἱερᾶται μόνον)," sounds a note of intertextual polemic.

not able to transcend their own nature. Philo turns from literal paraphrase to allegory. The daughter-senses cannot understand Moses's identity because the sense-perceptions do not have the epistemic capacities of "mind" (νοῦς).

§ 118. *situated ... at the borderland.* An elevated metaphor for the faculties of sense-perception. In § 110, "sense-perception" (αἴσθησις) is identified with "the irrational" (τὸ ἄλογον) part of the soul; this implies that it has no internal capacity to apprehend "intelligible objects" (νοητά), but is limited to receiving "sense-perceptible" ones (αἰσθητά). In §118, however, the sensing faculties sit "at the borderland" (μεθόριοι) between these two kinds of object. Philo does not specify how the senses may relate to intelligible objects; it would be naïve, however, in his estimation, to hope that the senses might be led by intelligible objects alone. They may, nevertheless, have some intrinsic capacity to be led by rational promptings. Arnaldez (1964, 85, n. 2) adds that Philo's description here recalls the Aristotelian understanding of the "mean" (μεσότης: see the detailed comment on §2).

human being. Having given a literal interpretation of "an Egyptian person" (ἄνθρωπος Αἰγύπτιος) in §117, Philo now clarifies the two titles given to Moses by the seven daughters in Exod 2:19aα at the allegorical level. These titles represent different things from "Moses," who like the shepherds, remains a "manner" of the soul. The title "human being" (ἄνθρωπος) refers to those objects which are capable of "being seen/contemplated by reason alone" (τὰ μόνῳ λόγῳ θεωρητά). Colson (PLCL 5:203, n. a) erroneously suggests that the term "human being" (ἄνθρωπος) here stands for the mind itself, as it does at *Agr.* 9; *Her.* 231; and *Fug.* 71. Arnaldez too (1964, 86, n. 1) takes Moses to stand for a kind of mind: "The daughters of Jethro see in Moses an Egyptian man. They cannot see God's human being. The Egyptian man is reason mixed with sensible objects, the rational animal, in opposition to animals without reason from the flock of instincts." In this instance, however, Raguel is the rational part of the soul, whereas "human being" stands for the noetic objects only partially recognizable by the soul's lower faculties.

Egyptian. Whereas the epithet, "human being," indicates "objects of noetic contemplation" (θεωρητά), the second geographic epithet, "Egyptian," symbolizes "sense-perceptible objects" (αἰσθητά).

§119. *"where is the human being?"* Philo modifies Jethro's question in Exod 2:20a, foregrounding the word "human being" (ἄνθρωπος), to ask what has become of the ideal world momentarily glimpsed by the senses.

"in what part of your members does the rational capacity dwell?" Raguel further asks how it is that the seven "irrational" faculties have become aware of the noetic objects of contemplation ("the human being"), in addition to their proper sense-perceptible objects and emissions ("the Egyptian"). By "rational capacity" (λογικὸν εἶδος; for εἶδος used in this sense, see §110), he means a faculty—proper to the rational part of the soul—which might be used to intuit the presence of the intelligibles. In speculating about whether the lower part(s) of the soul have some kind of rational endowment, Philo plausibly draws on the psychology of Chrysippus and the idea that the activities of the sense

perceptions, though properly irrational faculties, are simultaneously extensions or outgrowths of the "ruling portion" (ἡγεμονικόν [Aëtius 4.21.1–4; SVF 2.806; L&S 53H]) and ideally operate there as well (Aëtius 4.23.1; SVF 2.867; L&S 53M). The ability of the senses to "leave their father," to the contrary, would suggest the quasi-independence of their operations, more characteristic of the Platonist tripartite model of the soul. In this case, "mind" wonders whether such parts of the soul bear the stamp of reason within themselves.

"why have you left him behind so easily." Continuing his sequential exposition of the secondary lemma, Philo now rewrites Jethro's second question, drawn from Exod 2:20b.

§ 120. *"so that he may eat and be nourished."* Philo has transitioned from understanding "human being" (ἄνθρωπος) symbolically as the object(s) of intellection to an active "rational faculty" (λογικὸν εἶδος), more akin to the "Moses manner." This capacity is not the ruling mind *per se* (still signified by Raguel in § 116), but the "manner" by which the irrational capacities of the soul may be led by practical reason in some—perhaps extrinsic or habitual—way. In addition to the possible Chrysippean background for this notion given in the comment on § 119, Philo may be dependent on Platonist and Aristotelian psychology. For rationality as shared between mind and appetites in the Peripatetic tradition, see Korsgaard 2008 (133, n. 10). Arnaldez (1964, 86, n. 2) explains this interpenetration of the senses and reason as follows: "The senses come to be penetrated by reason and reason will dwell in them, under the law of Raguel, until it ⟨reason⟩ weds audible speech, 'nature winged and prophetic.'"

"perhaps he will … take in marriage … the prophetic class." Raguel suggests that the rational capacity (or Moses "manner") in the senses might be symbolically "married" to Zipporah—the prophetic class. Here, Philo's thesaurus of allegorical equivalents presents a minor difficulty, in that one of Raguel's seven daughters—a group identified collectively as the five senses, speech, and the reproductive organs (see § 110)—is identified as the irrational or supra-rational capacity for prophecy. (For "prophecy" [μαντικὴ τέχνη] as the god-sent form madness [μανικὴ τέχνη], see Plato, *Phaedr.* 244a–d.) Arnaldez (1964, 86, n. 2) resolves this tension by suggesting the Zipporah is the irrational capacity of "speech," elevated to the prophetic level. This is plausible, but perhaps unnecessary, as Philo has already taken the liberty in this allegoresis of aligning proper and common names, applied literally to the same figure, with different allegorical referents (e.g., "Egyptian" and "Moses").

As may be seen in the case of Moses, Philo's allegorical method admits midcourse shifts of referent as well as double referents. He is not the only Platonizing allegorist to make use of such semiotic polyvalence. Porphyry, for example, identifies Homer's "cave of the Nymphs" with the generated world, the powers in the world, and noetic substance all in the same treatise (*Antr. nymph.* 9). There remains, moreover, the distinct possibility in this case that Philo has combined two or more allegorical readings of the Jethro/Raguel episode in Exod 2 and only imperfectly harmonized them. If this is the case, the most likely source critical seam is at § 110, where the second etymology of "Midian" is introduced.

"winged, god-borne ... whose name is Zipporah." Philo's description of Zipporah as "winged" (πτηνός) arises from the etymology of her name, which in Hebrew means "bird" (צפור). For the explicit etymology, which Philo does not reprise here, see *Cher.* 41; *Her.* 128; and Grabbe 1988, 203. Philo's adjective invokes Plato's "winged chariot" (πτηνὸν ἅρμα) soul, which achieves the capacity to fly through erotic "desire" (ἵμερος) and is borne up to God in *Phaedr.* 246e5. The marriage of Moses and Zipporah, with which Philo's allegory culminates, thus represents the possible harmony between rational and irrational elements in the human soul, the wedding of philosophy and prophecy, and the love that the inspired soul might experience for the intelligible objects of contemplation, as she is swept up into the heavens to experience them further, assisted by the charioteer reason, and following in the train of her father "mind" (νοῦς).

Parallel Exegesis

§ 103. *Jethro means "excessive" ... pomposity.* Jethro is associated etymologically with excessiveness and allegorically with pomposity in *Sacr.* 50; *Gig.* 50; *Agr.* 43; and *Ebr.* 36–37. In *Sacr.* 50, Moses's shepherding of Jethro's sheep is allegorically interpreted without reference to his daughters. Philo looks more narrowly to Exod 3:1, where Moses leads Jethro's sheep "down into the wilderness." Similarly, in *Gig.* 50, Philo focuses on the amazement of Jethro, i.e., "excessive pomposity" (ὁ περισσὸς τῦφος), at the solitary nature of Moses in Exod 18:14—another verse not explicitly commented upon by Philo in *Mut.* 103–120. In *Agr.* 43, Moses is said to be appointed as the shepherd of the Jethro soul, again with Exod 3:1 as the primary link to the narrative. And in *Ebr.* 36–37, Philo focuses on Jethro's symbolism of the "seeming sophist" (δοκησίσοφος), weaving in a new tertiary lemma, Num 10:29, where Moses speaks therapeutically to Jethro's son, Hobab.

§ 104. *Exod 18:17–26 ("ought not teach")*. In addition to the passages mentioned in the previous note (*Gig.* 50; *Ebr.* 36–37), Moses's division of judicial labors (Exod 18:25–26) is briefly mentioned in *Leg.* 3.197 and *Congr.* 110, albeit with no reference to Jethro. Especially striking is the paraphrase of this passage in a different commentary series, the Exposition of the Law. In *Spec.* 4.173–175, Philo recounts that Jethro "counselled Moses most excellently" (ἄριστα συνεβούλευσεν) to divide his judicial labors. Moses's obedience to his father-in-law receives no reproof or correction; his words are presented by Philo as sage counsel. In fact, Philo makes a point that Moses's listening to Jethro is an example to other rulers that however wise they are, they ought not spurn counsel. This serves as a good illustration of how differently Philo may interpret the same text between these two commentary series. Like Joseph, Jethro is a figure portrayed negatively in the Allegorical Commentary and positively in the Exposition of the Law.

§ 105. *Raguel ... "shepherded by God."* Raguel is only mentioned in this treatise in the *corpus Philonicum*. Arnaldez (1964, 79, n. 3) observes that Jethro's departure from human society for the people of Israel, who are ruled by God, "aligns with *Fug.* 10" in terms of its political implications.

§ 106. *Midian ... means "from judgment."* Philo gives the same etymology, as well as its first interpretation of "selection and separation," only here in the Allegorical Commentary—a sign that he has drawn on an exegetical tradition. In *Leg.* 3.12, Midian is etymologized as "judgment of natural affairs" (ἡ κρίσις τῶν φύσεως πραγμάτων), and again in *Leg.* 3.13 simply as "discernment" (ἡ κρίσις), which Colson renders freely as "the sifting place." The only other place the name "Midian" appears is *Conf.* 55, where no etymology is given and the Phinehas episode is in view. Philo glosses the name negatively as "the nurture of things bodily" (ἡ τῶν σωματικῶν τροφή).

the so-called holy games. Colson (PLCL 5:589) points to the parallel at *Agr.* 116–119, in which Philo also casts shade on the purported holiness of the Panhellenic games. The Olympic contest escapes censure (*Agr.* 119), but only because Philo is making a moral allegory from it (Colson, PLCL 3:491).

§ 107. *Num 25:3–13 ("the unholy rites of Baal Peor")*. The story is paraphrased, but not treated allegorically, in *Mos.* 1.300–304; *Spec.* 1.56–57; and *Virt.* 41–42. For parallel symbolic interpretations, see *Conf.* 55–57 and esp. *Somn.* 1.89, were the Israelites' intermarriage with the Midianites is mentioned and the "daughters of Moab" (cf. the daughters of Raguel) are interpreted as daughters of the mind—i.e., the senses. Unlike *Mut.* 107, Philo finds no positive interpretation of such intermarriages between Israel/Moses and Midian in *Somn.* 1.89.

Baal Peor means "upper mouth of skin." The only other place where Philo mentions and interprets the name Baal Peor is *Conf.* 55. There, Baal Peor is interpreted as "the offspring" (ὁ ἔκγονος) of Midian, "the nurture (or nurse) of bodily things" (ἡ τῶν σωματικῶν τροφή). Some vestige of the etymology "upper mouth of skin" (ἀνωτέρω στόμα δέρματος) is felt in his interpretation as "leather-skin weight" (δερμάτινον ὄγκον), i.e., the weight produced on the soul encumbered with concerns for the material world.

§ 108. *Phinehas*. A figure repeatedly interpreted in Philonic allegory. In *Leg.* 3.242, Phinehas is contrasted with Joseph, as the type who vanquishes pleasure instead of the type who merely runs away from it. In *Post.* 182, Phinehas's etymology, "mouth muzzle" (στόματος φιμός), is interpreted to symbolize his role as "controller of the inlets and outlets of the body" (ὁ τῶν σωματικῶν στομίων καὶ τρημάτων δίοπος). In *Ebr.* 73, Phinehas's name is not mentioned, but his narrative is retold. Here, Philo understands him as the "mind" that enters into the "furnace" (κάμινος [cf. Num 25:8]) of human existence to pierce both the woman and the man—i.e., the pretention of thinking of human beings as the source of things, and all vain thoughts that follow from this. In *Conf.* 57, he is allegorized as "the most warlike reason" (ὁ πολεμικώτατος λόγος).

lance ... swift and sharpened reason. Like the priest himself, Phinehas's "lance" (σειρομάστης) is a favorite symbol in Philo's allegorical arsenal. The image of human "reason" (λόγος) as a "sharpened and swift" (ἠκονημένος καὶ ὀξύς) weapon used to excise the passions (cf. *Cher.* 31, where human reason is similarly likened to a μάχαιρα) mirrors the role of the divine Logos as "cutter" (τομεύς [*Her.* 133]; Dillon 1996, 160). Colson (PLCL 5:157, n. e) gives *Leg.* 3.242; *Post.* 183; and *Ebr.* 73 as important parallels. In *Leg.* 3.242, the lance is interpreted as "zealous reason" (ὁ ζηλωτικὸς λόγος). In *Post.* 182 and *Ebr.* 73, Philo glosses Phinehas's "taking the lance" (λαβὼν τὸν σειρομάστην) etymologically as the noetic act of "probing and searching" (ὁ μαστεύσας καὶ ἀναζητήσας) either "the nature of the realities" (τὴν τῶν ὄντων φύσιν [*Post.* 182]) or, alternatively, "the affairs of corruptible creation" (τὰ τῆς φθαρτῆς γενέσεως [*Ebr.* 73]). In the former quest, Phinehas discovers "virtue"; in the latter, he finds instead the "multitude of our transgressions." In *Conf.* 57, "taking of the lance" is not mentioned, but it would seem to be allegorized Phinehas's "taking the zeal of virtue" (ζῆλον τὸν ἀρετῆς λαβών), with which he "cuts up all created becoming" (ὅλην ἀνέτεμνε γένεσιν).

§ 110. *the discerning and judicial capacity*. For Midian positively as a judging capacity, see *Leg.* 3.12–13, and the Parallel Exegesis for *Mut.* 106.

Exod 2:16–21 ("the priest of Midian had seven daughters"). Philo only comments on Exod 2:16–20 allegorically in this chapter (for Exod 2:21, see the Parallel Exegesis on Zipporah). He does, however, offer an extended paraphrase of the narrative in *Mos.* 1.51–59, which shows a similar treatment of the text from the perspective of rewritten Bible. The passage reads like a literal retelling, of which *Mut.* 110–120 offers a correlated allegorical interpretation. There are, at the same time, important interpretive differences. In the *De vita Mosis*, Philo explains in detail the process of drawing water for animals. He then gives Moses an elongated, excoriating speech to the shepherds, which upbraids their fleshy attachments and makes a plea for justice. Philo adds the intriguing detail that in the process of speaking, Moses became "transfigured into a prophet" (μεταμορφούμενος εἰς προφήτην [*Mos.* 1.57]; see *Mut.* 103, 110, and 120). When the daughters arrive home to their father, who is unnamed, Philo sets an extended set of questions on his lips, which do not address the daughters as the sense perceptive faculties, but nevertheless clarify and elevate the set of concerns raised in *De mutatione nominum*. Raguel gives his most beautiful daughter in marriage to Moses, interpreted as a symbol of "the excellence" (τὸ κάλον) that is in need of no supplementation (cf. *Mut.* 120, where Moses "supplements" Raguel and his family).

§ 111. *away from their natural use.* Philo's notion that each of the senses has a "use which accords with nature" (ἡ κατὰ φύσιν χρῆσις) has an important parallel in *Leg.* 3.110. There, Philo says that the maimed and blinded sense faculties ought to follow reason, which can see, in "keeping with what accords with nature" (τοῦ κατὰ φύσιν ἀκολουθία). In *Sacr.* 73, he similarly speaks of the parts of the soul and body as possessing "natural" (κατὰ φύσιν) movements and states. In *Ebr.* 190, exploring the theme of the impairment of the mind and senses—fittingly, in a treatise on drunkenness—Philo mentions flavors "which accord with nature or do not" (ὅσοι κατὰ φύσιν ἢ παρὰ φύσιν). For further occurrences of the phrase in the Allegorical Commentary, see *Her.* 172, 237–238, especially the latter passage, in which the haunts of birds are described according to their natural or unnatural fitness. In the Exposition of the Law, Philo maintains his commitment to the natural law in suggesting that "life according to nature" (ὁ κατὰ φύσιν βίος [*Mos.* 2.182]) or "living according to nature" (ὁ βιῶν κατὰ φύσιν [*Ios.* 31]) is the highest form of life.

§ 113. *Moses ... the virtue-loving manner.* In addition to § 132, Moses's connection to the love of virtue is noted earlier in the Allegorical Commentary in *Leg.* 2.90 and 3.107. He is also described as "virtue-loving" in *Opif.* 128.

§ 114. *as in a tragedy.* Philo mentions the stage at least four more times in the Allegorical Commentary, and not always with such negative overtones. In *Leg.* 2.75, he lists the pleasures of both tragedy and comedy among the neutral delights of the senses, not yet fully enmeshed in the concerns of the body. In *Post.* 165 (Arnaldez [1964, 83, n. 3]), by contrast, we find a use more akin to *Mut.* 113. There, Philo excoriates those who think that life is a mere "dramatic performance" (τραγῳδία). Similarly, in *Congr.* 61, Philo invokes "tragedy" as the kind of bombastic show that the Esau soul (via the etymology ποίημα) prefers. By contrast, in the philosophical treatise, *Quod omnis probus liber sit*, Philo reveals not only that he attended tragedies of Euripides, but that he could draw from the Athenian dramatist's writings verses worthy of public reflection (*Prob.* 141). For Philo's commendation of the right use of poetry, see *Mut.* 220.

§ 115. *Ps 22(23):1 ("the Lord shepherds me")*. Philo's brief interpretation of Ps 22(23):1 can be compared with the beautiful and extended exegesis given to this verse in *Agr.* 50–54, which may record a part of a synagogue homily. Philo advises every lover of God to recite this psalm often. His first rationale is that God, as king of the universe who sets his Word over the world, ought to be confessed by the sum total of creation—His greatest and most perfect flock. Likewise, Philo maintains, ought every individual soul make this same confession and accept the shepherding of God in his or her own life.

§ 118. *situated ... at the borderland*. Philo uses the spatial metaphor of faculties or figures located "at the borderland" (μεθόριος) in rich and varied ways throughout his corpus. In *Leg.* 3.184—the only other place in his Greek writings where the perceptive faculties are described in this way—Philo interprets the enmity "between the woman and the serpent" (Gen 3:15) to signify a borderland between desire (the serpent) and sense-perception (the woman). The following examples will give a further, albeit incomplete, glimpse into the parallel ways Philo frames entities at various metaphysical border(land)s. In *Agr.* 161, Philo speaks of a special kind of Socratic ignorance that sits at the border of knowledge, such as is often possessed by the young sage. In *Plant.* 10, the divine Word is said to station himself at the border between the cosmic elements to maintain universal order. In *Migr.* 147, Philo describes "the Peripatetic mean" as at the border between two extremes. In that same treatise, the seventy-five-year-old Abraham, at the turning point in his conversion to philosophy, is said to sit at the borderland of perceptible and intelligible natures (*Migr.* 198). In *Her.* 45, Philo uses the word to describe the mixed life, which stands on the border of the active and contemplative lives; and later in the same treatise, he uses it to describe the border state between beginning the philosophical life and reaching perfection (*Her.* 121; cf. *Fug.* 213). In *Her.* 172, Philo notes that the fifth commandment (honor of parents) is set at the borderland between the first and second tables of the Decalogue. And in *Her.* 205, the divine Word is said to stand at the border of the created and uncreated. In *Congr.* 22, the middle cycle of education is said to be at the borderland of the first preliminaries and philosophy. Turning to the present treatise, in *Mut.* 45 Philo has already spoken of the human soul that stands at the border between the world and God (cf. *Opif.* 135, which speaks of the entire human being this way). In *Somn.* 2.188, the adjective is used to describe the high priest who in the holy of holies is himself at the border between humanity and God, being greater than the former and lesser than the latter. Examples could be multiplied, but it is fair to say that as a Platonist, Philo is concerned with the *metaxu* as an important space in many areas of his thought.

§ 120. *"the prophetic class ... Zipporah."* Earlier in the Allegorical Commentary, Philo lists Zipporah among the other matriarchs (**Sarah**, Rebecca, and Leah) as symbolizing virtues. There, she represents a power of noetic ascent: "Zipporah, the ⟨wife⟩ of Moses, speeding upward from the earth and contemplating the divine and happy natures there, is called 'bird' (ὀρνίθιον)" (*Cher*. 41). In that same treatise, Philo will assert that the matriarchal virtues conceive their children from God. So, "without supplication or entreaty did Moses, when he took Zipporah 'the winged and soaring virtue' (ἡ πτηνὴ καὶ μετάρσιος ἀρετή), find her pregnant through no mortal agency (Exod 2:22)" (*Cher*. 47). This is akin to, yet still different from, the winged prophetic "class" spoken of in *Mut*. 120. In *Post*. 77–78, Zipporah is again mentioned in a chain of matriarchs, this time symbolizing the "reason" and "knowledge" wedded by the sage. Cf. *Mut*. 119–120, where Moses is the rational power, which weds Zipporah, ecstatic winged prophecy. Finally, in *Her*. 128, Zipporah's avian-association is again productive of an allegory: for "it is the special property of divine knowledge that it ever soars aloft like a bird."

Nachleben

§ 103. *father-in-law.* Philo's Greek word "father-in-law" (πενθερός) is echoed by Josephus (*A.J.* 3.63; 4.42), who speaks of "Raguel the father-in-law of Moses" (Ῥαγουῆλος ὁ πενθερὸς αὐτοῦ).

sometimes ... other times. Jethro/Raguel is identified by Didymus the Blind (*Comm. Ps.* 29–34, 184.7 [B/C]) as one of the "double names" (διωνυμίαι) of Scripture. Others given by Didymus include Achish/Abimelech (in Ps 33[34]), Thomas/Didymus, and Matthew/Levi. Didymus accounts for such variations in terms of proper and catachrestic names, but does not offer an extended allegory of psychic progress or regress (*Comm. Ps.* 29–34, 184.15–23 [B/C]). Theodoret (*Quaest. Oct.* 202.27 [D]) also mentions several "double-named" (διώνυμος) figures in Scripture, which he treats as a matter of history, rather than of allegorical significance. For Cyril of Alexandria's interpretation, which develops the double-name in a Philonic way, see the following note.

Jethro means "excessive." Philo's etymology, "excessive" (περισσός / περιττός), is found also in Cyril of Alexandria: "Jethro symbolizes excessiveness, indeed ⟨his name⟩ is interpreted 'excessive'" (Ἰοθὸρ μὲν περιττότης, ἤτοι περιττὸς ἑρμηνεύεται, *Glaph. Pent*. 69.409.27 [A]). The phrase comes at the end of a homiletic passage, ostensibly a meditation on the Pauline idea in Phil 3 that humans have no homeland on earth. The pericope is worth citing in full for its proximity to its Philonic precursor:

> But observe how very economically indeed (ὅπως οἰκονομικῶς δὴ λίαν) the Holy Writ names the father of the seven young women "Jethro," before

assistance through Moses comes to them; but after this ⟨it calls him⟩ "Raguel." For Jethro symbolizes excessiveness (περιττότης), as indeed ⟨his name⟩ is interpreted "excessive" (περιττός), as also I said before; but Raguel means "shepherding of God" (ποιμασία Θεοῦ). I will make use of this language to derive some ⟨spiritual⟩ benefit. Casting ⟨Jethro⟩ as the personification of adornment, we were saying that truly excessive and purposeless (περιττὸς καὶ εἰκαῖος ἀληθῶς) is the distraction of adornment. Now, he was among these ⟨vanities⟩ before the chorus of young women was helped by Christ. But when they have been snatched away from greed and separated from the hand of the unholy shepherds, then indeed at that time is his name is changed to Raguel (τότε δὴ τότε μετωνόμασται Ῥαγουήλ), which is "sheep of God" (Θεοῦ ποίμνιον) or "shepherded ⟨by God⟩" (ποιμασία), according to the meaning of the allegorical interpretation (κατά γε τὴν τῆς ἑρμηνείας δύναμιν). For he has taken refuge under the hand of the chief shepherd of all (ὁ πάντων ἀρχιποίμην), by which I mean Christ. Through whom, with the Father and the Holy Spirit, be the glory unto the ages of ages.

Numerous points of connection between this passage and *Mut.* 103–120 make it obvious that Cyril knows Philo's allegory of Jethro and his daughters and has reinterpreted it, with Christ standing in for Moses. Particularly telling, in addition to the general schema of the allegory, are Philo's use of the twin etymologies, the Philonic verb for "name change" (μετωνόμασται), the rhetorical anaphora "then indeed at that time" (τότε δὴ τότε, used by Philo in *Spec.* 3.6), and the compound "chief shepherd" (ἀρχιποίμην), which mirrors Philo's compound "chief prophet" (ἀρχιπροφήτης [*Mut.* 103]).

Also aware of Philo's etymology of Jethro, and exceptionally interesting for its inversion rather than its adoption of the Alexandrian Jewish tradition, is the symbolic exegesis of Moses and Jethro in an anonymous *Dialogus cum Judaeis* [A/B], spuriously attributed to John of Damascus. A parallel to Philo's interpretation appears on the lips of Moses as a speech-in-character:

"For after I, ⟨Moses⟩, killed the murderer of my kinsman and fled Pharaoh, the scatterer of good things, and crowded Egypt, and led the flocks of the excessive Jethro (τοῦ περισσοῦ Ἰωθὼρ τὰ θρέμματα) from the wet and dissipated life to dryness in Horeb"—for the comprehending hearer assuredly knew that, in the Hebrew dialect, Pharaoh symbolizes "scatterer," and Egypt, "crowded," and Jethro, "excessive" (περιττός) or "watery" (δίυγρος), and Horeb, "dryness"—"after, therefore, I led the flocks of the father of the feminine reasonings (τὰ θρέμματα τοῦ πατρὸς τῶν θηλυκῶν λογισμῶν) from the wet life to the dryness of Horeb, then was I thought worthy to see the mystery of the bush, which was burning but not being consumed." (*Anon. dial. Jud.* 5.114–130)

Although no such allegory of Moses's migrations is laid out in Philo, the schema recalls the similar pattern used in the Alexandrian's sequential allegory of Abraham's movements in *De migratione Abrahami*. The use of the Philonic words "flocks" (τὰ θρέμματα [cf. *Mut.* 103]) and "feminine reasonings" (τῶν θηλυκῶν λογισμῶν [cf. *Mut.* 110–111]) show a strong affinity with the present passage. Also intriguing is the fact that the anonymous author of the Christian dialogue alternates between the sigmatic and Attic forms of "excessive" (περισσός / περιττός) in the same sequence used by Philo. At the traditional level, the anonymous author's insistence that the gift of Moses is not the wetness of the sense-perceptions rightly adjudicated (as in Philo), but its opposite, dryness, might indicate a polemic monastic rereading of the Philonic allegoresis, which would be in keeping with the *Adversus Iudaeos* genre. Given that John of Damascus is one of the most important tradents of the Philonic text, it would not surprise if this dialogue, which was attributed to him, was written by someone familiar with *De mutatione nominum*.

§ 105. *Raguel ... "shepherded by God."* Philo's etymology is known by Origen: "Raguel ⟨means⟩ strong friend, or shepherded by God" ('Ραγουὴλ φίλος ἰσχυρός, ἢ ποιμανσία [sic] Θεοῦ) (*Sel. Gen.* 12.121.4 [B/C], not mentioned by Van den Hoek 2000); and Cyril of Alexandria: "And Raguel ⟨means⟩ 'shepherded by God'" ('Ραγουὴλ δὲ ποιμασία Θεοῦ) (*Glaph. Pent.* 69.409.27 [A]; see Cyril's entire interpretation above). The alternative etymology, *amicus Dei* ("friend of God")—related to Origen's first etymology—is known to Jerome and possibly to Philo as an additional entry in his onomasticon.

§ 105. *Midian ... "from judgment."* Origen gives a related etymology for Midian in *Hom. Iud.* 8.1 [B/C] (Van den Hoek 2000, 87). His allegorical interpretation differs from Philo's.

§ 107. *Baal Peor.* See Origen, *Hom. Num.* 17.1 and *Hom. Num.* 20.3 [B/C], and the discussions in Van den Hoek (2000, 100, 102).

§ 108. *lance ... swift and sharpened reason.* The likening of reason to a "lance" or "sword" (μάχαιρα [*Cher.* 31]), in imitation of divine reason as a "cutter" (τομεύς [*Her.* 133]), is echoed in the Epistle to the Hebrews (4:12), where the "Word" (λόγος) of God is presented as "active and sharper than every sword" (ἐνεργὴς καὶ τομώτερος ὑπὲρ πᾶσαν μάχαιραν), piercing the thoughts of the heart. Origen (*Hom. Num.* 20.5 [B/C]) identifies Phinehas's lance as the "sword of the Spirit" ("gladius spiritus") (Van den Hoek 2000, 102).

§ 110. *the organs of procreation, the voice, and the five senses.* Van den Hoek (1988, 201) cites, as a possible reception and adaptation of Philo's sevenfold division of the irrational soul, the tenfold division of the human person found in Clement at *Strom.* 2.50.2–3 [D] and 6.134.2 [B/C]. The former text divides the soul according to the true "ten-fold measure" into "body and soul, and the five senses (αἵ τε πέντε αἰσθήσεις), and the vocal (τὸ φωνητικόν) and the procreative (σπερματικόν) and the rational or spiritual faculties." Closer to the Philonic account is the form of the tradition found at *Strom.* 6.134.2:

> There is also a kind of decade (δεκάς τις) about the human person himself: the five sense-faculties (τά τε αἰσθητήρια πέντε) and the vocal (τὸ φωνητικόν) and progenerative (τὸ σπερματικόν) faculties; then eighth comes the spiritual faculty according to its initial molding (cf. Gen 2:7); ninth is the governing faculty of the soul; and tenth is the specific possession of the Holy Spirit which is appended through faith.

Van den Hoek notes the inexactness of the connection between these texts and passages like *Mut.* 110, giving them a low likelihood of direct dependence [D]. While such a low grade seems warranted in the case of *Strom.* 2.50.2–3, *Strom.* 6.134.2 might deserve a better ranking [B/C] on the following grounds: First, the first seven divisions (of the irrational soul) are identical to Philo's and in the same sequence. These initial seven are clearly divided from the latter three, with (9) being the Stoic "eighth" governing/rational part; and (8) and (10) being derived from Scripture—the natural (Gen 2:7) and supernatural (e.g., John 20:22; Acts 19:2) capacities, respectively.

§ 111. *away from their natural use.* For a similar conceptuality of vice, see Rom 1:26, where Paul speaks of people who exchange "natural use" (ἡ φυσικὴ χρῆσις) of their bodies for "the use which is contrary to nature" (ἡ παρὰ φύσιν ⟨χρῆσις⟩).

§ 115. *Ps 22(23):1 ("the Lord shepherds me")*. For the Logos as divine shepherd and king, see John 10:11 (shepherd); 1:49 (king). For logocentric interpretations of the psalm, see Clement of Alexandria, *Paed.* 1.4.11.2; Origen, *Comm. Jo.* 33.211–212.

h   *Hoshea–Joshua (§§ 121–123a)*
     Analysis and General Comments

In the foregoing section on Jethro/Raguel (§§ 103–120), Philo moves his focus away from the triad of patriarchs in Genesis (Abraham, Isaac, and Jacob) to a new triad of patriarchal figures from Exodus-Numbers: Joshua (§§ 121–122), Caleb (§§ 123–124), and Moses (§§ 125–129). It is important to note that Philo's exemplaric triads in the Allegorical Commentary do not map identically onto those in the Exposition of the Law. The juxtaposition of Enoch and Abraham in §§ 34 and 39 as leaders of divergent companies of sages does suggest a schema similar to that in *Abr*. 48, but there are critical differences as well. In the Allegorical Commentary, the two groups signify not two differing stages on the road toward perfection but rather differing approaches to revelation and philosophy, as well as different relationships to public life and social virtue. The Enochic group is dependent on ecstatic experience and is relatively reclusive, whereas the Abrahamic group is more dialectical in its philosophy and visible to society. Joseph, Benjamin, and Jethro represent moral devolutions; Ephraim, Manasseh, and Raguel, their possible improvements. With Joshua, Caleb, and Moses, yet another triad emerges, though its cohesive characteristics are never explicitly thematized.

By including Moses in his allegoresis of Raguel (§§ 113–120), Philo bookends this second section of chapter five, with the "many-named" Moses (§ 125) serving as its frame. Like Philo's Genesis triad, the Exodus triad is composed of three figures, whose name changes are not of a piece: Joshua (like Abraham) has his name changed once; Caleb (like Isaac) does not have a change in name, though his spirit changes; and Moses has many titles. The Hoshea-Joshua section, which comes first, consists of two sub-sections:

(1) Philo adduces Num 13:16b as a secondary lemma. Hoshea is renamed Joshua by Moses. This shift is symbolically interpreted as the change from a temporary quality to a stable disposition. Philo supports this symbolic allegoresis etymologically: Hoshea means "this sort of person" (ποιὸς οὗτος); Joshua means "salvation of the Lord"—which is, according to Philo, the best kind of "stable disposition" (ἕξις) (§ 121).

(2) Having rendered Joshua's change of name as a shift from a qualitative predicate to a stable disposition, Philo then gives several examples of how a "stable disposition" (ἕξις) categorically exceeds the "quality" (ποῖος, i.e., a person who is of a certain sort). Philo relies on the Platonic difference between a skill and its practitioner. He then formulates the difference in a more Aristotelian way: that a "stable disposition" (ἕξις) is a kind of entelechy, or a habit that by definition entails its own virtuous end (§§ 122–123a).

Detailed Comments

(1) § 121. *these words will suffice.* Turning from the long digressive section on (g.) Jethro-Raguel (§§ 97–102), Philo considers a new instance of biblical name change in Num 13:16b: (h.) Moses's renaming of Hoshea as Joshua. The secondary lemma from Numbers is formally subordinated to the two texts from

Gen 17:5 and 15 earlier in chapter five. This short lemma and its exposition are about the same length as the secondary lemma and exposition in (d.) Joseph (§§ 89–91). The syntax of Num 13:16b ("And Moses named Hoshea son of Nun 'Joshua'" [καὶ ἐπωνόμασεν Μωυσῆς τὸν Αὐσὴ υἱὸν Ναυὴ Ἰησοῦν]) is similar to Gen 41:45 ("And Pharaoh called the name of Joseph 'Zaphenath-paneah'" [καὶ ἐκάλεσεν Φαραὼ τὸ ὄνομα Ἰωσὴφ Ψονθομφανήχ]). Both sentences involve a renaming by someone other than God. Moses is here a historical figure in the narrative, as well as the inspired author. Viewed from this form-critical angle, the (d.) Joseph–Zaphenath-paneah and (h.) Hoshea–Joshua subsections are antithetical versions of the same type of name change.

Moses also changes the name. Philo uses the verb "change the name" (μετονομάζειν) for the last time in the treatise. The verb is previously predicated only of a divine subject, regarding the name changes of Abraham, Sarah, and Israel (§§ 66, 76, 77, 81, 83, 87, 88)—a point which creates a strong, if implicit, analogy between God and Moses and highlights the latter's unique role as an inspired human namewright (ὀνοματουργός [Plato, *Crat.* 389a]).

Hoshea (Osēa) to Joshua (Iēsous) ... this exchange of letters. The transformation of *Hôšēʿa* (הושע) to *Yəhôšūʿa* (יהושע) in Hebrew happens by way of the addition of a single consonant, *yod*, and the repointing of some vowels. As the first letter of the Tetragrammaton, *yod* is a divine indicator, like the *he* added to the names of Abram and Sarai. Philo may know this tradition (without an extensive grasp of the Hebrew), as he uses the verb "to exchange letters" (μεταχαράττειν) to describe only the transformations of Abraham and Joshua in this treatise (§§ 71, 121, 123). In the latter case, the letter exchange is more obvious in Hebrew.

Philo is one of the only extant Greek interpreters to transliterate the Hebrew *Hôšēʿa* (הושע) as *Ōsēe* (Ὡσηέ). The Old Greek transliterates the name as *Hausē* (Αὐσή: note the more accurate rough breathing). Presumably, Philo drew this spelling from an onomasticon, although his etymology, as will be argued below, may come from Greek. It is also possible that the spelling comes from another Jewish source—perhaps an amulet or other popular medium with close relation to the Hebrew-speaking tradition. Alternatively, a proto-recensional spelling of the name could have been introduced to Philo's text by a scribe in Origen's scriptorium in Caesarea. Philo's preference for this spelling may be in part because the names Ὡσηέ and Ἰησοῦς share a sequence of three similar letters—thus making the idea of a "change of lettering" (μεταχαρακτηρισμός) a more explicable to a Greek audience. The three central characters are reversed, from ωση → ησο. Something similar is achieved, however, in the reversal from αυση → ησου as well; either spelling provides a literal, vocalic icon of the symbolic inversion of character.

a certain quality into a stable disposition. For the philosophical difference between a qualitative appellation and a stable disposition, see the detailed comment on § 122.

Hoshea is interpreted as "this person is of a certain sort." No account of the etymology "a person of a certain sort" (ποιός οὗτος) is entirely convincing. As a result, some scholars (e.g., Colson, PLCL 5:204, n. 1; followed by Arnaldez 1964, 86, n. 3) have resorted to emending the text. I present here several Hebrew and Greek analyses of the name, followed by Colson's proposal.

(a) After Siegfried's suggestion (1863, 21–22), the etymologist may have understood the Greek *Ōsēe* (Ὡσηέ) to transliterate a different Hebrew string of consonants—not *Hôšēʿa* (הושע) but *ʾay zeh* (אי זה), "where is this one." Grabbe (1988, 222) notes that LXX Esther 7:5 renders this same Hebrew question in Greek as "which sort is this man?" (ποῖος οὗτος;). On this interpretation, Philo read the interrogative "which sort" (ποῖος) incorrectly as an indefinite "of a certain sort" (ποιός). Although "ingenious," as Grabbe opines, this solution does not explain why Philo's tradition works from the Greek spelling to the Hebrew word, rather than beginning with the Hebrew word, according to the usual pattern.

(b) Grabbe (1988, 222) suggests an alternative Hebrew etymology: *Hôšēʿa* (הושע), as resolved into the words (1) "he" (*hûʾ*, הוא) and (2) the Hebrew relative pronoun (*š-*, -ש), giving the composite meaning "he who." This solution has the appeal of working in the usual manner from a Hebrew name to Hebrew etymology to Greek translation of the etymology. The problem occurs at stage three, as "he who" is not obviously rendered with "of a certain sort" (ποιός) or "which sort" (ποῖος).

(c) A third solution, apart from emending the text, which has not to my knowledge been suggested before, is that Philo or his tradition may be working *directly* from the Greek name *Ōsēe* (Ὡσηέ), without thinking of the Hebrew at all. This would explain his adoption of this rather odd spelling, which departs from the LXX. Philo might have resolved the name *Ōsēe* (Ὡσηέ) into two parts: (1) "thus" (ὡς) and (2) "was" (ἦν or ἦεν, as frequently in Homer), meaning "in this way he was." To rewrite a phrase of Siegfried, "*Griechisch* dachte sich Philo Ὡσηέ etwa = ὡς ἦεν" ("Philo was thinking in Greek"; cf. Siegfried 1863, 21–22, "Hebräisch dachte sich Philo Ὡσηέ etwa = אִיָּה," who suggests that Philo "was thinking in Hebrew.") Philo could then have paraphrased this all too transparent Greek interpretation of the name as "this person is of a certain sort" (ποιός οὗτος). In support of this suggestion, it is worth noting that Philo does at times offer non-Hebrew etymologies in his commentaries, such as the etymology of Moses from the Egyptian *mou* in *Mos.* 1.17 and, more proximately, the interpretation of "sheep" (πρόβατα) as "advances" (προβάσεις) in § 111.

(d) Colson (PLCL, 5:204, n. 1; 5:590), unhappy with the solution of (a) Siegfried and relying on the patristic tradition of linking the name Hoshea to the verb for "salvation" (יָשַׁע), suggests that the PCW text be amended to read "Hoshea ... is interpreted 'this sort of person ⟨is saved⟩'" ('Ωσηέ ... ἑρμηνεύεται ⟨σώζεται⟩ ποιὸς οὗτος). On this reading, the distinction between Hoshea, etymologized as the passive finite verb "he is saved" (σώζεται = Hophʻal, הוּשַׁע), and Joshua, etymologized as the noun "salvation" (σωτηρία), indicates the distinction between the particular and the generic, which Philo then distills into the difference between "quality" (τὸ ποιόν or ποιότης) and the "state" (ἕξις).

Colson's conjectural solution makes sense of the *crux* and is satisfying, especially insofar as it echoes the kind of grammatical analysis used earlier by Philo in §§ 78–79. There, Philo distinguishes between the symbolic meanings of Sarai (*Sara*), "my ruler" (ἀρχή μου), as particular virtue, and Sarah (*Sarra*), "ruling woman" (ἄρχουσα), as generic virtue. The cases are not identical, however. For whereas in § 78, the verbal form "ruling woman" (ἄρχουσα) symbolizes the generic, stable virtue, and the noun a particular instance of it, in § 121, the conjectured verb "is saved" (σώζεται) would indicate the individualized salvation, while the noun would indicate its firm possession as a state. Colson's emendation is too conjectural to gain wide acceptance without further textual evidence.

Joshua means "salvation of the Lord." Philo's etymology of *Yəhôšūʻa* (יהושע) follows the more typical pattern: it is a divided by the etymologist into two parts: (1) "by the LORD" and (2) "saved" or "salvation." It is not entirely clear exactly which letters belong to which part of the etymology. It could be resolved either (a) *y-* (י) + *Hôšēʻa* (הושע) or (b) *yâ* (יה) + *yēšaʻ* (יֶשַׁע), both of which give the required sense, "salvation of the Lord" (σωτηρία κυρίου). Option (a) pays attention to the addition of the single letter *yod*, taking the proper name Hoshea as a noun and the *yod* as an abbreviation of the Tetragrammaton. Option (b), preferred by Grabbe (1988, 168), provides the exact Hebrew equivalent *yēšaʻ* (יֶשַׁע) of the Greek "salvation" (σωτηρία) and the fuller form of the divine name *yâ* (יה).

the name of the best stable disposition. Philo's understanding of the noun "salvation," as indicating a "stable disposition" in the soul, may result from several considerations. First, if Hoshea is interpreted as "is saved" (σώζεται) per Colson's emendation, then Philo would be cashing in on the reifying function of the noun vs. the verb. "Salvation" symbolizes stability over and against "is saved," a moveable, impermanent predicate. A second way to derive this interpretation is derived from Aristotle's *Categories*. If Hoshea is etymologized as "a certain kind" (ποιός), according to the manuscript tradition, then his name would symbolize the "quality" (of being saved), in contrast with Joshua, whose name would symbolize the "essence" of salvation. A third interpretation, which applies regardless of what one does with Hoshea, trades on rereading the name "Lord" (κύριος) in Joshua's etymology to mean "proper." With this inexact gloss (cf. §§ 11–13), Philo finds the meaning "salvation, properly speaking" and in the generic sense, as opposed to the incidental salvation of this or that person.

(2) § 122. *thus music exceeds the musician ... every skill exceeds every practitioner.* Philo offers two proofs of his thesis, that the change from Hoshea to Joshua represents an improvement (i.e., that a stable disposition is better than a predicate of the same quality). His first argument is a Platonic one: everyone would agree that the generic craft, which is ideal, exceeds the individual craftsman, who practices his skill imperfectly on material objects. For the Platonic basis of this argument and further examples of Philonic meditation on the "skills" (τεχναί), see the detailed comment on § 80a above.

eternality and power and unfailing excellence. Philo specifies three respects in which a skill exceeds its practitioner. First, a skill is eternal, whereas its predication perishes with the practitioner; second, a skill is "active," empowering many individual practitioners, whereas the individual musician or doctor is passively empowered by his art; third, a skill is perfect, whereas a practitioner at best strives toward completion.

moreover, a stable disposition is infinite, actively self-fulfilling, and complete. In a dense but important note, Arnaldez (1964, 86–87, n. 4) sets out the principal problems of this passage:

> ⟨Philo's⟩ sense is clear, but the use of ἕξις ("stable disposition") is difficult. The term has multiple meanings: (1) the Stoic ⟨meaning⟩ in the progression *hexis, physis, psyche*; (2) the Aristotelian ⟨meaning⟩ in the opposition *hexis-energeia*, which leads to the meaning of *habitus*. Is ⟨Philo⟩ here speaking of the *habitus* of the skill (Fr. "science") in opposition to the ⟨mere⟩ exercise of the skill? But then the *habitus* would disappear with the individual, as the ποιότης with the ποιός. Does one need to understand *hexis* here in its relation to ἠρεμία ("rest")? This would be the reality from which one draws quality (Fr. "qualification"), but which remains *in rest* in itself, outside of the use, which the one that it qualifies makes of it. If the translation "state" (*habitus*) does not satisfy, since it is a question of a music and a science in itself, one can say in French that this *hexis* ⟨means⟩ those "habits" that permit one to name musicians or sages. Therefore, ἕξις ("a stable disposition") corresponds to a divine κλῆρος ("lot" / "inheritance").

Philo is trying to distinguish between the stable possession of a skill or "quality" (ἕξις) and its temporary manifestation in "the subject/so-and-so" (ὁ ποιός). The stable disposition is permanent, whereas the appellation (e.g., "musical") is true only so long as the musician's ears do not go deaf. Colson (PLCL 5:205, n. a) similarly observes that "ποιός (a person of a particular kind) ... may be used in antithesis of ποιότης .... cf. *Theaet.* 182a. In this case the ποιός is the concrete of the abstract ποιότης. Philo has used it in exactly the same way in *Leg.* 1.67 and also in *Leg.* 2.18."

As Arnaldez suggests, Philo's substitution of "stable disposition" (ἕξις) for "quality" (ποιότης) may give the passage an Aristotelian tone; however, the Alexandrian's usage of the term differs from that of the Stagirite in its most technical sense. Philo speaks of a "stable disposition" (ἕξις) as "self-fulfilling" (ἐνεργοῦν), that is, as an "activity" (ἐνέργεια). This conflicts with a famous passage in Aristotle's *Nicomachean Ethics*, in which a "stable disposition" (ἕξις) is defined precisely as the kind of activity that does *not* contain its own end in itself, in contrast to an "activity" (ἐνέργεια), which does (Aristotle, *Eth. nic.* 1098b–1099a). Philo has thus used "stable disposition" (ἕξις) in a less technical sense (see Aristotle, *Met.* 5.1022b), to indicate the unflagging activity of a virtue in an individual, linked in a Platonizing fashion to a generic universal.

§ 123a. *the coinage.* Philo refers to the human soul as a "stamped coin" (νόμισμα). The metaphor implies its ability to be minted, for better or worse, according to the type which both shapes and empowers it through its image—the Logos or one of his helpers (§ 31). "Joshua" is a symbol of the soul which has been stamped aright and acquired a stable disposition of salvation, rather than the Hoshea soul, of whom the appellative "saved" remained extrinsic and capable of being effaced or otherwise rendered non-efficacious.

has been reminted into a better form. The verb "remint" (μεταχαράττω) also carries the significance of "change alphabetical characters" and is thus a rough synonym of "change one's name" (μετονομάζω [§ 121]). It is used only three times in the present treatise—once in the case of the "remodeled" Abraham (§ 71) and twice in the discussion of Joshua (§§ 121, 123). Philo thus uses the verb to describe the first and last names changed in chapter five (Caleb and Moses do not have their names changed), creating a ring composition.

Parallel Exegesis

§ 121. *Num 13:16b ("Hoshea ... Joshua").* Philo treats Hoshea's change of name to Joshua only here in his extant corpus.

Joshua means "salvation of the Lord." The only other place in the Allegorical Commentary where Joshua is explicitly mentioned is *Ebr.* 96–98. There, Philo identifies him as the voice of "experience," which alerts the mind (Moses) to the unruly carousing of the body. There is not a connection with the etymology "salvation." Other references to Joshua in the Exposition of the Law remain at the level of literal paraphrase.

§ 123a. *the coinage*. Arnaldez (1964, 88, n. 1) points to Philo's use of the same image at *Leg.* 3.95.

Nachleben

§ 121. *Num 13:16b ("Hoshea ... Joshua")*. Several references to Hoshea's change of name to Joshua are to be found in Justin Martyr. In the first two instances in his *Dialogus cum Tryphone* (75.2; 106.3 [D]), no attempt to allegorize the change is made, nor is any etymology given. Something more Philonic appears in *Dial.* 113.1–3 [B/C], where Joshua's change of name is compared to Abraham's and Sarah's. Justin's framing of the argument is exceptionally interesting, and might even suggest that Trypho was among the Jewish thinkers who wondered about patriarchal name change (perhaps not unlike Philo's quarrelsome exegetes):

> You speculate theologically (θεολογεῖς) about why one alpha (ἓν ἄλφα) was added to the first in the name Abraham, and you likewise boast (ὁμοίως κομπολογεῖς) and answer as to why one rho (ἓν ῥῶ) is added to the name Sarah. But you do not seek with equal interest (οὐ ζητεῖς ὁμοίως) why the name of Hoshea, the son of Nun, given to him by his father, has been changed in its entirety (ὅλον μετωνόμασται) to Joshua.

Philonic echoes abound. The etymology "salvation," however, which was known in the Gospel of Matthew, does not surface in Justin's interpretation. Furthermore, if Justin had read *De mutatione nominum*, he has clearly forgotten that at least one Greek-speaking Jew did in fact wrestle with Hoshea's change of name—as well as the difference between the changing of letters and entire names. (For Justin's potential knowledge of Philo, see Runia 1993, 97–105.) Origen (*Sel. Num.* 12.576.36–40 [C]) offers a comment on this verse, but like Justin also connects Joshua to his leading Israel into the land, and the gaining of an inheritance—not to the essence of salvation.

Eusebius links the name of Jesus with the title "Savior" (σωτήρ) three times in the *Eclogae prophetae* (35.24; 36:10, 15 [C/D]), the third time using the Matthean (Matt 1:21) version of the etymology: "⟨Moses⟩ named his own successor 'Joshua,' through whom also he himself preserved (ἔσωζε) a type of our Savior, Jesus (τοῦ Σωτῆρος ἡμῶν Ἰησοῦ)." Of special interest is a passage in *Dem. ev.* 4.17.1, 3 [B], where Eusebius writes:

Again, Moses changed the name (μετωνόμασεν) of his successor, making use of another name (ἑτέρᾳ χρώμενος προσωνυμίᾳ), to Joshua. For it is written, "These are the names of the men, whom Moses sent to spy out the land, and Moses named (ἐπωνόμασεν) Hoshea (Gr. *Nausē* [sic]) son of Nun 'Joshua' and sent them" (Num 12:16) .... When he had recognized by divine wisdom and knowledge innumerable other ⟨truths⟩ concerning the power and nature of names, which were more divine than human; and since no one of those authors from before him had ever used the name Joshua, ⟨Moses⟩, having first been guided by the divine Spirit to determine the one who would be his successor in ruling the people (who had earlier made use of another name [ἑτέρῳ πρότερον ὀνόματι κεχρημένον]), changed his title and called him Joshua (μεταβαλὼν Ἰησοῦν καλεῖ), thinking that the epithet (προσηγορία) that he had been called from birth by his forebears was not sufficient. For those who bore him referred to him (ἐφώνουν) as Hoshea; but the prophet of God, having changed out his birth name (τὸ ἐκ γενετῆς ἀμείψας ὄνομα), calls (καλεῖ) the man Joshua according to the divine will (κατὰ τὸ θεῖον νεῦμα).

In this passage, which likely owes a debt to *De mutatione nominum*, Eusebius recounts Moses's philosophical intention in devising such name changes.

Joshua means "salvation of the Lord." Philo's etymology of "Joshua" (Ἰησοῦς) as "salvation" is known in Christian literature as early as the Gospel of Matthew (Matt 1:21; cf. Luke 1:69; Acts 4:12; Jude 5), where the angel of the Lord bids Joseph name Mary's child "Joshua" (Ἰησοῦς), "for he will save (σώσει) his people form their sins." This is not proof of Philonic influence on the first Gospel, but evidence of a common etymological tradition. In addition to Eusebius of Caesarea (*Ecl. proph.* 35.24; 36.10, 15 [D]), Cyril of Jerusalem (*Cat. Ill.* 10.11 [D]) also knows the etymology of Joshua, but contrasts it not primarily with his earlier name "Hoshea," but with the title "Christ": Jesus Christ is called by a "double name" (διώνυμος): Jesus, "because he saves" (διὰ τὸ σώζειν); Christ, "because he serves as a priest" (διὰ τὸ ἱερατεύειν). See Grabbe 1988, 168.

i   *Caleb (§§ 123B–124)*
       Analysis and General Comments
Having treated (h.) Hoshea-Joshua—the salvation of the soul—in §§ 121–123a, Philo now turns to the second member of his patriarchal triad from Exodus-Numbers: Caleb, the symbol of the penitent soul, which receives another nature. (For the "triad" language in the Allegorical Commentary, see the Analysis and General Comments to Hoshea–Joshua above.) Caleb, like Isaac, does not have his name changed. According to Num 14:24, however, Caleb receives

"another spirit." Philo finds in this detail, as well as in the etymology of his name ("all heart"), a symbol of the perfected soul, which gives reason to include him as the second member of his third patriarchal triad as a parallel to Isaac. In speaking of the soul at its eschatological zenith, Philo's allegory suddenly and without much exegetical fanfare reaches its summit.

This section can be divided into two parts:
(1) Philo first summarizes the significance of Caleb's "change of spirit," citing a secondary biblical lemma (Num 14:24) as evidence of this psychic transformation (§ 123b).
(2) Philo supports this interpretation of the secondary lemma by offering an etymological and allegorical analysis of Caleb's name. Caleb represents the soul that has become "all heart," mind, or spirit—the soul at the pinnacle of perfection, by way of repentance and the inner lustrations of wisdom (§ 124).

Detailed Comments

(1) § 123b. *Caleb, for his part, is entirely changed.* Philo's opening description of the Caleb soul summarizes his soteriology. The human person is in the process of "being changed" (ἀλλάττεται), such that the "heart" (καρδία) or "spirit" (πνεῦμα) or "the governing part" (τὸ ἡγεμονικόν) becomes the dominant portion of the soul.

Moses says, there came to be another spirit in him. Philo cites Num 14:24 as a secondary lemma. Besides replacing the aorist passive, "there became" (ἐγενήθη), with the more common aorist middle, "there came to be" (ἐγένετο), Philo's text follows the Septuagint. Given the connection of Joshua and Caleb with the themes of entering the promised land and perfection, these two figures amplify Philo's allegory of Abraham's achievement of the same, with which the treatise is concerned at the primary level.

the governing part of the soul changes into the pinnacle of perfection. Philo uses one of the typical Stoic titles (Reydams-Schils 2008, 183) for the rational soul—the "the governing part" (τὸ ἡγεμονικόν)—which often specifies the "mind" (νοῦς) or the "spirit" (πνεῦμα). He thus offers a portrait of the soul that reaches the "highest perfection" (ἄκρα τελειότης). This phrase is rare within the *corpus Philonicum*, used only three times. In *Fug.* 172, Philo uses it to describe the perfection, to which only God can lead the human soul. In *Mos.* 2.58, it describes the perfection *not* achieved by Lot. Only the Caleb soul, in the present treatise, is said explicitly to reach this height by way of transformation.

(2) § 124. *Caleb, etymologically, means "all heart."* The etymologist analyzes the Hebrew name "Caleb" (כלב) into two parts: (1) "all" (*kōl* [כל]); and (2) "heart" (*lēb* [לב]).

this is a symbol that the soul. Philo allegorically identifies the "heart" (καρδία) with the "soul" (ψυχή)—a subtle but important change of referent, which depends in part on the word "spirit" (πνεῦμα) in Philo's secondary biblical lemma. Stoics typically located the center of thought and agency in the heart (Reydams-Schils 2008, 184), Platonists, in the head. In Caleb's case, the heart signifies the soul in its entirety—the "ruling part" (νοῦς / πνεῦμα / τὸ ἡγεμονικόν) and its (seven) irrational or quasi-rational extensions working in complete unity.

half-way between two poles and vacillating back and forth. Cf. the earlier description of Jacob soul of §§ 84–85.

it has entirely and completely gone over. Philo's etymology, "all heart" (πᾶσα καρδία), is shorthand for psychic perfection. Becoming "all heart" is understood as synonymous with the scriptural notion of receiving "another spirit" (πνεῦμα ἕτερον) in Num 14:24. This formulation recalls to Philo the protological text, Gen 2:7, which presents the human soul at its most rational, prior to the coming of sense-perception (see *Leg.* 1.31–42; 2.24–25). Caleb's return to this state—becoming all heart or all spirit—signifies "the soul that has been completely transformed" (ὅλην δι' ὅλου τὴν ψυχὴν μεταβεβλῆσθαι) back to its protological condition. Whether this implies the "eviction" of the irrational capacities of the soul (hence, the soul's becoming "all mind/spirit" in the most literal sense—see Origen in the *Nachleben*) or the purification of these irrational faculties through the "eviction" of their objects is not entirely clear. The effect in either case would be the same, ethically speaking.

has evicted. To illustrate the total transformation of the Caleb soul, Philo draws on three different registers. The first involves the spatial metaphor of the soul as a house. The thoroughly transformed Caleb soul has "evicted" (ἐξοικίζειν) all emotions, opinions, and other sub-rational tenants. The process is the opposite of "appropriation" or "accommodation" (οἰκείωσις) of such extrinsic concerns and influences to the rational soul, as seen in the "drawing" of Raguel's daughters.

through words of repentance. The second register used to depict the soul's perfection is that of "repentance" (μετάνοια). Philo's thought is "conversionist" throughout, and it is critical that here he insists on "repentance" as a necessary part of the full, eschatological transformation of the soul into perfect spirit.

purged of all that stained it ... lustrations and purifications. The third register of transformation that Philo employs is that of ritual purity. This is common throughout the Allegorical Commentary—perhaps, on account of Philo's alleged priestly lineage, if there is any truth to that report. More importantly, Philo views the individual soul as a temple, such that its moral improvement through wisdom (as here) can be described with the language of priestly cleansing. See further Nikiprowetzsky 1967, 104; Cover 2024b.

Parallel Exegesis
§124. *Num 14:24 ("there came to be another spirit in him")*. Philo only adduces this lemma or mentions Caleb here in his entire corpus.

Caleb, etymologically, means "all heart." Philo uses this etymology uniquely here in his corpus (Grabbe 1988, 215–216).

Nachleben
§123b. *Caleb, for his part, is entirely changed.* Philo's individualist, realized eschatology in the description of the Caleb soul being "changed" (ἀλλάττεται) in the allegorical present may be fruitfully contrasted with Paul's corporate, future eschatology in 1Cor 15:51: "we will *all* be transformed" (πάντες δὲ ἀλλαγησόμεθα).

§124. *Caleb, etymologically, means "all heart."* Something similar to this Philonic interpretation may be found in Origen (*Hom. Jes. nav.* 407 [A/B]), who writes:

> ⟨Caleb⟩ is interpreted as "heart" (ὡς καρδία). This is the person who considers all things (πάντα) in his thoughts, who ⟨putting⟩ aside all the members (πάντα τὰ μέλη), which he has renounced, is deliberating as heart (ὡς καρδία) and is wholly resolved into the governing part ⟨of his soul⟩ (ὅλος ἀναστοιχειωθεὶς εἰς ἡγεμονικόν).

Although Origen does not give the etymology "all heart," the repetition of the words "all" (πάντα) and "whole" (ὅλος) suggest that he has the Philonic etymology in mind. The reference to Caleb's resolution into the "governing part" (ἡγεμονικόν [cf. *Mut.* 123]) further suggests a link between the text of Origen and *De mutatione nominum*. See also Origen, *Hom. Ios.* 18.3 [C] (Van den Hoek 2000, 85).

j   *The Many Names of Moses (§§125–129)*
      Analysis and General Comments

Having introduced Moses already in the Raguel section as a symbol of the "virtue-loving manner" (τρόπος ... φιλάρετος [§113]) or a virtuous "manner of drawing" (τρόπος ⟨ἀντλήσεως⟩ [cf. §111]) and brought the allegorical soul-narrative to its symbolic fulfilment in the total transformation of the Caleb (§§123–124), Philo's final subsection of chapter five on the many names of the "archprophet" (§103) represents something of a denouement. The section is added not to continue the exposition of the change of names, but to praise the "namewright" (ὀνοματούργος) as the image of perfection ("God's human being") and to give him the final word. For an important recent study of Moses in the Exposition of the Law, see Sterling 2022a.

This section divides into four parts:

(1) Philo notes the fittingness that Moses, the Jewish archprophet, should be "many-named" (πολυώνυμος). He proceeds to list three titles or epithets, and their symbolic meanings. He is called (a) "Moses," when he is acting as a prophet; he is called (b) "God's human being," when he is blessing the people in prayer; and he is called (c) "god of Pharaoh, the king of the land," when he is recompensing the wicked for their impieties. In these three titles, one sees an explication of Moses's role as prophet and his work as agent of the Logos, in its beneficent ("blessing") and punitive ("cursing") powers (§ 125).

(2) Philo first explains the meaning of the name (a) "Moses." This name, etymologically, means "receiving" or "touching"—a symbol of his ability as lawgiver and prophet to have divine revelation close to hand (§ 126).

(3) Second, Philo offers a clarification of the title (b) "God's human being." Blessings cannot efficaciously be offered by anyone, but remain the special work of those whose attentions are focused on God, rather than generated natures (§§ 127–128a).

(4) Third, Philo explains the meaning of Moses's title (c) "god of Pharaoh, the king of the land." Philo endorses the Stoic commonplace that every wise man is a king (or free), and every fool, a slave. If the fool is to be corrected, however, it is better that this happen by the sage, who will upbraid out of "love of humanity" (φιλανθρωπία) rather than vindictiveness. To make this kind reproof, for the sake of correction, is truly god-like (§ 128b).

Detailed Comments

(1) § 125. *the archprophet.* Philo only uses this title for Moses three times—twice in the present treatise (both in chapter five) and once in *Somn.* 2.189. See the detailed comment on § 103.

a man of many names. Philo applies to Moses the epithet "of many names" (πολυώνυμος), which is often applied to divinities. In Greek poetry, it is used as an epithet of Pluto (Homer, *Hymn.* 2.18, 32), Apollo (Homer, *Hymn.* 3.82), Nikē (Bacchylides, *Epigr.* 6.313.1), Dionysus (Sophocles, *Ant.* 1115), Zeus (Cleanthes, *Hymn.* 1), and Isis (*SEG* 8.548, 26), denoting fame, wide-repute, and the multiplication of local cult titles (Hornblower 2014). In Moses's case, it represents the archprophet's symbolic polyvalence.

Moses. Philo's first title for the archprophet, "Moses," does not refer to a scriptural lemma, but rather to the general way that he is referred to throughout the

Pentateuch. Philo is thinking especially of Moses's role of mediating the divine oracles to Israel.

God's human being. Philo's second title for the archprophet, "God's human being," is drawn from Deut 33:1—an implicit secondary lemma and the only place in the Pentateuch where this description is used of Moses. In this passage, Moses is preparing to bless the twelve tribes of Israel. Philo has shortened the biblical title, "human being of *the* God" (ἄνθρωπος τοῦ θεοῦ) to the anarthrous "God's human being" (ἄνθρωπος θεοῦ). This title recapitulates Moses's interpretation as the "human being" (i.e., the intelligible world) by Raguel's daughters in § 118 earlier in chapter five, although the allegorical significances of the word "human being" are not identical between the passages. In chapter one (§§ 24–26), Philo applies the title "God's human being" to Abraham, his principal protagonist. By attributing the same title to Moses, Philo forges a link between the first and final characters of chapter five. Arnaldez (1964 *passim*) sees the development of the figure of "God's human being" as one of Philo's most profound contributions in the treatise.

god of Pharaoh, the king of the land. Philo's third title for the archprophet likewise refers to an implicit secondary lemma, Exod 7:1. Philo paraphrases God's naming of Moses in the scriptural narrative, "Behold, I give you as a god to Pharaoh" (ἰδοὺ δέδωκά σε θεὸν Φαραώ) with the more expansive rendition, "... as a God of the ruler of the land, Pharaoh," (τοῦ βασιλεύοντος τῆς χώρας Φαραὼ θεός), foreshadowing his symbolic interpretation. Philo has already given a slightly different explication of this title from Exod 7:1, "god of Pharaoh," in § 19 (see also *Leg.* 1.40; *Sacr.* 9; *Det.* 161; *Migr.* 84), relating Moses to "mind" (νοῦς) and Pharaoh to "body" (σῶμα). The alternative interpretation that he offers here demonstrates that he is thinking more of the literal Moses, the Jewish lawgiver, than of his symbolic significance within the allegory of the soul. For the title "king of the land," see the detailed comment on § 89.

(2) § 126. *why is this?* Philo uses a favorite scholastic question to introduce a further allegorical clarification of his summary statement about the three names of Moses. For other uses of the question "why is this?" (διὰ τί;), see §§ 46, 81, 83, 88, 94, 116.

to transcribe laws for the benefit of those who will receive them. Despite Philo's conception of Moses as an author of allegories in his own right, the archprophet's work is here construed as "transcription" (μεταγράφειν). This accords with the first mode of Mosaic authorship later sketched by Philo in *Mos.* 2.188. There, Philo states that the divine utterances of Mosaic Scripture can be divided into three kinds: (1) those spoken by God in his own person; (2) those developed by Moses, in question and answer with God; and (3) those spoken by Moses in his own person.

one who can touch and always have at hand the divine things. Philo's tactile metaphor (see the etymology of Moses below) calls to mind both the receiving of manuscripts (and potentially, the concepts of heavenly scrolls and a noetic scriptorium—cf. Jubilees, "Prologue," 1:1–29), as well as the philosophical metaphor of "groping" for transcendent truths (see *Nachleben*).

one who has been called up by the oracle-speaking Lawgiver. The participle "called" (ἀνακεκλημένου) alludes to Exod 24:1 and Moses's being called to "come up to the Lord" (ἀνάβηθι πρὸς κύριον). It is noteworthy that Philo here refers to God as the "Lawgiver" (νομοθέτης). Frequently, he uses this as a title for Moses, speaking of him as a "lawgiver" alongside other human lawgivers (see the Parallel Exegesis). Philo's use of the title in §126 conforms to a second pattern in the Allegorical Commentary, in which the title "lawgiver" (νομοθέτης) refers to God's "legislative power" (ἡ νομοθετικὴ δύναμις [*Sacr.* 131]). This is the only use of the noun "lawgiver" in *De mutatione nominum*. Philo has Plato's *Cratylus* in mind—particularly, the notion that the giving of names is a skill belonging to the "lawgiver" (*Crat.* 389a)—and wants to assure his readers that the names of Scripture depend not simply on the wisdom of Moses, but on the Word that empowers him.

a great gift. Hearkening back to the covenantal paraphrase in §§52–53 and 57–59, Philo now adds that the holy laws themselves are instruments of grace.

the interpretation and exposition of the holy laws. Moses's primary role is not as author, but as divinely inspired interpreter and promulgator of the laws of God. "Prophecy" (προφητεία) here is understood as "authoritative interpretation" (ἑρμηνεία) rather than prediction.

Moses interpreted means "receiving." Philo gives the etymological rationale of his foregoing argument. According to Grabbe (1988, 188–189), Philo's primary etymology of Moses, "receiving" (λῆμμα), depends on deriving the biblical name *Mōšeh* (משה) from the Hebrew noun *maśśā'* (מַשָּׂא) "lifting up" (> נשא) rather than following the biblical etymology in Exod 2:10, which derives it from the verb *māšâ* (> משה, "to draw"; see the detailed comment at §113). Grabbe's suggestion seems possible enough (*maśśā'* is the most frequent *Vorlage* of the noun "receiving" [λῆμμα] in the Septuagint). Alternatively, it is possible that the etymologist is offering a different Greek translation of the Hebrew of Exod 2:5, "and she took it" (ותקחה). The principal verb of this statement, *lqḥ* (לקח), is often rendered with "take up" (ἀναλαμβάνειν [Gen 24:61; 45:18]) or "take" (λαμβάνειν [Gen 2:15, 21, *et passim*]) in the Septuagint. Whatever the source of the etymology, as Colson (PLCL 5:206, n. a) notes, in Philo's hands the name derives not from Moses being "received" by the daughter of Pharaoh, but from Moses's own being "called up" (cf. Exod 24:1) and "receiving" the Law on Sinai: "Moses is named after the gift which he has received." Compare the possible etymology of Moses as "drawing," hypothesized as lying behind the tradition in §§ 111–113, through which Moses is allegorized as a virtuous "manner of ⟨active⟩ drawing" (τρόπος ⟨ἀντλήσεως⟩) on objects of sensation and thought, for the health of the soul.

it is possible also that it means "touching." Grabbe (1988, 189) notes that "it is not entirely clearly whether ψηλάφημα ["touching"] is meant to be an etymology or not." Philo's appended phrase, "for the reasons just stated," might suggest that the word is a gloss on the principal etymology. Colson (PLCL 5:206, n. b), in support of this first option, comments: "Perhaps the fact that Moses 'handled' the laws shows that his name of 'receiving' must also be understood to include the kindred meaning of 'handling'." Alternatively, Grabbe (Ibid.) notes that the verb "to touch" (ψηλαφᾶν) often renders the Hebrew verb *māšaš* (משׁשׁ, "to grope or feel")—a root which is near enough to the name *Mōšeh* (משׁה) to make an etymological explanation probable. Colson's (Ibid.) note of the Egyptian etymology of Moses's name at *Mos.* 1.17 shows that multiple etymologies existed in Philo's repertoire.

(3) § 127. *to pray and to bless … any person who chances to be present.* Having interpreted the name "Moses," Philo turns to the archprophet's second title, "God's human being." Whereas frequently in the Allegorical Commentary, this title refers to the ethical perfection of the "mind" (νοῦς [*Gig.* 63; *Mut.* 24–25]), here Philo offers a more literal interpretation. To pronounce an efficacious blessing is not something God leaves up "the one who happens to be at hand" (ὁ τυχών [§ 91]), but to the human being who has forsaken human kinship and "cast his lot" (προσκεκληρωκώς) with God, the bestower of all blessings. As to the sense of this final idiom, Arnaldez (1964, 90, n. 1) comments succinctly: "God's human being is no longer related to the beings of this world; he comes to resemble God by κλῆρος ("lot" or "inheritance")."

§ 128a. *a blessing.* Philo uses an unusual word for "blessing": εὐλογιστία. This usually means "right reasoning" and Colson renders it such, but there is little contextual motive for Philo to have shifted from speaking about literal blessings to an allegorical discourse about right reason. Mangey would thus emend to the more usually word for "blessing" (εὐλογία), but it is preferable to let the *lectio difficilior* stand.

the promised reward. The reward likely refers to Deut 34:4, where God shows Moses the land (promised to Abraham). This will now be given through his mediation to Joshua, Caleb, and all of Israel. That Moses only sees the land with his eyes is not interpreted by Philo as a punishment, but as an indication of his noetic attainment of the promise, as he is resolved completely into "mind" (νοῦς [*Migr.* 44; *Mos.* 2.291]).

(4) §128b. ***this same man is even called god.*** Philo addresses Moses's third title, "god of Pharaoh." This gives a second sense in which he is "God's human being." Arnaldez (1964, 90, n. 3) comments on the linkage between the two titles: "The human being is God's human being insofar as he carries himself like God: divine adoption permits him to inherit, in place of creatures, the goods of the Creator—from whom he receives the storehouse in virtue. Cf. *Plant.* 67–68; Sir 27:37; 24:22–23; Wis 7:12."

he is wise and therefore ruler of every fool. Philo argues the Stoic thesis that the wise person is truly a king and ruler, while the fool (even if a king) is really a slave or subject, regardless of his apparent status in life. For this "Stoic paradox" elsewhere in Philo, see his philosophical treatise *Quod omnis probus liber sit*, as well as the further references in the Allegorical Commentary in the detailed comment on §152.

§129. ***imitating the merciful power of the Father, will apply punishments.*** Philo specifies an additional reason that the wise man is called "god": when given the opportunity to serve as an agent of God's punishment, he will do so in a manner that aims not at vengeance but the improvement of those punished—however heinous their crimes. In doing this, the sage represents God's power to make use of "punishments" (τιμωρίαι) for therapeutic ends and to "give benefits" (εὐεργετεῖν). Philo considers the distribution of benefits to be the proper work of God alone. The task is often executed by the wise human being, however, who shares the title "god" in an improper sense.

to show kindness is characteristic of a "god." Colson (PLCL 5:209, n. b) comments: "The thought is: Moses's 'godship' to Pharaoh was particularly shewn in his not punishing him summarily, but allowing him so many chances of repenting, and in interceding with God for him, e.g., Exod 9:29."

Parallel Exegesis

§125. ***a man of many names.*** Elsewhere in the Allegorical Commentary, Philo applies the epithet "of many names" to the heavenly Sophia (*Leg.* 1.43), to the true and perfect sage (*Ebr.* 92), to the Logos (*Conf.* 146), and to the divine powers (*Somn.* 2.254).

Exod 7:1 ("I will make you a god to Pharaoh"). See the Parallel Exegesis on §19.

Deut 33:1 ("God's human being"). See the Parallel Exegesis on §25.

§126. ***Lawgiver.*** Philo often speaks of Moses as the "lawgiver," alongside other human lawgivers, such as Solon (*Opif.* 1, 103). The first appearance of the title in the Allegorical Commentary (*Leg.* 2.14) follows this usage, and other passages relate the title "lawgiver" to Moses (*Leg.* 3.145; *Cher.* 53) as well. Philo's use of the title in *Mut.* 126 conforms to a second pattern in the Allegorical Commentary, in which the title "lawgiver" (νομοθέτης) refers to God's "legislative power" (ἡ νομοθετικὴ δύναμις): "for he himself is lawgiver (νομοθέτης) and fountain of laws (πηγὴ νόμων), from whom all other particular lawgivers (οἱ κατὰ μέρος νομοθέται) ⟨spring forth⟩" (*Sacr.* 131). Philo's "legislative power" (ἡ νομοθετικὴ δύναμις) represents a philosophical version of the angel of the presence in Jub. 1:27, who is told to "dictate" (trans. Vanderkam) world history and the laws to Moses. See further Sterling 2022a.

Moses interpreted means "receiving." Grabbe (1988, 188) finds the etymology of Moses as "receiving" (λῆμμα) only here in Philo's *œuvre*.

Nachleben

§ 125. *Exod 7:1 ("I will make you a god to Pharaoh")*. See the *Nachleben* on § 19.

Deut 33:1 ("God's human being"). For this title, see the *Nachleben* on § 25.

§ 126. *one who can touch and always have at hand the divine things*. For a parallel use of the philosophical metaphor of "groping" or "touching" divine realities, see Acts 17:27, where Paul speaks of the Athenians as "groping" (ψηλαφᾶν) after God and perhaps finding him.

Moses interpreted means "receiving." Grabbe (1988, 188) does not mention any other author who attests the Philonic etymology of Moses as "receiving" (λῆμμα). The etymology clearly existed before Philo and may be reflected in the final two iambs of Ezekiel, *frag.* 15.38, which read "Moses, taking / ⟨the staff⟩" (Μωσῆς, λαβών), though this formulation is scriptural. The only possible parallel I am able to find after Philo comes from the *Sortes Astrampsychi* (4.9 [D]), a third or fourth-century CE magical text, which reads in its ninth headings: "Moses, received from the water" (Μωυσῆς ληφθεὶς ἐξ ὕδατος), though there the etymology is passive rather than active.

127. *touching*. Philo's second etymology of Moses, "touching" (ψηλάφημα), finds an echo in the commentary of the fifth-century author Hesychius, who notes that "Moses is interpreted 'touching'" (Μωυσῆς γὰρ ἑρμηνεύεται ψηλάφημα) (*Comm. brev.* 76.21 [D]).

Part Three

[Chapter 6]
The Birth of Isaac (§§ 130–153)

Chapter six begins the third and longest part of *De mutatione nominum*—the one which is least directly connected with the title of the work. (So Kraus Reggiani 1994; cf. Arnaldez 1964, who divides the treatise into two parts [§§ 1–129; §§ 130–270]. In either case, § 130 marks the beginning of a major new unit.) Whereas part one (§§ 1–59) deals with the ineffability of God, who has no proper name and part two (§§ 60–129) presents Philo's study of the symbolic significances of scriptural name changes, the subject of part three (§§ 130–270) cannot be neatly summarized under a central heading. It continues the allegorical exposition of the perfection of the Abraham soul by exploring the symbolic significance of the births of Isaac and Ishmael. The continuity of the eight chapters in part three with the foregoing five is most clearly seen at the level of the commentary form: having interpreted Gen 17:1–5 and 15 in parts one and two, in part three Philo continues the sequential exegesis of Gen 17:16–22, treating roughly one verse per chapter (see Introduction 4. Exegetical Structure of the Treatise). Various thematic connections between part three and the preceding parts will be noted in the comments below. Philo's beginning with the birth of Isaac in chapter six, for example, resumes a principal theme already sounded in the overture to the treatise (§ 1), which up to this point has been only partly explored. The final chapter thirteen (§ 270), on God's departure from Abraham (Gen 17:22), likewise offers an intentional closure of the allegorical study of the patriarch begun in chapters one through five (esp. § 84).

The unit that I am calling "chapter six" is variously analyzed by other scholars into two (Schur), three (Cohn, Arnaldez), or four (Kraus Reggiani) chapters (see Introduction 3. Chapters of the Treatise). The decision to treat Philo's exposition of Gen 17:16 as a single chapter is made on several grounds. First, it accords with the principle that has been adopted throughout this commentary: to be guided, at the heuristic level, by Philo's lemmatic divisions in the *Quaestiones in Genesin*. §§ 130–153 cover the same lemma (Gen 17:16) as QG 3.54. Four additional pieces of internal evidence support this division. First, in § 130 (cf. § 177), Philo entitles the discourse that is to follow, "the birth of Isaac" (ἡ γένεσις Ἰσαάκ). This must refer, at minimum, to §§ 130–147, but the fact that §§ 151–153 also discusses Sarah's offspring (albeit in the plural) would suggest that the entirety is comprised by this heading. Second, the allegories of Sarah ("her") as "virtue" in §§ 142 and 148 show an organic connection and development. Third, in § 154 Philo speaks cumulatively of "these promises" (αὗται αἱ ὑποσχέσεις). This refers to chapters 4–6, but surely the entirety of §§ 130–153 is included. (See the parallel use of this formula in § 54, where it again marks the beginning of a new chapter.) Fourth, Philo omits the phrase "I will bless her" in §§ 130–147, although it appears in the primary lemma (Gen 17:16a). Presumably, this is because he will treat the identical phrase in Gen 17:16b in § 148—evidence that he considered it part of the same pericope. Thus, while a chapter division at § 148 (and § 151) is possible, on the strength of the foregoing considerations, I have treated §§ 130–153 as a unit entitled, "The Birth of Isaac."

Nevertheless, the judgments of previous commentators rightly ascertain subdivisions within this chapter, marked by Philo's explicit citation of his primary lemma (and use of the *quaestio*). Contrary to previous commentators, I find not two, three, or four, but five subdivisions: Philo's exposition of (a) Gen 17:16aα, "I will give to you" (§§ 130–140); (b) Gen 17:16aβ, "from her" (§§ 141–144); (c) Gen 17:16aγ, "a child" (§§ 145–147); (d) Gen 17:16b, "I will bless her, and she shall be for the nations" (§§ 148–150); (e) Gen 17:16c, "and kings of the nations shall be from her" (§§ 151–153). Together, these five subsections constitute chapter six.

a   *"I Will Give to You" (§§ 130–140)*
    Analysis and General Comments

Philo begins this first section by quoting the opening words of the chapter's primary lemma (Gen 17:16a), and then suggesting that "each part warrants careful investigation" (ἐν μέρει δ' ἕκαστον ἀκριβωτέον). He divides it into three parts, which constitute the first three subunits of the chapter: (a) "I will give to you"; (b) "from her"; (c) "a child." Having provided this framework, Philo proceeds to offer an interpretation of the first part of the primary lemma: "I will give to you." The phrase is odd, Philo points out, because Moses says that God is the one who gives the child (Isaac / joy), even though Abraham is the husband of Sarah. A child "given" by a father other than the mother's proper husband is usually called a bastard or illegitimate. To explain this apparent problem in the text of Genesis, Philo suggests that God is, in fact, the true husband of every virtue-loving "thought" (διάνοια). Not only Sarah, but Leia and Tamar—who all according to the Allegorical Commentary symbolize virtues (see Philo, *Cher.* 41)—truly have God as their husband and give birth to children through him. The first section divides into five units:

(1)   Philo begins by formally transitioning to the third part of the treatise by naming the next "chapter" (κεφάλαιον), "The Birth of Isaac." He quotes

Gen 17:16a, suggesting that each part of that primary lemma warrants investigation. He begins with Gen 17:16aα, "I will give to you." This signifies that it is God who gives Isaac, whose name means "laughter," the symbol of joy (§ 130).

(2) Philo turns to the first word in his primary biblical lemma: "I will give" (δώσω). God, he argues, is the subject of the giving, which means that Isaac points not to the biological child, but is the symbolic name of the good emotion, joy—a meaning already given in § 1 and here derived from the etymology of Isaac as "laughter" (γέλως) (§ 131).

(3) Philo raises a problem for the text: usually when a woman gives birth to a son from someone other than her husband, the child is considered illegitimate. Since this cannot be true, Moses must be asserting that God is the true husband of Sarah, allegorically construed, and that Isaac is her legitimate son, given to the Abraham mind as a gift. To prove this, Philo adduces the first of three secondary lemmata, Gen 29:31, in which Moses says that "God opened the womb of Leah" (§§ 132–133).

(4) Philo then adduces a much longer, implicit secondary lemma to illustrate the same point. Although Tamar allegedly bore children by Judah (Gen 38:15–26), these turn out, on the allegorical plane, also to be the legitimate children of God. In the course of speaking of Tamar's veiling, Philo alludes to two tertiary lemmata drawn from the Exodus cycle (Exod 3:6 and Exod 34:33–35)—demonstrating the parallel between Tamar and Moses, who veil their faces in approaching God (§§ 134–136).

(5) Philo then returns to his central subject—God's being the proper husband of Sarah (Gen 17:16aα)—by way of a third contextualizing secondary lemma, in which Sarah attributes Isaac's parentage to God (Gen 21:6). Philo admits that this is a strange teaching, and that not all will be able to accept it. To prove that this is Moses's meaning, Philo quotes, as a tertiary biblical lemma, Hos 14:9–10, in which the prophet proclaims (1) that true virtue is from God; and that (2) this is a difficult teaching for many to understand (§§ 137–140).

Detailed Comments

(1) § 130. *having said what was necessary*. Philo uses the adverb "from necessity" (ἀποχρώντως) to specify not what was logically required, but the sum total of comments he had intended to make on a particular pericope. For other uses of this *terminus technicus*, see the Parallel Exegesis.

the change and transposition of names. Philo names the foregoing chapter (five): "concerning the change and transposition of names" (περὶ τῆς τῶν ὀνομάτων ἀλλαγῆς τε καὶ μεταθέσεως), of which the Latin title, *De mutatione nominum*, is an abbreviation. The expanded title is meant to signify the range of topics in the foregoing chapter—not merely name change proper (μετάθεσις), as in the cases of Abraham, Jacob, and Joshua, but also the "alternation" (ἀλλαγή) of names, as in the case of Joseph, Benjamin, and Raguel (see esp. §89: "Joseph alternates ... his name" [⟨Ἰωσὴφ⟩ ἀλλάττει ... τοὔνομα]).

the chapters which come next in course. Philo refers to exegetical/thematic subunits within his commentary as κεφάλαια or "chapters," naming two of them: (5) "On the Alternation and Change of Names" and (6) "The Birth of Isaac." "In course" renders the noun ἔφοδος, which points to a textual "course," "method," or "scientific investigation." Philo's comments suggest that the title, "The Birth of Isaac" (ἡ γένεσις Ἰσαάκ), applies to chapter six. The reappearance of the words "birth" (γένεσις) and "has come into being" (γεγένηται) in chapter seven (§157) allude to the earlier chapter (§130), thus providing an internal cross-reference. Chapter eight, which treats the faith of Abraham, likewise references the earlier chapter (§177), but then moves on to a new topic. By chapter nine (Abraham's prayer for Ishmael), Isaac is no longer the focus.

I will give to you ⟨from her⟩ a child. Philo cites the first part of the primary lemma, Gen 17:16a. A synopsis of the Septuagint and Philo's citation evinces two important differences.

Gen 17:16a	§130
I will bless her and I will give to you from her a child.	I will give to you ... a child

First, Philo omits the opening clause, "I will bless her" (εὐλογήσω δὲ αὐτήν). This is because this promise is repeated in Gen 17:16b, and Philo intends to treat it in §§148–150. Second, Philo has omitted the prepositional phrase "from her" (ἐξ αὐτῆς). Wendland supplies it and Colson accepts the addition, but this is not strictly necessary. Philo will cite this part of the lemma in §141. Note that even here in this first part of chapter six, the entire lemma under consideration is not explicitly cited. The discernment of chapter divisions in the Allegorical Commentary is always a critical task, and not as simple as mapping pericope citations, which are often incomplete.

(2) §131. *each part of this sentence warrants detailed investigation.* Philo articulates his exegetical method, which is implicitly active elsewhere in the Allegorical Commentary: to break up the primary lemma into subunits and

give each an independent, sequential exegesis. These are: (a) "I will give to you" (δώσω σοι); (b) "from her" (ἐξ αὐτῆς); and (c) "a child" (τέκνον).

the one who just now gives, properly speaking. Philo's description of God as "the one who properly gives" (ὁ ... κυρίως διδούς) turns the principal verb of the primary lemma, "I will give" (δώσω), into a substantive noun.

something that is entirely his own. Only the one who truly possesses something can properly be named a giver. Taking into account what Philo says about divine relations in § 28, we must suppose that he is thinking of God's beneficent power.

if this statement is not false. Philo uses logic to clarify the proper subject and object of the sentence. If the "I" of "I will give" (δώσω) is God, then the gift must not be the literal Isaac, but Isaac as a symbol of the good emotion, "joy."

the best of the good emotions, joy. Echoing and developing the interpretation of Isaac given in § 1. By cross-referencing the beginning of the treatise, Philo demonstrates the unity of its first, second, and third parts. The perfection of Abraham—signified by his change of name—has as its natural consequence God's gift of "joy"—signified by the birth of Isaac.

laughter within the mind, a son of God. For Philo's etymological interpretation of Isaac as "laughter" or "joy," see the detailed comment on § 1 above. This translation depends upon accepting Colson's repunctuation of PCW. See the Notes on the Text.

(3) §132. *strange ... that by another she should produce children.* Philo addresses the seemingly "strange" (lit. "out of place" [ἄτοπον]) situation unearthed by his exegesis. Whereas Abraham is the literal husband of Sarah, God is said to "give" Isaac. This would, by common reasoning, mean that Isaac was an illegitimate son by a different father. Philo's solution is to claim that allegorically, God is the true "husband" of the virtue-loving thought, and therefore "gives" Isaac to Abraham through Sarah legitimately.

Philo uses the word "out of place" (ἄτοπον) to describe this situation in a double sense. On the surface, it means something like "wicked" or "unnatural" (see Plato, *Apol.* 27e), describing Isaac's superficial illegitimacy. Simultaneously, Philo draws on a Platonic use of this adjective, which describes something that appears paradoxical or unexpected, but turns out to be correct. Arnaldez (1964, 93, n. 2) comments that "the theme of the divine spouse and divine seed/offspring is frequent in Philo. 'Spouse' is often associated with the 'Father' (*Mut.* 205; *Somn.* 2.273)."

Moses writes that God is the husband of the virtue-loving thought. Philo argues that God is the true husband of every virtue-loving way of "thought" (διάνοια). In this symbolic analysis, "thought" (διάνοια) is the allegorical identity of Leah at the secondary level of exegesis; and of Sarah and Abraham

TABLE 6.1   Pattern of Exegesis in *Mut.* 133

Gen 29	LXX Text	*Mut.*
29:31aα	The Lord, seeing that Leah is hated	§133a
29:31b	(but Rachel was barren)	§133b
29:31aβ	opened her womb.	§133c

together—i.e., the thought of the soul (Abraham) that weds virtue (Sarah)—at the primary level. It is critical that both Abraham and Sarah symbolize grammatically feminine nouns, "soul" (ψυχή) and "virtue" (ἀρετή), to which God can serve as allegorical "husband" (ἀνήρ), reason.

the Lord, seeing that Leah was hated, opened her womb. Philo does not immediately apply his allegorical solution—that God, as giver, is the husband of the virtue-loving soul—to Sarah, but first illustrates his point through the exegesis of two secondary lemmata. The first, Gen 29:31, is adduced through a thematic connection with the primary lemma. This verse tells the story of God's favor toward Leah, the hated sister of Rachel. Rachel was already interpreted in §§ 94–96 as the soul who gives "ill-birth" to Joseph and Benjamin—symbols of patterns of reasoning which depend upon devotion to the body, the senses, and to popular opinion. Leah, by contrast, in §§ 132–133, is the virtuous antitype of her sister. Philo's text and that of the Septuagint are basically identical, although he does not quote Gen 29:31b (which he will interpret in the subsequent section). Table 6.1 represents his pattern of exegesis.

§ 133. ***on virtue, which is hated ... and on the soul that loves virtue.*** In interpreting Gen 29:31aα, Philo foregoes the use the Hebrew etymology of Leah's name (see § 254), since it does not advance his allegoresis. Rather, Philo reads Leah in this passage as a three-fold symbol: she is a "virtue" (ἀρετή), like Sarah (§§ 78, 137), but also a virtue-loving "soul" (ψυχή), like Abraham, and particularly, a manner of "thought" (διάνοια [§ 132]). In eliding these roles, Philo foregoes his usual pattern of allegorizing the patriarch as the soul (so Isaac in § 82) and the matriarch as its virtue (§ 78; see *Cher.* 40–41). Philo's interpretation of Leah as the virtuous soul picks up on the earlier allegoresis of Rachel in chapter five as the "soul that suffers" (ἡ παθοῦσα ψυχή [§ 94]) or experiences the bad emotions. In allegorical schema, Jacob represents "mind" (νοῦς), and Rachel and Leah represent two alternative (vicious or virtuous) dispositions of the entire soul.

He renders barren ... the nature that does ⟨not⟩ love the good. An allegorical interpretation of Gen 29:31b, "but Rachel was barren" (Ραχὴλ δὲ ἦν στεῖρα).

This description of Rachel's infertility is in keeping with Philo's presentation of her "soul death" in § 96 (Gen 35:16–19), but reflects an earlier stage in the narrative of her decline at Gen 29:31b. For the addition of "⟨not⟩," see the Notes to the Text and Translation.

opens the spring of good childbearing. Interpreting Gen 29:31aβ, Philo construes Leah as the soul that gives birth well to a virtuous life. The "good education" (εὐπαιδία) and "good childbearing" (εὐτοκία) that she offers are the opposites of Rachel's "ill-childbearing" (δυστοκήσασα) in Gen 35:16, cited by Philo in § 96. This clear cross-reference between §§ 96 and 133 demonstrates Philo's aim of weaving chapters five and six into a thematically related treatise, despite the limitations of the running commentary genre. For the question of the thematic unity of Philo's allegorical treatises, see Nikiprowetzky 1977; Runia 1984; 1987.

(4) § 134. ***Tamar too became pregnant from divine seeds.*** Philo adduces another secondary lemma, Gen 38:15–26, to demonstrate that God is the true "father" of all goods born from the matriarchal soul-virtues. Unlike the Leah lemma, which was thematically connected and explicitly cited, Philo introduces this much longer and extensively interpreted text by way of allusion. The Tamar lemma is lexically connected to the primary biblical lemma through the key verb "to give" (διδόναι): see Gen 17:16a, "I will give" (δώσω); Gen 38:16, "you will give" (δώσεις); Gen 38:17: "⟨if⟩ you give" (δῷς); Gen 38:18, "I will give" (δώσω) and "he gave" (ἔδωκεν); and Gen 38:26, "I gave" (ἔδωκα). The plural "seeds" is curious. It would seem that, just as the tokens given to Tamar are multiple, so are the divine graces given to Tamar (she does, after all, bear twins). Because of the extensive and complex use of the scriptural text in Philo's exegesis, a synopsis of the two texts is provided below:

Gen 38:15, 18ab, 25–26	§§ 134–136
15 And Judah, seeing her (ἰδὼν αὐτήν), thought that she was a prostitute; for she covered her face (κατεκαλύψατο τὸ πρόσωπον) and he did not recognize her.	§ 134. Tamar too became pregnant from divine seeds. And although she did not see (οὐκ ἰδοῦσα) the One who sowed them—for at that time, it is said that her face was veiled (ἐγκαλύψασθαι τὸ πρόσωπον), just as Moses was, when he turned aside, intent on seeing God (τὸν θεὸν ἰδεῖν).

PART THREE

(cont.)

Gen 38:15, 18ab, 25–26	§§ 134–136

^{18ab} He said, "What is the pledge that I will give (δώσω) to you?" And she said, "Your ring and the necklace and the staff in your hand."
And he gave (ἔδωκεν) them to her.

She nevertheless inspected the symbols and tokens left behind.
And judging within herself that a mortal does not give these (οὐ δίδωσιν)

²⁵ Then being led there she sent word to her father-in-law, saying,
"By the human being, to whom these things belong, from him I have conceived"
(ἐκ τοῦ ἀνθρώπου, τίνος ταῦτά ἐστιν, ἐγὼ ἐν γαστρὶ ἔχω).

she cried out,

"To whomsoever these things belong, from him I have conceived"
(οὗτινος ταῦτ' ἐστίν, ἐξ ἐκείνου ἐν γαστρὶ ἔχω).

And she said, "Recognize, whose is the ring (τίνος ὁ δακτύλιος)

§ 135. "Whose is the ring (τίνος ὁ δακτύλιος), the proof, the seal of the universe, the archetypal form, by which all things, being without form and symbolized without quality, were impressed into matter?

and the necklace (καὶ ὁ ὁρμίσκος)

Whose also is the necklace (τίνος δὲ καὶ ⟨ὁ⟩ ὁρμίσκος), Fate, the necessary sequence and analogy, which possesses the uninterrupted chain of all things?

and this staff (καὶ ἡ ῥάβδος αὕτη)."

And whose is the staff (τίνος δὲ καὶ ἡ ῥάβδος) the mainstay, the unshaken, the unturned, establishment of mind, temperance, and instruction? ...."

²⁶ Then Judah recognized ⟨the tokens⟩ and said,

§ 136. Therefore Judah, the thankful manner, delighted by her steadfast and godly reasoning, speaks frankly saying,

(cont.)

Gen 38:15, 18ab, 25–26	§§ 134–136
"Tamar is more justified than I (δεδικαίωται Θαμὰρ ἢ ἐγώ), for I did not give her to my son Shelah (οὗ εἵνεκεν οὐκ ἔδωκα αὐτὴν Σηλὼμ τῷ υἱῷ μου)."	"She is justified (δεδικαίωται), for I gave her to no mortal" (ἧς ἕνεκα αἰτίας ἐγὼ οὐδενὶ θνητῷ αὐτὴν ἔδωκα), thinking that it would be impious to pollute divine things with profane ones.

although she did not see the One who sowed them. As the synopsis shows, Philo ingeniously shifts the focalizer of the passage from Judah (in the LXX) to Tamar. This allows him to make some paraphrastic alterations to the text, which lay the groundwork for the ensuing allegory. Whereas Moses's Judah mistakenly "sees" (ἰδών [Gen 38:15]) the one he thinks is a prostitute, Philo's Tamar soul/virtue "does not see" (οὐκ ἰδοῦσα) the one who impregnates her. Tamar's lack of vision paradoxically belies her true spiritual sight, for she will recognize that the giver of her tokens "does not give" (οὐ δίδωσιν) as a human being "gives" (ἔδωκεν [Gen 38:18]), and must therefore be divine. Philo's interpretive negation of the biblical text demonstrates how careful he will attend to it in illustrating Tamar's *via negativa*. The germ of an apophatic theology of divine darkness is present in this allegoresis.

for at that time, it is said that her face was veiled. Philo offers the first of several citations of the secondary biblical lemma, beginning with Gen 38:15. Philo's verb, "to be veiled" (ἐγκαλύψασθαι), paraphrases the similar Septuagintal verb, "was veiled" (κατεκαλύψατο), which signifies at the allegorical level an internal, psychic veiling. Inverting the dynamics of the biblical narrative, where Tamar's veiling deceives Judah about his mistress's identity, in Philo's rewriting, the veiled Tamar soul-virtue is herself initially uncertain about the identity of her partner in spiritual intercourse.

just as Moses was, when he turned aside, intent on seeing God. Inspired by the image of the Tamar soul-virtue in veiled spiritual congress with her divine husband, Philo adduces a tertiary lemma, Exod 3:6—Moses's sheltering his face from the image of God in the burning bush. A synopsis of Exod 3:6 and Philo's text shows a pattern of allusion and amplification:

Exod 3:6	§ 134
Moses turned aside (ἀπέστρεψεν) his face, for he was being reverent to look down before God (εὐλαβεῖτο γὰρ κατεμβλέψαι ἐνώπιον τοῦ θεοῦ).	As Moses When he turned aside (ἡνίκα ἀπεστράφη) intent on seeing God (εὐλαβούμενος τὸν θεὸν ἰδεῖν).

Philo has Exod 3:6 before his eyes and makes some key modifications. Chief among these is the omission of the direct object, "his face" (τὸ πρόσωπον αὐτοῦ); the transformation of the active verb "turned aside" (ἀπέστρεψεν) into a passive, "was turned aside" or "turned ⟨himself⟩ aside" (ἀπεστράφη); and especially the change from Moses's "looking down" (κατεμβλέψαι) before God in the biblical text to Moses's intent "to see God" (ἰδεῖν) in Philo's rewriting. One effect of these changes is to render the comparison between Tamar and Moses less evident, as the lexical connection between the passages is grounded in the shared noun phrase, "her face / his face" (τὸ πρόσωπον αὐτῆς / αὐτοῦ) in Gen 38:15 ("for she covered her face" [κατεκαλύψατο γὰρ τὸ πρόσωπον αὐτῆς]) and Exod 3:6 ("and Moses turned aside his face" [ἀπέστρεψεν δὲ Μωυσῆς τὸ πρόσωπον αὐτοῦ]). Philo nonetheless weaves together these portraits of the Moses soul on Horeb and the Tamar soul at the roadside as two images of the veiled soul approaching a divine lover with a mystical, visionary "unknowing."

Philo's transformation of the syntax of Exod 3:6—removing the word "face" and focusing on "seeing" rather than bending the eyes downward in reverence—suggests that he wishes to connect Tamar with Moses not only on this first ascent of Horeb (Moses is not "veiled" in Exod 3), but also in his later ascent of the same mountain in Exod 34:33–35. There, Moses is explicitly said to wear a "veil" (κάλυμμα) when descending from seeing God on the mountain. § 134 reads: "For at that time, it is written that '⟨Tamar's⟩ face was veiled' (ἐγκαλύψασθαι), just as Moses ⟨was⟩, when he was turned aside, intent on seeing God." This is an intriguing conflation of Exod 3 and Exod 34. In Exod 34, Moses's veil is removed when he faces God, but only worn when he speaks to the people. In this passage, Philo presents a "veiled" Moses speaking to God on Horeb. It is worthy of note that Philo is generally wary of adducing Exod 34—perhaps on account of its image of "unveiled vision"—preferring to focus on Exod 3 and 33, and their more modest portraits of Mosaic vision (Cover 2015).

she nevertheless inspected the symbols and tokens. Philo alludes to the ring, the necklace, and the staff given to Tamar by Judah as a pledge in Gen 38:18ab. In keeping with his shift of focalizer, it is Tamar rather than Judah who inspects these symbols, in the quest to discover the giver and father of the child to be born from her.

judging within herself that a mortal does not give these. The verb "does not give" (οὐ δίδωσιν) alludes to Gen 38:18 and the various other references to Judah's giving in Gen 31:15–26, while simultaneously negating them on interpretive grounds (it is God who gives). Rather than replicating the future tense of "I will give" (δώσω), which would create a direct verbal parallel with the primary lemma (Gen 17:16a), or the aorist "he gave" (ἔδωκεν, cf. Gen 31:18), Philo uses the present tense of the verb to indicate the timeless allegorical significance of the story.

"to whomsoever these things belong, from him I have conceived." Philo now quotes the secondary biblical lemma (Gen 38:25a) again—this time rewriting it as part of the Tamar soul's speech in character. In the biblical narrative, Tamar's assertion, "by the human being to whom these things belong, from him I have conceived" (ἐκ τοῦ ἀνθρώπου, τίνος ταῦτά ἐστιν, ἐγὼ ἐν γαστρὶ ἔχω), is posed to Judah, in order to prove that he is the human father of her child. In Philo's rewritten version, the Tamar soul asks the question of herself, replacing the specifier "human being" (τοῦ ἀνθρώπου) with the indefinite relative pronoun "whomever" (οὗτινος), in order to make space for the divine husband and parent. This omission of the word "human being" (ἄνθρωπος) is the result of Tamar's prior conclusion, that no "mortal" (θνητός) gives gifts such as this.

§ 135. *"the ring ... the necklace ... the staff."* Philo has the Tamar soul cite the three symbols or tokens in the scriptural order (Gen 38:18, 25b). In the interstices between each token, Philo interpolates a catalogue of allegorical glosses, which suggest that God is the father.

"the proof, the seal of the universe ... were impressed." Tamar understands the ring to be a symbol of the Logos—the singular form and seal, in whom all the ideal forms are collected and by whom the material cosmos is stamped.

"fate, the necessary sequence ... the uninterrupted chain of all things." Tamar interprets the necklace as "fate" (εἱμαρμένη). This term, which signifies etymologically the necessary "chain of events," appears as early as Heraclitus, one of the most influential pre-Socratic philosophers on Philo's thought. His suggestion that fate possesses an "uninterrupted chain" (εἱρμόν ... ἀδιάλυτον) evinces his knowledge of a Greek etymological analysis of the name of fate. So, Colson (PLCL 5:590) notes on his translation of εἱμαρμένη as "chain of destiny" that "though there is no real philological connection between εἱρμός ("chain") and εἱμαρμένη ("fate"), it seems to have been regularly assumed. See

SVF 2.915–921." Fate's possession by God, the giver, suggests that the chain symbolizes not the material determinism of the Stoics, but the divine providence of Middle Platonizing Judaism (see Philo, *De providentia* 1–2).

"the mainstay, the unshaken, the unturned." Tamar's interpretation of the rod of Judah can be divided into two groups of three. The first triad (all neuter singular substantives) understands the rod to symbolize divine permanence and ontological stability. See notes on §§ 28, 54, and 87 for similar epithets applied directly to God. Alesse (2008, 6) points out that the second term, "the unshaken" (τὸ ἀκράδαντον), was characteristic of "Stoic-Academic epistemological debate."

"establishment of mind, temperance, and instruction." Tamar's second symbolic triad interpreting the rod of Judah is comprised of feminine and masculine nouns representing goods of the human psyche, which flow from divine stability. These goods are firmness of mind, the virtue of temperance, and sound instruction.

"the scepter, the kingdom, whose are these?" In addition to the first six interpretations of the rod of Judah, Tamar adds two additional significances. These point to the traditional Jewish ascription of kingship to God.

"do they not belong to God alone?" Tamar, in her internal monologue, echoes Philo's premise stated in § 131: "the one who ... gives, properly speaking, gives something that is entirely his own."

§ 136. *Judah, the thankful manner*. Having depicted the internal deliberations of the Tamar soul and her conclusion that God is the true father of her child, Philo now explains the symbolic identity of Judah, the literal father of Tamar's children according to the subsequent verse of the secondary lemma (Gen 38:26). Allegorically, Judah symbolizes "the thankful manner" (ὁ ἐξομολογήτικος τρόπος). For a parallel to this, see Philo's interpretation of Moses as the "virtue-loving manner" in § 113. This turn of phrase depends on a derivation of the Hebrew name *Yəhûdâ* (יהודה) from the root *yādâ* (ידה), which in the Hiphʻil can mean "confess" or "give thanks."

delighted by her steadfast and godly reasoning. Antithetically to the shame implicit in Judah's response in Gen 38:26, Judah's confession in Philo's allegorical account is characterized by delight.

speaks frankly. As a correlative to his symbolism of thankful confession, Judah also speaks, according to Philo, with "frankness" (παρρησία), a hallmark virtue of the soul of the sage (see *Her.* 5). For frank speech in antiquity and in Philo more generally, see Fitzgerald 1996; Bosman 2006.

"she is justified, for I gave her to no mortal." Philo quotes a third portion of the secondary lemma (Gen 38:26), again incorporating it into the speech of one of his allegorical figures. Judah's scriptural response, "Tamar is more just

than I (δεδικαίωται Θαμὰρ ἢ ἐγώ), for I did not give her (οὐκ ἔδωκα αὐτήν) to my son Shelah," is rewritten to read: "she is justified (δεδικαίωται), for I gave her to no mortal (οὐδενὶ θνητῷ αὐτὴν ἔδωκα)." Several modifications are made: (1) Tamar's "justification" is rendered as an absolute quality, rather than a comparative one; (2) her name and Shelah's are both removed, to make way for their allegorical referents; (3) the thankful manner "gives her" to God with *parrhesia*, rather than "not giving" her to a human son. These inversions of the literal sense are devised by Philo (or the tradition that he anthologizes) to re-focalize the text through the eyes of Tamar, the interpreter of Scripture and divine signs, transforming a thorny biblical text into an edifying allegory of the soul.

thinking that it would be impious to pollute divine things with profane ones. Philo's "thankful manner" recognizes the kinship between the Tamar soul's steadfast reasoning and divine immutability. The language of purity and pollution ironically reverses the themes of sexual and moral impurity found in the literal story in Gen 38.

(5) § 137. *so also Sarah.* Philo now returns to the subject matter of his primary lemma (Gen 17:16a [§ 130]) by adducing a later verse from the Abraham cycle, Gen 21:6, which he will interpret sequentially in §§ 137–139. While Gen 21:6 functions in many ways like the secondary lemmata of Leah and Tamar, its close connection to Gen 17:16a makes it better described as a "contextualizing secondary lemma" (SBL^c). For this and other categories of scriptural lemma, see Introduction 4. The Exegetical Structure of the Treatise.

practical wisdom. For Sarah as "practical wisdom" (φρόνησις), see the detailed comment on § 79 above.

the self-taught class. For Isaac as the "self-taught" class of soul, see the detailed comments on §§ 1 and 88 above.

"the Lord made laughter for me." Philo cites the first part of his contextualizing secondary lemma, Gen 21:6a. The citation is identical to the Septuagint, with the exception that Philo adds the definite article before "Lord" (κύριος). The contextualizing secondary lemma is linked to the primary lemma thematically rather than lexically—although there is a partial correspondence between the ethic dative "to you" (σοι), referring to Abraham in Gen 17:16a, and "for me" (μοι), referring to Sarah in Gen 21:6a. What the Lord "gives" to Abraham in Gen 17, he "makes" for Sarah in Gen 21.

this is the equivalent to saying. For this interpretive formula (ἴσον τῷ + sentence), see §§ 11, 21, 29, and 48.

"he molded Isaac, he fashioned him, he begot him." A pleonastic tricolon, in which the verbs "mold" (διαπλάττω), "fashion" (δημιουργέω), and "beget" (γεννάω) offer three different idioms for divine "filiation." The first, "mold" (δια-

πλάττω), recalls Gen 2:7 and the "molding" of Adam; the second, "fashion" (δημιουργέω), reflects the divine craftsmanship of the cosmos in Plato's *Timaeus*; the third, "beget" (γεννάω), is the more typical Pentateuchal verb for *human* siring of children, which Philo insists may be predicated of God through the scriptural verse.

Isaac is the same as laughter. For the etymological exegesis of Isaac as psychic joy, see the notes on §§ 1 and 131. It is curious that Philo repeats this etymological identification in § 137 so soon after § 131.

§ 138. *the great evil of superstition.* The problems caused by "superstition" (δεισιδαιμονία)—understood as an unwarranted fear of the numinous pantheon of lesser powers, elements, and "demons," rather than the rational worship of the one God—are commonly referenced by religious and philosophical writers. On δεισιδαιμονία, see Malherbe 2014, 2:751–778. Philo's concern is to divert mythological anxieties about the claim that Isaac is the son of God.

she adds. Philo deliberately leaves the female subject of the verb ambiguous. While ostensibly referring to Sarah, it simultaneously serves as the speech in character of personified "practical wisdom" (φρόνησις).

"whoever should hear this will rejoice with me." Philo cites a second bit of his secondary lemma, Gen 21:6b. His text is identical to that of the Septuagint. The purpose of extending Sarah's speech is twofold. First, the indefinite relative pronoun ("whoever") supports his contention that the doctrine that he is here propounding (that God is properly father and begetter of all) will be difficult for everyone to accept. Secondly, the compound verb "rejoice together with" (συγχαίρεσθαι) echoes Philo's interpretation of Isaac as "joy" in Gen 17:1 (§ 1) and 17:16a (§ 131).

it is the proper work of God alone. Arnaldez (1964, 94, n. 2) takes this text as proof of the "ontological" character of divine virtue in *De mutatione nominum*. It is a personal power of God, not merely a verbal abstraction arising from the presence of particular virtues.

§ 139. *an oracle to this effect.* In support of his argument that scriptural wisdom proclaims doctrines that are hard for the spiritually "deaf" to comprehend, Philo cites a tertiary lemma: Hos 14:9–10. Its connection with the SCL[c] is thematic, not lexical.

The citation of Hos 14 is a rare instance of Philo citing from outside the Pentateuch. Hos 14:9–10 is one of only two prophetic lemmata cited by Philo in the present treatise (excluding the dubious reference to Isa 57:21 in § 169), the other being 1 Sam 2:5 in § 143. Philo cites the latter prophets 12 times in his corpus (Cohen 2007, 66–68). § 139 represents one of three occasions where Hosea is quoted—the other two being *QE* 2.76 (Hos 14:6) and *Plant.* 138 (Hos 14:9–10; see Cohen 2007, 65–66). In all three of these instances, the lemma is drawn from Hos 14 and Hosea is called a prophet. Philo's possession of a scroll of the twelve minor prophets in his private library is improbable (Sterling 2024b); he may have perused a copy in a prayer house or the Alexandrian library. In both *Plant.* 138 and *Mut.* 139, the prophet is said to utter an "oracle." This is in keeping with Philo's description of the only other minor prophet that he cites (Zech 6:12 in *Conf.* 62) as one of the "oracles" (χρησμοί). Philo thus construes Hosea's inspiration as analogous to that of Moses (see the detailed comment on § 7). Surprisingly, the prophets Isaiah and Jeremiah—cited or alluded to five and four times, respectively, in the *corpus Philonicum*—are not said explicitly to utter oracles.

proclaimed once by a prophetic mouth, as if through flame. Only in § 139 (citing Hosea) and *Fug.* 197 (citing Jeremiah) does Philo use this expression, "the prophetic mouth" or "prophetic mouths." It seems to be reserved in his commentaries for descriptions of the latter prophets. The further detail that an oracle was spoken "through flame" (διάπυρος) is unique to the Allegorical Commentary and probably bespeaks a kind of inspiration not dissimilar from that of Moses on Sinai. The adjective also describes the fire of God's judgment on those who do not worship him (see LXX Hos 8:14; cf. Philo, *Mut.* 180, which uses the same adjective to describe the fiery transcendence of thought; and *Somn.* 2.67, where the adjective describes the "zeal" of Nadab and Abihu, in light of their fiery deaths). It provides a rare window into Philo's own religious experience of hearing or reading Hosea's oracular words ("I marveled at this, being also thoroughly overwhelmed by the content of the proclamation").

"from me, may your fruit be found ... know them." Philo cites the tertiary lemma, Hos 14:9b–10a, selecting only the parts of the prophecy to Ephraim that are applicable to his symbolic allegoresis of the offspring of Sarah. The text is nearly identical with that of the Septuagint; Philo has only omitted a disjunction ("or" [ἤ]) and simplified the compound verb "will recognize" (ἐπιγνώσεται) to "will know" (γνώσεται).

in these words, I intuited the unseen ⟨Word⟩. Philo does not clarify who the "Unseen one" (ὁ ... ἀόρατος) is, but the Logos or a divine power is intended. This unseen musician plays upon the instrument of the soul. (Cf. Philo's description of Abraham's reason and speech being empowered as an instrument by God in §§ 56 and 69.)

§ 140. *in the manner of a tree ... nature.* The metaphor of a tree and its fruit—more often applied by Philo to the human microcosm in an ethical register (§§ 73–74)—here describes the physical cosmos. Both understandings of the "fruit" of philosophical discourse, ethics and physics, are present in Hellenistic philosophy before Philo. See the detailed comments on §§ 74–76.

Parallel Exegesis

§ 130. *having said what was necessary*. Philo uses the adverb "from necessity" (ἀποχρώντως) as a formal term elsewhere in his exegesis in the Allegorical Commentary (*Sacr.* 72; *Post.* 98; *Deus.* 51; *Fug.* 143), as well as in comments on both legal (*Ios.* 80) and narrative (*Decal.* 32) texts in the Exposition of the Law.

Gen 17:16a ("I will give to you ⟨from her⟩ a child"). Philo also cites and interprets Gen 17:16 in QG 3.54. There, instead of dividing the primary lemma into five discrete subunits as he does in *Mut.* 130–153, in QG 3.54 Philo cites the entire verse as a single block and then offers interwoven literal and allegorical interpretations. Further complicating the situation are several critical differences between the Armenian text of Gen 17:16 and Philo's Greek lemma quoted in the Allegorical Commentary. As Marcus translates the Armenian in QG 3.54:

> "Why does he say, 'I will give ⟨to you⟩ from her children, and I will bless him (զնա) and he shall be for peoples, and the kings of the nations shall come from him (ի նմանէ)' (Gen 17:16)?"

The text of Gen 17:16 in QG 3.54 has "I will give you *children*" (մանկունս) rather than "a child" (մանուկ, τέκνον). The singular "child" is found in extant Hebrew (בן), LXX (τέκνον), and Armenian (որդի) versions of Gen 17:16, such that Philo's reading here is difficult to account for. His entire analysis, both literal and allegorical, in QG 3.54 depends upon the plural offspring of generic virtue (Sarah), such that it is impossible to resolve the issue by suggesting Armenian interference in the original text. The effect of this divergent Armenian text is to suggest a closer correspondence between Sarah's "children" and the plural "kings and nations" that will come from "her."

On this last point, a second textual issue arises regarding the gender of the pronouns in Gen 17:16b ("I will bless *her*," "*she* will be for nations," "kings of nations will be from *her*"). In the Hebrew Masoretic Text, a feminine pronoun or subject is required in all three clauses; in the LXX, the witnesses are mixed, but the Göttingen LXX prints the feminine. Philo's citation here, and his exegesis in §§ 148 and 151 also presume the feminine. As Marcus notes, however, Armenian has no distinction of gender—making the ultimate meaning of "he/she" (նա) a matter of interpretation. Intriguingly, both Aucher and Marcus render the pronouns masculine in the lemma cited in QG 3.54. Marcus (PLCLSup 1:255, n. c) decides for this translation in part on the mistaken grounds that the pronouns are masculine in the Septuagint (Wevers's edition of LXX Genesis [1974] did not appear until a quarter of a century after Marcus's translations [1951]). Although it matters little for his literal and allegorical interpretations, these pronouns are better translated as feminine in QG 3.54 for four reasons: (1) the new LXX evidence; (2) the plural "children" make a reference to a singular Isaac ("him") unintelligible; (3) the parallel forms in *De mutatione nominum* suggest that Philo's text read the feminine; and (4) the ensuing allegory of *QG* 3.54, in which "peoples" and "kings" are understood to be the offspring of souls and "each of the immortal virtues," which come "from Sarah." For other parallel Philonic interpretations of this verse, see *Leg.* 3.217; *Cher.* 4–10, 41; *Congr.* 3; *Abr.* 91.

§ 132. **Gen 29:31** (*"the Lord, seeing that Leah was hated, opened her womb"*). The verse and Leah's spurned identity are alluded to but not cited in *Cher.* 41. There, Philo is arguing that the patriarchal souls did not marry women, but virtues. He gives a catalogue of matriarchs (including Zipporah), all of whom are mentioned in *De mutatione nominum*. The opening of Leah's womb is specifically alluded to in *Congr.* 7, though not in conjunction with Rachel but Sarai. More germane to the present passage is *Leg.* 3.180, where Philo interprets the verse to teach that God opens the womb of every virtue—a point that Leah understands but Rachel does not. Philo also thematizes the distinction between God as "husband" and patriarch as surrogate "father," for whose benefit the offspring is born. The schema, reproduced in *Mut.* 132, was thus already worked out by Philo at the beginning of the Allegorical Commentary. In *Her.* 50–51, Philo introduces this tradition into an Abrahamic allegory, adducing Gen 29:31 as a secondary lemma to explain the difference between the "son of Masek" (Gen 15:2) and Sarah's son. The latter is compared with the newfound fruitfulness of Leah, the former (after a fashion) with the barrenness of Rachel. For additional allegorical interpretations of Leah and Rachel together, see *Leg.* 2.47 and *Post.* 135.

§ 134. **Gen 38:15–26** (*Tamar too became pregnant from divine seeds*). For Tamar as a virtue in the strictest sense, rather than virtuously disposed "thought" (διάνοια) as here, see *Congr.* 124–126. Colson (PLCL 5:211, n. a) notes that *Fug.* 149–156 offers a significant extended parallel to Philo's interpretation of Tamar in *Mut.* 134. In point of fact, the two exegeses are complementary. In *Fug.* 149–156, Tamar is interpreted as "unconquered virtue" (ἡ ἀνίκητος ἀρετή, *Fug.* 149), and the three pledges of Judah are allegorically interpreted in similar, but not identical, ways, to those in *De mutatione nominum* (see *Fug.* 150). This is the extent of the overlap. Philo's lemma in *Fug.* 149, Gen 38:20–23, is precisely the part of this pericope that is *not* cited by Philo in *De mutatione nominum*. The verses highlight the inability of Judah's servant to "find" Tamar, when he brings a goat to "test" her—themes specially chosen for *De fuga et inventione*. Philo also offers a short allegoresis of the Tamar episode in *Deus* 137, in the course of which he gives the etymology "palm" (φοῖνιξ) for Tamar. Gen 38:11 serves as tertiary lemma, cited to amplify 1 Kings 17:10, and is focused on the command of Tamar to remain at home. Finally, in *Somn.*

2.44–45, Philo makes an allegorical comparison of Judah's gifts to Tamar and Pharaoh's gifts to Joseph—the latter being false or failed imitations of the former.

Exod 3:6; 34:33–35 ("just as Moses was, when he turned aside, intent on seeing God"). Philo's interpretation of Exod 3:6 as indicating Moses's interest in "seeing God" in § 134 (see detailed comments) contrasts with the more traditional exegesis of the verse in *Fug.* 141. In the latter treatise, Philo finds a proof of the limitations set on the human ability to see and know God. The reference to Exod 34:33–35 in *Mut.* 134 would be the only one in the *corpus Philonicum*, of which I am aware, outside of the conflation of the literal narratives of Exod 24:18 with Exod 34:28–35 in *Mos.* 2.70 (cf. *Gig.* 54, which focuses on Exod 33). For Philo's interpretation of Exod 3:3, see Cover 2018a.

§ 136. *Judah, the thankful manner*. For Judah as a symbol of thanks and acknowledgement, see also *Leg.* 1.80–82; 2.95; 3.146; *Plant.* 134 ("thankful confession to the Lord" [κυρίῳ ἐξομολόγησις]); *Somn.* 1.37; 2.34; and Grabbe 1988, 170.

§ 138. *the great evil of superstition*. Colson (PLCL 5:590) comments: "It is noticeable that here also as in *Cher.* 48 Philo insists on the esoteric character of the doctrine, that God was the father of the child of a human mother, as something which should not be mentioned to profane ears. See *Leg.* 3.219. Presumably he felt that it easily lent itself to confusion with pagan myths."

§ 139. *Hos 14:9b–10a ("from me, may your fruit be found ... and will know them")*. Colson (PLCL 5:213, n. b) cross-references the parallel exegesis of this verse in *Plant.* 138. There, Philo's aim is similarly to show that the intellectual gifts of instruction and understanding come from God.

in these words, I intuited the unseen ⟨Word⟩. Arnaldez (1964, 96, n. 1) comments that one finds "an analogous idea of prophecy in *Migr.* 114: the one who prophesies is compelled to pronounce, with his mouth and his tongue, invocations whose scope surpasses all limits. The instrument is human, but its sound is super-human." As additional parallels, Arnaldez numbers (from the Exposition of the Law) *Praem.* 5; *Spec.* 2.80; and *Mos.* 1.274.

Nachleben

§ 131. *the one who just now gives, properly speaking*. Compare the exegesis triggered by the word "he gave" (ἔδωκεν) (Ps 78[79]:24) in John 6:31, which similarly involves the exegetical scrutiny of the proper subject of such giving (divine, not human) and the substantivizing of the verb as "the one who is giving life to the world" (ὁ ... ζωὴν διδοὺς τῷ κόσμῳ). See Cover 2015; Borgen 1965.

Gen 17:16a ("I will give to you ⟨from her⟩ a child"). Some early interpreters, such as John Chrysostom (*Hom. Gen.* 53.369 [D]), interpret this promise literally. John notes that the addition of "the element" (τὸ στοιχεῖον), the rho, to Sarai is a sign that God can overcome her biological infertility. Others, such as Cyril of Alexandria, wish to press beyond the "literal sense" (ἱστορία) to the underlying allegory, but not in a purely Philonic sense. On Cyril's interpretation (*Epist. pasch.* 5.4 [D])—which reads Gen 17:16 by way of Gal 4:21–31—"the birth of Isaac from the promise symbolizes nothing other than Christ born at the completion of the ages" (σημαίνει τοιγαροῦν ἕτερον οὐδὲν τοῦ ἐξ ἐπαγγελίας Ἰσαὰκ ἡ γέννησις ἢ τὸν ἐπὶ συντελείᾳ τῶν αἰώνων γεννηθέντα Χριστόν). Ishmael, by contrast, allegorically symbolizes "the falsely-named wisdom of the world" (ἡ ... ψευδώνυμος τοῦ κόσμου σοφία).

§ 132. *Gen 29:31 ("the Lord, seeing that Leah was hated, opened her womb")*. Philo's reading of Leah as virtuous thought, who gives birth to a child with God as her true husband, finds an indirect echo in Origen's comment on Gen 29:31 in *Sel. Gen.* 12.124 [B]:

> He opens her womb ⟨literally⟩ for the birth of the saints (ἐπὶ ἁγίων γεννήσει); but according to the spiritual law, he opens the womb of the soul (ψυχῆς ἀνοίγει μήτραν), so that she who will be his mother will give birth to the Word of God (ἵνα γεννήσῃ Θεοῦ Λόγον ἡ ἐσομένη αὐτοῦ μήτηρ).

Origen's spiritual allegoresis begins as Philo's might, with an interpretation of Leah as a symbol of the soul, opened by a divine agent. This reading, however, quickly gives way to a Mariological interpretation—even if, by the birth of the Word, Origen means its advent in the heart of Christian believers. Van den Hoek (2000, 64) ranks it at [B].

Likewise Philonic is the point made by John Chrysostom, when interpreting this same verse in his *In Gen.* 54.39–44 [B/C]:

> See how the divine Scripture shows that the Demiurge of nature does each work by his own power (ὁ τῆς φύσεως δημιουργὸς ἑκάτερα τῇ οἰκείᾳ δυνάμει ἐργαζόμενος), both rousing (τῆς μὲν τὴν μήτραν διεγείρων) the womb of the one woman (Leah), and staying (ἐπέχων) the womb of Rachel. For being the Lord of nature, he does all things with ease.

Although the souls of Leah and Rachel are not mentioned, a similar lesson (God's control over the gift of procreation) is made by Philo in *Leg.* 3.180 (see Parallel Exegesis).

§ 134. *Gen 38:15–26 (Tamar too became pregnant from divine seeds)*. The earliest Christian tradition mentioning Tamar (i.e., Matt 1:3) treats her as a literal matriarch. Justin Martyr (*Dial.* 86.6 [B/C]), who links this pericope with a number of other "staff" (ῥάβρος) passages in the Septuagint, considers the scene of typological value, as the staff shows Judah to be the father of Tamar's children "on account of a great mystery" (διὰ μέγα μυστήριον). But the emphasis is on Christological symbolism, not ethical allegory. Clement of Alexandria's single reference to this passage in *Strom.* 1.31.6, by contrast, sounds quite a bit like Philo. The verse is adduced as a secondary lemma explicating Clement's interpretation of Hagar as the preliminary studies, which he traces explicitly to Philo (*Strom.* 1.31.6 [A/B]):

> You would have another image of the things which have been said (i.e., the patriarchs devotion to the preliminary studies) in Tamar, when she sat at the crossroads donning the appearance of a harlot, whom Judah, the lover of learning (for it is possible to interpret him in this way) who left nothing unseen or investigated (ὁ φιλομαθὴς Ἰούδας [δυνατὸς δὲ ἑρμηνεύεται] ὁ μηδὲν ἄσκεπτον καὶ ἀδιερεύνητον καταλιπών), looked upon and "turned aside to her" (Gen 38:16), preserving his agreement with God.

No influence of *De mutatione nominum* can be felt. The interpretation, however, is clearly Philonic, probably dependent instead on *De congressu eruditionis gratia* (Van den Hoek 1988, 40–41). Origen explicitly denies the presence of any salutary meaning in "the literal sense" (ἡ ἱστορία) of this passage (*Engastr.* 2), which he considers an example of a "lawless" (οὐ νομίμως) union (*Hom. Luc.* 28.11 [C]), but does not offer much by way of an alternative. Eusebius of Caesarea, taking up the passage in his *Quaest. ev. Steph.* 7.1 (22.905.10 [C]), attempts primarily to absolve Tamar of the charge of harlotry. Philo's complex allegorical interpretation, which focalizes the story through the eyes of Tamar, was not widely received.

Exod 3:6; 34:33–35 ("just as Moses was, when he turned aside, intent on seeing God"). It would be difficult to overstate the influence (or at least resonance) that Philo's interpretation of Moses turning aside "to see God" (τὸν θεὸν ἰδεῖν [§ 134]) at both of the first and second Horeb/Sinai theophanies had on later Christian literature. The locus would become one of the standard paradigms for visionary and apophatic theology. Gregory of Nyssa (*Vit. Moys.* 2.162 [A]), for example, famously understood the two Sinai theophanies to depict a Moses's "seeing God" (τὸν θεὸν ἰδεῖν), first in brightness (Exod 3:6), then in divine darkness (Exod 33–34). Earlier examples of the Logocentric interpretation of Exod 3:6, reminiscent of Philo, may be found in Justin Martyr (*Apol.* 1.63 [C/D]) and Origen (*Comm. Jo.* 1.218 [B]).

Philo's particular genius in this passage is the interweaving of the veilings of Moses (in Exod 34) and Tamar (in Gen 38). In Cover 2023a, I outline both the formal and thematic parallels between *Mut.* 134–136 and 2 Cor 3:7–18, in which Paul investigates the meaning of the veiled Moses. Philo's use of Exod 34 is extremely rare, as he prefers to derive Moses's visionary type from Exod 33. This would leave later exegetes, like Gregory of Nyssa, the opportunity to synthesize Philo on Exod 33 and Paul on Exod 34 (Cover 2015, 296–303).

§ 137. *Isaac is the same as laughter.* For this allegorical identification, see Origen, *Cels.* 5.45; *Hom. Gen.* 7.1 ("laughter or joy" ["risus vel gaudium"] [C]) (Van den Hoek 2000, 51).

§ 138. *the great evil of superstition.* For "superstition" in the New Testament, see Acts 17:22.

b   *"From Her"* (§§ 141–144)
      Analysis and General Comments

Having interpreted the phrase "I will give to you" (δώσω σοι [Gen 17:16aα]), Philo continues in the sequence of the primary lemma (Gen 17:16aβ) to interpret the phrase "from her" (ἐξ αὐτῆς). These words were not cited with the primary biblical lemma in § 130, though Philo means to comment on them. He knows three possible symbolic interpretations of the phrase from his exegetical school, and while he does not reject any of them, the third option—that "from her" represents virtue as the mother of the good—best fits the allegoresis that he is developing. The section divides into three units.

(1)   Philo lists three possible interpretations of "from her" (ἐξ αὐτῆς): (1) that the phrase signifies that all goods, as external and extrinsic to the human soul ("⟨apart⟩ from her"), are gifts of God, and therefore are not truly possessed; (2) that the phrase, taken adverbially, signifies the supernatural speed with which divine gifts come to fruition; or (3) that virtue (Sarah) is the mother of all that is good. This last best fits Philo's current line of interpretation (§§ 141–142).

(2)   Philo entertains a question about Sarah: Given that the Scriptures speak of her as barren (see Gen 11:30), how can she now give birth? Philo answers that symbolic barrenness signifies barrenness *from* vice (cf. Rachel's barrenness *on account of* vice in § 133) (§ 143a).

(3)   To support this interpretation, Philo adduces a secondary lemma from the former prophets: 1 Sam (LXX 1 Kgdms) 2:5. This verse, taken from the song of Hannah, recalls another barren woman who gives birth with God's help. Hannah, unlike Sarah, Leah, and Zipporah, is not a symbol of virtue or the soul, but a symbol of grace herself—an allegoresis which Philo derives from the Hebrew etymology of her name (§§ 143b–144).

Detailed Comments

(1) § 141. *"from her," must now be indicated.* Philo turns to the next part of his primary lemma, "from her" (ἐξ αὐτῆς [Gen 17:16aβ]). This prepositional phrase is omitted from the initial citation of the lemma in § 130. Its inclusion as a formal lemmatic component in the commentary demonstrates that Philo sometimes had in mind longer or more complete lemmata than he explicitly cites. Here, the omission of "from her" in § 130 may also be due to scribal error, reflected in the weakness of the manuscript tradition.

some take this to signify what comes into existence "outside of her." Philo's first allegorical interpretation for the phrase "from her" is "that which comes from outside of her" (τὸ ἔξω γινόμενον), i.e., outside of or apart from the soul. The theme of human nothingness and dependence on God, which plays a major role in Philo's thought, emphasizes the preposition "from" (ἐξ). Philo attributes the interpretation to "some" other exegetes, perhaps members of his own school.

to judge by right reason. Philo invokes the term "right reason" (ὀρθὸς λόγος) as an epistemological criterion. The phrase is attributed by the Pyrrhonian skeptic, Sextus Empiricus, to the Presocratic philosopher Empedocles (Sextus 7.122–124) as the guarantor of truth. It is invoked by Plato in numerous dialogues, including the *Phaedo* (73a; 94a) and the *Timaeus* (56b). By the time of Aristotle, it had become a "commonplace" (κοινόν [*Eth. nic.* 2.1, 1103b31–32]).

the soul manifests nothing good ... appended to her from the outside. Adherents to this first interpretation understand the soul to possess goods only extrinsically, as gifts of divine grace with no proper appropriation by the soul. It is difficult to imagine any of the major Hellenistic schools as accepting this description, particularly the Peripatetics, Stoics, or Middle Platonists, each of which can speak without qualification of a soul's goodness. It is a recurring leitmotif in Philo's Allegorical Commentary.

God, who showers down gifts. The language of grace recalls Philo's earlier discourses on the covenant in chapter four. See esp. the detailed comments on §§ 52–53 and 58.

§ 142. *others ... "straightaway, immediately, unencumbered, without delay."* Philo knows a second group of exegetes, again probably from his school, who interpret "from her" to mean "with immediate speed" (παραυτίκα τάχος). Colson (PLCL 5:214, n. 1) comments that "speed" (τάχος) is drawn from Philo's poetical lexicon. The Alexandrian gives a variety of adverbial synonyms (translated above): παραχρῆμα, εὐθύς, ἀνυπερθέτως, ἄνευ μελλήσεως.

divine gifts. A common theme in all three interpretations of "from her," particularly the first two. See the note on § 141 for other references to the theme of divine grace in the treatise.

in this manner, outstripping even intervals of time. Philo specifies that the immediacy of divine gifts stems from their immateriality, and hence, their freedom from "natural intervals of time" (τὰ χρόνων διαστήματα). This reading follows Plato's distinction between the created "time" (χρόνος), governing the movements of perceptible bodies, and eternity (αἰών) in the *Timaeus* (37d). Cf. § 179, where Philo speaks in a similar way of human thought "compressing and traversing distances of unbelievable magnitude (τὰ ἀπειρομεγέθη διαστήματα)" and changing swiftly "in a certain manner, outside of time" (τρόπον τινὰ ἄχρονος).

third ... that virtue is the mother of the created good. Philo's third interpretive option for the phrase "from her," presented like the first two as stemming from another group, is the one he wishes to commend at present (so Arnaldez [1964, 97, n. 3]). It best fits his exegetical context (Gen 17), in which Sarah, the mother of Isaac, plays an important role, and is the only interpretation offered of Gen 17:16 in QG 3.54. As parallels to the preceding two interpretations, Arnaldez (ibid.) suggests Wis 7:15–16 and 6:13.

(2) § 143. ***to those who inquire whether a barren woman gives birth.*** Having provided three possible allegorical interpretations of "from her" (ἐξ αὐτῆς), Philo entertains a hypothetical question in the manner of a school commentary. The language of "inquiry" (ζήτησις) is a technical one, and kin to the rabbinic concept of *midrash* ("seeking," מדרש). With regard to the theme of the question, Arnaldez (1964, 97, n. 4) distinguishes two senses of barrenness: the physical and the psychological. He rightly argues that Philo's primary concern is with the latter, in which soul-barrenness is at issue. Philo, however, poses the question in such a way that both literal and allegorical answers can be anthologized.

relating at an earlier stage that Sarah is barren. Philo alludes to Gen 11:30, "And Sarai was barren and was not bearing children" (καὶ ἦν Σαρα στεῖρα καὶ οὐκ ἐτεκνοποίει), adduced here as a contextualizing secondary lemma.

now agree that she will become a mother. For the first time, Sarah is named as the mother of Abraham's promised offspring. Prior to this, in Gen 17, only Abraham's child had been mentioned.

the soul, on the other hand, which has become barren of wicked deeds. Philo provides a different allegorical interpretation of Sarai's barrenness in Gen 11:30 than he does of Rachel's in Gen 29:31 (see § 133, "he renders barren ..." [στεροῖ μέν ...]). Whereas the latter's barrenness is a symbol of her vicious disposition, Sarai's is taken to signify her inability to conceive vice (as, e.g., Rachel in Gen 35:16–19, according to § 96).

almost exclusively bears children well. Philo's description of the Sarah soul "bearing children well" (lit. "using *good* childbearing" [εὐτοκίᾳ χρῆται]) involves a paronomasia, which emphasizes the reversal of Sarai's hard fate in Gen 11:30. She who was *not* child-bearing (οὐκ ἐτεκνοποίει [Gen 11]) becomes "*good* child-bearing" (εὐτοκεῖν [Gen 17]). In this reversal, Sarah serves as the allegorical antithesis to Rachel, who in Gen 35:16 is described as "bearing children badly" (δυστοκήσασα [see § 96]).

most worthy of love, seven in number. This is the second group of seven children mentioned in *De mutatione nominum*. As a complement to Raguel's seven daughters, the faculties of the irrational soul (§ 110), Philo now refers to Sarah's seven sons. That Sarah bore seven "virtuous" male children to Abraham rather than just one (MT Gen 22:2; cf. LXX Gen 22:2, which does not suggest, even here, that Isaac is an "only son") is clearly a transference of information from the secondary lemma (1 Kgdms 2:5) to the primary one. At the primary level of exegesis, Philo may simultaneously reckon Isaac alongside the six sons of Keturah, born to Abraham after the death of Sarah. Gen 25:2 lists their names as Zimran (Ζεμράν), Jokshan (Ἰεξάν), Medan (Μαδάν), Midian (Μαδιάμ), Ishbak (Ἰεσβόκ), and Shuah (Σωύε). They could conceivably, like Isaac, stand for "good emotions" (εὐπάθειαι), but Philo does not say this in § 146. Rather, he identifies the seven sons as the four cardinal virtues and three propaedeutic sciences (music, grammar, and geometry). For more on Sarah's children, see the Parallel Exegesis.

according to the song which is sung. Philo adduces a secondary lemma from the former prophets, 1 Sam (1 Kgdms) 2:5, taken from the song of Hannah. The text is linked lexically to the primary biblical lemma (Gen 17:16) through the word "child" (τέκνον), and to the contextualizing secondary lemma (Gen 11:30) through the word "barren" (στεῖρα). Philo's use of a prophetic tertiary lemma in § 143 to support a contextualizing secondary lemma from the Pentateuch (about Sarah's barrenness and motherhood) mirrors his exegetical practice in § 139, where a prophetic tertiary lemma was adduced to develop the allegoresis of a contextual biblical lemma from the Pentateuch (about the God's true paternity of Isaac). Philo thus draws atypically on both law and prophets in chapter six to create "double proofs" explaining Isaac's parentage. The introductory formula, "according to the song which is sung" (κατὰ τὸ ᾀδόμενον ᾆσμα), recalls introductions to the Psalms as secondary or tertiary lemmata earlier in the treatise (see Ps 23 and the detailed comments on §§ 42 and 115). Philo probably attributes a similar authority to this text from the former prophets as he does to the Psalms, although the latter are explicitly connected with Moses's school.

by grace—Hannah. Philo interprets the Greek name "Hannah" (Ἄννα), according to its etymology on the onomasticon, as "her grace" (χάρις αὐτῆς [*Deus* 5]) or simply "grace" (χάρις [*Ebr.* 145; *Somn.* 1.254]). The etymologist understands the Hebrew name Ḥanâ (חנה) to derive from the verb ḥānan (חנן), "to show favor, grace." The longer etymology in *Deus* 5 stems from a resolution of the name into two parts: (1) "grace" (חן); and (2) -â (ה-), "her" (see further Grabbe 1988, 133; Cohen 2007, 127). This etymology fits well with Philo's theology of covenantal "grace," which he has been developing in the context of his allegoresis of the Abraham cycle (§§ 52–53, 57–59). Grace (Hannah) proclaims to lady virtue (Sarah) the birth of her sevenfold sons (Isaac + the six sons of Keturah).

a barren woman gave birth to seven ... became weak. Philo's secondary biblical lemma from 1Sam (1Kgdms) 2:5 agrees in all essential points with the Septuagint. Only the phrase, "and she who was great" (καὶ ἡ πολλή), has become ἡ δὲ πολλή and the verb, "she became weak" (ἠσθένησεν), lacks the final nu.

§ 144. *she calls "many" the intellect.* Hannah, as a symbol of personified "grace," speaks not of herself, but of Sarah and Hagar. The latter women are both understood as kinds of "intellect" or "thought" (διάνοια).

borne along by mixed and confused arguments. Philo turns first to 1Sam (1Kgdms) 2:5b: "she who was 'many' with children became weak." Although in context, this refers to those who mocked Hannah for her childlessness, in Philo's allegory it is transferred to Hagar—the kind of confused intellect which flourished at the expense of the Sarah mind.

on account of the greatness of the tumultuous crowds. The word "much" or "great" (πολλή) of 1Sam (1Kgdms) 2:5b—originally referring to fertility and success in childbearing—is interpreted to refer to the "greatness" (πλῆθος) or multitude of thoughts that plague the Hagar-intellect. Great crowds are pleased by the rhetoric of sophists trained in Hagar's arts, but they do not improve the soul in virtue.

gives birth to incurable evils. The phrase "gives birth to incurable evils" (ἀνήκεστα κακὰ τίκτει) inversely mirrors the description of the seven good sons of the Sarah/Keturah-thought, which are described in § 143 as "worthy of love" (τὰ ἀξιέραστα).

that has not admitted anything mortal as a productive seed. The suggestion of a non-human father for Sarah/Keturah's children picks up on Philo's allegoresis in §§ 131–140.

but snatching up and destroying. Philo's description of the virtuous intellect with two predicative participles, "snatching up and destroying" (ἀναλίσκουσα καὶ διαφθείρουσα), using a full conjunction ("but" [ἀλλά]) is grammatically emphatic, as ἀλλά typically introduces an independent clause.

she embraces the seven and its most peaceful character. The number seven, derived from the "seven" children of Abraham in § 143, is linked to peace on account of its connection with the Sabbath (see Gen 2:2; *Fug.* 173). Philo will return to the symbolic importance of the number seven toward the end of the present treatise (§ 260).

Parallel Exegesis

§ 141. *"from her."* Philo interprets Sarah in *QG* 3.54 as "divine and incorruptible (virtue)" (Marcus, PLCLSup). This parallel confirms Philo's implicit commendation of the third interpretation of "Sarah" in *Mut.* 141–142 as the one most relevant to his allegoresis.

§ 143. *Gen 11:30 ("Sarah is barren")*. Philo only cites and interprets this verse here in his extant writings. That it is a citation is proved by the fact that "the oracles" are explicitly mentioned as "introducing" the character of Sarah (this is her scriptural debut). Additionally, two words from the Septuagint ("Sarah," "barren") are cited in sequence and the verb "gives birth" (τίκτει) paraphrases the verb "bear children" (ἐτεκνοποίει) in Gen 11:30.

the soul, on the other hand, which has become barren of wicked deeds. See similarly *Congr.* 3, where Philo summarizes Sarah's paradoxical significance as the one who was "once barren and exceedingly prolific."

most worthy of love, seven in number. In the detailed comments, I wonder whether Philo (or the tradition that he anthologizes) may group Isaac with Keturah's six sons to come up with a group of seven virtues. For an alternative allegorical understanding of Keturah, as in league more closely with Hagar, see *Sacr.* 44. In *QG* 4.147, the three wives/consorts of Abraham—Sarah, Hagar, and Keturah—are allegorized as offering the goods of "sight," "hearing," and "smell," respectively. They are not harmonized, as Sarah and Keturah are potentially in *Mut.* 143.

The tradition of Abraham's seven children of promise may be related to the odd version of Gen 17:16 cited by Philo in *QG* 3.54, "I will give to you from her children" (տալ բեզ ի նմանէ մանկունս [δώσω σοι ἐξ αὐτῆς τέκνα / παιδία, retroverted]). This is, of course, not literally true, but only figuratively, so long as Sarah and Keturah are both considered symbols of virtue. In *QG* 3.54, however, Philo understands the other children to be Isaac's offspring, providing an alternative way of understanding the "seven" of § 143.

1 Sam (1 Kgdms) 2:5 ("a barren woman gave birth to seven ... became weak"). Philo only cites the former prophets 13 to 16 times in the Allegorical Commentary (see Cohen 2007, 104–105). Of these, 1 Sam (1 Kgdms) 1:1–2:10, a later haftarah for Rosh Hashanah, accounts for four instances (*Deus* 5–15; *Ebr.* 143–152; *Mut.* 143–144; and *QG* 4.138; so Cohen 2007, 104). Only *Deus* 10–15 and the present passage treat the lemma in detail.

In *QG* 3.54, Philo had raised the question of how it is that Sarah, as mother of one, was also mother of many "children." In *Deus* 11, Philo asks a related question of Hannah in 1 Sam 2:5: if Hannah is the mother of one (Samuel), "how then can she say that she has borne seven?" In the ensuing exegesis, Philo uses arithmological arguments—particularly the unity of the one and the seven—to explain Hannah's difficult boast without reference to either hyperbole or the conventions of Hebrew parallelism. *Mut.* 143–144, by contrast, shows no concern with the arithmological problem of Sarah or Hannah bearing more than one virtuous child, but focuses instead on the true meaning of barrenness and fertility.

§144. *she calls "many" the intellect.* Sarah and Hagar are interpreted as "minds" (rather than as virtue or the preliminary studies) in *Congr.* 180 as well. As is characteristic of Philo's exegesis, both male and female characters in the scriptural narrative may take on multiple allegorical significances.

she embraces the seven. Colson (PLCL 5:274, n. a) argues that "ἡ ἑβδόμη (the seventh) ⟨also⟩ seems to be used for ἑβδομάς (heptad/seven) in *Decal.* 159 and *Spec.* 2.40, as well as in §144 .... Presumably no noun but ἡμέρα (day) can be understood, but by frequent use it has come to be a noun, which Philo can extent to cover any sacred period, day, month, or year."

Nachleben

§141. *God, who showers down gifts.* Philo's image of God as "the one who showers down gifts/graces" (ὁ χάριτας ὀμβρῶν) is reminiscent of Jas 1:17, which similarly claims that every perfect "gift" (δόσις/δώρημα) is "coming down" (καταβαῖνον) from the father of lights, who is conceived as ontologically stable.

§143. *1 Sam (1 Kgdms) 2:5 ("A barren woman gave birth to seven ... became weak").* The limited reception of Philo's interpretation of the barren woman who has given birth to seven (1 Kgdms 2:5) cannot be understood apart from the reception of a similar text, Isa 54:1, which often attracted 1 Kgdms 2:5 into its orbit. The former text (Isa 54:1), cited by Paul in Gal 4:27 as part of his allegory of Sarah and Hagar, became dominant in Christian interpretation of this motif, and lends to the figure of the barren woman a typological relationship to the gentile church. Thus, in Origen, *Hom. Luc.* 33.187 [D], we see 1 Kgdms 2:5 attracted secondarily to Isa 54:1 in a double proof of the fruitfulness of the prophets for attracting the faith of gentile believers in Jesus. See similarly, Didymus the Blind, *Comm. Zacch.* 3.106 [D], where the Pauline interpretation is maintained.

Despite the dominant Galatians-inspired interpretation of 1 Kgdms 2:5, we also see vestiges of an alternative ethical interpretation (though not Philo's) of this verse in the *Vit. Mar. Mag.* 2 [C/D]. There, the hagiographer notes that the "seven spirits," which once possessed Mary Magdalene, were displaced, in her "healing" by Jesus, with a sevenfold gift of virtues. The anonymous author adduces 1 Kgdms 2:5 as proof that as many as were the demons of the "barren one" (Mary Magdalene), so many were the virtues restored to her. More redolent of Philonic tradition, and potentially inspired by it, is Origen's interpretation of 1 Kgdms 2:5 in the prologue (66.25–29) to his *Commentarium in Canticum Canticorum* [B] (not mentioned by Van den Hoek 2000). There, in expounding ways that Scripture speaks of the "womb of the soul" ("venter animae"), Origen adduces 1 Kgdms 2:5 as evidence that

> according to the inner human being ("secundum interiorem hominem" [see 2 Cor 4:16]) one person is childless and "barren" ("alius sine filiis et 'sterilis'"), while another "has plenty of offspring" ("abundans in filiis"); and we notice that the saying "the barren woman has born seven, and she that was abundant in children has become sick" ("sterilis peperit septem, et fecunda in filiis infirmata est" [1 Kgdms 2:5]) is in accord with this. (Trans. R.P. Lawson, adapted.)

Here, another Pauline text (2 Cor 4:16) points Origen toward an ethical rather than a typological interpretation of 1 Kgdms 2:5. Although the precise similarity to the Philonic template is not explicit, the reference to the "inner human being" (= "venter animae") suggests that Origen reads 1 Kgdms 2:5 as speaking of the psychic fertility of the corporally barren, and the psychic sterility of the soul which has acquired many external goods and pleasures.

c   *"A Child" (§§ 145–147)*
     Analysis and General Comments

Philo turns to the third part of the primary biblical lemma for this chapter cited in § 130 (Gen 17:16aγ). Whereas his interpretation of (a) "I will give" (Gen 17:16aα) focuses on God the giver, and (b) "from her" (Gen 17:16aβ) focuses on the virtue of the Abraham/Sarah soul, "a child" turns at last to the fruit of such virtue. Isaac has already been allegorically interpreted in two different ways in the present treatise: (1) as a symbol of "joy" (§§ 1, 131); and (2) as the autodidactic class of souls, which is perfect in nature rather than perfected through teaching or practice (§§ 1, 88, 137). In the present section, Isaac is presented as the power enabling all the virtues. Although Philo calls attention to the promise of a single child (§ 145), the subsequent text offers an implicit allegoresis of Isaac and six others—i.e., the "seven" of 1 Kgdms 2:5 (§ 143)—as seven excellences, comprised of three propaedeutic sciences (music, grammar, and geometry) and the four cardinal virtues (§ 146). This allegoresis of Abraham's seven sons mirrors and complements Philo's allegoresis of the seven daughters of Raguel in chapter five (§§ 110–120). Whereas the seven daughters symbolized faculties of the irrational soul, Abraham's seven sons typify rational skills or virtues. The section divides into two units:

(1) Philo begins with a scholastic question: "why" (διὰ τί;) is Sarah (i.e., virtue) said to bear a single child rather than many? (This allegorical aporia is the literal inverse of the question posed by Philo in QG 3.54, where apparently his biblical lemma reads in the plural: why does the verse [Gen 17:16] say, "I will give you children [!] from her." See the Parallel Exegesis above.) Philo answers that while particular examples of the exercise of virtues and excellences may be found empirically in abundance, the essence of each rests in a singular power and archetype. Philo gives seven "chance" examples of such singular powers: three propaedeutic sciences (music, grammar, geometry) and the four cardinal virtues—corresponding to the seven children referenced above in §143 (§§ 145–146).

(2) Philo answers a second, implicit question: why does Moses call Isaac "child" (τέκνον) and not a more generic term for offspring like "progeny" (τόκος)? The question is related to the problem of the three propaedeutic sciences listed among virtue's seven children. Do these not properly belong to Hagar rather than Sarah? Philo takes the opportunity to differentiate "legitimate" from "adopted-legal" or "illegitimate" offspring. At the symbolic level, Isaac's being called "child" (τέκνον) indicates that he and the six others are the natural offshoots of generic virtue, whether signifying (1) "good emotions" (εὐπάθειαι); (2) types of soul; or, as in this case, (3) forms of virtues and propaedeutic sciences, which are themselves derived from the singular filial power, Isaac (§147).

Detailed Comments

(1) §145. *God does not say that he will give many children.* Whereas in the parallel at QG 3.54, Philo is concerned about the literal meaning of his aberrant scriptural text ("Why does God promise Abraham 'children' through Sarah?"), in §145 he has the opposite problem. *Given* that many goods will be born to Abraham, the virtuous soul, through his symbolic mating with virtue, why does Moses indicate that God will only give Abraham *one* legitimate son from Sarah? Philo's answer, according to Arnaldez (1964, 98, n. 2), is both philosophical and theological/scriptural. God can only engender generic virtue, which is singular. This is symbolized both by Abraham's one true wife, and his one legitimate child. In Sarah, Arnaldez sees both generic virtue as a metaphysical actor, as well as the recipient soul. In Isaac, he discerns the singularity of generic virtue "in act" and the birth "of perfect nature" outside the realm of becoming.

granted graciously. Translating χαρίζω, as opposed to "give" (δίδωμι), which was used earlier in the sentence. Philo modifies his gift-giving vocabulary to emphasize God's singular gift of Isaac.

why is this? Philo uses this diatribal question at several other points in this treatise, most often to introduce secondary questions (see §§ 46, 81, 83, 88, 94, 116, 126, 177, 241, 246, 250). The form used here in § 145, "but why" (διὰ τί δέ;), appears also in § 126 and indicates that the most important questions about Isaac's symbolic meaning have already been answered. Philo is tying up loose ends.

not ... by its abundance, but by its power. Philo has already inveighed against "abundance" or "multiplicity" (τὸ πλῆθος) in the foregoing discussion of Hagar-thought, with its confusion on account of the "abundance" of arguments (§ 144). Sarah, by contrast, symbolizes the kind of thought that attends to virtue and wisdom alone. What was said of the mother in § 144 is extended to the child in § 145: Isaac is the unique child of virtue. His uniqueness is further elaborated through the philosophical vocabulary of "power" (Barnes 2001). What is truly good, according to Philo, derives from a singular stable power, not from what is multiple and mutable.

§ 146. *as it happens.* Rendering the phrase εἰ τύχοι (lit. "sometimes," "if perchance"). Philo's *exempla* turn out to be seven in number—precisely the number of spiritual children that archetypal virtue is said to bear in § 143. While with the one hand, Philo gestures to the single child born of Sarah (§ 145), with the other hand he simultaneously holds forth the seven-fold offspring of grace, "barren" of vice (§ 143 [1 Kgdms 2:5]). Four of these are generic virtues in their own right; the other three are propaedeutic studies—an unevenness that Philo will address in § 147, when he turns from the grammatical number of the "child" (τέκνον) to its allegorical significance.

music itself, grammar itself, geometry itself. Philo selects three of the propaedeutic studies for this list of the seven legitimate children of generic virtue. They are placed before the four cardinal virtues on account of their preparatory nature—"the great introductions" (μεγάλα τὰ προοίμια) to the virtues, as Philo will call them in *Congr.* 11. Philo has already used this threefold (rather than fivefold) presentation of the preliminary studies in *Mut.* 80.

justice itself, temperance itself, prudence itself, and courage itself. The four cardinal virtues, according to common philosophical tradition. For other lists of virtues in Philo, see the Parallel Exegesis. It is striking that here, unlike § 225, Philo has not added any supplementary Roman or Jewish virtues (e.g., "love of humanity" [φιλανθρωπία], "piety" [εὐσέβεια], or "holiness" [ὁσιότης]), but has chosen instead three preliminary excellences.

those unspeakably many particular examples. Colson (PLCL 5:591) considers this phrase a "recognized formula of the Platonic school," citing *Phileb.* 14c–15b.

(2) § 147. ***he has not said "child" carelessly or without circumspection.*** Philo turns from the grammatical number of "child" (τέκνον [Gen 17:16]) to its semiotic value. He attends to a second, implicit "Philonic question" posed of the primary lemma: Why has Moses said "child" (τέκνον) rather than "progeny" (τόκος)? Philo's answer, that τέκνον refers to a legitimate child, responds to a deeper, underlying issue: that among his list of seven symbolic "children" of generic virtue, three—the propaedeutic excellences—might potentially be considered children "adopted" from Hagar. Philo must find a way to "legitimize" all seven sons.

neither foreign, nor switched at birth ... but the legitimate and noble offspring. Philo's claim that several of the propaedeutic skills, symbolized in *Congr.* 11 by Hagar, are in fact the legitimate children of Abraham, represents something of a puzzlement. In an allegorical *tour de force*, he argues (as elsewhere) that these excellences really to belong to philosophy and wisdom (*Congr.* 79). Philo's rationale can be seen in an earlier Abrahamic treatise, *De congressu eruditionis gratia*. There, he argues that Hagar's lower arts, as "skills" (τεχναί), are incomplete (or incompletely grasped) versions of the children of Sarah, which are "sciences" (ἐπιστῆμαι) (*Congr.* 140). These "skills," moreover, perceive their objects only dimly and inaccurately. Philosophy or wisdom, by contrast, takes as its object "this world and every form of existence, visible and invisible" (*Congr.* 144). Thus, one may even say that the grammarian, in teaching nouns and verbs, "encroaches on, and casually appropriates the discoveries of philosophy" (*Congr.* 148).

the truly citizen soul. Philo adds to his primary metaphor—that of genuine and illegitimate children—a secondary one, which was important in his native Alexandria: that of full citizenship vs. resident alien status. (LSJ gives papyrus evidence for this terminology from Alexandria: *PGnom.* 38.) During the principates of Gaius and Claudius, Alexandria's Jewish population wrestled against native Greeks for various levels of citizenship recognition. Philo himself likely possessed full Greek citizenship, but not all other Jews enjoyed this privilege. Allegorically, the philosophical soul participates in something analogous: the cosmopolitan citizenship of the sage in the *polis* of virtue. Just as a city can recognize a foreigner as her true citizen, so virtue can recognize her true children, wherever they appear.

rather than "progeny," "child." Etymologically, both "child" (τέκνον) and "progeny" (τόκος) are related to the same verb, "to give birth" (τίκτειν). Symbolically, Philo sees in "child" (τέκνον) a closer kinship connection, including spiritual kinship and the natural appropriation of like to like.

affinity. Philo uses a term "affinity" / "kinship" (οἰκειότης), which may be a synonym for the Stoic term, "appropriation" (οἰκείωσις). The latter word refers to the various forms of association between two beings, ontologically and sociologically. In Philo's philosophical allegory, kindred excellences, habits, sciences, and skills form a family, in which the generic form (Sarah) recognizes and attaches to herself particular expressions in act. This is not "fictive kinship," but the generic appropriation of the species.

Parallel Exegesis

§145. *"a child."* As noted in the general comment on (a) §§130–140, Philo's text of Gen 17:16 in QG 3.54 reads "children" (͈ͅ͏ͅ͏ͅ͏ͅ) rather than "a child" (ͅ͏ͅ͏ͅ). The singular "child" is found in extant Hebrew (בן), Greek (τέκνον), and Armenian (որդի) versions of Gen 17:16, such that Philo's reading is difficult to account for. Philo answers the question "why God used the plural ... in speaking of their only beloved son," by noting that "the allusion is to his descendants ... peoples and kings" (Marcus, PLCLSup). Marcus (PLCLSup 1:255, n. b) points out a further difficulty: that in *Mut.* 145, "Philo not only follows the LXX in reading τέκνον [child] but emphasizes the singular number of the noun" ("it is first worthy of wonderment that God does not say that he will give him many children, but that only one will be granted"). One way to account for this *quaestio* in *Mut.* 145 is to suggest that it offers an amendment of the discussion in QG 3.54. The other place that Philo apparently treated Sarah's "child" is in the now lost treatise *De Isaaco* (see *Ios.* 1). This work, which would have comprised part of the "living laws" section of the Exposition, would have been placed between *De Abrahamo* and the lost *De Iacobo*.

§146. *music itself, grammar itself, geometry itself.* In *Congr.* 11, Philo describes the preliminary studies as "the great introductions" (μεγάλα τὰ προοίμια) to the virtues. In that passage, he lists five (rather than three) such excellences: "grammar" (γραμματική), "geometry" (γεωμετρία), "astronomy" (ἀστρονομία), "rhetoric" (ῥητορική), and "music" (μουσική). These studies are children of Hagar rather than powers extending from Isaac. Philo gives them in their feminine forms (sc. θεωρία ["area of study"]). Cf. *Mut.* 146, which instead has the neuter forms "the musical and the grammatical and the geometric" (τὸ μουσικὸν καὶ γραμματικὸν καὶ γεωμετρικόν), reflecting the neuter noun "child" (τέκνον [Gen 17:16]). Philo's reduction of these five areas of study to three is done out of exegetical necessity: he wants to create a list of "seven" (cf. 1 Kgdms 2:5). He thus eliminates two that can be related to the others. Astronomy, which is often lacking from Philo's lists, was considered a part of geometry. Rhetoric (with its twin, dialectic: see *Congr.* 18), which was denigrated at times in the Platonist tradition, is kindred to grammar. See also Philo, *Prob.* 157, where a similar three-fold division is attributed to Diogenes the Cynic.

justice itself, temperance itself, prudence itself, and courage itself. Philo refers to the four cardinal virtues numerous times throughout his corpus. QGE: *QG* 4.204; Allegorical Commentary: *Leg.* 1.63; 2.18; *Cher.* 5; *Sacr.* 54, 84; *Det.* 75; *Post.* 128; *Agr.* 19; *Ebr.* 23; *Sobr.* 38; *Migr.* 219; *Her.* 209; *Mut.* 146, 225; Exposition of the Law: *Mos.* 2.185, 216; *Opif.* 73; *Abr.* 219; *Spec.* 2.62; *Virt.* 167; *Praem.* 160; Philosophical Treatises: *Prob.* 67, 71; Apologetic Treatises: *Legat.* 312.

§147. *the truly citizen soul.* Colson (PLCL 5:217, n. c) adds: "for this play on ἀστῆς ("citizen") and ἀστεῖον ("good") (for which Mangey needlessly wished to substitute ἀστόν [male citizen]) cf. *Migr.* 99."

Nachleben
For the early Christian reception of Gen 17:16a and 1 Kgdms 2:5, see the Parallel Exegesis on sections (a) and (b) in the current chapter.

d   *"I Will Bless Her, and She Shall Be for the Nations" (§§148–150)*
     Analysis and General Comments

Having completed his exegesis of the text cited in §130, Philo turns in section (d) §§148–150 to the next full sentence in his primary lemma, Gen 17:16b: "I will bless her, and she shall be for the nations." This section is included in the present chapter on the basis of its thematic continuity with the earlier parts of this chapter (a further elaboration of the Isaac power) and its offering of the second of three "promises" mentioned in §154. Although some find a minor caesura in the chapter at §148, the integrality of §§130–153 is suggested by Philo's treatment of the whole of Gen 17:16 in *QG* 3.54. With this second promise, Philo continues his exposition of the symbolic significance of Sarah, generic virtue, and her child(ren). Generic virtue is subdivided into a host of particular virtues, which illuminate a variety of skills or actions. Although the technical rhetorical terms are not used (see §106), the section divides into two parts: a "summary" (κεφάλαιον) and its "proofs" (πίστεις).

(1) Philo begins by interpreting the primary lemma (Gen 17:16b) allegorically. "Nations" refer, symbolically, both to species and subspecies of "living organisms" (ζῷα), as well as to subgroupings of different "disciplines" or "realities" (πράγματα). Virtue—as an excellence or stable disposition—is a boon to each kind of figural "nation," the literal and the allegorical (§148).

(2) Having summarized his allegorical thesis, Philo offers a series of supporting proofs. The farmer, the charioteer, the ship's captain, the household manager, and the civil servant all do their actions better when assisted by the appropriate excellence. By contrast, the absence of that excellence in

each of these areas results in the privation of the goods acquired by it: wars, lawlessness, shipwrecks, etc. Virtue being "for the nations" is proved by the benefit she gives in a number of spheres (§§ 149–150).

Detailed Comments

(1) § 148. *"I will bless her, and she will be for nations."* Philo cites the next part of his primary biblical lemma, Gen 17:16b: "I will bless her/him, and he/she will be for nations" (εὐλογήσω αὐτήν/αὐτόν, καὶ ἔσται εἰς ἔθνη). While the gender of the first pronoun is contested in the Septuagint, Philo's version evidently read "I will bless *her*"—i.e., Sarah. The textual tradition reading "her" instead of "him" points Philo toward an allegorical understanding of Sarah's blessing of the nations.

into suitable species and subspecies, as if into nations. Philo offers a window into Hellenistic biological taxonomy, which apparently divided genera not only into species, but also "sub-species" (τὰ ὑπὸ τοῖς εἴδεσιν). This is the only reference to subspecies in Philo's Greek corpus. One wonders whether "nation" (ἔθνος) also belongs to Hellenistic scientific taxonomy, just as "family" or "kingdom" functions in Linnaean biology. If so, it is subordinated, rather than superordinated, to genus. Philo uses the biological analogy to direct his allegoresis away from literal nations to the allegorical species and subspecies of actions and their respective virtues.

"nations" of animals ... "nations" of actions. Although Philo often uses the term "things" (πράγματα) to indicate noetic realities, in opposition to "bodies" (σώματα) made of matter, here the term carries the more common meaning of "actions"—not dissimilar from Aristotle's "acts" (πράξεις).

it is a great benefit for excellence to be present. Having allegorically parsed the final word of the primary lemma, "nations" (ἔθνη), as species of "actions," Philo turns to the first word, "I will bless" (εὐλογήσω), and perhaps also to the preposition "for the benefit of" (εἰς), deriving from both the sense of "advantage." Sarah (generic virtue) distributes divine blessings through her resolution into the excellences that produce specific actions.

Philo's summary entails an allegoresis of the first and last words of the pericope. In the following proofs (§§ 149–150), he will put flesh and bone on this skeletal interpretation.

(2) § 149. *destitute and bereft of practical wisdom.* In this section, Philo slightly shifts the allegorical significance of Sarah from generic virtue to "wisdom" or "practical reason" (φρόνησις). For Sarah as "practical wisdom" (φρόνησις), see the detailed comments on §§ 79–80.

by excellence ... by excellence ... by excellence. Arnaldez (1964, 101, n. 2) points out that the Greek word ἀρετή is not used here of "moral excellence," but

TABLE 6.2   The Effects of Virtue and Vice

Areas improved by excellence	Detrimental effects of mismanagement
(a) agrarian	(h') war
(b) charioteer	(g') lawlessness
(c) ship's captain	(e') corrupt politics
(d) household	(d') confusions
(e) city	(c') ill sailing
(f) countryside	upheavals
(g) laws	perverse skills
(h) peace	deceitful cunning

of "skills" or "excellences" in general (see Plato, *Gorgias, passim*). Philo employs the literary device of anaphora—"the repetition, with emphasis, of the same word or phrase at the beginning of several successive clauses" (Smyth § 3010). The threefold "by excellence" (ἀρετῇ μέν ... ἀρετῇ δέ ... ἀρετῇ δέ) reflects stock rhetoric in the Alexandrian synagogue (see Parallel Exegesis).

the agrarian ... the charioteer ... the ship's captain. Although literal professions, Philo's first three practitioners of excellence are also metaphors for the ruling part of the soul. For a symbolic interpretation of the "agrarian," see the Noahic treatises of the Allegorical Commentary. The charioteer and ship's captain are stock Platonist and political metaphors used throughout the *corpus Philonicum*.

households, city, and country ... keepers of the common weal. Philo's second exemplary triad names three spheres of action in increasing scope of geographical territory (household, city, countryside). Those who govern them are titled, respectively, "managers," "statesmen," and "keepers of the common weal." Each of these tasks requires the use of a particular "excellence" and the exercise of "practical wisdom" (φρόνησις).

§ 150. *introduces the best laws and sows everywhere the seeds of peace.* To the six foregoing examples, Philo adds two more: good lawgiving and peace.

the opposite disposition to excellence. I.e., "vice" (κακία), as the opposite generic "disposition" (ἕξις). In this allegoresis, this means something akin to "mismanagement."

war, lawlessness ... deceitful cunning. Philo lists seven or eight outcomes of vicious mismanagement, corresponding with the eight blessings of virtue or excellence. As shown in table 6.2, these are presented in inverse order, giving an (imperfectly) chiastic verbal picture of the contrasting states.

sickness among the sciences ... "perverse skills." Philo observes a sickness in the rational sciences. "Deceitful cunning" (πανουργία) stands at the root of such perversions. See Colson (PLCL 5:591) for a similar thought in Quintilian, *Inst.* 2.15.2: "(rhetoricen) quidam pravitatem quondam artis, id est κακοτεχνίαν, nominaverunt" [some have called rhetoric a kind of privation of a skill, or in Greek 'a perverse skill]."

the "nations"—these great and numerous networks of animals and actions. Philo restates his central argument, now amplified by the proofs. The "nations" (ἔθνη) of Gen 17:16bβ are "animals and actions" (ζῷα ὁμοῦ τε πράγματα). This construction syntactically recalls the earlier Philonic merism, "bodies and realities" (σώματα τε ὁμοῦ καὶ πράγματα [§§ 8, 9, cf. 179]), which refers to material bodies and immaterial realities. Colson, sensing some connection between these phrases, renders the former in § 150 as "both of living creatures and of actions and ideas." Something like this may well be meant. There is a correspondence between the literal actions of embodied creatures, on the one hand, and the ideological improvement of the mind via practical reason, on the other.

to the benefit of those who receive them. Philo reiterates his interpretation of Gen 17:16bα, "I will bless" and Gen 17:16bβ, "she will be for." Arnaldez (1964, 102, n. 1) notes the collective implications of Philo's interpretation of the nations: "Philo conserves for it ⟨viz., the word "nations"⟩ its political and social sense. Virtue, generic and generative, does not only engender the particular moral virtues in the individual soul, but all the virtues which are at root from the development of society by the sciences, the arts, politics."

Parallel Exegesis

§ 148. ***Gen 17:16b ("I will bless her, and she shall be for nations")***. Both Aucher and Marcus translate the ambiguous Armenian of Philo's citation of Gen 17:16 in QG 3.54 to read "I will bless *him*, and *he* shall be for the nations." Philologically, both pronouns might be masculine, feminine, or one of each. The simplest solution is to read both as feminine rather than masculine. As in *Mut.* 148–150, so in QG 3.54 Philo sees generic virtue ("her") at work behind particular laws and specific virtues. These, according to Philo, "bear the likeness of peoples and kings." Beyond these two treatises, Philo does not explicitly interpret Gen 17:16.

§ 149. ***by excellence ... by excellence ... by excellence***. Cf. Heb 11:3–31, in which the dative πίστει ("by faith") is brought to the fore of a sentence no fewer than eighteen times. Philo's rhetoric betrays the influence of the synagogue homily; but the device is standard in ancient rhetoric more widely.

Nachleben

§ 148. ***Gen 17:16b ("I will bless her, and she shall be for nations")***. Many later interpretations of this verse (and of Gen 17:16c ["Kings of nations will be from her/him"]) depend upon texts that transmit the masculine rather than the feminine pronoun (John Chrysostom, *Hom. Gen.* 53.369–370 [D]; Cyril of Alexandria, *Epist. pasch.* 5.3, 5 [D]). This version may have prevailed on account of the Christological reading of the verse in Christian circles. Both Chrysostom's and Cyril's interpretations are literal/biological, and the Philonic identification of "nations" with virtues is lost.

e   *"Kings of Nations Will Be from Her" (§§ 151–153)*
      Analysis and General Comments

Philo concludes chapter six with a comment on Gen 17:16c. His allegorical exposition of (e) "kings of nations will be from her" recalls both his interpretation of the "nations" (Gen 17:16b) in (d) §§ 148–150 and his discussion of Sarah's child(ren) (Gen 17:16a) as archetype and particular virtues in (b) § 143 and (c) §§ 145–147. The section divides into two units:

(1)   Philo provides a summary of his interpretation of the verse. "Kings of nations" are those whom generic virtue "carries in the womb." These are not temporal rulers, appointed by people, but eternal rulers (the wise), appointed by Nature, i.e., God (§ 151).

(2)   Philo offers two proofs of this allegoresis. For the first, he adduces and interprets Gen 23:6 as a contextualizing secondary lemma. Abraham is considered a king by the Hittites not because of his material wealth, but because of the regal character of his mind. This leads them to the correct conclusion that "only the sage is a king." Philo then illustrates this conclusion, stating the ways in which a person who possesses each of the four cardinal virtues can be said to rule. To the four virtues listed in § 146, Philo adds a fifth, "holiness," which he construes as a particular "theological" virtue (§§ 152–153).

Detailed Comments

(1) § 151. *"also kings of nations will be from her."* Philo quotes the final part of the primary lemma for chapter six, Gen 17:16c. His text-type shows the same variation from certain LXX types as was witnessed in his citation of Gen 17:16b (§ 148), with the feminine "from her" (ἐξ αὐτῆς) being found instead of the more common "from him" (ἐξ αὐτοῦ).

those whom ⟨virtue⟩ carries in her womb and issues forth. Sarah's allegorical referent, who does the "carrying" and "issuing forth," is left ambiguous by Philo. While "nature" (φύσις) could be intended, it is more in keeping with the allegoresis of the chapter (see §§ 142–143) to supply "virtue."

established as rulers forever by nature herself. The rulers of nations, of whom Moses speaks, are according to Philo "rulers" permanently appointed by nature. In Stoic thought, nature is sometimes a circumlocution for God. In Philonic Middle Platonizing thought, nature is distinguished from God, but often associated with his rule through the concept of natural law (Dillon 1977, 145). Such rulers are, in Philo's allegoresis, not changeable human beings but the stable virtues, which rule in human affairs across space and time eternally. Arnaldez (1964, 102, n. 2), cross-referencing *Virt.* 100 and *Decal.* 155, sees here Philo's "condemnation of political regimes which are a deformation of true democracy …. The word φύσις ("nature") does not here designate nature at the level of becoming (viz., creation), but in a Stoic sense, God, or perfect nature born of God in the virtuous soul."

(2) § 152. *not a myth of my fabrication.* Philo alludes to the dialectic in Platonic tradition between *mythos* and *logos* (Brisson 1998). Unlike Plato, who occasionally crafted his own philosophical myths, Philo does not create a story to make his point, but finds the allegory of virtue and her children present in the oracles of Moses. Of course, Philo is an author of allegories in a different sense (Domaradzki 2019), and also drew upon pagan myth, when appropriate. For a recent discussion of Philo and Greek myth, see Alesse and De Luca 2019 (esp. 8 and 51, on this passage).

derives from the most holy oracles. Although Philo is speaking in a Platonist register, his distinction between authorial myth and Mosaic oracle has a polemical edge against the pagan philosophers. Unlike Plato's "likely accounts," Moses speaks inspired oracles. Philo is thus differentiating Moses's philosophical mythmaking from his and Plato's, attributing the greatest authority to the Jewish lawgiver.

"you are a king from God among us." In support of his claim that Gen 17:16c speaks not of human kings but of the kingly offspring of generic virtue, Philo adduces Gen 23:4–6 as a contextualizing secondary lemma, citing only the last verse. Here, after the death of Sarah, the Hittites come to Abraham and proclaim him a king. Philo's text is identical to the Septuagint. It is lexically linked with the primary lemma (Gen 17:16c) through the catchword "king" (βασιλεύς).

not after examining his material possessions … without a city in which to dwell. Philo's depiction of Abraham as a migrant bereft of possessions is derived from the patriarch's request to the Hittites in Gen 23:4: "I am a pilgrim and sojourner with you; give me possession of a grave among yourselves" (πάροικος καὶ παρεπίδημος ἐγώ εἰμι μεθ' ὑμῶν· δότε οὖν μοι κτῆσιν τάφου μεθ' ὑμῶν). Abraham's want of a "house," a "people," a city, and any "possession," are echoed in Philo's description in § 152.

the kingly disposition of Abraham's thought. For the philosophical term "disposition" (ἕξις), see the detailed comments on §150 and esp. §§121–122.

only the sage is a king. A Stoic commonplace. See the detailed comment on §128 above. Colson (PLCL 5:591) gives *SVF* 3.169 as illustration of this "Stoic paradox."

§153. *the prudent person ... knowing what it is necessary to do and not to do.* To illustrate the ruling capacity of virtuous souls, Philo offers shorthand definitions of the four cardinal virtues (plus holiness) similar to those found in the doxographies. See Diogenes Laertius (7.126) for the Stoic definitions. Colson (PLCL 5:591) gives *SVF* 3.262. For the cardinal virtues more generally in Philo, see the detailed comment on §146.

"Prudence" (φρόνησις) is excellence in practical reason—knowing how to use the other virtues at the appropriate time. Diogenes Laertius (7.126) gives the Stoic definition: "prudence concerns things that ought to be done, that ought not to be done, and that are indifferent" (ἡ φρόνησις περὶ τὰ ποιητέα καὶ μὴ καὶ οὐδέτερα). Philo in §153 notably omits the third category of "adiaphora" (οὐδέτερα). Arnaldez (1964, 103, n. 3) reiterates his claim that Philo uses the Stoic description of prudence in a non-Stoic context. Virtue is not merely a disposition of the soul, but a personified and living thing—a personal power of God, with whom human beings might have an interpersonal relationship.

the temperate person ... distinguishing carefully ... to choose and to abstain. "Temperance" (σωφροσύνη) is the mean between gluttony and abstinence; or more generally, between choosing too little of something and choosing too much.

the courageous person ... to stand one's ground, and when this cannot be done safely. "Courage" (ἀνδρεία) is the stable disposition between cowardice and recklessness.

the just person ... impartial fairness when there are portions to be assigned. "Justice" or "righteousness" (δικαιοσύνη) is not defined in terms of a mean, but of a "balance" (ἰσότης), according to the classical definition found in both Peripatetic (Ps.-Aristotle, *Mag. mor.* 1.33.5) and Stoic (Chrysippus, frag. 295) thought. Similarly, Diogenes Laertius (7.126) speaks of fairness as the result of justice: "equality and fairness follow in the train of justice" (τῇ δὲ δικαιοσύνῃ ἰσότης καὶ εὐγνωμοσύνη ⟨ἕπεται⟩).

the holy person ... the best conceptions about God. "Holiness" (ὁσιότης) is added to this list by Philo as a fifth, theological virtue. Unlike the preceding four cardinal virtues, it is primarily theoretical and vertical (like piety), rather than practical and horizontal—although it does have an ethical aspect. The selection of five "kingly" virtues is likely conditioned by Philo's Mosaic Judaism, with its five books of the Law. For more on Philo's supplementation of the four cardinal virtues, see the detailed comments on §50, where Philo adds the "entirely perfect good" (συνόλως ἀγαθὸν τέλειον); on §225, where he adds "love of humanity" (φιλανθρωπία); and esp. on §76, where he adds "piety" (εὐσέβεια).

Parallel Exegesis

§ 151. *Gen 17:16c ("kings of nations will be from her")*. As mentioned in the Parallel Exegesis on § 130, both Aucher and Marcus translate the ambiguous Armenian of Philo's citation of Gen 17:16 in QG 3.54 to read "kings of the nations shall be from *him*." Philologically, the pronoun might be either masculine or feminine. Philo's ensuing allegorical exegesis, that "each of the immortal virtues has very many voluntary laws, which bear the likeness of kings and peoples" (Marcus, PLCLSup) suggests the feminine (generic virtue or the soul) as the more obvious translation. On the regal nature of the virtues, Philo adds that "virtues and the generations of virtues are kingly affairs, being taught beforehand by nature what is sovereign and unservile" (Marcus, PLCLSup).

§ 152. *only the sage is a king*. Colson (PLCL 5:591) cross-references *Sobr.* 57; *Migr.* 197; and *Somn.* 2.244. Cf. *Quod omnis probus liber sit*, for the similar thesis that "every good person is free."

Nachleben

§ 151. *Gen 17:16c ("kings of nations will be from her")*. See the *Nachleben* for Gen 17:16b (§ 148).

§ 152. *Gen 23:6 ("you are a king from God among us")*. Van den Hoek (1988, 106, 184) points to Clement of Alexandria's statement in *Strom.* 2.100.2 [A] as parallel to the present passage:

> And again, teaching that the wise man is king, it introduces people of different race saying to him (Abraham) "you are a king before God among us" (Gen 23:6), since the subjects obey the good man voluntarily because of his desire for virtue.

The likelihood of Philonic influence is high.

[Chapter 7]
Abraham and Sarah Laugh (§§ 154–174)

Chapter seven is the first of two chapters about Abraham's response to the covenantal promises of God discussed in chapters four through six. Their themes are, respectively, joy (chapter seven) and faith (chapter eight). These chapters pick up where chapter three (Gen 17:3) left off: with the Abraham mind again falling (Gen 17:17a)—but this time, on account of a fuller understanding of the promises.

Chapter seven is comprised of Philo's comments on a single primary biblical lemma (Gen 17:17a). The same primary lemma is treated in *QG* 3.55 (see Parallel Exegesis). In §154, the lemma is not cited, but presumed. The chapter can be divided into four subsections: (a) a brief exegesis of Gen 17:17a (§§154–156); (b) a long *quaestio et solutio* on the logical and philosophical possibility of Abraham's "laughter" before the birth of Isaac ("laughter") (§§157–165); (c) the adduction of a contextualizing secondary lemma (Gen 18:12) relating Sarah's laughter (§§166–167); and (d) a final section on the false mirth of the vicious soul, facilitated by the exegesis of a mid-length tertiary biblical lemma, Exod 45:16–18 (§§168–174). In its basic structure—a primary biblical lemma about Abraham's laughter (Gen 17:17a), supplemented by a contextualizing secondary lemma about Sarah's laughter (Gen 18:12)—the chapter resembles the first twenty sections of chapter five (§§60–80), which interpret Abram's (Gen 17:5) and Sarai's (Gen 17:15) changes of name in tandem.

a   *"Abraham Falls and Laughs"* (§§154–156)
     Analysis and General Comments

The opening three sections (§§154–167) of chapter seven are comprised of a short sermon with an exhortation on Gen 17:17a: Abraham's falling and laughing, subsequent to God's promise of a son from Sarah. The characterization of the mind that rightly responds to the "promises" (ὑποσχέσεις [§154]) of God by recognizing its own nothingness mirrors Abram's response to the "divine promises" (ὑποσχέσεις θεῖαι [§§54–56]) in chapter three. The present section (§§154–156) transcends and develops that earlier one in its new focus on the "joy" of the soul that falls. The section divides into two parts:

(1)   Philo's allegorical exposition of the primary biblical lemma (Gen 17:17a), which understands Abraham as a kind of mind (§§154–155).
(2)   An exhortation to the soul to fall like Abraham fell (§156).

     Detailed Comments

(1) §154. *the mind.* Philo begins by interpreting the uncited primary lemma (Gen 17:17a) allegorically, without even naming Abraham. He picks up seamlessly from the allegoresis of Abram/Abraham as "mind" (νοῦς) begun in chapter five (§69).

swollen by these promises. Referring to the "promises" (ὑποσχέσεις [§154]) of chapters four through six, Philo intentionally recalls Abram's first fall in Gen

17:3. He interpreted this earlier fall as the soul's recognition of its own inherent nothingness, in light of the "divine promises" (ὑποσχέσεις θεῖαι [§ 54]) in chapters one and two. I have translated the participle ἐκφυσηθέντα as "swollen," although no strongly negative connotation is intended. Philo's point is that the Abrahamic mind is *rightly* elated and inflated by these promises—if ever a mind should have been.

would be lifted up into the air. Philo's description of the Abraham mind as becoming "lifted up into the air" (μετέωρον ἀρθῆναι) recalls the etymological symbolism of the Abram soul of § 66—the "elevated father" (μετέωρος πατήρ)—rather than the Abraham soul. Philo may be relating an alternative allegoresis of the etymology. "Abram" is now interpreted as the truly philosophical mind (rather than the merely astronomical one), which like the chariot soul of Plato's *Phaedrus* ascends beyond the visible stars to the invisible "place beyond heaven" (ὑπερουράνιος τόπος [*Phaedr.* 247de]).

to convict us, who are wont to become haughty. Philo contrasts the Abrahamic mind, which has every natural right to be uplifted, with the more typical, imperfect human mind, which becomes conceited and "puffed up" even at the smallest accomplishment.

falls and immediately laughs. Philo adduces the primary lemma, Gen 17:17a, by way of an allusion which could easily be missed. A comparison with the Septuagint shows slight modifications attuned to the developing allegoresis:

Gen 17:17a	§ 154
Abraham fell (ἔπεσεν) upon his face and laughed (ἐγέλασεν).	He falls (πίπτει) and immediately laughs (καὶ εὐθὺς γελᾷ).

Five points about Philo's paraphrase warrant mention. First, Philo omits the name of Abraham. This is because he is already speaking at the level of the allegory of the soul. Second, Philo shifts both aorist verbs into the present tense, signifying the perennially present time of his psychic allegory. Third, Philo forgoes commenting on Abraham's falling "upon his face." He does not wish to repeat the three-fold interpretation, which he has already given in § 56 ("fallen is sense perception, fallen is speech, fallen is king mind"). Fourth, Philo focuses on the coordination of falling and laughter. While it remains unspoken, there is a critical difference between the "fall of Abram" in §§ 54–56, and the "fall of Abraham" in §§ 154–156. The former was the fall of the mind still in the process of learning; the latter is the fall of the mind, whose name has been changed—of Abraham, standing on the brink of perfection. This perfected mind not only falls (more as an indictment of others), but also laughs—a sign that he has in some way already reached the joyful perfection symbolized by Isaac. Fifth, Philo's addition of the adjective "immediately" (εὐθύς) signifies the immediacy of divine gifts like joy, which are not hindered by the "intervals" (διαστήματα) of space and time (cf. § 142).

sullen in face, but smiling in thought. The distinction between the sage's outward appearance and mind amplifies his anti-sophistic portrayal. True happiness is internal. This contrast may be found in other philosophical Jewish authors, who emphasize the frequent conjoining of external suffering and internal flourishing among the wise.

a great and unmixed joy has come to dwell within him. "Joy" (χαρά), the best of the good emotions and divine gifts, heralded at the outset of the treatise (§ 1), is said to dwell in Abraham. Joy is depicted as an unmixed wine, a noetic intoxicant. The habitation of such joy within the sage recalls Philo's microcosmic analogy of the Mosaic mind as a small temple or house for the Logos—"the image-bearing mind" (ὁ ἀγαλματοφορούμενος νοῦς [§ 21]). In § 154, the Abrahamic mind becomes a temple in which Isaac as joy—God's divine son—comes to dwell.

§ 155. *both of these movements happen at the same time.* Philo clarifies that his allegoresis is not chronological—i.e., the Abraham mind does not fall first (having learned something new) and then react in incredulous laughter. Rather, both fall and laughter are simultaneous, rational responses of the virtuous soul possessed of self-knowledge and aware of the benefits it is receiving.

within the sage who is inheriting. The language of inheritance echoes earlier scriptural texts in the Abraham cycle (Gen 15:3, 4, 7).

goods greater than his hope. The phrase might also be translated "goods greater than hope." In favor of this latter translation is the fact that not all philosophical schools (e.g., Stoicism) have a place for "hope"; however, hope is clearly among the gifts that Abraham receives. Colson's translation, "good beyond his hope," gets at this sense very nicely, but masks the plurality of gifts about which Philo is speaking.

he falls on account of his belief. In § 54, Abram is said to fall (in Gen 17:3) on account of his "judgment" or "estimate" (ὑπόληψις) of himself. In § 155, by contrast, Abraham falls on account of his "faith" (πίστις) in God. While these may be inverse ways of saying the same thing, one is not wrong also to sense an important transformation here. Philo's reinforcement of Abraham's "faith" and its new Godward focus looks ahead to the subsequent discussion of this important topic in chapter eight.

that he should not boast. The combination of the themes of faith and boasting in the exegesis of an Abrahamic text may derive from a similar conceptual field as that employed by Paul in several of his letters. See the *Nachleben*.

through scorning his mortal nothingness. Philo reiterates the reason given for Abram's first fall in §54: that the sage recognized the inherent "nothingness" (οὐδένεια [§155]); cf. "the nothingness of the mortal race" (ἡ τοῦ θνητοῦ γένους οὐδένεια [§54]). In that earlier passage, Philo indicates that Abraham "came to recognize" (γνῶναι) his nothingness; here, he adds that boasting would result from "scorning" or "misevaluating" (διὰ κατάγνωσιν) the nothingness, which he has come to comprehend. Philo's concept of human "nothingness" (οὐδένεια) reflects the influence of philosophical scepticism on his thought—an anthropological system which elides nicely with his Jewish convictions about God and creation. See esp. Lévy 2018; 2024.

he laughs, to the contrary, on account of the firmness of his piety. The translation does not do justice to Philo's syntax, which foregrounds the virtue of piety in the phrase "on account of his piety's firmness" (εἰς εὐσεβείας βεβαίωσιν). Philo uses parallel constructions to depict Abraham's double movement: he falls on "account of his faith" (εἰς πίστιν)—the virtue which will be treated in chapter eight—and laughs on account of his piety's firmness. By highlighting the stability of Abraham's piety, Philo reemphasizes the content of the sage's humility: that only God is stable, whereas the human being is "in no way so firmly fixed" (ὁ δ' οὐδέποτε ταὐτῷ βεβαίως ἱδρυμένος [§55]).

that God alone is the cause of graces and goods. The rationale for Abraham's laughter differs from that of his falling. Whereas he falls on account of his own self-knowledge, he laughs out of an inner joy produced by knowing who God is—the God of the covenant, who gives grace and all other goods (see §§52–53, 57–59). Arnaldez (1964, 104, n. 1) adds that with this twofold motion, "the mystical experience arrives at its goal. The joy subsists in God through the annihilation of the mortal creature that the human being carries within himself. The death of the human being is the birth of God's human being."

(2) §156. ***therefore, let creation fall and be sullen.*** Philo closes this first section of chapter seven with a short exhortation to "creation" (γένεσις). Cf. §§54–56, which lacks such an exhortation. Philo adds this new section on the second occasion of Abraham's falling because the patriarch has now reached his exemplary pinnacle. The exhortation may also anthologize a piece of synagogue paraenesis, which Philo wishes to incorporate and preserve.

with regard to its natural capacity ... raised by God. Philo explores the distinction between nature and grace. The distance between the two in passages such as this one should not lead the reader to forget that the human soul is already "graced" by God, according to Philo, in creation by the gift of its fashioning after the divine image. Neither should God's gifts in Philo's thought be construed as solely or primarily protological. The Abrahamic allegory of the soul bears witness to a theory of divine grace given at particular points throughout a soul's journey—sometimes after significant periods of time.

unstable and destined for grief ... its stay and its joy. Philo further expounds the difference between the soul that trusts in its own natural capacity, but is unaware that it is ontologically "unstable" (ἀνίδρυτος) (cf. §55: "in no way situated with similar stability" [ὁ δ' οὐδέποτε ταὐτῷ βεβαίως ἱδρυμένος]) and destined for "grief" (λυπή), and the soul that finds its entire "joy" (χαρά) in God. Arnaldez (1964, 105, n. 2) adds an important *caveat*: "The joy of Abraham is not yet blessedness (he needs to receive Isaac, cf. *Cher*. 8). His joy remains tethered to a movement, that of liberation from the sensible. This is hope: joy before joy (*Praem*. 161; *infra* §163)."

Parallel Exegesis

§154. ***Gen 17:17a ("Abraham fell ... and laughed")***. Philo treats the same lemma, Gen 17:17a, in *QG* 3.55. While similar in thrust to the present treatise, his *solutio* in the earlier series is less exegetically and philosophically developed. In themes and structure, it largely reduplicates *QG* 3.41 (Abram's first fall in Gen 17:3). Philo gives Abraham's second fall a double interpretation. First (*QG* 3.55a), Abraham falls in worshipful obeisance, engendered by divine ecstasy. Philo then (*QG* 3.55b) interprets the fall secondarily as a "confession" that "God alone stands" (see *QG* 3.41c). Having interpreted the fall, Philo thirdly (*QG* 3.55c) interprets Abraham's falling on his "face" as his "sovereign part"—in this case, the "governing faculty" (ἡγεμονικόν) rather than the senses (cf. *QG* 3.41a). Finally (*QG* 3.55d), Philo turns to Abraham's laughter, interpreted as "hope" at the joy of the promise.

Elsewhere in the *QGE*, Philo expands on this interpretation. In *QG* 4.17, for instance, Philo asks why Sarah is rebuked for her laughter (Gen 18:13–14), but Abraham (Gen 17:17) is not. Philo answers that Abraham was "secured by an unswerving and inflexible conviction of faith, for to him who has faith in God all uncertainty is alien" (Marcus, PLCLSup). Important parallels also occur in the Allegorical Commentary. Especially curious is *Leg*. 3.85–87, where Philo initially describes Abraham as "not hoping" (οὐκ ἐλπίσας), but then goes on to offer an interpretation of Abraham's laughter as joy in advance. In the Exposition of the Law (*Abr*. 201), Philo paraphrases the verse briefly and reiterates joy's classification as a good emotion.

sullen in face, but smiling in thought. For the dissonance between the external appearance of the sage and his internal happiness, see Philo, *Prov.* 2.12–14, 24.

§ 155. *both of these movements happen at the same time.* Unlike QG 3.55, in which the falling and laughter of the sage are treated as differentiated allegorical movements, in *De mutatione nominum* Philo focuses on their synchronicity within the soul approaching perfection. His exegesis of Abraham's second fall in the Allegorical Commentary shows conscious development from his symbolic interpretation of Abraham's first fall, in order to avoid repeating material and to coordinate both Abrahamic falls as distinct stages in the patriarch's journey toward perfection.

within the sage who is inheriting. Philo's most sustained treatment of Abrahamic inheritance, as a feature of his allegory of the soul, may be found in the treatise *Quis rerum divinarum heres sit.* See esp. *Her.* 30–39, 63–74.

Nachleben

§ 154. *Gen 17:17a ("Abraham fell ... and laughed").* Especially worthy of comparison is the parallel found in John Chrysostom (*Hom. Gen.* 53.370 [A]), which shows Philonic influence on a number of points:

> Abraham saw the superabundance of the promise (ἡ ὑπερβολὴ τῆς ὑποσχέσεως) and, having recognized the greatness of the power of the one who was announcing it (τῆς δυνάμεως τοῦ ἐπαγγειλαμένου τὸ μέγεθος), he fell upon his face and laughed (Gen 17:17a), which might be paraphrased as, "he became exceedingly joyful" (περιχαρὴς ἐγένετο). For he was pondering in the reasonings of his thought (κατὰ τοὺς τῆς διανοίας λογισμούς) how this could be according to human logic, that a child should be born to a hundred-year-old and that his barren wife, who had remained childless even until ninety years of age, should suddenly be able to be quickened to childbearing. Reckoning these things in his thought (κατὰ τὴν διάνοιαν), he did not move to utter anything of the sort with his tongue (διὰ τῆς γλώττης προενεγκεῖν), but showing his discretion, offers a prayer for Ishmael.

Although the full scope of Philo's allegory of the soul is missing, Chrysostom's interpretation nevertheless reflects Philonic vocabulary and thought in several ways. First, the mention of divine "superabundance" (ὑπερβολή) in connection with the covenantal promises echoes *Mut.* 53. Chrysostom also thematizes God's speech as containing "the promise" (ἡ ὑπόσχεσις), though in the singular rather than the Philonic plural (*Mut.* 54, 154). Most germanely to the present passage, Chrysostom interprets Abraham's laughter as "joy," indicating that the mind of the sage became "exceedingly joyful" (περιχαρής), anticipating in some way the birth of Isaac. Chrysostom also defends Abraham's questioning "in his thought" (κατὰ τὴν διάνοιαν [see Gen 17:17b]) by noting that these queries do not reach his tongue—a point which Philo will make in chapter eight (*Mut.* 178). For more on the reception of Abraham's various "falls," see the *Nachleben* on *Mut.* 54–55 above.

sullen in face, but smiling in thought. For a parallel dissonance between the external appearance of the sage and his internal happiness, see 2 Cor 4:16–18.

§ 155. **that he should not boast.** Philo's admonition against boasting derives from a common Jewish tradition, which also shapes Paul's thought. See, e.g., 1 Cor 1:29; 3:21; and esp. Rom 5:1–2, which follows Paul's allegorical exegesis of Abraham in Rom 4. Paul, however, prefers the verb "to boast" καυχᾶσθαι (found in *Congr.* 107) and never uses Philo's verb here "put on airs" (μεγαλαυχεῖν). Although the precise definition of "boasting" may differ in each figure (Barclay 2015), there is a conceptual kinship between these ideas.

b   *Hope: Joy before Joy (§§ 157–165)*
         Analysis and General Comments

Having given his exposition of Abraham's second fall (Gen 17:17a) in §§ 154–156, Philo now entertains a hypothetical question, which he suggests may puzzle some readers: how can it be that Abraham's laughter in Gen 17:17a symbolizes a joyful disposition, when in fact "joy" itself has not been born (cf. the birth of Isaac only in Gen 21:2–3)? Philo answers this question with a series of analogical and propositional proofs. Chiefly, he argues that nature herself provides "signs" and intimations of future states. For example, chicks flutter as a portent of their capacity to fly. So should the reader understand Abraham's laughter as the soul's expectation of future joy—or, "joy before joy," which Philo names "hope." With this evocation of hope as a kind of "pre-emotion" (προπάθεια [*QG* 1.79; see Runia 2020, 262–263]), Philo develops a "now and not yet" eschatology on the individual, psychic level. This long *quaestio et solutio* divides into six sub-sections.

(1) Philo raises a question on behalf of a hypothetical interlocutor. How can it be that the soul feels joy *before* joy itself exists? That is like saying that the soul can see without eyes or smell without nostrils (§ 157).

(2) Philo makes a first attempt at answering this question drawing on a range of natural analogies from the animal world. Chicks stretch their wings before they can fly; rams and goats buck and fight before they have horns; a bull in the arena shakes its head antagonistically, but does not at first make an actual charge (§§ 158–160).

(3) Philo concludes: the soul also demonstrates premonitions of joy, without yet having fully tasted its fruit. Such is the meaning of Abraham's laughter before laughter (§ 161a).
(4) Wishing to amplify this first string of proofs and give more philosophical specification to "rejoicing before joy," Philo adduces a second set of natural analogies. Plants, as well as animals, portend their own fruit through the signs of flowers; likewise, the "deep dawn laughs" in advance of the full sunrise, by sending forth oblique rays of light (§§ 161b–162).
(5) These additional natural analogies lead Philo to a clearer philosophical exposition of his conclusion. "Joy" properly describes the soul's happiness at present goods, "hope," its enjoyment of goods expected in the future. Conversely, the soul is sorrowful for present evils, but fearful of evils in the future. In depicting Abraham's "joy before joy," Moses is showing the soul characterized by hope (§ 163).
(6) Wishing to bring his answer back to the initial analogy from the senses (§ 157), Philo adds that smell and sight are similarly "foretasters" of the goods of perception. He concludes implicitly that the soul is capable of tasting future joys through hope (§§ 164–165).

Detailed Comments

(1) § 157. *fittingly might someone be confused*. Naming an *aporia* is a typical way of introducing a scholastic question in the commentary tradition. It may represent either the teacher's note to himself or a gesture to an implied audience. Philo uses the verb "be confused" (ἀπορεῖν) here and in § 83 in the present treatise to introduce secondary questions after the exposition of a primary lemma.

according to our account ... the present study. Philo's terse phrase "according to our account" (καθ' ἡμᾶς) refers to the understanding of Isaac's birth as the advent of joy that spans the entirety of the present "study" (σκέψις) or treatise. The plural pronoun "us" may be an aggrandizing singular, but may also refer to the communal tradition that has produced the commentary. (Philo is capable of speaking of his own individual experience and exegetical efforts in the first person singular. See Cover 2020b.)

laughter has not yet come into existence. For Isaac is "laughter." Isaac is not born until Gen 21:2–3, but Abraham laughs in Gen 17:17a—whence, the exegetical and allegorical problem. Philo has already defined Isaac as laughter and joy at several places in this treatise (§§ 1, 131, and 137).

just as one cannot see without eyes ... nor again make use of any of the senses. Philo elaborates the exegetical objection, raised by the tension between

Gen 17:17a and Gen 21:2–3, through an analogy from the senses. Just as the organs which enable the senses must exist before particular instances of seeing or hearing take place, so the psychic capacity for laughter must precede particular cases of its enjoyment.

nor ... form mental conceptions apart from the reasoning faculty. Philo's argument follows both his Platonist preference for vision and the Stoic bifurcation of the soul into irrational and rational components. What the eye is to physical sight, the "reasoning faculty" (λογισμός) is to the process of comprehension. Thus, psychic laughter (joy) is not possible without the appropriate rational capacity ordered thereunto.

without laughter having first been fashioned. Although Philo does not give particulars, the verb "has been fashioned" (ἐδεδημιούργητο) is a divine passive, which alludes to Plato's mythic Demiurge in the *Timaeus*. Philo forges a link between the initial creation of the soul and its perfection at later stages through the gracious gift of new or perfected faculties.

(2) § 158. **what should be said to this objection?** Philo responds to the questioner's *aporia* with a rhetorical question: "What is it necessary to say?" (τί οὖν χρὴ λέγειν;). This looks as much like a reminder to the teacher to address the subject as a rebuttal to the student. Philo uses the same rhetorical question several times elsewhere in the Allegorical Commentary (see *Leg.* 1.60; 3.91; *Post.* 34; *Deus* 38; *Somn.* 1.229), but never in its interrogative form in the Exposition of the Law or his other extant Greek writings. The question belongs to the scholastic setting of Philo's private school.

nature foreshadows many things ... through certain symbols. Philo invokes a theory of natural symbolism to complement his Platonizing theory of inspired Scripture. For Philo, the same Logos speaks in both. Philo stands, thereby, at the beginning of a long tradition—honored particularly by early Byzantine and medieval Christian authors—of reading the "book of nature" alongside what was to become the Bible.

proclaiming beforehand its hope. One of three instances of the verb "proclaim beforehand" (προευαγγελίζειν) in Philo's extant Greek writings. The others are in *Opif.* 34 (with reference to dawn "pre-evangelizing" the sun) and *Abr.* 153 (where the eyes "proclaim beforehand" that there is a good feeling in the heart of a person seeing his friend).

do you not see the chick? Philo adduces the first of two proofs from the animal kingdom with a rhetorical question. The fluttering of wings portends the "hope of flight" (cf. Emily Dickenson, "'Hope' is the things with feathers")—a motif that is equally natural and Platonic, symbolizing contemplation. Here, Philo first introduces the theme of "hope," to which he will return in earnest in § 163.

§ 159. *have you not seen a ram or billy goat or newly born ox?* Philo's second proof, drawn from the world of mammalian biology, is likewise introduced with a rhetorical question. "Have you not seen" (οὐκ εἶδες) is set in parallel with "do you not see" (οὐχ ὁρᾷς [§ 158]), but may be read as a gnomic aorist. Philo's adduction of young fighting goats implicitly complements his first example of a young flying bird. Whereas the chick portends the individual "flight" of the soul and the contemplative life, the butting rams or oxen represent the communal "fight" of souls engaged in the *vita activa*.

§ 160. *even in the bullfights, mature bulls.* Not wishing his analogical proofs to rest on immature "young bucks," which would hardly be appropriate to illustrate the Abrahamic soul's premonitions of joy as it nears perfection, Philo offers the supplementary image of the fully mature bull in the arena. This is the seasoned fighter—the soon-to-be-perfected athlete of virtue—which despite his ability, still shows a kind of patience about receiving his reward.

Philo's proofs from the natural world are comparatively rare in the Allegorical Commentary, but neither are they atypical. He concatenates natural proofs much as he does scriptural ones—drawing intentionally on complementary motifs. Philo's chosen animals are all clean ones, fit for sacrifice. Cf. the animal imagery for the sage in Dio Chrysostom's description of Cynic sages as "dogs" (*Orat.* 8.11), which might give Philo pause on a number of counts.

bull-like. Or, even more literally, "bull-faced" (ταυρωπός).

those people, whose custom it is to coin words. Philo uses the rare verb "to coin words" or "to make names" (ὀνοματοποεῖν), which is found in his corpus only here and in § 262. The language is inspired by Plato's description of Homer in *Crat.* 407b3 as "the name maker" (ὁ τὰ ὀνόματα ποιῶν), in his alleged coining of "Athena." Plato (388e1–8) also speaks of the name-maker as a "lawgiver" (νομοθέτης), and specifically refers to the action of "setting names" (ὄνομα θέσθαι/κεῖσθαι), "calling names" (καλεῖν τὰ ὀνόματα: *Crat.* 392c), or simply "naming" ([ἐπ]ὀνομάζεσθαι [*Crat.* 396a9, etc.]). Plato also uses the terms "namewright" (ὀνοματουργός) and "craftsman of names" (δημιουργὸς ὀνομάτων [*Crat.* 390e2]), which echo the *Timaeus*. Whereas in *Mut.* 160, Philo shows sympathy with the "conventionalist" idea of naming (naming according to "custom" [ἔθος]), in *Mut.* 262 he will espouse a "naturalist" theory. Through this bifurcated approach, Philo supports the moderate position of Socrates (and Plato) in the *Cratylus*, in which both nature and convention are given their due.

getting charged up (orousis). LSJ gives "impulse," "appetition," or "charge" (ὁρμή) as rough synonyms for "eagerness" (ὄρουσις). Philo, by contrast, makes a distinction between these similarly sounding words, which he attributes to prior name-makers. Colson (PLCL 5:591) cites the Stoic definition of "eagerness" (ὄρουσις) as "a movement of the mind toward something in the future" (φορὰ διανοίας ἐπί τι μέλλον [SVF 3.169]) as a precedent, but sees the Stoic identification of a "design" (ἐπιβολή) as an "impulse before impulse" (ὁρμὴ πρὸ ὁρμῆς [SVF 3.173]) as non-identical with Philo's similarly worded "kind of charge before the charge" (ὁρμή τινα πρὸ ὁρμῆς). Arnaldez (1964, 106, n. 1) adduces the same two Stoic parallels, in which "eagerness" (ὄρουσις) is defined as "a form of active impulse" (τῆς πρακτικῆς ὁρμῆς ... εἶδος). I have translated the noun "eagerness" (ὄρουσις) as "getting charged up" (although this metaphor originates with batteries rather than bulls) to denote the premeditated excitement of the bull before it actually engages its opponent—a kind of visceral preening and strutting. In American slang, one might speak of athletes "getting hyped up, amped up, revved up, pumped up, or fired up."

(3) 161a. *in a similar way, the soul also experiences many things*. Philo reaches a preliminary conclusion from his analogical proofs. The behavior of animals, both young and mature, demonstrates how souls may express characteristics not-yet-possessed ahead of time. Philo's insistence that the soul of the sage "experiences" (πάσχει) these things indicates (as noted above in §1) that he does not adopt an "apathetic" view of the emotions, but divides them according to the philosophical *koine*, between the bad and the good, as well as between the "pre-emotions" (προπάθειαι) and full emotions (see QG 1.79; Runia 2020).

it becomes cheerful ahead of time. The compound verb, "to be cheerful ahead of time" (προγήθειν), is a Philonic *hapax* and appears only here in Greek literature. It denotes the identity of hope as a "pre-emotion" (προπάθεια [QG 1.79]; Runia 2020). Philo includes it as one of a string of "pre-" (προ-) compounds in this chapter, which he delights in inventing and concatenating like so many beads on a necklace or daisies in a chain.

with the result that, in a certain manner ... it makes merry before mirth. Philo is very cautious in his wording here. The natural result clause, introduced by ὥς, "denotes an anticipated or possible result" (Smyth §2260), thus rendering the soul's "rejoicing before joy" as a logical but unrealized predication. "In a certain manner" (τρόπον τινα) further indicates that Moses may be speaking catachrestically of Abraham's laughter in Gen 17:17a. It does not betoken the fullness of his joy; but neither is it unconnected with the promise of that coming reality in the soul of the sage.

(4) §161b. *perhaps someone would liken it also to what happens in plants*. Philo extends his stock of analogical proofs beyond the animal world, to include plants as well. He begins with fruit-bearing trees. These supply flowers as natural portents of the fruits they are about to bear. This metaphor is particularly apt to Philo's Abrahamic allegoresis, as the virtuous children of the soul have already been referred to as fruits in several places (§98 [Ephraim]; §§139–140

[Isaac/Cosmos]; cf. §§ 73–75). Arnaldez (1964, 107, n. 2) notes that Diogenes Laertius (7.86, "the plants bloom" [θάλλει τὰ φυτά]) has an analogue to the idea presented here.

put forth buds and flowers and green shoots ahead of time. Philo adds two more examples to his *catena* of "pre-" (προ-) compounds: "to put forth buds before" (προβλαστάνειν) and "to bloom before" (προανθεῖν). Both verbs are of Peripatetic provenance, attested in the writings of Theophrastus (e.g., *Caus. plant.* 1.13.12, where the two verbs are paired). Philo's use evinces the further flourishing of the botanical sciences in Hellenistic and Roman Alexandria.

§ 162. *so also, the day at deep morning laughs ahead of time.* Philo's description of daybreak echoes the pathetic fallacy of the Psalms (see LXX Ps 18:3: "Day utters a word [ἐρεύγεται ῥῆμα] to day, and night recounts its knowledge [ἀναγγέλλει γνῶσιν] to night"). In addition to the biological and botanical analogies, Philo includes an analogy to the cosmos as a whole. "Laugh beforehand" (προγελᾶν), like "be cheerful beforehand" (προγήθειν [§ 161]), is a Philonic hapax, occurring only elsewhere in the writings of John of Damascus. Philo's fashioning of these two words to express his allegory of the hope in the Abrahamic soul demonstrates his own power as a namewright and wordsmith in the Platonic and Jewish traditions.

(5) § 163. *joy ... hope.* Having completed his second wave of analogical proofs, Philo now draws a more specific conclusion: that "hope" is "rejoicing before joy." "Joy" (χαρά) and "hope" (ἐλπίς) stand together as kindred "good emotions" (εὐπάθειαι)—though hope may also be conceived as a "pre-emotion" (Runia 2020)—distinguishable only in terms of their temporal relationship to the good (present and future).

the opposite cases ... the expectation of evil begets fear. Philo names the "passions" (πάθη) corresponding to joy and hope: "grief" (λυπή) and "fear" (φόβος), respectively, which describe the experience of evil in the present and the future. Philo does not indicate that grief and fear are avoidable; rather, they are necessary responses to deprivations of the good. This position corresponds more with the Platonist and Peripatetic ethics, in which the aim is not to be ruled by such negative emotions. See also *Abr.* 157, which Colson (PLCL 6:598) connects with Crantor, Plutarch, and the notion of "moderation of the emotions" (μετριοπάθεια). Elsewhere, however, Philo will uphold the Stoic ideal of the "absence of emotions" (ἀπάθεια) as well—see, e.g., *Leg.* 3.128–129, in which Moses is said to "cut out ⟨the seat of⟩ anger entirely"—a higher ideal than the metriopathetic Aaron. Philo can thus vacillate between the views in his comments. See Birnbaum and Dillon 2021, 326–327; and Weisser 2021.

(6) § 164. *the senses also entail clear signs of the phenomenon under discussion.* Having stated his own position in § 163, Philo turns in these last two

sections to a third set of proofs from anthropology. In a scholarly style that foreshadows the structure of a Thomistic question, he responds to the objection from the senses leveled by the hypothetical questioner in § 157. Arnaldez (1964, 108, n. 1) highlights Philo's "very fluid and dynamic psychology of hope" here and draws attention to his use of the natural world to illustrate mystical (supernatural) progress.

smell ... tries ahead of time ... everything pertaining to food and drink. Responding to the argument of § 157, Philo's line of reasoning continues as follows: It is true that no sensing can take place without its appropriate sense faculty. However, the irrational soul possesses not one, but many such faculties. It is also the case that these multiple sensing faculties may share objects: for instance, smelling and tasting may both take food as their object. One can rightly say that, despite not yet having tasted a good wine, the soul has some apprehension of its taste through smelling. The same, analogically speaking, might be said of the rational soul's apprehension of its own goods, including joy, by means of adjacent faculties.

a "foretaster." Despite Philo's attribution of the term "foretaster" (προγευστρίς) to some meticulous or pedantic colleagues with a penchant for neologisms, the word is a *hapax*, occurring only here and at *Sacr.* 44 in extant Greek literature. David Hoeschel found the word interesting enough to make it a marginal subheading in his text and mentions it briefly in his *notatiunculae* (Hoeschel 1587, 51 [text], 231 [note, citing par. *Sacr.* 44]). This demonstrates that not all *verba Philonica* are of Philonic coinage, but stem from the productive scholarly and poetic culture of Hellenistic Alexandria. Philo applies the term here as an analogy for the good emotions; but in *Sacr.* 44, he uses it as an analogy for the relationship between preliminary education and wisdom, symbolized by Hagar and Keturah, on the one hand, and Sarah, on the other.

recommends it ... make it her firm possession. Hope's role, like that of smell, is not only passively to acknowledge a good that is destined for the soul's possession, but actively to recommend it. Hope, in this analogy, is elevated by Philo to a criterion of judgment, which might help the soul choose the good and avoid the bad.

§ 165. *again, when someone on a journey.* Philo's final proof is drawn from the consideration of travelers, or those making a "road trip" (ὁδοιπορία). The analogy is fitting to Philo's scriptural context, as Abraham himself is in the process of such a journey—both literally, as Philo has recently noted in chapter six (§ 152), as well as figuratively, in the developing allegoresis of the journey of the soul.

has grown hungry and thirsty and then suddenly espies. It is not only smell which is a "foretaster" in Philo's analysis, but sight as well. To argue that sight—

the most important of the senses for Philo—is in some way preliminary to the lower enjoyment of taste tacitly suggests a further analogy: that physical sight is itself a premonition of noetic sight—a foretaster of true knowledge and noetic enjoyment. In this analogy, Philo recapitulates two of the three senses specifically introduced by the objector in § 157 (sight and smell), creating a rhetorical ring composition.

nor drawn the water or plucked the fruit. Philo introduces a fourth sense, touch, which is an intermediary between seeing and tasting. In Philo's argument, touch is linked with taste on the "fulfilled" side of the sensual register.

he takes his fill of these beforehand. Philo's verb, "to fill beforehand" (προπληροῦν), appears to be a neologism, poetically crafted for the series of "pre-" (προ-) compounds in this section. It appears only here in his writings, and subsequently in the Greek medical corpus.

accordingly ... but that the aliments of thought are not sufficient? The implied answer to this rhetorical question is "no." Philo argues *a minore ad maius*: if one confesses that in the case of physical food, there can be a kind of foresensing, how much more so must it be the case with noetic objects?

to delight in beforehand. Philo's final "pre-" (προ-) compound in this subsection, "to delight in beforehand" (προευφραίνειν), translates the idea of somatic enjoyment of food into psychic delight or happiness. While the joining of sight, taste, and happiness in this manner reminds one very much of the later concept of the beatific vision, it should be noted that for Philo, the visual enjoyment of such goods remains preliminary to a final noetic tasting. The *verbum Philonicum* appears earlier in the Allegorical Commentary (*Leg.* 3.47; *Post.* 21).

Parallel Exegesis

§ 157. *laughter has not yet come into existence.* Philo's analysis of the allegorical problem of Abraham's laughter in chapter seven of *De mutatione nominum*— i.e., how can "joy" be produced in the Abraham soul before the birth of Isaac— finds no parallel in QG 3.55 (Philo's corresponding treatment of Gen 17:17a). His elegant solution in *Mut.* 157—that what is meant is hope, or "joy before joy"—is only weakly gestured to in Philo's comment in QG 3.55d: "rightly did he laugh in his joy over the promise, being filled "with great hope" (յուսովք մեծամեծաւք) and in the expectation that it would be fulfilled" (Marcus, PLCLSup). Neither Aucher's "spe magna" nor Marcus's "with great hope" fully captures the intensity of the Armenian doubled adjective մեծամեծաւք ("twice-great"), nor the plural (instrumental) case, which might be better rendered "with exceedingly great hopes" (does the Armenian plural look back to the plural "children" of QG 3.54?).

Runia (2020), however, in a recent article on hope in Philo's thought, highlights *QG* 1.79 as including a more relevant parallel at least philosophically speaking. Here, in interpreting Enosh's "hope to call upon the name of the Lord" (Gen 4:26)—the only place in the Pentateuch where the verb "to hope" (ἐλπίζω) appears—Philo explicitly calls hope "a kind of pre-emotion, joy before joy, being an expectation of goods" (προπάθεια τις, χαρὰ πρὸ χαρᾶς, ἀγαθῶν οὖσα προσδοκία [PAPM 33, 73]). Philo's argument in the Armenian portion of the *solutio*, that "irrational animals are destitute of hope" (անասուն կենդանիքը յուսոյ անբաժք են) is curious, given the string of analogical proofs from the animal kingdom that Philo adduces in *De mutatione nominum*. Granted, in no place does Philo say that these beasts have "hope" *per se*; however, the analogical proofs work in the opposite direction from the distancing of hope and irrational animals in *QG*. 1.79. Within the Allegorical Commentary, *Leg.* 3.85–87 brings together both this account of Abraham's hope and the birth of Isaac. The thought differs little from what is found in *Mut.* 157–165 and should be read as preparatory to the present passage. In the Exposition of the Law, see *Praem.* 161. For other important Philonic discussions of hope, see Runia 2020.

§ 165. *again, when someone on a journey*. Philo's word "journey" or "road trip" (ὁδοιπορία) is used in *Mos.* 1.215–217 of the Israelites in the wilderness, and in *Abr.* 107 of the journey of the three "men" espied by Abraham in Gen 18. It serves as a synecdoche, linking various Pentateuchal migrations or journeys.

Nachleben

§ 158. *proclaiming beforehand its hope*. The closest echo of Philo's interpretation of Abraham's laughter in Gen 17:17a as "joy before joy" in a psychological register may be that found in Eusebius, *Dem ev.* 4.17.3 [A] (for an introduction to this important passage, see the *Nachleben* to §§ 60, 77, and 81). There, after citing his title for Philo's work, Eusebius defends Moses's earnest philosophical interest of scriptural name change. In what amounts to an implicit precis of chapter five of *De mutatione nominum*, Eusebius intriguingly includes Isaac in a catalogue that also contains the names of Abram/Abraham, Sarai/Sarah, and Jacob/Israel. "And Isaac," he says, "came to be given the epithet "Laughter" before his birth" (καὶ Γέλωτα τὸν Ἰσαὰκ πρὸ γενέσεως ἐπικεκλημένον). Eusebius's inclusion of Isaac after this catalogue of those whose names are changed, his repetition of one of the Philonic etymologies of Isaac, and especially his emphasis of Isaac's identity as laughter "before his birth" (πρὸ γενέσεως) all suggest awareness of the traditions found in *De mutatione nominum*.

PART THREE   425

c   *The Laughter of Sarah (§§ 166–167)*
        Analysis and General Comments
Having (a) given an allegorical interpretation of Abraham's falling and laughing in §§ 154–156; and then (b) answered a scholastic question about this interpretation, using analogical proofs from the natural world in §§ 157–165; Philo next (c) adduces and interprets a contextualizing secondary lemma, Gen 18:12. Philo's contextualization of an Abrahamic allegoresis with a parallel Sarah narrative follows the same pattern as the central fifth chapter of the treatise, in which the interpretation of Abraham's name change is followed by a leap in the text to a related lemma about his wife (see § 77). The present section divides into two units:

(1)   Philo adduces a parallel lemma from the life of Sarah (Gen 18:12), in which her laughter reflects the laughter of Abraham (Gen 17:17a). Philo interprets the words in Gen 18:12a, "it has not yet happened to me," to mean that the Sarah soul is awe-struck that such good things should happen by grace alone, without her effort, when such a gift had not been given before. Philo then turns to Sarah's statement, "my lord is rather old" (Gen 18:12b), which she intends as reference to the antiquity (or better, the eternity) not of Abraham, her human "lord" and husband, but of the Lord (i.e., the Logos) who makes the promise. For this reason, she reckons his word is trustworthy (§ 166).
(2)   Philo returns to Gen 18:12a to comment on Sarah's laughter itself. In this second allegoresis of the text, Sarah is not a soul, but virtue. Virtue, Philo asserts, is pleasant, whereas vice is sorrowful (§ 167).

        Detailed Comments
(1) § 166. *fittingly*. The adverb "fittingly" (εἰκότως) echoes § 157, where Philo suggests that queries about the existence of laughing before laughter were warranted ("fittingly then might someone be puzzled" [εἰκότως δ' ἂν ἀπορήσειέ τις]). It signals the end of the foregoing subunit on Gen 17:17a, as Philo transitions to the contextualizing secondary lemma (Gen 18:12).

to have been sown. Philo's use of the verb "to be sown" (σπαρῆναι) echoes the "seed" promises to Abraham in scriptural texts like Gen 12:7; 13:15–16; 15:5, 18; and esp. 17:7–10, 12, 19.

not he alone, but his wife also laughs. Philo links the aorist verbs of Gen 17:17 ("he laughed" [ἐγέλασεν]) and Gen 18:12a ("she laughed" [ἐγέλασεν]). These pericopes (Gen 17:17; 18:12–13) offer the only three instances of the aorist active indicative form of "to laugh" (γελᾶν) in Genesis, giving Philo a textual reason to extend his allegoresis of Abraham's laughter to include Sarah's. In both §§ 154 and 166, he paraphrases the verb in the present tense ("laughs" [γελᾷ]) to actualize the "laughter of the soul" as a present psychic reality.

a little later. Both here and at § 83 (the only two occurrences in the treatise), the adverb "a little later" (αὖθις) is used to denote forward movement in the scriptural text. It works as an ancient narrative-critical marker, describing the commentator's mode of reading.

and Sarah laughed within ... "up until now." Philo cites the first part of his contextualizing secondary lemma (Gen 18:12a), which includes both the narrative frame and the first part of Sarah's speech: "Sarah laughed within herself, saying 'it has not yet happened to me up until now.'" After an allegorical paraphrase, he will also cite Gen 18:12b. This first part of the citation is in complete agreement with the Septuagint.

"that a good should come about automatically without assistance." Philo's paraphrase shifts the meaning of Sarah's scriptural statement. In Genesis, Sarah suggests that she has not conceived a child, although she has presumably had regular sexual relations with Abraham. Not wishing to present Sarah as a figure of doubt (see also §§ 154–156, 175–180), Philo clarifies that she had received many goods from God, but never one so graciously and freely bestowed and without some effort on her part. Note the compound adverb "automatically" (ἀπαυτοματίζον), indicating the total independence of divine power. The Sarah soul emerges as grateful and overawed at the efficacy of God's grace, rather than as a miracle sceptic.

"but the One who promises this, my Lord." Philo's citation of the second part of his contextualizing secondary lemma (Gen 18:12b) is impossible to disentangle syntactically from the surrounding paraphrase. In place of Sarah's expression of doubt in Genesis, "my lord is older than me" (ὁ δὲ κύριός μου πρεσβύτερος), Philo's cited text, "my Lord is indeed rather ancient" (κύριός μου καὶ πρεσβύτερος), keeps "my lord" (κύριός μου) and "rather ancient" (πρεσβύτερος) separate, giving the Alexandrian an occasion to reinterpret both phrases. By adding the participial phrase "the One who is promising" (ὁ δ' ὑποσχόμενος) before "my Lord" (κύριός μου), Philo reinterprets the "Lord" to be not Abraham, but the promiser himself—none other than the Lord-Logos and the divine creative power. Colson (PLCL 5:226, n. a) comments that "this perversion of the laughter of Abraham and Sarah has some excuse in the case of the latter in the obscurity of the LXX."

"is also older than all creation." In its Septuagintal syntax, the adjective "older" in Sarah's statement is directly tied to comparative genitive "than me," indicating that Abraham's impotence arises from his being older than Sarah. By replacing the Septuagint's postpositive "and" (δέ) with a different conjunction (καί), Philo severs this connection, making "my" a possessive genitive ("my Lord") and giving the sense "my Lord is indeed rather old" (κύριός μου καὶ πρεσβύτερος). Philo takes this opening to offer a new comparative genitive, and

writes "older *than all creation*" (πρεσβύτερος πάσης γενέσεως). Sarah means to say that the Logos (rather than Abraham) is "older than all creation"—and hence can do what he promises.

Sarah's statement that the Logos is comparatively older than "all creation" implies that the Logos is distinct from the created order. This represents Philo's more nuanced and mature position on the question. At the beginning of the Allegorical Commentary, in a text like *Leg.* 3.175, Philo can speak of "the Logos of God" as "above all the world and the oldest and most generic of everything which has come into existence" (ὁ λόγος δὲ τοῦ θεοῦ ὑπεράνω παντός ἐστι τοῦ κόσμου καὶ πρεσβύτατος καὶ γενικώτατος τῶν ὅσα γέγονε)—a text which can been read as indicating that the Logos is part of creation. In *Her.* 205–206, by contrast, Philo prefers to speak of the Logos as a kind of ontological borderland, "neither ungenerated as God nor generated as you" (οὔτε ἀγένητος ὡς ὁ θεός, οὔτε γενητὸς ὡς ὑμεῖς). His phrase in *Mut.* 166, "older than all creation" (πρεσβύτερος πάσης γενέσεως), seems to follow in the trajectory mapped by this later current, implicitly correcting or clarifying the phraseology of *Leg.* 3.175.

"it is necessary to believe him." Sarah, like Abraham, becomes an allegorical figure of psychic "trust" or "faith" (πιστεύειν) in the Logos. See Morgan 2015.

§ 167. *at the same time*. Philo offers a second interpretation of Sarah's laughter, taking her now as a symbol of virtue rather than of the soul.

these verses reiterate. Philo uses the same verb, "to reiterate/teach again" (ἀναδιδάσκειν), in § 80 when introducing a secondary allegoresis of Sarah in Gen 17:15. Whereas in § 80 Philo differentiates two different ethical significances of Sarah's new name, here he distinguishes between Sarah's symbolizing a soul (§ 166) and virtue (§ 167).

virtue is a delightful thing by nature ... vice ... a sorrowful thing. In his second allegoresis, Philo focuses not on the epistemology of Sarah's "belief" (πιστεύειν), but on the emotional impact of virtue. That the perfection of virtue produces good emotions has been a theme of the treatise and a key to Philo's allegorical psychagogy since the beginning, in the reference to Isaac as the joy to be born at the age of Abraham's perfection (§ 1). Philo now adds that vice (imperfection) produces the opposite bad emotion, "grief" (λυπή). Colson (PLCL 5:591) cross-references Cicero, *Tusc.* 5.43: "The wise person is always happy; and also, every good thing is gladsome" ("semper sapiens beatus est. atque etiam omne bonum laetabile est").

those among the philosophers ... virtue is a good emotion. Philo may be opposing the Stoics (so Arnaldez 1964, 108, n. 2): "Philo distances himself from the Stoic doctrine of absolute ἀπάθεια (lack of emotion)." Colson (PLCL 5:591), however, is doubtful that the Stoics are referred to:

Who are the philosophers alluded to? Hardly the Stoics. I have found no evidence that they identified εὐπάθεια ("good emotion") with ἀρετή ("virtue") .... I can hardly think, however, that he speaks without authority and should conjecture that there were philosophers who like him used it as = εὐδαιμονία ("happiness") and naturally therefore equated it with ἀρετή ("virtue"), perhaps also like him coloring it with the Stoic insistence on joy as "the best of the higher emotions."

Philo similarly links good emotion and virtue in *Leg.* 3.22 (Colson renders "good emotion" [εὐπάθεια] here as "well-being"). If some other background is sought, Eudorus and other Middle Platonists suggest themselves. (For the blending of Stoic and Platonist ethical vocabularies during this period, see Dillon 1977, 122.)

What is curious about Philo's claim is that virtue itself is apparently called a good emotion. This is not, at least by Aristotelian terms, the meaning of virtue. A virtue, for Aristotle, is a good "stable disposition" (ἕξις [see *Mut.* 121–122 and *QG* 4.16 in the Parallel Exegesis]). An emotion—even a good one—is by contrast a movement in the soul. As an example of the good emotions, Philo gives "joy," but not a virtue as such. Might Philo mean that there is a strong link between virtue and the good emotions, and that some philosophers have gone so far as to catachrestically identify them (although Philo himself would not blur the distinction)? For more, see Weisser 2021.

Whichever particular "philosophers" Philo refers to, his distance from an "absolute" theory of "absence of the emotions" (ἀπάθεια) merits further consideration. As Arnaldez (1964, 108, n. 2) explicates, Philo often connects the term "good emotion" (εὐπάθεια) with "joy" (χαρά), "peace" (εἰρήνη/ἡσυχία), "good fortune" (εὐτυχία), and "gentleness" (τρυφή). In the earliest works of the Allegorical Commentary, Arnaldez finds that "lack of emotion" (ἀπάθεια) remains for Philo "the most beautiful" (τὸ κάλλιστον [*Leg.* 2.100; cf. *Leg.* 3.131]), attained by the most perfect sage. "Good emotion" (εὐπάθεια) is nevertheless linked by Philo to the joy of the garden of Eden (*Cher.* 12), which gives it a place in Philo's protology. In *Leg.* 3.132, the sage's "absence of emotion" (ἀπάθεια) is contrasted with Aaron's "moderated emotion" (μετριοπάθεια). One feels a certain tension between the medial and final places of the good emotions across the Allegorical Commentary as a whole, and Philo's position vacillates (Birnbaum and Dillon 2021, 326–327)—making more space for the emotions as the series develops.

Parallel Exegesis

§ 166. *Gen 18:12* ("*Sarah laughed ... my Lord is older*"). Colson (PLCL 5:226, n. a) adduces *Leg.* 3.217–218 as a parallel Philonic treatment of Sarah's laughter. There, Sarah is interpreted as virtue as in § 167. Many elements of Philo's interpretation of Gen 17:5, 15, and 17, in *De mutatione nominum* are related in this parallel, including the identification of Sarah's "rather ancient Lord" (Gen 18:12) as the "divine Logos." *QG* 4.16 provides a complementary parallel. Here, Sarah is identified as a "mind" (մտքր) (Marcus, PLCLSup 1:289 n. h, gives "mind" [ὁ νοῦς] or "thought" [ἡ διάνοια]) as in §166, rather than as a virtue. Philo also differentiates in *QG* 4.16 between psychological "laughter" (ծաղր) and the "very strong and stable disposition" (մտքագոյն ևս մտասյալ հաստատունութիւն, [retr. ἀσφαλεστέρα καὶ ἄπταιστος βεβαίωσις or στάσις]) required to support it.

The subsequent *QG*. 4.17 is also worth mentioning, because here Philo takes up the question of why Sarah is rebuked for her laughter, but Abraham is not. This is a question that Philo tries to downplay in *De mutatione nominum*, as his aim is to depict Abraham and Sarah as similar minds. Nevertheless, in *QG* 4.17, even Sarah's rebuke redounds to her (and God's) praise. She, like Abraham, is on the road to perfection, but has not yet attained it. In the Exposition of the Law, *De Abrahamo* provides several parallel interpretations of Gen 18:12 as well. In *Abr.* 112, Sarah is said in fact to be "ashamed" (καταιδεσθεῖσα) of her laughter after being corrected by the three men—a fair representation of the literal sense. *Abr.* 206 gives the correlated allegorical interpretation: that in fact Sarah, as virtue, laughs because she does not wish to claim the laughter as her own, since joy belongs to God alone. She rightly shows caution at the promise, but upon being reassured, accepts it with gratitude.

Nachleben
§166. *Gen 18:12 ("Sarah laughed ... my Lord is older")*. Philo's reading of Gen 18:12 (*Abr.* 112; cf. *QG* 4.17), that Sarah is somehow blameworthy for her laughter, is found in early Christian sources, including Ps.-Gregory of Nyssa (*Lib. cogn. Dei* 130.316.45 [C]); Eusebius (*Frag. Luc.* 24.532 [C]); and Ps.-Athanasius (*Nav. praec.* 28.908 [C]). In this last, Elizabeth, the mother of John the Baptist, is praised for "not having laughed, as Sarah did, but believing like Hannah" (ἡ μὴ γελάσασα κατὰ τὴν Σάρραν, ἀλλὰ πιστεύσασα κατὰ τὴν Ἄνναν). Likewise, in a spurious text attributed to Didymus the Blind (*Trin.* 3 [39.92] [C]), Sarah is explicitly described as "unbelieving" (ἀπιστήσασα) on account of her two objections.

Contrary to these readings, and in tune with Philo's more positive interpretation of Sarah's laughter in *Mut.* 166–167 [B], is the interpretation of John Chrysostom in *Mut.* 2.3 (131.9–12):

Her laughter was a recollection of the grace of God (ὁ γέλως τῆς τοῦ Θεοῦ χάριτος ὑπόμνησις ἦν), and the nursing mother believed the wondrous deed (ἡ γαλακτοτροφία τὴν θαυματοποιίαν ἐπιστοῦτο). For this was not a work of nature, but all happened as a stroke of grace.

to have been sown. For similar "seed" promises to Abraham in the New Testament, see Gal 3:16; Rom 4:18.

it is necessary to believe him. The emphasis on "trust" or "faith" (πιστεύειν) in the Logos is reminiscent of the Fourth Gospel and the Johannine epistles. There, however, belief in Jesus as Logos is grounded in the vision and touch of his incarnate body, whereas Sarah's faith in §166 has its ground in philosophical knowledge of who the Logos is (i.e., he precedes creation; cf. John 1:3).

d   *The Mirth of the Sage (§§168–174)*
Analysis and General Comments

Before continuing his commentary on the primary text (Gen 17:17b [§175]), Philo reflects further on the theme of the laughter of the sage—the lexical and thematic point of connection between Abraham's and Sarah's reactions to God's promise of a child. He adduces three tertiarty lemmata. The first demonstrates the "joy" of the wise soul (Exod 4:14 [§168]); the second depicts the feigned "joy" of the foolish and vicious soul (Isa 57:21; cf. Isa 48:22 [§169]). The false joy of the wicked soul is then elaborated with the help of a third tertiary biblical lemma from the Joseph cycle (Gen 45:16–18 [§§170–174]). All three tertiary lemmata are linked with one another lexically through the catchword "rejoice" (χαίρειν), and thematically to the MBL and SBL[c] through the idea of the soul's laughter. This section divides into three parts:

(1) Philo says Moses himself believed that only the soul of the sage truly rejoices. He argues this not only on the witness of Gen 17:17a and Gen 18:12, but now also on the grounds of a tertiary biblical lemma drawn from the Moses cycle (Exod 4:14) (§168).

(2) To prove the correlated and opposite thesis—that the wicked man does not truly delight in anything—Philo adduces another tertiary lemma, this time from the prophet Isaiah (Isa 57:21; cf. Isa 48:22) (§169).

(3) To demonstrate the harmony of Isaiah's understanding of the false joy of the wicked man with the teaching of Moses, Philo adduces and interprets a third tertiary biblical lemma from the Pentateuch, Gen 45:16–18. This tertiary lemma is taken from the Joseph cycle and relates Pharaoh's alleged joy at the arrival of Jacob and his other sons. Philo cites and sequentially interprets three verses from this longer lemma: Gen 45:16, 18a, and 18b. He also adduces a contextualizing tertiary lemma (TBL[c]), Gen 37:36//39:1, 20–22, likewise drawn from the Joseph cycle (§§170–174).

Detailed Comments

(1) §168. ***Moses may be discovered as the patron.*** Philo introduces a tertiary-level discussion by highlighting Moses's role as a dogmatic theologian. As the writer of Gen 18:12, Moses becomes the "patron" (χορηγός), who furnishes scriptural capital to underwrite the doctrine that the wise person's soul is filled with joy.

introducing in the foregoing verse the good mind. Although both the foregoing primary (Gen 17:17a) and contextualizing (Gen 18:12) biblical lemmata have sparked these additional comments, Gen 18:12 is the more immediate trigger for the adduction of the tertiary biblical lemmata that follow. The link between Gen 18:12 and the tertiary chain is thematic, but the connection to Exod 4:14 is lexical as well ("in herself" [ἐν ἑαυτῇ]; "in himself" [ἐν αὐτῷ, see Notes to Text and Translation]). The tertiary lemmata are all lexically enchained to one another through the verb "rejoice." Sarah is allegorized as a masculine substantive, "the good" (ὁ ἀστεῖος). I have supplied "mind" (νοῦς) rather than "man" (ἄνηρ) as the implied noun in the translation (cf. *QG* 4.16) to indicate that Philo is speaking at the allegorical rather than the literal level.

rejoicing and laughing. With the paraphrase "rejoicing and laughing" (χαίρων καὶ γελῶν), Philo coordinates the catchword linking the primary and contextualizing secondary lemmata ("laughing" [γελῶντα]: Gen 17:17, Gen 18:12) with the catchword linking the subsequent tertiary biblical lemmata ("rejoicing" [χαίροντα]: Exod 4:14; Isa 57:21; Gen 45:16–18).

in another passage. Moses's authorship of the tertiary biblical lemma is highlighted, although here (Exod 4:14), he is also a character referenced in the verse.

but also those who are approaching this same goal with him. I.e., not only the one who has reached perfection, but those who are looking to the sage as a model of future beatitude.

for God says to Moses. The citation formula "says" (φησί) conceals the complication of this scriptural example: that Moses is both its author and the symbol of the perfected soul within it.

"when he (i.e., Aaron) sees you, he will rejoice in himself." Philo adduces Exod 4:14 as the first of three tertiary lemmata, which elaborate his exposition of Gen 18:12 (the contextualizing secondary lemma): that only the sage rejoices, and that the wicked cannot truly rejoice. His choice of Exod 4:14 as a complementary illustration of the first premise grounded in Gen 18:12, is traditional and based upon the syntactic similarity of the two portrayals of internal joy in Sarah and Aaron. Philo will return to the internal joy of Abraham in Gen 17:17b in the subsequent chapter (see §176). For the reading "in himself" rather than "in him," see the Notes to the Text and Translation.

for the advance vision of the good person. That is, Aaron's seeing of Moses in Exod 4:14. The phrase "seeing you" (ἰδών σε) includes both subject (the Aaron mind in progress) and object ("you," Moses, the virtuous mind). Aaron and Sarah are complementary images of the mind on the road to perfection.

is enough to fill the intellect with gladness. Aaron's joy (here, "gladness" [εὐφροσύνη]) is understood not as sensual but intellectual, belonging to "thought" (διάνοια). The absence of any internalization of joy in the following lemma (Isa 48:22) suggests the feigned joy of the wicked mind (Pharaoh), which it wears like a comic mask (see §§ 169–170), as opposed the real and penetrating joy of the sage (Abraham, Sarah, Moses, Aaron). Arnaldez (1964, 110, n. 1) adds that Philo's synonym for joy, "gladness" (εὐφροσύνη), has connections with the language of religious feasting (*Congr.* 166–167; *Spec.* 1.191), "the incorruptible nourishments of the soul."

that most hateful of psychic evils, sorrow. Whereas joy is presented as the best of the good emotions (§ 1), grief, its opposite, is identified superlatively as the worst of the passions.

(2) § 169. *no one wicked has been permitted to rejoice.* The impersonal verb, "has been permitted" (ἐφεῖται), might equally be translated "desires to." Philo's interpretation of the following secondary biblical lemma supports the translation.

as it is also sung in the prophetic verses. Philo notes the poetic form of Isaiah's prophecy. For his use of the Psalms and prophets as secondary and tertiary lemmata, see the detailed comments above on §§ 115, 139, and 143. Philo's reference to singing links this citation, in form, with that of Ps 22 cited in § 115.

"it does not belong to the impious to rejoice," says God. Contrary to what is indicated in PCW and PLCL, Cohen (2007, 79, 84–85) has convincingly demonstrated that Philo cites not Isa 48:22 but the very similar verse, Isa 57:21. Although the aphorism about the impious is the same in both texts, Isa 48:22 ends with the formula, "says the Lord" (λέγει κύριος), whereas Isa 57:21 ends with formula "says (the Lord) God" (εἶπεν [κύριος] ὁ θεός). The latter is clearly reflected in Philo's citation in § 169. The only other difference is Philo's foregrounding of the catchword "to rejoice" (χαίρειν), which is done to highlight the lexical connection between this verse, Exod 4:14, and Gen 45:16.

this saying is also truly a divine oracle. Philo does not presume his reader will accept Isaiah's prophetic verses as inspired, and so clarifies with the word "oracle" (χρησμός) that they are commensurate in authority with Moses's writings.

the life of every bad person is sullen and sorrowful and full of heavy spirits. That a wicked life is necessarily sorrowful is a philosophical commonplace. Philo defends a related Stoic thesis in a pair of treatises in his philosophical works: that every bad person is a slave (now lost), and that every good person is free (*Prob.* 1).

he should play at smiling with his face. The bad person may feign being joyful—even going so far as to wear a smile in order to convince others (and himself) that he is happy. Philo uses the language of the theater, here and in the subsequent section, to deconstruct this false joy of the wicked. It is only the donning of a comic mask, an exercise in play-acting.

(3) §170. ***that the Egyptians truly rejoiced ... in order to seem to rejoice.*** To further illustrated Moses's double doctrine, Philo adduces a third tertiary biblical lemma, Gen 45:16–18. At first blush, Gen 45:16 might appear to offer counterevidence to the thesis that Philo has been developing. If the wicked do not rejoice, how should one explain Moses's statement that "Pharaoh rejoiced and his retinue with him" (ἐχάρη δὲ Φαραὼ καὶ ἡ θεραπεία αὐτοῦ) when he heard of the arrival of Joseph's father? Philo answers the question in a Platonic fashion by distinguishing between being and seeming, as well as by appealing to sophistry and the theater. Pharaoh and his entourage are not truly happy, but only seem to be so for reasons that Philo will go on to explain.

never is a rebuke brought against fools to their delight. Having ventured an exegetical opinion, Philo now supports it with two proverbs. The first, which speaks of the distaste of "fools" (ἄφρονες) for "rebuke" (ἔλεγχος), is reminiscent of Prov 12:1: "He who loves instruction loves ⟨accurate⟩ perception; but the one who hates rebuke (ἐλέγχους) is a fool (ἄφρων)."

just as a doctor is not ineffectual when practicing upon a sick person. Philo's second aphorism stems from Greek medical tradition. Aesop tells several fables about doctors and their patients (*Fab.* 57, 116, 180). Doctor similes are also frequent in the philosophical and rhetorical tradition (e.g., Dio Chrysostom, *Or.* 9.4; 48.2). Ps.-Plutarch, for example, describes the ability of the early Attic orator, Antiphon of Rhamnus (5th Century BCE), to combat grief through poetry, just "as the healing from doctors works upon the sick" (D-K frag. 6: ὥσπερ τοῖς νοσοῦσιν ἡ παρὰ τῶν ἰατρῶν θεραπεία ὑπάρχει). The doctor's skill is also frequently adverted to in the writings of Plato (e.g., *Leg.* 857cd).

The parallelism between Philo's first and second aphorisms is not immediately clear. Colson (PLCL 5:229) does not translate ἀκρατεῖν ("to be ineffectual"), smoothing out the doublet to mean that a "dissolute" man is no more pleased by an effectual doctor than a fool by an effectual proverb. In point of fact, the doctor aphorism is more about the doctor's effectiveness than the sick man's disapproval. The point of comparison lies in the potency of the remedy in each case.

for hard work ... but ease attends those which are harmful. The antithesis between "toil" (πόνος) and "ease" (ῥᾳστώνη) is proverbial in Platonic tradition (*Leg.* 779a).

§171. *so when you hear that Pharaoh rejoiced and all his retinue.* Philo explicitly cites the tertiary biblical lemma, on which he has already been commenting in the preceding paragraph, as if in answer to an implicit objection. His citation is identical with LXX Gen 45:16c, with the inconsequential omission of the connecting "and" (δέ). The catchphrase "Pharaoh rejoiced" (ἐχάρη δὲ Φαραώ) connects this tertiary lemma with the preceding two tertiary lemmata (Exod 4:14: "he will rejoice in himself" [χαρήσεται ἐν ἑαυτῷ]; Isa 57:21: "it does not belong to the impious to rejoice" [οὐκ ἔστιν χαίρειν τοῖς ἀσεβέσιν]).

on account of the arrival of the brothers of Joseph. A paraphrase of the proclamation to Pharaoh in Gen 45:16b: "The brothers of Joseph have arrived" (ἥκασιν οἱ ἀδελφοὶ Ἰωσήφ).

do not suppose that they truly had any delight. The phrase "truly have delight" (πρὸς ἀλήθειαν ἥδεσθαι) in §171 echoes Philo's reference to "true rejoicing" (χαίρειν πρὸς ἀλήθειαν) in §170, creating chiastic arrangement and lexical *variatio*.

they expect to shift him (i.e., Joseph). Philo explains the apparent elation of Pharaoh and his retinue by offering an extended allegoresis of the scene. Pharaoh and the Egyptians symbolize the external stimuli that attempt to vitiate the Joseph soul. Colson (PLCL 5:228, n. 2), unable to make sense of the text as it stands, emends it *ex ingenio* from "him" (αὐτόν) to "again, his mind" (αὖ τὸν ⟨νοῦν⟩), which gives the sense of "*again* shifting his *attention*." This is clever, but unnecessary. Colson's interpretation of the scene—that Pharaoh intends to distract not Joseph but Jacob and his brothers—creates more problems than it solves. I take Philo to mean that the Joseph-mind is the primary target in Pharaoh's crosshairs. Arnaldez (1964, 111, n. 3) agrees, suggesting that Colson's emendation and interpretation "does violence to the sequence of ideas and cohesion of the images" in this passage. For Arnaldez, the allegoresis has two components: (1) The Egyptians' hope that Joseph will forget the goods of the soul (his father and brothers); and (2) that he will, in the process, corrupt these goods as well.

from the goods of the soul, on which he was reared. In Philo's allegoresis, Joseph's brothers are not murderous traitors, but positive symbols of the habits and qualities of mind typical of the Jacob/Israel soul, practicing and perfecting its virtue.

to the insatiable desires of the body. Pharaoh and the Egyptians symbolize the desires of the body. This allegoresis of Joseph and the Egyptians bears some similarity with that of the daughters of Raguel and the shepherds in §112. There, however, the concern was not with bodily pleasure *per se*, but with the ability of sense perception to distort dialectical knowledge.

once he had debased ... ancestral stamp of kindred virtue. Colson renders the ambiguous masculine "he" as "mind"; this is clearly what Philo intends at the allegorical level. The language of the "ancestral stamp of virtue" (τὸ ἀρχαῖον ... ἀρετῆς ... νόμισμα) on the soul recalls the "stamped" mind of Bezalel, as well as the mind patterned after the image of God (Gen 1:27) in *Leg*. 3.95–96. Philo explains that the "ancestral stamp of virtue" (τὸ ἀρχαῖον ... ἀρετῆς ... νόμισμα) on the soul can be debased within the human being by his own viciousness. Cf. § 31, where he attributes the poor stamping of the soul neither to God nor to the human will, but to God's lesser co-workers in creation.

§ 172. *having such hopes*. A paradoxical formulation. Since the wicked mind will have no joy, its share in the pre-emotion of hope is destined to be thwarted and fictitious at its root.

the mind that loves pleasure ... to snare. The Pharaoh-vice is like a fisherman, trying to catch the good mind and turn it away from the virtues to the bad emotions. In the subsequent exegesis, Philo will employ a rich set of hamartiological (sin) metaphors, including the debasement of a coin (§ 171), hooking on a fishline (§ 172), imprisonment (§ 173), and psychic dismemberment (§ 173).

those who have only recently ... enrolled in the gymnasia of temperance. A fitting metaphor for the sons of Jacob/Israel, the ascetic soul. Temperance serves as shorthand for all the virtues, while unnecessary luxuries (excessive food and wealth) will be the particular bait on the line for Joseph.

the older reason. I.e., the Jacob/Israel mind. Philo is implicitly interpreting Gen 45:17, where Pharaoh bids Joseph's eleven brothers return to Canaan for their father.

raving passions. The emotions are depicted as mad and frothing, like startled horses or rabid dogs. Below (§ 173), Philo will speak of these emotions being incited and tamed. Plato's tripartite soul, with its spirited and appetitive horses, influences the image, as does his description in the same dialogue of the enamored soul's "raving" (λυττᾷ [*Phaedr*. 251d]). Such madness, however, in this Philonic passage, has no redeeming qualities.

§ 173. *for he says again*. Philo defends his interpretation of Gen 45:16c by extending his treatment of the tertiary lemma to include Gen 45:18ab. The adverb "again" (αὖ), although it might be taken with "extending" (προτείνων), more likely modifies "says" (λέγει). As Pharaoh has not previously said anything in the pericope, "again" marks the extension of the biblical lemma.

extending detriments as if they were benefits. Just as Pharaoh and his retinue wear false smiles, betokening fraudulent joy, so they also offer "benefits" that turn out to be incitements to the contrary.

"bring your father and your possessions, and come to me." Philo's extension of the tertiary lemma skips Gen 45:17, where Pharaoh bids the brothers

return to Canaan for Jacob. This return, however, is included in the exegesis in § 172, where Pharaoh is said to set his sights on converting "the older Logos" to the pleasures of the body. The text of Philo's citation is identical with that of the Septuagint, but for the omission of the first possessive "your" (ὑμῶν) after "father."

that is, to Egypt and into the court of this fearful king. Philo's gloss of the reflexive object "me" widens the scope of the literal sense for allegorical purposes. Pharaoh indicates not merely the king, but via synecdoche his court as well, and indeed, the entirety of Egypt, which is allegorically the land of the body (see Pearce 2007; Adams 2018). The adjective "fearful" (φοβερός) describes the psychological torments of those souls who make their home in that country and bend their affections thither. Gen 39, with its depiction of the soul dungeon, is for Philo a "text of terror."

when our paternal ... faculties have moved out in advance of the body. A psychological allegoresis of Abraham's departure from Ur and Haran in the direction of Canaan.

for they are by nature free. The theme of the soul's freedom is characteristic of Stoic discourse at the time (see *Prob.* 1), but also looks ahead to the scriptural enslavement and liberation of the Israelites in Egypt.

draws them back again ... a very bitter prison. Philo combines the narrative of the enslavement of the Israelites in Exodus with the earlier imprisonment of Joseph in Gen 39:20–23. This allegoresis demonstrates Philo's acumen as a literary critic. As many commentators have noted (e.g., Levenson 1993), the sojourns of individual patriarch in Egypt—Abraham (Gen 12), Isaac (Gen 26), and Joseph—look ahead to the national epic in Exodus. Philo finds in these various patriarchal stories a singular, psychological allegoresis: that the soul is ever tempted, in time of spiritual famine, to flee to the goods of the body.

appointing as guard, as the verse says. Philo introduces Potiphar (*Pentephres*) as a further mythological character in his allegory of the soul's imprisonment. He is drawn from the contextualizing (tertiary) lemma, Gen 39:1. Philo's description of him as a "jail-guard" (εἰρκτοφύλαξ), one of the *verba Philonica*, paraphrases the Septuagintal term "chief prison-guard" (ἀρχιδεσμοφύλαξ), which in context specifies not Potiphar, but the jailer to whom Joseph is sent after his alleged assault on Potiphar's wife (Gen 39:22–23). Clearly, the "verse" (λόγιον), Gen 39:1, does not say precisely what Philo says it does. Keenly focused on the allegory of the soul, Philo has blended the figures of Potiphar (Gen 39:1) and the jailer (Gen 39:22) to create a kind of macabre Egyptian butcher-jailer, who stalks to and fro in his psychic dungeon, mutilating and dismembering souls and torturing them by incensing their passions. Philo's linkage of these two antagonists may have been facilitated by the similarity between Potiphar's title "chief-butcher" (ἀρχιμάγειρος) and the jailer's title "chief prison-guard" (ἀρχιδεσμοφύλαξ), both of which use the "chief" (ἀρχι-) prefix. With this depiction of the torment of wicked souls, Philo comes imaginatively near to the psychic infernos of Plutarch and Dante.

Potiphar, the eunuch and chief butcher. Philo's description of Potiphar as "the eunuch and chief butcher" (ὁ σπάδων καὶ ἀρχιμάγειρος), draws selectively on Gen 37:36 and Gen 39:1, where he is described as "Pharaoh's eunuch, chief-butcher, and Egyptian" (ὁ εὐνοῦχος Φαραώ, ἀρχιμάγειρος, ἀνὴρ Αἰγύπτιος). The more derogatory title, "plucked man" (σπάδων), from Gen 37:36 is preferred to the genteel biblical "eunuch" (εὐνοῦχος), which Philo uses in *Leg.* 3.236 to denote Potiphar's lack of reproductive organs and spiritual incontinence. The active violence echoed in this title is then realized in Philo's extrapolations about Potiphar's soul-butchering. For the parallel identifications of Potiphar as a eunuch (one who also strangely has a wife), see the Parallel Exegesis and *Nachleben.*

he is called "eunuch" on account of his dearth of good members. Philo interprets Potiphar's two titles, but not his proper name—possibly because the last is Egyptian and had no entry in his onomasticon. Philo follows an aberrant Greek spelling, "Pentephres" (Πεντεφρῆς), instead of the more usual "Petephres" (Πετεφρῆς), which might have made the name difficult to locate. "Eunuch" (σπάδων) points etymologically and allegorically to Potiphar's "dearth" (σπάνις) of virtues.

excision from himself of the procreative organs of the soul. The translation takes the participle "excised from himself" (ἐκτετμήμενος) as a middle (see Homer, *Od.* 24.364, in which context butchering is also mentioned). For procreation as a symbol of virtue, see §§ 94–96 (Rachel's barrenness), § 133 (Leah's "opening"), § 137 (Sarah giving birth to Isaac), §§ 143–144 (Sarah and Hannah).

being no longer able to sow or plant anything that has value for paideia. "Education"—perhaps an implicit gloss of Potiphar, the "Egyptian man" (Gen 39:1)—refers to the standard encyclical training. Elsewhere in the Philo's allegoresis of the Abraham cycle, the early phases of education are symbolized by another Egyptian, Hagar (see *Congr.* 1–10). It is natural that Philo connects secular education with Egypt, as Alexandria was his own native pedagogical context.

he is called "chief butcher" because ... he slaughters living creatures. I.e., living souls, on the allegorical level, which he similarly castrates, dismembers, and hangs from the psychic meat hooks.

cuts them up and divides them into portions and limbs. The butchering of souls, depicted here so graphically by Philo, recalls the torturing of the wicked souls by δαίμονες in Plutarch (*Sera* 567c–f), albeit with the eschatological element removed.

stalks among the lifeless corpses. The hendiadys, "among soulless things and corpses" (ἐν ἀψύχοις καὶ νεκροῖς), refers to "soulless bodies," which symbolize, paradoxically, lifeless souls.

not the bodies so much as the immaterial realities. Philo invokes the "body—reality" (σῶμα—πρᾶγμα) distinction to indicate the psychological rather than somatic nature of his allegory. For the philosophical roots of this distinction, see the detailed comments on §§8–9. Colson (PLCL 5:231, n. c) cross-references *Her.* 242 for Philo's use of spiritual dismemberment elsewhere in his allegorical writings.

rousing and titillating with superfluous seasonings. Philo interprets Potiphar's second title, "chief-butcher" (ἀρχιμάγειρος), much as he does in *Leg.* 3.236, to indicate an overemphasis on the pleasures of the body, especially the seasoning of food. Here, in Philo's more grotesque imagery, we can imagine this daemonic butcher "stalking about" (καλινδούμενος) his smokehouse, seasoning each dismembered part of the soul (whether there are three or eight) with its most appropriate (and painful) pleasure. Philo's soul torments are construed not as pains of fire and lead (as in Plutarch, *Sera* 567c–f), but as incitements of ungratified desires.

which he should instead have tamed and domesticated. The language recalls the animalistic representation of the soul's "raving passions" in §172.

§174. ***he also says.*** The speaker is Pharaoh, not Potiphar. Philo has returned from his contextualizing tertiary lemma (Gen 39:1) to his tertiary biblical lemma, and now adduces the third citation from it (Gen 45:18b).

"I will give to you ... the marrow of the earth." Philo's citation agrees verbatim with the Septuagint, with the exception of the definite article "the" (ἡ) before "earth" (γῆ), which Wendland supplies. Pharaoh's gift is understood allegorically as an offer of bodily goods (i.e., pleasures for the passions) to the soul, which will lead it to the aforementioned tortures of Potiphar.

but we will respond to him. Philo speaks in the first-person plural, reflecting the communal ethics of his private school.

"we who look to the goods of the soul ... some good for the body." Philo's scripted response to the enticements of Pharaoh is, in fact, the opposite of the biblical account. In Gen 45:21, "The sons of Israel did thus" (ἐποίησαν δὲ οὕτως οἱ υἱοὶ Ἰσραήλ). Philo's response, by contrast, on behalf of himself and his wards, resembles the flight of Joseph *from* Potiphar's wife. They do *not* "do thus" (ἐποίησαν δὲ οὕτως) as Pharaoh suggests, but instead imitate Joseph's resistance earlier in the scriptural narrative. Philo's identification of himself and his students as "those who look to the goods of the soul" tacitly interprets "the sons of

Israel" (οἱ υἱοὶ Ἰσραήλ) in Gen 45:21, meaning those who practice "to see God."

the three-fold desire of those goods. Philo's encouragement of the soul to rebuff "the bodily desires" (αἱ τοῦ σώματος ... ἐπιθυμίαι [§ 171]) is fortified by an appeal to psychic longing. Such "desire" (ἵμερος) is a Platonizing sublimation of the bodily impulse, as commended by Plato himself in the *Phaedrus* (251c–e; 255c), and akin to the Stoic good emotion, βούλησις. The adjective "thrice-desirable" (τριπόθητος) is a common Philonic superlative, a synonym of "worthy of love" (ἀξιέραστος, *Post*. 12), whose precise meaning as a description of the divine lover is unclear. It belongs to the lexicon of Philonic religious experience. For the history of "thrice-desirable" in Hellenistic literature, other Philonic occurrences, and its possible connection with the "three-fold vision" of Abraham, see the detailed comment on § 7.

Parallel Exegesis

§ 168. *Exod 4:14* ("*when he [i.e., Aaron] sees you, he will rejoice in himself*"). In *QG* 4.16, Philo adduces the same verse as a secondary lemma to explicate Sarah's internal joy in Gen 18:12. This shows that Philo often began composing the Allegorical Commentary with his treatment of the same pericope in the *QGE* in mind, even though the project of the Allegorical Commentary is different. (For the relationship between the two series, see Introduction 1. The Place of *De mutatione nominum* in the Allegorical Commentary.) In *QG* 4.16, Philo splices Exod 4:14 between his comments on Sarah's laughter and her subsequent interior dialogue. His interpretation runs as follows:

> Similarly does Scripture introduce the high priest rejoicing inwardly and released from all corporeal thoughts and entering into joy, for it says, "And seeing you he will rejoice within himself" (Exod 4:14).

This placement of the secondary lemma allows Philo to craft a positive portrait of the Sarah mind. Likening her to the high priest, Aaron, she is presented as a mind on the road to perfection, who is still awaiting the dawn of a more perfect joy.

Exod 4:14 is also adduced as a secondary or tertiary lemma in a number of other places in the Allegorical Commentary. Chief in importance is *Det*. 126–137, where Exod 4:14 serves as a tertiary lemma, adduced to amplify Sarah's statement in Gen 21:6 that "whoever shall hear me will rejoice with me" (*Det*. 123). Aaron is a symbol of speech, and in *Det*. 135–137, Philo addresses his internal joy, indicating that speech properly rejoices over the goods of the soul, rather than those of the body. Thus "it is 'in himself' (Exod 4:14), not in the accidents of his position ... for the things that are 'in himself' are the excellences of mind." Aaron's rejoicing is also interpreted in *Migr.* 79, though there it is said to stem from his discovery of the right words for an occasion.

§ 169. *Isa 51:27 ("it does not belong to the impious to rejoice")*. This is the only occurrence of Isa 51:27 (cf. Isa 48:22) in Philo's works. For the four other certain citations from Isaiah in his *œuvre*, and other possible references, see Cohen 2007, 72–87. References to Isaiah appear in all three commentary series (see *QG* 2.26, 43; *Praem.* 87). This suggests that despite the relative paucity of references, Philo "thought with" Isaiah and likely had access to the text (for the Septuagintal books in Philo's personal library, see Sterling 2024).

§ 170. *Gen 45:16–18 ("Pharaoh rejoiced and all his retinue")*. Outside of the present treatise, Gen 45:16–18 only appears in the Philonic corpus in the literal paraphrase of *Ios.* 250–251. There, Philo remarks that the Egyptians' joy reveals that they had not heard how Joseph's brothers sold him into slavery.

just as a doctor. For other doctor similes in Philo, see *QE* 2, frag. 25d, and *Sacr.* 121.

for hard work ... but ease attends those which are harmful. In *Sacr.* 35, Philo speaks similarly of effort and dishonorable ease as "enemies," with "hard work" (πόνος) being at the root of all honorable leisure.

§ 173. *Gen 37:36; 39:1, 20–23 ("Potiphar, the eunuch and chief butcher ... chief prison-guard")*. *Leg.* 3.236–242 offers a parallel exegesis of an extended version of this pericope, treating many of the same themes. There, Philo focuses on the oddity of Potiphar being a married eunuch with a wife. The latter, he interprets as "pleasure," in accord with Potiphar's interpretation as a mind devoted to the sensual appetites. *Deus* 111–115 presents a second important parallel. There it is Potiphar's wife, pleasure, who is said to be the "chief-butcheress" (ἡ ἀρχιμαγείρος); the "chief prison-guard" (ἀρχιδεσμοφύλαξ) is a secondary character. Philo ends this exegesis with an aside to the soul, imploring it—should it find itself in such dire straits as the Joseph soul—to endeavor to be a prisoner, rather than a prison-guard (*Deus* 114–115). See also the elaborate exegesis of the Gen 39 episode in *Ebr.* 210–221, and shorter allusions to the scene at *Conf.* 95 and *Migr.* 19. In the Exposition of the Law, the scene is treated extensively in *De Iosepho*. See especially the literal paraphrases in *Ios.* 27, 52, and the corresponding allegorical interpretations in *Ios.* 35–36, 58–79.

Nachleben

§ 168. *Exod 4:14 ("when he [i.e., Aaron] sees you, he will rejoice in himself")*. In Cyril of Alexandria (*Ador. cult.* 68.252–253 [D]), the surrounding pericope is cited and Christ (rather than Aaron) is identified as the "true Levite," "great high priest," and "mouth" of Moses, but his internal joy is not thematized. Cyril offers a similar exegesis of the verse in *Glaph. Pent.* 69.89 [D].

§ 169. *Isa 51:27/48:22 ("it does not belong to the impious to rejoice")*. Irenaeus (*Haer.* 1.9.3 [D]) cites this verse and interprets it as a reference to certain gnosticizing opponents, who suggest that God, the maker of heaven and earth, is an emanation of "defect." The verse here serves as a stock invective, with no direct link to the *corpus Philonicum*. More Philonic is Eusebius of Caesarea's interpretation of Isa 48:22 in *Comm. Is.* 2.34 [A/B]. Noting that the Word saw beforehand that many people would hear the words of the prophet in an unworthy manner, Eusebius writes that in order to safeguard against the Israelites also receiving the prophetic oracles indiscriminately,

> of necessity he adds to the promises (αἱ ἐπαγγελίαι) the verse, "'It does not belong to the impious to rejoice,' says the Lord" (Isa 48:22). For to the pious (εὐσεβοῦσι) will belong all the delight and joy and happiness of God (ἡ παρὰ θεοῦ τρυφὴ καὶ χαρὰ καὶ εὐφροσύνη) and whatever else has been promised, but for the impious (ἀσεβοῦσιν), there is no way to receive the promises.

Although Eusebius cites Isa 48:22 rather than Isa 57:21, his interpretation picks up on the Philonic theme of "promises" (αἱ ἐπαγγελίαι [cf. § 154]), "joy" (χαρά [§ 163]), and "happiness" (εὐφροσύνη [§ 168]), suggesting some direct or traditional link between these passages.

§ 170. *Gen 45:16–18 ("Pharaoh rejoiced and all his retinue")*. This pericope is not listed in *BiPa* 1–3, 5, including Clement, Origen, and the Cappadocians. Eusebius (*BiPa* 4:49; *Chron.* B 72,22 [D]) relates Jacob's meeting with his brothers in a single sentence as a matter of historical interest. Procopius (*Comm. Gen.* 45.1 [D]) notes that Pharaoh and his retinue were elated because they now perceived that they were not ruled by a slave, but a well-born son of Jacob's noble line. Ambrose (*Jos.* 13,74 [D]), confused by Pharaoh's uncharacteristically joyful ("et gavisus est Pharao") and hospitable attitude, looks for a deeper ecclesial meaning in this story:

> Whence this *humanitas* in a pagan (i.e., Pharaoh), unless this should show a great mystery ("magnum mysterium"): that now the Church is not envious, when the Jews are redeemed, and the Christian people rejoices at this inclusion ("et populus Christianus hac adjunctione laetatur")?

If Ambrose knew Philo's allegory of the feigned joy of Pharaoh, he has removed all traces of it from his ecclesiological allegoresis or is quietly arguing against it.

once he had debased ... ancestral stamp of kindred virtue. The idea that the soul, stamped by the divine image, can become debased is a theme that will return in the early Christian tradition. See, e.g., Athanasius, *Inc.* 7.4 [C/D], who notes that human beings "were deprived of the grace belonging to the one who is created according to the image ⟨of God⟩" (τὴν τοῦ κατ' εἰκόνα χάριν ἀφαιρεθέντες ἦσαν [cf. Athanasius, *Inc.* 14.1]).

§172. *those who have ... enrolled in the gymnasia of temperance*. For the sons of Jacob as athletes of virtue in Christian tradition, see Clement of Alexandria (cited in the *Nachleben* on §81).

§173. *Gen 37:36; 39:1, 20–23* ("*Potiphar, the eunuch and chief butcher ... chief prison-guard*"). Josephus (*A.J.* 2.39–59) retells the story of Joseph in Potiphar's house, showing some influence of Philonic vocabulary in making Joseph a symbol of "reason" (*A.J.* 2.53 [C]) and Potiphar's wife one of "pleasure" (ἡδονή) (*A.J.* 2.51 [C]) and emotion (πάθος) (*A.J.* 2.53 [C]), but no strong connection to *De mutatione nominum*. For Josephus's knowledge of Philo, see Sterling 2013a.

§174. *good for the body*. For Egypt as goods of the body, see Origen, *Hom. Num.* 26.4 [A/B] (Van den Hoek 2000, 106) and the discussion there. The reference may not be to this particular passage, but Philo is clearly in mind.

[Chapter 8]
The Faith and Doubt of Abraham (§§175–200)

Chapter eight of *De mutatione nominum*, which treats the faith and potential doubt of Abraham in Genesis 15 and 17, is one of the true gems of this treatise. Although Philo continues the running commentary on Gen 17 and develops elements of the discussion from the previous chapter—especially, the theme of the soul's internal laughter (§§166, 168)—chapter eight can simultaneously be read as an independent exegetical dissertation on the virtue or disposition of subjective human "faith" (πίστις) in Hellenistic Jewish thought. In its studied interweaving of Abrahamic proofs from the Yahwistic (Gen 15) and Priestly (Gen 17) covenantal narratives and its philosophical reflection on the anthropology of human faith, set in comparison with the peerless faithfulness of God, this chapter approaches the magnitude, scope, and sublimity of several passages in the New Testament letters: Gal 3, Jas 2, and especially Rom 3–4, which is its nearest kin and foil. As with Philo's ruminations on the namelessness and transcendence of God in chapter one, we are dealing here in chapter eight with a contribution of the greatest significance for the history of religions.

To be a little more specific: in his *Theology of the New Testament*, Rudolf Bultmann argues that the concepts of "faith" (πίστις) in Philo and in Paul are fundamentally different (1951–1955, 1:316):

Philo understands "faith" as a "propensity" (διάθεσις) of the soul, the soul's perfect state, an "excellence" (ἀρετή). In his thought, therefore, "faith" stands at the end "as the goal of life's movement toward God" (Schlatter), while for Paul it stands at the beginning furnishing the basis for the new life.

The current chapter contests Bultmann's sweeping generality: for Philo, faith is a disposition and a virtue in formation. It is an excellence of the Abraham soul *on the road* to ethical perfection, but by no means having yet attained it. (On this topic, see also the important essay of Hay 1989, with an emphasis on objective rhetorical "proofs" [πίστεις]).

All modern commentators agree that §§ 176–200 comprises a single chapter. The only point of contention regards whether § 175 is the close of the previous chapter on Abraham's laughter (§§ 154–175) or the incipit of the present one (§§ 175–200). This commentary takes the view that chapter eight begins at § 175. (For the positions of previous commentators, which are divided, see Introduction 3. Chapters of the Treatise.) A brief look at other transitional paragraphs in the treatise will provide support for this position. First, at the beginning of chapter two, which is universally agreed to be at § 39, Philo opens his discussion (as in § 175) by recapitulating the foregoing arguments. Second, at § 47, which most take to be the incipit of a self-standing chapter or subsection, Philo begins by citing the primary lemma of the foregoing exegetical unit before then citing the primary lemma for the present one, again as in § 175. Thus, there is reason and precedent to reckon § 175 as the beginning of the present chapter.

Chapter eight divides neatly into three subsections, all of which address a fundamental question: does Abraham's "internal speech" (λόγος ἐνδιάθετος) about his and Sarah's ages betoken doubt in God's promise of a child? The chapter begins with (a) the citation of the foregoing (Gen 17:17a) and current (Gen 17:17b) primary lemmata, with a special focus on Gen 17:17bα, "he said in his thought." This leads to a long, topical discourse on the nature of Abraham's faith and the possibility of his doubt. Philo gives a first answer to this question: Abraham's hesitation occurs in his thought, but never reaches his lips. Hence, it is not "doubt" in the proper sense (§§ 175–187).

Next, Philo considers (b) a second answer to the central question (does Abraham's internal speech betoken doubt?), which focuses on the second part of the primary biblical lemma, Gen 17:17bβ: "Will/would that (εἰ) a child be born to this one-hundred-year-old man?" Philo wonders, with some of his more creative interpretive colleagues, whether Abraham's cryptic words in Gen 17:17bβ might constitute a prayer rather than an expression of doubt (§§ 188–192).

Philo concludes with (c) the adduction and selective interpretation of a long secondary biblical lemma, Gen 34:1–39 (the rape and avenging of Dinah). In his allegoresis, Philo illustrates the difference between Abraham's possible hesitation about God's promises in *thought* and the truly wicked *deed* of Shechem (*Sychem*), who not only plots in his mind, but attempts through his acts to overthrow God's justice. By setting Abraham in juxtaposition to Shechem, the faithfulness of the former comes into sharper focus (§§ 193–200).

a   *The Faith and Doubt of Abraham (§§ 175–187)*
    Analysis and General Comments

In the first subsection, Philo addresses what he sees as a fundamental tension within Moses's Abraham cycle: the struggle between doubt and belief. Beginning with the primary lemma, Gen 17:17b, he notes that Abraham's internal questioning of whether a child can be born to a one-hundred-year-old man with a ninety-year-old wife looks indeed like a moment of doubt or hesitation. This would seem to contradict the earlier picture of Abraham's faith in God's promise of a child in Gen 15:4, 6, which is "reckoned to him as righteousness." In the subsequent discussion, Philo offers and defends against counter-objection a first solution to this scriptural problem: that Abraham's momentary hesitation, although real, is negligible for being swift and internal, and remains compatible with the greatest degree of faith possible for a created mind. Those who object to Abraham's momentary hesitation in Gen 17:17b are demanding a greater degree of "faith" (πίστις) from Abraham than is humanly possible—requiring of a mortal the faithfulness proper to God alone (Deut 32:4, cf. Rom 3:3). Margaret Graver (2008, 209) links Philo's assertion of the inevitability of human wavering to the Stoic idea of the "pre-emotions" (προπάθειαι):

> The *De mutatione nominum* passage [viz., §§ 177–187] is complex, combining several traditions of thought, and cannot by any means be treated as evidence for Stoic doctrine. But given the similarity of [Abraham's] "slight turning" to Epictetus's "rapid and unplanned movements," it seems safe to say that a significant element in Philo's thinking here is attributable to his knowledge of the προπάθεια ["pre-emotion"] doctrine.

The subsection divides into six parts:
(1) *Recapitulatio.* Philo begins by recapitulating the interpretation of Gen 17:17a offered in chapter seven (§§ 154–174): that Abraham "falls" on account of a new appreciation of his own nothingness and "laughs" for joy at the grace of God, extended to him in the covenant (§§ 175–176a).

(2) *Quaestio/ζήτημα* or *problema*. Philo cites the "immediately" following words of the primary lemma (Gen 17:17b), in which Abraham questions "in his thought/intellect" whether a child can be born to a hundred-year-old man with a ninety-year-old wife. Abraham's reaction appears to stand in tension with his seemingly unwavering faith in God's promise of a child in Gen 15:4, 6. Philo poses the implicit question: how can both statements be true? The detection of this kind of exegetical problem is to be found in a wide range of commentary literatures, from Alexandrian Homeric scholarship to the rabbinic middah, "two verses ⟨contradict each other⟩" (שני כתובים) (§§ 176b–177).

(3) *Solutio/λύσις A*. As a first solution to the problem of Abraham's apparent doubt in Gen 17:17bβ, Philo observes a peculiarity in Moses's citation formula, that Abraham spoke "in his thought" (τῇ διανοίᾳ). He introduces the term "hesitation/wavering" (ἐνδοιασμός), key to this *solutio*, which is neither "faith" (πίστις) nor "doubt" (ἀπιστία) proper. (§ 178)

(4) *Probatio A*. As a proof of this interpretation of Gen 17:17bα, Philo adduces a secondary classical lemma from Homer (*Od*. 7.36), which likens thoughts to wings as the swiftest of created things. Abraham's "hesitation" (ἐνδοιασμός) was similarly swift, even existing "outside of time itself" (§§ 179–180).

(5) *Objectio et probatio B*. Philo next raises a hypothetical but probable objection to his first *solutio*. Someone will likely say that Abraham's faith must by definition preclude even a "trace or shadow or whiff of doubt" (ἴχνος ἢ σκία ἢ αὔρα ἀπιστίας). To answer this objection, Philo adduces a secondary biblical lemma, Deut 32:4—a verse that heralds the singular faithfulness of God. Only God's virtues are "unmixed"; human faithfulness is but an "image" of divine virtue. Thus, while it is praiseworthy for human beings to imitate divine faithfulness, one should not expect that any created mind, however "perfect," will be able to remain unshakeable as God himself— especially given our mortal natures (§§ 181–185).

(6) *Solutio/λύσις A′*. Having dealt with this objection, Philo reprises his first solution by way of an interpretation of the contextualizing secondary lemma, Gen 15:6: Abraham "believed" in God, but in a way that was excellent for a created mind and not to the necessary exclusion of a momentary hesitation or shadow of a doubt (§§ 186–187).

Detailed Comments

(1) § 175. *the falsely named "joy" of fools is something of this sort*. A reference to Pharaoh and his Egyptian entourage (Gen 45:16–18) and Potiphar (Gen 39:1), read through the lens of Isa 57:21. See chapter seven (§§ 169–174).

the true joy has been spoken of earlier. In chapter seven, as exemplified by Abraham (Gen 17:17a), Sarah (Gen 18:12), and Aaron (Exod 4:14). See §§ 155, 166–168.

befitting the good alone. See § 169.

therefore, falling, he laughed. Philo paraphrases the primary biblical lemma of chapter seven. To highlight the importance of Abraham's laughter over his falling, Philo has lightly rewritten Gen 17:17a, "and Abraham fell upon his face and laughed" (καὶ ἔπεσεν Ἀβραὰμ ἐπὶ πρόσωπον καὶ ἐγέλασεν), rendering the aorist indicative "fell" (ἔπεσεν) as a participle "having fallen" (πεσών).

not from God's want of strength, but from his own. Philo's Greek is terse, saying literally that Abraham falls not "from God" but "from himself." The prepositions are to be taken in a causal sense.

he stood with the support of the Unturned. The predicate is difficult to render literally ("he stood around the unmoved"). Colson translates it "in clinging to the Unmovable." "Around the unturned" (περὶ τὸν ἄτρεπτον) may depict either the metaphor of a vine supported by a lattice or an abstract metaphysical geography. Philo elaborates the image in § 176, noting that the God-loving thought is "established about the Unbending alone" (ἱδρυθεὶς περὶ τὸ ἀκλινὴ μόνον). For "the Unmoved" (ὁ ἄτρεπτος) as a title for God and Aristotelian resonances with this conception, see the detailed comments on § 28; also in this treatise, §§ 24, 55, 87, 135.

he fell away from his personal self-conceit. The meaning of the prepositional phrase may be double: "because of" his self-conceit and "away from" self-conceit toward a fuller knowledge of his own nothingness, owing to a renewed consideration of the grace given by The One Who Is. See § 176, in which Philo speaks of "sophistic pretention" being brought low. This is the only appearance of the word "self-conceit" (οἴησις) in the present treatise. Elsewhere in the Allegorical Commentary (*Cher.* 57), Philo calls it "the greatest of all evils of the soul." Arnaldez (1964, 114–115, n. 1) comments:

> οἴησις is a very grave malady of the soul (*Spec.* 1.10), which makes it believe that everything belongs to itself. It causes it to steal from God's goodness and appropriate it to itself, and more, to disbelieve in God (atheism) …. On account of ⟨the soul's⟩ lack of education, it ⟨viz., οἴησις⟩ becomes a mistress, whom one serves as a slave. When the soul is liberated by God, its former slavery … falls to the ground.

§ 176a. *fixed about the Unbending alone.* For God as "Unbending" and "Unturned," see the detailed comments on §§ 28, 54, and 87.

(2) § 176b. *having laughed.* Just as Philo turns the Septuagintal verb "he fell" (ἔπεσεν [Gen 17:17aα]) into an aorist participle in § 175, so he now transforms "he laughed" (ἐγέλασεν [Gen 17:17aβ]) into a participle to shift the exegetical focus onto the new primary lemma of the present chapter, Gen 17:17b.

immediately. The addition of this adverb contrasts Philo's positive allegorical interpretation of Abraham's laughter with the more questionable internal speech that follows. Abraham's laughter in § 155 is a symbol of the joy resulting from "faith" (πίστις). Philo must now prove that Gen 17:17b is compatible with such an interpretation.

said in his thought ... Sarah, being ninety years old, give birth? Philo's citation of the primary biblical lemma shows only minor deviations from the LXX.

Gen 17:17b	§ 176
He spoke in his thought, (ἐν τῇ διανοίᾳ αὐτοῦ) wondering if (εἰ) this will happen to a hundred-year-old man? and if (εἰ) a child will be born to Sarah (Σάρρα), although she is ninety years old?	He spoke in thought (τῇ διανοίᾳ), whether (εἰ) this will happen to a hundred-year-old man? And will Sarah (ἡ Σάρρα) give birth, although she is ninety years old?

Philo has eliminated the preposition "in" (ἐν) out of consideration for Greek style (the bare dative sounds fine, less Semitizing) and to heighten the sense of internal dialogue ("Abraham spoke *to* his thought") or mental instrumentality ("*with* his thought," rather than "with his mouth"). He has also added the definite article before Sarah, emphasizing that it is "this Sarah whose name is being changed" about whom he wonders.

§ 177. *noble reader.* Rendering ὦ γενναῖε, with "reader" supplied from context. This is the second of five Philonic ὦ-asides in the present treatise (see the note on § 25). The construction of this fictive discussion partner is a hallmark of philosophical diatribes, such as those of Epictetus. It is noteworthy that the only two occurrences of this formula ("noble reader") in *De mutatione nominum* appear in this first section of chapter eight (§§ 175–187). This may indicate an originally independent source or tradition-critical unit; or, alternatively, Philo's appeal for special attention in this important section.

not with his mouth, but in thought. Philo takes full advantage of his omission of the preposition "in" (ἐν) from the biblical phrase "in his thought" (ἐν τῇ διανοίᾳ), rendering τῇ διανοίᾳ as dialogical ("to his thought") or instrumental ("with his thought").

is set down superfluously ... with studied intention. Philo calls attention to contrasting portraits of Abraham's faith in Gen 15 and Gen 17 and suggests a way to harmonize them. He argues that Abraham's speech in Gen 17:17b is internal and noetic. In this way, Philo defends the inspiration of every word written by Moses, as well as the need to seek for solutions to Mosaic problems within the scriptural text itself—interpreting Moses by Moses. The second adverb, "with studied intention" (ἐξητάσμενος), points to Moses's own authorial searching (analogous to the work of exegesis itself) for a resolution to the tension within revealed history, as well as to Moses's careful composition of a psychic allegory.

why is this? Philo introduces the primary *quaestio* of the chapter by way of his favorite diatribal/scholastic question, "for what reason?" (διὰ τί;). This is one of the seven primary *aporiae* identified by Runia (1988, 74) in the present treatise. Although elsewhere in *De mutatione nominum*, Philo uses this phrase to introduce a secondary or qualifying objection, here it is used to frame the primary question of the chapter. For this rhetorical question, see also §§ 46, 81, 83, 88, 94, 116, 126, 145, 158, 241, 246, 250.

it seems that, by asking ... "to this hundred-year-old man." Philo's formula highlighting the tension between Gen 15 and Gen 17 is similar to the rabbinic middah, "two verses ⟨contradict each other⟩" (שני כתובים), and foreshadows the form and arrangement of Medieval scholastic literature—particularly the *videtur quod* ("it seems that") of the Thomistic *quaestio*.

Abraham has begun to waver. I render the aorist infinitive "to waver" (ἐνδοιάσαι) as ingressive. Critically, Philo does not use the "doubt" (ἀπιστ-) root, but introduces a different verb to describe Abraham's internal questioning. This renaming of the alleged phenomenon (Abraham's apparent lack of faith) opens up a linguistic space, in which to explore attendant anthropological and theological questions.

concerning the birth of Isaac. Philo reiterates here the title of chapter six, "The Birth of Isaac" (ἡ γένεσις Ἰσαάκ [§ 130]). This cross-reference suggests that chapters six through eight comprise a multi-chapter discourse, subsequent to chapter five, which was titled "On the Change and Transformation of Names" (ἡ τῶν ὀνομάτων ἀλλαγή τε καὶ μετάθεσις [§ 130]). On this reading, § 177 references chapter six from the outside, from the perspective of a later chapter.

beforehand, however, it was said that he believed. "Beforehand" in chapter six (§ 155), in Philo's interpretation of Abraham's laughter; but also "beforehand" in the text of the Pentateuch (Gen 15:4–6).

as this oracle spoken a little earlier clarified. To defend his attribution of faith to Abraham in Gen 17:17a (§ 155), Philo adduces Gen 15:4–6 as a contextualizing secondary lemma. He does not, as a modern source critic, see the two covenantal scenes as alternative versions of the same story, but as linear developments within a single narrative. The tension is not merely that Abraham's behavior in the two scenes differs, but that Abraham has apparently begun to doubt *after* his name has been changed—a major hiccup in the consistency of Philo's allegory of the soul.

"this man will not ... but a child who will come forth from you." Because the function of this citation is primarily contextualization rather than thematic development, Philo offers little comment on Gen 15:4. The text of the citation is identical with that found in the Septuagint.

then immediately. Just as Abraham's internal speech follows "immediately" (εὐθύς) upon his laughter (§176), so his belief in God follows "immediately" (εὐθύς) upon hearing the promise (§177). Beneath this rhetorical similarity, however, lies an exegetical sleight of hand. Philo, in his interpretation of Abraham's faith, skips over Gen 15:5, which seems to provide extra content to the promise (seed like the numberless stars) and stimulus for believing. He suggests instead that Abraham's faith rests on the singular miracle of a son from Sarah.

and Abraham believed God ... it was reckoned to him as righteousness. Philo's citation of the second part of the contextualizing secondary lemma agrees with the Septuagint, with the minor exception of the spelling of the name "Abraham" (Ἀβραάμ). Philo clearly attended to the spelling of biblical names in sequence (see §83, where he comments on the issue of Moses's editorial consistency or inconsistency). The current text may reflect the spelling preferences of Philo's tradents in the schools of Origen and Eusebius rather than the Alexandrian's own practices. He may also have simply followed the more common spelling.

(3) §178. *it did not follow.* Philo presents an interesting window into Moses's compositional subjectivity. Apparently, the lawgiver knows what Abraham does and says, and anticipates its misinterpretation. Thus, in writing the narrative, he writes Abraham's words in such a way that their allegorical meaning may be clearly gleaned.

the one who had come to believe. Philo uses the perfect aspect "has/had come to believe" (πεπιστευκώς) to denote the completion and perfection of Abraham's faith, which is related to the topic of the present treatise.

to waver in earnest. Philo does not ask whether Abraham "loses faith" (ἀπιστεῖν), but whether he has "wavered" (ἐνδοιάσαι). Elsewhere in the chapter, he uses the distinction between "doubt" (ἀπιστία) and "wavering" (ἐνδοιασμός) constructively. In the present section, the words are roughly synonymous, although "wavering" remains connected with cognitive and verbal expression, whereas "doubt" extends to actions as well. Philo also distinguishes between varying durations and intensities of "wavering," the shortest of which he attributes to Abraham.

long-lasting, of the variety that reaches tongue and mouth. A long-lasting "wavering" (ἐνδοιασμός) is one that reaches the lips—that is, wavering in speech. This confirms the impression that Philo uses the term "wavering" to apply both to cognitive and verbal doubt, but not to a lack of faith that entails evil deeds. Philo reserves the third part of this chapter (§§ 193–200) for a discussion of doubt in action, or "doubt/faithlessness" (ἀπιστία) proper.

remains fixed in his swift-moving thought. Philo literally confines Abraham's "wavering" (ἐνδοιασμός) to his intellect. It is the shortest "flicker" of doubt imaginable. To express this notion, Philo takes the scriptural word "thought" (διάνοια) and adorns it with the epicizing epithet, "swift-moving" (ὀξυκίνητος). This reflects his poetic sensibilities as an author, and particularly his interest in Homer (Roskam 2017; Niehoff 2012). The adjective, which may be of Philonic coinage, appears also in a first-century CE medical text as a description of the eye (Erotianus, frag. 3)—the somatic counterpart of the intellect. Philo has chosen it here to anticipate the Homeric compound "swiftness of foot" (ποδώκεια) in the following line.

no other faculty. A Platonizing position. Other nouns modified by the adjective "swift-moving" in Greek literature include the eye, fastest of the sense organs according to Erotianus (see note above); fire, which Galen, in his commentary on Hippocrates, calls "most swift-moving" (ὀξυκινητότατος) of the elements (*Comm. nat. hom.*, Kühn vol. 15, p. 170); and, as Philo implies in this passage (thinking of Homer), birds. All three of these corporeal things cannot outstrip "thought" (διάνοια).

praised for its swiftness of foot. The noun ποδώκεια, which refers literally to human or animal feet, symbolizes mental swiftness. Philo works within the Platonist tradition, known also from Plutarch, of reading Homeric heroes allegorically as figures of the human soul. The noun "swiftness of foot" (ποδώκεια) first appears in Homer (*Il.* 2.792), echoing the poetic formula, "swift of feet" (πόδας ὠκέα), used of the goddess Iris (Ibid.), and πόδας ὠκύς, used in *Il.* 1.58 *et passim*, of Achilles. Philo's use of the word is inspired by the broader context of his Homeric citation about the wing, which speaks of the vessels of the Phaeacians as "swift ships" (νέες ὠκεῖαι). Philo thus embellishes his psychic allegory of Moses's sage with language that recalls the Homeric sagas.

thought has even outstripped all the winged natures. Thought is swifter than wings, and wings, in poetry, are swifter than feet. Hence, Abraham's doubt was a thing, something swifter than which cannot be imagined. Birds are referenced in anticipation of the citation of *Od.* 7.36.

§ 179. *the most revered of the Greek poets*. Philo refers to Homer with similar honorifics elsewhere in his corpus. See Roskam 2017 for a comprehensive list of Philo's citations of Homer, as well as citation formulae. Most comparable to the present locus are the references in *Conf*. 4 ("Homer, the greatest and most revered of the poets" [ὁ μέγιστος καὶ δοκιμώτατος τῶν ποιητῶν Ὅμηρος]); *Prov*. 2.15; and *QG* 4.2. Such titles show the cultural, philosophical, and theological esteem with which Philo looked on Homer, even if he did not accept the *Iliad* and *Odyssey* as divinely inspired in the same fashion as Moses's, Jeremiah's, or even Plato's writings. See further Koskenniemi 2019, who argues that Philo knows Homer well and uses him more sympathetically than Josephus does.

Uses the phrase. Philo adduces a secondary classical lemma, *Od*. 7.36. While some of Philo's classical allusions are primarily rhetorical adornment, Roskam is right in pointing out the special place of Homer in Philo's theological speculation. If the poets were "milk for children," then "Philo was an enthusiastic milk drinker and remained so all his life" (Roskam 2017, 2). Not only Philo's familiarity with these poems from his early education, but also the more advanced Platonist allegoresis of the Odysseus cycle, left a deep impression on him. Roskam (2017, 13) categorizes Philo's use of Homer in § 179 as one which "throws light on the meaning of Scripture. Philo's focus ⟨in such passages⟩ is then not so much on a general philosophical doctrine as on the exegesis of a particular passage from Scripture—although the difference between both is not always crystal clear."

As if a wing or a notion. Philo cites the final five words from *Od*. 7.36, which reads "whose ships are swift as a wing or a notion" (τῶν νέες ὠκεῖαι ὡς εἰ πτερὸν ἠὲ νόημα). Colson (PLCL 5:179, n. a) cross-references the statement of Thales (Diogenes Laertius 1.35): "The swiftest thing is mind; for it runs through all" (τάχιστον νοῦς· διὰ παντὸς γὰρ τρέχει). As noted above, the full line is clearly in Philo's ear, as the adjective "swift" (ὠκεῖαι) conditions his description of thought as possessing "swiftness of foot" (ποδώκεια) in § 178. Philo begins his citation of the verse at the word "as" (ὡς) in order to incorporate the citation into the syntax of his own sentence. In doing so he also demonstrates an intuitive knowledge of Greek meter, as he begins after the masculine caesura in the third foot:

– ᴗ ᴗ | – – | – : – | – ᴗ ᴗ | – ᴗ ᴗ | – x

τῶν νέες ὠκεῖαι : ὡς εἰ πτερὸν ἠὲ νόημα

he clarifies the speed of thought's sharpness. Roskam (2017, 15) argues that this verse contains "precisely what Philo needs in order to emphasize the swiftness and instantaneous character of Abraham's hesitation. In this case, there is no need of subtle allegorical interpretations, for the literal meaning of the phrase perfectly expresses the idea of speed." This underplays the import of the classical lemma. Philo is not simply drawing on the phrase "as a wing or a notion," but through the literary trope of metalepsis, interpreting the ships of the Phaeacians as allegorical symbols of psychic vessels sailing vertically toward the realm of the forms and ethical perfection. The fact that this line is originally part of the speech of a disguised Athena to Odysseus, in which she instructs the hero on how to pass through a land of xenophobic foreigners to reach the palace of Alcinous, further suggests that Philo is creating (or was familiar with) an allegoresis of this Homeric passage. It is not hard to imagine an interpretation, in which Wisdom (Athena) instructs the soul (Odysseus) about the noetic means of passing through the "foreign land," warning him not to speak with any of the local inhabitants (the pleasures). Cf. Porphyry, *Vit. Plot.* 22, in which the Neo-Platonist pupil compares his own master's psychic journey to that of Odysseus in *Od.* 5—in hexameters, no less, and placed on the lips of Apollo.

setting "notion" after "wing." Philo offers a close reading of Homer's poetic syntax. The sequence of nouns "wing or notion" (πτερὸν ἠὲ νόημα) is not accidental to the metrical arrangement, but bespeaks a hierarchy of speed, with the swiftest item in the list coming last. The comment indicates that Philo read the words as a merism, indicating the sum total of material ("wing") and immaterial ("notion") speed—both "bodies and realities." If it is too much to say that Philo here articulates a principle of poetics, his attention to the words in their sequence and use of their placement in the line to develop an anthropology of thought implies one.

surpassing intensity. I have rendered ἐπίτασις as "intensity," in order to relate the word's connotations of extension in both space and time (cf. "swiftness of foot" [ποδώκεια], which entails both axes). Thought travels not only swiftly, but also over great distances. See *Leg.* 1.62 for Philo's autobiographical meditation of his own power of thought.

by some ineffable motion. Philo's language of ineffability, as in chapter one, exposes the sceptical edge of his philosophy. Even the soul itself remains unknown to the human being (§ 10).

over many terrains, both immaterial and material alike. The allegorical aspect of Philo's interpretation of Homer's Phaeacian ships is evident. Thought is not merely a metaphor for their swiftness; rather, the ability of the Phaeacian ships to cross the seas is symbolic of the movement of thought through both "material distances" (σώματα) and the world of immaterial forms or "realities" (πράγματα).

arrives, in an instant, at the bounds of earth and sea. That is, crossing the lowest two elements. This detail may reflect an allegoresis of Athena's description of the ships of the Phaeacians "cross over the great gulf of the sea" (λαῖτμα μέγ' ἐκπερόωσιν [*Od.* 7.35]).

compressing and traversing distances of unbelievable magnitude. Philo is ambivalent as to whether the soul crosses distances, or rather compresses them such that they no longer need to be crossed. For the verb "traversing," or more literally, "cutting down" (τέμνουσα), Colson (PLCL 5:235, n. b) opines: "the sense of the word is not clear. Wendland suggests συντέμνουσα … 'making a short cut.'"

in this same quantity of time. I.e., "instantly" (αὐτίκα), as mentioned above. Philo vacillates between claiming that the soul moves in "not a long time" (οὐ πολυχρόνιον [§ 178]) and that the soul's motion happens "in a certain manner, outside of time" (τρόπον τινὰ ἄχρονος [§ 180]).

also lifts off of the earth, ascends from air to aether. Having transcended the first two elements (earth, water), thought now traverses a second two, moving directly from air to aether (cf. Plato, *Tim.* 58d) and skipping over fire (perhaps because the soul itself is described in § 180 as possessing fiery attributes—although in this case, metaphorically).

with great toil. For the adverb "with great toil" (μόλις), see Plato, *Phaedr.* 248a, where the best human soul is said similarly to be "looking with difficulty" (μόγις καθορῶσα) upon the world of "the realities" (τὰ ὄντα), unlike the gods who make the journey with ease. Pierre Boyancé likewise finds influence of the *Phaedrus* on the present passage, as shaped by the interpretation of the "post-Platonic Academy" (Alesse 2008, 3).

comes to stand at the furthest circuit of the fixed stars. Philo's description of the soul's ascent "around furthest circuit" (περὶ τὴν ἐσχάτην … ἁψῖδα) of the material universe echoes Plato's account of the ascent of the souls in the *Phaedrus* (247ba1), which "go even to the furthest reach of the arch under heaven" (ἄκραν ἐπὶ τὴν ὑπουράνιον ἁψῖδα πορεύονται). This is the only occurrence of the noun "circuit/arch" (ἁψίς) in Plato's writings. On the flight of the mind in Philo, see Sterling 2018a.

§ 180. *its hot and fiery aspect.* Supplying the neuter noun "part"/"aspect" (μέρος). Omitting fire from the list of physical elements traversed by mind, Philo reserves it as a metaphorical modifier of the mind itself. The description has Stoic overtones. Read through Philo's Platonizing spectacles, it may signify a break between the thinnest material stuff (aether) and the "fiery" immaterial soul.

does not allow it to rest. Plato says that soul, as immortal, is always in motion (*Phaedr.* 245c).

it is borne. Cf. Plato, *Phaedr.* 246c, where the same verb "is borne" (φέρεται) is used to describe the soul's downward fall.

transcending many material bodies. In Philo's description of the good person's itinerary, the soul, having traversed the "material things" (σώματα), moves into the world of ideal "realities" (πράγματα [§ 179]).

the fixed region of the forms by kindred attraction. Philo locates Plato's forms within the "noetic cosmos"—i.e., the Logos in its passive, paradigmatic aspect. This Logos is also called "the image of God." The human soul is kindred with this image, having been created "after the image" (Gen 1:27). Being unlike all material bodies, it naturally ascends to the realm where it belongs.

the change which happens in the good man. Philo returns from his exegesis of the secondary classical lemma (the swift, fiery nature of thought) and applies its results to the primary biblical lemma regarding the psychic wavering of Abraham.

immediate, immeasurable, not perceptible but only noetic. Philo strings together two negative adjectives, "immediate" (lit. "indivisible" [ἄτομος]) and "immeasurable" (lit. "without parts" [ἀμερής]), each of which refer to unity and simplicity. Without divisibility, there is no possibility of measurement or time. Hence, the soul's "movement" in this region should be conceived not only as bodiless, but also as timeless.

in a certain manner, outside of time itself. See the detailed comment on "in this same quantity of time" (§ 179) above.

(5) § 181. ***but perhaps someone would say.*** Philo, as is his wont, introduces an objection to his own solution. Although the "someone" is hypothetical, Philo has in mind the interpretive traditions of other Jewish colleagues, for whom the faith of Abraham was of paramount importance. One thinks, for instance, of Abraham's contribution to the "merits of the fathers" in rabbinic tradition or Paul's especially high valuation of Gen 15:6 in Rom 4:3, 23; and Gal 3:6—both of which are at least loosely connected with Palestinian Pharisaic tradition. Philo may also have in mind the radical allegorizers, for whom—given their almost exclusive focus on the symbolic meaning of the Pentateuch—the faith of Abraham might have played a central role. See Goulet's comments on potential traditional elements underlying Philo's interpretation of Abraham's faith in Gen 15:6 (1987, 270–273).

he who has come to believe. See § 178, where the same substantive perfect participle, "the one who has come to believe" (ὁ πεπιστευκώς), is used to denote Abraham's fullness of faith; *pace* Bultmann (1951–1955, 1:316), this does not yet designate the final perfection of every virtue, nor the full attainment of joy. Rather, in both subsections (3) and (5) of the present chapter, Philo interprets the primary biblical lemma (Gen 17:17b) in light of the conclusion of chapter five: that Abram's change of name to Abraham represents his nearing perfection in virtue, including in his faith.

a trace or shade or whiff of doubt. Philo clarifies the meaning of "wavering" (ἐνδοιασμός) to include any "trace or shade or whiff of doubt" (ἴχνος ἢ σκιὰ ἢ αὖρα ἀπιστίας). "Wavering" is not "faithlessness" (ἀπιστία) *tout court.* By using the noun "shadow" (σκιά), he suggests (using a Platonic metaphor) the relative unreality of such psychic movement vis-à-vis actual doubt. In framing this objection, Philo unveils his own answer to the question of §177 ("Does Abraham's question about his and Sarah's ages betoken doubt?"): if it is a question of Abraham's "faithlessness" (ἀπιστία), the answer is "no."

generated is ungenerated ... that a human being ... is a god. Philo states the logical conclusion of the hypothetical objector's faulty line of reasoning, of which he has as yet only supplied the second, minor premise (B). Philo will unveil the first premise (A) in §§182–184.

[A: Perfect, unwavering faithfulness is only possible for uncreated, immortal, and incorruptible natures, i.e., for god(s), and most properly for The One Who Is.]
B: Some human beings, as stated in Scripture (e.g., Abraham), have perfect faith (§§178, 181).
C: Therefore, some human beings are gods, resembling The One Who Is in stability (§§182–184).

Although Philo does think of Abraham has having perfect (human) faith, and does not hesitate to speak of Moses as "a god" in certain contexts, he resists in strongest terms the idea that created humans can be held to divine standards that approach the virtue of the transcendent God.

§182. *which a human being obtains.* Philo uses the verb "to obtain/to be allotted" (λαγχάνω) to define human faith ultimately as a passive gift. This is in keeping with his theology of divine grace and human nothingness throughout the Allegorical Commentary. Such derivative human faith must be different in order and kind from the unoriginated faithfulness of The One Who Is.

so firm. Faith continues to be described in terms of motion and stasis, which applies to both ontological and epistemological fixity or vacillation.

pertaining to The One Who Is. Philo does not say, "the faithfulness *of* The One Who Is," as this might erroneously imply some kind of real relation between the transcendent Being and other entities, which are not truly existent (see §27). Hedging against this possibility, he uses the phrase "the faithfulness *surrounding* The One Who Is" (ἡ περὶ τὸ ὂν ⟨πίστις⟩).

which befits the divine essence. The adjective "befitting" or "fitted to" (ἄρτιος) can simply mean "perfect," but here it distinguishes the "perfect" faithfulness of God from the qualified perfection of "the faithful" (ὁ πεπιστευκώς) Abraham. Each is perfect insofar as that is possible for their respective natures.

as Moses says in the Greater Song. Philo adduces a secondary biblical lemma to support his stance: Deut 32:4 (referenced erroneously as "Deut 32,8" in PCW). Philo mentions the name of Moses to facilitate his transition from the excursus on Homer, *Od.* 7.35–36. In naming the two authorities side by side, he constructs a literary parallelism between them (both are the authors of "songs" and singers of tales). At the same time, Philo establishes a clear inspirational hierarchy between them. Homer remains merely "most revered" (δοκιμώτατος [§ 179]), whereas Moses is "most holy" (ἱερώτατος [§ 187]). Deut 32:4 serves as the theological bedrock of the entire chapter and is deeply important to Philo's theology. For "the Greater Song" and Philo's other divisions of the book of Deuteronomy, see the detailed comment on § 42 ("In his *Exhortations*").

"God is faithful, and there is no injustice in him." Philo's citation of Deut 32:4b draws selectively on the first part of the verse in the Septuagint. To the words "God is faithful, and there is no injustice" (θεὸς πιστός, καὶ οὐκ ἔστιν ἀδικία), Philo adds the words "in him" (ἐν αὐτῷ). This may be drawn from LXX Ps 91:16: "The Lord my God is upright and there is not injustice in him" (εὐθὴς κύριος ὁ θεός μου καὶ οὐκ ἔστιν ἀδικία ἐν αὐτῷ). Arnaldez (1964, 116–117, n. 1) notes that the distinction between divine and human faithfulness is one of the great spiritual themes of the chapter. His comment warrants consideration in full:

> Human faith is not founded on itself, but on God and on the knowledge that God is πιστός ["faithful"]. Faith is an authentic good of the soul, in the sense of a quality that makes it, like God, worthy of confidence. In this sense, it is related to the consequent sequence of actions and words (cf. *infra* § 193) and the rule of right education (*Fug.* 152). Faith entails therefore, by its nature, some fixedness (*Fug.* 150, 154). It is the strongest disposition of the soul which joins it with God (*Conf.* 31). The surest faith implies the testimony of God (*Plant.* 82; *Somn.* 1.12). Faith is a reward for the one who practices a learned virtue (*Praem.* 27 ... *Migr.* 44). The human being cannot therefore discover within himself the unshakeable reasons to believe, rather the contrary. He is not rewarded for his faith; it is the inverse which is true: faith rewards positively the human being who doubts himself, but not God.

For faith in the early Roman and Christian context as a species of trust, see Morgan 2015.

§ 183. *to think that a human soul is capable of making space.* Although he has spoken of the soul's motion outside of time and measurable distance, Philo continues to use spatial metaphors to describe it. Here, he suggests that the ideal virtues (i.e., God's) are too great to be accommodated within the relatively small human soul (see also *Somn.* 1.64, in which Philo confesses autobiographically that he is not properly a "space" at all).

the unwavering and most securely fixed virtues of God. That is, the forms of the virtues. See §§ 78–79, where Philo speaks of Sarah as formal or "generic virtue," which is "imperishable" and the ground of all instances of virtue in particular existents. The idea is derived from Plato's mythological depiction of the "divine intellect" (θεοῦ διάνοια) and its stable vision of the ideal virtues: "it beholds ... justice itself" (e.g., καθορᾷ ... αὐτὴν δικαιοσύνην) in the super-heavenly realm (*Phaedr.* 247de).

images of these were able to be created. I.e., the impresses of the archetypal virtues on human souls. These are perishable "images of the images" (see *Leg.* 1.78).

their archetypes. The ideal virtues, which are encapsulated within the Image, the Logos.

§ 184. *God's virtues are unmixed.* That is, entirely noetic, ideal, and generic, with no specific, corporeal differentiation. Philo argues for this position on the grounds of God's ontological simplicity.

God himself is not composite, being a simple nature. The simplicity of God—an attribute retained in classical theism—is for Philo related to his transcendence. For other references to this doctrine in the *corpus Philonicum*, see the Parallel Exegesis. In the present context, God's "being" (ὤν) simple differentiates him from "we" who "become" (γεγόναμεν).

human virtues ... had to be mixed. A necessity due to human composite nature, which must deal with the body. Philo implies that not only the mind, but also the bodily or irrational appetites of the soul, are formed by and exhibit the virtues.

blended together and harmonized ... according to the logic of the perfect music. The composite nature of the human being is not purely negative in Philo's eyes (see also *Leg.* 2.71–75). This represents a point of difference between him and certain anti-corporeal passages in Plato, as well as later Gnostic authors. At its best, the human "mixture" (κρᾶμα) is a logical and proportional harmony of body and soul, which is aesthetically beautiful. If there is an ontological and ethical deficit involved in the human status as a mixture, this does not diminish the goodness of humanity or its capacity for perfection according to its kind.

that which is compounded ... proclivities toward each of its constituent parts. Philo understands the embodied human being to require virtues for governing both soul and body. While the mind, by its "kindred" (συγγενικῶς [§ 180]) relation to the forms, may sometimes in an ineffable movement transcend the entire material universe, it must also simultaneously stay put to look after the excellences of the body.

§ 185. *happy is the one*. Philo offers a Platonist beatitude, using "happy" (εὐδαίμων) rather than the more Septuagintal "blessed" (μακάριος [e.g., Ps 1:1]). Happiness is the goal of life in eudaemonist traditions (see the notes on §§ 51 and 216). Philo's statement offers a counterclaim to the position of some Stoics, referenced in chapter one (§ 36): "that it is impossible for someone bound in a mortal body to be entirely happy." Philo argues that there is such a thing as embodied happiness, just as there is such a thing as human faithfulness. The key is that each virtue or good emotion is predicated in a qualified way, to match the potential and limitation of its subject.

who can devote the greater part of his life ... the divine portion. Philo likens life to a set of scales, in which the divine and mortal parts of a person counterbalance one another, drawing the soul in opposite directions. The whole description—particularly the notion of "mixed" lives, wrought of happiness and grief, as well as mortality and immortality—is reminiscent of Achilles's speech to Priam in *Il.* 24.525–533 about the two jars of Zeus, from which he apportions mixed allotments to mortals. Arnaldez (1964, 118, n. 1) comments: "So long as the soul elevates itself, it remains human and exposed to being shaken, for only God is really unshakeable. One knows that mystical states do not last, and that in the time that they have ceased, the soul can conceive of doubts. Saint Teresa of Avila said it well."

it would be impossible for him to spend his entire life in this way. I.e., on the contemplative, divine side of the scales. Philo will later note autobiographically that in his earlier years, he possessed such happiness (*Spec.* 3.2: "I counted myself happy" [εὐδαιμονίζον ἐμαυτόν]), focusing in his writings and teachings on this divine portion. In the years after the Flaccus affair (38 CE)—although some dispute the exact time referred to in *Spec.* 3.1–6—a sense of solidarity with the plight of his Jewish kinsfolk would prompt him to set aside the happier portion, at least for a while, for the sake of the common weal.

the rival counterweight of his mortal part. The metaphor of counterweights privileges the mortal portion, as bodies have weight, whereas souls do not. In the struggle of the two portions, Philo emphasizes that disturbance from contemplation of the divine remains the rule for embodied souls.

like a wrestler ... lying in ambush. To further explore the divided character of composite existence, Philo mythologizes the mortal and immortal parts of the human being as enemies in a wrestling bout. "Body" (σῶμα) and "reasoning" (λογισμός) stand as opponents in the ring.

bides its time for those inopportune moments. Philo's wordplay is difficult to render into English. The mortal part of the human composite "bides its moments" (ἐκαιροφυλάκησε) against "right moments" (καιροί), when the immortal part might gain the upper hand. It lies in ambush, waiting for an "inopportune moment" (ἀκαιρία) for immortal reasoning, at which point it will attack.

§ 186. ***Abraham did come fully to believe in God.*** Philo cites the contextualizing secondary lemma (Gen 15:6) again, this time emending the principal verb from the aorist, "Abraham believed" (ἐπίστευσε[ν]), of the Septuagint (cited in § 177) to the perfect, "Abraham has come to believe" (πεπίστευκεν), to symbolize Abraham's full possession of a human faith. This is in keeping with the perfect participles already used in §§ 178 and 181. Pace Bultmann (1951–1955, 1:316), such perfected faith is for Philo the "basis" of Abraham's covenanted life leading toward moral perfection. Faith begins in Gen 15, but does not really reach completion until the birth of Isaac in Gen 21; and in Gen 17, it wavers and undergoes refinements. Faith, in short, is not a disposition achieved only at the end in Philo's religious anthropology.

as a human being comes to believe. Philo reiterates the point, made earlier, that faith can only be as perfect as the capacity of the believer.

so that you might become acquainted with what is characteristic of a mortal nature. Philo refers to the mortal human being, who in both body and soul is vulnerable to death (§ 184). The two second person singular verbs in the final clause, "so that you may know and learn" (ἵνα γνῷς καὶ μάθῃς), indicate the pedagogical situation and telos of this section. Philo aims to inculcate a new appreciation for the perfections and limits of the human belief in God. The implied interlocutor is the "noble" (γενναῖε) reader of §§ 177 and 187.

no different than that which stems from nature. Abraham's change of name and his reception of covenantal grace do not immediately overcome his mortal constitution. Although Philo speaks of a gracious "elevation" or "raising" of the Abraham soul (§ 176) in the context of a name change, symbolizing the gift of a new psychic power, such grace does not obliterate the distinction between creature and Creator.

§ 187. ***noble reader.*** The third of five Philonic ὦ-asides in the present treatise (see the note on § 25). For Philo's "noble reader" (ὦ γενναῖε), see the detailed comment on § 177, where this vocative is first used in the present treatise.

the most holy Moses. This superlative adjective distinguishes Moses from Homer (merely "most revered" [δοκιμώτατος] at § 178) as the greater theological authority.

no virtue in a mortal body which is nimble-footed. While human virtues may be agile, they are not divinely "nimble-footed" (ἀρτίπους [Ep. ἀρτίπος])— an adjective used by Homer to describe certain gods. Particularly relevant is Hephaestus's use of the word "nimble-footed" to describe Ares—a trait the lame blacksmith emphatically lacks (*Od.* 8.310). By invoking this epithet, Philo recalls the Homeric secondary classical lemma of § 178, particularly the reference to "swiftness of foot" (ποδώκεια), adding a second epic "foot" lexeme. In the echo of Hephaestus's complaint, Philo simultaneously prepares the way for an allegoresis of human psychic "lameness" (see below), in the figure of Jacob, the disjointed wrestler.

whenever it meets something of about equal strength in conflict. An allegory of the soul and its faith, which draws on both Homeric and Mosaic narratives, including the heroic battles of the *Iliad*, Menelaus wrestling with Proteus, and Philo's forthcoming interpretation of Jacob wrestling at the Jabbok. The verb "meets" (πάσχουσα) betokens the soul's susceptibility to "encountering" and "suffering" emotions, bad or good.

it grows stiff. A *Vorklang* of the secondary biblical lemma (Gen 32:25[26]) about to be cited.

becomes a little lame. The participle "becoming lame" (ὑποχωλαίνουσα) paraphrases Jacob's "limping" (ἐπέσκαζεν) at the Jabbok, after his all-night wrestling bout with the angel (Gen 32:25[26]). In its Homeric register, the epithet simultaneously evokes the "lame" (χωλεύων) god, Hephaestus (*Il.* 18.411, 417; 20.37; cf. *Od.* 8.310). At the level of allegorical portraiture, Philo blends to two figures— Jacob and Hephaestus—to create a psychic type of the limited human soul. Philo's choice of Hephaestus, rather than Achilles or Ares, as a parallel to Jacob shows the quality of his critical mind. He chooses the Homeric figure who best aligns with his biblical exemplar in the particular text that he is interpreting, in order to convey his theological and philosophical pessimism about human epistemic/moral potential.

the flat part of Jacob's thigh became stiff, on account of which he also limped. Philo adduces a double citation of a secondary biblical lemma, LXX Gen 32:25(26)–31(32) ("Gen 32,25, 31" in PCW), drawing only from the first and last verses. It is thematically rather than lexically connected to the matrix of primary and contextualizing secondary lemmata (in the same fashion as the secondary classical lemma in § 178). Philo has combined the two verses into a single sentence:

Gen 32:25(26), 31(32)	§187
25(26) And the flat part of Jacob's thigh (τοῦ μηροῦ) became stiff ... 31(32) Now he was limping on his thigh (τῷ μηρῷ αὐτοῦ) ...	The flat part of his thigh (τοῦ μηροῦ) ... became stiff ... on account of which (ᾧ) he also limped.

TABLE 8.1   References to Gen 32 in *De mutatione nominum*

Mut.	*Mut.* Chapter	Gen 32	2° Lemma
§14	Ch. 1	32:29(30)	"Announce your name to me." "Why do you ask?"
§44	Ch. 2	32:28b(29b)	"You were strong with God, and powerful with human beings."
§81	Ch. 5	32:28a(29a)	"Your name will no longer be Jacob, but Israel."
§187	Ch. 8	32:25(26), 31(32)	"The flat of Jacob's thigh became stiff and he limped upon it."

Philo has chosen this verse with special reference to its exegetical context. Jacob's psychic disability illustrates the partial failure of Abraham in Gen 17:17b.

This is not the only time that Philo has adduced Gen 32 in *De mutatione nominum*. He has cited verses from Gen 32 on four occasions in this treatise, all related to Jacob's nighttime encounter. These are shown in table 8.1 above.

In chapter one, Jacob's request to the angel, "Announce your name to me," in Gen 32:29(30) illustrates that neither God nor his Logos have a proper name, but that God has given a catachrestic name for use in prayer. In chapter two, Jacob (Gen 32:28b[29b]) serves as a type of the eschatological fulfillment of the covenant of Abraham and Moses, with its requirements to "Be well-pleasing" to both God and human beings. In chapter five, Philo adduces Gen 32:28a(29a), where Jacob's name is changed to Israel, as a part of his central chapter on this theme. Finally, here in chapter eight, Jacob's wrestling with the angel demonstrates the ineluctable lameness of human virtue, which owing to its composite foundation always stands at the borderland between its mortal and immortal capacities and perfections.

TABLE 8.2   Interpretation of Gen 32 in *De mutatione nominum*

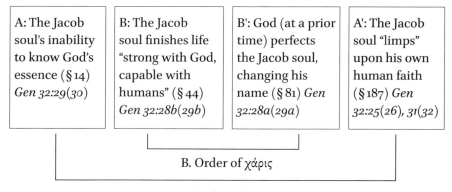

Although each secondary or tertiary lemma has its place within the proofs of its respective chapter, we may discover here also an architectonic ordering, which transcends the immediate setting and unifies four of the most important chapters of the treatise. Philo has worked backwards through the lemma, starting with Jacob's request for the angel's name and then "rewinding" from Gen 32:29(30) through Gen 32:28b(29b) and 32:28a(29a) to Gen 32:25(26). The final reference to this passage (in §187) alludes to the latest point in the pericope, Gen 32:31(32), which reaffirms the portrait of epistemological weakness occasioned by Gen 32:29(30) (§14). While in the two outer chapters, §§14 and 187, Philo uses Jacob to illustrate human failures of knowledge and faith vis-à-vis the divine, in the two inner chapters, God recognizes Jacob's covenantal faithfulness and perfection as belonging to the practicing soul which comes to see God. Across all four chapters, Philo has constructed a picture of God's recognition of human perfection in virtue (according to its created capacity), flanked on either side by illustrations of human epistemological limit. These are illustrated in table 8.2 above.

Ignorance and wavering of faith represent, for Philo, the natural human condition (A. Order of φύσις ["nature"]), which is elevated in the central two movements of the work not through human effort, but through grace (B. Order of χάρις ["grace"]).

Parallel Exegesis

The parallel *QGE* passage to *De mutatione nominum* chapter eight (*QG* 3.56), also interpreting Gen 17:17, is rich and complex. A complete commentary on this *quaestio et solutio* exceeds the scope of this section. The parallel is of particular importance for the arithmological interpretation in §§188–192. *QG* 3.56

divides into three parts: Philo begins by assessing the apparent "doubt" of Abraham, implied by his questioning of the divine promises (*QG* 3.56a; cf. *Mut.* 175–187). He then offers two long arithmological passages on the ages of Abraham (100) and Sarah (90) mentioned in Gen 17:17b. These occur in *QG* 3.56b (cf. *Mut.* 188–191) and the similarly lengthy *QG* 3.56c (cf. *Mut.* 192). For more Philonic passages related to the theme of Abraham (and Sarah) falling, see the Parallel Exegesis in chapter four.

§ 176. *fixed about the Unbending alone.* The title "Unbending" is also used for God in *Leg.* 2.83. Both it and "unturned" appear in *Conf.* 96 ("the unbending and unturned God" [ὁ ἀκλινὴς καὶ ἄτρεπτος θεός]).

§ 177. *Gen 17:17* ("*do not think … 'in thought' is set down superfluously*"). Philo's adjective "superfluously" (παρέργως) finds a close analogue in *QG* 3.56a "not ineptly or casually" (Marcus, PLCLSup). The Armenian, ոչ չպայրապար ևւ չպարկպարագի, might be retroverted as οὐκ εἰκῇ καὶ παρέργως. The point in both cases is to emphasize that Moses preempts potential charges of Abraham's faithlessness with the phrase "in thought" (ի մտի). Abraham's laughter is briefly alluded to in *Det.* 124, although Philo's focus in *Mut.* 177 is primarily on Sarah's laughter. Of greater interest is the parallel exegesis of Gen 17:17 in *Leg.* 3.85, where Philo interprets Abraham's laughter to signify that he was initially "not hoping" (οὐκ ἐλπίσαντι [*pace* Colson, PLCL, "unable to trust"]) in the birth of a son, and actually laughing "at the promise" (ἐπὶ τῇ ὑποσχέσει). Even here, however, Philo avoids describing Abraham as lacking faith—only hope. See also *Leg.* 3.218; and, in the Exposition of the Law, *Abr.* 201.

Gen 15:6 ("*Abraham believed*"). *QG* 3.56 does not adduce Gen 15:4–6 as a contextualizing secondary lemma. Philo's introduction of this text is a major advance of *De mutatione nominum* and demonstrates a certain proximity between Philo's and Paul's (see Rom 4) patterns of exegesis and religion. Philo earlier interprets Gen 15:6 as a primary lemma in *Her.* 90–95. There, Abraham is also said to have "come to believe" (πεπιστευκώς [*Her.* 90]) completely, using the perfect particle. Faith, moreover, is described by Philo there as "the most perfect of the virtues" (ἡ τελειοτάτη ἀρετῶν), the attainment of which is "not easy" (οὐ ῥᾴδιον) on account of our mortal nature. Gen 15:6 is also mentioned as a secondary lemma in *Deus* 4, where Philo alludes to Abraham's "perfect faith" (πεπιστευκέναι) in the "unwavering firmness" (ἡ … ἀνενδοίαστος … βεβαιότης) of The One Who Is; and in the Abraham cycle, in *Migr.* 44, where faith is interpreted as the "prize" (ἆθλον) and "perfect good" (ἀγαθὸν τέλειον). For the faithful soul treats things which are not yet present as "unwaveringly" (ἀνενδοίαστα) present through hope. See also *Leg.* 3.228; and in the Exposition of the Law, *Abr.* 262–274; *Virt.* 212–219 (esp. 216–218); and *Praem.* 27–30.

§ 177. *noble reader*. Philo makes an aside to the reader using the formula "noble one" (ὦ γενναῖε) fourteen times in his corpus. These include other instances in the Allegorical Commentary (*Leg.* 3.75; *Det.* 150; *Gig.* 40; *Her.* 91, 105; *Mut.* 177, 187; *Somn.* 2.253), the Exposition of the Law (*Spec.* 1.271; 2.84, 129; *Virt.* 127), and his philosophical works (*Aet.* 54; *Prov.* frag. 2).

§ 178. *Moses does not make Abraham's wavering long-lasting*. In *De mutatione nominum*, Philo vacillates between two positions: that Abraham had a momentary mental "wavering" (ἐνδοιασμός [§ 178]) and that Abraham's conditional ("if") marks not a question, but a petition of faith ("would that"), pertaining to the appropriate timing of the gift (§ 188). In the Greek parallel at *QG* 3.58b (cf. *Deus* 4; *Migr.* 44), a similar pair of interpretations is given and Philo clearly sides with the second position, noting God's affirmation to Abraham: "your faith is not ambivalent, but without wavering" (ἡ σὴ πίστις οὐκ ἀμφίβολος ἀλλ' ἀνενδοίαστος). Furthermore, in the *QG* parallel, God affirms that it is "on account of your faith in me" (διὰ τὴν πρὸς ἐμὲ πίστιν) that all the covenantal promises made regarding Isaac will come to pass. The possibility of any shade of doubt is foreclosed. In *Mut.* 178, by contrast, Philo inclines toward the first more nuanced (and "dubious") position, that Abraham hesitates in a created manner. As with his changing defense of the nature of God's gift to Abraham in chapter five, so in chapter eight, Philo parts ways with an earlier decision in the *QGE* to a follow a more nuanced philosophical tack in his allegory of the soul. His recording of both options in the present treatise illustrates his speculative flexibility, as well as the anthologizing nature of his writings.

§ 179. *the furthest circuit of the fixed stars*. Philo alludes to *Phaedr.* 247ba1 three other times: *Cher.* 23; *Det.* 85; and *Opif.* 71.

§ 180. *immediate, immeasurable, not perceptible but only noetic*. In *QG* 3.56a, Philo argues that thoughts are involuntary and thereby not culpable, unlike words and deeds, which require premeditation and will. (Philo will use the argument that unwilling thoughts are not punishable later in *Mut.* 241.) In *Mut.* 180, Philo mounts a different philosophical defense of Abraham's mental hesitation: that it is impossible for the created mind *not* to waver, on account of its mortal and complex nature.

§ 181. *but perhaps*. Philo's transition from the position (1) that Abraham's wavering is appropriate to the position (2) that Abraham does not actually doubt is made through the phrase ἀλλ' ἴσως in *De mutatione nominum*. Cf. *QG* 3.56a, in which the phrase "perhaps too" (ﬔրևս ևս) gives a similar sense, reflecting the literary connection between the two series on this question.

someone would say. In *De mutatione nominum*, Philo places the question about the possibility of Abraham's doubt on the lips of a misguided interlocutor. The person who would ask this question confuses human and divine powers of faithfulness. The format of the *quaestio et solutio* does not prohibit such an invective against a purported interlocutor (see QG 3.43 and 3.53), but in QG 3.56 Philo simply lets the question stand as a reasonable one.

a trace or shade or whiff of doubt at all? Cf. the *quaestio* of QG 3.56: "Why ⟨is it⟩ as if ⟨Abraham⟩ doubts (ըսդէր իբրև թերահաւատէ)?" The question, which might be retroverted διὰ τί ὥσπερ ἀπιστεῖ, reminds one of Philo's "as if" (ὡσανεί) with regard to predicates of divine "relation" (πρός τι) in *Mut.* 28. The force of the similitude is to imply the "impropriety" of the locution from Philo's point of view.

§ 182. *faithfulness in the case of The One Who Is*. In *De mutatione nominum*, Philo differentiates human and divine faith on subjective, ontological grounds. God's faithfulness (Deut 32:4) is primary and complete, and is the condition of all covenants with humans. The point is driven home in QG 3.58, where Philo interprets God's "yes" to Abraham as a sign of his covenantal faithfulness (cf. 2 Cor 2:17–18) with the words, "The agreement (ὁμολογία), my affirmation (ἡ ἐμὴ κατάφασις), is inviolate and unmixed with negation (ἀμιγὴς ἀρνήσεως)." God's "yes" (ἡ ἐμὴ κατάφασις) is the covenantal precondition of Abraham's "faithfulness" (ἡ σὴ πίστις), however important the latter is in confirming Abraham's receipt of the divine gift.

§ 184. *God himself is not composite, being a simple nature*. Philo speaks of God as a "simple nature" (φύσις ἁπλῆ) also in *Leg.* 2.2; *Deus* 56; *Plant.* 44; *Congr.* 36; *Fug.* 164; and *Num.* frag. 4d (Terian).

Nachleben

§ 177. *Gen 17:17* ("*falling on his face, he laughed*"). For the theme of Abraham's falling in later Christian authors, see the *Nachleben* in chapter four.

not with his mouth, but in thought. Ambrose (*Abr.* 2.87 [A]) similarly notes this important detail:

> The Greek interposes τῇ διανοίᾳ ("in thought"), so that we could understand that he spoke to his own heart, as if discoursing with himself.

> Graecus medie posuit τῇ διανοίᾳ, ut possimus aestimare quia cordi suo dixerit quasi alternanti secum.

It is especially noteworthy that Ambrose follows Philo's text of Gen 17:17 (τῇ διανοίᾳ), cited in Greek, rather than the Septuagint and the Latin versions. He also makes the same exegetical point: that "in thought" demonstrates the internal nature of Abraham's questioning. Ambrose goes on to write out the trusting dialogue between Abraham's "self and heart," in which the patriarch confesses almost instantaneously that all things are possible for God. Thus, Ambrose defends the perfection of his faith even at this moment. Philo's discussion clearly stands at the forefront of Ambrose's mind.

§ 178. *faith in me*. From the standpoint of the history of religions, it is worth noting that God's description of Abraham's faith as "faith in me" (ἡ πρὸς ἐμὲ πίστις) indicates that the terser phrase found in Paul's letters, the "faith in/of Jesus Christ" (πίστις Ἰησοῦ Χριστοῦ [Gal 3:22, etc.]) might well involve an objective genitive ("in Jesus Christ"). The point has been debated since the publication of Richard Hays's dissertation (1983), which argued for a reconsideration of the subjective genitive reading ("faithfulness of"). For Philo, Abraham's unwavering faith (and the faith of those who follow in his psychic footsteps) does not suffice to establish and maintain the covenant: God's "yes" and his own superior faithfulness (Deut 32:4 in *Mut.* 182) are its primary conditions. Philo would thus have no trouble affirming both the position that Abraham trusted in God, and that "The One Who Is" (*Migr.* 44) is unshakably faithful. That such fixed faithfulness extends to the Logos or second divine person (as in Paul), however, would not necessarily follow in Philo's theology, as the Logos at times in his writings occupies a status closer to creation on the ontological scale. This is an important distinction, as is the implication in Paul that the man Jesus might have a divine faithfulness.

does not make Abraham's wavering long-lasting. Philo's entertainment in § 178 (cf. *Leg.* 3.85) of the position that Abraham experienced a short-lived "wavering" (ἐνδοιασμός) of his faith (or hope), even if it is not to be reckoned "doubt" (ἀπιστία) *tout court*, had a mixed reception by later Christian authors. Under the influence of Paul, many follow the more positive assessments of *Deus* 4 and *Migr.* 44, that Abraham believed steadfastly. Thus, we find in the fourth century *Mart. Gur. Sam.* 37 [C] a description of God as "the one who empowered Abraham his servant ... unwaveringly (ἀνενδοιάστως) to offer the sacrifice of his son with his own hands" (cf. Gen 22). Similarly, in the sixth-century *Vit. Theod.* BHG 1776 [C], Abraham is said to have trusted in God "without wavering" (ἀνενδοιάστως). Philo's noun "wavering" (ἐνδοιασμός) itself does not appear in the extant Greek writings of Origen or the Cappadocians, and where it does resurface in Cyril of Alexandria, is used to describe the disciples' imperfect wavering of belief in the Resurrected Lord (*Comm. Jo.* 3.149 [C]), as distinguishable from perfect faith which exists "apart from any wavering" (ἐνδοιασμοῦ τινος δίχα) (*Frag. Rom.* 245.6 [C]). This latter phrase is a favorite of Cyril's and signifies the Alexandrian Christian rejection of Philo's anthropological space for any wavering between faith and doubt.

On the other side of the ledger are passages like that of John Chrysostom (*Hom. Gen.* 53.370 [A]; see the *Nachleben* for § 154 above), which clearly knows this Philonic tradition; and Eusebius (*Frag. Luc.* 24.531–532 [B/C]), who records a remarkable interpretation of Gen 17:17 in his comments on the incredulity of Zechariah in Luke 1:18:

> It was necessary for Zechariah to look intently not on his own old age and that of his wife, but on the power of the God who was making the promise. But great things are hard for human beings to understand, and God is forgiving. For also Abraham himself did not believe as was necessary (καὶ γὰρ οὐδ᾽ αὐτὸς Ἀβραὰμ ὡς ἐχρῆν ἐπίστευσεν), but at first laughed and said, "Will a son be born to a hundred-year-old man? (Gen 17:17)."

While not possessing any of Philo's nuance (nor showing direct dependence), Eusebius reads the passage straightforwardly and admits a kind of imperfect faith in Abraham on evidence in Gen 17:17. Likewise, Epiphanius, in his *Panarion* (1.371–372 [B/C]), can speak of the "uncertainty" (διστανμός) of Abraham in Gen 17:17 as the cause of circumcision and the sacrifices of Gen 15:9 as well.

Gen 15:6 ("Abraham believed in God"). By interweaving Abrahamic traditions from the Yahwistic (Gen 15:6) and Priestly (Gen 17:17) covenantal narratives, Philo's philosophical reflection on the weakness of human faith compared to the inimitable faithfulness of God approaches the magnitude, scope, and sublimity of several passages in the New Testament letters: Gal 3, Jas 2, and especially Rom 3–4, the last of which is the nearest kin and foil to the present passage. In Romans, Gen 15:6 plays a primary role (Rom 4:3), whereas Gen 17:5 is cited secondarily (Rom 4:17). Critically, Paul also alludes to Gen 17:17 (Rom 4:19), so that a similar constellation of texts forms the structure of both faith discourses. For more on the pattern of exegesis in Romans 4, see Cover 2015, 48–62. In addition to Bultmann's assessment (1951–1955, 1:316) of the difference between Paul and Philo, important related studies on faith in Philo and/or Paul include Böhm 2017; Hirsch-Luipold 2017; Schliesser 2011; and Hay 1989.

§ 179. *distances of unbelievable magnitude*. The noun "distances" (διαστήματα), used in this way of the intervals in space-time (for the temporal sense, see §§ 142, 267) traversed by the soul—particularly of intelligible distances—will become a hallmark of the later Christian philosophical vocabulary, especially in Gregory of Nyssa (Lourié 2016, 344–351).

§ 183. *to think that a human soul is capable of making space*. Although there is no clear genetic connection between the texts, Philo's formulation reminds one of Augustine's famous line in *Conf.* 1.2 [C/D]: "and what place is there in me in which my God might come into me?" ["et quis locus est in me quo veniat in me deus meus?"]. Here, Augustine, as Philo, speaks of the absence of a "space" within the human soul to contain God, despite the (paradoxical) dependence of the human being on God's presence within him.

§ 185. *like a wrestler ... lying in ambush.* Philo's depiction of "body" (σῶμα) and "reasoning" (λογισμός) as opponents in a wrestling ring finds an approximate analogue in Gal 5:17, where a similar tension is cast, albeit in the apocalyptic register of "flesh" (σάρξ) versus "spirit" (πνεῦμα).

§ 186. *so that you might become acquainted.* Philo's rhetorical address is not dissimilar to that of John 20:31 ("so that you may come to believe" [ἵνα πιστεύητε]). Characteristically, Philo addresses the ideal *individual* student rather than the community, addressed by the evangelist in the Fourth Gospel.

b   *The Prayer of the Centenarian (§§ 188–192)*
        Analysis and General Comments

Having offered a first answer to the problem of Abraham's doubt, through an exegesis of Gen 17:17bα ("he said in his thought") in §§ 175–187—that Abraham "wavers" insofar as a created mind would waver, but does not doubt in the full or proper sense of this word—Philo now addresses an alternative to this position, which turns out to be an interpretation of Gen 17:17bβ ("If this child will be born to this one-hundred-year-old man, and will Sarah, being ninety years old, give birth?"). He presents this alternative diatribally by ascribing it to someone of "better courage," who might suggest, in contradistinction to §§ 175–187, that Abraham's internal speech is *not* to be understood as the question of a waverer, but as the prayer of a faithful soul. On this reading, Abraham prays "whether" or "would that" (rather than "if") the child might be born when he himself is one-hundred and Sarah is ninety, on account of the symbolic excellence of these numbers. The second conditional "if" (εἰ) is thus re-read as a prayer—a marker of faith rather than an indication of doubt. While not giving this interpretation his full endorsement (as in QG 3.56), Philo seriously entertains it, offering a catena of scriptural proofs of the goodness of the numbers 100 and 90 in its support. Although there are vestiges of Neopythagorean tradition involved, Philo primarily relies on biblical examples to make his case exegetically rather than arithmologically—even to the point of stretching the plain sense of the biblical sense very far (e.g., the birth of Arphaxat). This section divides into three units:

(1) Philo introduces an alternative to his thesis about Abraham's momentary wavering: perhaps the forefather's internal speech is not a question of doubt, but a prayer of faith that joy may dawn on him and Sarah at these numerically significant ages? He attributes this position to some daring and creative colleagues (§ 188).

(2) Philo replies that this position has much scriptural support and catalogues some passages which speak in praise of the numbers 100 and 90, in turn. He begins with 100. Shem gives birth to Arphaxat when he is 100 years old (Gen 11:10); Abraham plants a field and measures the land with a one-hundred-fold rule (Gen 21:33); Isaac finds one hundred measures of barley (Gen 26:12); Moses commands the Tabernacle to be 100 cubits in length (Exod 27:9); and the priests offer a tithe of the tithe, equaling one hundredth—the perfect offering (Num 18:28) (§§ 189–191).

(3) Having adduced five secondary lemmata, all of which offer symbolic significances for the number 100—Abraham's age at the promised birth of Isaac—Philo turns to arguments for the symbolic significance of Sarah's age of 90. His first proof is both scriptural and arithmological, and picks up from his final example from the 100 section: ninety must be perfect, as the remainder of subtracting the regular Israelite tithe (10) from the priest's tithe (100). His second argument reiterates the penultimate proof from the 100 section: that the curtain separating the holy of holies from the sanctuary occurs at the ninetieth cubit mark. 90 is the borderland between those who are being perfected and the perfect (§ 192).

Detailed Comments

(1) § 188. *someone of better courage*. Philo again (see § 181) sets an alternative or objection to a first line of exegesis on the lips of an imagined interlocutor. Such questions indicate the "aporetic" character of this chapter, as suggested by Runia (1988). Philo seems initially sympathetic to this exegete "of better courage" (τῶν εὐθαρσεστέρων ... τις), finding the position important enough to anthologize and defend. On this point, LSJ suggests that the adjective "of good courage" (εὐθαρσής) can also denote "safety" and "security y" in one's physical, and by extension argumentative, position (so Xenophon). Philo elsewhere uses a related verb, "dare" (τολμῶ [*Spec.* 3.6]), positively to describe his own exegetical efforts.

not that of a doubter, but rather of one who prays. Philo's bold interpreter suggests that Abraham's internal speech in Gen 17:17bβ should be understood, not as a direct question ("how can it be, that ...?"), but as a prayer ("may it be, that ...!") or an indirect question ("⟨I ask⟩ *whether* a child may be born to a centenarian ... ."). Both readings are possible translations of an independent clause beginning with "if" (εἰ). The NETS follows the MT in understanding the conditional as a sign of a direct question, which is derived from the Hebrew *Vorlage* of the first part of the sentence, which has an interrogative marker (-ה).

TABLE 8.3 Gen 17:17bβ in MT and LXX

MT Gen 17:17bβ	Can a child be born to a man who is a hundred years old (הלבן מאה שנה יולד)? Can (אם) Sarah, who is ninety years old, bear a child?
LXX Gen 17:17bβ	Will (εἰ) this happen to a man who is a hundred years old? Will (εἰ) Sarah give birth, being ninety years old?

As table 8.3 shows, the Greek is more ambiguous. It lacks the explicit interrogative particle, as the Hebrew (-ה) at the outset of the double question and reads instead "if" (εἰ) at the beginning of both clauses, modeled on the second clause of MT Gen 17:17bβ. The effect is to render Abraham's speech in the Septuagint as two hanging protases, the apodosis of which must be supplied by the interpreter. Although the meaning of the phrase remains ambiguous, Philo's exegete paraphrases the verse in such a way that the first εἰ-clause is best understood as a true protasis ("if a child will be born ...") and the second εἰ-clause is understood as a petitionary final clause ("let it be born to no one other than ...") or indirect interrogative ("I ask *whether* it might be born to no one other than a centenarian ...").

if the best of the good emotions, joy, should soon be begotten. Philo's exegete of better courage understands the first εἰ as a true conditional and offers a paraphrase of the Septuagint:

Gen 17:17bβ1	§ 188
Will this happen (γενήσεται) to a one-hundred-year-old man?	If the best of the good emotions, joy, should soon be begotten (μέλλοι ... γεννᾶσθαι)

The exegete omits the age of Abraham in the paraphrase, focusing on supplying the implicit subject of the sentence, παῖς/υἱός, and allegorizing it as "joy, the best of the good emotions," as in §§ 1, 131, 155–157. Isaac's connection with joy has become so standard in this treatise that Philo here does not have to mention him by name. The second modification of the exegete, related to the first, is to clarify the significance of the verb "will happen" (γενήσεται), which might mean "shall this thing happen." Philo's exegete supplies instead "to be born" (γεννᾶσθαι)—the verb of begetting—as a paraphrastic equivalent to signal that the birth of a child is meant.

may it be born ... than ninety and one hundred. Philo's courageous exegete transforms the second biblical conditional into the apodosis of the sentence. It is no longer a direct question, but a prayerful petition. The exegete's paraphrastic technique can once again be illustrated through synopsis:

Gen 17:17bβ2	§188
Will Sarah give birth (τέξεται), being ninety years old?	May it not be born (μή ... τεχθῇ) to other numbers, rather than to ninety and one hundred.

The paraphrase of this second part of the verse is anchored in the reinterpretation of the final verb. "May it not be born" (μή ... τεχθῇ) replaces "will it be born" (τέξεται) to supply the missing petition: that joy might arrive in the soul in conjunction with the numbers 90 and 100, Sarah's and Abraham's respective ages, construed as arithmological symbols.

the perfect good would be born to perfect numbers. Philo's connection of the perfect good emotion with the perfect number 100 (and the near-perfect number 99) hearkens back to his opening section (§1), in which Abraham's age and the birth of Isaac were linked. Sarah's age/number, 90, is added out of exegetical necessity. This passage represents a part of the unfolding of this arithmological allegoresis of Gen 17 in this treatise. See also the notes on §61, where I speculated that faint traces of an arithmological interpretation of Abram's change of name—more fulsomely represented in *QG* 3.43—surface (also, Cover 2024c).

(2) §189. *especially according to the most holy Scriptures.* Philo offers a defense of the courageous exegete's paraphrase by adducing a catena of secondary biblical lemmata. One witnesses here, as in §1, not a full endorsement of arithmological speculation (which Philo seems to give in other writings), but a new scripturalization of the arithmological traditions of other Jewish exegetes. While not eschewing arithmology *tout court* in the Allegorical Commentary, Philo is more interested in arguments "according to the most holy Scriptures" (κατὰ τὰς ἱερωτάτας ἀναγραφάς).

first of all. I.e., "most immediately" (εὐθέως) or "first in order." Philo's catena of secondary lemmata is drawn from the Mosaic writings in narrative sequence. Aside from this first, they are not given elaboration in terms of the allegory of soul. Philo thus displays his interest in anthologizing Jewish exegetical traditions, albeit in a more anonymous manner than the redactor(s) of the Mishnah.

Shem, the son of the righteous Noah and ancestor of the visionary race. Philo's first example is Shem, a figure who links the Abraham cycle with the earlier Noah cycle. The fact that "Shem" means "name" makes him especially fitting for the current treatise, but arithmology is the primary reason for his selection.

one hundred years old when he gave birth to Arphaxat. Philo cites Gen 11:10 as a secondary lemma. His text form shows only minor variation from the Septuagint, which can be accounted for in terms of the exigencies of his paraphrase:

Gen 11:10	§189
Shem was one hundred years old (υἱὸς ἑκατὸν ἐτῶν) when he begot Arphaxat.	Shem, the son of the righteous Noah (ὁ υἱὸς τοῦ δικαίου Νῶε ...), is said to be one hundred years old (ἑκατὸν ἐτῶν εἶναι λέγεται) when he begot Arphaxat.

Philo takes advantage of the Hebraism, "son of one hundred years" (υἱὸς ἑκατὸν ἐτῶν), to elaborate on Shem's Noahic parentage and his place as forebear of Jacob/Israel. More immediately, he detects a literal similarity between Abraham's birth of Isaac and Shem's birth of Arphaxat at the age of 100. Only this text, among his five secondary lemmata, exactly mirrors the scenario of the primary biblical lemma (Gen 17:17b). Its place at the front of the catena thus stems both from priority in the scriptural sequence and degree of fit with the text being interpreted.

whose name means, "he confounded misery." Returning to the dominant heuristic technique of this treatise, Philo reports the etymology of Arphaxat found in his Hebrew-Greek onomasticon. This is the only place in Philo's works where this etymology is given. The precise Hebrew derivation is unclear (Royse 1988, 134–135). Siegfried (1875) analyzed the Hebrew consonants ארפכשד into רפה ("he relaxes / he lets go") and שׁוד ("devastation, ruin"). Jerome's etymology, "healing desolation" (*sanans depopulationem* = רפא שׁוד) would seem to confirm at least the second part of Siegfried's analysis.

a good offspring of the soul. "The destruction of misery"—technically speaking, a negative or neutral benefit, like Plato's "absence of pain" (*Resp.* 583c3–8; Erginel 2011)—is considered a good offspring of the soul, but not yet the best. This honor is reserved for Isaac, the positive emotion of joy. Shem, standing between Philo's two patriarchal triads in the Exposition (a: Enosh, Enoch, and Noah; and b: Abraham, Isaac, and Jacob), foreshadows the better birth that is to come (cf. Gen 12:2, which in Hebrew tradition creates a linguistic link between Shem [Gen 11:10] and God's promise to magnify Abraham's "name" [שם]). Philo's anthologizing of this tradition endows his timeless allegory of the soul with a hint of a salvation history, which finds in the scriptural genealogies a symbol of the birth of increasingly perfect fruits in the soul.

to disturb and confuse and destroy injustice, which is miserable. Philo allegorizes the etymology of Arphaxat's name, "he confounded misery" (συνετάραξε ταλαίπωρον), as signifying the destruction of "injustice, which is miserable" (τὴν ταλαίπωρον ἀδικίαν). According to Plato, the just person is happier than the unjust (*Resp.* 2). The elimination of misery and injustice thus go hand in hand; in both cases, the vice is destroyed, but the corresponding positive virtue is not born.

§ 190. *Abraham also plants a field.* Philo's next secondary lemma (Gen 21:33a) introduces an Abrahamic example related to the significance of 100. It is thematically rather than lexically linked in the constellation of secondary texts. Philo's quotation agrees substantially with the LXX, "And Abraham planted a field" (καὶ ἐφύτευσεν Ἀβραὰμ ἄρουραν), excepting a minor revision of syntax to foreground the critical word "field" and the transformation of the original aorist into a present tense, "plants" (ἄρουραν φυτεύει).

making use of a one-hundred-fold rule. Neither Gen 21:33 nor the broader pericope mentions the number 100. Colson (PLCL 5:239, n. a) explains the logic as follows: "Philo interprets ἄρουραν in the technical sense of a piece of land of 100 square cubits, cf. ἡ δὲ ἄρουρα ἑκατὸν πηχέων ἐστὶ Αἰγυπτίων πάντῃ ["An *aroura* is ⟨a square⟩ of one hundred Egyptian cubits in every direction"], Herodotus 2.168, *cf. De Plant.* 75." A similar explanation is given by Arnaldez (1964, 120, n. 1). The Egyptian provenance of Herodotus's report supports Philo's knowledge of this measurement.

Isaac finds a hundred measures of barley. Philo's third secondary lemma is Gen 26:12. This follows in chronological sequence after Gen 21:33a. Philo's text is again almost identical with the Septuagint, with the exception that an originally aorist verb, "he found," has been rendered in the present, and the syntax transposed to highlight the word which connects (lexically) to the theme of 100. He uses the same paraphrastic pattern:

Gen 26:12	§ 190
Isaac found (εὗρεν) in that year a hundred measures of barley (ἑκατοστεύουσαν κριθήν).	He finds a hundred measures of barley (ἑκατοστεύουσαν εὑρίσκει κριθήν).

Moses prepares the courtyard of the holy tabernacle. Philo's fourth secondary lemma in the constellation is Exod 27:9 (cf. Exod 27:18). There is some sleight of hand in the verb "prepares" (κατασκευάζει), which does not occur in the text alluded to. In Exod 27:9, God instructs Moses to "make" the tent and its courtyard, a task that Bezalel will later carry out. "Preparation" refers to Moses's mental construction and attention to the "paradigm of the tent" (τὸ παράδειγμα τῆς σκηνῆς) seen on the mountain. The verb "to prepare" (κατασκευάζειν) may be derived from Exod 27:19 in the summary of the courtyard, which God commands that "all of ⟨the courtyard's⟩ preparation (πᾶσα ἡ κατασκευή) ... shall be bronze." This phrase originally related to the bronze tent pegs of the courtyard.

at one hundred cubits, as he measures the distance from east to west. This length is mentioned in Exod 27:9 and again in Exod 27:18 as the length of the entire "courtyard" (αὐλή).

§ 191. ***the one-hundred-fold reckoning.*** Philo's fifth and final secondary lemma in this catena comes from the Levitical tithe, outlined in Num 18:25–32. The phrase "one-hundred-fold reckoning" (ὁ ἑκατοστὸς λόγος) is already found in § 2, where Philo employs the same secondary lemma to interpret Abraham's age of ninety-nine in Gen 17:1. If this constellation of texts is traditional, might it be the source upon which Philo draws earlier in the treatise? Source-critical questions aside, the title "one-hundred-fold reckoning" functions as an exegetical tag, which allows the arithmological import of this passage to be signaled.

the first fruit of the first fruit. This duplicated phrase, which does not appear in § 2, may well be derived from Num 18:28: "You shall give a deduction from the deductions to the Lord, to Aaron the priest" (δώσετε ἀπ' αὐτῶν ⟨i.e., τῶν ἀφαιρεμάτων⟩ ἀφαίρεμα κυρίῳ Ἀαρὼν τῷ ἱερεῖ [trans. NETS, adapted]), a phrase itself paralleling the earlier "tenth from the tenth" of Num 18:26 and looking ahead to the appearance of "first fruit" (ἀπαρχή) in Num 18:29–30. Philo has the entire pericope in view, even as he focuses his paraphrase on the syntax of Num 18:28.

which the Levites offer to the consecrated high priests. Num 18:28 says that the Levites "will give it to Aaron the priest" (δώσετε ... Ἀαρὼν τῷ ἱερεῖ). Philo's plural paraphrase "consecrated priests" reflects the institutionalization of Aaron's office and his symbolism of the order. Arnaldez (1964, 120, n. 2) cross-references *Spec.* 1.157, which states that these consecrated high priests belong to a higher tier in the sacerdotal hierarchy.

for when they receive the tenths from the nation. The syntax of this summary paraphrases Num 18:25–28a, "you take" (λάβητε). The word "tenth" (δεκάτη) departs slightly from the "tithe" (ἐπιδέκατον) of the Septuagint, presumably because the former is more standard in arithmological calculation.

(3) § 192. *what we have said will more than suffice.* Having anthologized the catena of lemmata in praise of one hundred, Philo returns to his primary text and prepares to discuss Sarah's age of 90, as mentioned by Abraham in Gen 17:17bβ.

if ... you subtract a holy tenth from the one-hundred. To reach the number ninety, Philo imagines a perfect soul and subtracts the spiritual tenth from the spiritual hundred. The protasis "if you subtract" (ἐάν ... ἀφέλῃς) echoes the conditionals of Num 18:25–32, as well as the verbs for "subtract" in Num 18:26, 28, 29 (ἀφελεῖτε), and 32 (ἀφαιρῆτε).

a first offering to God, who is bearing ... within the soul. Unlike the foregoing interpretation of 100, which reads like an anthology of texts, in his exegesis of the number ninety Philo integrates arithmological traditions seamlessly within his own allegory of the soul. The fruits are no longer merely ciphers, but products born, matured, and ripened to perfection within the human person. For other cases of the verb "bear" (φέρω) in this sense of "fruits," Colson (PLCL 5:241, n. a) points to *Her.* 36 and *Mut.* 256. "In *Mut.* 225 the use is somewhat different, as there φέρειν precedes τίκτειν" (ibid.).

fruits. That is, the virtues (see § 74) and the good emotions. Here, Philo speaks primarily of the joy represented by Isaac and born and perfected in Sarah.

another perfect number: ninety. Mangey added the adjective "perfect," which is accepted by PCW and PLCL, as being required by the following sentence. Many numbers can be "perfect," especially as regards their allegorical symbolism.

how could it not be perfect? The question reveals Philo's *a priori* commitment to the symbolism of Mosaic scripture. His interpretation makes less sense at the arithmological level; he is interpreting under scriptural constraint.

being a borderland. Philo construes the number ninety as a symbol of the curtain dividing the sanctuary from the holy of holies (see the detailed comment below on "in the manner of a middle curtain"). The sanctuary is a ritually liminal space between the courtyard, on the one hand, and the holy of holies or the inner adytum, on the other. Both sanctuary and adytum are "holy" and "perfect," but to differing degrees. When these spaces are transferred to

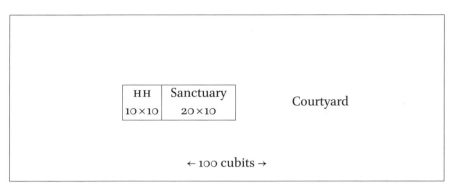

FIGURE 8.1 Exodus Tabernacle Court, Sanctuary, and Holy of Holies

the allegory of the soul, Sarah (90) represents the soul standing at the curtain, purified and perfect after a fashion, but not yet having entered into the most holy space. Abraham (100) is an image of the high priestly soul at the perfection of perfection, having entered the holy of holies to complete his work.

between the first and the ⟨second⟩ tenth. See the important textual note on this sentence. Accepting the reading of PCW, Philo may still have in mind a total length of 100 cubits in the east-west axis of the tabernacle "courtyard" (αὐλή [see § 190]). Consider Figure 8.1 above.

Viewed in terms of relative lengths, one can visualize how the holy of holies might constitute a "first tenth" (10 cubits) and the sanctuary/courtyard the remaining 9/10 (= 90 cubits). But this analysis is not entirely satisfactory for a number of reasons. First, Philo is thinking of the separation between the holy of holies and the sanctuary (not the sanctuary and the courtyard). Second, in *Mos.* 2.91, Philo states that the "tent" (σκηνή) is situated "in the middle" (μέση) of the 100-cubit layout, with 20 cubits toward the back and two long sides. Spatially, then, it is not the "first" tenth from either end, though in terms of the cult it remains the most important tenth. Something along these lines is in his mind, if sacred space (Wendland/Colson) rather than the sacred tithe (Arnaldez) is the operative symbol. It is also possible that Philo is thinking in purely arithmological terms.

the holy ⟨of holies⟩ is divided from the sanctuary. Philo alludes to Exod 26:33 as a secondary lemma to help interpret Sarah's age in Gen 17:17bβ. Although the Pentateuch calls the inner space τὸ ἅγιον τῶν ἁγίων, Philo routinely pluralizes the first word (see *Leg.* 2.55 [per Colson, PLCL 5:240, n. 3]).

in the manner of a middle curtain. Philo mentions the "middle curtain" (καταπέτασμα) of Exod 26:33, which divides the sanctuary from the holy of holies. The number 90 stands at this borderland between the first (in honor) and final (in sequence) decade and the remaining nine decades in 100, precisely where the curtain falls (for this interpretation, see the textual notes on §192). While Philo earlier linked the number 100 to the cubits of the temple "courtyard" (αὐλή), here, that number relates symbolically to the holy of holies, but *not* to the measurements of the sanctuary and holy of holies (which were 30×10 cubits together in area).

things of the same genus are sorted according to their divisions into species. Philo differentiates "species" or "kinds" of priests, who vary in their degree of sanctity. These symbolize, by allegorical extension, differing degrees of perfection in the souls represented by Sarah and Abraham. The "middle curtain" (καταπέτασμα) divides those capable of entering the adytum (having reached the culmination of perfection) from those who cannot yet enter. Holy is divided from holiest, the perfect from the most perfect, priest from high priest, Sarah from Abraham. Recall, however, that Sarah was earlier linked with Aaron as high priest in her laughter and joy (§168). Various figures in Philo's allegorical assembly may thus be recombined, depending on the point that needs proving.

Parallel Exegesis

For the structure of QG 3.56, see Parallel Exegesis on §175 above.

§188. *ninety and one hundred.* Philo gives expansive arithmological analyses of the numbers 100 and 90 in QG 3.56b and 3.56c, respectively—the same order as he treats them in *De mutatione nominum*. The discussion of 100 in *Mut.* 188–191 is richly scriptural and symbolic. The corresponding discourse in QG 3.56b is entirely arithmological. The difference is in keeping with Philo's discursive and scriptural focus in the Allegorical Commentary.

Gen 11:10 ("*Shem was one hundred years old when he gave birth to Arphaxat*"). Philo's first secondary lemma does not appear in QG 3.56. The only other place the verse may be referenced in Philo's œuvre is in *Sobr.* 65. There, Philo interprets Shem in connection to Abraham through agricultural imagery: "For in Shem we have the foundation, the root, as it were, of noble qualities and from that root sprung up wise Abraham, a tree yielding sweet nutriment, and his fruit was Isaac, the nature that needs no voice to teach him but his own ...." This description of the triad maps intriguingly onto the threefold division of philosophical discourse found in *Mut.* 74: Shem ("name"/logic), followed by Abraham (astronomy/physics), leading to fruit (Isaac).

§190. *Gen 21:33* ("*Abraham also plants a field*"). Although this text is not specifically adduced in QG 3.56c, Philo does mention the 100-fold ἄρουρα later in his discussion of the "fruitfulness" of the number ninety. See Marcus (PLCLSup 1:259, n. c) for further light shed on the Armenian text by the parallel here. This passage received an important treatment as a primary lemma in *Plant.* 73–77. There, the ἄρουρα is again interpreted in terms of 100 cubits square, to reach an area of 10,000 or one myriad. On this passage, see Geljon and Runia 2019, 193.

Gen 26:12 (*"Isaac found in that year a hundred measures of barley"*). The text is interpreted more fulsomely as a primary lemma in *QG* 4.189. The "year" is understood literally as "completed time," the number one hundred as "most perfect," and the whole verse interpreted allegorically as the fruitful production of the soul that receives the seed of virtue.

Exod 27:9 (*"Moses prepared the courtyard of the tabernacle"*). Moses's making of the tabernacle is recounted in *Mos.* 2.89–90, but nowhere else adduced by Philo as a secondary lemma.

§ 191. **Num 18:25–32** (*"the tithe of the tithe"*). See the parallel exegesis for § 2 above, the parallel at *QG* 3.39, and the comments on *QG* 3.56 in the following notes.

§ 192. *ninety*. Unlike his non-scriptural evaluation of 100 in *QG* 3.56b, Philo's examination of the number 90 (Sarah's age in Abraham's prayer in Gen 17:17) in *QG* 3.56c involves a mixture of scriptural and arithmological tradition, which comes much closer to what is found in *De mutatione nominum*. In fact, *QG* 3.56c is exegetically more expansive than *Mut.* 192. In the *QG* parallel, Philo adduces a long discussion of the first and second tenths of the priestly tithe—a point which comports with Arnaldez's interpretation of 90 in *Mut.* 192—after which follows a terse allusion to Abraham's 100-fold "field" in Gen 21:33. Philo then adds, without parallel in *De mutatione nominum*, that the ninth month is when women give birth. Philo thus specially emphasizes the natural "fruitfulness" of 90 in *QG* 3.56—a theme missing from the parallel in the present treatise.

if, however, you subtract a holy tenth. Philo speaks of subtracting the "tenth" in *De mutatione nominum* after a discussion of the Levitical tithe in § 191. The same process of subtraction is mentioned at the beginning of *QG* 3.56c, "insofar as a tenth is taken away" (ըստ ի բաց բառնալոյ զտասներորդ մասն). As argued in the detailed comments, however, Philo's thought in *Mut.* 192 swiftly shifts from sacred offering to sacred space, such that any vestige of the discussion of tithes in *QG* 3.56c is largely obscured. Further similarities between these parallel passages arise in the inherently "second" place that Sarah holds to Abraham in terms of psychic perfection. The exegetical rationale for this judgment, however, is different between the two series. In *QG* 3.56, it stems from the perfection of Abraham's offering, which contains both kinds of tithes; in *Mut.* 192, by contrast, it depends on the differing locations of Sarah and Abraham—at the curtain or within the adytum, respectively.

Nachleben

§ 188. *Gen 17:17b* ("*will a son be born to a hundred-year-old man?*"). For the reception of this verse, see the *Nachleben* for §§ 54–55, 154, and 175 above.

Gen 11:10 ("*Shem was one hundred years old when he gave birth to Arphaxat*"). Much interest in Arphaxat was spurred by his inclusion in Luke's genealogy of Jesus (3:36), where the hundred years are not mentioned. The first Greek author to pay close attention to Shem's age is Procopius, who in his *Comm. Gen.* 11.3 [D] is concerned primarily with reconciling the 100 years with other chronographic clues in Genesis, which might point to 102 years instead. Shem's place in the genealogy of Christ remains most important to Procopius. He notes that Scripture "perfectly traces the genealogy (τελείως γενεαλογεῖ) of Shem alone on account of Christ." In this connection of Shem with perfection, might one detect a faint Philonic echo?

§ 190. *Gen 21:33* ("*Abraham also plants a field*"). Abraham's planting of the field is commented upon by the Byzantine chronographer George Kedrenos (*Comp. hist.* 1.57 [D]), who notes that after the war with Abimelech

> Abraham, having planted a field or meadow (ἄρουραν ἢ λειμῶνα) at Beersheba, called upon the name of the Lord, "God eternal" (τὸ ὄνομα ἐπικέκληκε κυρίου, θεὸς αἰώνιος) ... and having reached the age of 176 [*sic*] (Gr. ρος´ [cf. Gen 25:7, 175]), he migrated toward God (μετέστη πρὸς τὸν θεόν).

Although various features of this account sound Philonic, direct dependence cannot be proven.

Gen 26:12 ("*Isaac found in that year a hundred measures of barley*"). Origen (*Hom. Gen.* 12.5 [C]) interprets the verse allegorically, in a way that shows dependence on *Spec.* 2.174 and perhaps QG 3.56 (Van den Hoek [2000, 71] ranks these passages at [B]), but not directly on *Mut.* 190. He interprets Isaac allegorically as the "word of God" ("sermo Dei") in Scripture, which in the Law of Moses "sows barley" ("hordeum seminat" [Gen 26:12]), but in the Gospels "sows wheat" (triticum ⟨sc. seminat⟩), the better food. Although the Law produces a hundred-fold fruit, Jesus in the Gospels gives bread to feed "so many thousands" ("quot milia"), thereby surpassing the Law. Rather than being a symbol of perfection, Origen reads the "hundredfold" ("centuplum") fruit of Isaac's field in Gen 26:12 as a preliminary yield, adumbrating the spiritual Gospel.

Exod 27:9 ("*Moses prepared the courtyard of the tabernacle*"). This passage of *De mutatione nominum* "as by Philo" (ὡς παρὰ Φίλωνι) is cited verbatim in the anonymous *Fragmentum lexici Graeci* (Cod. Paris. gr. 3027) 177.49–52 [A], attributed potentially to the 14th century astronomer and theologian,

Nicephoras Gregoras. The lexicographer's interest, however, is not in the one hundred cubits of the courtyard, but the middle verb "measure out" (ἐκμετροῦμαι).

§ 191. *Num 18:25–32 ("the tithe of the tithe")*. For the reception of the interpretation of this pericope by Origen, see the *Nachleben* on § 2 above.

§ 192. *fruits*. The metaphor of fruits for divine gifts and good emotions, taken over from Hellenistic philosophy, became a commonplace in Hellenistic Judaism (see Gal 5:22, esp. "joy" [χαρά]).

c   *The Faithlessness of Shechem (§§ 193–200)*
      Analysis and General Comments

In order further to explain the human perfection of Abraham in Gen 17:17b, despite his momentary "wavering" (ἐνδοιασμός) at the perfect covenant faithfulness of God, Philo adduces and interprets a long secondary biblical lemma, Gen 34:1–39 (the rape and avenging of Dinah). This passage was popular in Second Temple Jewish imagination, rewritten and envisaged *inter alios* by the author of Jubilees (30). In his allegoresis of this secondary lemma, Philo highlights the difference between Abraham's hesitation about God's promises in thought and the truly wicked deed of Shechem (*Sychem*), who not only plots in his mind, but attempts through his acts to overthrow God's justice. Only the latter constitutes "doubt" (ἀπιστία) proper. By setting Abraham in juxtaposition to Shechem, the faithfulness of the former is upheld. Between Abraham's thought and Shechem's deed is the ambiguous category of speech. Abraham's refusal to speak his doubt (§ 178), contrasted with Shechem's duplicitous speech (§§ 194–198), further clarifies the faithfulness of Abraham. (For "heart, mouth, and hand" as the three *loci* of sin in Philo's hamartiology, see §§ 197, 237–238.)

This section divides into four units:

(1) After a philosophical distinction between the one who wavers "in mind" and the one who doubts and sins in act, Philo offers an etymological and allegorical introduction to his primary case study: Shechem, the chief perpetrator in the rape of Dinah (§ 193).

(2) Philo presents an allegorical reading of Shechem's hypocritical attempt to speak "like a virgin" after his rape of Dinah, as well as of his bid to silence his victim (Gen 34:2, 3). As Dinah's name symbolizes, the "judgment" of God cannot be thwarted (§§ 194–195).

(3) Thinking of Shechem's duplicitous speech sends Philo into a quasi-personal tirade against the dangers of rhetorical sophistry in the public sphere (the "city" inflection may be derived from Gen 34:20, 27). He trots out a string of aphorisms, similar to those encountered in Jewish wisdom

literature—especially Ps.-Phocylides (see Cover 2020a)—placing them on the lips of a sophist (§§ 196–198).
(4) Philo returns to the main line of his exposition of the secondary lemma. Faithless hypocrites like Shechem will never silence divine justice. Her avengers will come—Simeon and Levi (Gen 34:25–26)—who symbolize the coordinated efforts of rational thought ("hearing") and action (§§ 199–200).

Detailed Comments

1. § 193. *the good man thus was speaking in thought*. Philo reiterates his previous interpretation (§§ 177–178) of "in thought" (Gen 17:17)—signifying a quick and passing idea that does not receive full cognitive assent. Colson (PLCL 5:241, n. b) disagrees, arguing that Philo's words "must under this second interpretation be understood not ... as indicating a passing thought, but as 'sincerely.'" It is possible that the phrase has a double meaning; but the former sense should not be lost, as we are still in the same interpretive chapter.

the bad man. I.e., Shechem. The narrative of Shechem's rape of Dinah is reinterpreted also in Jub. 30; the hexameter poet Theodotus, frags. 4–8 (Collins 1980); T. Levi 5–7; Jdt 9; Joseph and Aseneth; and Gen. Rab. 80 (Holladay 1989, 75).

though from time to time he gives utterance to entirely good things. An initial μέν ... δέ construction sets up the contrast between the "good" or "refined" (ἀστεῖος) person (Abraham), who thinks only good thoughts, insofar as he remains humanly steadfast in his "faith" (πίστις), and the bad person, Shechem, who may at times speak what is "entirely good," but thinks the opposite.

shamelessly does the most shameful things. The phrase, "but ⟨shamelessly⟩ does" (πράττει δέ), placed within the clause describing "the bad person" (ὁ δὲ φαῦλος), indicates an added difference between Abraham and Shechem. Whereas the former only wavers in his thought, the latter not only doubts and is ignorant in thought, but also acts viciously according to such ignorance.

Shechem, that spawn of ignorance. Philo expresses the antithesis between Abraham and Shechem through a philosophical wordplay. Abraham symbolizes the soul who hesitates "in thought" (τῇ διανοίᾳ [Gen 17:17b]); Shechem is the son of the "departure from thought" (ἄνοια). On the issue of ignorance and unintentional sin in Philo, see Francis 2015.

Hamor (Emōr) for his father, whose name, interpreted, means "ass." Philo further explains his allegoresis of Shechem by drawing a patronymic detail from the secondary lemma (Gen 34:2): "Shechem, the son of Hamor." (For a similar allegorical derivation of Abraham's spiritual symbolism, based on his relationship to Terah, see *Somn.* 1.58–60.) Returning to the primary technique of the treatise, etymology, Philo interprets Hamor as "ass" (ὄνος), trading on the homonymy of the proper name *Ḥămôr* (חמור) and its animal equivalent. The etymology is similarly linked with "ignorance/foolishness" (ἄνοια) in *Mut.* 193. To the rhetorical delight (and humor) of his reader, Philo "discovers" through paronomasia a parallelism between "ass" (ὄνος, the etymological equivalent) and "ignorance" (ἄνοια, the symbolic equivalent).

his name, Shechem, means "shoulder." Turning from father to son, Philo introduces a second etymology: Shechem means "shoulder" (ὦμος). This trades on the Hebrew homonymy between Shechem (שכם) as a toponym and as a proper name. Given that Abraham is characterized as "good" *qua* "refined" or "cultured" (ἀστεῖος), it is possible that Philo finds in this traditional definition some play on the homophony between the noun *ōmos* (ὦμος), meaning "shoulder," and the adjective *ōmos* (ὠμός), meaning "crude, savage, rough." *Migr.* 225 and *Mut.* 193 are the only places in which Σύχεμ is a proper name of a person (it is elsewhere a toponym).

a symbol of toil. Philo closes with a final antithesis: Just as the toil of "ignorance" (ἄνοια) is "wretched" (ἄθλιος), so the toil of "attentiveness" or "near presence of mind" (ἀγχίνοια) is "beneficial" (ὠφέλιμος) to the soul. The word "attentiveness" (ἀγχίνοια) renders in nominal form the description of Abraham in Gen 17:17bα as the one who is present to himself "in thought" (τῇ διανοίᾳ).

2. §194. **Shechem spoke according to the thought of the virgin.** The secondary lemma, portraying Shechem as a foil to Abraham in Gen 17:17b, is linked lexically to the primary lemma by the phrase "according to the thought of the virgin" (κατὰ τὴν διάνοιαν τῆς παρθένου [Gen 34:3]). Abraham wavers "in thoughtful consideration" (τῇ διανοίᾳ), whereas Shechem only pretends to speak "in accordance with" (κατά) the dictates of reason. His actions prove him the opposite sort of character: the son of ignorance and folly.

after he had formerly humbled her. Philo returns to Gen 34:2c to contextualize Shechem's speech. He treads lightly on the literal sense of this passage, not relating the more vivid "he slept with her" (ἐκοιμήθη μετ' αὐτῆς), but opting instead for the euphemistic paraphrase, "he humbled her" (ταπεινώσας αὐτήν), which is incidentally more violent.

was not this phrase ... pronounced deliberately. A marker of the intentionality of Moses in writing his allegory of souls, both wicked and good.

what had been done was the opposite of the words Shechem had spoken. Philo understands the phrase, "according to the mind of the virgin," to qualify Shechem's *own* speech. He accommodates his words to fit what Dinah would want to hear and speaks as though he were morally innocent. Moses—

a good dramatic author—uses the word "virgin" (παρθένος) to signal Shechem's hypocrisy, as Shechem knows well that "a virgin" is just what Dinah (physically speaking) and he (in his soul as well) are not. It is worth noting that in Hebrew, the Septuagintal *Vorlage*, *na'ărâ* ([ה]נער) simply means "young girl" and has no such overt connotation of virginity.

Dinah (Deina) is the judgment, which cannot be bribed. Philo offers two etymological interpretations of Dinah, "judgment" and "justice," both derived from the Hebrew root *dîn* (דין), (v.) "to judge" or (n.) "judgment." The first corresponds with just human "judgment" (κρίσις), which would see Shechem's attempt to cover up his wickedness as a legally duplicitous attempt to bribe a human court.

justice, co-regent with God. Philo's second allegoresis (an elaboration not found in the parallel at *Migr.* 223) understands Dinah simultaneously as a symbol of divine "justice" (δίκη). Philo has added a second feminine noun to further explicate the female figure of Dinah. With this second identification, she is now perceived as a divine "coregent" (πάρεδρος), in terms that recall divine scriptural Wisdom (see Wis 6:14, 9:4—the only two occurrences of "co-regent" [πάρεδρος] in the Septuagint). Both figures, legal "judgment" (κρίσις) and "coregent Wisdom" (πάρεδρος σοφία), occur close by one another in Wis 9:3–4, which speaks of God creating all things: "So that in uprightness of soul you might pass judgment, give to me Wisdom, co-regent of your throne" (⟨ἵνα⟩ ἐν εὐθύτητι ψυχῆς κρίσιν κρίνῃ / δός μοι τὴν τῶν σῶν θρόνων πάρεδρον σοφίαν). The implication is that Shechem's sophistry is ultimately sophomoric. He is no match for the justice he is vying against.

ever-virgin. Philo's addition of the epithet, "ever-virgin" (ἀειπάρθενος), signals an inversion of Shechem's feigned "virgin" speech. Philo retorts that divine justice—Dinah's allegorical referent—is always innocent of guilt, her virtue perpetually intact. The title was used by Philodemus to describe Athena and Artemis (*Mus.* 4, frag. 63.10). For its Christian use, see the *Nachleben*.

Dinah can be interpreted both ways. Philo may have found both equivalents, "judgment" (κρίσις) and "justice" (δίκη), in his onomasticon. Other names/figures in *De mutatione nominum* also receive multiple interpretations, usually by the listing of different titles or epithets. Etymology is not a limit to the range of possible meanings in Philonic allegoresis, but rather a vehicle for multiplying them.

§ 195. ***it is said, "Silence ⟨destroys⟩ half of evil."*** Not a known proverb. The Greek phrase, ἥμισυ κακοῦ ἡσυχία, is terse—performing, in its laconic economy, the wisdom of staying silent. Even if translated "Silence ⟨is⟩ half of evil," it remains a positive counsel of rest/silence, the very opposite of Shechem's and Hamor's loquaciousness. (Compare the rather different mod ern aphorism, that silence in the face of evil *is* sin.) Philo's exhortation to silence is partially suggested by Jacob's "silence" (παρεσιώπησεν) upon learning of the sin of Shechem and hearing his request in Gen 34:5.

Moses, rebuking ... worthy of second honors. Philo alludes to Gen 4:3–6 as a tertiary biblical lemma, offering an interpretation of the reason that God did not consider Cain's sacrifice as pleasing as Abel's. This supports Philo's interpretation of Gen 34 (SBL) rather than Gen 17:17b (MBL). Philo sees, in Abel's offering "from the firstborn (πρωτοτόκων) of his sheep," a reason for God's estimation of his sacrifice as worthy of "first honors" (πρεσβεῖα). The absence of such a description (e.g., "first fruit" [ἀπαρχή]) in Cain's offering suggests that God finds it belonging to the category of "second quality" (δευτερεῖα) gifts.

"you sinned, keep silent." Philo cites the culminating verse of the tertiary lemma, Gen 4:7, which is lexically linked to the secondary lemma through the word "silence" (ἡσυχία [Gen 34:5]). The Septuagintal text, "you sinned, keep silent" (ἥμαρτες, ἡσύχασον), differs significantly in meaning from the MT ("sin is lurking ⟨at your door⟩"), but can be derived by repointing the Hebrew consonants to read "you sinned, lie down ⟨i.e., don't move⟩" (חָטָאתָ רְבֹץ). The Greek syntax of the Septuagint is convoluted, and Philo has to ignore a more obvious reading, in which "you sinned" (ἥμαρτες) serves as part of the apodosis in the preceding conditional question ("Have you not ... sinned? Keep silent."), in order to discover a reading that suits his interpretation. See Colson (PLCL 3:470, n. b) for Philo's interpretation of the verse here and elsewhere.

3. §196. ***to boast or speak excessively about one's evils, like a tragic actor.*** Philo likens the behavior of the Shechem soul to an actor in a tragedy, who performs—often with dramatic irony for the audience/reader—the sins which will lead to his demise. Philo would have been to the theater, read tragedies and comedies, and was conversant with dramatic conventions (*Ebr.* 177; Koskenniemi 2019; Friesen 2019). The two verbs he uses here, "to boast as a tragedian" (ἐκτραγῳδεῖν) and "to speak excessively" (ἐπικομπάζειν), are rare in his corpus and occur only a handful of times ("boast as a tragedian" [ἐκτραγῳδεῖν]: *Mut.* 196 and *Somn.* 1.35; "speak excessively" [ἐπικομπάζειν]: *Fug.* 30; *Mut.* 196; and *Somn.* 1.131; 2.291). The clustering of these terms in treatises at the end of the Allegorical Commentary—as well as their largely negative connotation (cf. *Somn.* 1.35, where "speak as a tragic actor" [ἐκτραγῳδεῖν] is used quite positively)—may suggest that some events in Philo's life had turned his attention to public speech and dramatic performance.

these people always say things dear and just to virgin virtue. Philo generalizes the symbolic interchange between Shechem (the ignorant soul) and Dinah (human / divine justice). To express the hypocritical behavior of those who follow Shechem's pattern, he uses a contrastive μέν ... δέ construction. Speech "according to the thought of the virgin" in Gen 34:3 now indicates public praise of "virgin virtue."

they do not miss an opportunity to affront and harm her. While praising virtue publicly, in private these same speakers attempt to assault and "violate" the very virtue they commended.

what city is there ... sing a hymn to virtue, ever-virgin. Philo recalls his experience of hearing civic declamation and diatribe, in which public orators of all varieties would praise virtue. The same description, "ever-virgin," which he earlier ascribes to divine justice (§ 194), appears here on the lips of the hypocrites in a feigned encomium to virtue more generally. Arnaldez (1964, 124, n. 1) suggests that this rhetorical development "on human beings who do not understand what they are saying" in a civic context "recalls the Platonic theme of counterfeiting (*Resp.* 8.560d–e)." For Philo and civic sophism in Alexandria, see Wyss et al. 2017; Winter 1997.

§ 197. ***spewing out truisms.*** To lampoon the impotence and potential misdirection of public sapiential declamation, Philo writes a mock-wisdom poem, whose similarities to the Jewish poetic gnomic tradition are unmistakable. The poem consists of seven, non-metrical lines of poetry in antithetical parallelism. They treat the four cardinal virtues and three theological/philosophical ones. In form and language, they approach most proximately the *Sentences* of the Jewish poet, Ps.-Phocylides. The poem itself, while probably created by Philo as a *prosopopoeia* for this context, nevertheless reflects contemporaneous conventions of Jewish gnomic wisdom. Like the speech of Lysias in the *Phaedrus*, it is crafted for the sake of criticism by its author.

As indicated in table 8.4 below, the first five lines follow a chiastic pattern. Philo alternates between three syntactic types of antithetical parallelism. The simplicity of these antitheses lends the poem a satirical tone. Type A is comprised of an articular noun + adjectival predicate, reduplicated (Sub + Pred). Type B is the inverse: adjectival predicate + articular noun. Type C, which appears in the central line of the pentad, is a modification of Type B, but with a genitive noun added to lightly adorn the predicate. The first four lines praise the four cardinal virtues. Wis 8:7b also contains all four of these virtues (albeit, without the antithetical parallelism) in a different sequence: (2) "temperance" (σωφροσύνη), (1) "practical wisdom" (φρόνησις), (4) "justice" (δικαιοσύνη), and (3) "courage" (ἀνδρεία). Philo's hypocrite also praises holiness and piety in lines 5 and 6—notions that are at home in both Jewish and Roman ethics. These two lines follow the type-A syntactic pattern and form a secondary pair. The summary line 7 returns to the Type B syntax, but again amplifies it (as the third

TABLE 8.4   Philo's Mock Wisdom Poem

Stich	Verse	Syntax type	Virtue
1	ἡ φρόνησις ἀναγκαῖον, ἡ ἀφροσύνη βλαβερόν. Practical wisdom is necessary, the lack of wisdom it is harmful.	A	practical wisdom / prudence
2	αἱρετὸν ἡ σωφροσύνη, ἐχθρὸν ἡ ἀκολασία. Temperance is a choice virtue, incontinence is hateful.	B	temperance
3	ὑπομονῆς ἄξιον ἡ ἀνδρεία, φυγῆς ἡ δειλία. Courage is worthy of endurance, cowardice is worthy of flight.	C	courage
4	συμφέρον ἡ δικαιοσύνη, ἀσύμφορον ἡ ἀδικία. Justice is beneficial, injustice holds no reward.	B'	justice
5	τὸ ὅσιον καλόν, τὸ ἀνόσιον αἰσχρόν. Holiness is good, profanity is shameful.	A'	holiness
6	τὸ θεοσεβὲς ἐπαινετόν, τὸ ἀσεβὲς ψεκτόν. Piety is praiseworthy, impiety should be cursed.	A"	piety
7	[τὸ] οἰκειότατον ἀνθρώπου φύσει τὸ εὖ καὶ βουλεύεσθαι καὶ πράττειν καὶ λέγειν, ἀλλοτριώτατον τὸ κακῶς τούτων ἕκαστον. It is most appropriate for a human nature to think and act and speak well, but to do each of these badly is most alien to us.	B"/D	goodness in thought, action, speech

line), not only with a genitive in the predicate, but also by making the subjects articular infinitives.

Philo's supplementation of cardinal virtues with "holiness" and "piety" suggests that he is critiquing the gnomic wisdom tradition of biblical and Hellenistic Judaism, from Proverbs to Ps.-Phocylides, with a special eye to those varieties most easily parroted by Greeks and Romans. Although the content of his poem mirrors biblical wisdom in places, particularly in the book of Proverbs, the syntactic brevity Philo's lines imitates most closely the Ps.-Phocylidean *Sentences*. Ultimately, it is not the content of these pseudo-Pseudo-Phocylidean gnomes to which Philo objects, but their potential for sophistic abuse. Philo saw the Jewish adoption of this classicizing form as striking a dangerous bargain with Greco-Roman civic culture. Evidence of their deployment for deception in various public fora—courts, councils, chambers, theatres—suggests not merely a possible failure of gnomic wisdom poems as a form of *paideia* within Judaism, but the danger of their being coopted by pseudo-virtuous demagogues of every stripe, including (potentially) the likes of Flaccus and the Alexandrians during the pogrom of 38 CE. Obviously, other Jews would disagree with Philo. For the use of aphorisms in moral formation, see Morgan 2007.

practical wisdom is necessary, the lack of wisdom is harmful. The first stich treats the cardinal virtue of "practical wisdom" (φρόνησις). It occurs fittingly in the first position, because according to Aristotle (*Eth. nic.* 1144b), to have practical wisdom is to possess all the practical virtues. For this brief syntactic pattern, see Ps.-Phoc. 65: "Zeal for good things is good, zeal for bad things is very burdensome" (ζῆλος τῶν ἀγαθῶν ἐσθλός, φαύλων δ' ὑπέρογκος). On φρόνησις, see Prov 14:29: "The great-spirited man is great in practical wisdom, but the mean-spirited man is robustly a fool" (μακρόθυμος ἀνὴρ πολὺς ἐν φρονήσει / ὁ δὲ ὀλιγόψυχος ἰσχυρῶς ἄφρων).

temperance is a choice virtue, incontinence is hateful. Philo turns next to "temperance" (σωφροσύνη). For a near parallel, see Ps.-Phoc. 76: "Practice temperance, abstain from shameful works" (σωφροσύνην ἀσκεῖν, αἰσχρῶν δ' ἔργων ἀπέχεσθαι).

courage is worthy of endurance, cowardice is worthy of flight. There is no direct parallel to Philo's third stich on "courage" (ἀνδρεία) in Ps.-Phocylides's *Sentences*, Wisdom of Solomon, Ben Sira, or Proverbs. Its satirical character is clear in the admonition to flee cowardice—exactly the thing that a coward is both inclined and unable to do.

justice is beneficial, injustice holds no reward. Philo concludes his mock-commendation of the four cardinal virtues with justice, following Aristotle's division of the practical virtues in *Eth. nic.* 5 from the intellectual virtues in *Eth. nic.* 6. For similar sentences in Jewish wisdom texts, see esp. Prov 11:5: "Justice teaches its ways blamelessly and aright, but impiety stumbles on injustice" (δικαιοσύνη ἀμώμους ὀρθοτομεῖ ὁδούς / ἀσέβεια δὲ περιπίπτει ἀδικίᾳ). Cf. also Prov 10:2; 11:6; 13:6; 14:34; 15:6.

holiness is good, profanity is shameful. No close parallel to Philo's statement on "holiness" occurs in Ps.-Phocylides's *Sentences*. For "holy" and "shameful" as antithetical descriptions, see Ps.-Phoc. 67: "Love of virtue is holy, but the sensual lover increases shame" (σεμνὸς ἔρως ἀρετῆς, ὁ δὲ κύπριδος αἶσχος ὀφέλλει). Unlike the first four virtues, which are feminine singular nouns, the final three are set apart by their form as neuter singular substantives (or in the final case, neuter singular articular infinitives).

piety is praiseworthy, impiety should be cursed. Philo's sixth virtue, piety, is explicitly theological. Instead of the far more typical feminine noun "piety" (εὐσέβεια [see §§ 39, 76, 155]), Philo uses the rare neuter adjectival substantive, "the god-revering" (τὸ θεοσεβές), in keeping with the neuter singular form of virtues 5–7. The adjective, "god-revering" (θεοσεβής), *only* occurs here and in a Greek fragment of *QG* 1.66 (the related noun, "divine reverence" [θεοσέβεια], is only slightly more common) in Philo's *œuvre*. This raises the question of whether he is drawing on a poetic source or imitating the rhetoric of Jews other than himself. Philo surely approved, however, of "the queen of the virtues" coming near the end in a place of honor.

to think and act and speak well. The final stich presents not a virtue, but a string of three infinitives turned into a noun by the neuter singular article. They represent a typical Philonic division of anthropological activities into "thought, word, and deed" (§ 236). It is a summation that recalls the more immediate context of Philo's mock wisdom poem: the distinction between (1) Abraham's wavering "in thought" (§§ 178–187; 193a), and (2) Shechem's evil deed (§ 193b), which he masks with (3) duplicitous speech (§§ 194–196).

§ 198. *forever stringing together these and similar maxims.* Philo's critique of gnomic wisdom echoes Dio Chrysostom's (*Borysth.* 11–12) critique of those too fond of Homer. Ironically, Dio's satire comes in a *defense* of the poetic style of Phocylides, of whom Dio writes:

> For he's not one of those authors who strings together (οὐ ... εἰρόντες) long, continuous verse, in the way that your ⟨poet Homer⟩ will narrate a battle sequentially (ἑξῆς διέξεισι) in more than five-thousand lines; but with two or three lines, his composition takes its beginning and end.

Contrarily, Philo offers just such a satirical description in criticizing those who recite Phocylidean wisdom poems, chafing at the way such rhetors are "spewing out truisms" and "forever stringing together wisdom maxims." His preference is for Homer and for Moses, whose texts require studied allegory to plumb the depths of their wisdom. Despite his difference from Dio, Philo uses the same two verbs, "narrate sequentially" (διεξιέναι [§ 197]) and "string together" ([συν]είρειν [§ 198]) in his criticism. While Philo and Dio do not agree on who is the wiser poet, they do agree that not all poetic wisdom discourses are equally efficacious or desirable in the public square.

they deceive the courts and council chambers and theatres ... religious sodality. Philo lists a wide range of cultural spheres, most of which are not specifically Jewish. Egyptian Jews did have the ability to deal with some of their own legal matters in a given πολίτευμα, as the literary and papyrological evidence shows (e.g., *P. Polit. Iud.* 4 from Herakleopolis, on the breaking of an engagement). Philo's argument is that the rhapsodes of wisdom rhetoric, in any public sphere, are potentially play-acting and not to be trusted.

like those who put beautiful masks on the most shameful of faces. Philo describes these deceivers in ways that resemble stage actors (see §196, "boast like a tragedian" [ἐκτραγῳδεῖν]). Although he adopts a generally positive attitude toward the various arts (see Friesen 2019) and does not go so far as to suggest shutting down the theatres and banishing actors from the city (cf. Plato, *Resp.* 3, 398ab), Philo's critique of "mimesis" here is at least partially indebted to Plato's more austere reservations on the subject (see *Resp.* 10.598–601, 606e–607a). Paradoxically, gnomic wisdom poems like those of Phocylides are the kinds of things that Plato would permit (*Resp.* 3, 398ab)—over and against Philo's preference for the "mythological" accounts of Homer. At root, however, their basic concern is the same.

4. §199. *possessed by zeal for virtue*. Having completed the diatribe against gnomic wisdom performances, Philo returns to his allegory of the soul. Although no proper names are given at this point, the hale and hearty men who come concerned "about virtue" (περὶ ἀρετήν) are clearly Simeon and Levi. Their being "possessed by zeal for virtue" (τῷ περὶ ἀρετὴν ζήλῳ κατεσχημένοι) has connotations of priestly violence and its (positive) allegorical equivalent, recalling the description of Phinehas in §108 as "possessed by zeal for the good" (ζήλῳ τῶν καλῶν κατεσχημένος).

stripping off ... gazing upon her ... dragging out. Philo subtly shifts the object of the avengers' retribution from the theatrical pretenders, who are stripped of their theatrical garments, to the Shechem soul, which is stripped of its pretensions. Only at this point in the allegoresis does Philo "feminize" Shechem as a "soul" (ψυχή), to be treated roughly by Simeon and Levi, in inverse imitation of Shechem's "humiliation" of Dinah. In narratological terms, Shechem ceases to be the focalizer of the narrative and the allegory, and instead becomes subjected to the virtuous gaze of Dinah's (Justice's) brothers.

woven poorly with their speech. The verb "weave poorly" or "craft poorly" (κακοτεχνοῦντες) reflects Philo's own aesthetic judgment on the wisdom poem presented above.

the soul in its own nakedness. For background to the view that the soul is most authentic when "naked," sans body, clothes, and material attachments, which facilitate duplicitous mimesis, see *Leg.* 2.53–59.

§ 200. *such base and unclean characters.* Having transformed the plural hypocrites into the singular Shechem soul, Philo now allows his allegoresis to slip again, such that Simeon and Levi come to "ward off" several characters. This likely refers to Hamor (ignorance) and Shechem (toil) together, who both meet their end at the hands of the brothers in Gen 34:26. Philo categorizes them as "characters" or more literally "manners of living" (τρόποι), which the soul might adopt.

two in number—Simeon and Levi. Just as the perpetrators of Dinah's rape and kidnapping are two, so her avengers are two of her brothers, Simeon and Levi. They are mentioned in Gen 34:14, where they cannot countenance Jacob's suggestion of intermarriage, and again in Gen 34:25–26, where they slaughter the inhabitants of Shechem and take their goods and chattels as spoil.

but in judgment they are one. The paradoxical description, "two in number, in judgment one" (δύο μέν ... ἀριθμῷ ... γνώμῃ δὲ εἷς), is arranged as a chiasm. Philo unites the two brothers in a singular allegorical "substance" (see below), playing freely with metaphysical terms. In the present sentence, he foregrounds the arithmological relationship between the dyad and the monad, inflected with the Platonizing notion of procession and return. Such play is in service of Philo's ethical allegory, not a serious construction of a metaphysical system.

also in the Blessings. The title, the *"Blessings"* (εὐλογίαι), may be (1) generic (e.g., form-critical) or (2) titular, referring to a specific subdivision or anthology of Mosaic Scripture. For a fuller discussion of Philonic divisions of the Pentateuch, see the detailed comment on § 42, "In his *Exhortations*." The term reflects Jacob's role in Gen 49:28 and Moses's in Deut 33:1 (see *Det.* 67). Under this heading, Philo places the blessings of Simeon and Levi by Jacob (Gen 49:5) and by Moses (Deut 33:8). See Colson, PLCL 5:244, n. 5.

their father Jacob was numbering them in a single order. Of Jacob's twelve sons blessed in Gen 49, only Simeon and Levi are mentioned together (Gen 49:5–7). Philo has used scientific taxonomic language to construe this grouping as a priestly order within his table of allegorical symbols.

the harmony and singularity of their minds. As the author of Jub. 30, so in *Mut.* 200 Philo praises Simeon and Levi unequivocally as heroes and symbols of unity. Jacob's blessing of the brothers in Gen 49:5–7, by contrast, presents them as anything but examples of harmony. In that earlier, scriptural version of the story, Jacob responds negatively to the brothers' slaughter of the people of Shechem in Gen 34:30, and in his "blessing" describes the pair unfavorably— in fact, the father's words include a curse (Gen 49:7: "cursed [ἐπικατάρατος] be their anger!"). Philo says little about Jacob's final promise in Gen 49:7, that he will "divide" the brothers in Jacob, and "scatter" them in Israel. His interpretation of their "unity" stems instead from the first stich of the blessing (Gen

49:5a): "Simeon and Levi are brothers," i.e., they have the same mind, follow the same course, and share a "spirit" (θύμος). In context, this latter word is a poetic synonym for the "wrath" or "anger" (μῆνις) that Jacob despises. Both nouns are epic terms that link these two sons of Jacob with the famously wrathful "sons of Atreus," Agamemnon and Menelaus, who also followed a common spirit to sack a city on behalf of a wronged woman. Philo, however, reads the word "spirit" (θύμος) against the letter, in a Platonizing, psychological sense: Simeon and Levi share a singular spirit.

Moses no longer even mentions that they were two. The sons of Israel blessed by Moses in the Deut 33 include: Reuben (Deut 33:6), Judah (Deut 33:7), Levi (Deut 33:8), Benjamin (Deut 33:12), Joseph (Deut 33:13), Ephraim (Deut 33:17), Manasseh (Deut 33:17), Zebulun (Deut 33:18), Issachar (Deut 33:18), Gad (Deut 33:20), Dan (Deut 33:22), Naphtali (Deut 33:23), and Asher (Deut 33:24). There are thirteen in all, and Simeon is not mentioned. This is intriguing, given that Simeon stands at the head of the list of tribes in Deut 27:12.

but enrolls the entirety of Simeon in Levi ... stamped by a single form. The "stamping" connotation of the verb "enrolls" (ἐγχαράσσω) recalls the Platonic notion of the soul being stamped by the divine idea. This continues Philo's pattern, in the present pericope, of using technical philosophical vocabulary to depict the symbolic unity of the brothers. The metaphor is echoed in the participle "stamped" (τυπωθείς) later in the present sentence.

unifying hearing (i.e., Simeon) with acting (i.e., Levi). Philo at last unveils the answer to his long philosophical riddle. Simeon and Levi represent not some new metaphysical substance, but the perfect ethical harmony of thought and action. This is precisely the combination missed by Shechem and aimed at by Abraham in Gen 17:17b, when he falls and falters "in thought" (for further parallels, see Arnaldez 1964, 126, n. 1). Their unity provides a fitting end to the extended allegoresis of the secondary biblical lemma.

This final set of allegorical equivalents veils an etymological exegesis, which counterbalances the etymologies of Hamor and Shechem. Simeon stands for "hearing" (τὸ ἀκούειν), in accordance with the similarity between his Hebrew name *Šimʿôn* (שמעון) and the verb *šāmaʿ* (שמע), "to hear." The stock Greek equivalents, "obedience" (εἰσακοή [*Mut.* 99; *Somn.* 2.34]) and "hearing" (ἀκοή [*Ebr.* 94]), are given by Philo elsewhere in the Allegorical Commentary, but the infinitival construction here is Philo's own formulation. Grabbe (1988, 209–210) and Shaw (2015) do not include this instance of the etymology, and it should be added, especially because "hearing" (τὸ ἀκούειν) is a unique Philonic adaptation of the etymology.

That Levi is the symbol of "acting" (τὸ πράττειν) makes sense from a thematic plane: his name is closely linked with the verb "to serve" (עבד) and the noun "service" (עבודה), both indicating the "service" or "work" of the temple (in the Septuagint, most often rendered "service/liturgy" [λειτουργία] or "work" [ἔργον]). Did Philo also know an *etymological* basis for this allegorical equivalence? Levi's etymologically link with "acting" (τὸ πράττειν) is suggested by *Somn.* 2.31–36, esp. 2.33, where Philo asserts that "the name of each ⟨of Jacob's sons⟩ is the symbol" (ἑκάστου δὲ αὐτῶν τοὔνομα σύμβολον) of some kind of good action. Philo (*Somn.* 2.34) names Levi as the symbol of "activities (ἐνέργειαι) and good deeds (πράξεις σπουδαῖαι) and holy rites (λειτουργίαι ἅγιαι)." This symbolism is presented, however, without a specific etymological rationale, while others in this category, including Judah, Isaachar, Dan, and Gad, all have symbolic equivalents that relate to etymologies offered elsewhere in the Philonic corpus.

What might be the etymological basis for Philo's allegoresis of Levi as an "activity" (ἐνέργεια), "action" (πρᾶξις), or "service" (λειτουργία)? Grabbe (1988, 179) lists only one etymology for Levi in Philo (*Plant.* 64): *lî* (לי), comprised of the preposition "to" and the first person common singular pronominal suffix, meaning "to/for me" (μοι). Other later onomastic sources, according to Grabbe, give meanings based on the Hebrew root *lwh* (לוה), meaning either "join" or "escort." Neither of these, however, provides a strong link with the notion of action. While Philo may have simply settled for a symbolic equivalence, *sans* etymology, there are least three additional possibilities which warrant consideration, however speculative (I am grateful to Tzvi Novick and Joshua E. Burns for their suggestions):

(1) Philo may rely on an onomasticon that associated the name Levi with "action" on the basis of the Palestinian Aramaic root *l'y* (לעי), meaning "to work or toil." The strength of this solution lies in its recourse to the onomasticon technology and a Semitic derivation. Counting against it are the Aramaic provenance of the root, which does not appear to have been a usual source for derived meanings; and the presence of the guttural *'ayin* (ע), which does not occur in the name Levi (*Lwy*, לוי).

(2) Second, Philo may understand Levi's connection with work to be derived by way of a folk etymology, from the Greek noun *leitourgia* (λειτουργία), "rite" or "service." Adding an *upsilon* to the name, *Le⟨v⟩itourgia* (Λε⟨υ⟩ιτ-ουργία), one may even discover a compound word that means roughly "Levi works" or "the Levite works." Philo's use of Greek etymologies would not be without precedent. Runia (2004, 109) lists nine of them, four names of which (including "Leah") have *both* Hebrew and Greek etymologies. Philo's knowledge of a Greek etymology for Levi gains additional plausibility from the fact that Philo never uses the typical etymological formula for this name—a feature that Runia, Grabbe, and Winston all link with the Greek etymologies. Philo considers

Greek etymologies "not … on the same level as the Hebrew ones" and "fanciful or playful" (Runia 2004, 109). Such a description would surely fit the etymology of Levi derived from "Le⟨v⟩itourgia" (Λε⟨υ⟩ιτουργία)!

(3) Finally, it is worth mentioning the verbal similarity between the name Levi and the Latin verbs "laborare" (to work) and "levare" (to raise up). Philo does on at least one occasion (*Opif.* 127) make reference to the preferential spelling of the Latin name "septem" over the Greek *hepta* (ἑπτά), given the former's greater proximity to its roots in the words *semnos* (σεμνός ["holy"]) and *sebasmos* (σεβασμός ["majesty"]). Here, however, it is the name itself, rather than the definition, which is taken from Latin.

On balance, I find option two (the Greek folk etymology) most plausible. However, it also remains a possibility that Philo's allegoresis of the name Levi (alone among the tribes) has only a symbolic, and not an etymological, basis. Levi was, after all, unique.

Parallel Exegesis
§ 193. *Gen 34:2–3, 25 ("Shechem spoke according to the thought of a virgin").* The only other place where Philo treats the rape of Dinah is in *Migr.* 223–224. Gen 34:2–3, 25, appears there as a secondary lemma, amplifying Abraham's journey to Shechem in Gen 12:6 (*Migr.* 216). Philo presents in miniature the tradition which he expands in the present treatise.

Hamor (Emōr) for his father, whose name, interpreted, means "ass." Grabbe (1988, 155) notes that the etymology of Hamor as "ass" also occurs in *Migr.* 224, where it is understood symbolically as the "irrational nature" (ἄλογος φύσις).

his name, Shechem, means "shoulder." Grabbe (1988, 206–207) notes that Philo offers this etymology four times in the Allegorical Commentary, albeit with different spellings of the name, as well as different etymological significances. In *Leg.* 3.25, *Sikima* (Σίκιμα, toponym) is interpreted as "shouldering" (ὠμίασις). In *Det.* 9; *Migr.* 221 (224); and *Mut.* 193, *Sychem* (Σύχεμ, name or toponym) is interpreted as "shoulder" (ὦμος).

the symbol of toil. Although Shechem is etymologically understood as "toil" (πόνος) throughout the Allegorical Commentary, the connotation of this work and labor varies from the positive to the negative type, depending on Philo's exegetical needs. In *Leg.* 3.25, Jacob is said to hide the pleasures in Shechem, a symbol of those who guard their pleasures with great toil. This is close to the meaning here in *Mut.* 193, which speaks of the toil of folly and ignorance. In *Det.* 9, by contrast, Joseph hears that his brothers are tending their flocks in Shechem (Gen 37:15)—an inverse sign that they are virtuous, toiling at the moral life. Similarly, in *Migr.* 221, Shechem is initially the place of Abraham, the "lover of learning" (Gen 12:6), whose toil is the "toil of *paideia*" (*Migr.* 223). In

Migr. 224, however, the man who bears this name is interpreted as the son of the irrational nature and foolishness. See Arnaldez (1964, 123, n. 1), who cross-references *Sacrif.* 35–41, 112–114.

§ 194. ***Dinah (Deina) is the judgment, which cannot be bribed.*** Grabbe (1988, 150) notes that the same etymology is given in *Migr.* 223.

justice, co-regent with God. Philo will describe "justice" (δίκη) as God's "co-regent" (πάρεδρος) in *Mos.* 2.53 and *Ios.* 48.

ever-virgin. Philo elsewhere applies this remarkable epithet to the hebdomad (*Leg.* 1.15; *Her.* 170; *Mos.* 2.210; *Num.* frag. 43); to the womb of virtue, which God may yet open (*Congr.* 7); to divine wisdom, the daughter of God (*Fug.* 50); and here, to justice and virtue (*Mut.* 194, 196).

§ 195. ***Gen 4:7 ("you sinned, keep silent").*** The verse is interpreted as a primary lemma in *QG* 1.65, with the Greek *solutio* preserved much to the same effect. Best is not to sin, but "kindred" (συγγενές) to this, as a younger sibling, is the sinner who is "inwardly turned" (ἐντραπῆναι) and feels compunction. In *Sobr.* 50, Philo dives deeper into the philosophical rationale for this command: to sin is a kind of "movement" (κινεῖσθαι) or "activity" (ἐνεργεῖν). "Silence" or "stillness" (ἡσυχάζειν) places an important check on all movement, which immediately sets the guilty party on neutral footing, prevents him from sinning further, and provides a path to salvation. Gen 4:7 may also be alluded to as a secondary contextualizing lemma in *Det.* 96 (this treatise formally begins only with Gen 4:8), which speaks of Cain rejecting God's call to repentance.

§ 200. ***Gen 49:5 (Simeon and Levi are identified).*** According to *BiPaSup*, the verse is only interpreted here in Philo's works.

Deut 33:8 (Simeon enrolled in Levi). The verse is interpreted only here and at *Det.* 67, where Levi is similarly presented as a figure beyond reproach and worthy of emulation. No mention is made of Simeon.

Nachleben

§ 193. ***Gen 34:2–3, 25 ("Shechem spoke according to the thought of a virgin").*** Josephus's later retelling of Gen 34 in *A.J.* 1.337–340 [D] shows no literary dependence on the present passage. John Chrysostom (*Hom. Gen.* 54.516 [D]) takes up Philo's lemma, question, and answer at the literal level, when he writes:

> What is, "⟨And he spoke⟩ according to the thought of the virgin"? Since the maiden was young (νέα), it says, he discoursed with her using such words as were sufficient to snatch (ἐπισπάσασθαι) and seize (ἑλεῖν) her.

Chrysostom further takes the people of Shechem as examples of those overcome by desire, and exhorts parents to look after their own children to steer them away from such youthful follies.

Shechem means "shoulder." Philo's etymology of Shechem may be found in Origen (*Hom. Ex.* 13.7; *Hom. Lev.* 6.3; *Hom. Num.* 4.3; 5.1; *Hom. Ios.* 9.5 [C]) (Van den Hoek 2000, 90). It is also reproduced by Didymus the Blind in his *In Gen.* 215 [C], where he is commenting on Abraham's arrival at Shechem in Gen 12:6:

> "And he comes to Shechem" (cf. Gen 12:6), which is interpreted "shouldering" (ὠμίασις), thinking that this was on account of all these virtuous deeds. For the "shoulder" (ὦμος), from which ⟨is derived⟩ "shouldering" (ὠμίασις), is a symbol of "work" (ἔργον).

the attentive mind. For "attentiveness" (ἀγχίνοια) in later Byzantine tradition, see the *Nachleben* for § 220.

§ 194. *ever-virgin.* In Philo's application of this title to Dinah, one may detect a precursor to the position later advanced by Augustine—that those who are raped remain virgins in both mind and body (*Civ. Dei* 1.18). In later Greek Christian tradition, the adjective "ever-virgin" (ἀειπάρθενος) would be applied to the Virgin Mary in both liturgical and theological texts (e.g., Athanasius, *In Ps.* 27.373 [LXX 84:11]; Epiphanius, *Anchor.* 13.8; Ps.-Gregory of Nyssa, *Annunt.* 96 [D]).

§ 195. *Gen 4:7 ("you sinned, keep silent").* Eusebius of Caesarea (*Comm. Ps.* 347–348 [A/B]), commenting on LXX Ps 38, replicates the Philonic division of the lemma and his interpretation of the verse:

> Do you see in what manner ⟨David⟩ taught the reason not to dare to open one's mouth, when he said, "And I was silent from goods" (Ps 38:3a LXX: καὶ ἐσιώπησα ἐξ ἀγαθῶν) or, "I became silent, since I was not with good" (Ps 38:3a Σ: ἐσιωπήθην μὴ ὢν ἐν ἀγαθῷ), according to Symmachus? For when I am not among goods, nor speaking with *parrhesia*, I remember the one who said, "You have sinned, keep silent" (Gen 4:7: Ἥμαρτες, ἡσύχασον). Therefore, I keep silent (ἐσιώπησα) if I am not with the good.

Here, Philo's verbal interpretation of "be still" (ἡσύχασον) is recalled, as is his isolation of these two words as a single command.

[Chapter 9]
The Life of Ishmael (§§ 201–251)

In this chapter on Ishmael—the last of substantive length in the treatise—Philo turns from Abraham's faith in God's promise of the birth of Isaac (Gen 17:17b) to Abraham's prayer for the life of Ishmael (Gen 17:18). As Philo implies in § 218, this prayer could be seen as further evidence of Abraham's doubt: why, if Abraham believed that Isaac would fulfil God's promise of a son from Sarah would he pray for the life of Ishmael, his son by Hagar? Philo's answer is that although Ishmael, and by extension, Hagar, are not symbols of joy and the self-taught nature (Isaac) or wisdom (Sarah), they nonetheless represent important steps along the soul's journey. Ishmael is a symbol of "theological hearing" (§ 202), and Hagar (as we see in *Congr.* 255), of the preliminary studies. Focusing on the figure of Ishmael, Philo develops a theory of psychic accommodation in ethical instruction, by which souls weaker than the Isaac type, destined to become neither wholly vicious nor wholly virtuous, might still grow and develop according to their own potential.

The chapter (§§ 201–251) divides into three sections, delimited by Philo's sequential exegesis of Abraham's prayer in the primary lemma. Philo begins with (a) an interpretation of Gen 17:18a, "This Ishmael" (Ἰσμαὴλ οὗτος). Taking the two words in sequence, he first identifies the central figure, Ishmael, etymologically as the "hearing of God." He then interprets the demonstrative pronoun "this" as a marker of a word (i.e., "Ishmael") with multiple allegorical significances ("this" and "that"). Ishmael symbolizes two kinds of hearing souls: those that hear God and garner some profit from it ("this Ishmael"), and those that hear God, but gain no moral improvement (by grammatical extension: "that Ishmael"). Balaam (Num 24:16) is introduced as an illustration of the latter kind of soul, who hears but gains no profit (§§ 201–209a).

Second, Philo (b) interprets the imperative verb of Gen 17:18b, "Let him live" (ζήτω). In this section, he addresses a potential misinterpretation of Abraham's petition: that he is requesting corporeal immortality for Ishmael. To the contrary, argues Philo, Abraham is not concerned with physical life, nor the eschatological immortality of the soul, *per se*. Rather, Abraham seeks the rekindling of ethical life and fervor within the lukewarm soul, which like Ishmael has lost its spiritual hearing in the present moment. Jacob's prayer for Reuben's life (Deut 33:6) is adduced as a secondary parallel. Reuben stands for the soul in need of rekindled spiritual sight, just as Ishmael stands for the soul in need of rekindled spiritual hearing (§§ 209b–215).

Philo devotes (c) the third and longest section to the prepositional phrase of Gen 17:18c, "Before you" (ἐναντίον σου [§§ 216–251]). The lemma is cognate with Gen 17:1b, "Be well-pleasing before me" (ἐναντίον μου), discussed by Philo in chapter two (§§ 39–46). Philo argues that living "before God" constitutes the greatest human happiness (§§ 216–217). He then addresses whether Abraham's prayer for Ishmael constitutes a lack of faith in the birth of Isaac. In his estimation, it does not (Gen 15:6). Rather, Abraham prays that all souls, not only the perfect, may live before God; and that if they cannot yet ascend to the summit of virtue, at least they may attain some modicum of spiritual growth and refrain from becoming wholly vicious. Esau's request for a blessing in Gen 27:38 is adduced as a kindred example of God's ability to grant benefits proportionate to the capacity of various human souls. Through attention to the catchword "hand" (χείρ, interpreted as "power") in the first and final lemmata of this catena, Philo differentiates the limited potencies of human souls from the infinite and invariable mercies of God (§§ 218–232). In roughly the last twenty sections of the chapter, Philo explains the various spiritual sacrifices appropriate to each of three levels of perfection. He takes as his scriptural basis Lev 5:6–12, with its prescription to offer either a lamb, turtledoves, or flour, depending on the wealth of the supplicant. In Philo's allegory of the soul, this verse teaches that God's gifts are not reserved only for ascetics like the Therapeutae, but may be calibrated to accommodate souls in a variety of life-situations and degrees of perfection (§§ 233–251).

a   *"This Ishmael"* (*§§ 201–209a*)
     Analysis and General Comments
In this first section, Philo cites the entirety of the five-word primary lemma of the present chapter: "Let this Ishmael live before you" (Ἰσμαὴλ οὗτος ζήτω ἐνώπιόν σου [Gen 17:18]). He then analyses it into three parts: (a) "this ⟨Ishmael⟩" (⟨Ἰσμαὴλ⟩ οὗτος), (b) "let him live" (ζήτω), and (c) "before you" (ἐνώπιόν σου), and proceeds to interpret the subject (Ishmael) and its modifier. This first section divides into four units:

(1) Philo cites and analyzes the primary lemma of the chapter (Gen 17:18) into three parts. He notes that ambiguous words can cause problems if interpreted wrongly or according to homonyms (§ 201).

(2) Philo interprets the subject of the primary lemma, "Ishmael" (Ἰσμαήλ), to mean "hearing of God." The allegoresis in the entire chapter depends on this symbolic equivalence. Philo also addresses the meaning of the near demonstrative, "this" (οὗτος). In the Scriptures, Moses uses the word to distinguish between two things referred to by the same sign or name. Through a process of *diairesis*, Philo divides souls of the Ishmael-hearing type into two sub-categories: those who hear and gain some profit ("this Ishmael" or Ishmael$_1$) and those who hear but continue to plan vicious

actions (Ishmael₂). As an example of the latter, he adduces Balaam (Num 24:16) (§§ 202–205).

(3) To further illustrate this phenomenon, Philo adduces several secondary lemmata. First, to show how the demonstrative can distinguish the "vicious" member of a symbolic dyad, Philo adduces Deut 21:20. When the parents say, "*this* son of ours disobeys," they indicate that they have other children who obey (§ 206).

(4) Moses also uses the demonstrative to indicate the positive members of a class, as in the case of Exod 3:26–27. "This Aaron and Moses" refer to virtuous speech and thought, which alone can help the mind depart the land of the body—a feat that their vicious inverses, symbolized by Pharaoh's magicians (Exod 7:11), cannot accomplish (§§ 207–209a).

Detailed Comments

1. § 201. *the promise was articulating things full of reverence and piety.* God's promises teach Abraham a central lesson (found in chapter eight): that "God is faithful" and all human beings fall short of divine faithfulness. Abraham acquires "reverence" (αἰδώς) at the power of God's promise of psychic perfection and becomes newly aware of his own need for "discretion" or "caution" (εὐλαβεία) toward God. Both "reverence" (αἰδώς) and "discretion" (εὐλαβεία) are classed among the "good emotions" by the Stoics (so Konstan 2006, 96).

through his own thought. The phrase modifies Abraham's dawning "recognition" (ἔγνω) of what the promise reveals about God and himself. Arnaldez's (1964, 126, n. 2b) opinion, that "here, διὰ τὴν αὐτοῦ διάνοιαν ['through his own thought'] does not reprise the τῇ διανοίᾳ ['in thought'] of § 176 and § 193," but speaks in a more general and colloquial fashion, overstates the novelty of this phrase. Philo is crafting a more unified allegory of the soul.

faith toward God, and lack of faith toward what is generated. In response to Abraham's newly acquired "good emotions" (εὐπάθειαι) of reverence/piety (toward God) and caution (toward his own created capacities), Philo articulates a clear answer to the problem of Abraham's faith and faithlessness in chapter eight. With regard to God, Abraham has "faith" (πίστις); with regard to humans and all other generated "becomings," Abraham exercises an appropriately cautious "lack of faith" (ἀπιστία). Arnaldez (1964, 126, n. 2c) elaborates: "Abraham has no idea of the sum total of the free grace that God reserves for him. He can therefore only accept the tenderness of the words which are spoken to him, one of the marks of divine benevolence, and he demands naturally that this benevolence be exercised in favor of Ishmael."

he says in prayer. Philo adds the participle, "praying/in prayer" (δεόμενος), to predispose the reader to hear the words that follow favorably. This serves as one of several clues that Abraham's speech in Gen 17:18 (as in Gen 17:17) had caused problems or raised questions for contemporaneous commentators.

"let this Ishmael live before you." Philo's primary lemma agrees with the Septuagint, with the minor exception of his substitution of the preposition, "in the face of" (ἐνώπιον), for the LXX "opposite" (ἐναντίον). Both may be rendered "before." For Philo's substitution of the identical preposition in the text of Gen 17:1 (and a discussion of possible text-critical origins of this difference), see the detailed comment on § 39.

each of these words—"this ⟨Ishmael⟩," "let him live," and "before you." This short sentence is very valuable for the history of Alexandrian scholarship and commentary literature. Philo explicitly articulates his lemmatic pattern of interpretation, using three neuter definite articles to mark the individual text units ("this," "let him live," "before you"; τὸ «οὗτος», τὸ «ζήτω», τὸ «ἐνώπιόν σου»). He follows the same pattern tacitly throughout the Allegorical Commentary. It is striking that "Ishmael" is not included, even though Philo specifically interprets this name in the next section. Philo thus divides noun from adjective and predicate, treating the former as the allegorical subject of the later modifications.

more than a few people have been deceived. A second, more overt clue that Abraham's prayer for Ishmael has been the subject of scholarly debate in Jewish tradition.

like-sounding terms used to signify different realities. Just as Philo earlier used the technical rhetorical term *catachrēsis* (κατάχρησις [§§ 12–13]) to describe the creative and soteriological "misuses" of language in Scripture, so here he introduces another technical term, "equivocal nomenclature/ambiguity" (ὁμωνυμία), to explain mistaken interpretations of scriptural words and the "realities" (πράγματα) to which they point. Grammatical discussion of this term goes back at least as early as Aristotle's *Categories*, which begins famously with the words: "things are called equivocally [or ambiguously] (ὁμώνυμα), when they have the name only in common, the definition (lit. 'the statement of essence') corresponding with the name being different" (Cook, LCL [adapted]). Just as *catachrēsis* is the primary rhetorical vehicle for Philo's theological speculation in chapter one, so the discernment of homonymy will serve as the primary rhetorical method for deriving the ethical allegory of chapter nine.

2. § 202. *what I mean by this must be examined.* Philo often uses the Greek verbal adjectives (-τέος), such as "it must be examined" (σκεπτέον), to introduce exegetical questions. Here, he uniquely proposes that *his own writing*, rather than the writings of Moses or some other text, merits attention. While this falls short of an explicit claim to interpretive inspiration, Philo did conceive of him-

self as one who had "heard" from God and reaped some benefit, from which others might profit as well (see Hay 1995).

Ishmael is interpreted "hearing of God." Philo's onomasticon identifies Ishmael not simply with "hearing" (as Simeon in § 200), but more specifically with the "hearing of God" (ἀκοὴ θεοῦ). The etymologist resolved the name into two morphemes: *šāmaʿ* (שמע) "hear," and *ʾēl* (אל), "God." The genitive "of God" is ambiguous and might be either subjective, meaning "God heard" (as Gen 16:11: "the Lord heard" [ἐπήκουσεν κυρίος]); or, as here, objective, meaning "he heard God".

or do you not see? Philo poses a diatribal question to an imagined student in his private school. For further instances of this question in the present treatise, see §§ 11 and 158. The formula is comparatively rarer in the Exposition of the Law, being found only at *Mos.* 1.172 (in a speech in character for the Israelites at the Red Sea); *Spec.* 1.306 (speech in character for Moses); *Spec.* 1.322 (in his own person); *Virt.* 133 (in his own person). It is formally more at home in the philosophical school setting of the Allegorical Commentary (*Leg.* 2.46, 52, and passim).

Balaam. The use of Balaam as a foil to "this Ishmael" (Ishmael₁), the one who hears to his "benefit" (ὠφέλεια), might have been suggested by the etymological allegoresis of his name, "useless, worthless" (μάταιος). This etymology is not mentioned in § 202, but appears earlier in the Allegorical Commentary (*Cher.* 32; *Conf.* 159; and *Migr.* 113) as a stock equivalent. On the basis of the etymology given in *Cher.* 32, "vain people" (μάταιος λάος), Grabbe (1988, 138–139) suggests that Philo's onomasticon resolved the name *Bilʿām* (בלעם) into two constituents: (1a) ⟨h⟩*ebel* (⟨ה⟩בל), "vanity" (μάταιος); and (2a) *ʿam* (עַם), "people" (λάος). This agrees with one of Jerome's etymologies, "vanus populus" (ibid.). As a variant on this etymology, the author of the onomasticon might have pointed (2b) *ʿim* (עִם) as "with." He might then have read the preposition postpositively (cf. Homer *Od.* 9.332, with Greek σύν as a postpositive), to get "with vanity" or simply "vain" (μάταιος). Another etymology preserved by Jerome (Grabbe 1988, 139) suggests that the first two letters might also be read as (1b) *bly* (⟨י⟩בל) "not, without" (var. בבלי or מבלי). In this case, the second term being read as (2a) *ʿam* (עַם), "people," gives "without people" ("sine populo"). Alternatively, if (1c) בלי is understood nominally as "destruction" (Isa 38:17), the author of the onomasticon could have read (2b) עם "with" postpositively to reach "with destruction." This last strays far from the more basic meaning of μάταιος ("lazy, idle, useless"); but cf. Num 31:8 and Balaam's death "with the slain" (σὺν τοῖς τραυματίαις). See Arnaldez (1964, 127, n. 3) for further analysis.

the bird-augur. The word "bird-augur" (οἰωνόσκοπος) is not found in the Septuagint, but occurs elsewhere in Philo's corpus (see Parallel Exegesis). He uses it here pejoratively to paint Balaam as an illicit kind of prophet, after the model of Deut 18:10.

hearing the words of God and gaining knowledge from the Most High. Philo highlights the irony that despite being a mere bird-augur, Balaam heard divine words and gained some knowledge. As evidence, he adduces Num 24:16 (from the fourth song or oracle) as a secondary lemma. It is connected with the primary lemma (Gen 17:18) lexically, via the etymology of Ishmael, "hearing" (ἀκούων). Philo's text agrees exactly with the Septuagint, with the exception of the minor addition of the enclitic conjunction, "and" (τε), joining the two main participles.

§ 203. ***but what benefit did he accrue.*** The aorist form, "he accrued benefit" (*ōnato*, ὤνατο), is chosen in part on account of its paronomasia with the word Philo has used for Balaam's profession, *oiōnoskopos* (οἰωνοσκόπος). Might Philo have heard in latter title a verbal similarity to the phrase *ouk ōnato* (οὐκ ὤνατο), meaning "he did not accrued benefit"? While suggesting that Balaam's fourth oracle—so important to the apocalyptic and Messianic strands of Judaism in the Second Temple period—was indeed true, Philo relates the irony that Balaam, despite being the conduit of such "hearing" (ἀκρόασις), did not improve himself as a result, but died with the sinners of Midian.

to maim the best eye of the soul. "The best eye of the soul" is a reference to the etymological allegoresis of "Israel" to mean the one who "alone is taught to see God" (§ 81; cf. Ishmael as "the one who hears God"). It is primarily Balak who harbors this maiming intention, though Balaam is his instrument. Similarly Arnaldez (1964, 128, n. 1), who points to the parallel at *Somn.* 2.173.

he was not able, due to the indomitable might of the Savior. Balaam, despite being asked to curse Israel, four times blesses them. The identity of the "Savior" (σωτήρ) is ambiguous, as Balaam is said in the Septuagint to be compelled to speak these prophecies in favor of Israel by "a spirit of God" (πνεῦμα θεοῦ [Num 22:7]), by "the Lord" (κύριος [Num 22:8]), and by "God" (ὁ θεός [ibid.]) in the first oracle. All three titles continue to be used throughout the section. ("Savior" [σωτήρ] is used only of God in the LXX at Deut 32:15.) Philo's Savior in this passage is most likely the Logos or one of his powers. In *Migr.* 124, for instance, "the Savior God" is said to extend "the best remedy, his merciful power." This recalls the emanation of the powers from the Logos, not the transcendent One Who Is. On the title "Savior," see further the comment on § 56, and Geljon and Runia (2012, 176) on the "Savior" at in *Agr.* 80. Arnaldez (1964, 128, n. 2) suggests that "this ⟨Savior⟩ is the angel sent by God," referencing the parallel at *Det.* 71.

goaded on, nonetheless, by his own damaged mind. Philo interprets the repeated provocations of Balaam, the one who hears "in vain" (Ishmael$_2$), by

Balak, king of Moab (Num 22:4), as an intra-psychic process. Philo names the goad, "mind-harm" (φρενοβλάβεια). Might this conceal an etymological allegoresis of the name Balak? Grabbe (1988, 139) notes that Philo offers an etymology of Balak at *Conf.* 65, where it means "lack of attention" or "foolishness" (ἄνοια). Following Siegfried and Ginzberg (ibid.), he suggests that the name *Bālaq* (בלק) was understood by the author according to the identical verbal root to mean "lay waste, destroy." While "foolishness" (ἄνοια) hardly gets to this meaning, the notion of "damage" in "mind-harm" (φρενοβλάβεια) better reflects this etymology.

many injuries, he perished in the midst of wounded men. Philo alludes to the death of Balaam in Num 31:8: "And they killed Balaam, son of Beor, by the sword along with the wounded" (καὶ τὸν Βαλαὰμ υἱὸν Βεὼρ ἀπέκτειναν ἐν ῥομφαίᾳ σὺν τοῖς τραυματίαις). Philo infers from the "wounded men," in whose company Balaam dies, that the cause of Balaam's death was a series of inner "wounds" (τραύματα).

by mantic sophistry ... God-inspired prophecy. Philo juxtaposes Balaam's class of prophecy with that of Moses. Divinization and sophistry stand opposed to prophecy and philosophy in an absolute binary.

he had debased. The imagery of psychic stamping (and its "contrary" [παρά] perversion) is indicated by the rare verb, "debase" or "misstamp" (παραχαράσσω [see also *Spec.* 2.249; *Legat.* 116, 155]). Like an ill-struck coin, Balaam devalues his own currency and is thus eliminated from circulation.

§ 204. ***the good man necessarily prays that "this Ishmael" alone.*** Having etymologically interpreted the subject of Gen 17:18 ("Ishmael"), Philo turns to its modifier: the demonstrative "this" (οὗτος).

might be healthy. The Greek verb "be healthy" (ὑγιαίνω) serves as a paraphrase for the imperative "let him live" (ζήτω)—the first part of the predicate (Gen 17:18b), which Philo will formally interpret in (b) §§ 209b–215. With it, Philo extends his metaphor of psychic injury and healing, which he introduced in the allegoresis of Balaam as one who "dies among the wounded."

there are also those who do not rightly hear. An allusion to § 202 and the division between Ishmael$_1$ and Balaam (= Ishmael$_2$) as two kinds of God-hearers.

Moses openly forbade. To further explicate the wounded type of soul *not* indicated by Abraham's prayer in Gen 17:18a, Philo adduces Deut 23:2: "The eunuch and mutilated man will not enter into the assembly of the Lord" (οὐκ εἰσελεύσεται θλαδίας καὶ ἀποκεκομμένος εἰς ἐκκλησίαν κυρίου). The lemma amplifies the image of Balaam as one "wounded in thought" and thus is best classified as a tertiary biblical lemma. It is thematically, not lexically, connected with the "wounded ones" (τραυματίαις) of Num 31:8. Philo turns from Balaam to the whole "band" (θίασος) of "wounded men," among whose souls he has died.

from frequenting the assembly. Philo paraphrases the prohibition of "entrance" into the assembly—here a cipher for the Jewish prayer-house and the Philonic school—with the iterative verb, "to frequent, have congress" (φοιτᾶν). The verb is elsewhere used by Philo to mean "attend philosophical lectures" (*Fug.* 55).

the Ruler of all. A paraphrase of "Lord" (κύριος)—the Logos and his legislative power.

§ 205. *those who are permanent eunuchs.* Philo unpacks the meaning of the noun "eunuch" (θλαδίας)—the first category of prohibited persons in Deut 23:2a. They are not partially noetic and partially corporeal souls, but fully "castrated" (τεθλασμένοι)—the perfect participle denoting that this class of person has no possibility of improvement, education, or correction.

with regard to their generative thought-organs. Castration is taken as a symbol of the mind that cannot send forth productive thoughts—human counterparts of the divine σπερματικοὶ λόγοι.

completely castrated. Philo adds an interpretation of the second class of prohibited people in Deut 23:2b, which is similar to the first: the "mutilated" or "completely castrated" (ἀποκεκομμένος). Philo paraphrases such persons as "perfectly castrated" (τελείως ἀποκοπέντες), an aorist participle which on account of the adverb has the same force as the scriptural perfect, but ironically highlights the permanent "imperfection" and ethical impotence of this type of mind.

extol ... the sole causes of human affairs. That is, people who do not account for their own created "nothingness." For important studies of this term in the Allegorical Commentary, see Lévy (2018; 2024); Cover (2020a). To point to oneself as "cause" is fundamentally to disbelieve in God.

lovers of polytheism. Philo extrapolates beyond the biblical text. He may refer to the stereotypical self-castration practiced by priests of the cult of Cybele or *Magna Mater*, which although tolerated by Rome under Augustus, had the result of excluding Cybele's initiates from receiving full Roman citizenship. They too become a symbol of impotent souls without a share in the spiritual assembly. As to their precise allegorical referent, Runia (2008, 46–47) is wary of trying to pinpoint a particular philosophical school, noting that the description is too vague.

honor with complete conviction. Another perfect verb, "having honored with complete conviction" (ἐκτετιμηκότες), highlights the absolute commitment of the priests of Cybele and other consecrated eunuchs. The intensifying preposition *ek* (ἐκ), meaning "from" as *apo* (ἀπο) above, implies the eunuchs' "loss" of something valuable.

the one husband and father of the virtue-loving soul is God. In contradistinction to the sterility of these spiritual eunuchs, who self-castrate in worship of the *Magna Mater* (or themselves), Philo presents the God of Israel as the fertile lover (husband) and progenitor (father) of the virtuous soul. Cf. §§ 132–140, where God's fatherhood is also discussed.

are these not fittingly driven away and banished? Having interpreted the terms "eunuch and mutilated" (θλαδίας καὶ ἀποκεκομμένος) in Deut 23:2, Philo returns to the predicate with which he began. No longer does the negative (fut.) imperative, "he will not enter" (οὐκ εἰσελεύσεται), merely indicate exclusion from frequenting the school; it now also requires a more active excommunication, a "driving away" (ἐλαύνονται) or "sending into exile" (φυγαδεύονται). It is relevant that Roman citizens in Philo's time were forbidden from castrating themselves (the Galli of Cybele and Attis were honored non-citizens, but could not participate in Roman political life and "assembly" as such), and those who did could be exiled. Already here in the Allegorical Commentary, Philo echoes Roman imperial *mores*, speaking of polytheists as symbolic eunuchs also to be driven out.

3. § 206. **the parents who accuse their son of drunkenness in the Scriptures.** Philo completes the discussion of wounded souls *via* the secondary and tertiary biblical lemmata and returns to the problem of homonymous predication, indicated by Moses's use of the demonstrative pronoun "this" in Gen 17:18. As further proof that Abraham distinguishes "this Ishmael" (Ishmael₁) from other "hearers" of the word, who do not reap a benefit (Ishmael₂), Philo adduces another secondary lemma: the case of parents who accuse a son of "drunkenness" (οἰνοφλυγία) and have him stoned in Deut 21:18–21. The charge of drunkenness alludes to the third part of the parents' public accusation in Deut 21:20c: "Being given to feasting, he is a drunkard" (συμβολοκοπῶν οἰνοφλυγεῖ).

"this son of ours disobeys." Philo cites Deut 21:20a from the secondary lemma: "This son of ours disobeys" (ὁ υἱὸς ἡμῶν οὗτος ἀπειθεῖ). It is lexically and syntactically linked with the primary lemma, "this Ishmael" (Ἰσμαὴλ οὗτος), through the shared demonstrative pronoun placed after the main subject. The text agrees exactly with the Septuagint. Philo suggests that these parents use the demonstrative in a similar way to Abraham, to denote the negative (or positive) member of a filial pair. In both cases, the demonstrative indicates that homonymy is at play and that the interpreter needs to differentiate between two (or more) members of a class that bear the same name.

their other children are patient and temperate. As opposed to the group mentioned in Deut 21:20c, "given to feasting and being drunk"—with perhaps a backward glance at the charge in Deut 21:19, 20a, describing the same group also as "overly excitable" and "hot-headed" (ἐριθιστής / ἐρεθίζει). Both kinds of "son" (παῖς) are represented by the same word, requiring the demonstrative to distinguish the obedient and virtuous from the licentious and disobedient.

right reason and paideia ... the most truthful parents of a soul. Philo reads "his father and his mother" (ὁ πατὴρ αὐτοῦ καὶ ἡ μήτηρ αὐτοῦ) in Deut 21:19 allegorically to symbolize "right reason" (ὁ ὀρθὸς λόγος) and "education" (παιδεία)—one masculine and one feminine noun, corresponding to each parent.

4. § 207. *the phrases.* Philo adduces a cluster of two secondary lemmata, both descriptions of Moses and Aaron and linked to the primary biblical lemma through the demonstrative pronoun "this/these" (οὗτος, οὗτοι).

it is this Aaron and Moses ... to lead the sons of Israel out of Egypt. Philo first adduces Exod 6:26. His citation varies only slightly from the Septuagint.

Exod 6:26	§ 207
It is this Aaron and Moses, whom God commanded to lead out the sons of Israel from the land of Egypt	This is (ἐστιν) the Aaron and the Moses whom God commanded to lead out the sons of Israel from Egypt.

Most importantly, Philo's addition of the verb "is" (ἐστιν) allows him to highlight the demonstrative pronoun at the beginning of the sentence as a differentiation marker.

it is these who are disputing with king Pharoah. Philo next adduces Exod 6:27, which has a plural demonstrative. Both this Aaron and this Moses must work together symbolically. Philo's cited text is basically identical with the Septuagint, including the copula "they are" (εἰσίν), with the minor exception that in the Pentateuch, Pharaoh is given in the accusative case (following πρός) rather than in the Philo's dative (which is an improvement on the Greek).

let us not think that "these" are spoken superfluously. Philo's "these" references the two scriptural verses, not the demonstratives *per se*; he does not say "the demonstrative 'these'" (τὸ «οὗτοι») but simply "these things" (ταῦτα). Nevertheless, the translation given is a fair indication of Philo's intention: "this" and "these" are knowingly used by Moses in Exod 6:26–27 to signal the presence of ambiguous figures/symbols.

that the demonstratives ... the proper names. Philo's point—that the demonstratives indicate more than just the names and that the exact meaning of such names require further exegetical inquiry—is a fitting observation in a treatise dedicated to the etymological allegoresis of scriptural nomenclature. Philo argues that the demonstrative indicates not only the hidden symbolic referent, but also a referent with better and worse species. Colson (PLCL 5:592) devotes a short appendix entry to the technical terms for demonstrative pronouns, and suggests that in this case, perhaps "pronouns" in general could be a fitting translation. Philo, however, has the demonstrative pronouns of the biblical lemmata especially in view.

§ 208. *Moses is the purest sort of mind, and Aaron is its speech.* A stock pair of allegorical equivalents from Philo's symbolic arsenal—rooted in Exod 4:10–16 (the first of several underlying tertiary lemmata). Moses stands for "the mind" (ὁ νοῦς) or "immanent reason" (λόγος ἐνδιάθετος), and Aaron for the "the word borne forth" (ὁ προφορικὸς λόγος) or thought enunciated in speech.

the sophists, on the other hand, aping their behavior. The allegorical equivalent of Pharaoh's "magicians" (ἐπαοιδοί), literally called "sophists" (σοφισταί) in LXX Exod 7:11, who imitate the miracles of Aaron and Moses (Exod 7:11,22; 8:3).

counterfeiting their esteemed currency. One of Philo's favorite metaphors, on account of its anthropological overtones. Just as the sophist, symbolized by Balaam, "debases" (παρεχάραξε [§ 203]) the office of prophet; and the sophistic eunuchs of Cybele "mutilate" (ἀποκοπέντες [§ 205]) their psychic potency, so the Egyptian sophists "counterfeit" (παρακόπτοντες) the trusted currency of philosophical speech and rhetoric.

God gave a touchstone. Philo's image of the "touchstone" (βάσανος), employed to differentiate true virtuous currency from false, recalls Socrates's words in Plato, *Gorg.* 487d: "If my soul were wrought of gold, Callicles, do you not think I should be delighted to find one of those stones wherewith they test (βασανίζουσιν) gold ... which I could apply to it, and if it established that my soul had been well nurtured, I should be assured that I was in good condition and in need of no further test (ἄλλης βασάνου)?"

§ 209a. *What is the touchstone? The leading out from the land of the body.* Philo coordinates the Platonizing, alchemic image of the touchstone with the scriptural image of the Exodus (which, for its part, drew water from a rock). When they are united, philosophy and rhetoric produce psychic liberation from the passions.

the visionary, contemplative, and philosophical mind. Philo speaks now of Israel as the symbol of the human "mind." This is not in contradiction with § 208, where Moses was described as "pure mind"; rather, Philo draws on the double-meaning of "mind" (νοῦς) to signify both the thinking mind (Israel; LSJ I) and "thought" or "act of mind" (Moses; LSJ II). Technically, Philo thus involves the reader in a second, implicit instance of homonymy—not that between "this" pure thought and "that" impure one; but between the active and passive meanings of "mind" (νοῦς) as both thinker and thought.

the one who is able to do this is this Moses. As the allegory clarifies, Israel is the soul/mind led out of the land of the body, while "this Moses" (Exod 6:26) symbolizes the "pure thought" (νοῦς), "philosophy," or (as in §§ 103–120) "manner" (τρόπος) of life, which leads the mind ensnared by the body (either Jethro or Israel) into the realm of the ideas. In both contexts, "this Moses" (Moses₁) is opposed to an implied "that Moses" (Moses₂)—sophistry or the vicious way of life—though Philo does not name it such.

although he be clad in myriad reverent titles and names. Philo has already argued that Moses is a "polyonymous" (πολυώνυμος [§ 125]) figure in Scripture, with either positive or negative referent. In this discussion of *homonymy* (as the discourse on *catachrēsis* in chapter one), Philo evinces scepticism about the ultimate "power" of names. In the hands of Moses (as inspired author) or God, they become symbols of psychological change. In the hands of sophists, they remain masks, which hide the evil realities and intentions of disordered souls. Philo thus admits a fundamental ambiguity about the title of his treatise: that names can be as deceptive as they are revelatory. Such a studied and balanced assessment is in keeping with Plato's overall position in the *Cratylus*, which strikes a balance between the conventionalist position of Hermogenes and the naturalist position of Cratylus.

Parallel Exegesis

§ 201. ***Gen 17:18a ("this Ishmael").*** The parallel to the long ninth chapter of *De mutatione nominum*, QG 3.57, follows the same three basic subdivisions as §§ 201–251, albeit with characteristic brevity and economy. It also has a slightly different sequence, which does not hew as closely to the scriptural lemma. In the *quaestio et solutio*, Philo gives three answers to the questions surrounding Abraham's prayer for Ishmael: first he argues that this prayer does not constitute despair of the birth of Isaac, only the willingness to accept the gift of Ishmael (QG 3.57a). While this question underlies chapter nine as well, Philo does not render it explicit until § 218. Second, in the *quaestio*, Philo suggests that the phrase "before you" means a life of health and salvation (QG 3.57b). He offers an interpretation of the scriptural phrase identical to the one given in § 221. Finally, Philo interprets the name Ishmael as the one who hears God—not only with the ears, but also with the heart. This third section offers the strongest parallel to §§ 201–209a (QG 3.57c). If Philo used QG 3.57 in the composition of this chapter, he has rearranged it to better align with the scriptural sequence of the primary lemma and greatly expanded on the *theologoumena* and scriptural substructure of the earlier *solutio*. Gen 17:18a is not elsewhere interpreted by Philo.

like-sounding terms. Philo makes no reference to the rhetorical/Aristotelian notion of homonymy in QG 3.57. The inclusion and deployment of this term in *De mutatione nominum* results from Philo's focus on the philosophy of language in the present treatise.

§ 202. *Ishmael is interpreted "hearing of God."* The etymology is not explicit in QG 3.57c, but underlies the allegoresis found there. Grabbe (1988, 173) notes that the same etymology occurs at QG 3.32; 4.147; and *Fug.* 208.

some who hear to their benefit and others ... to the harm. Philo makes use of a rhetorical *diairesis* of the two types of hearing in both series, but in *De mutatione nominum*, he specifies those who hear to their benefit and those who hear to their detriment and the detriment of others. In QG 3.57c, Philo simply praises "hearing with the ears" as a good for the soul. The negative allegoresis of Ishmael's etymology—one who hears without understanding—is found in *Fug.* 208. An explicit basis for the sense-perceptual failure—that hearing is "second" to sight—is articulated, but no image of beneficial hearing is presented. *Mut.* 202 thus develops and synthesizes the symbolic interpretations in QG 3.57c (positive hearing) and *Fug.* 208 (negative hearing) into Philo's most complete discourse on the subject.

Num 24:16 ("hearing the words of God"). The verse is adduced only here in the *corpus Philonicum*.

the bird-augur. Outside of the present treatise, Philo uses the word "bird-augur" (οἰωνόσκοπος) only in the Exposition of the Law. See *Spec.* 1.61 and 4.48 for paraphrastic expansions of Deut 18:10–11 that rank "bird-auguring" (οἰωνιζόμενος) among the list of banished professions; and in the nominal form "bird-augury" (οἰωνοσκοπία, again of Balaam) in *Mos.* 1.264.

§ 203. *Num 31:8 ("he perished among the wounded")*. See also *Deus* 181–183, where Balaam's death "among the wounded" is similarly interpreted to indicate his inclusion with those who will not hear God. The verse is there linked to an entirely different chain of primary and secondary texts, and thus stems from a self-standing interpretive tradition, which Philo deploys in multiple contexts.

§ 205. *are these not fittingly driven away and banished?* Colson (PLCL 5:248, n. a) cross-references *Migr.* 69, where Deut 23:1–2 is adduced to condemn both (ancient) atheism and polytheism.

§ 206. *this son.* Philo makes no comment on the trigger word "this" (Gen 17:18) in QG 3.57, which prevents him from developing a large-scale network of secondary lemmata and scriptural-allegorical homonyms. Colson (PLCL 5:248, n. b; see also Arnaldez 1964, 139, n. 3) cross-references *Ebr.* 13–94 for Philo's "full development of this theme," drawn from Deut 21:20.

§ 207. *Exod 6:26–27 ("it is this Aaron and Moses ... to lead the sons of Israel out of Egypt")*. Philo only interprets these verses in the present treatise. They are especially selected for this discourse on homonymy.

§ 208. *Moses is the purest sort of mind, and Aaron is its speech*. This allegorical doublet of Moses and Aaron is famously explicated in *Migr.* 76–81. Moses stands for "the mind" (ὁ νοῦς) or "immanent reason" (λόγος ἐνδιάθετος), while Aaron is the "the word borne forth" (ὁ προφορικὸς λόγος) or thought enunciated.

Exod 7:11, 22; 8:3 (Pharaoh's sophists). The allegoresis of the battle between Moses and Aaron and Pharaoh's "sophists" (σοφισταί) is more fulsomely set out in *Migr.* 82–85.

Nachleben

§ 201. ***Gen 17:18a ("this Ishmael")***. A most intriguing parallel to Philo's discussion of scriptural homonymy may be found in Hilary of Poitiers (*Comm. Ps.* 51.17–18 [B]). While discussing Ps 114:9 ("I will please the Lord in the land of the living"), Hilary notes that the substantive adjective "living" may signify in two ways—those who are literally alive, and those who "live" to God. As evidence of the former, literal "living," he cites 1 Thess 4:16 ("we, who are alive ..."); as evidence of the latter, spiritual "living," he cites Matt 22:32 ("He is not God of the dead, but of the living"), followed by Deut 33:6 ("Let Reuben live and not die") and Gen 17:18 ("Let this Ishmael live"). The concatenation of these last two texts, Gen 17:18 (§ 201) and Deut 33:6 (§ 210) is strongly reminiscent of the present treatise, in which Philo also coordinates these two references. Hilary clarifies, moreover, that homonymy is the issue for the scriptural "reader" ("legenti") by noting parenthetically between his two sets of "living" texts that "⟨the word⟩ has a double signification of sense" ("duplicem sensus significationem habet" [*Comm. Ps.* 51.18]). Clearly, the word in question for Philo is "this," while for Hilary it is "live." The combination of shared elements, however, makes it possible that Philo's treatise stands in the back of Hilary's mind. For echoes of Philo's interpretation of Gen 17:18bc, see the *Nachleben* on subsequent chapters.

§ 202. ***Num 24:16 ("hearing the words of God")***. Balaam occurs as a type of injustice and evildoing in the New Testament Catholic Epistles, where the "way" (ὁδός), the "wandering" (πλάνη), and the "teaching" (διδαχή) of the diviner have become proverbial (2 Pet 2:15–16; Jude 11; Rev 2:14). For the interpretation of Balaam as "vain" or "vain people," which occurs in the parallel exegesis of this verse in *Cher.* 32; *Conf.* 159; and *Migr.* 113, see Jerome ("vanus populus," Grabbe 1988, 138–139), echoing Origen's reprisal of the Philonic etymology "vain people" (μάταιος λαός) in *Sel. Num.* 12.580–581 [B/C] (Van den Hoek 2000, 96). See Arnaldez (1964, 127, n. 3) for further analysis.

§ 203. *Num 31:8 ("he perished among the wounded")*. John Chrysostom (*In 1Cor.* 23.3 [61.193] [D]) cites the verse as evidence "that Balaam's counsel (συμβουλή) was evil," but this is a generic interpretation of the scene rather than a reprisal of Philo's interpretation.

but what benefit did he accrue. Philo's pun on the Balaam's role as *oiōnoskopos* (οἰωνοσκόπος) and his allegorical benefit (or not) *via* the similarly sounding aorist form *ōnato* (ὤνατο, "he accrued benefit") finds a rhetorical (but not exegetical) parallel in Paul's pun in Phlm 20, where the apostle links the name *Onēsimus* with the verb *oninēmi*, in a similar discussion about spiritual usefulness.

§ 205. *completely castrated.* Philo's pejorative, allegorical invective against the morally "mutilated" (ἀποκεκομμένος) person finds rhetorical (but not exegetical) resonance in Paul's invective against the circumcision party in Galatia, when he writes: "would that those who are upsetting you would mutilate themselves" (ὄφελον καὶ ἀποκόψονται οἱ ἀναστατοῦντες ὑμᾶς [Gal 5:12]). Although Paul speaks of physical mutilation, he also intimates that the circumcision party has its mind fixed in the wrong place, unable to hear the Law as it applies in the new Gentile context.

§ 208. *Moses is the purest sort of mind, and Aaron is its speech.* Philo's exegetical tradition is echoed in Ps.-Maximus the Confessor, *Capit. gnost.* 45 [B]:

> Mind (ὁ νοῦς) and speech (ὁ λόγος) precede all virtue and knowledge, the former knowing (ὁ μὲν νοῶν), and the latter teachings (ὁ δὲ διδάσκων), as Moses and Aaron (ὡς Μωϋσῆς καὶ Ἀαρών) ⟨did⟩ for Israel.

And again, in *Capit. gnost.* 47 [B]:

> Moses is the critical mind (Μωϋσῆς ἐστιν ὁ διαγνωστικὸς νοῦς), while Aaron is the speech that imparts knowledge (ὁ δὲ Ἀαρὼν ὁ ἐπιστημονικὸς λόγος).

b   *"Let Him Live"* (§§ 209b–215)
    Analysis and General Comments

Philo now turns to the verb of Gen 17:18b: "let him live" (ζήτω). This imperative seems problematic at face value for Philo's allegoresis, as Abraham, the soul being perfected in wisdom, should not be praying for the life of Ishmael the sophist, but should be expelling him forever from his company (so *Cher.* 9–10; cf. Gen 21:10, 12). Philo's response is ingenious: it is not "that" (i.e., "the former") Ishmael$_2$, symbol of the sophist in other treatises of the Allegorical Commentary, for whom the Abraham soul prays, but "this" Ishmael$_1$—that is, the soul which may yet hear the word of God and turn to gain some benefit (i.e., the Ishmael of Gen 16). The section divides into three units:

(1) Philo clarifies the meaning of the imperative "let him live" (ζήτω [Gen 17:18b]): Abraham does not pray for Ishmael's physical life. Neither does he pray for the life of "that" Ishmael$_2$, the sophist like Balaam, but "this" Ishmael$_1$, the soul that hears God and retains the possibility of improvement (§ 209b).

(2) To amplify this interpretation, Philo adduces a secondary lemma: Jacob's prayer for Reuben in Deut 33:6, "Let Reuben live and not die." Reuben is interpreted as the generic "good nature" (εὐφυΐα), which is not hard as stone and therefore fixed in its error, but soft as wax and capable of assenting to true impressions and turning toward virtue. It is for the life of such a hearing soul, possessed of such a malleable nature, that Abraham prays (§§ 210–213).

(3) Philo closes with a paraenetic interpretation of another secondary lemma: Jacob's cry to Joseph in Gen 46:30, "You are still alive!" Symbolically, this is not spoken by Jacob to Joseph, but by the Logos to every soul which can still change for the good. It warns them that to become enamored with their own material successes or entangled in the passions is to risk psychic shipwreck (§§ 214–215).

Detailed Comments

1. § 209b. *Abraham.* The subject of the sentence is not stated—often a sign that the allegorical figure rather than the scriptural person is meant. Supplying Abraham, understood as a mind, makes good sense, as Philo will mention "life with the body."

not because he himself is being converted. Philo uses the philosophical language of "conversion" (ἐπιστρεφόμενος), which can mean to turn in a positive or negative direction, although it usually signifies the former. The present aspect of the verb "being converted" denotes the instability of any perfection found in the soul while still embodied. Were "Ishmael" to be read as a symbol of the sophist, as he is earlier in the Allegorical Commentary (see *Cher.* 9–10), Abraham's prayer might be understood to symbolize a "deconversion" away from the life of virtue (Sarah) toward Hagar (the preliminary studies) and the pleasures of rhetoric and public office associated with her son ("that" Ishmael). Philo forecloses this possibility, offering an alternative interpretation.

life with the body ... the divine hearing. A nice shorthand for the two symbolic equivalents, "that Ishmael" (Ishmael$_2$) and "this Ismael" (Ishmael$_1$), respectively. The phrase "the divine hearing" (τὸ θεῖον ἄκουσμα) is an auditory counterpart to "the divine Logos" (ὁ θεῖος λόγος), both of which may signify the soul's subjective "hearing" of the divine Word and the Logos "sounding eternally in the soul."

might raise ... and rekindle the life within him. Philo speaks of the Ishmael₁ soul as though it were dead, but still capable of resurrection or reviving on account of the "eternal" (διαιωνίζον) presence of the "divine hearing" capacity. Cf. the "eternal exile" (φυγὴ ἀΐδιος) from virtue and wisdom, to which that Ishmael₂ soul of Gen 21:10 is sentenced in *Cher.* 9.

2. § 210. *the hearing of words and the learning of sacred doctrines.* Philo expands the etymological significance of the name Ishmael ("hearing of God") given in § 202 with the phrase, "learning of sacred doctrines" (μάθησις δογμάτων ἱερῶν). Such an interpretation is fitting of a lemma meant to amplify Philo's portrait of the Abraham soul, which is perfected through "learning" (see § 88 for Abraham as "the one being taught" [ὁ διδασκόμενος]).

the practicer Jacob. See § 88 and the detailed comment there on Jacob as "the one who uses training/practice" (ὁ δὲ ἀσκήσει χρώμενος). Philo erroneously but understandably ascribes the prayer for Reuben in Deut 33:6 to Jacob rather than Moses, conflating the speakers of the *Benedictions* in Gen 49 (Jacob; see Gen 49:3 for the blessing of Reuben) and Deut 33 (Moses). Such an oversight in attribution, which was not uncommon in antiquity (see Mark 1:2), could have been facilitated by Philo's categorization of these two chapters under the same taxonomic heading (*Benedictions*). (For Philo's divisions of the Pentateuch and "the *Benedictions*" as a title or taxonomic category, see the detailed comments on §§ 42 and 200.) Colson (PLCL 5:250, n. a) suggests that Philo "ascribes" the blessing "by inadvertence" to Jacob, and the oversight derives in equal measure from the fact that Reuben is Jacob's son.

prays the same for the good nature. Reuben is interpreted allegorically as a "good nature" (εὐφυΐα)—a meaning perhaps facilitated by the etymology of the second part of Reuben's name (*-ben*) as stemming from the Hebrew verb *bîn* (בין), "understanding." Earlier in the present treatise, Philo derives the same symbolic significance from a different etymology of Reuben, "seeing son," which is based on the derivation of the second element of his name from the Hebrew noun *ben* (בן), "son"; see the detailed comment on § 98.

he says, "Let Reuben live and not die." Philo adduces Moses's prayer for Reuben in Deut 33:6—attributed to Jacob/Israel, the seeing soul—as a secondary lemma. The text of his citation agrees verbatim with the Septuagint and is linked lexically to the primary lemma (Gen 17:18) through the shared imperative "let him live" (ζήτω). This is the fifth and final citation of Deut 33 (Moses's *Benedictions*) in *De mutatione nominum*. A synopsis of these uses is found in table 9.1.

Philo's use of Deut 33 as a secondary lemma shows a similar distribution to his use of Gen 32 (Jacob at the Jabbok: see the detailed comment on § 187),

PART THREE   513

TABLE 9.1   Deut 33 in *De mutatione nominum*

Mut. §	*Mut.* chapter	Deut 33	Principal character(s)	2° Lemma
§ 25	Ch. 1	33:1	Moses	"This is the blessing, with which Moses, God's human being, blessed."
§ 125	Ch. 5	33:1	Moses	"God's human being"
§ 127	Ch. 5	33:9	Moses	Moses, like Levi, is a human being "who has not seen" his parentage
§ 200	Ch. 8	33:8	Simeon and Levi	Simeon and Levi are conflated in a single blessing.
§ 210	Ch. 9	33:6	Reuben	"Let Reuben live and not die."

which also appears in four different chapters of the treatise. Although Philo does not develop the allegory of Deut 33 sequentially, as he does Gen 32, it is clear that Deut 33 and Gen 49 ("the *Benedictions*") represent a discrete cluster of texts in Philo's mind.

immortality and imperishability, a thing impossible for a human being. Philo means that the corporeal existence of the composite human being is not immortal, as the Pharisees and some other sects of apocalyptic Judaism held via belief in the resurrection of the body. Philo's Platonizing soteriology denies this possibility, even if he entertained the possibility of reincarnation (for the debate, see Yli-Karjanmaa 2015; Runia 2019).

what it is that he wishes to establish. The "he" of this statement—and hence, the author of the doctrine—may be either Jacob or Moses. Philo uses this formula often for the latter, and since Moses is both the author of the Jacob narrative and the literal speaker of the blessing in Deut 33:6, Moses is the most likely subject.

§ 211. ***all things that can be heard and learned***. Philo begins in grand philosophical style, offering an anthropological account of why certain souls "hear and learn" and others hear and do not learn (i.e., why there are two Ishmael's, "this one" and "that one"). Compare Philo's universal claim ("all things audible") with Socrates's description of the immortality of souls in *Phaedr*. 245c ("all soul is immortal" [ψυχὴ πᾶσα ἀθάνατος]). Philo's theory of learning is indebted to Socrates's image of memory as a wax tablet in *Theaet*. 191c–195b. Colson (PLCL 5:253, n. a) notes that Philo attributes this imagery to "some one of the ancients" in *Her*. 181. His redeployment of the image here without attribution reveals the depth to which it has been absorbed by his thought.

are built ... as upon a pre-constructed foundation. Philo likens learning and ethical improvement to the construction of a building. The stability of the foundation is of primary importance. Drawing on this analogy, Philo argues that the "natures" (φύσεις) of individuals in a given class (e.g., human) vary, such that some possess more stable and receptive foundations than others. Compare Plato, *Theaet.* 191c9, in which Socrates says that "within our souls" there are wax tablets of differing sizes.

upon a nature receptive to paideia. Alongside this metaphor of the soul as a building's foundation, Philo simultaneously suggests that human natures are variably receptive to the auditory and visual cues required for learning. Compare Plato, *Theaet.* 191c10–11, in which Socrates suggests that the wax tablets of human souls also differ in clarity and muddiness, hardness and softness, depth and width. This will be a critical *discrimen* in determining whether *paideia* can etch something within the soul of a given person.

if this kind of nature does not exist beforehand. Turning first to the architectural metaphor, Philo argues that each psychic nature must be properly prepared before education begins. Adapting one's nature later will not make up for a bad foundation. The verb "to exist beforehand" (προϋπάρχειν) is one of the *termini technici* that Alesse (2008, 3), following Theiler (1965), suggests that Philo gleaned from Antiochus of Ascalon via the school of Eudorus.

all these things lose their benefit. The adjective "without benefit" (ἀνωφελής) inverts the description of "this" Ishmael and his type in § 202: "those who hear to their benefit" (οἱ μὲν ἀκούουσιν ἐπ' ὠφελείᾳ).

differ nowise from an oak or a mute stone. Philo turns to his second criterion of learning: not only a nature's preparation, but its softness and ability to appropriate the learning it receives. Souls without such receptivity are presented as hard materials, such as wood or stone. Philo mines the merism "oak or a mute stone" (δρῦς ... ἢ λίθος κωφή) from epic poetry; it serves as a tertiary classical lemma. Hesiod (*Theog.* 35, "concerning an oak or concerning a rock" [περὶ δρῦν ἢ περὶ πέτρην]) uses the phrase as part of a proverb, which means "insignificant matters." In the *Iliad*, Hector uses it (*Il.* 22.126, "neither ... from an oak nor from a rock" [οὐ ... ἀπὸ δρυὸς ἢ οὐδ' ἀπὸ πέτρης]) to imagine a location for a private tête-à-tête with Achilles. Neither of these uses has direct relation to the present allusion.

The most relevant precursor for Philo's anthropological use of the merism, "of an oak or mute stone," is found in book 19 of Homer's *Odyssey*. There, Penelope, having confessed the secret of her weaving and unweaving to the disguised Odysseus, asks the stranger about his own lineage: "For you are not ⟨sprung⟩ from a proverbial oak or a rock" (*Od.* 19.163: οὐ γὰρ ἀπὸ δρυός ἐσσι παλαιφάτου οὐδ' ἀπὸ πέτρης). Although unaware that she has been speaking to her husband, Penelope guesses that he is not from crude or humble stock, but has nobility in his blood. The likelihood of an echo of this text in § 211 is suggested by several features. First, unlike in the previous two epic texts, here the phrase is used in an anthropological context. Penelope asks Odysseus—the symbol of the soul *par excellence* in Platonist allegoresis of Homer—what kind of stock he comes from. Second, in both *Od.* 19.163 and *Mut.* 211, the phrase "oak and a stone" refers to an undesirable lineage or constitution. It is not a far leap from the literal sense of Penelope's question to Philo's inquiry into the variable "natures" (φύσεις) of human souls. Just as Odysseus is not carved from wood or hewn from stone, but springs from something more refined and malleable, so Philo will argue that the cultivated or noble nature will not share the rigid, hard, and deflective characteristics of an oak or a stone, but will resemble a more receptive material (like Plato's medium, wax). Third, it is worth noting that only in *Od.* 19.163 (of the three texts surveyed) is the merism amplified with an adjective, as in *Mut.* 211.

Philo's allusion to *Od.* 19.163 (not mentioned in either Lincicum 2013 or Roskam 2017) in his portrait of the docile Jacob-like soul (Ishmael$_1$) accomplishes a powerful blending of Mosaic and Homeric figures. The spiritual itineraries of the hero and the patriarch are joined in a counter-image to the woody-rocky soul, which will never escape the trials of embodied life. Although Philo has "drunk deeply" from the epic metaphor and its Platonist reception, he does not leave Homer's merism unedited, but adapts it in two ways which reflect his Jewish tradition. First, in place of the standard second member of the merism, "rock" (πετρή), Philo substitutes the more Pentateuchal and prophetic noun, "stone" (λίθος); cf. *Theaet.* 194e: "something stony" (λιθῶδές τι). The word may recall the "stony" heart of Ezek 11:19, which is unreceptive to the "word of the Lord" (λόγος κυρίου) and God's commandments (Ezek 11:14, 20). Second, in place of the adjective "proverbial" (παλαίφατος [lit. "spoken of old"]), Philo inserts the adjective "mute" (κωφή). The description likely arises from Philo's association of the idiom ("oak or stone") with the idol polemic of texts like Deut 4:28, which inveigh against the worship of "other gods, the works of human hands, wood and stone (ξύλα καὶ λίθοι), which do not see nor hear (οὐδὲ μὴ ἀκούσωσιν) nor eat nor smell." See also Hab 2:18–19, which mocks those who pray to "mute idols" (εἴδωλα κωφά) of wood or stone. The oak and the rock may be fabled, but symbolically they are mute—reflective of those natures which cannot really hear what the Logos is teaching.

nothing could be rightly adjoined with them. The phrase echoes of the psychic "adjoining" (προσαρμόσαι) of a new impression to previous mnemonic imprints in *Theaet.* 193c4, although Philo is speaking of the initial process of making an impression in the memory.

everything rebounds and glances off, as from some solid surface. Philo likens the kind of nature with an overly rigid character to a "solid surface" (στερρόν, cf. στερεόν [§ 212]). Socrates describes this overly hard kind of soul in *Theaet.* 194e as "hard/harsh" (σκληρόν [used by Philo in *Her.* 181]), with a similar type of tablet being said to possess "something stony" (λιθῶδές τι). Those people with hard tablet souls possess their "impressions" (ἐκμαγεῖα) insecurely, "because there is no depth in them" (βάθος γὰρ οὐκ ἔνι). Cf. Philo, *Her.* 181, who speaks of depth—a concept missing in *Mut.* 211–212.

§ 212. *the souls of good natures have been mixed moderately.* Plato describes this kind of moderate, waxy "heart" at length in *Theaet.* 194c5–d7 (Lincicum 2013, 147, notes only *Theaet.* 191c; the extent of Philo's engagement with the text is wider than this). The wax of souls with the ideal depth, width, and smoothness are said to be "moderately softened" (μετρίως ὠργασμένος). Philo alludes to this passage by using the same adverb in his phrase "moderately mixed" (κεκερασμέναι μετρίως). Given the Homeric allusion that was traced in *Mut.* 211, it is worth noting that Plato (*Theaet.* 194c8–9, 194e1) develops his image of the wax tablet heart from the Homeric formula "shaggy heart" (λάσιον κέαρ/κῆρ [*Il.* 2.850; 16.553]), taking the Homeric word for "heart" (κέαρ/κῆρ) to be cognate with "wax" (κηρός). Both the image of the hard heart, like an oak or mute stone, as well as the moderately softened wax heart, have correlates in Platonist readings of the Homeric poems.

in the manner of smoothed wax. See the foregoing comment. This is Philo's second allusion to *Theaet.* 194c6. The phrase "smoothed ... wax" (κηρός ... λελειασμένος) echoes the Platonic adjective "smooth" (λεῖος). This intertext is missing in *Her.* 181, and demonstrates Philo's versatility when adducing a Platonic pericope.

neither too hard nor too soft. Philo's third allusion to Plato's wax tablet (see the foregoing two notes). The phrase "neither too hard nor too soft" (μήτε ἄγαν στερεὸν μήτε ἄγαν ἁπαλόν) echoes the syntax of *Theaet.* 194e3 and its description of the immoderately mixed wax, which is "either very pliant or ⟨very⟩ hard" (ἢ ὑγρὸν σφόδρα ἢ σκληρόν). These echoes are again missing from *Her.* 181.

readily receive all audible and visual stimuli. Philo refers to the audible words of God, which Ishmael₁ ("this Ishmael") and Reuben hear. The visual component in Philo's merism of perceptible objects, "the audible and the visible" (τὰ ἀκούσματα καὶ θεάματα), resonates with Reuben's etymological symbolism as the "seeing son" earlier in the treatise. It also finds inspiration in Socrates's introduction of the three-fold objects of memory at the outset of the wax tablet metaphor in *Theaet.* 191d6–7: "which things we ourselves may see or hear or understand" (ὧν ἴδωμεν ἢ ἀκούσωμεν ἢ αὐτοὶ ἐννοήσωμεν). In

Philo's allegory, audible and visual objects may refer to both sensual and noetic/spiritual perception. In *Theaet.* 194c–e, Socrates speaks of "the sense-perceptibles" (αἱ αἰσθήσεις). All these details are missing from the parallel in *Her.* 181.

perfectly impressing their forms on themselves. Unlike the hard and solid nature, which "could fit nothing to itself" (οὐδέν ... ⟨ἂν⟩ ἁρμόζοιτο [§ 211]), moderately soft natures are perfectly impressing (ἐναποματτόμεναι) their representations into their smooth waxy surface.

accurate images for memory. Philo's adjective "accurate" (ἐναργεῖς) paraphrases Plato's adjective "clean" (καθαρά [*Theaet.* 194d1]). The "images" (εἴδη) of which he speaks, Plato calls "thoughts" (ἔννοιαι) and "forms" (εἴδωλα)—the rational impressions which are "stamped" (ἀποτυποῦσθαι) on the wax tablet (*Theaet.* 191d7–10). Philo's final term, "memory" (μνήμη), recalls the main theme of Socrates's image of the tablet—the gift of "Memory" (Μνημοσύνη), the mother of the Muses (*Theaet.* 191d4–5).

§ 213. ***the rational class.*** Symbolized by Jacob, not Moses, despite the provenance of the secondary lemma (Deut 33:6). Philo uses the term "class" (γένος) to suggest a kind of genetic relationship between souls of this kind.

the good-natured offspring. Symbolized by Reuben, the seeing son. Philo uses the substantival phrase, "the good natured" (τὸ εὐφυές), rather than the noun, "good nature" (εὐφυΐα), to suggest both the child and the class.

the least false life ... the true life. Philo's first description—"the least false life"—maintains a humble pessimism about human potential. This is "the true life," insofar as it can be participated in by creatures. Properly speaking, "the true life," defined as a stable possession of the generic virtues, belongs only to God.

for whom it is possible to flee human pursuits and live for God alone. Philo expresses a preference for the contemplative life, as practiced by the Therapeutae, even as he also praises the "active life" of the Essenes elsewhere in his corpus. On these groups, see the *De vita contemplativa* (Therapeutae) and *Hypoth.* 8.11.1–18; *Prob.* 75–91 (Essenes). Arnaldez (1964, 132, n. 1), by contrast, sees this as "a new allusion to the distinction between the human being—God's human being :: those of the herd—those who live for God alone."

3. § 214. ***the ascetic and courageous man.*** Philo adduces a secondary lemma from the Jacob cycle (Gen 46:30) to further explicate Abraham's prayer for Ishmael$_1$ in Gen 17:18. Although often spoken of as the ascetic soul, Jacob is here linked with the virtue of courage as well.

being carried along in the midst of the river of life. Philo may think about the Nile and its various tributaries, particularly at flood time. The image is probably not of the soul as a swimmer but of the soul as a ship (see § 215).

is not totally submerged by its current. Continuing the line in § 213 that the person engaged in public life, and not devoted to God alone, cannot live a "true life."

torrent of unbounded pleasure ... storm of vain opinion. Pleasure comes like a current, pandering to the praise of the masses, like a storm. Philo describes two of the principal difficulties in sailing for commerce and applies them allegorically to the struggles of the political soul.

§ 215. *it is not Jacob who addresses Joseph.* Philo distinguishes sharply between the literal and allegorical meanings of the verse. He further intimates that the allegoresis is not of one soul (the Abraham or Jacob types) praying for a certain quality (psychic hearing or good-naturedness) in another (the Joseph soul, see §§ 89–91). What follows is a different kind of psychic allegory.

the holy Word who addresses every person. In this verse, Jacob is not a type of soul (§§ 81–88), but a symbol of the Logos—Philo's second god/divine person and God's active power in creating and sustaining the world. Joseph, for his part, becomes the symbol of "every human soul" that has not separated itself from human affairs, but being of good bodily constitution remains capable of standing against the twin dangers of pleasure-seeking and vainglory. This is a more positive image of Joseph than will emerge in other interpretations of him in the Allegorical Commentary, analogous to the unusually positive interpretation of Ishmael found in this chapter of the treatise. In the present context, Ishmael₁ and Joseph are both body-imperiled souls with open-ended potential, rather than souls irremediably bent on sophism.

he says, "You are still alive!" Philo cites from the secondary lemma after his introductory paraphrase. The text of Gen 46:30 (ἔτι γὰρ σὺ ζῇς)—Jacob's words to Joseph when the two are finally reunited after years of the father's believing that his son was dead—agrees with the Septuagint and is lexically linked with the primary lemma through the word "you are living" (ζῇς); cf. Gen 17:18, "let him live" (ζήτω). See the Notes to the Text and Translation for the question of whether Jacob's words ought to be punctuated as a statement or a question in Philo's interpretation.

felt the slightest breeze ... keenly puffed up ... great and taut airs. Philo returns to the image of the "river of life," now explicitly representing the soul as a ship. Colson freely adds more nautical imagery here, introducing "sails" being puffed up by the wind. I have preferred to keep closer to the anthropological idea of a soul's "inflation," although both nautical and psychic descriptions are being interwoven by Philo to good rhetorical effect.

borne toward the pleasures of the passions. This pericope, with its analogy of river, emotions, and desires, recalls (as myriad others in Philo's *œuvre*) Plato's winged chariot soul in *Phaedr.* 246–248, ascending to heaven and being pulled up and down to varying degrees by its spirited and desirous horses.

we run ashore the whole vessel of our soul and end in shipwreck. Philo only uses the phrase "vessel" or "ship of the soul" (τὸ ψυχῆς σκάφος) here in his corpus. He uses the noun "vessel/hull" (σκάφος)—a rough synonym for "ship" (ναῦς)—both of the soul (e.g., *Leg.* 2.104; 3.80) and of the cosmos (*Her.* 301) elsewhere in his corpus. In these passages, "ship" seems to refer to the outer bodily hull, not the captain mind. It has a close analogy in the slightly more frequent image "chariot" or "car of the soul" (τὸ τῆς ψυχῆς ὄχημα [*Leg.* 2.85; *Agr.* 77]). On the analogy with Plato, the "hull" would refer to the chariot, but not the charioteer.

These images of the chariot and the ship are simultaneously Platonic, Homeric, and Alexandrian (for Alexandria as a port city, see Schliesser et al. 2021). Earlier, in *Mut.* 149, Philo combines both the chariot and ship as his two principal psychic metaphors—these being the quintessential active vehicles of the *Iliad* and *Odyssey*, respectively (although admittedly, ships are important in the *Iliad* as well). The use of "sailing" as a psychic Odyssean symbol, which Philo wishes to combine with Pentateuchal figures, has already been seen in *Mut.* 35–36, where it is used for Enoch's ascent, and in *Mut.* 179, where it illuminates (in light of the explicit citation of *Od.* 7.36) the winged "sailing" of Abraham's soul-ship.

Parallel Exegesis
§ 209. ***Gen 17:18b*** (*"let him live"*). For the structure of QG 3.57, see the Parallel Exegesis on *Mut.* 201. Philo interprets the phrase, "Let him live" (Gen 17:18b), in QG 3.57ab as entailing similar themes to those found in the present section of *De mutatione nominum*. He does not interpret this verse elsewhere in his extant writings.

the divine hearing, sounding eternally in his soul. Philo mentions this idea of divine words entering the soul in QG 3.57c.

§ 210. **Deut 33:6** (*"let Reuben live"*). The only other adduction of this verse in the Philonic corpus appears in QG 4.123 (as a secondary lemma), where Philo comments on the connection between Reuben and Judah. The symbolic significance of Moses's specific petition for Reuben is withheld for a different discussion of "the *Blessings*" (see *Mut.* 42), which is not extant in the QGE.

§ 212. ***smoothed wax, neither too hard nor too soft.*** Partially analogous language for the plasticity of the soul occurs in QG 3.57c, where Philo speaks of true hearing penetrating the soul and "mold⟨ing⟩ and form⟨ing⟩ its most sovereign part" (Marcus, PLCLSup). The description of the soul in QG 3.57c uses Stoic-inflected vocabulary (τὸ ἡγεμονικώτατον μέρος [retrov. Marcus, PLCLSup]) and shows no sign of Philo's interpretation of the *Theaetetus* found in *Mut.* 213. The use of the *Theaetetus* in the Allegorical Commentary to unpack the more cursory/shorthand use of Stoic ideas in the QGE shows Philo's deeper commitment to former.

mixed moderately. Philo alludes to *Theaet.* 194c7 by echoing the adverb "moderately" (μετρίως) also in *Her.* 181. Noteworthy allusions to the *Theaetetus* present in *De mutatione nominum* but lacking from *Her.* 181 are referenced in the detailed comments.

accurate images for recollection. In *Her.* 181, Philo uses the terms "imprints" (χαρακτῆρες), "types" (τύποι, cf. *Theaet.* 194b6), and "forms" (εἴδη) for Plato's "signs" and "forms" (*Theaet.* 191d7–10). Colson (PLCL 5:253, n. a) references this same parallel, "where the simile is definitely referred to Plato (*Theaet.* 191c)."

§ 213. **without sickness and imperishable**. For parallel notions of spiritual health and salvation, see QG 3.57b.

the life that accords with virtue ... the least false life ... the true life. See QG 3.57b, where a similar interpretation of the spiritual/psychological "life" sought for Ishmael is given.

§ 215. **Gen 46:30** (*"you are still alive!"*). This verse is not adduced elsewhere in the *corpus Philonicum*.

Nachleben

§ 209. **Gen 17:18b** (*"let him live"*). Theodoret (*Quaest. Oct.* 73 [C]) comments that the "virtue" (ἀρετή) of Abraham is displayed in his kindness to Ishmael:

> Abraham was lovingly disposed in these respects toward Ishmael (φιλοστόργως περὶ τὸν Ἰσμαὴλ διακείμενος). For also, when God promised the production of a child from Sarah, he himself said, "Let this Ishmael live before you" (Gen 17:18).

See also the opinion of Ambrose (*Abr.* 2.88 [A]), who commenting on Abraham's prayer for Ishmael notes:

> It also is characteristic of a just man to make intercession for sinners ("iusti est etiam pro peccatoribus intervenire") ... because he also prays for them, if somehow they may come to believe. This is what it means to live in the sight of God ("vivere in conspectu Dei"), to do one's business in a manner worthy of the Word of God.

§ 210. **the practicer Jacob**. Philo's erroneous (but intuitive) attribution of Deut 33:6 to Jacob rather than Moses is followed by Hilary of Poitiers (*Comm. Ps.* 51.18 [B]: "and again, through Jacob" ["et rursum per Iacob"]).

Deut 33:6 ("*let Reuben live*"). The verse is commented upon by Origen (*Adnot. Deut.* 33 [D]), who contrasts Jacob's curse of Reuben (Gen 49:4; cf. 35:22) with Moses's blessing (Deut 33:6) and concludes that "both are just." In Origen's reasoning, Reuben's sin with his father's concubine, Bilhah, is offset by his later protection of Joseph. Philo's understanding of Reuben as symbol of a "good nature" progressing toward perfection does not surface in Origen's interpretation. Hilary of Poitiers (*Comm. Ps.* 51.17–18 [B]) also links Gen 17:18 with Deut 33:6 (see the *Nachleben* for the previous section).

§ 215. **Gen 46:30** ("*you are still alive!*"). Treated by Origen in *Sel. Gen.* 141.B15 [D], as stemming from Jacob's amazement that Joseph, though "being in Egypt, has not been harmed by the Egyptians, and that he has remained in the life in accordance with God (μεῖναι ἐν τῇ κατὰ Θεὸν ζωῇ).

c   "Before You" (§§ 216–251)
      Analysis and General Comments

Philo devotes the third and longest section of chapter nine to an analysis of Gen 17:18c, "before you" (ἐναντίον σου), cited by Philo as ἐνώπιόν σου (§§ 216–251). The lemma is similar to Gen 17:1b, "before me" (ἐναντίον μου), discussed in chapter two (§§ 39–46). Although the subsection begins with this part of the primary lemma (Gen 17:18c), interpreted in the first two sections (§§ 216–217), Philo's attention quickly returns to the theme of the imperfect Ishmael₁ soul of the preceding units.

The section divides into three parts, each of which admits of further subdivisions.

(1)   Philo first interprets the third part of the primary biblical lemma (Gen 17:18c), "before you" (ἐνώπιόν σου), as indicating that being overseen by God constitutes the greatest human happiness (§§ 216–217).
(2)   Philo asks whether Abraham's prayer for Ishmael betokens a lack of faith in the birth of Isaac (§§ 218–232).
      a.   Philo answers again: it does not (cf. Gen 15:6). Rather, Abraham prays that all souls, not only the most virtuous, may live before God. If they cannot yet ascend to the summit of virtue, he asks that they might at least attain some spiritual growth and learning, which would keep them from becoming wholly vicious (§§ 218–219).
      b.   Moses (Num 6:21) teaches that each soul ought to give thanks according to its own powers (§§ 220–223).
      c.   Joshua's spies (Num 13:24) likewise did not bring home *all* the fruits (of virtue), but only what they could carry (§§ 224–225).
      d.   No parent would commend only perfection or vice to his child (§§ 226–227).

e. Abraham's prayer for Sodom (Gen 18:24, 32), that God spare the city if there be 50 to 10 righteous people in it, teaches that a "mean" in virtue is better than none at all (§§ 228–230).
f. Esau's request for a blessing (Gen 27:38) likewise signals God's ability to grant various kinds of blessings, depending on the capacity of the human soul (§§ 230–231).
g. Through attention to the catchword "hand" (χείρ, interpreted as "power") in the second (Num 6:21) and final (Num 11:23) supplementary lemmata of this catena, Philo differentiates the varied and limited potencies of human souls from the infinite and invariable mercies of God (§ 232).

(3) The last subsection of this unit, although it remains of a piece with the foregoing catena of supplementary lemmata, is divided from the others because of its length and complexity. In it, Philo elaborates the various spiritual sacrifices appropriate to each of three levels of perfection, adducing and interpreting Lev 5:6–12 (with its prescription of an offering of a lamb, turtledoves, or flour, depending on the wealth of the supplicant) as a secondary lemma. This serves as a final defense of Abraham's prayer for Ishmael₁ in Gen 17:18c. Virtue is not reserved for devoted athletes like the Therapeutae alone, but can be practiced and acquired by souls in a variety of life-situations and degrees of perfection (§§ 233–251). This third section breaks down into three further units:
a. Philo offers a literal interpretation of Lev 5:6–7 on the three types of sin offering (lamb, birds, flour) (§§ 233–235).
b. Adducing Deut 30:12–14 as a tertiary lemma, Philo presents an allegorical reading of these three kinds of offering, based on the scriptural phrase, "in your mouth and your heart and your hands." The three purificatory offerings of Lev 5:6–7 are shown to correspond with three kinds of sins: those in thoughts, in words, and in deeds (§§ 236–244).
c. Philo returns to his secondary biblical lemma and interprets the remaining verses (Lev 5:7–12), explaining the symbolism of sheep, doves, flour, and the various priestly actions, again with the help of Deut 30:12–14 (§§ 245–251).

Detailed Comments

1. § 216. *he then adds, "before God let him live."* Having finished his defense of Abraham's prayer for Ishmael's life, "let him live" (ζήτω [Gen 17:18b]), Philo turns to the final words of the primary lemma of the chapter, "before you" (ἐνώπιόν σου [Gen 17:18c]). The form of the quotation varies slightly from the Septuagint,

including Philo's (or a later scribe's) preference for the preposition "in the face of" (ἐνώπιον) over the Septuagint's similar preposition "opposite to" (ἐναντίον); the substitution of the pronoun "you" for the LXX "God"; and Philo's reiteration of the verb "let him live" (ζήτω) at the end of the line. For a slightly different interpretation of the phrase "before me" (Gen 17:1), see §§ 39–46.

the goal of happiness. Philo's teleology, as that of many ancient philosophers, is eudaimonistic. Philo discovers this same teleology hidden in the Abraham narrative and exemplified by Isaac's identification with "joy," the offspring of the soul's ethical maturation and perfection. See the detailed comment on § 51.

for human thought. Philo's Platonizing eudaimonism in the Allegorical Commentary relates primarily to the mind and soul. In the Exposition of the Law, he makes space for the body as well—although Moses is ultimately absorbed into a psychic unity in *Mos.* 2.288.

to be worthy of the truly best Overseer and Guardian. Philo expresses a similar thought in chapter one—not, however, in his interpretation of the phrase "before me" in Gen 17:1 (§§ 39–46), but of the phrase "your God" (§§ 18–19, 24–25, and 32). The language of "worth" is similarly deployed there to denote a class of souls guided by God—both the perfect and those on their way to perfection.

§ 217. *if the ward does not wander ... school-slave is present.* Philo adduces a series of examples to produce an *a minore ad maius* argument that having a divine overseer is the greatest of blessings. He begins from the least natural and most forceful form of oversight, the "school-slave" (παιδαγωγός), whose job it is to lead the child to school, willing or no.

if an adviser being near benefits the learner. Philo's second example of a guardian is the "adviser" (ὑφηγητής)—an official, teacher, scribe, or expert, who assists a student on the material he is learning.

if, when an elder approaches, a youth dons reverence and temperance. Philo's third example of a guardian is a societal elder, before whom a youth feels a natural shame and modesty, despite lacking any familial relation.

if a father and mother hinder ... in silence. Philo's fourth and culminating examples of guardians are the natural father or mother, who are able to prevent a child's unjust actions merely by looking at him or her. As opposed to the school-slave, such positive influence is minimally coercive or verbal, and maximally natural.

supposes that he is always being seen by God. Philo ends with the *ad maius* conclusion: that the soul who is compelled by such lesser guardians will certainly be compelled by God himself. Becoming aware of God's ever-present gaze, he will have a treasure-house of virtues at his disposal. Rhetorically speaking, this elegantly constructed conditional is made up of five parts: four protases and one apodosis. The resulting number five recalls a table of the Decalogue. Arnaldez (1964, 134, n. 1), in his explication of Philonic mysticism, notes that "developing the sense of God's presence" represents "an important principle in the mystical life."

with fear and trembling. Philo's two participles, "fearing and trembling" (δεδιὼς καὶ τρέμων), are similar to Paul's more famous merism in Phil 3:12, "with fear and trembling" (μετὰ φόβου καὶ τρόμου), immortalized in modern Western philosophy by Søren Kierkegaard. Philo must mean something more like "caution," which is the moderate counterpart to the (negative) emotion of fear used by Paul, but which Philo here avoids (see also §163). According to Arnaldez, the "and" (καί) in this sentence does not join the two participles, but separates them. "Fearing" (δεδιώς) goes together with the preceding "looks about" (περιβλέπεται), while "trembling" (τρέμων) modifies the subsequent verb "will flee" (ἀποδράσεται). This is not impossible and would remove the necessity of an emendation (see the Notes on the Text and Translation). It would, however, require reading the two participles as disjoined, even while next to each other, and would sit uneasily with Philo's preference for parallel participial pairings (e.g., *Leg.* 1.3: "dividing and cutting" [διαιρουμένη καὶ τεμνομένη]). In terms of sense, the two participles better modify the verb of fleeing than the verb of seeing.

2a. §218. *when he prays that Ishmael might live.* In this paraphrase of the primary lemma (Gen 17:18ab), Philo omits the demonstrative "this" as well as "before you." His focus has shifted from the problem of Abraham's praying for Ishmael to the question of whether Abraham's prayer betokens a sign of doubt—the topic treated at length in chapter eight.

he does not despair ... as I also said before. See chapter eight.

the birth of Isaac. This is Philo's name for chapter six of the present treatise, and the promises unfolded therein. See the detailed comments on §§130 and 177.

he has come to believe in God. Philo cites again the secondary lemma (Gen 15:6) adduced in chapter eight (§177), modifying the aorist verb according to his "perfectionist" reading in §178 ("he believed" [ἐπίστευσε] → "he has come to believe" [πεπιστευκώς]) to reach the paraphrase "he has come to believe" (πεπίστευκε) in the present section. The point of this change in §§178 and 218 is the same: Abraham, who has come to believe perfectly (as he nears the age of one hundred), cannot relapse in his faith. Philo is left with the problem of why the Abraham soul should pray *both* for the Isaac and the Ishmael soul, when the former is clearly superior to the latter.

what God is able to give. Philo distinguishes between the limitless gifts that God could hypothetically give, and limited human potential to receive the same. For a discussion of God's gracious "superabundance" (ὑπερβολή), see the detailed comment on § 53 and Barclay 2015.

§ 219. *born automatically ... readily on their own*. It is difficult, Philo argues—again, *a minore ad maius*—to hold onto all the temporal goods that one acquires through human ingenuity and labor. How much more is this true of God-born goods—the virtues or knowledge of the forms—which are among those things that embodied humans find it most difficult to discover, let alone keep, even if God were to give them.

more divine and unmixed natures. Philo speaks of differing kinds of disembodied "natures," as he does in §§ 211–212, using the word as a rough synonym for "soul." With regard to the "findings" of such natures, Arnaldez (1964, 136, n. 1) comments, "We arrive here at the highest summit of the mystical life."

2b. § 220. *thankful confessions*. Philo's theology is irreducibly "eucharistic." For this theme, see Laporte 1983. Here, Philo is thinking of thanksgivings for the successful completion of a vow.

according to the power of hands. PCW and PLCL suggest that Philo alludes to the statement regarding the fulfillment of vows in LXX Num 6:21. Although I accept this, it remains a very tenuous allusion, as Philo's "according to the power of hands" (κατὰ δύναμιν τῶν χειρῶν) only partially echoes the suggested verse:

> This is the rule for the one who makes a vow, whoever vows his gift to the Lord, concerning his vow, apart from what his hand might find, according to the strength of his vow (ὧν ἂν εὕρῃ ἡ χεὶρ κατὰ δύναμιν τῆς εὐχῆς αὐτοῦ), which he vows according to the law of purity. (Num 6:21, trans. NETS)

As often in Philo's allegorical interpretations, the Greek word "hand" symbolizes a "power," either human or divine. This equivalence was made earlier by the Hellenistic Jewish philosopher and exegete, Aristobulus (*frag.* 1). Philo interprets it here to mean that each kind of psychic nature or expert in a given field must keep his vows and give thanks according to his or her capacity.

the rationally acute person. Philo begins his litany of the differing "powers of hands" with the acute or "near-minded" (ἀγχίνους) person—the one characterized by "presence of mind" (ἀγχίνοια) as opposed to the fool who is "without his mind" (ἄνοια). See § 193 for this dichotomy.

presenting ... as an offering ... consecrating. Philo uses two verbal synonyms for the verb "vow" (εὔχομαι) in Num 6:21: "devote" (ἀνατίθημι) and "consecrate" (ἀνιερέω). Both cultic actions take skills and arts, rather than of physical goods, as their metaphorical objects.

comprehension and practical wisdom. A merism indicating the two constituent parts of philosophical wisdom: theoretical knowledge, gained through contemplation; and the prudence to act according to the practical virtues.

the eloquent person ... song and prose encomia. Just as Aaron is second best to Moses, so second-best to the fruits of reason are "all the excellences in speech." Philo again uses a merism—poetry and prose—to indicate every written and spoken medium of communication. The Alexandrian remains more open to the contributions of poets, dramatists, and orators than Plato, critical passages like §§ 196–198 notwithstanding. The one caveat is that such songs be offered to The One Who Is.

according to his type. Philo offers a list of six additional occupations that should dedicate their successes to God.

§ 221. *sailor ... farmer ... herdsman ... doctor*. Philo begins his list with four private occupations: sailor, farmer, herdsman, and doctor. Each of these rightly gives thanks for success in his field, recalling that God is its ultimate source.

the leader of an army ... the statesman or the king. Philo appends two public occupations: the general and the statesman or king. The former rightly thanks God for victory in battle; the latter, for his ability to govern effectively and lawfully.

he who is not a lover of himself. "Self-love" (φιλαυτία), the sin of the "self-lover" (φίλαυτος), is for Philo amongst the most heretical and atheistic dispositions possible. Whoever is not in this category, however imperfect, still knows that he ought to give thanks to God according to his own power and trade. See Najman 2003 on Cain as a quintessential representative of this error.

§ 222. *despair of hope*. Both in terms of their material goods and ethical prospects. Philo is most concerned with the "Ishmael soul" and the "Joseph soul," which though they never become the Jacob or Isaac type, still ought to give thanks and strive for improvement.

let him ... give thanks according to his own power. An echo of the secondary biblical lemma, Num 6:21, which initiated the catena. For Philo's "eucharistic" theology, see the comment on "thankful confessions" in § 220.

§ 223. *he has received myriad*. Philo rehearses eight of the universal gifts of God to all human beings, the first five of which (birth, life, nourishment, soul, sense perception) require no further comment here.

impressions. Philo uses the term "impression" (φαντασία), which I have translated according to its shared Stoic and Academic meaning. An impression is an external stimulus, which imprints itself upon the soul and, if found trustworthy, may be assented to and "grasped." As Long and Sedley define it in Stoic terms, "An impression is not a belief. To have an impression is simply to entertain an idea, without any implication of commitment to it" (L&S § 39, 1:239). It is far from clear that Philo means it in the narrowly Stoic sense here. He will go on to describe the process of mental impressions and imaging in Platonic terms later in this same pericope. See further Sterling 2024b.

impulse. Philo's second of three Stoic terms is ὁρμή—"impulse," "instinct," or "appetition." Diogenes Laertius 7.84 (*SVF* 3.1; L&S § 56A) notes that the Stoics make impulse the first category in their discussion of ethics. Long and Sedley explain further: "Impulse, together with sensation, distinguishes animals quite generally (including man) from plants, and gives them the innate capacity to activate themselves in an animal's way of life" (L&S 1:350). See further Weisser 2021, 52.

reason. The third term in Philo's anthropological trifecta, "reasoning" (λογισμός), is shared by the Hellenistic philosophical schools. According to Aëtius (*SVF* 2.836; L&S § 53H), the Stoics used it as a technical term to designate the "ruling part" (τὸ ἡγεμονικόν) of the soul. When grouped with the previous two terms (impression and impulse), the three sound like a Stoic list of the "criteria of truth," required for assenting to a "cognitive impression." See, e.g., Diogenes Laertius 7.54 (L&S § 40A), who speaks of a Stoic named Boethus, who names four such criteria, the first three of which resemble Philo's list: "intellect (νοῦς) and sense-perception (αἴσθησις) and desire (ὄρεξις) and scientific knowledge (ἐπιστήμη)." It is important to note that "reasoning" (λογισμός) is equally at home in Platonism. Hence, Plato speaks both about an eternal "plan" or "reasoning" of God (*Tim.* 34a8) as well as "reasoning" within the human soul (*Resp.* 431c6). As is typical in his work, Philo weaves Stoic epistemological terms into a Middle Platonizing warp (so Reydams-Schils 2008, 191, regarding the present passage). For evidence of Philo's use of Stoic psychology elsewhere in the present treatise, see the detailed comment on § 111 "flock of reasoning."

although it is a small word. Or "small with respect to its name" (βραχὺ μὲν ὄνομα). Philo plays on the title and interpretive technique of the treatise. The small size of a name (or of a letter—an α or ρ, for example) should not be taken as an indication of its symbolic value or power.

the most perfect and divine operation. For God's reasoning, see, e.g., Plato, *Tim.* 34a8. Philo here speaks of human reasoning.

a fragment. Philo introduces a double description of human reason: it is both a "fragment" (ἀπόσπασμα) of the world soul and the image of God. The first description is philosophical, combining Stoic and Platonist vocabulary. Alesse (2008, 3) follows Theiler (1965) in suggesting that Philo borrows the word "fragment" from Antiochus of Ascalon, via the school of the Middle Platonist, Eudorus of Alexandria. The second description of the souls as "image" draws on Genesis 1:27 and is Platonizing. The double description of reason in § 223 as "fragment" (ἀπόσπασμα; cf. "reflection" [ἀπαύγασμα]) and "image" (εἰκών) reminds one of Wis 7:26, which describes God's wisdom as a "reflection of the eternal light ... and image of ⟨God's⟩ goodness" (ἀπαύγασμα ... φωτὸς ἀϊδίου ... καὶ εἰκὼν τῆς ἀγαθότητος αὐτοῦ). Philo's point is that just as Wisdom/Logos is derived from the reason of The One Who Is, so human reason is a fragment or reflection of the divine Wisdom/Logos.

the soul of the universe. Or more literally, "the soul of the whole" (ἡ τοῦ πάντος ψυχή). Philo does not often speak of Plato's "world soul," having generally ceded this role to the Logos (Radice 2009, 138; Runia 2002, 295).

more holy terms befitting ... philosophy according to Moses. Philo qualifies several aspects of his description of the relationship between human "reasoning" (λογισμός) and God, particularly his adoption of Plato's "world soul" into his cosmological system. Colson (PLCL 5:258, n. a) references Philo's caution with regard to this notion in *Leg.* 1.91 and *Migr.* 179. According to Radice (2009), this reticence results from the Logos largely displacing the World Soul in Philo's thought. The phrase "fragment" (ἀπόσπασμα) has its own philosophical complications, recalling a kind of Stoic partialism or monism that cannot easily account for the relationship between a transcendent God and humanity. So Arnaldez (1964, 137, n. 2) comments: "an interesting passage, which shows how Philo corrects a Stoic formula by a return to biblical thought." See further Tobin 1983.

corresponding to the divine image. Philo suggests that the best way to account for the genetic and analogical relationship between divine and human reason is to use the language of Gen 1:27. Here, Platonizing cosmology dies a little death at the hands of Moses. At the same time, Philo's word "impress" (ἐκμαγεῖον) echoes Plato's wax tablet soul in *Theaet.* 191–194 (see §§ 211–212), which is taken up by Philo into an explicitly theological register.

2C. § 224. *those spies sent by Moses.* Continuing to develop the theme of psychic progress accommodated to the power of individual souls, Philo alludes to the story of Moses's spies visiting Canaan in Num 13:1–33. Although this text illustrates Philo's interpretation of the secondary lemma, Num 6:21, it also echoes his explication of Gen 17:18c ("before you"), especially the discussions of limited human receptive capacities at § 219 (see also § 225). Hence, I have categorized it as the third of seven secondary biblical lemmata (see Introduction 4. Exegetical Structure of the Treatise). For the sending of the "spies" (κατάσκοποι), as Philo names them, see Num 13:1, 17, 25 ("those who were spying" [οἱ κατασκεψάμενοι]).

undertook to pull up the whole tree of virtue, root and branch. In Num 13:20, Moses asks the spies to see "whether there are trees (δένδρα) in ⟨the Land⟩ or not; and you shall persevere (προσκαρτερήσαντες) and take some of the fruit of the land" (NETS, adapted). Philo extrapolates from this statement that the spies "undertake" to uproot an entire tree or vine to carry back. The verb "undertaking" (ἐπιχειρήσαντες) picks up the metaphor of each soul gleaning virtue "according to the power of hands (κατὰ δύναμιν τῶν χειρῶν)" in §220. Philo uses the rare adjective, "root and branch" (αὐτόπρεμνος), which only elsewhere appears in his corpus at *Agr.* 7 and *Plant.* 24 (αὐτόπρεμνα δένδρα). Literally, the spies in Numbers attempt nothing of the sort. Allegorically, Philo means they tried initially to take all the virtues at once—not making progress gradually but seizing perfection instantaneously. For the philosophical background of the agrarian imagery of the tree bearing ethical fruit, see the detailed comment on §74.

but since they could not do this. Philo's phrase, "they were not able" (οὐκ ἠδυνήθησαν) continues his elaboration of the spies' failed attempt to take the whole tree at once. Although this detail (like the attempt on the tree) is not explicitly in the text, it is a reasonable extrapolation from the silences. Philo may have been inspired in this regard by the spies' report about the difficulties of the Canaanite cities and inhabitants in Num 13:27–28, as well as the people's response in Num 13:31 that they would "not be able" (οὐ μὴ δυνώμεθα) to go up against the strong nations in that land. The gigantic size of the Canaanites (Num 13:32–33) might also suggest that their trees were similarly apportioned.

Philo associates such a great tree or vine allegorically with the "tree of virtue," which is itself not easily attainably by most ordinary, progressing souls. This is in keeping with his metaphor of ethics as the fruit of philosophical discourse in §74, which can only be approached gradually and in stages. There, however, the tree itself is physics, not virtue. See Jastram 1989; 1991.

took instead a small vine and one grape cluster. See Num 13:23. Philo uses the diminutive "cluster" (κληματίς) in place of the LXX "vine" (κλῆμα), to emphasize that only a portion of virtue was received.

which was all they had the strength to carry. Philo's verb "had strength" (ἴσχυον) echoes the Israelite's description of their own want of strength in Num 13:31, when they worry that "⟨their nation⟩ is stronger than ours" (ὅτι ἰσχυρότερόν ἐστιν ἡμῶν μᾶλλον).

§225. ***greater than our human nature can bear.*** Or "greater than ⟨accords with⟩ human nature." Philo maintains his view from chapter eight: that human virtue is always *human* virtue, and thereby not as constant as divine virtue.

let us be happy. Philo's "let us be happy" (ἀγαπῶμεν) picks up the "gladness" (ἀγαπητόν) of §219, confirming that this exegesis of Num 13 amplifies the primary biblical lemma (Gen 17:18c).

the particular virtues. See *Leg.* 1.56 and *Mut.* 78–79 ("Sarai" as "particular wisdom"). Arnaldez (1964, 138, n. 1) comments that participation in the particular (cardinal) virtues is "still the same idea of a religious life measured according to effort and human powers. But to enter into the choir of virtue—this is, to the contrary, to be united with God by a grace which does not consider what the recipient being is capable of on its own."

practical wisdom or courage or justice or love of the human being. The classical list of four cardinal virtues, minus "temperance" (σωφροσύνη) and with "love of humanity" (φιλανθρωπία) serving as an index of additional Roman and Jewish virtues. For other lists of virtues in the present treatise, see comments on §§ 146 and 197.

2d. § 226. *will you yourself ... on your own son?* To strengthen the argument for gradual ethical progress derived from Gen 17:18c, Num 6:21, and Num 13, Philo extrapolates *ad absurdum* what would happen if a parent took a "perfection or nothing" stance in disciplining a child. His string of five conditionals is framed as one long rhetorical question, to which the fictive interlocutor is presumed to give a negative answer. The contents of the first three exhortations reflect concerns about social relationships, with the same stock categories present in the New Testament household codes (see Col 3:18–4:1; Eph 5:21–6:9; 1 Pet 2:18–3:7). Both the Decalogue and pagan Greco-Roman family values stand in the background. The final two mock exhortations form a secondary catena, structured around the vices of pleasure, greed, and pride. The broad form of this and the following section is the philosophical diatribe, common to texts composed for school settings. Philo effectively varies his rhetoric, moving from narrative to legal exegesis, and from the epideictic to the deliberative mode. His emphatic doubling of the second person pronoun, "you, yourself" (σύ, σεαυτοῦ) facilitates a sharper, address to the reader than the foregoing allegoresis.

"servants ... peers." Philo's first mock exhortation focuses on duties to one's more remote relations: servants and friends. These classes are of special concern in Greco-Roman ethics. The servants and peers may also allude to the "servant/maidservant" (παῖς/παιδίσκη) and the "neighbor" (πλήσιος) of the ninth and tenth commandments. The Pentateuch has plenty to say on the right treatment of slaves and neighbors elsewhere.

"your wife ... your parents." Philo's second mock exhortation turns to a more proximate set of human relations: wives and parents. The fifth and sixth commandments of the Decalogue are concerned with these groups. Philo construes duty toward one's parents as more consequential than duty toward one's spouse, on account of parents' god-like status in helping bring a person into existence (see the following comment). Both kinds of relations are naturally more obligatory than those listed in the first exhortation.

"mother and father, also act impiously toward God." Philo's third mock exhortation echoes the fifth commandment, "honor your father and mother" (τίμα τὸν πατέρα σου καὶ τὴν μητέρα), individuating the two parents. It also con-

nects the second table of the Decalogue with the first, forging an intrinsic link between the fifth commandment on parents and the preceding four on duties toward God (see *Spec.* 2.224).

"if you delight in pleasure, do not refrain from hoarding silver." Philo's fourth mock exhortation turns from social relations to personal vices, beginning—as he does the whole Allegorical Commentary—with problems related to pleasure (*Leg.* 2.71). The embodied state leads to physical attachments and greed. For desire and pleasure as the root of other vices in Philo, see Svebakken 2012.

much wealth ... vain opinion. With Philo's fifth mock exhortation, the downward ethical spiral reaches its satirical nadir. Neutral pleasure has led to covetousness (commandments nine and ten again), which infects the mind, turning it from knowledge to false opinion.

§ 227. *do you not think it worthwhile to walk a middle way?* Philo continues his diatribe to the fictitious father with two more rhetorical questions. Both are meant to exonerate the "middle way" (μετριάζειν) as a road to virtue. (NB: this is not the ethical "mean" as Aristotle exhorts, which is good for everyone; but a middle-point on the soul's journey up the mountain of virtue toward perfection, as symbolized by "this Ishmael.") Philo signals this theme in the opening of his treatise, when he writes "he who is at the mean always hastens toward the summit" (σπεύδει δὲ ὁ μέσος ἀεὶ πρὸς ἀκρότητα [§ 2]). In § 227, he nuances this position by suggesting that even if the soul never reaches the summit of virtue, it is better to attain the middle point than to remain mired in vice. For such souls, Philo counsels "moderation," echoing the description of the person who tries to moderate his grief in *Resp.* 603e, even if he cannot extricate it completely.

would not your son say. Philo sets the final rhetorical question on the lips of the fictive interlocutor's son. In dramatizing the diatribe, Philo increases its *pathos* and emphasizes the teleological aspect of his moral allegory—a characteristic that it shares Aristotelian virtue ethics. The best practice is not to compel everyone to follow the rules equally in the present, but to accommodate and improve a variety of characters as far as their souls and natures allow over time. One may hear this final objection as a speech in character for the Ishmael soul to the non-Abrahamic father—one who would not pray for the life of "this" son, but only for the self-perfecting nature, Isaac.

"either perfectly good or perfectly bad." A clever, paradoxical phrase, given that ethical perfection is the moral theme of the treatise, while being "perfectly bad" is an oxymoron.

"if he should reach the middle regions before he reaches the heights." Whereas Philo's rhetorical question in § 227a suggests that some souls may

never move beyond the middle, the son's question in § 227b implies that anyone ascending the mountain of virtue will need to pass by a middle plateau. The son's position is thus closer to that in § 2, cited above, than to Philo's more pessimistic statements at the beginning of this section and earlier in the discussion of different natures in §§ 31 and 211–212.

2e. § 228. *was it not also for this reason that Abraham.* Philo returns from his diatribe to an allegorical reading of several more secondary lemmata. He adduces first Abraham's prayer for Sodom (Gen 18:24, 32) as a parallel to his prayer for Ishmael in the primary lemma.

the destruction of the people of Sodom. Philo speaks literally of the inhabitants of Sodom, but the fifty and the ten also symbolize differing levels of virtue within the Sodom soul.

the all-perfect release into freedom ... the holy number fifty. While the number one hundred is the symbol of ethical perfection (§ 2), the number fifty is the symbol of "the all-perfect release/forgiveness into freedom" (ἡ παντελὴς εἰς ἐλευθερίαν ἄφεσις). Philo derives this significance from a tertiary biblical lemma, Lev 25:10, which speaks of the fiftieth year of Jubilee, in which Israel is to proclaim "release upon the land" (ἄφεσις ἐπὶ τῆς γῆς). Philo's arithmology in this passage owes more to Second Temple Judaism, with its calculation of the Jubilee following seven weeks of years (Lev 25:8), than it does with the Neopythagorean speculation about the decade. (NB: Philo combines scriptural and arithmological appreciations of the number fifty in *Spec.* 2.176–177; see the Parallel Exegesis.) This pairing of secondary and tertiary lemmata heightens the import of Abraham's prayer in Gen 17:18c, rendering it as a petition for the wayward soul—perhaps like that of his "apostatizing" nephew, Tiberias Julius Alexander, who features as a major character in his later philosophical dialogues, *De providentia* 1–2 and *De animalibus*.

at least the middle paideia, being reckoned as ten. This phrase provides the key to Philo's allegoresis of Gen 18:24–32, bringing together two important interpretive lines: (1) Fifty and ten are ethical "levels," the complete and the middle ways respectively. Perfect virtue (100) requires perfect education, assisted by complete forgiveness and release (50). In this schema, 10 is construed as the mean, just as the ordinary "tithe" must be multiplied by another "tenth" to reach the perfect Levitical tenth of a tenth in Num 18:26 (§ 2). (2) The number 10 as a virtuous halfway house is equated by Philo with Hagar—symbol of the preliminary studies (§ 255) and mother of "this Ishmael," for whom Abraham prays in Gen 17:18.

deliverance of the soul on the verge of condemnation. The themes of deliverance and release allude tersely to Lev 25:10 and the Jubilee year. Within the constellation of scriptural lemmata, these tertiary-level metaphors recall Ishmael's identity as a "slave" (primary-level, Gen 17 and 21), as well as the fact that the soul at mid-point, though not entirely destroyed (secondary-level, Gen 18), remains enslaved to certain emotions and unable to enjoy the complete freedom of the legitimate son of the sage.

§ 229. *tutored in the general arts and letters ... without schooling in instrument or muse.* Philo's imagery for the preliminary studies is inflected by musical metaphors, as the Muses were associated with learning and education. To lack such education renders one fundamentally "tone deaf" to virtue and aims one's pedagogical "point of departure" (ἀφορμή) in the wrong direction.

entirely scrubbed ... washed. Philo's two verbs, "scrubbed" (ἐξερρύψαντο) and "washed" (ἐρρύψαντο), emphasize the difference between complete washing of vices, indicated by the prepositional prefix "thoroughly/entirely" (ἐκ), and more rudimentary kinds of cleansing. This distinction is complemented by the adverbs "completely" (παντελῶς) and "moderately" (μετρίως/μέσως), which recall the foregoing discussion of the middle regions and the heights of the soul's journey.

bright from a fresh bath. Philo uses a relatively rare (though by no means atypical) verb from his repertoire, *phaedrunō* (φαιδρύνω ["brighten"]). Given his interest in names in this treatise, it is possible that Philo alludes to the preliminary education of Socrates's companion, Phaedrus (Φαῖδρος), which has initiated him into the arts and letters, but leaves him in danger of sophistic intrigues and requires further growth. Phaedrus's poetic starting point in ethical thinking is on display not only in the dialogue which eponymously bears his name, but also in his more famous speech in the *Symposium*, where he "begins" (ἀρξάμενος) the discussion on love with a markedly Homeric and Hesiodic contribution. If this is correct, then Philo adds Phaedrus to the column of characters that allegorically represent the soul at the mid-point of its ethical journey ("this" Ishmael$_1$, Joseph, Moses's spies, Sodom, Phaedrus). In the subsequent section, he will add Esau to this growing list.

2f. § 230. *"surely, you have not but one blessing, Father? bless me too, Father."* Philo adduces a fifth secondary lemma to amplify his interpretation of Abraham's prayer for Ishmael in Gen 17:18c. To the ever-increasing cast of characters representing the "middler" soul in the sphere of ethics, he now adds Esau, by way of the latter's belated petition for a blessing from Isaac (Gen 27:38). Philo's citation agrees with the Septuagint, excepting some minor differences such as the transposition of "one" (μία) and "you" (σοι) and the omission of "of course" (δή).

different blessings have been distinguished for different types of people. Philo summarizes his basic principle of psychagogic and therapeutic accommodation. The verb "distinguish" (ἀποκρίνομαι) is used in a medical register, on analogy with the physician's selection of differing treatments for different patients. Arnaldez (1964, 141, n. 1) comments: "At this level of the religious life, God adapts his gifts to the capacity of the one who should receive them; a person is not absolutely bereft. What each person needs is not to fall under the weight of this, but to carry what God has apportioned for him."

exercises. Philo plays on the homonymy between athletic "exercises" (γυμνάσματα) and the educational "preliminary studies/pre-exercises" (προγυμνάσματα).

so that they do not become wholly sick. The phrase "become wholly/soundly sick" (ὅλως νοσήσωσιν) conveys a similarly oxymoronic idea to that of becoming "perfectly vicious" (τέλειος κακός [§ 227]). Philo combines health and education as parallel soteriological metaphors.

§ 231. *since there are many goods in nature*. I.e., at God's disposal.

grant me, Lord. Philo's request, "grant this to me" (μοι τοῦτο χάρισαι), echoes Esau's request of Isaac, "bless me also, father" (εὐλόγησον κἀμέ, πάτερ), in the secondary lemma (§ 230). Whether Philo is speaking for himself here, or constructing a speech-in-character for Esau, is especially difficult to discern. In the following notes (as in Cover 2020b, 133), I identify Philo as the speaker because (1) as §§ 230–231 is an exegetical passage, it is natural to find scriptural vocabulary (Gen 27:38), even if they are offered in an autoreferential way; and (2) because much the same form is followed by Philo in the subsequent pericope (§ 232): a citation of Num 11:23 is followed by Philo's commentary in his own voice. In essence, the speaker is the "I" of the Philonic diatribe in §§ 226–227. He has, nonetheless, appropriated to himself some of the characteristics of the Esau soul—demonstrating that Philo does not see himself as having attained Abrahamic perfection.

which most seems to befit me. The language of "fit" or "accommodation" (ἐφαρμόττειν) recalls the verb "adjoined" (ἁρμόζοιτο) in § 211, used to describe a soul's or nature's ability (or not) to absorb and draw benefit from a certain teaching or grace. For links with the epistemology of the *Theaetetus*, see the detailed comment on § 211 *supra*.

I, unfortunate man that I am. Philo's self-estimation here as "the unfortunate one" (ὁ δυστυχής) is uncharacteristically pessimistic for his works overall (cf. *Spec*. 3.1, etc.), but in keeping with his general self-presentation as a human "nothing" in comparison to God (Lévy 2018; Cover 2020b). The speaker is a synthesis of (1) Philo's autobiographical/authorial self and (2) his persona in the diatribe—the latter being shaped by (3) the subjectivity of Esau in Gen 27:38, with whom Philo partially identifies. The overarching self-portraiture is dramatic, as the epithet "unfortunate" is used in tragedy (Euripides, *Med*. 1250; *Hipp*. 807; *Andr*. 386, 1201; Sophocles, *El*. 934), as well as in Aesop's fables (*Fab*.

8), where the dove says of its own deception by an image of water: "truly I am unfortunate" (δυστυχὴς ὄντως ἐγώ).

2g. § 232. *what else do we suppose.* Philo continues the diatribal exchange in the first-person plural (see §§ 225–226 for the inverse shift from the plural to the singular).

⟨*are you afraid*⟩ *that the hand of the Lord will not suffice?* Philo cites, as his sixth secondary lemma in this catena, Num 11:23—the words that God speaks to Moses when the Israelites complain in the wilderness. His text, identical with the Septuagint, is best understood as an implicit fearing clause. It has lexical affinities with another secondary lemma in this cluster, Num 6:21 (§ 220), through the shared word "hand."

the powers of The One Who Is extend everywhere. Philo interprets the "hand" of the Lord to mean his beneficent and merciful power(s). With this secondary lemma, he shifts the focus away from limited human capacities, discussed in the first five secondary lemmata, toward the infinite capacity of God. He answers the question of Abraham's prayer for Ishmael in Gen 17:18 from a new theological perspective: that God has plenteous gifts to bless both the Ishmael and the Isaac soul. To attempt to limit his blessing only to the latter would be to place a supposed limit on God's gracious power. Philo offers a similar line of argument at the beginning of the Allegorical Commentary in *Leg.* 1.34.

what is fitting. See the comment on § 231 for the notion of psychological fit or harmony.

with his own standard of equality ... the gift that is analogous. Because God is perfect number, he is also able to measure, with greater exactitude than a human doctor or craftsman, the apposite gift that each person can accommodate to its own wax-tablet soul. Philo's diasporic ethics tend to focus on the salvation of individuals or schools of individuals, even as a communal "salvation history" of the nation of Israel does surface in the Exposition of the Law (esp. *De praemiis et poenis*).

3a. § 233. *I am also amazed.* Or, more literally, "it also strikes me with amazement." The verb "it strikes" (καταπλήττει), spelled in this Atticizing fashion, is a favorite of Philo's in exegetical contexts.

not least of all. Philo saves his most important scriptural lemma for last. It will also receive the most detailed exegesis.

the law pertaining to those who ... resolve to repent. That is, via the sin offerings of Lev 5:6–12—the seventh secondary lemma. I have translated the verb δοκοῦσιν as "resolve" (see LSJ II.3) rather than "seem/appear" (Colson, PLCL), as feigned repentance is not the subject of Philo's comments.

to bring, as the first sacrificial animal, a blameless female sheep. Philo paraphrases the first part of his secondary lemma, Lev 5:6, as "a blameless female sheep" (θῆλυ πρόβατον ἄμωμον), expanding the LXX phrase, "a female from the sheep" (θῆλυ ἀπὸ τῶν προβάτων). The adjective "blameless/unblemished" (ἄμωμος) is not used in this pericope of the animals, but is a cultic qualifier found in surrounding passages of Leviticus. Philo paraphrases Lev 5:6 in order to allow the exegetical focus of his interpretation to fall on Lev 5:7 (see also Lev 5:11), which contains the catchword "hand" (χείρ). This links this lemma with the second and sixth secondary lemmata and recapitulates the theme of proportionate thanksgiving in §220 (Num 6:21) and §232 (Num 11:23).

but if ... as a whole burnt offering. Philo cites Lev 5:7 in its entirety. His text is identical to the Septuagint, with the exception of three omissions: (1) "the sheep" (⟨τὸ⟩ πρόβατον); (2) "his sin" (ἁμαρτίας ⟨αὐτοῦ⟩); and (3) "doves ⟨for the Lord⟩" (περιστερῶν ⟨κυρίῳ⟩).

§234. *but if his hand should not ... as a memorial upon the altar.* Philo continues his citation of the secondary lemma with Lev 5:11–12, without indicating that he is omitting Lev 5:8–10. The principle of selection binding Lev 5:7 and Lev 5:11 is the catchword "hand" (χείρ). Philo's citation of Lev 5:11–12 agrees closely with the Septuagint, but contains eight alterations or omissions, indicated in the synopsis below:

Lev 5:11–12	§234
¹¹But if his hand (αὐτοῦ ἡ χείρ) should not find a yoke of turtle doves or two young doves,	But if his hand (ἡ χεὶρ αὐτοῦ) should not find a yoke of turtle doves or two young doves,
then (καί) he will bring ⟨as⟩ his sin offering, the tenth of the (τοῦ) ephah of grain for his sin (περὶ ἁμαρτίας).	he will bring ⟨as⟩ the gift the tenth of an ephah of grain for his sin.
He will not pour oil upon it, nor will he set incense upon it, because it is for sin;	He will not pour oil upon it, nor will he set incense upon it, because it is for sin;
¹² And he will bring it to the priest. And the priest, grasping a full handful from it (ἀπ' αὐτῆς), will set its (αὐτῆς) memorial upon the altar of whole burnt offerings for the Lord (τῶν ὁλοκαυτωμάτων κυρίῳ); It is a sin offering (ἁμαρτία ἐστίν).	¹² And he will bring it to the priest. And the priest, grasping a full handful from it/him (ἀπ' αὐτοῦ), will set the memorial upon the altar.

In addition to foregrounding the word "hand," Philo redacts the word "sin ⟨offering⟩" (ἁμαρτία) out of the pericope twice, although it still occurs twice in the citation of Lev 5:7. His focus is on the soul, rather than the sin *per se*. Philo similarly emphasizes the priest's taking the handful "from it" (i.e., the tithe) or "from him" (i.e., the penitent)—in both cases focusing on the penitent soul— while in the Septuagint, the feminine pronoun in "from it" (ἀπ' αὐτῆς) most likely points to the "sin ⟨offering⟩" (ἁμαρτία).

§ 235. *atonement ... three named manners of repentance*. Philo blends cultic and moral vocabularies, taking into account the "many manners" (Homer, *Od.* 1.1) of souls, their imperfections, and their "modes of therapy" (θεραπεῖαι). He focuses on three types of offering (though his scriptural text gives him a fourth), looking ahead to the three-fold division of sin into "thought, words, and deeds" (§ 236), which will be developed through the interpretation of the tertiary lemma, Deut 30:12–14 (§ 237).

the power of the one who is being cleansed and repenting. "Power" is an allegorical gloss for the word "hand" in the secondary lemma (see the comment on § 220). Philo references the power of the soul, whose relative strength or weakness determines both the degree of the sin and the kind of therapy required. For the notion that different kinds of soul have differed powers (or gracious infusions of the divine spirit), see *Leg.* 1.42.

must be alike and equal. This important soteriological principle of equivalence is developed from what was, at the literal level, an accommodation for different economic classes of Israelites. Arnaldez (1964, 143, n. 2) comments: "⟨This is⟩ a Stoic idea of proportional justice applied to God; it is perfect justice."

3b. § 236. *why precisely*. Philo asks a clarifying question, which initiates a long discussion of the classification of different kinds of sin. This is not one of the seven major *aporiae* in this treatise identified by Runia (1984, 70), which are posed of the primary biblical lemma (Gen 17), but rather a question posed of a secondary biblical lemma (Lev 5:6–17). This text provides the framework for the whole third section (§§ 233–251) of chapter nine.

roughly. Philo admits that his schema could be developed with greater precision (see, e.g., the Exposition of the Law), but prefers a more general division in the current context.

three headings: thought, words, and deeds. This trichotomy of sins and corrections, "thought, words, and deeds" (διάνοια, λόγοι, πράξεις), reflects the three-fold schema in use by Philo throughout the treatise. It echoes his defense of Abraham's faith in chapter eight (§ 177), which wavers humanly "in thought" (τῇ διανοίᾳ) but not "in mouth" (τῷ στόματι) and stands juxtaposed to the Shechem soul, which speaks piously with its lips but acts according to the sin of its mind (§ 193). Unlike Thomas Cranmer's well-known trichotomy in the Confession from the 1549 *Book of Common Prayer* ("by thought, word and dede"), Philo emphasizes the unique singularity of (internal) sin in "thought," while conversely highlighting the plurality of (external) sins in "words" and "actions."

Moses also teaches in the Exhortations. For the *Exhortations* as a formal treatise, a cento of Mosaic texts, or a subdivision of the Pentateuch, see the comment on § 42.

the attainment of good is neither impossible nor overly difficult. Philo's summary of Moses's teaching, "that the attainment of good is neither impossible nor overly difficult" (ὅτι ἡ ἀγαθοῦ κτῆσις οὔτ' ἀδύνατος ... οὔτε δυσθήρατος), paraphrases Deut 30:11: "that the commandment ... is not overly burdensome and it is not far from you" (ὅτι ἡ ἐντολή ... οὐχ ὑπέρογχός ἐστιν οὐδὲ μακρὰν ἀπὸ σοῦ). The Septuagint's "commandment" is replaced by Philo's "attainment of good," representing the latter's shift from deontological law to philosophical ethics. Syntactically, Philo maintains the conjunction "that" (ὅτι) and the verb "is" (ἐστιν) from Deut 30:11, as well as a double adjective chain, wherein the first descriptor begins with a vowel and the second with a consonant. Philo's two adjectives, *adunatos* (ἀδύνατος ["impossible"]) and *dusthēratos* (δυσθήρατος ["overly difficult"]) are more closely bound together in terms of sound than their LXX equivalents. Both include the string *-du-* (δυ) at the beginning of both words, and have *-atos* (-ατος) at their endings. Despite these similarities, the *du-* (ἀδυ-) and *dus-/dys-* (δυσ-) morphemes also stand in antithetical parallelism, expressing potential (*dunamai* [δύναμαι]) and non-potential (*dus-* [δυσ-]), respectively.

§ 237. ***it is not necessary to fly up to heaven.*** After his artful paraphrase of the tertiary biblical lemma (Deut 30:11), Philo loosely quotes what Moses "says" (φησίν). Philo's wording, "it is not necessary to fly up to heaven" (οὐκ εἰς οὐρανὸν ἀναπτῆναι δεῖ), conflates the statements "it is not in heaven above" (οὐκ ἐν τῷ οὐρανῷ ἄνω) with the rhetorical question of Deut 30:12, "who will go up to heaven for us?" (τίς ἀναβήσεται ἡμῖν εἰς τὸν οὐρανόν;). By eliminating the first-person plural pronoun, Philo makes the statement more applicable to the individual soul.

This paraphrastic citation of Deut 30:11–14a focuses attention on the verbatim citation of Deut 30:14b (see below), which contains the catchword link to the secondary lemma chain, "hands" (χερσί). (For Philo's exegesis of this verse, especially in the Exposition of the Law, see Bekken 2007.) Philo uses a similar "funneling" pattern, beginning with paraphrase and narrowing to catchword citation of the secondary lemma, in his scriptural exegesis in §§ 233–234. There, the paraphrase of Lev 5:6 leads to a pointed citation and exegesis of the catchword "hand" (χείρ) in Lev 5:7 and Lev 5:12.

nor to go to the ends of earth and sea to acquire it. This next part of the citation consists of a paraphrase of Deut 30:13. Philo's "unto the ends of earth and sea" (ἄχρι περάτων γῆς καὶ θαλάττης) expands the scope of the Septuagint's maritime boundaries ("the place beyond the sea" [τὸ πέραν τῆς θαλάσσης]).

rather, the acquisition of the good is near; in fact, it is very near. The third and final clause of Philo's paraphrastic citation echoes Deut 30:14a, "the word is very near you" (ἐγγὺς σοῦ ἐστιν τὸ ῥῆμα σφόδρα). Philo clarifies that it is not merely the "word" or "command," but the acquisition of its benefits, which is "near, and very near" (ἐγγύς, καὶ σφόδρα ἐγγύς).

then he shows this. Philo introduces the direct citation of Moses's words in Deut 30:14b with a second citation formula. The verse offers proof of the foregoing vertical (heaven) and horizontal (earth/sea) cosmological claims.

every work. "Work" (ἔργον) paraphrases several occurrences of the verb "to make" (ποιεῖν) in Deut 30:11–14.

in your mouth and heart and hands. As the culmination of this long paraphrase, Philo cites Moses verbatim (Deut 30:14b), ending with the catchword "hands" (χερσί). The text of his citation agrees with the Septuagint, except for Philo's omission of the redundant "your" (σου) accompanying "heart" and "hands" in scriptural text. Here, the word "hands" does not mean psychic powers (as previously in the catena) but symbolizes sins in acts, as opposed to sins in thought and words.

symbolically "in words, in plans, in actions." Philo rephrases the allegorical equivalents of "mouth, heart, and hands," this time following the scriptural order of Deut 30:14b rather than the logical/philosophical order of § 236, in which "thought" comes before "words."

human happiness. For Philo's eudaimonism, see the detailed comment on § 51. The noun "happiness" (εὐδαιμονία) inspires the three following "good" (εὐ-) compound nouns.

good counsel and good speech and good work. Philo uses three nouns to indicate virtue in the three Deuteronomistic areas: "good counsel, good speech, good work" (εὐβουλία, εὐλογία, εὐπραξία). Note that the scriptural order of Deut 30:14b has been abandoned, as Philo reverts to the logical order of § 236.

§ 238. *in heart, mouth, and hand.* Philo still follows the logical order of sin-types, now rendering "hands" in the singular to make the three categories parallel.

the lightest ... the heaviest ... the middle kind of offense. Philo ranks the three domains of sin from the lightest to the heaviest—drawing on the Septuagintal metaphor of "sin as weight or burden." For the transformation of the older scriptural metaphor for sin as weight to sin as debt in Second Temple Judaism, see Anderson 2009.

§ 239. *the lightest kind of sin is also the most difficult to uproot.* Although sins of thought are "least serious" from a hamartiological perspective, they are also the most recalcitrant. They are the first sins to be committed by the soul, the last to be removed, and the final impediment to perfection. This judgment is in keeping with Philo's light estimation of Abraham's wavering in thought in chapter eight (§ 177).

to guide the turning of the soul toward rest. A description reminiscent of the Odysseus soul's "many turnings" (Homer, *Od.* 1.1), borrowed by Philo from Platonist allegoresis of Homer. "Rest" (ἠρεμία) here is a rough synonym of "happiness," given in psychological rather than ethical/emotional terms. As often in ancient psychology, "turning" (τροπή) serves as the negative or neutral antonym to a positive change or "conversion" (ἐπιστροφή)

more quickly stem the current of a swollen river. Earlier in the treatise, Philo likens the Joseph soul, immersed in external torrents of pleasure and vain opinion, to a ship on the "river of life" (§ 214). A similar metaphor is used here, with the besetting waves symbolizing the soul's "cares" or "desires" (ἐνθύμια = ἐπιθυμητικά), which keep it from rest.

§ 240. *most perfect form of purification ... anything out of place.* With the outline of this Deuteronomistic homily in place, Philo's thought returns to the catena of Levitical texts in §§ 233–235 (the seventh secondary lemma), as signaled by the word "purification" (κάθαρσις). The highest and most perfect form of purification is also the most difficult. In claiming that certain thoughts are "strange" or "out of place" (ἄτοποι), Philo borrows a Platonic metaphor. Not even Abraham (§ 177) is capable of maintaining divine purity in thought.

peace and lawfulness, whose leader is justice. "Justice" (δικαιοσύνη), as one of the cardinal virtues, stands at the head, with other specific virtues in its train.

the second form of purification is not to sin with words. If one cannot keep one's thoughts entirely ordered—which Philo presumes will be the case for most—the median form of purification is to keep one's speech in check. Underneath this second heading, Philo offers a series of six specific offences, which mirror a Greco-Roman "vice-list." Here, however, the vices are not presented as abstract nouns, but as participles modifying the imagined recipient of the command. The vice-list of speaking sins recalls the hypocrisy of Shechem in § 193, who sins in word (and deed).

a bridle. Philo's exhortation that the tongue be controlled with a "bridle" (χαλινός) is a stock trope in Hellenistic moral literature.

§ 241. *why speaking unfitting things is a heavier sin than thinking them.* A "why" (διὰ τί;) question is posed of the tertiary lemma, Deut 30:14b, to clarify Philo's ranking of the various weights of sins.

for such unwilling thoughts, there is no culpability. Philo ranks sins of thought as generically less evil than sins of speech, because in some cases one is assaulted by evil thoughts unintentionally. For the issue of intentional and unintentional sin in Philo more broadly, see Francis 2015; and Arnaldez (1964, 144, n. 1), who notes self-referentially: "On passivity and voluntary activity at the level of impressions, which sensation makes in thought, see R. Arnaldez (1963, 67; RR 6301)."

§ 242. *a person speaks willingly.* Philo remains a strong voluntarist, even while espousing a doctrine of divine providence and human nothingness. Speech, one of the seven irrational faculties of the soul, is always subject to rational control, even if bad emotions disturb or confuse it.

he does injustice and is unhappy. The imagined sinful speaker both misses the societal good of justice and the personal end of happiness.

a very secure solitude ... a voluntary silence. It is difficult to delineate the precise difference Philo intends between the two options, "to rest" (ἡσυχάζειν) and "to be silent" (σιωπᾶν). Both may mean "to be quiet," and in §§ 196–200 (the discussion of the Shechem soul), Philo uses the former verb apparently to mean "be quiet" with no indication of physical isolation. The differentiation presented in the translation reflects Colson's (PLCL 5:592) self-avowedly "desperate attempt to give some sense to the text as it stands." Another solution would be to read σιωπᾶν (in the text as it stands) invectively, which one might paraphrase as follows: "if the soul inclined to vicious speech cannot accept the goods of reflective silence, then he can at least voluntarily shut up."

§ 243. *they say, A word is a shadow of an act.* Just as a bad word is more serious than a bad thought and an evil act exceeds an evil word in moral gravity, so a body exceeds the shadow that it casts in ontological reality. Philo adduces, for proof of this position, a tertiary classical lemma from the atomist pre-Socratic philosopher, Democritus (frag. 105). Colson (PLCL 5:592; also Arnaldez 1964, 146, n. 1) notes that the saying is attributed to Democritus by Diogenes Laertius (9.37) and Ps.-Plutarch (*Lib. ed.* 14). It is thematically, rather than lexically, linked with the foregoing tertiary lemma (Deut 30:12–14b).

and if the shadow can harm, how is the act not more harmful. Philo extrapolates from the Democritean logion, arguing *a minore ad maius* that if the word (shadow) can cause damage, how much more the action (body)? Word and deed are joined strongly in this analogy. As it is impossible for there to be a shadow without a body, so it would seem impossible for there to be a word which did not also imply a deed.

Moses exonerates. Moses adds his voice to that of Democritus. For the remainder of §§ 243–244, Philo reiterates the rationales given for (1) the lightening of sins committed only in "judgment/thought" (γνώμη), (2) moral accountability for whatever comes out "through the mouth" (Deut 30:14b), and (3) greater punishments being assigned to evil actions that follow from evil thought and speech.

3c. § 245. *Moses has called ... a holy measure of flour.* Philo returns from interpreting the tertiary biblical and classical lemmata to the secondary biblical lemma, Lev 5:6–12. He now explicitly links the purification of the three kinds of sin (thought, words, and deeds) and their three corresponding domains (heart, mouth, and hands) with the three kinds of sacrifices mentioned by Moses in Lev 5: one sheep, two doves, and a handful of flour.

§ 246. *why is this?* A second question posed of the secondary biblical lemma (Lev 5:6–12), which continues and expands the question asked in § 236. This is not one of Runia's (1984) seven major *aporiae* posed of the primary biblical lemma (Gen 17).

the mind is the best faculty ... sheep best ... of irrational animals. A curious judgment for Philo to make, as the ewe is by no means the largest of the clean sacrificial animals, nor the one used on the Day of Atonement, nor the male ram discovered by Abraham in Gen 22. It might have been suggested to him by Abel's sacrifice of a sheep in Gen 4:4—the first recorded animal sacrifice. In what follows, Philo will adopt a naturalistic rationale for the scriptural order.

since a sheep is the tamest. Philo uses the particle "since" (ἄτε) with the circumstantial participle "being/existing" (ὑπάρχον) to indicate his own sense of a cause, rather than the reasoning of Moses. On this use of ἄτε (as opposed to ὡς), see Smyth § 2085.

the harmful effects of icy cold and summer heat. For a similar account of the purpose of clothing, see *Somn.* 2.52.

§ 247. *let the birds stand for the purification of speech.* Philo continues to develop his natural rationale for the three kinds of sin offering, moving on to the second term—the birds.

for speech is light and winged by nature. Earlier in § 179, Philo offers a Homeric analogy that likens thought to the winged bird, in contradistinction to speech that reaches the lips more slowly. Here, Philo reuses the analogy of the wing to characterize the swiftness of speech, rather than thought.

once it has been spoken ... immediately resounds. An intriguing summary of the physics of sound production, perhaps influenced by Philo's familiarity with medical writing in Alexandria.

§ 248. *speech is twofold—the true and the false.* Although Philo's formulation, "speech is twofold" (δίδυμος δὲ ὁ λόγος), appears to be unique in contemporaneous literature, the duplicity of speech has a long history in Greek thought. It is thematized especially by the tragedians (Sophocles, *Oed. tyr.* 525) as well as the pre-Socratics (see this pithy iambic trimeter by Critias [frag. 25.40]: "masking the truth with a false word" [ψευδεῖ καλύψας τὴν ἀλήθειαν λόγωι]) and the Attic orators (Isocrates, *Trapez.* 58). The most immediate precedent for Philo's formulation, "the true ⟨speech⟩, the false ⟨speech⟩" (ὁ μὲν ἀληθής, ὁ δὲ ψευδής), is Plato's *Cratylus* (385b5–6):

> Socrates: So one speech could be true, another false? (οὐκοῦν εἴη ἂν λόγος ἀληθής, ὁ δὲ ψευδής;)
> Hermogenes: Very much so.

for this reason, it seems to me, it was likened it to a pair of turtledoves. Having answered his first question ("Why is speech likened to a bird?") in § 247, Philo now explains why Moses requires two birds, but only one sheep. His answer is that one bird represents true speech, the other false speech—both may be complicit in sin, though in different ways.

the first of the birds, Moses says, ought to be for a sin offering. Philo uses a contrastive (μέν ... δέ) construction to divide the two birds, as he did of the two types of speech. Given that "true speech" (ὁ μὲν ἀληθής) was the first term in the initial dyad, one might suppose that the true speech corresponds with the first bird in Moses's pair for a sin-offering. However, the opposite turns out to be the case: the sin-offering bird is identified with "false speech," for "it has sinned and is in need of correction."

the second must be sacrificed as a whole burnt-offering. The second bird symbolizes the true speech. Philo again reverses the Platonic order to match the Mosaic order (Plato presents the true speech first, Moses presents it second). Philo clarifies his allegorical identifications by echoing the title "for the holocaust" (εἰς ὁλοκαύτωμα) in his description of the true speech as "completely (ὅλον δι' ὅλου) holy and perfect."

§ 249. *flour ... is a symbol of the purification of action.* Philo returns to the main question (§ 245) of how each sacrificial offering corresponds with the three areas of sin identified in Deut 30:12–14. Flour, so often handled, atones for sins of action. The noun "purification" (ἡ κάθαρσις) is supplied from § 247.

not without skill and active thought ... the hands of wheat-workers. Philo interprets the catchword "hands" (see Deut 30:14b [§ 237]) here to symbolize right actions, governed by "active thought" (ἐπίνοια), rather than "powers" (as earlier). A similar coordination of thought and deed is found in the following interpretation of Lev 5:12, in which the "priest" (mind) offers a "handful" of good action.

the priest, having grasped the full handful, will also elevate its memorial. Philo cites for a second time (cf. § 234) Lev 5:12, focusing on the two verbs, "grasp" (δραξάμενος) and "elevate" (ἀναφέρω). The first represents the "work" of the mind (the priest), the second, the work of "hands." The two-fold action stems from the mental offering, described as a "memorial" (μνημόσυνον)—memory being a key noetic faculty stimulating action. Although Philo knows the Septuagintal form of this verse, he paraphrases the second verb, replacing the phrase "he will set upon the altar" (ἐπιθήσει ἐπὶ τὸ θυσιαστήριον) with the verb "he will elevate" (ἀνοίσει). This shifts the direction of the priestly action, making it an upward elevation (with God as its referent) rather than a downward placing (focused upon the altar). The material world is lifted up to God.

showing symbolically, through the word handful, "handwork" and "action." Philo articulates the symbolic equivalence, "handful" (δράξ) = "action" (πρᾶξις), interposing "handwork/undertaking" (ἐγχείρημα) as a mediating term. This renders explicit the connection between Lev 5:12 (SBL) and the "hand" of Deut 30:14b (TBL).

§ 250. *very deliberately*. Nothing Moses says, including minor alternations of verb and phrase, is without potential allegorical meaning. In Lev 5:6–12, Philo notices a difference in the qualifying clauses that Moses uses regarding the hoofed-animal and the birds.

if the hand cannot acquire sufficient money for the sheep. Philo adduces Lev 5:7 from the secondary lemma. It was cited previously at § 233 in this form. Philo here omits the personal pronoun in the phrase "his hand," keeping only the catchword.

if he should not find. Philo next adduces Lev 5:11 from the secondary lemma, cited previously at § 234 in the same form. In this case, Philo omits the catchword "hand." The focus is on the contrast between the verbs "cannot" and "find."

why is this? Philo poses a third exegetical question (διὰ τί; ["Why?"]) of the secondary lemma: why is language of potential used of the sheep, whereas the verb for finding is used in the case of the turtle doves? The other two questions on Lev 5:6–12 occur at § 236 (τί δήποτ' οὖν; ["Why then indeed?"]) and § 246 (διὰ τί; ["Why?"]). For Philo's use of questions and Runia's (1984) seven major *aporiae* in the present treatise, see Introduction 2. The Genre, *Sitz im Leben*, and Rhetorical Structure of the Treatise.

because great strength and overwhelming power are necessary. Philo begins answering this third question by interpreting the verb "is strong/able" (ἰσχύῃ) from Lev 5:7. He reiterates a point made above in § 239: that thought is the most difficult faculty to cleanse. Even as sins of thought are "lightest" in culpability, they require the strongest "hand"—i.e., psychological power (see §§ 220, 222)—to purify. Their atonement thus "can" or "cannot" be mustered, depending on the strength of a soul. The purifications for erroneous speech, by contrast, are more easily "found."

to undo the ill turnings of thought. The word translated "turnings," "contortions," or "disturbances" (τροπαί) is in § 235 related to the three therapeutic "manners" (τρόποι) of repentance. Both terms recall the Platonizing allegoresis of the Odysseus soul as one of many "turnings" (*Od.* 1.1), which lead him off course and will need to be corrected by adopting more virtuous "modes" of behavior (cf. § 113, where Moses symbolizes "the virtue-loving manner [τρόπος]").

§ 251. ***a safeguard ... as I said earlier, is silence.*** Having interpreted Lev 5:7 and its significance for purifying the mind, Philo turns to the process of safeguarding speech. He refers to his earlier advocacy for "silence" (ἡσυχία) as a therapeutic strategy in chapters eight (§§ 195–196) and nine (§ 242).

which can easily be used by anyone. Philo is less optimistic about the "ease" (ῥᾴδιον) of this psychagogic method earlier in § 242, where he admits that some may not be strong enough to employ it, despite its relative "affordability" (λυσιτελές).

many ... do not find a limit to set upon their speech. The phrase "do not find" (οὐκ εὑρίσκουσι) echoes Lev 5:11, "if he should not find" (ἐὰν δὲ μὴ εὑρίσκῃ), which gives the exegetical basis of Philo's position on speech as well as on thought.

Parallel Exegesis

§ 216. ***Gen 17:18c ("let this Ishmael live before you").*** For the structure of QG 3.57, see the Parallel Exegesis section on § 201. Philo interprets the phrase "before you" in QG 3.57b as "a life before God, being one of wholeness and salvation, which is on par with immortality" (trans. Marcus, PLCLSup). In *De mutatione nominum*, he postpones treatment of this phrase until the final position, following the sequence of the primary biblical lemma. This is the only significant parallel interpretation of Gen 17:18 in the Philonic corpus.

§ 218. ***even the gifts that are extended.*** For Ishmael's life as a "gift" to be accepted, see QG 3.57a ("it is enough of a gift for me").

Gen 15:6 ("he has come to believe in God"). For Gen 15:6, see the Parallel Exegesis for § 177.

§ 220. ***Num 6:21 ("the power of hands").*** Philo does not interpret this verse elsewhere, according to BiPaSup.

§ 223. ***a fragment.*** The most important parallel to Philo's statement that the human soul is a "fragment" of the divine is found in *Opif.* 146 (see also *Somn.* 1.34): "every human being is kindred with the divine Word on account of his thought, having come into being as an impress or fragment or reflection of the blessed nature" (πᾶς ἄνθρωπος κατὰ μὲν τὴν διάνοιαν ᾠκείωται λόγῳ θείῳ, τῆς μακαρίας φύσεως ἐκμαγεῖον ἢ ἀπόσπασμα ἢ ἀπαύγασμα γεγονώς). Here, Philo gives "reflection" (ἀπαύγασμα) as a synonym for "fragment" (ἀπόσπασμα), which helps link the idea with the Wisdom of Solomon (see the detailed comment on § 223).

the soul of the universe. For similar formulations, which are rare, see *Gig.* 40: "the mind of the universe, God" (ὁ νοῦς τῶν ὅλων, ὁ θεός); *Migr.* 181: "the world soul" (ἡ τοῦ κόσμου ψυχή); and *Aet.* 47, 50, 51, 84. See also *Congr.* 133–134. These references to the world soul may not reflect Philo's own thought.

the divine image. See also *Her.* 58, 231; *Fug.* 13; *Somn.* 2.206; and Sterling 2013b.

§ 224. *Num 13:24(17–33)* (*Moses's spies*). The story of the spies is literally retold in *Mos.* 1.220–231. The most relevant parallel in the Allegorical Commentary occurs in *Somn.* 2.169–171. There, the allegorical reading is similar, though Philo speaks in the personae of the spies ("we were not able to carry ...."). Brief reference to the "spies" (κατάσκοποι) is made in *Post.* 60, but Philo is interested there not in the cluster of grapes but in the Canaanite cities that they visit.

§ 228. *Gen 18:24, 32* (*Abraham "begins with fifty, ends with ten"*). An important parallel to this tradition is found in *QG* 4.27. There, Philo interprets Gen 18:24 as a primary lemma and gives a more complete arithmological account, not only of 50 (connected with the right triangle [$3^2 + 4^2 = 5^2$: $9 + 16 + 25 = 50$], the power of the prophet, and release in the Jubilee year) and 10 (the "all perfect"), but also of 45, 30, 20, and 5. Although the question, "Why does he begin with fifty and end with ten?" is posed in the Armenian, Philo's answer from § 228—that ten represents the middle way of the Ishmael soul, falling short of the perfect 50—is not reflected. All the numbers are praised equally. Closer to the present passage is *Congr.* 109, which interprets Gen 18:24 in close proximity to Lev 25:9–11 (*Congr.* 108) and its promise of "release" (see the next note). There, as in § 228, Sodom is a kind of soul, and the number 10 is the number of accommodation for those who cannot yet reach perfection.

Lev 25:10 (*"release into freedom"*). "Release" is a major Philonic theme and Lev 25:9–11 appears in numerous places as a secondary lemma. In addition to *QG* 4.27, Philo also interprets this verse in *QG* 3.39, the *quaestio* which parallels the opening of *De mutatione nominum*; in *QG* 2.78, where it is used to explain the "fifty" in Noah's 150 years after the flood; and again, in *QG* 2.5, to explain the width of the ark being 50 cubits. In the Allegorical Commentary, important references to this verse occur at *Sacr.* 122 and *Congr.* 107–110. On the former, where Lev 25:10 is also linked with Abraham's prayer for Sodom, see Colson's comments (PLCL 5:261, n. a). Arnaldez (1964, 138, n. 2) highlights the parallel at *Congr.* 107–110. Abraham's prayer for psychic "deliverance" (ἀπόλυσις) is not the same as the Jubilee's "all-perfect release (ἄφεσις) into freedom," but a kind of temporary reprieve to stave off total soul death. Lev 25:10 is also adduced in *Her.*

273, where "release" is proclaimed as the desired end of our moral (and mortal) lives. Arnaldez (1964, 138, n. 2) further references the parallels at *Contempl.* 65 and *Spec.* 2.176–177 (also interpreting Lev 25:9–10), where fifty has this same significance. Elsewhere in the Exposition of the Law, the lemma is interpreted in *Decal.* 164 and *Spec.* 2.110, under the heading of the fourth commandment; and in *Virt.* 99 as an example of "love of humanity" (φιλανθρωπία). Additional examples might be added, but this sampling gives a picture of the breadth and frequency of Philo's engagement with this verse and theme.

§ 230. *Gen 27:38 ("bless me too, father")*. See the parallel at QG 4.231, where Philo says that even Esau knows divine grace is abundant and that God must have some portion for him. Philo also divides between the genus of "blessing" and its various species. A completely different interpretation is given in QG 4.227, where Esau is said to be envious as he seeks the blessing.

§ 232. *Num 11:23 ("will the hand of the Lord fail?")*. This part of the verse is interpreted only here by Philo.

§ 233. *Lev 5:6–12 ("sheep, turtle doves, flour")*. BiPaSup lists QG 2.38 as a parallel, but there is only the scarcest mention of doves being "among the sacrifices." *Spec.* 1.271 mentions briefly the flour/barley offering.

§ 237. *Deut 30:11–14 ("mouth, heart, and hands")*. In *Post.* 84–88, Philo interprets this passage in a similar fashion, pointing out the importance of unity between all three spheres of human volition (likewise, in *Somn.* 2.180). In the Exposition of the Law, Philo interprets this verse *Spec.* 1.301, but there his emphasis is on the nearness of the word, rather than the anthropological division of the person. In *Virt.* 183 and *Praem.* 80, by contrast, both the proximity motif and the anthropological symbolism are mentioned. Finally, the verse is adduced in one of the philosophical treatises, *Prob.* 68, which is remarkable given that Scripture does not figure heavily in this treatise. Philo evidently considered Deut 30:11–14 a statement of Moses's philosophical anthropology (the tripartite division) and ethics (it is not hard), and thereby found ways to incorporate the pericope in several different divisions of his writings. See further Bekken 2007.

Nachleben

§ 216. *Gen 17:18c ("before you")*. Origen, *Sel. Gen.* 12.116 [B], writes of this verse:

> Abraham said to God, "Let this Ishmael live before you" (Gen 17:18). Abraham requested something special (ἐξαίρετόν τι) for Ishmael, not being satisfied (οὐκ ἀρκούμενος) with "let him live" (Gen 17:18b); therefore, he added (προσέθηκεν), "before you" (Gen 17:18c). For "to live before the Lord" belongs to the blessed and saints alone (μακαρίων ... καὶ τῶν ἁγίων μόνων).

Philo's interpretation of Ishmael, like Esau, receiving a second-best portion is absent from Origen's interpretation. He suggests, rather, that "before you" (Gen 17:18c) indicates an unqualified inclusion of Ishmael among the saints and blessed. Even if this interpretation differs from Philo's, Origen's focus on the third part of the verse demonstrates a Philonic division of the pericope into smaller units. Van den Hoek (2000, 63) ranks this passage as probably dependent on Philo [B].

§ 218. *Gen 15:6 ("he has come to believe in God")*. For Gen 15:6, see the *Nachleben* for § 177.

§ 220. *Num 6:21 ("according to the power of hands")*. Eusebius (*Praep. ev.* 8.10.8 [B]) repeats the allegorical tradition that "hands ⟨stand⟩ for the power of God" (τὰς χεῖρας ἐπὶ δυνάμεως εἶναι θεοῦ), deriving this doctrine from several texts from Exodus.

the rationally acute person. Philo's philosophical interpretation of the adjective "near-minded" (ἀγχίνους) finds an analogy in the Byzantine tradition [D], where it was used as an epithet of Thomas Aquinas, the "rationally acute" theologian. The title *anchinous* (ἀγχίνους) was clearly chosen on account of its similarity to the angelic doctor's toponymic surname ("Aquinas"). See Plested 2012, 141.

§ 223. *impression, impulse*. See Origen's discussion of the "impressionable" (φανταστική) and "appetitive" (ὁρμητική) powers of the soul in *Princ.* 2.8.1 [C/D] (Van den Hoek 2000, 109–110).

§ 224. *Num 13:24(17–33)* (*Moses's spies*). Josephus, rewriting this scriptural narrative in *A.J.* 3.302 [C/D], echoes the Philonic paraphrase and has Moses say: "Let us send spies (κατασκόπους), who will learn the virtue of this land (τῆσδε τῆς γῆς ἀρετὴν κατανοήσουσι) and how great a power (πόση δύναμις) belongs to its inhabitants." "Virtue," however, in this context is meant in military and political terms, rather than moral ones. Treatments of the scene by Origen (*Hom. Num.* 8.1, 9.1 [D]) and Eusebius (*Dem. ev.* 4.17.1, 3 [D]) focus on the virtue of Joshua and Caleb relative to the other ten spies, or the typological significance of all twelve, without examining the latter as a symbol of ethical moderation.

§ 226. *servants ... peers*. The right treatment of slaves is also a moral and legal theme in the New Testament. See Col 4:1.

your wife ... your parents. See Col 3:18–21.

§ 228. *Gen 18:24, 32* (*Abraham "begins with fifty, ends with ten"*). Commenting on Num 4:3 (*Hom. Num.* 5.2 [B/C]), which specifies the age for a Levite beginning service between 25 and 50 years, Origen offers some theological notes on the number fifty. He shows potential knowledge of Philo's exegetical tradition, which links Gen 18:24 with Lev 25:10:

That the number fifty holds the mystery of forgiveness and mercy ("remissionis et indulgentiae ... sacramentum"), we have demonstrated often and abundantly in many places in Scripture. For it is the fiftieth year which is called the "Jubilee" among the Hebrews, on which occurs the release ("remissio") of possessions and servitude and debts (Lev 25:10 ["vocabis **remissionem** cunctis habitatoribus terrae tuae: ipse est enim jubilaeus"]). ... But in Genesis, where God was dealing with the forgiveness of the people of Sodom, if by chance they might be able to attain to mercy, the patriarch Abraham, aware of this kind of mystery, begins to make supplication to the Lord for the forgiveness of the people of Sodom from the number fifty ("a quinquagesimo numero incipit") ... (Gen 18:24).

Origen adduces Lev 25:10 before Gen 18:24, following the sequence of *Congr.* 108–109 rather than *Mut.* 228. The former Philonic passage may be the more direct pattern for Origen's homily. Especially striking is the way Origen's paraphrase, that Abraham "begins from the number fifty" ("a quinquagesimo numero incipit") echoes Philo's paraphrases in *Mut.* 228 ("beginning from fifty" [ἀρξάμενος ἀπὸ πεντηκοντάδος]) and *Congr.* 109 ("he begins his supplication from the number of release: fifty" [ἄρχεται μὲν οὖν τῆς ἱκεσίας ἀπὸ τοῦ τῆς ἀφέσεως ἀριθμοῦ, πεντηκοντάδος]). Van den Hoek (2000, 94) ranks this text, as well as *Hom. Gen.* 2.5; *Hom. Num.* 5.2; *Comm. Cant.* 1; and *Comm. Matt.* 11.3 (Van den Hoek 2000, 54, 67, 93, 96) at [C]; I rank it slightly higher [B/C].

Lev 25:10 ("release into freedom"). See the foregoing note.

§ 230. **Gen 27:38 (*"bless me too, father"*).** Hippolytus (*Bened. Is. Jac.* 34 [C/D]) interprets Isaac's response to Esau as a sign that the Word will become incarnate secretively in the form of a servant, to garner a blessing for sinners surreptitiously. John Chrysostom (*Hom. Gen.* 54.469.43–52 [D]) discusses Esau's good rationale for his petition, but Isaac's helplessness to grant it. Of greater interest is Cyril of Alexandria's interpretation of both of Isaac's blessings. In *Glaph. Pent.* 4.6 [B/C], after treating Isaac's blessing of Jacob, he turns to Isaac's blessing of Esau, his "firstborn," whom Cyril interprets as a "type of Israel" according to the old dispensation. On the authority of Matt 5 and Heb 1, Cyril holds that this Esau/the Israel of history receives a true blessing, even if it is not the fullness of Christ given first to "Jacob." The idea that Esau does indeed receive a grace proportionate to his time and nature represents the spirit of Philo's interpretation, even if Cyril's direct dependance upon his work is not demonstrable.

§ 231. **I, unfortunate man that I am.** Philo's autoreferential cry, "I, unfortunate man" (ὁ δυστυχής), which blends his voice with that of Esau, finds a parallel in Rom 7:24, where Paul declares, "I, wretch that I am" (ταλαίπωρος ἐγὼ ἄνθρωπος). Modern interpreters have likewise heard Paul blending or replacing his own voice with a scriptural speaker, such as Adam, Eve, or Cain; or with the universal human (or Gentile) speaker, much as Philo does here. See Tobin 2004, 228–238; Elder 2018.

§ 233. *Lev 5:6–12* (*"sheep, turtle doves, flour"*). Clement of Alexandria knows an anthropological reading of the two turtle doves, vaguely reminiscent of Philonic allegory, which he gives in *Paed.* 1.3 [C/D]:

> God commands through Moses that the young of two doves or a yoke of turtledoves are to be offered for sin, indicating that the sinlessness of sincere people (τὸ ἀναμάρτητον τῶν ἁπαλῶν) and young chicks' absence of evil and malice (ἄκακον καὶ ἀμνησίκακον τῶν νεοττῶν) well befit one another; for he thinks that like cleanses like. But also, the meekness of turtledoves symbolizes caution toward sins (τὴν πρὸς τὰς ἁμαρτίας εὐλάβειαν ὑποτυποῦται).

Origen offers several spiritual interpretations of the three kinds of offerings, though none exactly maps onto Philo's division. In *Hom. Lev.* 2.2 [C] (Van den Hoek 2000, 88), he notes that to offer a pair of doves is to be counted among the higher gifts of the mind. It means "not to be alone, but to associate one's mind with the Word of God, as with a true spouse." The sacrifice of flour, by contrast, is a gift of the soul ("anima") or "psychic human being," which devotes "this life in general ... stationed as one may be in agriculture or in sailing or in any other occupations of life, generally speaking." Here, Philo's allegorical hierarchy of gifts, with the quadrupeds and birds being higher than the agricultural offerings, is represented. Similarly, in *Frag. Luc.* 63 [D], Origen more tersely notes: "I think with the ⟨yoke of⟩ turtle doves, ⟨Moses⟩ signifies the wise and solitude-loving ⟨character⟩" (καὶ οἶμαι διὰ μὲν τῶν τρυγόνων τὸ σῶφρόν τε καὶ φιλέρημον δηλοῦσθαι).

In *Hom. Lev.* 2.4 [C], Origen gives another interpretation of all three kinds of sacrifice. To forgive one's brother or sister from the heart is to offer a ram or a sheep; to meditate on the Scriptures in peace and to a turn a sinner to the Lord is to offer a pair or turtles or two young doves; and to abound in charity is to offer the unmixed bread of sincerity and truth. Van den Hoek (2000, 56) ranks two similar passages (*Hom. Exod.* 3.3; *Hom. Ezech.* 10.1) at [D].

§ 237. *Deut 30:11–14* (*"mouth, heart, and hands"*). Clement of Alexandria relates this Philonic tradition in *Protr.* 10.109.2–3 [A], when he writes of "truth":

> Neither is ⟨truth⟩ difficult to approach, nor impossible to attain, but is very near us in our own homes, as the all-wise Moses says in riddles (ᾗ

φησὶν αἰνιττόμενος ὁ πάνσοφος Μωυσῆς), since it has its abode in three departments of our constitution—in "the hands, the mouth, and the heart" (χερσὶ καὶ στόματι καὶ καρδίᾳ [Deut 30:11–14]). This is a meet emblem this of truth, which is embraced by these three things in all—will and action and speech (βουλῇ καὶ πράξει καὶ λόγῳ). (Trans. W. Wilson, ANF 2, adapted)

it is not necessary to fly up to heaven. For a similar use of Philo's funneling commentary pattern, which begins with a paraphrase and leads to direct citation, see Paul's interpretation of Exod 34:29–35 in 2 Cor 3:7–18 (outlined in Cover 2015, 79).

§ 240. *most perfect form of purification ... nothing out of place.* See similarly Jas 3:2 (also Jas 2:12), in which perfection consists in controlling the tongue's speech, and thereby the actions of the body.

a bridle. As a parallel to Philo's "bridle" (χαλινός), see Jas 3:2 in which right speech enables the wise man to "lead the entire body by a bridle" (δυνατὸς χαλιναγωγῆσαι καὶ ὅλον τὸ σῶμα). Cf. Jas 3:8, which suggests that the tongue cannot truly be controlled.

§ 243. *a word is a shadow of an act.* For a similar halakhic appraisal of the seriousness of what comes "out of the mouth," see Matt 15:18 (cf. par. Mark 7:20, which does not mention the mouth).

[Chapter 10]
Sarah's Child (§§ 252–260)

Having interpreted Abraham's prayer for the life of Ishmael (Gen 17:18) in chapter nine, Philo turns in chapter ten to God's response in Gen 17:19a: "Yes, behold Sarah your wife will bear you a son." The second part of God's answer does not directly reply to Abraham's request—a point not lost on Philo, who takes this as an opportunity to distinguish allegorically between Hagar's child and Sarah's. All commentators agree that the chapter begins at § 252. Although some commentators (Kraus Reggiani and Schur) take §§ 261–263 to be part of the present chapter, I follow Arnaldez and Cohn in seeing §§ 261–263 as a separate chapter, interpreting Gen 17:19b. Alexandre, Jr (1999, 223–233) splits the difference between these views, suggesting that the entirety of §§ 252–263 is the elaboration of an "example story/anecdote" (χρεία), but that §§ 261–263 serves as an "Epilogue" (1999, 231). Further sub-divisions to the chapter are given in the Analysis/General Comments.

Analysis and General Comments

This short chapter divides into five sections. They are similar to the first five units identified by Alexandre, Jr. (1999, 226–233) in his rhetorical study of this section, but were arrived at independently. While I find Alexandre Jr.'s analysis helpful, his use of the later rhetorical pattern of Hermogenes's *Progymnasmata* remains wooden. I print his analysis alongside mine, to show both agreements and divergences.

(1) After reiterating the main argument of chapter nine and his interpretation of Gen 17:18, Philo notes that God answers Abraham's prayer not only by granting life to Ishmael, but also by reaffirming the birth of Isaac (Gen 17:19a). His comments in this first section focus on Gen 17:19aα: the single, ambiguous word "yes" (§§ 252–253). Cf. Alexandre, Jr. (1999, 226), who identifies §§ 252–253a as the first unit, (1) "Word of Praise."

(2) Philo turns to God's promise of a child from Sarah, who is still barren (Gen 17:19aβ). To demonstrate how many scoff at such promises, Philo alludes to a secondary lemma, Gen 29:31—recalling his explicit citation of this text in § 132—which narrates the hated status of another barren matriarch, Leah. Philo adds a new etymology of "Leah" here, which differs from those given elsewhere in the Allegorical Commentary (§§ 254–255a). Cf. Alexandre, Jr. (1999, 226), who identifies §§ 253b–255a as the second unit, (2) "Χρεία."

(3) Philo returns to Gen 17:19aβ and addresses the reader, indicating that virtue (Sarah), not only the middle *paideia* (Hagar), will have a child. Whereas Hagar's child will require further education, Sarah's child will not need a teacher (§ 255b). Cf. Alexandre, Jr. (1999, 227), who labels § 255b as (3) "Rationale and basic reason."

(4) To show that God does produce Isaac souls—however rare—Philo introduces two proofs. The first is drawn from the natural order. Just as there are many faculties in the soul which need no training, but immediately function, so also God can infuse virtue without the agency of a soul. See § 31 for the alternative side of this theology of psychic "election" (§§ 256–258a). Cf. Alexandre, Jr. (1999, 228), who isolates § 256a as (4) "Opposite" in Philo's elaboration of the "anecdote" (χρεία).

(5) Those who prefer scriptural to natural proofs need look no further than the writings of Moses, where God rains down heavenly nourishment on elect souls. Adducing Exod 16:14, 23, as a secondary lemma, Philo offers one of his many homiletical asides on the "bread from heaven," interpreted here as analogous with the grace and perfection afforded to Isaac at his birth. The verse is joined to the primary lemma through the shared word "behold" (§§ 258b–260). Cf. Alexandre, Jr. (1999, 229), who considers

§§ 256b–258a; 259b–260; 262 the fifth part of Philo's rhetorical schema, (5) "Analogy."

Detailed Comments

1. § 252. *divisions and specifications of realities.* Philo says that the Abraham soul has been trained in the philosophical processes of *diairesis* and *synthesis*—terms which were shared by the Hellenistic philosophical schools. Here, he focuses on certain subspecies of *diairesis*: "divisions" (τομαί) and "distinctions" (διαστολαί). Helpful in appreciating these logical processes is Diogenes Laertius's discussion of Stoic contradistinction: "contradistinction (ἀντιδιαίρεσις) is a dissection (τομή) of a genus into a species in relation to its opposite, such as by negation: for example, 'Of existing things, some are good, some are not good.'" (Diogenes Laertius 7.60–62; L&S 32C). This is the kind of division Philo makes between the good and bad "Ishmael" in chapter nine (§ 202), where some people "hear to their benefit," while others "hear to the harm of themselves and others."

to pray that "Ishmael might live." Arnaldez (1964, 148, n. 1) comments: "Ishmael is therefore, at the same time as he is the symbol of the middle education, the type of the human being who, unable to attain to perfect virtue, listens to the law of God and practices the purifications of repentance in order to escape from evil."

in case somehow he is not able to beget Isaac. Philo offers his interlocutor a hypothetical premise ("somehow" [πω]) of the kind used in Stoic logic. For Philo's potential use of hypothetical premises elsewhere in his corpus, see Sterling 1990; Vela 2010. His aim is not to reopen the question of whether Abraham doubted God's promise in a prolonged way (see chapters eight and nine), but rather to prove the reasonableness of his request, even in the extreme (and unreal) situation where such a doubt in the divine promises did exist.

Related to Philo's qualification ("somehow") is the lack of fit between the implied subject (Abraham) and the verb for "beget," literally "bear in the womb" (κυοφορῆσαι). Colson (PLCL 5:270, n. a) comments and wonders: "κυοφορῆσαι ('bear in the womb') rather strangely used for 'beget' (γεννᾶν). Has ἀρετή ('virtue') fallen out?" Arnaldez (1964, 150, n. 1) agrees that the usage is strange, but suggests that if there is a lacuna, "soul" (ψυχή) would more likely be the implicit subject (*Praem.* 63; *Congr.* 129; *Fug.* 211). He continues: "Applied to Abraham (rather than Sarah), the expression is without doubt audacious, and Philo is aware of this, as he adds πω ("somehow")." That Abraham has been a "soul" earlier in the treatise makes Arnaldez's suggestion appealing.

§ 253. *the propitious God.* Philo uses a rare epithet for God, which is a synonym for "gracious." He calls God "propitious" (χρηστός) only in three other places: *QG* 2.54a; *Det.* 46; *Abr.* 203. Alexandre, Jr. (1999, 226) notes that "after a brief *transitio* from the previous section (§ 252), Philo makes reference to the goodness and generosity of God," which serves as the opening "word of praise" preparing the way for an "anecdote" (χρεία).

he gives two ... the greater. Philo "divides" God's response in Gen 17:19a into two parts: (1) "yes" (ναί [Gen 17:19aα]); and (2) "behold, Sarah your wife will bear you a son" (ἰδοὺ Σάρρα ἡ γυνή σου τέξεταί σοι υἱόν [Gen 17:19β]). This is another example of diairetic "division" (τομή) or "distinction" (διαστολή), albeit not "contradistinction," as above in § 202. God's first answer, "yes," is "lesser" in Philo's reckoning, both in word-count and allegorical significance.

he said to Abraham: "Yes, behold Sarah your wife will bear you a son." Philo cites the primary lemma of chapter ten, Gen 17:19a. The text agrees exactly with the Septuagint, but diverges from the Hebrew of the MT (see the following note). According to Alexandre Jr.'s rhetorical analysis, this quotation serves as the *chreia* proper. "The way the text is cited satisfies the essential two attributes of an 'example story' (χρεία), for we are simultaneously in the presence of an action and a personal declaration." Moreover, "the allegorical interpretation that follows in the later section (§§ 255–262) makes manifest its ethical content, pedagogic function and paraenetic intention" (ibid.). NB: Alexandre Jr.'s inclusion of §§ 261–262 as allegorical elaboration of the citation in § 253 misses Philo's citation of a new primary lemma (Gen 17:19b) in § 261. Rhetorical and commentary methods of composition come into conflict with one another at this juncture.

God's symbolic answer, "Yes." God does not mean primarily that a particular child will live, but that God will give life to the hearing kind of soul, represented by Ishmael. NB: Most modern translations read the Hebrew MT particle, אבל, to mean "no" rather than "yes." On this translation, Philo's exegesis of the sentence, in which God reaffirms his promises to both Ishmael and Isaac, would be impossible.

responds directly. Philo's adjective "direct/straight-shooting" (εὐθύβολος) indicates the correspondence of God's first word in LXX Gen 17:19a ("yes") to Abraham's petition ("let this Ishmael live before you"). It also implies that Philo understands the second part of God's answer to respond to a different question—an unspoken or implicit petition by Abraham.

2. § 254. *those things to which God assents.* Including Abraham's requests for both the life of Ishmael and the birth of Isaac. The virtuous children of Sarah and Leah are especially in view, since these perfect virtues are more frequently rejected by the majority for their seeming difficulty.

the oracles introduce Leah as hated. Before mentioning Sarah and Gen 17:19aβ explicitly, Philo turns to her close symbolic counterpart, Leah, who also stands for unloved virtue. He adduces as a secondary lemma Gen 29:31a—a text he cites earlier in §132. The return of certain secondary lemmata in these final chapters of the treatise creates the feel of a "falling allegorical action" or denouement.

she also has the sort of name that signifies this. Despite having already interpreted Leah's character symbolically in §132, Philo here for the first time in the treatise addresses her "appellation" (πρόσρησις). He brings the treatise to a close by commenting on names in several contiguous chapters: Ishmael in chapter nine; Leah in chapter ten; and Isaac in chapter eleven.

the interpretation of Leah is "rejected" and "hard-laboring." Philo gives not one but two etymologies of Leah's name, both of which symbolize the average person's opinion of virtue: they reject it because its demands are too hard. It is unclear whether "rejected" (ἀνανευομένη) is meant as an etymology *per se* or a symbolic connotation arising from the primary etymology, "hard-laboring" or "tiresome" (κοπιῶσα), which is the etymology given at *Migr.* 145. Grabbe (1988, 178) sees Leah's primary etymology as derived from the Hebrew root *l'h* (לאה), "to be weary, impatient." It is possible that Philo's first etymology in § 254 picks up on this "impatient" definition. Alternatively, "'rejected' and 'hard-laboring'" (ἀνανευομένη καὶ κοπιῶσα) might also be rendered "denied, because 'laborious'." It is noteworthy that Philo also uses an additional Greek etymology for Leah twice in the Allegorical Commentary (*Leg.* 2.67; *Congr.* 25). This fact is not mentioned by Grabbe, but noted by Runia (2004, 109). The name Leah is understood to be derived from the Greek adjective *leia* (λεία), meaning "smooth"—almost the opposite of "laborious." Colson, in his comments on *Cher.* 41 (PLCL 2:483), unconvincingly derives this meaning ("smooth") from the Hebrew "not to be weary" (לא לאה) or "not to be faint" (לא להה).

§ 255a. **but she was thought worthy of so great a favor.** Contrary to the opinion of the majority of humanity, God sees virtue in a positive light and gives her the power to produce offspring.

once her womb had been opened by him. Philo alludes to the second part of his secondary lemma, Gen 29:31b.

she received the seed of divine progeny. As in §132, God is understood to be the husband of Sarah and Leah and father of their sons.

3. § 255b. **learn then, O soul.** The fourth of five Philonic ὦ-asides in the present treatise (see the note on §25). Philo returns to his primary biblical lemma, addressing the Abraham soul—and perhaps, his own as well. This is the only time in the present treatise where he speaks to "the soul" (ὦ ψυχή). Terian (1995, 57) argues that 39 such exclamations, including § 255 (Terian 1995, 72), are addressed by Philo to "his ⟨own⟩ mind, soul, or understanding." While

this might be true in other contexts, it would seem that Colson (PLCL) is right in this instance to translate "O soul of man." Philo speaks, in other words, not to his own soul, but to the putative soul of his hearer who identifies with the Abrahamic class (making progress through learning). Alexandre, Jr. (1999, 227) notes that this aside to the soul serves as the "rationale and basic reason" in Philo's rhetorical structure. It is the "reproduction of the χρεία in the form of an argumentative thesis and its primary defense."

that also. Philo's insertion of the word "also" (καί) into his paraphrase of God's response reaffirms the "double" character of Gen 17:19a: "yes" a child from Hagar; but "also" one from Sarah.

Sarah—virtue ... Hagar—the middle education. Philo interpolates the allegorical meanings of Sarah and Hagar into his citation of the primary biblical lemma. Sarah has already been treated as generic virtue or wisdom in §§ 77–78. The explicit reiteration of this allegorical identification creates a ring structure and contributes to the feel of allegorical falling action. Contrarily, although Ishmael has been treated as an allegorical figure in chapter nine, this is the first time Hagar's stock identification with the preliminary studies is mentioned in the present treatise (cf. *De congressu eruditionis gratia*). These features contribute to the growing sense of closure in the treatise, recalling the broader context of the Abrahamic cycle and pointing the reader's attention toward the allegorical matrix underlying the series as a whole.

Hagar's offspring must be taught. This is a curious as well as illuminating statement, as Ishmael's characterization as "taught" (διδακτός) sets him in a spiritual column with Abraham, separating them both from Isaac. See § 88, where Abraham also is presented as "the taught one" (ὁ διδασκόμενος). Philo's focus is on the two kinds of "births" that "taught virtue" produces—the imperfect (Ishmael) or the perfect (Isaac). He continues his positive estimation of Ishmael here, which was begun in chapter nine.

Sarah's offspring is entirely self-taught. The soul-child of virtue (Sarah) has no need of the preliminary studies; it is born with a natural affinity for its mother. This is in keeping with the understanding of Isaac presented in § 88.

4. § 256. *do not be amazed*. Philo opens and closes (§ 258a) his first proof from nature by forestalling the incredulity or "amazement" (θαυμάζειν) of his fictive interlocutor. Alexandre, Jr. (1999, 228) identifies this statement as the formal "opposite" in Philo's elaboration of the "anecdote" (χρεία). "Having just introduced the *locus a contrario* in the *ratio*, and returning to it consistently throughout his argumentative process, the Alexandrian here underscores the contrast between earthly and heavenly virtue."

if God ... also produces this latter kind ⟨of Isaac-soul⟩. Some Stoics denied that the truly wise person exists. Philo's counter-claim goes beyond mere contradiction: not only are there such wise souls on earth, but they are "born this way." To deny this possibility would be to limit the freedom and power of God.

rare on earth but abundant in heaven. Philo grants to the hypothetical Socratic or Stoic that there are very few Isaac souls on earth. Nevertheless, he claims, such souls are abundant in heaven. We are left to wonder whether heaven is populated with Isaac souls *because* they have no bodies, while Abraham and Jacob souls are the class generally characterizing the embodied; or whether they are scarce because God alone makes Isaac souls, whereas Abraham, Jacob, and other psychic types are fashioned imperfectly by Philo's "other craftsmen" (§ 31), who are more numerous.

you could learn why this is fitting from the other bodily members. Philo's first argument for the existence of the Isaac soul on earth is reasoned from analogy. Bodily members, including eyes, nostrils, hands, and feet, need no instruction in order to perform their tasks. Why, Philo asks his interlocutor, might not some souls likewise operate perfectly toward their natural end (virtue, knowledge, worship) without tutelage? Alexandre, Jr. (1999, 229) detects here the first of several arguments from "analogy," which occur in §§ 256b–258a, 259b–260, and 262: "Like the *a contrario* argument, the *similitudo* also permeates the central development of this elaboration. The first structure confirms the validity" of Philo's argument "by demonstrating the existence of autodidactic virtue and its divine origin" (Ibid.).

§ 257. **what about impulses and impressions ... our mind.** In addition to these first four physical faculties, Philo appends three cognitive functions (making a total list of seven): "impulse" (ὁρμή), "impression" (φαντασία), and "intellection" (νοῦς). All three of these are listed earlier among the eight universal gifts of God to human beings by Philo in § 223.

the first movements and dispositions of the soul. In Stoic psychology, impulse and impression precede noetic analysis and confirmation of data gathered by the irrational faculties. For an extended allegory illustrating these processes, see §§ 110–120.

all these ... make use of self-propelling nature. All three cognitive functions, including reason, require no teaching to perform their basic operations. Philo does not mean that all souls by nature reason rightly; most still need *paideia* in philosophy and dialectic. Rather, he means that their reason performs its basic tasks without extensive instruction. Likewise, in speaking of nature as "self-propelling" (ἀπαυτοματίζουσα), Philo does not imply complete autonomy, but indicates the gracious working of God in the natural order. Thus in § 259: "God alone works through his own power" (ὁ μόνος αὐτουργὸς θεός).

§ 258a. **why then do you still wonder?** An echo of the first question in § 256, creating a ring composition and drawing the first proof to a close. Arnaldez

(1964, 152, n. 1) summarizes the argument: "The intuition of the senses is the sign that renders comprehensible the possibility of the intelligible intuition of virtue, illustrative for those who have not yet experienced it."

if God will also shower down. Although Philo has not yet adduced the secondary lemma (Exod 16:4), his verb "shower down" (ὀμβρήσει) sounds as a *Vorklang* of "I am raining" (ὕω) in the verse about to be cited in the second proof.

virtue ... complete and perfect. In this passage, Isaac does not signify the self-taught mind, but perfect, self-taught virtue—an allegorical child of Sarah (generic virtue). It is this virtue that is born to the Abraham soul when he reaches the age of perfection. It is fitting that the birth of Isaac, with which the treatise also began (§ 1), which played a critical role in the eponymous fifth chapter (§ 88), and which provided the central theme of chapter six (§§ 145–147); should serve as the treatise's closing bookend as well.

from the beginning. A pregnant metaphysical and cosmological addition. Isaac is not only the symbol of the soul born perfect; as son of God (by Sarah), he also mirrors the Logos.

5. § 258b. *if you also wish to have a witness of this ... Moses.* In deliberative rhetorical style, Philo varies his proofs and introduces a witness to support his argument—in this case, the written witness of Moses. Alexandre, Jr. (1999, 230) says of this second proof from "analogy": "the comparison of education with agriculture is developed .... The heavenly bread, here analogically interpreted as 'virtue' and 'divine wisdom' poured out on the soul, is spontaneously engendered and automatically gathered as the perfect 'manna' of abundant philosophy" (Ibid.).

for other human beings, nourishments come from the earth. Philo means this primarily at the literal level: most human beings eat food produced from the earth. It is not entirely clear whether he has an explicit text of Moses in mind to this effect. More likely, his first claim is an inversion of the second—that only the seeing soul (= Israel [§ 81]) receives nourishments "from heaven"; therefore all others are naturally fed from earth. To support this interpretation, he draws on a well-worn secondary lemma, Exod 16:4. The plural "nourishments" (αἱ τροφαί) reflects the plural of the Exodus lemma, "breads" (ἄρτοι).

for one alone—the visionary class (i.e., Israel)—they come from heaven. The "one" is literally the people of Israel, but allegorically the Israel soul. Philo shifts his focus here to the allegorical level. He views God's provision of manna in the wilderness as provision to a singular Israel—the "seeing human being" (ὁρατικὸς ἄνθρωπος). This title is used earlier of Israel's firstborn, Reuben (§ 98), interpreted as "seeing son"; of the entire "seeing class" of Israelite souls (§ 109); of Shem, "firstborn of the seeing class" (§ 189); and of the "seeing mind"—Israel, liberated from Egypt by Moses (§ 209). Thinking especially of the last case,

Philo now turns to the seeing soul's peregrinations in the material wilderness, during which it is nourished with bread from heaven.

§ 259. *who alone works through his own power*. In § 257, Philo spoke of nature as "self-propelling" (ἀπαυτοματίζουσα). He now qualifies that epithet, noting that it is not truly nature that works, but "God, who alone works through his own power" (ὁ μόνος αὐτουργὸς θεός), animating nature.

without the collaboration of others. Philo's description of God's operation "apart from the collaboration of others" (χωρὶς συμπράψεως ἑτέρων) exhibits his monotheistic commitments. It stands in some tension with his suggestion in § 31 that God allows some human souls to be created by the "craftsmanship of others" (ἑτέρων ... δημιούργημα). The passages are not in strict contradiction, however, as the former merely states that God does not collaborate in any real relation with other powers or ministers. He might, nonetheless, appoint them certain tasks to carry out on their own.

sends down like snow. The verb "to snow down" (νίφειν) is a paraphrastic equivalent of "to rain" (ὕειν), reflecting the Israelites' description of manna in Exod 16:14 as "white like frost" (λευκὸν ὡσεὶ πάγος).

nourishments from heaven. Just as Philo speaks of many earthly "nourishments" (§ 257), so now he speaks of a plurality of heavenly "nourishments"—presumably, the various generic virtues. This is in keeping with the text of Exodus 16:4, which speaks of God giving "breads" (ἄρτοι), not simply "bread" (though the singular is kept in the translation).

"behold, I rain down on you bread from heaven." Philo cites the secondary lemma that he has already begun interpreting: Exod 16:4. The text of Philo's citation shows some minor differences from the Septuagint, as may be seen in the following synopsis.

Exod 16:4	§ 259
Behold, I myself (ἐγὼ ὕω) rain on you bread (ἄρτους) from heaven (ἐκ τοῦ οὐρανοῦ).	Behold I rain (ὕω) on you bread (ἄρτους) from heaven (ἀπ' οὐρανοῦ).

While such minor divergences do not affect Philo's exegesis greatly, in a text as well-commented upon as this one (see Borgen 1965), they are worth noting for comparative purposes. I have rendered "bread" singular in the translation, but from an exegetical standpoint, its plural number in the Septuagint shapes Philo's interpretation.

what nourishment is rightly said to be rained down. By speaking of "nourishment" (τροφή) now in the singular rather than "nourishments" (τροφαί) in the plural as previously, Philo makes an important point. While he has up till now been distinguishing physical, earthly "nourishments" from spiritual, heavenly "nourishments"—reflecting the plural noun "breads" (ἄρτοι) in Exod 16:4—he now references a singular heavenly "nourishment" (τροφή), which will signify a singular intellectual good. Philo finds a warrant for this alternation in Exod 16:15, where Moses explains to the wondering Israelites: "this is the bread, which the Lord gave you to eat" (οὗτος ὁ ἄρτος, ὃν ἔδωκεν κύριος ὑμῖν φαγεῖν). A play on the alternation between "breads" and "bread" was part of a Platonizing exegetical tradition in circulation in Second Temple Judaism. The thrust of this tradition is to focus on the divine singularity of the heavenly gift, which betokens formal reality and eternality, as opposed to created multiplicity, which is transient.

except the heavenly wisdom. Having transitioned from "nourishments" (Exod 16:4) to "nourishment" (Exod 16:15), Philo can now unveil the full allegorical significance of the manna as the singular and generic "heavenly wisdom" (ἡ οὐρανία σοφία [cf. *Leg.* 3.252]). Whereas "wisdom" elsewhere in Philo's Abrahamic cycle—particularly as a pedagogical good—is symbolized by Sarah (see *Congr.* 13), here it is Isaac who stands for the wisdom rained down from heaven. Sarah, in keeping with her primary allegorical equivalent (virtue), may be seen as the mother of such heavenly wisdom.

Excursus C: Allegorical Elasticity

I have noted the occasional inconsistency or slippage in Philo's various allegorical equivalences, including the example of heavenly wisdom (Sarah/Isaac) above. Because this phenomenon pervades Philo's works, a few words on this subject are in order. First, it is worth recalling the adage deployed by Emerson in *Self-Reliance*, that "a foolish consistency is the hobgoblin of little minds, adored by little statesmen and philosophers and divines." What we see in Philo's ability to associate *both* Sarah and Isaac with wisdom is not, to the contrary, a cavalier *inconsistency*, but rather the allegorical elasticity characteristic of a capacious and architectonic mind. This allows Philo to draw out a seemingly endless array of symbolic associations from the texts of Moses. In Philo's primary allegorical system in this treatise, Abraham is a soul/mind, Sarah is virtue, and Isaac is joy; but each can take on alternative roles when the reading calls for it. Second, it is worth remembering that part of the impetus of Philo's allegorical elasticity—in addition to his possessing a capacious and creative mind—is the hard fact that he is collecting and meshing together a variety of traditional exegeses of the Pentateuch, which do not always match up with each other. The source-critical horizon and Philo's anthological habit are not to be forgotten; but neither should they lead the critic to preclude Philo's intentional foregoing of a foolish consistency for the sake of creating a more fluid and expansive allegorical picture.

§ 260. *he, who has a plenteous abundance of practical wisdom*. God is imagined as a heavenly farmer growing the virtues in their generic form. "A fruitful abundance" renders the hendiadys "prosperity and good season" (εὐθηνία καὶ εὐετηρία). The latter word in this pairing looks ahead to the theme of allegorical "perfection time" in chapter twelve.

and waters all things. An allusion to the main verb of the secondary biblical lemma, "to rain" (ὕειν).

the souls which have a desire for virtue. For ἵμερος as Platonic "desire," redolent of the *Phaedrus*, see the comment on § 174.

this he does especially on the holy seventh day. Philo considers the Sabbath as a special day of grace and virtue—a point which he affirms in *Hypoth.* 8.7.13. In § 260, he refers to God's special providence for manna on the Sabbath (such that the Israelites do not have to collect it on the seventh day).

which Moses calls the Sabbath. An allusion, according to PCW, to the double-portion of manna given on Fridays in Exod 16:23–26. Moses mentions the Sabbath in these verses; however, Philo's ensuing description of *sua sponte* production of virtue on the Sabbath seems more general and not tied to the context of Exod 16. So Colson (PLCL 5:274–275, n. a) correctly: "Wendland gives the reference for this as Exod 16:23 ff. But this can hardly be right .... The reference is clearly to the Sabbatical year of Lev 25:4–5, definitely called "Sabbath," on which ⟨Philo⟩ has dwelt in *Fug.* 170 ff." Arnaldez (1964, 152, n. 2) follows Colson. Some blending of both texts and ideas is probable. For "Sabbath" (ἑβδόμη ⟨ἡμέρα⟩) used for "seven" (ἑβδομάς), see the note on § 144.

the production of goods ... automatically. An allusion to Exod 16:29, in which the Israelites are commanded *not* to go out and collect manna but to sit at home.

rising up from the earth not by any skill. For farming and agriculture as symbols of cultivating the virtues and weeding the vices in the soul, see the treatises of the Noahic cycle, esp. *De agricultura* and *De plantatione* (e.g., *Agr.* 7: "the ⟨skill⟩ of psychic agriculture" [ἡ ... ψυχῆς γεωργικὴ ⟨τεχνή⟩]).

blooming ... by means of self-begetting and self-perfecting nature. The Sabbath is presented as a kind of weekly golden age, begetting (from above) fruit-bearing plants of virtue in the soul *sua sponte*. Cf. Vergil, *Ecl.* 4.39–45: "the whole earth will put forth all things; / the ground will not endure rakes, nor the vine the pruning hook / .... *sua sponte*, vermilion will clothe the feeding lambs" ("... omnis feret omnia tellus; / non rastros patietur humus, non vinea falcem; / .... sponte sua sandyx pascentis vestiet agnos"). As in §257, where nature is described as "self-propelling" (ἀπαυτοματίζουσα), so here the epithets "self-begetting" (αὐτογενής) and "self-perfecting" (αὐτοτελής) do not imply that created nature has any truly self-sustaining autonomy of a Lucretian or Stoic fashion. God's grace, operative in nature, is presumed. Alesse (2008, 3) follows Theiler (1965) in identifying the epithet "self-begetting" (αὐτογενής) as a term drawn from Antiochus of Ascalon, via the school of Eudorus of Alexandria.

Parallel Exegesis

§ 253. *Gen 17:19 ("yes, behold Sarah your wife will bear you a son")*. We are in the fortunate position with QG 3.58, Philo's parallel exegesis of Gen 17:19 in this series, to possess what looks to be a relatively trustworthy and complete Greek text of the *solutio* in the writings of Procopius. The Armenian and the Greek are very close, with the ironic exception that Procopius omits the critical Greek word "yes" (ναί) from his initial lemma of Gen 17:19, writing instead "and" (καί), which may be an error or a recensional translation of the Hebrew אבל. Structurally, QG 3.58 addresses the text of Gen 17:19 in a less complete and systematic manner than chapter ten of the present treatise. Whereas Philo spends §§ 252–254 on "yes" (Gen 17:19aα) and §§ 255–260 on "behold, Sarah your wife will bear you a son" (Gen 17:19aβ), in QG 3.58 Philo's entire comment is framed on the word "yes," as indicated by the final line. That this is the subject of the *solutio* is also shown by the *quaestio*, only preserved in Armenian, which begins "Why is the divine oracle an assent (յաձանկալութիւն)?" Philo's answer is a two-fold ratification of the covenant: God's "yes" means that he himself is to keep the agreement about the birth of Isaac (QG 3.58a). Because Abraham's faith is in fact unwavering, he will receive the joy which was promised (QG 3.58b). Most importantly and divergently, Isaac (rather than Ishmael) is the object of God's "yes" in QG 3.58. Philo also interprets God's response to Abraham in Gen 17:19 in *Leg.* 3.85. There, he similarly sees God "ratifying and confirming" (καταφάσκει καὶ ἐπινεύει) the former covenant, with only the promise of Isaac, not of Ishmael, in view.

he gives two ... the lesser thing ... the greater. Because Philo understands the "yes" of God's reply to refer to Isaac in QG 3.58, he does not yet turn to God's double gift of Isaac and Ishmael together until QG 3.59a. There, presuming that God now properly addresses Abraham's petition in Gen 17:18, Philo summarizes God's speech to mean, "Both the first and the second good things ... I grant to you."

God's symbolic answer, "yes." Marcus renders the word յաձանկալութիւն as "agreement," but notes (PLCLSup 1:260, n. j) that "assent" (ἐπίνευσις) is an alternative translation (NBHL gives "agreement": յուււձւււսոոււքհււս, συνχώρησις, λῆψις, *acceptio*). The focus on God's "nod" in § 253 (see also *Leg.* 3.85: "ratifying and confirming" [καταφάσκει καὶ ἐπινεύει]) supports the general thrust of this suggestion and makes Marcus's proposed Greek probable.

§ 254. Gen 19:31 (*"the Lord, seeing that Leah was hated, opened her womb"*). See the Parallel Exegesis for § 132. Colson (PLCL 5:273, n. a) cross-references *Cher.* 41.

§ 255. *while Hagar's offspring must be taught, Sarah's offspring ... self-taught*. Philo's closest parallel to this statement is postponed until QG 3.59 for formal-exegetical reasons: "By nature is that which comes through the genuine Isaac, and by teaching is that which comes through the not-genuine Ishmael" (Marcus, PLCLSup). As Marcus (PLCLSup 1:261, n. g) points out, "in the parallel ⟨in *De mutatione nominum*⟩, Philo calls Ishmael ἔγγονον διδακτόν ("taught offspring") and Isaac αὐτομαθής ("self-taught")."

§ 259. Exod 16:4 (*"behold, I rain down on you bread from heaven"*). God's feeding of Israel with manna in the wilderness—"bread from heaven"—is a recurring exegetical theme in Philo's *œuvre*. It was the subject of an important monograph by Peder Borgen (1981). This study, which traces rabbinic and New Testament parallels, is still required reading for anyone interested in the subject. Major parallel interpretations of Exod 16:4 in Philo appear in *Leg.* 3.162–173 (cf. 3.174–176 on Deut 8:3); *Congr.* 173–174; *Fug.* 137–139; and in the Exposition of the Law, in *Mos.* 2.258–269 and *Decal.* 15–17.

what nourishment is rightly said to be rained down. For an important parallel to Philo's modulation to the singular heavenly "nourishment" (τροφή) in his allegorical exegesis, see *Leg.* 3.162, in which the "heavenly nourishments" (οὐράνιοι ... τροφαί) are interpreted as the singular Logos.

Nachleben

§ 253. *Gen 17:19 ("yes, behold Sarah your wife will bear you a son")*. As mentioned in the Parallel Exegesis, Philo's interpretation of God's "yes" in QG 3.58 is preserved by Procopius, *Comm. Gen.* 17.4:

> "Yes, behold Sarah your wife will bear you a son" (Gen 17:19). My confession (ἡ ὁμολογία), he says, is my unequivocal assent (ἡ ἐμὴ κατάφασις ... ἀκραιφνής), unmixed with denial (ἀμιγὴς ἀρνήσεως). And your faith is not uncertain (οὐκ ἀμφίβολος), but unwavering (ἀλλ' ἀνενδοίαστος), joined with reference and modesty. For this reason, the ⟨promise⟩ that you received from me beforehand, this will completely come to pass in accordance with your faith in me (διὰ τὴν πρὸς ἐμὲ πίστιν). This is what the "yes" signifies (τοῦτο γὰρ μηνύει τὸ «ναί»).

§ 254. *Gen 19:31 ("the Lord, seeing that Leah was hated, opened her womb")*. See the Nachleben for § 132.

§ 259. *Exod 16:4 ("behold, I rain down on you bread from heaven")*. Philo's interpretation of Exod 16:4, 15, would prove influential on later Christian authors. This is due, in part, to the importance of this pericope (as well as LXX Ps 77:24) for the Bread of Life Discourse in John 6:30–58. For the citation of the composite lemma, see John 6:31. At the level of exegetical pattern, the Philonic passages (see the Parallel Exegesis) have much in common with the Fourth Evangelist: see Borgen 1981 and Cover 2015, 182–195. Thematically, Philo shares the motif of heavenly nourishment with the first part of Jesus's homily (John 6:30–51b). John 5:51c–58, however, sets out in a different and decidedly Christian direction.

Philo and John did not know each other's works; neither do they comment on the same primary lemma. What they share is explainable in terms of common Jewish commentary tradition. This would not stop Origen (*Comm. Jo.* 6.45.236 [A]; not mentioned by Van den Hoek 2000) from harmonizing their interpretations. So, for example, commenting on John 6:49–51, he writes in both a Philonic and Pauline manner:

> The manna, if also it is given from God, was the bread of progress (ἄρτος ἦν προκοπῆς), bread supplied for those who are still being instructed (τοῖς ἔτι παιδαγωγουμένοις), bread most fitting for those under overseers and stewards.

Although the primary lens through which the Johannine pericope is read is Gal 3:23–25, the language of "progress" is unmistakably Philonic, and under its influence, Paul's image of the "school-slave" (παιδαγωγός) becomes an active participle denoting the process of education and instruction (see Philo, *Somn.* 2.165; *Spec.* 4.218).

Similarly, although he is involved in a polemic against Jewish interlocutors, Origen takes up Philonic tradition in his comments on Exod 16:4 in *Hom. Exod.* 7.5 [B/C] (Van den Hoek 2000, 58 [C]). He interprets the manna both as the Eucharist (it seems) and as a kind of daily "heavenly wisdom" (ἡ οὐράνιος σοφία [§ 259]):

> On our day (i.e., the Lord's Day), the Lord always "rains down manna from heaven" (Exod 16:4). But I also say that *today* (Heb 4:7) the Lord "rains down manna from heaven." For these declarations, which have been read by us, are heavenly ("coelestia ... sunt eloquia ista"); and the words ("verba"), which are recited by us, descended from God; and thus,

since we have received such manna, to us manna is always given from heaven ("semper ... datur de coelo").

Origen's "heavenly words" ("coelestia verba") echo Philo's "heavenly wisdom" (ἡ οὐράνιος σοφία), which "is given" ("datur" [John 6:32]; cf. *Mut.* 260, "he sends" [ἐπιπέμπει], for the allegorical present).

what nourishment is rightly said to be rained down. Philo's modulation to the singular "nourishment" (τροφή) from the plural "nourishments" finds a parallel in the exegesis of the author of the Fourth Gospel. In John 6:26, answering a hungry crowd seeking a sign from Exodus, Jesus says (echoing Philo's "nourishments from earth" [τροφαί ἀπὸ γῆς]), "you ate the breads (ἐκ τῶν ἄρτων) and were satisfied" (cf. Exod 16:4). Jesus then suggests to the crowds that they seek not "the food that is perishing but the food that leads to eternal life," in both cases shifting to the accusative singular noun "food" (βρῶσις [John 16:17; cf. Exod 16:15]). When the crowds reply with Scripture, "He gave them bread from heaven to eat," they have adopted Jesus's singular, meshing LXX Ps 77:24 with Exod 16:4, 15. This prepares the way for the Logocentric exegesis which follows.

the heavenly wisdom. A similar allegoresis of the manna appears in the Fourth Gospel: rather than the "bread" being Isaac, the heavenly "wisdom" (σοφία), it is Jesus, the incarnate "Word" (λόγος). Without positing a genetic connection, Philo's text leads us to the exegetical and Platonizing roots of Johannine Christology, even while revealing those roots to be ineluctably Jewish.

§ 260. *from above.* ἄνωθεν. Cf. John 3:3, 7.

[Chapter 11]
You Will Call His Name Joy (§§ 261–263)

This very short, antepenultimate chapter, despite its relative brevity, is rich in meaning and pathos. Treated by Kraus Reggiani and Schur as part of the foregoing chapter, and by Alexandre, Jr. (1999, 231) as a fifth section "(5) Analogy" and an "(6) Epilogue" of the same, Philo's introduction of a new primary lemma (Gen 17:19b) in § 261 and his separate treatment of this verse in QG 3.59 warrant partitioning these sections as an independent chapter. Philo's shift in thematic focus further validates this decision. Here at last, God reveals to Abraham in the primary biblical lemma what to name his promised son. In a treatise which begins with the namelessness of God (chapter one) and which centers on the change of Isaac's parents' names (chapter five), Philo's dedication of a chapter to the naming of Isaac—the child whose name does *not* change (since given by God)—can make some claim to being a kind of belated climax, despite the repetitious character of its content and the many indications of allegorical falling action already noted. Also indicative of the twilight of the treatise is the rapidity with which Philo treats the primary lemma, interpreting Gen 17:19–21a in a mere three sections.

Analysis and General Comments

This chapter divides into three parts, which align with the PCW treatise sections:

(1) Philo recapitulates, in a single verse, the principal point of his interpretation of Gen 17:19a in chapter ten: virtue will bear a son. Then, citing part of Gen 17:19b ("you shall call the name ⟨of him Isaac⟩") and interpreting Isaac's name in keeping with his previous etymological exegesis (§ 1, etc.), Philo explicates the significance of the emotion, "joy," within the soul of the perfected sage (§ 261).

(2) Philo defends the emotions more generally—continuing the apology for Abraham's experience of an emotion at such an advanced stage of perfection (§ 262).

(3) Despite the connective "therefore" (διό), which might link § 263 with the foregoing § 262, the last section of this chapter offers a *summa* of the foregoing two chapters (nine and ten), derived from Gen 17:20 and 21, respectively: Ishmael and Isaac represent two types or paths of virtue—Ishmael for souls of a weaker type, Isaac for those with innate virtue (§ 263).

Detailed Comments

1.§ 261. *"virtue, therefore, will bear you a son."* Philo summarizes the principal allegorical message derived from Gen 17:19a in chapter ten (esp. § 255).

"noble." The adjective "noble" (γενναῖος) means more than just "well-born" to a good family. In Philo's moral register, it denotes perfect natural constitution for virtue, which in Isaac's case is somewhat tautological. Philo devotes a sub-treatise to "nobility" (εὐγένεια) in *Virt.* 187–227, in which the adjective "noble" (γενναῖος) does not feature—the synonym, "well-born" (εὐγενής), being preferred. See Wilson 2011.

"male, removed from all female emotion." On the basis of other passages in the Allegorical Commentary, this pairing of gender descriptors might seem to suggest that "male" means "noetic" or "rational"; while "female" indicates "corporeal," "sensual," and "emotional." In fact, Philo makes a more nuanced distinction. Recall that Isaac symbolizes joy—"the best of the good emotions" (§ 1)—such that the complete excision of "emotion" (πάθος [§ 261]) in the Abrahamic soul cannot be Philo's intended meaning. Instead, Philo wants to distinguish between male and female emotions—with male being the specifier for

the "good" or "rational emotion" (εὐπάθεια). These are the forms of emotion, which are truly "felt" (as the following sentence will say), but which do not disturb the "governing faculty" (τὸ ἡγεμονικόν) or "mind" (νοῦς) in its steering the chariot soul in virtuous action.

"and you will call the name of your son ... joy." Philo now cites, without formula, a paraphrased portion of his primary biblical lemma for this chapter: Gen 17:19b. Whereas the Septuagint reads "and you will call his name Isaac" (καὶ καλέσεις τὸ ὄνομα αὐτοῦ Ἰσαάκ), Philo paraphrases this to read "you will call your son's name ... Joy" (καλέσεις τὸ ὄνομα τοῦ υἱοῦ ... χαράν). Immediately striking is the fact that "Isaac" has been omitted. Of course, the etymologizing of Isaac's name in this treatise is so frequent (§§ 1, 131, 161–163, 175, 188) that Philo can take the association for granted. Nevertheless, as this section contains the last two occurrences of the noun "name" (ὄνομα) referring to a human being in the treatise, the removal of "Isaac" requires some accounting for. One rationale is that while Philo cannot say that Isaac's name has changed (§ 88), in homage to the theme of his treatise, he has rhetorically "changed" Isaac's name in another way, by placing its allegorical equivalent directly in the verse. God tells Abraham not Isaac's literal name but the thing it stands for. It is as though, with this paraphrase, the reader hears through the veil beyond the human "name" (ὄνομα) to the "thing itself" (πρᾶγμα).

"the emotion which you feel for him (and you will feel it entirely)." In addition to calling "joy" (χαρά) an "emotion" (πάθος) rather than a "good emotion" (εὐπάθεια), as at §§ 1, 131, 188, Philo twice reiterates (in both the present and future tenses) the verb "suffer/endure" (πάσχειν). There can be no missing the paradox of his claim that the perfected soul still experiences certain emotions—a conviction which arises from his Jewish and Platonist commitments.

"you will also make his name a symbol of this emotion: laughter." This second command offers a window into Philo's understanding of God's speech to Abraham and the process of inspiration. Although God first reveals to Abraham the true meaning of his son, which is the philosophical good emotion ("joy"), Philo then suggests that God asks Abraham to use a slightly different name as a symbol: "laughter" (for this etymology, see §§ 131, 137, 154, 157). This is still not the Hebrew name, Isaac. Philo's God—who loves to hide himself (cf. § 60)—intentionally sets up the etymological riddle to be solved by those who hear Abraham's story.

2. § 262. *sorrow and fear*. For this pair of bad emotions, corresponding with joy and hope, see § 163. Alexandre, Jr. (1999, 231) treats this section as a further proof for the "anecdote" (χρεία) in chapter ten. In truth, however, it supports the proposition that Abraham's child will be named "laughter" (Gen 17:19b), not the proposition that "Sarah will bear a son" (Gen 17:19a).

their own appropriate shouts. Philo thinks, perhaps, of tragic/dramatic expressions like "alas!" (οἴμοι/ᾤμοι/ὤμοι), as well as less standardized cries and expletives. See Lateiner and Spatharas 2016.

coins. Philo uses the rare verb "to make a name" (ὀνοματοποεῖν), found only in this treatise (§§ 160, 262). For more on the use of this verb in the *Cratylus* and its significance for Philo's hermeneutics, see the detailed comment on § 160. Whereas in § 160, it is "custom" (ἔθος) which serves as name-maker, in § 262 this role is played by "nature" (φύσις). In espousing the partial truth of both the "conventionalist" and "naturalist" schools of language, Philo follows Plato's moderate approach, counterbalancing the conventionalism of Hermogenes with the naturalism of Cratylus. For the argument that names follow nature in some respect, see *Crat.* 389c3–8; 390e3. Socrates goes on to argue, in the first half of the dialogue (*Crat.* 394d), that certain naming patterns would be "according to nature" (κατὰ φύσιν) or "against nature" (παρὰ φύσιν).

by violence and force. Such exclamations are viewed by Philo as involuntary and, when governed by the bad emotions, irrational at best and vicious at worst.

good counsels and merriments ... natural expressions. Philo defends laughter as naturally connected to joy. By using the phrase "natural expressions" (φυσικαὶ ἐκφωνήσεις), Philo partially sides with the "naturalist" view of language, common to Cratylus (in the *Cratylus*) and the Stoics. He will go on to mention the Platonic view in this same sentence, admitting some truth to the "conventionalist" approach (see § 160). On the whole, then, Philo's philosophy of language is Platonist, with critical modifications made on behalf of his Jewish understanding of the inspiration of the Pentateuch.

one could not find more proper and accurate titles. Philo says that shouts like laughter resulting from joy in the soul are "more proper" (κυριώτεραι) than any rationally signifier. Like his discussion of the elusiveness of "proper names" (κύρια ὀνόματα) with regard to God (see §§ 11–13, 27), so here, with regard to the mystery of Abraham's son by virtue, the rational signifier is withheld. It is a part of the rhetorical unity of the work that discussions of proper names, related to God and Isaac, bookend the treatise.

even if one happens to be wise concerning appellations. Philo refers here to the "technical" understanding of name-giving, which is neither purely naturalist nor conventionalist, and perhaps most closely approximates Plato's view in the *Cratylus*. Thus, in 392c, he speaks of the Trojan men being "more prudent" (φρονιμώτεροι) and "wiser" (σοφώτεροι) with respect to names. Cf. *Crat.* 399a5, where Socrates speaks (with a touch of irony) of himself becoming "wiser" (σοφώτερος) in this same skill-set. Plato's ironic tone is imitated in Philo's conditional here.

3. § 263. *therefore, God says*. As noted in the general comment, "therefore" (διό) does not refer back to §§ 261–262, but to the cumulative arguments of chapter nine on Ishmael and chapter ten on Isaac.

"I have blessed him ... he will beget twelve nations." Philo continues at breakneck speed through his primary lemma, citing Gen 17:20 in a truncated form:

Gen 17:20	§ 263
And concerning Ishmael, see, I have heard you. See, I have blessed him and I will increase him and make him very numerous; he will beget twelve nations, and I will give him for a great nation.	I have blessed him I will increase him ... I will make ⟨him⟩ numerous; he will beget twelve nations.

Although Philo rightly reads this sentence as a summary of the foregoing promises to Ishmael, he pares down God's culminating words, removing the polysyndeton and the reference to the "great nation," which potentially overlap with the promise already made to Abraham through Isaac in Gen 17:5–6, 16.

the whole cyclical chorus of sophistic preliminary topics. This gloss suggests that a series of twelve disciplines or subtopics of study are signified by Ishmael's twelve nations. Was there any such ancient list of preliminary studies, or is this merely a convenient typological number? Before answering this question, a more basic issue must be settled: does the phrase "sophistic preliminary studies" (σοφιστικὰ προπαιδεύματα) refer to the general course of pre-philosophical topics, such as those mentioned in *Congr.* 11 and associated with Hagar? Or does Philo refer to the rhetorical *progymnasmata* specifically—such as those mentioned in the list of Aelius Theon? The latter makes more sense of the adjective "sophistic" (σοφιστικά) and more easily leads to the number twelve. However, as Philo routinely understands Hagar as the preliminary studies, both options will be considered below. For a treatment of this subject more broadly, see Mendelson 1982.

Option A ("Sophistic Preliminary Studies" = General Preliminary Studies [Hagar]): As already noted at § 146, Philo lists five or six basic subfields in *Congr.* 11: grammar, geometry, astronomy, rhetoric, music and "every other branch of rational inquiry." At *Congr.* 18, Philo speaks of "dialectic" as the twin of rhetoric. Grammar, in *Congr.* 74 and 148, is further divisible into reading, writing, poetry and prose literature. Music, in *Congr.* 76 (cf. *Agr.* 137) is further divisible into rhythm, harmony, and melody. This gives roughly eleven or twelve, as counted in *De congressu eruditionis gratia*. The weakness of this view, in addition to the subjectivity of subdividing major fields, is that this group is represented by Hagar (*Congr.* 11), not Ishmael (as in § 263).

Option B ("Sophistic Preliminary Studies" = Rhetorical *progymnasmata* [Ishmael]): This view takes Philo's statement to point to an early division of rhetorical *progymnasmata* into twelve subdivisions. There are five ancient handbooks, composed in different centuries, that are usually used to reconstruct these training exercises: Aelius Theon, Hermogenes, Aphthonius, Nicolaus, and Libanius. All five are succinctly summarized in Kennedy 2003. Aphthonius (4th century CE), whose list is the most widely used, lists fourteen kinds of exercise. Potentially the oldest list of these was written by Aelius Theon, an Alexandrian rhetorician who flourished, according to the traditional chronology, roughly during the first century CE (dated first century CE by, e.g., Kennedy [2003], 2; cf. Heath [2003] for a fifth-century CE dating). Following Kennedy's translation (2003, 4–5), Theon lists ten principal kinds of rhetorical *progymnasmata*, to be practiced by students: 1. "narration" (διήγησις); 2. "fable" (μῦθος); 3. "anecdote" (χρεία); 4. "commonplace" (τόπος); 5. "description" (ἔκφρασις); 6. "personification" (προσωποποιΐα); 7. "comparison" (σύγκρισις); 8. "thesis" (θέσις); 9. "laws" (νόμοι); 10. "encomium" (ἐγκώμιον). A simple way to reach 12 might be to add deliberative and judicial rhetoric (after epideictic rhetoric *qua* "encomium"), which Theon mentions in the preface. Theon seems to see these as more advanced, and hence not a proper part of the *progymnasmata*. Alternatively, one could subdivide "personification" into "speech in character" (προσωποποιΐα) and "construction of character" (ἠθοποιΐα), as the later lists, and add "invective" to "encomium" (ἐγκώμιον).

This second option has much to commend it. Not only does it naturally lead to a list of 10–12 studies; Philo's own description, "sophistic preliminary studies" (σοφιστικὰ προπαιδεύματα) points to rhetorical exercises, and Ishmael is a figure associated in the Allegorical Commentary with sophistry and verbal finesse. I thereby incline to the later explanation of the "twelve nations" of Ishmael.

but my covenant I will establish with Isaac. Having skipped over the similar promise of establishing a covenant with Isaac in Gen 17:19c, Philo now cites the analogous statement in Gen 17:21. The text agrees exactly with the Septuagint. For Philo's allegoresis of the covenant, see chapters two (§§ 39–53) and four (§§ 57–59).

he refashions the class of humans belonging to each virtue. In a novel allegorical move, Philo also "refashions" the allegorical significances of Ishmael and Isaac as two kinds of virtue, the taught (Abrahamic) and self-taught (Isaac) types.

Parallel Exegesis

§ 261. ***Gen 17:19b ("and you will call the name of your son ... joy").*** Philo's interpretation of Gen 17:19b in §§ 261–262 finds no parallel in the QGE. It occurs in *De mutatione nominum* as the culminating annunciation of the meaning of Isaac, toward which the whole treatise has been tending. A parallel interpretation is given in *Leg.* 3.85–87, including a treatment of Isaac's name (3.87). *Cher.* 8 also paraphrases this narrative, though there is no place left in that text for Ishmael "the sophist."

§ 263. ***Gen 17:20 ("I have blessed him ... he shall beget twelve nations.").*** In QG 3.59, Philo moves from Gen 17:19a to Gen 17:20. Here, the primary lemma adduced in § 263, the blessing of Ishmael, finds its parallel. Philo begins by interpreting the verse to mean that God gives "the first and the second good things" (Marcus, PLCLSup), namely the virtue that comes by nature and the virtue that comes by teaching. These goods are mapped allegorically onto Isaac and Ishmael, who differ in their modes of acquiring virtue as seeing differs from hearing (QG 3.59a). This interpretation is not self-evidently derived from the details of the text *per se*, but from the fact that Philo—who interprets the entirety of Gen 17:19a as refering to Isaac in this series—understands God in Gen 17:20 to be referring back to Abraham's prayer for Ishmael in Gen 17:18. The interpretation thus runs parallel to Philo's comments on "yes" (Gen 17:19aα) in chapter ten. Next, Philo turns to the significance of Ishmael's "twelve nations." He explains these as the "train of school studies" (Marcus, PLCLSup). This exegesis finds a parallel in § 263, where (as I argued in the detailed comments above), Philo's phrase "the whole cyclical chorus of sophistic preliminary topics" suggests Ishmael's association with the rhetorical *progymnasmata* (of Theon of Alexandria et al.). In QG 3.59, however, Philo spells out a different significance for the number twelve. On the analogy of the twelve months of the year and twelve hours in a day, Philo takes the number as a symbol of natural "cycles" (շրջապտութիւը: περίοδοι, ἀνακυκλώσεις), which resemble the "cycles" of preliminary education in all the typical range of subjects.

thus, he re-fashions the class of humans belonging to each virtue. In § 263, Philo differentiates the virtuous types that he has been presuming since chapter eight: the virtue that is self-taught (Isaac) and the virtue that is learned (Ishmael-Abraham). In the parallel at QG 3.59a, Philo articulates the additional etymological distinction in the allegory of Abraham's two sons, which never fully percolates to the surface in *De mutatione nominum*, but nonetheless forms a constituent part of the deep structural unity of chapters nine through eleven. Philo writes "for hearing (i.e., Ishmael) when compared to seeing (i.e., Isaac → Israel) is like the not genuine beside the genuine" (Marcus, PLCLSup; patriarchal glosses added). Comparing the respective interpretations in § 263 and QG 3.59 enables the Philonic interpreter to go "beyond" the surface level of the Allegorical Commentary without completely violating Runia's (1984/1987) principal of the "finality" of the Philonic text. We can be certain that this etymological contrast between Ishmael and Israel, though not enunciated in *De mutatione nominum*, is a part of Philo's allegorical reasoning.

Gen 17:21 ("but my covenant I will establish with Isaac"). See the important parallel interpretation of this verse QG 3.60. Philo distinguishes between Isaac, the "heir" of divine things, and Ishmael, who although not the heir will still receive gifts of divine grace.

Nachleben

§ 261. **Gen 17:19b ("and you will call the name of your son ... joy")**. Just as Philo reads "joy" as an *Ersatz* "changed name" for Isaac (according to § 88, his name doesn't change), so Eusebius (*Dem. ev.* 4.17.3 [B]) finds a kind of name change for Isaac, when he notes that "Isaac was given the surname 'Laughter' before his birth" (Γέλωτα τὸν Ἰσαὰκ πρὸ γενέσεως ἐπικεκλημένον). Cf. *Mut.* 261: "you will also make his name a symbol of this emotion: laughter" (καὶ τὸ σύμβολον αὐτῆς ὄνομα θήσεις, γέλωτα), which might be read: "you will also make the symbol of this emotion a name: Laughter."

§ 263. **Gen 17:20 ("I have blessed him ... he shall beget twelve nations.")**. There is an intriguing tradition found in the Shepherd of Hermas (Herm. 94–95, Sim. 9.17–18 [D]) that the peoples of the world may be divided into twelve tribes or "twelve nations." These are comprised of both bad and good groups of people, seemingly both inside and outside the church. This is one of the few places where the precise phrase "twelve nations" is to be found outside Gen 17:20, but a connection with Ishmael's offspring—and hence Philonic tradition—is not explicit. For this set of visions, see Harris 1887, 72–73. John Chrysostom (*Hom. Gen.* 53.371 [D]) interprets the blessing of Ishmael in the context of explaining God's covenant faithfulness to Isaac, but does not elaborate on the nature of the "twelve nations."

Gen 17:21 ("but my covenant I will establish with Isaac"). A passage of massive significance in later Christian tradition, on account of the identification of Isaac as a type of Christ. Very little of Philo's interpretation survives the journey to Clement and Origen. For whereas Philo (at least in the Allegorical Commentary) reads Isaac's covenantal primacy naturally and pedagogically, Christians read it in terms of salvation history. Thus, while for Philo, naming Isaac as "heir" meant the legitimacy of philosophical Judaism over secular education (Ishmael), Christians—following Paul's interpretation of the two brothers in Gal 4:21–31—would use this fraternal binary as a way of asserting the superiority of the church of the "new covenant" (Isaac) over the synagogue of the "old covenant" (Ishmael).

[Chapter 12]
God Is the Appropriate Time (§§ 264–269)

In this penultimate chapter, Philo turns from the anthropological to the theological aspects of his allegory of the soul—again, mirroring the beginning of the treatise at its close. The two-part reflection, which comments on Gen 17:21bα and Gen 17:21bβ in succession, offers a series of meditations on the subjects of time and perfection, which are richer than their brevity might suggest. God, who was presented as ineffable in the opening chapter (§§ 11–14), is now contemplated in his timelessness. The promises to Abraham, while partially recognizable in time, are only perfectly fulfilled in God's eternity.

The chapter subdivides evenly between the exegeses of the two portions of the primary lemma. In the first section, (a) Philo interprets Gen 17:21bα, identifying God as "the appropriate time" (§§ 264–266). He then (b) interprets the phrase "in the other/next year" as an indication of Abraham's perfection arriving only in the truly "other" noetic realm, not in the next (or any) calendrical year (§§ 267–269). Because Philo interprets two distinct phrases in the primary lemma, Kraus Reggiani and Cohn treat (b) §§ 267–269 (Gen 17:21bβ) as a separate chapter. Arnaldez and Schur consider §§ 264–269 a single chapter. My own judgment aligns with the latter position, following the chapter structure of QG 3.60, as well as the shared concern of both subunits with the theme of time.

a   *"At This Appropriate Time" (§§ 264–266)*
     Analysis and General Comments

The first subunit of this chapter offers an interpretation of Gen 17:21bα. Despite being only three sections long, it is unusually exegetically complex, as Philo adduces both a secondary (Num 14:9) and a tertiary (Lev 26:12) biblical lemma to elaborate his theology of God's timeless assistance to the soul. It divides into three shorter units, which align roughly with the PCW section divisions.

(1)   After citing Gen 17:21bα, Philo wonders, in an aside to God or Moses (the "most-wonderful"), what the expression "this appropriate time" (ὁ καιρὸς οὗτος) in the primary lemma means. In light of the demonstrative pronoun, he interprets it to mean God himself (§ 264).

574   PART THREE

(2) To support this reading of Gen 17:21bα, Philo adduces Num 14:9 as a secondary lemma, which is verbally linked to the primary lemma through the phrase "the appropriate time" (ὁ καιρός). Philo interprets *kairos* ("moment") in this verse as a parallel to *kurios* ("Lord"), transforming "the appropriate time" into a title or symbol of God (i.e., the Logos or legislative power). Picking up on the notion of God's special presence with the elect Israel in Num 14:9, Philo adduces a tertiary lemma (Lev 26:12), joined to Num 14:9 by thematic and verbal ("in us"—"in you") links (§§ 265–266a).

(3) Philo closes with a critical judgment: those who speak of "appropriate times" and "yearly seasons" in the plural are speaking catachrestically, using words in an improper or borrowed fashion. While there are indeed times and seasons, these are analogous uses of these terms applied to created time. The "reality" (πρᾶγμα) symbolized by these terms, however, is the singular "time" and "season": the Lord (§ 266b).

Detailed Comments

1. § 264. *"at this appropriate time, she will bear a son for you."* Philo begins the section by citing the primary lemma: Gen 17:21bα. He rewrites the syntax of the Septuagint to foreground the phrase "at this appropriate time," which will serve as the focus of his allegoresis.

Gen 17:21bα	§ 264
⟨to Isaac, whom⟩ Sarah will bear or you at this appropriate time.	At this appropriate time she will bear ⟨a son⟩ for you.

that is, wisdom will give birth to joy. Philo reiterates the interpretation presented in § 255.

what sort of appropriate time do you signify. The qualitative question, "which sort" (ποῖος), is triggered by the presence of the demonstrative pronoun "this ⟨appropriate time⟩" (⟨ὁ καιρὸς⟩ οὗτος), which Philo takes as a cue for further inquiry. For the importance of demonstratives as exegetical "markers," which prompt for "divisions" and "distinctions," see Philo's interpretation of "this Ishmael" in §§ 201–209.

O most-wonderful speaker? The fifth and final Philonic ὦ-aside in the present treatise (see the note on § 25 and Terian 1995). Philo's addressee is difficult to identify. Colson supposes in this case that the addressee is God himself—the literal speaker of the phrase. While this is possible, Moses is also possible, as he is (in Philo's view) simultaneously responsible for the locution and the craftsman of the allegory contained therein. Philo uses the identical superlative vocative, "O most-wonderful" (ὦ θαυμασιώτατε), on only one other occasion, *Agr.* 149, where it refers to a human interlocutor (see Geljon and Runia 2013, 238). I have left my translation intentionally ambiguous, as the Greek; however, I incline toward Moses as the addressee (see the note on Moses at § 265).

do you mean the appropriate time. Philo does not mention the noun "appropriate time" (καιρόν) here—a sign that he is beginning already to associate the noun with its allegorical referent, the Logos. I have supplied "appropriate time" in the translation as the most obvious masculine singular antecedent for the accusative definite article, "the" (τόν).

that alone cannot be referenced. Although he began by speaking of some eternal form of "time," the phrase "alone ... unable to be referenced" (μόνος ... ἄδεικτος) points to a divine figure. What "alone" cannot be pointed to (or indeed, named), other than God? The adjective "unable to be referenced" (ἄδεικτος) is paradoxical, echoing the foregoing verb from Philo's question to Moses or God, "you are referencing" (δεικνύεις). That there is one Being in creation that "cannot be referenced" (ἄδεικτος) recalls Philo's discussion of the ineffability of God and his powers in § 14. In § 266, Philo will use the discrimen of "proper" and "improper" to signify that "this appropriate time" rightly refers to the Logos, who paradoxically cannot be pointed to by created beings.

from the horizon of creation. Colson renders "under creation" (ὑπὸ γενέσεως) as agentive: "which no created being can set forth" (i.e., "which cannot be set forth *by* created being"). I have preferred to translate the preposition (ὑπό) in spatio-temporal terms: "from the horizon of creation"—*sub specie creationis* (i.e., *sub specie temporis*). Creatures, in their motion and limit, fall short of eternal, unchanging realities. As Philo will clarify in § 267, he arrives at this reading of the divine "appropriate time" (καιρός) by contrasting it with "secular time" (χρόνος), or time in motion, which remains relative to created material and immaterial objects.

for he himself. It is not quite right to translate the phrase "this would be the true appropriate time" (ὁ γὰρ ἀληθὴς αὐτὸς ⟨ἂν⟩ εἴη καιρός). The reflexive pronoun (αὐτός) must mean at this stage "He himself"—i.e., God, the Logos.

the true Appropriate Time, the dayspring of the universe. In identifying the Logos with an ideal "appropriate time" of creation, Philo echoes the allegorical equivalence between the Logos and the "day" of creation (Gen 2:4) in *Leg.* 1.21. In this exposition of the perfected state of the Abraham soul, he returns not only to creation, but also to the beginning of the Allegorical Commentary, noting that the true "appointed time" of eschatological perfection is the same as the protological "day of creation"—when viewed from the horizon of God's eternity (*sub specie aeternitatis*).

2. § 265. *for this reason, Moses also dared to say*. This translation of καί as "also" supports the interpretation of the "most-wonderful" (θαυμασιώτατος) addressed in § 264 as Moses.

those who fled ... against her antagonists. Philo alludes to the speech of Joshua in Num 14:7–9, in which he encourages the Israelites, upon hearing the report of the spies about the land of Canaan, not to fear conflict but to fight according to the command of the Lord. In adducing Num 14 as a secondary lemma, Philo returns to the same story cycle that he used in chapter nine in defense of the stepwise ascent to virtue modeled by the Ishmael soul (§ 224; cf. also §§ 121–124). In § 265, Philo suggests that the Israelites who do not flee but fight on behalf of virtue are also accompanied by the "appropriate time"—the Logos—and will ascend to higher flights of perfection.

"the appropriate time ... the Lord is among us." Philo now cites the secondary lemma, Num 14:9. Other than omitting the initial postpositive "for" (γάρ), his citation agrees exactly with the Septuagint. The secondary lemma is linked to the primary lemma lexically through the shared phrase, "the appropriate time" (ὁ καιρός).

not in a straightforward manner. Philo admits that the equivalence he derives between the "appropriate time" (*kairos*) and the "Lord" (*kurios*) is facilitated by a verbal similarity between the two terms, of the sort that the Socrates of the *Cratylus* would surely admire. Philo reads the phrase, "the appropriate time has departed from them, the Lord is with us" (ὁ καιρὸς ἀπ' αὐτῶν, ὁ δὲ κύριος ἐν ἡμῖν), as a narrative about a single subject: the departure of the "Lord," God's Logos or regal power, *from* the Israelites who do not defend virtue, as well as the Lord's presence *among* the Israelites who do hold fast.

that God alone is the Appropriate Time. Philo makes the allegorical equivalence explicit. The word "alone" (μόνον) might be read adverbially "only, not in a completely straightforward manner," but I have opted to translate it adjectivally, on analogy with the phrase "alone is unable to be demonstrated" (ἄδεικτος μόνος) in § 264.

who stands far off from all impiety, but walks among ... An allegorical reading of the secondary biblical lemma, Num 14:9, in which the verbs "stand far off" (ἀφέστηκεν) and "walk among" (ἐμπεριπατεῖ) are echoed in sequence, signaling through the prepositions "from" and "in" (ἀπό, ἐν) the movement of the Logos from one group of souls to another.

that conquer in virtue. My translation of the participle "conquer" (ἀρετῶσαι) reflects the martial significance of "virtue" in the Homeric epics. Philo endows his psychological allegory of the Israelite warrior souls with this connotation.

§ 266a. *for he says, "I will walk among you, and I will be your God."* The tertiary lemma from Lev 26:12 is adduced for rhetorical force, but does not receive an extended interpretation. Although Philo uses the double compound form "walk about among" (ἐμπεριπατεῖ) in discussing the verb, he cites the Septuagint with only the simple compound, "I will walk about" (περιπατήσω). The tertiary lemma is linked lexically with the secondary lemma through the prepositional phrase "among you" (ἐν ὑμῖν), which echoes the "among us" (ἐν ἡμῖν) of Joshua's speech. It complements Num 14:9 in affirming, from God's perspective, the faith of Joshua: that God walks "among" the virtuous souls.

3. § 266b. *but those who say that the seasons of the year are "appropriate times."* That is, those who adopt the literal sense of "appropriate times" as marked moments in a "secular timetable" (χρόνος). Philo adds this as a response to a possible objection to his allegorical reading of "appropriate time" (καιρός) as ideal, formal eternity (the Logos). Such literalists use their language "improperly" and miss the deeper intent of Moses's writing.

use the words inexactly. Philo has previously spoken of the "misuse" (καταχρῆσθαι, κατάχρησις) of language in §§ 12 and 14, indicating that God, the transcendent One Who Is, can only be "improperly" named. In § 27, he adds that "it is said catachrestically, not properly" (λέγεται καταχρηστικῶς, οὐ κυρίως) that God, The One Who Is, can be given predicates of relation. Here, Philo returns to this theory of language to argue *for* a particular title. On this reading, the word "appropriate time" (καιρός) belongs most properly to a divine power of the Logos, "the Lord" (κύριος), and only catachrestically to temporal seasons. This does not mean that the kingly power is fully disclosed in essence by the name, only that the name more properly refers to it than to anything in the created order. Philo's use of this philosophical category at the beginning and end of the treatise has the significance of first veiling The One Who Is in his transcendence (chapter one), and then unveiling the Logos in his economic power (chapter twelve). Not inconsequentially, the last instance of the noun "name" (ὄνομα) in the treatise appears here as well, in Philo's discussion of the misuse and misunderstanding of divine names, with which the work began. This is an elegant form of ring composition.

in an improper fashion. A synonym for "catachrestically," as § 27 indicates. Here, the phrase "not properly" (οὐ κυρίως) picks up on the noun "Lord" (ὁ κύριος) in the secondary lemma (Num 14:9). To summarize Philo's position, in a way that makes his wordplay clear: the title *kairos* ("appropriate time") belongs *kuriōs* ("properly") to the timeless and singular *kurios* ("Lord"). The word is only used of plural "moments" in secular time improperly. Arnaldez (1964, 156, n. 1) adds that "Philo, nevertheless, often uses the word ⟨καιρός⟩ in this ⟨temporal⟩ sense (*Opif.* 59; *Spec.* 1.181, 186; 3.188)."

the natures of realities. For the technical term πρᾶγμα as "reality," as opposed to "material bodies" or "names," see the detailed comments on §§ 8–9, 60, 173, 179 ("bodies and realities"); and on § 13 ("name and reality").

Parallel Exegesis

§ 264. *Gen 17:21bα ("at the appropriate time")*. Philo's parallel interpretation of Gen 17:21 in QG 3.60 divides into two parts: he first offers extensive comments on Gen 17:21a, in which he reiterates the allegorical distinction between the Ishmael and Isaac "testaments" and their related gifts (QG 3.60a). This amplifies the symbolic distinction between Isaac and Ishmael developed in QG 3.59, in relation to the covenant. Philo then offers a short interpretation of Gen 17:21bβ "in the other year," which provides the real parallel to chapter twelve, esp. §§ 267–269 (QG 3.60b). This phrase is interpreted as pointing to "another holy, great, sacred, and divine" time, which is different from the time of the gentiles (Marcus, PLCLSup). The phrase "at the appropriate time" (Gen 17:21bα) does not receive detailed treatment. The verse is only interpreted in these two *loci*.

§ 265. *Num 14:9 ("the appropriate time ... the Lord is among us")*. Colson (PLCL 5:276, n. a) and Arnaldez (1964, 154, n. 1) both point to the parallel interpretation of Num 14:9 at *Post.* 121–122, "where however the καιρός ("moment") is the false god who deserts his votaries" (Colson, Ibid.). See the similar interpretation of Num 14:9 in QG 1.100, where the verse is adduced as a secondary lemma to illuminate Gen 6:13, "the time (καιρός) of all humankind has come against me." In *Mut.* 265, by contrast, the "appropriate time" is identified with the "Lord." The syntax of the verse admits of both possibilities.

§ 266a. *Lev 26:12 ("for he says, 'I will walk among you, and I will be your God.'")* The tertiary lemma from Lev 26:12 is also interpreted allegorically in *Sacr.* 87; *Post.* 122 (in conjunction with Num 14:9); *Somn.* 1.148; 2.248; and *Praem.* 123–124. It this last text, the verse is taken to signify God's presence either in the mind of the sage or with the Jewish people collectively.

Nachleben

§ 264. *Gen 17:21bα ("at the appropriate time")*. John Chrysostom (*Hom. Gen.* 53.371.19–25 [C/D]) draws out the significance of Gen 17:21b for salvation history, albeit in a different way than Philo, when he writes:

> See here ⟨in Gen 17:21b⟩, beloved, how in one decisive and chosen moment (ἐν μιᾷ καιροῦ ῥοπῇ) the just man ⟨i.e., Abraham⟩ recovers the vicissitudes of all time (παντὸς τοῦ χρόνου τὰς ἀμοιβὰς ἐκομίσατο), and the word spoken by the Christ to his disciples was fulfilled: "whoever should leave father or mother ... will receive these back one hundred-fold, and will also inherit eternal life." (Matt 19:29).

The "appropriate time" that Philo identifies as the Logos, Chrysostom recognizes as the moment of Abraham's obedience (to leave his father and mother in Ur and Haran)—a single point of decision, but one that sums up all time and participates in an eternal pattern of obedience, commended also by Jesus to his disciples.

§ 266a. *Lev 26:12 ("for he says, 'I will walk among you, and I will be your God.'")* The verse passes on into Christian tradition in part by way of 2 Cor 6:16. A kindred interpretation to Philo's may be found in the Macarian writings (3.3.3 [C]):

> And thus the Lord, seeing the labor and competition of the soul, as it exerts itself in this age (ἐν τῷ αἰῶνι τούτῳ), then reveals himself in his heart as the one saying "I will dwell with you and walk about among you" (ἐνοικήσω καὶ ἐμπεριπατήσω ἐν ὑμῖν [2 Cor 6:16; cf. Lev 26:11–12]).

Here, the tradition is applied to the life of an ascetical monk. See also [Ps.-]Macarius 3.5.2. John Chrysostom applies the theme of God's walking "among you" to divine indwelling in baptism (*Cat. ill.* 1.46 [D]).

b   *"In the Other Year" (§§ 267–269)*
        Analysis and General Comments

The first part of the present chapter was primarily theological, focused on the allegorical meaning of the scriptural word "appropriate time" (καιρός) and its symbolism of the "Lord" (κύριος), God's kingly power. In the second half of the chapter, Philo turns to the next part of the primary lemma (Gen 17:21bβ), "in the other year," resuming his dominant ethical mode and assessing the perfection of the Abraham soul in light of the new focus on time and eternity.

The section is divisible into two smaller units.

(1) First, Philo (a) interprets the primary lemma, "in the other year" (Gen 17:21bβ), as indicating that the birth of Isaac will happen when the Abraham soul is "in the noetic realm." What is truly "other" than time is eternity. The phrases "appropriate time" and "other year" are related to one another, as the active Logos is related to the passive world of Ideas. The Logos is both (Radice 2009, 138, 142), containing the ideal world within himself (§ 267).

(2) Having laid out this explanation of the "location" of Abraham's perfection, Philo (b) adduces a secondary lemma, Gen 26:12, in which Isaac is said to "find" one-hundred-fold of what he sowed in his field. This secondary lemma shifts the emphasis from Abraham's perfection to the nature of his son. Self-taught virtue and joy yields one-hundred-fold—the same number as his father's soul-age at his birth (§§ 268–269).

Detailed Comments

1. § 267. *augmenting the goodness of the one being born.* The phrase indicates Philo's shift of interpretive focus from God (the "appropriate time") to Isaac.

God says that Isaac will be born "in the other year." Philo cites the primary biblical lemma, Gen 17:21bβ, in a form similar to the Septuagint, but in indirect discourse. The verb for "begetting" (γεννηθήσεσθαι), appropriate to a male subject (Isaac), has been substituted for the scriptural "she will bear" (τέξεται), which would point instead to Sarah.

indicating not the distances of time ... measured by lunar and solar circuits. For the technical term "distance, aperture, interval" (διάστημα) in its temporal and spatial meanings, see the detailed comments on §§ 142 and 179 respectively. Just as "the appropriate time" does not refer to a temporal season, so "in the other year" does not refer to a literal year.

the distance that is placeless and foreign and really new. Philo implies a different kind of "distance" (διάστημα)—one that has nothing to do with space-time, but is truly "outside of place" (ἔκτοπος).

"other" than what is seen and perceived. An echo of the primary biblical lemma. Philo develops a Platonizing discourse on "otherness," in which all differences this side of the line of perception are considered negligible. Only the intelligible order is truly "other."

the paradigm and archetype of time: namely, eternity. Philo alludes to Plato, *Tim.* 38b: "the pattern of eternal nature" (τὸ παράδειγμα τῆς διαιωνίας φύσεως, trans. Hamilton and Cairns); and esp. 37d: "a certain moving image of eternity ... which we have come to call time" (εἰκώ ... κινητόν τινα αἰῶνος ... ὃν δὴ χρόνον ὠνομάκαμεν) for this description of the relationship between time, which "comes into being with creation," and eternity, its everlasting form. It is noteworthy that in this latter passage (*Tim.* 37d), Plato describes created time as "days and nights and months and years (ἐνιαυτοί)" in the plural. Correspondingly, in Moses's phrase, "in the other year" (ἐν τῷ ἐνιαυτῷ τῷ ἑτέρῳ), Philo sees the "formal" year indicated by the singular rather than the plural. This meaning is further flagged by the marker "other" (ἕτερος), which like the demonstrative pronoun in Gen 17:21bα ("this acceptable time") indicates Moses's distinction of a formal reality from a material body.

eternity is ... the life of the noetic world, just as time ... the perceptible world. A fascinating phrase, which does not occur in *Tim.* 37cd, but arises from Middle Platonic developments. Runia's (1986, 221) comment on the passage merits citation:

> αἰών ["eternity"] is thus the βίος ["life"] of both God and the noetic cosmos. Such a formulation does not issue directly from *Tim.* 37c–38c ... Between

Plato and Philo important interpretive developments have taken place. A text such as *Soph.* 248e–249a stimulated the idea that (spiritual) life and motion and intelligence must be attributed to the world of ideas. Moreover, Aristotle's lyrical description of his highest god [see *Met.* 1072b] was influential: φαμὲν δὲ τὸν θεὸν εἶναι ζῷον ἀίδιον ἄριστον, ὥστε ζωὴ καὶ αἰὼν συνεχὴς καὶ ἀίδιος ὑπάρχει τῷ θεῷ· τοῦτο γὰρ ὁ θεός ["We say that God is the best eternal living thing, with the result that life and unbroken and perpetual eternity subsist in God; for this is what God is"].

See further the note of Arnaldez (1964, 156, n. 3), along similar lines; and Keizer 2000.

2. § 268. *in this year ... he finds the grain increased one-hundred fold*. Philo adduces Gen 26:12 as a secondary lemma. It is lexically linked with the primary lemma through the catchphrase "in that year" (ἐν τῷ ἐνιαυτῷ ἐκείνῳ), approximating Gen 17:21bβ, "in the other year" (ἐν τῷ ἐνιαυτῷ τῷ ἑτέρῳ). (NB: Philo's citation omits the demonstrative from Gen 26:12, replacing it with a relative pronoun, which is its functional equivalent.) "Other" and "that" serve as markers of allegorical content and modifiers of "year," the noetic realm. Philo's citation of the secondary lemma involves a few additional changes:

Gen 26:12	**§ 268**
And Isaac found (εὗρεν) in that year one-hundred fold grain.	In which year Isaac finds one-hundred fold grain (ἑκατοστεύουσαν εὑρίσκει κριθήν).

Note that, as is his wont, Philo has changed the tense of the main verb from the Septuagintal aorist, "found" (εὗρεν), to the allegorical present, "finds" (εὑρίσκει), illustrating the timeless character of the perfection reached by the Abraham and the Isaac souls.

Philo has already adduced Gen 26:12 as a secondary lemma in § 190 in the *catena* of texts illustrating the number 100 as a symbol of perfection. Here, Philo returns to this lemma and unveils a further significance of it. He connects Isaac's birth (the perfection of Abraham) with the noetic reality of Isaac's reaping one-hundred-fold (the perfect return on perfect spiritual planting). In the end of the treatise, both the "learning" and "self-taught" souls are united in this perfection, as the latter (Isaac) comes to symbolize the end of the former's (Abraham's) migrations.

he who has sown the graces of God ... more abundant goods. The implicit subject is the Isaac soul—the counterpart of his father's soul in its perfected status. For the related phrase "to return graces" (χάριτας ἀποδιδόναι) in Philo, see LaPorte 1983, 13.

as many ... worthy to partake may have a share in them. The Isaac soul's stewardship of divine gifts benefits other souls as well, not just itself. Philo introduces a corporate dimension to the soteriology of this treatise, which otherwise, like the Allegorical Commentary as a whole, focuses primarily on the individual.

§ 269. *it is the custom for the one who sows also to reap.* This is the proverbial Jewish and Greco-Roman wisdom that the worker merits the fruit of his labor. Having presented the noetic "location" of both Abraham's and Isaac's perfection, Philo makes one more important point, drawn from the curious verb "found/finds" (εὗρεν/εὑρίσκει) in the secondary lemma (see below).

he was sowing. Although the Isaac soul is the primary subject in Philo's exegesis of the secondary lemma, the significance applies to Abraham allegorically as well.

virtue is the enemy of jealousy and vice. The perfect soul does not care that it is God's seed (rather than its own) that it sows. Without jealousy, virtue serves the greater good of God.

he is said "to find," but not "to harvest." Philo responds to an implicit question: Ought not Moses have said that Isaac "harvested" (ἐθέρισεν)? Beneath this unexpected idiom, Philo discovers an important allegorical message. See the following note. (For Philo's similar attention to the phrase "find grace" in Gen 6:8, see *Deus* 86.)

he who made the ear of grain riper ... was Another. In his choice of the verb "find," Philo interprets Moses to imply that the Isaac soul does not properly "harvest," for that would imply that he caused the maturation of his own seeds. In fact, all that he has planted is "gift," such that the fruits of joy that grow from virtue can only be "found" by Isaac, as well as by others whom God intends to benefit. Only God, the divine Other, could properly be said to "harvest" what Isaac has sown and God has grown. Philo closes the treaties by reiterating his theology of divine grace and his emphasis on the "nothingness" of the human person—even the Isaac soul.

for those who seek to find. Philo signals the collective horizon of his allegory. The graces of God—the greater hopes and more abundant gifts—are for many to seek and find.

Parallel Exegesis

§ 267. *Gen 17:21bβ* (*"in the other year"*). The only parallel to chapter twelve of *De mutatione nominum* ("in the other year" [Gen 17:21bβ]) is to be found in QG 3.60b. For the structure of QG 3.60, see the Parallel Exegesis on § 264.

indicating not the distance of time. In QG 3.60b, Philo says that the birth of Isaac "is not the birth of the life of the time (ժամանակ) which now exists, but of another great, holy, sacred and divine ⟨moment⟩, which has abundant fullness and is not like that of the gentiles." The Armenian noun "time" (ժամանակ) used in the *solutio* can render either "appropriate time/moment" (καιρός) or "secular time" (χρόνος). Based on the parallel in *Mut.* 267, "secular time" (χρόνος) would seem more likely here, despite the probable appearance of "appropriate time" (καιρός) in the *quaestio*. Unique to Philo's interpretation in QG 3.60b is the additional detail that secular time belongs to the gentiles, while "the other year" points to God's holy time—perhaps meaning ritual or Sabbath time. In *De mutatione nominum*, Philo eschews such religious-ethnic distinctions (even if rendered symbolically) and interprets "the other year" to signify not what is religiously or ethnically other, but what is "truly other" from a philosophical and theological standpoint—the eternity which is beyond time itself. Philo's adduction of *Tim.* 37d as a secondary classical lemma in *Mut.* 267 supresses the ethnic elements of QG 3.60 and catapults the discourse from the religious to the philosophical and from the particular to the universal. One may speak here of an allegorical "universalizing" of the Jewish covenant. This should not be seen as a rejection of the former, but rather of a penetration of its inner- or under-sense. The precise relationship between Philo's allegoresis of the Jewish covenant and the literal observance of Jewish religion (cf. *Migr.* 89–92), as well as Philo's opposing hopes for Platonizing eternity (*Mut.* 267) and Messianic time (cf. *Mos.* 1.290; *Praem.* 95), remain unresolved issues in his thought and œuvre.

the paradigm and archetype of time: eternity. Colson (PLCL 5:279, n. a) cross-references the similar treatments of *Tim.* 37d at *Her.* 165 and *Deus* 32 (with note at PLCL 3:484).

§ 268. *Gen 26:12* (*"Isaac found the grain increased one-hundred-fold"*). See the Parallel Exegesis on § 190.

Nachleben
§ 267. *Gen 17:21bβ* (*"in the other year"*). Ambrose (*Abr.* 2.11 [C]) produces the following interpretation:

> The generation ⟨of Isaac⟩ is promised in the following year ("sequenti anno" [Gen 17:21bβ]), so that you may observe that the Lord promises a

birth—that is, not a birth from Sarah's corporeal womb ("non illam uteri corporalis Sarrae"), but that part of the church ("istum partum ecclesiae"), which is to come in the future ("qui esset futurus").

This may reflect a transposition of Philo's Platonic eschatology into a salvation-historical key, but Ambrose misses Philo's philosophical genius. "The following year" is not interpreted as eternity, but as a later Messianic age, in which a "part" of the church is to come. John Chrysostom's (*Hom. Gen.* 53.371 [D]) changing of the lemma to read "in the second year" (ἐν τῷ ἐνιαυτῷ τῷ δευτέρῳ) suggests that the phrase continued to puzzle ancient interpreters.

§ 268. *Gen 26:12 ("Isaac found the grain increased one-hundred fold")*. See the Nachleben on § 190.

§ 269. *It is the custom for the one who sows also to reap.* See 1 Cor 9:10–11.

[Chapter 13]
God's Departure (§ 270)

Philo's final chapter is only one PCW section long. He offers an exegesis of Gen 17:22ab (God stops speaking to Abraham): It has no parallel in the *QGE*, apparently because no serious problem is posed by it. The note that God "finished" speaking with Abraham, while of comparatively little interest as an independent lemma, provides a convenient place for Philo to wrap up his thematic allegorical treatise. This is not to insinuate that its content is superfluous. To the contrary, in this final chapter Philo reaffirms his compatibilist view of divine and human action: God's grace (see chapter twelve), which is the primary or original cause of all human agency, does not render human freedom negligible, but rather establishes the context in which created wills can act. God's departure from Abraham is thus not merely the end of the conversation, but the condition for the student—no longer in need of the teacher's oversight—to enact the potential power of virtue now emblazoned in his soul.

Analysis and General Comments

In the final chapter, Philo continues his rapid movement through the primary lemma, witnessed in chapter twelve. He interprets not one, but two portions of the lemma, taking Gen 17:22a and Gen 17:22b in turn. Because the chapter is a single section, no formal division for the detailed comments is necessary.

Detailed Comments

§ 270. *The phrase, God finished speaking to Abraham.* Philo cites the final primary lemma of the treatise, Gen 17:22a. The citation agrees exactly with the Septuagint, minus the connective "and" (δέ).

is equal to saying. For this interpretive formula, see comment on § 11.

"he perfected the hearer himself." "He perfected" (ἐτελείωσε) is paraphrase of the Pentateuchal words "he finished speaking" (συνετέλεσε λαλῶν). Philo creatively misreads the biblical helping verb "finished," sans supplementary participle, as indicative of God's making Abraham ethically "perfect" (τέλειος).

"who had been formerly empty ... filled him with immortal words." The second part of Philo's gloss—God's filling the empty Abraham soul with divine "words" (λόγοι)—takes its cue from the second part of the primary lemma: "speaking to him" (λαλῶν πρὸς αὐτόν). The resulting rereading inverts the literal sense. God does not "finish speaking" to Abraham, but rather "completes" Abraham *by* "speaking immortal words."

the Lord departed from Abraham. Philo turns to the final words of the primary lemma in the treatise: God's leave-taking of Abraham in Gen 17:22b. His text apparently reads "Lord" (κύριος) rather than the Septuagintal "God" (ὁ θεός) as departing from Abraham (cf. Gen 17:1, where it is the "Lord" who appears to Abraham initially). Citing the lemma in this fashion allows Philo to retain the theological nuance of his comments on the non-relationality of "God/The One Who Is" (ὁ θεός / τὸ ὄν) in § 27. Only the Logos is economically active in the perfection of the human soul.

not that they had been disjoined from one another. This cannot be the case, given what Philo has said about "the appropriate time" and "the other year." God's departure does not indicate a "distance" (διάστημα) between himself and the soul of the sage, nor a real "finishing" of their discourse, since neither God nor the soul are bound by space-time. His leave-taking must be understood in another way.

an attendant of God. Philo uses religious and cultic language to imagine the sage's dutiful presence near God. For this technical term, see the comment on § 45.

wish to establish the volition of his student. I translate the substantive "the willing capacity" (τὸ ἑκούσιον) as "volition," intentionally avoiding the vexed term "free will." Colson (PLCL) translates it "independence." The idea is a compatibilist one: God's grace precedes and grounds human action, but there is still a voluntary capacity within the human soul. Philo will go on to specify how God's non-diastemic departure can establish, rhetorically or otherwise, the perfected soul's voluntary action.

the teacher was no longer present. For the argument that parents, teachers, slaves, and other overseers often serve as ethical crutches or goads to the soul, see § 217.

an intentional and self-controlled forethought. Philo uses the technical term "forethought" (προθυμία) to relate the mind's premeditation of a particular course of action.

might act through his own agency. This phrase, "acting through his own agency" (ἐνεργῇ δι' ἑαυτοῦ), doubly emphasizes the volitional side of Philo's compatibilism. The action of the perfected soul constitutes an "activity" (ἐνέργεια)—a complete action, which contains its own end, insofar as it approximates an entelechy. Likewise, the perfected volition is the true instrumental cause of its own activity, acting "through itself" (δι' ἑαυτοῦ).

the teacher gives the student space for voluntary practice. What Philo means by saying that God provides the soul "space" or "place" (τόπος), in which to exercise its virtue—especially in light of the foregoing comments about the noetic and non-diastemic locale of such perfected activity—requires parsing. One thinks of Philo's statement in *Somn.* 1.64: "I, for my part, am not a place, but am *in* a place .... The Divine, on the other hand, is itself its own place" (ἐγὼ μὲν οὖν οὔκ εἰμι τόπος, ἀλλ' ἐν τόπῳ .... τὸ δὲ θεῖον ... ἐστὶν αὐτὸ τόπος ἑαυτοῦ). Philo thinks of God as a primary cause—but this is true both when God is actively teaching and not teaching. The "space" must thus also be a kind of divine silence, in which the psychic image of the Word is allowed to work without the God's direct intervention (i.e., "without external prompting").

engraving within the soul a most secure form of unforgetting memory. A powerful closing line, which highlights many of the treatise's main themes. First, the phrase, "unforgetting memory" (ἄληστος μνήμη), recalls Philo's adoption of Plato's wax-tablet soul from the *Theaetetus* in §§ 211–212 and the important role of memory in progress toward perfection. On this poignant turn of phrase, Arnaldez (1964, 158, n. 1) comments:

> Forgetting is a sickness of the memory, while memory is evidence of continual good health. To recollect oneself is like relieving a sickness (*Congr.* 39–40). 'Memory consists in guarding and keeping the precepts of the saints' (*Leg.* 1.55). This is the sense in which it is used here to close the treatise.

With architectonic balance, Philo stations memory at the beginning and (near) the end of the Allegorical Commentary.

More germane to the present treatise is the topic of changed letters and their allegorical significance, recapitulated in Philo's final three words: "engraving a most secure form" (ἐγχαράττων βεβαιότατον εἶδος). The verb "engraving" (ἐγχαράττων) serves as a reminder of the treatise's central, eponymous section (chapter five), in which God inscribes various "characters" or letters (§ 65) into scriptural names, conferring psychic powers that produce new types or "characters" of soul (§§ 70, 83). Finally, the phrase "most secure form" (βεβαιότατον εἶδος) ensures the reader that the transformation related in the name of Abraham is fixed and sure—that there is, so to speak, no further possibility of relapse, forgetting (as Socrates worries in the *Phaedrus*), or "cooling" (as Philo's later Alexandrian Christian recipient Origen would have it). The Abraham soul, once its name and powers have been changed for the best, receives a lasting mark, becoming "fixed" (βέβαιος) in faith and knowledge and virtue as firmly as is possible for any generated becoming (cf. the relapses of the Jacob soul intimated in § 83). Such a firm reshaping so conforms the Abraham mind to the power of the Logos that it can now "autonomously" sow the seeds of divine graces and find their fruits one-hundred-fold—Abraham's age at the birth of Isaac, the product of the priestly tithe, and the arithmological symbol of God's perfecting work.

Parallel Exegesis
§ 270. *Gen 17:22 ("God finished speaking to him Abraham")*. The verse is only interpreted in the present treatise.

Nachleben
§ 270. *Gen 17:22 ("the Lord departed from Abraham")*. Philo's Platonizing interpretation of God's non-diastemic "departing" or "going up" (ἀνέβη) from Abraham in Gen 17:22 is echoed by Origen in *Cels.* 4.12 (not mentioned by Van den Hoek 2000):

> If the words of the prophets speak of God as "coming down," we take this in a moral-allegorical sense (τροπολογοῦμεν) .... God comes down from his own greatness and majesty when he cares for the affairs of human beings (τὰ τῶν ἀνθρώπων ... οἰκονομεῖ.) .... Just as people commonly say that teachers "come down" to the level of children (συγκαταβαίνειν ... τοῖς νηπίοις τοὺς διδασκάλους), and wise men or advanced students ⟨"come down"⟩ to those only recently led to study philosophy, without meaning that they make a physical descent; so, if anywhere in the divine Scriptures God is said to "come down," it is to be understood in a similar sense to that common usage of a word (τῇ οὑτωσὶ χρωμένῃ τῷ ὀνόματι συνηθείᾳ). The same is also true of "going up" (ἀναβαίνειν [cf. Gen 17:22]). (Trans. Chadwick 1980, adapted)

Index of References to Scripture

Gen
- 1 — 237, 247
- 1:1–31 — 9
- 1:11 — 248
- 1:16–18 — 252, 302
- 1:25 — 248
- 1:26 — 24, 32, 78, 168, 179, 180, 181, 186
- 1:27 — 29, 35, 109, 180, 186, 435, 454, 528
- 2 — 247–248
- 2:1–17 — 9
- 2:1 — 10n22
- 2:2 — 394
- 2:4 — 575
- 2:7 — 24–25, 32, 77, 81, 168, 179, 180–181, 186, 227–230, 334, 352, 362, 383
- 2:8 — 248
- 2:9 — 248, 267, 277
- 2:15 — 366
- 2:17 — 24, 32, 78, 181
- 2:18–3:1 — 9
- 2:19 — 26, 32, 83, 243, 247–248, 262–263, 266, 269
- 2:20 — 248
- 2:21 — 366
- 3:8b–19 — 9
- 3:15 — 348
- 3:20–23 — 9, 10n22
- 3:22 — 24, 32, 181
- 3:24 — 10
- 4:1–4 — 10
- 4:3–6 — 484
- 4:4 — 542
- 4:7 — 29, 34, 104, 484, 494–495
- 4:8 — 494
- 4:8–15 — 10
- 4:16–25 — 10
- 4:17 — 187
- 4:26 — 424
- 5:18 — 187
- 5:24 — 25, 32, 78, 168, 183, 185, 187, 191
- 5:25 — 183
- 6:1–12 — 10
- 6:8 — 582
- 6:13 — 578
- 6:13–9:19 — 218
- 6:13–9:20 — 6, 10n24
- 6:13–22 — 10
- 6:16–18 — 10n24
- 9:3 — 138
- 9:8–17 — 10
- 9:20–21 — 4, 10
- 9:22–23 — 11
- 9:24–27 — 4n8, 11
- 10 — 11n27
- 11 — 393
- 11:1–9 — 11
- 11:10 — 28, 34, 103, 469, 472–473, 477, 479
- 11:28–32 — 159
- 11:30 — 27, 34, 96, 390–395
- 12 — 436
- 12–17 — 2
- 12:1 — 8n19, 183, 234
- 12:1–6 — 11
- 12:2 — 473
- 12:4 — 132
- 12:6 — 493, 495
- 12:7 — 425
- 12:10–20 — 8n15
- 13:15–16 — 425
- 15 — 133, 442, 448, 459
- 15:2 — 169, 386
- 15:2–18 — 11
- 15:3 — 412
- 15:4 — 28, 34, 101, 412, 444, 445, 449
- 15:4–6 — 448, 463
- 15:5 — 8n19, 425, 449
- 15:6 — 28–29, 34–35, 102–103, 108, 128, 444–445, 454, 459, 463, 467, 497, 521, 524, 545, 548
- 15:7 — 412
- 15:8 — 169

INDEX OF REFERENCES TO SCRIPTURE

Gen (*cont.*)		17:16	27–28, 33–34, 94–97, 241, 370–376, 380–409
15:9	205, 467		
15:18	425		
16	131, 277, 511	17:16–22	17, 370
16–22	11	17:17	8*n*19, 28–29, 34, 98, 101–104, 134–135, 226, 410–431, 443–448, 454, 461–499
16:1–2	277		
16:6, 8	234		
16:6–14	11		
16:11	500	17:18	29–30, 35, 106–108, 114, 496–512, 517–524, 528–535, 545–552, 562, 571
16:14–16	131		
17	2, 9, 12, 19, 38, 131, 140, 158, 219, 243, 382, 392–393, 442, 448, 459, 471, 533, 537, 542		
		17:19	8*n*19, 30, 35–36, 114–115, 293, 425, 551–556, 562–567, 570–572
17:1	24–25, 31–32, 73–80, 131–136, 141–142, 145, 149, 151, 154, 156, 158, 160–168, 173, 179, 182–187, 190–195, 204–210, 213–216, 224, 270, 383, 474, 497, 499, 521–523, 585	17:19–21	566
		17:20	30, 36, 115, 566, 569, 571–572
		17:21	30, 31, 36, 115–116, 570–583
		17:22	31, 36, 117, 370, 584, 585, 587
		17:23–27	31
		17:24–32	532
17:1–5	11, 17, 22, 370	18	140, 424, 533
17:1–22	4*n*7, 22*n*33, 240	18:1	12
17:2	25, 32, 81, 190, 216, 219–221, 224, 274	18:1–8	11, 161
		18:12	11*n*28, 28, 34, 99–100, 125, 410, 425–431, 439, 446
17:3	25, 32, 81, 222–227, 231, 410–414		
17:4	25, 32, 82, 231–241	18:12–15	135, 514, 525
17:5	9, 20, 26, 32, 41, 83, 173, 237–251, 262, 267, 269–273, 278, 354, 410, 429, 467	18:16	324
		18:20	324
		18:24, 32	29, 35, 110, 522, 532, 546, 548, 549
17:5–6	569	19:31	563–564
17:5–15	18, 241–242	20:3–8	11
17:6	241	21	277, 382, 459
17:6–14	12, 19, 27, 218–219, 239, 240–241, 272	21:2–3	416–418
		21:6	27, 33–34, 95, 135, 372, 382–383
17:7–10	425		
17:10	190	21:10	510, 512
17:12	425	21:12	278, 510
17:15	9, 11, 17, 22, 26–27, 32–33, 83–85, 94, 118, 239, 241, 248, 249, 262, 272–273, 277, 370, 410, 427	21:33	28, 34, 103, 469, 473, 477–479
		22	133, 261, 466, 533, 542
		22:2	393
		22:13	270

Gen (*cont.*)		32:29	24, 75, 86, 142, 157, 163, 202, 207–209, 284, 287, 461–462
23:4	407		
23:6	28, 34, 97, 406, 409		
23:9	206	32:30	158, 287, 461–462
24:3	174	32:31	28, 34, 103, 462
24:7	8n19	32:34	287
24:61	366	34	484, 494
24:63	8n19	34:1–39	444, 480
25:3	393	34:2	104, 481, 482
25:7	479	34:2–3	34, 104, 480, 493, 494
25:8	12	34:2–25	29
25:18	302	34:3	481, 485
25:26	86, 281	34:5–6	484, 490
26	436	34:14	105, 490
26:1	439	34:20	480
26:1–5	11	34:25	34, 493, 494
26:12	28, 31, 34, 36, 103, 116, 469–479, 579–584	34:25–26	105, 481, 490
		34:27	480
26:24–25	11	34:30	490
27:36	281	35	302
27:38	30, 35, 110, 497, 522, 533–534, 547–549	35:9–11	173
		35:11	24, 32, 76, 167, 173
28:9	12	35:16	26, 33, 88, 303–304, 376, 393
28:12–15	11		
29	375	35:16–19	300–302, 307, 323, 376, 392
29:31	27, 30, 33, 35, 94, 114, 372, 375, 376, 386, 388, 392, 552, 555	35:18	26, 33, 88, 301, 302, 303, 304, 305, 306
29:35	375	35:19	26, 33, 88, 304
30:24	26, 33, 87, 295, 298, 299	35:20	307
		35:22	521
31:10	206	37:7	11, 305
31:11–13	11	37:9	11
31:15–26	380	37:15	493
31:18	380	37:33	298
31:24	11n29, 26, 33	37:36	28, 34, 430, 437, 440, 442
32	158, 173, 201, 284, 460–462, 512–513	38	382, 389
32:1	290	38:11	386
32:24	287, 290	38:15	33, 94, 376–379
32:25	28, 34, 87, 103, 158, 202, 460–462	38:15–26	27, 372, 376, 386, 388
		38:16	376, 389
32:26–32	163, 202, 207, 460–461	38:17	376
		38:18	33, 94, 376–380
32:28	25–26, 32–33, 79, 163, 192, 201, 206–207, 281, 290, 461–462	38:20–23	386
		38:25	33, 94, 376–380
		38:26	33, 95, 376–381
		39	436, 440

INDEX OF REFERENCES TO SCRIPTURE

Gen (*cont.*)
39:1	28, 101, 430, 436–441, 445
39:20–23	28, 436, 440–441
39:22–23	436
40:9–17	11
41:11–24	11
41:41	294–296
41:41–49	26, 87, 295–296, 300, 323
41:42–43	300
41:45	33, 293–300, 354
41:49	295–296
41:51	313
41:52	311
45	302
45:16–18	28, 34, 100–101, 366, 430–435, 438, 440–441, 445
45:21	438–439
45:45	296
46:20	315
46:30	29, 35, 108, 127, 511, 517–521
48:5	26, 33, 89, 309–312, 315
48:14	316
48:15	25, 32, 79, 191, 195, 202, 206, 315
49	197, 340, 490, 512–513
49:3	512
49:4	521
49:5–7	29, 34, 105, 490–491, 494
49:17	290
49:28	490

Exod
2	330, 337, 344
2:5	366
2:10	337, 366
2:16	26, 33, 90–91, 319–321, 325, 328, 332–341
2:16–18	321, 327
2:16–20	346
2:16–21	319, 322, 331–333, 346
2:16–22	26
2:17	26, 33, 91, 334–337
2:18	26, 33, 91, 321, 325, 335, 339–341
2:18–21	26, 33, 92, 321, 340–343, 346
2:22	349
3	379
3:1	321, 344, 345
3:3	224
3:5	188
3:6	33, 94, 372, 378–379, 387–389
3:7	27
3:12	323
3:14	31, 74, 146, 151, 154, 162, 164
3:14–15	24, 142, 151–154, 156, 162
3:15	31, 74–75, 142, 151–155
3:26–27	498
4:10–16	29, 35, 107, 506
4:14	28, 34, 100, 125, 430–440, 446
4:18	322
6	155
6:3	24, 31, 75, 142, 154–156, 162
6:26–27	29, 35, 107, 505–509
6:29	24, 32, 76, 165, 171
7:1	24, 27, 32–33, 76, 93, 165, 170, 186, 188, 365, 368–369
7:11	29, 107, 498, 506, 509
7:16	170
7:17	24, 32, 76, 165, 170
7:22	29, 107, 506, 509
7:26	107
8:3	29, 107, 506, 509
8:16, 20	170
9:1, 13	170
9:29	24, 32, 76, 165, 171, 368
10:3	170
11:4	170
12:26	323
15	340
15:25	183
16:4	xiii, 30, 35, 558–565
16:14	115, 552, 559
16:15	560, 564–565

592　INDEX OF REFERENCES TO SCRIPTURE

Exod (*cont.*)		36:10, 17	198
16:23	30, 35, 115, 552, 561	45:16–18	410
16:23–26	561		
16:29	561	Lev	
17:2	336–337	5	542
18	319	5:6–17	30, 35, 111–113, 117, 335, 497, 522, 535–538, 542–547, 550
18:1–12	323		
18:14	344		
18:16–17	324	6:10	25, 32, 79, 192, 200–209
18:17–26	26, 33, 323, 345		
18:19–20	90, 319, 323–324	10:1–5	133
18:22–24	319, 324–325	16:2–14	133
18:25–26	345	16:4–5	25, 32, 79, 197, 201, 206, 209
18:26	325		
20	142, 148	16:12	79, 201
20:2	24, 32, 76, 168, 174	18:26	137
20:12	25, 32, 205	19:18	194
20:16	194	22:18	232
20:21	24, 31, 74, 142, 147, 160–165	24:2–3	208
		25:1–17	137
24:1	27, 33, 93, 366	25:4–5	561
24:12	225	25:8	532
24:18	387	25:9–11	546–547
25–33	200	25:10	30, 35, 110, 532, 546, 548, 549
25:10	25, 32, 192		
25:11	79, 200, 206, 208	25:11	197
26:33	25, 28, 32, 34, 79, 104, 192, 199–200, 206, 208, 476	26:11–12	579
		26:12	30, 36, 116, 573, 574, 576, 578, 579
27:9	28, 103, 160, 469, 474, 478–479		
		Num	
27:18–19	34, 474	4:3	548
28:4–8	25, 32, 79, 192, 200, 206, 209	6:21	29, 35, 109, 232, 521–530, 535–536, 545, 548
28:27–28	192, 200		
31:2	198	9:11	315
31:18	177	10:29	345
33	142, 148, 379, 387, 390	11:23	35, 111, 522, 534–536, 547
33–34	389		
33:7	133	11:33	30
33:13	31, 74, 149, 150, 160, 162	12:16	360
		13	529, 530
33:13–23	24, 142, 162	13:1–33	528
33:23	31, 74, 149, 150, 162	13:6	27, 93
34	379, 389, 390	13:16	27, 33, 92, 353, 354, 358, 359
34:28	137, 173		
34:28–35	387, 551	13:17	528
34:33–35	27, 33, 94, 372, 379, 387–389	13:20	528
		13:23	529

INDEX OF REFERENCES TO SCRIPTURE

Num (*cont.*)

13:24	29, 35, 109, 521, 546, 548	4:28	515
		4:29	197
13:27–28	529	5:16	25, 32, 205
13:28	528	6:4	232, 233
13:31	529	8:3	196, 563
13:32–22	529	8:15	197
14	576	10:1–2	200
14:7–9	576	12:8	197
14:9	30, 36, 116, 573–578	12:17	232
14:24	27, 33, 93, 360–363	12:28	25, 32, 79, 191–198, 206
18:25–28	475	17:15–16	197
18:25–32	474–475, 478, 480	18:10	501
18:26	475, 532	18:10–11	508
18:26–29	133–134, 139, 141	20:19	197, 504–505
18:26–30	139	21:18–21	504
18:26–32	24, 31, 73, 132	21:20	29, 35, 106, 498, 504, 508
18:28	29, 34, 103, 469, 474, 575	21:22–23	247
18:29	475	21:23	55, 246
18:29–30	474	23:1–2	29, 35, 106, 508
18:30	136	23:2	502, 503, 504
19:26	135, 136, 474	24:13–16	325
20:17	205	27:12	491
22:4	502	28:1–7	197
22:7–8	501	30:11	111, 538
24:16	29, 35, 106, 496, 498, 501, 508, 509	30:11–14	30, 35, 538–551
		30:12	538
25	319, 330	30:12–14	111, 197, 522, 537, 541–543
25:3	26, 33, 90, 328, 330		
25:3–13	320, 328, 330, 345	30:13	539
25:6–7	328	30:14	111, 538–544
25:7–8	26, 33, 90, 330	30:15, 19	196
25:8	346	32	197
25:11	328	32:4	28, 34, 102, 444–445, 456, 465–466
25:12–13	26, 33, 90, 329, 330		
25:14–15	328	32:8–12	237
27:1–3	315	32:15	501
31	319, 330	33	175, 197, 491, 512–513
31:1–3	328	33:1	24, 27, 32–33, 77, 93, 168, 175, 186–188, 364, 368–369, 490
31:8	29, 35, 106, 500, 502, 508, 510		
		33:6	29, 35, 107, 491, 496, 509, 511–521
31:49	26, 33, 90, 328, 330, 331		
		33:7	491
Deut		33:8	29, 34, 105, 490, 491, 494
1–30	197		
1:17	325	33:12–24	491
4:1	24, 32, 76, 168, 174, 188	34	197
		34:4	367

Judg		78:24	231, 387
13:8	175	79:6–7	340
		83:3	161
1 Kgdms		91:16	456
1:1–2:10	395	93:9	340
2:5	27, 34, 96, 383, 390–402	97:3	208, 291
		113:25	340
		114:9	509
3 Kgdms		120:4	194
13:1	175		
17:10	386	Prov	
		5:20	277, 278
2 Chron		8:22–30	160, 171, 203
2:12–13	198	10:2	487
		11:5–6	487
Esth		12:1	433
7:5	355	13:6	487
		14:29, 34	487
Iob		15:6	487
1:21	213	19:17	194
9:20	214		
14	213	Isa	
14:4	80, 210–211, 214	6	223
14:4–5	211, 213, 215	38:17	500
14:14	25, 32	48:22	28, 100, 430–432, 440–441
25:2	213		
28:24	213	54:1	396
38:4	213	57:21	28, 34, 383, 430, 431–434, 440–441, 445
Ps (LXX)			
1:1	458	Jer	
14:1–3	214	45(38):4	147
18:3	421		
22	432	Ezek	
22:1	26, 33, 91, 319–321, 340, 348	11:14–20	515
		Hos	
23	393	8:14	384
26:1	340	14	383–384
30:19	340	14:6	383
33	349	14:9–10	34, 95, 372, 383–384, 387
36:4	207, 340		
38:3	495	Hab	
38:6	227	2:18–19	515
41:4	340	Zach	
50:17	229	6:12	384
64:5	161	14:10	306
64:10	340		
73:16	188		
77:24	564, 565		

INDEX OF REFERENCES TO SCRIPTURE

Wis
- 6:14 — 483
- 7:10 — 194
- 7:12 — 368
- 7:15–16 — 392
- 7:26 — 29, 35, 109, 528
- 8:7 — 485
- 9:3–4 — 483
- 9:5–6 — 184
- 11:24 — 204

Sir
- 24:22–23 — 368
- 27:37 — 368

1 Macc
- 7:7 — 295

2 Macc
- 14:35 — 136

Matt
- 1–2 — 299
- 1:3 — 388
- 1:21 — 351, 360
- 3:3 — 208
- 5 — 549
- 7:16–20 — 271
- 15:18 — 551
- 19:29 — 578
- 22:32 — 509
- 27:51 — 208

Mark
- 1:2 — 512
- 7:20 — 551
- 12:28–34 — 193
- 14:38 — 268
- 14:58 — 189

Luke
- 1:18 — 467
- 1:69 — 360
- 6:43–45 — 271
- 24:13–27 — 189

John
- 1:3 — 430
- 1:5 — 163
- 3:3 — 565
- 3:3–8 — 188
- 3:7 — 565
- 5:35 — 208
- 5:51–58 — 564
- 6 — xiii
- 6:26 — 565
- 6:30–51 — 564
- 6:30–58 — 564
- 6:31 — 231, 387, 564
- 6:31–35 — 231
- 6:32 — 231, 565
- 6:33–34 — 231
- 6:49–51 — 564
- 16:17 — 565
- 18:5–6 — 166
- 20:22 — 352
- 20:31 — 468

Acts
- 2:47 — 299
- 4:12 — 360
- 7:48 — 189
- 17:22 — 390
- 17:24 — 189
- 17:27 — 369
- 19:2 — 352

Rom
- 1:26 — 352
- 3 — 214
- 3–4 — 442, 467
- 3:3 — 444
- 3:9–20 — 214
- 3:23 — 215
- 4 — 416, 463, 467
- 4:3 — 454, 467
- 4:17 — 209, 467
- 4:18 — 430
- 4:19 — 467
- 4:23 — 454
- 5:1–2 — 416
- 5:12 — 215
- 6:4 — 307
- 7:14 — 268
- 7:24 — 549
- 8:4–9 — 268
- 9:4 — 221
- 11:28 — 217
- 13:8–10 — 193
- 14:18 — 193

1 Cor

1:21	209
1:29	416
2:3–8	209
3:1	268
3:21	416
9:10–11	584
9:24–27	282
9:25	202, 292
9:27	209
10:25	292
11:4	209
15:14	209
15:44–49	188
15:51	363

2 Cor

2:17–28	465
3:7–18	319, 390, 551
3:12–18	268
3:17	269
4:16–18	397, 416
5:16	297
6:16	579
9:13	236

Gal

3	442, 467
3:6	454
3:16	430
3:19	189, 307
3:22	466
3:23–25	564
4:21–31	388, 573
4:27	396
4:29	268
5:12	510
5:17–23	268, 271, 468, 480

Eph

5:21–6:9	530

Phil

2:6–11	166
2:10	165
3	350
3:12	524

Col

1:18	166
3:18–21	548

3:18–4:1	530
4:1	548

1 Thess

4:16	509

1 Tim

4:13	317

Phlm

20	510

Heb

1	549
3:1	236
4:7	564
4:12	352
4:14	236
9:4	200
9:7	133
9:11	189
10:1–5	163
10:10	163
10:20	208
10:23	236
10:24	139
11:3–31	190, 405
12:2	269

Jas

1:17	396
1:22–25	317
2	442, 467
2:12	551
3:2	551
3:8	551

1 Pet

2:18–3:7	530

2 Pet

1:19	317
2:15–16	509

Jude

5	360
11	509

Rev

2:14	509

Index of References to Philo

Abr.
    title   xiv, 43, 260–261, 401, 429
    1   196
    2–5   xiv
    17–18   187, 191
    48   154, 191–192, 353
    51–52   162
    54   216
    57   290
    66–67   217
    68–80   159
    82   266–267
    91   386
    99   277
    103   230
    107   424
    112   429
    119–122   158, 162, 189
    123   148
    153   418
    157   421
    178–183   260–261
    198   133
    201   139, 414, 463
    203   554
    219   402
    262–274   463

Aet.
    title   xv
    19   196
    47   546
    50   546
    51   546
    54   464
    75   247
    84   546
    94   247

Agr.
    title   xiv, 3–6, 10–12, 15, 218, 239, 561
    1–2   131, 149, 152
    7   529, 561
    8–16   267, 342

    14   256–257
    19   402
    43   344
    44   265
    50–54   348
    57   230
    77   519
    78   197
    79–83   339, 501
    84   197
    116–119   345
    132   313
    137   570
    149   168, 575
    161   348
    172   197
    175   224

Cher.
    title   xiv, 10, 12, 44
    1   131
    3–10   8–9, 138–139, 214, 241, 243, 266–267, 272, 276–277, 386, 402, 414, 510–512, 571
    12–13   135, 139, 428
    23   464
    27   162, 181
    31   330, 346, 351
    32   500, 509
    40–41   344, 349, 371, 375, 386, 555, 563
    47   349
    48   387
    53   368
    56   266
    57   446
    75   168
    95   211
    96   144, 160
    123   176

Conf.
    title   xiv, 3, 10–12, 244
    1   131
    2–13   244, 451

Conf. (cont.)

19	172	166–167	432
31	456	173–174	563
39	339–340	180	396
52	339	255	496
55–57	331, 345–346		
59	330	*Contempl.*	
62	384	title	xv, 43, 327, 517
65	502	2	177
92	290	42	146–147
95	440	65	547
96	463		
119	168	*Decal.*	
123	187	title	xv, 137
146	290, 368	15–17	563
159	500, 509	20	137
169	181, 186	27	137–139
179	186, 290	32	385
		38	185
		88	168

Congr.

		106	193
title	xiv, 2, 131, 389, 400, 556, 570	106–120	205
		111	194
1	131	155	407
1–10	437	159	396
2	276–277	164	547
3	386, 395		
7	386, 494	*Deo*	
11	252, 399–401, 569–570	title	2, 11–12, 36, 42
		4	158, 162
13	560	5	162
14–18	145, 401, 570		
22	348	*Det.*	
25–27	305, 555	title	xiv, 10
34	291	1	131
36	135, 139, 465	4	168
39–43	314–316, 586	9	493
47	144	11	330
51	252, 290	16	365
61	347	22	160
64	246	38–40	230
71–88	8, 400, 570	46	554
107–110	226, 344, 416, 546, 549	52–53	205
		61	213
124–126	386	62	168
129	553	67	175, 197, 490, 494
133–134	546	68	149
135	160	71	501
140–148	144–145, 316, 400, 570	75	402
		80	240

INDEX OF REFERENCES TO PHILO

Det. (cont.)
85	464	92	368
92	162	94	316, 491
96	494	96–98	358
114	197, 224	111	230
119–120	135, 212	143–152	393, 395
123–137	125, 135, 139, 439, 463	177	484
139	162	190	347
140	214	202	256
150	464	210–221	440
159	162	220	230
160	162		
161–162	162, 170, 186	*Flacc.*	
		title	xv
		122	340

Deus
title	xiv, 3–6, 10–12, 43, 203, 218, 266	*Fug.*	
		title	xiv, 2–3, 11, 131, 231, 234, 386
1	131	1–3	131, 187, 229, 234
2	266	5	260
4	463–466	10	339, 345
5–15	211, 393–395	13	546
32	583	20	187
38	418	30	484
50	196	41	211
51	385	46	225
56	465	50	494
86–93	316, 582	55	503
87	224	59	339
109	172	60	186
111–115	440	68–71	186, 342
113	172	82	226
137	386	110–112	162
162	225	115	224
181–183	160, 508	120	229
		129	313
Ebr.		137–139	563
title	xiv, 4, 10–11	141	218, 387
1	131	142	197
2	224	143	385
11	331	149–156	386, 456
13–94	508	153	149
17	205	164	465
23	402	165	161–162
36–37	344	168	205
44	160	170	196–197, 561
73	346	172	361
79	213	173	394
80–87	168, 201, 206–207, 290	179	260, 263

599

Fug. (cont.)
197	384	170	494
208	290, 508	171–172	193, 205, 347–348
211	553	181	513, 516–517, 520
213	348	201	246
		205–206	202–203, 348, 427

Gig.
title	xiv, 5–6, 10–12	209	402
1	131	231	342, 546
19	265–266	237–238	347, 546–547
28–29	215, 265	242	438
40	464, 546	250	197, 205
50	344	251	196
54	387	252–256	307
61	201	258	277
62–64	9, 133, 185, 205–206, 213, 243, 266–267, 367	263	144
		264	205
		301	304, 519

Her.

Hypoth.
title	xiv	title	xv
1	131	8.7.13	561
5	381	8.11.1–18	517
14	196		
21	226, 326	*Ios.*	
29–31	225–226	title	xiv, 293, 298, 440
30–39	415, 475	1	154, 401
43	148	27	440
44	321	28	298
45–46	213, 348	31	298, 347
50–51	386	35–36	440
55	265	48	494
58	546	52	440
63–74	415	58–79	440
64	149	80	385
69	234	121	250, 299–300
70	162	147	205
75	126	151	230
78	290	250–251	440
89	160		
90–95	463–464	*Leg. 1–3*	
105	464	title	xiv, 3–4, 6, 9–12, 45, 224
113	211	1.1	131
121	348	1.3	524
127	205	1.8	252
128	344, 349	1.15	494
133	330, 346, 351	1.17	224
152	196	1.21	575
165	583		

INDEX OF REFERENCES TO PHILO

Leg. 1–3 (cont.)

1.31–43	179–180, 183, 186, 193, 212, 217, 227, 229, 362, 365, 368, 535, 537	3.12–13	345–346
		3.15	9, 290
		3.22	428
		3.25	493
		3.26	339
		3.39–43	8, 139
1.45	139, 324	3.47	423
1.55	586	3.61	247
1.56	267, 529	3.75	464
1.57	256	3.80	519
1.59	172, 267, 275, 277	3.83–87	8, 135, 139, 266, 414, 424, 463, 466, 562–563, 571
1.60	418		
1.61	275, 290		
1.62	452	3.88	230
1.63–67	275, 277, 358, 402	3.90–94	290, 314–315, 418
1.77	179	3.95–96	169, 359, 435
1.78	457	3.100	201
1.80–82	387	3.101	161–162
1.91	260, 528	3.105–107	135, 197, 224, 347
1.101–104	336	3.110	347
1.105–107	305	3.128–129	421
2.1	131	3.131–132	428
2.2	465	3.145	368
2.3	179, 212, 233	3.146	387
2.4–2.6	215, 329, 334	3.162–173	196, 563
2.8–9	335	3.175	172, 203, 427
2.14–15	249, 266, 276, 368	3.180	290, 386, 388
2.18	358, 402	3.184	348
2.24–25	362	3.197	344
2.34	290	3.217–219	8, 135, 139, 303, 386–387, 428, 463
2.38–39	334		
2.46	500	3.228	463
2.47	386	3.236–242	346, 437–438, 440
2.52	500	3.244–245	8–9, 266, 277–278
2.53–59	133, 201, 230, 476, 489	3.252	560
2.67	555	*Legat.*	
2.71–75	201, 230, 338, 347, 457, 531	title	xv, 3
		4	290
2.83	463	6	165
2.85	519	46	147
2.89	290	69	225
2.90	347	116	502
2.95	387	155	502
2.99	290	182	xii
2.100	428	195	168
2.104	519	312	402
2.105	196	370	xii
3.1	131	373	219

Migr.

title	xiv, 2–3, 5, 36, 231, 351
1	131
8	225
14–20	196, 296, 440
21	300
31–35	218
36	183
37	172
38	316
39	290
43	183
44	367, 456, 463–464, 466
49	160
69	508
76–81	125, 230, 290, 440, 509
82–85	509
84	186, 205, 365
87–88	158
89–93	xii, 189–190, 219, 589
99	402
103	220, 235
113	500, 509
114	387
115	158
124	228, 230, 501
136	213
138	225, 252
147	348
154	555
157	123, 135, 339
165	160
179	528
181	546
188	328
191	160
197	409
198–207	9, 132, 290, 315–316, 348
216	493
219	402
221	493
223–224	483, 493–494
225	482

Mos. 1–2

title	140, 260, 346
1.17	337, 355, 367
1.27	172
1.51–59	346–347
1.63	326
1.75–76	162
1.158	147, 160
1.172	500
1.185	205
1.220–231	546
1.248	260
1.264	508
1.273	226
1.274	387
1.290	583
1.300–304	345
2.7	199, 218
2.37	290
2.40	261
2.47–45	xiv
2.53	494
2.58	361
2.65	186
2.70	387
2.87	126
2.89–90	478
2.91	476
2.99	189
2.117	196
2.127–129	230, 253
2.182	347
2.185	402
2.188	340, 365
2.210	494
2.215–217	424
2.258–269	563
2.288	183, 523
2.290	197
2.291	367

Mut.

title	xiv, 2, 4, 10, 15, 125, 337
1–2	137, 139, 145, 264
3–10	143, 145, 148–149, 160–162, 194, 205
12	148, 153
7	140

INDEX OF REFERENCES TO PHILO

Mut. (cont.)

8	125, 160	115	339		
11–14	140, 153, 157–158, 162, 164–165, 461	121–122	9, 250, 269, 428		
		123	363		
		124	211		
15	138, 153, 163, 249	125	186, 188, 513		
18–19	147, 168, 186	126	368		
21–22	172	127	513		
24–25	174, 188, 367, 513	128	186		
26	177	130	1, 156		
27–29	162–163, 179, 189, 465	130–153	385–387, 390		
30–38	179, 183, 186–187, 519	131	135, 139, 164		
39–40	205, 259	133	375		
42	197, 519	139	384		
43	201, 209	141–144	395–396		
44	163, 207, 461	145–146	401–402		
45	348	148–150	405, 519		
46	204	154	123, 415		
48	213	155	226		
49	210–212	157–165	423–424		
50	205, 212	160	419		
51	213	166–167	11, 427, 429		
53	15, 218–219, 239, 272, 415	168	125		
		174	148		
54–56	149, 224–227, 229–230, 415–416	175–187	463		
		175	226		
57–59	162, 217, 234–236, 238	176	228		
60–76	1, 9, 247, 249–250, 262–263, 269	177–178	416, 463–464		
		179	519		
60–129	9–10	180	384, 464		
66	164	182	197, 466		
68	252	187	163, 461, 464		
70	159, 291	188–192	135, 139, 206, 463, 477–479		
73	267				
74	256, 477	193	482, 493		
76	9	194–196	484, 494		
77–80	9, 276–277, 279, 399, 529	199	199, 338		
		200	197, 490, 513		
81	9, 164, 292, 461	201–209	145, 160, 187, 374, 508, 519		
82	162				
83	9	210	315–316, 513		
85	285	211–212	284, 515–516		
87	9	213	519		
88	9, 249	216	127		
92	305–306, 328	220	338, 347		
98	315	225	402, 475		
99	491	227–228	180, 549		
100	313	241	464		
103–120	228, 344–351	255	180		
114	338	256	475		

Mut. (cont.)
260	565	10	348
261	139, 572	18–44	186
262	419	22	160
263	197	24	529
265	578	26	162, 196
267	155, 583	29	339–340
270	285	38	139
		44	465
		49	212

Num.
title	xv, 134, 139, 196, 264
frag. 4d (Terian)	465
frag. 43	494

64	492
67–68	368
71	168
73–77	478
75	473
82	456

Opif.
title	xiv, 186	108	168
1	368	134	387
16	201	138	383–384, 387
21	207	139–177	10
25	172	167–169	139
26	xii		
34	418		

Post.
title	xiv, 6, 10, 44, 187
1	131
9	160
12	148, 439
13–18	160–162
21	423
28	291
30	120
32	218
34	418
35–36	187
39	120
41–42	187
48	120
60	546
67	265
77–78	349
84–88	547
98	385
121–122	578
127	196
128	402
135	305, 386
165	338, 347
167	160
168	162
173	264

59	577
69	172, 186
71	186, 464
72	168, 186
73	402
75	179–180, 186
77	xii
82	172
103	368
113	252
117	334
127	493
128	347
134–135	179, 183, 274, 348
134–144	186
136	249
137	172
139	172
142	177
146	545
148–150	249, 266
151	215
154	180

Plant.
title	xiv, 4, 6, 10, 561
1	131

INDEX OF REFERENCES TO PHILO

Post. (cont.)
179   218, 298
181   168
182–183   329, 346

Praem.
title   43, 535
1–3   xiv
5   387
27–30   456, 463
40   177, 235
44   162, 290
50   290
63   553
80   547
87   440
95   583
123–124   578
160   402
161   414, 424

Prob.
title   xv, 347, 368, 409
1   433, 436
43   186
65   213
67   402
68   547
71   402
75–91   517
80   159
141   347
157   402

Prov. 1–2
title   xi, xv, 381, 532
2.12–14   415
2.15   451
2.24   415
frag. 2   464

QE 1–2
title   xiii, 5, 12–13, 16, 21, 31, 41, 48, 137, 186, 237, 263, 290, 327, 402, 414, 439, 462, 464, 519, 520, 571, 584
1.20   162
1 frag. (Cover)   224
2.3   162
2.11   162
2.14   162
2.16   162
2.28   160
2.47   162
2.51   162
2.54   206
2.61   162
2.62   162
2.63   162
2.66   162
2.68   157–158, 162, 174, 178
2.76   383
2.91   206
2.94   206
2.104   206
2.106   160, 206
2.108   207
2.122   162
2 frag. 25d   440

QG 1–4
title   xiii, 5, 12–13, 16, 21, 31, 41, 48, 137, 186, 218, 237, 263, 290, 327, 402, 414, 439, 462, 464, 519, 520, 571, 584
1.4   186
1.20–21   266
1.65   494
1.66   488
1.69   213
1.79   416, 420, 424
1.100   578
2.5   546
2.6   10
2.26   440
2.38   547
2.43   440
2.47   134
2.54   554
2.57   138
2.62   181, 186
2.78   546
3.32   508
3.38   139

QG 1–4 (cont.)		Sacr.	
3.39–60	45	title	xiv, 10, 44
3.39	24, 137, 139, 160–161,	1	131
	163, 185–186, 478, 546	9	162, 170, 186, 365
3.40	25, 185, 190, 205, 210,	28	172
	213, 216–221, 233, 235	35	440
3.41	25, 217, 221, 224–226,	36	144, 160
	229, 235, 238, 414	44	395, 422
3.42	25, 217, 231, 234–238	50	344
3.43	9, 26, 239, 243, 245,	54	402
	249, 254, 262–267,	56	226
	276, 465, 471	59	172
3.44–52	27, 239	61	313
3.49	290	69	160
3.53	9, 26, 139, 239, 245,	72	385
	262–263, 272, 276–	73	347
	277, 465	78	138, 160
3.54	27, 370, 385–386,	84	402
	392, 395, 398, 401,	87	578
	402, 405, 409, 423	101	162
3.55	28, 410, 414–415, 423	112	334
3.56	28, 137, 139, 462–464,	121	440
	465, 468, 477–479	122	546
3.57	29, 127, 507–508,	131	366, 369
	519–520, 545		
3.58	30, 464, 465, 562–563	Sobr.	
3.59	30, 562–563, 565,	title	xiv, 4–5, 6, 11, 239
	571–572, 578	1	11, 131
3.60	30, 572–573, 578, 583	3	160
3.61–62	31	16–17	292
4.2	162, 451	27–29	314–316
4.4	162	38	402
4.8	148, 161–162	50	494
4.16	428–429, 431, 439	55	201, 230
4.17	414, 429	57	409
4.22	162	65–66	290, 477
4.27	546		
4.80	206	Somn. 1–2	
4.123	197, 519	title	xiv, 3–4, 9, 11–13, 40,
4.138	395		45, 239, 293, 302, 306
4.147	395, 508	1.1	131
4.153	12	1.12	456
4.189	478	1.23	145
4.204	402	1.30–32	150, 162, 172
4.227	547	1.34	545
4.231	547	1.35	484
4.233	290	1.37	387
4 frag. 163	290	1.39	260
		1.53	145

INDEX OF REFERENCES TO PHILO 607

Somn. 1–2 (cont.)

1.57–60	225–226, 482	2.188	348
1.64	457, 586	2.189	186, 322, 364
1.67	152, 163, 165	2.206	546
1.71	135	2.211	295
1.72–119	302, 305	2.223	226
1.73–74	144, 267	2.224	409
1.75	339	2.227	162
1.77	328	2.237	162
1.78	298	2.242	240
1.82	138	2.245	340
1.89	345	2.248	578
1.105	213	2.253	464
1.117	160, 196	2.254	368
1.129	290	2.273	374
1.131	207, 484	2.279	135
1.143	127	2.291	484
1.148	578	2.292	162, 219
1.161	159		
1.164	160	*Spec. 1–4*	
1.171	290	title	xv, 320
1.183	168	1.10	446
1.190	169	1.31	161
1.203–205	206	1.40	161
1.208	172	1.41–50	162, 205, 225
1.212	225–226	1.56–57	345
1.213–218	206	1.61	508
1.220	225	1.81	162
1.226	127	1.84–85	206
1.229	162, 418	1.94	206
1.230	162	1.111	321
1.231	162	1.157	135, 139, 475
1.234	162	1.162–256	43
1.254	393	1.181	577
2.31–36	315–316, 387, 491–492	1.186	577
		1.191	432
2.36–41	304–305	1.247	224
2.44–45	290, 387	1.271	168, 464, 547
2.47	298, 300	1.278	168
2.52	542	1.295	213
2.63–66	298	1.301	547
2.67	384	1.306	500
2.125	177	1.322	500
2.160	160	1.330	205
2.165	564	1.336	256
2.169–171	546	2.40	396
2.170	127	2.52	213
2.173	290, 501	2.62	402
2.180	547	2.63	259
		2.75	168

Spec. 1–4 (cont.)

2.80	387	*Test. 1–2*	
2.84	464	title	10, 12, 19, 38, 190, 218, 240
2.96	168		
2.110	547	*Virt.*	
2.129	464	title	xv, 259
2.174	479	8	256
2.176–177	532, 547	41–42	345
2.192	213	47	197
2.224	531	50–51	259
2.249	502	58	265
3.1–6	xii, 350, 458, 469, 534	99	547
3.111	230	100	407
3.188	577	127	464
3.202	168	133	500
4.48	508	167	402
4.51	263	183	547
4.60	144, 160	187–227	566
4.69	230, 253	193	213
4.92	230	212–219	463
4.98	139		
4.131	197		
4.135	258, 277		
4.139	205		
4.173–175	344		
4.218	564		

Index of References to Other Ancient Sources

Aeschylus
Prom.
   309   222

Alexander Polyhistor
Frag.
   frag. 4   321
   frag. 14   318, 336

Ambrose
Abr.
   1.43   141
   1.27   214, 271
   2.11   583
   2.75–76   214
   2.85   141
   2.86   226, 236
   2.87   465
   2.88   520
Isaac
   1.1   141
Exp. Ps. 118
   8.21   188
Jac.
   2.7.34   307
Jos.
   7.40   299–300
   13.74   441

Andreas of Caesarea
Comm. Apoc.
   7.19   306, 317

Andronicus of Rhodes
Pass.
   SVF 3.391   135, 255

Anonymous
Acts John
   79   163, 165
Frag. lex. Graec.
   177.49–52   479
Tab. Ceb.
   2.14   283
   6.1–7.3   286
   7.1   297
   7.3   298

Anon. Theaet. Comm.
   5.19–23   145

Apostolic Fathers
Shepherd of Hermas
   94–95 (Sim. 9.17–18) 572

Aristophanes
Thesm.
   295–310   158

Aristotle
De an.
   420b   523
Cat.
   4   177
Cael.
   279a   155, 177
   288b   223
Eth. eud.
   1.1.4–5 (1214a)   154
Eth. nic.
   1.6 (1096a23)   148
   1.7–8 (1098b–1099a) 358
   2.1 (1103a)   154
   2.1 (1103b31–32) 391
   2.2   218
   2.6 (1107a2–8)   136
   3.2 (1111a–1113b) 285
   5   487
   5.5   335
   5.10–11 (1136a–b) 313
   6   487
   6.12 (1143b)   143
   6.13 (1144b)   487
   10.8   337
[*Mag. mor.*]
   1.9.11 (1187a)   286
   1.33.5   408
Pol.
   1.10   335
   7 (1332a)   154
Top.
   105b   256

Astrampsychus
Sort. Astr.
    4.9   369
    4.86   278

Athanasius
C. Ar.
    2.15   226
Inc.
    4.4–5   226
    7.4   442
    14.1   442
[*Nav. praec.*]
    28.908   429

Augustine
Civ.
    1.18   495
    16.28   270
Conf.
    1.2   467

Bacchylides
Epigr.
    6.313.1   364

Basil of Caesarea
[*En. in proph. Isa.*]
    3.99.16   278

Cleanthes
Hymn.
    1   364

Clement of Alexandria
Paed.
    1.3   550
    1.4.11.2   352
    1.7.56   221
    1.56.3   207
    1.57.2   291
Strom.
    1.31.1   277
    1.31.4   291
    1.31.6   389
    1.72.4   134
    1.182.2   236, 238
    1.182.3   189
    2.5.3–2.6.4   163
    2.6.1   163
    2.50.2–3   352
    2.100.2   409
    2.100.3   134
    3.99.1   271
    5.8.5–6   269–270
    5.65.2   165
    5.78.3   163, 165
    5.82.1   165
    6.60.3   292
    6.134.2   352

Cocondrius
Trop.
    3   156

Cyril of Alexandria
Ador. cult.
    68.252–253   440
Comm. Jo.
    1.522–523   208
    3.149   466
Contr. Jul.
    2.5   207
Epist. pasch.
    5.3   406
    5.4   388
    5.5   406
Frag. Rom.
    245.6   466
Glaph. Pent.
    4   549
    89   440
    125   278
    213   307
    224   307
    213   299
    224   299
    232   299
    296   299
    409.27   349, 351

Cyril of Jerusalem
Catech. illum.
    10.11   360

Damascius
Princ.
    3   157
    6.25   157

Didymus the Blind

Comm. Job

251	214

Comm. Ps.

20–21 (41.21)	207
29–34 (184.7–23)	165, 349

Comm. Zacch.

2.23	207
3.106	396
3.276	317
5.103–104	306

In Gen.

114.5	278
114.6–11	191
215	495
250.12	141
250.24–29	187, 207

Frag. Ps.

948	208, 291

[Trin.]

3 (39.92)	429

Dio Chrysostom (Dio of Prusa)

Borysth.

11–12	488

Or.

8	296
8.11–13	282–283, 287, 419
8.15	202, 283
8.20	282
8.26	282
9.4	433
48.2	433

Dionysius of Halicarnassus

Ant. rom.

2.3.7	212

Is.

14	326

[Rhet.]

10.6	326

Epictetus

Diatr.

1.14	194
4.12.19	184, 194

Epiphanius

Anchor.

13.8	495

Pan.

1.371–372	467

Euripides

Hel.

1165–1166	152

Med.

1250	534

Hipp.

807	534

Andr.

386	534
1201	534

Eusebius of Caesarea

Comm. Is.

2.34	441

Comm. Ps.

347–348	495

Dem. ev.

4.17.1–3	267, 270, 278, 291, 359, 548, 572

Ecl. proph.

35.24	360
36.10	360
36.15	360
125.18	317

Frag. Luc.

24.531–532	429, 467

Hist. eccl.

1.12.9	134
2.4.3	134
2.18.1–3	2, 10–11, 43, 240

Praep. ev.

3.6.6	165
8.10.8	548
11.4.6	208
11.6.25–27	270

Quaest. ev. Steph.

7.1 (22.905.10)	389

Eusebius of Emesa

Comm. in Gen.

frag. 74	300

Evagrius

Exp. Prov.

95.15	306

Galen
Comm. nat. hom.
15.170	450

George Kedrenos (Cedrenus)
Comp. hist.
1.57	479

Gregory of Nyssa
Antirrhet. adv. Apoll.
3.1	226

Eun. 1–3
2.1.100	226
2.1.124	227
2.1.398–402	269

Hom. opif.
11	164

[Lib. cogn. Dei]
130.316.45	429

Vit. Moys. 1–2
2.162	389

Hagiographiae et Martyria
Vit. Mar. Mag.
2	396

Mart. Gur. Sam.
37	466

Vit. Theod.
BGH 1776	466

Herodotus
Hist.
2.52	179
2.168	473
3.124	251

Hesychius
Comm. brev.
76.21	369
107.9	317

Hilary of Poitiers
Comm. Ps.
51.17–18	509, 520–521

Hippodamus
[Resp.]
101.11	326

Hippolytus
Ben. Is. Jac.
34	549
114	307

Homer
[Hymn.]
2.18	364
2.32	364
3.82	364

Il.
1.58	450
2.302	211
2.792	450
2.850	516
12.177–178	156
15.189	161
16.235	169
16.553	516
18.382–383	v, 218
18.400	xxii
18.411	460
18.417	460
20.37	460
20.74	38
22.126	107, 514
24.525–533	458

Od.
1.1	8, 174
1.6	289
1.235–236	184
5	452
7.35	453, 456
7.36	28, 34, 102, 445, 450–451, 456
8.18–19	218
8.310	460
8.499	198
19.163	29, 35, 107
24.364	437

Irenaeus
Frag. deperdit.
8	208

Haer.
1.2.1	163
1.9.3	441

INDEX OF REFERENCES TO OTHER ANCIENT SOURCES 613

Isocrates
Trapez. (Or. 17)
  58   543

Jerome
Nom. hebr.
  7.15   141

John Chrysostom
Catech. illum.
  1.46   579
Hom. Gen.
  53.363–371   226, 387, 406, 415,
                                466, 572, 578, 584
  54.469   549
  54.516   494
In 1 Cor.
  23.3   510
In Gen.
  54.39–44   388
Mut.
  title   140
  1.6 (123.19–22)   268, 278, 291
  2.2 (125.58–60)   269
  2.2 (126.5–11)   268
  2.2 (126.28–34)   268, 278, 291
  2.2 (126.45–47)   269
  2.3 (128.23–28)   292
  2.3 (128.44–54)   292
  2.4 (130.51–57)   293
  2.4 (131.9–12)   429
  2.4 (132)   271

John of Damascus
[*Anon. dial. Jud.*]
  5.114–130   351

Josephus
A.J.
  1.337–340   494
  2.39–59   442
  2.91   300
  3.63   322, 349
  3.302   548
  4.42   349
  18.159–160   xi
  18.259   xi
  19.276–277   xi
  20.100   xi

B.J.
  5.45–46   xi
  6.237   xi

Justin Martyr
Apol. 1–2
  1.63   389
[*Cohort. gent.*]
  20–21   165
Dial.
  57.2   168
  86.6   388
  113.1–3   269, 359
  126.2   165

Libanius
Progymn.
  6.1   207

Lucian
Hist. conscr.
  31   148

Ps.-Macarius
Serm.
  3.5.2   579

Maximus the Confessor
[*Capit. gnost.*]
  45   510
Exp. Ps. 59
  204–205   317

Menander
Sent.
  1.298   256

Nilus of Ancyra
Ep.
  90   299, 316–317

Origen
Adnot. Deut.
  33   521
Cels.
  4.12   587
  5.4   165
  5.45   141, 164, 270, 292, 390
Comm. Cant.
  1   549

Comm. Jo.
	1.9 141
	1.12–23 141
	1.35.260 292
	1.218 389
	6.45.236 564
	28.24.213–222 317
	33.211–212 352
Comm. Matt.
	11.3 549
	15.5 271
Comm. Rom.
	5.1 215
Engastr.
	2 389
Frag. Jer.
	56 317
Frag. Luc.
	63 550
Hom. Gen.
	2.5 549
	3 140
	3.3 267, 292
	4 140
	6.1 278
	7.1 390
	12.5 479
	15.3–4 291–292
Hom. Jer.
	9.3 187
Hom. Jes. nav.
	407 363
	436 299
Hom. Jos.
	7.40 299
	9.5 495
	14.2 317
	18.3 363
	21.2 317
	22.4 299
Hom. Lev.
	2.2 550
	2.4 550
	4.6 209
	6.3 209, 495
Hom. Luc.
	28.11 389
	33.187 396
Hom. Num.
	4.3 495
	5.1 495
	5.2 548–549
	8.1 548
	9.1 548
	17.1 351
	20.3 351
	20.5 351
	25.3 269–270
	26.4 442
Hom. Ps.
	11.2.18 188
	15.1.1 307
Princ.
	2.8.1 548
Sel. Gen.
	12.115–116 269–270
	12.124.4 351
Sel. Num.
	12.576.36–40 359
	12.580–581 509

Philodemus
Deis
	3.5 136
Ir.
	46.30 286
Mus.
	4 483

Ovid
Met.
	1.1–4 1
	15.871–879

Plato
Apol.
	27e 374
	31d 285
Charm.
	164d 222
Crat.
	383a–384d 243
	388e–389a 147, 150, 248, 354, 366
	389c 568
	390e 419, 568
	391b 155
	392c 419
	394d 568
	396a 419

INDEX OF REFERENCES TO OTHER ANCIENT SOURCES

Crat. (cont.)
   397d   179
   399a   568
   401b   249
   403c–d   7
   407b   419
   420d   285
   436a–d   153, 155
[*Epin.*]
   986c–d   252
Leg.
   589a   170
   779a   433
   857cd   433
   923a   223
   937d   212
Phaedr.
   229e   81, 223
   242b   285
   243b   219
   244ad   192, 343
   245c   146, 210, 233, 453, 513
   246b   159, 519
   246c   454
   246d   313
   246e   344
   247b   464
   247de   134, 411, 457
   248a   453
   249c   146
   250c   146
   251d   435
   252e   329
   253e   159
   255c   328
   257a   219
   264c   240
Phileb.
   28c   229
Pol.
   258a   153
   279b–287c   199
   292c6   285
   305e   199
Prot.
   343b   150, 223
   358bc   313
Resp.
   Book 7   146

   Book 10   304
   347c   134
   398ab   489
   404d   134
   431c   527
   505a   148
   508b–509e   142–146, 148
   511e   144
   516b   252
   518c   142–143
   529b   252
   530a   252
   533d   142–143
   560de   485
   583c   472
   598–601   489
   603e   531
   606–607   489
   615a   134
Symp.
   208a   313
   215b   172
Theaet.
   150c   271
   152a   161
   176b   181
   182a   358
   191c–195b   29, 35, 180, 284, 513–517, 520, 528
Tim.
   21a   124
   29de   204
   30d   144
   34a   527
   37c   172, 580
   37d   42, 580, 583
   38b   580
   41b–42d   180–181, 326
   45d   240
   51d   143
   52b   296
   58d   453
   64d   240
   75e   254

Plotinus
Enn.
   6.7   149

Plutarch
Adv. Col.
   1119e   273
Cim.
   2   211
Crass.
   6   212
Is. Os.
   title   xviii, 199
Quaest. conviv.
   9 (745d–f)   7
Stoic. rep.
   1035a–f   257
   1040f   184

Posidippus
Epigr.
   62   229

Porphyry
Antr. nymph.
   1   148
   9   344

Proclus
In Plat. rem publ.
   1.157   207
In Tim.
   3.265   326

Procopius
Comm. Gen.
   11.3   479
   17.4   563
   45.1   441

Quintilian
Inst.
   2.15   405
   5.1   326
   5.7   327
   8.6   153

Rabbinic Literature
Gen. Rab.
   43:6   133
   46:5   133
   55:6–7   133
   80   481

Mek.
   Pisḥa 11   169

Seneca
Ep.
   42.1   184

Sextus Empiricus
Math.
   7.2   256

Sophocles
Ant.
   1115   364
   1284   247
El.
   934   534
Oed. tyr.
   525   542

Stobaeus
Ecl.
   1.1.10   137

Theodoret
Quaest. Oct.
   73   520
   202   349

Theodotus
Exc.
   56.5   291

Theophrastus
Caus. plant.
   1.13.12   421

Tryphon
Trop.
   192.21   153

Vergil
Aen.
   1.10   259
   1.378   259
Ecl.
   4.39–45   561

Index of Modern Authors

Adams, Sean   15, 296, 436
Adler, Maximilian   4–11
Alesse, Francesca   1, 40, 136, 144, 310, 381, 407, 453, 514, 527, 562
Alexandre, Jr., Manuel   227, 551–558, 565, 567
Anderson, Gary   194, 203, 299, 539
Arnaldez, Roger   17–18, 20–22, 41, 44, 118–128, 143, 154–155, 159, 170, 174–175, 177–179, 182, 185, 187–188, 192–195, 203, 210–211, 217, 223, 237, 245, 252, 275, 286, 288, 295, 307–308, 314, 324, 326, 329, 339, 342–343, 357–358, 367–368, 370, 374, 383, 387, 398, 405, 407, 413–414, 422, 427–428, 446, 456, 458, 476, 478, 498, 517, 524–525, 529–530, 534, 541, 551, 553, 558, 586
Attridge, Harold   44, 163, 165
Aucher, Johann Baptist   127, 161, 220, 224, 229, 276, 385, 405, 409, 423
Auvinen, Risto   291

Barclay, John M.G.   176, 215, 217, 416, 525
Barnes, Michel   xx, 166, 399
Barthélemy, Dominique   149
Bekken, Per Jarle   538, 547
Berthelot, Katell   7–8
Birnbaum, Ellen   154, 216, 250–251, 261, 266–267, 282, 290, 421, 428
Bloch, René   262
Boccaccini, Gabriele   192
Borgen, Peder   231, 319, 387, 559, 563–564
Boys-Stones, George   39, 198, 249
Brenk, Frederick   xviii, xx, 15, 44, 199
Brisson, Luc   407
Brooke, George   251
Bultmann, Rudolf   442
Burns, Joshua   492

Cazeaux, Jacques   xix, 3, 5, 6, 13, 15–18, 20–22, 24, 44, 330
Cohen, Naomi   196, 211, 213, 340, 383, 394, 395, 432, 440
Cohn, Leopold   21–22, 45, 118, 121–124, 127–128, 190, 195, 370, 551, 573
Collins, John   xx, 193–194, 481

Colson, Francis   20, 22, 44, 118–128, 134, 137, 154, 157–158, 162, 171, 176, 179, 182, 184, 195–196, 204–205, 210, 216, 232–233, 244–246, 249–250, 259, 273, 276, 289–290, 296, 298, 303, 307–308, 324, 329, 331, 334–337, 339, 342, 345, 355–356, 358, 366–368, 374, 380, 387, 391, 396, 400, 402, 405, 412, 419, 421, 426–428, 433–435, 446, 451, 453, 463, 473, 476, 481, 506, 512–513, 518, 520, 541, 553, 555–556, 561, 574–575, 585
Cover, Michael   xix, 13, 20, 23, 44–46, 145–146, 149, 159, 162, 164–166, 169, 172, 176, 189, 201, 203, 217, 219, 224–226, 231, 247, 255, 261–262, 268–269, 283, 319, 363, 379, 387, 389–390, 417, 467, 471, 481, 534, 551, 564

Dillon, John   5, 10, 18, 37, 44, 136, 146, 149–150, 157, 163, 165, 178, 182, 216, 237, 250–251, 261, 266–267, 282, 329–330, 334–335, 346, 407, 421, 428
Doering, Lutz   xxi, 193

Edwards, Mark   156, 250
Elder, Nicholas   550
Engberg-Pedersen, Troels   218–219

Francis, Michael   227, 481, 541
Friesen, Courtney   46, 338, 484, 489

Geljon, Albert   2, 5, 6, 10, 14–15, 22, 46, 131, 136, 196, 218, 256, 478, 501, 575
Goodenough, Erwin Ramsdell   157–158, 174, 182, 326, 339
Goulet, Richard   6, 12, 14, 149, 260, 454
Grabbe, Lester   44, 123, 135, 179, 187, 250–251, 282, 290, 295–297, 311, 315–317, 323, 327, 329, 337, 344, 355–356, 360, 363, 366–367, 369, 387, 394, 491–494, 500, 502, 508–509, 555
Graver, Margaret   135, 444

Hamerton-Kelly, Robert   319
Harl, Marguerite   133, 149
Harris, J. Rendel   259, 572

Hay, David   259–260, 327, 443, 467, 500
Hays, Richard   466
Heath, Malcom   281, 570
Heath, Thomas   264–265
Hilgert, Earle   255, 293
Hirsch-Luipold, Rainer   150, 467
Hoeschel, David   xix, 43–45, 118, 121, 157, 165, 189, 422
Holladay, Carl   318, 481
Hornblower, Simon   2014

Ierodiakonou, Katerina   256–257
Inwood, Brad   40, 135

Jacobson, Howard   338

Kamesar, Adam   228
Katz, Peter   118, 149, 193
Kennedy, George   570
Kraus Reggiani, Clara   18, 20–22, 44, 47, 190, 195, 370, 551, 565, 573
Konstan, David   498
Koskenniemi, Erkki   451, 484

LaPorte, Jean   139, 525, 582
Legaspi, Michael   14
Levenson, Jon   8, 436
Levison, John   147
Lévy, Carlos   145, 150, 176, 203–204, 223, 226, 413, 503, 534
Lincicum, David   46, 515–516
Litwa, M. David   203
Long, Anthony   xviii, 39, 169, 250, 526–527

Mack, Burton   255
Malherbe, Abraham   383
Mansfeld, Jaap   39–40, 143
Marcus, Ralph   127, 138–139, 160, 190, 205, 224, 226, 229–230, 235–236, 263–265, 276–277, 385, 401, 405, 409, 423, 429, 519, 562–563
Markland, Jeremiah   45, 120–122
Martín, José Pablo   3, 44
Massebieau, Louis   3–4, 6, 10–11, 218
McFarland, Orrey   176, 217
Méasson, Anita   146, 159, 219
Meier, John P.   193
Michaelis, Johann David   14
Morgan, Teresa   427, 457, 487

Morris, Jenny   6, 218

Nagy, Gregory   3, 198
Najman, Hindy   526
Niehoff, Maren   7, 39, 44, 245, 259–260, 275, 293, 340, 450
Nieto Hernández, Pura   325
Nikiprowetzky, Valentin   4–5, 13, 15–18, 20, 281
Novick, Tzvi   492

Orlov, Andrei   xxi, 133, 151, 184

Pearce, Sarah   296, 436
Plested, Marcus   548

Reydams-Schils, Gretchen   334, 361–362, 527
Roskam, Geert   7, 450–451, 515
Royse, James   xx, 4, 9–12, 44–45, 131, 133, 218, 240, 259, 472
Runia, David   xviii, xx–xxi, 2, 5–6, 10, 14–16, 18–20, 22–23, 37, 40, 44, 46, 131, 133, 136, 149–150, 153, 162, 164–165, 169, 171–172, 179, 196, 215, 218, 252, 256, 269, 304, 340, 359, 376, 416, 420–421, 424, 448, 469, 478, 492–493, 501, 503, 513, 528, 537, 542, 544, 555, 572, 575, 580

Salvesen, Alison   296
Schäfer, Peter   157
Schironi, Francesca   239
Schliesser, Benjamin   467, 519
Schwartz, Daniel   201, 341
Scott, James   182
Sedley, David   169, 526–527
Segal, Alan   157, 166
Siegert, Folker   xxi, 2, 196–197, 255, 319
Sly, Dorothy   272
Sterling, Gregory   xix–xxi, 2–3, 5–6, 10, 44–45, 118, 131, 146, 179–180, 189, 193, 203, 209, 211, 223, 241, 243, 258–259, 277, 283, 318, 364, 369, 384, 440, 442, 453, 527, 546, 553
Struck, Peter   148

Taylor, Christopher   275
Taylor, Joan   327
Terian, Abraham   2, 5, 134, 137, 158, 175, 264–265, 465, 555, 574

INDEX OF MODERN AUTHORS

Theiler, Willy   20–22, 40, 136, 144, 310, 514, 527, 562
Tobin, Thomas   7, 9, 14, 40, 180, 212, 233, 528, 550
Topchyan, Aram   319
Torallas-Tovar, Sofía   11–12
[Turnebus] Turnèbe, Adrien   xix, 45

Van den Hoek, Annewies   46, 163–165, 189, 209, 236, 269–271, 277–278, 291–292, 299, 317, 351–352, 388–390, 397, 409, 442, 479, 495, 509, 548–550, 564, 587
Van Inwagen, Peter   204
Vela, Horacio   553

Wasserman, Emma   210, 304
Weisser, Sharon   37, 134–135, 255, 421, 428, 527
Wendland, Paul   45, 118–128, 171, 259, 321, 373, 438, 453, 476, 561
Wilson, Walter   135, 196, 259, 551, 566
Winston, David   10, 149, 182, 212, 237, 492
Winter, Bruce   150, 485
Wolfson, Harry Austryn   xx, 177–178, 182
Wyss, Beatrice   150, 485

Yadin-Israel, Azzan   169, 247, 268
Yli-Karjanmaa, Sami   179, 215, 304, 513

Zaleski, Richard   198

Index of Selected Greek Terms

ἀγαλματοφορέω 171–172, 412
ἀγχίνοια 482, 495, 525, 548
ἀγένητος 172, 203, 427
ἀειδής 147
ἀειπάρθενος 483, 495
αἰνίττομαι 147–148, 551
ἀνάμνησις 312–313, 316, 325
ἀνδρεία 207, 408, 485–487
αἴσθησις/αἰσθητός 143, 201, 238, 321, 334–335, 341–342, 352, 517, 527
αἰών 155, 225, 388, 392, 579–581
αἰώνιος 152, 154, 230, 253, 479
ἀκατονόμαστος 118, 152–153, 165
ἀκρότης 136, 212, 288, 531
ἀλλαγή/ἀλλάττω 1, 17, 43, 145, 156, 294, 361, 363, 372–373, 448
ἄλογος/τὸ ἄλογον 43, 135, 255, 303, 321, 334, 342, 493
ἀμερής 454
ἀμετάβλητος 121, 177, 223
ἀπάθεια/ἀπαθής 223, 255, 421, 427–428
ἀπαρτάω 12, 240
ἀπαρχή 126–127, 132, 136, 474, 484
ἀπαυτοματίζω 426, 557, 559, 562
ἀπιστέω/ἀπιστία 41, 128, 429
ἀπνευστί 246, 260, 265, 268–269
ἀπόσπασμα 527–528, 545–546
ἀπαύγασμα 527–528, 545–546
ἀρετή 154, 188, 256, 274–275, 277–278, 282–283, 286, 311, 316, 336, 346, 349, 375, 386, 403–404, 428, 435, 443, 463, 488–489, 520, 548, 553
ἄρρητος 152, 157, 164–165
ἀρχιδεσμοφύλαξ 436–437, 440
ἀρχιμάγειρος 437–438, 440
ἀρχιποίμην 350
ἀρχιπροφήτης 322, 350
ἀσώματος 147, 149, 220
ἄτρεπτος 121, 174–175, 223, 287, 291, 446, 463
αὐτόπρεμνος 529
ἀχειροποίητος 189
ἄχρονος 453
ἄψις 453

βέβαιος/βεβαίωσις 141, 144, 184, 298, 413–414, 429, 463, 587

βίος 43, 188, 211–213, 256, 347, 580
βούλησις 134, 138, 285–286, 439

γελάω/γέλως 123, 125, 135, 164, 372, 411, 424–425, 429, 431, 446–447, 572
γενητός 128, 172, 203, 427

δεισιδαιμονία 383
δημιούργημα 559
δημιουργός/δημιουργέω 169, 179, 239, 248, 382, 388, 418–419
διὰ τί 280–281, 283, 288, 291, 293, 301, 303, 306, 333, 340, 365, 398–399, 448, 465, 540, 544
διαθήκη 10, 216–217, 231, 234–236
διαιώνιος/διαιωνίζω 512, 580
διάνοια 160, 203, 228, 319, 371, 374–374, 386, 394, 415–416, 420, 429, 432, 445, 447, 450, 457, 465, 481–482, 498, 537, 545
διάστημα 392, 412, 580, 585
διασῴζω 245, 260
δίδωμι 170, 231, 365, 372, 374, 376, 377–378, 380, 382, 387, 390, 395, 399, 474, 560
δίκη 331, 333, 335, 483, 494
δικαιοσύνη 43, 259, 408, 457, 485–487, 540
δοκησίσοφος 44, 339, 344
δύναμις 163, 174, 179, 207, 236–237, 249, 340, 350, 366, 369, 388, 415, 525, 529, 538, 548

ἐγχαράττω 491, 587
εἶδος 147, 183, 220, 231, 233, 235, 274, 287, 320, 331–332, 342–343, 403, 420, 517, 520, 587
εἴδωλον 515, 517
εἰκών 188, 527–528, 580
τὸ ἑκούσιον 285–286, 290, 585
ἐκτραγῳδέω 484, 489
ἐλπίς 135, 421, 424, 463
ἐνδιάθετος 123, 228, 230, 253, 443, 506, 509
ἐνδοιασμός 41, 445, 449–450, 455, 463–464, 466, 480, 563
ἐνέργεια 214, 223, 292, 351, 358, 492, 494, 586
ἐνώπιον 191, 193, 195, 198, 227, 379, 497, 499, 521–523
ἐπαγγελία 388, 441

INDEX OF SELECTED GREEK TERMS 621

ἐπανόρθωσις 254, 291
ἐπιθυμία 134, 138, 255, 289, 439
ἐπικομπάζω 484
ἐπιστήμη 144–145, 199, 248, 270, 400, 510, 527
εὐαρεστέω 183, 191, 198, 206–207
εὐδαιμονία 212, 283, 428, 458, 539
εὐλάβεια 134, 138, 498
εὐπάθεια 134, 139, 214, 255, 393, 398, 421, 428, 498, 567
εὐσέβεια 258, 399, 413, 441, 488
εὐφημία 158
εὐχαριστία 139
ἕξις 353, 356–358, 404, 408, 428

ζωοπλάστης 229–230

τὸ ἡγεμονικόν 329, 335, 343, 361–363, 414, 519, 527, 567
ἡγέμων 203, 263, 277–278
ἡδονή 134, 148, 255, 442
ἡλιοειδέστατος 183
ἡσυχάζω/ἡσυχία 428, 483–484, 494–495, 541, 545

θεόπτης 142, 147
θεός 118–119, 123, 141–142, 145, 147, 153–154, 157–158, 164–171, 173, 174–175, 179, 183, 185–189, 193, 203, 205, 207, 217, 224, 229, 232–233, 247, 248, 269–270, 281, 287, 291–293, 295, 298–300, 304, 317, 323, 331, 336, 338–339, 340, 350–351, 365, 376, 379, 388–389, 427, 429, 432, 441, 456–457, 463, 479, 500–501, 521, 546, 548, 557, 559, 581, 585
θέσις 266, 269, 296, 570
θέω 179

ἰδέα 148, 163, 183, 220, 235
ἵστημι 120, 226, 232, 297

καιρός 42, 459, 573–579, 583
κακία 180–181, 286, 292, 404
κακοτεχνία 405, 489
καρδία 361–363, 551
καταληπτικός 146
κατάχρησις/καταχρῆσθαι 37, 153, 155, 165, 177, 499, 577

κέαρ/κῆρ 180, 211–213, 516
κεφάλαιον 319–320, 326, 338–340, 371, 373, 402
κῆρος 180, 516
κήρυγμα 192, 202, 209
κοσμοποιέω 169
κόσμος 119, 124, 201, 387–388, 427, 546
κύριος 37, 118–119, 128, 136, 142–143, 146, 150–151, 153–156, 158, 162, 165–166, 169–171, 177, 229, 232, 236, 248, 263, 298, 299, 340, 356–257, 266, 382, 387, 426, 432, 456, 474, 479, 500–503, 515, 536, 560, 568, 576–577, 579, 585
κυρίως 153, 374, 577

λύπη 134, 138–139, 255, 414, 421, 427
λογισμός 171–172, 282, 335–336, 351, 415, 418, 459, 468, 527–528
λόγος 43, 126, 145, 156, 186, 196, 220, 227–228, 230, 233, 240, 246, 253–255, 257, 267, 270, 305, 314, 330, 339, 340, 346, 351, 388, 391, 427, 443, 474, 493, 503, 505–506, 509–511, 515, 537, 542–543, 565, 585, 587
λυττάω 435

μανία 205, 207
μανικός 343
μεθόριος 126, 132, 203, 342, 348
μεσότης 342
μετάθεσις/μετατίθημι 1, 156, 372–373, 448
μεταχαρακτηρισμός 354
μεταχαράσσω 255, 358
μετεμψυχόομαι 185
μετεωρολέσχης/μετεωρολεσχέω 119, 159, 252–254
μετέωρος 250–253, 270, 411
μετονομάζω xviii, 9, 42–43, 185, 239, 249–250, 266–267, 291–294, 350, 358–360
μετριοπάθεια 421, 428
μνήμη 311–312, 314, 316, 517, 586

νομοθέτης 147, 239, 248, 326, 366, 369, 419
νοῦς 43, 169, 183, 253–254, 270, 291, 303, 311, 325, 328, 334–335, 339–341, 344, 361–362, 365, 367, 375, 410, 412, 429, 431, 434, 451, 506–507, 509–510, 527, 546, 557, 567

ὁμωνυμία 152, 499
ὄνομα 1, 17, 118–119, 142–143, 152, 155–156, 158, 177, 239, 248, 267, 269, 281, 287, 293, 295, 300, 306, 336–337, 354, 360, 372, 419, 448, 479, 527, 567–568, 572, 577, 587
ὀνοματοποιέω 419, 568
ὀνοματουργός 239, 248, 354, 364, 419
ὁράω 136, 142–143, 145, 149, 151, 155, 173, 281, 287, 291, 311, 316–317, 331, 334, 419
ὄρεξις 255, 527
ὄρουσις 419–420
ὁσιότης 259, 399, 408
οὐδένεια/οὐδενία 225–227, 413
οὐσία 121, 147, 163–164, 177, 223, 297
τὸ ὄν 18, 146, 151, 157, 177, 203–204, 288, 291, 455, 585

πάθος/πάσχω 134, 177, 255, 291, 316, 334, 341, 375, 420–421, 442, 460, 566–567
παιδεία 145, 505
παλινῳδέω/παλινῳδία 218–219, 240
παντέλεια 136–137
παράδειγμα 147, 220, 474, 580
παραχαράττω 502, 506
παρρησία 381
πατήρ 164, 178, 250–251, 253, 267, 270, 303, 351, 411, 505
περισσός/περιττός 322–323, 338, 344, 349–351
πίπτω 121, 125, 222, 228, 231, 411, 446–447
πίστις/πιστεύω 41, 268, 319–320, 326, 402, 405, 412–413, 427, 429–430, 442–445, 447, 449, 454–456, 459, 463–468, 481, 498, 524, 563
πιστός 188, 207, 264, 456
(δια)πλάττω 180, 229, 382–383
πνεῦμα 209, 361–362, 468, 501
ποδώκεια 450–452, 460
ποιός/ποῖος 123, 177, 353, 355–358, 574
πολύτροπος 8, 174, 325
πολυώνυμος 364, 507
πρᾶγμα 149–151, 155, 161, 163, 260, 266, 273, 345, 402–405, 438, 452, 454, 499, 567, 574, 577
πραγματεία 12, 19, 218–219, 239–240
προγελάω 421
προγευστρίς 422
προγήθω 420–421

προγύμνασμα 534
προευφραίνω 423
προπάθεια 416, 420, 424, 444
προπαιδεία/προπαίδευμα 227, 569, 570
προφορικός 123, 228, 230, 253, 506, 509
πρός τι (ὡσανεί) 37, 167, 177–178, 287, 465
προσηγορία 267, 292–293, 327, 360
πρόσθεμα/προσθήκη 295–296, 298–300
πρόσρησις 150–153, 327, 555
πτερνιστής 164, 280–282, 290–292, 316

σιωπάω 484, 495, 541
σοφία 271, 277, 388, 483, 560, 564–565
σοφιστής 506, 509, 569–570
σοφός 43, 199, 254, 270, 568
στοιχεῖον 122, 265, 363, 387
σύγγραμμα 15, 239
σύμβολον 148, 201, 492, 572
σῶμα 149, 155, 161, 163, 183, 213, 244, 260, 273, 329, 345–346, 365, 403, 405, 438–439, 452, 454, 459, 468, 551
σωτήρ 228, 230, 359, 501
σωτηρία 356
σωφροσύνη 408, 485–487, 530

τεκνοποιέω 392–393, 395
τέλειος 128, 409, 463, 479, 503, 534, 585
τελειόω 43, 289, 585
τελειότης 136, 278, 361
τέχνη 123, 144–145, 275–276, 353, 357, 400, 561
τρισευδαίμων 161
τρισμακάριος 161
τρισμέγιστος 148
τριπόθητος 148, 160–161, 439
τροπή 233, 540, 545
τρόπος 8, 154, 254–255, 278, 334–337, 339, 363, 367, 381, 392, 420, 453, 490, 507, 545

ὑποβολεύς 285–286, 290
ὑπόμνημα 13–15, 237, 239
ὑποχωλαίνω 460
(συν)ὑφαίνω 198–199

φαντασία 143–144, 146, 526, 557
φιλανθρωπία 226, 259, 364, 399, 409, 530, 547
φιλαπεχθήμων 260

INDEX OF SELECTED GREEK TERMS

φιλοσοφία/φιλόσοφος 254, 257, 270, 272
φόβος 134, 138, 171, 255, 421, 524
φρόνησις 138, 272, 275, 277, 282–283, 297, 382–383, 403–404, 408, 485–487
φυσικός 179–180, 256–257, 301, 352, 568
φυσιολογέω 247
φύσις 120–121, 124, 147, 150–151, 154, 160, 164, 183, 209, 223, 245, 266–267, 270, 296, 314, 335, 345–347, 352, 388, 406–407, 462, 465, 486, 493, 514–515, 545, 568, 580
φωνητήριον 229, 253

χαλινός 540, 551
χαρά 134, 138–139, 212, 311, 412, 414, 421, 424, 428, 441, 480, 567
χαρακτήρ 249–250, 520

χάρις/χαρίζομαι 176, 187, 205, 218, 220, 237, 274, 393, 396, 399, 429, 442, 462, 534, 582
χαλδαΐζειν 159
χειροποίητος 177
χρεία 551–552, 554, 556, 567, 570
χρησμολογέω 147
χρησμός 147, 327, 384, 432
χρόνος 392, 575, 577–578, 583

ψυχή 143, 183, 207, 213, 229, 248–249, 255, 283, 287, 303, 326, 329, 335, 362, 375, 388, 483, 489, 513, 519, 528, 546, 553, 555, 561

ὦ (vocative) 154, 175, 189, 239, 447, 459, 464, 555, 574–575
ὁ ὤν 118, 146, 151, 153, 157

Index of Subjects and Names

Aaron 34–35, 100, 125, 290, 324, 421, 431–432, 439–440, 446, 474, 477, 498, 505, 526
  as speech/*logos prophorikos* 107, 230, 439, 506, 509–510
  with moderated emotion 428
Abram/Abraham 2–3, 5, 10–11, 14, 19, 42, 118, 128, 131–132, 134–136, 141–142, 148, 155, 157–158, 164, 166, 171, 174–175, 182–183, 192–193, 199–201, 206, 212, 214, 220, 232, 238, 261, 272, 285–286, 289–293, 311–312, 318, 323, 348, 354, 358, 374–375, 392–393, 395–398, 400–401, 406–409, 468–480, 551–565, 584–587
  analogue to Odysseus xx, 7–8, 36, 218, 289
  change of name xviii, 1–2, 19–20, 36, 41, 237, 241–259, 263–272, 280, 284, 287, 322, 359, 373
  contrasted with Enoch 184–185, 191–192, 195, 353
  covenant with 38, 190, 202, 206, 216–217, 220–221, 234–237
  divine prompter of 285
  faith and doubt of xx, 41, 261, 442–468
  fall(s) 222–227, 229–230, 410–415
  God's human being 365
  God's name revealed to 37
  hope of 416–424
  learner 153–154, 207, 280, 282
  merit of 217, 219, 229
  migration 5, 8, 36, 217, 234, 351, 436
  pedagogical triad 173, 288
  perfection 14, 19, 36–37, 132, 159, 167, 170, 174, 212, 283, 370
  prayer for Ishmael 496–551
  as priest 132–133
  and Socrates (Terah) 223, 225, 227
  two sons 19
  as type of soul 118, 133, 173–174, 218, 228, 231, 257–258, 272
  as visionary 131–132, 147, 161, 168
Allegorical Commentary xiii–xiv, xix–xx, 1–16, 21, 23, 40, 44–46, 131, 133, 137–139, 141, 145, 148, 154, 158, 160, 162, 168, 172, 185–187, 191, 195–196, 201, 203, 205, 211, 213, 215–218, 220, 223, 225, 227, 230, 233, 237, 239–241, 243, 247, 250, 252, 257–258, 260–261, 263, 265–267, 272, 281, 288, 290, 298–300, 304–306, 311, 313, 315–316, 322, 325, 327, 330, 334, 336, 339, 345, 347, 349, 353, 358, 360, 362, 367–368, 367, 371, 373, 384–386, 391, 395, 402, 404, 414–415, 418–419, 423–424, 427–428, 439, 446, 455, 464, 471, 477, 484, 491, 493, 499–500, 503–504, 510–511, 518, 520, 523, 531, 535, 546, 552, 555, 566, 570, 572, 575, 582, 586
allegory/allegoresis xiii, 5, 89, 122, 154, 168, 171, 179–181, 199, 202, 208, 214, 218, 224, 263, 267, 270, 272, 275, 278, 280, 283–284, 287, 290, 296–298, 301–305, 308–310, 321–330, 488
  arithmological 40–41, 131–132
  of the cave (Plato) 146
  cosmological 186
  ethical/moral 180, 183, 490, 531
  etymology in/vs. 44, 250, 253, 353, 411, 571
  focalizer of 489
  Homeric parallels xx, 8, 218, 304, 450–453, 460
  Moses as author of 304, 407, 575
  pedagogical 277
  Platonist parallels 7–8, 199
  present tense in 145, 155, 250
  priestly/cultic 133, 192, 201, 550
  radical allegorizers 259–261
  of the soul 40, 133, 211, 217–218, 230, 257, 295, 382, 411, 414, 436, 476, 498
  Stoic influence 334
  theological 573
  "trigger" words 227, 287, 499
Alexandria xi–xii, xv, xviii, 3, 14, 150, 209, 228, 241–245, 260, 294, 304, 318, 336, 338, 341, 384, 400, 404, 421–422, 437, 445, 485, 487, 499, 519
Antiochus of Ascalon 39–40, 136, 144, 310, 514, 527, 562
apophaticism 177, 236, 378, 389
aporiae 19–20, 162, 283, 398, 417–418, 448, 537, 542, 544

INDEX OF SUBJECTS AND NAMES

Aristotle   3, 42, 120, 136, 143, 148, 154–155, 169, 177, 195–196, 218, 222–223, 246, 253, 256, 258, 275, 285–288, 296, 313, 326, 335, 337, 356, 358, 391, 403, 408, 428, 487, 497, 531, 581
arithmology   xv, 471–472
   fifty   137, 532, 546
   fifty-five   264
   five   132, 193, 197, 205, 305, 315, 321, 334, 401, 408, 524, 530
   mod 9   264–265
   Neo-Pythagorean   41, 136, 232, 264
   ninety   126, 468–469, 475, 477
   ninety-nine   131–134, 137, 474
   one   182–183, 232–233, 235, 264–265, 359
   one-hundred   133, 264–265, 474, 477–478
   seven   20, 42, 91, 96, 252, 321, 334, 393–401, 532, 557, 561
   seventy   132
   ten   125–126, 134, 136–137, 139, 177, 305, 532, 546
attributes, divine
   eternal   42, 154, 479, 512, 575, 580–581
   ineffable   18, 152, 165, 222
   incomprehensible   18, 150, 163–165, 234, 273
   invisible   74, 146–147, 168, 172, 222–223
   unchanging   120–121, 177, 223
   unmoved   120, 169, 175, 222–223, 287, 291
   unturned   223, 287, 291, 446

Balaam   498, 500–502, 506, 508–509, 511
Benjamin   241–242, 294, 300–310, 318–319, 353, 373
bodies and realities   149–151, 155, 161, 163, 244, 260, 273, 403, 405, 438, 452, 454, 577
body   7, 160, 162–163, 167, 171–172, 182–184, 186, 206, 209–210, 212, 265, 275, 294, 296, 298, 434, 457, 459, 511
   resurrection of   513
bread from heaven   xx, 552, 559, 563–565

Caleb   242, 302, 352–353, 358, 360–363
categories (Aristotle)   177, 353, 356, 499
chapter, Philonic   15–17, 20–22
commentary   xii–xiii, 2–15
covenant   38, 190–192, 215–221, 231–238
cycle, heroic   3*n*5

cycle, patriarchal   3
   Abrahamic   xiv, 2–3, 5–6, 8–10, 12, 36, 131–132, 174, 183, 186–187, 218, 228, 234, 242, 296, 382, 394, 437
   Adamic   6, 9
   Cain   10
   dreams   12
   Jacob   173
   Moses   174
   Noahic   5–6, 9, 10, 10*n*25, 11–13

Delphi   147, 328
   Delphic maxim   150, 222, 225
Dinah   444, 480–495
double name   349, 360
doubt   xx, 41, 426, 442–480
doxography   39–40, 150, 162, 252, 408

education   xii, 134, 136, 145–146, 154, 348, 376, 422, 437, 446, 451, 456, 505, 514, 532–534, 556, 558, 564, 571, 573
embassy to Rome   xv
emotions   37–37, 134–135, 138–139, 232, 286, 427, 435, 460, 524, 566–567
   bad   134, 138–139, 229, 255, 282, 303, 330, 375, 421, 432, 442, 566
   good   134–135, 138–139, 212, 214, 289, 374, 393, 398, 412, 421, 427–428, 439, 471, 475, 498, 566–567, 572
   lack of   420–421, 427–428
   moderation of   421, 428
   pre-emotion   416, 420–422, 424, 435, 444
Enoch   154, 168, 183–185, 187, 190–195, 234, 353, 473, 519
Ephraim   242, 294, 302, 307–317, 322, 325, 333, 353, 384, 420, 491
Epicureanism   136, 143, 243, 286
Esau   281, 314–315, 347, 497, 522, 533–534, 547–549
eschatology   42, 183, 304, 363, 416, 584
Essenes   xv, 517
eternity   2, 17, 42, 154–155, 223, 392, 425, 573, 575, 577, 579, 580–581, 583–584
etymology   xviii, 19, 38–40, 42, 44, 135, 141, 144, 153
   Aramaic/Syriac   311, 492
   Demotic/Coptic   337
   Greek   38–40, 144, 179, 180, 187, 272, 380, 492–493, 555

Hebrew   38–40, 187, 247, 250–251, 261–262, 265–266, 273–274, 276–278, 281–282, 293, 295, 297, 302, 311–313, 320, 322, 326, 328–329, 331, 337, 354–356, 361, 366, 375, 393–394, 472, 481–483, 491, 500, 502, 512, 555
  Latin   493
Eudorus of Alexandria   13, 40, 149, 427, 514, 542, 562
Exposition of the Law   xiii, xiv, 13, 133, 154, 160, 162, 168, 177, 185, 191–192, 205–206, 213, 216, 225, 230, 261, 290, 293, 298, 325, 344–345, 347, 353, 359, 364, 366, 402, 414, 418, 440, 464, 523, 535, 547
Ezekiel (tragedian)   xii, 318, 322, 327, 336, 338, 341, 369

faith   xx, 2, 41, 261, 268, 412–414, 427, 430, 442–471, 480, 498, 524, 562–563, 577, 587
fall   121, 125, 189, 211–212, 242, 454
  epistemic   224–232, 235, 410–416, 446, 454
  no "hard" fall from sin   215, 242
  result of embodiment   215, 242
flesh   182, 246, 260, 265, 267–268, 346, 468

grace   xx–xxii, 2, 38, 41, 175–176, 179, 183, 187, 195, 206, 209–210, 215–221, 230–231, 234, 236–238, 243–244, 279, 286, 366, 376, 390–391, 393–394, 396, 399, 413, 426, 429–430, 442, 455, 459, 462, 498, 530, 547, 549, 572, 582, 585, 587

Hagar   8, 19, 42, 145, 277–278, 314–315, 389, 394–396, 398–400, 402, 437, 496, 511, 532, 551–552, 556, 563, 569–570
Hannah   19, 96, 390, 393–394, 396, 429, 437
Hebrew, knowledge of   xviii, 38, 245–246, 248, 251, 261–262
Hephaestus   218, 460
hexameter   193–194, 451–452, 481
holy of holies   127, 137, 199–200, 206, 348, 469, 475–477
Homer   xx, 3*n*5, 7, 8*n*18, 23, 36, 38, 42, 148, 161, 169, 174, 180, 184, 198, 207, 211, 218, 245–246, 260, 325, 344, 355, 364, 419, 437, 445, 450–452, 456, 459–460, 488–489, 500, 514–516, 519, 533, 537, 540, 542, 576
homily   xx, 14, 140, 188, 268, 271, 318–319, 348, 405, 540, 549, 564
homomensura   161
homonymy   152, 187, 482, 497, 499, 504, 507–509, 534
hope   2, 36, 135, 412, 414, 416–418, 420–424, 435, 463, 466, 526, 567, 582
Hoshea   242, 250, 352–360

Isaac   xiv, 2, 10*n*24, 11–12, 14, 17, 19, 36, 42, 131–132, 134–141, 145, 153–155, 158, 164, 174, 195, 202, 214, 218, 228, 242, 249, 261, 271–272, 276, 280–281, 288–289, 291–294, 308, 311, 314, 352–353, 361, 370–375, 382–383, 386, 388, 390, 392–395, 397–399, 401–402, 410, 412, 414, 416–417, 421, 423–424, 436, 448, 459, 464, 469–475, 477–479, 492, 496, 507, 521, 523–524, 526, 531–535, 549, 552–560, 562–574, 578–584, 587
Ishmael   19, 42, 145, 187, 308, 315–316, 323, 370, 373, 388, 415, 496–504, 507–518, 520–522, 524, 526, 531–533, 535, 545–548, 551–556, 562–563, 566, 571–574, 576, 578
Israel   19, 181, 220, 290
  land   158
  nation/people   36, 151–152, 174, 190, 192, 237, 277, 299, 323, 328, 330, 345, 359, 365, 436, 438–439, 441, 532, 535, 561, 563
  practicer   195
  seer of God   42, 157, 173–174, 202, 207–208, 241–242, 268, 280–285, 290–295, 311, 319–320, 322, 331, 339, 354, 435, 461, 501, 506–507, 512, 558
  twelve tribes of   365, 491

Jacob   xiv, 7–11, 14, 42, 127, 134, 140, 142–143, 152–155, 157–158, 162–164, 167, 173–174, 184, 187, 192, 201–202, 206–209, 218, 241–242, 249, 280–294, 296–298, 300–303, 307–312, 314–319, 322, 338–339, 352, 362, 373, 375, 424, 430, 434–436, 441–442, 460–462, 472–473, 484, 490–493, 496, 511–513, 515, 517–518, 520–521, 526, 549, 557

INDEX OF SUBJECTS AND NAMES 627

name vacillates 284, 587
practicer 195, 283, 285, 316, 512, 520
parallel to Hephaestus 460
Jethro 122, 165, 242–243, 317–353, 507
Joseph 195, 241–242, 250, 261, 292–302,
304–310, 317–320, 322–323, 325, 329,
345–346, 353–354, 360, 373, 385, 387,
430, 434–436, 438, 440, 442, 481, 491,
493, 511, 518, 521, 526, 533, 540
Joshua 242, 250, 302, 317–319, 352–361, 367,
373, 521, 548, 576–577
joy 2, 36, 125, 132, 134–135, 138–139, 141, 145,
212–213, 217, 221, 255, 276, 289, 308, 311–
312, 371–372, 374, 383, 390, 397, 410,
412–424, 427–433, 435, 439–441, 444–
447, 454, 468, 470–472, 475, 477, 480,
496, 523, 560, 562, 565–568, 571–572,
574, 579, 582
Judaism xi–xii, xv, xix–xx, 42, 136, 182, 191–
194, 217, 221, 249, 273, 295, 408, 480,
486–487, 501, 532, 539, 560, 573
Alexandrian 245
apocalyptic 42, 513
Enochic 191–192
mystery religion 182
Palestinian 268
Platonizing 136, 381
rabbinic 217, 247

Keturah 393–395, 422

language (see names)
laughter 11n28, 123–125, 135, 139, 141, 164,
293, 372, 374, 382–383, 390, 410–418,
420, 423–430, 439, 442–443, 446–449,
463, 477, 567–568, 572
law xiv, 122, 132, 135–136, 139, 163, 173–174,
189–190, 192, 197, 200, 210, 220, 258,
263, 323–326, 339, 349, 388, 393, 479,
510, 525, 535, 538, 553
divine 258
natural 347, 407
Sinai 366
Torah 408
lawgiver 147, 186, 199, 239, 246, 248, 364–
366, 368–369, 407, 419, 449
Leah 19, 305, 308–310, 349, 372, 374–376,
382, 386, 388, 390, 492, 552, 554–555,
563–564

lemma 22–36
main/primary 5, 9–10, 13
secondary 14
tertiary 14
Levi 19, 38, 105, 133, 341, 481, 489–494, 513
Levite 127, 132–133, 135–137, 139, 141, 208,
341, 440, 474, 478, 492, 532, 548
Logos 39, 42, 124, 144, 149, 152–153, 157–159,
163, 165–166, 168–170, 172, 178–179, 181,
186, 193, 201–203, 209, 218, 220, 234–
235, 237, 243, 246, 248, 253–254, 268,
287–288, 295, 303, 325–326, 329, 330,
339, 340, 346, 352, 358, 364, 368, 380,
384, 407, 412, 418, 425–427, 429–430,
436, 454, 457, 461, 466, 501, 503, 511–
512, 515, 518, 528, 558, 563, 574–579, 585,
587

Manasseh 242, 294, 302, 307–318, 322, 325,
329, 333, 353, 491
memory 284, 307–309, 311–312, 314–317, 513,
515–517, 544, 586
Midian 90, 142, 318–320, 327–333, 335–336,
344–346, 351, 393, 501
Moses xii, xiv, 7–8, 19, 42, 122, 132, 134, 136–
137, 141–143, 147–151, 153, 155–157,
160–163, 167–168, 170–171, 173–176,
179, 183–184, 188, 192, 194–196, 199–
202, 206, 208–209, 224–225, 230, 232,
235–236, 242, 245–246, 248, 250, 253,
261, 267–268, 276, 278, 280, 284, 289–
290, 292, 302–304, 318–327, 330–333,
335–347, 349–355, 358–361, 363–369,
371–372, 374, 376, 378–379, 381, 384,
387, 389–390, 393, 398, 400, 407, 417,
420–421, 424, 431–433, 440, 445, 448–
451, 455–456, 459, 461, 463–464, 469,
474, 478–479, 482, 484, 488, 490–491,
497–500, 502, 504, 505–507, 509–510,
512–513, 517, 519–521, 523, 526, 528, 533,
535, 538–539, 541–548, 550, 552, 558,
560–561, 574–577, 580, 582
as archprophet 322
as author 39, 198, 304, 309–310, 354,
365–366
God's human being 175–176, 179, 186,
188, 342, 364–365, 367, 513
manner of life 335, 342, 363, 367
many-named 242, 353, 363–369, 507

namewright   239, 248, 354, 364
prophet   151, 242, 267, 360, 363–364

names
   change of   xviii–xix, xxii, 1–2, 17, 36, 40–41, 43, 121, 133–134, 140, 162, 173, 185, 189, 203, 206–207, 231, 237, 239–369, 373–374, 455, 459, 471
      divine (lack of)   18, 37, 75, 118, 137, 142–143, 146, 153, 158, 164–166, 168, 198, 221, 243, 247–248, 356, 577
      improper (*catachresis*)   18, 38, 153, 155, 158, 162, 165, 177, 284, 349, 420, 428, 461, 499, 507, 574, 577
      philosophy of   38–39, 44, 140, 143, 243, 249, 508, 568
      proper   37, 118–119, 142–143, 150–151, 153, 156–158, 162, 164–166, 177, 302, 327, 336, 338, 341, 356, 370, 437, 461, 482, 489, 505, 568
names and realities   261, 577
nothingness   41, 176, 203, 215, 223–227, 391, 410–411, 413, 444, 446, 455, 503, 541, 582
numerology (see arithmology)

Odysseus   xx, 7–8, 36, 174, 184, 218, 289, 304, 325, 451–452, 514–515, 540, 545
offering
   Abel and Cain   484
   first fruit (tithe)   132–133, 135, 141, 469, 475, 478
   sin   522, 525, 535–537, 542–544, 547, 550
   tamid   201
onomasticon   xviii, 38, 135, 261–262, 272, 280–281, 294–295, 298, 301, 310–313, 322–323, 326–328, 331, 337, 351, 354, 393, 437, 472, 483, 492, 500

passion (see emotions, bad)
Penelope   8, 514–515
Pentateuch   xiv, xix, 1, 8, 10, 12–15, 39–41, 127, 134, 148, 156, 168–169, 175, 184, 189, 196, 198, 232, 237, 242–243, 245–247, 255, 280–281, 292, 295, 340, 365, 383, 393, 424, 430, 448, 454, 476, 490, 505, 512, 515, 519, 530, 538, 560, 568, 585
perfection   xxi, 2, 14, 19, 36, 41–43, 132, 134, 136, 141, 154, 159, 167, 170, 173–174, 176, 185, 188, 190–191, 195, 202–203, 209, 211, 213–215, 217, 220, 222, 242–244, 250, 264–265, 275–276, 278, 281, 283, 285–286, 288–289, 294, 301, 312, 326, 348, 353, 361–362, 364, 367, 370, 374, 412, 415, 418–419, 427, 429, 431, 439, 443, 449, 452, 454–457, 459, 461–462, 466, 475–480, 497–498, 503, 511, 521–524, 529–534, 537, 540, 546, 551–552, 558, 561, 566, 573, 575–576, 579, 581–582, 585–586
Pharaoh   167, 169–173, 177, 186, 188, 230, 290, 294–295, 299–300, 322, 337, 350, 354, 364–366, 368–369, 387, 430, 432–438, 440–441, 445, 498, 505–506, 509
philosophy, divisions   257–258, 311, 384, 477, 529
piety   182, 193–194, 205, 258–259, 261, 271, 277, 399, 408–409, 413, 485–488, 498, 576
Platonism   xii–xiii, xvi, xviii–xx, 7–8, 14–15, 18, 36–37, 39–41, 134, 136, 143–146, 148–149, 155, 157, 159, 162–167, 169–170, 172, 174, 177, 179–181, 184–185, 189, 192, 198–199, 203, 207, 210, 212, 216–217, 219–220, 223, 226, 228, 232–233, 235, 237, 248, 250, 252–254, 257–259, 265, 273–275, 281, 283, 288, 296–297, 304, 312–314, 316, 325–326, 329, 334, 343, 348, 353, 357–358, 362, 374, 381, 391, 400–401, 404, 407, 418, 421, 428, 433, 439, 450–453, 455, 458, 485, 490–491, 506, 523, 516, 519, 523, 527–528, 540, 543, 545, 560–561, 565, 567–568, 580, 583–584, 587
Plutarch   xiii, xviii, 7–8, 15, 124, 147, 184, 199, 211–212, 256–257, 273, 285, 319, 335, 421, 433, 437–438, 450, 541
Potiphar   436–438, 440, 442, 445
preliminary studies   42, 145, 252, 277, 315, 389, 396, 401, 496, 511, 532–534, 556, 569–570
priest   14–15, 126–127, 132–136, 141, 198, 200–201, 206–207, 209, 318, 320, 327–336, 341, 346, 348, 360, 362–363, 439–440, 469, 474–478, 489–490, 503, 522, 536–537, 543–544, 587
   Aaron as   474
   Abraham as   133
   of Cybele   503

INDEX OF SUBJECTS AND NAMES

Fourth Evangelist as   141
high priest   14, 200, 253, 439
Levitical   132
Paul as   209
Philo as   201, 341
Phinehas as   320
Plutarch as   15
Raguel as   318
promises, divine   36, 186, 202, 220, 323, 361, 367, 371, 373, 387–388, 392, 397–398, 402, 409–411, 414–415, 420, 423, 425–427, 429–430, 441, 443–445, 449, 463–464, 467, 469, 473, 480, 496, 498, 520, 524, 546, 552–554, 562–563, 565, 569–570, 583
prophets   13, 23, 151, 169, 175, 208, 211, 263, 292, 321, 331–332, 343, 347, 349–350, 373, 383–384, 393, 395–396, 430, 432, 501, 506, 546, 587
Ps.-Phocylides   42, 193–194, 481, 485–489

QGE   5, 12–13, 16, 21, 24–31, 41, 45, 127, 134, 186, 237, 263, 290, 327, 402, 414, 439, 462, 464, 519–520
quarrelsome exegetes   241, 243–247, 249, 259–264, 266–268, 273–274, 359

Rachel   242, 294–295, 298, 300–308, 310, 375–376, 386, 388, 390, 392–393, 437
Raguel (see Jethro)
relation (category)   37, 167, 177–179, 204, 287, 374, 455, 465, 490, 528, 559, 577, 585
Reuben   19, 302, 307–318, 491, 496, 509, 511–513, 516–517, 519, 521, 558
rhetoric   xii, xviii, 5, 8, 13–18, 23, 37, 41–42, 135, 143, 145, 147, 156, 168, 170, 177, 185, 191, 198, 208–209, 211, 222, 224, 227, 246, 250, 255, 288, 297, 319–320, 326–327, 350, 394, 401–402, 404–405, 418–419, 433, 443, 448, 451, 468, 480, 482, 489, 499, 506, 508, 510–511, 518, 523, 530–531, 538, 551–558, 567–571
Rome   xi–xii, xviii, 1, 189, 318, 503

sanctuary (see also tabernacle)   127, 200–201, 469, 475–477
Sarah   xviii, 2, 8, 11, 19, 125, 127, 141, 161, 206, 241, 245, 262, 268, 272–274, 276–280, 293, 314–315, 317–318, 349, 354, 356, 359, 370–372, 375, 382–386, 390, 392–403, 406–407, 409–410, 414, 422, 424–432, 437, 439, 443, 446–447, 449, 455, 457, 463, 468–471, 475–478, 496, 511, 520, 551–565, 567, 574, 580, 584
Scripture (see Pentateuch, etc.)
Shem   103, 469, 472–473, 477, 479, 558
Simeon   19, 220, 242, 302, 307–318, 341, 489–491, 494, 500, 513
sin (see also, vice)   163, 210, 214–216, 227, 435, 480–481, 484, 494, 521–522, 526, 535–543, 550
Socrates   38, 148, 152–154, 172, 180, 223, 225, 227, 240, 271, 284–285, 313, 419, 514, 516–517, 543, 568, 576, 587
sophists   42, 112, 150, 187, 297, 339, 344, 481, 506, 510–511, 571
soul   2, 7, 15, 17, 37, 40–42, 119–120, 126, 132, 134–136, 148, 154–162, 167, 181, 201, 205, 210, 212, 222, 229, 250, 253, 282–283, 288, 311–312, 331, 340, 345, 362, 378, 388, 391–392, 457, 489, 533, 540, 555–557
   ascent of   xiv, 132, 328, 411, 419
   butcher of   436–437
   as chariot   329, 343–344, 404, 411, 567
   as coin   435, 491
   death of   210, 301, 304–306, 376, 546
   eight-part   37, 321, 334, 352, 393, 398, 541
   eye of the   142–146, 194, 205, 501
   fall of   212, 313, 328
   as house/temple   362
   immortality of   513
   movement of   453, 467
   as musical instrument   384
   rational and irrational   303, 305, 321, 330, 334, 342, 398, 418, 541
   reincarnation of   312
   as ship   517–519
   as wax tablet   180, 284, 515–517, 528, 535, 586
   world soul   169, 528, 546
Stoicism   xv, xix, 37–39, 134–135, 143, 145–146, 148, 157, 182, 184–185, 189, 192, 196, 198, 210, 212, 223, 228, 230, 249–250, 255–258, 266, 273, 310, 329, 334–335, 339, 352, 357, 361, 364, 368, 381, 401, 407–408, 418–421, 427–428, 432, 436, 439, 444, 453, 520, 526–528, 537, 553, 557, 562

tabernacle/temple 126, 133, 160, 192, 198–201, 206, 208, 220, 469, 474, 476, 478–479
technique, rhetorical xiii, xviii(*n*4), 8, 18–19, 38, 191, 222, 472, 482, 527
Tamar 371–372, 376, 378–382, 386–389
theater 146, 285, 338, 433, 484
Therapeutae 497, 517, 522
time 42, 154–155, 177, 223, 225, 234, 288, 305, 350, 392, 407–408, 411–412, 414–414, 420–422, 445, 452–454, 457–459, 467, 478, 561, 573–585
tithe, Levitical 126–127, 132, 134, 136–137, 139, 141, 265, 469, 474–476, 478, 480, 532, 537, 587

unity
    arithmological 396, 490
    of the forms 148, 160
    of minds 490–491
    rhetorical/thematic xiii–xiv, 4–5, 12–13, 15–17, 19, 219, 240, 374, 376, 568, 572
    of soul 362, 454, 523

verba Philonica 159, 171, 422–423, 436
vice (see also, sin) 172, 180–181, 205, 210, 271, 282, 286, 292, 298, 300–301, 308, 313, 321, 330, 336–339, 352, 390, 392, 399, 404–405, 425, 427, 435, 446, 473, 490, 521, 530–531, 533, 540, 561, 582

virtue xiv–xv, 41, 124, 132, 134, 136–137, 145–154, 175–176, 188, 191, 203–205, 210, 214, 250, 257–259, 267, 271–272, 277–289, 292, 303, 305, 308, 311–312, 316, 320, 325, 328, 335–338, 346–347, 349, 353, 358, 363, 368, 371–372, 374–376, 378, 385–386, 394, 402–407, 413, 419, 427–429, 435, 437, 441–442, 458–460, 463, 483–485, 494, 497, 520–523, 525–526, 528–533, 539–540, 545, 548, 552–561, 568, 571, 576, 579, 582, 584, 587
    cardinal 212, 275, 381, 393, 398–399, 402, 408, 486–488
    divine 18, 172, 275, 383, 445, 455, 457
    Jewish 259, 408–409, 486–488
    as queen 276
    Roman 259, 486–488
    specific/generic 274–275, 277, 356, 383, 398–400

wisdom 8, 38–42, 132, 134, 138, 144, 166, 169, 180, 182, 184, 193–195, 199, 202, 205, 209, 214, 221, 223, 225, 252, 254, 271–272, 275, 277, 282–283, 295, 297, 325, 360–361, 363, 366, 382–383, 388, 399–400, 403–404, 422, 452, 480, 483, 485–489, 494, 496, 510, 512, 526, 528–530, 546, 556, 558, 560–561, 564–565, 574, 582
Word (see Logos)

Zipporah 321–322, 331–333, 337–338, 341, 343–344, 346, 349, 386, 390